Beginning
Microsoft® Visual C#® 2008

Karli Watson

Christian Nagel

Jacob Hammer Pedersen

Jon D. Reid

Morgan Skinner

Eric White

WILEY

Wiley Publishing, Inc.

Beginning Microsoft® Visual C#® 2008

Published by

Wiley Publishing, Inc.
10475 Crosspoint Boulevard
Indianapolis, IN 46256
www.wiley.com

Published simultaneously in Canada

ISBN: 978-0-470-19135-4

Manufactured in the United States of America

10 9 8 7 6 5 4 3 2

Library of Congress Cataloging-in-Publication Data is available from the publisher.

Beginning
Microsoft® Visual C#® 2008

(Continued)

Thanks to everyone at Wiley for helping me through this project and reigning in my strange British stylings, to assorted clients for giving me the time to write, and to Donna for keeping me sane and coping with my temperamental back. Thanks also to friends and family for being patient with my deadline-laden lifestyle.
—Karli Watson

To my wife, Beth, and our children, Nathaniel, Timothy, and Walter. Thanks for your support and encouragement. Also a big thank-you to my co-authors and the team at Wrox/Wiley.
—Jon Reid

To Mum and Dad: No words can express how much I love and miss you. Thanks for everything, you were brilliant.
—Morgan Skinner

About the Authors

Karli Watson is a freelance IT specialist, author, and developer. He is also a technical consultant for 3form Ltd. (www.3form.net) and Boost.net (www.boost.net), and an associate technologist with Content Master (www.contentmaster.com). For the most part, he immerses himself in .NET (in particular, C#) and has written numerous books in the field. He specializes in communicating complex ideas in a way that is accessible to anyone with a passion to learn, and spends much of his time playing with new technology to find new things to teach people.

During those rare times when he isn't doing the above, Karli is probably wishing he were hurtling down a mountain on a snowboard or possibly trying to get his novel published. Either way, you'll know him by his brightly colored clothes.

Christian Nagel is a software architect, trainer, and consultant, and an associate of Thinktecture (www.thinktecture.com), offering training and coaching based on Microsoft .NET technologies. His achievements in the developer community have earned him a position as Microsoft Regional Director and MVP for ASP.NET. He enjoys an excellent reputation as an author of several .NET books, such as *Professional C#, Pro .NET Network Programming,* and *Enterprise Services with the .NET Frameworks,* and he speaks regularly at international industry conferences.

Christian has more than 15 years of experience as a developer and software architect. He started his computing career on PDP 11 and VAX/VMS, covering a variety of languages and platforms. Since 2000, he has been working with .NET and C#, developing and architecting distributed solutions. He can be reached at www.christiannagel.com.

Jacob Hammer Pedersen is a systems developer at Fujitsu Service, Denmark. He's been programming the PC since the early 1990s using various languages, including Pascal, Visual Basic, C/C++, and C#. Jacob has co-authored a number of .NET books and works with a wide variety of Microsoft technologies, ranging from SQL Server to Office extensibility. A Danish citizen, he works and lives in Aarhus, Denmark.

Jon D. Reid is the director of systems engineering at Indigo Biosystems, Inc. (www.indigobio.com), an independent software vendor for the life sciences, where he develops in C# for the Microsoft environment. He has co-authored many .NET books, including *Beginning Visual C# 2005, Beginning C# Databases: From Novice to Professional, Pro Visual Studio .NET, ADO.NET Programmer's Reference,* and *Professional SQL Server 2000 XML.*

Morgan Skinner started programming at school in 1980 and has been hooked on computing ever since. He now works for Microsoft as an application development consultant where he helps customers with their architecture, design, coding, and testing. He's been working with .NET since the PDC release in 2000, and has authored several MSDN articles and co-authored a couple of books on .NET. In his spare time he relaxes by fighting weeds on his allotment. You can reach Morgan at www.morganskinner.com.

Eric White is an independent software consultant with more than 20 years of experience in building management information systems and accounting systems. When he isn't hunched over a screen programming in C#, he is most likely to be found with an ice axe in hand, climbing some mountain.

Credits

Acquisitions Editor
Katie Mohr

Development Editor
Maryann Steinhart

Technical Editor
Douglas Parsons

Production Editor
William A. Barton

Copy Editor
Luann Rouff

Editorial Manager
Mary Beth Wakefield

Production Manager
Tim Tate

Vice President and Executive Group Publisher
Richard Swadley

Vice President and Executive Publisher
Joseph B. Wikert

Project Coordinator, Cover
Lynsey Stanford

Proofreaders
Jeremy Bagai,
Josh Chase,
David Fine,
Reed Kellman,
Scott Klemp,
Josh Peterson,
Todd Spencer,
Word One

Indexer
Robert Swanson

Contents

Contents

Contents

Contents

Contents

Contents

Contents

Contents

Contents

Contents

Contents

Contents

Contents

Contents

Introduction

C# is a relatively new language that was unveiled to the world when Microsoft announced the first version of its .NET Framework in July 2000. Since then its popularity has rocketed, and it has arguably become the language of choice for both Windows and Web developers who use the .NET Framework. Part of the appeal of C# comes from its clear syntax, which derives from C/C++ but simplifies some things that have previously discouraged some programmers. Despite this simplification, C# has retained the power of C++, and there is now no reason not to move into C#. The language is not difficult, making it a great one to learn elementary programming techniques with. This ease of learning, combined with the capabilities of the .NET Framework, make C# an excellent way to start your programming career.

The latest release of C#, C# 3.0, which is included with version 3.5 of the .NET Framework, builds on the existing successes and adds even more attractive features. Some of these, again, have their roots in C++ — at least superficially — but some are entirely new. The latest releases of Visual Studio and the Express line of development tools also bring many tweaks and improvements to make your life easier and dramatically increase your productivity.

This book is intended to teach you about all aspects of C# programming, from the language itself, through Windows and Web programming, to making use of data sources, and finally to some advanced techniques such as graphics programming. You'll also learn about the capabilities of Visual C# Express 2008, Visual Web Developer Express 2008, and Visual Studio 2008, and all the ways that these products can aid your application development. The book is written in a friendly, mentor-style fashion, with each chapter building on previous ones, and every effort is made to ease you into advanced techniques painlessly. At no point do technical terms appear from nowhere to discourage you from continuing; every concept is introduced and discussed as required. Technical jargon is kept to a minimum, but where it is necessary, it too is properly defined and laid out in context.

The authors of this book are all experts in their fields, and are enthusiastic in their passion for both the C# language and the .NET Framework. Nowhere will you find a group of people better qualified to take you under their collective wing and nurture your understanding of C# from first principles to advanced techniques. Along with the fundamental knowledge it provides, this book is packed full of helpful hints, tips, exercises, and full-fledged example code (available for download at p2p.wrox.com) that you will find yourself using time and again as your career progresses.

We pass this knowledge on without begrudging it, and hope that you will be able to use it to become the best programmer you can be. Good luck, and all the best!

Who This Book Is For

This book is for everyone who wants to learn how to program in C# using the .NET Framework. The early chapters cover the language itself, assuming no prior programming experience. If you have programmed in other languages before, then much of the material in these chapters will be familiar. Many aspects of C# syntax are shared with other languages, and many structures are common to practically all programming languages (such as looping and branching structures). However, even if you are an experienced programmer, you will benefit from looking through these chapters to learn the specifics of how these techniques apply to C#.

If you are new to programming, then you should start from the beginning. If you are new to the .NET Framework but know how to program, then you should read Chapter 1 and then skim through the next few chapters before beginning to apply the C# concepts you have learned. If you know how to program but haven't encountered an object-oriented programming language before, then read the chapters from Chapter 8 onward.

Alternatively, if you already know the C# language, then you may wish to concentrate on the chapters dealing with the most recent .NET Framework and C# language developments, specifically the chapters on collections, generics, and C# 3.0 language additions (Chapters 11 to 14), or skip the first section of the book completely and start with Chapter 15.

The chapters in this book are written with a dual purpose in mind: They can be read sequentially to provide a complete tutorial in the C# language, and they can be dipped into as required as reference material.

In addition to the core material, each chapter also includes a selection of exercises that you can work through to ensure that you have understood the material. The exercises range from simple multiple choice or true/false questions to more involved questions that require you to modify or build applications. The answers to all the exercises are provided as a download from the book's Web page at www.wrox.com.

How This Book Is Structured

This book is divided into six sections:

❑   **Introduction:** What this book is about and for whom it was written.

❑   **The C# Language:** Covers all aspects of the C# language, from the fundamentals to object-oriented techniques.

❑   **Windows Programming:** How to write Windows applications in C#, and how to deploy them.

❑   **Web Programming:** Web application development, Web services, and Web application deployment.

❑   **Data Access:** Using data in your applications, including data stored in files on your hard disk, data stored in XML format, and data in databases.

❑   **Additional Techniques:** This section examines some extra ways of using C# and the .NET Framework, including attributes, XML documentation, networking, and graphics programming with GDI+. It also looks at WPF, WCF, and WF — technologies introduced with .NET 3.0 and enhanced for .NET 3.5.

The following sections describe the chapters in the five major sections of this book.

The C# Language (Chapters 1–14)

Chapter 1 introduces you to C# and how it fits into the .NET landscape. You'll learn the fundamentals of programming in this environment, and how Visual C# Express (VCE) and Visual Studio (VS) fit in.

Chapter 2 starts you off with writing C# applications. You'll look at the syntax of C# and put the language to use with sample command-line and Windows applications. These examples demonstrate just how quick and easy it can be to get up and running, and along the way you'll be introduced to the VCE and VS development environments and the basic windows and tools that you'll be using throughout the book.

Next, you'll learn more about the basics of the C# language. In **Chapter 3,** you'll learn what variables are and how to manipulate them. You'll enhance the structure of your applications with flow control (looping and branching) in **Chapter 4,** and learn some more advanced variable types such as arrays in **Chapter 5.** In **Chapter 6,** you'll start to encapsulate your code in the form of functions, which make it much easier to perform repetitive operations, and make your code much more readable.

By the start of **Chapter 7** you'll have a handle on the fundamentals of the C# language, and will focus on debugging your applications. This involves looking at outputting trace information as your applications are executed, and at how VS can be used to trap errors and lead you to solutions for them with its powerful debugging environment.

From **Chapter 8** onward you'll learn about object-oriented programming (OOP), starting with a look at what this term means, and an answer to the eternal question, "What is an object?" OOP can seem quite difficult at first. The whole of Chapter 8 is devoted to demystifying it and explaining what makes it so great, and you won't actually deal with much C# code until the very end of the chapter.

Everything changes in **Chapter 9,** when you put theory into practice and start using OOP in your C# applications. This is where the true power of C# lies. You'll begin by looking at how to define classes and interfaces, and then move on to class members (including fields, properties, and methods) in **Chapter 10.** At the end of that chapter, you'll start to assemble a card game application, which is developed over several chapters and helps to illustrate OOP.

Once you've learned how OOP works in C#, you'll move on in **Chapter 11** to look at common OOP scenarios, including dealing with collections of objects, and comparing and converting objects. **Chapter 12** takes a look at a new and very useful feature of C# in .NET 2.0, generics, which enable, you to create very flexible classes. **Chapter 13** continues the discussion of the C# language and OOP with some additional techniques, and notable events, which become very important in, for example, Windows programming. Finally, **Chapter 14** focuses on C# language features that were introduced with version 3.0 of the language.

Windows Programming (Chapters 15–18)

Chapter 15 starts by introducing you to what is meant by Windows programming, and looks at how this is achieved in VCE and VS. As before, you'll start with the basics and build up your knowledge over the chapter. Then, in **Chapter 16,** you will see how you can use the wealth of controls supplied by the .NET Framework in your applications. You'll quickly understand how .NET enables you to build Windows applications in a graphical way, and assemble advanced applications with the minimum of effort and time.

Chapter 17 looks at some commonly used features that can add specialized features with ease, such as file management, printing, and so on. **Chapter 18** then discusses deploying your applications, including making installation programs to enable your users to get up and running with your applications as soon as possible.

Web Programming (Chapters 19–23)

This section is structured in a similar way to the Windows programming section. **Chapter 19** describes the controls that make up the simplest of Web applications, and how you can fit them together and make them perform tasks using ASP.NET. **Chapter 20** builds on this and introduces more advanced techniques, versatile controls, and state management in the context of the Web, as well as conforming to Web standards.

Chapter 21 is an excursion into the wonderful world of Web services, which provide programmatic access to information and capabilities across the Internet. Web services enable you to expose complex data and functionality to Web and Windows applications in a platform-independent way. This chapter discusses how to use and create Web services, and the additional tools that .NET provides, including security.

Chapter 22 looks at Ajax programming, which is a way to add dynamic, client-side functionality to Web applications. Version 3.5 of the .NET Framework provides Ajax functionality through ASP.NET Ajax, and this chapter explains how to use it.

Chapter 23 examines the deployment of Web applications and services — in particular, the new features of VS and VWD that enable you to publish applications to the Web with the click of a button.

Data Access (Chapters 24–29)

Chapter 24 looks at how your applications can save data to and retrieve it from a disk, both as simple text files and as more complex representations of data. You'll also see how to compress data, how to work with legacy data such as comma-separated value (CSV) files, and how to monitor and act on file system changes.

In **Chapter 25** you'll learn about what is fast becoming the de facto standard for data exchange — namely, XML. You will have touched on XML several times in preceding chapters, but this chapter lays out the ground rules and shows you what all the excitement is about.

The remainder of this section looks at LINQ, which is a query language built in to the latest versions of the .NET Framework. **Chapter 26** provides a general introduction to LINQ, and then you will use LINQ to access database data in **Chapter 27**. In **Chapter 28,** you will see how LINQ can be used alongside the older ADO.NET data access technology. Finally, in **Chapter 29** you will learn how to use LINQ with XML data.

Additional Techniques (Chapters 30–36)

The last section of the book looks at a wide variety of additional C# and .NET subjects. In **Chapter 30** you'll look at attributes, a powerful way to both include additional information about types in assemblies and add functionality that would otherwise be difficult to implement.

Chapter 31 deals with XML documentation and how you can document your applications at the source code level. You'll see how to add this information and how to use and extract it. You'll take this to the point where you can generate expansive, MSDN-style documentation from your code.

Next, you'll look at networking in **Chapter 32,** and how your applications can communicate with each other and with other services across various types of networks. **Chapter 33** provides a bit of light relief from many of the involved techniques you'll have seen earlier in the book, as it covers the subject of graphics programming with GDI+. You'll learn how to manipulate graphics and style your applications, opening the door to a vast array of C# applications and having a bit of fun along the way.

Finally, you will look at some exciting new technologies that have emerged with the latest .NET Framework release. In **Chapter 34,** you will get to play with Windows Presentation Foundation (WPF) and see how it promises enormous changes to both Windows and Web development. **Chapter 35** looks at Windows Communication Foundation (WCF), which extends and enhances the concept of Web services to an enterprise-level communication technology. The last chapter of the book, **Chapter 36,** looks at Windows Workflow Foundation (WF). WF enables you to implement workflow functionality in your applications, meaning that you can define operations that are performed in a specific order controlled by external interactions, which is very useful for many types of applications.

What You Need to Use This Book

The code and descriptions of C# and the .NET Framework in this book apply to .NET 3.5. You don't need anything other than the framework to understand this aspect of the book, but many of the examples require a development tool. This book uses Visual C# Express 2008 as its primary development tool, although some chapters use Visual Web Developer Express 2008. In addition, some functionality is only available in Visual Studio 2008, and where appropriate this is noted.

Conventions

A number of conventions are used throughout the book to help you get the most from the text and keep track of what's happening.

Try It Out

The *Try It Out* is an exercise you should work through, following the text in the book.

1. They usually consist of a set of steps.

2. Each step has a number.

3. Follow the steps through with your copy of the database.

How It Works

After most of the *Try It Out* sections, the code you have typed is explained in detail.

> **Boxes like this one hold important, not-to-be forgotten information that is directly relevant to the surrounding text.**

Tips, hints, tricks, and asides to the current discussion are offset and placed in italics like this.

As for styles in the text:

❑ New terms and important words are *italicized* when introduced.

❑ Keyboard strokes look like this: Ctrl+A.

❑ Filenames, URLs, and code within the text look like so: `persistence.properties`.

❑ Code is presented in two different ways:

```
Code examples nearly always look like this.
Gray highlighting is used to show where new code is added to existing code, or
to point out a specific section of code that's being explained in the text.
```

Source Code

As you work through the examples in this book, you may choose either to type in all the code manually or to use the source code files that accompany the book. All of the source code used in this book is available for download at `www.wrox.com`. Once at the site, simply locate the book's title (either by using the Search box or by using one of the title lists) and click the Download Code link on the book's detail page to obtain all the source code for the book.

Because many books have similar titles, you may find it easiest to search by ISBN; for this book, the ISBN is 978-0-470-19135-4

Once you download the code, just decompress it with your favorite compression tool. Alternatively, you can go to the main Wrox code download page at `www.wrox.com/dynamic/books/download.aspx` to see the code available for this book and all other Wrox books.

Errata

Every effort is made to ensure that there are no errors in the text or in the code. However, no one is perfect, and mistakes do occur. If you find an error such as a spelling mistake or a faulty piece of code in one of our books, we would be grateful for your feedback. By sending in errata, you may save another reader hours of frustration, and at the same time you will be helping us provide even higher quality information.

To find the errata page for this book, go to `www.wrox.com` and locate the title using the Search box or one of the title lists. Then, on the book details page, click the Book Errata link. On this page you can view all errata that have been submitted for this book and posted by Wrox editors. A complete book list, including links to each book's errata, is also available at `www.wrox.com/misc-pages/booklist.shtml`.

If you don't spot "your" error on the Book Errata page, go to `www.wrox.com/contact/techsupport .shtml` and complete the form there to send us the error you have found. We'll check the information and, if appropriate, post a message to the book's errata page and fix the problem in subsequent editions of the book.

p2p.wrox.com

For author and peer discussion, join the P2P forums at p2p.wrox.com. The forums are a Web-based system for you to post messages relating to Wrox books and related technologies and interact with other readers and technology users. The forums offer a subscription feature to e-mail you topics of interest of your choosing when new posts are made to the forums. Wrox authors, editors, other industry experts, and your fellow readers are present on these forums.

At http://p2p.wrox.com you will find a number of different forums that can help you not only as you read this book, but also as you develop your own applications. To join the forums, just follow these steps:

1. Go to p2p.wrox.com and click the Register link.

2. Read the terms of use and click Agree.

3. Complete the required information to join as well as any optional information you want to provide and click Submit.

4. You will receive an e-mail with information describing how to verify your account and complete the joining process.

You can read messages in the forums without joining P2P, but to post your own messages you must join.

Once you join, you can post new messages and respond to messages other users post. You can read messages at any time on the Web. If you would like to have new messages from a particular forum e-mailed to you, click the Subscribe to this Forum icon by the forum name in the forum listing.

For more information about how to use the Wrox P2P, be sure to read the P2P FAQs for answers to questions about how the forum software works as well as many common questions specific to P2P and Wrox books. To read the FAQs, click the FAQ link on any P2P page.

Part I
The C# Language

1

Introducing C#

Welcome to the first chapter of the first section of this book. This section will provide you with the basic knowledge you need to get up and running with C#. This chapter provides an overview of C# and the .NET Framework, including what these technologies are, the motivation for using them, and how they relate to each other.

First is a general discussion of the .NET Framework. This technology contains many concepts that are tricky to come to grips with initially. This means that the discussion, by necessity, covers many new concepts in a short amount of space. However, a quick look at the basics is essential to understanding how to program in C#. Later in the book you will revisit many of the topics covered here, exploring them in more detail.

After that general introduction, the chapter provides a basic description of C# itself, including its origins and similarities to C++. Finally, you look at the primary tools used throughout this book: Visual Studio 2008 (VS) and Visual C# 2008 Express Edition (VCE).

What Is the .NET Framework?

The .NET Framework is a new and revolutionary platform created by Microsoft for developing applications. The most interesting thing about this statement is how vague it is — but there are good reasons for this. For a start, note that it doesn't "develop applications on the Windows operating system." Although the Microsoft release of the .NET Framework runs on the Windows operating system, it is fast becoming possible to find alternative versions that will work on other systems. One example of this is Mono, an open-source version of the .NET Framework (including a C# compiler) that runs on several operating systems, including various flavors of Linux and Mac OS. More such projects are in the pipeline and may be available by the time you read this. In addition, you can use the Microsoft .NET Compact Framework (essentially a subset of the full .NET Framework) on personal digital assistant (PDA) class devices and even some smartphones. One of the key motivations behind the .NET Framework is its intended use as a means of integrating disparate operating systems.

In addition, the preceding definition of the .NET Framework includes no restriction on the type of applications that are possible. That's because there is no restriction — the .NET Framework allows the creation of Windows applications, Web applications, Web services, and pretty much anything else you can think of.

The .NET Framework has been designed so that it can be used from any language, including C# (the subject of this book) as well as C++, Visual Basic, JScript, and even older languages such as COBOL. For this to work, .NET-specific versions of these languages have also appeared, and more are being released all the time. Not only do all of these have access to the .NET Framework, but they can also communicate with each other. It is perfectly possible for C# developers to make use of code written by Visual Basic programmers, and vice versa.

All of this provides a hitherto unthinkable level of versatility and is part of what makes using the .NET Framework such an attractive prospect.

What's in the .NET Framework?

The .NET Framework consists primarily of a gigantic library of code that you use from your client languages (such as C#) using object-oriented programming (OOP) techniques. This library is categorized into different modules — you use portions of it depending on the results you want to achieve. For example, one module contains the building blocks for Windows applications, another for network programming, and another for Web development. Some modules are divided into more specific submodules, such as a module for building Web services within the module for Web development.

The intention is for different operating systems to support some or all of these modules, depending on their characteristics. A PDA, for example, would include support for all the core .NET functionality, but is unlikely to require some of the more esoteric modules.

Part of the .NET Framework library defines some basic *types*. A type is a representation of data, and specifying some of the most fundamental of these (such as "a 32-bit signed integer") facilitates interoperability between languages using the .NET Framework. This is called the *Common Type System (CTS)*.

As well as supplying this library, the .NET Framework also includes the .NET *Common Language Runtime (CLR)*, which is responsible for maintaining the execution of all applications developed using the .NET library.

Writing Applications Using the .NET Framework

Writing an application using the .NET Framework means writing code (using any of the languages that support the Framework) using the .NET code library. In this book you use VS and VCE for your development — VS is a powerful, integrated development environment that supports C# (as well as managed and unmanaged C++, Visual Basic, and some others). VCE is a slimmed down (and free) version of VS that supports C# only. The advantage of these environments is the ease with which .NET features can be integrated into your code. The code that you create will be entirely C# but will use the .NET Framework throughout, and you'll make use of the additional tools in VS and VCE where necessary.

For C# code to execute, it must be converted into a language that the target operating system understands, known as *native code*. This conversion is called *compiling* code, an act that is performed by a *compiler*. Under the .NET Framework, however, this is a two-stage process.

MSIL and JIT

When you compile code that uses the .NET Framework library, you don't immediately create operating system–specific native code. Instead, you compile your code into *Microsoft Intermediate Language (MSIL)* code. This code isn't specific to any operating system and isn't specific to C#. Other .NET languages — Visual Basic .NET, for example — also compile to this language as a first stage. This compilation step is carried out by VS or VCE when you develop C# applications.

Obviously, more work is necessary to execute an application. That is the job of a *Just-in-Time (JIT)* compiler, which compiles MSIL into native code that is specific to the OS and machine architecture being targeted. Only at this point can the OS execute the application. The *just-in-time* part of the name reflects the fact that MSIL code is only compiled as, and when, it is needed.

In the past, it was often necessary to compile your code into several applications, each of which targeted a specific operating system and CPU architecture. Often, this was a form of optimization (to get code to run faster on an AMD chipset, for example), but at times it was critical (for applications to work in both Win9*x* and WinNT/2000 environments, for example). This is now unnecessary, because JIT compilers (as their name suggests) use MSIL code, which is independent of the machine, operating system, and CPU. Several JIT compilers exist, each targeting a different architecture, and the appropriate one will be used to create the native code required.

The beauty of all this is that it requires a lot less work on your part — in fact, you can forget about system-dependent details and concentrate on the more interesting functionality of your code.

Assemblies

When you compile an application, the MSIL code created is stored in an *assembly*. Assemblies include both executable application files that you can run directly from Windows without the need for any other programs (these have a .exe file extension), and libraries (which have a .dll extension) for use by other applications.

In addition to containing MSIL, assemblies also include *meta* information (that is, information about the information contained in the assembly, also known as *metadata*) and optional *resources* (additional data used by the MSIL, such as sound files and pictures). The meta information enables assemblies to be fully self-descriptive. You need no other information to use an assembly, meaning you avoid situations such as failing to add required data to the system registry and so on, which was often a problem when developing with other platforms.

This means that deploying applications is often as simple as copying the files into a directory on a remote computer. Because no additional information is required on the target systems, you can just run an executable file from this directory and (assuming the .NET CLR is installed) you're good to go.

Of course, you won't necessarily want to include everything required to run an application in one place. You might write some code that performs tasks required by multiple applications. In situations like that, it is often useful to place the reusable code in a place accessible to all applications. In the .NET Framework, this is the *Global Assembly Cache (GAC)*. Placing code in the GAC is simple — you just place the assembly containing the code in the directory containing this cache.

Managed Code

The role of the CLR doesn't end once you have compiled your code to MSIL, and a JIT compiler has compiled that to native code. Code written using the .NET Framework is *managed* when it is executed (a stage usually referred to as *runtime*). This means that the CLR looks after your applications by managing memory, handling security, allowing cross-language debugging, and so on. By contrast, applications that do not run under the control of the CLR are said to be *unmanaged,* and certain languages such as C++ can be used to write such applications, which, for example, access low-level functions of the operating system. However, in C# you can write only code that runs in a managed environment. You will make use of the managed features of the CLR and allow .NET itself to handle any interaction with the operating system.

Garbage Collection

One of the most important features of managed code is the concept of *garbage collection*. This is the .NET method of making sure that the memory used by an application is freed up completely when the application is no longer in use. Prior to .NET this was mostly the responsibility of programmers, and a few simple errors in code could result in large blocks of memory mysteriously disappearing as a result of being allocated to the wrong place in memory. That usually meant a progressive slowdown of your computer followed by a system crash.

.NET garbage collection works by inspecting the memory of your computer every so often and removing anything from it that is no longer needed. There is no set time frame for this; it might happen thousands of times a second, once every few seconds, or whenever, but you can rest assured that it will happen.

There are some implications for programmers here. Because this work is done for you at an unpredictable time, applications have to be designed with this in mind. Code that requires a lot of memory to run should tidy itself up, rather than wait for garbage collection to happen, but that isn't as tricky as it sounds.

Fitting It Together

Before moving on, let's summarize the steps required to create a .NET application as discussed previously:

1. Application code is written using a .NET-compatible language such as C# (see Figure 1-1).

C#code

Figure 1-1

2. That code is compiled into MSIL, which is stored in an assembly (see Figure 1-2).

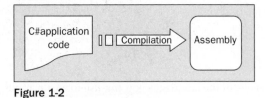

Figure 1-2

3. When this code is executed (either in its own right if it is an executable or when it is used from other code), it must first be compiled into native code using a JIT compiler (see Figure 1-3).

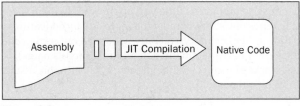

Figure 1-3

4. The native code is executed in the context of the managed CLR, along with any other running applications or processes, as shown in Figure 1-4.

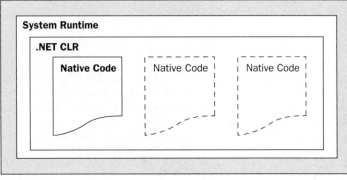

Figure 1-4

Linking

Note one additional point concerning this process. The C# code that compiles into MSIL in step 2 needn't be contained in a single file. It's possible to split application code across multiple source code files, which are then compiled together into a single assembly. This extremely useful process is known as *linking*. This is because it is far easier to work with several smaller files than one enormous one. You can separate out logically related code into an individual file so that it can be worked on independently and then practically forgotten about when completed. This also makes it easy to locate specific pieces of code when you need them and enables teams of developers to divide up the programming burden into manageable chunks, whereby individuals can "check out" pieces of code to work on without risking damage to otherwise satisfactory sections or sections other people are working on.

What Is C#?

C#, as mentioned earlier, is one of the languages you can use to create applications that will run in the .NET CLR. It is an evolution of the C and C++ languages and has been created by Microsoft specifically to work with the .NET platform. Because it is a recent development, the C# language has been designed with hindsight, taking into account many of the best features from other languages, while clearing up their problems.

Developing applications using C# is simpler than using C++, because the language syntax is simpler. Still, C# is a powerful language, and there is little you might want to do in C++ that you can't do in C#. Having said that, those features of C# that parallel the more advanced features of C++, such as directly accessing and manipulating system memory, can only be carried out using code marked as *unsafe*. This advanced programmatic technique is potentially dangerous (hence its name), because it is possible to overwrite system-critical blocks of memory with potentially catastrophic results. For this reason, and others, this book does not cover that topic.

At times, C# code is slightly more verbose than C++. This is a consequence of C# being a *type-safe* language (unlike C++). In layperson's terms, this means that once some data has been assigned to a type, it cannot subsequently transform itself into another unrelated type. Consequently, strict rules must be adhered to when converting between types, which means you will often need to write more code to carry out the same task in C# than you might write in C++, but you get two benefits: the code is more robust and debugging is simpler, and .NET can always track the type of a piece of data at any time. In C#, you therefore may not be able to do things such as "take the region of memory 4 bytes into this data and 10 bytes long and interpret it as X," but that's not necessarily a bad thing.

C# is just one of the languages available for .NET development, but it is certainly the best. It has the advantage of being the only language designed from the ground up for the .NET Framework and may be the principal language used in versions of .NET that are ported to other operating systems. To keep languages such as the .NET version of Visual Basic as similar as possible to their predecessors yet compliant with the CLR, certain features of the .NET code library are not fully supported. By contrast, C# can make use of every feature that the .NET Framework code library has to offer. The latest version of .NET includes several improvements to the C# language, partly in response to requests from developers, making it even more powerful.

Applications You Can Write with C#

The .NET Framework has no restrictions on the types of applications that are possible, as discussed earlier. C# uses the framework and therefore has no restrictions on possible applications. However, here are a few of the more common application types:

❑ **Windows applications:** These are applications, such as Microsoft Office, that have a familiar Windows look and feel about them. This is made simple by using the Windows Forms module of the .NET Framework, which is a library of *controls* (such as buttons, toolbars, menus, and so on) that you can use to build a Windows user interface (UI).

❑ **Web applications:** These are Web pages such as might be viewed through any Web browser. The .NET Framework includes a powerful system for generating Web content dynamically, allowing personalization, security, and much more. This system is called ASP.NET (Active Server Pages .NET), and you can use C# to create ASP.NET applications using Web Forms.

❑ **Web services:** These are a new and exciting way to create versatile distributed applications. Using Web services you can exchange virtually any data over the Internet, using the same simple syntax regardless of the language used to create a Web service or the system that it resides on.

Any of these types may also require some form of database access, which can be achieved using the ADO.NET (Active Data Objects .NET) section of the .NET Framework or through the new LINQ (Language Integrated Query) capabilities of C#. Many other resources can be drawn on, such as tools for creating networking components, outputting graphics, performing complex mathematical tasks, and so on.

C# in This Book

The first part of this book deals with the syntax and usage of the C# language without too much emphasis on the .NET Framework. This is necessary because you won't be able to use the .NET Framework at all without a firm grounding in C# programming. We'll start off even simpler, in fact, and leave the more involved topic of object-oriented programming (OOP) until you've covered the basics. These are taught from first principles, assuming no programming knowledge at all.

Once you have done that, you'll be ready to move on to developing the types of applications listed in the last part. Part 2 of this book looks at Windows Forms programming, Part 3 tackles Web application and Web service programming, Part 4 examines data access (for database, file system, and XML data), and Part 5 covers some other .NET topics of interest, such as more about assemblies and graphics programming.

Visual Studio 2008

In this book, you use the Visual Studio 2008 (VS) or Visual C# 2008 Express Edition (VCE) development tools for all of your C# programming, from simple command-line applications to more complex project types. A development tool, or Integrated Development Environment (IDE), such as VS isn't essential for developing C# applications, but it makes things much easier. You can (if you want to) manipulate C# source code files in a basic text editor, such as the ubiquitous Notepad application, and compile code into assemblies using the command-line compiler that is part of the .NET Framework. However, why do this when you have the power of an IDE to help you?

The following is a short list of some Visual Studio features that make it an appealing choice for .NET development:

❑ VS automates the steps required to compile source code but at the same time gives you complete control over any options used should you wish to override them.

❑ The VS text editor is tailored to the languages VS supports (including C#) so that it can intelligently detect errors and suggest code where appropriate as you are typing. This feature is called *IntelliSense*.

❑ VS includes designers for Windows Forms and Web Forms applications, enabling simple drag-and-drop design of UI elements.

❑ Many types of C# projects may be created with "boilerplate" code already in place. Instead of starting from scratch, you will often find that various code files are started for you, reducing the amount of time spent getting started on a project. This is especially true of the new "Starter Kit" project type, which enables you to develop from a fully functional application base. Some starter kits are included with the VS installation, and you can find plenty more online to play with.

❑ VS includes several wizards that automate common tasks, many of which can add appropriate code to existing files without you having to worry about (or even, in some cases, remember) the correct syntax.

❑ VS contains many powerful tools for visualizing and navigating through elements of your projects, whether they are C# source code files or other resources such as bitmap images or sound files.

❑ As well as simply writing applications in VS, you can create deployment projects, making it easy to supply code to clients and for them to install it without much trouble.

❑ VS enables you to use advanced debugging techniques when developing projects, such as the capability to step through code one instruction at a time while keeping an eye on the state of your application.

There is much more than this, but you get the idea!

Visual Studio 2008 Express Products

In addition to Visual Studio 2008, Microsoft also supplies several simpler development tools known as Visual Studio 2008 Express Products. These are freely available at `http://lab.msdn.microsoft.com/express`.

Two of these products, Visual C# 2008 Express Edition and Visual Web Developer 2008 Express Edition, together enable you to create almost any C# application you might need. They both function as slimmed-down versions of VS and retain the same look and feel. While they offer many of the same features as VS, some notable feature are absent, although not so many that they would prevent you from using these tools to work through this book.

In this book you'll use VCE to develop C# applications wherever possible, and only use VS where it is necessary for certain functionality.

Solutions

When you use VS or VCE to develop applications, you do so by creating *solutions*. A solution, in VS and VCE terms, is more than just an application. Solutions contain *projects*, which might be Windows Forms projects, Web Form projects, and so on. Because solutions can contain multiple projects, you can group together related code in one place, even if it will eventually compile to multiple assemblies in various places on your hard disk.

This is very useful because it enables you to work on shared code (which might be placed in the GAC) at the same time as applications that use this code. Debugging code is a lot easier when only one development environment is used, because you can step through instructions in multiple code modules.

Summary

In this chapter, you looked at the .NET Framework in general terms and discovered how it makes it easy for you to create powerful and versatile applications. You saw what is necessary to turn code in languages such as C# into working applications and what benefits you gain from using managed code running in the .NET Common Language Runtime.

You also learned what C# actually is and how it relates to the .NET Framework, and you were introduced to the tools that you'll use for C# development — Visual Studio 2008 and Visual C# 2008 Express Edition.

In this chapter, you learned the following:

❑ What the .NET Framework is, why it was created, and what makes it such an attractive environment to program in

❑ What C# is and what makes it an idea tool to program in the .NET Framework

❑ What you need to develop .NET applications effectively — namely, a development environment such as VS or VCE

In the next chapter, you get some C# code running, which will give you enough knowledge to sit back and concentrate on the C# language itself, rather than worry too much about how the IDE works.

Writing a C# Program

Now that you've spent some time learning what C# is and how it fits into the .NET Framework, it's time to get your hands dirty and write some code. You use Visual Studio 2008 (VS) and Visual C# 2008 Express Edition (VCE) throughout this book, so the first thing to do is have a look at some of the basics of these development environments.

VS is an enormous and complicated product, and it can be daunting to first-time users, but using it to create basic applications can be surprisingly simple. As you start to use VS in this chapter, you will see that you don't need to know a huge amount about it to start playing with C# code. Later in the book you'll see some of the more complicated operations that VS can perform, but for now a basic working knowledge is all that is required.

VCE is far simpler for getting started, and in the early stages of this book all the examples are described in the context of this IDE. However, if you choose to, you can use VS instead, and everything will work in more or less the same way. For that reason, you'll see both IDEs in this chapter, starting with VS.

Once you've had a look at the IDEs, you put together two simple applications. You don't need to worry too much about the code in these for now; you just prove that things work. By working through the application creation procedures in these early examples, they will become second nature before too long.

The first application you create is a simple *console application*. Console applications are those that don't make use of the graphical windows environment, so you won't have to worry about buttons, menus, interaction with the mouse pointer, and so on. Instead, you run the application in a command prompt window, and interact with it in a much simpler way.

The second application is a *Windows Forms application*. The look and feel of this is very familiar to Windows users, and (surprisingly) the application doesn't require much more effort to create. However, the syntax of the code required is more complicated, even though in many cases you don't actually have to worry about details.

You use both types of application over the next two parts of the book, with slightly more emphasis on console applications at the beginning. The additional flexibility of Windows applications isn't necessary when you are learning the C# language, while the simplicity of console applications enables you to concentrate on learning the syntax and not worry about the look and feel of the application.

In this chapter, you learn the following:

- ❑   A basic working knowledge of Visual Studio 2008 and Visual C# 2008 Express Edition.
- ❑   How to write a simple console application.
- ❑   How to write a Windows Form application.

The Development Environments

This section explores the VS and VCE development environments, starting with VS. These environments are similar, and you should read both sections regardless of which IDE you are using.

Visual Studio 2008

When VS is first loaded, it immediately presents you with a host of windows, most of which are empty, along with an array of menu items and toolbar icons. You will be using most of these in the course of this book, and you can rest assured that they will look far more familiar before too long.

If this is the first time you have run VS, you will be presented with a list of preferences intended for users who have experience with previous releases of this development environment. The choices you make here affect a number of things, such as the layout of windows, the way that console windows run, and so on. Therefore, choose Visual C# Development Settings; otherwise, you may find that things don't quite work as described in this book. Note that the options available vary depending on the options you chose when installing VS, but as long as you chose to install C# this option will be available.

If this isn't the first time that you've run VS but you chose a different option the first time, don't panic. To reset the settings to Visual C# Development Settings you simply have to import them. To do this, select Tools ⇨ Import and Export Settings and choose the Reset All Settings option, shown in Figure 2-1.

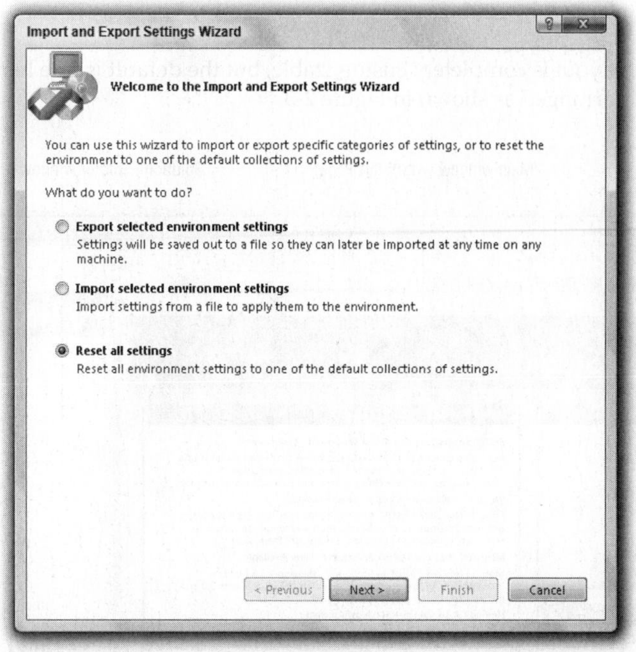

Figure 2-1

Click Next, and indicate whether you want to save your existing settings before proceeding. If you have customized things, you might want to do this; otherwise, select No and click Next again. From the next dialog, select Visual C# Development Settings, shown in Figure 2-2. Again, the available options may vary.

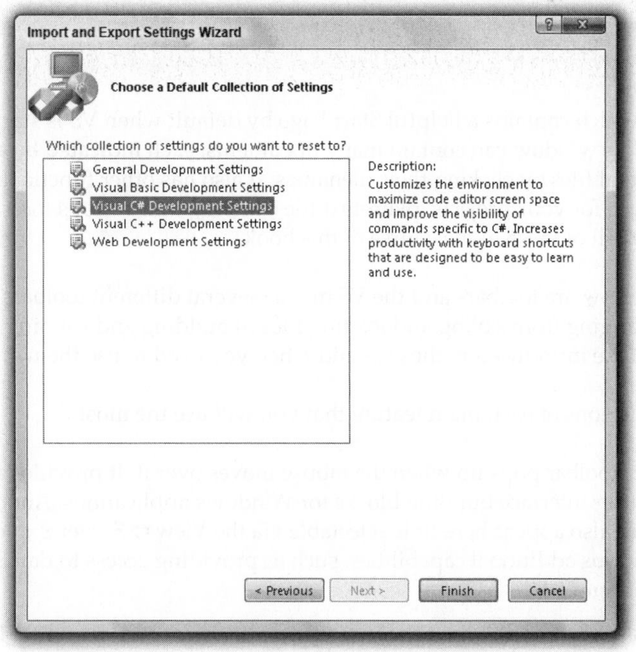

Figure 2-2

Finally, click Finish to apply the settings.

The VS environment layout is completely customizable, but the default is fine here. With C# Developer Settings selected, it is arranged as shown in Figure 2-3.

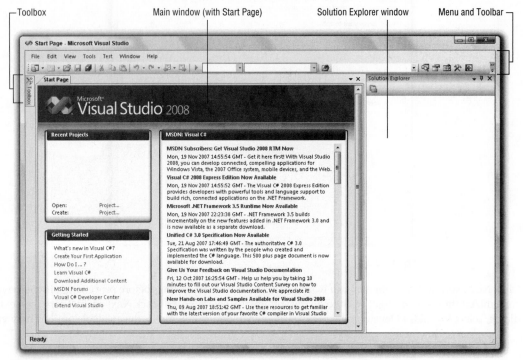

Figure 2-3

The main window, which contains a helpful Start Page by default when VS is started, is where all your code is displayed. This window can contain many documents, each indicated by a tab, so you can easily switch between several files by clicking their filenames. It also has other functions: It can display GUIs that you are designing for your projects, plain-text files, HTML, and various tools that are built into VS. You will come across all of these in the course of this book.

Above the main window are toolbars and the VS menu. Several different toolbars can be placed here, with functionality ranging from saving and loading files to building and running projects to debugging controls. Again, you are introduced to these as and when you need to use them.

Here are brief descriptions of each main feature that you will use the most:

❑ The Toolbox toolbar pops up when the mouse moves over it. It provides access to, among other things, the user interface building blocks for Windows applications. Another tab, Server Explorer, can also appear here (it is selectable via the View ⇨ Server Explorer menu option) and includes various additional capabilities, such as providing access to data sources, server settings, services, and more.

❑ The Solution Explorer window displays information about the currently loaded *solution*. A solution is VS terminology for one or more projects along with their configurations.

The Solution Explorer window displays various views of the projects in a solution, such as what files they contain and what is contained in those files.

❑ Just below the Solution Explorer window you can display a Properties window, not shown in Figure 2-3 because it appears only when you are working on a project (you can also toggle its display using View ➪ Properties Window). This window allows a more detailed view of the project's contents, enabling you to perform additional configuration of individual elements. For example, you can use this window to change the appearance of a button in a Windows form.

❑ Also not shown in the screenshot is another extremely important window: the Error List window, which you can display using View ➪ Error List. It shows errors, warnings, and other project-related information. The window updates continuously, although some information appears only when a project is compiled.

This may seem like a lot to take in, but it doesn't take long to get used to. You start by building the first of your example projects, which involves many of the VS elements just described.

VS is capable of displaying many other windows, both informational and functional. Many of these can share screen space with the windows mentioned here, and you can switch between them using tabs. Many of these windows are used later in the book, and you'll probably discover more yourself when you explore the VS environment in more detail.

Visual C# 2008 Express Edition

With VCE you don't have to worry about changing the settings. Obviously, this product isn't going to be used for Visual Basic programming, so there is no equivalent setting to worry about here. When you start VCE for the first time, you are presented with a screen that is very similar to the one in VS (see Figure 2-4).

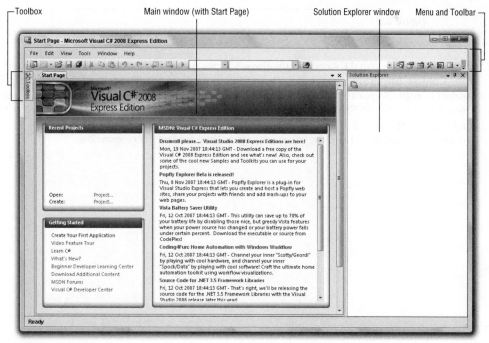

Figure 2-4

Console Applications

You use console applications regularly in this book, particularly at the beginning, so the following Try It Out provides a step-by-step guide to creating a simple one. This Try it Out includes instructions for both VS and VCE.

Try It Out   **Creating a Simple Console Application**

1. Create a new console application project by selecting File ⇨ New ⇨ Project in VS or File ⇨ New Project in VCE, as shown in Figure 2-5.

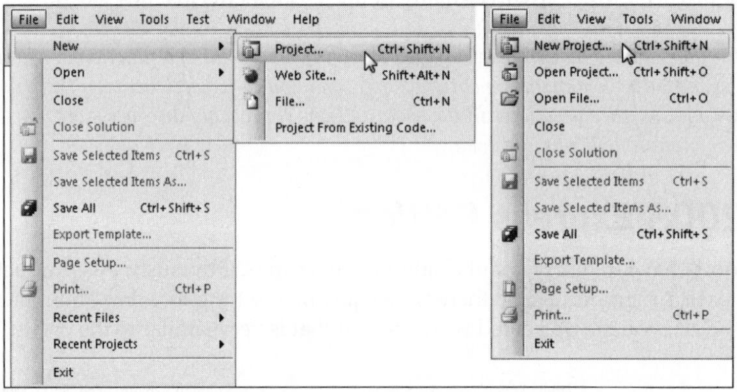

Figure 2-5

2. In VS, select the Visual C# node in the Project Types pane of the window that appears, and the Console Application project type in the Templates pane (see Figure 2-6). In VCE, simply select Console Application in the Templates pane (see Figure 2-7). In VS, change the Location text box to C:\BegVCSharp\Chapter02 (this directory is created automatically if it doesn't already exist). For both VS and VCE, leave the default text in the Name text box (ConsoleApplication1) and the other settings as they are (refer to Figure 2-6).

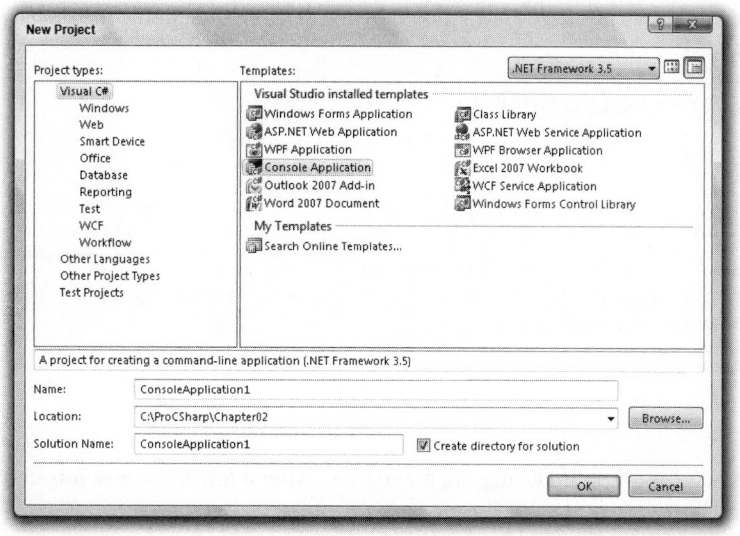

Figure 2-6

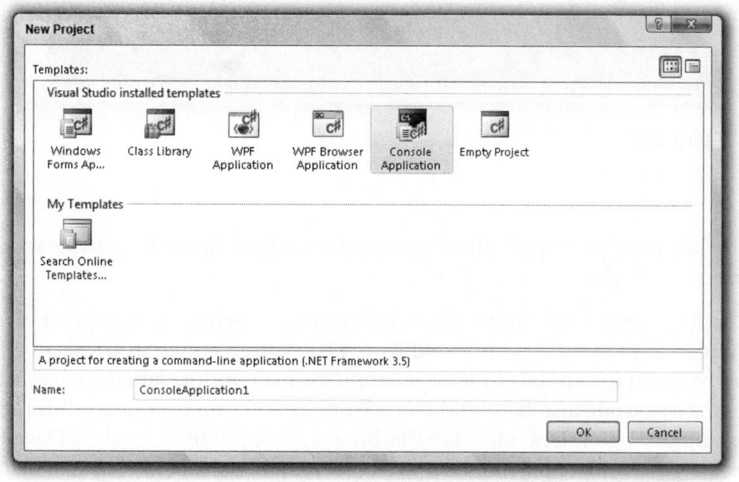

Figure 2-7

3. Click the OK button.

4. If you are using VCE, after the project is initialized click the Save All button on the toolbar or select Save All from the File menu, set the Location field to C:\BegVCSharp\Chapter02, and click OK.

5. Once the project is initialized, add the following lines of code to the file displayed in the main window:

```
namespace ConsoleApplication1
{
    class Program
    {
        static void Main(string[] args)
        {
            // Output text to the screen.
            Console.WriteLine("The first app in Beginning C# Programming!");
            Console.ReadKey();
        }
    }
}
```

6. Select the Debug ⇨ Start Debugging menu item. After a few moments you should see the window shown in Figure 2-8.

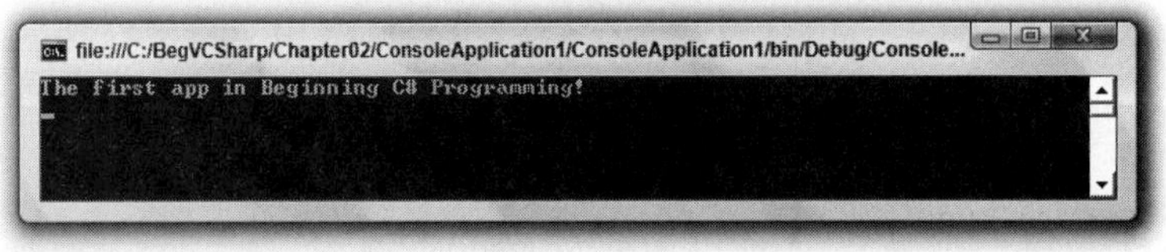

Figure 2-8

7. Press any key to exit the application (you may need to click on the console window to focus on it first).

The preceding display appears only if the Visual C# Developer Settings are applied, as described earlier in this chapter. For example, with Visual Basic Developer Settings applied, an empty console window is displayed, and the application output appears in a window labeled *Immediate*. In this case, the `Console.ReadKey()` code also fails, and you see an error. If you experience this problem, the best solution for working through the examples in this book is to apply the Visual C# Developer Settings — that way, the results you see match the results shown here. If this problem persists, then open the Tools ⇨ Options dialog and uncheck the Debugging ⇨ Redirect all output option, as shown in Figure 2-9.

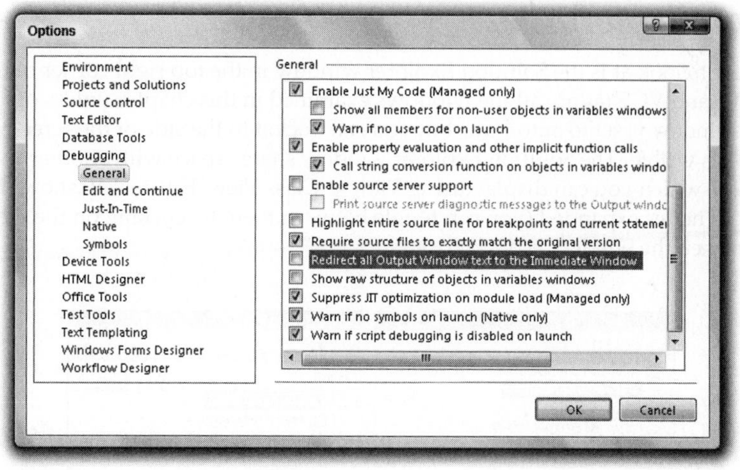

Figure 2-9

How It Works

For now, we won't dissect the code used thus far because the focus here is how to use the development tools to get code up and running. Clearly, both VS and VCE do a lot of the work for you and make the process of compiling and executing code simple. In fact, there are multiple ways to perform even these basic steps — e.g., you can create a new project by using the menu item mentioned earlier, by pressing Ctrl+Shift+N, or by clicking the corresponding icon in the toolbar.

Similarly, your code can be compiled and executed in several ways. The process you used previously — selecting Debug ⇨ Start Debugging — also has a keyboard shortcut (F5) and a toolbar icon. You can also run code without being in debugging mode using the Debug ⇨ Start Without Debugging menu item (or by pressing Ctrl+F5), or compile your project without running it (with debugging on or off) using Build ⇨ Build Solution or F6. Note that you can execute a project without debugging or build a project using toolbar icons, although these icons don't appear on the toolbar by default. Once you have compiled your code, you can also execute it simply by running the .exe file produced in Windows Explorer, or from the command prompt. To do this, open a command prompt window, change the directory to C:\BegVCSharp\Chapter02\ConsoleApplication1\ConsoleApplication1\ bin\Debug\, type **ConsoleApplication1**, and press Enter.

> *In future examples, when you see the instructions "create a new console project" or "execute the code," you can choose whichever method you want to perform these steps. Unless otherwise stated, all code should be run with debugging enabled. In addition, the terms "start," "execute," and "run" are used interchangeably in this book, and discussions following examples always assume that you have exited the application in the example.*

Console applications terminate as soon as they finish execution, which can mean that you don't get a chance to see the results if you run them directly through the IDE. To get around this in the preceding example, the code is told to wait for a key press before terminating, using the following line:

```
Console.ReadKey();
```

You will see this technique used many times in later examples. Now that you've created a project, you can take a more detailed look at some of the regions of the development environment.

The Solution Explorer

The first window to look at is the Solution Explorer window in the top right corner of the screen. It is the same for both VS and VCE (as are all the windows examined in this chapter unless otherwise specified). By default this window is set to auto-hide, but you can dock it to the side of the screen by clicking the pin icon when it is visible. The Solution Explorer window shares space with another useful window called Class View, which you can display using View ⇨ Class View. Figure 2-10 shows both of these windows with all nodes expanded (you can toggle between them by clicking on the tabs at the bottom of the window when the window is docked).

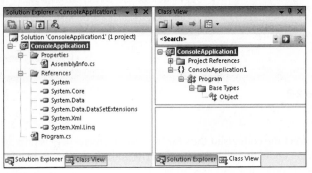

Figure 2-10

This Solution Explorer view shows the files that make up the ConsoleApplication1 project. The file to which you added code, `Program.cs`, is shown along with another code file, `AssemblyInfo.cs`, and several references.

> *All C# code files have a* `.cs` *file extension.*

You don't have to worry about the `AssemblyInfo.cs` file for the moment. It contains extra information about your project that doesn't concern us yet.

You can use this window to change what code is displayed in the main window by double-clicking `.cs` files; right-clicking them and selecting View Code; or selecting them and clicking the toolbar button that appears at the top of the window. You can also perform other operations on files here, such as renaming them or deleting them from your project. Other file types can also appear here, such as project resources (resources are files used by the project that might not be C# files, such as bitmap images and sound files). Again, you can manipulate them through the same interface.

The `References` entry contains a list of the .NET libraries you are using in your project. You'll look at this later; the standard references are fine for now. The other view, Class View, presents an alternative view of your project by showing the structure of the code you created. You'll come back to this later in the book; for now the Solution Explorer display is appropriate. As you click on files or other icons in these windows, you may notice that the contents of the Properties window (shown in Figure 2-11) changes.

The Properties Window

This window (select View ⇨ Properties Window if it isn't already displayed) shows additional information about whatever you select in the window above it. For example, the view shown in Figure 2-11 is displayed when the `Program.cs` file from the project is selected. This window also displays information about other selected items, such as user interface components (as shown in the "Windows Forms Applications" section of this chapter).

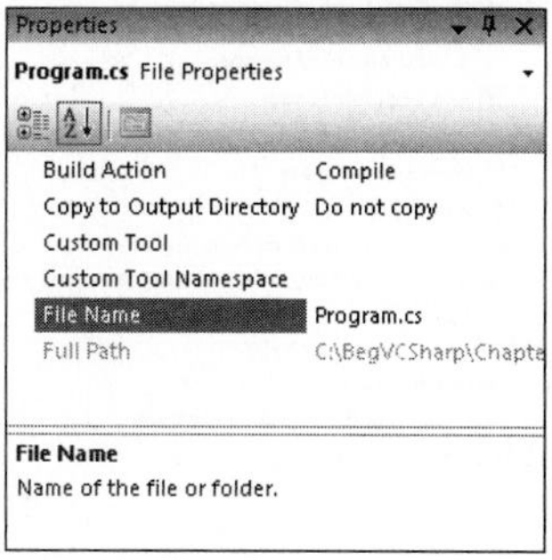

Figure 2-11

Often, changes you make to entries in the Properties window affect your code directly, adding lines of code or changing what you have in your files. With some projects, you spend as much time manipulating things through this window as making manual code changes.

The Error List Window

Currently, the Error List window (View ⇨ Error List) isn't showing much of interest because there is nothing wrong with the application. However, this is a very useful window indeed. As a test, remove the semicolon from one of the lines of code you added in the previous section. After a moment, you should see a display like the one shown in Figure 2-12.

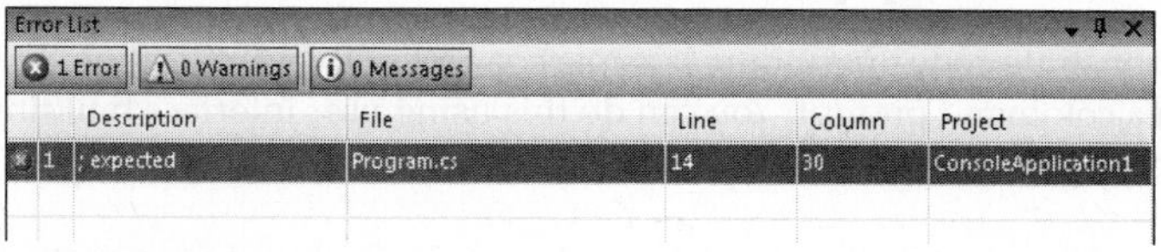

Figure 2-12

In addition, the project will no longer compile.

> *In Chapter 3, when you start looking at C# syntax, you will learn that semicolons are expected through-out your code — at the end of most lines, in fact.*

This window helps you eradicate bugs in your code because it keeps track of what you have to do to compile projects. If you double-click the error shown here, the cursor jumps to the position of the error in your source code (the source file containing the error will be opened if it isn't already open), so you can fix it quickly. You also see red wavy lines at the positions of errors in the code, so you can quickly scan the source code to see where problems lie.

Note that the error location is specified as a line number. By default, line numbers aren't displayed in the VS text editor, but this is something well worth turning on. To do so, tick the Line numbers check box in the Options dialog (selected via the Tools ⇨ Options menu item). It appears in the Text Editor ⇨ C# ⇨ General category, as shown in Figure 2-13.

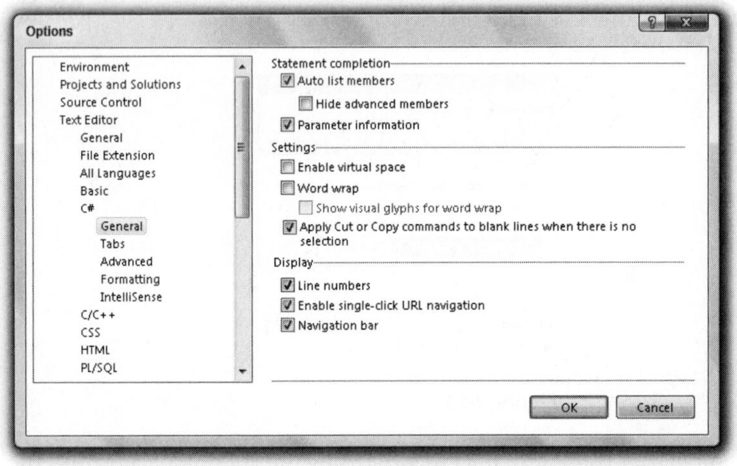

Figure 2-13

In VCE you must select Show All Settings for this option to become available, and the list of options looks slightly different from Figure 2-13.

Many useful options can be found through this dialog, and you will use several of them later in this book.

Windows Forms Applications

It is often easier to demonstrate code by running it as part of a Windows application than through a console window or via a command prompt. You can do this using user interface building blocks to piece together a user interface.

The following Try It Out shows just the basics of doing this, and you'll see how to get a Windows application up and running, without a lot of details about what the application is actually doing. Later you take a detailed look at Windows applications.

Try It Out   **Creating a Simple Windows Application**

1.   Create a new project of type Windows Forms Application (VS or VCE) in the same location as before (C:\BegVCSharp\Chapter02; and if you are using VCE, save the project to this location after you create it) with the default name WindowsFormsApplication1. If you are using VS and the first project is still open, make sure the Create New Solution option is selected to start a new solution. These settings are shown in Figures 2-14 and 2-15.

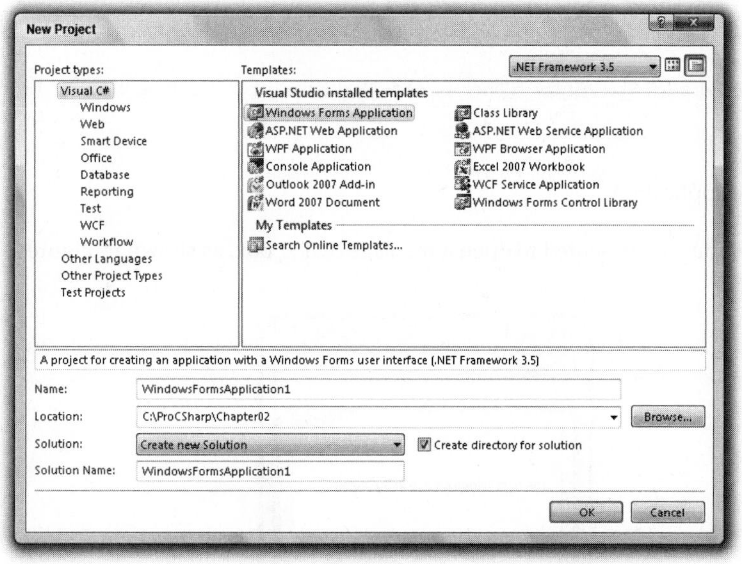

Figure 2-14

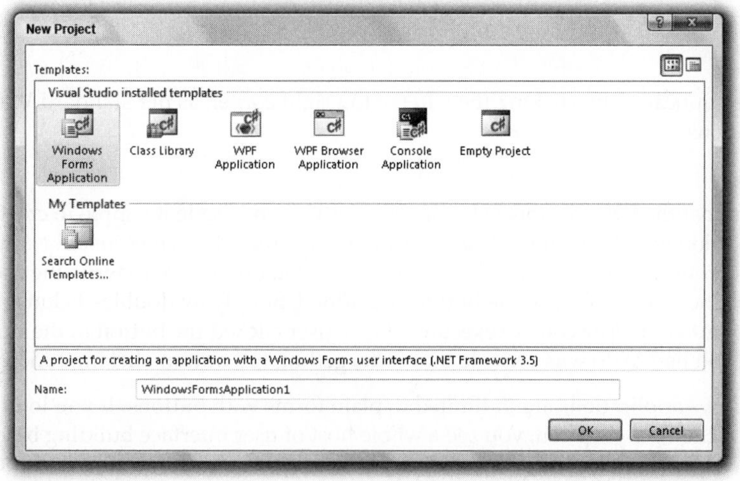

Figure 2-15

2. Click OK to create the project. You should see an empty Windows form. Move the mouse pointer to the Toolbox bar on the left of the screen, then to the Button entry of the All Windows Forms tab, and double-click the entry to add a button to the main form of the application (Form1).

3. Double-click the button that has been added to the form.

4. The C# code in `Form1.cs` should now be displayed. Modify it as follows (only part of the code in the file is shown here for brevity):

```
private void button1_Click(object sender, EventArgs e)
{
    MessageBox.Show("The first Windows app in the book!");
}
```

5. Run the application.

6. Click the button presented to open a message dialog box, as shown in Figure 2-16.

Figure 2-16

7. Exit the application by clicking the x in the top right corner, as per standard Windows applications.

How It Works

Again, it is plain that the IDE has done a lot of work for you and made it simple to create a functional Windows application with little effort. The application you created behaves just like other windows — you can move it around, resize it, minimize it, and so on. You don't have to write the code to do that — it works. The same is true for the button you added. Simply by double-clicking it, the IDE knew that you wanted to write code to execute when a user clicked the button in the running application. All you had to do was provide that code, getting full button-clicking functionality for free.

Of course, Windows applications aren't limited to plain forms with buttons. If you look at the toolbar where you found the Button option, you see a whole host of user interface building blocks, some of which may be familiar already. You will use most of these at some point in the book, and you'll find that they are all easy to use, saving you a lot of time and effort.

The code for your application, in `Form1.cs`, doesn't look much more complicated than the code in the previous section, and the same is true for the code in the other files in the Solution Explorer window. Much of the code generated is hidden by default. It is concerned with the layout of controls on the form, which is why you can view the code in Design View in the main window — it's a visual translation of this layout code. A button is an example of a control that you can use, as are the rest of the UI building blocks found in the Windows Forms section of the Toolbox bar.

You can take a closer look at the button as a control example. Switch back to the Design View of the form using the tab on the main window, and click once on the button to select it. When you do so, the Properties window in the bottom right corner of the screen shows the properties of the button control (controls have properties much like the files shown in the last example). Ensure that the application isn't currently running, scroll down to the `Text` property, which is currently set to `button1`, and change the value to `Click Me`, as shown in Figure 2-17.

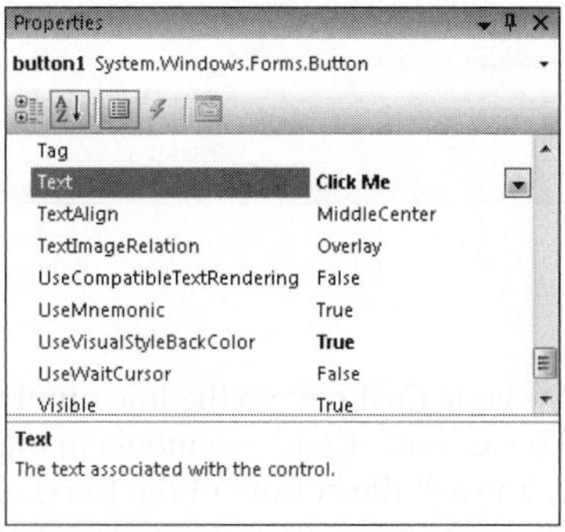

Figure 2-17

The text written on the button in Form1 should also reflect this change.

There are many properties for this button, ranging from simple formatting of the color and size to more obscure settings such as data binding settings, which enable you to establish links to databases. As briefly mentioned in the previous example, changing properties often results in direct changes to code, and this is no exception. However, if you switch back to the code view of `Form1.cs`, you won't see any change in the code.

To see the modified code, you need to look at the hidden code mentioned previously. To view the file that contains this code, expand `Form1.cs` in the Solution Explorer, which reveals a `Form1.Designer.cs` node. Double-click on this file to see what's inside.

At a cursory glance, you might not notice anything in this code reflecting the button property change at all. This is because the sections of C# code that deal with the layout and formatting of controls on a form are hidden (after all, you hardly need to look at the code if you have a graphical display of the results).

VS and VCE use a system of *code outlining* to achieve this subterfuge. You can see this in Figure 2-18.

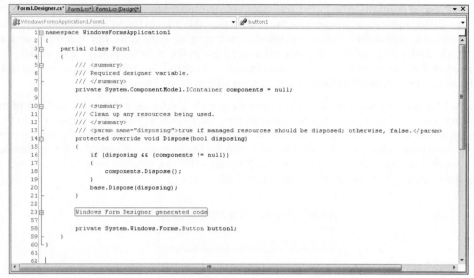

Figure 2-18

Looking down the lefthand side of the code (just next to the line numbers if you've turned them on), you may notice some gray lines and boxes with + and – symbols in them. These boxes are used to expand and contract regions of code. Toward the bottom of the file is a box with a + in it and a box in the main body of the code reading `Windows Form Designer generated code`. This label is basically saying, "Here is some code generated by VS that you don't need to know about." You can look at it if you want, however, and see what you have done by changing the button properties. Simply click on the box with the + in it and the code will become visible, and somewhere in there you should see the following line:

```
this.button1.Text = "Click Me";
```

Without worrying too much about the syntax used here, you can see that the text you typed in the Properties window has popped up directly in your code.

This outlining method can be very handy when you are writing code because you can expand and contract many other regions, not just those that are normally hidden. Just as looking at a book's table of contents can help you by providing a quick summary of the contents, looking at a series of collapsed regions of code can make it much easier to navigate through what can be vast amounts of C# code.

Summary

In this chapter you were introduced to some of the tools that you will use throughout the rest of this book. You have had a quick tour around the Visual Studio 2008 and Visual C# 2008 Express Edition development environments and used them to build two types of applications. The simpler of these, the console application, is quite enough for most of your needs and enables you to focus on the basics of C# programming. Windows applications are more complicated but are visually more impressive and intuitive to use for anyone accustomed to a Windows environment (and let's face it, that's most of us).

Now that you know how to create simple applications, you can get down to the real task of learning C#. After dealing with basic C# syntax and program structure, you move on to more advanced object-oriented methods. Once you've covered all that, you can begin to learn how to use C# to gain access to the power available in the .NET Framework.

In this chapter, you learned:

❑ How the Visual Studio 2008 and Visual C# 2008 Express Edition development environments work.

❑ How to create a simple console application.

❑ How to get a Windows application up and running.

For subsequent chapters, unless otherwise specified, instructions refer to VCE, although, as shown in this chapter, adapting these instructions for VS is not difficult, and you can use whichever IDE you prefer, or to which you have access.

3

Variables and Expressions

To use C# effectively, it's important to understand what you're actually doing when you create a computer program. Perhaps the most basic description of a computer program is that it is a series of operations that manipulate data. This is true even of the most complicated examples, such as vast, multifeatured Windows applications (e.g., Microsoft Office Suite). Although this is often completely hidden from users of applications, it is always going on behind the scenes.

To illustrate this further, consider the display unit of your computer. What you see onscreen is often so familiar that it is difficult to imagine it as anything other than a "moving picture." In fact, what you see is only a representation of some data, which in its raw form is merely a stream of 0s and 1s stashed away somewhere in the computer's memory. Any onscreen action — moving a mouse pointer, clicking on an icon, typing text into a word processor — results in the shunting around of data in memory.

Of course, simpler situations show this just as well. When using a calculator application, you are supplying data as numbers and performing operations on the numbers in much the same way as you would with paper and pencil — but a lot quicker!

If computer programs are fundamentally performing operations on data, then this implies that you need a way to store that data, and some methods to manipulate it. These two functions are provided by *variables* and *expressions*, respectively, and this chapter explores what that means, both in general and specific terms.

In this chapter, you learn about:

- ❏   Basic C# syntax
- ❏   Variables and how to use them
- ❏   Expressions and how to use them

Before starting that, though, you'll take a look at the basic syntax involved in C# programming, because you need a context in which you can learn about and use variables and expressions in the C# language.

Basic C# Syntax

The look and feel of C# code is similar to that of C++ and Java. This syntax can look quite confusing at first and it's a lot less like written English than some other languages. However, as you immerse yourself in the world of C# programming, you'll find that the style used is a sensible one, and it is possible to write very readable code without much effort.

Unlike the compilers of some other languages, C# compilers ignore additional spacing in code, whether it results from spaces, carriage returns, or tab characters (characters collectively known as *white space characters*). This means you have a lot of freedom in the way that you format your code, although conforming to certain rules can help make things easier to read.

C# code is made up of a series of *statements*, each of which is terminated with a semicolon. Because white space is ignored, multiple statements can appear on one line, although for readability it is usual to add carriage returns after semicolons, to avoid multiple statements on one line. It is perfectly acceptable (and quite normal), however, to use statements that span several lines of code.

C# is a *block-structured language*, meaning statements are part of a *block* of code. These blocks, which are delimited with curly brackets ({ and }), may contain any number of statements, or none at all. Note that the curly bracket characters do not need accompanying semicolons.

For example, a simple block of C# code could take the following form:

```
{
   <code line 1, statement 1>;
   <code line 2, statement 2>
      <code line 3, statement 2>;
}
```

Here the <code line x, statement y> sections are not actual pieces of C# code; this text is used as a placeholder where C# statements would go. In this case, the second and third lines of code are part of the same statement, because there is no semicolon after the second line.

The following simple example uses *indentation* to clarify the C# itself. This is actually standard practice, and in fact VS automatically does this for you by default. In general, each block of code has its own level of indentation, meaning how far to the right it is. Blocks of code may be *nested* inside each other (that is, blocks may contain other blocks), in which case nested blocks will be indented further:

```
{
   <code line 1>;
   {
      <code line 2>;
      <code line 3>;
   }
   <code line 4>;
}
```

In addition, lines of code that are continuations of previous lines are usually indented further as well, as in the third line of code in the first example above.

If you look in the VCE Options dialog (select Tools ⇨ Options), you can find the rules that VCE uses for formatting your code. There are very many of these, in subcategories of the Text Editor ⇨ C# ⇨ Formatting node. Most of the settings here reflect parts of C# that haven't been covered yet, but you might want to return to these settings later if you want to tweak them to suit your personal style better. For clarity, this book shows all code snippets as they would be formatted by the default settings.

Of course, this style is by no means mandatory. If you don't use it, however, you will quickly find that things can get very confusing as you move through this book!

Something else you often see in C# code are *comments*. A comment is not, strictly speaking, C# code at all, but it happily cohabits with it. Comments are self-explanatory: They enable you to add descriptive text to your code — in plain English (or French, German, Outer Mongolian, and so on) — which is ignored by the compiler. When you start dealing with lengthy code sections, it's useful to add reminders about exactly what you are doing, such as "this line of code asks the user for a number" or "this code section was written by Bob." C# has two ways of doing this. You can either place markers at the beginning and end of a comment, or you can use a marker that means "everything on the rest of this line is a comment." This latter method is an exception to the rule mentioned previously about C# compilers ignoring carriage returns, but it is a special case.

To indicate comments using the first method, you use /* characters at the start of the comment and */ characters at the end. These may occur on a single line, or on different lines, in which case all lines in between are part of the comment. The only thing you can't type in the body of a comment is */, because this is interpreted as the end marker. For example, the following are OK:

```
/* This is a comment */

/* And so...

                 ... is this! */
```

The following, however, cause problems:

```
/* Comments often end with "*/" characters */
```

Here the end of the comment (the characters after "*/") will be interpreted as C# code, and errors will occur.

The other commenting approach involves starting a comment with //. After that, you can write whatever you like — as long as you keep to one line! The following is OK:

```
// This is a different sort of comment.
```

The following fails, because the second line is interpreted as C# code:

```
// So is this,
   but this bit isn't.
```

This sort of commenting is useful to document statements, because both can be placed on a single line:

```
<A statement>;          // Explanation of statement
```

It was stated earlier that there are two ways of commenting C# code, but there is a third type of comment in C# — although strictly speaking this is an extension of the // syntax. You can use single-line comments that start with three / symbols instead of two, like this:

```
/// A special comment
```

Under normal circumstances, they are ignored by the compiler — just like other comments, but you can configure VS to extract the text after these comments and create a specially formatted text file when a project is compiled, which you can then use to create documentation. This is covered in detail in Chapter 31.

A *very* important point to note about C# code is that it is *case sensitive*. Unlike some other languages, you must enter code using exactly the right case, because using an uppercase letter instead of a lowercase one will prevent a project from compiling. For example, consider the following line of code, taken from Chapter 2:

```
Console.WriteLine("The first app in Beginning C# Programming!");
```

This code is understood by the C# compiler, as the case of the Console.WriteLine() command is correct. However, none of the following lines of code work:

```
console.WriteLine("The first app in Beginning C# Programming!");
CONSOLE.WRITELINE("The first app in Beginning C# Programming!");
Console.Writeline("The first app in Beginning C# Programming!");
```

Here the case used is wrong, so the C# compiler won't know what you want. Luckily, as you will soon discover, VCE is very helpful when it comes to entering code, and most of the time it knows (as much as a program can know) what you are trying to do. As you type, it suggests commands that you might like to use, and it tries to correct case problems.

Basic C# Console Application Structure

Let's take a closer look at the console application example from Chapter 2 (ConsoleApplication1), and break down the structure a bit. Here's the code:

```
using System;
using System.Collections.Generic;
using System.Linq;
using System.Text;

namespace ConsoleApplication1
{
    class Program
    {
        static void Main(string[] args)
        {
            // Output text to the screen.
            Console.WriteLine("The first app in Beginning C# Programming!");
            Console.ReadKey();
        }
    }
}
```

You can immediately see that all the syntactic elements discussed in the previous section are present here — semicolons, curly braces, and comments, along with appropriate indentation.

The most important section of code at the moment is the following:

```
static void Main(string[] args)
{
    // Output text to the screen.
    Console.WriteLine("The first app in Beginning C# Programming!");
    Console.ReadKey();
}
```

This is the code that is executed when you run your console application. Well, to be more precise, the code block enclosed in curly braces is executed. The comment line doesn't do anything, as mentioned earlier; it's just there for clarity. The other two code lines output some text to the console window and wait for a response, respectively, though the exact mechanisms of this don't concern us for now.

Note how to achieve the code outlining functionality shown in the previous chapter, albeit for a Windows application, since it is such a useful feature. You can do this with the `#region` and `#endregion` keywords, which define the start and end of a region of code that can be expanded and collapsed. For example, you could modify the generated code for ConsoleApplication1 as follows:

```
#region Using directives

using System;
using System.Collections.Generic;
using System.Linq;
using System.Text;

#endregion
```

This enables you to collapse this code into a single line and expand it again later should you want to look at the details. The `using` statements contained here, and the `namespace` statement just underneath, are explained at the end of this chapter.

> *Any keyword that starts with a # is actually a preprocessor directive and not, strictly speaking, a C# keyword. Other than the two described here, #region and #endregion, these can be quite complicated, and they have very specialized uses. This is one subject you might like to investigate yourself after you have worked through this book.*

For now, don't worry about the other code in the example, because the purpose of these first few chapters is to explain basic C# syntax, so the exact method of how the application execution gets to the point where `Console.WriteLine()` is called is of no concern. Later, the significance of this additional code is made clear.

Variables

As mentioned earlier, variables are concerned with the storage of data. Essentially, you can think of variables in computer memory as boxes sitting on a shelf. You can put things in boxes and take them out again, or you can just look inside a box to see if anything is there. The same goes for variables; you place data in them and can take it out or look at it, as required.

Although all data in a computer is effectively the same thing (a series of 0s and 1s), variables come in different flavors, known as *types*. Using the box analogy again, boxes come in different shapes and sizes, so some items fit only in certain boxes. The reasoning behind this type system is that different types of data may require different methods of manipulation, and by restricting variables to individual types you can avoid mixing them up. For example, it wouldn't make much sense to treat the series of 0s and 1s that make up a digital picture as an audio file.

To use variables, you have to *declare* them. This means that you have to assign them a *name* and a *type*. Once you have declared variables, you can use them as storage units for the type of data that you declared them to hold.

C# syntax for declaring variables merely specifies the type and variable name:

```
<type> <name>;
```

If you try to use a variable that hasn't been declared, your code won't compile, but in this case the compiler tells you exactly what the problem is, so this isn't really a disastrous error. Trying to use a variable without assigning it a value also causes an error, but, again, the compiler detects this.

There is an almost infinite number of types that you can use. This is because you can define your own types to hold whatever convoluted data you like. Having said this, though, there are certain types of data that just about everyone will need to use at some point or another, such as a variable that stores a number. Therefore, you should be aware of several simple, predefined types.

Simple Types

Simple types include types such as numbers and Boolean (true or false) values that make up the fundamental building blocks for your applications. Unlike complex types, simple types cannot have children or attributes. Most of the simple types available are numeric, which at first glance seems a bit strange — surely, you only need one type to store a number?

The reason for the plethora of numeric types is because of the mechanics of storing numbers as a series of 0s and 1s in the memory of a computer. For integer values, you simply take a number of *bits* (individual digits that can be 0 or 1) and represent your number in binary format. A variable storing N bits allows you to represent any number between 0 and ($2^N - 1$). Any numbers above this value are too big to fit into this variable.

For example, suppose you have a variable that can store 2 bits. The mapping between integers and the bits representing those integers is therefore as follows:

```
0 = 00
1 = 01
2 = 10
3 = 11
```

If you want to be able to store more numbers, then you need more bits (3 bits enable you to store the numbers from 0 to 7, for example).

The inevitable result of this system is that you would need an infinite number of bits to be able to store every imaginable number, which isn't going to fit in your trusty PC. Even if there were a quantity of bits you could use for every number, it surely wouldn't be efficient to use all these bits for a variable that, for example, was required to store only the numbers between 0 and 10 (because storage would be wasted). Four bits would do the job fine here, enabling you to store many more values in this range in the same space of memory.

Instead, a number of different integer types can be used to store various ranges of numbers, which take up differing amounts of memory (up to 64 bits). These types are shown in the following table.

Each of these types uses one of the standard types defined in the .NET Framework. As discussed in Chapter 1, this use of standard types is what allows language interoperability. The names you use for these types in C# are aliases for the types defined in the framework. The table lists the names of these types as they are referred to in the .NET Framework library.

Type	Alias For	Allowed Values
sbyte	System.SByte	Integer between –128 and 127
byte	System.Byte	Integer between 0 and 255
short	System.Int16	Integer between –32768 and 32767
ushort	System.UInt16	Integer between 0 and 65535
int	System.Int32	Integer between –2147483648 and 2147483647
uint	System.UInt32	Integer between 0 and 4294967295
long	System.Int64	Integer between –9223372036854775808 and 9223372036854775807
ulong	System.UInt64	Integer between 0 and 18446744073709551615

The u characters before some variable names are shorthand for *unsigned*, meaning that you can't store negative numbers in variables of those types, as shown in the Allowed Values column of the table.

Of course, you also need to store *floating-point* values, those that aren't whole numbers. You can use three floating-point variable types: float, double, and decimal. The first two store floating points in the form $+/-m \times 2e$, where the allowed values for m and e differ for each type. decimal uses the alternative form $+/-m \times 10e$. These three types are shown in the following table, along with their allowed values of m and e, and these limits in real numeric terms:

Type	Alias For	Min M	Max M	Min E	Max E	Approx. Min Value	Approx. Max Value
float	System. Single	0	224	−149	104	1.5×10^{-45}	3.4×10^{38}
double	System. Double	0	253	−1075	970	5.0×10^{-324}	1.7×10^{308}
decimal	System. Decimal	0	296	−26	0	1.0×10^{-28}	7.9×10^{28}

In addition to numeric types, three other simple types are available:

Type	Alias For	Allowed Values
char	System.Char	Single Unicode character, stored as an integer between 0 and 65535
bool	System.Boolean	Boolean value, true or false
string	System.String	A sequence of characters

Note that there is no upper limit on the amount of characters making up a string, because it can use varying amounts of memory.

The Boolean type bool is one of the most commonly used variable types in C#, and indeed similar types are equally prolific in code in other languages. Having a variable that can be either true or false has important ramifications when it comes to the flow of logic in an application. As a simple example, consider how many questions can be answered with true or false (or yes and no). Performing comparisons between variable values or validating input are just two of the programmatic uses of Boolean variables that you will examine very soon.

Now that you've seen these types, consider a short example that declares and uses them. In the following Try It Out you use some simple code that declares two variables, assigns them values, and then outputs these values.

Using Simple Type Variables

1. Create a new console application called Ch03Ex01 and save it in the directory C:\BegVCSharp\Chapter03.

2. Add the following code to `Program.cs`:

```
static void Main(string[] args)
{
    int myInteger;
    string myString;
    myInteger = 17;
    myString = "\"myInteger\" is";
    Console.WriteLine("{0} {1}.", myString, myInteger);
    Console.ReadKey();
}
```

3. Execute the code. The result is shown in Figure 3-1.

Figure 3-1

How It Works

The added code does three things:

❑ It declares two variables.

❑ It assigns values to those two variables.

❑ It outputs the values of the two variables to the console.

Variable declaration occurs in the following code:

```
int myInteger;
string myString;
```

The first line declares a variable of type `int` with a name of `myInteger`, and the second line declares a variable of type `string` called `myString`.

Variable naming is restricted; you can't use just any sequence of characters. You learn about this in the section on naming variables.

The next two lines of code assign values:

```
myInteger = 17;
myString = "\"myInteger\" is";
```

Here you assign two fixed values (known as *literal* values in code) to your variables using the = *assignment operator* (the "Expressions" section of this chapter has more details about operators). You assign the integer value 17 to `myInteger`, and the string `"myInteger"` (including the quotes) to `myString`. When you assign string literal values in this way, double quotation marks are required to enclose the string. Therefore, certain characters might cause problems if they are included in the string itself, such as the double quotation characters, and you must *escape* some characters by substituting a sequence of characters (an *escape sequence*) that represents the character(s) you want to use. In this example, you use the sequence \" to escape a double quotation mark:

```
myString = "\"myInteger\" is";
```

If you didn't use these escape sequences and tried coding this as

```
myString = ""myInteger" is";
```

you would get a compiler error.

Note that assigning string literals is another situation in which you must be careful with line breaks — the C# compiler rejects string literals that span more than one line. If you want to add a line break, then use the escape sequence for a carriage return in your string, which is \n. For example, the assignment

```
myString = "This string has a\nline break.";
```

would be displayed on two lines in the console view as follows:

```
This string has a
line break.
```

All escape sequences consist of the backslash symbol followed by one of a small set of characters (you'll see the full set later). Because this symbol is used for this purpose, there is also an escape sequence for the backslash symbol itself, which is simply two consecutive backslashes (\\).

Getting back to the code, there is one more new line to look at:

```
Console.WriteLine("{0} {1}.", myString, myInteger);
```

This looks similar to the simple method of writing text to the console that you saw in the first example, but now you are specifying your variables. To avoid getting ahead of ourselves here, we'll avoid a lot of the details about this line of code at this point. Suffice to say that it is the technique you will be using in the first part of this book to output text to the console window. Within the brackets you have two things:

❑   A string

❑   A list of variables whose values you want to insert into the output string, separated by commas

The string you are outputting, `"{0} {1}."`, doesn't seem to contain much useful text. As shown earlier, however, this is not what you actually see when you run the code. This is because the string is actually a template into which you insert the contents of your variables. Each set of curly brackets in the string is a placeholder that will contain the contents of one of the variables in the list.

Each placeholder (or format string) is represented as an integer enclosed in curly brackets. The integers start at 0 and are incremented by 1, and the total number of placeholders should match the number of variables specified in the comma-separated list following the string. When the text is output to the console, each placeholder is replaced by the corresponding value for each variable. In the preceding example, the {0} is replaced with the actual value of the first variable, myString, and {1} is replaced with the contents of myInteger.

This method of outputting text to the console is what you use to display output from your code in the examples that follow. Finally, the code has the line shown in the earlier example for waiting for user input before terminating:

```
Console.ReadKey();
```

Again, the code isn't dissected now, but you will see it frequently in later examples. For now, understand that it pauses code execution until you press a key.

Variable Naming

As mentioned in the previous section, you can't just choose any sequence of characters as a variable name. This isn't as worrying as it might sound at first, however, because you're still left with a very flexible naming system.

The basic variable naming rules are as follows:

❑ The first character of a variable name must be either a letter, an underscore character (_), or the *at* symbol (@).

❑ Subsequent characters may be letters, underscore characters, or numbers.

There are also certain keywords that have a specialized meaning to the C# compiler, such as the using and namespace keywords shown earlier. If you use one of these by mistake, the compiler complains, however, so don't worry about this.

For example, the following variable names are fine:

```
myBigVar
VAR1
_test
```

These are not, however:

```
99BottlesOfBeer
namespace
It's-All-Over
```

Remember that C# is case sensitive, so be careful not to forget the exact case used when you declare your variables. References to them made later in the program with even so much as a single letter in the wrong case prevents compilation. A further consequence of this is that you can have multiple variables whose names differ only in case. For example, the following are all separate names:

```
myVariable
MyVariable
MYVARIABLE
```

Naming Conventions

Variable names are something you will use *a lot*, so it's worth spending a bit of time learning the sort of names you should use. Before you get started, though, bear in mind that this is controversial ground. Over the years, different systems have come and gone, and many developers will fight tooth and nail to justify their personal system.

Until recently the most popular system was what is known as *Hungarian notation*. This system involves placing a lowercase prefix on all variable names that identify the type. For example, if a variable were of type int, then you might place an i (or n) in front of it, for example iAge. Using this system, it is easy to see a variable's type at a glance.

More modern languages, however, such as C#, make this system tricky to implement. For the types you've seen so far, you could probably come up with one- or two-letter prefixes signifying each type. However, because you can create your own types, and there are many hundreds of these more complex types in the basic .NET Framework, this quickly becomes unworkable. With several people working on a project, it would be easy for different people to come up with different and confusing prefixes, with potentially disastrous consequences.

Developers have realized that it is far better to name variables appropriately for their purpose. If any doubt arises, it is easy enough to work out what the type of a variable is. In VS and VCE, you just have to hover the mouse pointer over a variable name and a pop-up box tells you what the type is soon enough.

Currently, two naming conventions are used in the .NET Framework namespaces: *PascalCase* and *camelCase*. The case used in the names indicates their usage. They both apply to names that are made up of multiple words and they both specify that each word in a name should be in lowercase except for its first letter, which should be uppercase. For camelCase terms, there is an additional rule: The first word should start with a lowercase letter.

The following are camelCase variable names:

```
age
firstName
timeOfDeath
```

These are PascalCase:

```
Age
LastName
WinterOfDiscontent
```

For your simple variables, stick to camelCase. Use PascalCase for certain more advanced naming, which is the Microsoft recommendation. Finally, note that many past naming systems involved frequent use of the underscore character, usually as a separator between words in variable names, such as `yet_another_variable`. This usage is now discouraged (which is just as well; it looks ugly!).

Literal Values

The previous Try It Out showed two examples of literal values: `integer` and `string`. The other variable types also have associated literal values, as shown in the following table. Many of these involve *suffixes*, whereby you add a sequence of characters to the end of the literal value to specify the type desired. Some literals have multiple types, determined at compile time by the compiler based on their context (also shown in the table).

Type(s)	Category	Suffix	Example/Allowed Values
bool	Boolean	None	true or false
int, uint, long, ulong	Integer	None	100
uint, ulong	Integer	u or U	100U
long, ulong	Integer	l or L	100L
ulong	Integer	ul, uL, Ul, UL, lu, lU, Lu, or LU	100UL
float	Real	f or F	1.5F
double	Real	None, d, or D	1.5
decimal	Real	m or M	1.5M
Char	Character	None	'a', or escape sequence
String	String	None	"a...a", may include escape sequences

String Literals

Earlier in the chapter, you saw a few of the escape sequences you can use in `string` literals. Here is a full table of these for reference purposes:

Escape Sequence	Character Produced	Unicode Value of Character
\'	Single quotation mark	0x0027
\"	Double quotation mark	0x0022
\\	Backslash	0x005C
\0	Null	0x0000
\a	Alert (causes a beep)	0x0007
\b	Backspace	0x0008
\f	Form feed	0x000C
\n	New line	0x000A
\r	Carriage return	0x000D
\t	Horizontal tab	0x0009
\v	Vertical tab	0x000B

The Unicode Value column of the preceding table shows the hexadecimal values of the characters as they are found in the Unicode character set. As well as the preceding, you can specify any Unicode character using a Unicode escape sequence. These consist of the standard \ character followed by a u and a four-digit hexadecimal value (for example, the four digits after the x in the preceding table).

This means that the following strings are equivalent:

```
"Karli\'s string."
"Karli\u0027s string."
```

Obviously, you have more versatility using Unicode escape sequences.

You can also specify strings *verbatim*. This means that all characters contained between two double quotation marks are included in the string, including end-of-line characters and characters that would otherwise need escaping. The only exception to this is the escape sequence for the double quotation mark character, which must be specified to avoid ending the string. To do this, place the @ character before the string:

```
@"Verbatim string literal."
```

This string could just as easily be specified in the normal way, but the following requires this method:

```
@"A short list:
item 1
item 2"
```

Verbatim strings are particularly useful in filenames, as these use plenty of backslash characters. Using normal strings, you'd have to use double backslashes all the way along the string:

```
"C:\\Temp\\MyDir\\MyFile.doc"
```

With verbatim string literals you can make this more readable. The following verbatim string is equivalent to the preceding one:

```
@"C:\Temp\MyDir\MyFile.doc"
```

As shown later in the book, strings are reference types, unlike the other types you've seen in this chapter, which are value types. One consequence of this is that strings can also be assigned the value null, *which means that the string variable doesn't reference a string (or anything, for that matter).*

Variable Declaration and Assignment

To recap, recall that you declare variables simply using their type and name:

```
int age;
```

You then assign values to variables using the = assignment operator:

```
age = 25;
```

Remember that variables must be initialized before you use them. The preceding assignment could be used as an initialization.

There are a couple of other things you can do here that you are likely to see in C# code. One, you can declare multiple variables of the same type at the same time by separating their names with commas after the type, as shown here:

```
int xSize, ySize;
```

Here, xSize and ySize are both declared as integer types.

The second technique you are likely to see is assigning values to variables when you declare them, which basically means combining two lines of code:

```
int age = 25;
```

You can use both these techniques together:

```
int xSize = 4, ySize = 5;
```

Here, both `xSize` and `ySize` are assigned different values. Note that

```
int xSize, ySize = 5;
```

results in only `ySize` being initialized — `xSize` is just declared, and it still needs to be initialized before it's used.

Expressions

Now that you've learned how to declare and initialize variables, it's time to look at manipulating them. C# contains a number of *operators* for this purpose, including the = assignment operator you've used already. By combining operators with variables and literal values (together referred to as *operands* when used with operators), you can create *expressions*, which are the basic building blocks of computation.

The operators available range from the simple to the highly complex, some of which you might never encounter outside of mathematical applications. The simple ones include all the basic mathematical operations, such as the + operator to add two operands; the complex ones include manipulations of variable content via the binary representation of this content. There are also logical operators specifically for dealing with Boolean values, and assignment operators such as =.

This chapter focuses on the mathematical and assignment operators, leaving the logical ones for the next chapter, where you examine Boolean logic in the context of controlling program flow.

Operators can be roughly classified into three categories:

- ❑ **Unary:** Act on single operands
- ❑ **Binary:** Act on two operands
- ❑ **Ternary:** Act on three operands

Most operators fall into the binary category, with a few unary ones, and a single ternary one called the *conditional operator* (the conditional operator is a logical one and is discussed in Chapter 4). Let's start by looking at the mathematical operators, which span both the unary and binary categories.

Mathematical Operators

There are five simple mathematical operators, two of which (+ and -) have both binary and unary forms. The following table lists each of these operators, along with a short example of its use and the result when it's used with simple numeric types (integer and floating point).

Operator	Category	Example Expression	Result
+	Binary	var1 = var2 + var3;	var1 is assigned the value that is the sum of var2 and var3.
-	Binary	var1 = var2 - var3;	var1 is assigned the value that is the value of var3 subtracted from the value of var2.
*	Binary	var1 = var2 * var3;	var1 is assigned the value that is the product of var2 and var3.
/	Binary	var1 = var2 / var3;	var1 is assigned the value that is the result of dividing var2 by var3.
%	Binary	var1 = var2 % var3;	var1 is assigned the value that is the remainder when var2 is divided by var3.
+	Unary	var1 = +var2;	var1 is assigned the value of var2.
-	Unary	var1 = -var2;	var1 is assigned the value of var2 multiplied by -1.

The + (unary) operator is slightly odd, as it has no effect on the result. It doesn't force values to be positive, as you might assume — if var2 is -1, then +var is also -1. However, it is a universally recognized operator, and as such is included. The most useful fact about this operator is shown later in this book when you look at operator overloading.

The examples use simple numeric types because the result can be unclear when using the other simple types. What would you expect if you added two Boolean values together, for example? In this case, nothing, because the compiler complains if you try to use + (or any of the other mathematical operators) with bool variables. Adding char variables is also slightly confusing. Remember that char variables are actually stored as numbers, so adding two char variables together also results in a number (of type int, to be precise). This is an example of *implicit conversion*, which you'll learn a lot more about shortly (and *explicit conversion*), because it also applies to cases where var1, var2, and var3 are of mixed types.

The binary + operator *does* make sense when used with string type variables. In this case, the table entry should read as shown in the following table:

Operator	Category	Example Expression	Result
+	Binary	var1 = var2 + var3;	var1 is assigned the value that is the concatenation of the two strings stored in var2 and var3.

None of the other mathematical operators, however, work with strings.

The other two operators you should look at here are the increment and decrement operators, both of which are unary operators that can be used in two ways: either immediately before or immediately after the operand. The results obtained in simple expressions are shown in the next table:

Operator	Category	Example Expression	Result
++	Unary	`var1 = ++var2;`	var1 is assigned the value of var2 + 1. var2 is incremented by 1.
--	Unary	`var1 = --var2;`	var1 is assigned the value of var2 - 1. var2 is decremented by 1.
++	Unary	`var1 = var2++;`	var1 is assigned the value of var2. var2 is incremented by 1.
--	Unary	`var1 = var2--;`	var1 is assigned the value of var2. var2 is decremented by 1.

These operators always result in a change to the value stored in their operand:

❑   ++ always results in its operand being incremented by one.

❑   -- always results in its operand being decremented by one.

The differences between the results stored in var1 are a consequence of the fact that the placement of the operator determines when it takes effect. Placing one of these operators before its operand means that the operand is affected before any other computation takes place. Placing it after the operand means that the operand is affected after all other computation of the expression is completed.

This merits another example! Consider this code:

```
int var1, var2 = 5, var3 = 6;
var1 = var2++ * --var3;
```

What value will be assigned to var1? Before the expression is evaluated, the -- operator preceding var3 takes effect, changing its value from 6 to 5. You can ignore the ++ operator that follows var2, as it won't take effect until after the calculation is completed, so var1 will be the product of 5 and 5, or 25.

These simple unary operators come in very handy in a surprising number of situations. They are really just a shorthand for expressions such as this:

```
var1 = var1 + 1;
```

This sort of expression has many uses, particularly where *looping* is concerned, as shown in the next chapter. The following Try It Out provides an example of how to use the mathematical operators, and it introduces a couple of other useful concepts as well. The code prompts you to type in a string and two numbers and then demonstrates the results of performing some calculations.

Try It Out   **Manipulating Variables with Mathematical Operators**

1.   Create a new console application called Ch03Ex02 and save it to the directory
     C:\BegVCSharp\Chapter03.

2.   Add the following code to `Program.cs`:

```
static void Main(string[] args)
{
    double firstNumber, secondNumber;
    string userName;
    Console.WriteLine("Enter your name:");
    userName = Console.ReadLine();
    Console.WriteLine("Welcome {0}!", userName);
    Console.WriteLine("Now give me a number:");
    firstNumber = Convert.ToDouble(Console.ReadLine());
    Console.WriteLine("Now give me another number:");
    secondNumber = Convert.ToDouble(Console.ReadLine());
    Console.WriteLine("The sum of {0} and {1} is {2}.", firstNumber,
            secondNumber, firstNumber + secondNumber);
    Console.WriteLine("The result of subtracting {0} from {1} is {2}.",
            secondNumber, firstNumber, firstNumber - secondNumber);
    Console.WriteLine("The product of {0} and {1} is {2}.", firstNumber,
            secondNumber, firstNumber * secondNumber);
    Console.WriteLine("The result of dividing {0} by {1} is {2}.",
            firstNumber, secondNumber, firstNumber / secondNumber);
    Console.WriteLine("The remainder after dividing {0} by {1} is {2}.",
            firstNumber, secondNumber, firstNumber % secondNumber);
    Console.ReadKey();
}
```

3.   Execute the code. The display shown in Figure 3-2 appears.

Figure 3-2

4. Enter your name and press Enter, as shown in Figure 3-3.

Figure 3-3

5. Enter a number, press Enter, then another number, then Enter again, as shown in Figure 3-4.

Figure 3-4

How It Works

As well as demonstrating the mathematical operators, this code introduces two important concepts that you will often come across:

❑ User input

❑ Type conversion

User input uses a syntax similar to the `Console.WriteLine()` command you've already seen — you use `Console.ReadLine()`. This command prompts the user for input, which is stored in a `string` variable:

```
string userName;
Console.WriteLine("Enter your name:");
userName = Console.ReadLine();
Console.WriteLine("Welcome {0}!", userName);
```

This code writes the contents of the assigned variable, `userName`, straight to the screen.

You also read in two numbers in this example. This is slightly more involved, because the `Console.ReadLine()` command generates a string, but you want a number. This introduces the topic of *type conversion*. This is covered in more detail in Chapter 5, but let's have a look at the code used in this example.

First, you declare the variables you want to store the number input in:

```
double firstNumber, secondNumber;
```

Next, you supply a prompt and use the command `Convert.ToDouble()` on a string obtained by `Console.ReadLine()` to convert the string into a `double` type. You assign this number to the `firstNumber` variable you have declared:

```
Console.WriteLine("Now give me a number:");
firstNumber = Convert.ToDouble(Console.ReadLine());
```

This syntax is remarkably simple, and many other conversions can be performed in a similar way.

The remainder of the code obtains a second number in the same way:

```
Console.WriteLine("Now give me another number:");
secondNumber = Convert.ToDouble(Console.ReadLine());
```

Next, you output the results of adding, subtracting, multiplying, and dividing the two numbers, in addition to displaying the remainder after division, using the remainder (%) operator:

```
Console.WriteLine("The sum of {0} and {1} is {2}.", firstNumber,
        secondNumber, firstNumber + secondNumber);
Console.WriteLine("The result of subtracting {0} from {1} is {2}.",
        secondNumber, firstNumber, firstNumber - secondNumber);
Console.WriteLine("The product of {0} and {1} is {2}.", firstNumber,
        secondNumber, firstNumber * secondNumber);
Console.WriteLine("The result of dividing {0} by {1} is {2}.",
        firstNumber, secondNumber, firstNumber / secondNumber);
Console.WriteLine("The remainder after dividing {0} by {1} is {2}.",
        firstNumber, secondNumber, firstNumber % secondNumber);
```

Note that you are supplying the expressions, `firstNumber + secondNumber` and so on, as a parameter to the `Console.WriteLine()` statement, without using an intermediate variable:

```
Console.WriteLine("The sum of {0} and {1} is {2}.", firstNumber,
        secondNumber, firstNumber + secondNumber);
```

This kind of syntax can make your code very readable, and reduce the number of lines of code you need to write.

Assignment Operators

So far, you've been using the simple = assignment operator, and it may come as a surprise that any other assignment operators exist at all. There are more, however, and the biggest surprise is probably that they're quite useful! All of the assignment operators other than = work in a similar way. Like =, they all result in a value being assigned to the variable on their left side based on the operands and operators on their right side.

The following table describes the operators:

Operator	Category	Example Expression	Result
=	Binary	`var1 = var2;`	var1 is assigned the value of var2.
+=	Binary	`var1 += var2;`	var1 is assigned the value that is the sum of var1 and var2.
-=	Binary	`var1 -= var2;`	var1 is assigned the value that is the value of var2 subtracted from the value of var1.
*=	Binary	`var1 *= var2;`	var1 is assigned the value that is the product of var1 and var2.
/=	Binary	`var1 /= var2;`	var1 is assigned the value that is the result of dividing var1 by var2.
%=	Binary	`var1 %= var2;`	var1 is assigned the value that is the remainder when var1 is divided by var2.

As you can see, the additional operators result in var1 being included in the calculation, so code like

```
var1 += var2;
```

has exactly the same result as

```
var1 = var1 + var2;
```

> *The += operator can also be used with strings, just like +.*

Using these operators, especially when employing long variable names, can make code much easier to read.

Operator Precedence

When an expression is evaluated, each operator is processed in sequence, but this doesn't necessarily mean evaluating these operators from left to right. As a trivial example, consider the following:

```
var1 = var2 + var3;
```

Here, the + operator acts before the = operator. There are other situations where operator precedence isn't so obvious, as shown here:

```
var1 = var2 + var3 * var4;
```

In the preceding example, the * operator acts first, followed by the + operator, and finally the = operator. This is standard mathematical order, and it provides the same result as you would expect from working out the equivalent algebraic calculation on paper.

Similarly, you can gain control over operator precedence by using parentheses, as shown in this example:

```
var1 = (var2 + var3) * var4;
```

Here, the content of the parentheses is evaluated first, meaning that the + operator acts before the * operator.

The following table shows the order of precedence for the operators you've encountered so far, whereby operators of equal precedence (such as * and /) are evaluated from left to right:

Precedence	Operators
Highest	++, -- (used as prefixes); +, - (unary)
	*, /, %
	+, -
	=, *=, /=, %=, +=, -=
Lowest	++, -- (used as suffixes)

You can use parentheses to override this precedence order, as described previously. In addition, note that ++ and --, when used as suffixes, only have lowest priority in conceptual terms, as described in the table. They don't operate on the result of, say, an assignment expression, so you can consider them to have a higher priority than all other operators. However, because they change the value of their operand after expression evaluation, it's easier to think of their precedence as shown in the preceding table.

Namespaces

Before moving on, it's worthwhile to consider one more important subject — *namespaces*. These are the .NET way of providing containers for application code, such that code and its contents may be uniquely identified. Namespaces are also used as a means of categorizing items in the .NET Framework. Most of these items are type definitions, such as the simple types in this chapter (System.Int32 and so on).

C# code, by default, is contained in the *global namespace*. This means that items contained in this code are accessible from other code in the global namespace simply by referring to them by name. You can use the namespace keyword, however, to explicitly define the namespace for a block of code enclosed in curly brackets. Names in such a namespace must be *qualified* if they are used from code outside of this namespace.

A qualified name is one that contains all of its hierarchical information, which basically means that if you have code in one namespace that needs to use a name defined in a different namespace, you must include a reference to this namespace. Qualified names use period characters (.) between namespace levels, as shown here:

```
namespace LevelOne
{
    // code in LevelOne namespace

    // name "NameOne" defined
}

// code in global namespace
```

This code defines one namespace, LevelOne, and a name in this namespace, NameOne (no actual code is shown here to keep the discussion general; instead, a comment appears where the definition would go). Code written inside the LevelOne namespace can simply refer to this name using NameOne — no classification is necessary. Code in the global namespace, however, must refer to this name using the classified name LevelOne.NameOne.

Within a namespace, you can define nested namespaces, also using the namespace keyword. Nested namespaces are referred to via their hierarchy, again using periods to classify each level of the hierarchy. This is best illustrated with an example. Consider the following namespaces:

```
namespace LevelOne
{
    // code in LevelOne namespace

    namespace LevelTwo
    {
        // code in LevelOne.LevelTwo namespace

        // name "NameTwo" defined
    }
}

// code in global namespace
```

Here, NameTwo must be referred to as LevelOne.LevelTwo.NameTwo from the global namespace, LevelTwo.NameTwo from the LevelOne namespace, and NameTwo from the LevelOne.LevelTwo namespace.

The important point here is that names are uniquely defined by their namespace. You could define the name NameThree in the LevelOne and LevelTwo namespaces:

```
namespace LevelOne
{
    // name "NameThree" defined

    namespace LevelTwo
    {
        // name "NameThree" defined
    }
}
```

This defines two separate names, `LevelOne.NameThree` and `LevelOne.LevelTwo.NameThree`, which can be used independently of each other.

After namespaces are set up, you can use the `using` statement to simplify access to the names they contain. In effect, the `using` statement says, "OK, I'll be needing names from this namespace, so don't bother asking me to classify them every time." For example, the following code says that code in the `LevelOne` namespace should have access to names in the `LevelOne.LevelTwo` namespace without classification:

```
namespace LevelOne
{
    using LevelTwo;

    namespace LevelTwo
    {
        // name "NameTwo" defined
    }
}
```

Code in the `LevelOne` namespace can now refer to `LevelTwo.NameTwo` by simply using `NameTwo`.

Sometimes, as with the `NameThree` example shown previously, this can lead to problems with clashes between identical names in different namespaces (if you use such a name, then your code won't compile — and the compiler will let you know that there is an ambiguity). In cases such as these, you can provide an *alias* for a namespace as part of the `using` statement:

```
namespace LevelOne
{
    using LT = LevelTwo;

    // name "NameThree" defined

    namespace LevelTwo
    {
        // name "NameThree" defined
    }
}
```

Here, code in the `LevelOne` namespace can refer to `LevelOne.NameThree` as `NameThree` and `LevelOne.LevelTwo.NameThree` as `LT.NameThree`.

`using` statements apply to the namespace they are contained in, and any nested namespaces that might also be contained in this namespace. In the preceding code, the global namespace can't use `LT.NameThree`. However, if this `using` statement were declared as

```
using LT = LevelOne.LevelTwo;

namespace LevelOne
{
    // name "NameThree" defined

    namespace LevelTwo
    {
        // name "NameThree" defined
    }
}
```

then code in the global namespace and the LevelOne namespace can use LT.NameThree.

Note one more important point here: The using statement doesn't in itself give you access to names in another namespace. Unless the code in a namespace is in some way linked to your project, by being defined in a source file in the project or being defined in some other code linked to the project, you won't have access to the names contained. In addition, if code containing a namespace is linked to your project, then you have access to the names contained in that code, regardless of whether you use using. using simply makes it easier for you to access these names and can shorten otherwise lengthy code to make it more readable.

Going back to the code in ConsoleApplication1 shown at the beginning of this chapter, the following lines that apply to namespaces appear:

```
using System;
using System.Collections.Generic;
using System.Text;

namespace ConsoleApplication1
{
    ...
}
```

The three lines that start with the using keyword are used to declare that the System, System .Collections.Generic, and System.Text namespaces will be used in this C# code and should be accessible from all namespaces in this file without classification. The System namespace is the root namespace for .NET Framework applications and contains all the basic functionality you need for console applications. The other two namespaces are very often used in console applications, so they are there just in case.

Finally, a namespace is declared for the application code itself, ConsoleApplication1.

Summary

In this chapter, you covered a fair amount of ground on the way to creating usable (if basic) C# applications. You've looked at the basic C# syntax and analyzed the basic console application code that VS and VCE generate for you when you create a console application project.

The major part of this chapter concerned the use of variables. You have seen what variables are, how you create them, how you assign values to them, and how you manipulate them and the values that they contain. Along the way, you've also looked at some basic user interaction, which showed how you can output text to a console application and read user input back in. This involved some very basic type conversion, a complex subject that is covered in more depth in Chapter 5.

You also learned how you can assemble operators and operands into expressions, and looked at the way these are executed and the order in which this takes place.

Finally, you looked at namespaces, which will become increasingly important as the book progresses. By introducing this topic in a fairly abstract way here, the groundwork is completed for later discussions.

This chapter covered all of the following:

❑　　How basic C# syntax works

❑　　What Visual Studio does when you create a console application project

❑　　How to understand and use variables

❑　　How to understand and use expressions

❑　　What a namespace is

So far, all of your programming has taken the form of line-by-line execution. In the next chapter, you learn how to make your code more efficient by controlling the flow of execution using looping techniques and conditional branching.

Exercises

1. In the following code, how would you refer to the name `great` from code in the namespace `fabulous`?

```
namespace fabulous
{
   // code in fabulous namespace
}

namespace super
{
   namespace smashing
   {
      // great name defined
   }
}
```

2. Which of the following is not a legal variable name:

- ❏ myVariableIsGood
- ❏ 99Flake
- ❏ _floor
- ❏ time2GetJiggyWidIt
- ❏ wrox.com

3. Is the string `"supercalifragilisticexpialidocious"` too big to fit in a `string` variable? If so, why?

4. By considering operator precedence, list the steps involved in the computation of the following expression:

```
resultVar += var1 * var2 + var3 % var4 / var5;
```

5. Write a console application that obtains four `int` values from the user and displays the product. Hint: You may recall that the `Convert.ToDouble()` command was used to convert the input from the console to a `double`; the equivalent command to convert from a `string` to an `int` is `Convert.ToInt32()`.

4

Flow Control

All of the C# code you've seen so far has had one thing in common. In each case, program execution has proceeded from one line to the next in top-to-bottom order, missing nothing. If all applications worked like this, then you would be very limited in what you could do. This chapter describes two methods for controlling program flow — that is, the order of execution of lines of C# code: *branching* and *looping*. Branching executes code conditionally, depending on the outcome of an evaluation, such as "only execute this code if the variable myVal is less than 10." Looping repeatedly executes the same statements (a certain number of times or until a test condition has been reached).

Both of these techniques involve the use of *Boolean logic*. In the last chapter you saw the bool type, but didn't actually do much with it. This chapter uses it a lot, so the chapter begins by discussing what is meant by Boolean logic so that you can use it in flow control scenarios.

This chapter covers the following main topics:

❑   Boolean logic and how to use it.

❑   How to control the execution of your code.

Boolean Logic

The bool type introduced in the previous chapter can hold one of only two values: true or false. This type is often used to record the result of some operation, so that you can act on this result. In particular, bool types are used to store the result of a *comparison*.

> *As a historical aside, it is the work of the mid-nineteenth-century English mathematician George Boole that forms the basis of Boolean logic.*

For instance, consider the situation (mentioned in the chapter introduction) in which you want to execute code based on whether a variable, myVal, is less than 10. To do this, you need some indication of whether the statement "myVal is less than 10" is true or false — that is, you need to know the Boolean result of a comparison.

Boolean comparisons require the use of Boolean *comparison operators* (also known as *relational operators*), which are shown in the following table. In all cases here, var1 is a bool type variable, whereas the types of var2 and var3 may vary.

Operator	Category	Example Expression	Result
==	Binary	var1 = var2== var3;	var1 is assigned the value true if var2 is equal to var3, or false otherwise.
!=	Binary	var1 = var2 != var3;	var1 is assigned the value true if var2 is not equal to var3, or false otherwise.
<	Binary	var1 = var2 < var3;	var1 is assigned the value true if var2 is less than var3, or false otherwise.
>	Binary	var1 = var2 > var3;	var1 is assigned the value true if var2 is greater than var3, or false otherwise.
<=	Binary	var1 = var2 <= var3;	var1 is assigned the value true if var2 is less than or equal to var3, or false otherwise.
>=	Binary	var1 = var2 >= var3;	var1 is assigned the value true if var2 is greater than or equal to var3, or false otherwise.

You might use operators such as these on numeric values in code:

```
bool isLessThan10;
isLessThan10 = myVal < 10;
```

This code results in isLessThan10 being assigned the value true if myVal stores a value less than 10, or false otherwise.

You can also use these comparison operators on other types, such as strings:

```
bool isKarli;
isKarli = myString == "Karli";
```

Here, isKarli is true only if myString stores the string "Karli".

You can also focus on Boolean values:

```
bool isTrue;
isTrue = myBool == true;
```

Here, however, you are limited to the use of == and != operators.

A common code error occurs if you unintentionally assume that because val1 < val2 *is false,* val1 > val2 *is true. If* val1 == val2, *then both these statements are false.*

Some other Boolean operators are intended specifically for working with Boolean values, as shown in the following table:

Operator	Category	Example Expression	Result
!	Unary	var1 = ! var2;	var1 is assigned the value true if var2 is false, or false if var2 is true. (Logical NOT)
&	Binary	var1 = var2 & var3;	var1 is assigned the value true if var2 and var3 are both true, or false otherwise. (Logical AND)
|	Binary	var1 = var2 | var3;	var1 is assigned the value true if either var2 or var3 (or both) is true, or false otherwise. (Logical OR)
^	Binary	var1 = var2 ^ var3;	var1 is assigned the value true if either var2 or var3, but not both, is true, or false otherwise. (Logical XOR or exclusive OR)

Therefore, the previous code snippet could also be expressed as follows:

```
bool isTrue;
isTrue = myBool & true;
```

The & and | operators also have two similar operators, known as *conditional Boolean* operators, shown in the following table:

Operator	Category	Example Expression	Result
&&	Binary	var1 = var2 && var3;	var1 is assigned the value true if var2 and var3 are both true, or false otherwise. (Logical AND)
||	Binary	var1 = var2 || var3;	var1 is assigned the value true if either var2 or var3 (or both) is true, or false otherwise. (Logical OR)

The result of these operators is exactly the same as & and |, but note an important difference in the way this result is obtained, which can result in better performance. Both of these look at the value of their first operands (var2 in the preceding table) and, based on the value of this operand, may not need to process the second operators (var3 in the preceding table) at all.

If the value of the first operand of the && operator is false, then there is no need to consider the value of the second operand, because the result will be false regardless. Similarly, the || operator returns true if its first operand is true, regardless of the value of the second operand. This isn't the case for the & and | operators shown earlier. With these, both operands are always evaluated.

Because of this conditional evaluation of operands, you get a small performance increase if you use && and || instead of & and |. This is particularly apparent in applications that use these operators a lot. As a rule of thumb, *always* use && and || where possible. These operators really come into their own in more complicated situations, where computation of the second operand is possible only with certain values of the first operand, as shown in this example:

```
var1 = (var2 != 0) && (var3 / var2 > 2);
```

Here, if var2 is zero, then dividing var3 by var2 results in either a "division by zero" error or var1 being defined as infinite (the latter is possible, and detectable, with some types, such as float).

Bitwise Operators

At this point, you may be asking why the & and | operators exist at all. The reason is that these operators may be used to perform operations on numeric values. In fact, they operate on the series of bits stored in a variable, rather than the value of the variable.

Let's consider these in turn, starting with &. Each bit in the first operand is compared with the bit in the same position in the second operand, resulting in the bit in the same position in the resultant value being assigned a value, as shown in the following table:

Operand 1 Bit	Operand 2 Bit	& Result Bit
1	1	1
1	0	0
0	1	0
0	0	0

| is similar, but the result bits are different, as shown in this table:

Operand 1 Bit	Operand 2 Bit	| Result Bit
1	1	1
1	0	1
0	1	1
0	0	0

For example, consider the operation shown here:

```
int result, op1, op2;
op1 = 4;
op2 = 5;
result = op1 & op2;
```

In this case, you must consider the binary representations of op1 and op2, which are 100 and 101, respectively. The result is obtained by comparing the binary digits in equivalent positions in these two representations as follows:

❑ The leftmost bit of result is 1 if the leftmost bits of op1 and op2 are both 1, or 0 otherwise.

❑ The next bit of result is 1 if the next bits of op1 and op2 are both 1, or 0 otherwise.

❑ Continue for all remaining bits.

In this example, the leftmost bits of op1 and op2 are both 1, so the leftmost bit of result will be 1, too. The next bits are both 0, and the third bits are 1 and 0, respectively, so the second and third bits of result will be 0. The final value of result in binary representation is therefore 100, so the result is assigned the value 4. This is shown graphically in the following table:

	1	0	0			4
&	1	0	1		&	5
	1	0	0			4

The same process occurs if you use the | operator, except that in this case each result bit is 1 if either of the operand bits in the same position is 1, as shown in the following table:

	1	0	0			4
|	1	0	1		|	5
	1	0	1			5

You can also use the ^ operator in the same way, where each result bit is 1 if one or other of the operand bits in the same position is 1, but not both, as shown in the following table:

Operand 1 Bit	Operand 2 Bit	^ Result Bit
1	1	0
1	0	1
0	1	1
0	0	0

C# also allows the use of a unary bitwise operator (~), which acts on its operand by inverting each of its bits, such that the result is a variable having values of 1 for each bit in the operand that is 0, and vice versa. This is shown in the following table:

Operand Bit	~ Result Bit
1	0
0	1

The way integer numbers are stored in .NET, known as Two's Complement, means that using the ~ unary operator can lead to results that look a little odd. If you remember that an int type is a 32-bit number, for example, then knowing that the ~ operator acts on all 32 of those bits can help you to see what is going on. For example, the number 5 in its full binary representation is as follows:

```
00000000000000000000000000000101
```

The number –5 is this:

```
11111111111111111111111111111011
```

In fact, by the Two's Complement system, (–x) is defined as (~x + 1). That may seem odd, but this system is very useful when it comes to adding numbers. For example, adding 10 and –5 (that is, subtracting 5 from 10) looks like this in binary format:

```
    00000000000000000000000000001010
+   11111111111111111111111111111011
=  100000000000000000000000000000101
```

By ignoring the 1 on the far left, you are left with the binary representation for 5. So while results such as ~1 = –2 may look odd, the underlying structures force this result.

The bitwise operations you've seen in this section are quite useful in certain situations, because they enable an easy method of making use of individual variable bits to store information. Consider a simple representation of a color using three bits to specify red, green, and blue content. You can set these bits independently to change the three bits to one of the configurations shown in the following table:

Bits	Decimal Representation	Meaning
000	0	black
100	4	red
010	2	green
001	1	blue
101	5	magenta

Bits	Decimal Representation	Meaning
110	6	yellow
011	3	cyan
111	7	white

Suppose you store these values in a variable of type `int`. Starting from a black color — that is, an `int` variable with the value of 0 — you can perform operations like this:

```
int myColor = 0;
bool containsRed;
myColor = myColor | 2;           // Add green bit, myColor now stores 010
myColor = myColor | 4;           // Add red bit, myColor now stores 110
containsRed = (myColor & 4) == 4; // Check value of red bit
```

The final line of code assigns a value of `true` to `containsRed`, as the red bit of `myColor` is 1. This technique can be quite useful for making efficient use of information, particularly because the operations involved can be used to check the values of multiple bits simultaneously (32 in the case of `int` values). However, there are better ways to store extra information in single variables (making use of the advanced variable types discussed in the next chapter).

In addition to these four bitwise operators, this section considers two others, shown in the following table:

Operator	Category	Example Expression	Result
>>	Binary	`var1 = var2 >> var3;`	var1 is assigned the value obtained when the binary content of var2 is shifted var3 bits to the right.
<<	Binary	`var1 = var2 << var3;`	var1 is assigned the value obtained when the binary content of var2 is shifted var3 bits to the left.

These operators, commonly called *bitwise shift operators*, are best illustrated with a quick example:

```
int var1, var2 = 10, var3 = 2;
var1 = var2 << var3;
```

Here, `var1` is assigned the value 40. This can be explained by considering that the binary representation of 10 is 1010, which shifted to the left by two places is 101000 — the binary representation of 40. In effect, you have carried out a multiplication operation. Each bit shifted to the left multiplies the value by 2, so two bit-shifts to the left result in multiplication by 4. Conversely, each bit shifted to the right has the effect of dividing the operand by 2, with any integer remainder being lost:

```
int var1, var2 = 10;
var1 = var2 >> 1;
```

In this example, `var1` contains the value 5, whereas the following code gives a value of 2:

```
int var1, var2 = 10;
var1 = var2 >> 2;
```

You are unlikely to use these operators in most code, but it is worth being aware of their existence. Their primary use is in highly optimized code, where the overhead of other mathematical operations just won't do. For this reason, they are often used in, for example, device drivers or system code.

Boolean Assignment Operators

The last operators to look at in this section are those that combine some of the operators you've seen previously with assignment, much like the mathematical assignment operators in the preceding chapter (+=, *=, and so on). These are shown in the following table:

Operator	Category	Example Expression	Result
&=	Binary	var1 &= var2;	var1 is assigned the value that is the result of var1 & var2.
|=	Binary	var1 |= var2;	var1 is assigned the value that is the result of var1 | var2.
^=	Binary	var1 ^= var2;	var1 is assigned the value that is the result of var1 ^ var2.

These work with both Boolean and numeric values in the same way as &, |, and ^.

Note that &= and |= use & and |, not && and ||, and that they have the overhead associated with these simpler operators.

The bitwise shift operators also have assignment operators, as shown in the following table:

Operator	Category	Example Expression	Result
>>=	Unary	var1 >>= var2;	var1 is assigned the value obtained when the binary content of var1 is shifted var2 bits to the right.
<<=	Unary	var1 <<= var2;	var1 is assigned the value obtained when the binary content of var1 is shifted var2 bits to the left.

Now it's time for an example. In the Try It Out that follows, you type in an integer and then the code performs various Boolean evaluations using that integer.

Using the Boolean and Bitwise Operators

1.   Create a new console application called Ch04Ex01 and save it in the directory
      C:\BegVCSharp\Chapter04.

2.   Add the following code to `Program.cs`:

```
static void Main(string[] args)
{
    Console.WriteLine("Enter an integer:");
    int myInt = Convert.ToInt32(Console.ReadLine());
    Console.WriteLine("Integer less than 10? {0}", myInt < 10);
    Console.WriteLine("Integer between 0 and 5? {0}",
                     (0 <= myInt) && (myInt <= 5));
    Console.WriteLine("Bitwise AND of Integer and 10 = {0}", myInt & 10);
    Console.ReadKey();
}
```

3.   Execute the application and enter an integer when prompted. The result is shown in Figure 4-1.

Figure 4-1

How It Works

The first two lines of code prompt for and accept an integer value using techniques you've already seen:

```
Console.WriteLine("Enter an integer:");
int myInt = Convert.ToInt32(Console.ReadLine());
```

You use `Convert.ToInt32()` to obtain an integer from the string input, which is simply another conversion command in the same family as the `Convert.ToDouble()` command used previously.

The remaining three lines of code perform various operations on the number obtained and display the results. You work through this code assuming that the user enters 6, as shown in the screenshot.

The first output is the result of the operation `myInt<10`. If `myInt` is 6, which is less than 10, then the result is `true`, which is what you see displayed. Values of `myInt` of 10 or higher result in `false`.

The second output is a more involved calculation: `(0 <= myInt) && (myInt <= 5)`. This involves two comparison operations, to determine whether `myInt` is greater than or equal to 0 and less than or equal to 5, and a Boolean AND operation on the results obtained. With a value of 6, `(0 <= myInt)` returns `true`, and `(myInt <= 5)` returns `false`. The result is then `(true)&&(false)`, which is `false`, as you can see from the display.

Finally, you perform a bitwise AND on the value of myInt. The other operand is 10, which has the binary representation 1010. If myInt is 6, which has the binary representation 110, then the result of this operation is 10, or 2 in decimal, as shown in the following table:

	0	1	1	0			6
&	1	0	1	0		&	10
	0	0	1	0			2

Operator Precedence Updated

Now that you have a few more operators to consider, the operator precedence table from the previous chapter should be updated to include them. The new order is shown in the following table:

Precedence	Operators
Highest	++, -- (used as prefixes); (), +, - (unary), !, ~
	*, /, %
	+, -
	<<, >>
	<, >, <=, >=
	==, !=
	&
	^
	|
	&&
	||
	=, *=, /=, %=, +=, -=, <<=, >>=, &=, ^=, |=
Lowest	++, -- (used as suffixes)

This adds quite a few more levels, but explicitly defines how expressions such as the following will be evaluated, where the && operator is processed after the <= and >= operators:

```
var1 = var2 <= 4 && var2 >= 2;
```

Note that it doesn't hurt to add parentheses to make expressions such as this one clearer. The compiler knows what order to process operators in, but we humans are prone to forget such things (and you might want to change the order). Writing the previous expression as

```
var1 = (var2 <= 4) && (var2 >= 2);
```

solves this problem by explicitly ordering the computation.

The goto Statement

C# enables you to label lines of code and then jump straight to them using the goto statement. This has its benefits and problems. The main benefit is that it's a simple way to control what code is executed when. The main problem is that excessive use of this technique can result in difficult-to-understand *spaghetti* code.

The goto statement is used as follows:

```
goto <labelName>;
```

Labels are defined as follows:

```
<labelName>:
```

For example, consider the following:

```
int myInteger = 5;
goto myLabel;
myInteger += 10;
myLabel:
Console.WriteLine("myInteger = {0}", myInteger);
```

Execution proceeds as follows:

❑   myInteger is declared as an int type and assigned the value 5.

❑   The goto statement interrupts normal execution and transfers control to the line marked myLabel:.

❑   The value of myInteger is written to the console.

The line highlighted in the following code is never executed:

```
int myInteger = 5;
goto myLabel;
myInteger += 10;
myLabel:
Console.WriteLine("myInteger = {0}", myInteger);
```

In fact, if you try this out in an application, this is noted in the Error List window as a warning when you try to compile the code, labeled "Unreachable code detected," along with location details. You will also see a wavy green line under myInteger on the unreachable line of code.

goto statements have their uses, but they can make things very confusing indeed. The following example shows some spaghetti code arising from the use of goto:

```
start:
int myInteger = 5;
goto addVal;
writeResult:
Console.WriteLine("myInteger = {0}", myInteger);
goto start;
addVal:
myInteger += 10;
goto writeResult;
```

This is perfectly valid code but very difficult to read! Try it out for yourself and see what happens. Before doing that, though, try to first determine what this code will do by looking at it, and then give yourself a pat on the back if you're right. You'll come back to this statement a little later, because it has implications for use with some of the other structures in this chapter.

Branching

Branching is the act of controlling which line of code should be executed next. The line to jump to is controlled by some kind of conditional statement. This conditional statement is based on a comparison between a test value and one or more possible values using Boolean logic.

This section describes three branching techniques available in C#:

❑ The ternary operator

❑ The if statement

❑ The switch statement

The Ternary Operator

The simplest way to perform a comparison is to use the *ternary* (or *conditional*) operator mentioned in the last chapter. You've already seen unary operators that work on one operand, and binary operators that work on two operands, so it won't come as a surprise that this operator works on three operands. The syntax is as follows:

```
<test> ? <resultIfTrue> : <resultIfFalse>
```

Here, <test> is evaluated to obtain a Boolean value, and the result of the operator is either <resultIfTrue> or <resultIfFalse> based on this value.

You might use this as follows:

```
string resultString = (myInteger < 10) ? "Less than 10"
                                        : "Greater than or equal to 10";
```

The result of the ternary operator is one of two strings, both of which may be assigned to `resultString`. The choice of which string to assign is made by comparing the value of `myInteger` to 10, where a value of less than 10 results in the first string being assigned, and a value of greater than or equal to 10 results in the second string being assigned. For example, if `myInteger` is 4, then `resultString` will be assigned the string `Less than 10`.

This operator is fine for simple assignments such as this, but it isn't really suitable for executing larger amounts of code based on a comparison. A much better way to do this is to use the `if` statement.

The if Statement

The `if` statement is a far more versatile and useful way to make decisions. Unlike `?:` statements, `if` statements don't have a result (so you can't use them in assignments); instead, you use the statement to conditionally execute other statements.

The simplest use of an `if` statement is as follows, where `<test>` is evaluated (it must evaluate to a Boolean value for the code to compile) and the line of code that follows the statement is executed if `<test>` evaluates to `true`:

```
if (<test>)
    <code executed if<test>is true>;
```

After this code is executed, or if it isn't executed due to `<test>` evaluating to `false`, program execution resumes at the next line of code.

You can also specify additional code using the `else` statement in combination with an `if` statement. This statement is executed if `<test>` evaluates to `false`:

```
if (<test>)
  <code executed if <test> is true>;
else
  <code executed if <test> is false>;
```

Both sections of code can span multiple lines using blocks in braces:

```
if (<test>)
{
    <code executed if<test>is true>;
}
else
{
    <code executed if <test> is false>;
}
```

As a quick example, you could rewrite the code from the last section that used the ternary operator:

```
string resultString = (myInteger < 10) ? "Less than 10"
                                        : "Greater than or equal to 10";
```

Because the result of the `if` statement cannot be assigned to a variable, you have to assign a value to the variable in a separate step:

```
string resultString;
if (myInteger < 10)
    resultString = "Less than 10";
else
    resultString = "Greater than or equal to 10";
```

Code such as this, although more verbose, is far easier to read and understand than the equivalent ternary form, and allows far more flexibility.

Try It Out   **Using the if Statement**

1. Create a new console application called Ch04Ex02 and save it in the directory C:\BegVCSharp\Chapter04.

2. Add the following code to `Program.cs`:

```
static void Main(string[] args)
{
    string comparison;
    Console.WriteLine("Enter a number:");
    double var1 = Convert.ToDouble(Console.ReadLine());
    Console.WriteLine("Enter another number:");
    double var2 = Convert.ToDouble(Console.ReadLine());
    if (var1 < var2)
        comparison = "less than";
    else
    {
        if (var1 == var2)
            comparison = "equal to";
        else
            comparison = "greater than";
    }
    Console.WriteLine("The first number is {0} the second number.",
                      comparison);
    Console.ReadKey();
}
```

3. Execute the code and enter two numbers at the prompts (see Figure 4-2).

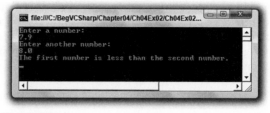

Figure 4-2

How It Works

The first section of code is very familiar. It simply obtains two `double` values from user input:

```
string comparison;
Console.WriteLine("Enter a number:");
double var1 = Convert.ToDouble(Console.ReadLine());
Console.WriteLine("Enter another number:");
double var2 = Convert.ToDouble(Console.ReadLine());
```

Next, you assign a string to the `string` variable `comparison` based on the values obtained for `var1` and `var2`. First you check whether `var1` is less than `var2`:

```
if (var1 < var2)
    comparison = "less than";
```

If this isn't the case, then `var1` is either greater than or equal to `var2`. In the `else` section of the first comparison, you need to nest a second comparison:

```
else
{
    if (var1 == var2)
        comparison = "equal to";
```

The `else` section of this second comparison is reached only if `var1` is greater than `var2`:

```
    else
        comparison = "greater than";
}
```

Finally, you write the value of `comparison` to the console:

```
Console.WriteLine("The first number is {0} the second number.",
                  comparison);
```

The nesting used here is just one method. You could equally have written this:

```
if (var1 < var2)
    comparison = "less than";
if (var1 == var2)
    comparison = "equal to";
if (var1 > var2)
     comparison = "greater than";
```

The disadvantage with this method is that you are performing three comparisons regardless of the values of var1 and var2. With the first method, you only perform one comparison if var1<var2 is true, and two comparisons otherwise (you also perform the var1 == var2 comparison), resulting in fewer lines of code being executed. The difference in performance here is slight, but would be significant in applications where speed of execution is crucial.

Checking More Conditions Using if Statements

In the preceding example, you checked for three conditions involving the value of var1. This covered all possible values for this variable. Sometimes, you might want to check for specific values — for example, if var1 is equal to 1, 2, 3, or 4, and so on. Using code such as the preceding can result in annoyingly nested code:

```
if (var1 == 1)
{
    // Do something.
}
else
{
    if (var1 == 2)
    {
        // Do something else.
    }
    else
    {
        if (var1 == 3 || var1 == 4)
        {
            // Do something else.
        }
        else
        {
            // Do something else.
        }
    }
}
```

It's a common mistake to write conditions such as the third condition as if (var1 == 3 || 4). *Here, owing to operator precedence, the* == *operator is processed first, leaving the* || *operator to operate on a Boolean and a numeric operand, which causes an error.*

In these situations, consider using a slightly different indentation scheme and contracting the block of code for the else blocks (that is, using a single line of code after the else blocks, rather than a block of code). That way, you end up with a structure involving else if statements:

```
if (var1 == 1)
{
    // Do something.
}
else if (var1 == 2)
```

```
    {
        // Do something else.
    }
    else if (var1 == 3 || var1 == 4)
    {
        // Do something else.
    }
    else
    {
        // Do something else.
    }
```

These `else if` statements are really two separate statements, and the code is functionally identical to the previous code, but much easier to read. When making multiple comparisons such as this, consider using the `switch` statement as an alternative branching structure.

The switch Statement

The `switch` statement is similar to the `if` statement in that it executes code conditionally based on the value of a test. However, `switch` enables you to test for multiple values of a test variable in one go, rather than just a single condition. This test is limited to discrete values, rather than clauses such as "greater than X," so its use is slightly different. But it can be a powerful technique.

The basic structure of a `switch` statement is as follows:

```
    switch (<testVar>)
    {
        case <comparisonVal1>:
            <code to execute if <testVar> == <comparisonVal1> >
            break;
        case <comparisonVal2>:
            <code to execute if <testVar> == <comparisonVal2> >
            break;
        ...
        case <comparisonValN>:
            <code to execute if <testVar> == <comparisonValN> >
            break;
        default:
            <code to execute if <testVar>!= comparisonVals>
            break;
    }
```

The value in `<testVar>` is compared to each of the `<comparisonValX>` values (specified with `case` statements), and if there is a match, then the code supplied for this match is executed. If there is no match, then the code in the `default` section is executed if this block exists.

On completion of the code in each section, you have an additional command, `break`. It is illegal for the flow of execution to reach a second `case` statement after processing one `case` block.

This behavior is one area in which C# differs from C++, where the processing of `case` *statements is allowed to run from one to another.*

The `break` statement here simply terminates the `switch` statement, and processing continues on the statement following the structure.

There are alternative methods of preventing flow from one `case` statement to the next in C# code. You can use the `return` statement, which results in termination of the current function, rather than just the `switch` structure (see Chapter 6 for more details about this), or a `goto` statement. `goto` statements (as detailed earlier) work here because `case` statements actually define labels in C# code. Here is an example:

```
switch (<testVar>)
{
    case <comparisonVal1>:
        <code to execute if <testVar> == <comparisonVal1> >
        goto case <comparisonVal2>;
    case <comparisonVal2>:
        <code to execute if <testVar> == <comparisonVal2> >
        break;
    ...
```

Note one exception to the rule that the processing of one `case` statement can't run freely into the next: If you place multiple `case` statements together (*stack* them) before a single block of code, then you are in effect checking for multiple conditions at once. If any of these conditions is met, then the code is executed. Here's an example:

```
switch (<testVar>)
{
    case <comparisonVal1>:
    case <comparisonVal2>:
        <code to execute if <testVar> == <comparisonVal1> or
                             <testVar> == <comparisonVal2> >
        break;
    ...
```

Note that these conditions also apply to the `default` statement. There is no rule stipulating that this statement must be the last in the list of comparisons, and you can stack it with `case` statements if you want. Adding a breakpoint with `break`, `goto`, or `return` ensures that a valid execution path exists through the structure in all cases.

Each of the `<comparisonValX>` comparisons must be a constant value. One way of doing this is to provide literal values, like this:

```
switch (myInteger)
{
    case 1:
        <code to execute if myInteger == 1>
        break;
    case -1:
        <code to execute if myInteger == -1>
        break;
    default:
        <code to execute if myInteger != comparisons>
        break;
}
```

Another way is to use *constant variables*. Constant variables (also known as just "constants," avoiding the oxymoron) are just like any other variable except for one key factor: the value they contain never changes. Once you assign a value to a constant variable, that is the value it has for the duration of code execution. Constant variables can come in handy here, because it is often easier to read code where the actual values being compared are hidden from you at the time of comparison.

You declare constant variables using the `const` keyword in addition to the variable type, and you *must* assign them values at this time, as shown here:

```
const int intTwo = 2;
```

The preceding code is perfectly valid, but if you try

```
const int intTwo;
intTwo = 2;
```

you will get an error and won't be able to compile your code. This also happens if you try to change the value of a constant variable through any other means after initial assignment.

The following Try It Out uses a `switch` statement to write different strings to the console, depending on the value you enter for a test string.

Try It Out   Using the switch Statement

1. Create a new console application called Ch04Ex03 and save it to the directory C:\BegVCSharp\Chapter04.

2. Add the following code to `Program.cs`:

```
static void Main(string[] args)
{
    const string myName = "karli";
    const string sexyName = "angelina";
    const string sillyName = "ploppy";
    string name;
    Console.WriteLine("What is your name?");
    name = Console.ReadLine();
    switch (name.ToLower())
    {
        case myName:
            Console.WriteLine("You have the same name as me!");
            break;
        case sexyName:
            Console.WriteLine("My, what a sexy name you have!");
            break;
        case sillyName:
            Console.WriteLine("That's a very silly name.");
            break;
    }
    Console.WriteLine("Hello {0}!", name);
    Console.ReadKey();
}
```

3. Execute the code and enter a name. The result is shown in Figure 4-3.

Figure 4-3

How It Works

The code sets up three constant strings, accepts a string from the user, and then writes out text to the console based on the string entered. Here, the strings are names.

When you compare the name entered (in the variable name) to your constant values, you first force it into lowercase with name.ToLower(). This is a standard command that works with all string variables, and it comes in handy when you're not sure what the user entered. Using this technique, the strings Karli, kArLi, karli, and so on all match the test string karli.

The switch statement itself attempts to match the string entered with the constant values you have defined, and, if successful, writes out a personalized message to greet the user. If no match is made, you offer a generic greeting.

switch statements place no limit on the amount of case: sections they contain, so you could extend this code to cover every name you can think of should you want . . . but it might take a while!

Looping

Looping refers to the repeated execution of statements. This technique comes in very handy because it means that you can repeat operations as many times as you want (thousands, even millions, of times) without having to write the same code each time.

As a simple example, consider the following code for calculating the amount of money in a bank account after 10 years, assuming that interest is paid each year and no other money flows into or out of the account:

```
double balance = 1000;
double interestRate = 1.05; // 5% interest/year
balance *= interestRate;
balance *= interestRate;
balance *= interestRate;
balance *= interestRate;
balance *= interestRate;
balance *= interestRate;
balance *= interestRate;
balance *= interestRate;
balance *= interestRate;
balance *= interestRate;
```

Writing the same code 10 times seems a bit wasteful, and what if you wanted to change the duration from 10 years to some other value? You'd have to manually copy the line of code the required amount of times, which would be a bit of a pain! Luckily, you don't have to do this. Instead, you can have a loop that executes the instruction you want the required number of times.

Another important type of loop is one in which you loop until a certain condition is fulfilled. These loops are slightly simpler than the situation detailed previously (although no less useful), so they're a good starting point.

do Loops

do loops operate as follows. The code you have marked out for looping is executed, a Boolean test is performed, and the code executes again if this test evaluates to true, and so on. When the test evaluates to false, the loop exits.

The structure of a do loop is as follows, where <Test> evaluates to a Boolean value:

```
do
{
    <code to be looped>
} while (<Test>);
```

The semicolon after the while *statement is required.*

For example, you could use the following to write the numbers from 1 to 10 in a column:

```
int i = 1;
do
{
    Console.WriteLine("{0}", i++);
} while (i <= 10);
```

Here, you use the suffix version of the ++ operator to increment the value of i after it is written to the screen, so you need to check for i <= 10 to include 10 in the numbers written to the console.

The following Try It Out uses this for a slightly modified version of the code shown earlier, where you calculated the balance in an account after 10 years. Here, you use a loop to calculate how many years it will take to get a specified amount of money in your account, based on a starting amount and an interest rate.

Try It Out   Using do Loops

1. Create a new console application called Ch04Ex04 and save it to the directory C:\BegVCSharp\Chapter04.

2. Add the following code to Program.cs:

```
static void Main(string[] args)
{
    double balance, interestRate, targetBalance;
    Console.WriteLine("What is your current balance?");
    balance = Convert.ToDouble(Console.ReadLine());
```

```
         Console.WriteLine("What is your current annual interest rate (in %)?");
         interestRate = 1 + Convert.ToDouble(Console.ReadLine()) / 100.0;
         Console.WriteLine("What balance would you like to have?");
         targetBalance = Convert.ToDouble(Console.ReadLine());

         int totalYears = 0;
         do
         {
            balance *= interestRate;
            ++totalYears;
         }
         while (balance < targetBalance);
         Console.WriteLine("In {0} year{1} you'll have a balance of {2}.",
                      totalYears, totalYears == 1 ? "" : "s", balance);
         Console.ReadKey();
      }
```

3.   Execute the code and enter some values. The result is shown in Figure 4-4.

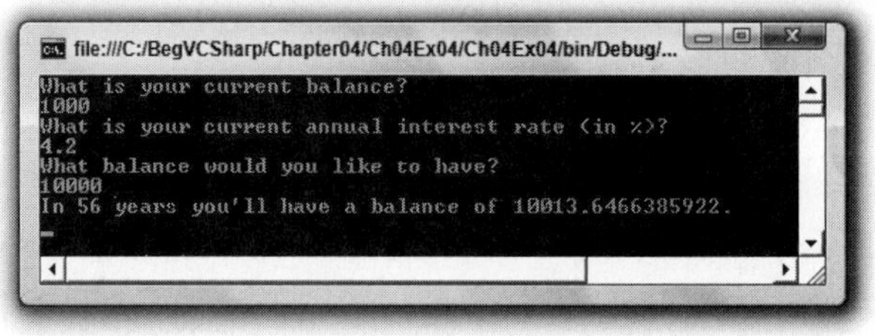

Figure 4-4

How It Works

This code simply repeats the simple annual calculation of the balance with a fixed interest rate as
many times as is necessary for the balance to satisfy the terminating condition. You keep a count of
how many years have been accounted for by incrementing a counter variable with each loop cycle:

```
         int totalYears = 0;
         do
         {
            balance *= interestRate;
            ++totalYears;
         }
         while (balance < targetBalance);
```

You can then use this counter variable as part of the result output:

```
         Console.WriteLine("In {0} year{1} you'll have a balance of {2}.",
                      totalYears, totalYears == 1 ? "" : "s", balance);
```

This is perhaps the most common usage of the ? : *(ternary) operator — to conditionally format text with
the minimum of code. Here, you output an "s" after "year" if* totalYears *isn't equal to 1.*

Unfortunately, this code isn't perfect. Consider what happens when the target balance is less than the current balance. The output will be similar to what is shown in Figure 4-5.

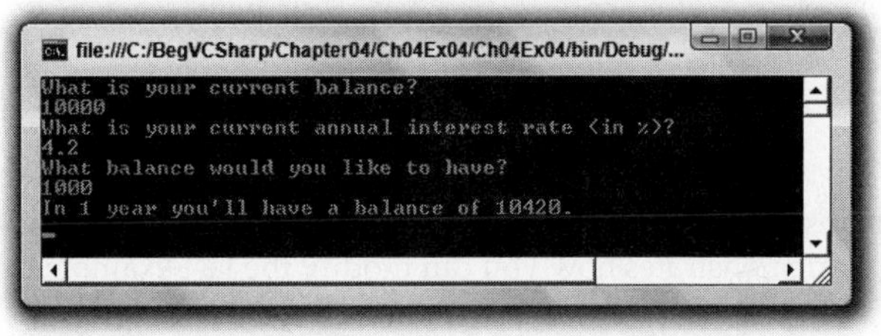

Figure 4-5

do loops always execute at least once. Sometimes, as in this situation, this isn't ideal. Of course, you could add an `if` statement:

```
int totalYears = 0;
if (balance < targetBalance)
{
    do
    {
        balance *= interestRate;
        ++totalYears;
    }
    while (balance < targetBalance);
}
Console.WriteLine("In {0} year{1} you'll have a balance of {2}.",
                  totalYears, totalYears == 1 ? "" : "s", balance);
```

Clearly, this does seem to add unnecessary complexity. A far better solution is to use a `while` loop.

while Loops

`while` loops are very similar to do loops, but they have one important difference: The Boolean test in a `while` loop takes place at the start of the loop cycle, not the end. If the test evaluates to `false`, then the loop cycle is never executed. Instead, program execution jumps straight to the code following the loop.

Here's how `while` loops are specified:

```
while (<Test>)
{
    <code to be looped>
}
```

They can be used in almost the same way as do loops:

```
int i = 1;
while (i <= 10)
{
    Console.WriteLine("{0}", i++);
}
```

This code has the same result as the do loop shown earlier; it outputs the numbers 1 to 10 in a column. The following Try It Out demonstrates how you can modify the last example to use a while loop.

Try It Out   Using while Loops

1. Create a new console application called Ch04Ex05 and save it to the directory C:\BegVCSharp\Chapter04.

2. Modify the code as follows (use the code from Ch04Ex04 as a starting point, and remember to delete the while statement at the end of the original do loop):

```
static void Main(string[] args)
{
    double balance, interestRate, targetBalance;
    Console.WriteLine("What is your current balance?");
    balance = Convert.ToDouble(Console.ReadLine());
    Console.WriteLine("What is your current annual interest rate (in %)?");
    interestRate = 1 + Convert.ToDouble(Console.ReadLine()) / 100.0;
    Console.WriteLine("What balance would you like to have?");
    targetBalance = Convert.ToDouble(Console.ReadLine());

    int totalYears = 0;
    while (balance < targetBalance)
    {
        balance *= interestRate;
        ++totalYears;
    }
    Console.WriteLine("In {0} year{1} you'll have a balance of {2}.",
                    totalYears, totalYears == 1 ? "" : "s", balance);
    Console.ReadKey();
}
```

3. Execute the code again, but this time use a target balance that is less than the starting balance, as shown in Figure 4-6.

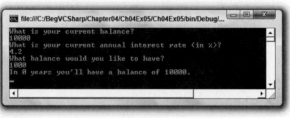

Figure 4-6

How It Works

This simple change from a `do` loop to a `while` loop has solved the problem in the last example. By moving the Boolean test to the beginning, you provide for the circumstance where no looping is required, and you can jump straight to the result.

There are, of course, other alternatives in this situation. For example, you could check the user input to ensure that the target balance is greater than the starting balance. In that case, you can place the user input section in a loop as follows:

```
Console.WriteLine("What balance would you like to have?");
do
{
    targetBalance = Convert.ToDouble(Console.ReadLine());
    if (targetBalance <= balance)
        Console.WriteLine("You must enter an amount greater than " +
                    "your current balance!\nPlease enter another value.");
}
while (targetBalance <= balance);
```

This rejects values that don't make sense, so the output looks like Figure 4-7.

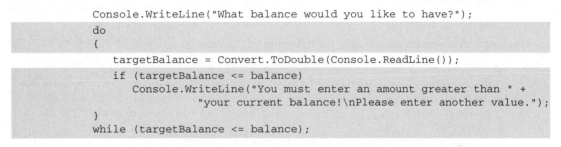

Figure 4-7

This *validation* of user input is an important topic when it comes to application design, and many examples of it appear throughout this book.

---

for Loops

The last type of loop to look at in this chapter is the `for` loop. This type of loop executes a set number of times and maintains its own counter. To define a `for` loop you need the following information:

❑ A starting value to initialize the counter variable.

❑ A condition for continuing the loop, involving the counter variable.

❑ An operation to perform on the counter variable at the end of each loop cycle.

For example, if you want a loop with a counter that increments from 1 to 10 in steps of one, then the starting value is 1; the condition is that the counter is less than or equal to 10; and the operation to perform at the end of each cycle is to add 1 to the counter.

This information must be placed into the structure of a `for` loop as follows:

```
for (<initialization>; <condition>; <operation>)
{
    <code to loop>
}
```

This works in exactly the same way as the following `while` loop:

```
<initialization>
while (<condition>)
{
    <code to loop>
    <operation>
}
```

The format of the `for` loop makes the code easier to read, however, because the syntax involves the complete specification of the loop in one place, rather than dividing it over several statements in different areas of the code.

Earlier, you used `do` and `while` loops to write out the numbers from 1 to 10. The code that follows shows what is required to do this using a `for` loop:

```
int i;
for (i = 1; i <= 10; ++i)
{
    Console.WriteLine("{0}", i);
}
```

The counter variable, an integer called `i`, starts with a value of 1 and is incremented by 1 at the end of each cycle. During each cycle, the value of `i` is written to the console.

When the code resumes after the loop, `i` has a value of 11. That's because at the end of the cycle where `i` is equal to 10, `i` is incremented to 11. This happens before the condition `i <= 10` is processed, at which point the loop ends. As with `while` loops, `for` loops execute only if the condition evaluates to `true` before the first cycle, so the code in the loop doesn't necessarily run at all.

As a final note, you can declare the counter variable as part of the `for` statement, rewriting the preceding code as follows:

```
for (int i = 1; i <= 10; ++i)
{
    Console.WriteLine("{0}", i);
}
```

If you do this, though, then the variable `i` won't be accessible from code outside this loop (see the section "Variable Scope" in Chapter 6).

The next Try It Out uses `for` loops, and because you have already used several loops now, this example is a bit more interesting: It displays a Mandelbrot set (but using plain-text characters, so it won't look that spectacular).

Try It Out   **Using for Loops**

1. Create a new console application called Ch04Ex06 and save it to the directory C:\BegVCSharp\Chapter04.

2. Add the following code to `Program.cs`:

```
static void Main(string[] args)
{
    double realCoord, imagCoord;
    double realTemp, imagTemp, realTemp2, arg;
    int iterations;
    for (imagCoord = 1.2; imagCoord >= -1.2; imagCoord -= 0.05)
    {
        for (realCoord = -0.6; realCoord <= 1.77; realCoord += 0.03)
        {
            iterations = 0;
            realTemp = realCoord;
            imagTemp = imagCoord;
            arg = (realCoord * realCoord) + (imagCoord * imagCoord);
            while ((arg < 4) && (iterations < 40))
            {
                realTemp2 = (realTemp * realTemp) - (imagTemp * imagTemp)
                            - realCoord;
                imagTemp = (2 * realTemp * imagTemp) - imagCoord;
                realTemp = realTemp2;
                arg = (realTemp * realTemp) + (imagTemp * imagTemp);
                iterations += 1;
            }
            switch (iterations % 4)
            {
                case 0:
                    Console.Write(".");
                    break;
                case 1:
                    Console.Write("o");
                    break;
                case 2:
                    Console.Write("O");
                    break;
                case 3:
                    Console.Write("@");
                    break;
            }
        }
        Console.Write("\n");
    }
    Console.ReadKey();
}
```

3. Execute the code. The result is shown in Figure 4-8.

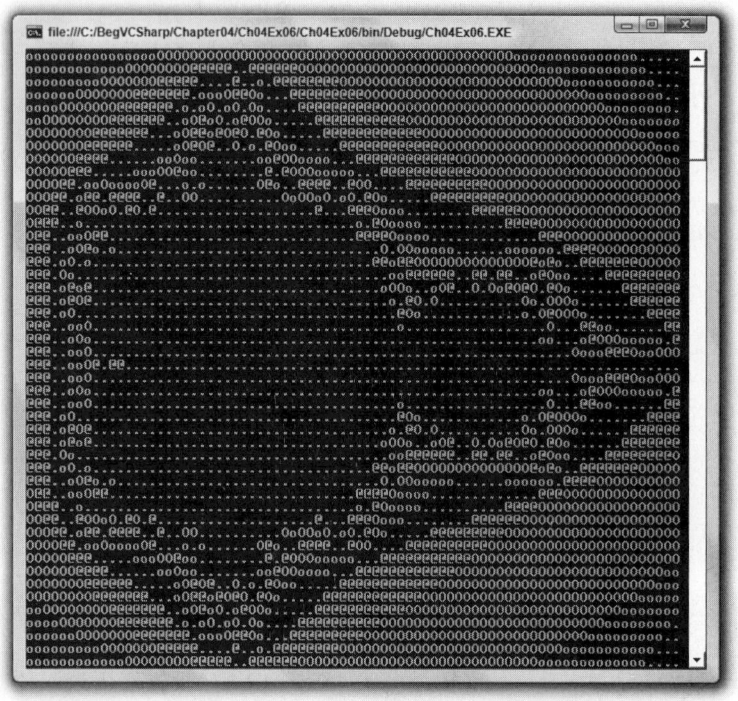

Figure 4-8

How It Works

Details about calculating Mandelbrot sets are beyond the scope of this chapter, but you should understand why you need the loops used in this code. Feel free to skim through the following two paragraphs if the mathematics doesn't interest you; it's an understanding of the code that is important here.

Each position in a Mandelbrot image corresponds to an imaginary number of the form $N = x + y*i$, where the real part is x, the imaginary part is y, and i is the square root of -1. The x and y coordinates of the position in the image correspond to the x and y parts of the imaginary number.

For each position on the image, you look at the argument of N, which is the square root of $x*x + y*y$. If this value is greater than or equal to 2, then you say that the position corresponding to this number has a value of 0. If the argument of N is less than 2, then you change N to a value of $N*N - N$ (giving you $N = (x*x-y*y-x) + (2*x*y-y)*i$), and check the argument of this new value of N again. If this value is greater than or equal to 2, then you say that the position corresponding to this number has a value of 1. This process continues until you either assign a value to the position on the image or perform more than a certain number of iterations.

Based on the values assigned to each point in the image, you would, in a graphical environment, place a pixel of a certain color on the screen. However, because you are using a text display, you simply place characters onscreen instead.

Now, back to the code, and the loops contained in it. You begin by declaring the variables you need for your calculation:

```
double realCoord, imagCoord;
double realTemp, imagTemp, realTemp2, arg;
int iterations;
```

Here, `realCoord` and `imagCoord` are the real and imaginary parts of N, and the other `double` variables are for temporary information during computation. `iterations` records how many iterations it takes before the argument of N (`arg`) is 2 or greater.

Next, you start two `for` loops to cycle through coordinates covering the whole of the image (using a slightly more complex syntax for modifying your counters than ++ or --, a common and powerful technique):

```
for (imagCoord = 1.2; imagCoord >= -1.2; imagCoord -= 0.05)
{
    for (realCoord = -0.6; realCoord <= 1.77; realCoord += 0.03)
    {
```

Here, appropriate limits have been used to show the main section of the Mandelbrot set. Feel free to play around with these if you want to try "zooming in" on the image.

Within these two loops you have code that pertains to a single point in the Mandelbrot set, giving you a value for N to play with. This is where you perform your calculation of iterations required, giving you a value to plot for the current point.

First, initialize some variables:

```
iterations = 0;
realTemp = realCoord;
imagTemp = imagCoord;
arg = (realCoord * realCoord) + (imagCoord * imagCoord);
```

Next, you have a `while` loop to perform your iterating. Use a `while` loop rather than a do loop, in case the initial value of N has an argument greater than 2 already, in which case `iterations = 0` is the answer you are looking for and no further calculations are necessary.

Note that you're not quite calculating the argument fully here. You're just getting the value of $x*x + y*y$ and checking whether that value is less than 4. This simplifies the calculation, because you know that 2 is the square root of 4 and don't have to calculate any square roots yourself:

```
while ((arg < 4) && (iterations < 40))
{
    realTemp2 = (realTemp * realTemp) - (imagTemp * imagTemp)
            - realCoord;
    imagTemp = (2 * realTemp * imagTemp) - imagCoord;
    realTemp = realTemp2;
    arg = (realTemp * realTemp) + (imagTemp * imagTemp);
    iterations += 1;
}
```

The maximum number of iterations of this loop, which calculates values as detailed above, is 40.

Once you have a value for the current point stored in `iterations`, you use a `switch` statement to choose a character to output. You just use four different characters here, instead of the 40 possible values, and use the modulus operator (`%`) so that values of 0, 4, 8, and so on give one character; values of 1, 5, 9, and so on give another character and so forth:

```
switch (iterations % 4)
{
    case 0:
        Console.Write(".");
        break;
    case 1:
        Console.Write("o");
        break;
    case 2:
        Console.Write("O");
        break;
    case 3:
        Console.Write("@");
        break;
}
```

You use `Console.Write()` here, rather than `Console.WriteLine()`, because you don't want to start a new line every time you output a character. At the end of one of the innermost `for` loops, you do want to end a line, so you simply output an end-of-line character using the escape sequence shown earlier:

```
    }
    Console.Write("\n");
}
```

This results in each row being separated from the next and lining up appropriately. The final result of this application, though not spectacular, is fairly impressive, and certainly shows how useful looping and branching can be.

Interrupting Loops

Sometimes you want finer-grained control over the processing of looping code. C# provides four commands to help you here, three of which were shown in other situations:

❑   `break` — Causes the loop to end immediately.

❑   `continue` — Causes the current loop cycle to end immediately (execution continues with the next loop cycle).

❑   `goto` — Allows jumping out of a loop to a labeled position (not recommended if you want your code to be easy to read and understand).

❑   `return` — Jumps out of the loop and its containing function (see Chapter 6).

The break command simply exits the loop, and execution continues at the first line of code after the loop, as shown in the following example:

```
int i = 1;
while (i <= 10)
{
    if (i == 6)
        break;
    Console.WriteLine("{0}", i++);
}
```

This code writes out the numbers from 1 to 5 because the break command causes the loop to exit when i reaches 6.

continue only stops the current cycle, not the whole loop, as shown here:

```
int i;
for (i = 1; i <= 10; i++)
{
    if ((i % 2) == 0)
        continue;
    Console.WriteLine(i);
}
```

In the preceding example, whenever the remainder of i divided by 2 is zero, the continue statement stops the execution of the current cycle, so only the numbers 1, 3, 5, 7, and 9 are displayed.

The third method of interrupting a loop is to use goto, as shown earlier:

```
int i = 1;
while (i <= 10)
{
    if (i == 6)
        goto exitPoint;
    Console.WriteLine("{0}", i++);
}
Console.WriteLine("This code will never be reached.");
exitPoint:
Console.WriteLine("This code is run when the loop is exited using goto.");
```

Note that exiting a loop with goto is legal (if slightly messy), but it is illegal to use goto to jump into a loop from outside.

Infinite Loops

It is possible, through both coding errors and design, to define loops that never end, so-called *infinite loops*. As a very simple example, consider the following:

```
while (true)
{
    // code in loop
}
```

This can be useful, and you can always exit such loops using code such as `break` statements or manually by using the Windows Task Manager. However, when this occurs by accident, it can be annoying. Consider the following loop, which is similar to the `for` loop in the previous section:

```
int i = 1;
while (i <= 10)
{
    if ((i % 2) == 0)
        continue;
    Console.WriteLine("{0}", i++);
}
```

Here, `i` isn't incremented until the last line of code in the loop, which occurs after the `continue` statement. If this `continue` statement is reached (which it will be when `i` is 2), the next loop cycle will be using the same value of `i`, continuing the loop, testing the same value of `i`, continuing the loop, and so on. This will cause the application to freeze. Note that it's still possible to quit the frozen application in the normal way, so you won't have to reboot if this happens.

Summary

In this chapter, you increased your programming knowledge by considering various structures that you can use in your code. The proper use of these structures is essential when you start making more complex applications, and you will see them used throughout this book.

First, you spent some time looking at Boolean logic, with a bit of bitwise logic thrown in for good measure. Looking back on this after working through the rest of the chapter should confirm the suggestion that this topic is very important when it comes to implementing branching and looping code in your programs. It is essential to become very familiar with the operators and techniques detailed in this section.

Branching enables you to conditionally execute code, which, when combined with looping, enables you to create convoluted structures in your C# code. When you have loops inside loops inside `if` structures inside loops, you start to see why code indentation is so useful! If you shift all your code to the left of the screen, it instantly becomes difficult to parse by eye, and even more difficult to debug. Make sure you've got the hang of indentation at this stage — you'll appreciate it later! VS does a lot of this for you, but it's a good idea to indent code as you type it anyway.

The next chapter covers variables in more depth.

Exercises

1.   If you have two integers stored in variables `var1` and `var2`, what Boolean test can you perform to determine whether one or the other (but not both) is greater than 10?

2.   Write an application that includes the logic from Exercise 1, obtains two numbers from the user, and displays them, but rejects any input where both numbers are greater than 10 and asks for two new numbers.

3. What is wrong with the following code?

```
int i;
for (i = 1; i <= 10; i++)
{
    if ((i % 2) = 0)
        continue;
    Console.WriteLine(i);
}
```

4. Modify the Mandelbrot set application to request image limits from the user and display the chosen section of the image. The current code outputs as many characters as will fit on a single line of a console application; consider making every image chosen fit in the same amount of space to maximize the viewable area.

More About Variables

Now that you've seen a bit more of the C# language, it's time to go back and tackle some of the more involved topics concerning variables.

The first subject you look at in this chapter is *type conversion*, whereby you convert values from one type into another. You've already seen a bit of this, but you look at it formally here. A grasp of this topic gives you both a greater understanding of what happens when you mix types in expressions (intentionally or unintentionally) as well as tighter control over the way that data is manipulated. This helps you to streamline your code and avoid nasty surprises.

Then you'll look at a few more types of variables that you can use:

❑ **Enumerations**: Variable types that have a user-defined discrete set of possible values that can be used in a human-readable way.

❑ **Structs:** Composite variable types made up of a user-defined set of other variable types.

❑ **Arrays**: Types that hold multiple variables of one type, allowing index access to the individual value.

These are slightly more complex than the simple types you've been using up to now, but they can make your life much easier. Finally, you'll tackle another useful subject concerning strings: basic string manipulation.

Type Conversion

Earlier in this book you saw that all data, regardless of type, is simply a sequence of bits — that is, a sequence of zeros and ones. The meaning of the variable is determined by the way in which this data is interpreted. The simplest example of this is the char type. This type represents a character in the Unicode character set using a number. In fact, this number is stored in exactly the same way as a ushort — both of them store a number between 0 and 65535.

However, in general, the different types of variables use varying schemes to represent data. This implies that even if it were possible to place the sequence of bits from one variable into a variable of a different type (perhaps they use the same amount of storage, or perhaps the target type has enough storage space to include all the source bits), the results might not be what you expect!

Instead of this one-to-one mapping of bits from one variable into another, you need to use *type conversion* on the data. Type conversion takes two forms:

❑ **Implicit conversion:** Conversion from type A to type B is possible in all circumstances, and the rules for performing the conversion are simple enough for you to trust in the compiler.

❑ **Explicit conversion:** Conversion from type A to type B is only possible in certain circumstances or where the rules for conversion are complicated enough to merit additional processing of some kind.

Implicit Conversions

Implicit conversion requires no work on your part and no additional code. Consider the code shown here:

```
var1 = var2;
```

This assignment may involve an implicit conversion if the type of var2 can be implicitly converted into the type of var1, but it could just as easily involve two variables with the same type, and no implicit conversion is necessary. For example, the values of ushort and char are effectively interchangeable, because both store a number between 0 and 65535. You can convert values between these types implicitly, as illustrated by the following code:

```
ushort destinationVar;
char sourceVar = 'a';
destinationVar = sourceVar;
Console.WriteLine("sourceVar val: {0}", sourceVar);
Console.WriteLine("destinationVar val: {0}", destinationVar);
```

Here, the value stored in sourceVar is placed in destinationVar. When you output the variables with the two Console.WriteLine() commands, you get the following output:

```
sourceVar val: a
destinationVar val: 97
```

Even though the two variables store the same information, they are interpreted in different ways using their type.

There are many implicit conversions of simple types; bool and string have no implicit conversions, but the numeric types have a few. For reference, the following table shows the numeric conversions that the compiler can perform implicitly (remember that chars are stored as numbers, so char counts as a numeric type):

Type	Can Safely Be Converted To
Byte	short, ushort, int, uint, long, ulong, float, double, decimal
Sbyte	short, int, long, float, double, decimal
Short	int, long, float, double, decimal
Ushort	int, uint, long, ulong, float, double, decimal
Int	long, float, double, decimal
Uint	long, ulong, float, double, decimal
Long	float, double, decimal
Ulong	float, double, decimal
Float	double
Char	ushort, int, uint, long, ulong, float, double, decimal

Don't worry — you don't need to learn this table by heart, because it's actually quite easy to work out which conversions the compiler can do implicitly. Back in Chapter 3, you saw a table showing the range of possible values for every simple numeric type. The implicit conversion rule for these types is this: Any type *A* whose range of possible values completely fits inside the range of possible values of type *B* can be implicitly converted into that type.

The reasoning for this is simple. If you try to fit a value into a variable but that value is outside the range of values the variable can take, then there will be a problem. For example, a short type variable is capable of storing values up to 32767, and the maximum value allowed into a byte is 255, so there could be problems if you try to convert a short value into a byte value. If the short holds a value between 256 and 32767, then it simply won't fit into a byte.

If you know that the value in your short type variable is less than 255, then you should be able to convert the value, right? The simple answer is that, of course, you can. The slightly more complex answer is that, of course, you can, but you must use an *explicit* conversion. Performing an explicit conversion is a bit like saying "OK, I know you've warned me about doing this, but I'll take responsibility for what happens."

Explicit Conversions

As the name suggests, an explicit conversion occurs when you explicitly ask the compiler to convert a value from one data type to another. Because of this, they require extra code, and the format of this code may vary, depending on the exact conversion method. Before you look at any of this explicit conversion code, you should look at what happens if you *don't* add any.

For example, the following modification to the code from the last section attempts to convert a `short` value into a `byte`:

```
byte destinationVar;
short sourceVar = 7;
destinationVar = sourceVar;
Console.WriteLine("sourceVar val: {0}", sourceVar);
Console.WriteLine("destinationVar val: {0}", destinationVar);
```

If you attempt to compile this code, you will receive the following error:

```
Cannot implicitly convert type 'short' to 'byte'. An explicit conversion
exists (are you missing a cast?)
```

Luckily for you, the C# compiler can detect missing explicit conversions!

To get this code to compile, you need to add the code to perform an explicit conversion. The easiest way to do that in this context is to *cast* the `short` variable into a `byte` (as suggested by the preceding error string). Casting basically means forcing data from one type into another, and it uses the following simple syntax:

```
(destinationType)sourceVar
```

This will convert the value in `sourceVar` into `destinationType`.

This is only possible in some situations. Types that bear little or no relation to each other are likely not to have casting conversions defined.

You can, therefore, modify your example using this syntax to force the conversion from a `short` to a `byte`:

```
byte destinationVar;
short sourceVar = 7;
destinationVar = (byte)sourceVar;
Console.WriteLine("sourceVar val: {0}", sourceVar);
Console.WriteLine("destinationVar val: {0}", destinationVar);
```

This results in the following output:

```
sourceVar val: 7
destinationVar val: 7
```

What happens when you try to force a value into a variable into which it won't fit? Modifying your code as follows illustrates this:

```
byte destinationVar;
short sourceVar = 281;
destinationVar = (byte)sourceVar;
Console.WriteLine("sourceVar val: {0}", sourceVar);
Console.WriteLine("destinationVar val: {0}", destinationVar);
```

This results in the following:

```
sourceVar val: 281
destinationVar val: 25
```

What happened? Well, look at the binary representations of these two numbers, along with the maximum value that can be stored in a byte, which is 255:

```
281 = 100011001
 25 = 000011001
255 = 011111111
```

You can see that the leftmost bit of the source data has been lost. This immediately raises a question: How can you tell when this happens? Obviously, there will be times when you will need to explicitly cast one type into another, and it would be nice to know if any data has been lost along the way. Not detecting this could cause serious errors — for example, in an accounting application or an application determining the trajectory of a rocket to the moon.

One way to do this is simply to check the value of the source variable and compare it with the known limits of the destination variable. Another technique is to force the system to pay special attention to the conversion at runtime. Attempting to fit a value into a variable when that value is too big for the type of that variable results in an *overflow*, and this is the situation you want to check for.

Two keywords exist for setting what is called the *overflow checking context* for an expression: checked and unchecked. You use these in the following way:

```
checked(expression)
unchecked(expression)
```

You can force overflow checking in the last example:

```
byte destinationVar;
short sourceVar = 281;
destinationVar = checked((byte)sourceVar);
Console.WriteLine("sourceVar val: {0}", sourceVar);
Console.WriteLine("destinationVar val: {0}", destinationVar);
```

When this code is executed, it will crash with the error message shown in Figure 5-1 (this was compiled in a project called OverflowCheck).

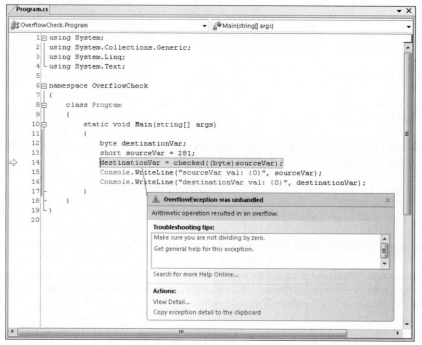

Figure 5-1

However, if you replace checked with unchecked in this code, you get the result shown earlier, and no error occurs. This is identical to the default behavior you saw earlier.

As well as these two keywords, you can configure your application to behave as if every expression of this type includes the checked keyword, unless that expression explicitly uses the unchecked keyword (in other words, you can change the default setting for overflow checking). To do this, you modify the properties for your project in VS by right-clicking on the project in the Solution Explorer window and selecting the Properties option. Click Build on the left side of the window. This will bring up the Build settings, as shown in Figure 5-2.

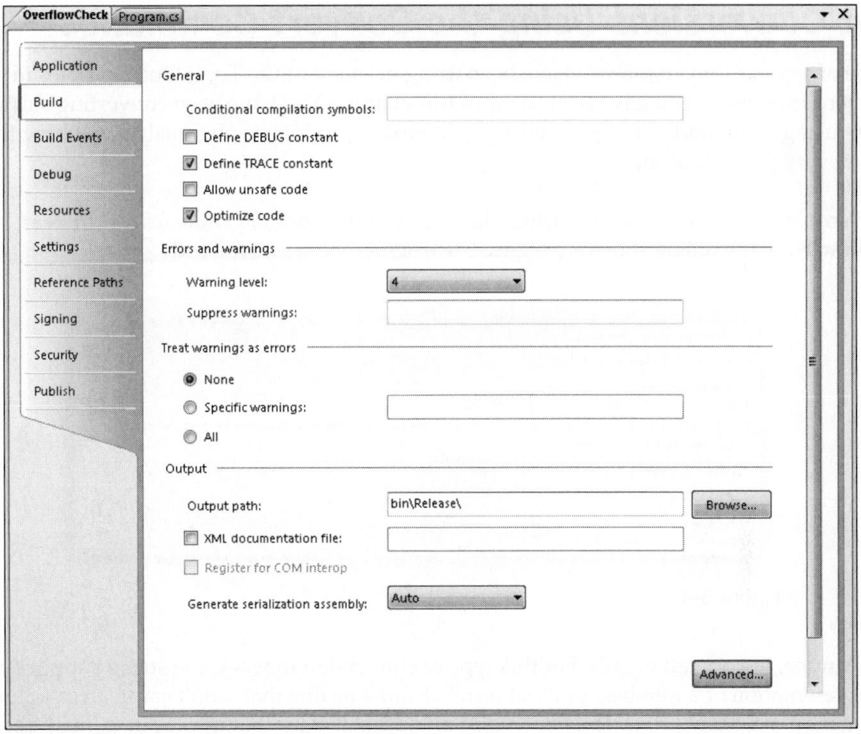

Figure 5-2

The property you want to change is one of the Advanced settings, so you click the Advanced button. In the dialog that appears, enable the Check for arithmetic overflow/underflow option, as shown in Figure 5-3. By default, this setting is disabled, but enabling it provides the checked behavior detailed previously.

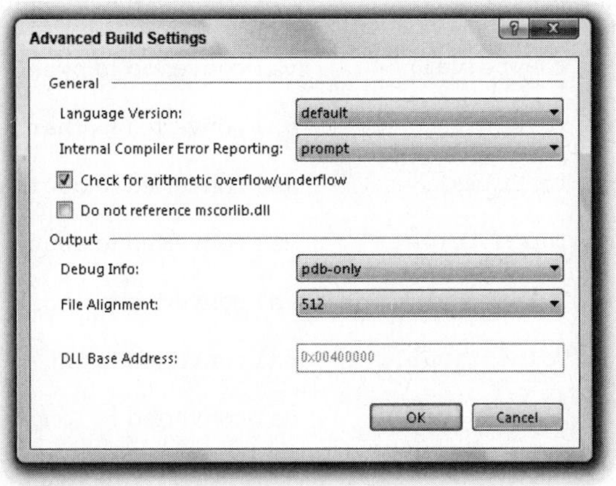

Figure 5-3

Explicit Conversions Using the Convert Commands

The type of explicit conversion you have been using in many of the Try It Out examples in this book is a bit different from those you have seen so far in this chapter. You have been converting string values into numbers using commands such as `Convert.ToDouble()`, which is obviously something that won't work for every possible string.

If, for example, you try to convert a string like `Number` into a double value using `Convert.ToDouble()`, then you will see the dialog shown in Figure 5-4 when you execute the code.

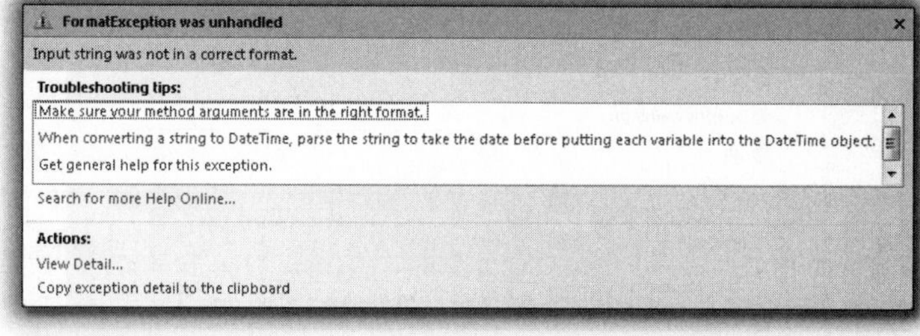

Figure 5-4

As you can see, the operation fails. For this type of conversion to work, the string supplied *must* be a valid representation of a number, and that number must be one that won't cause an overflow. A valid representation of a number is one that contains an optional sign (that is, plus or minus), zero or more digits, an optional period followed by one or more digits, and an optional "e" or "E" followed by an optional sign and one or more digits and *nothing else except spaces* (before or after this sequence). Using all of these optional extras, you can recognize strings as complex as $-1.2451e-24$ as being a number.

There are many such explicit conversions that you can specify in this way, as the following table shows:

Command	Result
`Convert.ToBoolean(val)`	val converted to `bool`
`Convert.ToByte(val)`	val converted to `byte`
`Convert.ToChar(val)`	val converted to `char`
`Convert.ToDecimal(val)`	val converted to `decimal`
`Convert.ToDouble(val)`	val converted to `double`
`Convert.ToInt16(val)`	val converted to `short`
`Convert.ToInt32(val)`	val converted to `int`
`Convert.ToInt64(val)`	val converted to `long`

Command	Result
`Convert.ToSByte(val)`	`val` converted to `sbyte`
`Convert.ToSingle(val)`	`val` converted to `float`
`Convert.ToString(val)`	`val` converted to `string`
`Convert.ToUInt16(val)`	`val` converted to `ushort`
`Convert.ToUInt32(val)`	`val` converted to `uint`
`Convert.ToUInt64(val)`	`val` converted to `ulong`

Here `val` can be most types of variable (if it's a type that can't be handled by these commands, the compiler will tell you).

Unfortunately, as the table shows, the names of these conversions are slightly different from the C# type names; for example, to convert to an `int` you use `Convert.ToInt32()`. That's because these commands come from the .NET Framework `System` namespace, rather than being native C#. This enables them to be used from other .NET-compatible languages besides C#.

The important thing to note about these conversions is that they are *always* overflow-checked, and the `checked` and `unchecked` keywords and project property settings have no effect.

The next Try It Out is an example that covers many of the conversion types from this section. It declares and initializes a number of variables of different types and then converts between them implicitly and explicitly.

Try It Out   Type Conversions in Practice

1. Create a new console application called `Ch05Ex01` and save it in the directory C:\BegVCSharp\Chapter05.

2. Add the following code to `Program.cs`:

```
static void Main(string[] args)
{
    short   shortResult, shortVal = 4;
    int     integerVal = 67;
    long    longResult;
    float   floatVal = 10.5F;
    double  doubleResult, doubleVal = 99.999;
    string  stringResult, stringVal = "17";
    bool    boolVal = true;

    Console.WriteLine("Variable Conversion Examples\n");

    doubleResult = floatVal * shortVal;
    Console.WriteLine("Implicit, -> double: {0} * {1} -> {2}", floatVal,
```

```
            shortVal, doubleResult);

        shortResult = (short)floatVal;
        Console.WriteLine("Explicit, -> short:  {0} -> {1}", floatVal,
            shortResult);

        stringResult = Convert.ToString(boolVal) +
            Convert.ToString(doubleVal);
        Console.WriteLine("Explicit, -> string: \"{0}\" + \"{1}\" -> {2}",
            boolVal, doubleVal, stringResult);

        longResult = integerVal + Convert.ToInt64(stringVal);
        Console.WriteLine("Mixed,    -> long:   {0} + {1} -> {2}",
            integerVal, stringVal, longResult);
        Console.ReadKey();
    }
}
```

3. Execute the code. The result is shown in Figure 5-5.

Figure 5-5

How It Works

This example contains all of the conversion types you've seen so far, both in simple assignments as in the short code examples in the preceding discussion and in expressions. You need to consider both cases, because the processing of *every* non-unary operator may result in type conversions, not just assignment operators. For example:

```
shortVal * floatVal
```

Here, you are multiplying a `short` value by a `float` value. In situations such as this, where no explicit conversion is specified, implicit conversion will be used if possible. In this example, the only implicit conversion that makes sense is to convert the `short` into a `float` (as converting a `float` into a `short` requires explicit conversion), so this is the one that will be used.

However, you can override this behavior should you wish, as shown here:

```
shortVal * (short)floatVal
```

This doesn't mean that a short *will be returned from this operation. Because the result of multiplying two* short *values is quite likely to exceed 32767 (the maximum value a* short *can hold), this operation actually returns an* int.

Explicit conversions performed using this casting syntax take the same operator precedence as other unary operators (such as ++ used as a prefix) — that is, the highest level of precedence.

When you have statements involving mixed types, conversions occur as each operator is processed, according to operator precedence. This means that "intermediate" conversions may occur:

```
doubleResult = floatVal + (shortVal * floatVal);
```

The first operator to be processed here is *, which, as discussed previously, will result in shortVal being converted to a float. Next, you process the + operator, which won't require any conversion because it acts on two float values (floatVal and the float type result of shortVal * floatVal). Finally, the float result of this calculation is converted into a double when the = operator is processed.

This conversion process can seem complex at first glance, but as long as you break expressions down into parts by taking the operator precedence order into account, you should be able to work things out.

Complex Variable Types

So far you've looked at all the simple variable types that C# has to offer. This section looks at three slightly more complex (but very useful) sorts of variable: enumerations, structures, and arrays.

Enumerations

Each of the types you've seen so far (with the exception of string) has a clearly defined set of allowed values. Admittedly, this set is so large in types such as double that it can practically be considered a continuum, but it *is* a fixed set nevertheless. The simplest example of this is the bool type, which can only take one of two values: true or false.

There are many other situations in which you might want to have a variable that can take one of a fixed set of results. For example, you might want to have an orientation type that can store one of the values north, south, east, or west.

In situations like this, *enumerations* can be very useful. Enumerations do exactly what you want in this orientation type: They allow the definition of a type that can take one of a finite set of values that you supply. What you need to do, then, is create your own enumeration type called orientation that can take one of the four possible values.

Note that there is an additional step involved here — you don't just declare a variable of a given type; you declare and detail a user-defined type and then you declare a variable of this new type.

Defining Enumerations

Enumerations can be defined using the enum keyword as follows:

```
enum typeName
{
    value1,
    value2,
    value3,
    ...
    valueN
}
```

Next, you can declare variables of this new type as follows:

```
typeName varName;
```

You can assign values using the following:

```
varName = typeName.value;
```

Enumerations have an *underlying type* used for storage. Each of the values that an enumeration type can take is stored as a value of this underlying type, which by default is int. You can specify a different underlying type by adding the type to the enumeration declaration:

```
enum typeName : underlyingType
{
    value1,
    value2,
    value3,
    ...
    valueN
}
```

Enumerations can have underlying types of byte, sbyte, short, ushort, int, uint, long, and ulong.

By default, each value is assigned a corresponding underlying type value automatically according to the order in which it is defined, starting from zero. This means that value1 gets the value 0, value2 gets 1, value3 gets 2, and so on. You can override this assignment by using the = operator and specifying actual values for each enumeration value:

```
enum typeName : underlyingType
{
    value1 = actualVal1,
    value2 = actualVal2,
    value3 = actualVal3,
    ...
    valueN = actualValN
}
```

In addition, you can specify identical values for multiple enumeration values by using one value as the underlying value of another:

```
enum typeName : underlyingType
{
    value1 = actualVal1,
    value2 = value1,
    value3,
    ...
    valueN = actualValN
}
```

Any values left unassigned are given an underlying value automatically, whereby the values used are in a sequence starting from 1 greater than the last explicitly declared one. In the preceding code, for example, `value3` will get the value `value1 + 1`.

Note that this can cause problems, with values specified after a definition such as `value2 = value1` being identical to other values. For example, in the following code `value4` will have the same value as `value2`:

```
enum typeName : underlyingType
{
    value1 = actualVal1,
    value2,
    value3 = value1,
    value4,

    . . .
    valueN = actualValN
}
```

Of course, if this is the behavior you want then this code is fine. Note also that assigning values in a circular fashion will cause an error:

```
enum typeName : underlyingType
{
    value1 = value2,
    value2 = value1
}
```

The following Try It Out shows an example of all of this. The code defines an enumeration called `orientation` and then demonstrates its use.

Try It Out   Using an Enumeration

1. Create a new console application called `Ch05Ex02` and save it in the directory C:\BegVCSharp\Chapter05.

2. Add the following code to `Program.cs`:

```
namespace Ch05Ex02
{
    enum orientation : byte
    {
        north = 1,
        south = 2,
        east  = 3,
        west  = 4
    }

    class Program
    {
        static void Main(string[] args)
```

```
            orientation myDirection = orientation.north;
            Console.WriteLine("myDirection = {0}", myDirection);
            Console.ReadKey();
        }
    }
}
```

3. Execute the application. You should see the output shown in Figure 5-6.

Figure 5-6

4. Quit the application and modify the code as follows:

```
        byte directionByte;
        string directionString;
        orientation myDirection = orientation.north;
        Console.WriteLine("myDirection = {0}", myDirection);
        directionByte = (byte)myDirection;
        directionString = Convert.ToString(myDirection);
        Console.WriteLine("byte equivalent = {0}", directionByte);
        Console.WriteLine("string equivalent = {0}", directionString);
        Console.ReadKey();
```

5. Execute the application again. The output is shown in Figure 5-7.

Figure 5-7

How It Works

This code defines and uses an enumeration type called `orientation`. The first thing to notice is that the type definition code is placed in your namespace, `Ch05Ex02`, but not in the same place as the rest of your code. This is because definitions are not executed as such; that is, at runtime you don't step through the code in a definition as you do the lines of code in your application. Application execution starts in the place you're used to and has access to your new type because it belongs to the same namespace.

The first iteration of the example demonstrates the basic method of creating a variable of your new type, assigning it a value and outputting it to the screen. Next, you modify the code to show the conversion of enumeration values into other types. Note that you must use explicit conversions here. Even though the underlying type of `orientation` is `byte`, you still have to use the `(byte)` cast to convert the value of `myDirection` into a `byte` type:

```
directionByte = (byte)myDirection;
```

The same explicit casting is necessary in the other direction, too, if you want to convert a `byte` into an `orientation`. For example, you could use the following code to convert a `byte` variable called `myByte` into an orientation and assign this value to `myDirection`:

```
myDirection = (orientation)myByte;
```

Of course, care must be taken here because not all permissible values of `byte` type variables map to defined `orientation` values. The `orientation` type can store other `byte` values, so you won't get an error straight away, but this may break logic later in the application.

To get the string value of an enumeration value you can use `Convert.ToString()`:

```
directionString = Convert.ToString(myDirection);
```

Using a `(string)` cast won't work because the processing required is more complicated than just placing the data stored in the enumeration variable into a `string` variable. Alternatively, you can use the `ToString()` command of the variable itself. The following code gives you the same result as using `Convert.ToString()`:

```
directionString = myDirection.ToString();
```

Converting a `string` to an enumeration value is also possible, except that here the syntax required is slightly more complex. A special command exists for this sort of conversion, `Enum.Parse()`, which is used in the following way:

```
(enumerationType)Enum.Parse(typeof(enumerationType), enumerationValueString);
```

This uses another operator, `typeof`, which obtains the type of its operand. You could use this for your `orientation` type as follows:

```
string myString = "north";
orientation myDirection = (orientation)Enum.Parse(typeof(orientation),
                                                  myString);
```

Of course, not all string values will map to an `orientation` value! If you pass in a value that doesn't map to one of your enumeration values, you will get an error. Like everything else in C#, these values are case sensitive, so you still get an error if your string agrees with a value in everything but case (for example, if `myString` is set to `North` rather than `north`).

Structs

The next sort of variable that you will look at is the *struct* (short for structure). Structs are just that. That is, data structures are composed of several pieces of data, possibly of different types. They enable you to define your own types of variables based on this structure. For example, suppose that you want to store the route to a location from a starting point, where the route consists of a direction and a distance in miles. For simplicity you can assume that the direction is one of the compass points (such that it can be represented using the `orientation` enumeration from the last section) and that distance in miles can be represented as a `double` type.

You could use two separate variables for this using code you've seen already:

```
orientation myDirection;
double      myDistance;
```

There is nothing wrong with using two variables like this, but it is far simpler (especially where multiple routes are required) to store this information in one place.

Defining Structs

Structs are defined using the `struct` keyword as follows:

```
struct <typeName>
{
    <memberDeclarations>
}
```

The `<memberDeclarations>` section contains declarations of variables (called the *data members* of the struct) in almost the same format as usual. Each member declaration takes the following form:

```
<accessibility> <type> <name>;
```

To allow the code that calls the struct to access the struct's data members, you use the keyword `public` for `<accessibility>`. For example:

```
struct route
{
    public orientation direction;
    public double      distance;
}
```

Once you have a struct type defined, you use it by defining variables of the new type:

```
route myRoute;
```

In addition, you have access to the data members of this composite variable via the period character:

```
myRoute.direction = orientation.north;
myRoute.distance = 2.5;
```

This is illustrated in the following Try It Out, where the `orientation` enumeration from the last Try It Out is used with the `route` struct shown previously. This struct is then manipulated in code to give you a feel for how structs work.

Try It Out   **Using a Struct**

1. Create a new console application called Ch05Ex03 and save it in the directory
   C:\BegVCSharp\Chapter05.

2. Add the following code to Program.cs:

```
namespace Ch05Ex03
{
    enum orientation : byte
    {
        north = 1,
        south = 2,
        east  = 3,
        west  = 4
    }

    struct route
    {
        public orientation direction;
        public double      distance;
    }

    class Program
    {
        static void Main(string[] args)
        {
            route myRoute;
            int myDirection = -1;
            double myDistance;
            Console.WriteLine("1) North\n2) South\n3) East\n4) West");
            do
            {
                Console.WriteLine("Select a direction:");
                myDirection = Convert.ToInt32(Console.ReadLine());
            }
            while ((myDirection < 1) || (myDirection > 4));
            Console.WriteLine("Input a distance:");
            myDistance = Convert.ToDouble(Console.ReadLine());
            myRoute.direction = (orientation)myDirection;
            myRoute.distance = myDistance;
            Console.WriteLine("myRoute specifies a direction of {0} and a " +
                "distance of {1}", myRoute.direction, myRoute.distance);
            Console.ReadKey();
        }
    }
}
```

3. Execute the code, select a direction by entering a number between 1 and 4, and then enter a
   distance. The result is shown in Figure 5-8.

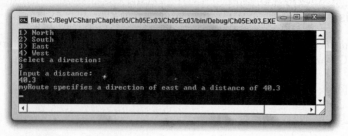

Figure 5-8

How It Works

Structs, like enumerations, are declared outside of the main body of the code. You declare your `route` struct just inside the namespace declaration, along with the `orientation` enumeration that it uses:

```
enum orientation : byte
{
    north = 1,
    south = 2,
    east  = 3,
    west  = 4
}

struct route
{
    public orientation direction;
    public double      distance;
}
```

The main body of the code follows a structure similar to some of the example code you've already seen, requesting input from the user and displaying it. You perform some simple validation of user input by placing the direction selection in a `do` loop, rejecting any input that isn't an integer between 1 and 4 (with values chosen such that they map onto the enumeration members for easy assignment).

Input that cannot be interpreted as an integer will result in an error. You'll see why this happens, and what to do about it, later in the book.

The interesting point to note is that when you refer to members of `route` they are treated exactly the same way that variables of the same type as the member would be. The assignment is as follows:

```
myRoute.direction = (orientation)myDirection;
myRoute.distance = myDistance;
```

You could simply take the input value directly into `myRoute.distance` with no ill effects as follows:

```
myRoute.distance = Convert.ToDouble(Console.ReadLine());
```

The extra step allows for more validation, although none is performed in this code. Any access to members of a structure is treated in the same way. Expressions of the form `structVar.memberVar` can be said to evaluate to a variable of the type of `memberVar`.

Arrays

All the types you've seen so far have one thing in common: Each of them stores a single value (or a single set of values in the case of structs). Sometimes, in situations where you want to store a lot of data, this isn't very convenient. Sometimes you want to store several values of the same type at the same time, without having to use a different variable for each value.

For example, suppose you want to perform some processing that involves the names of all of your friends. You could use simple string variables:

```
string friendName1 = "Robert Barwell";
string friendName2 = "Mike Parry";
string friendName3 = "Jeremy Beacock";
```

But this looks like it will require a lot of effort, especially because you need to write different code to process each variable. You couldn't, for example, iterate through this list of strings in a loop.

The alternative is to use an *array*. Arrays are indexed lists of variables stored in a single array type variable. For example, you might have an array called `friendNames` that stores the three names shown above. You can access individual members of this array by specifying their index in square brackets, as shown here:

```
friendNames[<index>]
```

This index is simply an integer, starting with 0 for the first entry, using 1 for the second, and so on. This means that you can go through the entries using a loop:

```
int i;
for (i = 0; i < 3; i++)
{
    Console.WriteLine("Name with index of {0}: {1}", i, friendNames[i]);
}
```

Arrays have a single *base type* — that is, individual entries in an array are all of the same type. This `friendNames` array has a base type of `string` because it is intended for storing `string` variables. Array entries are often referred to as *elements*.

Declaring Arrays

Arrays are declared in the following way:

```
<baseType>[] <name>;
```

Here, `<baseType>` may be any variable type, including the enumeration and struct types you've seen in this chapter. Arrays must be initialized before you have access to them. You can't just access or assign values to the array elements like this:

```
int[] myIntArray;
myIntArray[10] = 5;
```

Arrays can be initialized in two ways. You can either specify the complete contents of the array in a literal form, or you can specify the size of the array and use the new keyword to initialize all array elements.

Specifying an array using literal values simply involves providing a comma-separated list of element values enclosed in curly braces:

```
int[] myIntArray = {5, 9, 10, 2, 99};
```

Here, myIntArray has five elements, each with an assigned integer value.

The other method requires the following syntax:

```
int[] myIntArray = new int[5];
```

Here, you use the new keyword to explicitly initialize the array, and a constant value to define the size. This method results in all the array members being assigned a default value, which is 0 for numeric types. You can also use nonconstant variables for this initialization:

```
int[] myIntArray = new int[arraySize];
```

In addition, you can combine these two methods of initialization if you wish:

```
int[] myIntArray = new int[5] {5, 9, 10, 2, 99};
```

With this method the sizes *must* match. You can't, for example, write

```
int[] myIntArray = new int[10] {5, 9, 10, 2, 99};
```

Here, the array is defined as having 10 members, but only 5 are defined, so compilation will fail. A side effect of this is that if you define the size using a variable, then that variable must be a constant:

```
const int arraySize = 5;
int[] myIntArray = new int[arraySize] {5, 9, 10, 2, 99};
```

If you omit the const keyword, this code will fail.

As with other variable types, there is no need to initialize an array on the same line that you declare it. The following is perfectly legal:

```
int[] myIntArray;
myIntArray = new int[5];
```

Now it's time to try out some code. In the following Try It Out you create and use an array of strings, using the example from the introduction to this section.

Try It Out   **Using an Array**

1. Create a new console application called Ch05Ex04 and save it in the directory
   C:\BegVCSharp\Chapter05.

2. Add the following code to Program.cs:

```
static void Main(string[] args)
{
    string[] friendNames = {"Robert Barwell", "Mike Parry",
                            "Jeremy Beacock"};
    int i;
    Console.WriteLine("Here are {0} of my friends:",
                      friendNames.Length);
    for (i = 0; i < friendNames.Length; i++)
    {
        Console.WriteLine(friendNames[i]);
    }
    Console.ReadKey();
}
```

3. Execute the code. The result is shown in Figure 5-9.

Figure 5-9

How It Works

This code sets up a string array with three values and lists them in the console in a for loop. Note that you have access to the number of elements in the array using friendNames.Length:

```
Console.WriteLine("Here are {0} of my friends:", friendNames.Length);
```

This is a handy way to get the size of an array. Outputting values in a for loop is easy to get wrong. For example, try changing < to <= as follows:

```
for (i = 0; i <= friendNames.Length; i++)
{
    Console.WriteLine(friendNames[i]);
}
```

Compiling this results in the dialog shown in Figure 5-10.

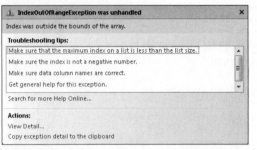

Figure 5-10

Here, you have attempted to access `friendNames[3]`. Remember that array indices start from 0, so the last element is `friendNames[2]`. If you attempt to access elements outside of the array size, then the code will fail. It just so happens that there is a more resilient method of accessing all the members of an array: using `foreach` loops.

foreach Loops

A `foreach` loop enables you to address each element in an array using this simple syntax:

```
foreach (<baseType> <name> in <array>)
{
    // can use <name> for each element
}
```

This loop will cycle through each element, placing each one in the variable `<name>` in turn, without danger of accessing illegal elements. You don't have to worry about how many elements are in the array, and you can be sure that you'll get to use each one in the loop. Using this approach, you can modify the code in the last example as follows:

```
static void Main(string[] args)
{
    string[] friendNames = {"Robert Barwell", "Mike Parry",
                            "Jeremy Beacock"};
    Console.WriteLine("Here are {0} of my friends:",
                      friendNames.Length);
    foreach (string friendName in friendNames)
    {
        Console.WriteLine(friendName);
    }
    Console.ReadKey();
}
```

The output of this code will be exactly the same as that of the previous Try It Out. The main difference between using this method and a standard `for` loop is that `foreach` gives you *read-only* access to the array contents, so you can't change the values of any of the elements. You couldn't, for example, do the following:

```
foreach (string friendName in friendNames)
{
    friendName = "Rupert the bear";
}
```

If you try this, then compilation will fail. If you use a simple `for` loop, however, then you can assign values to array elements.

Multidimensional Arrays

A multidimensional array is simply one that uses multiple indices to access its elements. For example, suppose you want to plot the height of a hill against the position measured. You might specify a position using two coordinates, x and y. You want to use these two coordinates as indices, such that an array called `hillHeight` would store the height at each pair of coordinates. This involves using multidimensional arrays.

A two-dimensional array such as this is declared as follows:

```
<baseType>[,] <name>;
```

Arrays of more dimensions simply require more commas:

```
<baseType>[,,,] <name>;
```

This would declare a four-dimensional array. Assigning values also uses a similar syntax, with commas separating sizes. To declare and initialize the two-dimensional array `hillHeight`, with a base type of `double`, an x size of 3, and a y size of 4 requires the following:

```
double[,] hillHeight = new double[3,4];
```

Alternatively, you can use literal values for initial assignment. Here, you use nested blocks of curly braces, separated by commas:

```
double[,] hillHeight = {{1, 2, 3, 4}, {2, 3, 4, 5}, {3, 4, 5, 6}};
```

This array has the same dimensions as the previous one — that is, three rows and four columns. By providing literal value these dimensions are defined implicitly.

To access individual elements of a multidimensional array, you simply specify the indices separated by commas:

```
hillHeight[2,1]
```

You can then manipulate this element just as you can other elements. This expression will access the second element of the third nested array as defined previously (the value will be 4). Remember that you start counting from 0 and that the first number is the nested array. In other words, the first number specifies the pair of curly braces, and the second number specifies the element within that pair of braces. You can represent this array visually, as shown in Figure 5-11.

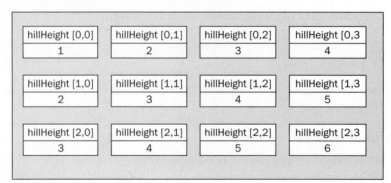

Figure 5-11

The `foreach` loop gives you access to all elements in a multidimensional way, just as with single-dimensional arrays:

```
double[,] hillHeight = {{1, 2, 3, 4}, {2, 3, 4, 5}, {3, 4, 5, 6}};
foreach (double height in hillHeight)
{
    Console.WriteLine("{0}", height);
}
```

The order in which the elements are output is the same as the order used to assign literal values:

```
hillHeight[0,0]
hillHeight[0,1]
hillHeight[0,2]
hillHeight[0,3]
hillHeight[1,0]
hillHeight[1,1]
hillHeight[1,2]
```

Arrays of Arrays

Multidimensional arrays, as discussed in the last section, are said to be *rectangular* because each "row" is the same size. Using the last example, you can have a y coordinate of 0 to 3 for any of the possible x coordinates.

It is also possible to have *jagged* arrays, whereby "rows" may be different sizes. For this, you need an array in which each element is another array. You could also have arrays of arrays of arrays if you want, or even more complex situations. However, all this is only possible if the arrays have the same base type.

The syntax for declaring arrays of arrays involves specifying multiple sets of square brackets in the declaration of the array, as shown here:

```
int[][] jaggedIntArray;
```

Unfortunately, initializing arrays such as this isn't as simple as initializing multidimensional arrays. You can't, for example, follow the preceding declaration with this:

```
jaggedIntArray = new int[3][4];
```

Even if you could do this, it wouldn't be that useful because you can achieve the same effect with simple multidimensional arrays with less effort. Nor can you use code such as this:

```
jaggedIntArray = {{1, 2, 3}, {1}, {1, 2}};
```

You have two options. You can initialize the array that contains other arrays (I'll call these sub-arrays for clarity) and then initialize the subarrays in turn:

```
jaggedIntArray = new int[2][];
jaggedIntArray[0] = new int[3];
jaggedIntArray[1] = new int[4];
```

Alternately, you can use a modified form of the preceding literal assignment:

```
jaggedIntArray = new int[3][] {new int[] {1, 2, 3}, new int[] {1},
                               new int[] {1, 2}};
```

This can be simplified if the array is initialized on the same line as it is declared, as follows:

```
int[][] jaggedIntArray = {new int[] {1, 2, 3}, new int[] {1}, new int[] {1, 2}};
```

You can use `foreach` loops with jagged arrays, but you often need to nest these to get to the actual data. For example, suppose you have the following jagged array that contains 10 arrays, each of which contains an array of integers that are divisors of an integer between 1 and 10:

```
int[][] divisors1To10 = {new int[] {1},
                         new int[] {1, 2},
                         new int[] {1, 3},
                         new int[] {1, 2, 4},
                         new int[] {1, 5},
                         new int[] {1, 2, 3, 6},
                         new int[] {1, 7},
                         new int[] {1, 2, 4, 8},
                         new int[] {1, 3, 9},
                         new int[] {1, 2, 5, 10}};
```

The following code will fail:

```
foreach (int divisor in divisors1To10)
{
    Console.WriteLine(divisor);
}
```

117

This is because the array `divisors1To10` contains `int[]` elements, not `int` elements. Instead, you have to loop through every sub-array as well as through the array itself:

```
foreach (int[] divisorsOfInt in divisors1To10)
{
    foreach(int divisor in divisorsOfInt)
    {
        Console.WriteLine(divisor);
    }
}
```

As you can see, the syntax for using jagged arrays can quickly become complex! In most cases, it is easier to use rectangular arrays or a simpler storage method. However, there may well be situations in which you are forced to use this method, and a working knowledge can't hurt!

String Manipulation

Your use of strings so far has consisted of writing strings to the console, reading strings from the console, and concatenating strings using the + operator. In the course of programming more interesting applications, you will soon discover that manipulating strings is something that you end up doing *a lot*. Because of this, it is worth spending a few pages looking at some of the more common string manipulation techniques available in C#.

To start with, note that a `string` type variable can be treated as a read-only array of `char` variables. This means that you can access individual characters using syntax like the following:

```
string myString = "A string";
char myChar = myString[1];
```

However, you can't assign individual characters in this way. To get a `char` array that you can write to, you can use the following code. This uses the `ToCharArray()` command of the array variable:

```
string myString = "A string";
char[] myChars = myString.ToCharArray();
```

Then you can manipulate the `char` array in the standard way. You can also use strings in `foreach` loops, as shown here:

```
foreach (char character in myString)
{
    Console.WriteLine("{0}", character);
}
```

As with arrays, you can also get the number of elements using `myString.Length`. This gives you the number of characters in the string:

```
string myString = Console.ReadLine();
Console.WriteLine("You typed {0} characters.", myString.Length);
```

Other basic string manipulation techniques use commands with a format similar to this `<string>`
`.ToCharArray()` command. Two simple, but useful, ones are `<string>.ToLower()` and
`<string>.ToUpper()`. These enable strings to be converted into lowercase and uppercase, respectively.
To see why this is useful, consider the situation in which you want to check for a specific response from a
user — for example, the string `yes`. If you convert the string entered by the user into lowercase, then you can
also check for the strings `YES`, `Yes`, `yeS`, and so on — you saw an example of this in the previous chapter:

```
string userResponse = Console.ReadLine();
if (userResponse.ToLower() == "yes")
{
    // Act on response.
}
```

This command, like the others in this section, doesn't actually change the string to which it is applied.
Instead, combining this command with a string results in the creation of a new string, which you can
compare to another string (as shown here) or assign to another variable. The other variable may be the
same one that is being operated on:

```
userResponse = userResponse.ToLower();
```

This is an important point to remember, because just writing

```
userResponse.ToLower();
```

doesn't actually achieve very much!

There are other things you can do to ease the interpretation of user input. What if the user accidentally
put an extra space at the beginning or end of their input? In this case, the preceding code won't work.
You need to trim the string entered, which you can do using the `<string>.Trim()` command:

```
string userResponse = Console.ReadLine();
userResponse = userResponse.Trim();
if (userResponse.ToLower() == "yes")
{
    // Act on response.
}
```

Using this, you will also be able detect strings like this:

```
" YES"
"Yes "
```

You can also use these commands to remove any other characters, by specifying them in a `char` array,
for example:

```
char[] trimChars = {' ', 'e', 's'};
string userResponse = Console.ReadLine();
userResponse = userResponse.ToLower();
userResponse = userResponse.Trim(trimChars);
if (userResponse == "y")
{
    // Act on response.
}
```

This eliminates any occurrences of spaces, the letter "e," and the letter "s" from the beginning or end of your string. Providing there aren't any other characters in the string, this will result in the detection of strings such as

```
"Yeeeees"
" y"
```

and so on.

You can also use the `<string>.TrimStart()` and `<string>.TrimEnd()` commands, which will trim spaces from the beginning and end of a string, respectively. These can also have `char` arrays specified.

There are two other string commands that you can use to manipulate the spacing of strings: `<string>`. `.PadLeft()` and `<string>.PadRight()`. These enable you to add spaces to the left or right of a string to force it to the desired length. You use these as follows:

```
<string>.PadX(<desiredLength>);
```

Here is an example:

```
myString = "Aligned";
myString = myString.PadLeft(10);
```

This would result in three spaces being added to the left of the word `Aligned` in `myString`. These methods can be helpful when aligning strings in columns, which is particularly useful for positioning strings containing numbers.

As with the trimming commands, you can also use these commands in a second way, by supplying the character to pad the string with. This involves a single `char`, not an array of `chars` as with trimming:

```
myString = "Aligned";
myString = myString.PadLeft(10, '-');
```

This would add three dashes to the start of `myString`.

There are many more of these string manipulation commands, many of which are only useful in very specific situations. These are discussed as you use them in the forthcoming chapters. Before moving on, though, it is worth looking at one of the features contained in both Visual C# 2008 Express Edition and Visual Studio 2008 that you may have noticed over the course of the last few chapters, and especially this one. In the following Try It Out, you examine auto-completion, whereby the IDE tries to help you out by suggesting what code you might like to insert.

Try It Out   **Statement Auto-Completion in VS**

1. Create a new console application called Ch05Ex05 and save it in the directory C:\BegVCSharp\Chapter05.

2. Type the following code to `Program.cs`, exactly as written, noting windows that pop up as you do so:

```
static void Main(string[] args)
{
    string myString = "This is a test.";
    char[] separator = {' '};
    string[] myWords;
    myWords = myString.
}
```

3. As you type the final period, the window shown in Figure 5-12 appears.

Figure 5-12

4. Without moving the cursor, type **s**. The pop-up window changes, and a tooltip pop-up appears (it is yellow, which can't be seen in Figure 5-13).

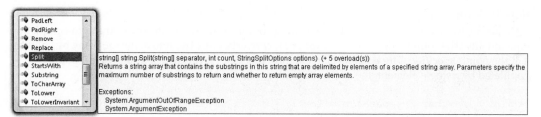

Figure 5-13

5. Type the following characters: `(separator);`. The code should look as follows, and the pop-up windows should disappear:

```
static void Main(string[] args)
{
    string myString = "This is a test.";
    char[] separator = {' '};
    string[] myWords;
    myWords = myString.Split(separator);
}
```

6. Add the following code, noting the windows as they pop up:

```csharp
static void Main(string[] args)
{
    string myString = "This is a test.";
    char[] separator = {' '};
    string[] myWords;
    myWords = myString.Split(separator);
    foreach (string word in myWords)
    {
        Console.WriteLine("{0}", word);
    }
    Console.ReadKey();
}
```

7. Execute the code. The result is shown in Figure 5-14.

Figure 5-14

How It Works

Note two main aspects of this code: the new string command used and the use of the auto-completion functionality. The command, `<string>.Split()`, converts a `string` into a `string` array by splitting it at the points specified. These points take the form of a `char` array, which in this case is simply populated by a single element, the space character:

```csharp
char[] separator = {' '};
```

The following code obtains the substrings you get when the string is split at each space — that is, you get an array of individual words:

```csharp
string[] myWords;
myWords = myString.Split(separator);
```

Next, you loop through the words in this array using `foreach` and write each one to the console:

```csharp
foreach (string word in myWords)
{
    Console.WriteLine("{0}", word);
}
```

Each word obtained has no spaces, neither embedded in the word nor at either end. The separators are removed when you use `Split()`.

Next, on to auto-completion. Both VS and VCE are very intelligent packages that work out a lot of information about your code as you type it in. Even as you type the first character on a new line, the IDE tries to help you by suggesting a keyword, a variable name, a type name, and so on. Only three letters into the preceding code (str), the IDE correctly guessed that you want to type string. Even more useful is when you type variable names. In long pieces of code, you often forget the names of variables you want to use. Because the IDE pops up a list of these as you type, you can find them easily, without having to refer to earlier code.

By the time you type the period after myString, it knows that myString is a string, detects that you want to specify a string command, and presents the available options. At this point, you can stop typing if desired, and select the command you want using the up and down arrow keys. As you move through the available options, the IDE describes the currently selected command and indicates what syntax it uses.

As you start typing more characters, the IDE moves the selected command to the top of the commands you might mean automatically. Once it shows the command you want, you can simply carry on typing as if you'd typed the whole name, so typing " (" takes you straight to the point where you specify the additional information that some commands require — and the IDE even tells you the format this extra information must be in, presenting options for those commands that accept varying amounts of information.

This feature of the IDE (known as IntelliSense) can come in very handy, enabling you to find information about strange types with ease. You might find it interesting to look at all the commands that the string type exposes and experiment — nothing you do is going to break the computer, so play away!

> Sometimes the displayed information can obscure some of the code you have already typed, which can be annoying. This is because the hidden code may be something that you need to refer to when typing. However, you can press the Ctrl key to make the command list transparent, enabling you to see what was hidden. This extremely useful technique is new in the 2008 editions of VS and VCE.

Summary

In this chapter, you've spent some time expanding your current knowledge of variables and filling in some of the blanks left from earlier. Perhaps the most important topic covered in this chapter is type conversion, because this is one that will come back to haunt you throughout this book. Getting a sound grasp of the concepts involved now will make things a lot easier later.

You've also seen a few more variable types that you can use to help you store data in a more developer-friendly way. You've learned how enumerations can make your code much more readable with easily discernable values; how structs can be used to combine multiple, related data elements in one place; and how you can group similar data together in arrays. You see all of these types used many times throughout the rest of this book.

Finally, you looked at string manipulation, including some of the basic techniques and principles involved. Many individual string commands are available, and you only examined a few, but you now know how to view the available commands in your IDE. Using this technique, you can have some fun trying things out. At least one of the following exercises can be solved using one or more string commands you haven't seen yet, but you'll have to figure out which!

This chapter extended your knowledge of variables to cover the following:

- ❑ Type conversions
- ❑ Enumerations
- ❑ Structs
- ❑ Arrays
- ❑ String manipulation

Exercises

1. Which of the following conversions can't be performed implicitly:

    a. `int` to `short`

    b. `short` to `int`

    c. `bool` to `string`

    d. `byte` to `float`

2. Show the code for a `color` enumeration based on the `short` type containing the colors of the rainbow plus black and white. Can this enumeration be based on the `byte` type?

3. Modify the Mandelbrot set generator example from the last chapter to use the following struct for complex numbers:

```
struct imagNum
{
    public double real, imag;
}
```

4. Will the following code compile? Why or why not?

```
string[] blab = new string[5]
string[5] = 5th string.
```

5. Write a console application that accepts a string from the user and outputs a string with the characters in reverse order.

6. Write a console application that accepts a string and replaces all occurrences of the string `no` with `yes`.

7. Write a console application that places double quotes around each word in a string.

Functions

All the code you have seen so far has taken the form of a single block, perhaps with some looping to repeat lines of code, and branching to execute statements conditionally. If you needed to perform an operation on your data, then this has meant placing the code required right where you want it to work.

This kind of code structure is limited. Often, some tasks — such as finding the highest value in an array, for example — may need to be performed at several points in a program. You can place identical (or near identical) sections of code in your application whenever necessary, but this has its own problems. Changing even one minor detail concerning a common task (to correct a code error, for example) may require changes to multiple sections of code, which may be spread throughout the application. Missing one of these could have dramatic consequences and cause the whole application to fail. In addition, the application could get very lengthy.

The solution to this problem is to use *functions*. Functions in C# are a means of providing blocks of code that can be executed at any point in an application.

> *Functions of the specific type examined in this chapter are known as methods, but this term has a very specific meaning in .NET programming that will only become clear later in this book. So for now this term is not to be used.*

For example, you could have a function that calculates the maximum value in an array. You can use this function from any point in your code, and use the same lines of code in each case. Because you only need to supply this code once, any changes you make to it will affect this calculation wherever it is used. This function can be thought of as containing *reusable* code.

Functions also have the advantage of making your code more readable, as you can use them to group related code together. This way, your application body itself can be made very short, as the inner workings of the code are separated out. This is similar to the way in which you can collapse regions of code together in the IDE using the outline view, and it gives a more logical structure to your application.

Functions can also be used to create multipurpose code, enabling them to perform the same operations on varying data. You can supply a function with information to work with in the form of parameters, and you can obtain results from functions in the form of return values. In the preceding example, you could supply an array to search as a parameter and obtain the maximum value in the array as a return value. This means that you can use the same function to work with a different array each time. The name and parameters of a function (but not its return type) collectively define the *signature* of a function.

This chapter covers all of the following topics:

❑ How to define and use simple functions that don't accept or return any data.

❑ How to transfer data to and from functions.

❑ Variable scope, which reflects how data in a C# application is localized to specific regions of code, an issue that becomes especially important when you are separating your code into multiple functions.

❑ An in-depth look at an important function in C# applications: `Main()`. You will learn how you can use the built-in behavior of this function to make use of *command-line arguments*, which enable you to transfer information into applications when you run them.

❑ Another feature of the struct type shown in the last chapter: the fact that you can supply functions as members of struct types.

The chapter ends with two more advanced topics: *function overloading* and *delegates*. Function overloading is a technique that enables you to provide multiple functions with the same name but different parameters. A delegate is a variable type that enables you to use functions indirectly. A delegate can be used to call any function that matches the return type and parameters defined by the delegate, giving you the ability to choose between several functions at runtime.

Defining and Using Functions

This section describes how you can add functions to your applications and then use (call) them from your code. Starting with the basics, you look at simple functions that don't exchange any data with code that calls them, and then look at more advanced function usage. The following Try It Out gets things moving.

Try It Out   Defining and Using a Basic Function

1. Create a new console application called Ch06Ex01 and save it in the directory C:\BegVCSharp\Chapter06.

2. Add the following code to `Program.cs`:

```
class Program
{
    static void Write()
    {
        Console.WriteLine("Text output from function.");
    }
```

```
static void Main(string[] args)
{
    Write();
    Console.ReadKey();
}
}
```

3.   Execute the code. The result is shown in Figure 6-1.

Figure 6-1

How It Works

The following four lines of your code define a function called `Write()`:

```
static void Write()
{
    Console.WriteLine("Text output from function.");
}
```

The code contained here simply outputs some text to the console window, but this behavior isn't that important at the moment, because the focus here is on the mechanisms behind function definition and use.

The function definition here consists of the following:

❑   Two keywords: static and void

❑   A function name followed by parentheses, `Write()`

❑   A block of code to execute enclosed in curly braces

   Function names are usually written in PascalCasing.

The code that defines the `Write()` function looks very similar to some of the other code in your application:

```
static void Main(string[] args)
{
    ...
}
```

This is because all the code you have written so far (apart from type definitions) has been part of a function. This function, `Main()`, is the *entry point* function for a console application. When a C# application is executed, the entry point function it contains is called; and when this function is completed, the application terminates. All C# executable code must have an entry point.

The only difference between the `Main()` function and your `Write()` function (apart from the lines of code they contain) is that there is some code inside the parentheses after the function name `Main`. This is how you specify parameters, which you see in more detail shortly.

As mentioned earlier, both `Main()` and `Write()` are defined using the `static` and `void` keywords. The `static` keyword relates to object-oriented concepts, which you come back to later in the book. For now, you only need to remember that all the functions you use in your applications in this section of the book must use this keyword.

`void`, in contrast, is much simpler to explain. It's used to indicate that the function does not return a value. Later in this chapter, you see the code that you need to use when a function has a return value.

Moving on, the code that calls your function is as follows:

```
Write();
```

You simply type the name of the function followed by empty parentheses. When program execution reaches this point, the code in the `Write()` function runs.

> The parentheses used both in the function definition and where the function is called are mandatory. Try removing them if you like — the code won't compile.

Return Values

The simplest way to exchange data with a function is to use a return value. Functions that have return values *evaluate* to that value, in exactly the same way that variables evaluate to the values they contain when you use them in expressions. Just like variables, return values have a type.

For example, you might have a function called `GetString()` whose return value is a string. You could use this in code, such as the following:

```
string myString;
myString = GetString();
```

Alternatively, you might have a function called `GetVal()` that returns a `double` value, which you could use in a mathematical expression:

```
double myVal;
double multiplier = 5.3;
myVal = GetVal() * multiplier;
```

When a function returns a value, you have to modify your function in two ways:

❑ Specify the type of the return value in the function declaration instead of using the `void` keyword.

❑ Use the `return` keyword to end the function execution and transfer the return value to the calling code.

In code terms, this looks like the following in a console application function of the type you've been looking at:

```
static <returnType> <functionName>()
{
    ...
    return <returnValue>;
}
```

The only limitation here is that `<returnValue>` must be a value that either is of type `<returnType>` or can be implicitly converted to that type. However, `<returnType>` can be any type you want, including the more complicated types you've seen. This might be as simple as the following:

```
static double GetVal()
{
    return 3.2;
}
```

However, return values are usually the result of some processing carried out by the function; the preceding could be achieved just as easily using a `const` variable.

When the `return` statement is reached, program execution returns to the calling code immediately. No lines of code after this statement are executed, although this doesn't mean that `return` statements can only be placed on the last line of a function body. You can use `return` earlier in the code, perhaps after performing some branching logic. Placing `return` in a `for` loop, an `if` block, or any other structure causes the structure to terminate immediately and the function to terminate, as shown here:

```
static double GetVal()
{
    double checkVal;
    // CheckVal assigned a value through some logic (not shown here).
    if (checkVal < 5)
        return 4.7;
    return 3.2;
}
```

Here, one of two values may be returned, depending on the value of `checkVal`. The only restriction in this case is that a `return` statement must be processed before reaching the closing `}` of the function. The following is illegal:

```
static double GetVal()
{
    double checkVal;
    // CheckVal assigned a value through some logic.
    if (checkVal < 5)
        return 4.7;
}
```

If `checkVal` is `>= 5`, then no `return` statement is met, which isn't allowed. All processing paths must reach a `return` statement. In most cases, the compiler detects this and gives you the error "not all code paths return a value."

As a final note, `return` can be used in functions that are declared using the `void` keyword (that don't have a return value). In that case, the function simply terminates. When you use `return` in this way, it is an error to provide a return value in between the `return` keyword and the semicolon that follows.

Parameters

When a function is to accept parameters, you must specify the following:

❏   A list of the parameters accepted by the function in its definition, along with the types of those parameters.

❏   A matching list of parameters in each function call.

This involves the following code, where you can have any number of parameters, each with a type and a name:

```
static <returnType> <functionName>(<paramType> <paramName>, ...)
{
    ...
    return <returnValue>;
}
```

The parameters are separated using commas, and each of these parameters is accessible from code within the function as a variable. For example, a simple function might take two `double` parameters and return their product:

```
static double Product(double param1, double param2)
{
    return param1 * param2;
}
```

The following Try It Out provides a more complex example.

Try It Out   Exchanging Data with a Function (Part 1)

1.   Create a new console application called Ch06Ex02 and save it in the directory C:\BegVCSharp\Chapter06.

2.   Add the following code to `Program.cs`:

```
class Program
{
    static int MaxValue(int[] intArray)
    {
        int maxVal = intArray[0];
        for (int i = 1; i < intArray.Length; i++)
        {
            if (intArray[i] > maxVal)
                maxVal = intArray[i];
        }
```

```
        return maxVal;
    }

static void Main(string[] args)
{
    int[] myArray = {1, 8, 3, 6, 2, 5, 9, 3, 0, 2};
    int maxVal = MaxValue(myArray);
    Console.WriteLine("The maximum value in myArray is {0}", maxVal);
    Console.ReadKey();
}
}
```

3. Execute the code. The result is shown in Figure 6-2.

Figure 6-2

How It Works

This code contains a function that does what the example function at the beginning of this chapter hoped to do. It accepts an array of integers as a parameter and returns the highest number in the array. The function definition is as follows:

```
static int MaxValue(int[] intArray)
{
    int maxVal = intArray[0];
    for (int i = 1; i < intArray.Length; i++)
    {
        if (intArray[i] > maxVal)
            maxVal = intArray[i];
    }
    return maxVal;
}
```

The function, MaxValue(), has a single parameter defined, an int array called intArray. It also has a return type of int. The calculation of the maximum value is simple. A local integer variable called maxVal is initialized to the first value in the array, and then this value is compared with each of the subsequent elements in the array. If an element contains a higher value than maxVal, then this value replaces the current value of maxVal. When the loop finishes, maxVal contains the highest value in the array, and is returned using the return statement.

The code in Main() declares and initializes a simple integer array to use with the MaxValue() function:

```
int[] myArray = {1, 8, 3, 6, 2, 5, 9, 3, 0, 2};
```

The call to `MaxValue()` is used to assign a value to the `int` variable `maxVal`:

```
int maxVal = MaxValue(myArray);
```

Next, you write this value to the screen using `Console.WriteLine()`:

```
Console.WriteLine("The maximum value in myArray is {0}", maxVal);
```

Parameter Matching

When you call a function, you must match the parameters as specified in the function definition exactly. This means matching the parameter types, the number of parameters, and the order of the parameters. For example, the function:

```
static void MyFunction(string myString, double myDouble)
{
    ...
}
```

can't be called using the following:

```
MyFunction(2.6, "Hello");
```

Here, you are attempting to pass a `double` value as the first parameter and a `string` value as the second parameter, which is not the order in which the parameters are defined in the function definition.

You also can't use:

```
MyFunction("Hello");
```

Here, you are only passing a single `string` parameter, where two parameters are required. Attempting to use either of the two preceding function calls will result in a compiler error, because the compiler forces you to match the signatures of the functions you use.

Recall from the introduction that the signature of a function is defined by the name and parameters of the function.

Going back to the example, `MaxValue()` can only be used to obtain the maximum `int` in an array of `int` values. If you replace the code in `Main()` with:

```
static void Main(string[] args)
{
    double[] myArray = {1.3, 8.9, 3.3, 6.5, 2.7, 5.3};
    double maxVal = MaxValue(myArray);
    Console.WriteLine("The maximum value in myArray is {0}", maxVal);
    Console.ReadKey();
}
```

then the code won't compile because the parameter type is wrong. In the "Overloading Functions" section later in this chapter, you'll learn a useful technique for getting around this problem.

Parameter Arrays

C# enables you to specify one (and only one) special parameter for a function. This parameter, which must be the last parameter in the function definition, is known as a *parameter array*. Parameter arrays enable you to call functions using a variable amount of parameters and are defined using the `params` keyword.

Parameter arrays can be a useful way to simplify your code because you don't have to pass arrays from your calling code. Instead, you pass several parameters of the same type, which are placed in an array you can use from within your function.

The following code is required to define a function that uses a parameter array:

```
static <returnType> <functionName>(<p1Type> <p1Name>, ... ,
                                  params <type>[] <name>)
{
    ...
    return <returnValue>;
}
```

You can call this function using code like the following:

```
<functionName>(<p1>, ... , <val1>, <val2>, ...)
```

Here `<val1>`, `<val2>`, and so on are values of type `<type>`, which are used to initialize the `<name>` array. The number of parameters that you can specify here is almost limitless; the only restriction is that they must all be of type `<type>`. You can even specify no parameters at all.

This final point makes parameter arrays particularly useful for specifying additional information for functions to use in their processing. For example, suppose you have a function called `GetWord()` that takes a `string` value as its first parameter and returns the first word in the string:

```
string firstWord = GetWord("This is a sentence.");
```

Here, `firstWord` will be assigned the string `This`.

You might add a `params` parameter to `GetWord()`, enabling you to optionally select an alternative word to return by its index:

```
string firstWord = GetWord("This is a sentence.", 2);
```

Assuming that you start counting at 1 for the first word, this would result in `firstWord` being assigned the string `is`.

You might also add the capability to limit the number of characters returned in a third parameter, also accessible through the `params` parameter:

```
string firstWord = GetWord("This is a sentence.", 4, 3);
```

Here, firstWord would be assigned the string sen.

Here's a complete example. The following Try It Out defines and uses a function with a params type parameter.

Try It Out   Exchanging Data with a Function (Part 2)

1. Create a new console application called Ch06Ex03 and save it in the directory
   C:\BegVCSharp\Chapter06.

2. Add the following code to Program.cs:

```
class Program
{
    static int SumVals(params int[] vals)
    {
        int sum = 0;
        foreach (int val in vals)
        {
            sum += val;
        }
        return sum;
    }

    static void Main(string[] args)
    {
        int sum = SumVals(1, 5, 2, 9, 8);
        Console.WriteLine("Summed Values = {0}", sum);
        Console.ReadKey();
    }
}
```

3. Execute the code. The result is shown in Figure 6-3.

file:///C:/BegVCSharp/Chapter06/Ch06Ex03/...

Summed Values = 25

Figure 6-3

How It Works

In this example, the function SumVals() is defined using the params keyword to accept any number of int parameters (and no others):

```
static int SumVals(params int[] vals)
{
    ...
}
```

The code in this function simply iterates through the values in the `vals` array and adds the values together, returning the result.

In `Main()`, you call this function with five integer parameters:

```
int sum = SumVals(1, 5, 2, 9, 8);
```

Note that you could just as easily call this function with none, one, two, or a hundred integer parameters — there is no limit to the number you can specify.

Reference and Value Parameters

All the functions defined so far in this chapter have had value parameters. That is, when you have used parameters, you have passed a value into a variable used by the function. Any changes made to this variable in the function have no effect on the parameter specified in the function call. For example, consider a function that doubles and displays the value of a passed parameter:

```
static void ShowDouble(int val)
{
    val *= 2;
    Console.WriteLine("val doubled = {0}", val);
}
```

Here, the parameter, `val`, is doubled in this function. If you call it in the following way:

```
int myNumber = 5;
Console.WriteLine("myNumber = {0}", myNumber);
ShowDouble(myNumber);
Console.WriteLine("myNumber = {0}", myNumber);
```

The text output to the console is as follows:

```
myNumber = 5
val doubled = 10
myNumber = 5
```

Calling `ShowDouble()` with `myNumber` as a parameter doesn't affect the value of `myNumber` in `Main()`, even though the parameter it is assigned to, `val`, is doubled.

That's all very well, but if you *want* the value of `myNumber` to change, you have a problem. You could use a function that returns a new value for `myNumber`, like this:

```
static int DoubleNum(int val)
{
    val *= 2;
    return val;
}
```

You could call this function using the following:

```
int myNumber = 5;
Console.WriteLine("myNumber = {0}", myNumber);
myNumber = DoubleNum(myNumber);
Console.WriteLine("myNumber = {0}", myNumber);
```

However, this code is hardly intuitive and won't cope with changing the values of multiple variables used as parameters (as functions have only one return value).

Instead, you want to pass the parameter by *reference*. This means that the function will work with exactly the same variable as the one used in the function call, not just a variable that has the same value. Any changes made to this variable will therefore be reflected in the value of the variable used as a parameter. To do this, you simply use the `ref` keyword to specify the parameter:

```
static void ShowDouble(ref int val)
{
    val *= 2;
    Console.WriteLine("val doubled = {0}", val);
}
```

Then, specify it again in the function call (this is mandatory):

```
int myNumber = 5;
Console.WriteLine("myNumber = {0}", myNumber);
ShowDouble(ref myNumber);
Console.WriteLine("myNumber = {0}", myNumber);
```

The text output to the console is now as follows:

```
myNumber = 5
val doubled = 10
myNumber = 10
```

This time `myNumber` has been modified by `ShowDouble()`.

Note two limitations on the variable used as a `ref` parameter. First, the function may result in a change to the value of a reference parameter, so you must use a *nonconstant* variable in the function call. The following is therefore illegal:

```
const int myNumber = 5;
Console.WriteLine("myNumber = {0}", myNumber);
ShowDouble(ref myNumber);
Console.WriteLine("myNumber = {0}", myNumber);
```

Second, you must use an initialized variable. C# doesn't allow you to assume that a `ref` parameter will be initialized in the function that uses it. The following code is also illegal:

```
int myNumber;
ShowDouble(ref myNumber);
Console.WriteLine("myNumber = {0}", myNumber);
```

Out Parameters

In addition to passing values by reference, you can also specify that a given parameter is an *out* parameter by using the out keyword, which is used in the same way as the ref keyword (as a modifier to the parameter in the function definition and in the function call). In effect, this gives you almost exactly the same behavior as a reference parameter in that the value of the parameter at the end of the function execution is returned to the variable used in the function call. However, there are important differences:

❑ Whereas it is illegal to use an unassigned variable as a ref parameter, you can use an unassigned variable as an out parameter.

❑ An out parameter must be treated as an unassigned value by the function that uses it.

This means that while it is permissible in calling code to use an assigned variable as an out parameter, the value stored in this variable is lost when the function executes.

As an example, consider an extension to the MaxValue() function shown earlier, which returns the maximum value of an array. Modify the function slightly so that you obtain the index of the element with the maximum value within the array. To keep things simple, obtain just the index of the first occurrence of this value when there are multiple elements with the maximum value. To do this, you add an out parameter by modifying the function as follows:

```
static int MaxValue(int[] intArray, out int maxIndex)
{
    int maxVal = intArray[0];
    maxIndex = 0;
    for (int i = 1; i < intArray.Length; i++)
    {
        if (intArray[i] > maxVal)
        {
            maxVal = intArray[i];
            maxIndex = i;
        }
    }
    return maxVal;
}
```

You might use this function as shown here:

```
int[] myArray = {1, 8, 3, 6, 2, 5, 9, 3, 0, 2};
int maxIndex;
Console.WriteLine("The maximum value in myArray is {0}",
                MaxValue(myArray, out maxIndex));
Console.WriteLine("The first occurrence of this value is at element {0}",
                maxIndex + 1);
```

This results in the following:

```
The maximum value in myArray is 9
The first occurrence of this value is at element 7
```

Note that you must use the out keyword in the function call, just as with the ref keyword.

One has been added to the value of maxIndex *returned here when it is displayed onscreen. This is to translate the index to a more readable form, so that the first element in the array is referred to as element 1, rather than element 0.*

Variable Scope

Throughout the last section, you may have been wondering why exchanging data with functions is necessary. The reason is that variables in C# are only accessible from localized regions of code. A given variable is said to have a *scope* from where it is accessible.

Variable scope is an important subject and one best introduced with an example. The following Try It Out illustrates a situation in which a variable is defined in one scope, and an attempt to use it is made in a different scope.

Try It Out   **Defining and Using a Basic Function**

1. Make the following changes to Ch06Ex01 in Program.cs:

```
class Program
{
    static void Write()
    {
        Console.WriteLine("myString = {0}", myString);
    }

    static void Main(string[] args)
    {
        string myString = "String defined in Main()";
        Write();
        Console.ReadKey();
    }
}
```

2. Compile the code and note the error and warning that appear in the task list:

```
The name 'myString' does not exist in the current context
The variable 'myString' is assigned but its value is never used
```

How It Works

What went wrong? Well, the variable myString defined in the main body of your application (the Main() function) isn't accessible from the Write() function.

The reason for this inaccessibility is that variables have a scope within which they are valid. This scope encompasses the code block that they are defined in and any directly nested code blocks. The blocks of code in functions are separate from the blocks of code from which they are called. Inside Write(), the name `myString` is undefined, and the `myString` variable defined in `Main()` is *out of scope* — it can only be used from within `Main()`.

In fact, you can have a completely separate variable in `Write()` called `myString`. Try modifying the code as follows:

```
class Program
{
    static void Write()
    {
        string myString = "String defined in Write()";
        Console.WriteLine("Now in Write()");
        Console.WriteLine("myString = {0}", myString);
    }

    static void Main(string[] args)
    {
        string myString = "String defined in Main()";
        Write();
        Console.WriteLine("\nNow in Main()");
        Console.WriteLine("myString = {0}", myString);
        Console.ReadKey();
    }
}
```

This code does compile, resulting in the output shown in Figure 6-4.

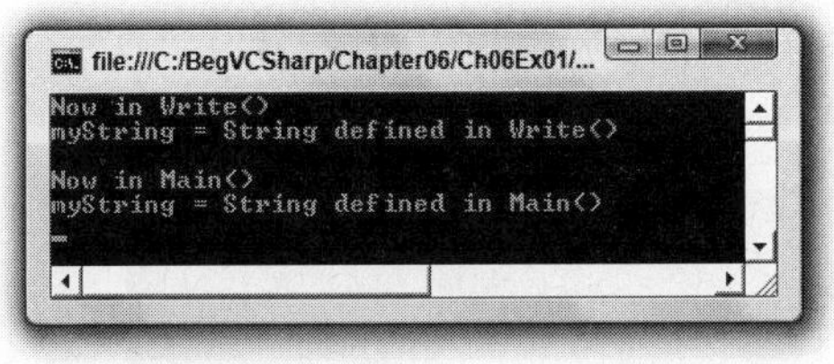

Figure 6-4

The operations performed by this code are as follows:

❑   `Main()` defines and initializes a string variable called `myString`.

❑   `Main()` transfers control to `Write()`.

❑   `Write()` defines and initializes a string variable called `myString`, which is a different variable than the `myString` defined in `Main()`.

❑   `Write()` outputs a string to the console containing the value of `myString` as defined in `Write()`.

❑   `Write()` transfers control back to `Main()`.

❑   `Main()` outputs a string to the console containing the value of `myString` as defined in `Main()`.

Variables whose scopes cover a single function in this way are known as *local variables*. It is also possible to have *global* variables, whose scopes cover multiple functions. Modify the code as follows:

```
class Program
{
    static string myString;

    static void Write()
    {
        string myString = "String defined in Write()";
        Console.WriteLine("Now in Write()");
        Console.WriteLine("Local myString = {0}", myString);
        Console.WriteLine("Global myString = {0}", Program.myString);
    }

    static void Main(string[] args)
    {
        string myString = "String defined in Main()";
        Program.myString = "Global string";
        Write();
        Console.WriteLine("\nNow in Main()");
        Console.WriteLine("Local myString = {0}", myString);
        Console.WriteLine("Global myString = {0}", Program.myString);
        Console.ReadKey();
    }
}
```

The result is now as shown in Figure 6-5.

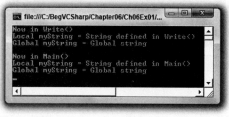

Figure 6-5

Here, you have added another variable called `myString`, this time further up the hierarchy of names in the code. This variable is defined as follows:

```
static string myString;
```

Note that again the `static` keyword is required here. Without going into too much detail, understand that in this type of console application, you must use either the `static` or `const` keyword for global variables of this form. If you want to modify the value of the global variable, you need to use `static` because `const` prohibits the value of the variable from changing.

To differentiate between this variable and the local variables in `Main()` and `Write()` with the same names, you have to classify the variable name using a fully qualified name, as described in Chapter 3.

Here, you refer to the global version as `Program.myString`. This is only necessary when you have global and local variables with the same name; if there were no local `myString` variable, you could simply use `myString` to refer to the global variable, rather than `Program.myString`. When you have a local variable with the same name as a global variable, the global variable is said to be *hidden*.

The value of the global variable is set in `Main()` with

```
Program.myString = "Global string";
```

and accessed in `Write()` with

```
Console.WriteLine("Global myString = {0}", Program.myString);
```

You might be wondering why you shouldn't just use this technique to exchange data with functions, rather than the parameter passing shown earlier. There are indeed situations where this is the preferable way to exchange data, but there are just as many (if not more) where it isn't. The choice of whether to use global variables depends on the intended use of the function in question. The problem with using global variables is that they are generally unsuitable for "general-purpose" functions, which are capable of working with whatever data you supply, not just data in a specific global variable. You look at this in more depth a little later.

Variable Scope in Other Structures

Before moving on, note that one of the points made in the last section has consequences above and beyond variable scope between functions. It was stated that the scopes of variables encompass the code blocks in which they are defined and any directly nested code blocks. This also applies to other code blocks, such as those in branching and looping structures. Consider the following code:

```
int i;
for (i = 0; i < 10; i++)
{
    string text = "Line " + Convert.ToString(i);
    Console.WriteLine("{0}", text);
}
Console.WriteLine("Last text output in loop: {0}", text);
```

Here, the string variable `text` is local to the `for` loop. This code won't compile because the call to `Console.WriteLine()` that occurs outside of this loop attempts to use the variable `text`, which is out of scope outside of the loop. Try modifying the code as follows:

```
int i;
string text;
for (i = 0; i < 10; i++)
{
    text = "Line " + Convert.ToString(i);
    Console.WriteLine("{0}", text);
}
Console.WriteLine("Last text output in loop: {0}", text);
```

This code will also fail because variables must be declared and initialized before use, and `text` is only initialized in the `for` loop. The value assigned to `text` is lost when the loop block is exited. However, you can make the following change:

```
int i;
string text = "";
for (i = 0; i < 10; i++)
{
    text = "Line " + Convert.ToString(i);
    Console.WriteLine("{0}", text);
}
Console.WriteLine("Last text output in loop: {0}", text);
```

This time `text` is initialized outside of the loop, and you have access to its value. The result of this simple code is shown in Figure 6-6.

Figure 6-6

Here, the last value assigned to `text` in the loop is accessible from outside the loop. As you can see, this topic requires a bit of effort to come to grips with. It is not immediately obvious why, in light of the earlier example, `text` doesn't retain the empty string it is assigned before the loop in the code after the loop.

The explanation for this behavior is related to memory allocation for the `text` variable, and indeed any variable. Merely declaring a simple variable type doesn't result in very much happening. It is only when values are assigned to the variables that values are allocated a place in memory to be stored. When this allocation takes place inside a loop, the value is essentially defined as a local value and goes out of scope outside of the loop.

Even though the variable itself isn't localized to the loop, the value it contains is. However, assigning a value outside of the loop ensures that the value is local to the main code, and is still in scope inside the loop. This means that the variable doesn't go out of scope before the main code block is exited, so you have access to its value outside of the loop.

Luckily for you, the C# compiler detects variable scope problems, and responding to the error messages it generates certainly helps you to understand the topic of variable scope.

Finally, you should be aware of best practices. In general, it is worth declaring and initializing all variables before any code blocks that use them. An exception to this is when you declare looping variables as part of a loop block:

```
for (int i = 0; i < 10; i++)
{
   ...
}
```

Here, i is localized to the looping code block, but that's fine because you will rarely require access to this counter from external code.

Parameters and Return Values Versus Global Data

This section takes a closer look at exchanging data with functions via global data and via parameters and return values. To recap, consider the following code:

```
class Program
{
    static void ShowDouble(ref int val)
    {
        val *= 2;
        Console.WriteLine("val doubled = {0}", val);
    }

    static void Main(string[] args)
    {
        int val = 5;
        Console.WriteLine("val = {0}", val);
        ShowDouble(ref val);
        Console.WriteLine("val = {0}", val);
    }
}
```

This code is slightly different from the code shown earlier in this chapter, when you used the variable name myNumber *in* Main(). *This illustrates the fact that local variables can have identical names and yet not interfere with each other. It also means that the two code samples shown here are more similar, allowing you to focus more on the specific differences without worrying about variable names.*

Compare it with this code:

```
class Program
{
    static int val;

    static void ShowDouble()
    {
        val *= 2;
        Console.WriteLine("val doubled = {0}", val);
    }
```

```
static void Main(string[] args)
{
    val = 5;
    Console.WriteLine("val = {0}", val);
    ShowDouble();
    Console.WriteLine("val = {0}", val);
}
}
```

The results of both of these ShowDouble() functions are identical.

There are no hard-and-fast rules for using one technique rather than another, and both techniques are perfectly valid, but you may want to consider the following guidelines.

To start with, as mentioned when this topic was first introduced, the ShowDouble() version that uses the global value only uses the global variable val. To use this version, you must use this global variable. This limits the versatility of the function slightly and means that you must continuously copy the global variable value into other variables if you intend to store the results. In addition, global data might be modified by code elsewhere in your application, which could cause unpredictable results (values might change without you realizing it until it's too late).

However, this loss of versatility can often be a bonus. Sometimes you only want to use a function for one purpose, and using a global data store reduces the possibility that you will make an error in a function call, perhaps passing it the wrong variable.

Of course, it could also be argued that this simplicity actually makes your code more difficult to understand. Explicitly specifying parameters enables you to see at a glance what is changing. If you see a call that reads myFunction(val1, out val2), you instantly know that val1 and val2 are the important variables to consider and that val2 will be assigned a new value when the function is completed. Conversely, if this function took no parameters, then you would be unable to make any assumptions about what data it manipulated.

Finally, remember that using global data isn't always possible. Later in this book, you will see code written in different files and/or belonging to different namespaces communicating with each other via functions. In these cases, the code is often separated to such a degree that there is no obvious choice for a global storage location.

To summarize, feel free to use either technique to exchange data. In general, use parameters rather than global data. But there are certainly cases where global data might be more suitable, and it certainly isn't an error to use this technique.

The Main() Function

Now that you've covered most of the simple techniques used in the creation and use of functions, it's time to take a closer look at the Main() function.

Earlier, you saw that `Main()` is the entry point for a C# application and that execution of this function encompasses the execution of the application. That is, when execution is initiated, the `Main()` function executes, and when the `Main()` function finishes, execution ends.

The `Main()` function can return either `void` or `int`, and can optionally include a `string[] args` parameter, so you can use any of the following versions:

```
static void Main()
static void Main(string[] args)
static int Main()
static int Main(string[] args)
```

The third and fourth versions return an `int` value, which can be used to signify how the application terminates, and often is used as an indication of an error (although this is by no means mandatory). In general, returning a value of 0 reflects normal termination (that is, the application has completed and can terminate safely).

The optional `args` parameter of `Main()` provides you with a way to obtain information from outside the application, specified at runtime. This information takes the form of *command-line parameters*.

You may well have come across command-line parameters already. When you execute an application from the command line, you can often specify information directly, such as a file to load on application execution. For example, consider the Notepad application in Windows. You can run Notepad simply by typing **Notepad** in a command prompt window or in the window that appears when you select the Run option from the Windows Start menu. You can also type something like **Notepad "myfile.txt"** in these locations. The result is that Notepad will either load the file `myfile.txt` when it runs or offer to create this file if it doesn't already exist. Here, "myfile.txt" is a command-line argument. You can write console applications that work similarly by making use of the `args` parameter.

When a console application is executed, any specified command-line parameters are placed in this `args` array. You can then use these parameters in your application. The following Try It Out shows this in action. You can specify any number of command-line arguments, each of which will be output to the console.

Try It Out   Command-Line Arguments

1. Create a new console application called Ch06Ex04 and save it in the directory C:\BegVCSharp\Chapter06.

2. Add the following code to `Program.cs`:

```
class Program
{
    static void Main(string[] args)
    {
        Console.WriteLine("{0} command line arguments were specified:",
                            args.Length);
        foreach (string arg in args)
            Console.WriteLine(arg);
        Console.ReadKey();
    }
}
```

3. Open the property pages for the project (right-click on the Ch06Ex04 project name in the Solution Explorer window and select Properties).

4. Select the Debug page and add any command-line arguments you want to the Command line arguments setting. An example is shown in Figure 6-7.

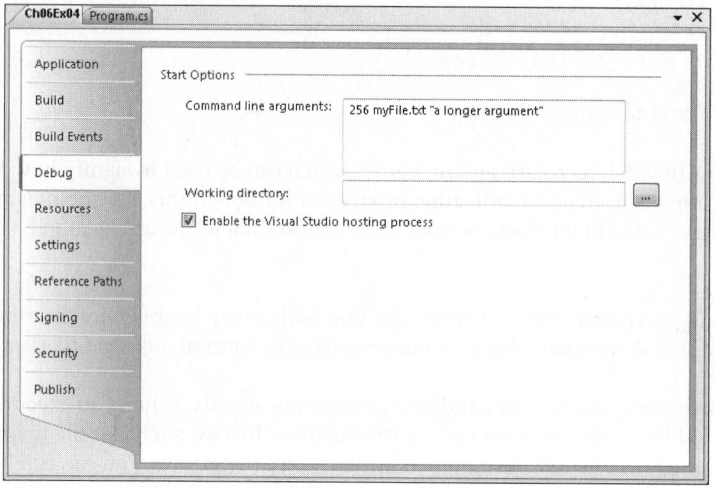

Figure 6-7

5. Run the application. The output is shown in Figure 6-8.

Figure 6-8

How It Works

The code used here is very simple:

```
Console.WriteLine("{0} command line arguments were specified:",
                  args.Length);
foreach (string arg in args)
   Console.WriteLine(arg);
```

You're just using the `args` parameter as you would any other string array. You're not doing anything fancy with the arguments; you're just writing whatever is specified to the screen. You supplied the arguments via the project properties in the IDE. This is a handy way to use the same command-line arguments whenever you run the application from the IDE, rather than type them at a command-line prompt every time. The same result can be obtained by opening a command prompt window in the same directory as the project output (C:\BegCSharp\Chapter6\Ch06Ex04\Ch06Ex04\bin\Debug) and typing this:

```
Ch06Ex04 256 myFile.txt "a longer argument"
```

Each argument is separated from the next by spaces. To supply an argument that includes spaces, you can enclose it in double quotation marks, which prevents it from being interpreted as multiple arguments.

Struct Functions

The last chapter covered struct types for storing multiple data elements in one place. Structs are actually capable of a lot more than this. For example, they can contain functions as well as data. That may seem a little strange at first, but it is in fact very useful. As a simple example, consider the following struct:

```
struct customerName
{
    public string firstName, lastName;
}
```

If you have variables of type `customerName` and you want to output a full name to the console, you are forced to build the name from its component parts. You might use the following syntax for a `customerName` variable called `myCustomer`, for example:

```
customerName myCustomer;
myCustomer.firstName = "John";
myCustomer.lastName = "Franklin";
Console.WriteLine("{0} {1}", myCustomer.firstName, myCustomer.lastName);
```

By adding functions to structs, you can simplify this by centralizing the processing of common tasks. For example, you can add a suitable function to the struct type as follows:

```
struct customerName
{
    public string firstName, lastName;

    public string Name ()
    {
        return firstName + " " + lastName;
    }
}
```

This looks much like any other function you've seen in this chapter, except that you haven't used the `static` modifier. The reasons for this will become clear later in the book; for now it is enough to know that this keyword isn't required for struct functions. You can use this function as follows:

```
customerName myCustomer;
myCustomer.firstName = "John";
myCustomer.lastName = "Franklin";
Console.WriteLine(myCustomer.Name());
```

This syntax is much simpler, and much easier to understand, than the previous syntax. Note here that the `Name()` function has direct access to the `firstName` and `lastName` struct members. Within the `customerName` struct, they can be thought of as global.

Overloading Functions

Earlier in this chapter, you saw how you must match the signature of a function when you call it. This implies that you need to have separate functions to operate on different types of variables. Function overloading provides you with the capability to create multiple functions with the same name, but each working with different parameter types. For example, earlier you used the following code, which contained a function called `MaxValue()`:

```
class Program
{
    static int MaxValue(int[] intArray)
    {
        int maxVal = intArray[0];
        for (int i = 1; i < intArray.Length; i++)
        {
            if (intArray[i] > maxVal)
                maxVal = intArray[i];
        }
        return maxVal;
    }

    static void Main(string[] args)
    {
        int[] myArray = {1, 8, 3, 6, 2, 5, 9, 3, 0, 2};
        int maxVal = MaxValue(myArray);
        Console.WriteLine("The maximum value in myArray is {0}", maxVal);
        Console.ReadKey();
    }
}
```

This function can only be used with arrays of `int` values. You could provide different named functions for different parameter types, perhaps renaming the preceding function as `IntArrayMaxValue()` and adding functions such as `DoubleArrayMaxValue()` to work with other types. Alternatively, you could just add the following function to your code:

```
...
static double MaxValue(double[] doubleArray)
{
    double maxVal = doubleArray[0];
    for (int i = 1; i < doubleArray.Length; i++)
    {
        if (doubleArray[i] > maxVal)
            maxVal = doubleArray[i];
    }
    return maxVal;
}
...
```

The difference here is that you are using `double` values. The function name, `MaxValue()`, is the same, but (crucially) its *signature* is different. That's because the signature of a function, as shown earlier, includes both the name of the function and its parameters. It would be an error to define two functions with the same signature, but because these two functions have different signatures, this is fine.

> *The return type of a function isn't part of its signature, so you can't define two functions that differ only in return type; they would have identical signatures.*

After adding the preceding code, you have two versions of `MaxValue()`, which accept `int` and `double` arrays, returning an `int` or `double` maximum, respectively.

The beauty of this type of code is that you don't have to explicitly specify which of these two functions you want to use. You simply provide an array parameter, and the correct function is executed depending on the type of parameter used.

Note another aspect of the IntelliSense feature in VS and VCE: When you have the two functions shown previously in an application and then proceed to type the name of the function, e.g., `Main()`, the IDE shows you the available overloads for the function. For example, if you type

```
double result = MaxValue(
```

the IDE gives you information about both versions of `MaxValue()`, which you can scroll between using the up and down arrow keys, as shown in Figure 6-9.

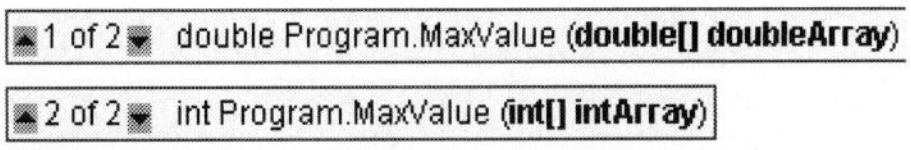

| ▲1 of 2▼ | double Program.MaxValue (**double[] doubleArray**) |

| ▲2 of 2▼ | int Program.MaxValue (**int[] intArray**) |

Figure 6-9

All aspects of the function signature are included when overloading functions. You might, for example, have two different functions that take parameters by value and by reference, respectively:

```
static void ShowDouble(ref int val)
{
    ...
}
static void ShowDouble(int val)
{
    ...
}
```

Deciding which version to use is based purely on whether the function call contains the ref keyword. The following would call the reference version:

```
ShowDouble(ref val);
```

This would call the value version:

```
ShowDouble(val);
```

Alternatively, you could have functions that differ in the number of parameters they require, and so on.

Delegates

A *delegate* is a type that enables you to store references to functions. Although this sounds quite involved, the mechanism is surprisingly simple. The most important purpose of delegates will become clear later in the book when you look at events and event handling, but it will be useful to briefly consider them here. Delegates are declared much like functions, but with no function body and using the delegate keyword. The delegate declaration specifies a return type and parameter list. After defining a delegate, you can declare a variable with the type of that delegate. You can then initialize the variable as a reference to any function that has the same return type and parameter list as that delegate. Once you have done this, you can call that function by using the delegate variable as if it were a function.

When you have a variable that refers to a function, you can also perform other operations that would be otherwise impossible. For example, you can pass a delegate variable to a function as a parameter, and then that function can use the delegate to call whatever function it refers to, without knowing what function will be called until runtime. The following Try It Out demonstrates using a delegate to access one of two functions.

Using a Delegate to Call a Function

1. Create a new console application called Ch06Ex05 and save it in the directory C:\BegVCSharp\Chapter06.

2. Add the following code to Program.cs:

```
class Program
{
    delegate double ProcessDelegate(double param1, double param2);

    static double Multiply(double param1, double param2)
    {
        return param1 * param2;
    }

    static double Divide(double param1, double param2)
    {
        return param1 / param2;
    }

    static void Main(string[] args)
    {
        ProcessDelegate process;
        Console.WriteLine("Enter 2 numbers separated with a comma:");
        string input = Console.ReadLine();
        int commaPos = input.IndexOf(',');
        double param1 = Convert.ToDouble(input.Substring(0, commaPos));
        double param2 = Convert.ToDouble(input.Substring(commaPos + 1,
                                            input.Length - commaPos - 1));
        Console.WriteLine("Enter M to multiply or D to divide:");
        input = Console.ReadLine();
        if (input == "M")
            process = new ProcessDelegate(Multiply);
        else
            process = new ProcessDelegate(Divide);
        Console.WriteLine("Result: {0}", process(param1, param2));
        Console.ReadKey();
    }
}
```

3. Execute the code. The result is shown in Figure 6-10.

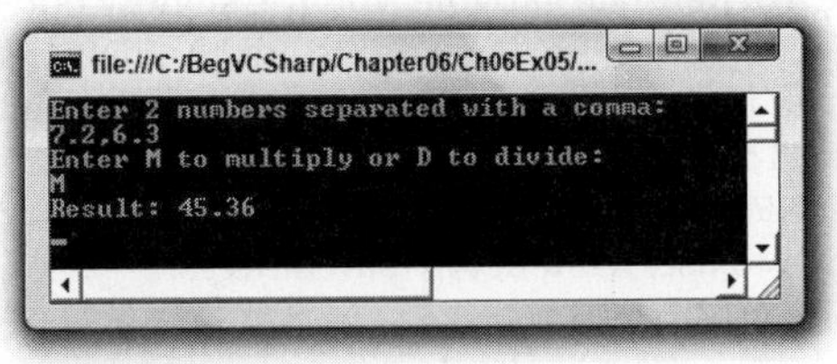

Figure 6-10

151

How It Works

This code defines a delegate (`ProcessDelegate`) whose return type and parameters match those of the two functions (`Multiply()` and `Divide()`). The delegate definition is as follows:

```
delegate double ProcessDelegate(double param1, double param2);
```

The `delegate` keyword specifies that the definition is for a delegate, rather than a function (the definition appears in the same place that a function definition might). Next, the definition specifies a `double` return value and two `double` parameters. The actual names used are arbitrary; you can call the delegate type and parameter names whatever you like. Here, we've used a delegate name of `ProcessDelegate` and double parameters called `param1` and `param2`.

The code in `Main()` starts by declaring a variable using the new delegate type:

```
static void Main(string[] args)
{
    ProcessDelegate process;
```

Next you have some fairly standard C# code that requests two numbers separated by a comma, and then places these numbers in two `double` variables:

```
Console.WriteLine("Enter 2 numbers separated with a comma:");
string input = Console.ReadLine();
int commaPos = input.IndexOf(',');
double param1 = Convert.ToDouble(input.Substring(0, commaPos));
double param2 = Convert.ToDouble(input.Substring(commaPos + 1,
                                      input.Length - commaPos - 1));
```

For demonstration purposes, no user input validation is included here. If this were "real" code, you'd spend much more time ensuring that you had valid values in the local param1 *and* param2 *variables.*

Next, you ask the user to multiply or divide these numbers:

```
Console.WriteLine("Enter M to multiply or D to divide:");
input = Console.ReadLine();
```

Based on the user's choice, you initialize the `process` delegate variable:

```
if (input == "M")
    process = new ProcessDelegate(Multiply);
else
    process = new ProcessDelegate(Divide);
```

To assign a function reference to a delegate variable, you use slightly odd-looking syntax. Much like assigning array values, you must use the `new` keyword to create a new delegate. After this keyword, you specify the delegate type and supply a parameter referring to the function you want to use — namely, the `Multiply()` or `Divide()` function. This parameter doesn't match the parameters of the delegate type or the target function; it is a syntax unique to delegate assignment. The parameter is simply the name of the function to use, without any parentheses.

Finally, call the chosen function using the delegate. The same syntax works here, regardless of which function the delegate refers to:

```
        Console.WriteLine("Result: {0}", process(param1, param2));
        Console.ReadKey();
    }
```

Here, you treat the delegate variable as if it were a function name. Unlike a function, though, you can also perform additional operations on this variable, such as passing it to a function via a parameter, as shown in this simple example:

```
    static void ExecuteFunction(ProcessDelegate process)
    {
        process(2.2, 3.3);
    }
```

This means that you can control the behavior of functions by passing them function delegates, much like choosing a "snap-in" to use. For example, you might have a function that sorts a string array alphabetically. You can use several techniques to sort lists, with varying performance depending on the characteristics of the list being sorted. By using delegates, you can specify the function to use by passing a sorting algorithm function delegate to a sorting function.

There are many such uses for delegates, but, as mentioned earlier, their most prolific use is in event handling, the subject of Chapter 13.

Summary

This chapter provided a fairly complete overview of the use of functions in C# code. Many of the additional features that functions offer (delegates in particular) are more abstract, and you need to understand them in regard to object-oriented programming, the subject of Chapter 8.

Following are the highlights of this chapter:

- ❏ Defining and using functions in console applications.
- ❏ Exchanging data with functions via return values and parameters.
- ❏ Passing parameter arrays to functions.
- ❏ Passing values by reference or by value.
- ❏ Specifying parameters for additional return values.
- ❏ The concept of variable scope, whereby variables can be hidden from sections of code where they aren't required.
- ❏ Details of the Main() function, including command-line parameter usage.

- ❑ Using functions in struct types.

- ❑ Function overloading, whereby you can supply different parameters to the same function to get additional functionality.

- ❑ Delegates and how to dynamically select functions for runtime execution.

Knowing how to use functions is central to all of the programming you are likely to do. Later chapters, particularly when you get to OOP (from Chapter 8 onward), explain a more formal structure for functions and how they apply to classes. You will likely find that the capability to abstract code into reusable blocks is the most useful aspect of C# programming.

Exercises

1. The following two functions have errors. What are they?

```
static bool Write()
{
    Console.WriteLine("Text output from function.");
}
static void myFunction(string label, params int[] args, bool showLabel)
{
    if (showLabel)
        Console.WriteLine(label);
    foreach (int i in args)
        Console.WriteLine("{0}", i);
}
```

2. Write an application that uses two command-line arguments to place values into a string and an integer variable, respectively. Then display these values.

3. Create a delegate and use it to impersonate the `Console.ReadLine()` function when asking for user input.

4. Modify the following struct to include a function that returns the total price of an order:

```
struct order
{
    public string itemName;
    public int     unitCount;
    public double unitCost;
}
```

5. Add another function to the order struct that returns a formatted string as follows (where italic entries enclosed in angle brackets are replaced by appropriate values):

Order Information: <unit count> <item name> items at $<unit cost> each, total cost $<total cost>

7

Debugging and Error Handling

So far in this book, you have covered all the basics of simple programming in C#. Before moving on to object-oriented programming in the next part, you need to look at debugging and error handling in C# code.

Errors in code are something that will always be with you. No matter how good a programmer is, problems will always slip through, and part of being a good programmer is realizing this and being prepared to deal with it. Of course, some problems are minor and don't affect the execution of an application, such as a spelling mistake on a button, but glaring errors are also possible, those that cause applications to fail completely (usually known as *fatal errors*). Fatal errors include simple errors in code that prevent compilation (syntax errors), or more serious problems that occur only at runtime. Some errors are subtle. Perhaps your application fails to add a record to a database because a requested field is missing, or adds a record with the wrong data in other restricted circumstances. Errors such as these, where application logic is in some way flawed, are known as *semantic errors*, or *logic errors*.

Often, you won't know about a subtle errors until a user of your application complains that something isn't working properly. This leaves you with the task of tracing through your code to find out what's happening and fixing it so that it does what it was intended to do. In these situations, the debugging capabilities of VS and VCE are a fantastic help. The first part of this chapter looks at some of the techniques available and applies them to some common problems.

Then, you'll learn the error-handling techniques available in C#. These enable you to take precautions in cases where errors are likely, and to write code that is resilient enough to cope with errors that might otherwise be fatal. These techniques are part of the C# language, rather than a debugging feature, but the IDE provides some tools to help you here, too.

This chapter covers two main topics:

❑   Debugging methods available in Visual Studio.

❑   Error-handling techniques available in C#.

Debugging in VS and VCE

Earlier, you learned that you can execute applications in two ways: with debugging enabled or without debugging enabled. By default, when you execute an application from VS or VCE, it executes with debugging enabled. This happens, for example, when you press F5 or click the green Play arrow in the toolbar. To execute an application without debugging enabled, choose Debug ⇨ Start Without Debugging.

Both VS and VCE allow you to build applications in two configurations: *Debug* (the default) and *Release*. (In fact, you can define additional configurations, but that's an advanced technique not covered here.) You can switch between these configurations using the Solution Configurations drop-down in the Standard toolbar.

> *In VCE this drop-down list is inactive by default. To work through this chapter, enable it by selecting Tools ⇨ Options. In the Options dialog, ensure that Show All Settings is selected, choose the General subcategory of the Projects and Solutions category, and enable the Show Advanced Build Configurations option.*

When you build an application in debug configuration and execute it in Debug mode, more is going on than the execution of your code. Debug builds maintain *symbolic information* about your application, so that the IDE knows exactly what is happening as each line of code is executed. Symbolic information means keeping track of, for example, the names of variables used in uncompiled code, so they can be matched to the values in the compiled machine code application, which won't contain such human-readable information. This information is contained in .pdb files, which you may have seen in your computer's Debug directories. This enables you to perform many useful operations:

❑   Outputting debugging information to the IDE.

❑   Looking at (and editing) the values of variables in scope during application execution.

❑   Pausing and restarting program execution.

❑   Automatically halting execution at certain points in the code.

❑   Stepping through program execution one line at a time.

❑   Monitoring changes in variable content during application execution.

❑   Modifying variable content at runtime.

❑   Performing test calls of functions.

In the release configuration, application code is optimized, and you cannot perform these operations. However, release builds also run faster, and when you have finished developing an application you will typically supply users with release builds because they won't require the symbolic information that debug builds include.

This section describes debugging techniques you can use to identify and fix areas of code that don't work as expected, a process known as *debugging*. The techniques are grouped into two sections according to how they are used. In general, debugging is performed either by interrupting program execution or by making notes for later analysis. In VS and VCE terms, an application is either running or is in Break mode — that is, normal execution is halted. You'll look at the Nonbreak mode (runtime or normal) techniques first.

Debugging in Nonbreak (Normal) Mode

One of the commands you've been using throughout this book is the `Console.WriteLine()` function, which outputs text to the console. As you are developing applications, this function comes in handy for getting extra feedback on operations:

```
Console.WriteLine("MyFunc() Function about to be called.");
MyFunc("Do something.");
Console.WriteLine("MyFunc() Function execution completed.");
```

This code snippet shows how you can get extra information concerning a function called `MyFunc()`. This is all very well, but it can make your console output a bit cluttered, and when you develop other types of applications, such as Windows forms applications, you won't have a console to output information to. As an alternative, you can output text to a separate location — the Output window in the IDE.

In Chapter 2, which described the Error List window, it was mentioned that other windows can also be displayed in the same place. One of these, the Output window, can be very useful for debugging. To display this window, select View ⇨ Output. This window provides information related to compilation and execution of code, including errors encountered during compilation. You can also use this window, shown in Figure 7-1, to display custom diagnostic information by writing to it directly.

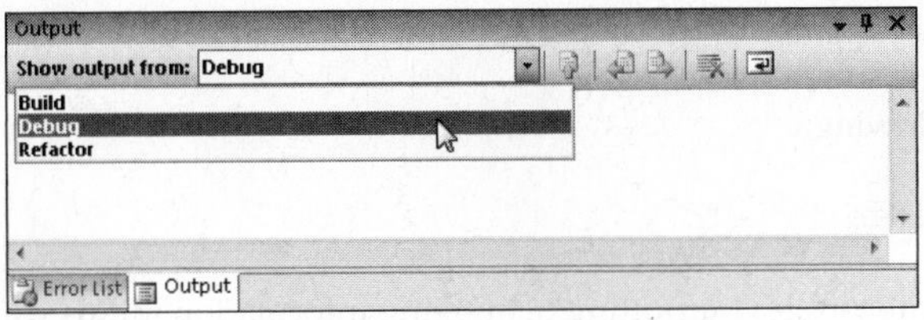

Figure 7-1

This window contains a drop-down menu from which different modes can be selected, including Build and Debug. These modes display compilation and runtime information, respectively. When you read "writing to the Output window" in this section, it actually means "writing to the Debug mode view of the Output window."

Alternatively, you might want to create a logging file, which has information appended to it when your application is executed. The techniques for doing this are much the same as those for writing text to the Output window, although the process requires an understanding of how to access the file system from C# applications. For now, leave that functionality on the back burner because there is plenty you can do without getting bogged down by file-access techniques.

Outputting Debugging Information

Writing text to the Output window at runtime is easy. You simply replace calls to `Console.WriteLine()` with the required call to write text where you want it. There are two commands you can use to do this:

❑   `Debug.WriteLine()`

❑   `Trace.WriteLine()`

These commands function in almost exactly the same way — with one key difference: The first command works in debug builds only; the latter works for release builds as well. In fact, the `Debug.WriteLine()` command won't even be compiled into a release build; it just disappears, which certainly has its advantages (the compiled code will be smaller, for one thing). You can, in effect, create two versions of your application from a single source file. The debug version displays all kinds of extra diagnostic information, whereas the release version won't have this overhead, and won't display messages to users that might otherwise be annoying!

These functions don't work exactly like `Console.WriteLine()`. They work with only a single string parameter for the message to output, rather than letting you insert variable values using `{X}` syntax. This means you must use an alternative technique to embed variable values in strings — for example, the + concatenation. You can also (optionally) supply a second string parameter, which displays a category for the output text. This enables you to see at a glance what output messages are displayed in the Output window, which is useful when similar messages are output from different places in the application.

The general output of these functions is as follows:

```
<category>: <message>
```

For example, the following statement, which has `"MyFunc"` as the optional category parameter,

```
Debug.WriteLine("Added 1 to i", "MyFunc");
```

would result in the following:

```
MyFunc: Added 1 to i
```

The next Try It Out demonstrates outputting debugging information in this way.

Try It Out **Writing Text to the Output Window**

1.   Create a new console application called Ch07Ex01 and save it in the directory C:\BegVCSharp\Chapter07.

2.   Modify the code as follows:

```
using System;
using System.Collections.Generic;
using System.Linq;
using System.Text;
using System.Diagnostics;

namespace Ch07Ex01
```

```csharp
{
    class Program
    {
        static void Main(string[] args)
        {
            int[] testArray = {4, 7, 4, 2, 7, 3, 7, 8, 3, 9, 1, 9};
            int[] maxValIndices;
            int maxVal = Maxima(testArray, out maxValIndices);
            Console.WriteLine("Maximum value {0} found at element indices:",
                                maxVal);
            foreach (int index in maxValIndices)
            {
                Console.WriteLine(index);
            }
            Console.ReadKey();
        }

        static int Maxima(int[] integers, out int[] indices)
        {
            Debug.WriteLine("Maximum value search started.");
            indices = new int[1];
            int maxVal = integers[0];
            indices[0] = 0;
            int count = 1;
            Debug.WriteLine(string.Format(
                "Maximum value initialized to {0}, at element index 0.", maxVal));
            for (int i = 1; i < integers.Length; i++)
            {
                Debug.WriteLine(string.Format(
                    "Now looking at element at index {0}.", i));
                if (integers[i] > maxVal)
                {
                    maxVal = integers[i];
                    count = 1;
                    indices = new int[1];
                    indices[0] = i;
                    Debug.WriteLine(string.Format(
                        "New maximum found. New value is {0}, at element index {1}.",
                        maxVal, i));
                }
                else
                {
                    if (integers[i] == maxVal)
                    {
                        count++;
                        int[] oldIndices = indices;
                        indices = new int[count];
                        oldIndices.CopyTo(indices, 0);
                        indices[count - 1] = i;
```

```
                            Debug.WriteLine(string.Format(
                                "Duplicate maximum found at element index {0}.", i));
                        }
                    }
                }
                Trace.WriteLine(string.Format(
                    "Maximum value {0} found, with {1} occurrences.", maxVal, count));
                Debug.WriteLine("Maximum value search completed.");
                return maxVal;
            }
        }
    }
```

3. Execute the code in Debug mode. The result is shown in Figure 7-2.

Figure 7-2

4. Terminate the application and check the contents of the Output window (in Debug mode). A truncated version of the output is shown here:

```
...

Maximum value search started.
Maximum value initialized to 4, at element index 0.
Now looking at element at index 1.
New maximum found. New value is 7, at element index 1.
Now looking at element at index 2.
Now looking at element at index 3.
Now looking at element at index 4.
Duplicate maximum found at element index 4.
Now looking at element at index 5.
Now looking at element at index 6.
Duplicate maximum found at element index 6.
Now looking at element at index 7.
New maximum found. New value is 8, at element index 7.
Now looking at element at index 8.
Now looking at element at index 9.
New maximum found. New value is 9, at element index 9.
Now looking at element at index 10.
Now looking at element at index 11.
Duplicate maximum found at element index 11.
Maximum value 9 found, with 2 occurrences.
Maximum value search completed.
```

```
The thread '<No Name>' (0xcc8) has exited with code 0 (0x0).
The thread '<No Name>' (0xccc) has exited with code 0 (0x0).
The program '[3648] Ch07Ex01.vshost.exe: Managed' has exited with code 0 (0x0).
```

5. Change to Release mode using the drop-down menu on the Standard toolbar, as shown in Figure 7-3.

Figure 7-3

6. Run the program again, this time in Release mode, and recheck the Output window when execution terminates. The output (again truncated) is as follows:

```
. . .
Maximum value 9 found, with 2 occurrences.
The thread '<No Name>' (0xe2c) has exited with code 0 (0x0).
The thread '<No Name>' (0xd2c) has exited with code 0 (0x0).
The program '[1736] Ch07Ex01.vshost.exe: Managed' has exited with code 0 (0x0).
```

How It Works

This application is an expanded version of one shown in Chapter 6, using a function to calculate the maximum value in an integer array. This version also returns an array of the indices where maximum values are found in an array, so that the calling code can manipulate these elements.

First, an additional `using` directive appears at the beginning of the code:

```
using System.Diagnostics;
```

This simplifies access to the functions discussed earlier because they are contained in the `System.Diagnostics` namespace. Without this `using` directive, code such as

```
Debug.WriteLine("Bananas");
```

would need further qualification, and would have to be rewritten as

```
System.Diagnostics.Debug.WriteLine("Bananas");
```

The `using` directive keeps your code simple and reduces verbosity.

The code in `Main()` simply initializes a test array of integers called `testArray`; it also declares another integer array called `maxValIndices` to store the index output of `Maxima()` (the function that performs the calculation), and then calls this function. Once the function returns, the code simply outputs the results.

`Maxima()` is slightly more complicated, but it doesn't use much code that you haven't already seen. The search through the array is performed in a similar way to the `MaxVal()` function Chapter 6, but a record is kept of the indices of maximum values.

Especially note (other than the lines that output debugging information) the function used to keep track of the indices. Rather than return an array that would be large enough to store every index in the source array (needing the same dimensions as the source array), Maxima() returns an array just large enough to hold the indices found. It does this by continually recreating arrays of different sizes as the search progresses. This is necessary because arrays can't be resized once they are created.

The search is initialized by assuming that the first element in the source array (called integers locally) is the maximum value and that there is only one maximum value in the array. Values can therefore be set for maxVal (the return value of the function and the maximum value found) and indices, the out parameter array that stores the indices of the maximum values found. maxVal is assigned the value of the first element in integers, and indices is assigned a single value, simply 0, which is the index of the array's first element. You also store the number of maximum values found in a variable called count, which enables you to keep track of the indices array.

The main body of the function is a loop that cycles through the values in the integers array, omitting the first one because it has already been processed. Each value is compared to the current value of maxVal and ignored if maxVal is greater. If the currently inspected array value is greater than maxVal, then maxVal and indices are changed to reflect this. If the value is equal to maxVal, then count is incremented and a new array is substituted for indices. This new array is one element bigger than the old indices array, containing the new index found.

The code for this last piece of functionality is as follows:

```
if (integers[i] == maxVal)
{
    count++;
    int[] oldIndices = indices;
    indices = new int[count];
    oldIndices.CopyTo(indices, 0);
    indices[count - 1] = i;
    Debug.WriteLine(string.Format(
        "Duplicate maximum found at element index {0}.", i));
}
```

This works by backing up the old indices array into oldIndices, an integer array local to this if code block. Note that the values in oldIndices are copied into the new indices array using the <array>.CopyTo() function. This function simply takes a target array and an index to use for the first element to copy to and pastes all values into the target array.

Throughout the code, various pieces of text are output using the Debug.WriteLine() and Trace.WriteLine() functions. These functions use the string.Format() function to embed variable values in strings in the same way as Console.WriteLine(). This is slightly more efficient than using the + concatenation operator.

When you run the application in Debug mode, you see a complete record of the steps taken in the loop that give you the result. In Release mode, you see just the result of the calculation, because no calls to Debug.WriteLine() are made in release builds.

In addition to these WriteLine() functions are a few more you should be aware of. To start with, there are equivalents to Console.Write():

❏   Debug.Write()

❏   Trace.Write()

Both functions use the same syntax as the `WriteLine()` functions (one or two parameters, with a message and an optional category), but differ in that they don't add end-of-line characters.

There are also the following commands:

- ❑ `Debug.WriteLineIf()`
- ❑ `Trace.WriteLineIf()`
- ❑ `Debug.WriteIf()`
- ❑ `Trace.WriteIf()`

Each of these has the same parameters as the non-`If` counterparts, with the addition of an extra, mandatory parameter that precedes them in the parameter list. This parameter takes a `Boolean` value (or an expression that evaluates to a `Boolean` value) and results in the function only writing text if this value evaluates to `true`. You can use these functions to conditionally output text to the Output window.

For example, you might require debugging information to be output in only certain situations, so you can have a great many `Debug.WriteLineIf()` statements in your code that all depend on a certain condition being met. If this condition doesn't occur, then they aren't displayed, which prevents the Output window from being cluttered with superfluous information.

Tracepoints

Tracepoints are a feature only available in VS, not in VCE. If you are using VCE, you may choose to skip this section.

An alternative to writing information to the Output window is to use *tracepoints*. These are a feature of VS, rather than C#, but they serve the same function as using `Debug.WriteLine()`. Essentially, they enable you to output debugging information without modifying your code.

To demonstrate tracepoints, you can use them to replace the debugging commands in the previous example. (See the `Ch07Ex01TracePoints` file in the downloadable code for this chapter.) The process for adding a tracepoint is as follows:

1. Position the cursor at the line where you want the tracepoint to be inserted. The tracepoint will be processed *before* this line of code is executed.

2. Right-click the line of code and select Breakpoint ⇨ Insert Tracepoint.

3. Type the string to be output in the Print a Message text box in the When Breakpoint Is Hit dialog that appears. If you want to output variable values, enclose the variable name in curly braces.

4. Click OK.

5. A red diamond appears to the left of the line of code containing a tracepoint, and the line of code itself is shown with red highlighting.

As implied by the title of the dialog for adding tracepoints, and the menu selections required for them, tracepoints are a form of breakpoints (and can cause application execution to pause, just like a breakpoint, if desired). You look at breakpoints, which typically serve a more advanced debugging purpose, a little later in the chapter.

Figure 7-4 shows the breakpoint required for line 31 of Ch07Ex01TracePoints, where line numbering applies to the code after the existing Debug.WriteLine() statements have been removed.

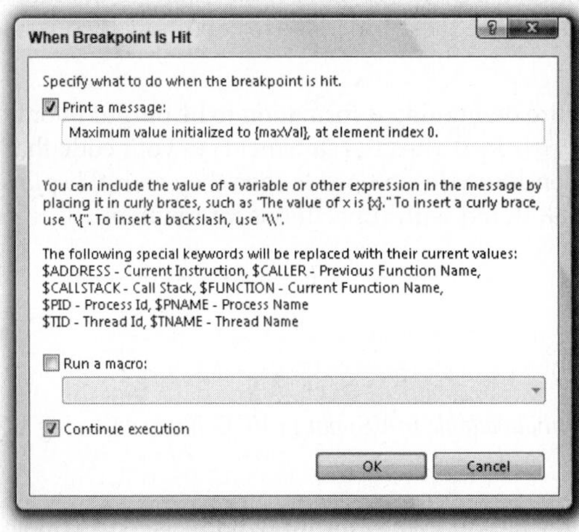

Figure 7-4

As shown in the text in Figure 7-4, tracepoints allow you to insert other useful information concerning the location and context of the tracepoint. You should experiment with these values, particularly $FUNCTION and $CALLER, to see what additional information you can glean. You can also see that it is possible for the tracepoint to execute a macro, an advanced feature that isn't covered here.

There is another window you can use to quickly see the tracepoints in an application. To display this window, select Debug ⇨ Windows ⇨ Breakpoints from the VS menu. This is a general window for displaying breakpoints (tracepoints, as noted earlier, are a form of breakpoint). You can customize the display to show more tracepoint-specific information by adding the When Hit column from the Columns drop-down in this window. Figure 7-5 shows the display with this column configured and all the tracepoints added to Ch07Ex01TracePoints.

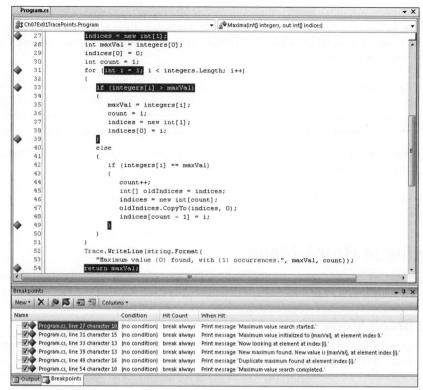

```
Program.cs
Ch07Ex01TracePoints.Program                                    Maxima(int[] integers, out int[] indices)
    27        indices = new int[1];
    28        int maxVal = integers[0];
    29        indices[0] = 0;
    30        int count = 1;
    31        for (int i = 1; i < integers.Length; i++)
    32        {
    33            if (integers[i] > maxVal)
    34            {
    35                maxVal = integers[i];
    36                count = 1;
    37                indices = new int[1];
    38                indices[0] = i;
    39            }
    40            else
    41            {
    42                if (integers[i] == maxVal)
    43                {
    44                    count++;
    45                    int[] oldIndices = indices;
    46                    indices = new int[count];
    47                    oldIndices.CopyTo(indices, 0);
    48                    indices[count - 1] = i;
    49                }
    50            }
    51        }
    52        Trace.WriteLine(string.Format(
    53            "Maximum value {0} found, with {1} occurrences.", maxVal, count));
    54        return maxVal;
```

```
Breakpoints
New ▾  ✕  | Columns ▾
Name                                    Condition        Hit Count      When Hit
  ☑  Program.cs, line 27 character 10   (no condition)   break always   Print message 'Maximum value search started.'
  ☑  Program.cs, line 31 character 15   (no condition)   break always   Print message 'Maximum value initialized to {maxVal}, at element index 0.'
  ☑  Program.cs, line 33 character 13   (no condition)   break always   Print message 'Now looking at element at index {i}.'
  ☑  Program.cs, line 39 character 13   (no condition)   break always   Print message 'New maximum found. New value is {maxVal}, at element index {i}.'
  ☑  Program.cs, line 49 character 16   (no condition)   break always   Print message 'Duplicate maximum found at element index {i}.'
  ☑  Program.cs, line 54 character 10   (no condition)   break always   Print message 'Maximum value search completed.'
  Output   Breakpoints
```

Figure 7-5

Executing this application in Debug mode has the same result as before. You can remove or temporarily disable tracepoints by right-clicking on them in the code window or via the Breakpoints window. In the Breakpoints window, the check box to the left of the tracepoint shows if the tracepoint is enabled; disabled tracepoints are unchecked and displayed in the code window as diamond outlines, rather than solid diamonds.

Diagnostics Output Versus Tracepoints

Now that you have seen two methods of outputting essentially the same information, consider the pros and cons of each. First, tracepoints have no equivalent to the `Trace` commands; that is, there is no way to output information in a release build using tracepoints. This is because tracepoints are not included in your application. Tracepoints are handled by Visual Studio, and as such do not exist in the compiled version of your application. You will see tracepoints doing something only when your application is running in the VS debugger.

The chief disadvantage of tracepoints is also their major advantage, which is that they are stored in VS. This makes them quick and easy to add to your applications as and when you need them, but also all too easy to delete. Deleting a tracepoint is as simple as clicking on the red diamond indicating its position, which can be annoying if you are outputting a complicated string of information.

One bonus of tracepoints, though, is the additional information that can be easily added, such as $FUNCTION, as noted in the previous section. While this information is available to code written using Debug and Trace commands, it is trickier to obtain. In summary, use these two methods of outputting debug information as follows:

❑ **Diagnostics output:** Use when debug output is something you always want to output from an application, particularly where the string you want to output is complex, involving several variables or a lot of information. In addition, Trace commands are often the only option should you want output during execution of an application built in Release mode.

❑ **Tracepoints:** Use these when debugging an application to quickly output important information that may help you resolve semantic errors.

There is also the obvious difference that tracepoints are only available in VS, whereas diagnostics output is available in both VS and VCE.

Debugging in Break Mode

The rest of the debugging techniques described in this chapter work in Break mode. This mode can be entered in several ways, all of which result in the program pausing in some way.

Entering Break Mode

The simplest way to enter Break mode is to click the pause button in the IDE while an application is running. This pause button is found on the Debug toolbar, which you should add to the toolbars that appear by default in VS. To do this, right-click in the toolbar area and select Debug, as shown in Figure 7-6.

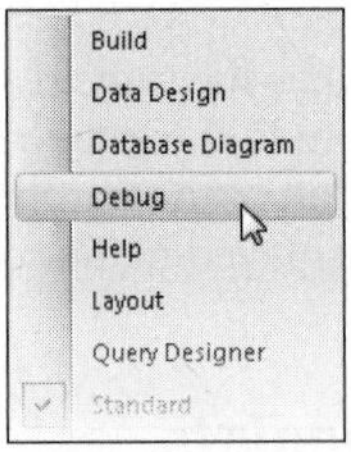

Build
Data Design
Database Diagram
Debug
Help
Layout
Query Designer
Standard

Figure 7-6

Figure 7-7 shows the Debug toolbar that appears.

Start

Figure 7-7

The first four buttons on the toolbar allow manual control of breaking. In Figure 7-7, three of these are grayed out, because they won't work with a program that isn't currently executing. The one that is enabled, Start, is identical to the button that exists on the standard toolbar. The following sections describe the rest of the buttons as needed.

When an application is running, the toolbar changes to look like Figure 7-8.

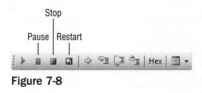

Figure 7-8

The three buttons next to Start that were grayed out now enable you to do the following:

❑   Pause the application and enter Break mode.

❑   Stop the application completely (this doesn't enter Break mode, it just quits).

❑   Restart the application.

Pausing the application is perhaps the simplest way to enter Break mode, but it doesn't give you fine-grained control over exactly where to stop. You are likely to stop in a natural pause in the application, perhaps where you request user input. You might also be able to enter Break mode during a lengthy operation, or a long loop, but the exact stop point is likely to be fairly random. In general, it is far better to use breakpoints.

Breakpoints

A *breakpoint* is a marker in your source code that triggers automatic entry into Break mode. Breakpoints are available in both VS and VCE, but they are more flexible in VS. Breakpoints may be configured to do the following:

❑   Enter Break mode immediately when the breakpoint is reached.

❑   (VS only.) Enter Break mode when the breakpoint is reached if a Boolean expression evaluates to true.

❑   (VS only.) Enter Break mode once the breakpoint is reached a set number of times.

❑   (VS only.) Enter Break mode once the breakpoint is reached and a variable value has changed since the last time the breakpoint was reached.

❑   (VS only.) Output text to the Output window or execute a macro (see the section "Tracepoints" earlier in the chapter).

These features are available only in debug builds. If you compile a release build, all breakpoints are ignored.

There are several ways to add breakpoints. To add simple breakpoints that break when a line is reached, simply left-click on the gray area to the left of the line of code, right-click on the line, and select Breakpoint ➪ Insert Breakpoint; select Debug ➪ Toggle Breakpoint from the menu; or press F9. Figure 7-9 shows the right-clicking on a line option for VS (in VCE the menu is slightly different, and the Insert Tracepoint menu item does not appear).

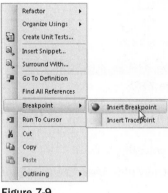

Figure 7-9

The breakpoint appears as a red circle next to the line of code, which is highlighted, as shown in Figure 7-10.

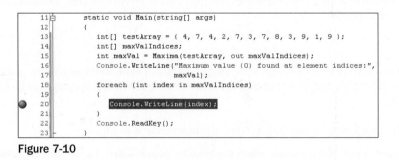

Figure 7-10

The remainder of this section applies only to VS and not VCE. If you are using VCE, then feel free to skip ahead to the section "Other Ways to Enter Break Mode."

In VS you can also see information about a file's breakpoints using the Breakpoints window (you saw how to enable this window earlier). You can use the Breakpoints window to disable breakpoints (by removing the tick to the left of a description; a disabled breakpoint shows up as an unfilled red circle), to delete breakpoints, and to edit the properties of breakpoints.

The columns shown in this window, Condition and Hit Count, are only two of the available ones, but they are the most useful. You can edit these by right-clicking a breakpoint (in code or in this window) and selecting Condition or Hit Count.

Selecting Condition opens the dialog shown in Figure 7-11.

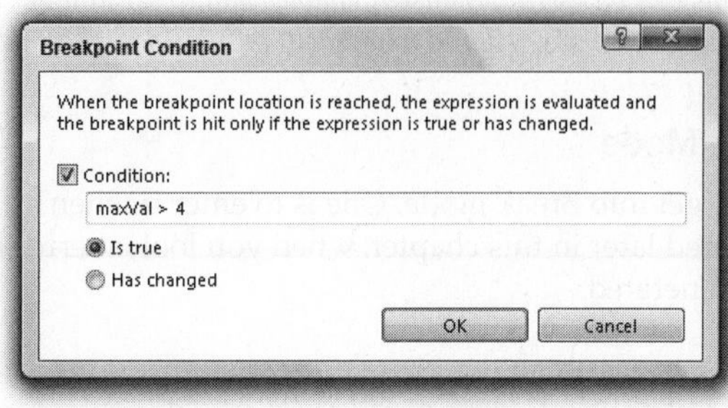

Breakpoint Condition

When the breakpoint location is reached, the expression is evaluated and the breakpoint is hit only if the expression is true or has changed.

☑ Condition:

maxVal > 4

◉ Is true
◯ Has changed

OK   Cancel

Figure 7-11

Here, you can type any Boolean expression, which may involve any variables in scope at the breakpoint. Figure 7-11 shows a breakpoint that triggers when it is reached and the value of maxVal is greater than 4. You can also check whether this expression has changed and only trigger the breakpoint then (you might trigger it if maxVal changed from 2 to 6 between breakpoint encounters, for example).

Selecting Hit Count opens the dialog shown in Figure 7-12.

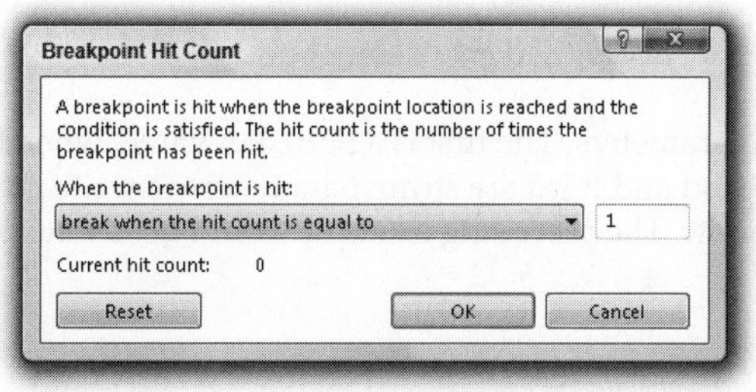

Breakpoint Hit Count

A breakpoint is hit when the breakpoint location is reached and the condition is satisfied. The hit count is the number of times the breakpoint has been hit.

When the breakpoint is hit:

break when the hit count is equal to   1

Current hit count: 0

Reset   OK   Cancel

Figure 7-12

Here you can specify how many times a breakpoint needs to be hit before it is triggered. The drop-down list offers the following options:

❑   Break always

❑   Break when the hit count is equal to

❑   Break when the hit count is a multiple of

❑   Break when the hit count is greater than or equal to

The option chosen, combined with the value entered in the text box next to the list, determines the behavior of the breakpoint. The hit count is useful in long loops, when you might want to break after, say, the first 5000 cycles. It would be a pain to break and restart 5000 times if you couldn't do this!

A breakpoint with additional properties set (such as a condition or hit count) is displayed slightly differently. Instead of a simple red circle, a configured breakpoint consists of a red circle containing a white + (plus) symbol. This can be useful because it enables you to see at a glance which breakpoints will always cause Break mode to be entered and which will only do so in certain circumstances.

Other Ways to Enter Break Mode

There are two more ways to get into Break mode. One is to enter it when an unhandled exception is thrown. This subject is covered later in this chapter, when you look at error handling. The other way is to break when an *assertion* is generated.

Assertions are instructions that can interrupt application execution with a user-defined message. They are often used during application development to test whether things are going smoothly. For example, at some point in your application you might require a given variable to have a value less than 10. You can use an assertion to confirm that this is true and interrupt the program if it isn't. When the assertion occurs, you have the option to Abort, which terminates the application; Retry, which causes Break mode to be entered; or Ignore, which causes the application to continue as normal.

As with the debug output functions shown earlier, there are two versions of the assertion function:

❑   `Debug.Assert()`

❑   `Trace.Assert()`

Again, the debug version is only compiled into debug builds.

These functions take three parameters. The first is a `Boolean` value, whereby a value of `false` causes the assertion to trigger. The second and third are string parameters to write information both to a pop-up dialog and the Output window. The preceding example would need a function call such as the following:

```
Debug.Assert(myVar < 10, "myVar is 10 or greater.",
             "Assertion occurred in Main().");
```

Assertions are often useful in the early stages of user adoption of an application. You can distribute release builds of your application containing `Trace.Assert()` functions to keep tabs on things. Should an assertion be triggered, the user will be informed, and this information can be passed on to you. You can then determine what has gone wrong even if you don't know how it went wrong.

You might, for example, provide a brief description of the error in the first string, with instructions as to what to do next as the second string:

```
Trace.Assert(myVar < 10, "Variable out of bounds.",
             "Please contact vendor with the error code KCW001.");
```

Should this assertion occur, the user will see the dialog shown in Figure 7-13.

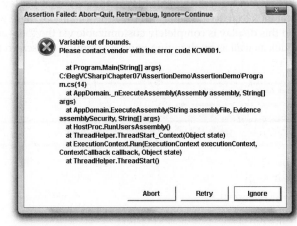

Figure 7-13

Admittedly, this isn't the most user-friendly dialog in the world, as it contains a lot of information that could confuse users, but if they send you a screenshot of the error, you could quickly track down the problem.

Now it's time to look at what you can actually do after application execution is halted and you are in Break mode. In general, you enter Break mode to find an error in your code (or to reassure yourself that things are working properly). Once you are in Break mode, you can use various techniques, all of which enable you to analyze your code and the exact state of the application at the point in its execution where it is paused.

Monitoring Variable Content

Monitoring variable content is just one example of how VS and VCE help you a great deal by making things simple. The easiest way to check the value of a variable is to hover the mouse over its name in the source code while in Break mode. A yellow tooltip showing information about the variable appears, including the variable's current value.

You can also highlight entire expressions to get information about their results in the same way. For more complex values, such as arrays, you can even expand values in the tooltip to see individual element entries.

You may have noticed that when you run an application, the layout of the various windows in the IDE changes. By default, the following changes are likely to occur at runtime (this behavior may vary slightly depending on your installation):

❑ The Properties window disappears, along with some other windows, probably including the Solution Explorer window.

❑ The Error List window is replaced with two new windows across the bottom of the IDE window.

❑ Several new tabs appear in the new windows.

The new screen layout is shown in Figure 7-14. This may not match your display exactly, and some of the tabs and windows may not look exactly the same, but the functionality of these windows as described later will be the same, and this display is completely customizable via the View and Debug ⇨ Windows menus (during Break mode), as well as by dragging windows around the screen to reposition them.

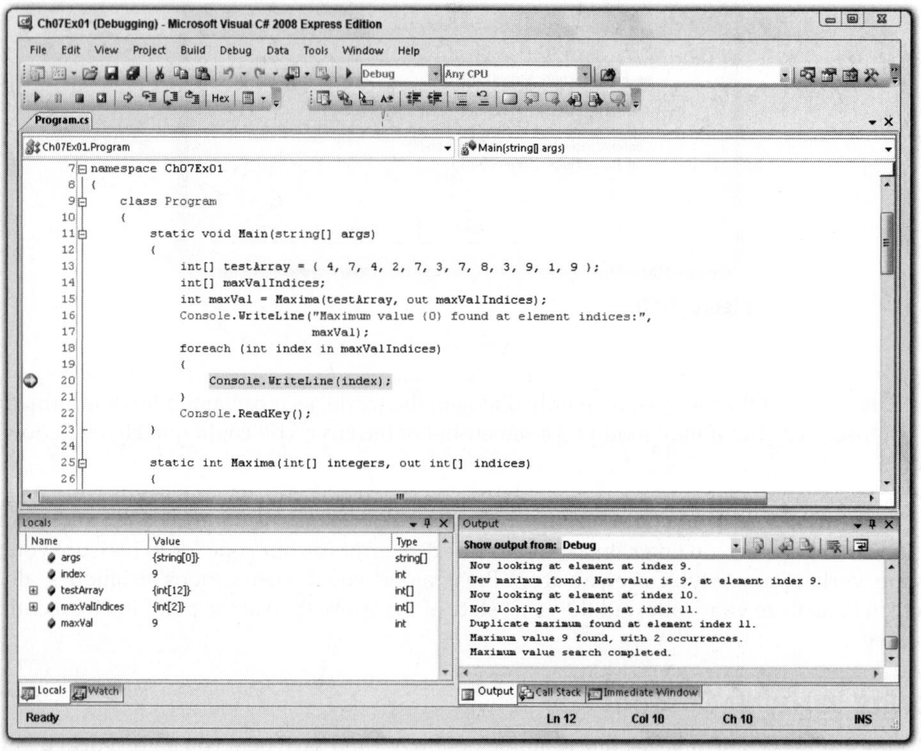

Figure 7-14

The new window that appears in the bottom left corner is particularly useful for debugging. It enables you to keep tabs on the values of variables in your application when in Break mode. The tabs displayed here vary between VS and VCE:

❑ **Autos (VS only):** Variables in use in the current and previous statements (Ctrl+D, A)

❑ **Locals:** All variables in scope (Ctrl+D, L)

❑ **Watch N:** Customizable variable and expression display (where N is 1 to 4, found on Debug ⇨ Windows ⇨ Watch)

All these tabs work in more or less the same way, with various additional features depending on their specific function. In general, each tab contains a list of variables, with information on each variable's name, value, and type. More complex variables, such as arrays, may be further examined using the + and – tree expansion/contraction symbols to the left of their names, allowing a tree view of their content. For example, Figure 7-15 shows the Locals tab obtained by placing a breakpoint in the example code. It shows the expanded view for one of the array variables, maxValIndices.

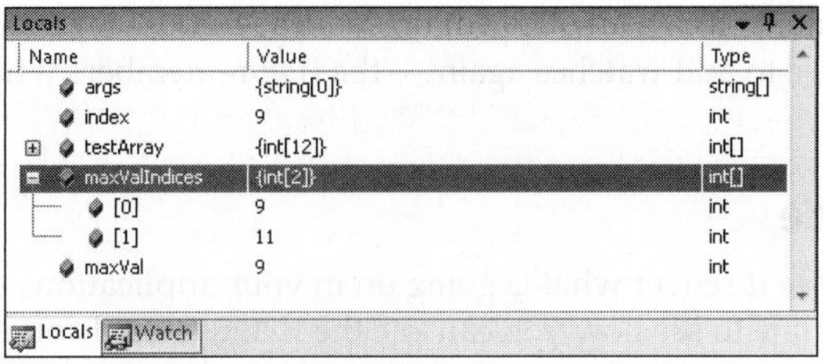

Figure 7-15

You can also edit the content of variables from this view. This effectively bypasses any other variable assignment that might have happened in earlier code. To do this, simply type a new value into the Value column for the variable you want to edit. You might do this to try out some scenarios that would otherwise require code changes, for example.

The Watch window (or Watch windows in VS, which can display up to four) enables you to monitor specific variables or expressions involving specific variables. To use this window, simply type the name of a variable or expression into the Name column and view the results. Note that not all variables in an application are in scope all the time and are labeled as such in a Watch window. For example, Figure 7-16 shows a Watch window with a few sample variables and expressions in it.

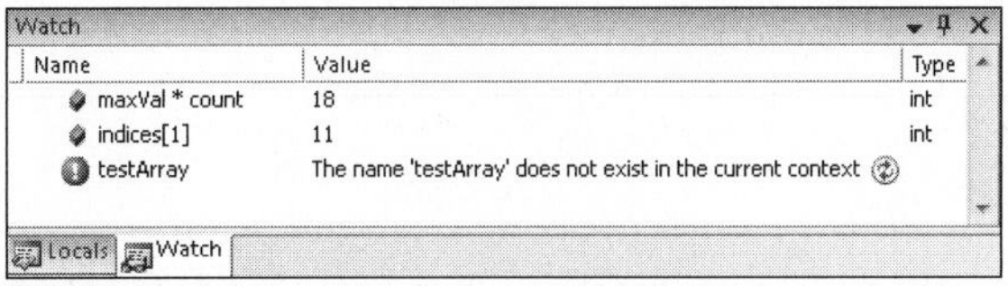

Figure 7-16

The `testArray` array is local to `Main()`, so you don't see a value here. Instead, you get a message informing you that the variable isn't in scope.

You can also add variables to a Watch window by dragging them from the source code into the window.

One nice feature about the various displays of variables accessible in this window is that they show you variables that have changed between breakpoints. Any new value is shown in red, rather than black, making it easy to see whether a value has changed.

As mentioned earlier, to add more Watch windows in VS, in Break mode you can use the Debug ⇨Windows ⇨ Watch ⇨ Watch N menu options to toggle the four possible windows on or off. Each window may contain an individual set of watches on variables and expressions, so you can group related variables together for easy access.

As well as these windows, VS also has a QuickWatch window that provides detailed information about a variable in the source code. To use this, simply right-click the variable you want to examine and select the QuickWatch menu option. In most cases, though, it is just as easy to use the standard Watch windows.

Note that watches are maintained between application executions. If you terminate an application and then rerun it, you don't have to add watches again — the IDE remembers what you were looking at the last time.

Stepping through Code

So far, you've learned how to discover what is going on in your applications at the point where Break mode is entered. Now it's time to see how you can use the IDE to step through code while remaining in Break mode, which enables you to see the exact results of the code being executed. This is an extremely valuable technique for those of us who can't think as fast as computers can.

When Break mode is entered, a cursor appears to the left of the code view (which may initially appear inside the red circle of a breakpoint if a breakpoint was used to enter Break mode), by the line of code that is about to be executed, as shown in Figure 7-17.

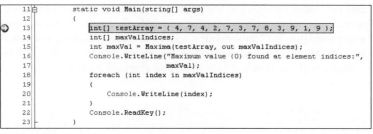

```
11   static void Main(string[] args)
12   {
13       int[] testArray = { 4, 7, 4, 2, 7, 3, 7, 8, 3, 9, 1, 9 };
14       int[] maxValIndices;
15       int maxVal = Maxima(testArray, out maxValIndices);
16       Console.WriteLine("Maximum value {0} found at element indices:",
17                       maxVal);
18       foreach (int index in maxValIndices)
19       {
20           Console.WriteLine(index);
21       }
22       Console.ReadKey();
23   }
```

Figure 7-17

This shows you what point execution has reached when Break mode is entered. At this point, you can have execution proceed on a line-by-line basis. To do so, you use some of the Debug toolbar buttons shown in Figure 7-18.

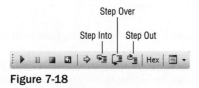

Figure 7-18

The sixth, seventh, and eighth icons control program flow in Break mode. In order, they are as follows:

❑ **Step Into:** Execute and move to the next statement to execute.

❑ **Step Over:** This is similar to Step Into, but won't enter nested blocks of code, including functions.

❑ **Step Out:** This will run to the end of the code block and resume Break mode at the statement that follows.

To look at every single operation carried out by the application, you can use Step Into to follow the instructions sequentially. This includes moving inside functions, such as `Maxima()` in the preceding example. Clicking this icon when the cursor reaches line 15, the call to `Maxima()`, results in the cursor moving to the first line inside the `Maxima()` function. Alternatively, clicking Step Over when you reach line 15 moves the cursor straight to line 16, without going through the code in `Maxima()` (although this code is still executed). If you do step into a function that you aren't interested in, you can click Step Out to return to the code that called the function. As you step through code, the values of variables are likely to change. If you keep an eye on the monitoring windows just discussed, you can clearly see this happening.

In code that has semantic errors, this technique may be the most useful one at your disposal. You can step through code right up to the point where you expect problems to occur, and the errors will be generated as if you were running the program normally. Along the way, watch the data to see just what is going wrong. Later in this chapter, you use this technique to find out what is happening in an example application.

Immediate and Command Windows

The Command (VS only) and Immediate windows (found on the Debug ⇨ Windows menu) enable you to execute commands while an application is running. The Command window enables you to perform VS operations manually (such as menu and toolbar operations), and the Immediate window enables you to execute additional code besides the source code lines being executed and to evaluate expressions.

In VS, these windows are intrinsically linked (in fact, earlier versions of VS treated them as the same thing). You can even switch between them by entering commands: `immed` to move from the Command window to the Immediate window and `>cmd` to move back.

This section concentrates on the Immediate window because the Command window is only really useful for complex operations and is only available in VS, whereas the Immediate window is available in both VS and VCE. The simplest use of this window is to evaluate expressions, a bit like a one-shot use of the Watch windows. To do this, type an expression and press Return. The information requested will then be displayed. An example is shown in Figure 7-19.

Figure 7-19

You can also change variable content here, as demonstrated in Figure 7-20.

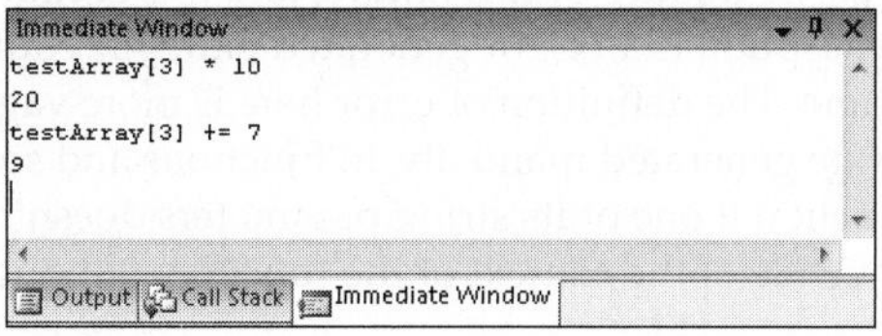

Figure 7-20

In most cases, you can get the effects you want more easily using the variable monitoring windows shown earlier, but this technique is still handy for tweaking values, and it's good for testing expressions for which you are unlikely to be interested in the results later.

The Call Stack Window

The final window to look at shows you the way in which the current location was reached. In simple terms, this means showing the current function along with the function that called it, the function that called that, and so on (that is, a list of nested function calls). The exact points where calls are made are also recorded.

In the earlier example, entering Break mode when in Maxima(), or moving into this function using code stepping, reveals the information shown in Figure 7-21.

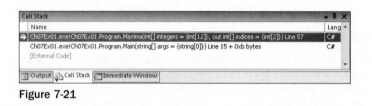

Figure 7-21

If you double-click an entry, you are taken to the appropriate location, enabling you to track the way code execution has reached the current point. This window is particularly useful when errors are first detected, because you can see what happened immediately before the error. Where errors occur in commonly used functions, this helps you determine the source of the error.

Sometimes this window shows some very confusing information. For example, errors may occur outside of your applications due to using external functions in the wrong way. In such cases, this window could contain a long list of entries, but only one or two might look familiar. You can see external references (should you ever need to) by right-clicking in the window and selecting Show External Code.

Error Handling

The first part of this chapter explained how to find and correct errors during application development so that they won't occur in release-level code. Sometimes, however, you know that errors are likely to occur and there is no way to be 100 percent sure that they won't. In these situations, it may be preferable to anticipate problems and write code that is robust enough to deal with these errors gracefully, without interrupting execution.

Error handling is the term for all techniques of this nature, and this section looks at exceptions and how you can deal with them. An exception is an error generated either in your code or in a function called by your code that occurs at runtime. The definition of error here is more vague than it has been up until now, because exceptions may be generated manually, in functions and so on. For example, you might generate an exception in a function if one of its string parameters doesn't start with the letter "a." Strictly speaking, this isn't an error outside of the context of the function, although it is treated as one by the code that calls the function.

You've seen exceptions a few times already in this book. Perhaps the simplest example is attempting to address an array element that is out of range:

```
int[] myArray = {1, 2, 3, 4};
int myElem = myArray[4];
```

This outputs the following exception message and then terminates the application:

```
Index was outside the bounds of the array.
```

You've already seen some examples of the window that is displayed. It has a line connecting it to the offending code and includes links to reference topics in the .NET help files, as well as a View Detail link to more information about the exception.

Exceptions are defined in namespaces, and most have names that make their purpose clear. In this example, the exception generated is called `System.IndexOutOfRangeException`, which makes sense because you have supplied an index that is not in the range of indices permissible in `myArray`. This message appears, and the application terminates, only when the exception is unhandled. In the next section, you'll see exactly what you have to do to handle an exception.

try . . . catch . . . finally

The C# language includes syntax for *structured exception handling (SEH)*. Three keywords mark code as being able to handle exceptions, along with instructions as to what to do when an exception occurs: `try`, `catch`, and `finally`. Each of these has an associated code block and must be used in consecutive lines of code. The basic structure is as follows:

```
try
{
   . . .
}
catch (<exceptionType> e)
{
   . . .
}
finally
{
   . . .
}
```

It is also possible, however, to have a `try` block and a `finally` block with no `catch` block, or a `try` block with multiple `catch` blocks. If one or more `catch` blocks exist, then the `finally` block is optional; otherwise, it is mandatory. The usage of the blocks is as follows:

❑   **try**: Contains code that might throw exceptions ("throw" is the C# way of saying "generate" or "cause" when talking about exceptions).

❑   **catch**: Contains code to execute when exceptions are thrown. `catch` blocks may be set to respond only to specific exception types (such as `System.IndexOutOfRangeException`) using `<exceptionType>`, hence the ability to provide multiple `catch` blocks. It is also possible to omit this parameter entirely, to get a general `catch` block that responds to all exceptions.

❑   **finally**: Contains code that is always executed, either after the `try` block if no exception occurs, after a `catch` block if an exception is handled, or just before an unhandled exception terminates the application (the fact that this block is processed at this time is the reason for its existence; otherwise, you might just as well place code after the block).

Here's the sequence of events that occurs after an exception occurs in code in a `try` block:

❑   The `try` block terminates at the point where the exception occurred.

❑   If a `catch` block exists, then a check is made to determine whether the block matches the type of exception that was thrown. If no `catch` block exists, then the `finally` block (which must be present if there are no `catch` blocks) executes.

❑   If a `catch` block exists but there is no match, then a check is made for other `catch` blocks.

❑   If a `catch` block matches the exception type, then the code it contains executes, and then the `finally` block executes if it is present.

❑   If no `catch` blocks match the exception type, then the `finally` block of code executes if it is present.

The following Try It Out demonstrates handling exceptions, throwing and handling them in several ways so you can see how things work.

Try It Out   Exception Handling

1.   Create a new console application called Ch07Ex02 and save it in the directory C:\BegVCSharp\Chapter07.

2.   Modify the code as follows (the line number comments shown here will help you match up your code to the discussion afterward, and are duplicated in the downloadable code for this chapter for your convenience):

```
class Program
{
    static string[] eTypes = {"none", "simple", "index", "nested index"};

    static void Main(string[] args)
    {
        foreach (string eType in eTypes)
        {
            try
            {
                Console.WriteLine("Main() try block reached.");        // Line 23
                Console.WriteLine("ThrowException(\"{0}\") called.", eType);
                                                                       // Line 24
                ThrowException(eType);
                Console.WriteLine("Main() try block continues.");      // Line 26
            }
            catch (System.IndexOutOfRangeException e)                  // Line 28
```

```
            {
                Console.WriteLine("Main() System.IndexOutOfRangeException catch"
                            + " block reached. Message:\"\n\"{0}",
                            e.Message);
            }
            catch                                                   // Line 34
            {
                Console.WriteLine("Main() general catch block reached.");
            }
            finally
            {
                Console.WriteLine("Main() finally block reached.");
            }
            Console.WriteLine();
        }
        Console.ReadKey();
    }
```

```
        static void ThrowException(string exceptionType)
        {
                                                                    // Line 49
            Console.WriteLine("ThrowException(\"{0}\") reached.", exceptionType);
            switch (exceptionType)
            {
                case "none" :
                    Console.WriteLine("Not throwing an exception.");
                    break;                                          // Line 54
                case "simple" :
                    Console.WriteLine("Throwing System.Exception.");
                    throw (new System.Exception());                 // Line 57
                case "index" :
                    Console.WriteLine("Throwing System.IndexOutOfRangeException.");
                    eTypes[4] = "error";                            // Line 60
                    break;
                case "nested index" :
                    try                                             // Line 63
                    {
                        Console.WriteLine("ThrowException(\"nested index\") " +
                                    "try block reached.");
                        Console.WriteLine("ThrowException(\"index\") called.");
                        ThrowException("index");                    // Line 68
                    }
                    catch                                           // Line 70
                    {
                        Console.WriteLine("ThrowException(\"nested index\") general"
                                    + " catch block reached.");
                    }
                    finally
                    {
                        Console.WriteLine("ThrowException(\"nested index\") finally"
                                    + " block reached.");
                    }
                    break;
            }
        }
    }
```

3. Run the application. The result is shown in Figure 7-22.

Figure 7-22

How It Works

This application has a `try` block in `Main()` that calls a function called `ThrowException()`. This function may throw exceptions, depending on the parameter it is called with:

❑   **ThrowException("none")**: Doesn't throw an exception

❑   **ThrowException("simple")**: Generates a general exception

❑   **ThrowException("index")**: Generates a `System.IndexOutOfRangeException` exception

❑   **ThrowException("nested index")**: Contains its own try block, which contains code that calls `ThrowException("index")` to generate a `System.IndexOutOfRangeException` exception

Each of these `string` parameters is held in the global `eTypes` array, which is iterated through in the `Main()` function to call `ThrowException()` once with each possible parameter. During this iteration, various messages are written to the console to indicate what is happening. This code gives you an excellent opportunity to use the code-stepping techniques shown earlier in the chapter. By working your way through the code one line at a time, you can see exactly how code execution progresses.

Add a new breakpoint (with the default properties) to line 23 of the code, which reads as follows:

```
Console.WriteLine("Main() try block reached.");
```

Here, code is referred to by line numbers as they appear in the downloadable version of this code. If you have line numbers turned off, remember that you can turn them back on (Tools ⇨ Options or the Text Editor ⇨ C# ⇨ General option section). Comments are included in the preceding code so that you can follow the text without having the file open in front of you.

Run the application in Debug mode. Almost immediately, the program will enter Break mode, with the cursor on line 23. If you select the Locals tab in the variable monitoring window, you should see that eType is currently "none". Use the Step Into button to process lines 23 and 24, and confirm that the first line of text has been written to the console. Next, use the Step Into button to step into the ThrowException() function on line 25.

Once in the ThrowException() function (on line 49), the Locals window changes. eType and args are no longer in scope (they are local to Main()); instead, you see the local exceptionType argument, which is of course "none". Keep pressing Step Into and you'll reach the switch statement that checks the value of exceptionType and executes the code that writes out the string Not throwing an exception to the screen. When you execute the break statement (on line 54), you exit the function and resume processing in Main() at line 26. Because no exception was thrown, the try block continues.

Next, processing continues with the finally block. Click Step Into a few more times to complete the finally block and the first cycle of the foreach loop. The next time you reach line 25, ThrowException() is called using a different parameter, simple.

Continue using Step Into through ThrowException(), and you'll eventually reach line 57:

```
throw (new System.Exception());
```

Here you use the C# throw keyword to generate an exception. This keyword simply needs to be provided with a new-initialized exception as a parameter, and it will throw that exception. Here, you are using another exception from the System namespace, System.Exception.

No break; statement is necessary in this case: block–throw is enough to end execution of the block.

When you process this statement with Step Into, you find yourself at the general catch block starting on line 34. There was no match with the earlier catch block starting on line 28, so this one is processed instead. Stepping through this code takes you through this block, through the finally block, and back into another loop cycle that calls ThrowException() with a new parameter on line 25. This time the parameter is "index".

Now ThrowException() generates an exception on line 60:

```
eTypes[4] = "error";
```

The eTypes array is global, so you have access to it here. However, here you are attempting to access the fifth element in the array (remember counting starts at 0), which generates a System .IndexOutOfRangeException exception.

This time there is a matched catch block in Main(), and stepping into the code takes you to this block, starting at line 28. The Console.WriteLine() call in this block writes out the message stored in the exception using e.Message (you have access to the exception through the parameter of the catch block). Again, stepping through takes you through the finally block (but not the second catch block, as the exception is already handled) and back into the loop cycle, again calling ThrowException() on line 25.

When you reach the switch structure in ThrowException(), this time you enter a new try block, starting on line 63. When you reach line 68, you perform a nested call to ThrowException(), this time with the parameter "index". You can use the Step Over button to skip the lines of code that are executed here because you've been through them already. As before, this call generates a System .IndexOutOfRangeException exception, but this time it's handled in the nested try...catch... finally structure, the one in ThrowException(). This structure has no explicit match for this type of exception, so the general catch block (starting on line 70) deals with it.

As with the earlier exception handling, you now step through this catch block and the associated finally block, and reach the end of the function call, but with one crucial difference: Although an exception was thrown, it was also handled — by the code in ThrowException(). This means there is no exception left to handle in Main(), so you go straight to the finally block, and then the application terminates.

Listing and Configuring Exceptions

The .NET Framework contains a whole host of exception types, and you are free to throw and handle any of these in your own code, or even throw them from your code so that they may be caught in more complex applications. The IDE supplies a dialog for examining and editing the available exceptions, which can be called up with the Debug ⇨ Exceptions menu item (or by pressing Ctrl+D, E). This dialog is shown in Figure 7-23 (the entries in the list may vary if you use VS).

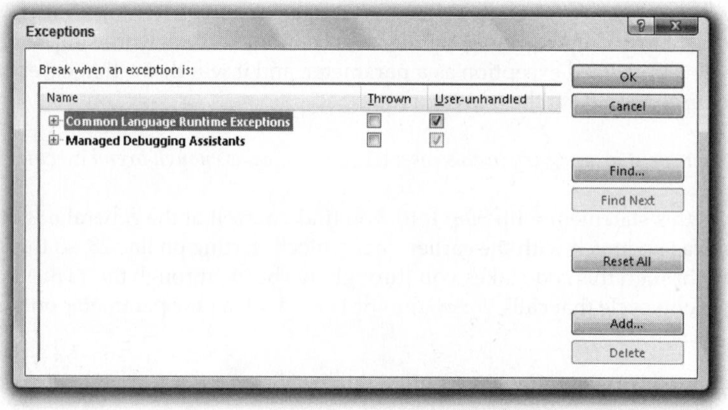

Figure 7-23

Exceptions are listed by category and .NET library namespace. You can see the exceptions in the System namespace by expanding the Common Language Runtime Exceptions tab, and then the System tab. This list includes the System.IndexOutOfRangeException exception you used earlier.

Each exception may be configured using the check boxes shown. You can use the first option, (break when) Thrown, to cause a break into the debugger even for exceptions that are handled. The second option enables you to ignore unhandled exceptions, and suffer the consequences. In most cases, this results in Break mode being entered, so you will likely need to do this only in exceptional circumstances.

Typically, the default settings here are fine.

Notes on Exception Handling

You must always supply `catch` blocks for more specific exceptions before more general catching. If you get this wrong, the application will fail to compile. Note also that you can throw exceptions from within `catch` blocks, either in the ways used in the previous example or simply by using the following expression:

```
throw;
```

This expression results in the exception handled by the `catch` block being rethrown. If you throw an exception in this way, it will not be handled by the current `try...catch...finally` block, but by parent code (although the `finally` block in the nested structure will still execute).

For example, if you changed the `try...catch...finally` block in `ThrowException()` as follows:

```
try
{
    Console.WriteLine("ThrowException(\"nested index\") " +
                            "try block reached.");
    Console.WriteLine("ThrowException(\"index\") called.");
    ThrowException("index");
}
catch
{
    Console.WriteLine("ThrowException(\"nested index\") general"
        + " catch block reached.");
    throw;
}
finally
{
    Console.WriteLine("ThrowException(\"nested index\") finally"
        + " block reached.");
}
```

then execution would proceed first to the `finally` block shown here, then with the matching `catch` block in `Main()`. The resulting console output changes, as shown in Figure 7-24.

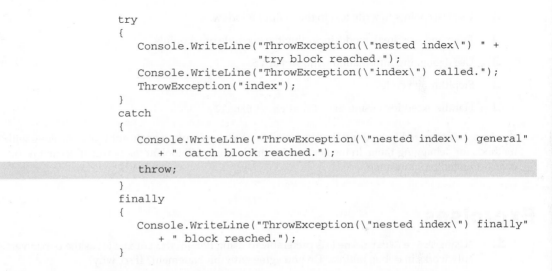

Figure 7-24

This screenshot shows extra lines of output from the Main() function, as the System .IndexOutOfRangeException is caught in this function.

Summary

This chapter has concentrated on techniques that you can use to debug your applications. A variety of techniques are possible here, most of which are available for whatever type of project you are creating, not just console applications.

In this chapter, you learned to do the following:

❑   Use Debug.WriteLine() and Trace.WriteLine() to write text to the Output window.

❑   Use tracepoints to write text to the Output window.

❑   Enter and use Break mode, including the versatile breakpoints.

❑   Use debugging information windows in VS.

❑   Step through code.

❑   Handle exceptions using try...catch...finally.

You have now covered everything that you need to produce simple console applications, along with the methods for debugging them. In the next part of this book, you'll look at the powerful technique of object-oriented programming.

Exercises

1.   "Using Trace.WriteLine() is preferable to using Debug.WriteLine(), as the Debug version only works in debug builds." Do you agree with this statement? If so, why?

2.   Provide code for a simple application containing a loop that generates an error after 5000 cycles. Use a breakpoint to enter Break mode just before the error is caused on the 5000th cycle. (Note: A simple way to generate an error is to attempt to access a nonexistent array element, such as myArray[1000] in an array with a hundred elements.)

3.   "finally code blocks only execute if a catch block isn't executed." True or false?

4.   Given the enumeration data type orientation defined in the following code, write an application that uses structured exception handling (SEH) to cast a byte type variable into an orientation type variable in a safe way. (Note: You can force exceptions to be thrown using the checked keyword, an example of which is shown here. This code should be used in your application.)

```
enum orientation : byte
{
    north = 1,
    south = 2,
    east  = 3,
    west  = 4
}
myDirection = checked((orientation)myByte);
```

Introduction to Object-Oriented Programming

At this point in the book, you've covered all the basics of C# syntax and programming, and have learned how to debug your applications. Already, you can assemble usable console applications. However, to access the real power of the C# language and the .NET Framework, you need to make use of *object-oriented programming* (*OOP*) techniques. In fact, as you will soon see, you've been using these techniques already, although to keep things simple we haven't focused on this.

This chapter steers away from code temporarily and focuses instead on the principles behind OOP. This leads you back into the C# language, because it has a symbiotic relationship with OOP. All of the concepts introduced in this chapter are revisited in later chapters, with illustrative code — so don't panic if you don't grasp everything in the first read-through of this material.

To start with, you'll look at the basics of OOP, which include answering that most fundamental of questions, "What is an *object*?" You will quickly find that there is a lot of terminology related to OOP that can be quite confusing at first, but plenty of explanations are provided. You will also see that using OOP requires you to look at programming in a different way.

As well as discussing the general principles of OOP, this chapter also looks at an area requiring a thorough understanding of OOP: Windows Forms applications. This type of application (which makes use of the Windows environment, with features such as menus, buttons, and so on) provides plenty of scope for description, and you will be able to illustrate OOP points effectively in the Windows Forms environment.

In this chapter you learn the following:

- ❑ What object-oriented programming is.
- ❑ OOP techniques.
- ❑ How Windows Forms applications rely on OOP.

OOP as presented in this chapter is really .NET OOP, and some of the techniques presented here don't apply to other OOP environments. When programming in C#, you use .NET-specific OOP, so it makes sense to concentrate on these aspects.

What Is Object-Oriented Programming?

Object-oriented programming is a relatively new approach to creating computer applications that seeks to address many of the problems with traditional programming techniques. The type of programming you have seen so far is known as *functional* (or *procedural*) programming, often resulting in so-called monolithic applications, meaning all functionality is contained in a few modules of code (often just one). With OOP techniques, you often use many more modules of code, each offering specific functionality, and each module may be isolated or even completely independent of others. This modular method of programming gives you much more versatility and provides more opportunity for code reuse.

To illustrate this further, imagine that a high-performance application on your computer is a top-of-the-range racecar. Written with traditional programming techniques, this sports car is basically a single unit. If you want to improve this car, then you have to replace the whole unit by sending it back to the manufacturer and getting their expert mechanics to upgrade it, or by buying a new one. If OOP techniques are used, then you can simply buy a new engine from the manufacturer and follow their instructions to replace it yourself, rather than take a hacksaw to the bodywork.

In a more traditional application, the flow of execution is often simple and linear. Applications are loaded into memory, begin executing at point A, end at point B, and are then unloaded from memory. Along the way various other entities might be used, such as files on storage media, or the capabilities of a video card, but the main body of the processing occurs in one place. The code along the way is generally concerned with manipulating data through various mathematical and logical means. The methods of manipulation are usually quite simple, using basic types such as integers and Boolean values to build more complex representations of data.

With OOP, things are rarely so linear. Although the same results are achieved, the way of getting there is often very different. OOP techniques are firmly rooted in the structure and meaning of data, and the interaction between that data and other data. This usually means putting more effort into the design stages of a project, but it has the benefit of extensibility. After an agreement is made as to the representation of a specific type of data, that agreement can be worked into later versions of an application, and even entirely new applications. The fact that such an agreement exists can reduce development time dramatically. This explains how the racecar example works. The agreement here is how the code for the "engine" is structured, such that new code (for a new engine) can be substituted with ease, rather than requiring a trip back to the manufacturer. Conversely, it also means that the engine, once created, can be used for other purposes. You could put it in a different car, or use it to power a submarine, for example.

As well as providing an agreed-on approach to data representation, OOP programming often simplifies things by providing an agreement on the structure and usage of more abstract entities. For example, an agreement can be made not just on the format of data that should be used to send output to a device such as a printer, but also on the methods of data exchange with that device, including what instructions it understands, and so on. Going back to the racecar analogy, the agreement would include how the engine connects to the fuel tank, how it passes drive power to the wheels, and so on.

As the name of the technology suggests, this is achieved using *objects*.

What Is an Object?

An *object* is a building block of an OOP application. This building block encapsulates part of the application, which may be a process, a chunk of data, or a more abstract entity.

In the simplest sense, an object may be very similar to a struct type such as those shown earlier in the book, containing members of variable and function types. The variables contained make up the data stored in the object, and the functions contained allow access to the functionality of the object. Slightly more complex objects might not maintain any data; instead, they can represent a process by containing only functions. For example, an object representing a printer might be used, which would have functions enabling control over a printer (so you can print a document, a test page, and so on).

Objects in C# are created from types, just like the variables you've seen already. The type of an object is known by a special name in OOP, its *class*. You can use class definitions to *instantiate* objects, which means to create a real, named *instance* of a class. The phrases *instance of a class* and *object* mean the same thing here; but note at this point that *class* and *object* mean fundamentally different things.

> *The terms* class *and* object *are often confused, and it is important to understand the distinction. It may help you to visualize these terms using the earlier racecar analogy. Think of a class as the template for the car, or perhaps the plans used to build the car. The car itself is an instance of those plans, so it could be referred to as an object.*

In this chapter, you work with classes and objects using *Universal Modeling Language* (*UML*) syntax. UML is a language designed for modeling applications, from the objects that build them, to the operations they perform, and to the use cases that are expected. Here, you use only the basics of this language, which are explained as you go along. Not covered are more complex aspects because UML is a specialized subject to which entire books are devoted.

> *VS has a class viewer that is a powerful tool in its own right.*

Figure 8-1 shows a UML representation of your printer class, called `Printer`.

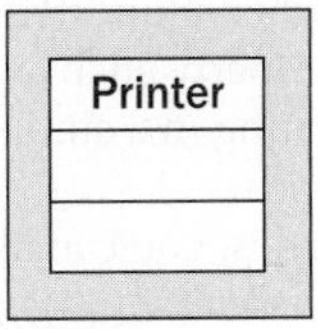

Figure 8-1

The class name is shown in the top section of this box (you learn about the bottom two sections a little later). Figure 8-2 shows a UML representation of an instance of this `Printer` class called `myPrinter`.

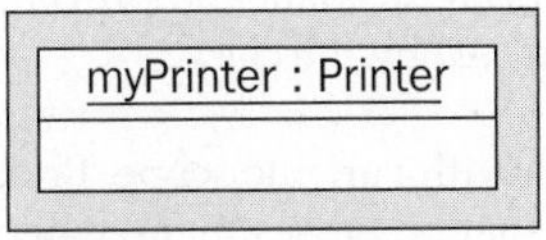

Figure 8-2

Here, the instance name is shown first in the top section, followed by the name of its class. These two names are separated by a colon.

Properties and Fields

Properties and fields provide access to the data contained in an object. This object data is what differentiates separate objects, because it is possible for different objects of the same class to have different values stored in properties and fields.

The various pieces of data contained in an object together make up the *state* of that object. Imagine an object class that represents a cup of coffee, called `CupOfCoffee`. When you instantiate this class (that is, create an object of this class), you must provide it with a state for it to be meaningful. In this case, you might use properties and fields to enable the code that uses this object to set the type of coffee used, whether the coffee contains milk and/or sugar, whether the coffee is instant, and so on. A given coffee cup object would then have a given state, such as `"Columbian filter coffee with milk and two sugars."`

Both fields and properties are typed, so you can store information in them as `string` values, as `int` values, and so on. However, properties differ from fields in that they don't provide direct access to data. Objects can shield users from the nitty-gritty details of their data, which needn't be represented on a one-to-one basis in the properties that exist. If you used a field for the number of sugars in a `CupOfCoffee` instance, then users could place whatever values they liked in the field, limited only by the limits of the type used to store this information. If, for example, you used an `int` to store this data, then users could use any value between –2147483648 and 2147483647, as shown in Chapter 3. Obviously, not all values make sense, particularly the negative ones — some of the large positive amounts might require an inordinately large cup. Still, if you used a property for this information, then you could limit this value to, say, a number between 0 and 2.

In general, it is better to provide properties, rather than fields, for state access, because you have more control over various behaviors. This choice doesn't affect code that uses object instances, because the syntax for using properties and fields is the same.

Read/write access to properties may also be clearly defined by an object. Certain properties may be read-only, allowing you to see what they are but not change them (at least not directly). This is often a useful technique for reading several pieces of state simultaneously. You might have a read-only property of the `CupOfCoffee` class called `Description`, returning a string representing the state of an instance of this class (such as the string given earlier) when requested. You might be able to assemble the same data by interrogating several properties, but a property such as this one may save you time and effort. You might also have write-only properties operating in a similar way.

As well as this read/write access for properties, you can also specify a different sort of access permission for both fields and properties, known as *accessibility*. Accessibility determines which code can access these members — that is, whether they are available to all code (public), only to code within the class (private), or use a more complex scheme (covered in more detail later in the chapter, when it becomes pertinent). One common practice is to make fields private and provide access to them via public properties. This means that code within the class has direct access to data stored in the field, while the public property shields external users from this data and prevents them from placing invalid content there. Public members are said to be *exposed* by the class.

One way to visualize this is to equate it with variable scope. Private fields and properties, for example, can be thought of as local to the object that possesses them, whereas the scope of public fields and properties also encompasses code external to the object.

In the UML representation of a class, you use the second section to display properties and fields, as shown in Figure 8-3.

CupOfCoffee
+BeanType : string
+Instant : bool
+Milk : bool
+Sugar : byte
+Description : string

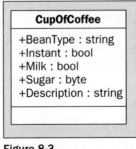

Figure 8-3

This is a representation of the `CupOfCoffee` class, with five members (properties or fields, because no distinction is made in UML) defined as discussed earlier. Each of the entries contains the following information:

- Accessibility: A + symbol is used for a public member, a - symbol is used for a private member. In general, though, private members are not shown in the diagrams in this chapter, because this information is internal to the class. No information is provided as to read/write access.
- The member name.
- The type of the member.

A colon is used to separate the member names and types.

Methods

Method is the term used to refer to functions exposed by objects. These may be called in the same way as any other function and may use return values and parameters in the same way — you looked at functions in detail in Chapter 6.

Methods are used to provide access to the object's functionality. Like fields and properties, they can be public or private, restricting access to external code as necessary. They often make use of an object's state to affect their operations, and have access to private members such as private fields if required. For example, the `CupOfCoffee` class might define a method called `AddSugar()`, which would provide a more readable syntax for incrementing the amount of sugar than setting the corresponding `Sugar` property.

In UML, class boxes show methods in the third section, as shown in Figure 8-4.

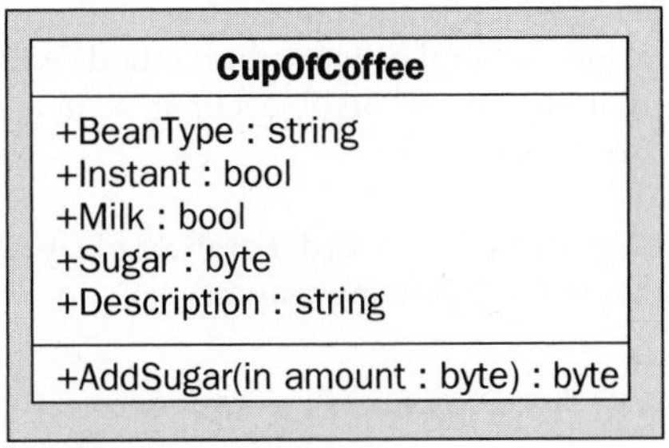

CupOfCoffee
+BeanType : string
+Instant : bool
+Milk : bool
+Sugar : byte
+Description : string
+AddSugar(in amount : byte) : byte

Figure 8-4

The syntax here is similar to that for fields and properties, except that the type shown at the end is the return type and method parameters are shown. Each parameter is displayed in UML with one of the following identifiers: `in`, `out`, or `inout`. These are used to signify the direction of data flow, where `out` and `inout` roughly correspond to the use of the C# keywords `out` and `ref` described in Chapter 6. `in` roughly corresponds to the default C# behavior, where neither the `out` nor `ref` keyword is used.

Everything's an Object

At this point, it's time to come clean: You have been using objects, properties, and methods throughout this book. In fact, everything in C# and the .NET Framework is an object! The `Main()` function in a console application is a method of a class. Every variable type you've looked at is a class. Every command you have used has been a property or a method, such as `<String>.Length`, `<String>.ToUpper()`, and so on. (The period character here separates the object instance's name from the property or method name.)

Objects really are everywhere, and the syntax to use them is often very simple. It has certainly been simple enough for you to concentrate on some of the more fundamental aspects of C# up until now. From this point on, you'll begin to look at objects in detail. Bear in mind that the concepts introduced here have far-reaching consequences — applying even to that simple little `int` variable you've been happily playing around with.

The Life Cycle of an Object

Every object has a clearly defined life cycle. Apart from the normal state of "being in use," this life cycle includes two important stages:

❑ **Construction:** When an object is first instantiated it needs to be initialized. This initialization is known as *construction* and is carried out by a constructor function.

❑ **Destruction:** When an object is destroyed, there are often some clean-up tasks to perform, such as freeing memory. This is the job of a destructor function.

Constructors

Basic initialization of an object is automatic. For example, you don't have to worry about finding the memory to fit a new object into. However, at times you will want to perform additional tasks during an object's initialization stage, such as initializing the data stored by an object. A constructor function is what you use to do this.

All objects have a *default constructor*, which is a parameterless method with the same name as the class itself. A class definition might include several constructor methods with parameters, known as *nondefault constructors*. These enable code that instantiates an object to do so in many ways, perhaps providing initial values for data stored in the object.

In C#, constructors are called using the `new` keyword. For example, you could instantiate a `CupOfCoffee` object using its default constructor in the following way:

```
CupOfCoffee myCup = new CupOfCoffee();
```

Objects may also be instantiated using nondefault constructors. For example, the `CupOfCoffee` class might have a nondefault constructor that uses a parameter to set the bean type at instantiation:

```
CupOfCoffee myCup = new CupOfCoffee("Blue Mountain");
```

Constructors, like fields, properties, and methods, may be public or private. Code external to a class can't instantiate an object using a private constructor; it must use a public constructor. In this way, you can, for example, force users of your classes to use a nondefault constructor (by making the default constructor private).

Some classes have no public constructors, meaning that it is impossible for external code to instantiate them (they are said to be *noncreatable*). However, this doesn't make them completely useless, as you will see shortly.

Destructors

Destructors are used by the .NET Framework to clean up after objects. In general, you don't have to provide code for a destructor method; instead, the default operation does the work for you. However, you can provide specific instructions if anything important needs to be done before the object instance is deleted.

When a variable goes out of scope, for example, it may not be accessible from your code, but it may still exist somewhere in your computer's memory. Only when the .NET runtime performs its garbage collection cleanup is the instance completely destroyed.

> *Don't rely on the destructor to free up resources used by an object instance, as this may occur long after the object is of no further use to you. If the resources in use are critical, then this can cause problems. However, there is a solution to this — described in "Disposable Objects" later in this chapter.*

Static and Instance Class Members

As well as having members such as properties, methods, and fields that are specific to object instances, it is also possible to have *static* (also known as *shared*, particularly to our Visual Basic brethren) members, which may be methods, properties, or fields. Static members are shared between instances of a class, so they can be thought of as global for objects of a given class. Static properties and fields enable you to access data that is independent of any object instances, and static methods enable you to execute commands related to the class type but not specific to object instances. When using static members, in fact, you don't even need to instantiate an object.

For example, the `Console.WriteLine()` and `Convert.ToString()` methods you have been using are static. At no point do you need to instantiate the `Console` or `Convert` classes (indeed, if you try, you'll find that you can't, as the constructors of these classes aren't publicly accessible, as discussed earlier).

There are many situations such as these where static properties and methods can be used to good effect. For example, you might use a static property to keep track of how many instances of a class have been created. In UML syntax, static members of classes appear with underlining, as shown in Figure 8-5.

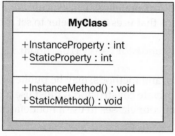

Figure 8-5

Static Constructors

When using static members in a class, you may want to initialize these members beforehand. You can supply a static member with an initial value as part of its declaration, but sometimes you may want to perform a more complex initialization, or perhaps perform some operations before assigning values or allowing static methods to execute.

You can use a static constructor to perform initialization tasks of this type. A class can have a single static constructor, which must have no access modifiers and cannot have any parameters. A static constructor can never be called directly; instead, it is executed when one of the following occurs:

❑ When an instance of the class containing the static constructor is created.

❑ When a static member of the class containing the static constructor is accessed.

In both cases, the static constructor is called first, before the class is instantiated or static members accessed. No matter how many instances of a class are created, its static constructor will only be called once. To differentiate between static constructors and the constructors described earlier in this chapter, all non-static constructors are also known as *instance constructors*.

Static Classes

Often, you will want to use classes that contain only static members and cannot be used to instantiate objects (such as `Console`). A shorthand way to do this, rather than make the constructors of the class private, is to use a *static class*. A static class can contain only static members and can't have instance constructors, since by implication it can never be instantiated. Static classes can, however, have a static constructor, as described in the preceding section.

> *If you are completely new to OOP, then you might like to take a break before embarking on the remainder of this chapter. It is important to fully grasp the fundamentals before learning about the more complicated aspects of this methodology.*

OOP Techniques

Now that you've covered the basics and know what objects are and how they work, you should spend some time looking at some of the other features of objects. This section covers all of the following:

❑ Interfaces

❑ Inheritance

❑ Polymorphism

❑ Relationships between objects

❑ Operator overloading

❑ Events

❑ Reference versus value types

Interfaces

An interface is a collection of public methods and properties that are grouped together to encapsulate specific functionality. After an interface has been defined, you can implement it in a class. This means that the class will then support all of the properties and members specified by the interface.

Note that interfaces cannot exist on their own. You can't "instantiate an interface" as you can a class. In addition, interfaces cannot contain any code that implements its members; it just defines the members themselves. The implementation must come from classes that implement the interface.

In the earlier coffee example, you might group together many of the more general-purpose properties and methods into an interface, such as AddSugar(), Milk, Sugar, and Instant. You could call this interface something like IHotDrink (interface names are normally prefixed with a capital I). You could use this interface on other objects, perhaps those of a CupOfTea class. You could therefore treat these objects in a similar way, and they may still have their own individual properties (BeanType for CupOfCoffee and LeafType for CupOfTea, for example).

Interfaces implemented on objects in UML are shown using a *lollipop* syntax. In Figure 8-6, members of IHotDrink are split into a separate box using class-like syntax.

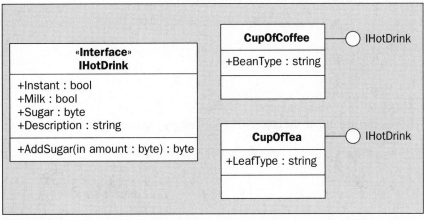

Figure 8-6

A class can support multiple interfaces, and multiple classes can support the same interface. The concept of an interface, therefore, makes life easier for users and other developers. For example, you might have some code that uses an object with a certain interface. Provided that you don't use other properties and methods of this object, it is possible to replace one object with another (code using the IHotDrink interface shown earlier could work with both CupOfCoffee and CupOfTea instances, for example). In addition, the developer of the object itself could supply you with an updated version of an object, and as long as it supports an interface already in use it would be easy to use this new version in your code.

Once an interface is published — that is, it has been made available to other developers or end users — it is good practice not to change it. One way of thinking about this is to imagine the interface as a contract between class creators and class consumers. You are effectively saying, "Every class that supports interface X will support these methods and properties." If the interface changes later, perhaps due to an upgrade of the underlying code, this could cause consumers of that interface to run it incorrectly, or even fail. Instead, you should create a new interface that extends the old one, perhaps including a version number, such as X2. This has become the standard way of doing things, and you are likely to come across numbered interfaces frequently.

Disposable Objects

One interface of particular interest is IDisposable. An object that supports the IDisposable interface must implement the Dispose() method — that is, it must provide code for this method. This method can be called when an object is no longer needed (just before it goes out of scope, for example) and should be used to free up any critical resources that might otherwise linger until the destructor method is called on garbage collection. This gives you more control over the resources used by your objects.

C# enables you to use a structure that makes excellent use of this method. The using keyword enables you to initialize an object that uses critical resources in a code block, where Dispose() is automatically called at the end of the code block:

```
<ClassName> <VariableName> = new <ClassName>();

. . .

Using (<VariableName>)
{
   . . .
}
```

Alternatively, you can instantiate the object <VariableName> as part of the using statement:

```
using (<ClassName> <VariableName> = new <ClassName>())
{
   . . .
}
```

In both cases, the variable <VariableName> will be usable within the using code block and will be disposed of automatically at the end (that is, Dispose() is called when the code block finishes executing).

Inheritance

Inheritance is one of the most important features of OOP. Any class may *inherit* from another, which means that it will have all the members that the class it inherits from has. In OOP terminology, the class being inherited from (*derived* from) is the *parent* class (also known as the *base* class). Note that classes in C# may derive only from a single base class directly, although of course that base class may have a base class of its own, and so on.

Inheritance enables you to extend or create more specific classes from a single, more generic base class. For example, consider a class that represents a farm animal (as used by ace octogenarian developer Old MacDonald in his livestock application). This class might be called `Animal` and possess methods such as `EatFood()` or `Breed()`. You could create a derived class called `Cow`, which would support all of these methods, but might also supply its own, such as `Moo()` and `SupplyMilk()`. You could also create another derived class, `Chicken`, with `Cluck()` and `LayEgg()` methods.

In UML, you indicate inheritance using arrows, as shown in Figure 8-7.

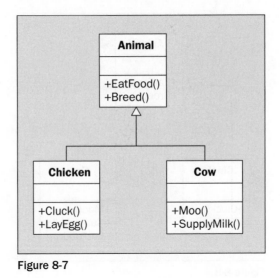

Figure 8-7

In Figure 8-7, the member return types are omitted for clarity.

When using inheritance from a base class, the question of member accessibility becomes an important one. Private members of the base class are not accessible from a derived class, but public members are. However, public members are accessible to both the derived class and external code. Therefore, if you could use only these two levels of accessibility, you couldn't have a member that was accessible both by the base class and the derived class but not external code.

To get around this, there is a third type of accessibility, *protected*, in which only derived classes have access to a member. As far as external code is aware, this is identical to a private member — it doesn't have access in either case.

As well as defining the protection level of a member, you can also define an inheritance behavior for it. Members of a base class may be *virtual,* which means that the member can be overridden by the class that inherits it. Therefore, the derived class may provide an alternative implementation for the member. This alternative implementation doesn't delete the original code, which is still accessible from within the class, but it does shield it from external code. If no alternative is supplied, then any external code that uses the member through the derived class automatically uses the base class implementation of the member.

> *Virtual members cannot be private because that would cause a paradox — it is impossible to say that a member can be overridden by a derived class at the same time you say that it is inaccessible from the derived class.*

In the animals example, you could make `EatFood()` virtual and provide a new implementation for it on any derived class — for example, just on the `Cow` class, as shown in Figure 8-8. This displays the `EatFood()` method on the `Animal` and `Cow` classes to signify that they have their own implementations.

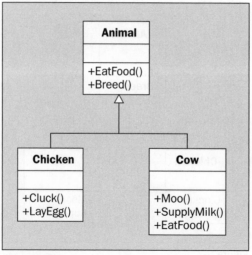

Figure 8-8

Base classes may also be defined as *abstract* classes. An abstract class can't be instantiated directly; to use it you need to inherit from it. Abstract classes may have abstract members, which have no implementation in the base class, so an implementation must be supplied in the derived class. If `Animal` were an abstract class, then the UML would look as shown in Figure 8-9.

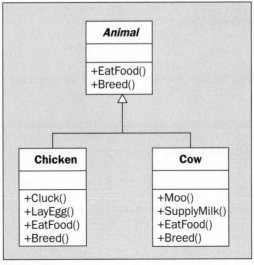

Figure 8-9

Abstract class names are shown in italics (or with a dashed line for their boxes).

In Figure 8-9, both EatFood() and Breed() are shown in the derived classes Chicken and Cow, implying that these methods are either abstract (and, therefore, must be overridden in derived classes) or virtual (and, in this case, have been overridden in Chicken and Cow). Of course, abstract base classes can provide implementation of members, which is very common. The fact that you can't instantiate an abstract class doesn't mean you can't encapsulate functionality in it.

Finally, a class may be *sealed*. A sealed class may not be used as a base class, so no derived classes are possible.

C# provides a common base class for all objects called object (which is an alias for the System .Object class in the .NET Framework). You take a closer look at this class in Chapter 9.

Interfaces, described earlier in this chapter, may also inherit from other interfaces. Unlike classes, interfaces may inherit from multiple base interfaces (in the same way that classes can support multiple interfaces).

Polymorphism

One consequence of inheritance is that classes deriving from a base class have an overlap in the methods and properties that they expose. Because of this, it is often possible to treat objects instantiated from classes with a base type in common using identical syntax. For example, if a base class called Animal has a method called EatFood(), then the syntax for calling this method from the derived classes Cow and Chicken will be similar:

```
Cow myCow = new Cow();
Chicken myChicken = new Chicken();
myCow.EatFood();
myChicken.EatFood();
```

Polymorphism takes this a step further. You can assign a variable that is of the base type to a variable of one of the derived types, as shown here:

```
Animal myAnimal = myCow;
```

No casting is required for this. You can then call methods of the base class through this variable:

```
myAnimal.EatFood();
```

This results in the implementation of EatFood() in the derived class being called. Note that you can't call methods defined on the derived class in the same way. The following code won't work:

```
myAnimal.Moo();
```

However, you can cast a base type variable into a derived class variable and call the method of the derived class that way:

```
Cow myNewCow = (Cow)myAnimal;
myNewCow.Moo();
```

This casting causes an exception to be raised if the type of the original variable was anything other than Cow or a class derived from Cow. There are ways to determine what type an object is, which you'll learn in the next chapter.

Polymorphism is an extremely useful technique for performing tasks with a minimum of code on different objects descending from a single class. Note that it isn't just classes sharing the same parent class that can make use of polymorphism. It is also possible to treat, say, a child and a grandchild class in the same way, as long as there is a common class in their inheritance hierarchy.

As a further note here, remember that in C# all classes derive from the base class object at the root of their inheritance hierarchies. It is therefore possible to treat all objects as instances of the class object. This is how Console.WriteLine() is able to process an almost infinite number of parameter combinations when building strings. Every parameter after the first is treated as an object instance, allowing output from any object to be written to the screen. To do this, the method ToString() (a member of object) is called. You can override this method to provide an implementation suitable for your class, or simply use the default, which returns the class name (qualified according to any namespaces it is in).

Interface Polymorphism

Earlier, you were introduced to the concept of interfaces for grouping together related methods and properties. Although you can't instantiate interfaces in the same way as objects, you can have a variable of an interface type. You can then use this variable to access methods and properties exposed by this interface on objects that support it.

For example, suppose that instead of an Animal base class being used to supply the EatFood() method, you place this EatFood() method on an interface called IConsume. The Cow and Chicken classes could both support this interface, the only difference being that they are forced to provide an implementation for `EatFood()` (as interfaces contain no implementation). You can then access this method using code such as the following:

```
Cow myCow = new Cow();
Chicken myChicken = new Chicken();
IConsume consumeInterface;
consumeInterface = myCow;
consumeInterface.EatFood();
consumeInterface = myChicken;
consumeInterface.EatFood();
```

This provides a simple way for multiple objects to be called in the same manner, and it doesn't rely on a common base class. In this code, calling `consumeInterface.EatFood()` results in the `EatFood()` method of the `Cow` or `Chicken` class being called, depending on which instance has been assigned to the interface type variable.

Note here that derived classes inherit the interfaces supported by their base classes. In the preceding example, it may be that either `Animal` supports `IConsume` or that both `Cow` and `Chicken` support `IConsume`. Remember that classes with a base class in common do not necessarily have interfaces in common, and vice versa.

Relationships Between Objects

Inheritance is a simple relationship between objects that results in a base class being completely exposed by a derived class, where the derived class may also have some access to the inner workings of its base class (through protected members). There are other situations in which relationships between objects become important.

This section takes a brief look at the following:

❑ **Containment:** One class contains another. This is similar to inheritance but allows the containing class to control access to the members of the contained class and even perform additional processing before using members of a contained class.

❑ **Collections:** One class acts as a container for multiple instances of another class. This is similar to having arrays of objects, but collections have additional functionality, including indexing, sorting, resizing, and more.

Containment

Containment is simple to achieve by using a member field to hold an object instance. This member field might be public, in which case users of the container object have access to its exposed methods and properties, much like with inheritance. However, you won't have access to the internals of the class via the derived class, as you would with inheritance.

Alternatively, you can make the contained member object a private member. If you do this, then none of its members will be accessible directly by users, even if they are public. Instead, you can provide access to these members using members of the containing class. This means that you have complete control over which members of the contained class to expose, if any, and you can perform additional processing in the containing class members before accessing the contained class members.

For example, a Cow class might contain an Udder class with the public method Milk(). The Cow object could call this method as required, perhaps as part of its SupplyMilk() method, but these details will not be apparent (or important) to users of the Cow object.

Contained classes may be visualized in UML using an association line. For simple containment, you label the ends of the lines with 1s, showing a one-to-one relationship (one Cow instance will contain one Udder instance). You can also show the contained Udder class instance as a private field of the Cow class for clarity (see Figure 8-10).

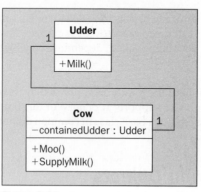

Figure 8-10

Collections

Chapter 5 described how you can use arrays to store multiple variables of the same type. This also works for objects (remember, the variable types you have been using are really objects, so this is no real surprise). Here's an example:

```
Animal[] animals = new Animal[5];
```

A collection is basically an array with bells and whistles. Collections are implemented as classes in much the same way as other objects. They are often named in the plural form of the objects they store — for example, a class called Animals might contain a collection of Animal objects.

The main difference from arrays is that collections usually implement additional functionality, such as Add() and Remove() methods to add and remove items to and from the collection. There is also usually an Item property that returns an object based on its index. More often than not this property is implemented in such a way as to allow more sophisticated access. For example, it would be possible to design Animals so that a given Animal object could be accessed by its name.

In UML you can visualize this as shown in Figure 8-11.

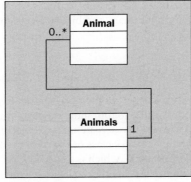

Figure 8-11

Members are not included in Figure 8-11 because it's the relationship that is being illustrated. The numbers on the ends of the connecting lines show that one `Animals` object will contain zero or more `Animal` objects. You'll take a more detailed look at collections in Chapter 11.

Operator Overloading

Earlier in the book, you saw how operators can be used to manipulate simple variable types. There are times when it is logical to use operators with objects instantiated from your own classes. This is possible because classes can contain instructions regarding how operators should be treated.

For example, you might add a new property to the `Animal` class called `Weight`. You could then compare animal weights using the following:

```
if (cowA.Weight > cowB.Weight)
{
    . . .
}
```

Using operator overloading, you can provide logic that used the `Weight` property implicitly in your code, so that you can write code such as:

```
if (cowA > cowB)
{
    . . .
}
```

Here, the greater-than operator (>) has been *overloaded*. An overloaded operator is one for which you have written the code to perform the operation involved — this code is added to the class definition of one of the classes that it operates on. In the preceding example, you are using two `Cow` objects, so the operator overload definition is contained in the `Cow` class. You can also overload operators to work with different classes in the same way, where one (or both) of the class definitions contains the code to achieve this.

Note that you can only overload existing C# operators in this way; you can't create new ones. However, you can provide implementations for both unary and binary usages of operators such as +. You'll see how to do this in C# in Chapter 13.

Events

Objects may raise (and consume) *events* as part of their processing. Events are important occurrences that you can act on in other parts of code, similar to (but more powerful than) exceptions. You might, for example, want some specific code to execute when an `Animal` object is added to an `Animals` collection, where that code isn't part of either the `Animals` class or the code that calls the `Add()` method. To do this, you need to add an *event handler* to your code, which is a special kind of function that is called when the event occurs. You also need to configure this handler to listen for the event you are interested in.

Using events, you can create *event-driven applications,* which are far more prolific than you might think. For example, bear in mind that Windows-based applications are entirely dependent on events. Every button click or scrollbar drag you perform is achieved through event handling, as the events are triggered by the mouse or keyboard.

Later in this chapter you will see how this works in Windows applications, and there is a more in-depth discussion of events in Chapter 13.

Reference Versus Value Types

Data in C# is stored in a variable in one of two ways, depending on the type of the variable. This type will fall into one of two categories: reference or value. The difference is as follows:

❑ Value types store themselves and their content in one place in memory.

❑ Reference types hold a reference to somewhere else in memory (called the heap) where content is stored.

In fact, you don't have to worry about this too much when using C#. So far, you've used `string` variables (which are reference types) and other simple variables (most of which are value types, such as `int`) in pretty much the same way.

One key difference between value types and reference types is that value types always contain a value, whereas reference types can be `null`, reflecting the fact that they contain no value. It is, however, possible to create a value type that behaves like a reference type in this respect (that is, it can be `null`) by using *nullable types,* which are a form of *generic.* Generics are an advanced technique described in Chapter 12.

The only simple types that are reference types are `string` and `object`, although arrays are implicitly reference types as well. Every class you create will be a reference type, which is why this is stressed here.

Structs

The key difference between struct types and classes is that struct types are value types. The fact that struct types and classes are similar may have occurred to you, particularly when you saw in Chapter 6 how you can use functions in struct types. You'll learn more about this in Chapter 9.

OOP in Windows Applications

In Chapter 2, you created a simple Windows application in C#. Windows applications are heavily dependent on OOP techniques, and this sections takes a look at this to illustrate some of the points made in this chapter. The following Try It Out enables you to work through a simple example.

Try It Out — Objects in Action

1. Create a new Windows application called Ch08Ex01 and save it in the directory C:\BegVCSharp\Chapter08.

2. Add a new Button control using the Toolbox, and position it in the center of Form1, as shown in Figure 8-12.

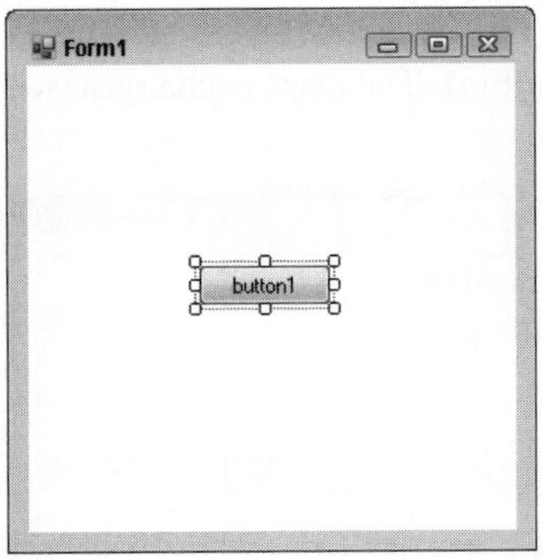

Figure 8-12

3. Double-click on the button to add code for a mouse click. Modify the code that appears as follows:

```
private void button1_Click(object sender, System.EventArgs e)
{
    ((Button)sender).Text = "Clicked!";
    Button newButton = new Button();
    newButton.Text = "New Button!";
    newButton.Click += new EventHandler(newButton_Click);
    Controls.Add(newButton);
}
private void newButton_Click(object sender, System.EventArgs e)
{
    ((Button)sender).Text = "Clicked!!";
}
}
```

4. Run the application. The form is shown in Figure 8-13.

Figure 8-13

5. Click the button marked button1. The display changes (see Figure 8-14).

Figure 8-14

6. Click the button marked New Button! The display changes (see Figure 8-15).

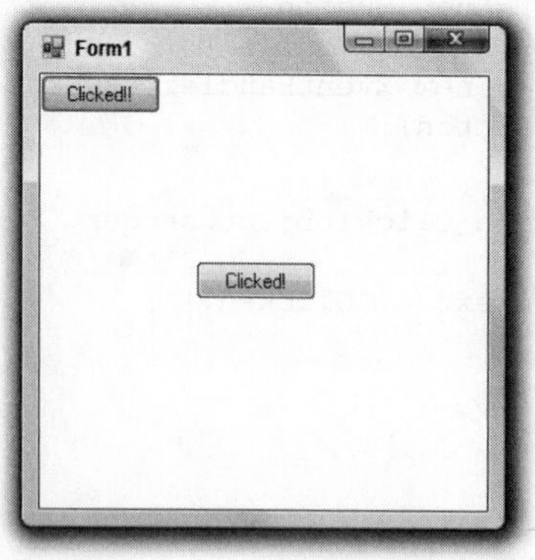

Figure 8-15

How It Works

By adding just a few lines of code you've created a Windows application that does something, while at the same time illustrating some OOP techniques in C#. The phrase "everything's an object" is even more true when it comes to Windows applications. From the form that runs to the controls on the form, you need to make use of OOP techniques all the time. This example has highlighted some of the concepts you looked at earlier in this chapter to show how everything fits together.

The first thing you did in your application was add a new button to the Form1 form. This button is an object, called `Button`. Next, by double-clicking the button, you added an event handler to listen for the `Click` event that the `Button` object generates. This event handler is added into the code for the `Form` object that encapsulates your application, as a private method:

```
private void button1_Click(object sender, System.EventArgs e)
{
}
```

This code uses the C# keyword `private` as a qualifier. Don't worry too much about this for now; the next chapter explains the C# code required for the OOP techniques you've seen in this chapter.

The first line of code you added changes the text on the button that is clicked. This makes use of polymorphism, described earlier in this chapter. The `Button` object representing the button that you click is sent to the event handler as an `object` parameter, which you cast into a `Button` type (this is possible because the `Button` object inherits from `System.Object`, which is the .NET class that `object` is an alias for). You then change the `Text` property of the object to change the text displayed:

```
((Button)sender).Text = "Clicked!";
```

Next, you create a new `Button` object with the `new` keyword (note that namespaces are set up in this project to enable this simple syntax; otherwise, you'd need to use the fully qualified name of this object, `System.Windows.Forms.Button`):

```
Button newButton = new Button();
newButton.Text = "New Button!";
```

Elsewhere in the code a new event handler is added, which you use to respond to the `Click` event generated by the new button:

```
private void newButton_Click(object sender, System.EventArgs e)
{
    ((Button)sender).Text = "Clicked!!";
}
```

You then register this event handler as a listener for the `Click` event, using overloaded operator syntax. Along the way, you create a new `EventHandler` object using a nondefault constructor, with the name of the new event handler function:

```
newButton.Click += new EventHandler(newButton_Click);
```

Finally, you make use of the `Controls` property. This property is an object representing a collection of all the controls on your form, and you use its `Add()` method to add your new button to the form:

```
Controls.Add(newButton);
```

The `Controls` property illustrates that properties don't have to be simple types such as strings or integers but can be any kind of object. This short example used almost all the techniques introduced in this chapter. As you can see, OOP programming needn't be complicated — it just requires a different point of view to get right.

Summary

This chapter has presented a full description of object-oriented techniques. You have worked through this in the context of C# programming, but this has mainly been illustrative. The vast majority of this chapter is relevant to OOP in any language.

You first covered the basics, such as what is meant by the term *object* and how an object is an instance of a class. Next, you learned how objects can have various members, such as fields, properties, and methods. These members can have restricted accessibility, and you learned what is meant by public and private members. Later, you saw that members can also be protected, as well as being virtual and abstract (where abstract methods are only permissible for abstract classes). You also learned the difference between static (shared) and instance members, and why you might want to use static classes.

Next, you took a quick look at the life cycle of an object, including how constructors are used in object creation and destructors are used in object deletion. Later, after examining groups of members in interfaces, you looked at more advanced object destruction with disposable objects supporting the `IDisposable` interface.

Most of the remainder of the chapter covered the features of OOP, many of which you'll explore in more depth in the chapters that follow. You looked at inheritance, whereby classes inherit from base classes; two versions of polymorphism, through base classes and shared interfaces; and how objects can be used to contain one or more other objects (through containment and collections). Finally, you saw how operator overloading can be used to simplify the syntax of object usage and how objects often raise events.

The last part of this chapter demonstrated much of the theory in this chapter, using a Windows application example. The next chapter looks at defining classes using C#.

Exercises

1. Which of the following are real levels of accessibility in OOP?

   a. Friend

   b. Public

   c. Secure

   d. Private

   e. Protected

   f. Loose

   g. Wildcard

2. "You must call the destructor of an object manually or it will waste memory." True or false?

3. Do you need to create an object to call a static method of its class?

4. Draw a UML diagram similar to the ones shown in this chapter for the following classes and interface:

   ❑ An abstract class called HotDrink that has the methods Drink, AddMilk, and AddSugar, and the properties Milk and Sugar.

   ❑ An interface called ICup that has the methods Refill and Wash, and the properties Color and Volume.

   ❑ A class called CupOfCoffee that derives from HotDrink, supports the ICup interface, and has the additional property BeanType.

   ❑ A class called CupOfTea that derives from HotDrink, supports the ICup interface, and has the additional property LeafType.

5. Write some code for a function that will accept either of the two cup objects in the preceding example as a parameter. The function should call the AddMilk, Drink, and Wash methods for any cup object it is passed.

Defining Classes

In Chapter 8, you looked at the features of object-oriented programming (OOP). In this chapter, you put theory into practice and define classes in C#. You won't go so far as to define class members in this chapter but will concentrate on the class definitions themselves. That may sound a little limiting, but don't worry — there's plenty here to get your teeth into!

To start, you explore the basic class definition syntax, the keywords you can use to determine class accessibility and more, and the way in which you can specify inheritance. You also look at interface definitions, because they are similar to class definitions in many ways.

The rest of the chapter covers various related topics that apply when defining classes in C#, including the following:

- ❑ The `System.Object` class.
- ❑ Helpful tools provided by VS and VCE.
- ❑ Class libraries.
- ❑ A comparison between interfaces and abstract classes.
- ❑ Struct types.
- ❑ Copying objects.

Class Definitions in C#

C# uses the `class` keyword to define classes:

```
class MyClass
{
    // Class members.
}
```

This code defines a class called `MyClass`. Once you have defined a class, you are free to instantiate it anywhere else in your project that has access to the definition. By default, classes are declared as *internal*, meaning that only code in the current project will have access to them. You can specify this explicitly using the `internal` access modifier keyword as follows (although you don't have to):

```
internal class MyClass
{
   // Class members.
}
```

Alternatively, you can specify that the class is public and should also be accessible to code in other projects. To do so, you use the `public` keyword:

```
public class MyClass
{
   // Class members.
}
```

Classes declared in their own right like this cannot be private or protected, but you can use these modifiers to declare classes as class members, as shown in the next chapter.

In addition to these two access modifier keywords, you can also specify that the class is either *abstract* (cannot be instantiated, only inherited, and can have abstract members) or *sealed* (cannot be inherited). To do this, you use one of the two mutually exclusive keywords, `abstract` or `sealed`. An abstract class is declared as follows:

```
public abstract class MyClass
{
   // Class members, may be abstract.
}
```

Here, `MyClass` is a public abstract class, while internal abstract classes are also possible.

Sealed classes are declared as follows:

```
public sealed class MyClass
{
   // Class members.
}
```

As with abstract classes, sealed classes may be public or internal.

Inheritance can also be specified in the class definition. You simply put a colon after the class name, followed by the base class name:

```
public class MyClass : MyBase
{
   // Class members.
}
```

Only one base class is permitted in C# class definitions; and if you inherit from an abstract class, you must implement all the abstract members inherited (unless the derived class is also abstract).

The compiler does not allow a derived class to be more accessible than its base class. This means that an internal class can inherit from a public base, but a public class can't inherit from an internal base. This code is legal:

```
public class MyBase
{
    // Class members.
}
```

```
internal class MyClass : MyBase
{
    // Class members.
}
```

The following code won't compile:

```
internal class MyBase
{
    // Class members.
}
```

```
public class MyClass : MyBase
{
    // Class members.
}
```

If no base class is used, the class inherits only from the base class `System.Object` (which has the alias `object` in C#). Ultimately, all classes have `System.Object` at the root of their inheritance hierarchy. You take a closer look at this fundamental class a little later.

In addition to specifying base classes in this way, you can also specify interfaces supported after the colon character. If a base class is specified, it must be the first thing after the colon, with interfaces specified afterward. If no base class is specified, you specify the interfaces immediately after the colon. Commas must be used to separate the base class name (if there is one) and the interface names from one another.

For example, you could add an interface to `MyClass` as follows:

```
public class MyClass : IMyInterface
{
    // Class members.
}
```

All interface members must be implemented in any class that supports the interface, although you can provide an "empty" implementation (with no functional code) if you don't want to do anything with a given interface member, and you can implement interface members as abstract in abstract classes.

The following declaration is invalid, because the base class `MyBase` isn't the first entry in the inheritance list:

```
public class MyClass : IMyInterface, MyBase
{
   // Class members.
}
```

The correct way to specify a base class and an interface is as follows:

```
public class MyClass : MyBase, IMyInterface
{
   // Class members.
}
```

Remember that multiple interfaces are possible, so the following is also valid:

```
public class MyClass : MyBase, IMyInterface, IMySecondInterface
{
   // Class members.
}
```

The following table shows the allowed access modifier combinations for class definitions:

Modifier	Meaning
none or `internal`	Class accessible only from within the current project.
`public`	Class accessible from anywhere.
`abstract` or `internal abstract`	Class accessible only from within the current project, and cannot be instantiated, only derived from.
`public abstract`	Class accessible from anywhere, and cannot be instantiated, only derived from.
`sealed` or `internal sealed`	Class accessible only from within the current project, and cannot be derived from, only instantiated.
`public sealed`	Class accessible from anywhere, and cannot be derived from, only instantiated.

Interface Definitions

Interfaces are declared in a similar way to classes, but using the `interface` keyword, rather than `class`:

```
interface IMyInterface
{
    // Interface members.
}
```

The access modifier keywords `public` and `internal` are used in the same way; and as with classes, interfaces are defined as internal by default. To make an interface publicly accessible you must use the `public` keyword:

```
public interface IMyInterface
{
    // Interface members.
}
```

The keywords `abstract` and `sealed` are not allowed because neither modifier makes sense in the context of interfaces (they contain no implementation, so they can't be instantiated directly, and they must be inheritable to be useful).

Interface inheritance is also specified in a similar way to class inheritance. The main difference here is that multiple base interfaces can be used, as shown here:

```
public interface IMyInterface : IMyBaseInterface, IMyBaseInterface2
{
    // Interface members.
}
```

Interfaces are not classes, and thus do not inherit from `System.Object`. However, the members of `System.Object` are available via an interface type variable, purely for convenience. In addition, as already discussed, it is impossible to instantiate an interface in the same way as a class. The following Try It Out provides an example of some class definitions, along with some code that uses them.

Try It Out   Defining Classes

1. Create a new console application called Ch09Ex01 and save it in the directory C:\BegVCSharp\Chapter09.

2. Modify the code in `Program.cs` as follows:

```
namespace Ch09Ex01
{
    public abstract class MyBase
    {
    }
```

```
internal class MyClass : MyBase
{
}

public interface IMyBaseInterface
{
}

internal interface IMyBaseInterface2
{
}

internal interface IMyInterface : IMyBaseInterface, IMyBaseInterface2
{
}

internal sealed class MyComplexClass : MyClass, IMyInterface
{
}

class Program
{
    static void Main(string[] args)
    {
        MyComplexClass myObj = new MyComplexClass();
        Console.WriteLine(myObj.ToString());
        Console.ReadKey();
    }
}
}
```

3. Execute the project. The output is shown in Figure 9-1.

Figure 9-1

How It Works

This project defines classes and interfaces in the inheritance hierarchy shown in Figure 9-2.

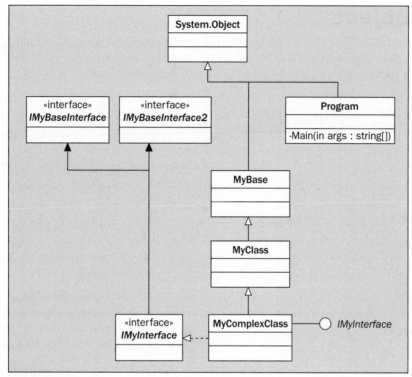

Figure 9-2

Here, Program is included because it is a class defined in the same way as the other classes, even though it isn't part of the main class hierarchy. The Main() method possessed by this class is the entry point for your application.

MyBase and IMyBaseInterface are public definitions, so they are available from other projects. The other classes and interfaces are internal, and only available in this project.

The code in Main() calls the ToString() method of myObj, an instance of MyComplexClass:

```
MyComplexClass myObj = new MyComplexClass();
Console.WriteLine(myObj.ToString());
```

This is one of the methods inherited from System.Object (not shown in the diagram because I've omitted the members of this class for clarity) and simply returns the class name of the object as a string, qualified by any relevant namespaces.

This example may not actually do a lot, but you will return to it later in this chapter, where it is used to demonstrate several key concepts and techniques.

System.Object

Because all classes inherit from `System.Object`, all classes have access to the protected and public members of this class. Therefore, it is worthwhile to take a look at what is available there. `System.Object` contains the methods described in the following table:

Method	Return Type	Virtual	Static	Description
Object()	N/A	No	No	Constructor for the `System.Object` type. Automatically called by constructors of derived types.
~Object() (also known as `Finalize()`— see the next section)	N/A	No	No	Destructor for the `System.Object` type. Automatically called by destructors of derived types; cannot be called manually.
Equals(object)	bool	Yes	No	Compares the object for which this method is called with another object and returns `true` if they are equal. The default implementation checks whether the object parameter refers to the same object (because objects are reference types). This method can be overridden if you want to compare objects in a different way, e.g., to compare the state of two objects.
Equals(object, object)	bool	No	Yes	This method compares the two objects passed to it and checks whether they are equal. This check is performed using the `Equals(object)` method. If both objects are null references, then this method returns `true`.
ReferenceEquals (object, object)	bool	No	Yes	This method compares the two objects passed to it and checks whether they are references to the same instance.

Method	Return Type	Virtual	Static	Description
ToString()	string	Yes	No	Returns a string corresponding to the object instance. By default, this is the qualified name of the class type, but this can be overridden to provide an implementation appropriate to the class type.
MemberwiseClone()	object	No	No	Copies the object by creating a new object instance and copying members. This member copying does not result in new instances of these members. Any reference type members of the new object refer to the same objects as the original class. This method is protected, so it can only be used from within the class or from derived classes.
GetType()	System .Type	No	No	Returns the type of the object in the form of a System.Type object.
GetHashCode()	int	Yes	No	Used as a hash function for objects where this is required. A hash function is one that returns a value identifying the object state in some compressed form.

These are the basic methods that must be supported by object types in the .NET Framework, although you might never use some of them (or use them only in special circumstances, such as GetHashCode).

GetType is helpful when you are using polymorphism because it enables you to perform different operations with objects depending on their type, rather than the same operation for all objects, as is often the case. For example, if you have a function that accepts an object type parameter (meaning you can pass it just about anything), you might perform additional tasks if certain objects are encountered. Using a combination of GetType and typeof (a C# operator that converts a class name into a System.Type object), you can perform comparisons such as the following:

```
if (myObj.GetType() == typeof(MyComplexClass))
{
    // myObj is an instance of the class MyComplexClass.
}
```

The `System.Type` object returned is capable of a lot more than that, but only this is covered here. It can also be very useful to override the `ToString` method, particularly in situations where the contents of an object can be easily represented with a single human-readable string. You see these `System.Object` methods repeatedly in subsequent chapters, so you'll learn more details as necessary.

Constructors and Destructors

When you define a class in C#, it's often unnecessary to define associated constructors and destructors, because the compiler adds them for you when you build your code if you don't supply them. However, you can provide your own, if required, which enables you to initialize and clean up after your objects, respectively.

A simple constructor can be added to a class using the following syntax:

```
class MyClass
{
    public MyClass()
    {
        // Constructor code.
    }
}
```

This constructor has the same name as the class that contains it, has no parameters (making it the default constructor for the class), and is public so that objects of the class may be instantiated using this constructor (refer to Chapter 8 for more information about this).

You can also use a private default constructor, meaning that object instances of this class cannot be created using this constructor (it is *noncreatable* — again, see the discussion in Chapter 8):

```
class MyClass
{
    private MyClass()
    {
        // Constructor code.
    }
}
```

Finally, you can add nondefault constructors to your class in a similar way, simply by providing parameters:

```
class MyClass
{
    public MyClass()
    {
        // Default constructor code.
    }

    public MyClass(int myint)
    {
        // Nondefault constructor code (uses myint).
    }
}
```

You can supply an unlimited number of constructors (apart from running out of memory or distinct sets of parameters, so maybe "almost no limit" is more appropriate).

Destructors are declared using a slightly different syntax. The destructor used in .NET (and supplied by the System.Object class) is called Finalize, but this isn't the name you use to declare a destructor. Instead of overriding Finalize, you use the following:

```
class MyClass
{
    ~MyClass()
    {
        // Destructor body.
    }
}
```

Thus, the destructor of a class is declared by the class name (like the constructor is), with the tilde (~) prefix. The code in the destructor is executed when garbage collection occurs, enabling you to free resources. After the destructor is called, implicit calls to the destructors of base classes also occur, including a call to Finalize in the System.Object root class. This technique enables the .NET Framework to ensure that this occurs because overriding Finalize would mean that base class calls would need to be explicitly performed, which is potentially dangerous (you learn how to call base class methods in the next chapter).

Constructor Execution Sequence

If you perform multiple tasks in the constructors of a class, it can be handy to have this code in one place, which has the same benefits as splitting code into functions, as shown in Chapter 6. You could do this using a method (see Chapter 10), but C# provides a nice alternative. You can configure any constructor to call any other constructor before it executes its own code.

First, though, you need to take a closer look at what happens by default when you instantiate a class instance. Apart from facilitating the centralization of initialization code as noted previously, this is worth knowing about in its own right. During development, objects often don't behave quite as you expect them to due to errors during constructor calling — usually due to a base class somewhere in the inheritance hierarchy of your class that you are not instantiating correctly, or because information is not being properly supplied to base class constructors. Understanding what happens during this phase of an object's life cycle can make it much easier to solve this sort of problem.

For a derived class to be instantiated, its base class must be instantiated. For this base class to be instantiated, its own base class must be instantiated, and so on all the way back to System.Object (the root of all classes). As a result, whatever constructor you use to instantiate a class, System.Object .Object is always called first.

Regardless of which constructor you use in a derived class (the default constructor or a nondefault constructor), unless you specify otherwise, the default constructor for the base class is used. (You'll see how to change this behavior shortly.) Here's a short example illustrating the sequence of execution. Consider the following object hierarchy:

```
public class MyBaseClass
{
    public MyBaseClass()
    {
    }

    public MyBaseClass(int i)
    {
    }
}

public class MyDerivedClass : MyBaseClass
{
    public MyDerivedClass()
    {
    }

    public MyDerivedClass(int i)
    {
    }

    public MyDerivedClass(int i, int j)
    {
    }
}
```

You could instantiate `MyDerivedClass` as follows:

```
MyDerivedClass myObj = new MyDerivedClass();
```

In this case, the following sequence of events will occur:

❑   The `System.Object.Object` constructor will execute.

❑   The `MyBaseClass.MyBaseClass` constructor will execute.

❑   The `MyDerivedClass.MyDerivedClass` constructor will execute.

Alternatively, you could use the following:

```
MyDerivedClass myObj = new MyDerivedClass(4);
```

Here, the sequence is as follows:

❑   The `System.Object.Object` constructor will execute.

❑   The `MyBaseClass.MyBaseClass` constructor will execute.

❑   The `MyDerivedClass.MyDerivedClass(int i)` constructor will execute.

Finally, you could use this:

```
MyDerivedClass myObj = new MyDerivedClass(4, 8);
```

This results in the following sequence:

❏   The `System.Object.Object` constructor will execute.

❏   The `MyBaseClass.MyBaseClass` constructor will execute.

❏   The `MyDerivedClass.MyDerivedClass(int i, int j)` constructor will execute.

This system works fine most of the time, but sometimes you will want a little more control over the events that occur. For example, in the last instantiation example, you might want to have the following sequence:

❏   The `System.Object.Object` constructor will execute.

❏   The `MyBaseClass.MyBaseClass(int i)` constructor will execute.

❏   The `MyDerivedClass.MyDerivedClass(int i, int j)` constructor will execute.

Using this you could place the code that uses the `int i` parameter in `MyBaseClass(int i)`, meaning that the `MyDerivedClass(int i, int j)` constructor would have less work to do — it would only need to process the `int j` parameter. (This assumes that the `int i` parameter has an identical meaning in both scenarios, which might not always be the case; but in practice, with this kind of arrangement, it usually is.) C# allows you to specify this kind of behavior if you want.

To do this, you can use a *constructor initializer*, which consists of code placed after a colon in the method definition. For example, you could specify the base class constructor to use in the definition of the constructor in your derived class as follows:

```
public class MyDerivedClass : MyBaseClass
{
    ...

    public MyDerivedClass(int i, int j) : base(i)
    {
    }
}
```

The `base` keyword directs the .NET instantiation process to use the base class constructor, which has the specified parameters. Here, you are using a single `int` parameter (the value of which is the value that is passed to the `MyDerivedClass` constructor as the parameter `i`), so `MyBaseClass(int i)` will be used. Doing this means that `MyBaseClass` will not be called, giving you the sequence of events listed prior to this example — exactly what you want here.

You can also use this keyword to specify literal values for base class constructors, perhaps using the default constructor of `MyDerivedClass` to call a nondefault constructor of `MyBaseClass`:

```
public class MyDerivedClass : MyBaseClass
{
    public MyDerivedClass() : base(5)
    {
    }
    ...
}
```

This gives you the following sequence:

❑ The `System.Object.Object` constructor will execute.

❑ The `MyBaseClass.MyBaseClass(int i)` constructor will execute.

❑ The `MyDerivedClass.MyDerivedClass()` constructor will execute.

As well as this `base` keyword, you can use one more keyword as a constructor initializer: `this`. This keyword instructs the .NET instantiation process to use a nondefault constructor on the current class before the specified constructor is called:

```
public class MyDerivedClass : MyBaseClass
{
    public MyDerivedClass() : this(5, 6)
    {
    }

    ...

    public MyDerivedClass(int i, int j) : base(i)
    {
    }
}
```

Here, you have the following sequence:

❑ The `System.Object.Object` constructor will execute.

❑ The `MyBaseClass.MyBaseClass(int i)` constructor will execute.

❑ The `MyDerivedClass.MyDerivedClass(int i, int j)` constructor will execute.

❑ The `MyDerivedClass.MyDerivedClass` constructor will execute.

The only limitation here is that you can only specify a single constructor using a constructor initializer. However, as demonstrated in the last example, this isn't much of a limitation, because you can still construct fairly sophisticated execution sequences.

If you don't specify a constructor initializer for a constructor, the compiler adds one for you: `base()`. *This results in the default behavior described earlier in this section.*

OOP Tools in VS and VCE

Because OOP is such a fundamental subject in the .NET Framework, several tools are provided by VS and VCE to aid development of OOP applications. This section describes some of these.

The Class View Window

In Chapter 2, you saw that the Solution Explorer window shares space with a window called Class View. This window shows you the class hierarchy of your application and enables you to see at a glance the characteristics of the classes you use. Figure 9-3 shows the view for the example project in the previous Try It Out.

Figure 9-3

The window is divided into two main sections; the bottom section shows members of types. To see this in action with this example project, and to see what else is possible with the Class View window, you need to show some items that are currently hidden. To do this, tick the items in the Class View Grouping drop-down at the top of the Class View window, as shown in Figure 9-4.

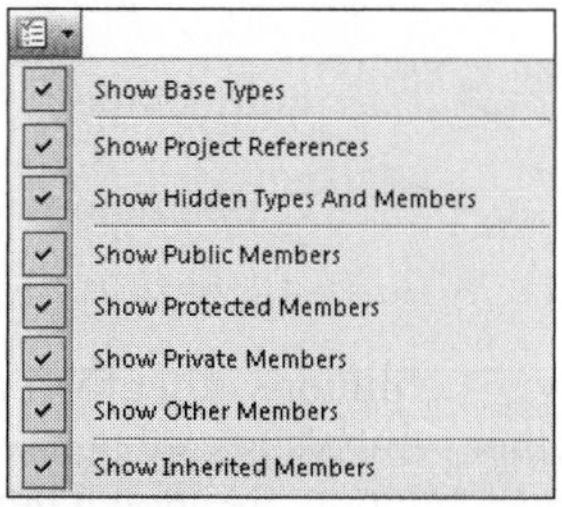

Figure 9-4

Now you can see members and additional information, as shown in Figure 9-5.

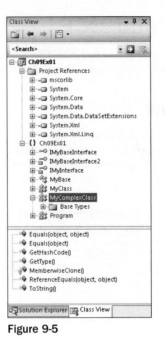

Figure 9-5

Many symbols may be used here, including the following icons:

Icon	Meaning	Icon	Meaning	Icon	Meaning
	Project		Property		Event
{}	Namespace		Field		Delegate
	Class		Struct		Assembly
	Interface		Enumeration		
	Method		Enumeration item		

Note that some of these are used for type definitions other than classes, such as enumerations and struct types. Some of the entries may have other symbols placed below them signifying their access level (no symbol appears for public entries). These symbols are shown here:

Icon	Meaning	Icon	Meaning	Icon	Meaning
	Private		Protected		Internal

No symbols are used to denote abstract, sealed, or virtual entries.

As well as being able to look at this information here, you can also access the relevant code for many of these items. Double-clicking on an item, or right-clicking and selecting Go To Definition, takes you straight to the code in your project that defines the item, if it is available. If the code isn't available, such as code in an inaccessible base type (e.g., System.Object), you instead have the option to select Browse Definition, which will take you to the Object Browser view (described in the next section).

One other entry that appears in Figure 9-5 is Project References. This enables you to see what assemblies are referenced by your projects, which in this case includes the core .NET types in mscorlib and system, data access types in system.data, and XML manipulation types in system.xml. The references here can be expanded, showing you the namespaces and types contained within these assemblies.

There is also a function available from the Class View that enables you to find occurrences of types and members in your code. These are available by right-clicking on an item and selecting Find All References. Either option provides a list of search results in the Find Symbol Results window, which appears at the bottom of the screen as a tabbed window in the Error List display area. You can also rename items using the Class View. If you do this, you're given the option to rename references to the item wherever it occurs in your code. This means you have no excuse for spelling mistakes in class names because you can change them as often as you like!

The Object Browser

The Object Browser is an expanded version of the Class View window, enabling you to view other classes available to your project, and even completely external classes. It is entered either automatically (e.g., in the situation noted in the last section) or manually via View ➪ Other Windows ➪ Object Browser. The view appears in the main window, and you can browse it in the same way as the Class View window.

This window provides the same information as Class View but also shows you more of the .NET types. When an item is selected, you also get information about it in a third window, as shown in Figure 9-6.

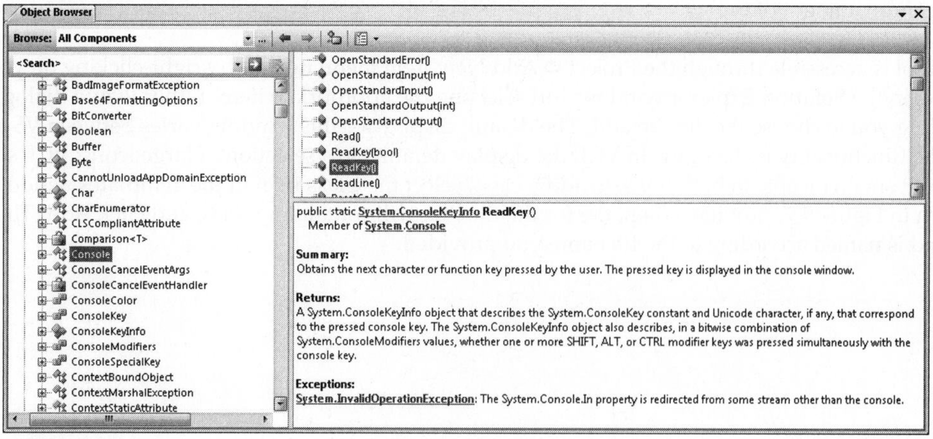

Figure 9-6

225

Here, the ReadKey method of the Console class has been selected. (Console is found in the System namespace in the mscorlib assembly.) The information window in the bottom, right corner shows you the method signature, the class to which the method belongs, and a summary of the method function. This information can be useful when you are exploring the .NET types, or if you are just refreshing your memory about what a particular class can do.

In addition, you can make use of this information window in types that you create. Make the following change to the code in Ch09Ex01:

```
/// <summary>
/// This class contains my program!
/// </summary>
class Program
{
    static void Main(string[] args)
    {
        MyComplexClass myObj = new MyComplexClass();
        Console.WriteLine(myObj.ToString());
        Console.ReadKey();
    }
}
```

Return to the Object Browser. The change is reflected in the information window. This is an example of XML documentation, the subject of Chapter 31.

*If you made this code change manually, then you noticed that simply typing the three slashes ///
causes the IDE to add most of the rest of the code for you. It automatically analyzes the code to which
you are applying XML documentation and builds the basic XML documentation — more evidence,
should you need any, that VS and VCE are great tools to work with!*

Adding Classes

VS and VCE contain tools that can speed up some common tasks, and some of these are applicable to OOP. One of these tools, the Add New Item Wizard, enables you to add new classes to your project with a minimum amount of typing.

This tool is accessible through the Project ⇨ Add New Item menu item or by right-clicking on your project in the Solution Explorer window and selecting the appropriate item. Either way, a dialog appears, enabling you to choose the item to add. The default display for this window varies between VS and VCE but the functionality is the same. In VCE the display defaults to a selection of large icons; VCE shows a list with smaller icons. In both IDEs, to add a class, select the Class item in the Templates window, as shown in Figure 9-7, provide a filename for the file that will contain the class, and click Add. The class created is named according to the filename you provided.

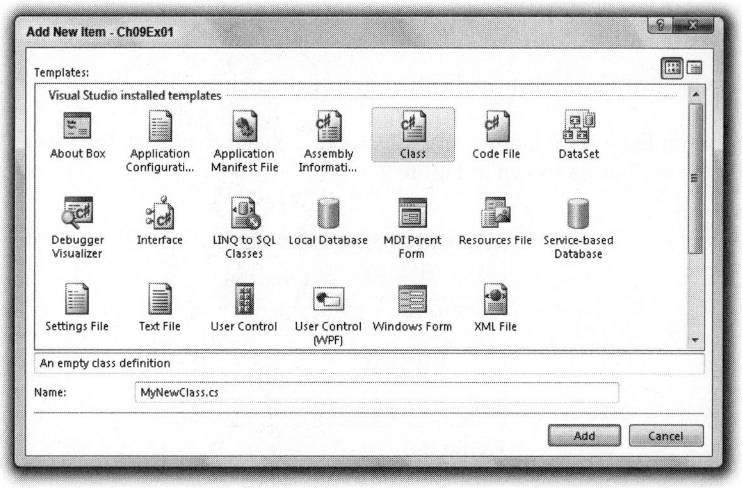

Figure 9-7

In the Try It Out earlier in this chapter, you added class definitions manually to your `Program.cs` file. Often, keeping classes in separate files makes it easier to keep track of your classes. Entering the information in the Add New Item dialog when the Ch09Ex01 project is open results in the following code being generated in `MyNewClass.cs`:

```
using System;
using System.Collections.Generic;
using System.Linq;
using System.Text;

namespace Ch09Ex01
{
    class MyNewClass
    {
    }
}
```

This class, `MyNewClass`, is defined in the same namespace as your entry point class, `Program`, so you can use it from code just as if it were defined in the same file. As shown in the code, the class generated for you contains no constructor. Recall that if a class definition doesn't include a constructor, then the compiler adds a default constructor when you compile your code.

Class Diagrams

One powerful feature of VS that you haven't looked at yet is the capability to generate class diagrams from code and use them to modify projects. The class diagram editor in VS enables you to generate UML-like diagrams of your code with ease. You'll see this in action in the following Try It Out when you generate a class diagram for the Ch09Ex01 project you created earlier.

Unfortunately, class diagrams are a feature that is missing from VCE, so you can only follow this Try It Out if you have VS.

Try It Out   **Generating a Class Diagram**

1. Open the Ch09Ex01 project created earlier in this chapter.

2. In the Solution Explorer window, select `Program.cs` and then click the View Class Diagram button in the toolbar, as shown in Figure 9-8.

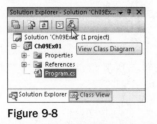

Figure 9-8

3. A class diagram appears, called ClassDiagram1.cd.

4. Click on the IMyInterface lollipop and, using the Properties window, change its `Position` property to Right.

5. Right-click on MyBase and select Show Base Type from the context menu.

6. Move the objects in the drawing around by dragging them to achieve a more pleasing layout. At this point, the diagram should look a little like Figure 9-9.

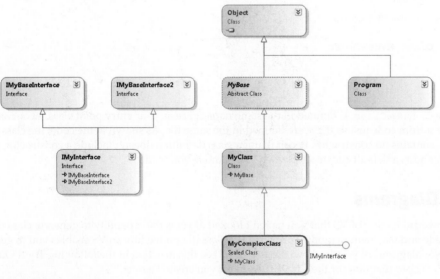

Figure 9-9

How It Works

With very little effort, you have created a class diagram not unlike the UML diagram presented in Figure 9-2 (which doesn't show the color, of course). The following features are evident:

❑ Classes are shown as blue boxes, including their name and type.

❑ Interfaces are shown as green boxes, including their name and type.

❑ Inheritance is shown with arrows with white heads (and in some cases text inside class boxes).

❑ Classes implementing interfaces have lollipops.

❑ Abstract classes are shown with a dotted outline and italicized name.

❑ Sealed classes are shown with a thick black outline.

Clicking on an object shows you additional information in a Class Details window at the bottom of the screen. Here, you can see (and modify) class members. You can also modify class details in the Properties window.

> *Chapter 10 takes a detailed look at adding members to classes using the class diagram.*

From the Toolbox, you can add new items such as classes, interfaces, and enums to the diagram, and define relationships between objects in the diagram. When you do this, the code for the new items is automatically generated for you.

Using this editor, you can design whole families of types graphically, without ever having to use the code editor. Obviously, when it comes to actually adding the functionality you have to do things by hand, but this is a great way to get started. You'll return to this view in subsequent chapters and learn more about what it can do for you, including using the Object Test Bench to test your classes before using them in your code. For now, though, you can explore things on your own.

Class Library Projects

As well as placing classes in separate files within your project, you can also place them in completely separate projects. A project that contains nothing but classes (along with other relevant type definitions, but no entry point) is called a *class library*.

Class library projects compile into .dll assemblies, and you can access their contents by adding references to them from other projects (which might be part of the same solution, but doesn't have to be). This extends the encapsulation that objects provide because class libraries may be revised and updated without touching the projects that use them, enabling you to easily upgrade services provided by classes (which might affect multiple consumer applications).

The following Try It Out provides an example of a class library project and a separate project that makes use of the classes that it contains.

Try It Out   Using a Class Library

1. Create a new project of type Class Library called Ch09ClassLib and save it in the directory C:\BegVCSharp\Chapter09, as shown in Figure 9-10.

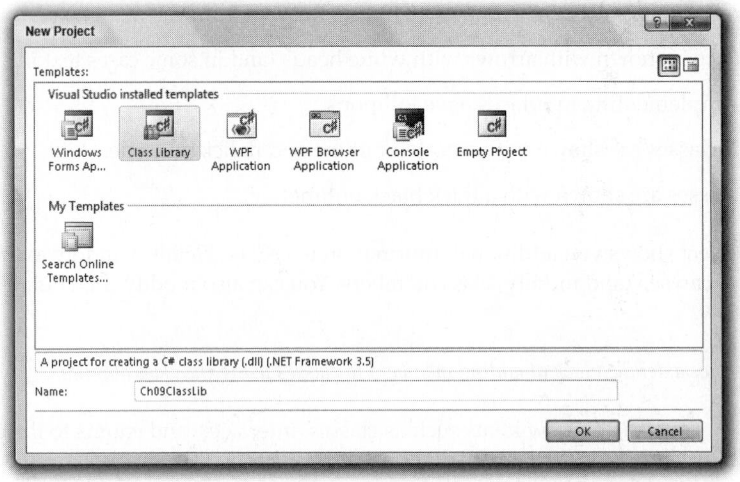

Figure 9-10

2. Rename the file `Class1.cs` to `MyExternalClass.cs` (by right-clicking on the file in the Solution Explorer window and selecting Rename). Click Yes on the dialog that appears.

3. The code in `MyExternalClass.cs` automatically changes to reflect the class name change:

```
class MyExternalClass
{
}
```

4. Add a new class to the project, using the filename `MyInternalClass.cs`.

5. Modify the code to make the class `MyInternalClass` explicitly internal:

```
internal class MyInternalClass
{
}
```

6. Compile the project (this project has no entry point, so you can't run it as normal — instead, you can build it by selecting Build ⇨ Build Solution).

7. Create a new console application project called Ch09Ex02 and save it in the directory C:\BegVCSharp\Chapter09.

8. Select Project ⇨ Add Reference, or select the same option after right-clicking on References in the Solution Explorer window.

9. Click the Browse tab, navigate to C:\BegVCSharp\Chapter09\Chapter09\Ch09ClassLib\ bin\Debug\, and double-click on `Ch09ClassLib.dll`.

10. When the operation completes, confirm that a reference was added in the Solution Explorer window, as shown in Figure 9-11.

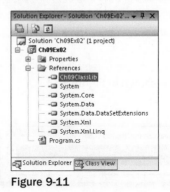

Figure 9-11

11. Open the Object Browser window and examine the new reference to see what objects it contains (see Figure 9-12).

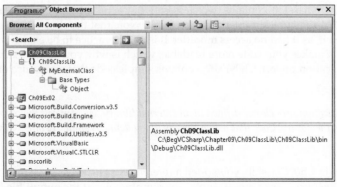

Figure 9-12

12. Modify the code in `Program.cs` as follows:

```
using System;
using System.Collections.Generic;
using System.Linq;
using System.Text;
using Ch09ClassLib;

namespace Ch09Ex02
```

```
{
    class Program
    {
        static void Main(string[] args)
        {
            MyExternalClass myObj = new MyExternalClass();
            Console.WriteLine(myObj.ToString());
            Console.ReadKey();
        }
    }
}
```

13.   Run the application. The result is shown in Figure 9-13.

Figure 9-13

How It Works

This example created two projects: a class library project and a console application project. The class library project, Ch09ClassLib, contains two classes: `MyExternalClass`, which is publicly accessible, and `MyInternalClass`, which is internally accessible. Note that the class was implicit by default when you created it, as it had no access modifier. It is good practice to be explicit about accessibility, though, because it makes your code more readable, which is why you add the `internal` keyword. The console application project, Ch09Ex02, contains simple code that makes use of the class library project.

> *When an application uses classes defined in an external library, you can call that application a client application of the library. Code that uses a class that you define is similarly often referred to as client code.*

To use the classes in Ch09ClassLib, you added a reference to `Ch09ClassLib.dll` to the console application. For the purposes of this example, you simply point at the output file for the class library, although it would be just as easy to copy this file to a location local to Ch09Ex02, enabling you to continue development of the class library without affecting the console application. To replace the old assembly version with the new one, simply copy the newly generated DLL file over the old one.

After adding the reference you took a look at the available classes using the object browser. Because the `MyInternalClass` is internal, you can't see it in this display — it isn't accessible to external projects. However, `MyExternalClass` is accessible, and it's the one you use in the console application.

You could replace the code in the console application with code attempting to use the internal class as follows:

```
static void Main(string[] args)
{
    MyInternalClass myObj = new MyInternalClass();
    Console.WriteLine(myObj.ToString());
    Console.ReadKey();
}
```

If you attempt to compile this code, you receive the following compilation error:

```
'Ch09ClassLib.MyInternalClass' is inaccessible due to its protection level
```

This technique of making use of classes in external assemblies is key to programming with C# and the .NET Framework. It is, in fact, exactly what you are doing when you use any of the classes in the .NET Framework because they are treated in the same way.

Interfaces Versus Abstract Classes

This chapter has demonstrated how you can create both interfaces and abstract classes (without members for now — you get to them in Chapter 10). The two types are similar in a number of ways, so it would be useful to know how to determine when you would want to use one technique or the other.

First the similarities: Both abstract classes and interfaces may contain members that can be inherited by a derived class. Neither interfaces nor abstract classes may be directly instantiated, but you can declare variables of these types. If you do, you can use polymorphism to assign objects that inherit from these types to variables of these types. In both cases, you can then use the members of these types through these variables, although you don't have direct access to the other members of the derived object.

Now the differences: Derived classes may only inherit from a single base class, which means that only a single abstract class can be inherited directly (although it is possible for a chain of inheritance to include multiple abstract classes). Conversely, classes can use as many interfaces as they want, but this doesn't make a massive difference — similar results can be achieved either way. It's just that the interface way of doing things is slightly different.

Abstract classes may possess both *abstract members* (these have no code body and must be implemented in the derived class unless the derived class is itself abstract) and *non-abstract members* (these possess a code body, and can be virtual so that they may be overridden in the derived class). *Interface members*, conversely, must be implemented on the class that uses the interface — they do not possess code bodies. Moreover, interface members are by definition public (because they are intended for external use), but members of abstract classes may also be private (as long as they aren't abstract), protected, internal, or protected internal (where protected internal members are accessible only from code within the application or from a derived class). In addition, interfaces can't contain fields, constructors, destructors, static members, or constants.

This indicates that the two types are intended for different purposes. Abstract classes are intended for use as the base class for families of objects that share certain central characteristics, such as a common purpose and structure. Interfaces are intended for use by classes that might differ on a far more fundamental level, but can still do some of the same things.

For example, consider a family of objects representing trains. The base class, `Train`, contains the core definition of a train, such as wheel gauge and engine type (which could be steam, diesel, and so on). However, this class is abstract, because there is no such thing as a "generic" train. To create an "actual" train, you add characteristics specific to that train. For example, you derive classes such as `PassengerTrain`, `FreightTrain`, and `424DoubleBogey`, as shown in Figure 9-14.

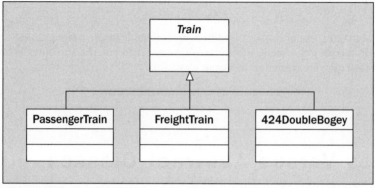

Figure 9-14

A family of car objects might be defined in the same way, with an abstract base class of `Car` and derived classes such as `Compact`, `SUV`, and `PickUp`. `Car` and `Train` might even derive from a common base class, such as `Vehicle`. This is shown in Figure 9-15.

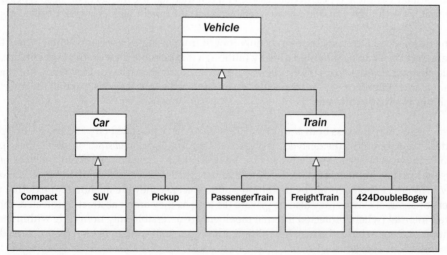

Figure 9-15

Some of the classes lower in the hierarchy may share characteristics because of their purpose, not just because of what they are derived from. For example, `PassengerTrain`, `Compact`, `SUV`, and `Pickup` are all capable of carrying passengers, so they might possess an `IPassengerCarrier` interface. `FreightTrain` and `PickUp` can carry heavy loads, so they might both have an `IHeavyLoadCarrier` interface as well. This is illustrated in Figure 9-16.

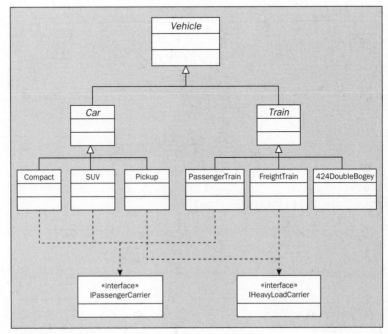

Figure 9-16

By breaking down an object system in this way before going about assigning specifics, you can clearly see which situations should use abstract classes rather than interfaces, and vice versa. The result of this example couldn't be achieved using only interfaces or only abstract inheritance.

Struct Types

Chapter 8 noted that structs and classes are very similar but that structs are value types and classes are reference types. What does this actually mean to you? Well, the easiest way of looking at this is with an example, such as the following Try It Out.

Try It Out   Classes versus Structs

1. Create a new console application project called Ch09Ex03 and save it in the directory
    C:\BegVCSharp\Chapter09.

2. Modify the code as follows:

```
namespace Ch09Ex03
{
    class MyClass
    {
        public int val;
    }

    struct myStruct
    {
        public int val;
    }

    class Program
    {
        static void Main(string[] args)
        {
            MyClass objectA = new MyClass();
            MyClass objectB = objectA;
            objectA.val = 10;
            objectB.val = 20;
            myStruct structA = new myStruct();
            myStruct structB = structA;
            structA.val = 30;
            structB.val = 40;
            Console.WriteLine("objectA.val = {0}", objectA.val);
            Console.WriteLine("objectB.val = {0}", objectB.val);
            Console.WriteLine("structA.val = {0}", structA.val);
            Console.WriteLine("structB.val = {0}", structB.val);
            Console.ReadKey();
        }
    }
}
```

3. Run the application. The output is shown in Figure 9-17.

Figure 9-17

How It Works

This application contains two type definitions: one for a struct called `myStruct`, which has a single public `int` field called `val`, and one for a class called `MyClass` that contains an identical field (you look at class members such as fields in Chapter 10; for now just understand that the syntax is the same here). Next, you perform the same operations on instances of both of these types:

1. Declare a variable of the type.

2. Create a new instance of the type in this variable.

3. Declare a second variable of the type.

4. Assign the first variable to the second variable.

5. Assign a value to the `val` field in the instance in the first variable.

6. Assign a value to the `val` field in the instance in the second variable.

7. Display the values of the `val` fields for both variables.

Although you are performing the same operations on variables of both types, the outcome is different. When you display the values of the `val` field, both object types have the same value, whereas the struct types have different values. What has happened?

Objects are *reference* types. When you assign an object to a variable you are actually assigning that variable with a *pointer* to the object it refers to. A pointer, in real code terms, is an address in memory. In this case, the address is the point in memory where the object is found. When you assign the first object reference to the second variable of type `MyClass` with the following line, you are actually copying this address:

```
MyClass objectB = objectA;
```

This means that both variables contain pointers to the same object.

Structs are *value* types. Instead of the variable holding a pointer to the struct, the variable contains the struct itself. When you assign the first struct to the second variable of type `myStruct` with the following line, you are actually copying all the information from one struct to the other:

```
myStruct structB = structA;
```

You saw behavior like this earlier in this book for simple variable types such as `int`. The upshot is that the two struct type variables contain different structs. The entire technique of using pointers is hidden from you in managed C# code, making your code much simpler. It is possible to access lower-level operations such as pointer manipulation in C# using unsafe code, but that is an advanced topic not covered here.

Shallow Copying versus Deep Copying

Copying objects from one variable to another by value instead of by reference (that is, copying them in the same way as structs) can be quite complex. Because a single object may contain references to many other objects, such as field members and so on, a lot of processing may be involved. Simply copying each member from one object to another may not work because some of these members might be reference types in their own right.

The .NET Framework takes this into account. Simple object copying by members is achievable through the method MemberwiseClone, inherited from System.Object. This is a protected method, but it would be easy to define a public method on an object that called this method. This copying method is known as a *shallow copy,* in that it doesn't take reference type members into account. This means that reference members in the new object refer to the same objects as equivalent members in the source object, which isn't ideal in many cases. If you want to create new instances of the members in question by copying the values across (rather than the references), you need to perform a *deep copy.*

There is an interface you can implement that enables you to do this in a standard way: ICloneable. If you use this interface, then you must implement the single method it contains, Clone. This method returns a value of type System.Object. You can use whatever processing you want to obtain this object, by implementing the method body however you choose. That means you can implement a deep copy if you want to (although the exact behavior isn't mandatory, so you could perform a shallow copy if desired). You take a closer look at this in Chapter 11.

Summary

This chapter showed how you can define classes and interfaces in C#, putting the theory from the last chapter into a more concrete form. You've learned the C# syntax required for basic declarations as well as the accessibility keywords you can use, the way in which you can inherit from interfaces and other classes, how to define abstract and sealed classes to control this inheritance, and how to define constructors and destructors.

You then looked at System.Object, the root base class of any class that you define. It supplies several methods, some of which are virtual, so you can override their implementation. This class also enables you to treat any object instance as an instance of this type, enabling polymorphism with any object.

You also examined some of the tools supplied by VS and VCE for OOP development, including the Class View window, the Object Browser window, and a quick way to add new classes to a project. As an extension of this multifile concept, you learned how to create assemblies that can't be executed, but that contain class definitions that you can use in other projects.

After that, you took a more detailed look at abstract classes and interfaces, including their similarities and differences, and situations in which you use one or the other.

Finally, you revisited the subject of reference and value types, looking at structs (the value type equivalent of objects) in slightly more detail. This led to a discussion about shallow and deep copying of objects, a subject covered in more detail later in the book.

The next chapter looks at defining class members, such as properties and methods, which will enable you to take OOP in C# to the level required to create real applications.

Exercises

1. What is wrong with the following code?

```
public sealed class MyClass
{
   // Class members.
}

public class myDerivedClass : MyClass
{
   // Class members.
}
```

2. How would you define a noncreatable class?

3. Why are noncreatable classes still useful? How do you make use of their capabilities?

4. Write code in a class library project called Vehicles that implements the `Vehicle` family of objects discussed earlier in this chapter. There are nine objects and two interfaces that require implementation.

5. Create a console application project, Traffic, that references `Vehicles.dll` (created in question 4). Include a function called `AddPassenger` that accepts any object with the `IPassengerCarrier` interface. To prove that the code works, call this function using instances of each object that supports this interface, calling the `ToString` method inherited from `System.Object` on each one and writing the result to the screen.

10

Defining Class Members

This chapter continues exploring class definitions in C# by looking at how you define field, property, and method class members. You start by examining the code required for each of these types, and learn how to generate the structure of this code using wizards. You also learn how to modify members quickly by editing their properties.

After covering the basics of member definition, you'll learn some advanced techniques involving members: hiding base class members, calling overridden base class members, nested type definitions, and partial class definitions.

Finally, you put theory into practice by creating a class library that you can build on and use in later chapters.

In this chapter you learn how to do the following:

- ❑ Work with fields, properties, and method class members.
- ❑ Create a class library.

Member Definitions

Within a class definition, you provide definitions for all members of the class, including fields, methods, and properties. All members have their own accessibility levels, defined in all cases by one of the following keywords:

- ❑ `public` — Members are accessible from any code.
- ❑ `private` — Members are accessible only from code that is part of the class (the default if no keyword is used).
- ❑ `internal` — Members are accessible only from code within the project (assembly) where they are defined.
- ❑ `protected` — Members are accessible only from code that is part of either the class or a derived class.

The last two of these can be combined, so `protected internal` members are also possible. These are only accessible from code-derived classes within the project (more accurately, the assembly).

Fields, methods, and properties can also be declared using the keyword `static`, which means that they are static members owned by the class, rather than by object instances, as discussed in Chapter 8.

Defining Fields

Fields are defined using standard variable declaration format (with optional initialization), along with the modifiers discussed previously:

```
class MyClass
{
    public int MyInt;
}
```

Public fields in the .NET Framework are named using PascalCasing, rather than camelCasing, and that's the casing methodology used here. That's why the field in this example is called `MyInt` *instead of* `myInt`*. This is only a suggested casing scheme, but it makes a lot of sense. There is no recommendation for private fields, which are usually named using camelCasing.*

Fields can also use the keyword `readonly`, meaning that the field may be assigned a value only during constructor execution or by initial assignment:

```
class MyClass
{
    public readonly int MyInt = 17;
}
```

As noted in the chapter introduction, fields may be declared as static using the `static` keyword:

```
class MyClass
{
    public static int MyInt;
}
```

Static fields are accessed via the class that defines them (`MyClass.MyInt` in the preceding example), not through object instances of that class. You can use the keyword `const` to create a constant value. `const` members are static by definition, so you don't need to use the `static` modifier (in fact, it is an error).

Defining Methods

Methods use standard function format, along with accessibility and optional `static` modifiers, as shown in this example:

```
class MyClass
{
    public string GetString()
    {
        return "Here is a string.";
    }
}
```

Like fields, public methods in the .NET Framework are named using PascalCasing.

Remember that if you use the static keyword, then this method is accessible only through the class, not the object instance. You can also use the following keywords with method definitions:

- ❏   virtual — The method may be overridden.

- ❏   abstract — The method must be overridden in non-abstract derived classes (only permitted in abstract classes).

- ❏   override — The method overrides a base class method (it must be used if a method is being overridden).

- ❏   extern — The method definition is found elsewhere.

Here's an example of a method override:

```
public class MyBaseClass
{
    public virtual void DoSomething()
    {
        // Base implementation.
    }
}

public class MyDerivedClass : MyBaseClass
{
    public override void DoSomething()
    {
        // Derived class implementation, overrides base implementation.
    }
}
```

If override is used, then sealed may also be used to specify that no further modifications can be made to this method in derived classes — that is, the method can't be overridden by derived classes. Here is an example:

```
public class MyDerivedClass : MyBaseClass
{
    public override sealed void DoSomething()
    {
        // Derived class implementation, overrides base implementation.
    }
}
```

Using `extern` enables you to provide the implementation of a method externally to the project, but this is an advanced topic not covered here.

Defining Properties

Properties are defined in a similar way to fields, but there's more to them. Properties, as already discussed, are more involved than fields in that they can perform additional processing before modifying state — and, indeed, might not modify state at all. They achieve this by possessing two function-like blocks: one for getting the value of the property and one for setting the value of the property.

These blocks, also known as *accessors*, defined using `get` and `set` keywords, respectively, may be used to control the access level of the property. You can omit one or the other of these blocks to create read-only or write-only properties (where omitting the `get` block gives you write-only access, and omitting the `set` block gives you read-only access). Of course, that only applies to external code because code elsewhere within the class will have access to the same data that these code blocks have. You can also include accessibility modifiers on accessors — making a `get` block public while the `set` block is protected, for example. You must include at least one of these blocks to obtain a valid property (and, let's face it, a property you can't read or change wouldn't be very useful).

The basic structure of a property consists of the standard access modifying keyword (`public`, `private`, and so on), followed by a type name, the property name, and one or both of the `get` and `set` blocks that contain the property processing:

```
public int MyIntProp
{
   get
   {
      // Property get code.
   }
   set
   {
      // Property set code.
   }
}
```

Public properties in .NET are also named using PascalCasing, rather than camelCasing, and, as with fields and methods, PascalCasing is used here.

The first line of the definition is the bit that is very similar to a field definition. The difference is that there is no semicolon at the end of the line; instead, you have a code block containing nested `get` and `set` blocks.

`get` blocks must have a return value of the type of the property. Simple properties are often associated with a single private field controlling access to that field, in which case the `get` block may return the field's value directly:

```
// Field used by property.
private int myInt;

// Property.
public int MyIntProp
{
    get
    {
        return myInt;
    }
    set
    {
        // Property set code.
    }
}
```

Code external to the class cannot access this `myInt` field directly due to its accessibility level (it is private). Instead, external code must use the property to access the field. The `set` function assigns a value to the field similarly. Here, you can use the keyword `value` to refer to the value received from the user of the property:

```
// Field used by property.
private int myInt;

// Property.
public int MyIntProp
{
    get
    {
        return myInt;
    }
    set
    {
        myInt = value;
    }
}
```

`value` equates to a value of the same type as the property, so if the property uses the same type as the field, then you never have to worry about casting in situations like this.

This simple property does little more than shield direct access to the `myInt` field. The real power of properties is apparent when you exert a little more control over the proceedings. For example, you might implement your `set` block as follows:

```
set
{
    if (value >= 0 && value <= 10)
        myInt = value;
}
```

Here, you modify `myInt` only if the value assigned to the property is between 0 and 10. In situations like this, you have an important design choice to make: What should you do if an invalid value is used? You have four options:

❑   Do nothing (as in the preceding code).

❑   Assign a default value to the field.

❑   Continue as if nothing had gone wrong but log the event for future analysis.

❑   Throw an exception.

In general, the last two options are preferable. Deciding between them depends on how the class will be used and how much control should be assigned to the users of the class. Exception throwing gives users a fair amount of control and lets them know what is going on so that they can respond appropriately. You can use one of the standard exceptions in the `System` namespace for this:

```
set
{
    if (value >= 0 && value <= 10)
        myInt = value;
    else
        throw (new ArgumentOutOfRangeException("MyIntProp", value,
                   "MyIntProp must be assigned a value between 0 and 10."));
}
```

This can be handled using `try ... catch ... finally` logic in the code that uses the property, as you saw in Chapter 7.

Logging data, perhaps to a text file, can be useful, such as in production code where problems really shouldn't occur. It enables developers to check on performance and perhaps debug existing code if necessary.

Properties can use the `virtual`, `override`, and `abstract` keywords just like methods, something that isn't possible with fields. Finally, as mentioned earlier, accessors can have their own accessibilities, as shown here:

```
// Field used by property.
private int myInt;

// Property.
public int MyIntProp
{
    get
    {
        return myInt;
    }
    protected set
    {
        myInt = value;
    }
}
```

Here, only code within the class or derived classes can use the `set` accessor.

The accessibilities that are permitted for accessors depend on the accessibility of the property, and it is forbidden to make an accessor more accessible than the property to which it belongs. This means that a private property cannot contain any accessibility modifiers for its accessors, whereas public properties can use all modifiers on their accessors. The following Try It Out enables you to experiment with defining and using fields, methods, and properties.

Try It Out   Using Fields, Methods, and Properties

1. Create a new console application called Ch10Ex01 and save it in the directory C:\BegVCSharp\Chapter10.

2. Add a new class called `MyClass`, using the `Add Class` shortcut, which will cause the new class to be defined in a new file called `MyClass.cs`.

3. Modify the code in `MyClass.cs` as follows:

```
public class MyClass
{
    public readonly string Name;
    private int intVal;

    public int Val
    {
        get
        {
            return intVal;
        }
        set
        {
            if (value >= 0 && value <= 10)
                intVal = value;
            else
                throw (new ArgumentOutOfRangeException("Val", value,
                    "Val must be assigned a value between 0 and 10."));
        }
    }
    public override string ToString()
    {
        return "Name: " + Name + "\nVal: " + Val;
    }

    private MyClass() : this("Default Name")
    {
    }

    public MyClass(string newName)
    {
        Name = newName;
        intVal = 0;
    }
}
```

4. Modify the code in `Program.cs` as follows:

```csharp
static void Main(string[] args)
{
    Console.WriteLine("Creating object myObj...");
    MyClass myObj = new MyClass("My Object");
    Console.WriteLine("myObj created.");
    for (int i = -1; i <= 0; i++)
    {
        try
        {
            Console.WriteLine("\nAttempting to assign {0} to myObj.Val...",
                              i);
            myObj.Val = i;
            Console.WriteLine("Value {0} assigned to myObj.Val.", myObj.Val);
        }
        catch (Exception e)
        {
            Console.WriteLine("Exception {0} thrown.", e.GetType().FullName);
            Console.WriteLine("Message:\n\"{0}\"", e.Message);
        }
    }
    Console.WriteLine("\nOutputting myObj.ToString()...");
    Console.WriteLine(myObj.ToString());
    Console.WriteLine("myObj.ToString() Output.");
    Console.ReadKey();
}
```

5. Run the application. The result is shown in Figure 10-1.

Figure 10-1

How It Works

The code in `Main()` creates and uses an instance of the `MyClass` class defined in `MyClass.cs`. Instantiating this class must be performed using a nondefault constructor because the default constructor of `MyClass` is private:

```csharp
private MyClass() : this("Default Name")
{
}
```

Using `this("Default Name")` ensures that `Name` gets a value if this constructor is ever called, which is possible if this class is used to derive a new class. This is necessary because not assigning a value to the `Name` field could be a source of errors later.

The nondefault constructor used assigns values to the `readonly` field `Name` (you can only do this by assignment in the field declaration or in a constructor) and the private field `intVal`.

Next, `Main()` attempts two assignments to the `Val` property of `myObj` (the instance of `MyClass`). A `for` loop is used to assign the values `-1` and `0` in two cycles, and a `try ... catch` structure is used to check for any exception thrown. When `-1` is assigned to the property, an exception of type `System.ArgumentOutOfRangeException` is thrown, and code in the `catch` block outputs information about the exception to the console window. In the next loop cycle, the value `0` is successfully assigned to the `Val` property, and through that property to the private `intVal` field.

Finally, you use the overridden `ToString()` method to output a formatted string representing the contents of the object:

```
public override string ToString()
{
    return "Name: " + Name + "\nVal: " + Val;
}
```

This method must be declared using the `override` keyword, because it is overriding the virtual `ToString()` method of the base `System.Object` class. The code here uses the property `Val` directly, rather than the private field `intVal`. There is no reason why you shouldn't use properties from within classes in this way, although there may be a small performance hit (so small that you are unlikely to notice it). Of course, using the property also gives you the validation inherent in property use, which may be beneficial for code within the class as well.

Adding Members from a Class Diagram

The last chapter described how you can use the class diagram to explore the classes in a project. You also learned that the class diagram can be used to add members, and this is what you will look at in this section.

The class diagram is a feature of VS only and is not available in VCE.

All the tools for adding and editing members are shown in the Class Details window in the Class Diagram view. To see this in action, create a class diagram for the `MyClass` class created in `Ch10Ex01`. You can see the existing members by expanding the view of the class in the class designer (by clicking on the icon that looks like two downward pointing chevrons). The resulting view is shown in Figure 10-2.

Figure 10-2

In the Class Details window, you can see the information shown in Figure 10-3 when the class is selected.

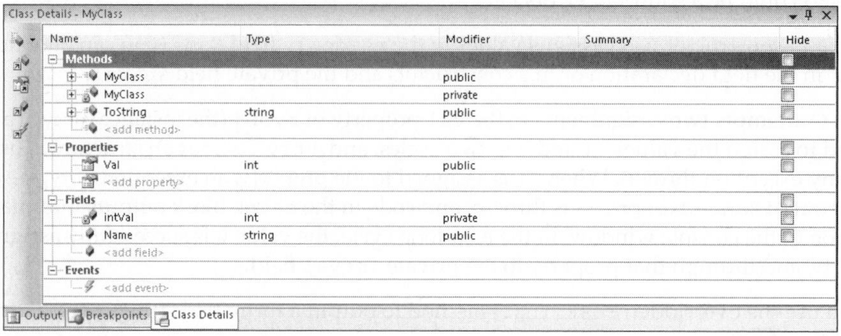

Figure 10-3

The window shows all the currently defined members for the class and includes spaces so you can add new members simply by typing them in.

Adding Methods

To add a method to your class, simply type it in the box labeled <add method>. After you have named a method, you can use the Tab key to navigate to subsequent settings, starting with the return type of the method, and moving on to the accessibility of the method, summary information (which translates to XML documentation, covered in Chapter 31), and whether to hide the method in the class diagram.

Once you have added a method, you can expand the entry and add parameters in the same way. For parameters, you also have the option to use the modifiers out, ref, and params. Figure 10-4 shows an example of a new method.

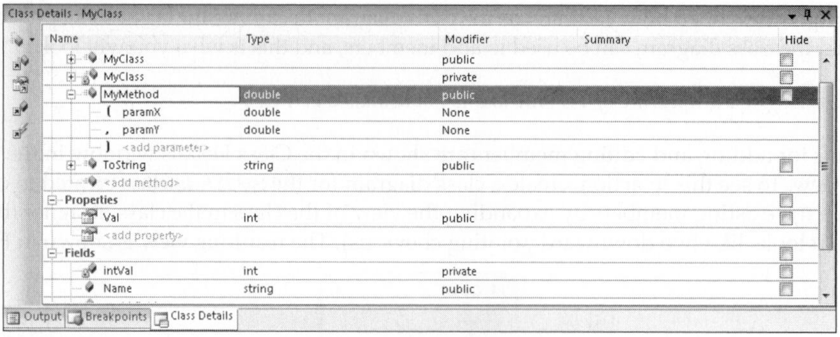

Figure 10-4

With this new method, the following code is added to your class:

```
public double MyMethod(double paramX, double paramY)
{
    throw new System.NotImplementedException();
}
```

You can configure other method settings in the Properties window, shown in Figure 10-5.

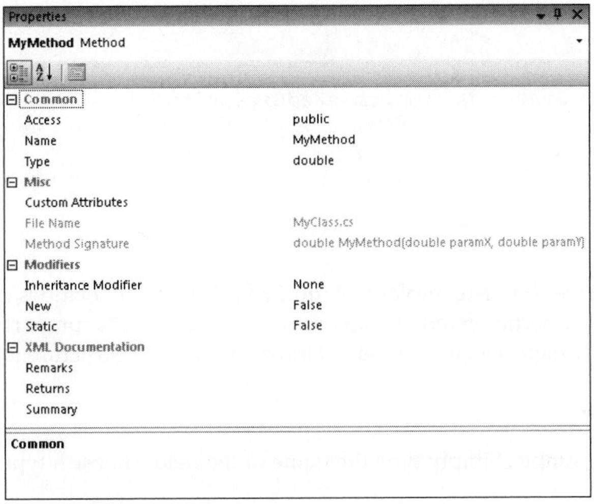

Figure 10-5

Among other things, you can make the method static here. Obviously, this technique can't provide the method implementation for you, but it does provide the basic structure, and certainly reduces typing errors!

Adding Properties

Adding properties is achieved in much the same way. Figure 10-6 shows a new property added using the Class Details window.

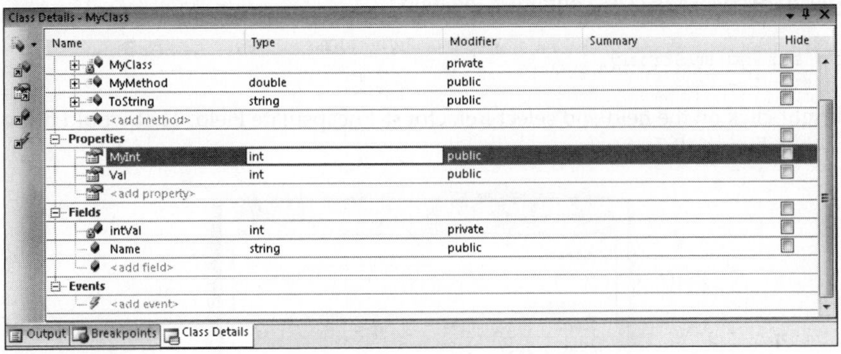

Figure 10-6

This adds the property shown here:

```
public int MyInt
{
    get
    {
        throw new System.NotImplementedException();
    }
    set
    {
    }
}
```

You are left to provide the complete implementation yourself, which includes matching the property with a field for simple properties, removing an accessor if you want the property to be read- or write-only, or applying accessibility modifiers to accessors. However, the basic structure is provided for you.

Adding Fields

Adding fields is just as simple. Simply type the name of the field, choose a type and access modifier, and away you go.

Refactoring Members

One technique that comes in handy when adding properties is the capability to generate a property from a field. This is an example of *refactoring*, which in general simply means modifying your code using a tool, rather than by hand. This can be accomplished when using a class diagram by right-clicking on a member or simply by right-clicking on a member in code view.

> *VCE includes limited refactoring capabilities, which unfortunately do not include the field encapsulation described here. VS has many more options than VCE in this area.*

For example, if the `MyClass` class contained the field

```
public string myString;
```

you could right-click on the field and select Refactor ⇨ Encapsulate Field. That would bring up the dialog shown in Figure 10-7.

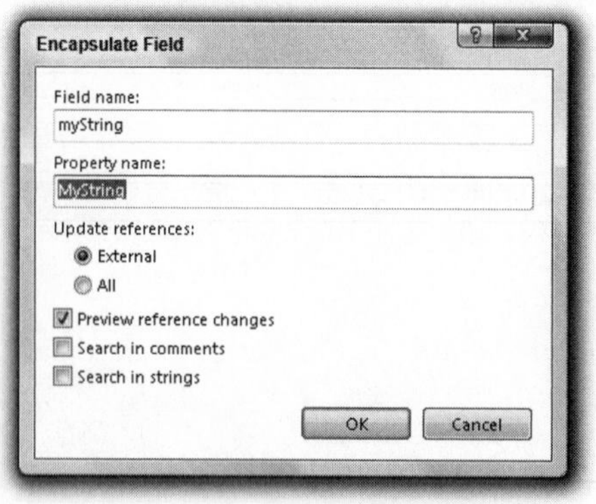

Encapsulate Field

Field name:
myString

Property name:
MyString

Update references:
- ● External
- ○ All

☑ Preview reference changes
☐ Search in comments
☐ Search in strings

[OK] [Cancel]

Figure 10-7

Accepting the default options modifies the code for `MyClass` as follows:

```
private string myString;
public string MyString
{
    get
    {
        return myString;
    }

    set
    {
        myString = value;
    }
}
```

Here, the `myString` field has had its accessibility changed to `private`, and a public property called `MyString` has been created and automatically linked to `myString`. Clearly, reducing the time required to monotonously create properties for fields is a big plus!

Automatic Properties

Properties are the preferred way to access the state of an object because they shield external code from the implementation of data storage within the object. They also give you greater control over how internal data is accessed, as you have seen several times in this chapter's code. However, you'll typically define properties in a very standard way — that is, you will have a private member that is accessed directly through a public property. The code for this is almost invariably similar to the code in the previous section, which was autogenerated by the VS refactoring tool.

Refactoring certainly speeds things up when it comes to typing, but C# has another trick up its sleeve: automatic properties. With an *automatic property*, you declare a property with a simplified syntax and the C# compiler fills in the blanks for you. Specifically, the compiler declares a private field that is used for storage and uses that field in the `get` and `set` blocks of your property — without you having to worry about the details.

Use the following code structure to define an automatic property:

```
public int MyIntProp
{
    get;
    set;
}
```

You define the accessibility, type, and name of the property in the usual way, but you don't provide any implementation for the `get` or `set` block. The implementations of these blocks (and the underlying field) is provided by the compiler.

When you use an automatic property you only have access to the data through the property because you will not be able to access the underlying private field without knowing its name, which is defined during compilation. However, that's not really a limitation because using the property name directly is fine. The only limitation of automatic properties is that they must include both a `get` and `set` accessor — you cannot define read- or write-only properties in this way.

Additional Class Member Topics

Now that you've covered the basics of member definition, it's time to look at some more advanced member topics. This section tackles the following:

❑   Hiding base class methods.

❑   Calling overridden or hidden base class methods.

❑   Nested type definitions.

Hiding Base Class Methods

When you inherit a (non-abstract) member from a base class, you also inherit an implementation. If the inherited member is virtual, then you can override this implementation with the `override` keyword. Regardless of whether the inherited member is virtual, you can, if you want, *hide* the implementation. This is useful when, for example, a public inherited member doesn't work quite as you want it to.

You can do this simply by using code such as the following:

```
public class MyBaseClass
{
   public void DoSomething()
   {
      // Base implementation.
   }
}
public class MyDerivedClass : MyBaseClass
{
   public void DoSomething()
   {
      // Derived class implementation, hides base implementation.
   }
}
```

Although this code works fine, it generates a warning that you are hiding a base class member. That gives you the chance to correct things if you have accidentally hidden a member that you actually want to use. If you really do want to hide the member, you can use the new keyword to explicitly indicate that this is what you want to do:

```
public class MyDerivedClass : MyBaseClass
{
   new public void DoSomething()
   {
      // Derived class implementation, hides base implementation.
   }
}
```

This works in exactly the same way but won't show a warning. At this point, it's worthwhile to note the difference between hiding and overriding base class members. Consider the following code:

```
public class MyBaseClass
{
    public virtual void DoSomething()
    {
        Console.WriteLine("Base imp");
    }
}

public class MyDerivedClass : MyBaseClass
{
    public override void DoSomething()
    {
        Console.WriteLine("Derived imp");
    }
}
```

Here, the overriding method replaces the implementation in the base class, such that the following code will use the new version even though it does so through the base class type (using polymorphism):

```
MyDerivedClass myObj = new MyDerivedClass();
MyBaseClass myBaseObj;
myBaseObj = myObj;
myBaseObj.DoSomething();
```

This results in the following output:

```
Derived imp
```

Alternatively, you could hide the base class method:

```
public class MyBaseClass
{
    public virtual void DoSomething()
    {
        Console.WriteLine("Base imp");
    }
}

public class MyDerivedClass : MyBaseClass
{
    new public void DoSomething()
    {
        Console.WriteLine("Derived imp");
    }
}
```

The base class method needn't be virtual for this to work, but the effect is exactly the same and the preceding code only requires changes to one line. The result, for a virtual or nonvirtual base class method, is as follows:

```
Base imp
```

Although the base implementation is hidden, you still have access to it through the base class.

Calling Overridden or Hidden Base Class Methods

Whether you override or hide a member, you still have access to the base class member from the derived class. There are many situations in which this can be useful, such as the following:

❑　When you want to hide an inherited public member from users of a derived class but still want access to its functionality from within the class.

❑　When you want to add to the implementation of an inherited virtual member rather than simply replace it with a new overridden implementation.

To achieve this, you use the base keyword, which refers to the implementation of the base class contained within a derived class (in a similar way to its use in controlling constructors, as shown in the last chapter):

```
public class MyBaseClass
{
    public virtual void DoSomething()
    {
        // Base implementation.
    }
}

public class MyDerivedClass : MyBaseClass
{
    public override void DoSomething()
    {
        // Derived class implementation, extends base class implementation.
        base.DoSomething();
        // More derived class implementation.
    }
}
```

This code executes the version of DoSomething contained in MyBaseClass, the base class of MyDerivedClass, from within the version of DoSomething contained in MyDerivedClass. As base works using object instances, it is an error to use it from within a static member.

The this Keyword

As well as using base in the last chapter, you also used the this keyword. As with base, this can be used from within class members, and, like base, this refers to an object instance, although it is the current object instance (which means you can't use this keyword in static members because static members are not part of an object instance).

The most useful function of the `this` keyword is the capability to pass a reference to the current object instance to a method, as shown in this example:

```
public void doSomething()
{
    MyTargetClass myObj = new MyTargetClass();
    myObj.DoSomethingWith(this);
}
```

Here, the `MyTargetClass` that is instantiated has a method called `DoSomethingWith`, which takes a single parameter of a type compatible with the class containing the preceding method. This parameter type might be of this class type, a class type from which this class derives, an interface implemented by the class, or (of course) `System.Object`.

Nested Type Definitions

As well as defining types such as classes in namespaces, you can also define them inside other classes. If you do this, then you can use the full range of accessibility modifiers for the definition, rather than just `public` and `internal`, and you can use the `new` keyword to hide a type definition inherited from a base class. For example, the following code defining `MyClass` also defines a nested class called `myNestedClass`:

```
public class MyClass
{
    public class myNestedClass
    {
        public int nestedClassField;
    }
}
```

To instantiate `myNestedClass` from outside `MyClass`, you must qualify the name, as shown here:

```
MyClass.myNestedClass myObj = new MyClass.myNestedClass();
```

However, you may not be able to do this at all if the nested class is declared as `private` or another accessibility level that is incompatible with the code at the point at which this instantiation is performed. The main reason for the existence of this feature is to define classes that are private to the containing class so that no other code in the namespace has access to them.

Interface Implementation

Before moving on, we'll take a closer look at how you go about defining and implementing interfaces. In the last chapter, you learned that interfaces are defined in a similar way as classes, using code such as the following:

```
interface IMyInterface
{
    // Interface members.
}
```

Interface members are defined like class members except for a few important differences:

❏ No access modifiers (`public`, `private`, `protected`, or `internal`) are allowed — all interface members are implicitly public.

❏ Interface members can't contain code bodies.

❏ Interfaces can't define field members.

❏ Interface members can't be defined using the keywords `static`, `virtual`, `abstract`, or `sealed`.

❏ Type definition members are forbidden.

You can, however, define members using the `new` keyword if you want to hide members inherited from base interfaces:

```
interface IMyBaseInterface
{
    void DoSomething();
}

interface IMyDerivedInterface : IMyBaseInterface
{
    new void DoSomething();
}
```

This works in exactly the same way as hiding inherited class members.

Properties defined in interfaces define either or both of the access blocks, `get` and `set`, which are permitted for the property, as shown here:

```
interface IMyInterface
{
    int MyInt
    {
        get;
        set;
    }
}
```

Here the `int` property `MyInt` has both `get` and `set` accessors. Either of these may be omitted for a property with more restricted access.

This syntax is similar to automatic properties, but remember that automatic properties are defined for classes, not interfaces, and that automatic properties must have both `get` and `set` accessors.

Interfaces do not specify how the property data should be stored. Interfaces cannot specify fields, for example, that might be used to store property data. Finally, interfaces, like classes, may be defined as members of classes (but not as members of other interfaces because interfaces cannot contain type definitions).

Implementing Interfaces in Classes

A class that implements an interface must contain implementations for all members of that interface, which must match the signatures specified (including matching the specified `get` and `set` blocks), and must be public, as shown here:

```
public interface IMyInterface
{
   void DoSomething();
   void DoSomethingElse();
}

public class MyClass : IMyInterface
{
   public void DoSomething()
   {
   }

   public void DoSomethingElse()
   {
   }
}
```

It is possible to implement interface members using the keyword `virtual` or `abstract`, but not `static` or `const`. Interface members can also be implemented on base classes:

```
public interface IMyInterface
{
   void DoSomething();
   void DoSomethingElse();
}
public class MyBaseClass
{
   public void DoSomething()
   {
   }
}

public class MyDerivedClass : MyBaseClass, IMyInterface
{
   public void DoSomethingElse()
   {
   }
}
```

Inheriting from a base class that implements a given interface means that the interface is implicitly supported by the derived class. Here's an example:

```csharp
public interface IMyInterface
{
    void DoSomething();
    void DoSomethingElse();
}
```

```csharp
public class MyBaseClass : IMyInterface
{
    public virtual void DoSomething()
    {
    }

    public virtual void DoSomethingElse()
    {
    }
}

public class MyDerivedClass : MyBaseClass
{
    public override void DoSomething()
    {
    }
}
```

Clearly, it is useful to define implementations in base classes as virtual so that derived classes can replace the implementation, rather than hide it. If you were to hide a base class member using the new keyword, rather than override it in this way, the method IMyInterface.DoSomething would always refer to the base class version even if the derived class were being accessed via the interface.

Explicit Interface Member Implementation

Interface members can also be implemented *explicitly* by a class. If you do this, the member can only be accessed through the interface, not the class. *Implicit* members, which you used in the code in the last section, can be accessed either way.

For example, if the class MyClass implemented the DoSomething method of IMyInterface implicitly, as in the preceding example, then the following code would be valid:

```csharp
MyClass myObj = new MyClass();
myObj.DoSomething();
```

This would also be valid:

```csharp
MyClass myObj = new MyClass();
IMyInterface myInt = myObj;
myInt.DoSomething();
```

Alternatively, if MyDerivedClass implements DoSomething explicitly, then only the latter technique is permitted. The code for doing this is as follows:

```
public class MyClass : IMyInterface
{
    void IMyInterface.DoSomething()
    {
    }

    public void DoSomethingElse()
    {
    }
}
```

Here, DoSomething is implemented explicitly, and DoSomethingElse implicitly. Only the latter is accessible directly through an object instance of MyClass.

Adding Property Accessors with Nonpublic Accessibility

Earlier it was stated that if you implement an interface with a property, you must implement matching get/set accessors. That isn't strictly true — it is possible to add a get block to a property in a class where the interface defining that property only contains a set block, and vice versa. However, this is only possible if you add the accessor with an accessibility modifier that is more restrictive than the accessibility modifier on the accessor defined in the interface. Because the accessor defined by the interface is, by definition, public, you can only add nonpublic accessors. Here's an example:

```
public interface IMyInterface
{
    int MyIntProperty
    {
        get;
    }
}

public class MyBaseClass : IMyInterface
{
    protected int myInt;

    public int MyIntProperty
    {
        get
        {
            return myInt;
        }
        protected set
        {
            myInt = value;
        }
    }
}
```

Partial Class Definitions

When you create classes with a lot of members of one type or another, things can get quite confusing, and code files can get very long. One thing that can help, which you've looked at in earlier chapters, is to use code outlining. By defining regions in code, you can collapse and expand sections to make things easier to read. For example, you might have a class defined as follows:

```csharp
public class MyClass
{
    #region Fields
    private int myInt;
    #endregion

    #region Constructor
    public MyClass()
    {
        myInt = 99;
    }
    #endregion

    #region Properties
    public int MyInt
    {
        get
        {
            return myInt;
        }

        set
        {
            myInt = value;
        }
    }
    #endregion

    #region Methods
    public void DoSomething()
    {
        // Do something...
    }
    #endregion
}
```

Here, you can expand and contract fields, properties, the constructor, and methods for the class, enabling you to focus only on what you are interested in. It is even possible to nest regions this way, so some regions are only visible when the region that contains them is expanded.

However, if you're even using this technique, things can still get out of hand. One alternative is to use *partial class definitions*. Put simply, you use partial class definitions to split the definition of a class across multiple files. You could, for example, put the fields, properties, and constructor in one file and the methods in another. To do that, you just use the `partial` keyword with the class in each file that contains part of the definition, as follows:

```
public partial class MyClass
{
    . . .
}
```

If you use partial class definitions, the `partial` keyword must appear in this position in every file containing part of the definition.

Partial classes are used to great effect in Windows applications to hide from you the code relating to the layout of forms. You've already seen this, in fact, in Chapter 2. A Windows form, in a class called `Form1`, for example, has code stored in both `Form1.cs` and `Form1.Designer.cs`. This enables you to concentrate on the functionality of your forms, without worrying about your code being cluttered with information that doesn't really interest you.

One final note about partial classes: Interfaces applied to one partial class part apply to the whole class, meaning that this definition:

```
public partial class MyClass : IMyInteface1
{
    . . .
}

public partial class MyClass : IMyInteface2
{
    . . .
}
```

is equivalent to this one:

```
public class MyClass : IMyInteface1, IMyInteface2
{
    . . .
}
```

This also applies to attributes, covered in Chapter 27.

Partial Method Definitions

Partial classes may also define partial methods. Partial methods are defined in one partial class definition without a method body, and implemented in another partial class definition. In both places, the `partial` keyword is used:

```
public partial class MyClass
{
    partial void MyPartialMethod();
}

public partial class MyClass
{
    partial void MyPartialMethod()
    {
        // Method implementation
    }
}
```

Partial methods can also be static, but they are always private and can't have a return value. Any parameters they use can't be `out` parameters, although they can be `ref` parameters. They also can't use the `virtual`, `abstract`, `override`, `new`, `sealed`, or `extern` modifier.

Given these limitations, it is not immediately obvious what purpose partial methods fulfill. In fact, they are important when it comes to code compilation, rather than usage. Consider the following code:

```
public partial class MyClass
{
    partial void DoSomethingElse();

    public void DoSomething()
    {
        Console.WriteLine("DoSomething() execution started.");
        DoSomethingElse();
        Console.WriteLine("DoSomething() execution finished.");
    }
}

public partial class MyClass
{
    partial void DoSomethingElse()
    {
        Console.WriteLine("DoSomethingElse() called.");
    }
}
```

Here, the partial method `DoSomethingElse` is defined and called in the first partial class definition, and implemented in the second. The output, when `DoSomething` is called from a console application, is what you might expect:

```
DoSomething() execution started.
DoSomethingElse() called.
DoSomething() execution finished.
```

If you were to remove the second partial class definition or partial method implementation entirely (or comment out the code), the output would be as follows:

```
DoSomething() execution started.
DoSomething() execution finished.
```

You might assume that what is happening here is that when the call to `DoSomethingElse` is made, the runtime discovers that the method has no implementation and therefore continues executing the next line of code. What actually happens is a little subtler. When you compile code that contains a partial method definition without an implementation, the compiler actually removes the method entirely. It also removes any calls to the method. When you execute the code, no check is made for an implementation because there is no call to check. This results in a slight — but nevertheless significant — improvement in performance.

As with partial classes, partial methods are useful when it comes to customizing autogenerated or designer-created code. The designer may declare partial methods that you can choose to implement or not depending on the situation. If you don't implement them, you incur no performance hit because effectively the method does not exist in the compiled code.

Consider at this point why partial methods can't have a return type. If you can answer that to your own satisfaction, you can be sure that you fully understand this topic — so that is left as an exercise for you.

Example Application

To illustrate some of the techniques you've been using so far, in this section you'll develop a class module that you can build on and make use of in subsequent chapters. The class module will contain two classes:

❑ `Card` — Representing a standard playing card, with a suit of club, diamond, heart, or spade, and a rank that lies between ace and king.

❑ `Deck` — Representing a full deck of 52 cards, with access to cards by position in the deck and the ability to shuffle the deck.

You'll also develop a simple client to ensure that things are working, but you won't use the deck in a full card game application — yet.

Planning the Application

The class library for this application, Ch10CardLib, will contain your classes. Before you get down to any code, though, you should plan the required structure and functionality of your classes.

The Card Class

The Card class is basically a container for two read-only fields: suit and rank. The reason for making the fields read-only is that it doesn't make sense to have a "blank" card, and cards shouldn't be able to change once they have been created. To facilitate this, you'll make the default constructor private, and provide an alternative constructor that builds a card from a supplied suit and rank.

Other than that, the Card class will override the ToString method of System.Object, so that you can easily obtain a human-readable string representing the card. To make things a little simpler, you'll provide enumerations for the two fields suit and rank.

The Card class is shown in Figure 10-8.

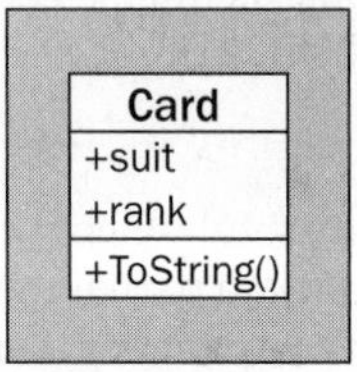

Figure 10-8

The Deck Class

The Deck class will maintain 52 Card objects. You can just use a simple array type for this. This array won't be directly accessible because access to the Card object is achieved through a GetCard method, which returns the Card object with the given index. This class should also expose a Shuffle method to rearrange the cards in the array. The Deck class is shown in Figure 10-9.

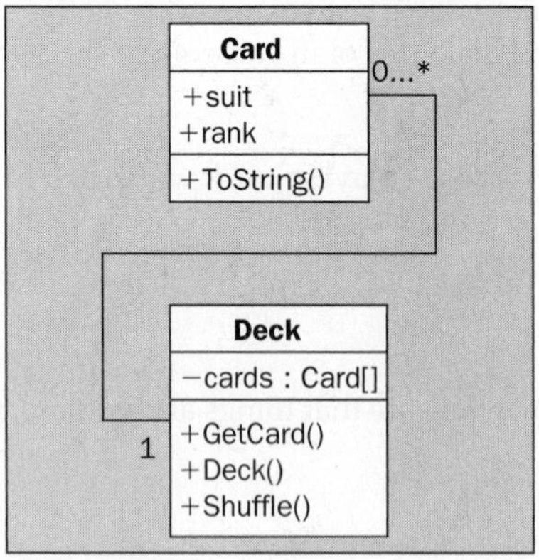

Figure 10-9

Writing the Class Library

For the purposes of this example, it is assumed that you are familiar enough with the IDE to bypass the standard Try It Out format, so the steps aren't listed explicitly, as they are the same steps you've used many times. The important thing here is a detailed look at the code. Nonetheless, several pointers are included to ensure that you don't run into any problems along the way.

Both your classes and your enumerations will be contained in a class library project called Ch10CardLib. This project will contain four .cs files: Card.cs, which contains the Card class definition, Deck.cs, which contains the Deck class definition, and Suit.cs and Rank.cs files containing enumerations.

You can put together a lot of this code using the VS class diagram tool.

> *Don't worry if you are using VCE and don't have the class diagram tool at your disposal. Each of the following sections also includes the code generated by the class diagram, so you'll be able to follow along just fine. There are no differences in the code for this project between the IDEs.*

To get started, you need to do the following:

1. Create a new class library project called Ch10CardLib and save it in the directory C:\BegVCSharp\Chapter10.

2. Remove Class1.cs from the project.

3. If you are using VS, open the class diagram for the project using the Solution Explorer window (you must have the project selected, rather than the solution, for the class diagram icon to appear). The class diagram should be blank to start with because the project contains no classes.

> *If you can see the Resources and Settings classes in this view, they can be hidden by right-clicking on them and selecting Remove from Diagram.*

Adding the Suit and Rank Enumerations

You can add an enumeration to the class diagram by dragging an Enum from the Toolbox into the diagram, and then filling in the dialog that appears. For example, for the Suit enumeration, fill out the dialog as shown in Figure 10-10.

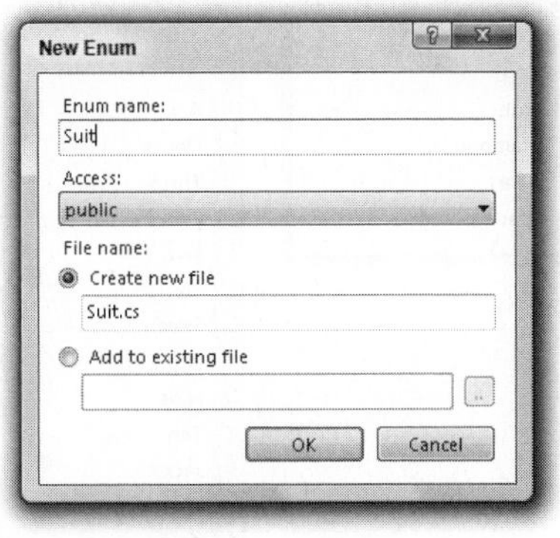

Figure 10-10

Next, add the members of the enumeration using the Class Details window. The values required are shown in Figure 10-11.

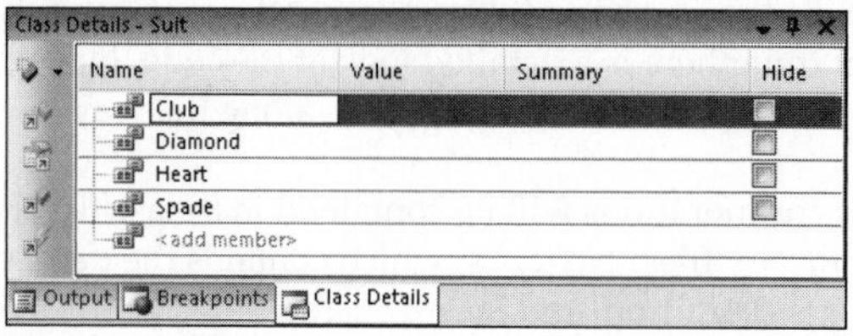

Figure 10-11

Add the `Rank` enumeration from the Toolbox in the same way. The values required for the `Rank` enumeration are shown in Figure 10-12.

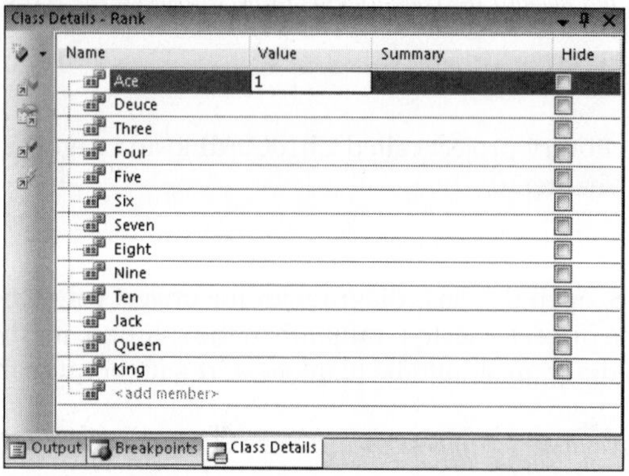

Figure 10-12

The value entry for the first member is `Ace` so that the underlying storage of the enum matches the rank of the card, such that Six is stored as 6, for example.

When you've finished, the diagram should look as shown in Figure 10-13.

Figure 10-13

The code generated for these two enumerations, in the code files `Suit.cs` and `Rank.cs`, is as follows:

```csharp
using System;
using System.Collections.Generic;
using System.Text;

namespace Ch10CardLib
{
    public enum Suit
    {
        Club,
        Diamond,
        Heart,
        Spade,
    }
}

using System;
using System.Collections.Generic;
using System.Text;


namespace Ch10CardLib
{
    public enum Rank
    {
        Ace = 1,
        Deuce,
        Three,
        Four,
        Five,
        Six,
        Seven,
        Eight,
        Nine,
        Ten,
        Jack,
        Queen,
        King,
    }
}
```

If you are using VCE you can add this code manually by adding `Suit.cs` and `Rank.cs` code files and then entering the code. Note that the extra commas added by the code generator after the last enumeration member do not prevent compilation and do not result in an additional "empty" member being created — although they are a little messy.

Adding the Card Class

This section adds the `Card` class, using a mix of the class designer and code editor in VS, or just the code editor in VCE. Adding a class in the class designer is much like adding an enumeration — you drag the appropriate entry from the Toolbox into the diagram. In this case, you drag a `Class` into the diagram, and name the new class `Card`.

Use the Class Details window to add the fields `rank` and `suit`, and then use the Properties window to set the `Constant Kind` of the field to `readonly`. You also need to add two constructors: a default constructor (private), and one that takes two parameters, `newSuit` and `newRank`, of types `Suit` and `Rank`, respectively (public). Finally, you override `ToString`, which requires modifying the `Inheritance Modifier` in the Properties window to `override`.

Figure 10-14 shows the Class Details window and the `Card` class with all the information entered.

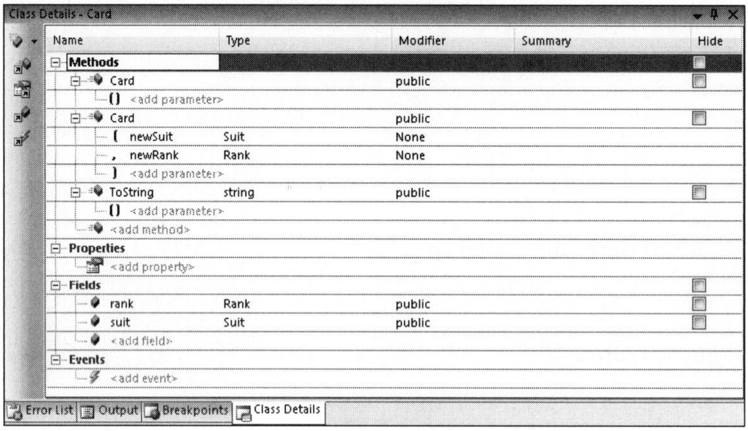

Figure 10-14

Next, modify the code for the class in `Card.cs` as follows (or add the code shown to a new class called `Card` in the `Ch10CardLib` namespace if you are using VCE):

```
public class Card
{
    public readonly Suit suit;
    public readonly Rank rank;

    public Card(Suit newSuit, Rank newRank)
    {
        suit = newSuit;
        rank = newRank;
    }

    private Card()
    {

    }

    public override string ToString()
    {
        return "The " + rank + " of " + suit + "s";
    }
}
```

The overridden ToString method writes the string representation of the enumeration value stored to the returned string, and the nondefault constructor initializes the values of the suit and rank fields.

Adding the Deck Class

The Deck class needs the following members defined using the class diagram:

❑ A private field called cards, of type Card[].

❑ A public default constructor.

❑ A public method called GetCard, which takes one int parameter called cardNum and returns an object of type Card.

❑ A public method called Shuffle, which takes no parameters and returns void.

When these are added, the Class Details for the Deck class will appear as shown in Figure 10-15.

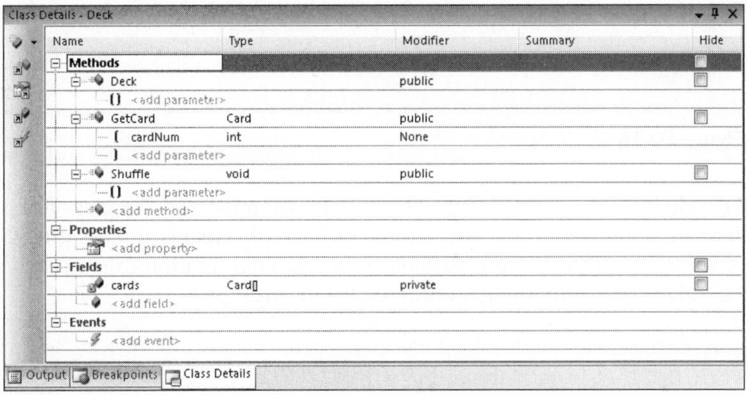

Figure 10-15

To make things clearer in the diagram, you can show the relationships among the members and types you have added. In the class diagram, right-click on each of the following in turn, and select Show as Association from the menu:

❑ cards in Deck

❑ suit in Card

❑ rank in Card

When you have finished, the diagram should look like Figure 10-16.

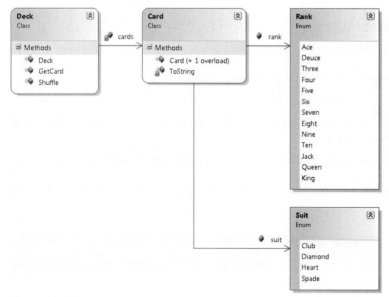

Figure 10-16

Next, modify the code in Deck.cs (if you are using VCE, you must add this class first with the code shown here). First you implement the constructor, which simply creates and assigns 52 cards in the cards field. You iterate through all combinations of the two enumerations, using each to create a card. This results in cards initially containing an ordered list of cards:

```csharp
using System;
using System.Collections.Generic;
using System.Text;

namespace Ch10CardLib
{
    public class Deck
    {
        private Card[] cards;

        public Deck()
        {
            cards = new Card[52];
            for (int suitVal = 0; suitVal < 4; suitVal++)
            {
                for (int rankVal = 1; rankVal < 14; rankVal++)
                {
                    cards[suitVal * 13 + rankVal -1] = new Card((Suit)suitVal,
                                                        (Rank)rankVal);
                }
            }
        }
```

Next, you implement the GetCard method, which either returns the Card object with the requested index or throws an exception as shown earlier:

```
public Card GetCard(int cardNum)
{
    if (cardNum >= 0 && cardNum <= 51)
        return cards[cardNum];
    else
        throw (new System.ArgumentOutOfRangeException("cardNum", cardNum,
                "Value must be between 0 and 51."));
}
```

Finally, you implement the Shuffle method. This method works by creating a temporary card array and copying cards from the existing cards array into this array at random. The main body of this function is a loop that counts from 0 to 51. On each cycle, you generate a random number between 0 and 51, using an instance of the System.Random class from the .NET Framework. Once instantiated, an object of this class generates a random number between 0 and X, using the method Next(X). When you have a random number, you simply use that as the index of the Card object in your temporary array in which to copy a card from the cards array.

To keep a record of assigned cards, you also have an array of bool variables and assign these to true as each card is copied. When you are generating random numbers, you check against this array to see whether you have already copied a card to the location in the temporary array specified by the random number. If so, you simply generate another.

This isn't the most efficient way of doing things because many random numbers may be generated before a vacant slot to copy a card into is found. However, it works, it's very simple, and C# code executes so quickly you will hardly notice a delay.

The code is as follows:

```
public void Shuffle()
{
    Card[] newDeck = new Card[52];
    bool[] assigned = new bool[52];
    Random sourceGen = new Random();
    for (int i = 0; i < 52; i++)
    {
        int destCard = 0;
        bool foundCard = false;
        while (foundCard == false)
        {
            destCard = sourceGen.Next(52);
            if (assigned[destCard] == false)
                foundCard = true;
        }
        assigned[destCard] = true;
        newDeck[destCard] = cards[i];
    }
    newDeck.CopyTo(cards, 0);
}
```

The last line of this method uses the CopyTo method of the System.Array class (used whenever you create an array) to copy each of the cards in newDeck back into cards. This means you are using the same set of Card objects in the same cards object, rather than creating any new instances. If you had instead used cards = newDeck, then you would be replacing the object instance referred to by cards with another. This could cause problems if code elsewhere were retaining a reference to the original cards instance — which wouldn't be shuffled!

That completes the class library code.

A Client Application for the Class Library

To keep things simple, you can add a client console application to the solution containing the class library. To do so, simply right-click on the solution in Solution Explorer and select Add ⇨ New Project. The new project is called Ch10CardClient.

To use the class library you have created from this new console application project, add a reference to your Ch10CardLib class library project. Once the console project has been created, you can do this though the Projects tab of the Add Reference dialog, as shown in Figure 10-17.

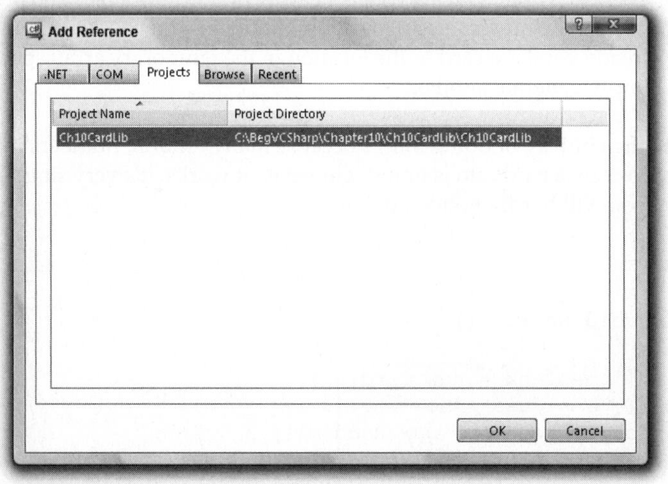

Figure 10-17

Select the project, click OK, and the reference is added.

Because this new project was the second one created, you also need to specify that it is the start-up project for the solution, meaning it is the one that will be executed when you click Run. To do this, simply right-click on the project name in the Solution Explorer window and select the Set as StartUp Project menu option.

Next, add the code that uses your new classes. That doesn't require anything particularly special, so the following code will do:

```
using System;
using System.Collections.Generic;
using System.Linq;
using System.Text;
using Ch10CardLib;

namespace Ch10CardClient
{
    class Class1
    {
        static void Main(string[] args)
        {
            Deck myDeck = new Deck();
            myDeck.Shuffle();
            for (int i = 0; i < 52; i++)
            {
                Card tempCard = myDeck.GetCard(i);
                Console.Write(tempCard.ToString());
                if (i != 51)
                    Console.Write(", ");
                else
                    Console.WriteLine();
            }
            Console.ReadKey();
        }
    }
}
```

The result is shown in Figure 10-18.

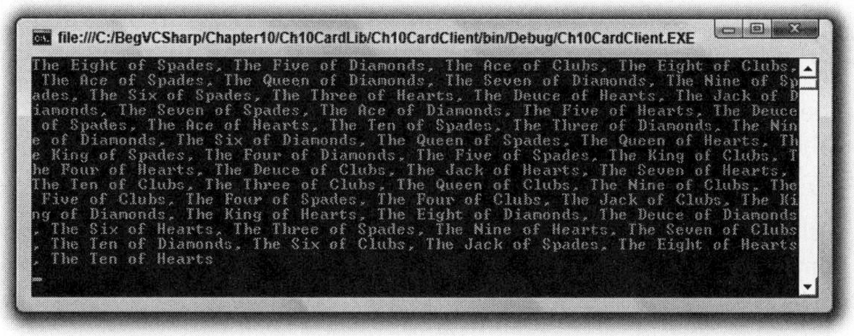

Figure 10-18

This is a random arrangement of the 52 playing cards in the deck. You'll continue to develop and use this class library in later chapters.

Summary

This chapter completed the discussion of how to define basic classes. There's still plenty to cover, but the techniques covered so far enable you to create quite complicated applications already.

You looked at how to define fields, methods, and properties, including the various access levels and modifier keywords. You also looked at the tools you can use to get the outline of a class together in half the time.

You explored inheritance behavior in detail, learning how to hide unwanted inherited members with the `new` keyword, and extending base class members rather than replacing their implementation, using the `base` keyword. You also looked at nested class definitions, had a detailed look at interface definition and implementation, including the concepts of explicit and implicit implementation, and learned how to split definitions between code files using partial class and method definitions.

Finally, you developed and used a simple class library representing a deck of playing cards, making use of the handy class diagram tool to make things easier. You'll make further use of this library in later chapters.

This chapter covered the following main topics:

- ❑ How to define fields, methods, and properties.
- ❑ Tools available for creating the outline of a class.
- ❑ More about inheritance behavior.
- ❑ Interface definition and implementation.
- ❑ Partial classes and method definitions.
- ❑ Creating and deploying a simple class library.

In the next chapter, you look at collections, a type of class you will frequently use in your development.

Exercises

1. Write code that defines a base class, `MyClass`, with the virtual method `GetString`. This method should return the string stored in the protected field `myString`, accessible through the write-only public property `ContainedString`.

2. Derive a class, `MyDerivedClass`, from `MyClass`. Override the `GetString` method to return the string from the base class, using the base implementation of the method, but add the text `"(output from derived class)"` to the returned string.

3. Partial method definitions must use the `void` return type. Provide a reason why this might be so.

4. Write a class called `MyCopyableClass` that is capable of returning a copy of itself using the method `GetCopy`. This method should use the `MemberwiseClone` method inherited from `System.Object`. Add a simple property to the class, and write client code that uses the class to confirm that everything is working.

5. Write a console client for the Ch10CardLib library that draws five cards at one time from a shuffled `Deck` object. If all five cards are the same suit, then the client should display the card names onscreen along with the text `Flush!`; otherwise, it should quit after 50 cards with the text `No flush.`

Collections, Comparisons, and Conversions

You've covered all the basic OOP techniques in C# now, but there are some more advanced techniques that are worth becoming familiar with. In this chapter, you look at the following:

- ❑ **Collections** — Collections enable you to maintain groups of objects. Unlike arrays, which you've used in earlier chapters, collections can include more advanced functionality, such as controlling access to the objects they contain, searching and sorting, and so on. You'll learn how to use and create collection classes and learn about some powerful techniques for getting the most out of them.

- ❑ **Comparisons** — When dealing with objects, you often want to make comparisons between them. This is especially important in collections, because it is how sorting is achieved. You'll look at how to compare objects in a number of ways, including operator overloading, and how to use the IComparable and IComparer interface to sort collections.

- ❑ **Conversions** — Earlier chapters showed how to cast objects from one type into another. In this chapter, you'll learn how to customize type conversions to suit your needs.

Collections

In Chapter 5, you learned how you can use arrays to create variable types that contain a number of objects or values. Arrays, however, have their limitations. The biggest is that once arrays have been created, they have a fixed size, so you can't add new items to the end of an existing array without creating a new one. This often means that the syntax used to manipulate arrays can become overly complicated. OOP techniques enable you to create classes that perform much of this manipulation internally, simplifying the code that uses lists of items or arrays.

Arrays in C# are implemented as instances of the System.Array class and are just one type of what are known as *collection* classes. Collection classes in general are used for maintaining lists of objects and may expose more functionality than simple arrays. Much of this functionality comes through implementing interfaces from the `System.Collections` namespace, thus standardizing collection syntax. This namespace also contains some other interesting things, such as classes that implement these interfaces in ways other than `System.Array`.

Because the collection's functionality (including basic functions such as accessing collection items by using `[index]` syntax) is available through interfaces, you aren't limited to using basic collection classes such as `System.Array`. Instead, you can create your own customized collection classes. These can be made more specific to the objects you wish to enumerate (that is, the objects you want to maintain collections of). One advantage of doing this, as you will see, is that custom collection classes can be *strongly typed*. That is, when you extract items from the collection, you don't need to cast them into the correct type. Another advantage is the capability to expose specialized methods. For example, you can provide a quick way to obtain subsets of items. In the deck of cards example, you could add a method to obtain all `Card` items of a particular suit.

Several interfaces in the `System.Collections` namespace provide basic collection functionality:

❑ `IEnumerable` — Provides the capability to loop through items in a collection.

❑ `ICollection` — Provides the capability to obtain the number of items in a collection and copy items into a simple array type (inherits from `IEnumerable`).

❑ `IList` — Provides a list of items for a collection along with the capabilities for accessing these items, and some other basic capabilities related to lists of items (inherits from `IEnumerable` and `ICollection`).

❑ `IDictionary` — Similar to `IList`, but provides a list of items accessible via a key value, rather than an index (inherits from `IEnumerable` and `ICollection`).

The `System.Array` class implements `IList`, `ICollection`, and `IEnumerable`. However, it doesn't support some of the more advanced features of `IList`, and it represents a list of items by using a fixed size.

Using Collections

One of the classes in the `Systems.Collections` namespace, `System.Collections.ArrayList`, also implements `IList`, `ICollection`, and `IEnumerable`, but does so in a more sophisticated way than `System.Array`. Whereas arrays are fixed in size (you can't add or remove elements), this class may be used to represent a variable-length list of items. To give you more of a feel for what is possible with such a highly advanced collection, the following Try It Out uses this class, as well as a simple array.

Try It Out   **Arrays versus More Advanced Collections**

1. Create a new console application called Ch11Ex01 and save it in the directory C:\BegVCSharp\Chapter11.

2. Add three new classes, `Animal`, `Cow`, and `Chicken`, to the project by right-clicking on the project in the Solution Explorer window and selecting Add ➪ Class for each.

3. Modify the code in `Animal.cs` as follows:

```
namespace Ch11Ex01
{
    public abstract class Animal
    {
        protected string name;

        public string Name
        {
            get
            {
                return name;
            }
            set
            {
                name = value;
            }
        }

        public Animal()
        {
            name = "The animal with no name";
        }

        public Animal(string newName)
        {
            name = newName;
        }

        public void Feed()
        {
            Console.WriteLine("{0} has been fed.", name);
        }
    }
}
```

4. Modify the code in `Cow.cs` as follows:

```
namespace Ch11Ex01
{
    public class Cow : Animal
    {
        public void Milk()
        {
            Console.WriteLine("{0} has been milked.", name);
        }

        public Cow(string newName) : base(newName)
        {
        }
    }
}
```

5. Modify the code in `Chicken.cs` as follows:

```
namespace Ch11Ex01
{
    public class Chicken : Animal
    {
        public void LayEgg()
        {
            Console.WriteLine("{0} has laid an egg.", name);
        }

        public Chicken(string newName) : base(newName)
        {
        }
    }
}
```

6. Modify the code in `Program.cs` as follows:

```
using System;
using System.Collections;
using System.Collections.Generic;
using System.Linq;
using System.Text;

namespace Ch11Ex01

{
    class Program
    {
        static void Main(string[] args)
        {
            Console.WriteLine("Create an Array type collection of Animal " +
                              "objects and use it:");

            Animal[] animalArray = new Animal[2];
            Cow myCow1 = new Cow("Deirdre");
            animalArray[0] = myCow1;
            animalArray[1] = new Chicken("Ken");

            foreach (Animal myAnimal in animalArray)
            {
                Console.WriteLine("New {0} object added to Array collection, " +
                                  "Name = {1}", myAnimal.ToString(), myAnimal.Name);
            }

            Console.WriteLine("Array collection contains {0} objects.",
                              animalArray.Length);
            animalArray[0].Feed();
            ((Chicken)animalArray[1]).LayEgg();
            Console.WriteLine();

            Console.WriteLine("Create an ArrayList type collection of Animal " +
                              "objects and use it:");
```

```
ArrayList animalArrayList = new ArrayList();
Cow myCow2 = new Cow("Hayley");
animalArrayList.Add(myCow2);
animalArrayList.Add(new Chicken("Roy"));

foreach (Animal myAnimal in animalArrayList)
{
   Console.WriteLine("New {0} object added to ArrayList collection," +
                     " Name = {1}", myAnimal.ToString(), myAnimal.Name);
}
Console.WriteLine("ArrayList collection contains {0} objects.",
      animalArrayList.Count);
((Animal)animalArrayList[0]).Feed();
((Chicken)animalArrayList[1]).LayEgg();
Console.WriteLine();

Console.WriteLine("Additional manipulation of ArrayList:");
animalArrayList.RemoveAt(0);
((Animal)animalArrayList[0]).Feed();
animalArrayList.AddRange(animalArray);
((Chicken)animalArrayList[2]).LayEgg();
Console.WriteLine("The animal called {0} is at index {1}.",
                  myCow1.Name, animalArrayList.IndexOf(myCow1));
myCow1.Name = "Janice";
Console.WriteLine("The animal is now called {0}.",
                  ((Animal)animalArrayList[1]).Name);
Console.ReadKey();
      }
   }
}
```

7. Run the application. The result is shown in Figure 11-1.

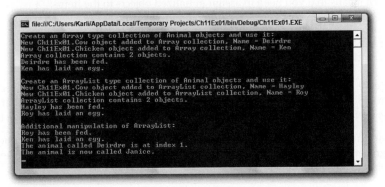

Figure 11-1

How It Works

This example creates two collections of objects: the first uses the `System.Array` class (that is, a simple array), and the second uses the `System.Collections.ArrayList` class. Both collections are of `Animal` objects, which are defined in `Animal.cs`. The `Animal` class is abstract, so it can't be instantiated, although you can have items in your collection that are instances of the `Cow` and `Chicken` classes, which are derived from `Animal`. You achieve this by using polymorphism, discussed in Chapter 8.

Once created in the `Main()` method in `Class1.cs`, these arrays are manipulated to show their characteristics and capabilities. Several of the operations performed apply to both `Array` and `ArrayList` collections, although their syntax differs slightly. Some, however, are only possible by using the more advanced `ArrayList` type.

We'll cover the similar operations first, comparing the code and results for both types of collection. First, collection creation. With simple arrays you must initialize the array with a fixed size in order to use it. You do this to an array called `animalArray` by using the standard syntax shown in Chapter 5:

```
Animal[] animalArray = new Animal[2];
```

`ArrayList` collections, conversely, don't need a size to be initialized, so you can create your list (called `animalArrayList`) as follows:

```
ArrayList animalArrayList = new ArrayList();
```

You can use two other constructors with this class. The first copies the contents of an existing collection to the new instance by specifying the existing collection as a parameter; the other sets the *capacity* of the collection, also via a parameter. This capacity, specified as an `int` value, sets the initial number of items that can be contained in the collection. This is not an absolute capacity, however, because it is doubled automatically if the number of items in the collection ever exceeds this value.

With arrays of reference types (such as the `Animal` and `Animal`-derived objects), simply initializing the array with a size doesn't initialize the items it contains. To use a given entry, that entry needs to be initialized, which means that you need to assign initialized objects to the items:

```
Cow myCow1 = new Cow("Deirdre");
animalArray[0] = myCow1;
animalArray[1] = new Chicken("Ken");
```

The preceding code does this in two ways: once by assignment using an existing `Cow` object, and once by assignment through the creation of a new `Chicken` object. The main difference here is that the former method creates a reference to the object in the array — a fact that you make use of later in the code.

With the `ArrayList` collection, there are no existing items, not even `null`-referenced ones. This means you can't assign new instances to indices in the same way. Instead, you use the `Add()` method of the `ArrayList` object to add new items:

```
Cow myCow2 = new Cow("Hayley");
animalArrayList.Add(myCow2);
animalArrayList.Add(new Chicken("Roy"));
```

Apart from the slightly different syntax, you can add new or existing objects to the collection in the same way. Once you have added items in this way, you can overwrite them by using syntax identical to that for arrays:

```
animalArrayList[0] = new Cow("Alma");
```

You won't do that in this example, though.

Chapter 5 showed how the `foreach` structure can be used to iterate through an array. This is possible because the `System.Array` class implements the `IEnumerable` interface, and the only method on this interface, `GetEnumerator()`, allows you to loop through items in the collection. You'll look at this in more depth a little later in the chapter. In your code, you write out information about each `Animal` object in the array:

```
foreach (Animal myAnimal in animalArray)
{
    Console.WriteLine("New {0} object added to Array collection, " +
                    "Name = {1}", myAnimal.ToString(), myAnimal.Name);
}
```

The `ArrayList` object you use also supports the `IEnumerable` interface and can be used with `foreach`. In this case, the syntax is identical:

```
foreach (Animal myAnimal in animalArrayList)
{
    Console.WriteLine("New {0} object added to ArrayList collection, " +
                    "Name = {1}", myAnimal.ToString(), myAnimal.Name);
}
```

Next, you use the `Length` property of the array to output to the screen the number of items in the array:

```
Console.WriteLine("Array collection contains {0} objects.",
                    animalArray.Length);
```

You can achieve the same thing with the `ArrayList` collection, except that you use the `Count` property that is part of the `ICollection` interface:

```
Console.WriteLine("ArrayList collection contains {0} objects.",
                    animalArrayList.Count);
```

Collections — whether simple arrays or more complex collections — aren't very useful unless they provide access to the items that belong to them. Simple arrays are strongly typed — that is, they allow direct access to the type of the items they contain. This means you can call the methods of the item directly:

```
animalArray[0].Feed();
```

The type of the array is the abstract type `Animal`; therefore, you can't call methods supplied by derived classes directly. Instead you must use casting:

```
((Chicken)animalArray[1]).LayEgg();
```

The `ArrayList` collection is a collection of `System.Object` objects (you have assigned `Animal` objects via polymorphism). This means that you must use casting for all items:

```
((Animal)animalArrayList[0]).Feed();
((Chicken)animalArrayList[1]).LayEgg();
```

The remainder of the code looks at some of the `ArrayList` collection's capabilities that go beyond those of the `Array` collection. First, you can remove items by using the `Remove()` and `RemoveAt()` methods, part of the `IList` interface implementation in the `ArrayList` class. These remove items from an array based on an item reference or index, respectively. This example uses the latter method to remove the list's first item, the `Cow` object with a `Name` property of `Hayley`:

```
animalArrayList.RemoveAt(0);
```

Alternatively, you could use

```
animalArrayList.Remove(myCow2);
```

because you already have a local reference to this object — you added an existing reference to the array via `Add()`, rather than create a new object. Either way, the only item left in the collection is the `Chicken` object, which you access as follows:

```
((Animal)animalArrayList[0]).Feed();
```

Any modifications to items in the `ArrayList` object resulting in N items being left in the array will be executed in such a way as to maintain indices from 0 to N-1. For example, removing the item with the index 0 results in all other items being shifted one place in the array, so you access the `Chicken` object with the index 0, not 1. You no longer have an item with an index of 1 (because you only had two items in the first place), so an exception would be thrown if you tried the following:

```
((Animal)animalArrayList[1]).Feed();
```

`ArrayList` collections enable you to add several items at once with the `AddRange()` method. This method accepts any object with the `ICollection` interface, which includes the `animalArray` array created earlier in the code:

```
animalArrayList.AddRange(animalArray);
```

To check that this works, you can attempt to access the third item in the collection, which will be the second item in `animalArray`:

```
((Chicken)animalArrayList[2]).LayEgg();
```

The AddRange() method isn't part of any of the interfaces exposed by ArrayList. This method is specific to the ArrayList class and demonstrates the fact that you can exhibit customized behavior in your collection classes, beyond what is required by the interfaces you have looked at. This class exposes other interesting methods too, such as InsertRange(), for inserting an array of objects at any point in the list, and methods for tasks such as sorting and reordering the array.

Finally, you make use of the fact that you can have multiple references to the same object. Using the IndexOf() method (part of the IList interface), you can see not only that myCow1 (an object originally added to animalArray) is now part of the animalArrayList collection, but also its index:

```
Console.WriteLine("The animal called {0} is at index {1}.",
                  myCow1.Name, animalArrayList.IndexOf(myCow1));
```

As an extension of this, the next two lines of code rename the object via the object reference and display the new name via the collection reference:

```
myCow1.Name = "Janice";
Console.WriteLine("The animal is now called {0}.",
                  ((Animal)animalArrayList[1]).Name);
```

Defining Collections

Now that you know what is possible using more advanced collection classes, it's time to learn how to create your own strongly typed collection. One way of doing this is to implement the required methods manually, but this can be a time-consuming and complex process. Alternatively, you can derive your collection from a class, such as System.Collections.CollectionBase, an abstract class that supplies much of the implementation of a collection for you. This option is strongly recommended.

The CollectionBase class exposes the interfaces IEnumerable, ICollection, and IList but only provides some of the required implementation — notably, the Clear() and RemoveAt() methods of IList and the Count property of ICollection. You need to implement everything else yourself if you want the functionality provided.

To facilitate this, CollectionBase provides two protected properties that provide access to the stored objects themselves. You can use List, which gives you access to the items through an IList interface, and InnerList, which is the ArrayList object used to store items.

For example, the basics of a collection class to store Animal objects could be defined as follows (you'll see a fuller implementation shortly):

```
public class Animals : CollectionBase
{
    public void Add(Animal newAnimal)
    {
        List.Add(newAnimal);
    }

    public void Remove(Animal oldAnimal)
```

```
    {
        List.Remove(oldAnimal);
    }

    public Animals()
    {
    }
}
```

Here, Add() and Remove() have been implemented as strongly typed methods that use the standard Add() method of the IList interface used to access the items. The methods exposed will now only work with Animal classes or classes derived from Animal, unlike the ArrayList implementations shown earlier, which work with any object.

The CollectionBase class enables you to use the foreach syntax with your derived collections. For example, you can use code such as this:

```
Console.WriteLine("Using custom collection class Animals:");
Animals animalCollection = new Animals();
animalCollection.Add(new Cow("Sarah"));
foreach (Animal myAnimal in animalCollection)
{
    Console.WriteLine("New {0} object added to custom collection, " +
                        "Name = {1}", myAnimal.ToString(), myAnimal.Name);
}
```

You can't, however, do the following:

```
animalCollection[0].Feed();
```

To access items via their indices in this way, you need to use an indexer.

Indexers

An *indexer* is a special kind of property that you can add to a class to provide array-like access. In fact, you can provide more complex access via an indexer, because you can define and use complex parameter types with the square bracket syntax as you wish. Implementing a simple numeric index for items, however, is the most common usage.

You can add an indexer to the Animals collection of Animal objects as follows:

```
public class Animals : CollectionBase
{
    ...

    public Animal this[int animalIndex]
    {
        get
        {
            return (Animal)List[animalIndex];
        }
        set
```

```
            {
                List[animalIndex] = value;
            }
        }
    }
```

The `this` keyword is used along with parameters in square brackets, but otherwise this looks much like any other property. This syntax is logical, because you access the indexer by using the name of the object followed by the index parameter(s) in square brackets (for example, `MyAnimals[0]`).

This code uses an indexer on the `List` property (that is, on the `IList` interface that provides access to the `ArrayList` in `CollectionBase` that stores your items):

```
return (Animal)List[animalIndex];
```

Explicit casting *is* necessary here, as the `IList.List` property returns a `System.Object` object. The important thing to note here is that you define a type for this indexer. This is the type that will be obtained when you access an item by using this indexer. This means that you can write code such as

```
animalCollection[0].Feed();
```

rather than

```
((Animal)animalCollection[0]).Feed();
```

This is another handy feature of strongly typed custom collections. In the following Try It Out, you expand the last example properly to put this into action.

Try It Out   **Implementing an Animals Collection**

1. Create a new console application called Ch11Ex02 and save it in the directory
    C:\BegVCSharp\Chapter11.

2. Right-click on the project name in the Solution Explorer window and select Add ⇨ Existing Item.

3. Select the `Animal.cs`, `Cow.cs`, and `Chicken.cs` files from the C:\BegVCSharp\Chapter11\
    Ch11Ex01\Ch11Ex01 directory, and click Add.

4. Modify the namespace declaration in the three files you added as follows:

    ```
    namespace Ch11Ex02
    ```

5. Add a new class called `Animals`.

6. Modify the code in `Animals.cs` as follows:

```csharp
using System;
using System.Collections;
using System.Collections.Generic;
using System.Linq;
using System.Text;

#endregion

namespace Ch11Ex02
{
    public class Animals : CollectionBase
    {
        public void Add(Animal newAnimal)
        {
            List.Add(newAnimal);
        }

        public void Remove(Animal newAnimal)
        {
            List.Remove(newAnimal);
        }

        public Animals()
        {
        }

        public Animal this[int animalIndex]
        {
            get
            {
                return (Animal)List[animalIndex];
            }
            set
            {
                List[animalIndex] = value;
            }
        }
    }
}
```

7. Modify `Program.cs` as follows:

```csharp
static void Main(string[] args)
{
    Animals animalCollection = new Animals();
    animalCollection.Add(new Cow("Jack"));
    animalCollection.Add(new Chicken("Vera"));
    foreach (Animal myAnimal in animalCollection)
```

```
        {
            myAnimal.Feed();
        }
        Console.ReadKey();
    }
```

8. Execute the application. The result is shown in Figure 11-2.

Figure 11-2

How It Works

This example uses code detailed in the last section to implement a strongly typed collection of `Animal` objects in a class called `Animals`. The code in `Main()` simply instantiates an `Animals` object called `animalCollection`, adds two items (an instance of `Cow` and `Chicken`), and uses a `foreach` loop to call the `Feed()` method that both objects inherit from their base class, `Animal`.

Adding a Cards Collection to CardLib

In the last chapter, you created a class library project called Ch10CardLib that contained a `Card` class representing a playing card, and a `Deck` class representing a deck of cards — that is, a collection of `Card` classes. This collection was implemented as a simple array.

In this chapter, you'll add a new class to this library, renamed Ch11CardLib. This new class, `Cards`, will be a custom collection of `Card` objects, giving you all the benefits described earlier in this chapter. Create a new class library called Ch11CardLib in the C:\BegVCSharp\Chapter11 directory, select the Project ⇨ Add Existing Item menu item, select the `Card.cs`, `Deck.cs`, `Suit.cs`, and `Rank.cs` files from the C:\BegVCSharp\Chapter10\Ch10CardLib\Ch10CardLib directory, and add the files to your project. As with the previous version of this project, introduced in Chapter 10, these changes are presented without using the standard Try It Out format. Should you want to jump straight to the code, feel free to open the version of this project included in the downloadable code for this chapter.

> *Don't forget that when copying the source files from* Ch10CardLib *to* Ch11CardLib, *you must change the namespace declarations to refer to* Ch11CardLib. *This also applies to the* Ch10CardClient *console application that you will use for testing.*

> *The downloadable code for this chapter includes a project that contains all the code you need for the various expansions to* Ch11CardLib. *The code is divided into regions, and you can uncomment the section you want to experiment with.*

If you decide to create this project yourself, add a new class called `Cards` and modify the code in `Cards.cs` as follows:

```csharp
using System;
using System.Collections;
using System.Collections.Generic;
using System.Linq;
using System.Text;

namespace Ch11CardLib
{
    public class Cards : CollectionBase
    {
        public void Add(Card newCard)
        {
            List.Add(newCard);
        }

        public void Remove(Card oldCard)
        {
            List.Remove(oldCard);
        }

        public Cards()
        {
        }

        public Card this[int cardIndex]
        {
            get
            {
                return (Card)List[cardIndex];
            }
            set
            {
                List[cardIndex] = value;
            }
        }

        // Utility method for copying card instances into another Cards
        // instance - used in Deck.Shuffle(). This implementation assumes that
        // source and target collections are the same size.
        public void CopyTo(Cards targetCards)
        {
            for (int index = 0; index < this.Count; index++)
            {
                targetCards[index] = this[index];
            }
        }

        // Check to see if the Cards collection contains a particular card.
        // This calls the Contains method of the ArrayList for the collection,
        // which you access through the InnerList property.
```

```
        public bool Contains(Card card)
        {
            return InnerList.Contains(card);
        }
    }
}
```

Next, modify `Deck.cs` to use this new collection, rather than an array:

```
using System;
using System.Collections.Generic;
using System.Linq;
using System.Text;

namespace Ch11CardLib
{
    public class Deck
    {
        private Cards cards = new Cards();

        public Deck()
        {
            // Line of code removed here
            for (int suitVal = 0; suitVal < 4; suitVal++)
            {
                for (int rankVal = 1; rankVal < 14; rankVal++)
                {
                    cards.Add(new Card((Suit)suitVal, (Rank)rankVal));
                }
            }
        }

        public Card GetCard(int cardNum)
        {
            if (cardNum >= 0 && cardNum <= 51)
                return cards[cardNum];
            else
                throw (new System.ArgumentOutOfRangeException("cardNum", cardNum,
                    "Value must be between 0 and 51."));
        }

        public void Shuffle()
        {
            Cards newDeck = new Cards();
            bool[] assigned = new bool[52];
            Random sourceGen = new Random();
            for (int i = 0; i < 52; i++)
            {
                int sourceCard = 0;
                bool foundCard = false;
                while (foundCard == false)
```

291

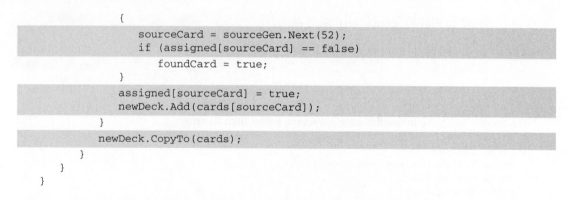

```
        {
            sourceCard = sourceGen.Next(52);
            if (assigned[sourceCard] == false)
                foundCard = true;
        }
        assigned[sourceCard] = true;
        newDeck.Add(cards[sourceCard]);
    }
    newDeck.CopyTo(cards);
  }
 }
}
```

Not many changes are necessary here. Most of them involve changing the shuffling logic to allow for the fact that cards are added to the beginning of the new `Cards` collection `newDeck` from a random index in `cards`, rather than to a random index in `newDeck` from a sequential position in `cards`.

The client console application for the Ch10CardLib solution, Ch10CardClient, may be used with this new library with the same result as before, as the method signatures of `Deck` are unchanged. Clients of this class library can now make use of the `Cards` collection class, however, rather than rely on arrays of `Card` objects — for example, to define hands of cards in a card game application.

Keyed Collections and IDictionary

Instead of the `IList` interface, it is also possible for collections to implement the similar `IDictionary` interface, which allows items to be indexed via a key value (such as a string name), rather than an index. This is also achieved using an indexer, although here the indexer parameter used is a key associated with a stored item, rather than an `int` index, which can make the collection a lot more user-friendly.

As with indexed collections, there is a base class you can use to simplify implementation of the `IDictionary` interface: `DictionaryBase`. This class also implements `IEnumerable` and `ICollection`, providing the basic collection manipulation capabilities that are the same for any collection.

`DictionaryBase`, like `CollectionBase`, implements some (but not all) of the members obtained through its supported interfaces. Like `CollectionBase`, the `Clear` and `Count` members are implemented, although `RemoveAt()` isn't because it's a method on the `IList` interface and doesn't appear on the `IDictionary` interface. `IDictionary` does, however, have a `Remove()` method, which is one of the methods you should implement in a custom collection class based on `DictionaryBase`.

The following code shows an alternative version of the `Animals` class, this time derived from `DictionaryBase`. Implementations are included for `Add()`, `Remove()`, and a key-accessed indexer:

```
public class Animals : DictionaryBase
{
    public void Add(string newID, Animal newAnimal)
    {
        Dictionary.Add(newID, newAnimal);
    }

    public void Remove(string animalID)
```

```
      {
         Dictionary.Remove(animalID);
      }

      public Animals()
      {
      }

      public Animal this[string animalID]
      {
         get
         {
            return (Animal)Dictionary[animalID];
         }
         set
         {
            Dictionary[animalID] = value;
         }
      }
   }
```

The differences in these members are as follows:

❏   **Add()** — Takes two parameters, a key and a value, to store together. The dictionary collection has a
    member called Dictionary inherited from DictionaryBase, which is an IDictionary interface.
    This interface has its own Add() method, which takes two object parameters. Your implementation
    takes a string value as a key and an Animal object as the data to store alongside this key.

❏   **Remove()** — Takes a key parameter, rather than an object reference. The item with the key value
    specified is removed.

❏   **Indexer** — Uses a string key value, rather than an index, which is used to access the stored item
    via the Dictionary inherited member. Again, casting is necessary here.

One other difference between collections based on DictionaryBase and collections based on
CollectionBase is that foreach works slightly differently. The collection from the last section allowed
you to extract Animal objects directly from the collection. Using foreach with the DictionaryBase
derived class gives you DictionaryEntry structs, another type defined in the System.Collections
namespace. To get to the Animal objects themselves, you must use the Value member of this struct, or
you can use the Key member of the struct to get the associated key. To get code equivalent to the earlier

```
      foreach (Animal myAnimal in animalCollection)
      {
         Console.WriteLine("New {0} object added to custom collection, " +
                           "Name = {1}", myAnimal.ToString(), myAnimal.Name);
      }
```

you need the following:

```
      foreach (DictionaryEntry myEntry in animalCollection)
      {
         Console.WriteLine("New {0} object added to custom collection, " +
                           "Name = {1}", myEntry.Value.ToString(),
                           ((Animal)myEntry.Value).Name);
      }
```

It is possible to override this behavior so that you can access `Animal` objects directly through `foreach`. There are several ways to do this, the simplest being to implement an iterator.

Iterators

Earlier in this chapter, you saw that the `IEnumerable` interface enables you to use `foreach` loops. It's often beneficial to use your classes in `foreach` loops, not just collection classes such as those shown in previous sections.

However, overriding this behavior, or providing your own custom implementation of it, is not always simple. To illustrate this, it's necessary to take a detailed look at `foreach` loops. The following steps show what actually happens in a `foreach` loop iterating through a collection called `collectionObject`:

1. `collectionObject.GetEnumerator()` is called, which returns an `IEnumerator` reference. This method is available through implementation of the `IEnumerable` interface, although this is optional.

2. The `MoveNext()` method of the returned `IEnumerator` interface is called.

3. If `MoveNext()` returns `true`, then the `Current` property of the `IEnumerator` interface is used to get a reference to an object, which is used in the `foreach` loop.

4. The preceding two steps repeat until `MoveNext()` returns `false`, at which point the loop terminates.

To enable this behavior in your classes, you must override several methods, keep track of indices, maintain the `Current` property, and so on. This can be a lot of work to achieve very little.

A simpler alternative is to use an iterator. Effectively, using iterators generates a lot of the code for you behind the scenes and hooks it all up correctly. Moreover, the syntax for using iterators is much easier to come to grips with.

A good definition of an iterator is a block of code that supplies all the values to be used in a `foreach` block in sequence. Typically, this block of code is a method, although you can also use property accessors and other blocks of code as iterators. To keep things simple, you'll just look at methods here.

Whatever the block of code is, its return type is restricted. Perhaps contrary to expectations, this return type isn't the same as the type of object being enumerated. For example, in a class that represents a collection of `Animal` objects, the return type of the iterator block can't be `Animal`. Two possible return types are the interface types mentioned earlier, `IEnumerable` or `IEnumerator`. You use these types as follows:

❑   To iterate over a class, use a method called `GetEnumerator()` with a return type of `IEnumerator`.

❑   To iterate over a class member, such as a method, use `IEnumerable`.

Within an iterator block, you select the values to be used in the `foreach` loop by using the `yield` keyword. The syntax for doing this is as follows:

```
yield return value;
```

That information is all you need to build a very simple example, as follows:

```
public static IEnumerable SimpleList()
{
    yield return "string 1";
    yield return "string 2";
    yield return "string 3";
}

public static void Main(string[] args)
{
    foreach (string item in SimpleList())
        Console.WriteLine(item);

    Console.ReadKey();
}
```

> *To test this code yourself, remember to add a* using *statement for the* System.Collections
> *namespace or fully qualify the* System.Collections.IEnumerable *interface. Alternately, you can
> find this code in the* SimpleIterators *project in the downloadable code for this chapter.*

Here, the static method `SimpleList()` is the iterator block. Because it is a method, you use a return type of `IEnumerable`. `SimpleList()` uses the `yield` keyword to supply three values to the `foreach` block that uses it, each of which is written to the screen. The result is shown in Figure 11-3.

Figure 11-3

Obviously, this iterator isn't a particularly useful one, but it does show how this works in action and how simple the implementation can be. Looking at the code, you might wonder how the code knows to return `string` type items. In fact, it doesn't; it returns `object` type values. As you know, `object` is the base class for all types, so you can return anything from the `yield` statements.

However, the compiler is intelligent enough to enable you to interpret the returned values as whatever type you want in the context of the `foreach` loop. Here, the code asks for `string` type values, so that is what the values you get to work with are. Should you change one of the `yield` lines so that it returns, say, an integer, you would get a bad cast exception in the `foreach` loop.

Note one more thing about iterators. It is possible to interrupt the return of information to the `foreach` loop by using the following statement:

```
yield break;
```

When this statement is encountered in an iterator, the iterator processing terminates immediately, as does the `foreach` loop using it.

Now it's time for a more complicated — and useful! — example. In this Try It Out, you'll implement an iterator that obtains prime numbers.

Try It Out   Implementing an Iterator

1. Create a new console application called Ch11Ex03 and save it in the directory
    C:\BegVCSharp\Chapter11.

2. Add a new class called `Primes` and modify the code as follows:

```csharp
using System;
using System.Collections;
using System.Collections.Generic;
using System.Linq;
using System.Text;

namespace Ch11Ex03
{
    public class Primes
    {
        private long min;
        private long max;

        public Primes() : this(2, 100)
        {
        }

        public Primes(long minimum, long maximum)
        {
            if (min < 2)
                min = 2;
            else
                min = minimum;

            max = maximum;
        }

        public IEnumerator GetEnumerator()
        {
            for (long possiblePrime = min; possiblePrime <= max; possiblePrime++)
            {
                bool isPrime = true;
                for (long possibleFactor = 2; possibleFactor <=
                    (long)Math.Floor(Math.Sqrt(possiblePrime)); possibleFactor++)
                {
                    long remainderAfterDivision = possiblePrime % possibleFactor;
                    if (remainderAfterDivision == 0)
```

```
                    {
                        isPrime = false;
                        break;
                    }
                }
            }
            if (isPrime)
            {
                yield return possiblePrime;
            }
        }
    }
}
```

3.   Modify the code in `Program.cs` as follows:

```
static void Main(string[] args)
{
    Primes primesFrom2To1000 = new Primes(2, 1000);
    foreach (long i in primesFrom2To1000)
        Console.Write("{0} ", i);

    Console.ReadKey();
}
```

4.   Execute the application. The result is shown in Figure 11-4.

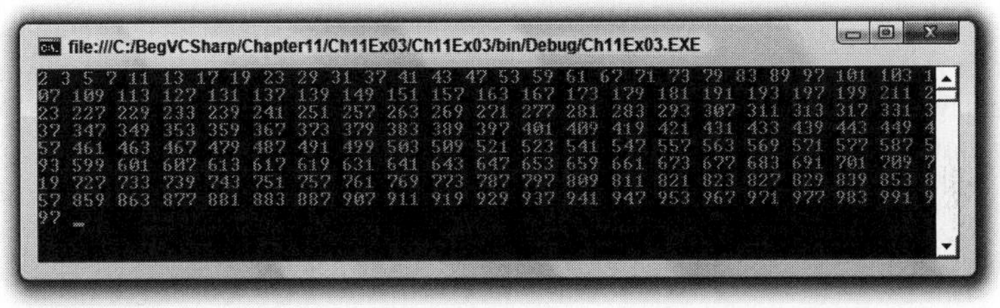

Figure 11-4

How It Works

This example consists of a class that enables you to enumerate over a collection of prime numbers between an upper and lower limit. The class that encapsulates the prime numbers uses an iterator to provide this functionality.

The code for `Primes` starts off with the basics: two fields to hold the maximum and minimum values to search between, and constructors to set these values. Note that the minimum value is restricted — it can't be less than 2. This makes sense, because 2 is the lowest prime number. The interesting code is all in the `GetEnumerator()` method. The method signature fulfils the rules for an iterator block in that it returns an `IEnumerator` type:

```
public IEnumerator GetEnumerator()
{
```

To extract prime numbers between limits, you need to test each number in turn, so you start with a `for` loop:

```
for (long possiblePrime = min; possiblePrime <= max; possiblePrime++)
{
```

Because you don't know whether a number is prime or not, you first assume that it is and then check to see if it isn't. That means checking whether any number between 2 and the square root of the number to be tested is a factor. If this is true, then the number isn't prime, so you move on to the next one. If the number is indeed prime, then you pass it to the `foreach` loop using `yield`:

```
bool isPrime = true;
for (long possibleFactor = 2; possibleFactor <=
    (long)Math.Floor(Math.Sqrt(possiblePrime)); possibleFactor++)
{
    long remainderAfterDivision = possiblePrime % possibleFactor;
    if (remainderAfterDivision == 0)
    {
        isPrime = false;
        break;
    }
}
if (isPrime)
{
    yield return possiblePrime;
}
}
}
```

An interesting fact reveals itself through this code if you set the minimum and maximum limits to very big numbers. When you execute the application, the results appear one at a time, with pauses in between, rather than all at once. This is evidence that the iterator code returns results one at a time, despite the fact that there is no obvious place where the code terminates between `yield` calls. Behind the scenes, calling `yield` does interrupt the code, which resumes when another value is requested — that is, when the `foreach` loop using the iterator begins a new cycle.

Iterators and Collections

Earlier you were promised an explanation of how iterators can be used to iterate over the objects stored in a dictionary-type collection without having to deal with `DictionaryItem` objects. Recall the collection class `Animals`:

```
public class Animals : DictionaryBase
{
    public void Add(string newID, Animal newAnimal)
    {
        Dictionary.Add(newID, newAnimal);
    }

    public void Remove(string animalID)
```

```
    {
        Dictionary.Remove(animalID);
    }

    public Animals()
    {
    }

    public Animal this[string animalID]
    {
        get
        {
            return (Animal)Dictionary[animalID];
        }
        set
        {
            Dictionary[animalID] = value;
        }
    }
}
```

You can add this simple iterator to the code to get the desired behavior:

```
public new IEnumerator GetEnumerator()
{
    foreach (object animal in Dictionary.Values)
        yield return (Animal)animal;
}
```

Now you can use the following code to iterate through the `Animal` objects in the collection:

```
foreach (Animal myAnimal in animalCollection)
{
    Console.WriteLine("New {0} object added to custom collection, " +
                      "Name = {1}", myAnimal.ToString(), myAnimal.Name);
}
```

In the downloadable code for this chapter you will find this code in the DictionaryAnimals project.

Deep Copying

Chapter 9 described how you can perform shallow copying with the `System.Object.MemberwiseClone()` protected method, by using a method like the `GetCopy()` one shown here:

```
public class Cloner
{
    public int Val;

    public Cloner(int newVal)
    {
        Val = newVal;
    }
```

```
        public object GetCopy()
        {
            return MemberwiseClone();
        }
    }
```

Suppose you have fields that are reference types, rather than value types (for example, objects):

```
public class Content
{
    public int Val;
}
```

```
public class Cloner
{
    public Content MyContent = new Content();

    public Cloner(int newVal)
    {
        MyContent.Val = newVal;
    }
    public object GetCopy()
    {
        return MemberwiseClone();
    }
}
```

In this case, the shallow copy obtained though GetCopy() has a field that refers to the same object as the original object. The following code, which uses this Cloner class, illustrates the consequences of shallow copying reference types:

```
Cloner mySource = new Cloner(5);
Cloner myTarget = (Cloner)mySource.GetCopy();
Console.WriteLine("myTarget.MyContent.Val = {0}", myTarget.MyContent.Val);
mySource.MyContent.Val = 2;
Console.WriteLine("myTarget.MyContent.Val = {0}", myTarget.MyContent.Val);
```

The fourth line, which assigns a value to mySource.MyContent.Val, the Val public field of the MyContent public field of the original object, also changes the value of myTarget.MyContent.Val. This is because mySource.MyContent refers to the same object instance as myTarget.MyContent. The output of the preceding code is as follows:

```
myTarget.MyContent.Val = 5
myTarget.MyContent.Val = 2
```

To get around this, you need to perform a deep copy. You could just modify the GetCopy() method used previously to do this, but it is preferable to use the standard .NET Framework way of doing things: Implement the ICloneable interface, which has the single method Clone(). This method takes no parameters and returns an object type result, giving it a signature identical to the GetCopy() method used earlier.

To modify the preceding classes, try using the following deep copy code:

```
public class Content
{
    public int Val;
}
```

```
public class Cloner : ICloneable
{
    public Content MyContent = new Content();

    public Cloner(int newVal)
    {
        MyContent.Val = newVal;
    }
```

```
    public object Clone()
    {
        Cloner clonedCloner = new Cloner(MyContent.Val);
        return clonedCloner;
    }
}
```

This created a new `Cloner` object by using the `Val` field of the `Content` object contained in the original `Cloner` object (`MyContent`). This field is a value type, so no deeper copying is necessary.

Using code similar to that just shown to test the shallow copy but using `Clone()` instead of `GetCopy()` gives you the following result:

```
myTarget.MyContent.Val = 5
myTarget.MyContent.Val = 5
```

This time, the contained objects are independent. Note that sometimes calls to `Clone()` are made recursively, in more complex object systems. For example, if the `MyContent` field of the `Cloner` class also required deep copying, then you might need the following:

```
public class Cloner : ICloneable
{
    public Content MyContent = new Content();

    ...
```

```
    public object Clone()
    {
        Cloner clonedCloner = new Cloner();
        clonedCloner.MyContent = MyContent.Clone();
        return clonedCloner;
    }
}
```

You're calling the default constructor here to simplify the syntax of creating a new `Cloner` object. For this code to work, you would also need to implement `ICloneable` on the `Content` class.

Adding Deep Copying to CardLib

You can put this into practice by implementing the capability to copy Card, Cards, and Deck objects by using the ICloneable interface. This might be useful in some card games, where you might not necessarily want two decks with references to the same set of Card objects, although you might conceivably want to set up one deck to have the same card order as another.

Implementing cloning functionality for the Card class in Ch11CardLib is simple, because shallow copying is sufficient (Card only contains value-type data, in the form of fields). Just make the following changes to the class definition:

```
public class Card : ICloneable
{
    public object Clone()
    {
        return MemberwiseClone();
    }
```

Note that this implementation of ICloneable is just a shallow copy. There is no rule determining what should happen in the Clone() method, and this is sufficient for your purposes.

Next, implement ICloneable on the Cards collection class. This is slightly more complicated because it involves cloning every Card object in the original collection — so you need to make a deep copy:

```
public class Cards : CollectionBase, ICloneable
{
    public object Clone()
    {
        Cards newCards = new Cards();
        foreach (Card sourceCard in List)
        {
            newCards.Add(sourceCard.Clone() as Card);
        }
        return newCards;
    }
```

Finally, implement ICloneable on the Deck class. Note a slight problem here: The Deck class has no way to modify the cards it contains, short of shuffling them. There is no way, for example, to modify a Deck instance to have a given card order. To get around this, define a new private constructor for the Deck class that allows a specific Cards collection to be passed in when the Deck object is instantiated. Here's the code to implement cloning in this class:

```
public class Deck : ICloneable
{
    public object Clone()
    {
        Deck newDeck = new Deck(cards.Clone() as Cards);
        return newDeck;
    }
```

```
        private Deck(Cards newCards)
        {
            cards = newCards;
        }
```

Again, you can test this out with some simple client code (as before, place this code within the `Main()` method of a client project for testing):

```
Deck deck1 = new Deck();
Deck deck2 = (Deck)deck1.Clone();
Console.WriteLine("The first card in the original deck is: {0}",
                  deck1.GetCard(0));
Console.WriteLine("The first card in the cloned deck is: {0}",
                  deck2.GetCard(0));
deck1.Shuffle();
Console.WriteLine("Original deck shuffled.");
Console.WriteLine("The first card in the original deck is: {0}",
                  deck1.GetCard(0));
Console.WriteLine("The first card in the cloned deck is: {0}",
                  deck2.GetCard(0));
Console.ReadKey();
```

The output will be something like what is shown in Figure 11-5.

Figure 11-5

Comparisons

This section covers two types of comparisons between objects:

❑ Type comparisons

❑ Value comparisons

Type comparisons — that is, determining what an object is, or what it inherits from — are important in all areas of C# programming. Often when you pass an object — to a method, for example — what happens next depends on what type the object is. You've seen this in passing in this and earlier chapters, but here you will see some more useful techniques.

Value comparisons are also something you've seen a lot of, at least with simple types. When it comes to comparing values of objects, things get a little more complicated. You have to define what is meant by a comparison for a start, and what operators such as > mean in the context of your classes. This is especially important in collections, for which you might want to sort objects according to some condition, perhaps alphabetically or according to a more complicated algorithm.

Type Comparison

When comparing objects, you often need to know their type, which may enable you to determine whether a value comparison is possible. In Chapter 9 you saw the `GetType()` method, which all classes inherit from `System.Object`, and how this method can be used in combination with the `typeof()` operator to determine (and take action depending on) object types:

```
if (myObj.GetType() == typeof(MyComplexClass))
{
    // myObj is an instance of the class MyComplexClass.
}
```

You've also seen how the default implementation of `ToString()`, also inherited from `System.Object`, will get you a string representation of an object's type. You can compare these strings too, although that's a rather messy way to accomplish this.

This section demonstrates a handy shorthand way of doing things: the `is` operator. This allows for much more readable code and, as you will see, has the advantage of examining base classes. Before looking at the `is` operator, though, you need to be aware of what often happens behind the scenes when dealing with value types (as opposed to reference types): boxing and unboxing.

Boxing and Unboxing

In Chapter 8, you learned the difference between reference types and value types, which was illustrated in Chapter 9 by comparing structs (which are value types) with classes (which are reference types). *Boxing* is the act of converting a value type into the `System.Object` type or to an interface type that is implemented by the value type. *Unboxing* is the opposite conversion.

For example, suppose you have the following struct type:

```
struct MyStruct
{
    public int Val;
}
```

You can box a struct of this type by placing it into an `object`-type variable:

```
MyStruct valType1 = new MyStruct();
valType1.Val = 5;
object refType = valType1;
```

Here, you create a new variable (`valType1`) of type `MyStruct`, assign a value to the `Val` member of this struct, and then box it into an `object`-type variable (`refType`).

The object created by boxing a variable in this way contains a reference to a copy of the value-type variable, not a reference to the original value-type variable. You can verify this by modifying the original struct's contents and then unboxing the struct contained in the object into a new variable and examining its contents:

```
valType1.Val = 6;
MyStruct valType2 = (MyStruct)refType;
Console.WriteLine("valType2.Val = {0}", valType2.Val);
```

This code gives you the following output:

```
valType2.Val = 5
```

When you assign a reference type to an object, however, you get a different behavior. You can illustrate this by changing `MyStruct` into a class (ignoring the fact that the name of this class isn't appropriate now):

```
class MyStruct
{
    public int Val;
}
```

With no changes to the client code shown previously (again ignoring the misnamed variables), you get the following output:

```
valType2.Val = 6
```

You can also box value types into interface types, so long as they implement that interface. For example, suppose the `MyStruct` type implements the `IMyInterface` interface as follows:

```
interface IMyInterface
{
}
```

```
struct MyStruct : IMyInterface
{
    public int Val;
}
```

You can then box the struct into an `IMyInterface` type as follows:

```
MyStruct valType1 = new MyStruct();
IMyInterface refType = valType1;
```

You can unbox it by using the normal casting syntax:

```
MyStruct ValType2 = (MyStruct)refType;
```

As you can see from these examples, boxing is performed without your intervention — that is, you don't have to write any code to make this possible. Unboxing a value requires an explicit conversion, however, and requires you to make a cast (boxing is implicit and doesn't have this requirement).

You might be wondering why you would actually want to do this. There are actually two very good reasons why boxing is extremely useful. First, it enables you to use value types in collections (such as `ArrayList`) where the items are of type `object`. Second, it's the internal mechanism that enables you to call `object` methods on value types, such as `ints` and `structs`.

As a final note, it is worth remarking that unboxing is necessary before access to the value type contents is possible.

The is Operator

Despite its name, the is operator isn't a way to tell whether an object *is* a certain type. Instead, the is operator enables you to check whether an object either is or *can be converted into* a given type. If this is the case, then the operator evaluates to true.

Earlier examples showed a Cow and a Chicken class, both of which inherit from Animal. Using the is operator to compare objects with the Animal type will return true for objects of all three of these types, not just Animal. This is something you'd have a hard time achieving with the GetType() method and typeof() operator shown previously.

The is operator has the following syntax:

```
<operand> is <type>
```

The possible results of this expression are as follows:

❑   If <type> is a class type, then the result is true if <operand> is of that type, if it inherits from that type, or if it can be boxed into that type.

❑   If <type> is an interface type, then the result is true if <operand> is of that type or it is a type that implements the interface.

❑   If <type> is a value type, then the result is true if <operand> is of that type or it is a type that can be unboxed into that type.

The following Try It Out shows how this works in practice.

Try It Out   **Using the is Operator**

1.   Create a new console application called Ch11Ex04 in the directory C:\BegVCSharp\Chapter11.

2.   Modify the code in Program.cs as follows:

```
namespace Ch11Ex04
{
    class Checker
    {
        public void Check(object param1)
        {
            if (param1 is ClassA)
                Console.WriteLine("Variable can be converted to ClassA.");
            else
                Console.WriteLine("Variable can't be converted to ClassA.");
            if (param1 is IMyInterface)
                Console.WriteLine("Variable can be converted to IMyInterface.");
            else
```

```
                    Console.WriteLine("Variable can't be converted to IMyInterface.");

            if (param1 is MyStruct)
                Console.WriteLine("Variable can be converted to MyStruct.");
            else
                Console.WriteLine("Variable can't be converted to MyStruct.");
        }
    }

interface IMyInterface
{
}

class ClassA : IMyInterface
{
}

class ClassB : IMyInterface
{
}

class ClassC
{
}

class ClassD : ClassA
{
}

struct MyStruct : IMyInterface
{
}

class Program
{
    static void Main(string[] args)
    {
        Checker check = new Checker();
        ClassA try1 = new ClassA();
        ClassB try2 = new ClassB();
        ClassC try3 = new ClassC();
        ClassD try4 = new ClassD();
        MyStruct try5 = new MyStruct();
        object try6 = try5;
        Console.WriteLine("Analyzing ClassA type variable:");
        check.Check(try1);

        Console.WriteLine("\nAnalyzing ClassB type variable:");
        check.Check(try2);
        Console.WriteLine("\nAnalyzing ClassC type variable:");
        check.Check(try3);
        Console.WriteLine("\nAnalyzing ClassD type variable:");
        check.Check(try4);
```

```
          Console.WriteLine("\nAnalyzing MyStruct type variable:");
          check.Check(try5);
          Console.WriteLine("\nAnalyzing boxed MyStruct type variable:");
          check.Check(try6);
          Console.ReadKey();
       }
     }
   }
```

3.   Execute the code. The result is shown in Figure 11-6.

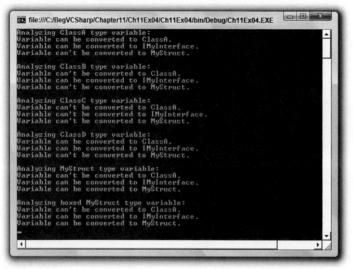

Figure 11-6

How It Works

This example illustrates the various results possible when using the `is` operator. Three classes, an interface, and a structure are defined and used as parameters to a method of a class that uses the `is` operator to determine whether they can be converted into the `ClassA` type, the interface type, and the struct type.

Only `ClassA` and `ClassD` (which inherits from `ClassA`) types are compatible with `ClassA`. Types that don't inherit from a class are not compatible with that class.

The `ClassA`, `ClassB`, and `MyStruct` types all implement `IMyInterface`, so these are all compatible with the `IMyInterface` type. `ClassD` inherits from `ClassA`, so that it too is compatible. Therefore, only `ClassC` is incompatible.

Finally, only variables of type `MyStruct` itself and boxed variables of that type are compatible with `MyStruct`, because you can't convert reference types to value types (although, of course, you can unbox previously boxed variables).

Value Comparison

Consider two `Person` objects representing people, each with an integer `Age` property. You might want to compare them to see which person is older. You can simply use the following code:

```
if (person1.Age > person2.Age)
{
    ...
}
```

This works fine, but there are alternatives. You might prefer to use syntax such as the following:

```
if (person1 > person2)
{
    ...
}
```

This is possible using operator overloading, which you'll look at in this section. This is a powerful technique, but it should be used judiciously. In the preceding code, it is not immediately obvious that ages are being compared — it could be height, weight, IQ, or just general "greatness."

Another option is to use the `IComparable` and `IComparer` interfaces, which enable you to define how objects will be compared to each other in a standard way. This technique is supported by the various collection classes in the .NET Framework, making it an excellent way to sort objects in a collection.

Operator Overloading

Operator overloading enables you to use standard operators, such as +, >, and so on, with classes that you design. This is called "overloading" because you are supplying your own implementations for these operators when used with specific parameter types, in much the same way that you overload methods by supplying different parameters for methods with the same name.

Operator overloading is useful because you can perform whatever processing you want in the implementation of the operator overload, which might not be as simple as, for example, +, meaning "add these two operands together." Later, you'll see a good example of this in a further upgrade of the `CardLib` library, whereby you'll provide implementations for comparison operators that compare two cards to see which would beat the other in a trick (one round of card game play).

Because a trick in many card games depends on the suits of the cards involved, this isn't as straightforward as comparing the numbers on the cards. If the second card laid down is a different suit from the first, then the first card wins regardless of its rank. You can implement this by considering the order of the two operands. You can also take a trump suit into account, where trumps beat other suits even if that isn't the first suit laid down. This means that calculating that `card1 > card2` is `true` (that is, `card1` will beat `card2` if `card1` is laid down first), doesn't necessarily imply that `card2 > card1` is `false`. If neither `card1` nor `card2` are trumps and they belong to different suits, then both these comparisons will be `true`.

To start with, though, here's a look at the basic syntax for operator overloading. Operators may be overloaded by adding operator type members (which must be `static`) to a class. Some operators have multiple uses (such as -, which has unary and binary capabilities); therefore, you also specify how many operands you are dealing with and what the types of these operands are. In general, you will have operands that are the same type as the class in which the operator is defined, although it is possible to define operators that work on mixed types, as you will see shortly.

As an example, consider the simple type `AddClass1`, defined as follows:

```
public class AddClass1
{
    public int val;
}
```

This is just a wrapper around an `int` value but it illustrates the principles. With this class, code such as the following will fail to compile:

```
AddClass1 op1 = new AddClass1();
op1.val = 5;
AddClass1 op2 = new AddClass1();
op2.val = 5;
AddClass1 op3 = op1 + op2;
```

The error you get informs you that the + operator cannot be applied to operands of the `AddClass1` type. This is because you haven't defined an operation to perform yet. Code such as the following works, but it won't give you the result you might want:

```
AddClass1 op1 = new AddClass1();
op1.val = 5;
AddClass1 op2 = new AddClass1();
op2.val = 5;
bool op3 = op1 == op2;
```

Here, op1 and op2 are compared by using the `==` binary operator to determine whether they refer to the same object, and *not* to verify whether their values are equal. op3 will be `false` in the preceding code, even though op1.val and op2.val are identical.

To overload the + operator, use the following code:

```
public class AddClass1
{
    public int val;

    public static AddClass1 operator +(AddClass1 op1, AddClass1 op2)
    {
        AddClass1 returnVal = new AddClass1();
        returnVal.val = op1.val + op2.val;
        return returnVal;
    }
}
```

As you can see, operator overloads look much like standard `static` method declarations, except that they use the keyword `operator` and the operator itself, rather than a method name. You can now successfully use the + operator with this class, as in the previous example:

```
AddClass1 op3 = op1 + op2;
```

Overloading all binary operators fits the same pattern. Unary operators look similar but have only one parameter:

```
public class AddClass1
{
    public int val;

    public static AddClass1 operator +(AddClass1 op1, AddClass1 op2)
    {
        AddClass1 returnVal = new AddClass1();
        returnVal.val = op1.val + op2.val;
        return returnVal;
    }

    public static AddClass1 operator -(AddClass1 op1)
    {
        AddClass1 returnVal = new AddClass1();
        returnVal.val = -op1.val;
        return returnVal;
    }
}
```

Both these operators work on operands of the same type as the class and have return values that are also of that type. Consider, however, the following class definitions:

```
public class AddClass1
{
    public int val;

    public static AddClass3 operator +(AddClass1 op1, AddClass2 op2)
    {
        AddClass3 returnVal = new AddClass3();
        returnVal.val = op1.val + op2.val;
        return returnVal;
    }
}

public class AddClass2
{
    public int val;
}

public class AddClass3
{
    public int val;
}
```

This will allow the following code:

```
AddClass1 op1 = new AddClass1();
op1.val = 5;
AddClass2 op2 = new AddClass2();
op2.val = 5;
AddClass3 op3 = op1 + op2;
```

When appropriate, you can mix types in this way. Note, however, that if you added the same operator to `AddClass2`, then the preceding code would fail, because it would be ambiguous as to which operator to use. You should, therefore, take care not to add operators with the same signature to more than one class.

In addition, if you mix types, then the operands *must* be supplied in the same order as the parameters to the operator overload. If you attempt to use your overloaded operator with the operands in the wrong order, then the operation will fail. For example, you can't use the operator like

```
AddClass3 op3 = op2 + op1;
```

unless, of course, you supply another overload with the parameters reversed:

```
public static AddClass3 operator +(AddClass2 op1, AddClass1 op2)
{
    AddClass3 returnVal = new AddClass3();
    returnVal.val = op1.val + op2.val;
    return returnVal;
}
```

The following operators can be overloaded:

❑ **Unary operators**: +, -, !, ~, ++, --, true, false

❑ **Binary operators**: +, -, *, /, %, &, |, ^, <<, >>

❑ **Comparison operators**: ==, !=, <, >, <=, >=

If you overload the `true` *and* `false` *operators, then you can use classes in Boolean expressions, such as* `if (op1) {}`.

You can't overload assignment operators, such as +=, but these operators use their simple counterparts, such as +, so you don't have to worry about that. Overloading + means that += will function as expected. The = operator can't be overloaded because it has such a fundamental usage, but this operator is related to the user-defined conversion operators, which you'll look at in the next section.

You also can't overload && and ||, but these operators use the & and | operators to perform their calculations, so overloading these is enough.

Some operators, such as < and >, must be overloaded in pairs. That is to say, you can't overload < unless you also overload >. In many cases, you can simply call other operators from these to reduce the code required (and the errors that might occur), as shown in this example:

```
public class AddClass1
{
    public int val;

    public static bool operator >=(AddClass1 op1, AddClass1 op2)
    {
        return (op1.val >= op2.val);
    }
```

```
    public static bool operator <(AddClass1 op1, AddClass1 op2)
    {
        return !(op1 >= op2);
    }

    // Also need implementations for <= and > operators.
}
```

In more complex operator definitions, this can reduce the lines of code. It also means that you have less code to change if you decide to change the implementation of these operators.

The same applies to == and !=, but with these operators it is often worth overriding `Object`
`.Equals()` and `Object.GetHashCode()`, because both of these functions may also be used to compare objects. By overriding these methods, you ensure that whatever technique users of the class use, they get the same result. This isn't essential, but is worth adding for completeness. It requires the following nonstatic override methods:

```
public class AddClass1
{
    public int val;

    public static bool operator ==(AddClass1 op1, AddClass1 op2)
    {
        return (op1.val == op2.val);
    }

    public static bool operator !=(AddClass1 op1, AddClass1 op2)
    {
        return !(op1 == op2);
    }

    public override bool Equals(object op1)
    {
        return val == ((AddClass1)op1).val;
    }

    public override int GetHashCode()
    {
        return val;
    }
}
```

`GetHashCode()` is used to obtain a unique `int` value for an object instance based on its state. Here, using `val` is fine, because it is also an `int` value.

Note that Equals() uses an object type parameter. You need to use this signature or you will be overloading this method, rather than overriding it, and the default implementation will still be accessible to users of the class. Instead, you must use casting to get the required result. It is often worth checking the object type using the is operator discussed earlier, in code such as this:

```
public override bool Equals(object op1)
{
    if (op1 is AddClass1)
    {
        return val == ((AddClass1)op1).val;
    }
    else
    {
        throw new ArgumentException(
            "Cannot compare AddClass1 objects with objects of type "
            + op1.GetType().ToString());
    }
}
```

In this code, an exception is thrown if the operand passed to Equals is of the wrong type or cannot be converted into the correct type. Of course, this behavior may not be what you want. You may want to be able to compare objects of one type with objects of another type, in which case more branching would be necessary. Alternatively, you may want to restrict comparisons to those in which both objects are of exactly the same type, which would require the following change to the first if statement:

```
if (op1.GetType() == typeof(AddClass1))
```

Adding Operator Overloads to CardLib

Now you'll upgrade your Ch11CardLib project again, adding operator overloading to the card class. First, though, you'll add the extra fields to the Card class that allow for trump suits and a choice to place Aces high. You make these static, because when they are set, they apply to all Card objects:

```
public class Card
{
    // Flag for trump usage. If true, trumps are valued higher
    // than cards of other suits.
    public static bool useTrumps = false;

    // Trump suit to use if useTrumps is true.
    public static Suit trump = Suit.Club;

    // Flag that determines whether aces are higher than kings or lower
    // than deuces.
    public static bool isAceHigh = true;
```

Note that these rules apply to all Card objects in every Deck in an application. It's not possible to have two decks of cards with cards contained in each that obey different rules. This is fine for this class library, however, as you can safely assume that if a single application wants to use separate rules, then it could maintain these itself, perhaps setting the static members of Card whenever decks are switched.

Because you have done this, it is worth adding a few more constructors to the `Deck` class to initialize decks with different characteristics:

```
public Deck()
{
    for (int suitVal = 0; suitVal < 4; suitVal++)
    {
        for (int rankVal = 1; rankVal < 14; rankVal++)
        {
            cards.Add(new Card((Suit)suitVal, (Rank)rankVal));
        }
    }
}
```

```
// Nondefault constructor. Allows aces to be set high.
public Deck(bool isAceHigh) : this()
{
    Card.isAceHigh = isAceHigh;
}
```

```
// Nondefault constructor. Allows a trump suit to be used.
public Deck(bool useTrumps, Suit trump) : this()
{
    Card.useTrumps = useTrumps;
    Card.trump = trump;
}
```

```
// Nondefault constructor. Allows aces to be set high and a trump suit
// to be used.
public Deck(bool isAceHigh, bool useTrumps, Suit trump) : this()
{
    Card.isAceHigh = isAceHigh;
    Card.useTrumps = useTrumps;
    Card.trump = trump;
}
```

Each of these constructors is defined by using the : this() syntax shown in Chapter 9, so in all cases, the default constructor is called before the nondefault one, initializing the deck.

Now add your operator overloads (and suggested overrides) to the `Card` class:

```
public Card(Suit newSuit, Rank newRank)
{
    suit = newSuit;
    rank = newRank;
}
```

```
public static bool operator ==(Card card1, Card card2)
{
    return (card1.suit == card2.suit) && (card1.rank == card2.rank);
}
```

```csharp
    public static bool operator !=(Card card1, Card card2)
    {
        return !(card1 == card2);
    }
```

```csharp
    public override bool Equals(object card)
    {
        return this == (Card)card;
    }
    public override int GetHashCode()
    {
        return 13*(int)rank + (int)suit;
    }
```

```csharp
    public static bool operator >(Card card1, Card card2)
    {
        if (card1.suit == card2.suit)
        {
            if (isAceHigh)
            {
                if (card1.rank == Rank.Ace)
                {
                    if (card2.rank == Rank.Ace)
                        return false;
                    else
                        return true;
                }
                else
                {
                    if (card2.rank == Rank.Ace)
                        return false;
                    else
                        return (card1.rank > card2.rank);
                }
            }
            else
            {
                return (card1.rank > card2.rank);
            }
        }
        else
        {
            if (useTrumps && (card2.suit == Card.trump))
                return false;
            else
                return true;
        }
    }
```

```csharp
    public static bool operator <(Card card1, Card card2)
    {
        return !(card1 >= card2);
    }

    public static bool operator >=(Card card1, Card card2)
```

```
        {
            if (card1.suit == card2.suit)
            {
                if (isAceHigh)
                {
                    if (card1.rank == Rank.Ace)
                    {
                        return true;
                    }
                    else
                    {
                        if (card2.rank == Rank.Ace)
                            return false;
                        else
                            return (card1.rank >= card2.rank);
                    }
                }
                else
                {
                    return (card1.rank >= card2.rank);
                }
            }
            else
            {
                if (useTrumps && (card2.suit == Card.trump))
                    return false;
                else
                    return true;
            }
        }
```

```
    public static bool operator <=(Card card1, Card card2)
    {
        return !(card1 > card2);
    }
```

There's not much to note here, except perhaps the slightly lengthy code for the > and >= overloaded operators. If you step through the code for >, you can see how it works and why these steps are necessary.

You are comparing two cards, `card1` and `card2`, where `card1` is assumed to be the first one laid down on the table. As discussed earlier, this becomes important when you are using trump cards, because a trump will beat a nontrump even if the nontrump has a higher rank. Of course, if the suits of the two cards are identical, then whether the suit is the trump suit or not is irrelevant, so this is the first comparison you make:

```
public static bool operator >(Card card1, Card card2)
{
    if (card1.suit == card2.suit)
    {
```

If the static `isAceHigh` flag is true, then you can't compare the cards' ranks directly via their value in the `Rank` enumeration, because the rank of ace has a value of 1 in this enumeration, which is less than that of all other ranks. Instead, use the following steps:

❑ If the first card is an ace, then check whether the second card is also an ace. If it is, then the first card won't beat the second. If the second card isn't an ace, then the first card wins:

```
if (isAceHigh)
{
    if (card1.rank == Rank.Ace)
    {
        if (card2.rank == Rank.Ace)
            return false;
        else
            return true;
    }
```

❑ If the first card isn't an ace, then you also need to check whether the second one is. If it is, then the second card wins; otherwise, you can compare the rank values because you know that aces aren't an issue:

```
    else
    {
        if (card2.rank == Rank.Ace)
            return false;
        else
            return (card1.rank > card2.rank);
    }
}
```

❑ If aces aren't high, then you can just compare the rank values:

```
else
{
    return (card1.rank > card2.rank);
}
```

The remainder of the code concerns the case where the suits of `card1` and `card2` are different. Here, the static `useTrumps` flag is important. If this flag is `true` and `card2` is of the trump suit, then you can say definitively that `card1` isn't a trump (because the two cards have different suits), and trumps always win, so `card2` is the higher card:

```
else
{
    if (useTrumps && (card2.suit == Card.trump))
        return false;
```

If `card2` isn't a trump (or `useTrumps` is `false`), then `card1` wins, because it was the first card laid down:

```
    else
        return true;
    }
}
```

Only one other operator (>=) uses code similar to this, and the other operators are very simple, so there's no need to go into more detail about them.

The following simple client code tests these operators (place it in the `Main()` function of a client project to test it, like the client code shown earlier in the earlier `CardLib` examples):

```
Card.isAceHigh = true;
Console.WriteLine("Aces are high.");
Card.useTrumps = true;
Card.trump = Suit.Club;
Console.WriteLine("Clubs are trumps.");

Card card1, card2, card3, card4, card5;
card1 = new Card(Suit.Club, Rank.Five);
card2 = new Card(Suit.Club, Rank.Five);
card3 = new Card(Suit.Club, Rank.Ace);
card4 = new Card(Suit.Heart, Rank.Ten);
card5 = new Card(Suit.Diamond, Rank.Ace);
Console.WriteLine("{0} == {1} ? {2}",
    card1.ToString(), card2.ToString(), card1 == card2);
Console.WriteLine("{0} != {1} ? {2}",
    card1.ToString(), card3.ToString(), card1 != card3);
Console.WriteLine("{0}.Equals({1}) ? {2}",
    card1.ToString(), card4.ToString(), card1.Equals(card4));
Console.WriteLine("Card.Equals({0}, {1}) ? {2}",
    card3.ToString(), card4.ToString(), Card.Equals(card3, card4));
Console.WriteLine("{0} > {1} ? {2}",
    card1.ToString(), card2.ToString(), card1 > card2);
Console.WriteLine("{0} <= {1} ? {2}",
    card1.ToString(), card3.ToString(), card1 <= card3);
Console.WriteLine("{0} > {1} ? {2}",
    card1.ToString(), card4.ToString(), card1 > card4);
Console.WriteLine("{0} > {1} ? {2}",
    card4.ToString(), card1.ToString(), card4 > card1);
Console.WriteLine("{0} > {1} ? {2}",
    card5.ToString(), card4.ToString(), card5 > card4);
Console.WriteLine("{0} > {1} ? {2}",
    card4.ToString(), card5.ToString(), card4 > card5);
Console.ReadKey();
```

The results are as shown in Figure 11-7.

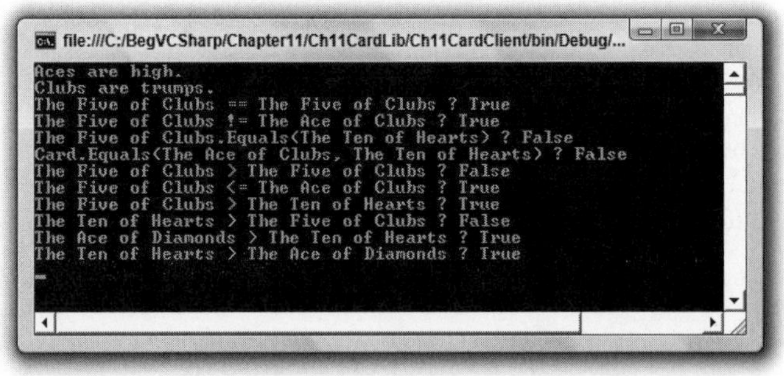

Figure 11-7

In each case, the operators are applied taking the specified rules into account. This is particularly apparent in the last four lines of output, demonstrating how trump cards always beat nontrumps.

The IComparable and IComparer Interfaces

The `IComparable` and `IComparer` interfaces are the standard way to compare objects in the .NET Framework. The difference between the interfaces is as follows:

❑ `IComparable` is implemented in the class of the object to be compared and allows comparisons between that object and another object.

❑ `IComparer` is implemented in a separate class, which allows comparisons between any two objects.

Typically, you give a class default comparison code by using `IComparable`, and nondefault comparisons using other classes.

`IComparable` exposes the single method `CompareTo()`, which accepts an object. You could, for example, implement it in a way that enables you to pass a `Person` object to it and determine whether that person is older or younger than the current person. In fact, this method returns an `int`, so you could also determine how much older or younger the second person is:

```
if (person1.CompareTo(person2) == 0)
{
    Console.WriteLine("Same age");
}
else if (person1.CompareTo(person2) > 0)
{
    Console.WriteLine("person 1 is Older");
}
else
{
    Console.WriteLine("person1 is Younger");
}
```

`IComparer` exposes the single method `Compare()`, which accepts two objects and returns an integer result just like `CompareTo()`. With an object supporting `IComparer`, you could use code like the following:

```
if (personComparer.Compare(person1, person2) == 0)
{
    Console.WriteLine("Same age");
}
else if (personComparer.Compare(person1, person2) > 0)
{
    Console.WriteLine("person 1 is Older");
}
else
{
    Console.WriteLine("person1 is Younger");
}
```

In both cases, the parameters supplied to the methods are of the type `System.Object`. This means that you can compare one object to another object of any other type, so you usually have to perform some type comparison before returning a result, and maybe even throw exceptions if the wrong types are used.

The .NET Framework includes a default implementation of the `IComparer` interface on a class called `Comparer`, found in the `System.Collections` namespace. This class is capable of performing culture-specific comparisons between simple types, as well as any type that supports the `IComparable` interface. You can use it, for example, with the following code:

```
string firstString = "First String";
string secondString = "Second String";
Console.WriteLine("Comparing '{0}' and '{1}', result: {2}",
    firstString, secondString,
    Comparer.Default.Compare(firstString, secondString));

int firstNumber = 35;
int secondNumber = 23;
Console.WriteLine("Comparing '{0}' and '{1}', result: {2}",
    firstNumber, secondNumber,
    Comparer.Default.Compare(firstNumber, secondNumber));
```

This uses the `Comparer.Default` static member to obtain an instance of the `Comparer` class, and then uses the `Compare()` method to compare first two strings, and then two integers.

The result is as follows:

```
Comparing 'First String' and 'Second String', result: -1
Comparing '35' and '23', result: 1
```

Because F comes before S in the alphabet, it is deemed "less than" S, so the result of the first comparison is -1. Similarly, 35 is greater than 23, hence the result of 1. Note that the results do not indicate the magnitude of the difference.

When using `Comparer`, you must use types that can be compared. Attempting to compare `firstString` with `firstNumber`, for example, will generate an exception.

Note a few more points about the behavior of this class:

❑   Objects passed to `Comparer.Compare()` are checked to determine whether they support `IComparable`. If they do, then that implementation is used.

❑   Null values are allowed, and are interpreted as being "less than" any other object.

❑   Strings are processed according to the current culture. To process strings according to a different culture (or language), the `Comparer` class must be instantiated using its constructor, which enables you to pass a `System.Globalization.CultureInfo` object specifying the culture to use.

❑   Strings are processed in a case-sensitive way. To process them in a non-case-sensitive way, you need to use the `CaseInsensitiveComparer` class, which otherwise works exactly the same.

Sorting Collections Using the *IComparable* and *IComparer* Interfaces

Many collection classes allow sorting, either by default comparisons between objects or by custom methods. `ArrayList` is one example. It contains the method `Sort()`, which can be used without parameters, in which case default comparisons are used, or it can be passed an `IComparer` interface to use to compare pairs of objects.

When you have an `ArrayList` filled with simple types, such as integers or strings, the default comparer is fine. For your own classes, you must either implement `IComparable` in your class definition or create a separate class supporting `IComparer` to use for comparisons.

Note that some classes in the `System.Collection` namespace, including `CollectionBase`, don't expose a method for sorting. If you want to sort a collection you have derived from this class, then you have to do a bit more work and sort the internal `List` collection yourself.

The following Try It Out shows how to use a default and nondefault comparer to sort a list.

Try It Out   Sorting a List

1. Create a new console application called Ch11Ex05 in the directory C:\BegVCSharp\Chapter11.

2. Add a new class called `Person`, and modify the code as follows:

```
namespace Ch11Ex05
{
    class Person : IComparable
    {
        public string Name;
        public int Age;

        public Person(string name, int age)
        {
            Name = name;
            Age = age;
        }

        public int CompareTo(object obj)
        {
            if (obj is Person)
            {
                Person otherPerson = obj as Person;
                return this.Age - otherPerson.Age;
            }
            else
            {
                throw new ArgumentException(
                    "Object to compare to is not a Person object.");
            }
        }
    }
}
```

3. Add another new class called `PersonComparerName` and modify the code as follows:

```
using System;
using System.Collections;
using System.Collections.Generic;
using System.Linq;
using System.Text;

namespace Ch11Ex05
{
    public class PersonComparerName : IComparer
    {
        public static IComparer Default = new PersonComparerName();

        public int Compare(object x, object y)
        {
            if (x is Person && y is Person)
            {
                return Comparer.Default.Compare(
                    ((Person)x).Name, ((Person)y).Name);
            }
            else
            {
                throw new ArgumentException(
                    "One or both objects to compare are not Person objects.");
            }
        }
    }
}
```

4. Modify the code in `Program.cs` as follows:

```
using System;
using System.Collections;
using System.Collections.Generic;
using System.Linq;
using System.Text;

namespace Ch11Ex05
{
    class Program
    {
        static void Main(string[] args)
        {
            ArrayList list = new ArrayList();
            list.Add(new Person("Jim", 30));
            list.Add(new Person("Bob", 25));
            list.Add(new Person("Bert", 27));
            list.Add(new Person("Ernie", 22));

            Console.WriteLine("Unsorted people:");
            for (int i = 0; i < list.Count; i++)
```

```
        {
            Console.WriteLine("{0} ({1})",
                (list[i] as Person).Name, (list[i] as Person).Age);
        }
        Console.WriteLine();

        Console.WriteLine(
            "People sorted with default comparer (by age):");
        list.Sort();
        for (int i = 0; i < list.Count; i++)
        {
            Console.WriteLine("{0} ({1})",
                (list[i] as Person).Name, (list[i] as Person).Age);
        }
        Console.WriteLine();

        Console.WriteLine(
            "People sorted with nondefault comparer (by name):");
        list.Sort(PersonComparerName.Default);
        for (int i = 0; i < list.Count; i++)
        {
            Console.WriteLine("{0} ({1})",
                (list[i] as Person).Name, (list[i] as Person).Age);
        }

        Console.ReadKey();
    }
  }
}
```

5. Execute the code. The result is shown in Figure 11-8.

Figure 11-8

How It Works

An `ArrayList` containing `Person` objects is sorted in two different ways here. By calling the `ArrayList.Sort()` method with no parameters, the default comparison is used, which is the `CompareTo()` method in the `Person` class (because this class implements `IComparable`):

```
public int CompareTo(object obj)
{
    if (obj is Person)
    {
        Person otherPerson = obj as Person;
        return this.Age - otherPerson.Age;
    }
    else
    {
        throw new ArgumentException(
            "Object to compare to is not a Person object.");
    }
}
```

This method first checks whether its argument can be compared to a `Person` object — that is, whether the object can be converted into a `Person` object. If there is a problem, then an exception is thrown. Otherwise, the `Age` properties of the two `Person` objects are compared.

Next, a nondefault comparison sort is performed using the `PersonComparerName` class, which implements `IComparer`. This class has a `public static` field for ease of use:

```
public static IComparer Default = new PersonComparerName();
```

This enables you to get an instance using `PersonComparerName.Default`, just like the `Comparer` class shown earlier. The `CompareTo()` method of this class is as follows:

```
public int Compare(object x, object y)
{
    if (x is Person && y is Person)
    {
        return Comparer.Default.Compare(
            ((Person)x).Name, ((Person)y).Name);
    }
    else
    {
        throw new ArgumentException(
            "One or both objects to compare are not Person objects.");
    }
}
```

Again, arguments are first checked to determine whether they are `Person` objects. If they aren't, then an exception is thrown. If they are, then the default `Comparer` object is used to compare the two string `Name` fields of the `Person` objects.

Conversions

Thus far, you have used casting whenever you have needed to convert one type into another, but this isn't the only way to do things. Just as an `int` can be converted into a `long` or a `double` implicitly as part of a calculation, you can define how classes you have created may be converted into other classes (either implicitly or explicitly). To do this, you overload conversion operators, much like other operators were overloaded earlier in this chapter. You'll see how in the first part of this section. You'll also see another useful operator, the `as` operator, which in general is preferable to casting when using reference types.

Overloading Conversion Operators

As well as overloading mathematical operators, as shown earlier, you can define both implicit and explicit conversions between types. This is necessary if you want to convert between types that aren't related — if there is no inheritance relationship between them and no shared interfaces, for example.

Suppose you define an implicit conversion between `ConvClass1` and `ConvClass2`. This means that you can write code such as the following:

```
ConvClass1 op1 = new ConvClass1();
ConvClass2 op2 = op1;
```

Alternatively, you can define an explicit conversion:

```
ConvClass1 op1 = new ConvClass1();
ConvClass2 op2 = (ConvClass2)op1;
```

As an example, consider the following code:

```
public class ConvClass1
{
    public int val;

    public static implicit operator ConvClass2(ConvClass1 op1)
    {
        ConvClass2 returnVal = new ConvClass2();
        returnVal.val = op1.val;
        return returnVal;
    }
}

public class ConvClass2
{
    public double val;

    public static explicit operator ConvClass1(ConvClass2 op1)
    {
        ConvClass1 returnVal = new ConvClass1();
        checked {returnVal.val = (int)op1.val;};
        return returnVal;
    }
}
```

Here, `ConvClass1` contains an int value and `ConvClass2` contains a double value. Because int values may be converted into double values implicitly, you can define an implicit conversion between `ConvClass1` and `ConvClass2`. The reverse is not true, however, and you should define the conversion operator between `ConvClass2` and `ConvClass1` as explicit.

You specify this using the `implicit` and `explicit` keywords as shown. With these classes, the following code is fine:

```
ConvClass1 op1 = new ConvClass1();
op1.val = 3;
ConvClass2 op2 = op1;
```

A conversion in the other direction, however, requires the following explicit casting conversion:

```
ConvClass2 op1 = new ConvClass2();
op1.val = 3e15;
ConvClass1 op2 = (ConvClass1)op1;
```

Because you have used the `checked` keyword in your explicit conversion, you will get an exception in the preceding code, as the `val` property of op1 is too large to fit into the `val` property of op2.

The as Operator

The `as` operator converts a type into a specified reference type, using the following syntax:

```
<operand> as <type>
```

This is only possible in certain circumstances:

❑   If <operand> is of type <type>.

❑   If <operand> can be implicitly converted to type <type>.

❑   If <operand> can be boxed into type <type>.

If no conversion from <operand> to <type> is possible, then the result of the expression will be `null`.

Note that conversion from a base class to a derived class is possible by using an explicit conversion, but it won't always work. Consider the two classes `ClassA` and `ClassD` from an earlier example, where `ClassD` inherits from `ClassA`:

```
class ClassA : IMyInterface
{
}

class ClassD : ClassA
{
}
```

The following code uses the as operator to convert from a ClassA instance stored in obj1 into the ClassD type:

```
ClassA obj1 = new ClassA();
ClassD obj2 = obj1 as ClassD;
```

This will result in obj2 being null.

However, it is possible to store ClassD instances in ClassA-type variables by using polymorphism. The following code illustrates this and uses the as operator to convert from a ClassA-type variable containing a ClassD-type instance into the ClassD type:

```
ClassD obj1 = new ClassD();
ClassA obj2 = obj1;
ClassD obj3 = obj2 as ClassD;
```

This time the result is that obj3 ends up containing a reference to the same object as obj1, not null.

This functionality makes the as operator very useful, because the following code (which uses simple casting) results in an exception being thrown:

```
ClassA obj1 = new ClassA();
ClassD obj2 = (ClassD)obj1;
```

The as equivalent of this code results in a null value being assigned to obj2 — no exception is thrown. This means that code such as the following (using two of the classes developed earlier in this chapter, Animal and a class derived from Animal called Cow) is very common in C# applications:

```
public void MilkCow(Animal myAnimal)
{
    Cow myCow = myAnimal as Cow;
    if (myCow != null)
    {
        myCow.Milk();
    }
    else
    {
        Console.WriteLine("{0} isn't a cow, and so can't be milked.",
            myAnimal.Name);
    }
}
```

This is much simpler than checking for exceptions!

Summary

This chapter covered many of the techniques that you can use to make your OOP applications far more powerful — and more interesting. Although these techniques take a little effort to accomplish, they can make your classes much easier to work with and therefore simplify the task of writing the rest of the code.

Each of the topics covered has many uses. You're likely to come across collections of one form or another in almost any application, and creating strongly typed collections can make your life much easier if you need to work with a group of objects of the same type. You also learned how you can add indexers and iterators to get easy access to objects within the collection.

Comparisons and conversions are another topic that crops up repeatedly. You learned how to perform various comparisons, and saw some of the underlying functionality of boxing and unboxing. You also learned how to overload operators for both comparisons and conversions, and how to link things together with list sorting.

The next chapter covers something entirely new — generics. These enable you to create classes that automatically customize themselves to work with dynamically chosen types. This is especially useful with collections, and you'll see how a lot of the code in this chapter can be simplified dramatically using generic collections.

Exercises

1. Create a collection class called `People` that is a collection of the `Person` class shown below. The items in the collection should be accessible via a string indexer that is the name of the person, identical to the `Person.Name` property:

```
public class Person
{
    private string name;
    private int age;

    public string Name
    {
        get
        {
            return name;
        }
        set
        {
            name = value;
        }
    }

    public int Age
    {
        get
        {
            return age;
        }
        set
        {
            age = value;
        }
    }
}
```

2. Extend the `Person` class from the preceding exercise so that the `>`, `<`, `>=`, and `<=` operators are overloaded, and compare the `Age` properties of `Person` instances.

3. Add a `GetOldest` method to the `People` class that returns an array of `Person` objects with the greatest `Age` property (one or more objects, as multiple items may have the same value for this property), using the overloaded operators defined previously.

4. Implement the `ICloneable` interface on the `People` class to provide deep copying capability.

5. Add an iterator to the `People` class that enables you to get the ages of all members in a `foreach` loop as follows:

```
foreach (int age in myPeople.Ages)
{
    // Display ages.
}
```

12

Generics

One of the (admittedly few) criticisms leveled against the first version of C# was its lack of support for *generics*. Generics in C++ (known as *templates* in that language) had long been regarded as an excellent way of doing things, as it allowed a single type definition to spawn a multitude of specialized types at compile time and thus save an awful lot of time and effort. For whatever reason, generics didn't quite make it into the first release of C#, and the language suffered because of it. Perhaps it was because generics are often seen as being quite difficult to get a handle on, or maybe it was decided that they weren't necessary. Fortunately, with C# version 2.0 generics have joined the party. Even better, they aren't very difficult to use, although they do require a slightly different way of looking at things.

In this chapter you do all of the following:

❑ Examine what a generic is. You learn about generics in fairly abstract terms at first, because learning the concepts behind generics is crucial to being able to use them effectively.

❑ See some of the generic types in the .NET Framework in action. This will help you to understand their functionality and power, as well as the new syntax required in your code.

❑ Define your own generic types, including generic classes, interfaces, methods, and delegates. You also learn additional techniques for further customizing generic types: the `default` keyword and type constraints.

What Is a Generic?

To best illustrate what a generic is, and why they are so useful, recall the collection classes from the last chapter. You saw how basic collections can be contained in classes such as `ArrayList`, but that such collections suffer from being untyped, so you need to cast `object` items into whatever type of objects you actually stored in the collection. Because anything that inherits from `System.Object` (that is, practically anything) can be stored in an `ArrayList`, you need to be careful. Assuming that certain types are all that is contained in a collection can lead to exceptions being thrown, and code logic breaking down. You learned some techniques to deal with this, including the code required to check the type of an object.

However, you discovered that a much better solution is to use a strongly typed collection class initially. By deriving from `CollectionBase` and providing your own methods for adding, removing, and otherwise accessing members of the collection, you learned how you could restrict collection members to those derived from a certain base type or supporting a certain interface. This is where you encounter a problem. Every time you create a new class that needs to be held in a collection, you must do one of the following:

❑ Use a collection class you've already made that can contain items of the new type.

❑ Create a new collection class that can hold items of the new type, implementing all the required methods.

Typically, with a new type you need extra functionality, so more often that not you need a new collection class anyway. Therefore, making collection classes may take up a fair amount of your time!

Generic classes, conversely, make things a lot simpler. A generic class is one that is built around whatever type, or types, you supply during instantiation, enabling you to strongly type an object with hardly any effort at all. In the context of collections, creating a "collection of type `T` objects" is as simple as saying it aloud — and achievable in a single line of code. Instead of code such as:

```
CollectionClass col = new CollectionClass();
col.Add(new ItemClass());
```

You can use:

```
CollectionClass<ItemClass> col = new CollectionClass<ItemClass>();
col.Add(new ItemClass());
```

The angle bracket syntax is the way you pass variable types to generic types. In the preceding code, read `CollectionClass<ItemClass>` as `CollectionClass` of `ItemClass`. You will, of course, examine this syntax in more detail later in the chapter.

There's more to the subject of generics than just collections, but they are particularly suited to this area, as you will see later in the chapter when you look at the `System.Collections.Generic` namespace. By creating a generic class, you can generate methods that have a signature that can be strongly typed to any type you wish, even catering to the fact that a type may be a value or reference type, and deal with individual cases as they occur. You can even allow only a subset of types to be used, by restricting the types used to instantiate a generic class to those that support a given interface or are derived from a certain type. Moreover, you're not restricted to generic classes — you can create generic interfaces, generic methods (which can be defined on nongeneric classes), and even generic delegates. All this adds a great deal of flexibility to your code, and judicious use of generics can eliminate hours of development time.

You're probably wondering how all this is possible. Usually, when you create a class it is compiled into a type that you can then use in your code. You might think that when you create a generic class it would have to be compiled into a plethora of types, so that you could instantiate it. Fortunately, that's not the case — and given the infinite amount of classes possible in .NET, that's just as well. Behind the scenes, the .NET runtime allows generic classes to be dynamically generated as and when you need them. A given generic class *A* of *B* won't even exist until you ask for it by instantiating it.

For those who are familiar with C++, or are interested, this is one difference between C++ templates and C# generic classes. In C++ the compiler detects where you used a specific type of template — for example, A of B — and compiles the code necessary to create this type. In C# everything happens at runtime.

To summarize, generics enable you to create flexible types that process objects of one or more specific types, where these types are determined when you instantiate or otherwise use the generic. Now it's time to see them in action.

Using Generics

Before you look at how to create your own generics, it's worth looking at those that are supplied by the .NET Framework. These include the types in the `System.Collections.Generic` namespace, a namespace that you've seen several times in your code because it is included by default in console applications. You haven't yet used any of the types in this namespace, but that's about to change. This section looks at the types in this namespace and how you can use them to create strongly typed collections and improve the functionality of your existing collections.

First, though, you'll look at another, simpler generic type that gets around a minor issue with value types: *nullable types.*

Nullable Types

In earlier chapters, you saw that one of the ways in which value types (which include most of the basic types such as `int` and `double` as well as all structs) differ from reference types (`string` and any class) is that they must contain a value. They can exist in an unassigned state, just after they are declared and before a value is assigned, but you can't make use of this in any way. Conversely, reference types may be `null`.

There are times, and they crop up more often than you might think (particularly when you work with databases), when it is useful to have a value type that can be `null`. Generics give you a way to do this using the `System.Nullable<T>` type, as shown in this example:

```
System.Nullable<int> nullableInt;
```

This code declares a variable called `nullableInt`, which can have any value that an `int` variable can, plus the value `null`. This enables you to write code such as the following:

```
nullableInt = null;
```

If `nullableInt` were an `int` type variable, then the preceding code wouldn't compile.

The preceding assignment is equivalent to the following:

```
nullableInt = new System.Nullable<int>();
```

As with any other variable, you can't just use it before some kind of initialization, whether to `null` (through either syntax shown above) or by assigning a value.

You can test nullable types to determine whether they are `null`, just like you test reference types:

```
if (nullableInt == null)
{
    ...
}
```

Alternatively, you can use the `HasValue` property:

```
if (nullableInt.HasValue)
{
    ...
}
```

This wouldn't work for reference types, even one with a `HasValue` property of its own, because having a `null` valued reference type variable means that no object exists through which to access this property, and an exception would be thrown.

You can also look at the value of a nullable type by using the `Value` property. If `HasValue` is `true`, then you are guaranteed a non-null value for `Value`. But if `HasValue` is `false` — that is, `null` has been assigned to the variable — then accessing `Value` will result in an exception of type `System` `.InvalidOperationException`.

Note that nullable types are so useful that they have resulted in a modification of C# syntax. Rather than use the syntax shown above to declare a nullable type variable, you can instead use the following:

```
int? nullableInt;
```

`int?` is simply a shorthand for `System.Nullable<int>` but is much more readable. In subsequent sections, you'll use this syntax.

Operators and Nullable Types

With simple types, such as `int`, you can use operators such as +, -, and so on to work with values. With nullable type equivalents, there is no difference: The values contained in nullable types are implicitly converted to the required type and the appropriate operators are used. This also applies to structs with operators that you have supplied:

```
int? op1 = 5;
int? result = op1 * 2;
```

Note that here the `result` variable is also of type `int?`. The following code will not compile:

```
int? op1 = 5;
int result = op1 * 2;
```

To get this to work you must perform an explicit conversion:

```
int? op1 = 5;
int result = (int)op1 * 2;
```

This works fine as long as `op1` has a value — if it is `null`, then you will get an exception of type `System.InvalidOperationException`.

This raises the obvious question: What happens when one or both values in an operator evaluation are `null`, such as `op1` in the preceding code? The answer is that for all simple nullable types other than `bool?`, the result of the operation is `null`, which you can interpret as "unable to compute." For structs you can define your own operators to deal with this situation (as shown later in the chapter), and for `bool?` there are operators defined for `&` and `|` that may result in non-`null` return values. These are shown in the following table:

OP1	OP2	OP1 & OP2	OP1 | OP2
true	true	true	true
true	false	false	true
true	null	null	true
false	true	false	true
false	false	false	false
false	null	false	null
null	true	null	true
null	false	false	null
null	null	null	null

The results in the table make perfect sense logically — if there is enough information to work out the answer of the computation without needing to know the value of one of the operands, then it doesn't matter if that operand is `null`.

The ?? Operator

To further reduce the amount of code you need in order to deal with nullable types, and to make it easier to deal with variables that can be `null`, you can use the `??` operator. Known as the *null coalescing operator*, it is a binary operator that enables you to supply an alternative value to use for expressions that might evaluate to `null`. The operator evaluates to its first operand if the first operand is not `null`, or to its second operator if the first operand is `null`. Functionally, the following two expressions are equivalent:

```
op1 ?? op2
op1 == null ? op2 : op1
```

In this code, `op1` can be any nullable expression, including a reference type and, importantly, a nullable type. This means that you can use the `??` operator to provide default values to use if a nullable type is `null`, as shown here:

```
int? op1 = null;
int result = op1 * 2 ?? 5;
```

Because in this example op1 is null, op1 * 2 will also be null. However, the ?? operator detects this and assigns the value 5 to result. Importantly, note here that no explicit conversion is required to put the result in the int type variable result. The ?? operator handles this conversion for you. Alternatively, you can pass the result of a ?? evaluation into an int? with no problems:

```
int? result = op1 * 2 ?? 5;
```

This makes the ?? operator a versatile one to use when dealing with nullable variables, and a handy way to supply defaults without using either a block of code in an if structure or the often confusing tertiary operator.

Use the following Try It Out to experiment with a nullable Vector type.

Try It Out   Nullable Types

1. Create a new console application project called Ch12Ex01 and save it in the directory C:\BegVCSharp\Chapter12.

2. Add a new class called Vector in the file Vector.cs.

3. Modify the code in Vector.cs as follows:

```
public class Vector
{
    public double? R = null;
    public double? Theta = null;

    public double? ThetaRadians
    {
        get
        {
            // Convert degrees to radians.
            return (Theta * Math.PI / 180.0);
        }
    }

    public Vector(double? r, double? theta)
    {
        // Normalize.
        if (r < 0)
        {
            r = -r;
            theta += 180;
        }
        theta = theta % 360;

        // Assign fields.
        R = r;
```

```
        Theta = theta;
   }

   public static Vector operator +(Vector op1, Vector op2)
   {
      try
      {
         // Get (x, y) coordinates for new vector.
         double newX = op1.R.Value * Math.Sin(op1.ThetaRadians.Value)
            + op2.R.Value * Math.Sin(op2.ThetaRadians.Value);
         double newY = op1.R.Value * Math.Cos(op1.ThetaRadians.Value)
            + op2.R.Value * Math.Cos(op2.ThetaRadians.Value);

         // Convert to (r, theta).
         double newR = Math.Sqrt(newX * newX + newY * newY);
         double newTheta = Math.Atan2(newX, newY) * 180.0 / Math.PI;

         // Return result.
         return new Vector(newR, newTheta);
      }
      catch
      {
         // Return "null" vector.
         return new Vector(null, null);
      }
   }

   public static Vector operator -(Vector op1)
   {
      return new Vector(-op1.R, op1.Theta);
   }

   public static Vector operator -(Vector op1, Vector op2)
   {
      return op1 + (-op2);
   }

   public override string ToString()
   {
      // Get string representation of coordinates.
      string rString = R.HasValue ? R.ToString() : "null";
      string thetaString = Theta.HasValue ? Theta.ToString() : "null";

      // Return (r, theta) string.
      return string.Format("({0}, {1})", rString, thetaString);
   }
}
```

4. Modify the code in `Program.cs` as follows:

```
class Program
{
    static void Main(string[] args)
    {
        Vector v1 = GetVector("vector1");
        Vector v2 = GetVector("vector1");
        Console.WriteLine("{0} + {1} = {2}", v1, v2, v1 + v2);
        Console.WriteLine("{0} - {1} = {2}", v1, v2, v1 - v2);
        Console.ReadKey();
    }

    static Vector GetVector(string name)
    {
        Console.WriteLine("Input {0} magnitude:", name);
        double? r = GetNullableDouble();
        Console.WriteLine("Input {0} angle (in degrees):", name);
        double? theta = GetNullableDouble();
        return new Vector(r, theta);
    }

    static double? GetNullableDouble()
    {
        double? result;
        string userInput = Console.ReadLine();
        try
        {
            result = double.Parse(userInput);
        }
        catch
        {
            result = null;
        }
        return result;
    }
}
```

5. Execute the application and enter values for two vectors. Sample output is shown in Figure 12-1.

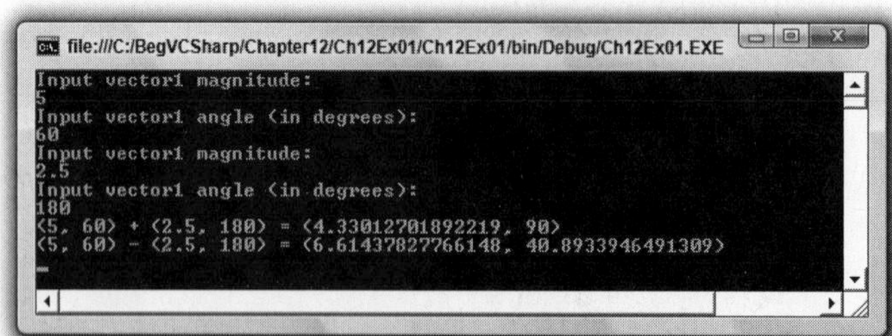

Figure 12-1

6. Execute the application again, but this time skip at least one of the four values. Sample output is shown in Figure 12-2.

Figure 12-2

How It Works

This example created a class called `Vector` that represents a vector with polar coordinates (that is, with a magnitude and an angle), as shown in Figure 12-3.

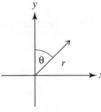

Figure 12-3

The coordinates *r* and *θ* are represented in code by the public fields `R` and `Theta`, where `Theta` is expressed in degrees. `ThetaRad` is supplied to obtain the value of `Theta` in radians — this is necessary because the `Math` class uses radians in its static methods. Both `R` and `Theta` are of type `double?`, so they can be `null`:

```
public class Vector
{
    public double? R = null;
    public double? Theta = null;

    public double? ThetaRadians
    {
        get
        {
            // Convert degrees to radians.
            return (Theta * Math.PI / 180.0);
        }
    }
}
```

The constructor for `Vector` normalizes the initial values of `R` and `Theta` and then assigns the public fields:

```
public Vector(double? r, double? theta)
{
    // Normalize.
    if (r < 0)
    {
        r = -r;
        theta += 180;
    }
    theta = theta % 360;

    // Assign fields.
    R = r;
    Theta = theta;
}
```

The main functionality of the `Vector` class is to add and subtract vectors using operator overloading, which requires some fairly basic trigonometry not covered here. The important thing about the code is that if an exception is thrown when obtaining the `Value` property of `R` or `ThetaRadians` — that is, if either is `null` — then a "null" vector is returned:

```
public static Vector operator +(Vector op1, Vector op2)
{
    try
    {
        // Get (x, y) coordinates for new vector.
        ...
    }
    catch
    {
        // Return "null" vector.
        return new Vector(null, null);
    }
}
```

If either of the coordinates making up a vector is `null`, then the vector is invalid, which is signified here by a `Vector` class with `null` values for both `R` and `Theta`. The rest of the code in the `Vector` class overrides the other operators required to extend the addition functionality to include subtraction, and overrides `ToString()` to obtain a string representation of a `Vector` object.

The code in `Program.cs` tests the `Vector` class by enabling the user to initialize two vectors, and then adds and subtracts them to and from one another. Should the user omit a value, it will be interpreted as `null`, and the rules mentioned previously apply.

The System.Collections.Generics Namespace

In practically every application used so far in this book, you have seen the following namespaces:

```
using System;
using System.Collections.Generic;
using System.Linq;
using System.Text;
```

The System namespace contains most of the basic types used in .NET applications. The System.Text namespace includes types relating to string processing and encoding. The System.Linq namespace you'll look at later in this book, from Chapter 26 onward. But what about System.Collections .Generic, and why is it included by default in console applications?

The answer is that this namespace contains generic types for dealing with collections, and it is likely to be used so often that it is configured with a using statement, ready for you to use without qualification.

As promised earlier in the chapter, you'll now look at these types, which are guaranteed to make your life easier. They make it possible for you to create strongly typed collection classes with hardly any effort. The following table lists two types from the System.Collections.Generics namespace that are covered in this section. More of the types in this namespace are covered later in this chapter.

Type	Description
List<T>	Collection of type T objects
Dictionary<K, V>	Collection of items of type V, associated with keys of type K

This section also describes various interfaces and delegates used with these classes.

List<T>

Rather than derive a class from CollectionBase and implement the required methods as you did in the last chapter, it can be quicker and easier simply to use the List<T> generic collection type. An added bonus here is that many of the methods you'd normally have to implement, such as Add(), are implemented for you.

Creating a collection of type T objects requires the following code:

```
List<T> myCollection = new List<T>();
```

That's it. You don't have to define any classes, implement any methods, or do anything else. You can also set a starting list of items in the collection by passing a `List<T>` object to the constructor. An object instantiated using this syntax supports the methods and properties shown in the following table (where the type supplied to the `List<T>` generic is `T`):

Member	Description
`int Count`	Property providing the number of items in the collection.
`void Add(T item)`	Adds an item to the collection.
`void AddRange(IEnumerable<T>)`	Adds multiple items to the collection.
`IList<T> AsReadOnly()`	Returns a read-only interface to the collection.
`int Capacity`	Gets or sets the number of items that the collection can contain.
`void Clear()`	Removes all items from the collection.
`bool Contains(T item)`	Determines whether the item is contained in the collection.
`void CopyTo(T[] array, int index)`	Copies the items in the collection into the array `array`, starting from index `index` in the array.
`IEnumerator<T> GetEnumerator()`	Obtains an `IEnumerator<T>` instance for iteration through the collection. Note that the interface returned is strongly typed to `T`, so no casting is required in `foreach` loops.
`int IndexOf(T item)`	Obtains the index of the item, or –1 if the item is not contained in the collection.
`void Insert(int index, T item)`	Inserts the item into the collection at the specified index.
`bool Remove(T item)`	Removes the first occurrence of the item from the collection and returns `true`. If the item is not contained in the collection, it returns `false`.
`void RemoveAt(int index)`	Removes the item at index `index` from the collection.

`List<T>` also has an `Item` property, enabling array-like access:

```
T itemAtIndex2 = myCollectionOfT[2];
```

This class supports several other methods, but that's plenty to get you started. The following Try It Out demonstrates how to use `Collection<T>` in practice.

Try It Out   Using List<T>

1. Create a new console application called Ch12Ex02 and save it in the directory
C:\BegVCSharp\Chapter12.

2. Right-click on the project name in the Solution Explorer window, and select the Add ⇨ Add
Existing Item option.

3. Select the `Animal.cs`, `Cow.cs`, and `Chicken.cs` files from the C:\BegVCSharp\Chapter11\
Ch11Ex01\Ch11Ex01 directory and click Add.

4. Modify the namespace declaration in the three files you added as follows:

```
namespace Ch12Ex02
```

5. Modify `Program.cs` as follows:

```
static void Main(string[] args)
{
    List<Animal> animalCollection = new List<Animal>();
    animalCollection.Add(new Cow("Jack"));
    animalCollection.Add(new Chicken("Vera"));
    foreach (Animal myAnimal in animalCollection)
    {
        myAnimal.Feed();
    }
    Console.ReadKey();
}
```

6. Execute the application. The result is exactly the same as the result for Ch11Ex02 in the last
chapter.

How It Works

There are only two differences between this example and Ch11Ex02. The first is that the line of code

```
Animals animalCollection = new Animals();
```

has been replaced with

```
List<Animal> animalCollection = new List<Animal>();
```

The second, and more crucial, difference is that there is no longer an `Animals` collection class in the
project. All that hard work you did earlier to create this class was achieved in a single line of code by
using a generic collection class.

An alternate way to get the same result is to leave the code in `Program.cs` as it was in the last chapter,
and use the following definition of `Animals`:

```
public class Animals : List<Animal>
{
}
```

Doing this has the advantage that the code in `Program.cs` is slightly easier to read, plus you can add additional members to the `Animals` class as you see fit.

You may, of course, be wondering why you'd ever want to derive classes from `CollectionBase`, which is a good question. In fact, there aren't many situations where you would. It's certainly a good thing to know how things work internally because `List<T>` works in much the same way, but `CollectionBase` is basically there for backward compatibility. The only situation in which you might want to use `CollectionBase` is when you want much more control over the members exposed to users of the class. For example, if you wanted a collection class with an internal access modifier on its `Add()` method, then using `CollectionBase` might be the best option.

> You can also pass an initial capacity to use to the constructor of `List<T>` (as an int), or an initial list of items using an `IEnumerable<T>` interface. Classes supporting this interface include `List<T>`.

Sorting and Searching Generic Lists

Sorting a generic list is much the same as sorting any other list. The last chapter described how you can use the `IComparer` and `IComparable` interfaces to compare two objects and thereby sort a list of that type of object. The only difference here is that you can use the generic interfaces `IComparer<T>` and `IComparable<T>`, which expose slightly different, type-specific methods. The following table explains these differences:

Generic Method	Nongeneric Method	Difference
`int IComparable<T>.CompareTo(T otherObj)`	`int IComparable.CompareTo(object otherObj)`	Strongly typed in generic versions
`bool IComparable<T>.Equals(T otherObj)`	N/A	Doesn't exist on a nongeneric interface; can use inherited `object.Equals()` instead
`int IComparer<T>.Compare(T objectA, T objectB)`	`int IComparer.Compare(object objectA, object object B)`	Strongly typed in generic versions
`bool IComparer<T>.Equals(T objectA, T objectB)`	N/A	Doesn't exist on a nongeneric interface; can use inherited `object.Equals()` instead
`int IComparer<T>.GetHashCode(T objectA)`	N/A	Doesn't exist on a nongeneric interface; can use inherited `object.GetHashCode()` instead

To sort a `List<T>` you can supply an `IComparable<T>` interface on the type to be sorted, or supply an `IComparer<T>` interface. Alternatively, you can supply a *generic delegate* as a sorting method. From the perspective of seeing how things are done, this is far more interesting because implementing the interfaces shown above is really no more effort than implementing their nongeneric cousins.

In general terms, all you need to sort a list is a method that compares two objects of type T; and to search, all you need is a method that checks an object of type T to determine whether it meets certain criteria. It is a simple matter to define such methods, and to aid you there are two generic delegate types that you can use:

❑   `Comparison<T>` — A delegate type for a method used for sorting, with the following return type and parameters:

```
int method(T objectA, T objectB)
```

❑   `Predicate<T>` — A delegate type for a method used for searching, with the following return type and parameters:

```
bool method(T targetObject)
```

You can define any number of such methods, and use them to "snap-in" to the searching and sorting methods of `List<T>`. The next Try It Out illustrates this.

Try It Out   **Sorting and Searching List<T>**

1.   Create a new console application called Ch12Ex03 and save it in the directory C:\BegVCSharp\Chapter12.

2.   Right-click on the project name in the Solution Explorer window and select the Add ➪ Add Existing Item option.

3.   Select the `Vector.cs` file from the C:\BegVCSharp\Chapter12\Ch12Ex01\Ch12Ex01 directory and click Add.

4.   Modify the namespace declaration in the file you added as follows:

```
namespace Ch12Ex03
```

5.   Add a new class called `Vectors`.

6.   Modify `Vectors.cs` as follows:

```
public class Vectors : List<Vector>
{
    public Vectors()
    {
    }

    public Vectors(IEnumerable<Vector> initialItems)
    {
        foreach (Vector vector in initialItems)
        {
            Add(vector);
```

```
        }
    }

    public string Sum()
    {
        StringBuilder sb = new StringBuilder();
        Vector currentPoint = new Vector(0.0, 0.0);
        sb.Append("origin");
        foreach (Vector vector in this)
        {
            sb.AppendFormat(" + {0}", vector);
            currentPoint += vector;
        }
        sb.AppendFormat(" = {0}", currentPoint);
        return sb.ToString();
    }
}
```

7. Add a new class called `VectorDelegates`.

8. Modify `VectorDelegates.cs` as follows:

```
public static class VectorDelegates
{
    public static int Compare(Vector x, Vector y)
    {
        if (x.R > y.R)
        {
            return 1;
        }
        else if (x.R < y.R)
        {
            return -1;
        }
        return 0;
    }

    public static bool TopRightQuadrant(Vector target)
    {
        if (target.Theta >= 0.0 && target.Theta <= 90.0)
        {
            return true;
        }
        else
        {
            return false;
        }
    }
}
```

9. Modify `Program.cs` as follows:

```
static void Main(string[] args)
{
    Vectors route = new Vectors();
    route.Add(new Vector(2.0, 90.0));
    route.Add(new Vector(1.0, 180.0));
    route.Add(new Vector(0.5, 45.0));
    route.Add(new Vector(2.5, 315.0));

    Console.WriteLine(route.Sum());

    Comparison<Vector> sorter = new Comparison<Vector>(VectorDelegates.Compare);
    route.Sort(sorter);
    Console.WriteLine(route.Sum());

    Predicate<Vector> searcher =
        new Predicate<Vector>(VectorDelegates.TopRightQuadrant);
    Vectors topRightQuadrantRoute = new Vectors(route.FindAll(searcher));
    Console.WriteLine(topRightQuadrantRoute.Sum());

    Console.ReadKey();
}
```

10. Execute the application. The result is shown in Figure 12-4.

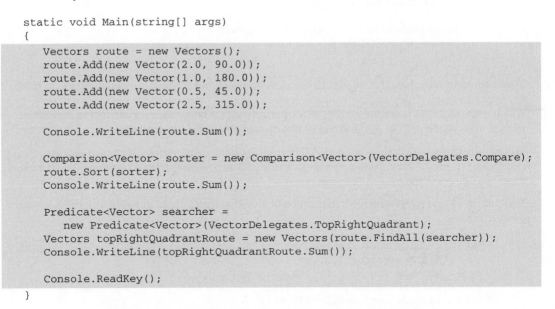

Figure 12-4

How It Works

In this example, you have created a collection class, `Vectors`, for the `Vector` class created in Ch12Ex01. You could just use a variable of type `List<Vector>`, but because you want additional functionality you use a new class, `Vectors`, and derive from `List<Vector>`, which enables you to add whatever additional members you want.

One member, `Sum()`, returns a string listing each vector in turn, along with the result of summing them all together (using the overloaded + operator from the original `Vector` class). Because each vector can be thought of as a direction and a distance, this effectively constitutes a route with an endpoint:

```
public string Sum()
{
    StringBuilder sb = new StringBuilder();
    Vector currentPoint = new Vector(0.0, 0.0);
    sb.Append("origin");
    foreach (Vector vector in this)
    {
```

```
        sb.AppendFormat(" + {0}", vector);
        currentPoint += vector;
    }
    sb.AppendFormat(" = {0}", currentPoint);
    return sb.ToString();
}
```

This method uses the handy `StringBuilder` class, found in the `System.Text` namespace, to build the response string. This class has members such as `Append()` and `AppendFormat()` (used here), which make it easy to assemble a string — the performance is better than concatenating individual strings. You use the `ToString()` method of this class to obtain the resultant string.

You also create two methods to be used as delegates, as static members of `VectorDelegates`. `Compare()` is used for comparison (sorting), and `TopRightQuadrant()` for searching. You'll look at these as you review the code in `Program.cs`.

The code in `Main()` starts with the initialization of a `Vectors` collection, to which are added several `Vector` objects:

```
Vectors route = new Vectors();
route.Add(new Vector(2.0, 90.0));
route.Add(new Vector(1.0, 180.0));
route.Add(new Vector(0.5, 45.0));
route.Add(new Vector(2.5, 315.0));
```

The `Vectors.Sum()` method is used to write out the items in the collection as noted earlier, this time in their initial order:

```
Console.WriteLine(route.Sum());
```

Next, you create the first of your delegates, `sorter`. This delegate is of type `Comparison<Vector>` and, therefore, can be assigned a method with the following return type and parameters:

```
int method(Vector objectA, Vector objectB)
```

This matches `VectorDelegates.Compare()`, which is the method you assign to the delegate:

```
Comparison<Vector> sorter = new Comparison<Vector>(VectorDelegates.Compare);
```

`Compare()` compares the magnitudes of two vectors as follows:

```
public static int Compare(Vector x, Vector y)
{
    if (x.R > y.R)
    {
        return 1;
    }
    else if (x.R < y.R)
    {
        return -1;
    }
    return 0;
}
```

This enables you to order the vectors by magnitude:

```
route.Sort(sorter);
Console.WriteLine(route.Sum());
```

The output of the application gives the result you'd expect — the result of the summation is the same because the endpoint of following the "vector route" is the same regardless of the order in which you carry out the individual steps.

Next, you obtain a subset of the vectors in the collection by searching. This uses VectorDelegates .TopRightQuadrant():

```
public static bool TopRightQuadrant(Vector target)
{
    if (target.Theta >= 0.0 && target.Theta <= 90.0)
    {
        return true;
    }
    else
    {
        return false;
    }
}
```

This method returns true if its Vector argument has a value of Theta between 0 and 90 degrees — that is, it points up and/or right in a diagram of the sort shown earlier.

In the Main() method, you use this method via a delegate of type Predicate<Vector> as follows:

```
Predicate<Vector> searcher =
    new Predicate<Vector>(VectorDelegates.TopRightQuadrant);
Vectors topRightQuadrantRoute = new Vectors(route.FindAll(searcher));
Console.WriteLine(topRightQuadrantRoute.Sum());
```

This requires the constructor defined in Vectors:

```
public Vectors(IEnumerable<Vector> initialItems)
{
    foreach (Vector vector in initialItems)
    {
        Add(vector);
    }
}
```

Here, you initialize a new Vectors collection using an interface of IEnumerable<Vector>, which is necessary because List<Vector>.FindAll() returns a List<Vector> instance, not a Vectors instance.

The result of the searching is that only a subset of Vector objects is returned, so (again, as you'd expect) the result of the summation is different. The use of these generic delegate types to sort and search generic collections can take a little while to get used to, but the result is code that is streamlined and efficient, and which has a highly logical structure. It is well worth investing the time to learn the techniques presented in this section.

Dictionary<K, V>

The Dictionary<K, V> type enables you to define a collection of key-value pairs. Unlike the other generic collection types you've looked at in this chapter, this class requires instantiating two types: the types for both the key and value that represent each item in the collection.

Once a Dictionary<K, V> object is instantiated, you can perform much the same operations on it as you can on a class that inherits from DictionaryBase, but with type-safe methods and properties already in place. You can, for example, add key-value pairs using a strongly typed Add() method:

```
Dictionary<string, int> things = new Dictionary<string, int>();
things.Add("Green Things", 29);
things.Add("Blue Things", 94);
things.Add("Yellow Things", 34);
things.Add("Red Things", 52);
things.Add("Brown Things", 27);
```

You can iterate through keys and values in the collection by using the Keys and Values properties:

```
foreach (string key in things.Keys)
{
    Console.WriteLine(key);
}

foreach (int value in things.Values)
{
    Console.WriteLine(value);
}
```

In addition, you can iterate through items in the collection by obtaining each as a KeyValuePair<K, V> instance, much like you can with the DictionaryEntry objects shown in the last chapter:

```
foreach (KeyValuePair<string, int> thing in things)
{
    Console.WriteLine("{0} = {1}", thing.Key, thing.Value);
}
```

One thing to note about Dictionary<K, V> is that the key for each item must be unique. Attempting to add an item with an identical key to one already added will cause an ArgumentException exception to be thrown. Because of this, Dictionary<K, V> allows you to pass an IComparer<K> interface to its constructor. This may be necessary if you use your own classes as keys and they don't support an IComparable or IComparable<K> interface, or should you want to compare objects using a nondefault process. For instance, in the preceding example shown, you could use a case-insensitive method to compare string keys:

```
Dictionary<string, int> things =
    new Dictionary<string, int>(StringComparer.CurrentCultureIgnoreCase);
```

Now you'll get an exception if you use keys such as this:

```
things.Add("Green Things", 29);
things.Add("Green things", 94);
```

You can also pass an initial capacity (with an `int`) or set of items (with an `IDictionary<K,V>` interface) to the constructor.

Modifying CardLib to Use a Generic Collection Class

One simple modification you can make to the CardLib project you've been building over recent chapters is to change the `Cards` collection class to use a generic collection class, thus saving many lines of code. The required modification to the class definition for `Cards` is as follows:

```
public class Cards : List<Card>, ICloneable
{
    ...
}
```

You can also remove all the methods of `Cards` except `Clone()`, which is required for `ICloneable`, and `CopyTo()`, because the version of `CopyTo()` supplied by `List<Card>` works with an array of `Card` objects, not a `Cards` collection. `Clone()` requires a minor modification because the `List<T>` class does not define a `List` property to use:

```
public object Clone()
{
    Cards newCards = new Cards();
    foreach (Card sourceCard in this)
    {
        newCards.Add(sourceCard.Clone() as Card);
    }
    return newCards;
}
```

Rather than show the code here for what is a very simple modification, the updated version of CardLib, called Ch12CardLib, is included in the downloadable code for this chapter, along with the client code from the last chapter.

Defining Generics

You've now learned enough about generics to create your own. You've seen plenty of code involving generic types and have had plenty of practice using generic syntax. In this section, you'll look at defining the following:

- ❑ Generic classes
- ❑ Generic interfaces
- ❑ Generic methods
- ❑ Generic delegates

You'll also look at the following more advanced techniques for dealing with the issues that come up when defining generic types:

❑   The default keyword

❑   Constraining types

❑   Inheriting from generic classes

❑   Generic operators

Defining Generic Classes

To create a generic class, merely include the angle bracket syntax in the class definition:

```
class MyGenericClass<T>
{
    ...
}
```

Here, T can be any identifier you like, following the usual C# naming rules, such as not starting with a number and so on. Typically, though, you can just use T. A generic class can have any number of types in its definition, separated by commas:

```
class MyGenericClass<T1, T2, T3>
{
    ...
}
```

Once these types are defined, you can use them in the class definition just like any other type. You can use them as types for member variables, return types for members such as properties or methods, and parameter types for method arguments:

```
class MyGenericClass<T1, T2, T3>
{
    private T1 innerT1Object;

    public MyGenericClass(T1 item)
    {
        innerT1Object = item;
    }

    public T1 InnerT1Object
    {
        get
        {
            return innerT1Object;
        }
    }
}
```

Here, an object of type T1 can be passed to the constructor, and read-only access is permitted to this object via the property InnerT1Object. Note that you can make practically no assumptions as to what the types supplied to the class are. The following code, for example, will not compile:

```
class MyGenericClass<T1, T2, T3>
{
    private T1 innerT1Object;

    public MyGenericClass()
    {
        innerT1Object = new T1();
    }

    public T1 InnerT1Object
    {
        get
        {
            return innerT1Object;
        }
    }
}
```

Because you don't know what T1 is, you can't use any of its constructors — it might not even have any, or it may have no publicly accessible default constructor. Without more complicated code involving the techniques shown later in this section, you can pretty much make only the following assumption about T1: You can treat it as a type that either inherits from or can be boxed into System.Object.

Obviously, this means that you can't really do anything very interesting with instances of this type, or any of the other types supplied to the generic class MyGenericClass. Without using *reflection*, which is an advanced technique used to examine types at runtime (and not covered in this chapter), you're limited pretty much to code as complicated as the following:

```
public string GetAllTypesAsString()
{
    return "T1 = " + typeof(T1).ToString()
        + ", T2 = " + typeof(T2).ToString()
        + ", T3 = " + typeof(T3).ToString();
}
```

There is a bit more that you can do, particularly in terms of collections, because dealing with groups of objects is a pretty simple process and doesn't need any assumptions about the object types — which is one good reason why the generic collection classes you've seen in this chapter exist.

Another limitation that you need to be aware of is that using the operator `==` or `!=` is only permitted when comparing a value of a type supplied to a generic type to `null`. That is, the following code works fine:

```
public bool Compare(T1 op1, T1 op2)
{
    if (op1 != null && op2 != null)
    {
        return true;
    }
    else
    {
        return false;
    }
}
```

Here, if `T1` is a value type, then it is always assumed to be non-`null`, so in the preceding code `Compare` will always return `true`. However, attempting to compare the two arguments `op1` and `op2` fails to compile:

```
public bool Compare(T1 op1, T1 op2)
{
    if (op1 == op2)
    {
        return true;
    }
    else
    {
        return false;
    }
}
```

This is because this code assumes that `T1` supports the `==` operator. In short, to do anything really interesting with generics, you need to know a bit more about the types used in the class.

The default Keyword

One of the most basic things you might want to know about types used to create generic class instances is whether they are reference types or value types. Without knowing this you can't even assign `null` values with code such as this:

```
public MyGenericClass()
{
    innerT1Object = null;
}
```

If T1 is a value type, then innerT1Object can't have the value null, so this code won't compile. Luckily, this problem has been addressed, resulting in a new use for the default keyword (which you've seen being used in switch structures earlier in the book). This is used as follows:

```
public MyGenericClass()
{
    innerT1Object = default(T1);
}
```

The result of this is that innerT1Object is assigned a value of null if it is a reference type, or a default value if it is a value type. This default value is 0 for numeric types, while structs have each of their members initialized to 0 or null in the same way. The default keyword gets you a bit further in terms of doing a little more with the types you are forced to use, but to truly get ahead you need to constrain the types that are supplied.

Constraining Types

The types you have used with generic classes until now are known as *unbounded* types because no restrictions are placed on what they can be. By *constraining* types, it is possible to restrict the types that can be used to instantiate a generic class. There are a number of ways to do this. For example, it's possible to restrict a type to one that inherits from a certain type. Referring back to the Animal, Cow, and Chicken classes used earlier, you could restrict a type to one that was or inherited from Animal, so this code would be fine:

```
MyGenericClass<Cow> = new MyGenericClass<Cow>();
```

The following, however, would fail to compile:

```
MyGenericClass<string> = new MyGenericClass<string>();
```

In your class definitions this is achieved using the where keyword:

```
class My GenericClass<T> where T : constraint
{
    . . .
}
```

Here, constraint defines what the constraint is. You can supply a number of constraints in this way by separating them with commas:

```
class MyGenericClass<T> where T : constraint1, constraint2
{
    . . .
}
```

You can define constraints on any or all of the types required by the generic class by using multiple where statements:

```
class MyGenericClass<T1, T2> where T1 : constraint1 where T2 : constraint2
{
    . . .
}
```

Any constraints that you use must appear after the inheritance specifiers:

```
class MyGenericClass<T1, T2> : MyBaseClass, IMyInterface
   where T1 : constraint1 where T2 : constraint2
{
   . . .
}
```

The available constraints are shown in the following table:

Constraint	Definition	Example Usage
struct	Type must be a value type	In a class that requires value types to function — for example, where a member variable of type T being 0 means something
class	Type must be a reference type	In a class that requires reference types to function — for example, where a member variable of type T being null means something
base-class	Type must be, or inherit from, base-class. You can supply any class name as this constraint	In a class that requires certain baseline functionality inherited from base-class in order to function
interface	Type must be, or implement, interface	In a class that requires certain baseline functionality exposed by interface in order to function
new()	Type must have a public, parameterless constructor	In a class where you need to be able to instantiate variables of type T, perhaps in a constructor

If new() is used as a constraint, it must *be the last constraint specified for a type.*

It is possible to use one type parameter as a constraint on another through the base-class constraint as follows:

```
class MyGenericClass<T1, T2> where T2 : T1
{
   . . .
}
```

Here, T2 must be the same type as T1 or inherit from T1. This is known as a *naked type constraint*, meaning that one generic type parameter is used as a constraint on another.

Circular type constraints, as shown here, are forbidden:

```
class MyGenericClass<T1, T2> where T2 : T1 where T1 : T2
{
   . . .
}
```

This code will not compile. In the following Try It Out, you'll define and use a generic class that uses the `Animal` family of classes shown in earlier chapters.

Try It Out   **Defining a Generic Class**

1.   Create a new console application called Ch12Ex04 and save it in the directory C:\BegVCSharp\Chapter12.

2.   Right-click on the project name in the Solution Explorer window and select the Add ⇨ Add Existing Item option.

3.   Select the `Animal.cs`, `Cow.cs`, and `Chicken.cs` files from the C:\BegVCSharp\Chapter12\ Ch12Ex02\Ch12Ex02 directory, and click Add.

4.   Modify the namespace declaration in the file you have added as follows:

```
namespace Ch12Ex04
```

5.   Modify `Animal.cs` as follows:

```
public abstract class Animal
{
    ...

    public abstract void MakeANoise();
}
```

6.   Modify `Chicken.cs` as follows:

```
public class Chicken : Animal
{
    ...

    public override void MakeANoise()
    {
        Console.WriteLine("{0} says 'cluck!'", name);
    }
}
```

7.   Modify `Cow.cs` as follows:

```
public class Cow : Animal
{
    ...

    public override void MakeANoise()
    {
        Console.WriteLine("{0} says 'moo!'", name);
    }
}
```

8. Add a new class called `SuperCow` and modify the code in `SuperCow.cs` as follows:

```csharp
public class SuperCow : Cow
{
    public void Fly()
    {
        Console.WriteLine("{0} is flying!", name);
    }

    public SuperCow(string newName) : base(newName)
    {
    }

    public override void MakeANoise()
    {
        Console.WriteLine("{0} says 'here I come to save the day!'", name);
    }
}
```

9. Add a new class called `Farm` and modify the code in `Farm.cs` as follows:

```csharp
using System;
using System.Collections;
using System.Collections.Generic;
using System.Linq;
using System.Text;

namespace Ch12Ex04
{
    public class Farm<T> : IEnumerable<T>
        where T : Animal
    {
        private List<T> animals = new List<T>();

        public List<T> Animals
        {
            get
            {
                return animals;
            }
        }

        public IEnumerator<T> GetEnumerator()
        {
            return animals.GetEnumerator();
        }

        IEnumerator IEnumerable.GetEnumerator()
        {
            return animals.GetEnumerator();
        }

        public void MakeNoises()
```

```
    {
        foreach (T animal in animals)
        {
            animal.MakeANoise();
        }
    }

    public void FeedTheAnimals()
    {
        foreach (T animal in animals)
        {
            animal.Feed();
        }
    }

    public Farm<Cow> GetCows()
    {
        Farm<Cow> cowFarm = new Farm<Cow>();
        foreach (T animal in animals)
        {
            if (animal is Cow)
            {
                cowFarm.Animals.Add(animal as Cow);
            }
        }
        return cowFarm;
    }
}
}
```

10.   Modify `Program.cs` as follows:

```
static void Main(string[] args)
{
    Farm<Animal> farm = new Farm<Animal>();
    farm.Animals.Add(new Cow("Jack"));
    farm.Animals.Add(new Chicken("Vera"));
    farm.Animals.Add(new Chicken("Sally"));
    farm.Animals.Add(new SuperCow("Kevin"));
    farm.MakeNoises();

    Farm<Cow> dairyFarm = farm.GetCows();
    dairyFarm.FeedTheAnimals();

    foreach (Cow cow in dairyFarm)
    {
        if (cow is SuperCow)
        {
            (cow as SuperCow).Fly();
        }
    }
    Console.ReadKey();
}
```

11. Execute the application. The result is shown in Figure 12-5.

Figure 12-5

How It Works

In this example, you have created a generic class called `Farm<T>`, which, rather than inheriting from a generic list class, exposes a generic list class as a public property. The type of this list is determined by the type parameter `T` that is passed to `Farm<T>` and is constrained to be or inherit from `Animal`:

```
public class Farm<T> : IEnumerable<T>
    where T : Animal
{
    private List<T> animals = new List<T>();

    public List<T> Animals
    {
        get
        {
            return animals;
        }
    }
}
```

`Farm<T>` also implements `IEnumerable<T>`, where `T` is passed into this generic interface and is therefore also constrained in the same way. You implement this interface to make it possible to iterate through the items contained in `Farm<T>` without needing to explicitly iterate over `Farm<T>.Animals`. This is simple to achieve: You simply return the enumerator exposed by `Animals`, which is a `List<T>` class that also implements `IEnumerable<T>`:

```
public IEnumerator<T> GetEnumerator()
{
    return animals.GetEnumerator();
}
```

Because `IEnumerable<T>` inherits from `IEnumerable`, you also need to implement `IEnumerable.GetEnumerator()`:

```
IEnumerator IEnumerable.GetEnumerator()
{
    return animals.GetEnumerator();
}
```

Next, `Farm<T>` includes two methods that make use of methods of the abstract `Animal` class:

```
public void MakeNoises()
{
    foreach (T animal in animals)
    {
        animal.MakeANoise();
    }
}

public void FeedTheAnimals()
{
    foreach (T animal in animals)
    {
        animal.Feed();
    }
}
```

Because `T` is constrained to `Animal`, this code compiles fine — you are guaranteed to have access to these methods whatever `T` actually is.

The next method, `GetCows()`, is more interesting. This method simply extracts all the items in the collection that are of type `Cow` (or that inherit from `Cow`, such as the new `SuperCow` class):

```
public Farm<Cow> GetCows()
{
    Farm<Cow> cowFarm = new Farm<Cow>();
    foreach (T animal in animals)
    {
        if (animal is Cow)
        {
            cowFarm.Animals.Add(animal as Cow);
        }
    }
    return cowFarm;
}
```

What is interesting here is that this method seems a bit wasteful. If you wanted other methods of the same sort, such as `GetChickens()` and so on, you'd need to implement them explicitly too. In a system with many more types, you'd need many more methods. A far better solution here would be to use a *generic method*, which you'll implement a little later in the chapter.

The client code in `Program.cs` simply tests the various methods of `Farm` and doesn't really contain much you haven't already seen, so there's no need to examine this code in any greater detail — despite the flying cow.

Inheriting from Generic Classes

The `Farm<T>` class in the preceding example, as well as several other classes you've seen in this chapter, inherit from a generic type. In the case of `Farm<T>`, this type was an interface: `IEnumerable<T>`. Here, the constraint on `T` supplied by `Farm<T>` resulted in an additional constraint on `T` used in `IEnumerable<T>`. This can be a useful technique for constraining otherwise unbounded types. However, some rules need to be followed.

First, you can't "unconstrain" types that are constrained in a type you are inheriting from. In other words, a type T that is used in a type you are inheriting from must be constrained at least as much as it is in that type. For example, the following code is fine:

```
class SuperFarm<T> : Farm<T>
     where T : SuperCow
{
}
```

This works because T is constrained to Animal in Farm<T>, and constraining it to SuperCow is constraining T to a subset of these values. However, the following won't compile:

```
class SuperFarm<T> : Farm<T>
     where T : struct
{
}
```

Here, you can say definitively that the type T supplied to SuperFarm<T> cannot be converted into a T usable by Farm<T>, so the code won't compile.

Even situations where the constraint is a superset have the same problem:

```
class SuperFarm<T> : Farm<T>
     where T : class
{
}
```

Even though types such as Animal would be allowed by SuperFarm<T>, other types that satisfy the class constraint won't be allowed in Farm<T>. Again, compilation will fail. This rule applies to all the constraint types shown earlier in this chapter.

Also note that if you inherit from a generic type, then you must supply all the required type information, either in the form of other generic type parameters, as shown above, or explicitly. This also applies to nongeneric classes that inherit from generic types, as you've seen elsewhere. Here's an example:

```
public class Cards : List<Card>, ICloneable
{
}
```

This is fine, but attempting the following will fail:

```
public class Cards : List<T>, ICloneable
{
}
```

Here, no information is supplied for T, so no compilation is possible.

If you supply a parameter to a generic type, as in List<Card> *above, then you can refer to the type as* closed. *Similarly, inheriting from* List<T> *is inheriting from an* open *generic type.*

Generic Operators

Operator overrides are implemented in C# just like other methods and can be implemented in generic classes. For example, you could define the following implicit conversion operator in Farm<T>:

```
public static implicit operator List<Animal>(Farm<T> farm)
{
    List<Animal> result = new List<Animal>();
    foreach (T animal in farm)
    {
        result.Add(animal);
    }
    return result;
}
```

This allows the Animal objects in a Farm<T> to be accessed directly as a List<Animal> should you require it. This comes in handy if you want to add two Farm<T> instances together, such as with the following operators:

```
public static Farm<T> operator +(Farm<T> farm1, List<T> farm2)
{
    Farm<T> result = new Farm<T>();
    foreach (T animal in farm1)
    {
        result.Animals.Add(animal);
    }
    foreach (T animal in farm2)
    {
        if (!result.Animals.Contains(animal))
        {
            result.Animals.Add(animal);
        }
    }
    return result;
}

public static Farm<T> operator +(List<T> farm1, Farm<T> farm2)
{
    return farm2 + farm1;
}
```

You could then add instances of Farm<Animal> and Farm<Cow> as follows:

```
Farm<Animal> newFarm = farm + dairyFarm;
```

In this code, dairyFarm (an instance of Farm<Cow>) is implicitly converted into List<Animal>, which is usable by the overloaded + operator in Farm<T>.

You might think that this could be achieved simply by using the following:

```
public static Farm<T> operator +(Farm<T> farm1, Farm<T> farm2)
{
    Farm<T> result = new Farm<T>();
    foreach (T animal in farm1)
    {
        result.Animals.Add(animal);
    }
    foreach (T animal in farm2)
    {
        if (!result.Animals.Contains(animal))
        {
            result.Animals.Add(animal);
        }
    }
    return result;
}
```

However, because `Farm<Cow>` cannot be converted into `Farm<Animal>`, the summation will fail. To take this a step further, you could solve this using the following conversion operator:

```
public static implicit operator Farm<Animal>(Farm<T> farm)
{
    Farm <Animal> result = new Farm <Animal>();
    foreach (T animal in farm)
    {
        result.Animals.Add(animal);
    }
    return result;
}
```

With this operator, instances of `Farm<T>`, such as `Farm<Cow>`, can be converted into instances of `Farm<Animal>`, solving the problem. You can use either of the methods shown, although the latter is preferable for its simplicity.

Generic Structs

You learned in earlier chapters that structs are essentially the same as classes, barring some minor differences and the fact that a struct is a value type, not a reference type. Because this is the case, *generic structs* can be created in the same way as generic classes, as shown here:

```
public struct MyStruct<T1, T2>
{
    public T1 item1;
    public T2 item2;
}
```

Defining Generic Interfaces

You've now seen several generic interfaces in use — namely, those in the `Systems.Collections` `.Generic` namespace such as `IEnumerable<T>` used in the last example. Defining a generic interface involves the same techniques as defining a generic class:

```
interface MyFarmingInterface<T>
   where T : Animal
{
   bool AttemptToBreed(T animal1, T animal2);

   T OldestInHerd
   {
      get;
   }
}
```

Here, the generic parameter `T` is used as the type of the two arguments of `AttemptToBreed()` and the type of the `OldestInHerd` property.

The same inheritance rules apply as for classes. If you inherit from a base generic interface, you must obey the rules, such as keeping the constraints of the base interface generic type parameters.

Defining Generic Methods

The last Try It Out used a method called `GetCows()`, and in the discussion of the example it was stated that you could make a more general form of this method using a *generic method*. In this section you'll see how this is possible. A generic method is one in which the return and/or parameter types are determined by a generic type parameter or parameters:

```
public T GetDefault<T>()
{
   return default(T);
}
```

This trivial example uses the default keyword you looked at earlier in the chapter to return a default value for a type `T`. This method is called as follows:

```
int myDefaultInt = GetDefault<T>();
```

The type parameter `T` is provided at the time the method is called.

This `T` is quite separate from the types used to supply generic type parameters to classes. In fact, generic methods can be implemented by nongeneric classes:

```
public class Defaulter
{
   public T GetDefault<T>()
   {
      return default(T);
   }
}
```

If the class is generic, though, then you must use different identifiers for generic method types. The following code won't compile:

```
public class Defaulter<T>
{
    public T GetDefault<T>()
    {
        return default(T);
    }
}
```

The type T used by either the method or the class must be renamed.

Constraints can be used by generic method parameters in the same way that they are for classes, and in this case you can make use of any class type parameters:

```
public class Defaulter<T1>
{
    public T2 GetDefault<T2>()
        where T2 : T1
    {
        return default(T2);
    }
}
```

Here, the type T2 supplied to the method must be the same as, or inherit from, T1 supplied to the class. This is a common way to constrain generic methods.

In the Farm<T> class shown earlier, you could include the following method (included, but commented out, in the downloadable code for Ch12Ex04):

```
public Farm<U> GetSpecies<U>() where U : T
{
    Farm<U> speciesFarm = new Farm<U>();
    foreach (T animal in animals)
    {
        if (animal is U)
        {
            speciesFarm.Animals.Add(animal as U);
        }
    }
    return speciesFarm;
}
```

This can replace GetCows() and any other methods of the same type. The generic type parameter used here, U, is constrained by T, which is in turn constrained by the Farm<T> class to Animal. This enables you to treat instances of T as instances of Animal, should you wish to do so.

In the client code for Ch12Ex04, in `Program.cs`, using this new method requires one modification:

```
Farm<Cow> dairyFarm = farm.GetSpecies<Cow>();
```

You could equally write:

```
Farm<Chicken> dairyFarm = farm.GetSpecies<Chicken>();
```

or any other class that inherits from `Animal`.

Note here that having generic type parameters on a method changes the signature of the method. This means you can have several overloads of a method differing only in generic type parameters, as shown in this example:

```
public void ProcessT<T>(T op1)
{
    ...
}
```

```
public void ProcessT<T, U>(T op1)
{
    ...
}
```

Which method should be used is determined by the amount of generic type parameters specified when the method is called.

Defining Generic Delegates

The last generic type to consider is the *generic delegate*. You saw these in action earlier in the chapter when you learned how to sort and search generic lists. You used the `Comparison<T>` and `Predicate<T>` delegates, respectively, for this.

Chapter 7 described how to define delegates using the parameters and return type of a method, the delegate keyword, and a name for the delegate:

```
public delegate int MyDelegate(int op1, int op2);
```

To define a generic delegate, you simply declare and use one or more generic type parameters:

```
public delegate T1 MyDelegate<T1, T2>(T2 op1, T2 op2) where T1 : T2;
```

As you can see, constraints can be applied here too, where the same rules apply to the constraints. You'll learn a lot more about delegates in the next chapter, including how you can use them in a common C# programming technique — events.

Summary

In this chapter, you examined how to use generic types in C# and learned how to create your own generic types, including classes, interfaces, methods, and delegates. You also looked at how to use structs, including how to create nullable types, and how to use the classes in the System.Collecitons .Generic namespace.

Generics, as you saw, are an extremely powerful new technique in C#. You can use them to create classes that satisfy several purposes at the same time, and they can be used in a variety of situations. Even if you don't have any reason to create your own generic types, you're almost certain to use the generic collection classes repeatedly.

In the next chapter, you'll continue your examination of the basic C# language by tying up a few loose ends and looking at events.

Exercises

1. Which of the following can be generic?

   a. classes

   b. methods

   c. properties

   d. operator overloads

   e. structs

   f. enumerations

2. Extend the Vector class in Ch12Ex01 such that the * operator returns the dot product of two vectors.

   The dot product of two vectors is defined as the product of their magnitudes multiplied by the cosine of the angle between them.

3. What is wrong with the following code? Fix it.

```
public class Instantiator<T>
{
    public T instance;

    public Instantiator()
    {
        instance = new T();
    }
}
```

4. What is wrong with the following code? Fix it.

```
public class StringGetter<T>
{
    public string GetString<T>(T item)
    {
        return item.ToString();
    }
}
```

5. Create a generic class called `ShortCollection<T>` that implements `IList<T>` and consists of a collection of items with a maximum size. This maximum size should be an integer that can be supplied to the constructor of `ShortCollection<T>` or defaults to 10. The constructor should also be able to take an initial list of items via a `List<T>` parameter. The class should function exactly like `Collection<T>` but throw an exception of type `IndexOutOfRangeException` if an attempt is made to add too many items to the collection, or if the `List<T>` passed to the constructor contains too many items.

Additional OOP Techniques

In this chapter, you continue exploring the C# language by looking at a few bits and pieces that haven't quite fit in elsewhere. This isn't to say that these techniques aren't useful — just that they don't fall under any of the headings you've worked through so far.

Specifically, you will look at the following:

❑   The : : operator and the global namespace qualifier

❑   Custom exceptions and exception recommendations

❑   Events

❑   Anonymous methods

You also make some final modifications to the CardLib code that you've been building in the last few chapters, and even use CardLib to create a card game.

The :: Operator and the Global Namespace Qualifier

The : : operator provides an alternative way to access types in namespaces. This may be necessary if you want to use a namespace alias and there is ambiguity between the alias and the actual namespace hierarchy. If that's the case, then the namespace hierarchy is given priority over the namespace alias. To see what this means, consider the following code:

```
using MyNamespaceAlias = MyRootNamespace.MyNestedNamespace;

namespace MyRootNamespace
{
   namespace MyNamespaceAlias
   {
```

```
            public class MyClass
            {
            }
        }

        namespace MyNestedNamespace
        {
            public class MyClass
            {
            }
        }
    }
```

Code in `MyRootNamespace` might use the following to refer to a class:

```
MyNamespaceAlias.MyClass
```

The class referred to by this code is the `MyRootNamespace.MyNamespaceAlias.MyClass` class, not the `MyRootNamespace.MyNestedNamespace.MyClass` class. That is, the namespace `MyRootNamespace.MyNamespaceAlias` has hidden the alias defined by the `using` statement, which refers to `MyRootNamespace.MyNestedNamespace`. You can still access the `MyRootNamespace`.`MyNestedNamespace` namespace and the class contained within, but you require different syntax:

```
MyNestedNamespace.MyClass
```

Alternatively, you can use the `::` operator:

```
MyNamespaceAlias::MyClass
```

Using this operator forces the compiler to use the alias defined by the `using` statement, and therefore the code refers to `MyRootNamespace.MyNestedNamespace.MyClass`.

You can also use the keyword `global` with the `::` operator, which is essentially an alias to the top-level, root namespace. This can be useful to make it clearer which namespace you are referring to, as shown here:

```
global::System.Collections.Generic.List<int>
```

This is the class you'd expect it to be, the generic `List<T>` collection class. It definitely isn't the class defined with the following code:

```
namespace MyRootNamespace
{
    namespace System
    {
        namespace Collections
        {
```

```
namespace Generic
{
    class List<T>
    {
    }
}
        }
    }
}
```

Of course, you should avoid giving your namespaces names that already exist as .NET namespaces, although this problem may arise in large projects, particularly if you are working as part of a large team. Using the :: operator and the global keyword may be the only way you can access the types you want.

Custom Exceptions

Chapter 7 covered exceptions and explained how you can use try ... catch ... finally blocks to act on them. You also saw several standard .NET exceptions, including the base class for exceptions, System.Exception. Sometimes it's useful to derive your own exception classes from this base class for use in your applications, instead of using the standard exceptions. This enables you to be more specific with the information you send to whatever code catches the exception, and it enables catching code to be more specific about which exceptions it handles. For example, you might add a new property to your exception class that permits access to some underlying information, making it possible for the exception's receiver to make the required changes, or just provide more information about the exception's cause.

Once you have defined an exception class, you can add it to the list of exceptions recognized by VS using the Debug ⇨ Exceptions dialog's Add button, and then define exception-specific behavior as shown in Chapter 7.

Exception Base Classes

While you can derive exceptions from System.Exception as described in the previous section, best practices dictate that you don't. Instead, you should derive custom exceptions from System .ApplicationException.

Two fundamental exception classes exist in the System namespace and derive from Exception: ApplicationException and SystemException. SystemException is used as the base class for exceptions that are predefined by the .NET Framework. ApplicationException is provided for developers to derive their own exception classes. If you follow this model, then you will always be able to differentiate between predefined and custom exceptions by catching exceptions that derive from one of these two base classes.

Neither ApplicationException nor SystemException extend the functionality of the Exception class in any way. They exist purely so that you can differentiate between exceptions in the manner described here.

Adding Custom Exceptions to CardLib

How to use custom exceptions is, once again, best illustrated by upgrading the CardLib project. The `Deck.GetCard()` method currently throws a standard .NET exception if an attempt is made to access a card with an index less than 0 or greater than 51, but you'll modify that to use a custom exception.

First, you need to create a new class library project called Ch13CardLib and copy the classes from Ch12CardLib as before, changing the namespace to Ch13CardLib as applicable. Next, define the exception. You do this with a new class defined in a new class file called `CardOutOfRangeException` `.cs`, which you can add to the Ch13CardLib project with Project ⇨ Add Class:

```
public class CardOutOfRangeException : ApplicationException
{
    private Cards deckContents;

    public Cards DeckContents
    {
        get
        {
            return deckContents;
        }
    }

    public CardOutOfRangeException(Cards sourceDeckContents) :
        base("There are only 52 cards in the deck.")
    {
        deckContents = sourceDeckContents;
    }
}
```

An instance of the `Cards` class is required for the constructor of this class. It allows access to this `Cards` object through a `DeckContents` property and supplies a suitable error message to the base `Exception` constructor, so that it is available through the `Message` property of the class.

Next, add code to throw this exception to `Deck.cs` (replacing the old standard exception):

```
public Card GetCard(int cardNum)
{
    if (cardNum >= 0 && cardNum <= 51)
        return cards[cardNum];
    else
        throw new CardOutOfRangeException(cards.Clone() as Cards);
}
```

The `DeckContents` property is initialized with a deep copy of the current contents of the `Deck` object, in the form of a `Cards` object. This means that you see what the contents were at the point where the exception was thrown, so subsequent modification to the deck contents won't "lose" this information.

To test this, use the following client code (in Ch13CardClient in the downloadable code for this chapter):

```
Deck deck1 = new Deck();
try
{
    Card myCard = deck1.GetCard(60);
}
catch (CardOutOfRangeException e)
{
    Console.WriteLine(e.Message);
    Console.WriteLine(e.DeckContents[0]);
}
Console.ReadKey();
```

This code results in the output shown in Figure 13-1.

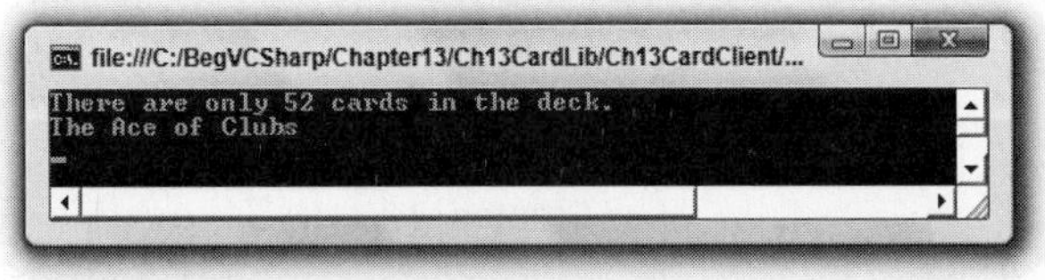

Figure 13-1

Here, the catching code has written the exception `Message` property to the screen. You also displayed the first card in the `Cards` object obtained through `DeckContents`, just to prove that you can access the `Cards` collection through your custom exception object.

Events

This section covers one of the most frequently used OOP techniques in .NET: *events*. You start, as usual, with the basics — looking at what events actually are. After that, you'll see some simple events in action and learn what you can do with them. Then you learn how you can create and use events of your own.

At the end of this chapter you'll complete your CardLib class library by adding an event. Finally, because this is the last port of call before arriving at some advanced topics, you'll have a bit of fun creating a card game application that uses this class library.

What Is an Event?

Events are similar to exceptions in that they are *raised* (thrown) by objects, and you can supply code that acts on them. However, there are several important differences, the most important of which is that there is no equivalent to the `try...catch` structure for handling events. Instead, you must *subscribe* to them. Subscribing to an event means supplying code that will be executed when an event is raised, in the form of an *event handler*.

Many handlers can be subscribed to an event, all of which are called when the event is raised. This may include event handlers that are part of the class of the object that raises the event, but event handlers are just as likely to be found in other classes.

Event handlers themselves are simply functions. The only restriction on an event handler function is that it must match the return type and parameters required by the event. This restriction is part of the definition of an event and is specified by a *delegate*.

> *The fact that delegates are used in events is what makes delegates so useful. This is why some space was devoted to them in Chapter 6. You may want to review that material to refresh your memory about delegates and how you use them.*

The basic sequence of processing is as follows: First, an application creates an object that can raise an event. For example, suppose an instant messaging application creates an object that represents a connection to a remote user. That connection object might raise an event when a message arrives through the connection from the remote user (see Figure 13-2).

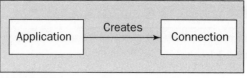

Figure 13-2

Next, the application subscribes to the event. Your instant messaging application would do this by defining a function that could be used with the delegate type specified by the event, passing a reference to this function to the event. The event handler function might be a method on another object, such as an object representing a display device to display instant messages when they arrive (see Figure 13-3).

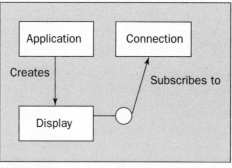

Figure 13-3

When the event is raised, the subscriber is notified. When an instant message arrives through the connection object, the event handler method on the display device object is called. Because you are using a standard method, the object that raises the event may pass any relevant information via parameters, making events very versatile. In the example case, one parameter might be the text of the instant message, which the event handler could display on the display device object. This is shown in Figure 13-4.

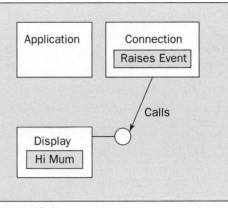

Figure 13-4

Handling Events

As previously discussed, to handle an event you need to subscribe to it by providing an event handler function whose return type and parameters match that of the delegate specified for use with the event. The following example uses a simple timer object to raise events, which results in a handler function being called.

Try It Out   **Handling Events**

1.   Create a new console application called Ch13Ex01 and save it in the directory
C:\BegVCSharp\Chapter13.

2.   Modify the code in `Program.cs` as follows:

```
using System;
using System.Collections.Generic;
using System.Linq;
using System.Text;
using System.Timers;

namespace Ch13Ex01
{
    class Program
    {
        static int counter = 0;

        static string displayString =
                        "This string will appear one letter at a time. ";

        static void Main(string[] args)
```

```
    {
        Timer myTimer = new Timer(100);
        myTimer.Elapsed += new ElapsedEventHandler(WriteChar);
        myTimer.Start();
        Console.ReadKey();
    }

    static void WriteChar(object source, ElapsedEventArgs e)
    {
        Console.Write(displayString[counter++ % displayString.Length]);
    }
    }
}
```

3. Run the application (once it is running, pressing a key will terminate the application). The result, after a short period, is shown in Figure 13-5.

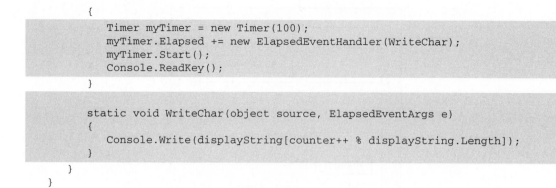

Figure 13-5

How It Works

The object you are using to raise events is an instance of the System.Timers.Timer class. This object is initialized with a time period (in milliseconds). When the Timer object is started using its Start() method, a stream of events is raised, spaced out in time according to the specified time period. Main() initializes a Timer object with a timer period of 100 milliseconds, so it will raise events 10 times a second when started:

```
        static void Main(string[] args)
        {
            Timer myTimer = new Timer(100);
```

The Timer object possesses an event called Elapsed, and the event handler required by this event must match the return type and parameters of the System.Timers.ElapsedEventHandler delegate type, which is one of the standard delegates defined in the .NET Framework. This delegate specifies the following return type and parameters:

```
    void functionName(object source, ElapsedEventArgs e);
```

The Timer object sends a reference to itself in the first parameter and an instance of an ElapsedEventArgs object in its second parameter. It is safe to ignore these parameters for now; you'll take a look at them a little later.

In your code you have a suitable method:

```
static void WriteChar(object source, ElapsedEventArgs e)
{
    Console.Write(displayString[counter++ % displayString.Length]);
}
```

This method uses the two static fields of Class1, counter and displayString, to display a single character. Every time the method is called the character displayed is different.

The next task is to hook this handler up to the event — to subscribe to it. To do this, you use the += operator to add a handler to the event in the form of a new delegate instance initialized with your event handler method:

```
static void Main(string[] args)
{
    Timer myTimer = new Timer(100);
    myTimer.Elapsed += new ElapsedEventHandler(WriteChar);
```

This command (which uses slightly strange-looking syntax, specific to delegates) adds a handler to the list that will be called when the Elapsed event is raised. You can add as many handlers as you like to this list as long as they all meet the criteria required. Each handler is called in turn when the event is raised.

All that remains for Main() to do is to start the timer running:

```
    myTimer.Start();
```

You don't want the application terminating before you have handled any events, so you put the Main() function on hold. The simplest way to do this is to request user input, as this command won't finish processing until the user has pressed a key:

```
    Console.ReadKey();
```

Although processing in Main() effectively ceases here, processing in the Timer object continues. When it raises events it calls the WriteChar() method, which runs concurrently with the Console .ReadLine() statement.

Defining Events

Now it's time to define and use your own events. The following Try It Out implements an example version of the instant messaging scenario introduced earlier in this chapter, creating a Connection object that raises events that are handled by a Display object.

Try It Out   **Defining Events**

1. Create a new console application called Ch13Ex02 and save it in the directory C:\BegVCSharp\Chapter13.

2. Add a new class called `Connection` and modify `Connection.cs` as follows:

```csharp
using System;
using System.Collections.Generic;
using System.Linq;
using System.Text;
using System.Timers;

namespace Ch13Ex02
{
    public delegate void MessageHandler(string messageText);

    public class Connection
    {
        public event MessageHandler MessageArrived;

        private Timer pollTimer;

        public Connection()
        {
            pollTimer = new Timer(100);
            pollTimer.Elapsed += new ElapsedEventHandler(CheckForMessage);
        }

        public void Connect()
        {
            pollTimer.Start();
        }

        public void Disconnect()
        {
            pollTimer.Stop();
        }

        private static Random random = new Random();

        private void CheckForMessage(object source, ElapsedEventArgs e)
        {
            Console.WriteLine("Checking for new messages.");
            if ((random.Next(9) == 0) && (MessageArrived != null))
            {
                MessageArrived("Hello Mum!");
            }
        }
    }
}
```

3. Add a new class called `Display` and modify `Display.cs` as follows:

```csharp
namespace Ch13Ex02
{
    public class Display
    {
        public void DisplayMessage(string message)
        {
            Console.WriteLine("Message arrived: {0}", message);
        }
    }
}
```

4. Modify the code in `Program.cs` as follows:

```csharp
static void Main(string[] args)
{
    Connection myConnection = new Connection();
    Display myDisplay = new Display();
    myConnection.MessageArrived +=
            new MessageHandler (myDisplay.DisplayMessage);
    myConnection.Connect();
    Console.ReadKey();
}
```

5. Run the application. The result is shown in Figure 13-6.

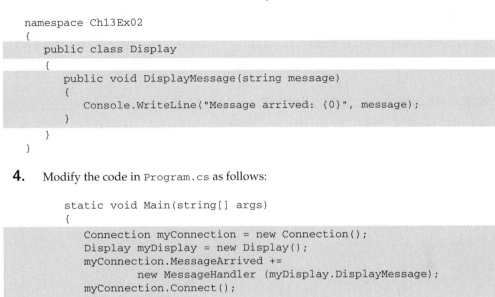

Figure 13-6

How It Works

The `Connection` class does most of the work in this application. Instances of this class make use of a `Timer` object much like the one shown in the first example of this chapter, initializing it in the class constructor and providing access to its state (enabled or disabled) via `Connect()` and `Disconnect()`:

```
public class Connection
{
    private Timer pollTimer;

    public Connection()
    {
        pollTimer = new Timer(100);
        pollTimer.Elapsed += new ElapsedEventHandler(CheckForMessage);
    }

    public void Connect()
    {
        pollTimer.Start();
    }
    public void Disconnect()
    {
        pollTimer.Stop();
    }

    . . .

}
```

Also in the constructor, you register an event handler for the `Elapsed` event, just as you did in the first example. The handler method, `CheckForMessage()`, raises an event on average once every 10 times it is called. You will look at the code for this, but first it would be useful to look at the event definition itself.

Before you define an event, you must define a delegate type to use with the event — that is, a delegate type that specifies the return type and parameters that an event handling method must conform to. You do this using standard delegate syntax, defining it as public inside the `Ch13Ex02` namespace to make the type available to external code:

```
namespace Ch13Ex02
{
    public delegate void MessageHandler(string messageText);
```

This delegate type, called `MessageHandler` here, is a `void` function that has a single `string` parameter. You can use this parameter to pass an instant message received by the `Connection` object to the `Display` object. Once a delegate has been defined (or a suitable existing delegate has been located), you can define the event itself, as a member of the `Connection` class:

```
public class Connection
{
    public event MessageHandler MessageArrived;
```

You simply name the event (here it is `MessageArrived`) and declare it by using the `event` keyword and specifying the delegate type to use (the `MessageHandler` delegate type defined earlier). After you have declared an event in this way, you can raise it simply by calling it by name as if it were a method with the return type and parameters specified by the delegate. For example, you could raise this event using the following:

```
MessageArrived("This is a message.");
```

If the delegate had been defined without any parameters, then you could simply use the following:

```
MessageArrived();
```

Alternatively, you could have defined more parameters, which would have required more code to raise the event. The `CheckForMessage()` method looks like this:

```
private static Random random = new Random();

private void CheckForMessage(object source, ElapsedEventArgs e)
{
    Console.WriteLine("Checking for new messages.");
    if ((random.Next(9) == 0) && (MessageArrived != null))
    {
        MessageArrived("Hello Mum!");
    }
}
```

You use an instance of the `Random` class shown in earlier chapters to generate a random number between 0 and 9, and raise an event if the number generated is 0, which should happen 10 percent of the time. This simulates polling the connection to determine whether a message has arrived, which won't be the case every time you check. To separate the timer from the instance of `Connection`, you use a private static instance of the `Random` class.

Note that you supply additional logic. You only raise an event if the expression `MessageArrived != null` evaluates to `true`. This expression, which again uses the delegate syntax in a slightly unusual way, means: "Does the event have any subscribers?" If there are no subscribers, then `MessageArrived` evaluates to `null`, and there is no point in raising the event.

The class that will subscribe to the event is called `Display` and contains the single method, `DisplayMessage()`, defined as follows:

```
public class Display
{
    public void DisplayMessage(string message)
    {
        Console.WriteLine("Message arrived: {0}", message);
    }
}
```

This method matches the delegate type (and is public, which is a requirement of event handlers in classes other than the class that generates the event), so you can use it to respond to the `MessageArrived` event.

All that is left now is for the code in `Main()` to initialize instances of the `Connection` and `Display` classes, hook them up, and start things going. The code required here is similar to that from the first example:

```
static void Main(string[] args)
{
    Connection myConnection = new Connection();
    Display myDisplay = new Display();
    myConnection.MessageArrived +=
            new MessageHandler(myDisplay.DisplayMessage);
    myConnection.Connect();
    Console.ReadKey();
}
```

Again, you call `Console.ReadKey()` to pause the processing of `Main()` once you have started things moving with the `Connect()` method of the `Connection` object.

Multipurpose Event Handlers

The delegate you saw earlier, for the `Timer.Elapsed` event, contained two parameters that are of a type often seen in event handlers:

❑ object source — A reference to the object that raised the event

❑ `ElapsedEventArgs e` — Parameters sent by the event

The reason why the `object` type parameter is used in this event, and indeed in many other events, is that you often need to use a single event handler for several identical events generated by different objects and still tell which object generated the event.

To explain and illustrate this, we'll extend the last example a little.

Try It Out   Using a Multipurpose Event Handler

1. Create a new console application called Ch13Ex03 and save it in the directory C:\BegVCSharp\Chapter13.

2. Copy the code across for `Program.cs`, `Connection.cs`, and `Display.cs` from Ch13Ex02, making sure that you change the namespaces in each file from Ch13Ex02 to Ch13Ex03.

3. Add a new class called `MessageArrivedEventArgs` and modify `MessageArrivedEventArgs.cs` as follows:

```
namespace Ch13Ex03
{
    public class MessageArrivedEventArgs : EventArgs
```

```
    {
        private string message;

        public string Message
        {
            get
            {
                return message;
            }
        }

        public MessageArrivedEventArgs()
        {
            message = "No message sent.";
        }

        public MessageArrivedEventArgs(string newMessage)
        {
            message = newMessage;
        }
    }
}
```

4. Modify `Connection.cs` as follows:

```
namespace Ch13Ex03
{
    public delegate void MessageHandler(Connection source,
                                        MessageArrivedEventArgs e);

    public class Connection
    {
        public event MessageHandler MessageArrived;

        private string name;

        public string Name
        {
            get
            {
                return name;
            }
            set
            {
                name = value;
            }
        }
```

```
    ...

    private void CheckForMessage(object source, EventArgs e)
    {
        Console.WriteLine("Checking for new messages.");
        if ((random.Next(9) == 0) && (MessageArrived != null))
        {
            MessageArrived(this, new MessageArrivedEventArgs("Hello Mum!"));
        }
    }

    ...


    }
}
```

5. Modify `Display.cs` as follows:

```
    public void DisplayMessage(Connection source, MessageArrivedEventArgs e)
    {
        Console.WriteLine("Message arrived from: {0}", source.Name);
        Console.WriteLine("Message Text: {0}", e.Message);
    }
```

6. Modify `Program.cs` as follows:

```
    static void Main(string[] args)
    {
        Connection myConnection1 = new Connection();
        myConnection1.Name = "First connection.";
        Connection myConnection2 = new Connection();
        myConnection2.Name = "Second connection.";
        Display myDisplay = new Display();
        myConnection1.MessageArrived +=
                    new MessageHandler(myDisplay.DisplayMessage);
        myConnection2.MessageArrived +=
                    new MessageHandler(myDisplay.DisplayMessage);
        myConnection1.Connect();
        myConnection2.Connect();
        Console.ReadKey();
    }
```

7. Run the application. The result is shown in Figure 13-7.

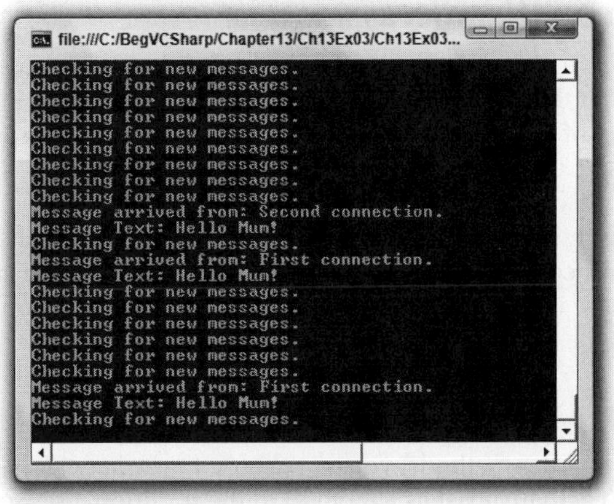

Figure 13-7

How It Works

By sending a reference to the object that raises an event as one of the event handler parameters you can customize the response of the handler to individual objects. The reference gives you access to the source object, including its properties.

By sending parameters that are contained in a class that inherits from System.EventArgs (as ElapsedEventArgs does), you can supply whatever additional information is necessary as parameters (such as the Message parameter on the MessageArrivedEventArgs class).

In addition, these parameters will benefit from polymorphism. You could define a handler for the MessageArrived event such as this:

```
public void DisplayMessage(object source, EventArgs e)
{
    Console.WriteLine("Message arrived from: {0}",
                      ((Connection)source).Name);
    Console.WriteLine("Message Text: {0}",
                      ((MessageArrivedEventArgs)e).Message);
}
```

Then you could modify the delegate definition in Connection.cs as follows:

```
public delegate void MessageHandler(object source, EventArgs e);
```

The application will execute exactly as it did before, but you have made the DisplayMessage() function more versatile (in theory at least — more implementation would be needed to make this production quality). This same handler could work with other events, such as the Timer.Elapsed, although you'd have to modify the internals of the handler a bit more such that the parameters sent when this event is raised are handled properly (casting them to Connection and MessageArrivedEventArgs objects in this way will cause an exception; you should use the as operator instead and check for null values).

387

Return Values and Event Handlers

All the event handlers you've seen so far have had a return type of void. It is possible to provide a return type for an event, but this can lead to problems because a given event may result in several event handlers being called. If all of these handlers return a value, then it may be unclear which value was actually returned.

The system deals with this by only allowing you access to the last value returned by an event handler. That will be the value returned by the last event handler to subscribe to an event. Although this functionality might be of use in some situations, it is recommended that you use void type event handlers, and avoid out type parameters.

Anonymous Methods

Instead of defining event handler methods, you can choose to use *anonymous methods*. An anonymous method is one that doesn't actually exist as a method in the traditional sense — that is, it isn't a method on any particular class. Instead, an anonymous method is created purely for use as a target for a delegate.

To create an anonymous method, you need the following code:

```
delegate(parameters)
{
    // Anonymous method code.
};
```

parameters is a list of parameters matching those of the delegate type you are instantiating, as used by the anonymous method code:

```
delegate(Connection source, MessageArrivedEventArgs e)
{
    // Anonymous method code matching MessageHandler event in Ch13Ex03.
};
```

For example, you could use this code to completely bypass the Display, DisplayMessage() method in Ch13Ex03:

```
myConnection1.MessageArrived +=
    delegate(Connection source, MessageArrivedEventArgs e)
{
    Console.WriteLine("Message arrived from: {0}", source.Name);
    Console.WriteLine("Message Text: {0}", e.Message);
};
```

An interesting point about anonymous methods is that they are effectively local to the code block that contains them, and they have access to local variables in this scope. If you use such a variable, then it becomes an *outer* variable. Outer variables are not disposed of when they go out of scope like other local variables are; instead, they live on until the anonymous methods that use them are destroyed. This may be some time later than you expect, so it's definitely something to be careful about.

Expanding and Using CardLib

Now that you've had a look at defining and using events, you can use them in Ch13CardLib. The event you'll add to your library will be generated when the last Card object in a Deck object is obtained by using GetCard, and will be called LastCardDrawn. The event enables subscribers to reshuffle the deck automatically, cutting down on the processing necessary by a client. The delegate defined for this event (LastCardDrawnHandler) needs to supply a reference to the Deck object such that the Shuffle() method will be accessible from wherever the handler is. Add the following code to Deck.cs:

```
namespace Ch13CardLib
{
    public delegate void LastCardDrawnHandler(Deck currentDeck);
```

The code to define the event and raise it is simple:

```
    public event LastCardDrawnHandler LastCardDrawn;

    public Card GetCard(int cardNum)
    {
        if (cardNum >= 0 && cardNum <= 51)
        {
            if ((cardNum == 51) && (LastCardDrawn != null))
                LastCardDrawn(this);
            return cards[cardNum];
        }
        else
            throw new CardOutOfRangeException((Cards)cards.Clone());
    }
```

This is all the code required to add the event to the Deck class definition.

A Card Game Client for CardLib

After spending all this time developing the CardLib library, it would be a shame not to use it. Before finishing this section on OOP in C# and the .NET Framework, it's time to have a little fun and write the basics of a card game application that uses the familiar playing card classes.

As in previous chapters, you'll add a client console application to the Ch13CardLib solution, and add a reference to the Ch13CardLib project and make it the startup project. This application will be called Ch13CardClient.

To begin, you'll create a new class called Player in a new file in Ch13CardClient, Player.cs. This class will contain a private Cards field called hand, a private string field called name, and two read-only properties: Name and PlayHand. The properties simply expose the private fields. Although the PlayHand property is read-only, you will have write access to the reference to the hand field returned, enabling you to modify the cards in the player's hand.

You'll also hide the default constructor by making it private, and supply a public nondefault constructor that accepts an initial value for the Name property of Player instances.

Finally, you'll provide a `bool` type method called `HasWon()`, which returns `true` if all the cards in the player's hand are of the same suit (a simple winning condition, but that doesn't matter too much).

Here's the code for `Player.cs`:

```
using System;
using System.Collections.Generic;
using System.Linq;
using System.Text;
using Ch13CardLib;

namespace Ch13CardClient
{
    public class Player
    {
        private Cards hand;
        private string name;
        public string Name
        {
            get
            {
                return name;
            }
        }

        public Cards PlayHand
        {
            get
            {
                return hand;
            }
        }

        private Player()
        {
        }

        public Player(string newName)
        {
            name = newName;
            hand = new Cards();
        }

        public bool HasWon()
        {
            bool won = true;
            Suit match = hand[0].suit;
            for (int i = 1; i < hand.Count; i++)
```

```
            {
                won &= hand[i].suit == match;
            }
            return won;
        }
    }
}
```

Next, define a class that will handle the card game itself, called Game. This class is found in the file Game.cs of the Ch13CardClient project. The class has four private member fields:

❑ playDeck — A Deck type variable containing the deck of cards to use.

❑ currentCard — An int value used as a pointer to the next card in the deck to draw.

❑ players — An array of Player objects representing the players of the game.

❑ discardedCards — A Cards collection for the cards that have been discarded by players but not shuffled back into the deck.

The default constructor for the class initializes and shuffles the Deck stored in playDeck, sets the currentCard pointer variable to 0 (the first card in playDeck), and wires up an event handler called Reshuffle() to the playDeck.LastCardDrawn event. The handler simply shuffles the deck, initializes the discardedCards collection, and resets currentCard to 0, ready to read cards from the new deck.

The Game class also contains two utility methods: SetPlayers() for setting the players for the game (as an array of Player objects) and DealHands() for dealing hands to the players (7 cards each). The allowed number of players is restricted from 2 to 7 to ensure that there are enough cards to go around.

Finally, there is a PlayGame() method that contains the game logic itself. You'll come back to this function shortly, after you've looked at the code in Program.cs. The rest of the code in Game.cs is as follows:

```
using System;
using System.Collections.Generic;
using System.Linq;
using System.Text;
using Ch13CardLib;

namespace Ch13CardClient
{
    public class Game
    {
        private int currentCard;
        private Deck playDeck;
        private Player[] players;
        private Cards discardedCards;

        public Game()
        {
            currentCard = 0;
            playDeck = new Deck(true);
```

```csharp
        playDeck.LastCardDrawn += new LastCardDrawnHandler(Reshuffle);
        playDeck.Shuffle();
        discardedCards = new Cards();
    }

    private void Reshuffle(Deck currentDeck)
    {
        Console.WriteLine("Discarded cards reshuffled into deck.");
        currentDeck.Shuffle();
        discardedCards.Clear();
        currentCard = 0;
    }

    public void SetPlayers(Player[] newPlayers)
    {
        if (newPlayers.Length > 7)
            throw new ArgumentException("A maximum of 7 players may play this" +
                                        " game.");

        if (newPlayers.Length < 2)
            throw new ArgumentException("A minimum of 2 players may play this" +
                                        " game.");

        players = newPlayers;
    }

    private void DealHands()
    {
        for (int p = 0; p < players.Length; p++)
        {
            for (int c = 0; c < 7; c++)
            {
                players[p].PlayHand.Add(playDeck.GetCard(currentCard++));
            }
        }
    }

    public int PlayGame()
    {
        // Code to follow.
    }
    }
}
```

`Program.cs` contains the `Main()` function, which initializes and runs the game. This function performs the following steps:

- ❑ An introduction is displayed.
- ❑ The user is prompted for a number of players between 2 and 7.
- ❑ An array of `Player` objects is set up accordingly.
- ❑ Each player is prompted for a name, used to initialize one `Player` object in the array.

❑   A `Game` object is created and players are assigned using the `SetPlayers()` method.

❑   The game is started by using the `PlayGame()` method.

❑   The `int` return value of `PlayGame()` is used to display a winning message (the value returned is the index of the winning player in the array of `Player` objects).

The code for this (commented for clarity) follows:

```csharp
static void Main(string[] args)
{
    // Display introduction.
    Console.WriteLine("KarliCards: a new and exciting card game.");
    Console.WriteLine("To win you must have 7 cards of the same suit in" +
                      " your hand.");
    Console.WriteLine();

    // Prompt for number of players.
    bool inputOK = false;
    int choice = -1;
    do
    {
        Console.WriteLine("How many players (2-7)?");
        string input = Console.ReadLine();
        try
        {
            // Attempt to convert input into a valid number of players.
            choice = Convert.ToInt32(input);
            if ((choice >= 2) && (choice <= 7))
                inputOK = true;
        }
        catch
        {
            // Ignore failed conversions, just continue prompting.
        }
    } while (inputOK == false);

    // Initialize array of Player objects.
    Player[] players = new Player[choice];

    // Get player names.
    for (int p = 0; p < players.Length; p++)
    {
        Console.WriteLine("Player {0}, enter your name:", p + 1);
        string playerName = Console.ReadLine();
        players[p] = new Player(playerName);
    }

    // Start game.
    Game newGame = new Game();
    newGame.SetPlayers(players);
    int whoWon = newGame.PlayGame();

    // Display winning player.
    Console.WriteLine("{0} has won the game!", players[whoWon].Name);
}
```

Now you come to `PlayGame()`, the main body of the application. Space limitations preclude a lot of detail about this method, but it is commented to make it more comprehensible. None of the code is complicated; there's just quite a bit of it.

Play proceeds with each player viewing his or her cards and an upturned card on the table. They may either pick up this card or draw a new one from the deck. After drawing a card, each player must discard one, replacing the card on the table with another one if it has been picked up, or placing the discarded card on top of the one on the table (also adding the discarded card to the `discardedCards` collection).

As you consider this code, bear in mind how the `Card` objects are manipulated. The reason why these objects are defined as reference types, rather than value types (using a struct) should now be clear. A given `Card` object may appear to exist in several places at once because references can be held by the `Deck` object, the `hand` fields of the `Player` objects, the `discardedCards` collection, and the `playCard` object (the card currently on the table). This makes it easy to keep track of the cards and is used in particular in the code that draws a new card from the deck. The card is accepted only if it isn't in any player's hand or in the `discardedCards` collection.

The code is as follows:

```
public int PlayGame()
{
    // Only play if players exist.
    if (players == null)
        return -1;

    // Deal initial hands.
    DealHands();

    // Initialize game vars, including an initial card to place on the
    // table: playCard.
    bool GameWon = false;
    int currentPlayer;
    Card playCard = playDeck.GetCard(currentCard++);
    discardedCards.Add(playCard);

    // Main game loop, continues until GameWon == true.
    do
    {
        // Loop through players in each game round.
        for (currentPlayer = 0; currentPlayer < players.Length;
            currentPlayer++)
        {
            // Write out current player, player hand, and the card on the
            // table.
            Console.WriteLine("{0}'s turn.", players[currentPlayer].Name);
            Console.WriteLine("Current hand:");
            foreach (Card card in players[currentPlayer].PlayHand)
            {
                Console.WriteLine(card);
            }
```

```
             Console.WriteLine("Card in play: {0}", playCard);

// Prompt player to pick up card on table or draw a new one.
bool inputOK = false;
do
{
    Console.WriteLine("Press T to take card in play or D to " +
                     "draw:");
    string input = Console.ReadLine();
    if (input.ToLower() == "t")
    {
        // Add card from table to player hand.
        Console.WriteLine("Drawn: {0}", playCard);
        // Remove from discarded cards if possible (if deck
        // is reshuffled it won't be there any more)
        if (discardedCards.Contains(playCard))
        {
            discardedCards.Remove(playCard);
        }
        players[currentPlayer].PlayHand.Add(playCard);
        inputOK = true;
    }
    if (input.ToLower() == "d")
    {
        // Add new card from deck to player hand.
        Card newCard;
        // Only add card if it isn't already in a player hand
        // or in the discard pile
        bool cardIsAvailable;
        do
        {
            newCard = playDeck.GetCard(currentCard++);
            // Check if card is in discard pile
            cardIsAvailable = !discardedCards.Contains(newCard);
            if (cardIsAvailable)
            {
                // Loop through all player hands to see if newCard is
                // already in a hand.
                foreach (Player testPlayer in players)
                {
                    if (testPlayer.PlayHand.Contains(newCard))
                    {
                        cardIsAvailable = false;
                        break;
                    }
                }
            }
        } while (!cardIsAvailable);
        // Add the card found to player hand.
        Console.WriteLine("Drawn: {0}", newCard);
        players[currentPlayer].PlayHand.Add(newCard);
        inputOK = true;
    }
```

```
        } while (inputOK == false);

        // Display new hand with cards numbered.
        Console.WriteLine("New hand:");
        for (int i = 0; i < players[currentPlayer].PlayHand.Count; i++)
        {
            Console.WriteLine("{0}: {1}", i + 1,
                            players[currentPlayer].PlayHand[i]);
        }

        // Prompt player for a card to discard.
        inputOK = false;
        int choice = -1;
        do
        {
            Console.WriteLine("Choose card to discard:");
            string input = Console.ReadLine();
            try
            {
                // Attempt to convert input into a valid card number.
                choice = Convert.ToInt32(input);
                if ((choice > 0) && (choice <= 8))
                    inputOK = true;
            }
            catch
            {
                // Ignore failed conversions, just continue prompting.
            }
        } while (inputOK == false);

        // Place reference to removed card in playCard (place the card
        // on the table), then remove card from player hand and add
        // to discarded card pile.
        playCard = players[currentPlayer].PlayHand[choice - 1];
        players[currentPlayer].PlayHand.RemoveAt(choice - 1);
        discardedCards.Add(playCard);
        Console.WriteLine("Discarding: {0}", playCard);

        // Space out text for players
        Console.WriteLine();

        // Check to see if player has won the game, and exit the player
        // loop if so.
        GameWon = players[currentPlayer].HasWon();
        if (GameWon == true)
            break;
    }
} while (GameWon == false);

// End game, noting the winning player.
return currentPlayer;
}
```

Figure 13-8 shows a game in progress.

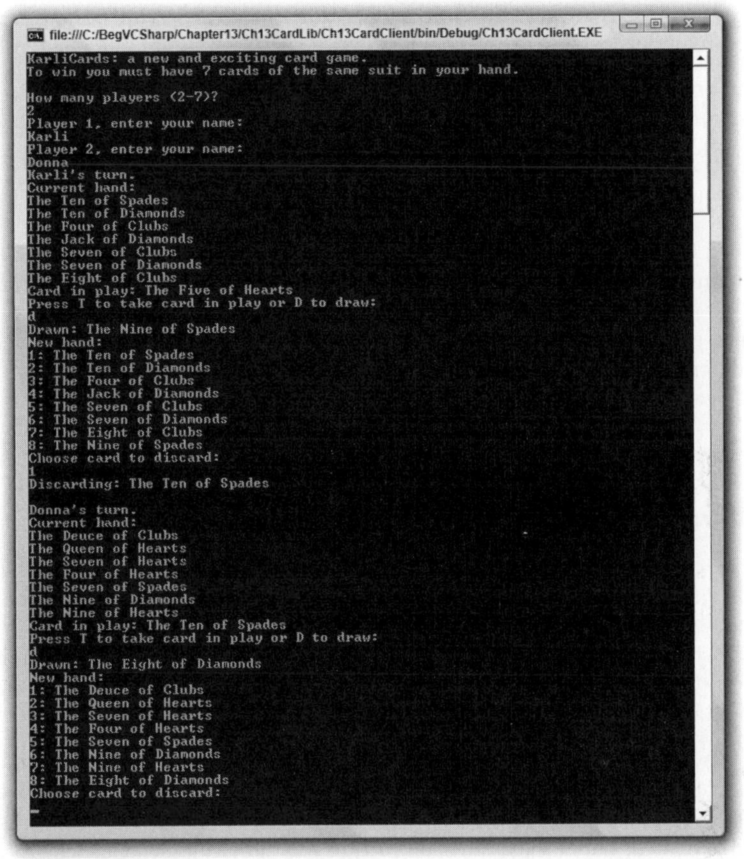

Figure 13-8

Have fun playing the game — and make sure that you spend some time going through it in detail. Try putting a breakpoint in the `Reshuffle()` method and play the game with seven players. If you keep drawing cards and discarding the cards drawn, it won't take long for reshuffles to occur because with seven players there are only three cards to spare. This way, you can prove to yourself that things are working properly by noting the three cards when they reappear.

Summary

This chapter explained some advanced techniques that extend your knowledge of the C# language. It contained the following highlights:

❑   The qualification of type names in namespaces (in more detail than you saw in earlier chapters)

❑   How to use the `::` operator and `global` keyword to ensure that references to types are references to the types you want

❑ How to implement your own exception objects and pass more detailed information to the exception handler

❑ Using a custom exception in the code for CardLib — the card game library you've been developing in the last few chapters

❑ The important topic of events and event handling. Although quite subtle, and initially difficult to get your head around, the code involved is quite simple — and you'll certainly be using event handlers a lot in the rest of the book.

❑ Some simple illustrative examples of events and how to handle them

You also modified the CardLib library and used it to create a simple card game application. This application demonstrates nearly all the techniques you've looked at so far in this book.

With this chapter, you have completed not only a full description of OOP as applied to C# programming but also a full description of version 2.0 of the C# language. The next chapter describes the new features of C# that have been added with version 3.0.

Exercises

1. Show the code for an event handler that uses the general-purpose `(object sender, EventArgs e)` syntax that will accept either the `Timer.Elapsed` event or the `Connection.MessageArrived` event from the code shown earlier in this chapter. The handler should output a string specifying which type of event has been received, along with the `Message` property of the `MessageArrivedEventArgs` parameter or the `SignalTime` property of the `ElapsedEventArgs` parameter, depending on which event occurs.

2. Modify the card game example to check for the more interesting winning condition of the popular card game rummy. This means that a player wins the game if his or her hand contains two "sets" of cards, one of which consists of three cards and one of which consists of four cards. A set is defined as either a sequence of cards of the same suit (such as 3H, 4H, 5H, 6H) or several cards of the same rank (such as 2H, 2D, 2S).

C# 3.0 Language Enhancements

The C# language is not static. Anders Hejlsberg (the inventor of C#) and others at Microsoft continue to update and refine the language. At the time of this writing, the most recent changes are part of version 3.0 of the C# language, which is released as part of the Visual Studio 2008 product line. At this point in the book you may be wondering what else could be needed; indeed, previous versions of C# lack little in terms of functionality. However, this doesn't mean that it isn't possible to make some aspects of C# programming easier, or that the relationships between C# and other technologies can't be streamlined.

Perhaps the best way to understand this is to consider an addition that was made between versions 1.0 and 2.0 of the language — generics. You could argue that while generics are extremely useful, they don't actually provide any functionality that you couldn't achieve before. True, they simplify things a great deal, and you would have to write a lot more code without them. None of us would want to go back to the days before generic collection classes. Nonetheless, generics aren't an essential part of C#. They are, though, a definite improvement to the language.

The C# 3.0 language enhancements are much the same. They provide new ways of achieving things that would have been difficult to accomplish before without lengthy and/or advanced programming techniques.

You've already seen two of the new features of C# 3.0: automatic properties and partial methods (Chapter 10). In both cases you may have noticed that the changes affect the compilation of C# code, rather than do something completely new. That's a common aspect of C# language improvements, reinforcing the point that these improvements do not reflect enormous changes.

In this chapter you look at the following:

- ❑ Initializers
- ❑ Type inference
- ❑ Anonymous types

❑   Extension methods

❑   Lambda expressions

Probably the biggest change to the C# language is the Language Integrated Query (LINQ) technology, which is covered later in Chapters 26–29. LINQ is a new way to manipulate collections of objects that can come from a variety of sources — most importantly, database or XML data. Many of the enhancements covered in this chapter are primarily used in association with LINQ, although they are also enhancements in their own rights.

Initializers

In earlier chapters you learned to instantiate and initialize objects in various ways. Invariably, that has required you either to add additional code to class definitions to enable initialization or to instantiate and initialize objects with separate statements. You have also learned how to create collection classes of various types, including generic collection classes. Again, you may have noticed that there was no easy way to combine the creation of a collection with adding items to the collection.

Object initializers provide a way to simplify your code by enabling you to combine instantiation and initialization of objects. Collection initializers give you a simple, elegant syntax to create and populate collections in a single step. This section explains how to use both of these new features.

Object Initializers

Consider the following simple class definition:

```
public class Curry
{
    public string MainIngredient {get; set;}
    public string Style {get; set;}
    public int Spiciness {get; set;}
}
```

This class has three properties that are defined using the automatic property syntax shown in Chapter 10. If you want to instantiate and initialize an object instance of this class, you must execute several statements:

```
Curry tastyCurry = new Curry();
tastyCurry.MainIngredient = "panir tikka";
tastyCurry.Style = "jalfrezi";
tastyCurry.Spiciness = 8;
```

This code uses the default, parameterless constructor that is supplied by the C# compiler if you don't include a constructor in your class definition. To simplify this initialization, you can supply an appropriate nondefault constructor:

```
public class Curry
{
    public Curry(string mainIngredient, string style, int spiciness)
    {
```

```
        MainIngredient = mainIngredient;
        Style = style;
        Spiciness = spiciness;
    }

    ...
}
```

That enables you to write code combining instantiation with initialization:

```
Curry tastyCurry = new Curry("panir tikka", "jalfrezi", 8);
```

This works fine, although it forces code that uses this class to use this constructor, which would prevent the previous code, which used a parameterless constructor, from working. Often, particularly where classes must be serializable, it is necessary to provide a parameterless constructor:

```
public class Curry
{
    public Curry()
    {
    }

    ...
}
```

Now you have a situation where you can instantiate and initialize the Curry class any way you like, although you have added several lines of code to the initial class definition, that doesn't do anything much other than provide the basic plumbing required for this to work.

Enter *object initializers,* which are a way to instantiate and initialize objects without having to add additional code (such as the constructors detailed here) to a class. When you instantiate an object, you supply values for publicly accessible properties or fields using a name-value pair for each property you want to initialize. The syntax for this is as follows:

```
className variableName = new className
{
    propertyOrField1 = value1,
    propertyOrField2 = value2,
    ...
    propertyOrField N = valueN
};
```

For example, you could rewrite the code shown earlier, which instantiates and initializes an object of type Curry, as follows:

```
Curry tastyCurry = new Curry
{
    MainIngredient = "panir tikka",
    Style = "jalfrezi",
    Spiciness = 8
};
```

Often you can put code like that on a single line without seriously degrading readability.

When you use an object initializer, you cannot explicitly call a constructor of the class (no parentheses are permitted in the object initializer syntax). Instead, the default parameterless constructor is called automatically. This happens before any parameter values are set by the initializer, which enables you to provide default values for parameters in the default constructor if desired. If you do not provide a constructor for a class, then the compiler-provided public default constructor will work just fine.

Because of this automatic constructor call, you must have access to the default constructor of the class in order for object initializers to work. Therefore, if you have added a nondefault constructor with parameters, you also require a default constructor — just as in the preceding case that used constructors to initialize properties.

If one of the properties you want to initialize with an object initializer is more complex than the simple types used in this example, then you may find yourself using a *nested object initializer*. That simply means using the exact same syntax you've already seen:

```
Curry tastyCurry = new Curry
{
  MainIngredient = "panir tikka",
  Style = "jalfrezi",
  Spiciness = 8,
  Origin = new Restaurant {Name = "King's Balti", Location = "York Road", Rating = 5}
};
```

Here, a property called `Origin` of type `Restaurant` (not shown here) is initialized. The code initializes three properties of the `Origin` property, `Name`, `Location`, and `Rating`, with values of type `string`, `string`, and `int`, respectively. This initialization uses a nested object initializer.

Note that object initializers are not a replacement for nondefault constructors. The fact that you can use object initializers to set property and field values when you instantiate an object does not mean that you will always know what state needs initializing. With constructors you can specify exactly what values are required for an object to function, and then execute code in response to those values immediately.

Collection Initializers

Chapter 5 described how arrays can be initialized with values using the following syntax:

```
int[] myIntArray = new int[5] {5, 9, 10, 2, 99};
```

This is a quick and easy way to combine the instantiation and initialization of an array. Collection initializers simply extend this syntax to collections:

```
List<int> myIntCollection = new List<int> {5, 9, 10, 2, 99};
```

By combining object and collection initializers, it is possible to configure collections with simple and elegant code. Rather than code like this:

```
List<Curry> curries = new List<Curry>();
curries.Add(new Curry("Chicken", "Pathia", 6));
curries.Add(new Curry("Vegetable", "Korma", 3));
curries.Add(new Curry("Prawn", "Vindaloo", 9));
```

You can use the following:

```
List<Curry> moreCurries = new List<Curry>
{
    new Curry {MainIngredient = "Chicken", Style = "Pathia", Spiciness = 6},
    new Curry {MainIngredient = "Vegetable", Style = "Korma", Spiciness = 3},
    new Curry {MainIngredient = "Prawn", Style = "Vindaloo", Spiciness = 9}
};
```

This works very well for types that are primarily used for data representation, and as such, collection initializers are a great accompaniment for the LINQ technology described later in the book.

Try It Out   **Initializers**

1. Create a new console application called Ch14Ex01 and save it in the directory C:\BegVCSharp\Chapter14.

2. Right-click on the project name in the Solution Explorer window, and select the Add ⇨ Existing Item option.

3. Select the `Animal.cs`, `Cow.cs`, `Chicken.cs`, `SuperCow.cs`, and `Farm.cs` files from the C:\BegVCSharp\Chapter12\Ch12Ex04\Ch12Ex04 directory, and click Add.

4. Modify the namespace declaration in the file you have added as follows:

```
namespace Ch14Ex01
```

5. Add a default constructor to the `Cow`, `Chicken`, and `SuperCow` classes. For example, for `Cow` add the following code:

```
namespace Ch14Ex01
{
    public class Cow : Animal
    {
        public Cow()
        {
        }

        . . .
```

6. Modify the code in `Program.cs` as follows:

```
static void Main(string[] args)
{
    Farm<Animal> farm = new Farm<Animal>
    {
        new Cow { Name="Norris" },
        new Chicken { Name="Rita" },
        new Chicken(),
        new SuperCow { Name="Chesney" }
    };
    farm.MakeNoises();
    Console.ReadKey();
}
```

7. Build the application. You should receive the build errors shown in Figure 14-1.

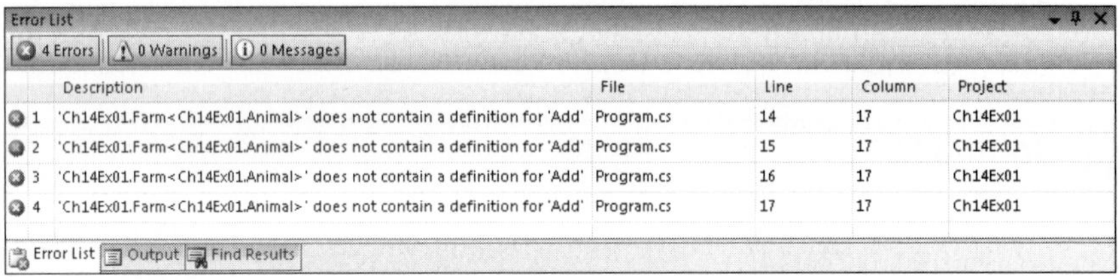

Error List
4 Errors
0 Warnings
0 Messages
Description | File | Line | Column | Project
1 'Ch14Ex01.Farm<Ch14Ex01.Animal>' does not contain a definition for 'Add' | Program.cs | 14 | 17 | Ch14Ex01
2 'Ch14Ex01.Farm<Ch14Ex01.Animal>' does not contain a definition for 'Add' | Program.cs | 15 | 17 | Ch14Ex01
3 'Ch14Ex01.Farm<Ch14Ex01.Animal>' does not contain a definition for 'Add' | Program.cs | 16 | 17 | Ch14Ex01
4 'Ch14Ex01.Farm<Ch14Ex01.Animal>' does not contain a definition for 'Add' | Program.cs | 17 | 17 | Ch14Ex01
Error List
Output
Find Results

Figure 14-1

8. Add the following code to `Farm.cs`:

```
namespace Ch14Ex01
{
   public class Farm<T> : IEnumerable<T>
     where T : Animal
  {
      public void Add(T animal)
      {
         animals.Add(animal);
      }

      ...
```

9. Run the application. The result is shown in Figure 14-2.

file:///C:/BegVCSharp/Chapter14/Ch14Ex01/Ch14Ex01...
Norris says 'moo!'
Rita says 'cluck!'
The animal with no name says 'cluck!'
Chesney says 'here I come to save the day!'

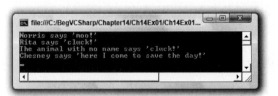

Figure 14-2

How It Works

This example combined object and collection initializers to create and populate a collection of objects in a single step. It used the farmyard collection of objects that you have seen in previous chapters, although two modifications are necessary for initializers to be used with these classes.

First, you add default constructors to the classes derived from the base `Animal` class. That's necessary because, as shown earlier in this chapter, default constructors are called when object initializers are used. When using these default constructors, the `Name` property is initialized according to the default constructor in the base class, which has code as follows:

```
public Animal()
{
    name = "The animal with no name";
}
```

However, when an object initializer is used with a class that derives from `Animal`, recall that any properties set by the initializer are set after the object is instantiated, and therefore after this base class constructor is executed. If a value for the `Name` property is supplied as part of an object initializer, it will override this default value. In the example code, the `Name` property is set for all but one of the items added to the collection.

Second, you add an `Add()` method to the `Farm` class. This is in response to a series of compiler errors of the following form:

```
'Ch14Ex01.Farm<Ch14Ex01.Animal>' does not contain a definition for 'Add'
```

This error exposes part of the underlying functionality of collection initializers. Behind the scenes, the compiler calls the `Add()` method of a collection for each item that you supply in a collection initializer. The `Farm` class exposes a collection of `Animal` objects through a property called `Animals`. The compiler cannot guess that this is the property you want to populate (through `Animals.Add()`), so the code fails. To correct this problem, you add an `Add()` method to the class, which is initialized through the object initializer.

Alternatively, you could modify the code in the example to provide a nested initializer for the `Animals` property as follows:

```
static void Main(string[] args)
{
    Farm<Animal> farm = new Farm<Animal>
    {
        Animals =
        {
            new Cow { Name="Norris" },
            new Chicken { Name="Rita" },
            new Chicken(),
            new SuperCow { Name="Chesney" }
        }
    };
    farm.MakeNoises();
    Console.ReadKey();
}
```

405

With this code there is no need to provide an Add() method for the Farm class. This alternative technique is appropriate when you have a class that contains multiple collections. In this case, there is no obvious candidate for a collection to add to with an Add() method of the containing class.

Type Inference

Earlier in this book you saw how C# is a *strongly typed* language, meaning that every variable has a fixed type and can only be used in code that takes that type into account. In every code example you've seen so far you've declared variables with code of the following form:

```
type varName;
```

or

```
type varName = value;
```

The following code shows at a glance what type of variable varName is:

```
int myInt = 5;
Console.WriteLine(myInt);
```

You can also see that the IDE is aware of the variable type simply by hovering the mouse pointer over the variable identifier, as shown in Figure 14-3.

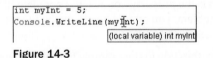

```
int myInt = 5;
Console.WriteLine(myInt);
                     (local variable) int myInt
```

Figure 14-3

C# 3.0 introduces the new keyword var, which you can use as an alternative for type in the preceding code:

```
var varName = value;
```

In this code, the variable varName is *implicitly typed* to the type of value. Note that there is no type called var. In the code

```
var myVar = 5;
```

myVar is a variable of type int, not of type var. Again, as shown in Figure 14-4, the IDE is aware of this.

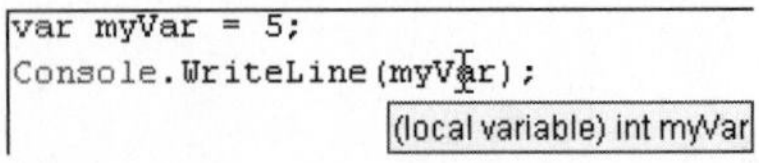

```
var myVar = 5;
Console.WriteLine(myVar);
                     (local variable) int myVar
```

Figure 14-4

This is an extremely important point. When you use var you are not declaring a variable with no type, or even a type that can change. If that were the case, C# would no longer be a strongly typed language. All you are doing is relying on the compiler to determine the type of the variable.

If the compiler is unable to determine the type of variable declared using var, then your code will not compile. Therefore, you can't declare a variable using var without initializing the variable at the same time, because if you did there would be no value that the compiler could use to determine the type of the variable. The following code, therefore, will not compile:

```
var myVar;
```

The var keyword can also be used to infer the type of an array through the array initializer:

```
var myArray = new[] {4, 5, 2};
```

In this code, the type of myArray is implicitly int[]. When you implicitly type an array in this way, the array elements used in the initializer must be one of the following:

❑   All the same type.

❑   All the same reference type or null.

❑   All elements that can be implicitly converted to a single type.

If the last of these rules is applied, the type that elements can be converted to is referred to as the *best type* for the array elements. If there is any ambiguity as to what this best type might be — that is, if there are two or more types that all the elements can be implicitly converted to — your code will not compile. Instead, you receive the error indicating that no best type is available:

```
var myArray = new[] {4, "not an int", 2};
```

Note also that numeric values are never interpreted as nullable types, so the following code will not compile:

```
var myArray = new[] {4, null, 2};
```

You can, however, use a standard array initializer to make this work:

```
var myArray = new int?[] {4, null, 2};
```

A final point: The identifier var is not a forbidden identifier to use for a class name. This means, for example, that if your code has a class called var in scope (in the same namespace or in a referenced namespace), then you cannot use implicit typing with the var keyword.

In itself, type inference is not particularly useful because in the code you've seen in this section it only serves to complicate things. Using var makes it more difficult to see at a glance what type a given variable is. However, as you will see later in this chapter, the concept of inferred types is important because it underlies other techniques. The next subject, anonymous types, is one for which inferred types are essential.

Anonymous Types

After programming for a while you may find, especially in database applications, that you spend a lot of time creating simple, dull classes for data representation. It is not unusual to have families of classes that do absolutely nothing other than expose properties. The Curry class shown earlier in this chapter is a perfect example:

```
public class Curry
{
    public string MainIngredient {get; set;}
    public string Style {get; set;}
    public int Spiciness {get; set;}
}
```

This class doesn't actually do anything — it merely stores structured data. In database or spreadsheet terms, you could think of this class as representing a row in a table. A collection class that was capable of holding instances of this class would be a representation of multiple rows in a table or spreadsheet.

This is a perfectly acceptable use of classes, but writing the code for these classes can become monotonous, and any modifications to the underlying data schema requires you to add, remove, or modify the code that defines the classes.

Anonymous types are a way to simplify this programming model. The idea behind anonymous types is that rather than define these simple data storage types, you can instead use the C# compiler to automatically create types based on the data that you want to store in them.

The preceding Curry type can be instantiated as follows:

```
Curry curry = new Curry { MainIngredient = "Lamb", Style = "Dhansak", Spiciness = 5 };
```

Alternatively, you could use an anonymous type, as in the following code:

```
var curry = new { MainIngredient = "Lamb", Style = "Dhansak", Spiciness = 5 };
```

There are two differences here. First, the var keyword is used. That's because anonymous types do not have an identifier that you can use. Internally they do have an identifier, as you will see in a moment, but it is not available to you in your code. Second, no type name is specified after the new keyword. That is how the compiler knows that you want to use an anonymous type.

The IDE detects the anonymous type definition and updates IntelliSense accordingly. With the preceding declaration, you can see the anonymous type as shown in Figure 14-5.

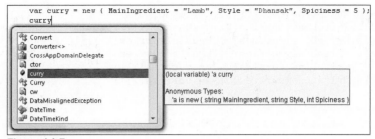

Figure 14-5

Here, internally, the type of the variable `curry` is `'a`. Obviously, you can't use this type in your code — it's not even a legal identifier name. The `'` is simply the symbol used to denote an anonymous type in IntelliSense. IntelliSense also enables you to inspect the members of the anonymous type, as shown in Figure 14-6.

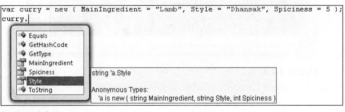

Figure 14-6

Note that the properties shown here are defined as *read-only* properties. This means that if you want to be able to change the values of properties in your data storage objects, you cannot use anonymous types.

The other members of anonymous types are implemented, as you will see in the following Try It Out.

Try It Out   Anonymous Types

1. Create a new console application called Ch14Ex02 and save it in the directory C:\BegVCSharp\Chapter14.

2. Modify the code in `Program.cs` as follows:

```
static void Main(string[] args)
{
    var curries = new[]
    {
        new { MainIngredient = "Lamb", Style = "Dhansak", Spiciness = 5 },
        new { MainIngredient = "Lamb", Style = "Dhansak", Spiciness = 5 },
        new { MainIngredient = "Chicken", Style = "Dhansak", Spiciness = 5 }
    };
    Console.WriteLine(curries[0].ToString());
    Console.WriteLine(curries[0].GetHashCode());
```

```
        Console.WriteLine(curries[1].GetHashCode());
        Console.WriteLine(curries[2].GetHashCode());
        Console.WriteLine(curries[0].Equals(curries[1]));
        Console.WriteLine(curries[0].Equals(curries[2]));
        Console.WriteLine(curries[0] == curries[1]);
        Console.WriteLine(curries[0] == curries[2]);

        Console.ReadKey();
}
```

3. Run the application. The result is shown in Figure 14-7.

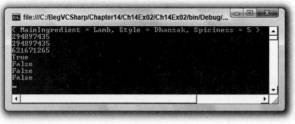

Figure 14-7

How It Works

In this example you create an array of anonymous type objects that you then proceed to use to perform tests of the members supplied by anonymous types. The code to create the array of anonymously typed objects is as follows:

```
var curries = new[]
{
    new { MainIngredient = "Lamb", Style = "Dhansak", Spiciness = 5 },
    new { MainIngredient = "Lamb", Style = "Dhansak", Spiciness = 5 },
    new { MainIngredient = "Chicken", Style = "Dhansak", Spiciness = 5 }
};
```

This uses an array that is implicitly typed to an anonymous type, using a combination of syntax from this section and the "Type Inference" section earlier in this chapter. The result is that the `curries` variable contains three instances of an anonymous type.

The first thing the code does after creating this array is to output the result of calling `ToString()` on the anonymous type:

```
Console.WriteLine(curries[0].ToString());
```

This results in the following output:

```
{ MainIngredient = Lamb, Style = Dhansak, Spiciness = 5 }
```

The implementation of `ToString()` in an anonymous type is to output the values of each property defined for the type.

The code next calls `GetHashCode()` on each of the array's three objects:

```
Console.WriteLine(curries[0].GetHashCode());
Console.WriteLine(curries[1].GetHashCode());
Console.WriteLine(curries[2].GetHashCode());
```

When implemented, `GetHashCode()` should return a unique integer for an object based on the state of the object. The first two objects in the array have the same property values, and therefore the same state. The result of these calls is the same integer for each of these objects, but a different integer for the third object. The output is as follows:

```
294897435
294897435
621671265
```

Next, the `Equals()` method is called to compare the first object with the second object, and then to compare the first object with the third object:

```
Console.WriteLine(curries[0].Equals(curries[1]));
Console.WriteLine(curries[0].Equals(curries[2]));
```

The result is as follows:

```
True
False
```

The implementation of `Equals()` in anonymous types compares the state of objects. The result is `true` where every property of one object contains the same value as the comparable property on another object.

That is not what happens when you use the `==` operator, however. The `==` operator, as shown in previous chapters, compares object references. The last section of code performs the same comparisons as the previous section of code, but uses `==` instead of `Equals()`:

```
Console.WriteLine(curries[0] == curries[1]);
Console.WriteLine(curries[0] == curries[2]);
```

Each entry in the `curries` array refers to a different instance of the anonymous type, so the result is `false` in both cases. The output is as expected:

```
False
False
```

Interestingly, when you created instances of the anonymous types, the compiler noticed that the parameters are the same and created three instances of the *same* anonymous type — not three separate anonymous types. However, this doesn't mean that when you instantiate an object from an anonymous type the compiler looks for a type to match it with. Even if you have defined a class elsewhere that has matching properties, if you use anonymous type syntax, an anonymous type will be created (or reused as in this example).

Extension Methods

Extension methods are a way to extend the functionality of types without modifying the types themselves. You can even use extension methods to extend types that you cannot modify — including types defined in the .NET Framework. Using an extension method, for example, you could even add functionality to something as fundamental as the System.String type.

In this context, to *extend the functionality* of a type means to provide a method that can be called through an instance of that type. The method you create to do this, known as the extension method, can take any number of parameters and return any return type (including void). To create and use an extension method, you must do the following:

1. Create a non-generic static class.

2. Add the extension method to the class you have created as a static method, using extension method syntax (described shortly).

3. Ensure that the code where you want to use the extension method imports the namespace containing the extension method class with a using statement.

4. Call the extension method through an instance of the extended type as if you were calling any other method of the extended type.

The C# compiler works its magic between step 3 and step 4. The IDE is instantly aware that you have created an extension method, and even displays it in IntelliSense, as shown in Figure 14-8.

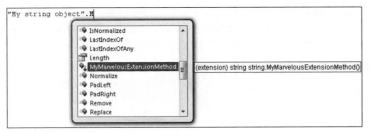

Figure 14-8

In Figure 14-8, an extension method called MyMarvelousExtensionMethod() is available through a string object (here just a literal string). This method, which is denoted with a slightly different method icon that includes a blue, downward-pointing arrow, takes no additional parameters and returns a string.

To define an extension method you define a method in the same way as any other method, but that method must meet the requirements of extension method syntax. These requirements are as follows:

❑ The method must be static.

❑ The method must include a parameter to represent the instance of the type that the extension method will be called on. (This parameter will be referred to here as the instance parameter.)

❑ The instance parameter must be the first parameter defined for the method.

❑ The instance parameter must have no other modifier other than the this keyword.

The syntax for an extension method is as follows:

```
public static class ExtensionClass
{
    public static ReturnType ExtensionMethodName(this TypeToExtend instance)
    {
        ...
    }
}
```

Once you have imported the namespace containing the static class that includes this method (which is known as making the extension method available), you can write code as follows:

```
TypeToExtend myVar;
// myVar is initialized by code not shown here.
myVar.ExtensionMethodName();
```

You can also include any additional parameters you want in the extension method, and make use of its return type.

Effectively, this call is identical to the following, but with simpler syntax:

```
TypeToExtend myVar;
// myVar is initialized by code not shown here.
ExtensionClass.ExtensionMethodName(myVar);
```

The other advantage is that, once imported, you can find the functionality you need much more easily by looking at extension methods through IntelliSense. Extension methods may be spread across multiple extension classes, or even libraries, but they will all show up in the member list of the extended type.

When you define an extension method that can be used with a particular type, you can use it with any types that derive from this type. Referring back to an example used earlier in this chapter, if you defined an extension method for the `Animal` class, you could call it on, for example, a `Cow` object.

Extension methods provide a fantastic way to provide libraries of utility code that you can reuse across your applications. They are also used extensively in LINQ, which you will learn about later in this book. To better understand them, work through a full Try It Out example.

Try It Out   Extension Methods

1. Create a new console application called `Ch14Ex03` and save it in the directory C:\BegVCSharp\Chapter14.

2. Add a new class library project to the solution called `ExtensionLib`.

3. Remove the existing `Class1.cs` class file from `ExtensionLib` and add a new class called `ExtensionLibExtensions`.

4. Modify the code in `ExtensionLibExtensions.cs` as follows:

```
public static class ExtensionLibExtensions
{
    public static string ToTitleCase(this string inputString, bool forceLower)
    {
        inputString = inputString.Trim();
        if (inputString == "")
        {
            return "";
        }
        if (forceLower)
        {
            inputString = inputString.ToLower();
        }

        string[] inputStringAsArray = inputString.Split(' ');
        StringBuilder sb = new StringBuilder();
        for (int i = 0; i < inputStringAsArray.Length; i++)
        {
            if (inputStringAsArray[i].Length > 0)
            {
                sb.AppendFormat("{0}{1} ",
                    inputStringAsArray[i].Substring(0, 1).ToUpper(),
                    inputStringAsArray[i].Substring(1));
            }
        }
        return sb.ToString(0, sb.Length - 1);
    }

    public static string ReverseString(this string inputString)
    {
        return new string(inputString.ToCharArray().Reverse().ToArray());
    }

    public static string ToStringReversed(this object inputObject)
    {
        return inputObject.ToString().ReverseString();
    }
}
```

5. Add a project reference to the `ExtensionLib` project to the `Ch14Ex03` project.

6. Modify the code in `Program.cs` as follows:

```
using System;
using System.Collections.Generic;
using System.Linq;
using System.Text;
using ExtensionLib;

namespace Ch14Ex03
{
```

```
class Program
{
    static void Main(string[] args)
    {
        Console.WriteLine("Enter a string to convert:");
        string sourceString = Console.ReadLine();
        Console.WriteLine("String with title casing: {0}",
            sourceString.ToTitleCase(true));
        Console.WriteLine("String backwards: {0}", sourceString.ReverseString());
        Console.WriteLine("String length backwards: {0}",
            sourceString.Length.ToStringReversed());
        Console.ReadKey();
    }
}
}
```

7. Run the application. When prompted, type in a string (at least 10 characters long and more than one word for the best effect). An example result is shown in Figure 14-9.

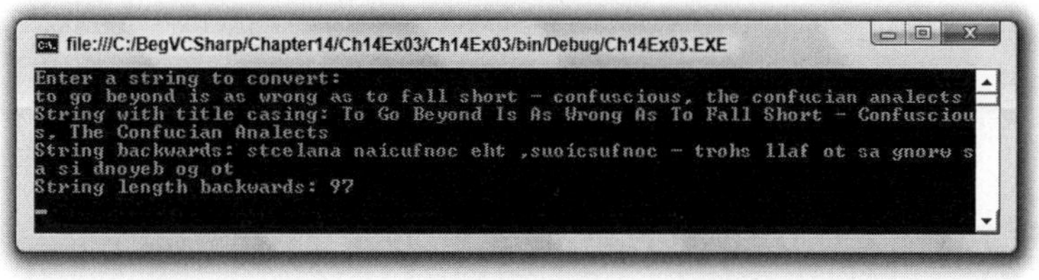

Figure 14-9

How It Works

This example created a class library containing utility extension methods, which you used on a simple client application. The class library includes a static class called `ExtensionLibExtensions` that contains the extension methods, and you imported the `ExtensionLib` namespace that contains this class into the client application, thus making the extension methods available.

You created the three extension methods shown in the following table:

Method	Usage
`ToTitleCase()`	Capitalizes each word in a `string`, and returns a `string`. Has a `bool` parameter, which if `true` changes the string into lowercase before starting.
`ReverseString()`	Reverses the order of letters in a `string`, and returns a `string`.
`ToStringReversed()`	Uses `Reverse()` to reverse the order of letters in the `string` returned by calling `ToString()` on an `object`. Returns a `string`.

The client code used each of these methods in turn, using the string you input as a starting point.

The first of these extension methods, `ToTitleCase()`, contains the most code but is the simplest method to understand. It is defined by using the extension method syntax shown earlier. You can see that this extension method will apply to `string` objects because the instance parameter is a string. There is also a second parameter defined, `forceLower`. When you call this extension method, though, only one parameter is used because the instance parameter comes from the object from which the extension method is called.

The code for this method starts by preparing the input string by trimming whitespace and (optionally) converting it to lowercase:

```
public static string ToTitleCase(this string inputString, bool forceLower)
{
    inputString = inputString.Trim();
    if (inputString == "")
    {
        return "";
    }
    if (forceLower)
    {
        inputString = inputString.ToLower();
    }
```

Next, the string is split into an array of single words, and the array is parsed in a `for` loop that assembles the result string in a `StringBuilder` object:

```
    string[] inputStringAsArray = inputString.Split(' ');
    StringBuilder sb = new StringBuilder();
    for (int i = 0; i < inputStringAsArray.Length; i++)
    {
        if (inputStringAsArray[i].Length > 0)
        {
            sb.AppendFormat("{0}{1} ",
                inputStringAsArray[i].Substring(0, 1).ToUpper(),
                inputStringAsArray[i].Substring(1));
        }
    }
```

Finally, the result string is returned. The last character of the string is a space because of the processing in the `for` loop, so that character is trimmed when the string is returned:

```
    return sb.ToString(0, sb.Length - 1);
}
```

The next extension method, `ReverseString()`, looks simple, but looks can be deceptive. The sequence of operations carried out by this method is straightforward: A string is compared to a `char` array, the elements in this array are reversed, and the reversed array is converted back into a `string`, which is then returned. However, the method that reverses the elements in the `char` array is itself an extension method. This method is `Reverse()`, and is defined in the `System.Linq` namespace as follows:

```
public static IEnumerable<TSource> Reverse<TSource>(this IEnumerable<TSource> source);
```

This looks more complicated than it is, as it uses generics. Extension methods can use generic type parameters much like any other method. The Reverse() method uses a single generic type parameter, TSource, where the instance parameter used by the generic method must support the IEnumerable<TSource> interface. In the ReverseString() method, the Reverse() method is called on an object of type char[]. An array of type TSource supports the IEnumerable<TSource> interface by definition, so an array of type char supports the IEnumerable<char> interface. The version of Reverse() that is called is therefore as follows:

```
public static IEnumerable<char> Reverse<char>(this IEnumerable<char> source);
```

In ReverseString() the resultant IEnumerable<char> interface is converted back into a char[] object by calling its ToArray() method, and this char[] object is used in the constructor of a new string object. This string object, finally, is returned:

```
public static string ReverseString(this string inputString)
{
    return new string(inputString.ToCharArray().Reverse().ToArray());
}
```

The System.Linq namespace contains a large array of extension methods, most of which are designed for use with LINQ, as you will see later in the book. Many, however, can be useful in other situations, as shown here.

You can see these extension methods through IntelliSense if you have the System.Linq *namespace imported — which it is by default. However, don't concern yourself with them at this point because many of these extension methods use lambda expressions, which are covered in the next section.*

The final extension method in the example, ToStringReversed(), is an example of a more general extension method. Rather than require a string type instance parameter, this method instead has an instance parameter of type object. This means that this extension method can be called on *any* object and will show up in IntelliSense on every object you use. There isn't a lot you can do in this extension method, as you cannot assume very much about the object that might be used. You could use the is operator or try conversion to find out what the instance parameter type is and act accordingly, or you could do what is done in this example and use basic functionality that is supported by all objects — the ToString() method:

```
public static string ToStringReversed(this object inputObject)
{
    return inputObject.ToString().ReverseString();
}
```

This method simply calls the ToString() method on its instance parameter and reverses it using the ReverseString() method described earlier. In the example client application, the ToStringReversed() method is called on an int variable, which results in a string representation of the integer with its digits reversed.

Extension methods that can be used with multiple types can be very useful. Remember as well that you can define generic extension methods, which can have constraints applied to the types that can be used, as shown in Chapter 12.

Lambda Expressions

Lambda expressions are a new construct in C# 3.0 that you can use to simplify certain aspects of C# programming, in particular when combined with LINQ. They can be difficult to grasp at first, mainly because they are so flexible in their usage. Lambda expressions are extremely useful when combined with other C# language features, such as anonymous methods. Without looking at LINQ, a subject left until later in the book, anonymous methods are the best entry point for examining this subject. Start with a quick refresher.

Anonymous Methods Recap

In Chapter 13 you learned about anonymous methods, methods that you supply inline, where a delegate type variable would otherwise be required. When you add an event handler to an event, the sequence of events is as follows:

1. Define an event handler method whose return type and parameters match those of the delegate required for the event you want to subscribe to.

2. Declare a variable of the delegate type used for the event.

3. Initialize the delegate variable to an instance of the delegate type that refers to the event handler method.

4. Add the delegate variable to the list of subscribers for the event.

In practice, things are a bit simpler than this because you typically won't bother with a variable to store the delegate — you will just use an instance of the delegate when you subscribe to the event.

This was the case when you used the following code in Chapter 13:

```
Timer myTimer = new Timer(100);
myTimer.Elapsed += new ElapsedEventHandler(WriteChar);
```

This code subscribes to the `Elapsed` event of a `Timer` object. This event uses the `ElapsedEventHandler` delegate type, which is instantiated using a method identifier, `WriteChar`. The result here is that when the `Timer` raises the `Elapsed` event, the `WriteChar()` method is called. The parameters passed to `WriteChar()` depend on the parameter types defined by the `ElapsedEventHandler` delegate and the values passed by the code in `Timer` that raises the event.

In fact, the C# compiler can achieve the same result with even less code:

```
myTimer.Elapsed += WriteChar;
```

The C# compiler knows the delegate type required by the `Elapsed` event, so it can fill in the blanks. However, this isn't advisable in most circumstances because it makes it harder to read your code and know exactly what is happening. When you use an anonymous method, the sequence of events shown earlier is reduced to a single step:

1. Use an inline, anonymous method that matches the return type and the parameters of the delegate required by an event to subscribe to that event.

The inline, anonymous method is defined by using the `delegate` keyword:

```
myTimer.Elapsed += delegate(object source, ElapsedEventArgs e)
{
    Console.WriteLine("Event handler called after {0} milliseconds.",
        (source as Timer).Interval);
};
```

This code works just as well as using the event handler separately. The main difference is that the anonymous method used here is effectively hidden from the rest of your code. You cannot, for example, reuse this event handler elsewhere in your application. In addition, the syntax used here is, for want of a better description, a little clunky. The `delegate` keyword is instantly confusing because it is effectively being overloaded — you use it both for anonymous methods and for defining delegate types.

Lambda Expressions for Anonymous Methods

This brings us to lambda expressions. Lambda expressions are a way to simplify the syntax of anonymous methods. In fact, they are more than that, but let's keep things simple for now. Using a lambda expression, you can rewrite the code at the end of the previous section as follows:

```
myTimer.Elapsed += (source, e) => Console.WriteLine(
    "Event handler called after {0} milliseconds.", (source as Timer).Interval);
```

At first glance this looks . . . well, a little baffling (unless you are familiar with so-called functional programming languages such as Lisp or Haskell, that is). However, if you look closer you can see, or at least infer, how this works and how it relates to the anonymous method that it replaces. The lambda expression is made up of three parts:

❑   A list of (untyped) parameters in parentheses

❑   The => operator

❑   A C# statement

The types of the parameters are inferred from the context, using the same logic shown in the section "Anonymous Types" earlier in this chapter. The => operator simply separates the parameter list from the expression body. The expression body is executed when the lambda expression is called.

The compiler takes this lambda expression and creates an anonymous method that works exactly the same way as the anonymous method in the previous section. In fact, it will be compiled into the same or similar Microsoft Intermediate Language (MSIL) code.

To clarify what occurs in lambda expressions, here's another Try It Out.

Try It Out   **Simple Lambda Expressions**

1. Create a new console application called Ch14Ex04 and save it in the directory
    C:\BegVCSharp\Chapter14.

2. Modify the code in `Program.cs` as follows:

```csharp
namespace Ch14Ex04
{
    delegate int TwoIntegerOperationDelegate(int paramA, int paramB);

    class Program
    {
        static void PerformOperations(TwoIntegerOperationDelegate del)
        {
            for (int paramAVal = 1; paramAVal <= 5; paramAVal++)
            {
                for (int paramBVal = 1; paramBVal <= 5; paramBVal++)
                {
                    int delegateCallResult = del(paramAVal, paramBVal);
                    Console.Write("f({0},{1})={2}",
                        paramAVal, paramBVal, delegateCallResult);
                    if (paramBVal != 5)
                    {
                        Console.Write(", ");
                    }
                }
                Console.WriteLine();
            }
        }

        static void Main(string[] args)
        {
            Console.WriteLine("f(a, b) = a + b:");
            PerformOperations((paramA, paramB) => paramA + paramB);
            Console.WriteLine();
            Console.WriteLine("f(a, b) = a * b:");
            PerformOperations((paramA, paramB) => paramA * paramB);
            Console.WriteLine();
            Console.WriteLine("f(a, b) = (a - b) % b:");
            PerformOperations((paramA, paramB) => (paramA - paramB) % paramB);
            Console.ReadKey();
        }
    }
}
```

3. Run the application. The result is shown in Figure 14-10.

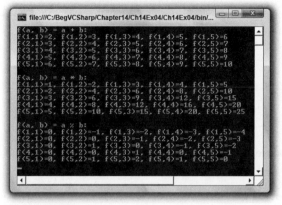

Figure 14-10

How It Works

This example uses lambda expressions to generate functions that can be used to return the result of performing specific processing on two input parameters. Those functions then operate on 25 pairs of values and output the results to the console.

You start by defining a delegate type called TwoIntegerOperationDelegate to represent a method that takes two int parameters and returns an int result:

```
delegate int TwoIntegerOperationDelegate(int paramA, int paramB);
```

This delegate type is used later when you define your lambda expressions. These lambda expressions compile into methods whose return type and parameter types match this delegate type, as you will see shortly.

Next, you add a method called PerformOperations(), which takes a single parameter of type TwoIntegerOperationDelegate:

```
static void PerformOperations(TwoIntegerOperationDelegate del)
{
```

The idea behind this method is that you can pass it a delegate instance (or an anonymous method or lambda expression because these constructs compile to delegate instances) and the method will call the method represented by the delegate instance with an assortment of values:

```
for (int paramAVal = 1; paramAVal <= 5; paramAVal++)
{
    for (int paramBVal = 1; paramBVal <= 5; paramBVal++)
    {
        int delegateCallResult = del(paramAVal, paramBVal);
```

The parameters and results are then output to the console:

```
Console.Write("f({0},{1})={2}",
    paramAVal, paramBVal, delegateCallResult);
if (paramBVal != 5)
{
    Console.Write(", ");
}
}
Console.WriteLine();
}
}
```

In the `Main()` method you create three lambda expressions and use them to call `PerformOperations()` in turn. The first of these calls is as follows:

```
Console.WriteLine("f(a, b) = a + b:");
PerformOperations((paramA, paramB) => paramA + paramB);
```

The lambda expression used here is as follows:

```
(paramA, paramB) => paramA + paramB
```

Again, this breaks down into three parts:

1. A parameter definition section. Here there are two parameters, `paramA` and `paramB`. These parameters are untyped, meaning the compiler can infer the types of these parameters according to the context. In this case the compiler can determine that the `PerformOperations()` method call requires a delegate of type `TwoIntegerOperationDelegate`. This delegate type has two `int` parameters, so by inference both `paramA` and `paramB` are typed as `int` variables.

2. The `=>` operator. This separates the lambda expression parameters from the lambda expression body.

3. The expression body. This specifies a simple operation, which is the summation of `paramA` and `paramB`. Notice that there is no need to specify that this is a return value. The compiler knows that to create a method that can be used with `TwoIntegerOperationDelegate`, the method must have a return type of `int`. Because the operation specified, `paramA + paramB`, evaluates to an `int`, and there is no additional information supplied, the compiler infers that the result of this expression should be the return type of the method.

In longhand then, you can expand the code that uses this lambda expression to the following code that uses an anonymous method:

```
Console.WriteLine("f(a, b) = a + b:");
PerformOperations(delegate(int paramA, int paramB)
{
    return paramA + paramB;
});
```

The remaining code performs operations using two different lambda expressions in the same way:

```
Console.WriteLine();
Console.WriteLine("f(a, b) = a * b:");
PerformOperations((paramA, paramB) => paramA * paramB);
Console.WriteLine();
Console.WriteLine("f(a, b) = (a - b) % b:");
PerformOperations((paramA, paramB) => (paramA - paramB) % paramB);
Console.ReadKey();
```

The last lambda expression involves more calculations but is no more complicated than the others. The syntax for lambda expressions enables you to perform far more complicated operations, as you will see shortly.

Lambda Expression Parameters

In the code you have seen so far, the lambda expressions have used type inference to determine the types of the parameters passed. In fact, this is not mandatory; you can define types if you wish. For example, you could use the following lambda expression:

```
(int paramA, int paramB) => paramA + paramB
```

This has the advantage of making your code more readable, although you lose out in both brevity and flexibility. You could use the implicitly typed lambda expressions from the previous Try It Out for delegate types that used other numeric types, such as `long` variables.

Note that you cannot use implicit and explicit parameter types in the same lambda expression. The following lambda expressions will not compile because `paramA` is explicitly typed and `paramB` is implicitly typed:

```
(int paramA, paramB) => paramA + paramB
```

Parameter lists in lambda expressions always consist of a comma-separated list of either all implicitly typed or all explicitly typed parameters. If you have only one parameter, then you can omit the parentheses; otherwise, they are required as part of the parameter list, as shown earlier. For example, you could have the following as a single-parameter, implicitly typed lambda expression:

```
param1 => param1 * param1
```

You can also define lambda expressions that have no parameters. This is denoted by using empty parentheses, `()`:

```
() => Math.PI
```

This could be used where a delegate requiring no parameters but returning a `double` value is required.

Lambda Expression Statement Bodies

In all the code that you have seen so far, a single expression has been used in the statement body of lambda expressions. You have also seen how this single expression has been interpreted as the return value of the lambda expression, which is, for example, how you can use the expression paramA + paramB as the statement body for a lambda expression for a delegate with a return type of int (assuming both paramA and paramB are implicitly or explicitly typed to int values, as they were in the example code).

An earlier example showed how a delegate with a void return type was less fussy about the code used in the statement body:

```
myTimer.Elapsed += (source, e) => Console.WriteLine(
    "Event handler called after {0} milliseconds.", (source as Timer).Interval);
```

Here, the statement doesn't evaluate to anything, so it is simply executed without any return value being used anywhere.

Given that lambda expressions can be visualized as an extension of the anonymous method syntax, you may not be surprised to learn that you can also include multiple statements as a lambda expression statement body. To do so, you simply provide a block of code enclosed in curly braces, much like any other situation in C# where you must supply multiple lines of code:

```
(param1, param2) =>
{
    // Multiple statements ahoy!
}
```

If you use a lambda expression in combination with a delegate type that has a non-void return type, then you must return a value with the return keyword, just like any other method:

```
(param1, param2) =>
{
    // Multiple statements ahoy!
    return returnValue;
}
```

For example, earlier you saw how you could rewrite the following code from the Try It Out:

```
PerformOperations((paramA, paramB) => paramA + paramB);
```

as

```
PerformOperations(delegate(int paramA, int paramB)
{
    return paramA + paramB;
});
```

Alternatively, you could rewrite the code as follows:

```
PerformOperations((paramA, paramB) =>
{
    return paramA + paramB;
});
```

This is more in keeping with the original code because it maintains implicit typing of the paramA and paramB parameters.

For the most part, lambda expressions are at their most useful — and certainly their most elegant — when used with single expressions. To be honest, if you require multiple statements, your code may read much better if you define a separate, non-anonymous method to use instead of a lambda expression; that also makes your code more reusable.

Lambda Expressions as Delegates and Expression Trees

You have already seen some of the differences between lambda expressions and anonymous methods where lambda methods have more flexibility — for example, implicitly typed parameters. At this point it is worth noting another key difference, although the implications of this will not become apparent until later in the book when you learn about LINQ.

You can interpret a lambda expression in two ways. The first way, which you have seen throughout this chapter, is as a delegate. That is, you can assign a lambda expression to a delegate type variable, as you did in the previous Try It Out.

In general terms, you can represent a lambda expression with up to four parameters as one of the following generic types, all defined in the System namespace:

- ❑   Action<> for lambda expressions with no parameters and a return type of void.
- ❑   Action<> for lambda expressions with up to four parameters and a return type of void.
- ❑   Func<> for lambda expressions with up to four parameters and a return type that is not void.

Action<> has up to four generic type parameters, one for each parameter, and Func<> has up to five generic type parameters, used for up to four parameters and the return type. In Func<>, the return type is always the last in the list.

For example, the following lambda expression, which you saw earlier:

```
(int paramA, int paramB) => paramA + paramB
```

can be represented as a delegate of type Func<int, int, int> because it has two parameters and a return type all of type int.

The second way is to interpret the lambda expression as what is known as an *expression tree*. An expression tree is an abstract representation of a lambda expression, and as such cannot be executed directly. Instead, you can use the expression tree to analyze the lambda expression programmatically and perform actions in response to the lambda expression.

This is, obviously, a complicated subject. However, expression trees are critical to the LINQ functionality you will learn about later in this book. To give a more concrete example, the LINQ framework includes a generic class called Expression<>, which you can use to encapsulate a lambda expression. One of the ways in which this class is used is to take a lambda expression that you have written in C# and convert it into an equivalent SQL script representation for executing directly in a database.

You don't need to know any more about that at this point. When you encounter this functionality later in the book, you will be better equipped to understand what is going on, as you now have a thorough grounding in the key concepts that C# 3.0 provides.

Lambda Expressions and Collections

Now that you have learned about the Func<> generic delegate, you can understand more of the list of extension methods that the System.Linq namespace provides for array types. For example, there is an extension method called Aggregate(), which is defined with three overloads as follows:

```
public static TSource Aggregate<TSource>(
   this IEnumerable<TSource> source,
   Func<TSource, TSource, TSource> func);

public static TAccumulate Aggregate<TSource, TAccumulate>(
   this IEnumerable<TSource> source,
   TAccumulate seed,
   Func<TAccumulate, TSource, TAccumulate> func);

public static TResult Aggregate<TSource, TAccumulate, TResult>(
   this IEnumerable<TSource> source,
   TAccumulate seed,
   Func<TAccumulate, TSource, TAccumulate> func,
   Func<TAccumulate, TResult> resultSelector);
```

As with the extension method shown earlier, this looks at first glance to be impenetrable, but if you break it down you can work it out easily enough. The IntelliSense for this function tells you that it does the following:

```
Applies an accumulator function over a sequence.
```

This means an accumulator function (which you can supply in the form of a lambda expression) will be applied for each pair of elements in a collection from beginning to end, with the output of each evaluation becoming one of the inputs of the next.

In the simplest of the three overloads there is only one generic type specification, which can be inferred from the type of the instance parameter. For example, in the following code the generic type specification will be int (the accumulator function is left blank for now):

```
int[] myIntArray = {2, 6, 3};
int result = myIntArray.Aggregate(...);
```

This is equivalent to the following:

```
int[] myIntArray = {2, 6, 3};
int result = myIntArray.Aggregate<int>(...);
```

The lambda expression that is required here can be deduced from the extension method specification. Because in this code the type TSource is int, you must supply a lambda expression for the delegate Func<int, int, int>. For example, you could use one you've seen before:

```
int[] myIntArray = {2, 6, 3};
int result = myIntArray.Aggregate((paramA, paramB) => paramA + paramB);
```

This call results in the lambda expression being called twice, first with paramA = 2 and paramB = 6, and once with paramA = 8 (the result of the first calculation) and paramB = 3. The final result assigned to the variable result will be the int value 11 — the summation of all the elements in the array.

The other two overloads of the Aggregate() extension method are similar, but enable you to perform slightly more complicated processing. This is illustrated in the following short Try It Out.

Try It Out   Lambda Expressions and Collections

1. Create a new console application called Ch14Ex05 and save it in the directory C:\BegVCSharp\Chapter14.

2. Modify the code in Program.cs as follows:

```
static void Main(string[] args)
{
    string[] curries = { "pathia", "jalfreze", "korma" };
    Console.WriteLine(curries.Aggregate(
        (a, b) => a + " " + b));
    Console.WriteLine(curries.Aggregate<string, int>(
        0,
        (a, b) => a + b.Length));
    Console.WriteLine(curries.Aggregate<string, string, string>(
        "Some curries:",
        (a, b) => a + " " + b,
        a => a));
    Console.WriteLine(curries.Aggregate<string, string, int>(
        "Some curries:",
        (a, b) => a + " " + b,
        a => a.Length));
    Console.ReadKey();
}
```

3. Run the application. The result is shown in Figure 14-11.

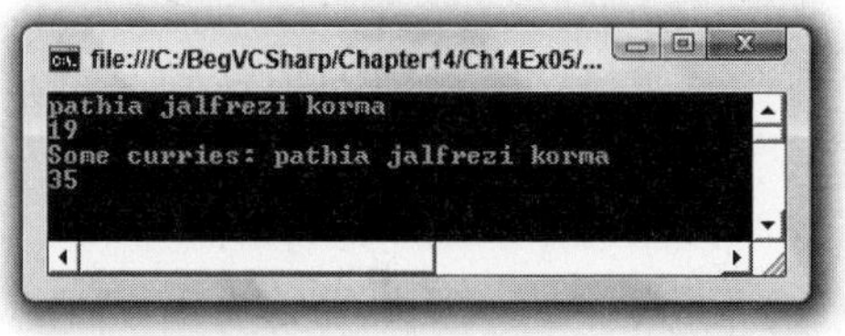

Figure 14-11

How It Works

In this example you experiment with each of the overloads of the `Aggregate()` extension method, using a string array with three elements as source data.

First, a simple concatenation is performed:

```
Console.WriteLine(curries.Aggregate(
    (a, b) => a + " " + b));
```

The first pair of elements is concatenated into a string using simple syntax. This is far from the best way to concatenate strings — ideally you would use `string.Concat()` or `string.Format()` to optimize performance — but here it provides a very simple way to see what is going on. After this first concatenation, the result is passed back into the lambda expression along with the third element in the array, in much the same way as you saw `int` values being summed earlier. The result is a concatenation of the entire array, with spaces separating entries.

Next, the second overload of the `Aggregate()` function, which has the two generic type parameters `TSource` and `TAccumulate`, is used. In this case the lambda expression must be of the form `Func<TAccumulate, TSource, TAccumulate>`. In addition, a seed value of type `TAccumulate` must be specified. This seed value is used in the first call to the lambda expression, along with the first array element. Subsequent calls take the accumulator result of previous calls to the expression. The code used is as follows:

```
Console.WriteLine(curries.Aggregate<string, int>(
    0,
    (a, b) => a + b.Length));
```

The accumulator (and, by implication, the return value) is of type `int`. The accumulator value is initially set to the seed value of 0, and with each call to the lambda expression is summed with the length of an element in the array. The final result is the sum of the lengths of each of the elements in the array.

Next you come to the last overload of `Aggregate()`. This takes three generic type parameters and differs from the previous version only in that the return value can be a different type from both the type of the elements in the array and the accumulator value. First, this overload is used to concatenate the string elements with a seed string:

```
Console.WriteLine(curries.Aggregate<string, string, string>(
    "Some curries:",
    (a, b) => a + " " + b,
    a => a));
```

The final parameter of this method, `resultSelector`, must be specified even if (as in this example) the accumulator value is simply copied to the result. This parameter is a lambda expression of type `Func<TAccumulate, TResult>`.

In the final section of code, the same version of `Aggregate()` is used again, but this time with an `int` return value. Here, `resultSelector` is supplied with a lambda expression that returns the length of the accumulator string:

```
Console.WriteLine(curries.Aggregate<string, string, int>(
    "Some curries:",
    (a, b) => a + " " + b,
    a => a.Length));
```

This example hasn't done anything spectacular, but it demonstrates how you can use more complicated extension methods that involve generic type parameters, collections, and seemingly complex syntax. You'll see more of this later in the book.

Summary

This chapter examined the new features that are included in version 3.0 of the C# language, which is the version that you use in Visual Studio 2008 and Visual C# Express Edition 2008. You learned how these features simplify some of the coding required to achieve certain commonly used and/or advanced functionality.

Highlights of this chapter included the following:

❑ How to use object and collection initializers to instantiate and initialize objects and collections in one step.

❑ How the IDE and C# compiler are capable of inferring types from context, and how to use the var keyword to permit type inference to be used with any variable type.

❑ How to create and use anonymous types, which combine the initializer and type inference topics already covered.

❑ How to create extension methods that can be called on instances of other types without adding code to the definition of these types, and how this technique can be used to supply libraries of utility methods.

❑ How to use lambda methods to provide anonymous methods to delegate instances, and how the extended syntax of lambda methods makes additional functionality possible.

Most of the C# features that you learned about in this chapter have been added specifically to cater to the new LINQ capabilities of the .NET Framework. Much of the elegance and many of the subtleties of the code that you have seen will only become apparent later. Having said that, you have learned some extremely powerful techniques that you can put to work straight away to improve your C# programming skills.

You have now covered the entire C# language as it stands with version 3.0. However, this is not the same thing as knowing everything about programming with the .NET Framework. The C# language gives you all the tools you need to write .NET applications, but it is the classes available to you in the .NET Framework that give you the raw materials to build with. From this point on in the book you will become increasingly immersed in these classes, and you will learn how to perform a multitude of tasks with them. The next chapter moves away from the console applications you have thus far spent most of your time working with, and starts to use the rich functionality offered by Windows Forms to create graphical user interfaces. As you do this, remember that the underlying principles are the same regardless of the type of application you create. The skills you learned in the first part of this book will serve you well as you progress through the following chapters.

Exercises

1. Why can't you use an object initializer with the following class? After modifying this class to enable the use of an object initializer, give an example of the code you would use to instantiate and initialize this class in one step:

```
public class Giraffe
{
    public Giraffe(double neckLength, string name)
    {
        NeckLength = neckLength;
        Name = name;
    }
    public double NeckLength {get; set;}
    public string Name {get; set;}
}
```

2. True or false: If you declare a variable of type `var` you will then be able to use it to hold any object type.

3. When you use anonymous types, how can you compare two instances to determine whether they contain the same data?

4. Try to correct the following code for an extension method, which contains an error:

```
public string ToAcronym(this string inputString)
{
    inputString = inputString.Trim();
    if (inputString == "")
    {
        return "";
    }
    string[] inputStringAsArray = inputString.Split(' ');
    StringBuilder sb = new StringBuilder();
    for (int i = 0; i < inputStringAsArray.Length; i++)
    {
        if (inputStringAsArray[i].Length > 0)
        {
            sb.AppendFormat("{0}", inputStringAsArray[i].Substring(0, 1).ToUpper());
        }
    }
    return sb.ToString();
}
```

5. How would you ensure that the extension method in question 4 was available to your client code?

6. Rewrite the `ToAcronym` method shown here as a single line of code. The code should ensure that strings including multiple spaces between words do not cause errors. Hint: You will require the `?:` tertiary operator, the `string.Aggregate<string, string>()` extension function, and a lambda expression to achieve this.

Part II
Windows Programming

15

Basic Windows Programming

About 10 years ago, Visual Basic won great acclaim for providing programmers with tools for creating highly detailed user interfaces via an intuitive form designer, along with an easy to learn programming language that together produced probably the best environment out there for Rapid Application Development (RAD). One of the advantages offered by RAD tools such as Visual Basic is that they provide access to a number of prefabricated controls that can be used to quickly build the user interface for an application.

At the heart of the development of most Visual Basic Windows applications is the Forms Designer. You create a user interface by dragging and dropping controls from a Toolbox to your form, placing them where you want them to appear when you run the program; double-clicking the control adds a handler for that control. The controls provided by Microsoft, along with additional custom controls that could be bought at reasonable prices, have supplied programmers with an unprecedented pool of reusable, thoroughly tested code that is no more than a mouse click away. Such application development is now available to C# developers through Visual Studio.

In this chapter, you work with Windows Forms, and use some of the many controls that ship with Visual Studio. These controls cover a wide range of functionality, and through the design capabilities of Visual Studio, developing user interfaces and handling user interaction is very straightforward — and fun! Presenting all of Visual Studio's controls is impossible within the scope of this book, so this chapter looks at some of the most commonly used controls, ranging from labels and text boxes to list views and tab controls.

In this chapter you learn about the following:

- ❑ The Windows Forms Designer.
- ❑ Controls for displaying information to the user, such as the Label and LinkLabel controls.
- ❑ Controls for triggering events, such as the Button control.
- ❑ Controls that enable users of your application to enter text, such as the TextBox control.

- ❏ Controls that enable you to inform users of the current state of the application and allow the user to change that state, such as the `RadioButton` and `CheckButton` controls.

- ❏ Controls that enable you to display lists of information, such as the `ListBox` and `ListView` controls.

- ❏ Controls that enable you to group other controls together, such as the `TabControl` and `Groupbox`.

Controls

You may not notice it, but when you work with Windows Forms, you are working with the `System.Windows.Forms` namespace. This namespace is included in the `using` directives in one of the files that holds the `Form` class. Most controls in .NET derive from the `System.Windows.Forms.Control` class. This class defines the basic functionality of the controls, which is why many properties and events in the controls you'll see are identical. Many of these classes are themselves base classes for other controls, as is the case with the `Label` and `TextBoxBase` classes (see Figure 15-1).

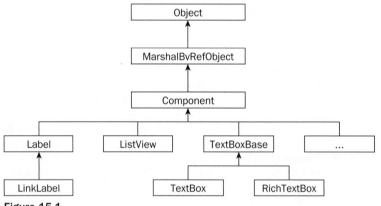

Figure 15-1

Properties

All controls have a number of properties that are used to manipulate the behavior of the control. The base class of most controls, `System.Windows.Forms.Control`, has several properties that other controls either inherit directly or override to provide some kind of custom behavior.

The following table shows some of the most common properties of the `Control` class. These properties are present in most of the controls in this chapter, so they are not explained in detail again unless the behavior changes for the control in question. Note that this table is not exhaustive; if you want to see all of the properties in the class, please refer to the .NET Framework SDK documentation.

Property	Description
Anchor	Specifies how the control behaves when its container is resized. See the next section for a detailed explanation of this property.
BackColor	The background color of a control.
Bottom	Specifies the distance from the top of the window to the bottom of the control. This is not the same as specifying the height of the control.
Dock	Docks a control to the edges of its container. See the next section for a more detailed explanation of this property.
Enabled	Setting `Enabled` to `true` usually means that the control can receive input from the user. Setting `Enabled` to `false` usually means that it cannot.
ForeColor	The foreground color of the control.
Height	The distance from the top to the bottom of the control.
Left	The left edge of the control relative to the left edge of its container.
Name	The name of the control. This name can be used to reference the control in code.
Parent	The parent of the control.
Right	The right edge of the control relative to the left edge of its container.
TabIndex	The number the control has in the tab order of its container.
TabStop	Specifies whether the control can be accessed by the Tab key.
Tag	This value is usually not used by the control itself. It enables you to store information about the control on the control itself. When this property is assigned a value through the Windows Forms Designer, you can only assign a string to it.
Text	Holds the text that is associated with this control.
Top	The top edge of the control relative to the top of its container.
Visible	Specifies whether the control is visible at runtime.
Width	The width of the control.

Anchoring, Docking, and Snapping Controls

With Visual Studio 2005, the Forms Designer default was changed from using a gridlike surface on which you could lay out your controls to a clean surface that uses snap-lines to position the controls. You can change between the two design styles by choosing Options on the Tools menu. Select the Windows Forms Designer node in the tree to the left and set the Layout Mode. Which tool is best is very much a question of personal preference. The following Try It Out uses the default.

Try It Out   Using Snap-Lines

Follow these steps to experiment working with snap-lines in the Windows Forms Designer:

1.   Create a new Windows Forms application, and name it **SnapLines**.

2.   Drag a single button control from the Toolbox to the middle of the form.

3.   Drag the button toward the upper-left corner of the form. Notice that when you are close to the edge of the form, lines appear from the left and top of the form and the controls snap into position. You can move the control beyond the snap-lines or leave it in position. Figure 15-2 shows the snap-lines that are displayed by Visual Studio when the button is moved to the top-left corner.

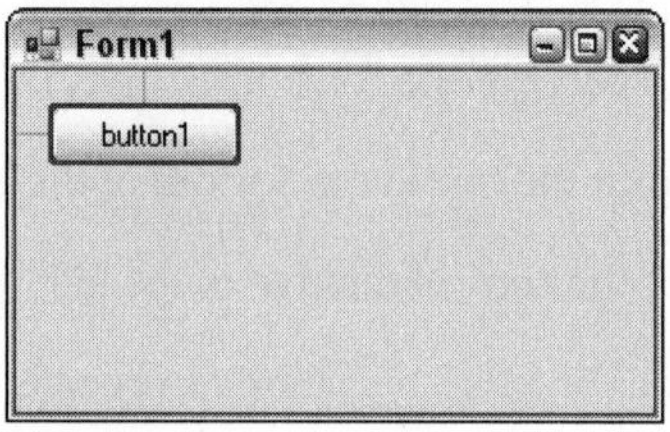

Figure 15-2

4.   Move the button back to the center of the form and drag another button from the Toolbox onto the form. Move it under the existing button. Snap-lines appear as you move the button below the existing button. These snap-lines enable you to line up the controls so that they are positioned directly above or at exactly the same height as another. If you move the new button up toward the existing button, another snap-line enables you to position the buttons with a preset space between them. Figure 15-3 shows the two buttons as they are being moved close to each other.

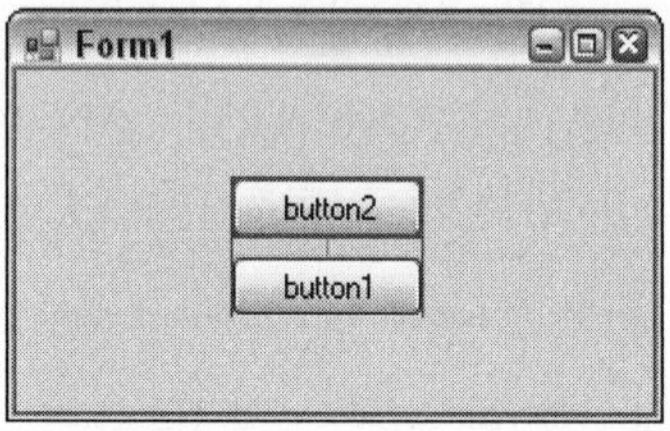

Figure 15-3

5.   Resize button1 to make it wider than button2. Then resize button2 as well and notice that when button2 is the same width as button1, a snap-line appears to enable you to set the width of the controls to the same value.

6.   Below the buttons, add a TextBox to the form and change the Text property of it to **Hello World!**

7.   Add a Label to the form and move it to the left of the TextBox. Note that as you move the control, the two snap-lines that enable you to snap to the top and bottom of the TextBox

appear, but between them is a third snap-line. This snap-line, shown in Figure 15-4, enables you to place the Label on the form so that the text of the TextBox and the Label are at the same height.

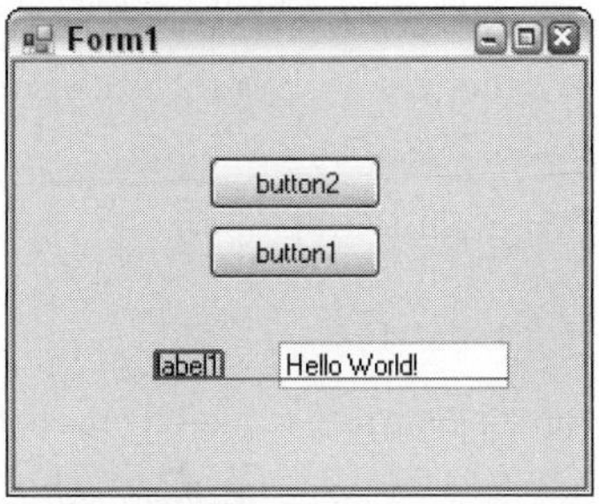

Figure 15-4

Anchor and Dock Properties

These two properties are especially useful when you are designing your form. Ensuring that a window doesn't become a mess to look at if the user decides to resize the window is far from trivial, and previously numerous lines of code had to be written to achieve this. Many programs solve the problem by simply disallowing window resizing, which is the easiest way around the problem but not always the best. The Anchor and Dock properties that have been introduced with .NET enable you to solve this problem without writing a single line of code.

The Anchor property specifies how the control behaves when a user resizes the window. You can specify that the control should resize itself, anchoring itself in proportion to its own edges, or stay the same size, anchoring its position relative to the window's edges.

The Dock property specifies that a control should dock to an edge of its container. If a user resizes the window, then the control continues to be docked to the edge of the window. If, for instance, you specify that a control should dock with the bottom of its container, then the control resizes and/or moves itself to always occupy the bottom part of the window, no matter how the window is resized.

You'll learn more about the Anchor property later in this chapter.

Events

In Chapter 13, you learned what events are and how to use them. This section covers particular kinds of events — specifically, the events generated by Windows Forms controls. These events are usually associated with user actions. For example, when the user clicks a button, that button generates an event indicating what just happened to it. Handling the event is the means by which the programmer can provide some functionality for that button.

The Control class defines a number of events that are common to the controls you use in this chapter. The following table describes a number of these events. Again, this is just a selection of the most common events; to see the entire list, refer to the .NET Framework SDK documentation.

Event	Description
Click	Occurs when a control is clicked. In some cases, this event also occurs when a user presses the Enter key.
DoubleClick	Occurs when a control is double-clicked. Handling the Click event on some controls, such as the Button control, means that the DoubleClick event can never be called.
DragDrop	Occurs when a drag-and-drop operation is completed — in other words, when an object has been dragged over the control, and the user releases the mouse button.
DragEnter	Occurs when an object being dragged enters the bounds of the control.
DragLeave	Occurs when an object being dragged leaves the bounds of the control.
DragOver	Occurs when an object has been dragged over the control.
KeyDown	Occurs when a key is pressed while the control has focus. This event always occurs before KeyPress and KeyUp.
KeyPress	Occurs when a key is pressed while a control has focus. This event always occurs after KeyDown and before KeyUp. The difference between KeyDown and KeyPress is that KeyDown passes the keyboard code of the key that has been pressed, whereas KeyPress passes the corresponding char value for the key.
KeyUp	Occurs when a key is released while a control has focus. This event always occurs after KeyDown and KeyPress.
GotFocus	Occurs when a control receives focus. Do not use this event to perform validation of controls. Use Validating and Validated instead.
LostFocus	Occurs when a control loses focus. Do not use this event to perform validation of controls. Use Validating and Validated instead.
MouseDown	Occurs when the mouse pointer is over a control and a mouse button is pressed. This is not the same as a Click event because MouseDown occurs as soon as the button is pressed and *before* it is released.
MouseMove	Occurs continually as the mouse travels over the control.
MouseUp	Occurs when the mouse pointer is over a control and a mouse button is released.
Paint	Occurs when the control is drawn.
Validated	Fires when a control with the CausesValidation property set to true is about to receive focus. It fires after the Validating event finishes and indicates that validation is complete.
Validating	Fires when a control with the CausesValidation property set to true is about to receive focus. Note that the control to be validated is the control that is losing focus, not the one that is receiving it.

You will see many of these events in the examples in this chapter. All the examples follow the same format: You first create the form's visual appearance, choosing and positioning controls, and so on, before moving on to adding the event handlers — which is where the main work of the examples takes place.

There are three basic ways to handle a particular event. The first is to double-click a control, which takes you to the event handler for the control's default event — this event is different for different controls. If that's the event you want, then you're fine. If you want an event other than the default, then you have two possible ways to proceed.

One way is to use the Events list in the Properties window, which is displayed when you click the lightning bolt button, shown in Figure 15-5.

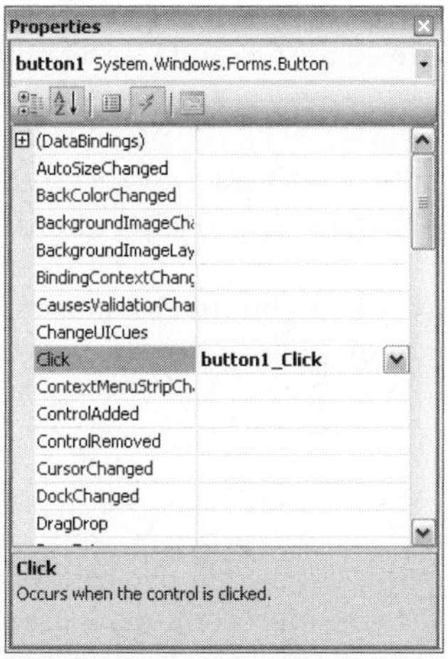

Figure 15-5

The grayed event is the control's default event. To add a handler for a particular event, double-click that event in the Events list, and the code to subscribe the control to the event is generated, along with the method signature to handle the event. Alternatively, you can type a name for the method to handle the particular event next to that event in the Events list, and when you press the Enter key, the event handler is generated with your chosen name.

Another option is to add the code to subscribe to the event yourself — you do this often in this and the next chapter by adding the code to the form's constructor after the `InitializeComponent()` call. Even when you type the code that is needed to subscribe to an event, Visual Studio detects what you are doing and offers to add the method signature to the code, just as it would do from the Forms Designer.

Each of these two options requires two steps — subscription to the event and the correct signature for the method handler. If you double-click a control and try to handle another event by editing the method signature of the default event for the event that you actually want handled, then you will fail — you also need to alter the event subscription code in `InitializeComponent()`, so this cheating method is not really a quick way to handle particular events.

You are now ready to start looking at the controls themselves, and you start with one that you've undoubtedly used countless times when working with Windows applications: the `Button` control.

The Button Control

When you think of a button, you probably think of a rectangular button that can be clicked to perform some task. However, the .NET Framework provides a class derived from Control — System.Windows .Forms.ButtonBase — that implements the basic functionality needed in Button controls, so programmers can derive from this class and create their own custom Button controls.

The System.Windows.Forms namespace provides three controls that derive from ButtonBase: Button, CheckBox, and RadioButton. This section focuses on the Button control (which is the standard, well-known rectangular button); the other two are covered later in this chapter.

The Button control exists on just about any Windows dialog you can think of. A button is primarily used to perform three kinds of tasks:

❑   To close a dialog with a state (e.g., the OK and Cancel buttons).

❑   To perform an action on data entered on a dialog (e.g., clicking Search after entering some search criteria).

❑   To open another dialog or application (e.g., Help buttons).

Working with the Button control is very straightforward. It usually consists of adding the control to your form and double-clicking it to add the code to the Click event, which is probably enough for most applications you work on.

Button Properties

This section looks at some of the properties of the Button control. This will give you an idea of what can be done with it. The following table lists the most commonly used properties of the Button class, even if technically they are defined in the ButtonBase base class. Only the most commonly used properties are described here. Please see the .NET Framework SDK documentation for a complete listing.

Property	Description
FlatStyle	Changes the style of the button. If you set the style to Popup, the button appears flat until the user moves the mouse pointer over it. When that happens, the button pops up to a 3-D look.
Enabled	Although this is derived from Control, it's mentioned here because it's a very important property for a button. Setting it to false means that the button becomes grayed out and nothing happens when you click it.
Image	Specifies an image (bitmap, icon, and so on) that will be displayed on the button.
ImageAlign	Specifies where the image on the button appears.

Button Events

By far, the most frequently used event of a button is the `Click` event. This event happens whenever a user clicks the button, which means pressing the left mouse button and releasing it while the pointer is over the button. Therefore, if you left-click the button and then draw the mouse away from the button before releasing it, then the `Click` event will not be raised. In addition, the `Click` event is raised when the button has focus and the user presses the Enter key. If you have a button on a form, you should always handle this event.

In the following Try It Out, you create a dialog with three buttons. Two of the buttons change the language used from English to Danish and back. (Feel free to use whatever language you prefer.) The last button closes the dialog.

Try It Out   **Working with Buttons**

Follow these steps to create a small Windows application that uses three buttons to change the text in the caption of the dialog:

1. Create a new Windows application called "ButtonTest" in the directory C:\BegVCSharp\Chapter15.

2. Pin the Toolbox down by clicking the pin icon next to the x in the top-right corner of the window, and double-click the `Button` control three times. Move the buttons and resize the form as shown in Figure 15-6.

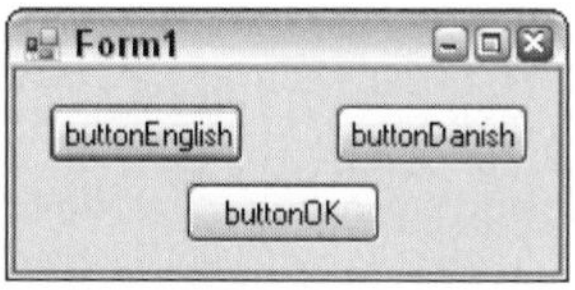

Figure 15-6

3. Right-click a button and select Properties. Change the name of each button as indicated in Figure 15-6 by selecting the (Name) edit field in the Properties window and typing the relevant text.

4. Change the `Text` property of each button to be the same as the name, but omit the `button` prefix for the `Text` property value.

5. You want to display a flag in front of the text to make it clear what you are talking about. Select the English button and find the `Image` property. Click to the right of it to bring up a dialog where you can add images to the resource file of the form. Click the Import button and browse to the icons. The icons you want to display are included in the project ButtonTest, which you can download from the Wrox home page. Select the icons `UK.PNG` and `DK.PNG`.

6. Select UK and click OK. Then select buttonDanish, click the (...) on the Image property and choose DK before clicking OK.

7. At this point, the button text and icon are placed on top of each other, so you need to change the alignment of the icon. For both the English and Danish buttons, change the `ImageAlign` property to `MiddleLeft`.

8. You may want to adjust the width of the buttons so that the text doesn't start right where the images end. Do this by selecting each of the buttons and pulling the notch on the right edge of the button.

9. Finally, click the form and change the `Text` property to `Do you speak English?`

That's it for the user interface of your dialog. You should now have something that looks like Figure 15-7.

Figure 15-7

Now you are ready to add the event handlers to the dialog. Double-click the English button. This takes you directly to the event handler for the control's default event — the `Click` event is the default event for the button, so that is the handler created.

Adding the Event Handlers

After double-clicking the English button, add the following code to the event handler:

```
private void buttonEnglish_Click(object sender, EventArgs e)
{
    this.Text = "Do you speak English?";
}
```

When Visual Studio creates a method to handle such an event, the method name is a concatenation of the name of the control, followed by an underscore and the name of the event that is handled.

For the `Click` event, the first parameter, `object sender`, holds the control that was clicked. For this example, that will always be the control indicated by the name of the method. In other cases, many controls may use the same method to handle an event; and in those cases you can find out exactly which control is calling by checking this value. The "TextBox Control" section later in this chapter demonstrates how to use a single method for multiple controls. The other parameter, `System.EventArgs e`, holds information about what actually happened. In this case, you won't need any of that information.

Return to the Design View and double-click the Danish button. You will be taken to the event handler for that button. Here is the code:

```
private void buttonDanish_Click(object sender, EventArgs e)
{
    this.Text = "Taler du dansk?";
}
```

This method is identical to btnEnglish_Click except that the text is in Danish. Finally, you add the event handler for the OK button just as you've done twice now. The code is a little different, though:

```
private void buttonOK_Click(object sender, EventArgs e)
{
    Application.Exit();
}
```

After this you exit the application and, with it, this first example. Compile it, run it, and click a few of the buttons. You should get output similar to what is displayed in Figure 15-8.

Figure 15-8

The Label and LinkLabel Controls

The Label control is probably the most frequently used control of them all. Look at any Windows application and you see a label on just about every dialog you find. Label is a simple control with one purpose only — to display text on the form.

The .NET Framework includes two label controls that present themselves in two distinct ways:

❑   Label, the standard Windows label.

❑   LinkLabel, a label similar to the standard one (and derived from it) but that presents itself as an Internet link (a hyperlink).

Figure 15-9 shows each type of label on a form.

Figure 15-9

Usually, you don't need to add event handling code for a standard `Label`, although it does support events like all controls. In the case of the `LinkLabel`, however, some extra code is needed to enable users clicking it to go to the target of the `LinkLabel`.

You can set a surprising number of properties for the `Label` control. Most of these are derived from `Control`, but some are new. The following table lists the most common properties. Unless stated otherwise, the properties are common to both the `Label` and `LinkLabel` controls.

Property	Description
BorderStyle	Specifies the style of the border around the label. The default is no border.
FlatStyle	Determines how the control is displayed. Setting this property to Popup makes the control appear flat until the user moves the mouse pointer over the control, at which time the control appears raised.
Image	Specifies a single image (bitmap, icon, and so on) to be displayed in the label.
ImageAlign	Specifies where in the Label the image is shown.
LinkArea	(LinkLabel only) This specifies the range in the text that should be displayed as a link.
LinkColor	(LinkLabel only) This indicates the color of the link.
Links	(LinkLabel only) It is possible for a LinkLabel to contain more than one link. This property enables you to find the link you want. The control keeps track of the links displayed in the text. Not available at design time.
LinkVisited	(LinkLabel only) Setting this to true means that the link is displayed in a different color if it has been clicked.
TextAlign	Specifies where in the control the text is shown.
VisitedLinkColor	(LinkLabel only) This specifies the color of the LinkLabel after the user has clicked it.

The TextBox Control

Text boxes should be used whenever you want users to enter text that you have no knowledge of at design time (e.g., the user's name). The primary function of a text box is for users to enter text, but any characters can be entered, and you can force users to enter numeric values only.

The .NET Framework comes with two basic controls to take text input from users: `TextBox` and `RichTextBox`. Both controls are derived from a base class called `TextBoxBase`, which itself is derived from `Control`.

TextBoxBase provides the base functionality for text manipulation in a text box, such as selecting text, cutting to and pasting from the clipboard, and a wide range of events. Right now you won't focus so much on what is derived from where, but instead look at the simpler of the two controls first — TextBox. You first build one example that demonstrates the TextBox properties, and then build on that to demonstrate the RichTextBox control later.

TextBox Properties

Again, there are simply too many properties to describe them all, so the following table includes only the most common ones:

Property	Description
CausesValidation	When a control with this property set to true is about to receive focus, two events are fired: Validating and Validated. You can handle these events in order to validate data in the control that is losing focus. This may cause the control never to receive focus. The related events are discussed below.
CharacterCasing	A value indicating whether the TextBox changes the case of the text entered. The possible values are as follows: Lower: All text entered is converted to lowercase. Normal: No changes are made to the text. Upper: All text entered is converted to uppercase.
MaxLength	A value that specifies the maximum length, in characters, of any text entered into the TextBox. Set this value to zero if the maximum limit is limited only by available memory.
Multiline	Indicates whether this is a multiline control, meaning it is able to show multiple lines of text. When Multiline is set to true, you'll usually want to set WordWrap to true as well.
PasswordChar	Specifies whether a password character should replace the actual characters entered into a single-line TextBox. If the Multiline property is true, then this has no effect.
ReadOnly	A Boolean indicating whether the text is read-only.
ScrollBars	Specifies whether a multiline TextBox should display scroll bars.
SelectedText	The text that is selected in the TextBox.
SelectionLength	The number of characters selected in the text. If this value is set to be larger than the total number of characters in the text, then it is reset by the control to be the total number of characters minus the value of SelectionStart.
SelectionStart	The start of the selected text in a TextBox.
WordWrap	Specifies whether a multiline TextBox should automatically wrap words if a line exceeds the width of the control.

TextBox Events

Careful validation of the text in the TextBox controls on a form can make the difference between happy users and angry users. You have probably experienced how annoying it is when a dialog only validates its contents when you click OK. This approach to validating the data usually results in a message box being displayed informing you that the data in "TextBox number three" is incorrect. You can then continue to click OK until all the data is correct. Clearly, this is not a good approach to validating data, so what can you do instead?

The answer lies in handling the validation events a TextBox control provides. To ensure that invalid characters are not entered in the text box or that only values within a certain range are allowed, you need to indicate to the user of the control whether the value entered is valid.

The TextBox control provides the following events (all of which are inherited from Control):

Event	Description
Enter Leave Validating Validated	These four events occur in the order in which they are listed here. They are known as *focus events* and are fired whenever a control's focus changes, with two exceptions. Validating and Validated are only fired if the control that receives focus has the CausesValidation property set to true. The reason why it's the receiving control that fires the event is that there are times when you do not want to validate the control, even if focus changes. An example of this is when a user clicks a Help button.
KeyDown KeyPress KeyUp	These three are known as *key events*. They enable you to monitor and change what is entered into your controls. KeyDown and KeyUp receive the key code corresponding to the key that was pressed. This enables you to determine whether special keys such as Shift *or* Ctrl and F1 were pressed. KeyPress, conversely, receives the character corresponding to a keyboard key. This means that the value for the letter *a* is not the same as the letter *A*. It is useful if you want to exclude a range of characters — for example, only allowing numeric values to be entered.
TextChanged	Occurs whenever the text in the text box is changed, no matter what the change.

In the following Try It Out, you create a dialog in which you can enter your name, address, occupation, and age. The purpose of this example is to give you a good grounding in manipulating properties and using events, not to create something truly useful.

Try It Out   Working with a TextBox Control

You build the user interface first:

1. Create a new Windows application called "TextBoxTest" in the directory
    C:\BegVCSharp\Chapter15.

2. Create the form shown in Figure 15-10 by dragging Label, TextBox, and Button controls
    onto the design surface. Before you can resize the two TextBox controls textBoxAddress
    and textBoxOutput as shown, you must set their Multiline property to true. Do this by
    right-clicking the controls and selecting Properties.

3. Name the controls as indicated in Figure 15-10.

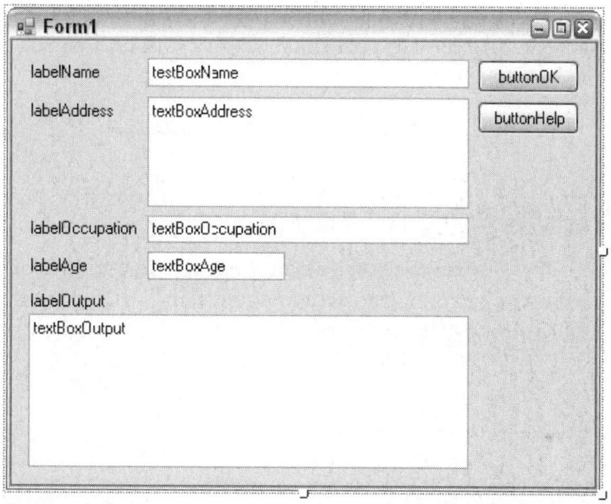

Figure 15-10

4. Set the Text property of all the other controls to match the name of the control, except for the
    prefixes that indicate the type of the control (that is, Button, TextBox, and Label). Set the
    Text property of the form to TextBoxTest.

5. Set the Scrollbars property of the two controls txtOutput and txtAddress to Vertical.

6. Set the ReadOnly property of the txtOutput control to true.

7. Set the CausesValidation property of the btnHelp Button to false. Remember from the
    discussion of the Validating and Validated events that setting this to false enables users
    to click this button without having to worry about entering invalid data.

8. When you have sized the form to fit snugly around the controls, it is time to anchor the
    controls so that they behave properly when the form is resized. Set the Anchor property for
    each type of control in one go: First, select all the TextBox controls except textBoxOutput by
    holding down the Ctrl key while you select each TextBox in turn. Once you've selected them

all, set the Anchor property to Top, Left, Right from the Properties window; the Anchor property for each of the selected TextBox controls will be set as well. Select just the textBoxOutput control and set the Anchor property to Top, Bottom, Left, Right. Now set the Anchor property for both Button controls to Top, Right.

The reason txtOutput is anchored, rather than docked, to the bottom of the form is that you want the output text area to be resized as you pull the form. If you docked the control to the bottom of the form, it would be moved to stay at the bottom, but it would not be resized.

9.   One final thing should be set. On the form, find the Size and MinimumSize properties. Your form has little meaning if it is sized to something smaller than it is now; therefore, set the MinimumSize property to the same as the Size property.

How It Works

The job of setting up the visual part of the form is now complete. If you run it nothing happens when you click the buttons or enter text, but if you maximize or pull in the dialog, the controls behave exactly as you want them to in a proper user interface, staying put and resizing to fill the whole area of the dialog.

Adding the Event Handlers

From Design View, double-click the buttonOK button. Repeat this with the other button. As shown in the button example earlier in this chapter, this causes event handlers for the Click event of the buttons to be created. When the OK button is clicked, you want to transfer the text in the input text boxes to the read-only output box.

Here is the code for the two Click event handlers:

```
private void buttonOK_Click(object sender, EventArgs e)
{
    // No testing for invalid values are made, as that should
    // not be necessary

    string output;

    // Concatenate the text values of the four TextBoxes.
    output = "Name: " + this.textBoxName.Text + "\r\n";
    output += "Address: " + this.textBoxAddress.Text + "\r\n";
    output += "Occupation: " + this.textBoxOccupation.Text + "\r\n";
    output += "Age: " + this.textBoxAge.Text;

    // Insert the new text.
    this.textBoxOutput.Text = output;
}
```

```
private void buttonHelp_Click(object sender, EventArgs e)
{
    // Write a short description of each TextBox in the Output TextBox.
    string output;

    output = "Name = Your name\r\n";
    output += "Address = Your address\r\n";
    output += "Occupation = Only allowed value is 'Programmer'\r\n";
    output += "Age = Your age";

    // Insert the new text.
    this.textBoxOutput.Text = output;
}
```

In both functions, the `Text` property of each `TextBox` is used. The `Text` property of the `textBoxAge` control is used to get the value entered as the age of the person, and the same property on the `textBoxOutput` control is used to display the concatenated text.

You insert the information the user has entered without bothering to check whether it is correct. This means that you must do the checking elsewhere. In this example, there are a number of criteria to enforce to ensure that the values are correct:

❑   The name of the user cannot be empty.

❑   The age of the user must be a number greater than or equal to zero.

❑   The occupation of the user must be "Programmer" or be left empty.

❑   The address of the user cannot be empty.

From this, you can see that the check that must be done for two of the text boxes (`textBoxName` and `textBoxAddress`) is the same. In addition, you should prevent users from entering anything invalid into the Age box, and you must check whether the user claims to be a programmer.

To prevent users from clicking OK before anything is entered, start by setting the OK button's `Enabled` property to `false` — this time you do it in the constructor of your form, rather than from the Properties window. If you do set properties in the constructor, make sure you don't set them until after the generated code in `InitializeComponent()` has been called:

```
public Form1()
{
    InitializeComponent();
    this.buttonOK.Enabled = false;
}
```

Now you create the handler for the two text boxes that must be checked to see whether they are empty. You do this by subscribing to the `Validating` event of the text boxes. You inform the control that the event should be handled by a method named `txtBoxEmpty_Validating()`, so that's a single event-handling method for two different controls.

You also need a way to know the state of your controls. For this purpose, use the `Tag` property of the `TextBox` control. Recall from the discussion of this property earlier in the chapter that only strings can be assigned to the `Tag` property from the Forms Designer. However, as you are setting the `Tag` value from code, you can do pretty much what you want with it, as the `Tag` property takes an `object`, and it is more appropriate to enter a Boolean value here.

Add to the constructor the following statements:

```
this.buttonOK.Enabled = false;
```

```
// Tag values for testing if the data is valid
    this.textBoxAddress.Tag = false;
    this.textBoxAge.Tag = false;
    this.textBoxName.Tag = false;
    this.textBoxOccupation.Tag = false;

// Subscriptions to events
    this.textBoxName.Validating += new System.ComponentModel.@@ta
CancelEventHandler(this.textBoxEmpty_Validating);
    this.textBoxAddress.Validating += new

System.ComponentModel.CancelEventHandler(this.textBoxEmpty_Validating);
```

Note as you type the += part of the event handler code, Visual Studio detects that you are adding event handlers to an object and suggests the remaining text. If you press Tab once, the text, including the new statement, is inserted with a suggested method name. If you press Tab again, the method that actually handles the event is inserted, using whatever name you have used. Very often you will simply press Tab twice, but in this case remember to change the name of the method to `textBoxEmpty_Validating` before pressing Tab the second time, in order to have the same method handle both events.

Unlike the button event handler shown previously, the event handler for the `Validating` event is a specialized version of the standard handler `System.EventHandler`. This event needs a special handler because if the validation fails, then there must be a way to prevent any further processing. If you were to cancel further processing, then that would effectively mean that it would be impossible to leave a text box until the data entered is valid.

The `Validating` and `Validated` events combined with the `CausesValidation` property fix a nasty problem that occurred when using the `GotFocus` and `LostFocus` events to perform validation of controls in earlier versions of Visual Studio. The problem occurred when the `GotFocus` and `LostFocus` events were continually fired because validation code was attempting to shift the focus between controls, which created an infinite loop.

Replace the `throw` statement in the event handler generated by Visual Studio with the following code:

```
private void textBoxEmpty_Validating (object sender,
                                  System.ComponentModel.CancelEventArgs e)
{
    // We know the sender is a TextBox, so we cast the sender object to that.
    TextBox tb = (TextBox)sender;

    // If the text is empty we set the background color of the
    // Textbox to red to indicate a problem. We use the tag value
    // of the control to indicate if the control contains valid
    // information.
```

```
        if (tb.Text.Length == 0)
        {
            tb.BackColor = Color.Red;
            tb.Tag = false;

            // In this case we do not want to cancel further processing,
            // but if we had wanted to do this, we would have added this line:
            // e.Cancel = true;
        }
        else
        {
            tb.BackColor = System.Drawing.SystemColors.Window;
            tb.Tag = true;
        }

        // Finally, we call ValidateOK which will set the value of
        // the OK button.
        ValidateOK();
    }
```

Because more than one text box is using this method to handle the event, you cannot be sure which is calling the function. You do know, however, that the effect of calling the method should be the same no matter who is calling, so you can simply cast the sender parameter to a TextBox and work on that:

```
        TextBox tb = (TextBox)sender;
```

If the length of the text in the text box is zero, then set the background color to red and the Tag to false. If it is not, then set the background color to the standard Windows color for a window.

Always use the colors found in the System.Drawing.SystemColors *enumeration when you want to set a standard color in a control. If you simply set the color to white, your application will look strange if the user has changed the default color settings.*

The description of the ValidateOK() function appears at the end of this example. Keeping with the Validating event, the next handler you'll add is for the Occupation text box. The procedure is exactly the same as for the two previous handlers, but the validation code is different because occupation must be Programmer or an empty string to be valid. Therefore, add a new line to the constructor:

```
        this.textBoxOccupation.Validating += new
            System.ComponentModel.CancelEventHandler(this.textBoxOccupation_Validating);
```

Then add the handler itself:

```
    private void textBoxOccupation_Validating(object sender,
                                    System.ComponentModel.CancelEventArgs e)
    {
        // Cast the sender object to a textbox.
        TextBox tb = (TextBox)sender;

        // Check if the values are correct.
```

```
        if (tb.Text.CompareTo("Programmer") == 0 || tb.Text.Length == 0)
        {
            tb.Tag = true;
            tb.BackColor = System.Drawing.SystemColors.Window;
        }
        else
        {
            tb.Tag = false;
            tb.BackColor = Color.Red;
        }

        // Set the state of the OK button.
        ValidateOK();
    }
```

Your second to last challenge is the Age text box. You don't want users to type anything but positive numbers (including 0 to make the test simpler). To achieve this, you use the KeyPress event to remove any unwanted characters before they are shown in the text box. You'll also limit the number of characters that can be entered into the control to three.

First, set the MaxLength of the textBoxAge control to 3. Then subscribe to the KeyPress event by double-clicking the KeyPress event in the Events list of the Properties window (select the Events lists by clicking the lightning bolt icon). The KeyPress event handler is specialized as well. The System .Windows.Forms.KeyPressEventHandler is supplied because the event needs information about the key that was pressed.

Add the following code to the event handler itself:

```
        private void textBoxAge_KeyPress(object sender, KeyPressEventArgs e)
        {
            if ((e.KeyChar < 48 || e.KeyChar > 57) && e.KeyChar != 8)
                e.Handled = true; // Remove the character
        }
```

The ASCII values for the characters between 0 and 9 lie between 48 and 57, so you make sure that the character is within this range — with one exception. The ASCII value 8 is the backspace key, and for editing reasons, you allow this to slip through. Setting the Handled property of KeyPressEventArgs to true tells the control that it shouldn't do anything else with the character, so if the key pressed isn't a digit or a backspace, it is not shown.

As it is now, the control is not marked as invalid or valid. This is because you need another check to determine whether anything was entered at all. This is easy, as you've already written the method to perform this check. Simply subscribe to the Validating event for the Age control as well by adding the following line to the constructor:

```
    this.textBoxAge.Validating += new
            System.ComponentModel.CancelEventHandler(this.textBoxEmpty_Validating);
```

One last case must be handled. If the user has entered valid text in all the text boxes and then changes something, making the text invalid, the OK button remains enabled. Therefore, you have to handle one last event handler for all of the text boxes: the Change event, which will disable the OK button should any text field contain invalid data.

The `TextChanged` event is fired whenever the text in the control changes. You subscribe to the event by selecting all four text boxes you've been working on and, in the Events list, typing the name `textBox_TextChanged`. This results in a single handler for all four events.

The `TextChanged` event uses the standard event handler you know from the `Click` event. Finally, add the event itself:

```
private void textBox_TextChanged(object sender, System.EventArgs e)
{
    // Cast the sender object to a Textbox
    TextBox tb = (TextBox)sender;

    // Test if the data is valid and set the tag and background
    // color accordingly.
    if (tb.Text.Length == 0 && tb != textBoxOccupation)
    {


        tb.Tag = false;
        tb.BackColor = Color.Red;
    }
    else if (tb == textBoxOccupation &&
            (tb.Text.Length != 0 && tb.Text.CompareTo("Programmer") != 0))
    {
        // Don't set the color here, as it will color change while the user
        // is typing.
        tb.Tag = false;
    }
    else
    {
        tb.Tag = true;
        tb.BackColor = SystemColors.Window;
    }

    // Call ValidateOK to set the OK button.
    ValidateOK();
}
```

This time, you must find out exactly which control is calling the event handler, because you don't want the background color of the Occupation text box to change to red when the user starts typing. You do this by checking the `Name` property of the text box that was passed to you in the `sender` parameter.

Only one thing remains: the `ValidateOK` method that enables or disables the OK button:

```
private void ValidateOK()
{
    // Set the OK button to enabled if all the Tags are true.
    this.buttonOK.Enabled = ((bool)(this.textBoxAddress.Tag) &&
                             (bool)(this.textBoxAge.Tag) &&
                             (bool)(this.textBoxName.Tag) &&
                             (bool)(this.textBoxOccupation.Tag));
}
```

The method simply sets the value of the Enabled property of the OK button to true if all of the Tag properties are true. You need to cast the value of the Tag properties to a Boolean because it is stored as an object type.

When you test the program now, you should see something like what is shown in Figure 15-11 (without the red background, of course). Notice that you can click the Help button while in a text box with invalid data without the background color changing to red.

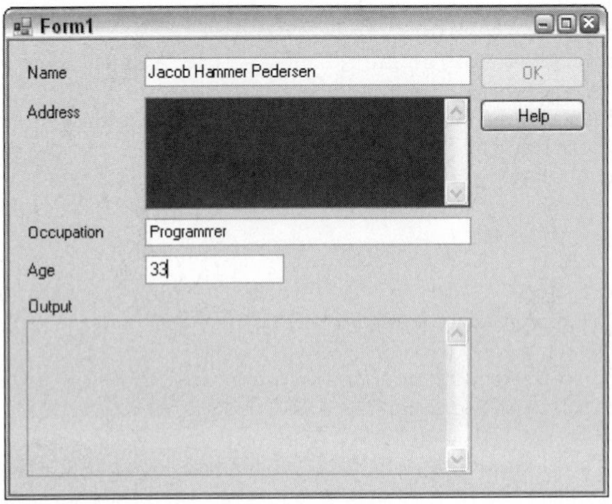

Figure 15-11

The example you just completed is quite long compared to the others in this chapter because you build on this example, rather than start from scratch with each example.

Remember that you can download the source code for all the examples in this book from www.wrox.com.

The RadioButton and CheckBox Controls

As mentioned earlier, the RadioButton and CheckBox controls share their base class with the Button control, although their appearance and use differs substantially from the Button.

Radio buttons traditionally display themselves as a label with a tiny circle to the left of it, which can be either selected or not. You should use the radio buttons when you want to give users a choice between several mutually exclusive options — for example, the user's gender.

To group radio buttons together so they create one logical unit you must use a GroupBox control or some other container. When you first place a GroupBox onto a form and then place the RadioButton controls you need within the borders of the GroupBox, the RadioButton controls will automatically change their state to reflect that only one option within the group box can be selected. If you do not place the controls within a GroupBox, only one RadioButton on the *form* can be selected at any given time.

A CheckBox control traditionally displays itself as a label with a small box on its immediate left. Use a check box when you want to enable users to choose one or more options — for example, a questionnaire asking which operating systems the user has tried (e.g., Windows XP, Windows Vista, Linux, and so on).

After looking next at the important properties and events of these two controls, starting with the RadioButton, you'll move on to a quick example of their use.

RadioButton Properties

Because the RadioButton control derives from ButtonBase and because you've already seen this in the example that used the Button control earlier, there are only a few properties to describe (shown in the following table). For a complete list, please refer to the .NET Framework SDK documentation.

Property	Description
Appearance	A radio button can be displayed either as a label with a circular check to the left, middle, or right of it, or as a standard button. When it is displayed as a button, the control appears depressed when selected, and not depressed otherwise.
AutoCheck	When true, a black point is displayed when the user clicks the radio button. When false, the radio button must be manually checked in code from the Click event handler.
CheckAlign	This is used to change the alignment of the check box portion of the radio button. The default is ContentAlignment.MiddleLeft.
Checked	Indicates the status of the control. It is true if the control is displaying a black point, and false otherwise.

RadioButton Events

You will typically use only one event when working with RadioButton controls, but many others can be subscribed to. Only the two described in the following table are covered in this chapter, and the second event is mentioned only to highlight a subtle difference between the two.

Event	Description
CheckedChanged	Sent when the check of the RadioButton changes
Click	Sent every time the RadioButton is clicked. This is not the same as the CheckedChange event, because clicking a RadioButton two or more times in succession changes the Checked property only once — and only if it wasn't checked already. Moreover, if the AutoCheck property of the button being clicked is false, then the button will not be checked at all, and only the Click event will be sent.

CheckBox Properties

As you would imagine, the properties and events of this control are very similar to those of the RadioButton, but the following table describes two new ones:

Property	Description
CheckState	Unlike the radio button, a check box can have three states: Checked, Indeterminate, and Unchecked. When the state of the check box is Indeterminate, the control check next to the label is usually grayed, indicating that either the current value of the check is not valid; for some reason cannot be determined (e.g., the check indicates the read-only state of files, and two are selected, of which one is read-only and the other is not); or has no meaning under the current circumstances.
ThreeState	When false, the user will not be able to change the CheckState state to Indeterminate. You can, however, still change the CheckState property to Indeterminate from code.

CheckBox Events

You'll normally use only one or two events on this control. Although the CheckChanged event exists on both the RadioButton and the CheckBox controls, the effects of the events differ. The following table describes the CheckBox events:

Event	Description
CheckedChanged	Occurs whenever the Checked property of the check box changes. Note that in a CheckBox where the ThreeState property is true, it is possible to click the check box without changing the Checked property. This happens when the check box changes from Checked to Indeterminate status.
CheckStateChanged	Occurs whenever the CheckedState property changes. As Checked and Unchecked are both possible values of the CheckedState property, this event is sent whenever the Checked property changes. In addition, it is also sent when the state changes from Checked to Indeterminate.

This concludes the events and properties of the RadioButton and CheckBox controls. But before looking at an example using these, let's take a look at the GroupBox control, which was mentioned earlier.

The GroupBox Control

The GroupBox control is often used to logically group a set of controls such as the RadioButton and CheckBox, and to provide a caption and a frame around this set.

Using the group box is as simple as dragging it onto a form and then dragging the controls it should contain onto it (but not the reverse — that is, you can't lay a group box over preexisting controls). The effect of this is that the parent of the controls becomes the group box, rather than the form, so it is possible to have more than one radio button selected at any given time. Within the group box, however, only one radio button can be selected.

The relationship between parent and child probably needs to be explained a bit more. When a control is placed on a form, the form is said to become the parent of the control, and hence the control is the child of the form. When you place a GroupBox on a form, it becomes a child of a form. Because a group box can itself contain controls, it becomes the parent of these controls. The effect of this is that moving the GroupBox control moves all of the controls placed on it.

Another effect of placing controls on a group box is that it enables you to affect the contained controls by setting the corresponding property on the group box. For instance, if you want to disable all the controls within a GroupBox control, you can simply set the Enabled property of the GroupBox to false.

The GroupBox control is demonstrated in the following Try It Out.

Try It Out   **Using RadioButton and CheckBox Controls**

In this exercise, you modify the TextBoxTest example you created earlier with the demonstration of text boxes. In that example, the only possible occupation was programmer. Instead of forcing users to type this out in full, you will change this text box to a check box. To demonstrate the radio button, you ask users to provide one more piece of information: their gender.

Change the text box example as follows:

1.   Remove the label named labelOccupation and the text box named textBoxOccupation.

2.   Add a CheckBox, a GroupBox and two RadioButton controls, and name the new controls as shown in Figure 15-12. Notice that the GroupBox control is located on the Containers tab in the Toolbox panel. Unlike the other controls you've used so far, GroupBox is located in the Containers section of the Toolbox.

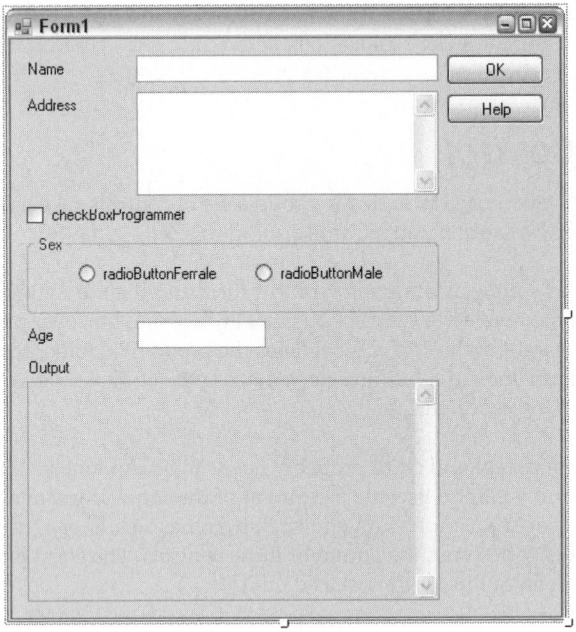

Figure 15-12

3. The `Text` property of the `RadioButton` and `CheckBox` controls should be the same as the names of the controls without the first three letters, and for the `GroupBox` the `Text` property should be `Sex`.

4. Set the `Checked` property of the `checkBoxProgrammer` check box to `true`. Note that the `CheckState` property changes automatically to `Checked`.

5. Set the `Checked` property of either `radioButtonMale` or `radioButtonFemale` to `true`. Note that you cannot set both to `true`. If you try to do this with a second button, then the value of the first `RadioButton` automatically changes to `false`.

No more needs to be done for the visual part of the example, but there are a number of changes in the code. First, you need to remove all the references to the text box that you've removed. Using the existing code, complete the following steps:

1. In the constructor of the form, remove the two lines that refer to `textBoxOccupation`. This includes subscriptions to the `Validating` event and the line that sets the `Tag` property to `false`.

2. Remove the `txtOccupation_Validating()` method entirely.

How It Works

The `txtBox_TextChanged` method included tests to determine whether the calling control was the `textBoxOccupation` TextBox. You now know that it will not be (because you removed it), so you change the method by removing the `else if` block and modify the `if` test as follows:

```
private void textBox_TextChanged(object sender, System.EventArgs e)
{
    // Cast the sender object to a Textbox.
    TextBox tb = (TextBox)sender;

    // Test if the data is valid and set the tag's background.
    // color accordingly.
    if (tb.Text.Length == 0)
    {
        tb.Tag = false;
        tb.BackColor = Color.Red;
    }
    else
    {
        tb.Tag = true;
        tb.BackColor = SystemColors.Window;
    }

    // Call ValidateOK to set the OK button.
    ValidateOK();
}
```

Another place where you check the value of the text box you've removed is in the `ValidateOK()` method. Remove the check entirely so the code is as follows:

```
private void ValidateOK()
{
    // Set the OK button to enabled if all the Tags are true.
    this.buttonOK.Enabled = ((bool)(this.textBoxAddress.Tag) &&
                             (bool)(this.textBoxAge.Tag) &&
                             (bool)(this.textBoxName.Tag));
}
```

Because you are using a check box, rather than a text box, you know that the user cannot enter any invalid information, because he or she will always be either a programmer or not.

You also know that the user is either male or female, and because you set the property of one of the radio buttons to `true`, the user is prevented from choosing an invalid value. Therefore, the only thing left to do is change the help text and the output. You do this in the button event handlers:

```
private void buttonHelp_Click(object sender, System.EventArgs e)
{
    // Write a short description of each TextBox in the Output TextBox.
    string output;
```

```
    output = "Name = Your name\r\n";
    output += "Address = Your address\r\n";
    output += "Programmer = Check 'Programmer' if you are a programmer\r\n";
    output += "Sex = Choose your sex\r\n";
    output += "Age = Your age";

    // Insert the new text.
    this.textBoxOutput.Text = output;
}
```

Only the help text is changed, so there is nothing surprising in the help method. Slightly more interesting is the OK method:

```
private void buttonOK_Click(object sender, EventArgs e)
{
    // No testing for invalid values is done, as that should
    // not be necessary.

    string output;

    // Concatenate the text values of the four TextBoxes.
    output = "Name: " + this.textBoxName.Text + "\r\n";
    output += "Address: " + this.textBoxAddress.Text + "\r\n";
    output += "Occupation: " + (string)(this.checkBoxProgrammer.Checked ?
            "Programmer" : "Not a programmer") + "\r\n";
    output += "Sex: " + (string)(this.radioButtonFemale.Checked ? "Female" :
                                                    "Male") + "\r\n";
    output += "Age: " + this.textBoxAge.Text;

    // Insert the new text.
    this.textBoxOutput.Text = output;
}
```

The first of the highlighted lines is the line in which the user's occupation is printed. You investigate the Checked property of the CheckBox and if it is true, then you write the string Programmer. If it is false, then you write Not a programmer.

The second line examines only the radio button radioButtonFemale. If the Checked property is true on that control, then you know that the user claims to be female. If it is false, then you know that the user claims to be male. It is possible to have radio buttons without any of them being checked when you start the program — but because you checked one of the radio buttons at design time, you can be certain that one of the two radio buttons will always be checked.

When you run the example now, you should get a result similar to what is shown in Figure 15-13.

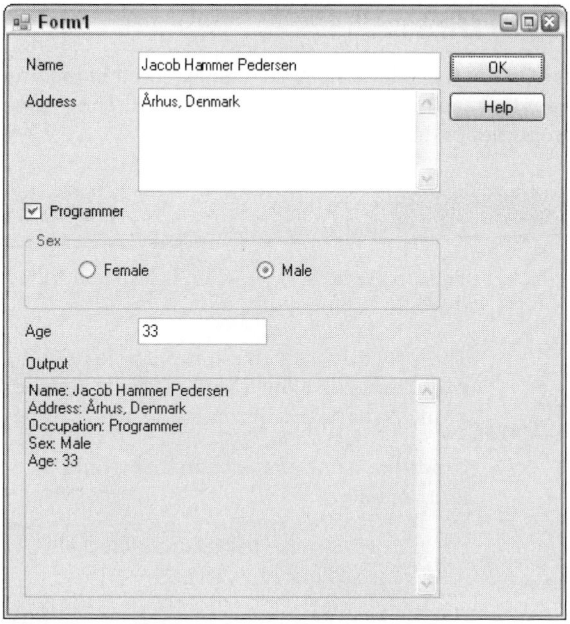

Figure 15-13

The RichTextBox Control

Like the normal `TextBox`, the `RichTextBox` control is derived from `TextBoxBase`. Because of this, it shares a number of features with the `TextBox`, but is much more diverse. Whereas a `TextBox` is commonly used for the purpose of obtaining short text strings from the user, the `RichTextBox` is used to display and enter formatted text (e.g., **bold**, <u>underline</u>, and *italic*). It does so using a standard for formatted text called Rich Text Format, or RTF.

In the previous example, you used a standard `TextBox`. You could just as well have used a `RichTextBox` to do the job. In fact, as shown in the example later, you can remove the `TextBox` name `textBoxOutput` and insert a `RichTextBox` in its place with the same name, and the example behaves exactly as it did before.

RichTextBox Properties

If this kind of text box is more advanced than the one you explored in the previous section, you'd expect there to be more properties that can be used, and you'd be correct. The following table describes the most commonly used properties of the RichTextBox:

Property	Description
CanRedo	This property is true when the last undone operation can be reapplied using Redo.
CanUndo	This property is true if it is possible to undo the last action on the RichTextBox. Note that CanUndo is defined in TextBoxBase, so it is available to TextBox controls as well.
RedoActionName	Holds the name of an action that would be performed by the Redo method.
DetectUrls	Set to true to make the control detect URLs and format them (underline, as in a browser).
Rtf	Corresponds to the Text property, except that this holds the text in RTF.
SelectedRtf	Use to get or set the selected text in the control, in RTF. If you copy this text to another application — Word, for example — it will retain all formatting.
SelectedText	As with SelectedRtf, you can use this property to get or set the selected text. However, unlike the RTF version of the property, all formatting is lost.
SelectionAlignment	Represents the alignment of the selected text. It can be Center, Left, or Right.
SelectionBullet	Use this to determine whether the selection is formatted with a bullet in front of it, or use it to insert or remove bullets.
BulletIndent	Specifies the number of pixels a bullet should be indented.
SelectionColor	Changes the color of the text in the selection.
SelectionFont	Changes the font of the text in the selection.
SelectionLength	Set or retrieve the length of a selection.
SelectionType	Holds information about the selection. It will tell you if one or more OLE objects are selected or if only text is selected.

Property	Description
ShowSelectionMargin	If true, a margin will be shown at the left of the RichTextBox. This makes it easier for the user to select text.
UndoActionName	Gets the name of the action that will be used if the user chooses to undo something.
SelectionProtected	You can specify that certain parts of the text should not be changed by setting this property to true.

As you can see from the preceding list, most of the new properties are related to a selection. This is because any formatting you will be applying when a user is working on his or her text will probably be done on a selection made by that user. In case no selection is made, the formatting starts from the point in the text where the cursor is located, called the insertion point.

RichTextBox Events

Most of the events used by the RichTextBox control are the same as those used by the TextBox control, but the following table presents a few new ones of interest:

Event	Description
LinkClicked	Sent when a user clicks on a link within the text.
Protected	Sent when a user attempts to modify text that has been marked as protected.
SelectionChanged	Sent when the selection changes. If for some reason you don't want the user to change the selection, you can prevent the change here.

In the next Try It Out, you create a very basic text editor. The example demonstrates how to change basic formatting of text and how to load and save the text from the RichTextBox. For the sake of simplicity, the example loads from and saves to a fixed file.

Try It Out   Using a RichTextBox

As always, you start by designing the form:

1. Create a new C# Windows application called "RichTextBoxTest" in the C:\BegVCSharp\ Chapter15 directory.

2. Create the form as shown in Figure 15-14. The text box named txtSize should be a TextBox control. The text box named RichTextBoxText should be a RichTextBox control.

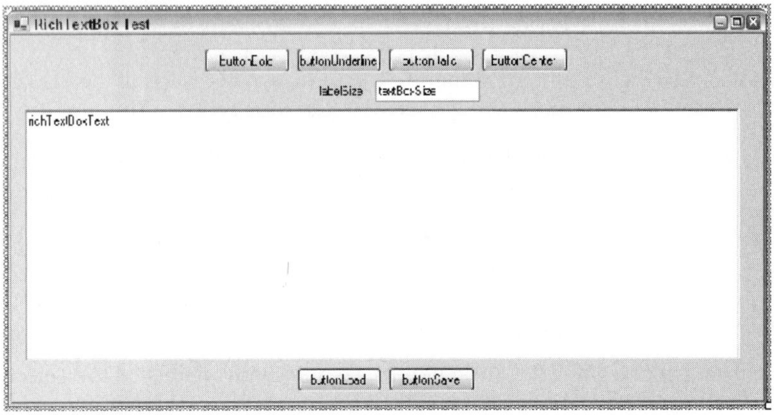

Figure 15-14

3. Name the controls as indicated in Figure 15-14.

4. Apart from the text boxes, set the `Text` of all controls to match the names, except for the first part of the name describing the type of the control.

5. Change the `Text` property of the `textBoxSize` text box to `10`.

6. Anchor the controls as shown in the following table:

Control Name	Anchor Value
`buttonLoad` and `buttonSave`	`Bottom`
`richTextBoxText`	`Top, Left, Bottom, Right`
All others	`Top`

7. Set the `MinimumSize` property of the form to match the `Size` property.

How It Works
That concludes the visual part of the example. Moving straight to the code, double-click the Bold button to add the `Click` event handler to the code. Here is the code for the event:

```
private void buttonBold_Click(object sender, EventArgs e)
{
    Font oldFont;
    Font newFont;

    // Get the font that is being used in the selected text
    oldFont = this.richTextBoxText.SelectionFont;

    // If the font is using bold style now, we should remove the
    // Formatting.
```

```
    if (oldFont.Bold)
        newFont = new Font(oldFont, oldFont.Style & ~FontStyle.Bold);
    else
        newFont = new Font(oldFont, oldFont.Style | FontStyle.Bold);

    // Insert the new font and return focus to the RichTextBox.
    this.richTextBoxText.SelectionFont = newFont;
    this.richTextBoxText.Focus();
}
```

Begin by getting the font that is used in the current selection and assigning it to a local variable, oldFont. Then, check whether this selection is already bold. If it is, remove the bold setting; otherwise, set it. You create a new font using oldFont as the prototype but add or remove the bold style as needed.

Finally, you assign the new font to the selection and return focus to the RichTextBox — you learn more about the Font object in Chapter 33.

The event handlers for buttonItalic and buttonUnderline are the same as shown earlier, except that you are checking the appropriate styles. Double-click the two buttons Italic and Underline and add this code:

```
private void buttonUnderline_Click(object sender, EventArgs e)
{
    Font oldFont;
    Font newFont;

    // Get the font that is being used in the selected text.
    oldFont = this.richTextBoxText.SelectionFont;

    // If the font is using Underline style now, we should remove it.
    if (oldFont.Underline)
        newFont = new Font(oldFont, oldFont.Style & ~FontStyle.Underline);
    else
        newFont = new Font(oldFont, oldFont.Style | FontStyle.Underline);

    // Insert the new font.
    this.richTextBoxText.SelectionFont = newFont;
    this.richTextBoxText.Focus();
}

private void buttonItalic_Click(object sender, EventArgs e)
{
    Font oldFont;
    Font newFont;

    // Get the font that is being used in the selected text.
    oldFont = this.richTextBoxText.SelectionFont;

    // If the font is using Italic style now, we should remove it.
    if (oldFont.Italic)
```

```
              newFont = new Font(oldFont, oldFont.Style & ~FontStyle.Italic);
          else
              newFont = new Font(oldFont, oldFont.Style | FontStyle.Italic);

          // Insert the new font.
          this.richTextBoxText.SelectionFont = newFont;
          this.richTextBoxText.Focus();
      }
```

Double-click the last formatting button, Center, and add the following code:

```
      private void buttonCenter_Click(object sender, EventArgs e)
      {
          if (this.richTextBoxText.SelectionAlignment == HorizontalAlignment.Center)
              this.richTextBoxText.SelectionAlignment = HorizontalAlignment.Left;
          else
              this.richTextBoxText.SelectionAlignment = HorizontalAlignment.Center;
          this.richTextBoxText.Focus();
      }
```

Here, you must check another property, `SelectionAlignment`, to determine whether the text in the selection is already centered. You do this because you want the button to behave like a toggle button — if the text is centered it becomes left-justified; otherwise, it becomes centered. `HorizontalAlignment` is an enumeration with values `Left`, `Right`, `Center`, `Justify`, and `NotSet`. In this case, you simply check whether `Center` is set; and if it is, then you set the alignment to left. If it isn't, then you set it to `Center`.

The final formatting your little text editor will be able to perform is setting the size of text. You'll add two event handlers for the text box `Size`: one for controlling the input, and one to detect when the user has finished entering a value.

Find and double-click the `KeyPress` and `Validated` events for the `textBoxSize` control in the Events list of the Properties window to add the handlers to the code.

Unlike the `Validating` event you used earlier, the `Validated` event occurs after all validation has completed. Both of the events use a helper method called `ApplyTextSize` that takes a string with the size of the text:

```
      private void textBoxSize_KeyPress(object sender, KeyPressEventArgs e)
      {
          // Remove all characters that are not numbers, backspace, or enter.
          if ((e.KeyChar < 48 || e.KeyChar > 57) &&
                                        e.KeyChar != 8 && e.KeyChar != 13)
          {
              e.Handled = true;
          }
          else if (e.KeyChar == 13)
          {
              // Apply size if the user hits enter
              TextBox txt = (TextBox)sender;
```

```
      if (txt.Text.Length > 0)
        ApplyTextSize(txt.Text);
      e.Handled = true;
      this.richTextBoxText.Focus();
    }
  }

  private void textBoxSize_Validated(object sender, EventArgs e)
  {
    TextBox txt = (TextBox)sender;

    ApplyTextSize(txt.Text);
    this.richTextBoxText.Focus();
  }

  private void ApplyTextSize(string textSize)
  {
    // Convert the text to a float because we'll be needing a float shortly.
    float newSize = Convert.ToSingle(textSize);
    FontFamily currentFontFamily;
    Font newFont;

    // Create a new font of the same family but with the new size.
    currentFontFamily = this.richTextBoxText.SelectionFont.FontFamily;
    newFont = new Font(currentFontFamily, newSize);

    // Set the font of the selected text to the new font.
    this.richTextBoxText.SelectionFont = newFont;
  }
```

The KeyPress event prevents the user from typing anything but an integer and calls ApplyTextSize if the user presses Enter. The work you are interested in takes place in the helper method ApplyTextSize(). It starts by converting the size from a string to a float. As stated previously, you prevented users from entering anything but integers, but when you create the new font, you need a float, so convert it to the correct type.

After that, you get the family to which the font belongs and create a new font from that family with the new size. Finally, you set the font of the selection to the new font.

That's all the formatting you can do, but some is handled by the RichTextBox itself. If you try to run the example now, you will be able to set the text to bold, italic, and underline, and you can center the text. That is what you expect, but note something else that is interesting: Try to type a Web address — for example, www.wrox.com — in the text. The text is recognized by the control as an Internet address, is underlined, and the mouse pointer changes to a hand when you move it over the text. If you assume that you can click it and be brought to the page, you are almost correct. You first need to handle the event that is sent when the user clicks a link: LinkClicked.

Find the `LinkClicked` event in the Events list of the Properties window and double-click it to add an event handler to the code. You haven't seen this event handler before — it is used to provide the text of the link that was clicked. The handler is surprisingly simple:

```
private void richTextBoxText_LinkClicked (object sender,
                                  System.Windows.Forms.LinkClickedEventArgs e)
{
    System.Diagnostics.Process.Start(e.LinkText);
}
```

This code opens the default browser if it isn't open already and navigates to the site to which the link that was clicked is pointing.

The editing part of the application is now done. All that remains is to load and save the contents of the control. You use a fixed file to do this. Double-click the Load button and add the following code:

```
private void buttonLoad_Click(object sender, EventArgs e)
{
    // Load the file into the RichTextBox.
    try
    {
        richTextBoxText.LoadFile("Test.rtf");
    }
    catch (System.IO.FileNotFoundException)
    {
        MessageBox.Show("No file to load yet");
    }
}
```

That's it! Nothing else has to be done. Because you are dealing with files, there is always a chance that you might encounter exceptions, and you have to handle these. In the Load method, you handle the exception that is thrown if the file doesn't exist. It is equally simple to save the file. Double-click the Save button and add this:

```
private void buttonSave_Click(object sender, EventArgs e)
{
    // Save the text.
    try
    {
        richTextBoxText.SaveFile("Test.rtf");
    }
    catch (System.Exception err)
    {
        MessageBox.Show(err.Message);
    }
}
```

Run the example now, format some text, and click Save. Clear the text box and click Load, and the text you just saved should reappear.

That concludes the `RichTextBox` example. When you run it, you should be able to produce something like what is shown in Figure 15-15.

Figure 15-15

The ListBox and CheckedListBox Controls

List boxes are used to show a list of strings from which one or more can be selected at a time. Just like check boxes and radio buttons, the list box provides a way to ask users to make one or more selections. You should use a list box when at design time you don't know the actual number of values the user can choose from (e.g., a list of co-workers). Even if you know all the possible values at design time, you should consider using a list box if there are a large number of values.

The `ListBox` class is derived from the `ListControl` class, which provides the basic functionality for list-type controls that ship with the .NET Framework.

Another kind of list box available is called `CheckedListBox`. Derived from the `ListBox` class, it provides a list just like the `ListBox` does, but in addition to the text strings it provides a check for each item in the list.

ListBox Properties

The properties described in the following table exist in both the `ListBox` class and `CheckedListBox` class unless indicated:

Property	Description
SelectedIndex	This value indicates the zero-based index of the selected item in the list box. If the list box can contain multiple selections at the same time, then this property holds the index of the first item in the selected list.
ColumnWidth	In a list box with multiple columns, this property specifies the width of the columns.
Items	The `Items` collection contains all of the items in the list box. You use the properties of this collection to add and remove items.
MultiColumn	A list box can have more than one column. Use this property to get or set whether values should be displayed in columns.
SelectedIndices	A collection that holds all of the zero-based indices of the selected items in the list box.
SelectedItem	In a list box where only one item can be selected, this property contains the selected item, if any. In a list box where more than one selection can be made, it will contain the first of the selected items.
SelectedItems	A collection that contains all currently selected items.
SelectionMode	You can choose from four different modes of selection from the `ListSelectionMode` enumeration in a list box: `None`: No items can be selected. `One`: Only one item can be selected at any time. `MultiSimple`: Multiple items can be selected. With this style, when you click an item in the list it becomes selected and stays selected even if you click another item until you click it again. `MultiExtended`: Multiple items can be selected. You use the Ctrl, Shift, and arrows keys to make selections. Unlike `MultiSimple`, if you simply click an item and then another item afterwards, only the second item clicked is selected.
Sorted	When set to `true`, the `ListBox` alphabetically sorts the items it contains.
Text	You saw `Text` properties on a number of controls, but this one works differently from any you've seen so far. If you set the `Text` property of the `ListBox` control, it searches for an item that matches the text and selects it. If you get the `Text` property, the value returned is the first selected item in the list. This property cannot be used if the `SelectionMode` is `None`.

Property	Description
CheckedIndices	(CheckedListBox only) This property is a collection that contains indexes of all the items in the CheckedListBox that have a Checked or Indeterminate state.
CheckedItems	(CheckedListBox only) A collection of all the items in a CheckedListBox that are in a Checked or Indeterminate state.
CheckOnClick	(CheckedListBox only) If true, then an item will change its state whenever the user clicks it.
ThreeDCheckBoxes	(CheckedListBox only) You can choose between CheckBoxes that are flat or normal by setting this property.

ListBox Methods

To work efficiently with a list box, you should know a number of methods that can be called. The following table describes the most common methods. Unless indicated, the methods belong to both the ListBox and CheckedListBox classes.

Method	Description
ClearSelected()	Clears all selections in the ListBox.
FindString()	Finds the first string in the ListBox beginning with a string you specify (e.g., FindString("a") will find the first string in the ListBox beginning with a).
FindStringExact()	Like FindString, but the entire string must be matched.
GetSelected()	Returns a value that indicates whether an item is selected.
SetSelected()	Sets or clears the selection of an item.
ToString()	Returns the currently selected item.
GetItemChecked()	(CheckedListBox only) Returns a value indicating whether an item is checked.
GetItemCheckState()	(CheckedListBox only) Returns a value indicating the check state of an item.
SetItemChecked()	(CheckedListBox only) Sets the item specified to a Checked state.
SetItemCheckState()	(CheckedListBox only) Sets the check state of an item.

ListBox Events

Normally, the events you will want to be aware of when working with a ListBox or CheckedListBox are those related to the selections being made by the user. The following table describes ListBox events:

Event	Description
ItemCheck	(CheckedListBox only) Occurs when the check state of one of the list items changes.
SelectedIndexChanged	Occurs when the index of the selected item changes.

In the following Try It Out, you create both a ListBox and a CheckedListBox. Users can check items in the CheckedListBox and then click a button that moves the checked items to the normal ListBox.

Try It Out   **Working with a ListBox Control**

You create the dialog as follows:

1. Create a new Windows application called **Lists** in the directory C:\BegVCSharp\Chapter15.

2. Add a ListBox, a CheckedListBox, and a Button to the form and change the names as shown in Figure 15-16.

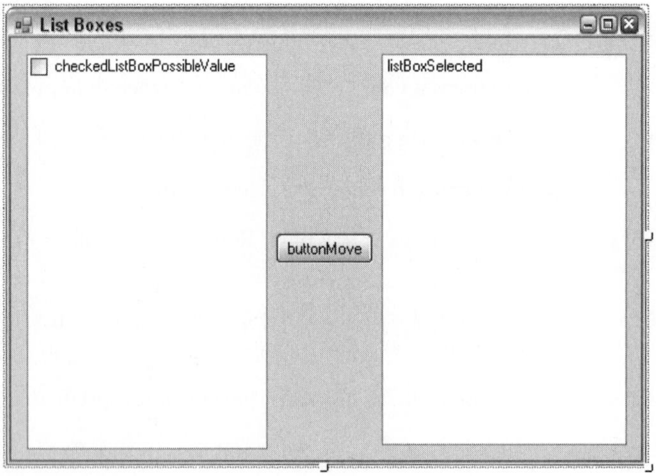

Figure 15-16

3. Change the Text property of the button to Move.

4. Change the CheckOnClick property of the CheckedListBox to true.

How It Works

You start by checking the Count property of the CheckedItems collection. This will be greater than zero if any items in the collection are checked. You then clear all items in the listBoxSelected list box, and loop through the CheckedItems collection, adding each item to the listBoxSelected list box. Finally, you remove all the checks in the CheckedListBox.

Now, you just need something in the CheckedListBox to move. You can add the items while in Design View by selecting the Items property in the Properties window and adding the items as shown in Figure 15-17.

Figure 15-17

You can also add items in code — for example, in the constructor of your form:

```
public Form1()
{
    //
    // Required for Windows Form designer support.
    //
    InitializeComponent();

    // Add a tenth element to the CheckedListBox.
    this.checkedListBoxPossibleValue.Items.Add("Ten");
}
```

Here you add a tenth element to the CheckedListBox, as you have already entered nine from the designer.

This concludes the list box example. If you run it now, you will see something like what is shown in Figure 15-18. Two, Four, and Six were selected, and the Move button pressed, to produce the image.

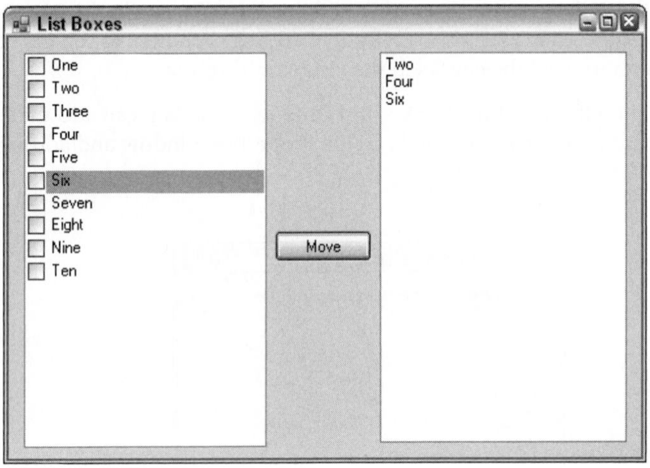

Figure 15-18

Adding the Event Handlers

Now you can add some code. When the user clicks the Move button, you want to find the items that are checked and copy those into the right-hand list box. Double-click the button and enter this code:

```
private void buttonMove_Click(object sender, EventArgs e)
{
    // Check if there are any checked items in the CheckedListBox.
    if (this.checkedListBoxPossibleValue.CheckedItems.Count > 0)
    {
        // Clear the ListBox we'll move the selections to
        this.listBoxSelected.Items.Clear();

        // Loop through the CheckedItems collection of the CheckedListBox
        // and add the items in the Selected ListBox
        foreach (string item in this.checkedListBoxPossibleValue.CheckedItems)
        {
            this.listBoxSelected.Items.Add(item.ToString());
        }

        // Clear all the checks in the CheckedListBox
        for (int i = 0; i < this.checkedListBoxPossibleValue.Items.Count; i++)
            this.checkedListBoxPossibleValue.SetItemChecked(i, false);
    }
}
```

The ListView Control

Figure 15-19 shows what is probably the most commonly known `ListView` in Windows. Even if Windows now provides a number of additional possibilities for displaying files and folders, you will recognize some of the options you have in a `ListView`, such as displaying large icons, details view, and so on.

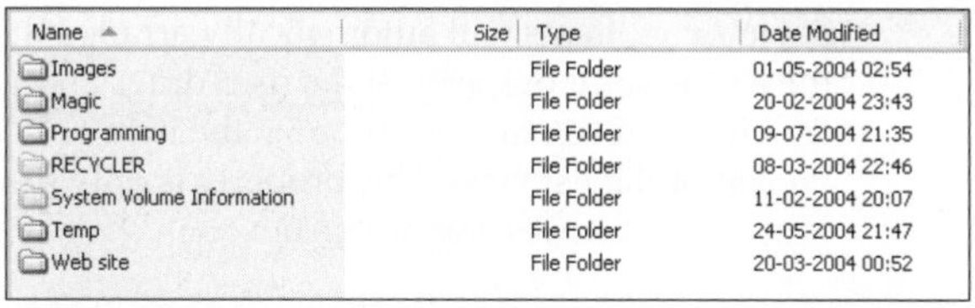

Name ▲	Size	Type	Date Modified
📁 Images		File Folder	01-05-2004 02:54
📁 Magic		File Folder	20-02-2004 23:43
📁 Programming		File Folder	09-07-2004 21:35
📁 RECYCLER		File Folder	08-03-2004 22:46
📁 System Volume Information		File Folder	11-02-2004 20:07
📁 Temp		File Folder	24-05-2004 21:47
📁 Web site		File Folder	20-03-2004 00:52

Figure 15-19

The list view is usually used to present data for which the user is allowed some control over the detail and style of its presentation. It is possible to display the data contained in the control as columns and rows much like in a grid, as a single column, or with varying icon representations. The most commonly used list view is like the one shown earlier, which is used to navigate the folders on a computer.

The `ListView` control is easily the most complex control you encounter in this chapter, and covering all of its aspects is beyond the scope of this book. This chapter provides a solid base for you to work on by writing an example that utilizes many of the most important features of the `ListView` control, including thorough descriptions of the numerous properties, events, and methods that can be used. You also look at the `ImageList` control, which is used to store the images used in a `ListView` control.

ListView Properties

The following table describes `ListView` properties:

Property	Description
Activation	Controls how a user activates an item in the list view. The possible values are as follows: Standard: This setting reflects what the user has chosen for his or her machine. OneClick: Clicking an item activates it. TwoClick: Double-clicking an item activates it.
Alignment	Controls how the items in the list view are aligned. The four possible values are as follows: Default: If the user drags and drops an item, it remains where he or she dropped it. Left: Items are aligned to the left edge of the `ListView` control. Top: Items are aligned to the top edge of the `ListView` control. SnapToGrid: The `ListView` control contains an invisible grid to which the items will snap.

(continued)

Property	Description
AllowColumnReorder	Set to true, this property enables users to change the order of the columns in a list view. If you do so, be sure that the routines that fill the list view are able to insert the items properly, even after the order of the columns is changed.
AutoArrange	Set to true, items will automatically arrange themselves according to the Alignment property. If the user drags an item to the center of the list view and Alignment is Left, the item will automatically jump to the left of the list view. This property is only meaningful if the View property is LargeIcon or SmallIcon.
CheckBoxes	Set to true, every item in the list view will have a CheckBox displayed to the left of it. This property is only meaningful if the View property is Details or List.
CheckedIndices CheckedItems	Gives you access to a collection of indices and items, respectively, containing the checked items in the list.
Columns	A list view can contain columns. This property gives you access to the collection of columns through which you can add or remove columns.
FocusedItem	Holds the item that has focus in the list view. If nothing is selected, it is null.
FullRowSelect	When this property is true and an item is clicked, the entire row in which the item resides is highlighted. If it is false, then only the item itself is highlighted.
GridLines	Set to true, the list view draws grid lines between rows and columns. This property is only meaningful when the View property is Details.
HeaderStyle	Controls how the column headers are displayed. There are three styles: Clickable: The column header works like a button. NonClickable: The column headers do not respond to mouse clicks. None: The column headers are not displayed.
HoverSelection	When this property is true, the user can select an item in the list view by hovering the mouse pointer over it.
Items	The collection of items in the list view.
LabelEdit	When true, the user can edit the content of the first column in a Details view.
LabelWrap	If true, then labels will wrap over as many lines as needed to display all of the text.
LargeImageList	Holds the ImageList, which holds large images. These images can be used when the View property is LargeIcon.
MultiSelect	Set to true to allow the user to select multiple items.
Scrollable	Set this property to true to display scroll bars.

Property	Description
SelectedIndices SelectedItems	Contains the collections that hold the indices and items that are selected, respectively.
SmallImageList	When the View property is SmallIcon, this property holds the ImageList that contains the images used.
Sorting	Enables the list view to sort the items it contains. There are three possible modes: Ascending Descending None
StateImageList	The ImageList contains masks for images that are used as overlays on the LargeImageList and SmallImageList images to represent custom states.
TopItem	Returns the item at the top of the list view.
View	A list view can display its items in four different modes: LargeIcon: All items are displayed with a large icon (32 × 32) and a label. SmallIcon: All items are displayed with a small icon (16 × 16) and a label. List: Only one column is displayed. That column can contain an icon and a label. Details: Any number of columns can be displayed. Only the first column can contain an icon. Tile (only available on Windows XP and newer Windows platforms): Displays a large icon with a label and sub-item information to the right of the icon.

ListView Methods

For a control as complex as the ListView, there are surprisingly few methods specific to it:

Name	Description
BeginUpdate()	Tells the list view to stop drawing updates until EndUpdate() is called. This is useful when you are inserting many items at once because it stops the view from flickering and dramatically increases speed.
Clear()	Clears the list view completely. All items and columns are removed.
EndUpdate()	Call this method after calling BeginUpdate. When you call this method, the list view draws all of its items.
EnsureVisible()	Tells the list view to scroll itself to make the item with the index you specified visible.
GetItemAt()	Returns the ListViewItem at position x, y in the list view.

ListView Events

The `ListView` control events that you might want to handle are described in the following table:

Event	Description
`AfterLabelEdit`	Occurs after a label has been edited.
`BeforeLabelEdit`	Occurs before a user begins editing a label.
`ColumnClick`	Occurs when a column is clicked.
`ItemActivate`	Occurs when an item is activated.

ListViewItem

An item in a list view is always an instance of the `ListViewItem` class. The `ListViewItem` holds information such as text and the index of the icon to display. `ListViewItem` objects have a `SubItems` property that holds instances of another class, `ListViewSubItem`. These sub-items are displayed if the `ListView` control is in Details or Tile mode. Each of the sub-items represents a column in the list view. The main difference between the sub-items and the main items is that a sub-item cannot display an icon.

You add `ListViewItems` to the `ListView` through the `Items` collection, and `ListViewSubItems` to a `ListViewItem` through the `SubItems` collection on the `ListViewItem`.

ColumnHeader

To make a list view display column headers, you add instances of a class called `ColumnHeader` to the `Columns` collection of the `ListView`. `ColumnHeaders` provide a caption for the columns that can be displayed when the `ListView` is in Details mode.

The ImageList Control

The `ImageList` control provides a collection that can be used to store images used in other controls on your form. You can store images of any size in an image list, but within each control every image must be of the same size. In the case of the `ListView`, this means that you need two `ImageList` controls to be able to display both large and small images.

The `ImageList` is the first control you visit in this chapter that does not display itself at runtime. When you drag it to a form you are developing, it is not placed on the form itself, but below it in a tray, which contains all such components. This nice feature is provided to prevent controls that are not part of the user interface from cluttering up the Forms Designer. The control is manipulated in exactly the same way as any other control, except that you cannot move it onto the form.

You can add images to the `ImageList` at both design time and runtime. If you know at design time what images you want to display, then you can add the images by clicking the button at the right side of the `Images` property. This will bring up a dialog in which you can browse to the images you want to insert. If you choose to add the images at runtime, you add them through the `Images` collection.

The best way to learn about using a `ListView` control and its associated image lists is through an example. In the following Try It Out, you create a dialog with a list view and two image lists. The list view will display files and folders on your hard drive. For the sake of simplicity, you will not extract the correct icons from the files and folders, but instead will use a standard folder icon for the folders and a text icon for files.

By double-clicking the folders, you can browse to the folder tree, and a Back button is provided to move up the tree. Five radio buttons are used to change the mode of the list view at runtime. If a file is double-clicked, you'll attempt to execute it.

Try It Out   Working with the ListView Control

As always, you start by creating the user interface:

1.   Create a new Windows application called **ListView** in the C:\BegVCSharp\Chapter15 directory.

2.   Add a `ListView`, a `Button`, a `Label`, and a `GroupBox` control to the form. Then add five radio buttons to the group box. Your form should look like the one shown in Figure 15-20. To set the width of the `Label` control, set its `AutoSize` property to `False`. Make the `Label` control as wide as the `ListView` control.

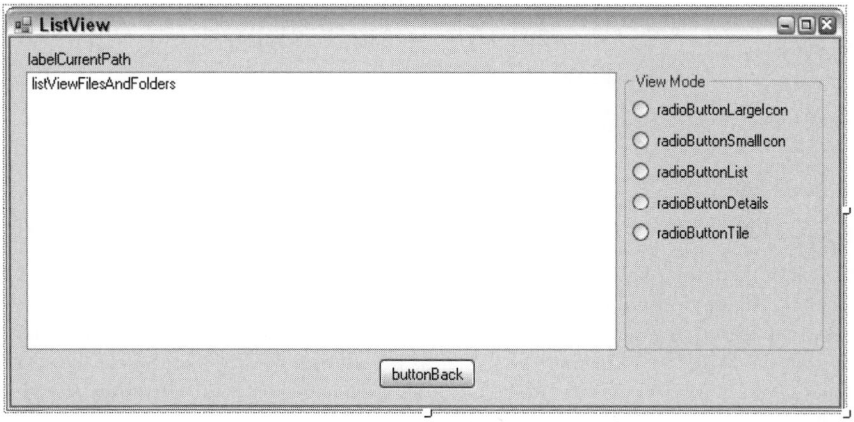

Figure 15-20

3.   Name the controls as shown in Figure 15-20. The `ListView` will not display its name as in the figure; an extra item is added just to show the name here — you don't need to add this item.

4.   Change the `Text` properties of the radio buttons and button to be the same as the name, except for the control names, and set the `Text` property of the form to `ListView`.

5.   Clear the `Text` property of the label.

6. Add two `ImageList` controls to the form by double-clicking this control's icon in the Toolbox — it is located in the Components section. Rename the controls `imageListSmall` and `imageListLarge`.

7. Change the `Size` property of the `ImageList` named `imageListLarge` to 32, 32.

8. Click the button to the right of the `Images` property of the `imageListLarge` image list to bring up the dialog from which you can browse to the images you want to insert.

9. Click Add and browse to the folder ListView in the code for this chapter. The files are `Folder 32x32.ico` and `Text 32x32.ico`.

10. Make sure that the folder icon is at the top of the list.

11. Repeat steps 8 and 9 with the other `ImageList`, `imageListSmall`, choosing the 16 × 16 versions of the icons.

12. Set the `Checked` property of the radio button `radioButtonDetails` to true.

13. Set the properties shown in the following table on the list view:

Property	Value
LargeImageList	imageListLarge
SmallImageList	imageListSmall
View	Details

How It Works

Before the first of the two `foreach` blocks, you call `BeginUpdate()` on the `ListView` control. Remember that the `BeginUpdate()` method on the `ListView` signals the `ListView` control to stop updating its visible area until `EndUpdate()` is called. If you did not call this method, then filling the list view would be slower and the list may flicker as the items are added. Just after the second `foreach` block, you call `EndUpdate()`, which causes the `ListView` control to draw the items you filled it with.

The two `foreach` blocks contain the code you are interested in. You start by creating a new instance of a `ListViewItem` and then setting the `Text` property to the name of the file or folder you are going to insert. The `ImageIndex` of the `ListViewItem` refers to the index of an item in one of the image lists. Therefore, it is important that the icons have the same indexes in the two image lists. You use the `Tag` property to save the fully qualified path to both folders and files, for use when the user double-clicks the item.

Next, you create the two sub-items. These are simply assigned the text to display and then added to the `SubItems` collection of the `ListViewItem`.

Finally, the `ListViewItem` is added to the `Items` collection of the `ListView`. The `ListView` is smart enough to simply ignore the sub-items if the view mode is anything but Details, so you add the sub-items no matter what the view mode is now.

Note that some aspects of the code are not discussed here — namely, the lines that actually obtain information about the files:

```
// Get information about the root folder.
DirectoryInfo dir = new DirectoryInfo(root);

// Retrieve the files and folders from the root folder.
DirectoryInfo[] dirs = dir.GetDirectories(); // Folders
FileInfo[] files = dir.GetFiles();           // Files
```

These lines use classes from the `System.IO` namespace for accessing files, so you need to add the following to the `using` region at the top of the code:

```
using System;
using System.Collections.Generic;
using System.ComponentModel;
using System.Data;
using System.Drawing;
using System.Windows.Forms;
using System.IO;
```

You learn more about file access and `System.IO` in Chapter 24, but to give you an idea of what's going on, the `GetDirectories()` method of the `DirectoryInfo` object returns a collection of objects that represents the folders in the directory you're looking in, and the `GetFiles()` method returns a collection of objects that represents the files in the current directory. You can loop through these collections, as you just did, using the object's `Name` property to return the name of the relevant directory or file, and create a `ListViewItem` to hold this string.

All that remains to be done in order for the `ListView` to display the root folder is to call the two functions in the constructor of the form. At the same time, you instantiate the `folderCol` `StringCollection` with the root folder:

```
InitializeComponent();

// Init ListView and folder collection
folderCol = new System.Collections.Specialized.StringCollection();
CreateHeadersAndFillListView();
PaintListView(@"C:\");
folderCol.Add(@"C:\");
```

To enable users to double-click an item in the `ListView` to browse the folders, you need to subscribe to the `ItemActivate` event. Select the `ListView` in the designer and double-click the `ItemActivate` event in the Events list of the Properties window.

The corresponding event handler looks like this:

```
private void listViewFilesAndFolders_ItemActivate(object sender, EventArgs e)
{
    // Cast the sender to a ListView and get the tag of the first selected
    // item.
    System.Windows.Forms.ListView lw = (System.Windows.Forms.ListView)sender;
    string filename = lw.SelectedItems[0].Tag.ToString();

    if (lw.SelectedItems[0].ImageIndex != 0)
    {
        try
        {
            // Attempt to run the file.
            System.Diagnostics.Process.Start(filename);
        }
        catch
        {
            // If the attempt fails we simply exit the method.
            return;
        }
    }
    else
    {
        // Insert the items.
        PaintListView(filename);
        folderCol.Add(filename);
    }
}
```

The `Tag` of the selected item contains the fully qualified path to the file or folder that was double-clicked. You know that the image with index 0 is a folder, so you can determine whether the item is a file or a folder by looking at that index. If it is a file, then you attempt to load the file. If it is a folder, then you call `PaintListView()` with the new folder and then add the new folder to the `folderCol` collection.

Before you move on to the radio buttons, complete the browsing capabilities by adding the `Click` event to the `Back` button. Double-click the button and fill the event handle with the following code:

```
private void buttonBack_Click(object sender, EventArgs e)
{
    if (folderCol.Count > 1)
    {
        PaintListView(folderCol[folderCol.Count - 2].ToString());
        folderCol.RemoveAt(folderCol.Count - 1);

    }
    else
    {
        PaintListView(folderCol[0].ToString());
    }
}
```

If there is more than one item in the `folderCol` collection, then you are not at the root of the browser, and you call `PaintListView()` with the path to the previous folder. The last item in the `folderCol` collection is the current folder, which is why you need to take the second to last item. You then remove the last item in the collection and make the new last item the current folder. If there is only one item in the collection, then you simply call `PaintListView()` with that item.

Now you just need to be able to change the view type of the `ListView`. Double-click each of the radio buttons and add the following code:

```csharp
private void radioButtonLargeIcon_CheckedChanged(object sender, EventArgs e)
{
    RadioButton rdb = (RadioButton)sender;
    if (rdb.Checked)
        this.listViewFilesAndFolders.View = View.LargeIcon;
}

private void radioButtonList_CheckedChanged(object sender, EventArgs e)
{
    RadioButton rdb = (RadioButton)sender;
    if (rdb.Checked)
        this.listViewFilesAndFolders.View = View.List;
}

private void radioButtonSmallIcon_CheckedChanged(object sender, EventArgs e)
{
    RadioButton rdb = (RadioButton)sender;
    if (rdb.Checked)
        this.listViewFilesAndFolders.View = View.SmallIcon;
}

private void radioButtonDetails_CheckedChanged(object sender, EventArgs e)
{
    RadioButton rdb = (RadioButton)sender;
    if (rdb.Checked)
        this.listViewFilesAndFolders.View = View.Details;
}
private void radioButtonTile_CheckedChanged(object sender, EventArgs e)
{
    RadioButton rdb = (RadioButton)sender;
    if (rdb.Checked)
        this.listViewFilesAndFolders.View = View.Tile;
}
```

You check the radio button to see whether it has been changed to `Checked` — if it has, then you set the `View` property of the `ListView` accordingly.

That concludes the `ListView` example. When you run it, you should see something like what is shown in Figure 15-21.

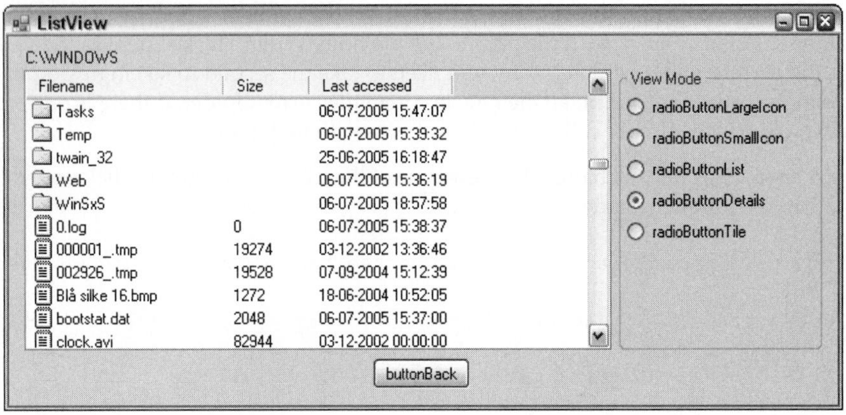

Figure 15-21

Adding the Event Handlers

That concludes the user interface, and you can move on to the code. First, you need a field to hold the folders you browsed through in order to be able to return to them when the Back button is clicked. You will store the absolute path of the folders, so choose a `StringCollection` for the job:

```
partial class Form1 : Form
{
    // Member field to hold previous folders
    private System.Collections.Specialized.StringCollection folderCol;
```

You didn't create any column headers in the Forms Designer, so you have to do that now, using a method called `CreateHeadersAndFillListView()`:

```
private void CreateHeadersAndFillListView()
{
    ColumnHeader colHead;

    // First header
    colHead = new ColumnHeader();
    colHead.Text = "Filename";
    this.listViewFilesAndFolders.Columns.Add(colHead); // Insert the header

    // Second header
    colHead = new ColumnHeader();
    colHead.Text = "Size";
    this.listViewFilesAndFolders.Columns.Add(colHead); // Insert the header

    // Third header
    colHead = new ColumnHeader();
    colHead.Text = "Last accessed";
    this.listViewFilesAndFolders.Columns.Add(colHead); // Insert the header
}
```

You start by declaring a single variable, `colHead`, which is used to create the three column headers. For each of the three headers, you declare the variable as new and assign the `Text` to it before adding it to the `Columns` collection of the `ListView`.

The final initialization of the form as it is displayed the first time is to fill the list view with files and folders from your hard disk. This is done in another method:

```
private void PaintListView(string root)
{
  try
  {
    // Two local variables that are used to create the items to insert
    ListViewItem lvi;
    ListViewItem.ListViewSubItem lvsi;

    // If there's no root folder, we can't insert anything.
    if (root.CompareTo("") == 0)
      return;

    // Get information about the root folder.
    DirectoryInfo dir = new DirectoryInfo(root);

    // Retrieve the files and folders from the root folder.
    DirectoryInfo[] dirs = dir.GetDirectories(); // Folders
    FileInfo[] files = dir.GetFiles();           // Files

    // Clear the ListView. Note that we call the Clear method on the
    // Items collection rather than on the ListView itself.
    // The Clear method of the ListView remove everything, including column
    // headers, and we only want to remove the items from the view.
    this.listViewFilesAndFolders.Items.Clear();

    // Set the label with the current path.
    this.labelCurrentPath.Text = root;

    // Lock the ListView for updates.
    this.listViewFilesAndFolders.BeginUpdate();


    // Loop through all folders in the root folder and insert them.
    foreach (DirectoryInfo di in dirs)
    {
      // Create the main ListViewItem.
      lvi = new ListViewItem();
      lvi.Text = di.Name; // Folder name
      lvi.ImageIndex = 0; // The folder icon has index 0
      lvi.Tag = di.FullName; // Set the tag to the qualified path of the
      // folder

      // Create the two ListViewSubItems.
      lvsi = new ListViewItem.ListViewSubItem();
      lvsi.Text = ""; // Size - a folder has no size and so this column
      // is empty
```

```
                lvi.SubItems.Add(lvsi); // Add the subitem to the ListViewItem

                lvsi = new ListViewItem.ListViewSubItem();
                lvsi.Text = di.LastAccessTime.ToString(); // Last accessed column
                lvi.SubItems.Add(lvsi); // Add the subitem to the ListViewItem.

                // Add the ListViewItem to the Items collection of the ListView.
                this.listViewFilesAndFolders.Items.Add(lvi);
            }

            // Loop through all the files in the root folder.
            foreach (FileInfo fi in files)
            {
                // Create the main ListViewItem.
                lvi = new ListViewItem();
                lvi.Text = fi.Name; // Filename
                lvi.ImageIndex = 1; // The icon we use to represent a folder has
                // index 1.
                lvi.Tag = fi.FullName; // Set the tag to the qualified path of the
                // file.

                // Create the two subitems.
                lvsi = new ListViewItem.ListViewSubItem();
                lvsi.Text = fi.Length.ToString(); // Length of the file
                lvi.SubItems.Add(lvsi); // Add to the SubItems collection

                lvsi = new ListViewItem.ListViewSubItem();
                lvsi.Text = fi.LastAccessTime.ToString(); // Last Accessed Column
                lvi.SubItems.Add(lvsi); // Add to the SubItems collection

                // Add the item to the Items collection of the ListView.
                this.listViewFilesAndFolders.Items.Add(lvi);
            }

            // Unlock the ListView. The items that have been inserted will now
            // be displayed.
            this.listViewFilesAndFolders.EndUpdate();
        }
        catch (System.Exception err)
        {
            MessageBox.Show("Error: " + err.Message);
        }
    }
```

The TabControl Control

The TabControl control provides an easy way to organize a dialog into logical parts that can be accessed through tabs located at the top of the control. A TabControl contains TabPages that essentially work like a GroupBox control, in that they group controls together, although they are somewhat more complex.

Figure 15-22 shows the Tools ⇨ Options dialog in Word 2003. Notice the three rows of tabs at the top of the dialog. Clicking each of them will show a different selection of controls in the rest of the dialog. This is a very good example of how to use a `TabControl` control to group related information, making it easy for users to find the information they want.

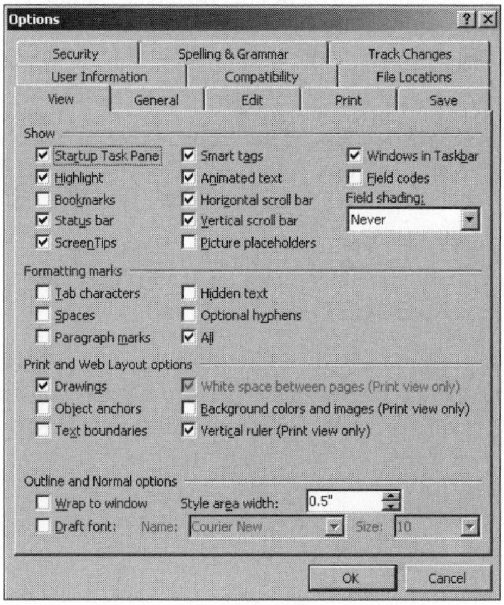

Figure 15-22

Using the `TabControl` is easy. You simply add the number of tabs you want to display to the control's collection of `TabPage` objects and then drag the controls you want to display to the respective pages.

TabControl Properties

The properties of the `TabControl` (shown in the following table) are largely used to control the appearance of the container of `TabPage` objects — in particular, the tabs displayed:

Name	Description
Alignment	This property controls where on the `TabControl` the tabs are displayed. The default is at the top.
Appearance	The `Appearance` property controls how the tabs are displayed. The tabs can be displayed as normal buttons or with flat style.
HotTrack	If this property is set to `true`, the appearance of the tabs on the control changes as the mouse pointer passes over them.
Multiline	If this property is set to `true`, it is possible to have several rows of tabs.

(continued)

Name	Description
RowCount	RowCount returns the number of rows of tabs currently displayed.
SelectedIndex	This property returns or sets the index of the selected tab.
SelectedTab	SelectedTab returns or sets the selected tab. Note that this property works on the actual instances of the TabPages.
TabCount	TabCount returns the total number of tabs.
TabPages	This property is the collection of TabPage objects in the control. Use this collection to add and remove TabPage objects.

Working with the TabControl

The TabControl works slightly differently from all other controls you've seen so far. The control itself is little more than a container for the tab pages that is used to display the pages. When you double-click a TabControl in the Toolbox, you are presented with a control that already has two TabPages, as shown in Figure 15-23.

Figure 15-23

When the mouse moves over the control, a small button with a triangle appears at the control's upper-right corner. When you click this button, a small window is unfolded. Called the Actions Window, this is provided to enable you to easily access selected properties and methods of the control. You may have noticed this earlier, as many controls in Visual Studio include this feature, but the TabControl is the first of the controls in this chapter that actually enables you to do anything interesting in the Actions Window. The Actions Window of the TabControl enables you to easily add and remove TabPages at design time.

The procedure outlined in the preceding paragraph for adding tabs to the TabControl is provided in order to quickly get you up and running with the control. However, if you want to change the behavior or style of the tabs, you should use the TabPages dialog — accessed through the button when you select TabPages in the Properties window. The TabPages property is also the collection used to access the individual pages on a TabControl.

Once you've added the TabPages you need, you can add controls to the pages in the same way you did earlier with the GroupBox. The following Try It Out demonstrates the basics of the control.

Try It Out Working with TabPages

Follow these steps to create a Windows application that demonstrates how to develop controls located on different pages on the TabControl:

1. Create a new Windows application called **TabControl** in the directory C:\BegVCSharp\Chapter15.

2. Drag a TabControl control from the Toolbox to the form. Like the GroupBox, the TabControl is found on the Containers tab in the Toolbox.

3. Find the TabPages property and click the button to the right of it after selecting it, to bring up the dialog shown in Figure 15-24.

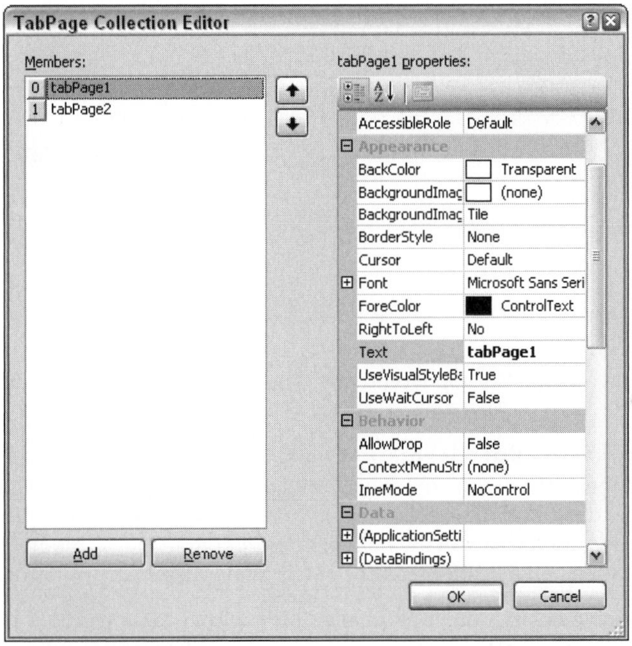

Figure 15-24

4. Change the Text property of the tab pages to Tab One and Tab Two, respectively, and click OK to close the dialog.

5. You can select the tab pages to work on by clicking on the tabs at the top of the control. Select the tab with the text Tab One. Drag a button on to the control. Be sure to place the button within the frame of the TabControl. If you place it outside, then the button will be placed on the form, rather than on the control.

6. Change the name of the button to buttonShowMessage and change the Text of the button to **Show Message**.

7. Click on the tab with the Text property Tab Two. Drag a TextBox control onto the TabControl surface. Name this control textBoxMessage and clear the Text property.

8. The two tabs should look as shown in Figure 15-25 and Figure 15-26.

Figure 15-25

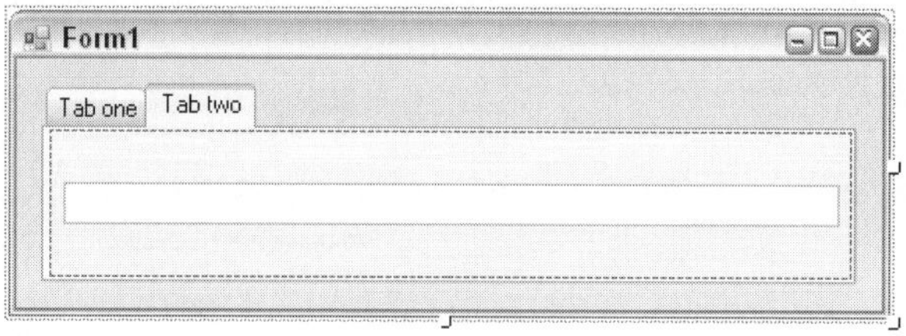

Figure 15-26

How It Works

You access a control on a tab just as you would any other control on the form. You get the Text property of the TextBox and display it in a message box.

Earlier in the chapter, you saw that it is only possible to have one radio button selected at a time on a form (unless you put them in a group box). The TabPages work in precisely the same way as group boxes, so it is possible to have multiple sets of radio buttons on different tabs without the need for group boxes. In addition, as you saw in the buttonShowMessage_Click method, it is possible to access the controls located on tabs other than the one that the current control is on.

The last thing you must know in order to be able to work with a TabControl is how to determine which tab is currently being displayed. You can use two properties for this purpose: SelectedTab and SelectedIndex. As the names imply, SelectedTab returns the TabPage object to you or null if no tab is selected, and SelectedIndex returns the index of the tab or –1 if no tab is selected. It is left to you in Exercise 2 to experiment with these properties.

Adding the Event Handler

You are now ready to access the controls. If you run the code as it is, you will see the tab pages displayed properly. All that remains to do to demonstrate the TabControl is to add some code such that when users click the Show Message button on one tab, the text entered in the other tab will be displayed in a message box. First, you add a handler for the `Click` event by double-clicking the button on the first tab and adding the following code:

```
private void buttonShowMessage_Click(object sender, EventArgs e)
{
    // Access the TextBox.

    MessageBox.Show(this.textBoxMessage.Text);
}
```

Summary

In this chapter, you visited some of the controls most commonly used for creating Windows applications, and you saw how they can be used to create simple, yet powerful, user interfaces. The chapter covered the properties and events of these controls, provided examples demonstrating their use, and explained how to add event handlers for the particular events of a control.

In this chapter, you learned how to do the following:

❑   Use the `Label` and `LinkedLabel` controls to display information to users.

❑   Use the `Button` control and the corresponding `Click` event to enable users to tell the application that they want some action to run.

❑   Use the `TextBox` and `RichTextBox` controls to enable users to enter text as either plain or formatted.

❑   Distinguish between the `CheckBox` and the `RadioButton` and how to use them. You also learned how to group the two with the `GroupBox` control and how that affected the behavior of the controls.

❑   Use the `CheckedListBox` to provide lists from which the user can select items by checking a check box. You also learned how to use the more common `ListBox` control to provide a list similar to that of the `CheckedListBox` control, but without the check boxes.

❑   Use the `ListView` and `ImageList` controls to provide a list that the users are able to view in a number of different ways.

❑   Use the `TabControl` to group controls on different pages on the same form that the user is able to select at will.

In the next chapter, you look at some of the more complex controls and features of creating Windows Forms applications.

Exercises

1. In previous versions of Visual Studio, it was quite difficult to get your own applications to display their controls in the style of the current Windows version. For this exercise, locate where, in a Windows Forms application, visual styles are enabled in a new Windows Forms project. Experiment with enabling and disabling the styles and see how what you do affects the controls on the forms.

2. Modify the `TabControl` example by adding a couple of tab pages and displaying a message box with the following text: **You changed the current tab to <Text of the current tab> from <Text of the tab that was just left>**.

3. In the `ListView` example, you used the `tag` property to save the fully qualified path to the folders and files in the `ListView`. Change this behavior by creating a new class that is derived from `ListViewItem` and use instances of this new class as the items in the `ListView`. Store the information about the files and folders in the new class using a property named `FullyQualifiedPath`.

Advanced Windows Forms Features

In the previous chapter, you looked at some of the controls most commonly used in Windows application development. With controls such as these, it is possible to create impressive dialogs, but very few full-scale Windows applications have a user interface consisting solely of a single dialog. Rather, these applications use a Single Document Interface (SDI) or a Multiple Document Interface (MDI). Applications of either of these types usually make heavy use of menus and toolbars, neither of which were discussed in the previous chapter, but I'll make amends for that now.

> With the addition of the Windows Presentation Foundation to the .NET Framework, a few new types of Windows applications were introduced. They are examined in detail in Chapter 34.

This chapter begins where the last left off, by looking at controls, starting with the menu control and then moving on to toolbars, where you will learn how to link buttons on toolbars to specific menu items, and vice versa. Then you move on to creating SDI and MDI applications, with the focus on MDI applications because SDI applications are basically subsets of MDI applications.

So far, you've consumed only those controls that ship with the .NET Framework. As you saw, these controls are very powerful and provide a wide range of functionality, but there are times when they are not sufficient. For those cases, it is possible to create custom controls, and you look at how that is done toward the end of this chapter.

In this chapter, you will see how to do the following:

- ❑ Use three common controls to create rich-looking menus, toolbars, and status bars.
- ❑ Create MDI applications.
- ❑ Create your own controls.

Menus and Toolbars

How many Windows applications can you think of that do not contain a menu or toolbar of some kind? None, right? Menus and toolbars are likely to be important parts of any application you will write for the Windows operating system. To assist you in creating them for your applications, Visual Studio 2008 provides two controls that enable you to create, with very little difficulty, menus and toolbars that look like the menus you find in Visual Studio.

Two Is One

The two controls you are going to look at over the following pages were introduced in Visual Studio 2005, and they represent a handsome boost of power to the casual developer and professional alike. Building applications with professional-looking toolbars and menus used to be reserved for those who would take the time to write custom paint handlers and those who bought third-party components. Creating what previously could take weeks is now a simple task that, quite literally, can be done in seconds.

The controls you will use can be grouped into a family of controls that has the suffix `Strip`. They are the `ToolStrip`, `MenuStrip`, and `StatusStrip`. You return to the `StatusStrip` later in the chapter. If you want to look at it in its purest form, the `ToolStrip` and the `MenuStrip` are in fact the same control, as `MenuStrip` derives directly from the `ToolStrip`. This means that anything the `ToolStrip` can do, the `MenuStrip` can do. Obviously, it also means that the two work really well together.

Using the MenuStrip Control

In addition to the `MenuStrip` control, several additional controls are used to populate a menu. The three most common of these are the `ToolStripMenuItem`, `ToolStripDropDown`, and the `ToolStripSeparator`. All of these controls represent a particular way to view an item in a menu or toolbar. The `ToolStripMenuItem` represents a single entry in a menu, the `ToolStripDropDown` represents an item that when clicked displays a list of other items, and the `ToolStripSeparator` represents a horizontal or vertical dividing line in a menu or toolbar.

There is another kind of menu that is discussed briefly after the discussion of the `MenuStrip` — the `ContextMenuStrip`. A context menu appears when a user right-clicks on an item, and typically displays information relevant to that item.

Without further ado, in the following Try It Out, you create the first example of the chapter.

Try It Out   Professional Menus in Five Seconds

This first example is very much a teaser, and you are simply going to introduce an aspect of the new controls that is truly wonderful if you want to create standard menus with the right look and feel.

1. Create a new Windows application and name it "Professional Menus" in the directory C:\BegVCSharp\Chapter16.

2. Drag an instance of the `MenuStrip` control from the Toolbox onto the design surface.

3. Click the triangle to the far right of the MenuStrip at the top of the dialog to display the Actions Window.

4. Click the small triangle in the upper right corner of the menu and click the Insert Standard Items link.

That's it. If you drop down the File menu, you will see the menu shown in Figure 16-1. There is no functionality behind the menu yet — you will have to fill that in. You can edit the menu as you see fit; and to do so, please read on.

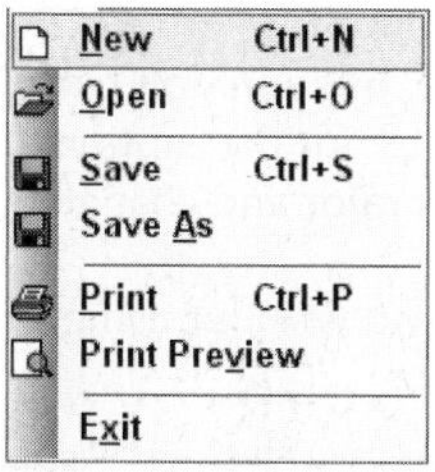

🗋	**New**	Ctrl+N
📂	**Open**	Ctrl+O
💾	**Save**	Ctrl+S
💾	Save **As**	
🖨	**Print**	Ctrl+P
🗐	Print Pre**v**iew	
	E**x**it	

Figure 16-1

Creating Menus Manually

When you drag the MenuStrip control from the Toolbox to the design surface, you will see that this control places itself both on the form itself and in the control tray, but it can be edited directly on the form. To create new menu items, you simply place the pointer in the box marked Type Here (see Figure 16-2).

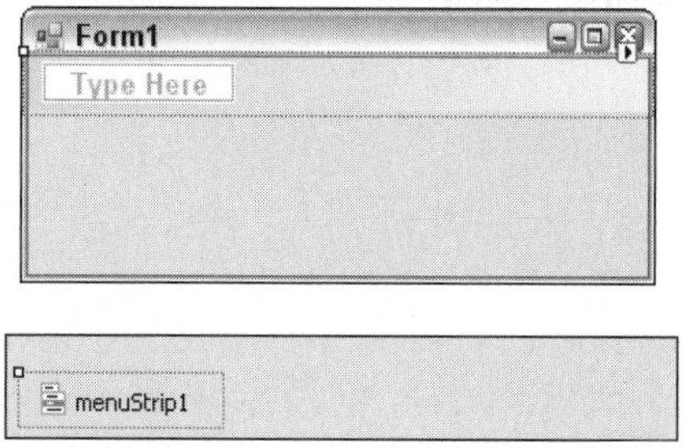

Figure 16-2

When you enter the caption of the menu in the highlighted box, you may include an ampersand (&) in front of a letter that you want to function as the shortcut key character for the menu item — this is the character that appears underlined in the menu item and that can be selected pressing Alt and the key together.

Note that it is quite possible to create several menu items in the same menu with the same shortcut key character. The rule is that a character can be used for this purpose only once for each pop-up menu (for example, once in the Files pop-up menu, once in the View menu, and so on). If you accidentally assign the same shortcut key character to multiple menu items in the same pop-up menu, you'll find that only the one closest to the top of the control responds to the character.

When you select the item, the control automatically displays items under the current item and to the right of it. When you enter a caption into either of these controls, you create a new item in relation to the one you started out with. That's how you create drop-down menus.

To create the horizontal lines that divide menus into groups, you must use the `ToolStripSeparator` control instead of the `ToolStripMenuItem`, but you don't actually insert a different control. Instead, you simply type a "−" (dash) as the only character for the caption of the item and Visual Studio will then automatically assume that the item is a separator and change the type of the control.

In the following Try It Out, you create a menu without using Visual Studio to generate the items on it.

Try It Out Creating Menus from Scratch

In this example, you are going to create the File and Help menus from scratch. The Edit and Tools menus are left for you to do by yourself.

1. Create a new Windows Application project, name it "Manual Menus," and save it to the C:\ BegVCSharp\Chapter16 folder.

2. Drag a `MenuStrip` control from the Toolbox onto the design surface.

3. Click in the text area of the `MenuStrip` control where it says Type Here, type **&File**, and press the Enter key.

4. Type the following into the text areas below the File item:

   ❑ &New

   ❑ &Open

   ❑ -

   ❑ &Save

   ❑ Save &As

   ❑ -

   ❑ &Print

   ❑ Print Preview

   ❑ -

   ❑ E&xit

Your menu should now look like the one shown in Figure 16-3. Notice how the dashes are automatically changed by Visual Studio to a line that separates the elements.

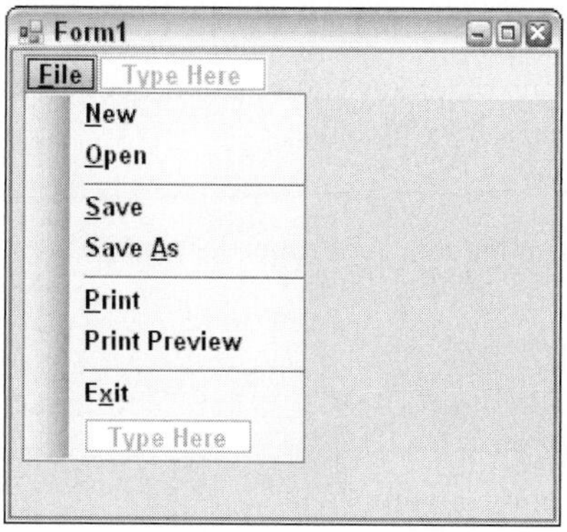

Figure 16-3

5. Click in the text area to the right of Files and type **&Help**.

6. Type the following into the text areas below the Help item:

    ❑   Contents

    ❑   Index

    ❑   Search

    ❑   -

    ❑   About

Your menu now looks like the one shown in Figure 16-4.

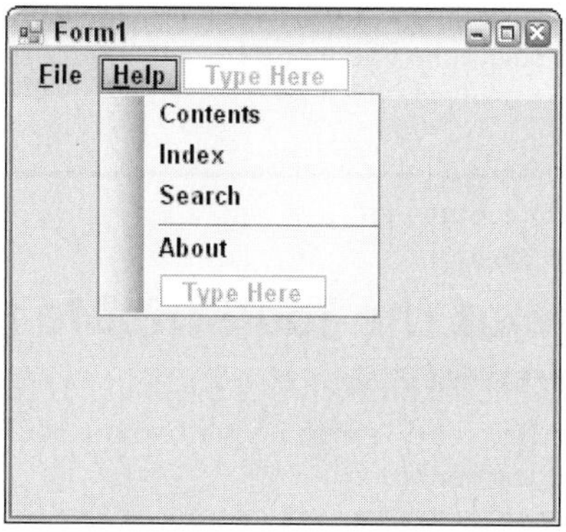

Figure 16-4

7. Return to the File menu and set the shortcut keys for the items. To do this, select the item you want to set and find the `ShortcutKeys` property in the properties panel. When you click the drop-down arrow, you are presented with a small window where you can set the key combination you want to associate with the menu item. Because this menu is a standard menu, you should use the standard key combinations, but if you are creating something else, please feel free to select any other key combination. Set the `ShortcutKeys` properties in the File menu as shown in the following table:

Item Name	Properties and Values
&New	Ctrl + N
&Open	Ctrl + O
&Save	Ctrl + S
&Print	Ctrl + P

8. Now for the finishing touch: the images. Select the New item in the File menu and click on the ellipses (...) to the left of the Image property in the Properties panel to bring up the Select Resource dialog.

    Arguably the most difficult thing about creating these menus is obtaining the images you want to display. In this case, you can get the images by downloading the source code for this book at www.wrox.com, but normally you will need to draw them yourself or get them in some other way.

9. Because there are currently no resources in the project, the Entry list box is empty, so click Import. The images for this example can be found in the source code for this book under Chapter16\Manual Menus\Images. Select all of the files there and click Open. You are currently editing the New item, so select the New image in the Entry list and click OK.

10. Repeat step 9 for the images for the Open, Save, Save As, Print, and Print Preview buttons.

11. Run the project. You can select the File menu by clicking it or by pressing Alt+F, and you can access the Help menu with Alt+H.

Additional Properties of the ToolStripMenuItem

You should be aware of a few additional properties of the `ToolStripMenuItem` when you are creating your menus. The list in the table that follows is in no way exhaustive — for a complete listing, please refer to .NET Framework SDK documentation.

Property	Description
Checked	Indicates whether the menu is checked.
CheckOnClick	When this property is true, a check mark is either added to or removed from the position to the left of the text in the item that is otherwise occupied by an image. Use the Checked property to determine the state of the menu item.
Enabled	An item with Enabled set to false will be grayed out and cannot be selected.
DropDownItems	Returns a collection of items that is used as a drop-down menu in relation to the menu item.

Adding Functionality to Menus

Now you can produce menus that look every bit as good as the ones you find in Visual Studio, so the only task left is to make something happen when you click on them. Obviously, what happens is up to you, but in the following Try It Out you create a very simple example that builds on the previous example.

To respond to selections made by the user, you should implement handlers for one of two events that the ToolStripMenuItems sends:

Event	Description
Click	Sent whenever the user clicks on an item. In most cases this is the event you want to respond to.
CheckedChanged	Sent when an item with the CheckOnClick property is clicked.

You are going to extend the Manual Menus example from the previous Try It Out by adding a text box to the dialog and implementing a few event handlers. You will also add another menu between Files and Help called Format. In the code download, this project is named "Extended Manual Menus."

Try It Out   **Handling Menu Events**

1. Drag a RichTextBox onto the design surface and change its name to **richTextBoxText**. Set its Dock property to Fill.

2. Select the MenuStrip and then enter **Format** into the text area next to the Help menu item and press the Enter key.

3. Select the Format menu item and drag it to a position between Files and Help.

4. Add a menu item to the Format menu with the text **Show Help Menu**.

5. Set the `CheckOnClick` property of the Show Help Menu to `true`. Set its `Checked` property to `true`.

6. Change the names of the following five menu items:

Menu Item	Name
New	MenuItemNew
Open	MenuItemOpen
Save	MenuItemSave
Show Help Menu	MenuItemShowHelpMenu
Help	MenuItemHelp

7. Select `MenuItemShowHelpMenu` and add an event handler for the `CheckedChanged` event by double-clicking the event in the Events part of the Properties panel.

8. Add this code to the event handler:

```
private void MenuItemShowHelpMenu _CheckedChanged (object sender, EventArgs e)
{
   ToolStripMenuItem item = (ToolStripMenuItem)sender;
   MenuItemHelp.Visible = item.Checked;
}
```

9. Double-click `MenuItemNew`, `MenuItemSave` and `MenuItemOpen`. Double-clicking a `ToolStripMenuItem` in Design View causes the `Click` event to be added to the code. Enter this code:

```
private void MenuItemNew_Click(object sender, EventArgs e)
{
   richTextBoxText.Text = "";
}

private void MenuItemOpen_Click(object sender, EventArgs e)
{
   try
   {
      richTextBoxText.LoadFile(@".\Example.rtf");
   }
   catch
   {
      // Ignore errors
   }
}
```

```
private void MenuItemSave_Click(object sender, EventArgs e)
{
    try
    {
        richTextBoxText.SaveFile(@".\Example.rtf");
    }
    catch
    {
        // Ignore errors
    }
}
```

10. Run the application. When you click the Show Help Menu, the Help menu disappears or appears, depending on the state of the Checked property, and you should be able to open, save, and clear the text in the text box.

How It Works

The MenuItemShowHelpMenu_CheckedChanged event is handled first. The event handler for this event sets the Visible property of MenuItemHelp to true if the Checked property is true; otherwise, it should be false. This causes the menu item to behave like a toggle button for the Help menu.

Finally, the three event handlers for the Click events clear the text in the RichTextBox, save the text in the RichTextBox to a predetermined file, and open said file, respectively. Notice that the Click and CheckedChanged events are identical in that they both handle the event that happens when a user clicks a menu item, but the behavior of the menu items in question are quite different and should be handled according to the purpose of the menu item.

Toolbars

While menus are great for providing access to a multitude of functionality in your application, some items benefit from being placed in a toolbar as well as on the menu. A toolbar provides one-click access to such frequently used functionality as Open, Save, and so on.

Figure 16-5 shows a selection of toolbars within Word 2003.

Figure 16-5

A button on a toolbar usually displays a picture and no text, though it is possible to have buttons with both. Examples of toolbars with no text are those found in Word (refer to Figure 16-5), and examples of toolbars that include text can be found in Internet Explorer. In addition to buttons, you will occasionally see combo boxes and text boxes in the toolbars too. If you let the mouse pointer hover above a button in a toolbar, it will often display a tooltip, which provides information about the purpose of the button, especially when only an icon is displayed.

The `ToolStrip`, like the `MenuStrip`, has been made with a professional look and feel in mind. When users see a toolbar, they expect to be able to move it around and position it wherever they want it. The `ToolStrip` enables users to do just that — that is, if you allow them to.

When you first add a `ToolStrip` to the design surface of your form it looks very similar to the `MenuStrip` shown earlier, except for two things: To the far left are four vertical dots, just as you know them from the menus in Visual Studio. These dots indicate that the toolbar can be moved around and docked in the parent application window. The second difference is that by default a toolbar displays images, rather than text, so the default of the items in the bar is a button. The toolbar displays a drop-down menu that enables you to select the type of the item.

One thing that is exactly like the `MenuStrip` is that the Actions window includes a link called Insert Standard Items. When you click this, you don't get quite the same number of items as you did with the `MenuStrip`, but you get the buttons for New, Open, Save, Print, Cut, Copy, Paste, and Help. Instead of going through a full Try It Out example as you did earlier, let's take a look at some of the properties of the `ToolStrip` itself and the controls used to populate it.

ToolStrip Properties

The properties of the `ToolStrip` control manage how and where the control is displayed. Remember that this control is actually the base for the `MenuStrip` control shown earlier, so there are many shared properties between them. Again, the table that follows shows only a few properties of special interest — if you want a complete listing please refer to .NET Framework SDK documentation.

Property	Description
GripStyle	Controls whether the four vertical dots are displayed at the far left of the toolbar. The effect of hiding the grip is that users can no longer move the toolbar.
LayoutStyle	Controls how the items in the toolbar are displayed. The default is horizontally.
Items	Contains a collection of all the items in the toolbar.
ShowItemToolTip	Determines whether tooltips should be shown for the items in the toolbar.
Stretch	By default, a toolbar is only slightly wider or taller than the items contained within it. If you set the `Stretch` property to `true`, the toolbar will fill the entire length of its container.

ToolStrip Items

You can use numerous controls in a `ToolStrip`. Earlier, it was mentioned that a toolbar should be able to contain buttons, combo boxes, and text boxes. As you would expect, there are controls for each of these items, but there are also quite a few others, described in the following table:

Control	Description
ToolStripButton	Represents a button. You can use this for buttons with or without text.
ToolStripLabel	Represents a label. It can also display images, which means that this control can be used to display a static image in front of another control that doesn't display information about itself, such as a text box or combo box.
ToolStripSplitButton	Displays a button with a drop-down button to the right that, when clicked, displays a menu below it. The menu does not unfold if the button part of the control is clicked.
ToolStripDropDownButton	Similar to the ToolStripSplitButton. The only difference is that the drop-down button has been removed and replaced with an image of a down array. The menu part of the control unfolds when any part of the control is clicked.
ToolStripComboBox	Displays a combo box.
ToolStripProgressBar	Embeds a progress bar in your toolbar.
ToolStripTextBox	Displays a text box.
ToolStripSeparator	Creates horizontal or vertical dividers for the items. You saw this control earlier.

In the following Try It Out, you will extend your menus example to include a toolbar. The toolbar will contain the standard controls of a toolbar and three additional buttons: Bold, Italic, and Underline. There will also be a combo box for selecting a font. (The images you use in this example for the button that selects the font can be found in the code download.)

Try It Out   Extend Your Toolbar

Follow these steps to extend the previous example with toolbars:

1. Remove the `ToolStripMenuItem` that was used in the Format menu. Select the Show Help Menu option and press the Delete key. Add three `ToolStripMenuItems` in its place and change each of their `CheckOnClick` properties to `true`:

   ❑ Bold

   ❑ Italic

   ❑ Underline

2. Name the three controls `ToolStripMenuItemBold`, `ToolStripMenuItemItalic`, and `ToolStripMenuItemUnderline`.

3. Add a `ToolStrip` to the form. In the Actions Window, click Insert Standard Items. Select and delete the items for Cut, Copy, Paste, and the Separator after them. When you insert the `ToolStrip`, the `RichTextBox` may fail to dock properly. If that happens, change the `Dock` style to `none` and manually resize the control to fill the form. Then change the `Anchor` property to `Top, Bottom, Left, Right`.

4. Create three new buttons and a separator at the end of the toolbar by selecting `Button` three times and `Separator` once. (Click on the last item in the `ToolStrip` to bring up those options.)

5. Create the final two items by selecting ComboBox from the drop-down list and then adding a separator as the last item.

6. Select the Help item and drag it from its current position to the position as the last item in the toolbar.

7. The first three buttons are going to be the Bold, Italic, and Underline buttons, respectively. Name the controls as shown in the following table:

ToolBarButton	Name
Bold button	ToolStripButtonBold
Italic button	ToolStripButtonItalic
Underline button	ToolStripButtonUnderline
ComboBox	ToolStripComboBoxFonts

8. Select the Bold button, click on the ellipses (...) in the Image property, select the Project Resource File radio button, and click Import. If you've downloaded the source code for this book, use the three images found in the folder Chapter16\Toolbars\ Images: BLD.ico, ITL.ico, and UNDRLN.ico. Note that the default extensions suggested by Visual Studio do not include ICO, so when browsing for the icons you will have to choose Show All Files from the drop-down.

9. Select BLD.ico for the image of the Bold button.

10. Select the Italic button and change its image to ITL.ico.

11. Select the Underline button and change its image to UNDRLN.ico.

12. Select the `ToolStripComboBox`. In the Properties panel, set the properties shown in the following table:

Property	Value
Items	MS Sans Serif Times New Roman
DropDownStyle	DropDownList

13. Set the `CheckOnClick` property for each of the Bold, Italic, and Underline buttons to `true`.

14. To select the initial item in the ComboBox, enter the following into the constructor of the class:

```
public Form1()
{
   InitializeComponent();

   this.ToolStripComboBoxFonts.SelectedIndex = 0;
}
```

15. Press F5 to run the example. You should see a dialog that looks like Figure 16-6.

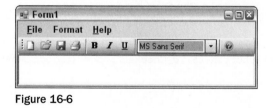

Figure 16-6

Adding Event Handlers

You are now ready to add the event handlers for the items on the menu and toolbars. You already have handlers for the Save, New, and Open items on the menu, and obviously the buttons on the toolbar should behave in exactly the same way as the menu. This is easily achieved by assigning the `Click` events of the buttons on the toolbars to the same handlers that are used by the buttons on the menu. Set the events as follows:

ToolStripButton	Event
New	MenuItemNew_Click
Open	MenuItemOpen_Click
Save	MenuItemSave_Click

Now it's time to add handlers for the Bold, Italic, and Underline buttons. As these buttons are check buttons, you should use the `CheckedChanged` event instead of the `Click` event, so go ahead and add that event for each of the three buttons. Add the following code:

```
private void ToolStripButtonBold_CheckedChanged(object sender, EventArgs e)
{
    Font oldFont;
    Font newFont;

    bool checkState = ((ToolStripButton)sender).Checked;

    // Get the font that is being used in the selected text.
    oldFont = this.richTextBoxText.SelectionFont;

    if (!checkState)
      newFont = new Font(oldFont, oldFont.Style & ~FontStyle.Bold);
    else
      newFont = new Font(oldFont, oldFont.Style | FontStyle.Bold);

    // Insert the new font and return focus to the RichTextBox.
    this.richTextBoxText.SelectionFont = newFont;
    this.richTextBoxText.Focus();

    this.ToolStripMenuItemBold.CheckedChanged -= new ←
EventHandler(ToolStripMenuItemBold_CheckedChanged);
    this.ToolStripMenuItemBold.Checked = checkState;
    this.ToolStripMenuItemBold.CheckedChanged += new ←
EventHandler(ToolStripMenuItemBold_CheckedChanged);
}

private void ToolStripButtonItalic_CheckedChanged(object sender, EventArgs e)
{
    Font oldFont;
    Font newFont;

    bool checkState = ((ToolStripButton)sender).Checked;

    // Get the font that is being used in the selected text.
    oldFont = this.richTextBoxText.SelectionFont;

    if (!checkState)
      newFont = new Font(oldFont, oldFont.Style & ~FontStyle.Italic);
    else
      newFont = new Font(oldFont, oldFont.Style | FontStyle.Italic);

    // Insert the new font.
    this.richTextBoxText.SelectionFont = newFont;
    this.richTextBoxText.Focus();

    this.ToolStripMenuItemItalic.CheckedChanged -= new ←
EventHandler(ToolStripMenuItemItalic_CheckedChanged);
```

```
        this.ToolStripMenuItemItalic.Checked = checkState;
        this.ToolStripMenuItemItalic.CheckedChanged += new ←
EventHandler(ToolStripMenuItemItalic_CheckedChanged);
    }

    private void ToolStripButtonUnderline_CheckedChanged(object sender, ←
EventArgs e)
    {
        Font oldFont;
        Font newFont;

        bool checkState = ((ToolStripButton)sender).Checked;

        // Get the font that is being used in the selected text.
        oldFont = this.richTextBoxText.SelectionFont;

        if (!checkState)
          newFont = new Font(oldFont, oldFont.Style & ~FontStyle.Underline);
        else
          newFont = new Font(oldFont, oldFont.Style | FontStyle.Underline);

        // Insert the new font.
        this.richTextBoxText.SelectionFont = newFont;
        this.richTextBoxText.Focus();

        this.ToolStripMenuItemUnderline.CheckedChanged -= new ←
EventHandler(ToolStripMenuItemUnderline_CheckedChanged);
        this.ToolStripMenuItemUnderline.Checked = checkState;
        this.ToolStripMenuItemUnderline.CheckedChanged += new ←
EventHandler(ToolStripMenuItemUnderline_CheckedChanged);
    }
```

The event handlers simply set the correct style to the font used in the RichTextBox. The three final lines in each of the three methods deal with the corresponding item in the menu. The first line removes the event handler from the menu item. This ensures that no events trigger when the next line runs, which sets the state of the Checked property to the same value as the toolbar button. Finally, the event handler is reinstated.

The event handlers for the menu items should simply set the Checked property of the buttons on the toolbar, allowing the event handlers for the toolbar buttons to do the rest. Add the event handlers for the CheckedChanged event and enter this code:

```
    private void ToolStripMenuItemBold_CheckedChanged(object sender, EventArgs e)
    {
        this.ToolStripButtonBold.Checked = ToolStripMenuItemBold.Checked;
    }

    private void ToolStripMenuItemItalic_CheckedChanged(object sender, EventArgs e)
```

```
    {
        this.ToolStripButtonItalic.Checked = ToolStripMenuItemItalic.Checked;
    }


    private void ToolStripMenuItemUnderline_CheckedChanged(object sender, ↵
EventArgs e)
    {
        this.ToolStripButtonUnderline.Checked = ToolStripMenuItemUnderline.Checked;
    }
```

The only thing left to do is allow users to select a font family from the ComboBox. Whenever a user changes the selection in the ComboBox, the SelectedIndexChanged is raised, so add an event handler for that event:

```
    private void toolStripComboBoxFonts_SelectedIndexChanged(object sender,
    EventArgs e)
    {
        string text = ((ToolStripComboBox)sender).SelectedItem.ToString();
        Font newFont = null;

        // Create a new font with the correct font family.
        if (richTextBoxText.SelectionFont == null)
          newFont = new Font(text, richTextBoxText.Font.Size);
        else
          newFont = new Font(text, richTextBoxText.SelectionFont.Size,
                             richTextBoxText.SelectionFont.Style);
        richTextBoxText.SelectionFont = newFont;      }
```

Now run the code. You should be able to create a dialog that looks something like what is shown in Figure 16-7. The toolbar has been moved a bit to the right to also show the menu.

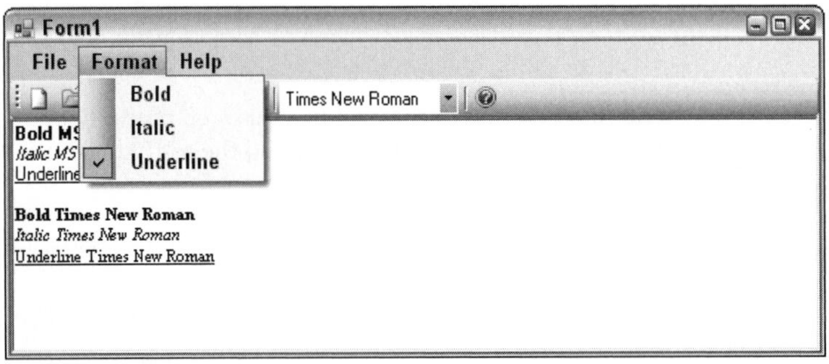

Figure 16-7

StatusStrip

The last of the small family of strip controls is the `StatusStrip`. This control represents the bar that you find at the bottom of the dialog in many applications. The bar is typically used to display brief information about the current state of the application — a good example is Word's display of the current page, column, line, and so on in the status bar as you are typing.

The `StatusStrip` is derived from the `ToolStrip`, and you should be quite familiar with the view that is presented as you drag the control onto your form. Three of the four possible controls that can be used in the `StatusStrip` — `ToolStripDropDownButton`, `ToolStripProgressBar`, and `ToolStripSplitButton` — were presented earlier. That leaves just one control that is specific to the `StatusStrip`: the `StatusStripStatusLabel`, which is also the default item you get.

StatusStripStatusLabel Properties

The `StatusStripStatusLabel` is used to present the user with information about the current state of the application, with text and images. Because the label is actually a pretty simple control, not a lot of properties are covered here. The following two are not specific to the label, but nevertheless can and should be used with some effect:

Property	Value
`AutoSize`	`AutoSize` is on by default, which isn't really very intuitive because you don't want the labels in the status bar to jump back and forth just because you changed the text in one of them. Unless the information in the label is static, always change this property to `false`.
`DoubleClickEnable`	Specifies whether the `DoubleClick` event will fire, which means your users get a second place to change something in your application. An example of this is allowing users to double-click on a panel containing the word Bold to enable or disable bolding in the text.

In the following Try It Out, you create a simple status bar for the example you've been working on. The status bar has four panels, three of which display an image and text; the last panel displays only text.

Try It Out   StatusStrip

Follow these steps to extend the small text editor you've been working on:

1. Double-click the `StatusStrip` in the `ToolBox` to add it to the dialog. You may need to resize the `RichTextBox` on the form.

2. In the Properties panel, click the ellipses (...) in the `Items` property of the `StatusStrip`. This brings up the Items Collection Editor.

3. Click the Add button four times to add four panels to the StaturStrip. Set the following properties on the panels:

Panel	Property	Value
1	Name	toolStripStatusLabelText
	Text	Clear this property
	AutoSize	False
	DisplayStyle	Text
	Font	Arial; 8,25pt; style=Bold
	Size	259,17
	TextAlign	Middle Left
2	Name	toolStripStatusLabelBold
	Text	Bold
	DisplayStyle	ImageAndText
	Enabled	False
	Font	Arial; 8.25pt; style=Bold
	Size	47, 17
	Image	BLD
	ImageAlign	Middle-Center
3	Name	toolStripStatusLabelItalic
	Text	Italic
	DisplayStyle	ImageAndText
	Enabled	False
	Font	Arial; 8.25pt; style=Bold
	Size	48, 17
	Image	ITL
	ImageAlign	Middle-Center

Panel	Property	Value
4	Name	toolStripStatusLabelUnderline
	Text	Underline
	DisplayStyle	ImageAndText
	Enabled	False
	Font	Arial; 8.25pt; style=Bold
	Size	76, 17
	Image	UNDRLN
	ImageAlign	Middle-Center

4. Add this line of code to the event handler at the end of the `ToolStripButtonBold_CheckedChanged` method:

```
toolStripStatusLabelBold.Enabled = checkState;
```

5. Add this line of code to the event handler at the end of the `ToolStripButtonItalic_CheckedChanged` method:

```
toolStripStatusLabelItalic.Enabled = checkState;
```

6. Add this line of code to the event handler at the end of the `ToolStripButtonUnderline_CheckedChanged` method:

```
toolStripStatusLabelUnderline.Enabled = checkState;
```

7. Select the `RichTextBox` and add the `TextChanged` event to the code. Enter the following code:

```
private void richTextBoxText_TextChanged(object sender, EventArgs e)
{
    toolStripStatusLabelText.Text = "Number of characters: " +
richTextBoxText.Text.Length;
}
```

When you run the application you should have a dialog that looks like the one shown in Figure 16-8.

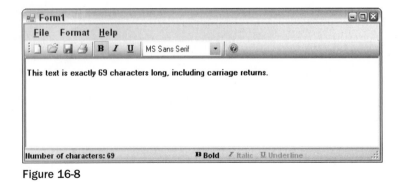

Figure 16-8

SDI and MDI Applications

Traditionally, three kinds of applications can be programmed for Windows:

❑ **Dialog-based applications**: These present themselves to the user as a single dialog from which all functionality can be reached.

❑ **Single-document interfaces (SDI)**: These present themselves to the user with a menu, one or more toolbars, and one window in which the user can perform some task.

❑ **Multiple-document interfaces (MDI)**: These present themselves to the user in the same manner as an SDI, but are capable of holding multiple open windows at one time.

Dialog-based applications are usually small, single-purpose applications aimed at a specific task that needs a minimum of data to be entered by the user or that target a very specific type of data. An example of such an application is shown in Figure 16-9 — the Windows Calculator.

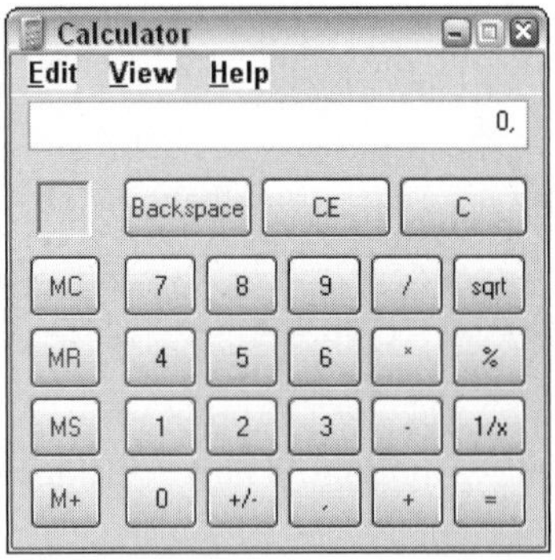

Figure 16-9

Single-document interfaces are each usually aimed at solving one specific task because they enable users to load a single document into the application to be worked on. This task, however, usually involves a lot of user interaction, and users often want the capability to save or load the result of their work. Good examples of SDI applications are WordPad (shown in Figure 16-10) and Paint, both of which come with Windows.

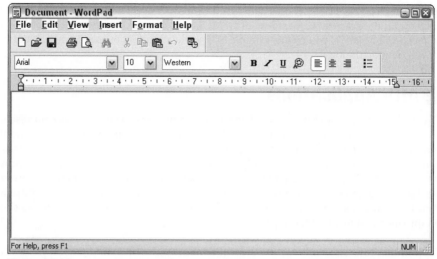

Figure 16-10

However, only one document can be open at any one time, so if a user wants to open a second document, then a fresh instance of the SDI application must be opened, and it will have no reference to the first instance. Any configuration you do to one instance is not carried over into the other. For example, in one instance of Paint you might set the drawing color to red, and when you open a second instance of Paint, the drawing color is the default, which is black.

Multiple-document interfaces are much the same as SDI applications, except that they are able to hold more than one document open in different windows at any given time. A telltale sign of an MDI application is the inclusion of the Window menu just before the Help menu on the menu bar. An example of an MDI application is Adobe Reader, shown in Figure 16-11.

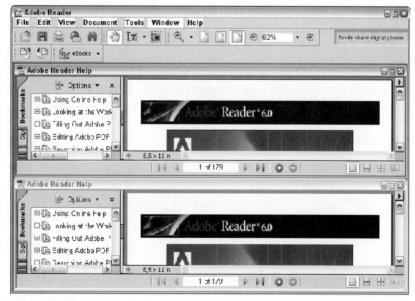

Figure 16-11

This chapter focuses on the tasks necessary for creating an MDI application. The reasoning behind this is that any SDI application is basically a subset of an MDI, so if you can create an MDI you can also create an SDI. In fact, in Chapter 17, you create a simple SDI application that is used to demonstrate how to use the Windows common dialogs.

Building MDI Applications

What is involved in creating an MDI? First, the task you want users to be able to accomplish should be one for which they would want to have multiple documents open at one time. A good example of this is a text editor or a text viewer. Second, you provide toolbars for the most commonly used tasks in the application, such as setting the font style, and loading and saving documents. Third, you provide a menu that includes a Window menu item that enables users to reposition the open windows relative to each other (tile and cascade) and that presents a list of all open windows. Another feature of MDI applications is that when a window is open and that window contains a menu, that menu should be integrated into the main menu of the application.

An MDI application consists of at least two distinct windows. The first window you create is called an *MDI container*. A window that can be displayed within that container is called an *MDI child*. This chapter refers to the MDI container as the MDI container or main window interchangeably, and to the MDI child as the MDI child or child window.

The following Try It Out is a small example that takes you through these steps. Then you move on to more complicated tasks.

Try It Out   Creating an MDI Application

To create an MDI application, begin as you do for any other application — by creating a Windows Forms application in Visual Studio.

1. Create a new Windows application called MDIBasic in the directory C:\BegVCSharp\Chapter16.

2. To change the main window of the application from a form to an MDI container, simply set the IsMdiContainer property of the form to true. The background of the form changes color to indicate that it is now merely a background that you should not place visible controls on (although it is possible to do so and might even be reasonable under certain circumstances).

    Select the form and set the following properties:

Property	Value
Name	frmContainer
IsMdiContainer	True
Text	MDI Basic
WindowState	Maximized

3. To create a child window, add a new form to the project by choosing a Windows Form from the dialog that appears by selecting Project ⇨ Add New Item. Name the form `frmChild`.

4. The new form becomes a child window when you set the `MdiParent` property of the child window to a reference to the main window. You cannot set this property through the Properties panel; you have to do this using code. Change the constructor of the new form like this:

```
public frmChild(MdiBasic.frmContainer parent)
{
    InitializeComponent();

    // Set the parent of the form to the container.
    this.MdiParent = parent;
}
```

5. Two things remain before the MDI application can display itself in its most basic mode. You must tell the MDI container which windows to display, and then you must display them. Simply create a new instance of the form you want to display, and then call `Show()` on it. The constructor of the form to display as a child should hook itself up with the parent container. You can arrange this by setting its `MdiParent` property to the instance of the MDI container. Change the constructor of the MDI parent form like this:

```
public frmContainer()
{
    InitializeComponent();

    // Create a new instance of the child form.
    MdiBasic.frmChild child = new MdiBasic.frmChild(this);

    // Show the form.
    child.Show();
}
```

How It Works

All the code that you need to display a child form is found in the constructors of the form. First, look at the constructor for the child window:

```
public frmChild(MdiBasic.frmContainer parent)
{
    InitializeComponent();

    // Set the parent of the form to the container.
    this.MdiParent = parent;
}
```

To bind a child form to the MDI container, the child must register itself with the container. This is done by setting the form's `MdiParent` property as shown in the preceding code. Notice that the constructor you are using includes the parameter `parent`.

Because C# does not provide default constructors for a class that defines its own constructor, the preceding code prevents you from creating an instance of the form that is not bound to the MDI container.

Finally, you want to display the form. You do so in the constructor of the MDI container:

```
public frmContainer()
{
    InitializeComponent();

    // Create a new instance of the child form.
    MdiBasic.frmChild child = new MdiBasic.frmChild(this);

    // Show the form.
    child.Show();
}
```

You create a new instance of the child class and pass this to the constructor, where this represents the current instance of the MDI container class. Then you call Show() on the new instance of the child form. That's it! If you want to show more than one child window, simply repeat the two highlighted lines in the preceding code for each window.

Run the code now. You should see something like what is shown in Figure 16-12 (although the MDI Basic form will initially be maximized, it's resized here to fit on the page).

Figure 16-12

It's not the most stunning user interface ever designed, but it is clearly a solid start. In the next Try It Out you produce a simple text editor based on what you have already achieved in this chapter using menus, toolbars, and status bars.

Try It Out   **Creating an MDI Text Editor**

Let's create the basic project first and then discuss what is happening:

1. Return to the earlier status bar example. Rename the form `frmEditor` and change its `Text` property to `Editor`.

2. Add a new form with the name `frmContainer.cs` to the project and set the following properties on it:

Property	Value
Name	frmContainer
IsMdiContainer	True
Text	Simple Text Editor
WindowState	Maximized

3. Open the `Program.cs` file and change the line containing the `Run` statement in the `Main` method as follows:

```
Application.Run(new frmContainer());
```

4. Change the constructor of the `frmEditor` form to this:

```
public frmEditor(frmContainer parent)
{
    InitializeComponent();

    this.ToolStripComboBoxFonts.SelectedIndex = 0;
    // Bind to the parent.
    this.MdiParent = parent;
}
```

5. Change the `MergeAction` property of the menu item with the text `&File` to `Replace` and the same property of the item with the text `&Format` to `MatchOnly`.

Change the `AllowMerge` property of the toolbar to `False`.

6. Add a `MenuStrip` to the `frmContainer` form. Add a single item to the `MenuStrip` with the text `&File`.

7. Change the constructor of the `frmContainer` form as follows:

```
public frmContainer()
{
    InitializeComponent();

    frmEditor newForm = new frmEditor(this);
    newForm.Show();
}
```

Run the application to see something like what is shown in Figure 16-13.

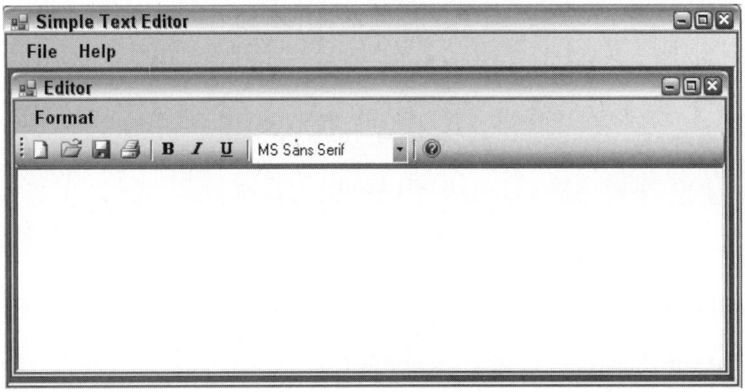

Figure 16-13

How It Works

Notice that a bit of magic has happened. The File menu and Help menu appear to have been removed from the `frmEditor`. Select the File menu in the container window and you will see that the menu items from the `frmEditor` dialog can now be found there.

The menus that should be contained on child windows are those that are specific to that window. The File menu should be general for all windows and shouldn't be contained in the child windows as the only place it is found. The reason for this becomes apparent if you close the Editor window — the File menu now contains no items! You want to be able to insert the items in the File menu that are specific to the child window when the child is in focus, and leave the rest of the items to the main window to display.

The following properties control the behavior of menu items:

Property	Description
MergeAction	Specifies how an item should behave when it is to be merged into another menu. The possible values are as follows: Append — Causes the item to be placed last in the menu. Insert — Inserts the item immediately before the item that matches the criterion for where this is inserted. This criterion is either the text in the item or an index. MatchOnly — A match is required, but the item will not be inserted. Remove — Removes the item that matches the criterion for inserting the item. Replace — The matched item is replaced and the drop-down items are appended to the incoming item.
MergeIndex	Represents the position of a menu item in regard to other menu items that are being merged. Set this to a value greater than or equal to 0 if you want to control the order of the items that are being merged; otherwise, set it to -1. When merges are being performed, this value is checked and if it is not -1, this is used to match items, rather than the text.
AllowMerge	Setting AllowMerge to false means the menus will not be merged.

In the following Try It Out, you continue with your text editor by changing how the menus are merged to reflect which menus belong where.

Try It Out   Merging Menus

Follow these steps to change the text editor to use menus in both the container and child windows:

1. Add the following four menu items to the File menu on the frmContainer form. Notice the jump in MergeIndex values.

Item	Property	Value
&New	Name	ToolStripMenuItemNew
	MergeAction	MatchOnly
	MergeIndex	0
	ShortcutKeys	Ctrl + N

Item	Property	Value
&Open	Name	ToolStripMenuItemOpen
	MergeAction	MatchOnly
	MergeIndex	1
	ShortcutKeys	Ctrl + O
–	MergeAction	MatchOnly
	MergeIndex	10
E&xit	Name	ToolStripMenuItemNewExit
	MergeAction	MatchOnly
	MergeIndex	11

2. You need a way to add new windows, so double-click the menu item New and add the following code. It is the same code you entered into the constructor for the first dialog to be displayed.

```
private void ToolStripMenuItemNew_Click(object sender, EventArgs e)
{
    frmEditor newForm = new frmEditor(this);
    newForm.Show();
}
```

3. In the frmEditor form, delete the Open menu item from the File menu. Change the other menu item properties as follows:

Item	Property	Value
&File	MergeAction	MatchOnly
	MergeIndex	-1
&New	MergeAction	MatchOnly
	MergeIndex	-1
–	MergeAction	Insert
	MergeIndex	2
&Save	MergeAction	Insert
	MergeIndex	3

Item	Property	Value
Save &As	MergeAction	Insert
	MergeIndex	4
-	MergeAction	Insert
	MergeIndex	5
&Print	MergeAction	Insert
	MergeIndex	6
Print Preview	MergeAction	Insert
	MergeIndex	7
-	MergeAction	Insert
	MergeIndex	8
E&xit	Name	ToolStripMenuItemClose
	Text	&Close
	MergeAction	Insert
	MergeIndex	9

4. Run the application. The two File menus have been merged, but there's still a File menu on the child dialog that contains one item: New.

How It Works

The items that are set to MatchOnly are not moved between the menus, but in the case of the &File menu item, the fact that the text of the two items matches means that their menu items are merged.

The items in the File menus are merged based on the MergedIndex properties for the items that you are interested in. The ones that should remain in place have their MergeAction properties set to MatchOnly; the rest are set to Insert.

What is now very interesting is what happens when you click the menu items New and Save on the two different menus. Remember that the New menu on the child dialog just clears the text box, whereas the other should create a new dialog. Not surprisingly, because the two menus should belong to different windows, both work as expected. But what about the Save item? That has been moved off of the dialog and into its parent.

Open a few dialogs, enter some text into them, and then click Save. Open a new dialog and click Open (remember that Save always saves to the same file). Select one of the other windows, click Save, return to the new dialog, and click Open again. What you are seeing is that the Save menu items always follow the dialog that is in focus. Every time a dialog is selected, the menus are merged again.

You just added a bit of code to the New menu item of the File menu in the frmContainer dialog, and you saw that the dialogs were created. One menu that is present in most if not all MDI applications is the Window menu. It enables you to arrange the dialogs and often lists them in some way. In the following Try It Out, you add this menu to your text editor.

Try It Out   Tracking Windows

Follow these steps to extend the application to include the capability to display all open dialogs and arrange them:

1. Add a new top-level menu item to the frmContainer menu called &Window. Name it ToolStripMenuItemWindow.

2. Add the following three items to the new menu:

Name	Text
ToolStripMenuItemTile	&Tile
ToolStripMenuItemCascade	&Cascade
-	-

3. Select the MenuStrip itself, not any of the items that are displayed in it, and change the MDIWindowListItem property to ToolStripMenuItemWindow.

4. Double-click first the tile item and then the cascade item to add the event handlers and enter the following code:

```
private void ToolStripMenuItemTile_Click(object sender, EventArgs e)
{
    LayoutMdi(MdiLayout.TileHorizontal);
}

private void ToolStripMenuItemCascasde_Click(object sender, EventArgs e)
{
    LayoutMdi(MdiLayout.Cascade);
}
```

5. Change the constructor of the `frmEditor` dialog as follows:

```
public frmEditor(frmContainer parent, int counter)
{
  InitializeComponent();

  this.ToolStripComboBoxFonts.SelectedIndex = 0;

  // Bind to the parent.
  this.MdiParent = parent;
  this.Text = "Editor " + counter.ToString();
}
```

6. Add a private member variable to the top of the code for `frmContainer` and change the constructor and the event handler for the menu item New to the following:

```
public partial class frmContainer : Form
{
  private int mCounter;

  public frmContainer()
  {
    InitializeComponent();

    mCounter = 1;
    frmEditor newForm = new frmEditor(this, mCounter);
    newForm.Show();
  }

  private void ToolStripMenuItemNew_Click(object sender, EventArgs e)
  {
    frmEditor newForm = new frmEditor(this, ++mCounter);
    newForm.Show();
  }
```

How It Works

The most interesting part of this example concerns the Window menu. To have a menu display a list of all the dialogs that are opened in a MDI application, you only have to create a menu at the top level for it and set the `MdiWindowListItem` property to point to that menu.

The framework will then append a menu item to the menu for each of the dialogs currently displayed. The item that represents the current dialog will have a check mark next to it, and you can select another dialog by clicking it in the list.

The other two menu items — Tile and Cascade — demonstrate a method of the form: `MdiLayout`. This method enables you to arrange the dialogs in a standard manner.

The changes to the constructors and New item simply ensure that the dialogs are numbered. Run the application now and you should see something like what is shown in Figure 16-14.

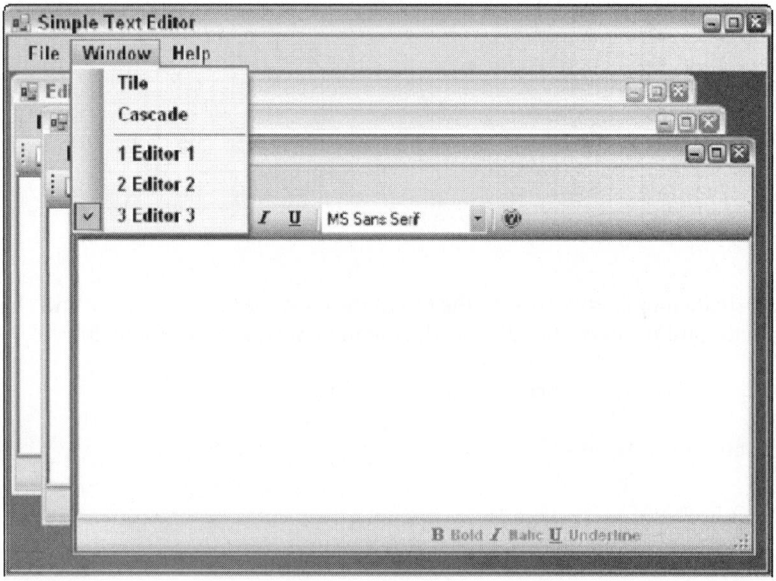

Figure 16-14

Creating Controls

Sometimes the controls that ship with Visual Studio just won't meet your needs. The reasons for this can be many — they don't draw themselves in the way you want them to, they are restrictive in some way, or the control you need simply doesn't exist. Recognizing this, Microsoft has provided the means to create controls that do meet your needs. Visual Studio provides a project type named Windows Control Library, which you use when you want to create a control yourself.

Two distinct kinds of homemade controls can be developed:

❑ **User or composite controls**: These build on the functionality of existing controls to create a new control. Such controls are generally made to encapsulate functionality with the user interface of the control, or to enhance the interface of a control by combining several controls into one unit.

❑ **Custom controls**: You can create these controls when no existing control fits your needs — that is, you start from scratch. A custom control draws its entire user interface itself and no existing controls are used in its creation. You normally need to create a control like this when the user interface control you want to create is unlike that of any available control.

This chapter focuses on user controls, because designing and drawing a custom control from scratch is beyond the scope of this book. Chapter 33, on GDI+, gives you the means to draw items by yourself, and from there you should then be able to move on to custom controls easily.

ActiveX controls as used in Visual Studio 6 existed in a special kind of file with the extension .ocx. These files were essentially COM DLLs. In .NET, a control exists in exactly the same way as any other assembly, so the .ocx extension has disappeared, and controls exist in DLLs.

User controls inherit from the System.Windows.Forms.UserControl class. This base class provides the control you are creating with all the basic features a control in .NET should include, leaving you only the task of creating the control. Virtually anything can be created as a control, from a label with a nifty design to full-blown grid controls. In Figure 16-15, the box at the bottom, UserControl1, represents a new control.

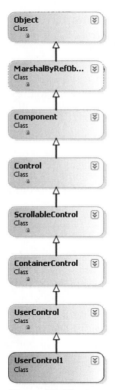

Figure 16-15

User controls inherit from the System.Windows.Forms.UserControl class, but custom controls derive from the System.Windows.Forms.Control class.

A couple of things are assumed when working with controls. If your control doesn't fulfill the following expectations, the chances are good that people will be discouraged from using it:

❑ The behavior of the design-time control should be very similar to its behavior at runtime. This means that if the control consists of a `Label` and a `TextBox` that have been combined to create a `LabelTextbox`, the `Label` and `TextBox` should both be displayed at design time and the text entered for the `Label` should also be shown at design time. While this is fairly easy to achieve in this example, it can present problems in more complex cases, where you'll need to find an appropriate compromise.

❑ Access to the properties of the control should be possible from the Forms Designer in a logical manner. A good example of this is the `ImageList` control, which presents a dialog from which users can browse to the images they want to include, and once the images are imported, they are shown in a list in the dialog.

The next few pages introduce you to the creation of controls by means of an example. The example creates the `LabelTextbox`, and it demonstrates the basics of creating a user control project, creating properties and events, and debugging controls.

As the name of the control in the following section implies, this control combines two existing controls to create a single one that performs, in one go, a task extremely common in Windows programming: adding a label to a form, and then adding a text box to the same form and positioning the text box in relation to the label. Here's what a user of this control will expect from it:

❑ The user will want to be able to position the text box either to the right of the label or below it. If the text box is positioned to the right of the label, then it should be possible to specify a fixed distance from the left edge of the control to the text box to align text boxes below each other.

❑ Availability of the usual properties and events of the text box and label.

A LabelTextbox Control

Now that you know your mission, start Visual Studio and create a new project.

1. Create a new Windows Forms Control Library project called "LabelTextbox" and save it in C:\BegVCSharp\Chapter16.

If you are using the Express edition of Visual Studio, then you might not see this option. In that case, create a new Class Library instead and add a user control to the project manually from the Project menu.

As shown in Figure 16-16, the Forms Designer presents you with a design surface that looks somewhat different from what you're used to. First, the surface is much smaller. Second, it doesn't look like a dialog at all. Don't let this new look discourage you in any way — things still work as usual. The main difference is that up until now you have been placing controls on a form, but now you are creating a control to be placed on a form.

Figure 16-16

2. Click the design surface and bring up the properties for the control. Change the name property of the control to `ctlLabelTextbox`.

3. Double-click a `Label` in the Toolbox to add it to the control, placing it in the top left corner of the surface. Change its `Name` property to `lblTextBox`. Set the `Text` property to `Label`.

4. Double-click a `TextBox` in the Toolbox to add it to the control. Change its `Name` property to `txtLabelText`.

At design time, you don't know how the user will want to position these controls, so you are going to write code that will position the `Label` and `TextBox`. That same code will determine the position of the controls when a `LabelTextbox` control is placed on a form.

Figure 16-17 shows that the design of the control looks anything but encouraging — not only is the `TextBox` obscuring part of the label, but the surface is too large. However, this is of no consequence, because, unlike what you've been used to until now, what you see is *not* what you get! The code you are about to add to the control will change the appearance of the control, but only when the control is added to a form.

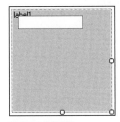

Figure 16-17

First, position the controls relative to each other. The user should be able to decide how the controls are positioned, and for that you add not one but two properties to the control. The `Position` property enables the user to choose between two options: `Right` and `Below`. If the user chooses `Right`, then the other property comes into play. This property is called `TextboxMargin` and is an `int` that represents the number of pixels from the left edge of the control to where the `TextBox` should be placed. If the user specifies `0`, then the `TextBox` is placed with its right edge aligned with the right edge of the control.

Adding Properties

To give the user a choice between `Right` and `Below`, start by defining an enumeration with these two values. Return to the control project, go to the code editor, and add this code:

```
public partial class ctlLabelTextbox : UserControl
{
    // Enumeration of the two possible positions
    public enum PositionEnum
    {
        Right,
        Below
    }
```

This is just a normal enumeration, as shown in Chapter 5. Now for the magic: You want the position to be a property the user can set through code and the designer. You do this by adding a property to the `ctlLabelTextbox` class. First, however, you create two member fields that will hold the values the user selects:

```
// Member field that will hold the choices the user makes
private PositionEnum mPosition = PositionEnum.Right;
private int mTextboxMargin = 0;

public ctlLabelTextbox()
{
    ...
```

Then add the `Position` property as follows:

```
public PositionEnum Position
{
    get
    {
        return mPosition;
    }
    set
    {
        mPosition = value;
        MoveControls();
    }
}
```

The property is added to the class like any other property. If you are asked to return the property, you return the `mPosition` member field; and if you are asked to change the `Position`, you assign the value to `mPosition` and call the method `MoveControls()`. You'll return to `MoveControls()` in a bit — for now it is enough to know that this method positions the two controls by examining the values of `mPosition` and `mTextboxMargin`.

The `TextboxMargin` property is the same, except it works with an integer:

```
public int TextboxMargin
{
    get
    {
        return mTextboxMargin;
    }
    set
    {
        mTextboxMargin = value;
        MoveControls();
    }
}
```

Adding the Event Handlers

Before you move on to test the two properties, you add two event handlers as well. When the control is placed on the form, the `Load` event is called. You should use this event to initialize the control and any resources the control may use. You handle this event in order to move the control and to size the control to fit neatly around the two controls it contains. The other event you add is the `SizeChanged` event. This event is called whenever the control is resized, and you should handle the event to enable the control to draw itself correctly. Select the control and add the two events: `SizeChanged` and `Load`.

Then add the event handlers:

```
private void ctlLabelTextbox_Load(object sender, EventArgs e)
{
    lblTextBox.Text = this.Name; // Add a text to the label
    // Set the height of the control.
    this.Height = txtLabelText.Height > lblTextBox.Height ? txtLabelText .Height ↵
: lblTextBox.Height;
    MoveControls(); // Move the controls.
}


private void ctlLabelTextbox_SizeChanged(object sender, System.EventArgs e)
{
    MoveControls();
}
```

Again, you call `MoveControls()` to take care of positioning the controls. It is time to see this method, before you test the control again:

```
private void MoveControls()
{
    switch (mPosition)
    {
    case PositionEnum.Below:
        // Place the top of the Textbox just below the label.
        this.txtLabelText.Top = this.lblTextBox.Bottom;
```

```
        this.txtLabelText.Left = this.lblTextBox.Left;

        // Change the width of the Textbox to equal the width of the control.
        this.txtLabelText.Width = this.Width;

        this.Height = txtLabelText.Height + lblTextBox.Height;
        break;
    case PositionEnum.Right:
        // Set the top of the textbox to equal that of the label.
        txtLabelText.Top = lblTextBox.Top;

        // If the margin is zero, we'll place the text box next to the label.
        if (mTextboxMargin == 0)
        {
            int width = this.Width-lblTextBox.Width-3;
            txtLabelText.Left = lblTextBox.Right + 3;
            txtLabelText.Width = width;
        }
        else
        {
            // If the margin isn't zero, we place the text box where the user
            // has specified.
            txtLabelText.Left = mTextboxMargin;
            txtLabelText.Width = this.Right-mTextboxMargin;
        }
        this.Height = txtLabelText.Height > lblTextBox.Height ?
                            txtLabelText.Height : lblTextBox.Height;
        break;
    }
}
```

The value in `mPosition` is tested in a `switch` statement to determine whether you should place the text box below or to the right of the label. If the user chooses `Below`, you move the top of the text box to the position that is at the bottom of the label. You then move the left edge of the text box to the left edge of the control and set its width to the width of the control.

If the user chooses `Right`, then there are two possibilities. If the `TextboxMargin` is zero, start by determining the width that is left in the control for the text box. Then set the left edge of the text box to just a nudge right of the text and set the width to fill the remaining space. If the user specifies a margin, place the left edge of the text box at that position and set the width again.

You are now ready to test the control. Before moving on, build the project.

Debugging User Controls

Debugging a user control is quite different from debugging a Windows application. Normally, you would just add a breakpoint somewhere, press F5, and see what happens. If you are still unfamiliar with debugging, then refer to Chapter 7 for a detailed explanation.

A control needs a container in which to display itself, and you have to supply it with one. You do that in the following Try It Out by creating a Windows application project.

Try It Out	Debugging User Controls

1. From the File menu choose Add ⇨ New Project. In the Add New Project dialog, create a new Windows application called "LabelTextboxTest." Because this application is only to be used to test the user control, it's a good idea to create the project inside the LabelTextBox project.

   In the Solution Explorer, you should now see two projects open. The first project you created, `LabelTextbox`, is written in boldface. That means if you try to run the solution, the debugger will attempt to use the control project as the start-up project. This will fail because the control isn't a standalone type of project. To fix this, right-click the name of the new project — `LabelTextboxTest` — and select Set as StartUp Project. If you run the solution now, the Windows application project will be run and no errors will occur.

2. At the top of the Toolbox you should now see a tab named LabelTextBox Components. Visual Studio recognizes that there is a Windows Control Library in the solution and that it is likely that you want to use the controls provided by this library in other projects. Double-click on `ctlLabelTextbox` to add it to the form. Note that the References node in the Solution Explorer is expanded. That happens because Visual Studio just added a reference to the LabelTextBox project for you.

3. While in the code, search for the new `ctlLabel`. Search in the entire project. You will get a hit in the "behind the scenes" file `Form.Designer.cs` where Visual Studio hides most of the code it generates for you. Note that you should never edit this file directly.

4. Place a breakpoint on the following line:

```
this.ctlLabelTextbox1 = new LabelTextbox.ctlLabelTextbox();
```

5. Run the code. As expected, the code stops at the breakpoint you placed. Now step into the code (if you are using the default keyboard maps, press F11 to do so). When you step into the code you are transferred to the constructor of your new control, which is exactly what you want in order to debug the component. You can also place breakpoints. Press F5 to run the application.

Extending the LabelTextbox Control

Finally, you are ready to test the properties of the control. Figure 16-18 shows the label displaying the name of the control and the text box occupying the remaining area of the control. Notice that the controls within the `LabelTextbox` control move to the correct positions when the control is added to the form.

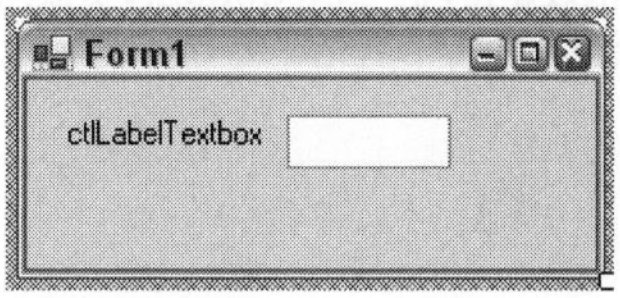

Figure 16-18

Adding More Properties

You can't do much with the control at the moment because, sadly, it is missing the capability to change the text in the label and text box. You add two properties to handle this: `LabelText` and `TextboxText`. The properties are added just as you added the two previous properties — open the project and add the following:

```
{
    get
    {
        return mLabelText;
    }
    set
    {
        mLabelText = value;
        lblTextBox.Text = mLabelText;          MoveControls();
    }
}

public string TextboxText
{
    get
    {
        return txtLabelText.Text;
    }
    set
    {
        txtLabelText.Text = value;
    }
}
```

You also need to declare the member variable `mLabelText` to hold the text:

```
    private string mLabelText = "";

    public ctlLabelTextbox()
    {
```

You simply assign the text to the `Text` property of the `Label` and `TextBox` controls if you want to insert the text, and return the value of the `Text` properties. If the label text is changed, then you need to call `MoveControls()` because the label text may influence where the text box is positioned. Text inserted into the text box, conversely, does not move the controls; and if the text is longer than the text box, it disappears.

Adding More Event Handlers

Now it is time to consider which events the control should provide. Because the control is derived from the `UserControl` class, it has inherited a lot of functionality that you don't need to handle. However, there are several events that you don't want to hand to the user in the standard way. Examples of this include the `KeyDown`, `KeyPress`, and `KeyUp` events. You need to change these events because users will expect them to be sent when they press a key in the text box. As they are now, the events are sent only when the control itself has focus and the user presses a key.

To change this behavior, you must handle the events sent by the text box and pass them on to the user. Add the `KeyDown`, `KeyUp`, and `KeyPress` events for the text box and enter the following code:

```csharp
private void txtLabelText_KeyDown(object sender, KeyEventArgs e)
{
    OnKeyDown(e);
}

private void txtLabelText_KeyUp(object sender, KeyEventArgs e)
{
    OnKeyUp(e);
}

private void txtLabelText_KeyPress(object sender, KeyPressEventArgs e)
{
    OnKeyPress(e);
}
```

Calling the `OnKeyXXX` method invokes a call to any methods subscribed to the event.

Adding a Custom Event Handler

When you want to create an event that doesn't exist in one of the base classes, you must do a bit more work. Create an event called `PositionChanged` that will occur when the `Position` property changes. To create this event, you need three things:

❑   An appropriate delegate that can be used to invoke the methods the user assigns to the event.

❑   The user must be able to subscribe to the event by assigning a method to it.

❑   You must invoke the method the user has assigned to the event.

The delegate you use is the `EventHandler` delegate provided by the .NET Framework. As you learned in Chapter 12, this is a special kind of delegate that is declared by its very own keyword, `event`. The following line declares the event and enables the user to subscribe to it:

```csharp
public event System.EventHandler PositionChanged;

// Constructor
public ctlLabelTextbox()
{
```

All that remains to do is raise the event. Because it should occur when the `Position` property changes, you raise the event in the `set` accessor of the `Position` property:

```
public PositionEnum Position
{
    get
    {
        return mPosition;
    }
    set
    {
        mPosition = value;
        MoveControls();
        if (PositionChanged != null) // Make sure there are subscribers
        {
            PositionChanged(this, new EventArgs());
        }
    }
}
```

First, make sure that there are some subscribers by checking whether `PositionChanged` is `null`. If it isn't, then you invoke the methods.

You subscribe to the new custom event as you would any other, but there is a small catch: Before the event is displayed in the events windows, you must build the control. After the control is built, select the control on the form in the LabelTextboxTest project and double-click the `PositionChanged` event in the Events part of the Properties panel. Then, add the following code to the event handler:

```
private void ctlLabelTextbox1_PositionChanged(object sender, EventArgs e)
{
    MessageBox.Show("Changed");
}
```

Your custom event handler doesn't really do anything sparkling — it simply points out that the position has changed.

Finally, add a button to the form, double-click it to add its `Click` event handler to the project, and add this code:

```
private void buttonToggle_Click(object sender, EventArgs e)
{
    ctlLabelTextbox1.Position = ctlLabelTextbox1.Position ==
LabelTextbox.ctlLabelTextbox.PositionEnum.Right ?
LabelTextbox.ctlLabelTextbox.PositionEnum.Below :
LabelTextbox.ctlLabelTextbox.PositionEnum.Right;
}
```

When you run the application you can change the position of the text box at runtime. Every time the text box moves, the `PositionChanged` event is called and a `messagebox` is displayed.

That completes the example. It could be refined a bit, but that's left as an exercise for you.

Summary

In this chapter, you started where you left off in the previous chapter, by examining the `MainMenu` and `ToolBar` controls. You learned how to create MDI and SDI applications and how menus and toolbars are used in those applications. You then moved on to create a control of your own: designing properties, a user interface, and events for the control. The next chapter completes the discussion of Windows Forms by looking at the one special type of form only glossed over so far: Windows common dialogs.

In this chapter, you learned to do the following:

❑   Use the three strip controls that enable you to work with menus, toolbars, and status bars in Windows Forms.

❑   Create MDI applications, which are used to extend the text editor even further.

❑   Create controls of your own by building on existing controls.

Exercises

1.   Using the `LabelTextbox` example as the base, create a new property called `MaxLength` that stores the maximum number of characters that can be entered into the text box. Then create two new events called `MaxLengthChanged` and `MaxLengthReached`. The `MaxLengthChanged` event should be raised when the `MaxLength` property is changed, and `MaxLengthReached` should be raised when the user enters a character making the length of the text in the text box equal to the value of `MaxLength`.

2.   The `StatusBar` includes a property that enables users to double-click on a field on the bar and trigger an event. Change the `StatusBar` example in such a way that users can set bold, italic, and underline for the text by double-clicking on the status bar. Ensure that the display on the toolbar, menu, and status bar is always in sync by changing the text "Bold" to be bold when it is enabled and otherwise not. Do the same with Italic and Underlined.

17

Using Common Dialogs

The last three chapters looked at various aspects of programming Windows Forms applications, and how to implement such things as menus, toolbars, and SDI and MDI forms. Now you know how to display simple message boxes to get information from the user and how to create more sophisticated custom dialogs to ask the user for specific information. However, for common tasks such as opening and saving files, you can use prewritten dialog classes instead of having to create your own custom dialog.

This not only has the advantage of requiring less code, but also it uses the familiar Windows dialogs, giving your application a standard look and feel. The .NET Framework has classes that hook up to the Windows dialogs to open and create directories, to open and save files, to access printers, and to select colors and fonts.

In this chapter, you learn how to use these standard dialog classes. In particular, you will learn how to do the following:

❑ Use the `OpenFileDialog` and `SaveFileDialog` classes

❑ Learn about the .NET printing class hierarchy and use the `PrintDialog`, `PageSetupDialog`, and `PrintPreviewDialog` classes to implement printing and print preview

❑ Change fonts and colors with the `FontDialog` and `ColorDialog` classes

❑ Use the `FolderBrowserDialog` class

Common Dialogs

A dialog is a window that is displayed within the context of another window. With a dialog, you can ask the user to enter some data before the flow of the program continues. A common dialog is one that is used to get information from the user that most applications typically require, such as the name of a file, and is a part of the Windows operating system.

The classes included with the Microsoft .NET Framework are shown in Figure 17-1.

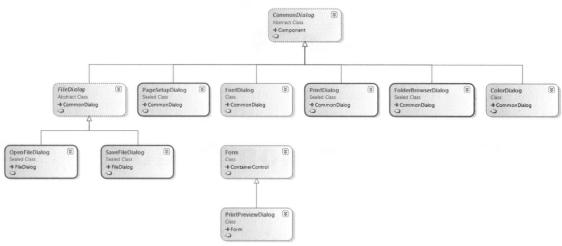

Figure 17-1

All of these dialog classes except the `PrintPreviewDialog` derive from the abstract `CommonDialog` base class, which has methods to manage a Windows common dialog. The `CommonDialog` class defines the following methods and events common to all common dialog classes:

Public Instance Methods and Events	Description
`ShowDialog()`	This method is implemented from the derived class to display a common dialog.
`Reset()`	Every derived dialog class implements the `Reset()` method to set all properties of the dialog class to their default values.
`HelpRequest`	This event is thrown when the user clicks the Help button on a common dialog.

All these dialog classes wrap up a Windows common dialog to make the dialog available for .NET applications. `PrintPreviewDialog` is an exception because it adds its own elements to a Windows Form to control the preview of a print, and hence is not really a dialog at all. The `OpenFileDialog` and `SaveFileDialog` classes derive from the abstract base class `FileDialog`, which adds file features that are common to both the opening and closing file dialogs.

The following list provides an overview of how the different dialogs can be used:

❑ To enable users to select and browse files to open, use the `OpenFileDialog`. This dialog can be configured to allow the selection of a single file or multiple files.

❑ With the `SaveFileDialog`, users can specify a filename and browse for a directory in which to save files.

- ❑ The `PrintDialog` is used to select a printer and set the printing options.

- ❑ To configure the margins of a page, the `PageSetupDialog` is usually used.

- ❑ The `PrintPreviewDialog` provides an onscreen preview of what is to be printed on paper, with options such as zoom.

- ❑ The `FontDialog` lists all installed Windows fonts, with styles and sizes, and provides a preview to select the font of choice.

- ❑ The `ColorDialog` class makes it easy to select a color.

- ❑ For selecting and creating directories, the dialog `FolderBrowserDialog` can be used.

Some applications (developed by the same company) not only do not reuse common dialogs, but also do not use a style guide for building custom dialogs. The functionality of these dialogs is inconsistent, with some buttons and other controls found in different locations, such as the OK and Cancel buttons reversed between dialogs. Sometimes this inconsistency can be found within one application. Not only is it frustrating for the user, it increases the time required to complete a task.

> **Be consistent in the dialogs you build and use! Consistency can be easily attained by using the common dialogs.**

How to Use Dialogs

Because `CommonDialog` is the base class for the dialog classes, all the dialog classes can be used similarly. Public instance methods are `ShowDialog()` and `Reset()`. `ShowDialog()` invokes the protected `RunDialog()` instance method to display the dialog, returning a `DialogResult` instance with information about how the user interacted with the dialog. `Reset()`, in contrast, sets properties of the dialog class to their default values.

The following code segment shows an example of how a dialog class can be used (later, you take a more detailed look at each of the steps):

```
OpenFileDialog dlg = new OpenFileDialog();
dlg.Title = "Sample";
dlg.ShowReadOnly = true;

if (dlg.ShowDialog() == DialogResult.OK)
{
    string fileName = dlg.FileName;
}
```

1. A new instance of the dialog class is created.

2. You set some properties to enable and disable optional features and set dialog state. In this case, you set the `Title` property to `"Sample"`, and the `ShowReadOnly` property to `true`.

3. By calling the ShowDialog() method, the dialog is displayed, waiting for, and reacting to user inputs.

4. If the user presses the OK button, the dialog closes, and you check for the OK by comparing the result of the dialog with DialogResult.OK. After that you can get the values from the user input by querying for the specific property values. In this case, the value of the FileName property is stored in the fileName variable.

It's really that easy! Of course, every dialog has its own configurable options, which you look at in the following sections.

If you use a dialog from within a Windows Forms application in Visual Studio, it's even easier than the preceding few lines of code. The Windows Forms Designer creates the code to instantiate a new instance, and the property values can be set from the Properties window. You just have to call ShowDialog() and get to the changed values, as you shall see.

File Dialogs

With a file dialog, the user can select a drive and browse through the file system to select a file. From the file dialog, all you want returned is a filename from the user.

The OpenFileDialog enables users to select by name the file they want to open. The SaveFileDialog, in contrast, enables users to specify a name for a file they want to save. These dialog classes are similar because they derive from the same abstract base class, though there are some properties unique to each class. In this section, you look first at the features of the OpenFileDialog, then at how the SaveFileDialog differs, and you develop a sample application that uses both of them.

OpenFileDialog

The OpenFileDialog class enables users to select a file to open. As shown in the preceding example, a new instance of the OpenFileDialog class is created before the ShowDialog() method is called:

```
OpenFileDialog dlg = new OpenFileDialog();
dlg.ShowDialog();
```

Running a Windows application program with these two code lines will result in the dialog shown in Figure 17-2.

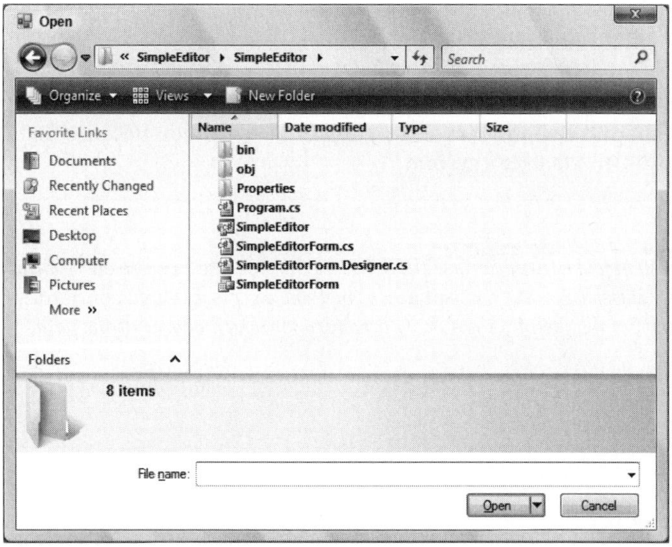

Figure 17-2

As shown earlier, you can set the properties of this class before calling `ShowDialog()`, which changes the behavior and appearance of this dialog, or limits the files that can be opened. The following sections describe some possible modifications.

To use the `OpenFileDialog` *with console applications, the* `System.Windows.Forms` *assembly must be referenced and the* `System.Windows.Forms` *namespace must be included.*

Dialog Title

The default title for the `OpenFileDialog` is Open. However, Open is not always the best name. For example, if in your application you want to analyze log files or get file sizes, perform whatever processing is required, and then close the files immediately afterward, a title of Analyze Files would be better because the files don't stay open for the user. Fortunately, you can change the dialog's title by setting the `Title` property. Visual Studio itself has different titles for the file open dialogs to differentiate the file types that are opened: Open Project, Open File, and Open Web Site.

This code segment shows how a different title can be set:

```
OpenFileDialog dlg = new OpenFileDialog();
dlg.Title = "Open File";
dlg.ShowDialog();
```

Specifying Directories

The directory that is opened by default is the directory that was opened by the user the last time the application was run. Setting the `InitialDirectory` property changes this behavior. The default value of `InitialDirectory` is an empty string representing the user's directory, which is shown the first time the dialog is used in the application. The second time the dialog is opened, the directory shown is the same as for the previously opened file. The Windows common dialog called by the `OpenFileDialog` uses the registry to locate the name of the previously opened file.

> **Never use a hard-coded directory string in your application because that directory might not exist on the user's system.**

To get special system folders you can use the static method `GetFolderPath()` *of the* `System.Environment` *class. The* `GetFolderPath()` *method accepts an* `Environment.SpecialFolder` *enumeration member that defines the system directory for which you want the path.*

In the following code example, the common user directory for templates is set as `InitialDirectory`:

```
string directory = Environment.GetFolderPath(Environment.SpecialFolder.Templates);
dlg.InitialDirectory = directory;
```

Setting the File Filter

The file filter defines the file types the user can select to open. A simple filter string looks like this:

```
Text Documents (*.txt)|*.txt|All Files|*.*
```

The filter is used to display the entries in the Files of Type: list box. Microsoft WordPad displays the entries as shown in Figure 17-3.

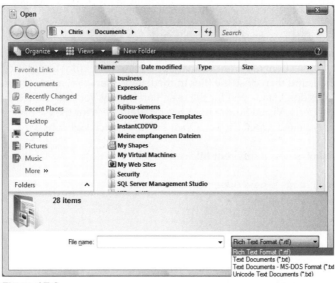

Figure 17-3

A filter has multiple segments separated with the pipe character (|). Two strings are required for each entry, so the number of segments should always be an even number. The first string for each entry defines the text presented in the list box; the second string specifies the extension of the files to be displayed in the dialog. You can set the filter string with the `Filter` property, as shown in the following code:

```
dlg.Filter = "Text documents (*.txt)|*.txt|All Files|*.*";
```

A blank before or after the filter is not allowed.

A wrong `Filter` value results in a runtime exception — `System.ArgumentException` — with the error message `The provided filter string is invalid`.

The `FilterIndex` property specifies the number of the default selection in the list box. With WordPad, the default selection is Rich Text Format (`*.rtf`) (highlighted in Figure 17-3). If you have multiple file types to choose from, you can set the `FilterIndex` to the default file type. Note that the `FilterIndex` is one-based!

Validation

The `OpenFileDialog` can do some automatic validation of the file before you attempt to open it. When the `ValidateNames` property is `true`, the filename entered by the user is checked to determine whether it is a valid Windows filename. Clicking the OK button of the dialog with an invalid filename displays the dialog shown in Figure 17-4, and the user must correct the filename or click Cancel to leave the `OpenFileDialog`. Invalid characters for a filename include characters such as \\, /, and :.

Figure 17-4

With `ValidateNames` set to `true`, you can use `CheckFileExists` and `CheckPathExists` for additional validation. With `CheckPathExists`, the path is validated, whereas `CheckFileExists` validates the file. If the file doesn't exist, then the dialog shown in Figure 17-5 is displayed after the user clicks OK.

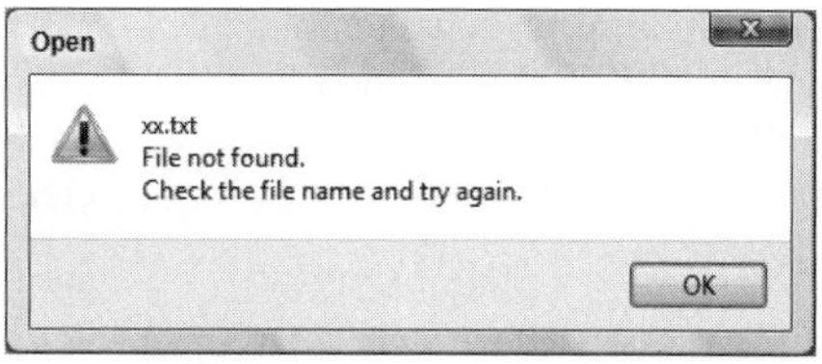

Figure 17-5

The default for these three properties is true, so the validation happens automatically.

Help

The OpenFileDialog class supports a Help button that is, by default, invisible. Setting the ShowHelp property to true makes this button visible, and you can add an event handler to the HelpRequest event to display help information to the user.

Results

The ShowDialog() method of the OpenFileDialog class returns a DialogResult enumeration value. The DialogResult enumeration defines the members Abort, Cancel, Ignore, No, None, OK, Retry, and Yes.

None is the default value that is set as long as the user hasn't closed the dialog. When a button is clicked, the corresponding result is returned. With the OpenFileDialog, only DialogResult.OK and DialogResult.Cancel are returned.

If the user clicks the OK button, then the selected filename can be accessed by using the FileName property. If the user cancels the dialog, then the FileName is just an empty string. If the Multiselect property is set to true so that the user can select more than one file, you get all the selected filenames by accessing the FileNames property, which returns a string array.

Note that the FileNames property contains the files in the reverse order to which they were selected — thus, the first string in the FileNames array is the last file selected. In addition, the FileNames property always contains the filename of the last file selected.

The following code extract shows how multiple filenames can be retrieved from an OpenFileDialog:

```
OpenFileDialog dlg = new OpenFileDialog();
dlg.Multiselect = true;

if (dlg.ShowDialog() == DialogResult.OK)
{
    foreach (string s in dlg.FileNames)
    {
        // Now display the filenames in a list box.
        this.listBox1.Items.Add(s);
    }
}
```

The ShowDialog() method opens the dialog. Because the Multiselect property is set to true, the user can select multiple files. Clicking the OK button of the dialog ends the dialog if all goes well, and DialogResult.OK is returned. With the foreach statement, you go through all strings in the string array returned from the FileNames property to display every selected file.

OpenFileDialog Properties

In summary, Figure 17-6 shows the `OpenFileDialog` with its properties — you can easily see what properties influence which user interface elements.

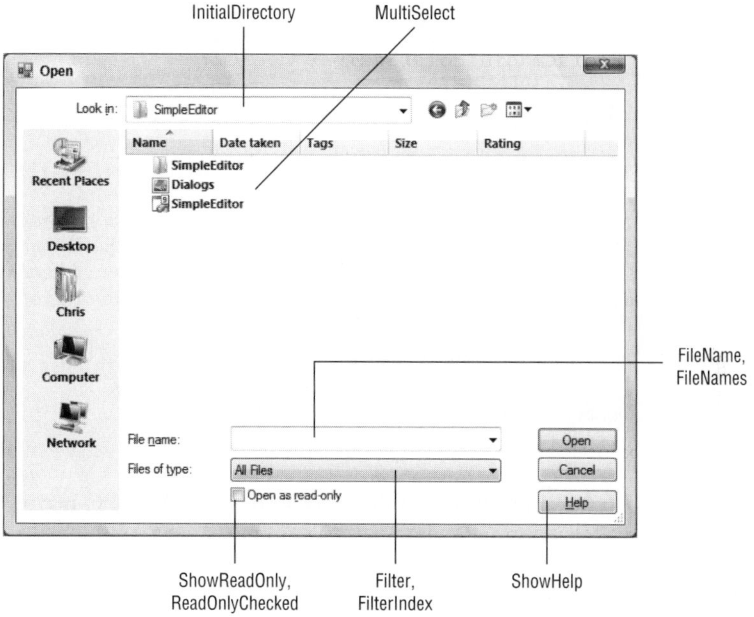

Figure 17-6

To demonstrate the use of the standard dialogs, in the following Try It Out you create a simple text editor Windows application called SimpleEditor, which enables users to load, save, and edit text files. As you progress further through the chapter, you will also see how to print the text file. In the following exercise, you start by using the Open and Save file dialogs.

Try It Out   **Creating the Simple Text Editor Windows Application**

1.   Create a new Windows Forms application called "SimpleEditor" in the directory C:\BegVCSharp\Chapter17.

2.   Rename the generated file `Form1.cs` to `SimpleEditorForm.cs`. Answer Yes to rename all references to the form. This way, Visual Studio 2008 also changes the name of the class to `SimpleEditorForm`.

3. Set the Text property of the form to SimpleEditor, and change its Size to 570,270. A multiline text box will serve as the area to read and modify the data of the file, so add a TextBox from the Toolbox to the Windows Forms Designer. The text box should be multiline and should cover the complete area of the application, so set these properties to the values specified in the following table:

Property	Value
(Name)	textBoxEdit
Text	
Multiline	True
Dock	Fill
ScrollBars	Both
AcceptsReturn	True
AcceptsTab	True

4. Add a MenuStrip to the application. Set the name of the MenuStrip to **mainMenu**. The menu should have a File entry with submenus New, Open . . . Save, and Save As . . . , as shown in Figure 17-7.

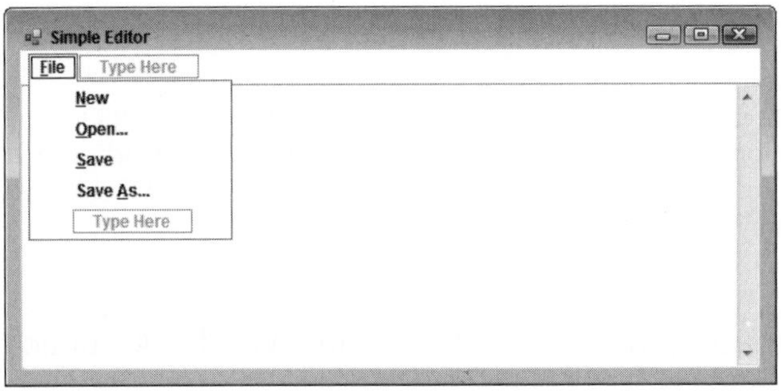

Figure 17-7

The ellipses (. . .) in the Text property of the Open and Save As menu entries advise users that they will be asked for some data before the action happens. When choosing the File, New, and Save menus, the action happens without additional intervention. The table that follows lists the names of the menu items, as well as the values for the Text properties. You should also define the Click event handler with the names shown in the table. To define the Click event handler, select the menu in the dialog, click the Events button in the Properties window, select the Click event, and enter the name of the handler method.

Menu Item Name	Text	Handler Method
miFile	&File	
miFileNew	&New	OnFileNew
miFileOpen	&Open...	OnFileOpen
miFileSave	&Save	OnFileSave
miFileSaveAs	Save &As...	OnFileSaveAs

5. The handler for the menu entry &New should clear the data of the text box by calling the Clear() method of the TextBox:

```
private void OnFileNew(object sender, System.EventArgs e)
{
    fileName = "Untitled";
    textBoxEdit.Clear();
}
```

6. Set the filename member variable to "Untitled". You must declare and initialize this member variable in the SimpleEditorForm class:

```
public partial class SimpleEditorForm : Form
{
    private string fileName = "Untitled";
```

With the SimpleEditor it should be possible to pass a filename as an argument when starting the application. The filename passed should be used to open the file and display it in the text box.

7. Change the implementation of the SimpleEditorForm constructor to use a string where the filename is passed:

```
public SimpleEditorForm(string fileName)
{
    InitializeComponent();

    if (fileName != null)
    {
        this.fileName = fileName;
        OpenFile();
    }
}
```

8. Now you can change the implementation of the `Main()` method in the file `Program.cs` so that an argument can be passed:

```
static void Main(string[] args)
{
    string fileName = null;
    if (args.Length != 0)
        fileName = args[0];

    Application.EnableVisualStyles();
    Application.SetCompatibleTextRenderingDefault(false);
    Application.Run(new SimpleEditorForm(fileName));
}
```

9. Implement the `OpenFile()` method, which opens a file and fills the text box with data from the file:

The `OpenFile()` method actually accesses the file in question and uses methods not discussed at length here, but file access is covered fully in Chapter 24.

```
private void OpenFile()
{
    try
    {
        textBoxEdit.Clear();
        textBoxEdit.Text = File.ReadAllText(filename);
    }
    catch (IOException ex)
    {
        MessageBox.Show(ex.Message, "Simple Editor",
            MessageBoxButtons.OK, MessageBoxIcon.Exclamation);
    }
}
```

This code uses the `File` class to read the file — this class is in the `System.IO` namespace, so you also need to add the following `using` directive at the beginning of the file `SimpleEditorForm.cs`:

```
using System.IO;
```

The `File` class and the `System.IO` namespace are explored in Chapter 24 along with other file access classes.

10. As shown in Chapter 7, it's possible to define command-line parameters within Visual Studio for debugging purposes. In the Solution Explorer, right-click on the project and select Properties. From the Properties dialog, select the Debug tab on the left. In the dialog that appears, you can enter the command-line arguments. For testing purposes here, enter the following:

```
C:\BegVCSharp\Chapter17\SimpleEditor\SimpleEditor\SimpleEditorForm.cs
```

11. Run the application. The `SimpleEditorForm.cs` file of your current project will be opened immediately and displayed, as shown in Figure 17-8.

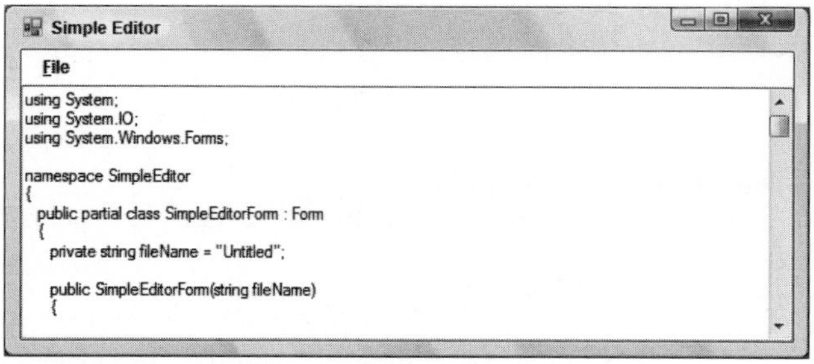

Figure 17-8

How It Works

The first six steps simply set up the form — you should be familiar with this process if you worked through the previous two chapters. Step 7 is where the meat of the application begins. By adding the `string[]` to the parameters of the `Main()` method, you can use any command-line arguments that the user supplies when starting the application:

```
static void Main(string[] args)
```

In the `Main()` method, you check to see whether arguments were passed by using the `Length` property. If at least one argument was passed, the first argument is set to the `fileName` variable, which is then passed to the constructor of the `SimpleEditorForm`:

```
{
    string fileName = null;
    if (args.Length != 0)
        fileName = args[0];

    Application.EnableVisualStyles();
    Application.SetCompatibleTextRenderingDefault(false);
    Application.Run(new SimpleEditorForm(fileName));
}
```

In the `SimpleEditorForm` constructor, you check whether the `fileName` variable already has a value set. If it has, then the member variable `fileName` is set and the method `OpenFile()` is invoked to open the file. Use a separate `OpenFile()` method, and don't write the calls to open the file and fill the text box directly in the constructor of the class, because `OpenFile()` can be used again in other parts of the program:

```
if (fileName != null)
{
    this.fileName = fileName;
    OpenFile();
}
```

In the `OpenFile()` method you read the data from the file. You use the static method `ReadAllText()` of the `File` class to get all lines returned in an array of strings.

Because file operations can easily generate exceptions (caused, for example, by the user not having the right access permissions to the file), the code is wrapped in a try block. In the case of an I/O exception, a message box appears to inform the user about the problem, but the application keeps running:

```
protected void OpenFile()
{
    try
    {
        textBoxEdit.Clear();
        textBoxEdit.Text = File.ReadAllText(fileName);
    }
    catch (IOException ex)
    {
        MessageBox.Show(ex.Message, "Simple Editor",
            MessageBoxButtons.OK, MessageBoxIcon.Exclamation);
    }
}
```

If you enter a nonexistent filename for the command-line argument when starting the application, the message box shown in Figure 17-9 is displayed.

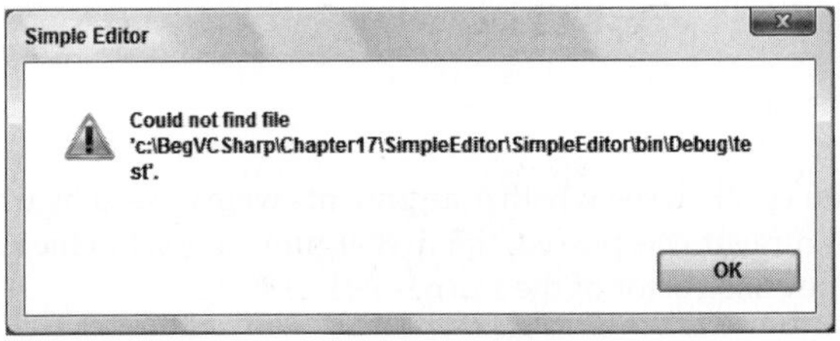

Figure 17-9

Now you can read files with the simple editor by passing a filename when starting the application. Of course, using common dialog classes is preferred, and you add those to the application in the following Try It Out

---

Try It Out   **Adding and Using an OpenFileDialog**

1. In the Windows Forms category of the Toolbox, find the OpenFileDialog component. Drag it from the Toolbox and drop it in the gray area on the bottom of the Forms Designer. Change three properties: the name for the instance to dlgOpenFile, the Filter property to the following string, and the FilterIndex property to 2 to make Wrox Documents the default selection:

    ```
    Text Documents (*.txt)|*.txt|Wrox Documents (*.wroxtext)|*.wroxtext|All
    Files|*.*
    ```

2. Earlier you added a Click event handler named OnFileOpen to the Open menu entry. To add the implementation to this event handler, using the Forms Designer, double-click the Open

menu entry. Here, the implementation for the dialog is displayed and the selected file is read with this code:

```
private void OnFileOpen(object sender, System.EventArgs e)
{
    if (dlgOpenFile.ShowDialog() == DialogResult.OK)
    {
        fileName = dlgOpenFile.FileName;
        OpenFile();
    }
}
```

How It Works

By adding the `OpenFileDialog` component to the Windows Forms Designer, a new private member is added to the `SimpleEditorForm` class. You can see the private member in the file `SimpleEditorForm.Designer.cs`. This file appears only when you click the Show All Files button in the Solution Explorer:

```
partial class SimpleEditorForm
{
    private System.Windows.Forms.TextBox textBoxEdit;
    private System.Windows.Forms.MenuStrip mainMenu;
    private System.Windows.Forms.ToolStripMenuItem miFile;
    private System.Windows.Forms.ToolStripMenuItem miFileNew;
    private System.Windows.Forms.ToolStripMenuItem miFileOpen;
    private System.Windows.Forms.ToolStripMenuItem miFileSave;
    private System.Windows.Forms.ToolStripMenuItem miFileSaveAs;
    private System.Windows.Forms.OpenFileDialog dlgOpenFile;
```

In the region of designer code by the Windows Forms, in `InitializeComponent()`, a new instance of this `OpenFileDialog` class is created, and the specified properties are set. Click on the + character of the line of Windows Forms Designer–generated code and then on the + character of the line `private void InitializeComponent()` to see the following code:

```
private void InitializeComponent()
{
    this.textBoxEdit = new System.Windows.Forms.TextBox();
    this.mainMenu = new System.Windows.Forms.MenuStrip();
    this.miFile = new System.Windows.Forms.ToolStripMenuItem();
    this.miFileNew = new System.Windows.Forms.ToolStripMenuItem();
    this.miFileOpen = new System.Windows.Forms.ToolStripMenuItem();
    this.miFileSave = new System.Windows.Forms.ToolStripMenuItem();
    this.miFileSaveAs = new System.Windows.Forms.ToolStripMenuItem();
    this.dlgOpenFile = new System.Windows.Forms.OpenFileDialog();
    // ...
    //
    // dlgOpenFile
    //
    this.dlgOpenFile.Filter =
        "Text Documents (*.txt)|*.txt|Wrox Documents" +
            "(*.wroxtext)|*.wroxtext|All Files|*.*";
    this.dlgOpenFile.FilterIndex = 2;
```

Of course, what has happened here is exactly what you would expect if you dragged any another standard control onto the form, but with the support of the Windows Forms Designer you have created a new instance of the OpenFileDialog and set the properties. Now you can display the dialog.

The ShowDialog() method displays the File Open dialog and returns the button that the user pressed. Nothing should be done if the user presses anything other than the OK button. That's the reason to check for DialogResult.OK in the if statement. If the user cancels the dialog, then nothing should happen.

```
if (dlgOpenFile.ShowDialog() == DialogResult.OK)
{
```

Next, you get the selected filename by accessing the FileName property of the OpenFileDialog class and setting the member variable fileName to this value. This is the value that's used by the OpenFile() method. You could also open the file directly with the File class, but because you already have an OpenFile() method that opens and reads a file, you will use this:

```
fileName = dlgOpenFile.FileName;
OpenFile();
```

Now start the SimpleEditor program, shown in Figure 17-10. Only the New and Open... menu entries are functional at the moment. Save and Save As... will be implemented in the next section.

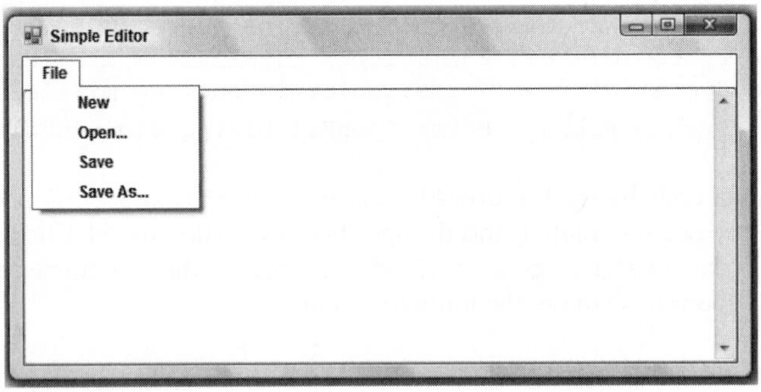

Figure 17-10

If you select the menu entry File ⇨ Open, the OpenFileDialog appears (see Figure 17-11) and you can select a file. I assume you currently don't have files with the file extension .wroxtext. Until now, you have not been able to save files, so you can choose a different file type in the dialog editor to open a file, or you can rename a text file to a file with the extension .wroxtext.

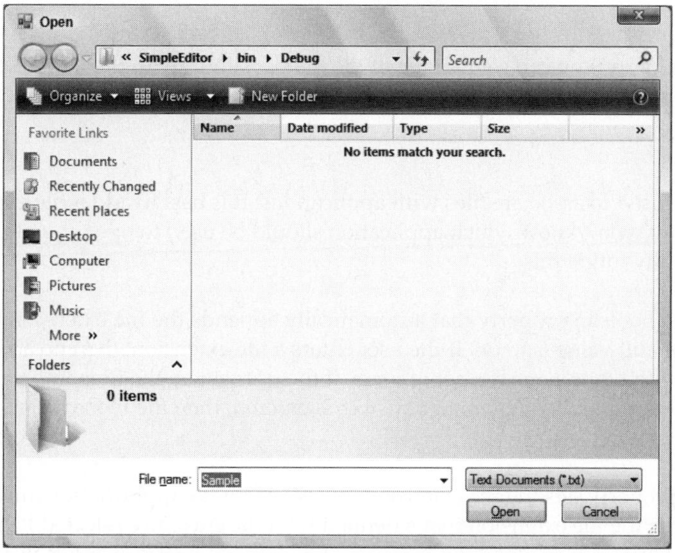

Figure 17-11

Select a text file, click the Open button, and the text shows up in the text box of the dialog. I selected a sample text file, Thinktecture.txt, on my local system, as shown in Figure 17-12.

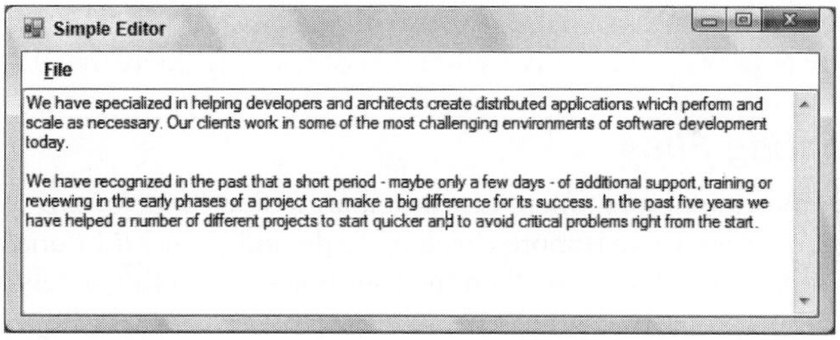

Figure 17-12

At this point, you can only read existing files. It would be great to create new files and modify existing ones. You will use the SaveFileDialog to do this.

SaveFileDialog

The SaveFileDialog class is very similar to the OpenFileDialog, and they have a set of common properties. This section focuses on the properties specific to the Save dialog, and explains how the application of the common properties differs.

Dialog Title

With the `Title` property, you can set the title of the dialog, similarly to the `OpenFileDialog`. If nothing is set, then the default title is Save As.

File Extensions

File extensions are used to associate files with applications. It is best to add a file extension to a file — otherwise, Windows won't know which application should be used to open the file, and it's likely that you would eventually forget this.

`AddExtension` is a Boolean property that automatically appends the file extension to the filename the user enters. The default value is `true`. If the user enters a file extension, then no additional extension is appended. Thus, with `AddExtension` set to `true`, if the user enters the filename `test`, then the filename `test.txt` will be stored. If the filename `test.txt` is entered, then the filename will still be `test.txt`, and not `test.txt.txt`.

The `DefaultExt` property sets the file extension that is used if the user doesn't enter one. If you leave the property blank, then the file extension that's defined with the currently selected `Filter` will be used instead. If you set both a `Filter` and the `DefaultExt`, then the `DefaultExt` is used regardless of the `Filter`.

Validation

For automatic filename validation, the properties `ValidateNames`, `CheckFileExists`, and `CheckPathExists` are used, similar to those for `OpenFileDialog`. The difference between `OpenFileDialog` and `SaveFileDialog` is that with the `SaveFileDialog`, the default value for `CheckFileExists` is `false`, which means that you can supply the name of a brand-new file to save.

Overwriting Existing Files

As you have seen, the validation of filenames is similar to that of the `OpenFileDialog`. However, for the `SaveFileDialog` class, there is more checking to do and some additional properties to set. If the `CreatePrompt` property is set to `true`, then the user is asked whether a new file should be created. If the `OverwritePrompt` property is set to `true`, then the user is asked if they really want to overwrite an already existing file. The default setting for `OverwritePrompt` is `true`, and `CreatePrompt` is `false`. With this setting, the dialog shown in Figure 17-13 is displayed if the user wants to save an already existing file.

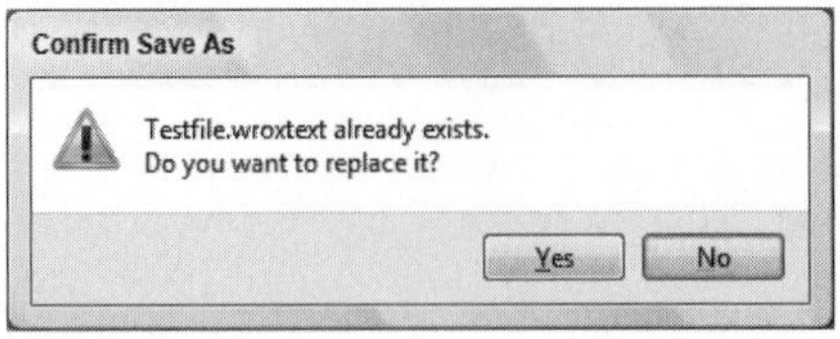

Figure 17-13

SaveFileDialog Properties

Figure 17-14 summarizes the properties of the SaveFileDialog.

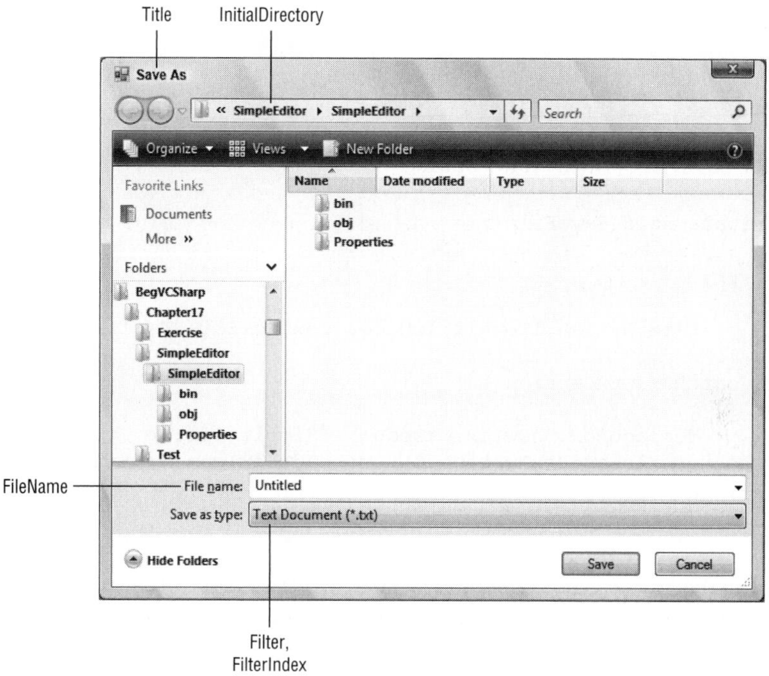

Title   InitialDirectory

FileName

Filter,
FilterIndex

Figure 17-14

In the following Try It Out, you add a Save File dialog to the sample application.

Adding and Using a SaveFileDialog

1. In the same way that you added an OpenFileDialog to the form, you can add a
   SaveFileDialog: Select the SaveFileDialog component from the Toolbox and drop it onto
   the gray area of the Forms Designer. Change the name to **dlgSaveFile**, FileName to **Untitled**, the
   FilterIndex to 2, and the Filter property to the following string, as you did with
   the OpenFileDialog earlier. (Because you allow only the file extensions .txt and .wroxtext
   to be saved with this editor, *.* will now be left out.)

```
Text Document (*.txt)|*.txt|Wrox Document (*.wroxtext)|*.wroxtext
```

2. Add a handler to the Click event of the Save As menu entry with the name OnFileSaveAs.
   In this code, you will display the SaveFileDialog with the ShowDialog() method. As with
   the OpenFileDialog, you are only interested in the results if the user has clicked the OK
   button. (You call the SaveFile() method, which stores the file to the disk. This method is
   implemented in the next step.)

```
        private void OnFileSaveAs(object sender, EventArgs e)
        {
            if (dlgSaveFile.ShowDialog() == DialogResult.OK)
            {
                fileName = dlgSaveFile.FileName;
                SaveFile();
            }
        }
```

3. Add the `SaveFile()` method to your file:

```
        private void SaveFile()
        {
            try
            {
                File.WriteAllText(fileName, textBoxEdit.Text);
            }
            catch (IOException ex)
            {
                MessageBox.Show(ex.Message, "Simple Editor",
                    MessageBoxButtons.OK, MessageBoxIcon.Exclamation);
            }
        }
```

Similar to the `OpenFile()` method, here the `File` class is used. The static method
`WriteAll()` writes a string to a file. The first parameter defines the name of the file; the
second parameter defines the string that should be written to the file.

You can read more about the classes used for file access in Chapter 24.

4. After building the project, start the application (select Debug ⇨ Start in Visual Studio). Write
    some text to the text box and then choose File ⇨ Save As (see Figure 17-15).

Figure 17-15

The `SaveFileDialog` (shown in Figure 17-16) will appear. Now you can save the file and open it again to make more changes.

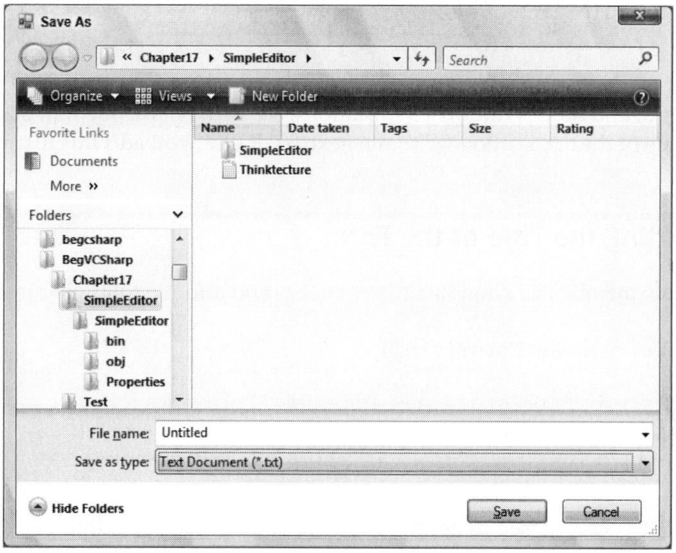

Figure 17-16

5. Now you can do a Save As, but the simple Save isn't available at the moment. Add a handler to the `Click` event of the Save menu entry and add the following code:

```
private void OnFileSave(object sender, EventArgs e)
{
    if (fileName == "Untitled")
    {
        OnFileSaveAs(sender, e);
    }
    else
    {
        SaveFile();
    }
}
```

How It Works

With the Save menu, the file should be saved without opening any dialog — with one exception to this rule: If the user creates a new document but does not supply a filename, then the Save handler should work like the Save As handler does and display the Save File dialog.

With the `filename` member variable you can easily check whether a file is open or the filename is still set to the initial value `Untitled` after creating a new document. If the `if` statement returns `true`, then the handler `OnFileSaveAs()` is called, which you implemented previously for the Save As menu.

In the other case, if a file was opened and the user now chooses the Save menu, then the thread of execution passes into the else *block. You can use the same* SaveFile() *method that you implemented previously.*

With Notepad, Word, and other Windows applications, the name of the file that's currently edited is displayed in the title of the application. With the next Try It Out, you add this feature, too.

Setting the Title of the Form

1. Create a new member function SetFormTitle() and add the following implementation:

```
private void SetFormTitle()
{
    FileInfo fileInfo = new FileInfo(fileName);
    Text = fileInfo.Name + " - Simple Editor";
}
```

The FileInfo class is used to get the filename without the preceding path that's stored in the fileName variable. The FileInfo class is covered in Chapter 24.

2. Add a call to this method in the OnFileNew(), OnFileOpen, and OnFileSaveAs() handlers after setting the member variable fileName as shown in the following code segments:

```
private void OnFileNew(object sender, System.EventArgs e)
{
    fileName = "Untitled";
    SetFormTitle();
    textBoxEdit.Clear();
}
private void OnFileOpen(object sender, System.EventArgs e)
{
    if (dlgOpenFile.ShowDialog() == DialogResult.OK)
    {
        fileName = dlgOpenFile.FileName;
        SetFormTitle();
        OpenFile();
    }
}
private void OnFileSaveAs(object sender, System.EventArgs e)
{
    if (dlgSaveFile.ShowDialog() == DialogResult.OK)
    {
        fileName = dlgSaveFile.FileName;
        SetFormTitle();
        SaveFile();
    }
}
```

How It Works

Every time the filename changes, the `Text` property of the actual form is changed to the filename appended with the name of the application.

The application now starts with the screen shown in Figure 17-17, where I'm editing the file `sample.txt`, as shown in the title of the form.

Figure 17-17

Now you have a simple editor — you can open, create, and save files (and edit them too). So, are we finished? Not really. Because the paperless office still doesn't exist, you should add some print functionality!

Printing

With printing there are many things to worry about, such as the selection of a printer, page settings, and how to print multiple pages. By using classes from the `System.Drawing.Printing` namespace, you can get a lot of help with these challenges, and print documents from your own applications with ease.

Before looking at the `PrintDialog` class that makes it possible to select a printer, take a quick look at how .NET handles printing. The foundation of printing is the `PrintDocument` class, which has a `Print()` method that starts a chain of calls culminating in a call to `OnPrintPage()`, which is responsible for passing the output to the printer. However, before learning how to implement printing code, first consider the .NET printing classes.

Printing Architecture

Figure 17-18 shows the major parts of the printing architecture to illustrate the relationship between the classes and some of the properties and methods.

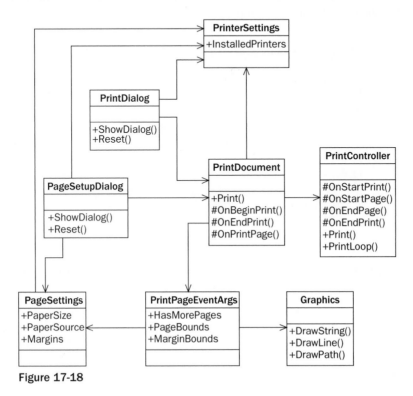

Figure 17-18

Let's look at the functionality of these classes:

❑ The `PrintDocument` class is the most important class. In Figure 17-18, you can see that nearly all other classes are related to this class. To print a document, an instance of `PrintDocument` is required. The following section looks at the printing sequence initiated by this class.

❑ The `PrintController` class controls the flow of a print job. The print controller has events for the start of the printing, for each page, and for the end of the printing. The class is abstract because the implementation of normal printing is different from that of print preview. Concrete classes that derive from `PrintController` are `StandardPrintController` and `PreviewPrintController`.

You will not find the methods `Print()` and `PrintLoop()` in the documentation because these methods are internal to the assembly and can be invoked only by other classes in the same assembly, such as the `PrintDocument` class. However, these methods help you understand the printing process, which is why they are shown here.

❑ The `PrinterSettings` class can get and set the printer configurations, such as duplex printing, landscape or portrait, and number of copies.

❑ The PrintDialog class contains options for selecting which printer to print to and how the PrinterSettings should be configured. This class is derived from CommonDialog like the other dialog classes already described.

❑ The PageSettings class specifies the sizes and boundaries of a page, and whether the page is in black and white or color. You can configure this class with the PageSetupDialog class, which is a CommonDialog.

Printing Sequence

Now that you know about the roles of the classes in the printing architecture, let's look at the main printing sequence. Figure 17-19 shows the major players — your application, an instance of the PrintDocument class, and a PrintController, in a timely sequence.

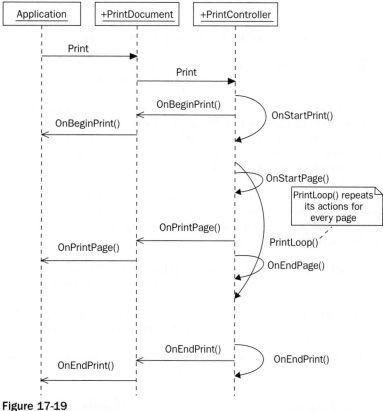

Figure 17-19

The application has to call the Print() method of the PrintDocument. This starts the printing sequence. As the PrintDocument itself is not responsible for the printing flow, the job is given to the PrintController by calling the Print() method of this class. The PrintController takes the action and informs the PrintDocument that the printing has started by calling OnBeginPrint(). If your application should do something at the start of a print job, then you have to register an event handler in the PrintDocument so that you are informed in your application class. In Figure 17-19, it is assumed that you registered the handler OnBeginPrint(), so this handler is called from the PrintDocument class.

After the beginning phase has ended, the `PrintController` goes into a `PrintLoop()` to call the `OnPrintPage()` method in the `PrintDocument` class for every page to print. `OnPrintPage()` invokes all `PrintPage` event handlers. You have to implement such a handler in every case; otherwise, nothing would be printed. In Figure 17-19, the handler is called `OnPrintPage()`.

After the last page is printed, the `PrintController` calls `OnEndPrint()` in the `PrintDocument` class. Optionally, you can implement a handler to be invoked here, too.

To summarize, the most important thing to know is that you can implement the printing code in the `PrintDocument.PrintPage` event handler. This handler will be called for every page that is to be printed. If there's printing code that should be called only once for a print job, then you have to implement the `BeginPrint` and `EndPrint` event handlers.

PrintPage Event

At this point, you know that you have to implement an event handler for the `PrintPage` event. The delegate `PrintPageEventHandler` defines the arguments of the handler:

```
public delegate void PrintPageEventHandler(object sender,
                                           PrintPageEventArgs e);
```

As shown here, you receive an object of type `PrintPageEventArgs`. You can refer to the class diagram to see the main properties of this class, which has associations to the `PageSettings` and `Graphics` classes. The first enables you to set the paper size and the margins, and you can get device information from the printer. The `Graphics` class, conversely, makes it possible to access the device context of the printer and send such things as strings, lines, and curves to the printer.

> GDI (graphics device interface) makes it possible to perform some graphical output to a device such as the screen or a printer. GDI+, the drawing technology of the .NET Framework, is the next generation of GDI, adding features such as gradient brushes and alpha blending. Chapter 30 has more details about drawing with GDI+ and the `Graphics` class.

If at this point you think that printing is complex, don't be worried! The following example should convince you that adding printing features to an application is quite an easy task.

Before you can add the `PrintDialog`, you have to add some menu entries for printing. Add two separators and Print, Print Preview, Page Setup, and Exit menu items to the SimpleEditor application.

The following table lists the `Name` and `Text` properties and handler methods of the new menu items:

Menu Item Name	Text	Handler
miFilePrint	&Print...	OnFilePrint
miFilePrintPreview	Print Pre&view...	OnFilePrintPreview
miFilePageSetup	Page Set&up...	OnFilePageSetup
miFileExit	E&xit	OnExit

The menu should look like the one shown in Figure 17-20.

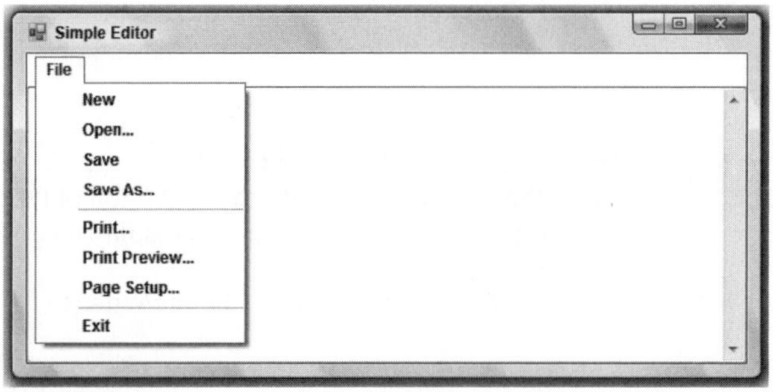

Figure 17-20

The following Try It Out adds printing functionality to the sample application by adding a `PrintDocument` component.

Try It Out   **Adding a PrintDocument Component**

1. Add the following `using` directive to the start of your code so that you can make use of the classes for printing:

```
using System.Drawing;
using System.Drawing.Printing;
```

2. Drag a `PrintDocument` component from the Toolbox and drop it on the gray area below the form. Change the `Name` to `printDocument` and add an event handler `OnPrintPage` to the `PrintPage` event by selecting the Events button in the Properties window. Then add the following code to the implementation of the event handler:

```
private void OnPrintPage(object sender, PrintPageEventArgs e)
{
    string[] lines = textBoxEdit.Text.Split('\n');

    int i = 0;

    foreach (string s in lines)
    {
        lines[i++] = s.TrimEnd('\r');
    }

    int x = 20;
    int y = 20;
    foreach (string line in lines)
    {
```

```
    e.Graphics.DrawString(line, new Font("Arial", 10),
        Brushes.Black, x, y);
    y += 15;
}
```
}

3. Add a handler to the `Click` event of the Print menu to call the `Print()` method of the `PrintDocument` class. In case there's no valid printer, an exception of type `InvalidPrinterException` is thrown, which is caught to display an error message:

```
private void OnFilePrint(object sender, EventArgs e)
{
    try
    {
        printDocument.Print();
    }
    catch (InvalidPrinterException ex)
    {
        MessageBox.Show(ex.Message, "Simple Editor",
            MessageBoxButtons.OK, MessageBoxIcon.Error);
    }
}
```

Now you can build and start the application and print a document. Of course, you must have a printer installed for the example to work.

How It Works

The `printDocument` object's `Print()` method invokes the `PrintPage` event with the help of the `PrintController` class:

```
printDocument.Print();
```

In the `OnPrintPage()` handler, you split up the text in the text box line by line using the `String.Split()` method and the newline character, `\n`. The resultant strings are written to the string array `lines`:

```
string[] lines = textBoxEdit.Text.Split('\n');
```

Depending on how the text file was created, the lines are not only separated with the `\n` (newline) character, but also the `\r` (return) character. The `TrimEnd()` method of the `String` class removes the character `\r` from every string:

```
int i = 0;
foreach(string s in lines)
{
    lines[i++] = s.TrimEnd('\r');
}
```

In the second `foreach` statement in the following code, you iterate through all the lines, and send each one to the printer by a call to `e.Graphics.DrawString()`. `e`, which is a variable of type `PrintPageEventArgs`, where the property `Graphics` is connected to the printer context. The printer context makes it possible to draw to a printing device. The `Graphics` class has some methods to draw into this context.

You can't select a printer yet, so the default printer (whose details are stored in the Windows registry) is used.

With the `DrawString()` method, you use the Arial font with a size of 10 points and a black brush for the print output. The position for the output is defined with the x and y variables. The horizontal position is fixed to 20 pixels, and the vertical position is incremented with every line:

```
int x = 20;
int y = 20;
foreach (string line in lines)
{
    e.Graphics.DrawString(line, new Font("Arial", 10),
                          Brushes.Black, x, y);
    y += 15;
}
```

The printing done so far has the following problems:

❏   Printing multiple pages doesn't work. If the document to print spans multiple pages, only the first page is printed. It would also be nice if a header (e.g., the filename) and footer (e.g., the page number) were printed.

❏   Page boundaries are fixed to hard-coded values in your program. To enable users to set values for other page boundaries, you use the `PageSetupDialog` class.

❏   The print output is sent to the default printer, set through the Control Panel by the user. It would be better if the application enabled the user to choose a printer. You will use the `PrintDialog` class to correct this.

❏   The font is fixed. To enable the user to choose the font, you can use the `FontDialog` class, described in more detail later.

Let's continue with the printing process to get these items fixed.

Printing Multiple Pages

The `PrintPage` event is called for every page that prints. In the following Try It Out, you inform the `PrintController` that the current page printed was not the last page by setting the `HasMorePages` property of the `PrintPageEventArgs` class to `true`.

Try It Out   **Modifying OnPrintPage() for Multiple Pages**

1. First, declare a member variable `lines` of type `string[]` and a variable `linesPrinted` of type `int` in the class `SimpleEditorForm`:

```
// Variables for printing
private string[] lines;
private int linesPrinted;
```

2. Modify the `OnPrintPage()` handler. In the previous implementation of `OnPrintPage()` the text was split into lines. Because the `OnPrintPage()` method is called with every page, and splitting the text into lines is needed just once at the beginning of the printing operation, remove all the code from `OnPrintPage()` and replace it with the new implementation:

```
private void OnPrintPage(object sender, PrintPageEventArgs e)
{
    int x = 20;
    int y = 20;

    while (linesPrinted < lines.Length)
    {
        e.Graphics.DrawString (lines[linesPrinted++],
                new Font("Arial", 10), Brushes.Black, x, y);
        y += 15;
        if (y = e.PageBounds.Height - 80)
        {
            e.HasMorePages = true;
            return;
        }
    }

    linesPrinted = 0;
    e.HasMorePages = false;
}
```

3. Add an event handler to the `BeginPrint` event of the `printDocument` object called `OnBeginPrint`. `OnBeginPrint` is called just once for each print job and here you create your `lines` array:

```
private void OnBeginPrint(object sender, PrintEventArgs e)
{
    lines = textBoxEdit.Text.Split('\n');

    int i = 0;
    foreach (string s in lines)
    {
        lines[i++] = s.TrimEnd('\r');
    }
}
```

4. Add an event handler to the `EndPrint` event of the `printDocument` called `OnEndPrint`. Here, you can release the resources that have been allocated in the `OnBeginPrint` method.

With the sample, an array of strings was allocated and referenced in the variable `lines`. In the `OnEndPrint` method, the reference of the variable `lines` is set to `null`, so that the garbage collector can release the string array:

```
private void OnEndPrint(object sender, PrintEventArgs e)
{
    lines = null;
}
```

5.   After building the project, you can start a print job for a multipage document.

How It Works

Starting the print job with the `Print()` method of the `PrintDocument` in turn calls `OnBeginPrint()` once, and `OnPrintPage()` for every page.

In `OnBeginPrint()` you split up the text of the text box into a string array. Every string in the array represents a single line because you split it up at the newline (`\n`) character and removed the carriage return character (`\r`), as you've done before:

```
lines = textBoxEdit.Text.Split('\n');
int i = 0;
foreach (string s in lines)
{
    lines[i++] = s.TrimEnd('\r');
}
```

`OnPrintPage()` is called after `OnBeginPrint()`. You want to continue printing as long as the number of lines printed is less than the total number of lines you have to print. The `lines.Length` property returns the number of strings in the array `lines`. The `linesPrinted` variable is incremented with every line you send to the printer:

```
while (linesPrinted < lines.Length)
{
    e.Graphics.DrawString(lines[linesPrinted++],
            new Font("Arial", 10), Brushes.Black, x, y);
```

After printing a line, you check whether the newly calculated vertical position is outside of the page boundaries. Additionally, you decrement the boundaries by 80 pixels, because you don't really want to print to the very end of the paper, particularly because many printers can't do this anyway. If this position is reached, then the `HasMorePages` property of the `PrintPageEventArgs` class is set to `true` to inform the controller that the `OnPrintPage()` method must be called again and another page needs to be printed — remember that `PrintController` has the `PrintLoop()` method, which has a sequence for every page to print, and `PrintLoop()` will stop if `HasMorePages` is `false`. (The default value of the `HasMorePages` property is `false` so that only one page is printed.)

```
y += 15;
if (y = e.PageBounds.Height - 80)
{
    e.HasMorePages = true;
    return;
}
```

PageSetupDialog

Currently, the margins of the page are hard-coded. Let's modify the application to enable users to set the margins on a page. To make this possible, another dialog class is available: `PageSetupDialog`.

This class enables the configuration of paper sizes and sources, orientation, and paper margins; and because these options depend on a printer, the printer can be selected from this dialog too.

Figure 17-21 provides an overview of the properties that enable or disable specific options of this dialog, and what properties can be used to access the values. I will discuss these properties in a moment.

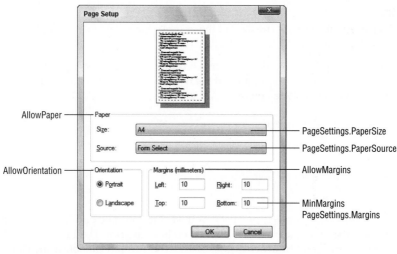

Figure 17-21

Paper

A value of `true` for the `AllowPaper` property means that users can choose the paper size and paper source. The `PageSetupDialog.PageSettings.PaperSize` property returns a `PaperSize` instance in which you can read the height, width, and name of the paper with the properties `Height`, `Width`, and `PaperName`, respectively. `PaperName` specifies names such as Letter or A4. The `Kind` property returns an enumeration from which you can get a value of the `PaperKind` enumeration. The `PaperKind` enumeration consists of many different paper values that define the size of the paper, such as A3, A4, A5, Letter, LetterPlus, and LetterRotated.

The `PageSetupDialog.PageSettings.PaperSource` property returns a `PaperSource` instance in which you can read the name of the printer paper source and the type of paper that fits in there (as long as the printer is correctly configured with the printer settings).

Margins

Setting the `AllowMargins` property to `true` enables users to set the margin value for the printout. You can define minimum values for the user to enter by specifying the `MinMargins` property. To read the margins, use the `PageSetupDialog.PageSettings.Margins` property. The returned `Margins` object has `Bottom`, `Left`, `Right`, and `Top` properties.

Orientation

The `AllowOrientation` property defines whether or not users can choose between portrait and landscape printing. The selected value can be read by querying the value of `PageSetupDialog`. `PageSettings.Landscape`, which is a Boolean value that specifies landscape mode with `true` and portrait mode with `false`.

Printer

The `AllowPrinter` property defines whether or not users can choose a printer. Depending on the value of this property, the Printer button is enabled (`true`) or disabled (`false`). The handler to this button in turn opens the `PrintDialog` that you will use next. In the next Try It Out, you add the capability to configure page setup options for printing.

Try It Out · Adding a PageSetupDialog

1. Drag a `PageSetupDialog` component from the Toolbox and drop it onto the form in the Forms Designer. Set its `Name` to `dlgPageSetup` and the `Document` property to `printDocument` to associate the dialog with the document to print.

2. Add a `Click` event handler to the Page Setup menu entry, and add the following code to display the dialog using the `ShowDialog()` method. It's not necessary to check the return value of `ShowDialog()` here because the implementation of the handler for the OK `Click` event already sets the new values in the associated `PrintDocument` object:

```
private void OnFilePageSetup(object sender, EventArgs e)
{
    dlgPageSetup.ShowDialog();
}
```

3. Now change the implementation of `OnPrintPage()` to use the margins set by the `PageSetupDialog`. In your code, the x and y variables are set to the properties `MarginBounds.Left` and `MarginBounds.Top` of the `PrintPageEventArgs` class. Check the boundary of a page with `MarginBounds.Bottom`:

```
private void OnPrintPage(object sender, PrintPageEventArgs e)
{
    int x = e.MarginBounds.Left;
    int y = e.MarginBounds.Top;

    while (linesPrinted < lines.Length)
    {
        e.Graphics.DrawString(lines[linesPrinted++],
            new Font("Arial", 10), Brushes.Black, x, y);

        y += 15;
        if (y >= e.MarginBounds.Bottom)
        {
            e.HasMorePages = true;
```

```
            return;
    }
  }

  linesPrinted = 0;
  e.HasMorePages = false;
}
```

4. Now, you can build the project and run the application. Selecting File ⇨ Page Setup displays the dialog shown in Figure 17-22. You can change the boundaries and print with the configured boundaries.

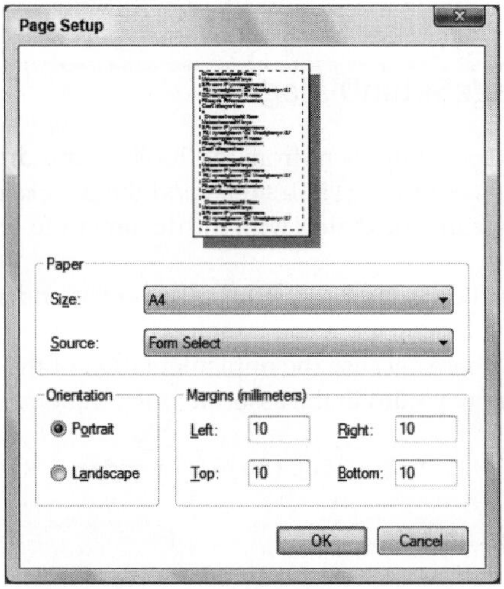

Figure 17-22

PrintDialog

The PrintDialog class enables users to select a printer from the installed printers and choose a number of copies and some printer settings, such as the layout and paper sources of the printer. Because the PrintDialog is very easy to use, you will immediately start by adding the PrintDialog to the Editor application with the following Try It Out.

Adding a PrintDialog

1. Add a `PrintDialog` component from the Toolbox to the form. Set the `Name` to `dlgPrint` and the `Document` property of this object to `printDocument`.

   Change the implementation of the event handler to the `Click` event of the Print menu as follows:

   ```
   private void OnFilePrint(object sender, EventArgs e)
   {
       try
       {
           if (dlgPrint.ShowDialog() == DialogResult.OK)
           {
               printDocument.Print();
           }
       }
       catch (InvalidPrinterException ex)
       {
           MessageBox.Show(ex.Message, "Simple Editor",
               MessageboButtons.OK, MessageBoxIcon.Error);
       }
   }
   ```

2. Build and run the application. Selecting File ➪ Print opens the `PrintDialog`. Now you can select a printer to print the document, as shown in Figure 17-23.

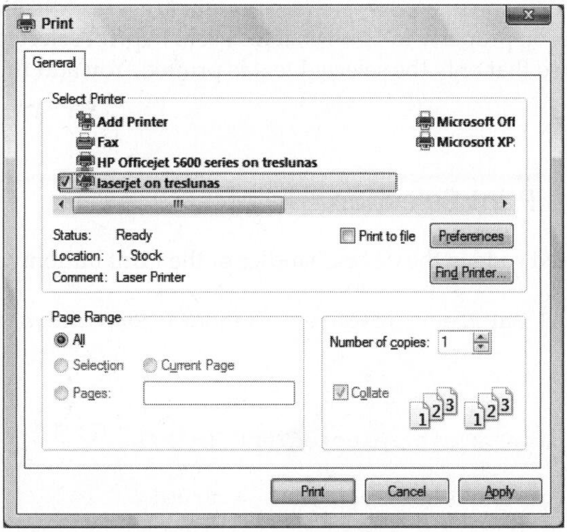

Figure 17-23

Options for the PrintDialog

In the SimpleEditor program you didn't change any of the properties of the PrintDialog, but this dialog has some options, too. The dialog shown in Figure 17-23 contains three groups: Printer, Page Range, and Copies:

❑ In the Printer group, not only the printer can be chosen; there's also a Print to File option. By default, this option is enabled, but it is not checked. Selecting this check box enables the user to write the printing output to a file instead of to the printer. You can disable this option by setting the AllowPrintToFile property to false.

❑ If the user selects this option, the dialog shown in Figure 17-24 is opened by the printDocument.Print() call, requesting an output filename for the printout.

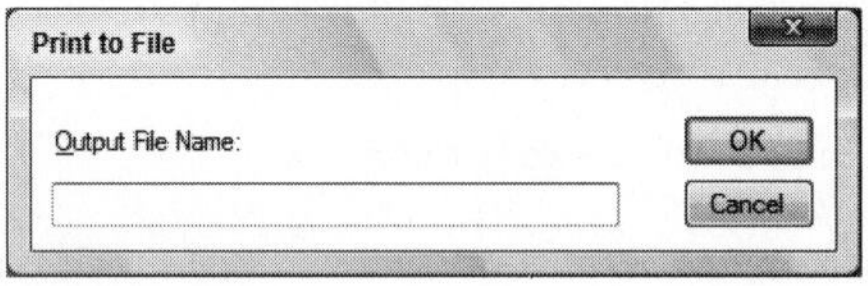

Figure 17-24

❑ In the Page Range section of the dialog, only All can be selected — Pages and Selection are disabled by default. The following section shows how these options can be implemented.

❑ The Copies group enables users to select the number of copies to be printed.

Printing Selected Text

Setting the AllowSelection property to true enables users to print selected text, but you need to change the printing code so that only the selected text is printed. You add this functionality in the next Try It Out.

Try It Out **Adding a Print Selection**

1. Add the highlighted code to the Click handler of the Print button:

```
private void OnFilePrint(object sender, EventArgs e)
{
    try
    {
        if (textBoxEdit.SelectedText != "")
        {
            dlgPrint.AllowSelection = true;
        }
        if (dlgPrint.ShowDialog() == DialogResult.OK)
        {
            printDocument.Print();
        }
    }
```

```
            catch (InvalidPrinterException ex)
            {
                MessageBox.Show(ex.Message, "Simple Editor",
                    MessageboButtons.OK, MessageBoxIcon.Error);
            }
        }
```

2. In this program all the lines that will be printed are set up in the OnBeginPrint() handler. Change the implementation of this method:

```
        private void OnBeginPrint(object sender, PrintEventArgs e)
        {
            char[] param = {'\n'};

            if (dlgPrint.PrinterSettings.PrintRange == PrintRange.Selection)
            {
                lines = textBoxEdit.SelectedText.Split(param);
            }
            else
            {
                lines = textBoxEdit.Text.Split(param);
            }

            int i = 0;
            char[] trimParam = {'\r'};
            foreach (string s in lines)
            {
                lines[i++] = s.TrimEnd(trimParam);
            }
        }
```

3. Now you can build and start the program. Open a file, select some text, start the Print dialog with the menu File ➪ Print, and choose the Selection option from the Page Range group. With this selected, pressing the Print button will print only the selected text.

How It Works

The AllowSelection property is set to true only if some text is selected. Before the PrintDialog is shown, a check must be done to determine whether any text is selected. If so, then the SelectedText property of the text box is not null. If some text is selected, the property AllowSelection is set to true:

```
        if (textBoxEdit.SelectedText != "")
        {
            dlgPrint.AllowSelection = true;
        }
```

OnBeginPrint() is called at the start of every print job. Accessing the printDialog.
PrinterSettings.PrintRange property, you discover whether the user has chosen the Selection option. The PrintRange property takes a value from the PrintRange enumeration: AllPages, Selection, or SomePages:

```
        if (printDialog.PrinterSettings.PrintRange == PrintRange.Selection)
        {
```

If the option is indeed `PrintRange.Selection`, then you get the selected text from the `SelectedText` property of the `TextBox`. This string is split up the same way as the complete text:

```
        lines = textBoxEdit.SelectedText.Split(param);
    }
```

Printing Page Ranges

Printing a range of pages can be implemented similarly to printing a selection. The option button can be enabled by setting the `AllowSomePages` property to `true`, which enables users to select the page range to print. However, where are the page boundaries in SimpleEditor? What's the last page? You set the last page by setting the `PrintDialog.PrinterSettings.ToPage` property. How does the user know which page numbers should be printed? With a document processing application such as Microsoft Word, users can select the Print Layout option to view the onscreen text, which indicates page numbers. With the simple `TextBox` that's used with SimpleEditor, the number of pages is not known, so you won't implement this feature here.

Of course, you could implement page range printing capability as an exercise. To do that, the `AllowSomePages` property must be set to `true`. Before displaying the `PrintDialog`, you can also set the `PrinterSettings.FromPage` to 1 and the `PrinterSettings.ToPage` to the maximum page number.

PrintDialog Properties

Figure 17-25 shows the properties discussed in this section and how they influence the layout of the `PrintDialog`.

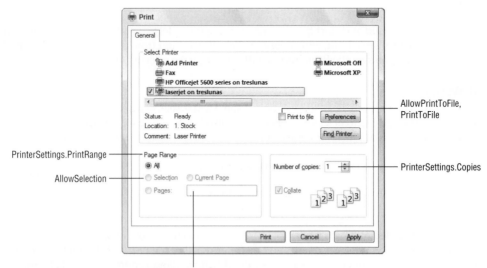

Figure 17-25

Print Preview

You can use Print Preview so that users can see what the printout will look like. Implementing Print Preview is easy in .NET — you can use a `PrintPreviewControl` class to preview the document inside a form to show how it will be printed. The `PrintPreviewDialog` is a dialog that wraps the control.

PrintPreviewDialog

If you look at the properties and inheritance list from the MSDN documentation of the `PrintPreviewDialog` class, you can see that it is actually a `Form` and not a wrapped common dialog — the class derives from `System.Windows.Forms.Form`, and you can work with it as you did with the forms you created in Chapter 15. In the following Try It Out, you add a `PrintPreviewDialog` class to the SimpleEditor application.

Try It Out   Adding a PrintPreviewDialog

1.   Add a `PrintPreviewDialog` component from the Toolbox to the Windows Forms Designer. Set the `Name` to `dlgPrintPreview` and the `Document` property to `printDocument`.

2.   Add and implement a handler for the `Click` event of the Print Preview menu entry:

```
private void OnFilePrintPreview(object sender, EventArgs e)
{
    dlgPrintPreview.ShowDialog();
}
```

3.   Start the application to see the Print preview, shown in Figure 17-26.

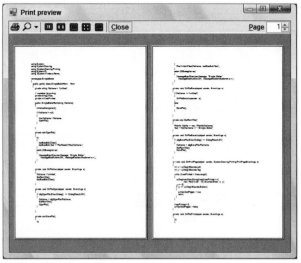

Figure 17-26

PrintPreviewControl

Print Preview in Microsoft Word and WordPad is different from the PrintPreviewDialog in that the preview in these applications doesn't show up in its own dialog, but in the main window of the application.

To do the same, you can place the PrintPreviewControl class in your form. The Document property must be set to the printDocument object, and the Visible property to false. When you want to display the print preview, you simply set the Visible property to true. Then the PrintPreviewControl is in front of the other control, as shown in Figure 17-27.

Figure 17-27

You can see from the title and the single File menu item that the main window of the SimpleEditor application is displayed. You still need to add some elements to control the PrintPreviewControl class to do zooming, printing, and to display several pages of text at once. A specific toolbar can be used to make these features available. The PrintPreviewDialog class already has this implemented, as shown in the four-page preview shown in Figure 17-28.

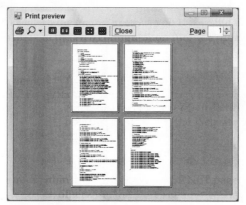

Figure 17-28

FontDialog and ColorDialog

The last dialogs you look at in this chapter are the `FontDialog` and the `ColorDialog`.

This chapter discusses these dialogs in terms of setting font and color. The Font *and* Color *classes are covered in Chapter 30.*

FontDialog

The `FontDialog` enables users to choose a font, including style, size, and color. Figure 17-29 shows the properties that change the behavior of the elements in the dialog.

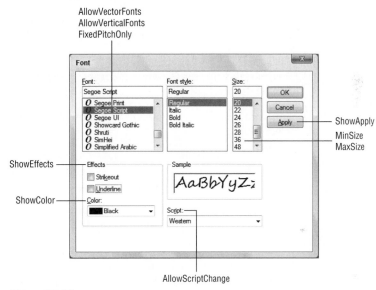

Figure 17-29

How to Use the FontDialog

The dialog can be used in the same way as the previous dialogs. In the Windows Forms Designer, the dialog can be dragged from the Toolbox and dropped to the form so that an instance of the `FontDialog` is created.

The code to use the `FontDialog` looks like this:

```
if (dlgFont.ShowDialog() == DialogResult.OK)
{
    textBoxEdit.Font = dlgFont.Font;
}
```

The `FontDialog` is displayed by calling the `ShowDialog()` method. If the user presses the OK button, `DialogResult.OK` is returned from the method. The selected font can be read by using the `Font` property of the `FontDialog` class; this font is then passed to the `Font` property of the `TextBox`.

Properties of the FontDialog

You have already seen an image showing the properties of the `FontDialog` class, but the following table shows how these properties are used:

Property	Description
AllowVectorFonts	Boolean value that defines whether vector fonts can be selected in the font list. The default is `true`.
AllowVerticalFonts	Boolean value that defines whether vertical fonts can be selected in the font list. Vertical texts are used in Far Eastern countries. There probably isn't a vertical font installed on your system. The default is `true`.
FixedPitchOnly	Setting the property `FixedPitchOnly` displays only fixed-pitch fonts in the font list. With a fixed-pitch font, every character is the same size. The default is `false`.
MaxSize	Specifying a value for the `MaxSize` property defines the maximum font size the user can select.
MinSize	Similar to `MaxSize`, you can set the minimum font size the user can select with `MinSize`.
ShowApply	If the Apply button should be displayed, then you have to set the `ShowApply` property to `true`. By pressing the Apply button, users can see an updated font in the application without leaving the font dialog.
ShowColor	By default, the color selection is not shown in the dialog. If you want users to select the font color in the font dialog, then set the `ShowColor` property to `true`.
ShowEffects	By default, users can select the Strikeout and Underline check boxes to manipulate the font. If you don't want these options to be displayed, then set the `ShowEffects` property to `false`.
AllowScriptChange	Setting the `AllowScriptChange` property to `false` prevents users from changing the script of a font. The available scripts depend on the selected font. For example, the font Arial supports Western, Hebrew, Arabic, Greek, Turkish, Baltic, Central European, Cyrillic, and Vietnamese scripts.

Enabling the Apply Button

Unlike the other dialogs presented so far, the `FontDialog` supports an Apply button, which is not displayed by default. If the user presses the Apply button, then the dialog stays open, but the font should be applied.

By selecting the `FontDialog` in the Windows Forms Designer, you can set the `ShowApply` property in the Properties window to `true`. How are you informed when the user presses the Apply button? The dialog is still open, so the `ShowDialog()` method will not return. Instead, you can add an event handler to the `Apply` event of the `FontDialog` class. To do this, press the Events button in the Properties window, and write a handler name to the `Apply` event.

As shown in the following code, I have entered the name `OnApplyFontDialog`. In this handler, you can access the selected font of the `FontDialog` using the member variable of the `FontDialog` class:

```
private void OnApplyFontDialog(object sender, System.EventArgs e)
{
    textBoxEdit.Font = dlgFont.Font;
}
```

ColorDialog

There isn't as much to configure in the `ColorDialog` as there was for the `FontDialog`. The `ColorDialog` makes it possible to configure custom colors if none of the basic colors are wanted. This is done by setting the `AllowFullOpen` property. The custom color configuration part of the dialog can also be automatically expanded with the `FullOpen` property. If `AllowFullOpen` is false, then the value of `FullOpen` will be ignored. The `SolidColorOnly` property specifies that only solid colors can be selected. The `CustomColors` property can be used to get and set the configured custom color values.

Figure 17-30 shows the color dialog and the properties that influence the dialog.

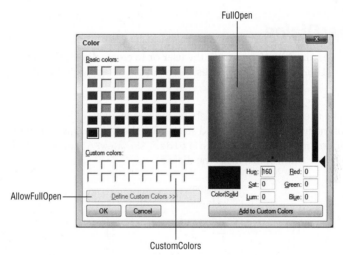

Figure 17-30

How to Use the ColorDialog

The `ColorDialog` can be dragged from the Toolbox and dropped onto the form in the Windows Forms Designer, as you have done with the other dialogs. `ShowDialog()` displays the dialog until the user presses the OK or Cancel button. You can read the selected color by accessing the `Color` property of the dialog, as shown in the following code example:

```
if (dlgColor.ShowDialog() == DialogResult.OK)
{
    textBoxEdit.ForeColor = dlgColor.Color;
}
```

Properties of the ColorDialog

The properties used to influence the look of the dialog are summarized in the following table:

Properties	Description
AllowFullOpen	Setting this property to `false` disables the Define Custom Colors button, thus preventing users from defining custom colors. The default value of this property is `true`.
FullOpen	Setting the `FullOpen` property to `true` before the dialog is displayed opens the dialog with the custom color selection automatically displayed.
AnyColor	Setting this property to `true` shows all available colors in the list of basic colors.
CustomColors	With the `CustomColors` property you can preset an array of custom colors, and you can read the custom colors defined by the user.
SolidColorOnly	By setting the `SolidColorOnly` property to `true` the user can select solid colors only.

FolderBrowserDialog

A simple dialog to get directory names from the user or to create directories is the `FolderBrowserDialog`. Just a few properties are available to configure this dialog, shown in Figure 17-31.

`Description` can be used to define the text above the tree view. `RootFolder` defines the folder where the user's search of the folder to select should start. With the `RootFolder` property, you can set a value from the enumeration `Environment.SpecialFolder`. `ShowNewFolderButton` defines whether the user is allowed to create a new folder with the dialog.

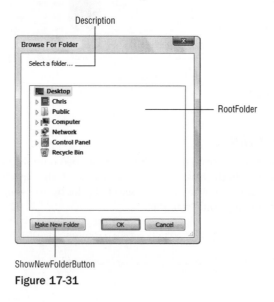

Figure 17-31

How to Use the Folder Browser Dialog

The `FolderBrowserDialog` can be dragged from the Toolbox and dropped onto the form in the Windows Forms Designer, as you have done previously. `ShowDialog()` displays the dialog until the user presses either OK or Cancel. You can read the path selected by the user using the `SelectedPath` property, as shown in the following code example:

```
dlgFolderBrowser.Description = "Select a directory";
if (dlgFolderBrowser.ShowDialog() == DialogResult.OK)
{
    MessageBox.Show("The folder " +
        dlgFolderBrowser.SelectedPath + " was selected");
}
```

Properties of the Folder Browser Dialog

The properties influencing the behavior of the dialog are summarized in the following table:

Property	Description
Description	With the `Description` property you can define the text that appears above the tree view of the dialog.
RootFolder	With the `RootFolder` property you can set the path where the browsing should start.
SelectedPath	The property `SelectedPath` returns the path of the directory selected by the user.
ShowNewFolderButton	By setting the `ShowNewFolderButton` to true, the user can create a new folder.

Summary

This chapter has explained how to use the dialog classes in applications. You looked at how to open and save files, and after reviewing the .NET Framework printing classes, you learned how to add printing capabilities to your applications. To summarize, the SimpleEditor application used the following dialog classes:

❑   `FileOpenDialog` — to enable users to open a file.

❑   `FileSaveDialog`–to ask for a filename to save the data.

❑   `PrintDialog`–to enable the printer and the printing configurations.

❑   `PageSetupDialog`–to modify the margins of the page to be printed.

❑   `PrintPreviewDialog`–to view a preview of the printed page so that users know in advance how the page will look.

❑   `FolderBrowserDialog`–to select and create directories.

The chapter also described the basics of the `FontDialog` and `ColorDialog` classes. In the exercises, you can extend the SimpleEditor application to use these dialogs as well.

The next chapter shows how Windows applications such as the SimpleEditor can be deployed on target systems using ClickOnce and the Windows installer.

Exercises

Because the `FontDialog` and the `ColorDialog` function like the other dialogs discussed in this chapter, it's an easy job to add these dialogs to the SimpleEditor application:

1.   Enable users to change the font of the text box. Add to the main menu a new menu item, F&ormat, and a submenu for Format: &Font.... Add a handler to this menu item. Next, add a `FontDialog` to the application with the help of the Windows Forms Designer. Display this dialog in the menu handler, and set the `Font` property of the text box to the selected font.

You also have to change the implementation of the `OnPrintPage()` method to use the selected font for a printout. In the previous implementation you created a new `Font` object in the `DrawString()` method of the `Graphics` object. Now, use the font of the `textBoxEdit` object by accessing the `Font` property instead. Be aware of a font location problem if the user chooses a big font. To prevent one line from partly overwriting the line above/below, change the fixed value you used to change the vertical position of the lines. A better way to do this would be to use the size of the font to change the vertical increment: Use the `Height` property of the `Font` class.

2.   Another great extension to the SimpleEditor application would be to change the font color. Add a second submenu to the Format menu entry: Color.... Add a handler to this menu entry that opens a `ColorDialog`. If the user presses the OK button, set the selected color of the `ColorDialog` to the `ForeColor` property of the text box.

In the `OnPrintPage()` method, make sure that the chosen color is used only if the printer supports colors. Check the color support of the printer with the `PageSettings.Color` property of the `PrintPageEventArgs` argument. You can create a brush object with the color of the text box with the following:

```
Brush brush = new SolidBrush(textBoxEdit.ForeColor);
```

This brush can then be used as an argument in the `DrawString()` method instead of the black brush used previously.

Deploying Windows Applications

There are several ways to install Windows applications. Simple applications can be installed with a basic xcopy deployment, but for installation to hundreds of clients, an xcopy deployment is not really useful. For that situation, you have two options: ClickOnce deployment or the Microsoft Windows Installer.

With ClickOnce deployment, the application is installed by clicking a link to a Web site. In situations where the user should select a directory in which to install the application, or when some registry entries are required, the Windows Installer is the deployment option to use.

This chapter covers both options for installing Windows applications. In particular, you will look at the following:

❑ Deployment basics

❑ ClickOnce deployment

❑ Visual Studio deployment and setup project types

❑ Features of the Windows Installer

❑ Creating Windows Installer packages using Visual Studio 2008

Deployment Overview

Deployment is the process of installing applications to the target systems. Traditionally, such an installation has been done by invoking a setup program. If a hundred or thousand clients must be installed, the installation can be very time-consuming. To alleviate this, the system administrator can create batch scripts to automate this activity. However, particularly if the application logic changes regularly, problems can occur with clients that don't have network access, along with incompatibilities among different library versions, resulting in a condition known as *DLL hell*.

DLL hell describes the problems that occur when each of several installed applications requires different versions of the same DLL. If one application installs a DLL that overwrites a different version of the same DLL, applications requiring the overwritten DLL might break.

Because of these problems, many companies have converted their intranet applications to Web applications, even though Windows applications offer a much richer user interface. Web applications just need to be deployed to the server, and the client automatically gets the up-to-date user interface.

With .NET, DLL hell is avoided by using private and shared assemblies. Private assemblies are copied with every application, so there can't be a conflict with assemblies from other applications. Shared assemblies have a strong name that includes the version number. Multiple versions of the same assembly can coexist on the same system.

.NET 1.0 supported a technology known as *no-touch deployment*. With no-touch deployment, it was possible for users to automatically install an application by clicking a link on a Web page. However, .NET 1.0 no-touch deployment had some security issues, and it was missing many features that are required with many client applications — clearly, this was a version 1 release. These issues were solved with the ClickOnce deployment technology that was new with .NET 2.0.

Like no-touch deployment, with ClickOnce deployment the application can be installed by clicking a link inside a Web page. The user on the client system doesn't need administrative privileges, as the application is installed in a user-specific directory. With ClickOnce, you can install applications with a rich user interface. The application is installed to the client, so there's no need to remain connected with the client system after the installation is completed. In other words, the application can be used offline. Now, an application icon is available from the Start menu, the security issues are easier to resolve, and the application can easily be uninstalled.

A nice feature of ClickOnce is that updates can happen automatically when the client application starts or as a background task while the client application is running.

However, there are some restrictions accompanying ClickOnce deployment: ClickOnce cannot be used if you need to install shared components in the global assembly cache, if the application needs COM components that require registry settings, or if you want users to decide in what directory the application should be installed. In such cases, you must use the Windows Installer, which is the traditional way to install Windows applications. Before working with the Windows Installer packages, however, we'll take a look at ClickOnce deployment.

ClickOnce Deployment

With ClickOnce deployment there is no need to start a setup program on the client system. All the client system's user has to do is click a link on a Web page, and the application is automatically installed. After the application is installed, the client can be offline — it doesn't need to access the server from which the application was installed.

ClickOnce installation can be done from a Web site, a UNC share, or a file location (e.g., a CD). With ClickOnce, the application is installed on the client system, it is available with Start menu shortcuts, and it can be uninstalled from the Add/Remove Programs dialog.

ClickOnce deployment is described by *manifest files*. The application manifest describes the application and permissions required by the application. The deployment manifest describes deployment configuration such as update policies. In the Try It Out examples of the ClickOnce section, you configure ClickOnce deployment for the simple editor you created in Chapter 17.

Successfully deploying the assembly across the network requires the manifest that is used with the installation to have a certificate showing the user installing the application the organization that created the installation program. In the following Try It Out, you create a certificate that is associated with the ClickOnce manifests.

Try It Out　　**Signing the ClickOnce Manifests**

1. Open the SimpleEditor sample from Chapter 17 with Visual Studio. If you didn't create the sample yourself, copy it from the downloadable files.

2. Select Properties for the project in the Solution Explorer, and select the Signing tab, shown in Figure 18-1.

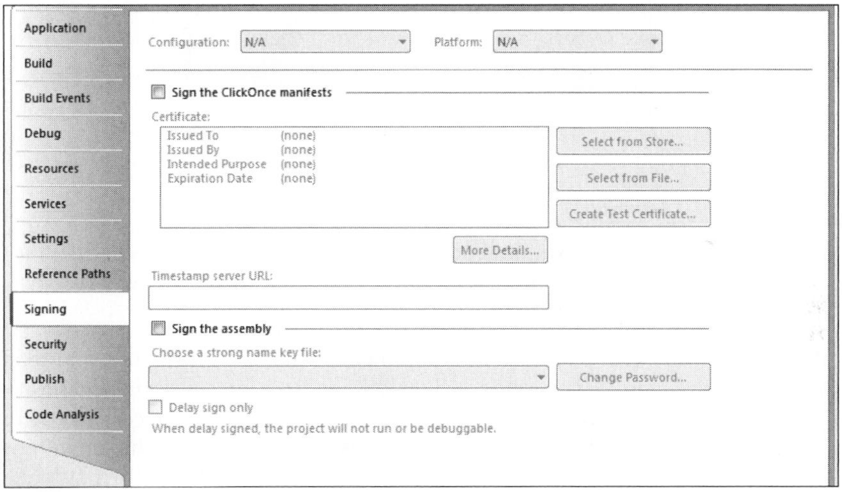

Figure 18-1

3. Check the Sign the ClickOnce Manifests check box.

4. Click the Create Test Certificate button to create a test certificate that is associated with the ClickOnce manifests. Enter a password for the certificate as requested. You must remember the password for later settings. Then click OK.

5. Click the More Details button for certificate information (see Figure 18-2).

Figure 18-2

How It Works

A certificate is used so that the user installing the application can identify the creator of the installation package. By reading the certificate, the users can decide if they can trust the installation to approve the security requirements.

With the test certificate you just created, the user doesn't get real trust information and receives a warning that this certificate cannot be trusted, as you will see later. Such a certificate is for testing only. Before you make the application ready for deployment, you have to get a real certificate from a certification authority such as VeriSign. If the application is only deployed within an intranet, then you can also get a certificate from a local certificate server if one is installed with your local network. The Microsoft Certificate Server can be installed with Windows Server 2003 or 2008. If you have such a certificate, you can configure it by clicking Select from File within the Signing tab.

In the next Try It Out, you configure the permission requirements of the assembly. When the assembly is installed on the client, the required permissions must be approved.

Try It Out	**Defining the Permission Requirements**

1. Select Properties for the project in the Solution Explorer, select Security, as shown in Figure 18-3, and select Enable ClickOnce Security Settings.

Figure 18-3

2. Click the This Is A Partial Trust Application radio button.

3. Select the zone (Custom), as special security permissions are required by the application.

4. Click the Calculate Permissions button to calculate the permissions that are required by the application.

5. If the permission `FileIOPermission` is not included with the calculation, change the setting to include it.

How It Works

Security is an important aspect of .NET applications. .NET uses evidence-based security to define what assemblies are allowed to do.

On the one hand, resources should be secured. Examples of such resources are files and directories, networking sockets, and environment variables. For all these resources, .NET permissions exist that allow access to them. One example is the `FileIOPermission` class, which can be used to allow access to the complete file system or to specific files and directories.

On the other hand, you must define who is allowed to use these resources. Here, assemblies are grouped into different categories, such as assemblies that are installed locally, and assemblies that are loaded from the network. You can also define a category of assemblies from a specific manufacturer.

For more information about evidence-based security, see the book Professional C# 2008 *(Wiley, 2008).*

The Calculate Permissions button from the Security properties of Visual Studio analyzes the code used by the application to check the application's permission requirements. The result of this analysis is an application manifest that includes all required permissions. With Visual Studio 2008, you can see the application manifest, named `app.manifest`, below Properties in the Solution Explorer. The content of this file is shown here:

```xml
<?xml version="1.0" encoding="utf-8"?>
<asmv1:assembly manifestVersion="1.0" xmlns="urn:schemas-microsoft-com:asm.v1"
xmlns:asmv1="urn:schemas-microsoft-com:asm.v1" xmlns:asmv2="urn:schemas-
microsoft-com:asm.v2" xmlns:xsi="http://www.w3.org/2001/XMLSchema-instance">
  <assemblyIdentity version="1.0.0.0" name="MyApplication.app" />
  <trustInfo xmlns="urn:schemas-microsoft-com:asm.v2">
    <security>
      <requestedPrivileges xmlns="urn:schemas-microsoft-com:asm.v3">
        <!-- UAC Manifest Options
            If you want to change the Windows User Account Control level
            replace the requestedExecutionLevel node with one of the following.

        <requestedExecutionLevel  level="asInvoker" />
        <requestedExecutionLevel  level="requireAdministrator" />
        <requestedExecutionLevel  level="highestAvailable" />

            If you want to utilize File and Registry Virtualization for backward
            compatibility then delete the requestedExecutionLevel node.
        -->
        <requestedExecutionLevel level="asInvoker" />
      </requestedPrivileges>
      <applicationRequestMinimum>
        <defaultAssemblyRequest permissionSetReference="Custom" />
        <PermissionSet class="System.Security.PermissionSet" version="1"
            ID="Custom" SameSite="site">
          <IPermission class="System.Security.Permissions.FileIOPermission,
              mscorlib, Version=2.0.0.0, Culture=neutral,
              PublicKeyToken=b77a5c561934e089" version="1" Unrestricted="true" />
          <IPermission class="System.Security.Permissions.ReflectionPermission,
              mscorlib, Version=2.0.0.0, Culture=neutral,
              PublicKeyToken=b77a5c561934e089" version="1" Unrestricted="true" />
          <IPermission class="System.Security.Permissions.SecurityPermission,
              mscorlib, Version=2.0.0.0, Culture=neutral,
              PublicKeyToken=b77a5c561934e089" version="1"
              Flags="UnmanagedCode, Execution, ControlEvidence" />
          <IPermission class="System.Security.Permissions.UIPermission,
              mscorlib, Version=2.0.0.0, Culture=neutral,
              PublicKeyToken=b77a5c561934e089" version="1" Window="AllWindows"
              Clipboard="OwnClipboard" />
          <IPermission class="System.Security.Permissions.KeyContainerPermission,
```

```
                    mscorlib, Version=2.0.0.0, Culture=neutral,
                    PublicKeyToken=b77a5c561934e089" version="1" Unrestricted="true" />
            </PermissionSet>
          </applicationRequestMinimum>
        </security>
      </trustInfo>
    </asmv1:assembly>
```

The XML element `<applicationRequestMinimum>` defines all required permissions of the application. The `FileIOPermission` is required because the application reads and writes files using classes from the `System.IO` namespace. By selecting a different zone in the Security dialog, you can verify whether the application needs permissions that are not available within the zone.

With the defined security requirements, you can start to publish the application by creating a deployment manifest. This can easily be done with the Publish Wizard, as shown in the following Try It Out.

Try It Out   More Publish Configuration Options

1.   Select the Publish tab with the project properties. Click the Options button to open the Publish Options dialog (see Figure 18-4). Enter the product name, the publisher name, a support URL, and a deployment Web page.

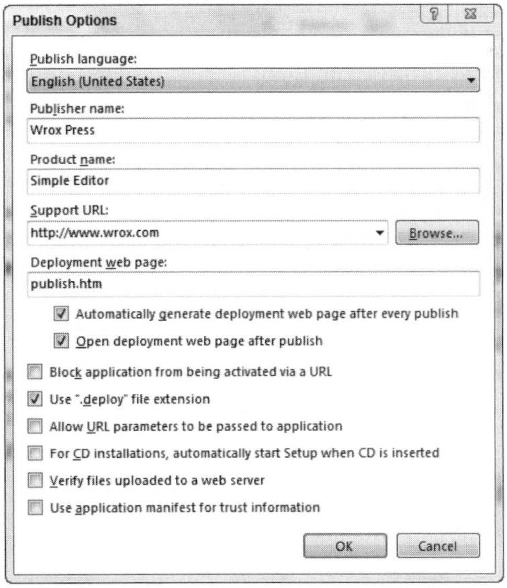

Figure 18-4

2. Configure the Update options by selecting the Updates button and select the The Application Should Check for Updates check box, as shown in Figure 18-5.

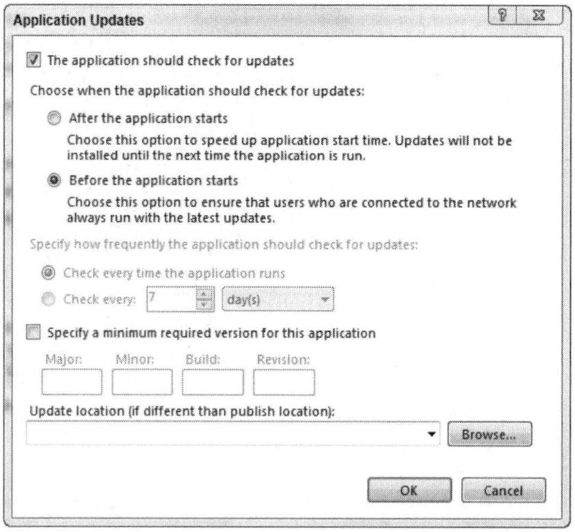

Figure 18-5

Try It Out   **Using the Publish Wizard**

1. Start the Publish Wizard by selecting Build ⇨ Publish SimpleEditor. Enter a path to the Web site `http://localhost/SimpleEditor`, as shown in Figure 18-6. Click the Next button.

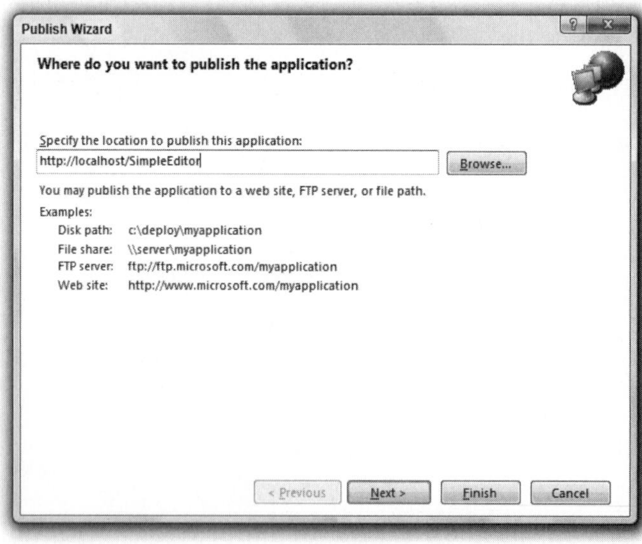

Figure 18-6

To publish the application to a Web server on Windows Vista, Visual Studio 2008 must be started in elevated mode with administrative privileges; and Internet Information Server (IIS) needs to be installed. If you do not have IIS installed, select publishing to the local file system.

2. At step 2 in the Publish Wizard, select "Yes, this application will be available online or offline," as shown in Figure 18-7. Click the Next button.

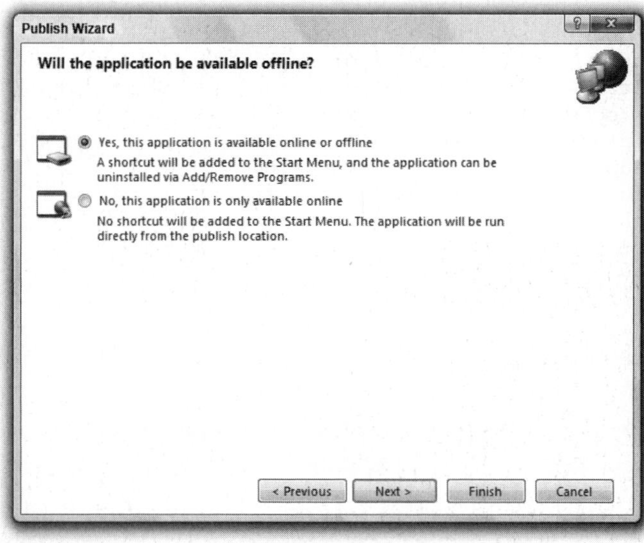

Figure 18-7

3. The last dialog gives summary information, as you are Ready to Publish! (see Figure 18-8). Click the Finish button.

Figure 18-8

How It Works

The Publish Wizard creates a Web site on the local Internet Information Services Web server. The assemblies of the application (executables and libraries), as well as the application and deployment manifests, a `setup.exe`, and a sample Web page, `publish.htm`, are copied to the Web server. The deployment manifest describes installation information, as shown here. With Visual Studio, you can open the deployment manifest by opening the file `SimpleEditor.application` in the Solution Explorer. With this manifest you can see a dependency to the application manifest with the XML element `<dependentAssembly>`:

```xml
<assemblyIdentity name="SimpleEditor.application" version="1.0.0.0"
publicKeyToken="74fe8381193333a9" language="en-US" processorArchitecture="msi
l" xmlns="urn:schemas-microsoft-com:asm.v1" />
  <description asmv2:publisher="Wrox Press" asmv2:product="SimpleEditor"
    asmv2:supportUrl="http://www.wrox.com"
    xmlns="urn:schemas-microsoft-com:asm.v1" />
  <deployment install="true" mapFileExtensions="true">
    <subscription>
      <update>
        <beforeApplicationStartup />
      </update>
    </subscription>
  </deployment>
  <dependency>
    <dependentAssembly dependencyType="install"
        codebase="Application Files\SimpleEditor_1_0_0_0\SimpleEditor.exe.manifest"
        size="8241">
    <assemblyIdentity name="SimpleEditor.exe" version="1.0.0.0"
        publicKeyToken=" 7815ea8568895047" language="neutral"
        processorArchitecture="msil" type="win32" />
    <hash>
      <dsig:Transforms>
        <dsig:Transform Algorithm=
            "urn:schemas-microsoft-com:HashTransforms.Identity" />
      </dsig:Transforms>
      <dsig:DigestMethod Algorithm="http://www.w3.org/2000/09/xmldsig#sha1" />
      <dsig:DigestValue>yMedux2GteUPg/c/LbS9WgXXeqs=</dsig:DigestValue>
    </hash>
    </dependentAssembly>
  </dependency>
```

By selecting the option shown in Figure 18-7, you specify that the application will be available online and offline. That way, the application is installed on the client system and can be accessed from the Start menu. You can also use Add/Remove Programs to uninstall the application. If you instead indicate that the application should be available only online, users must always click the Web site link to load the application from the server and start it locally.

The files that belong to the application are defined by the project output. To see the application files with the Properties of the application in the Publish settings, click the Application Files button. The Application Files dialog opens (see Figure 18-9).

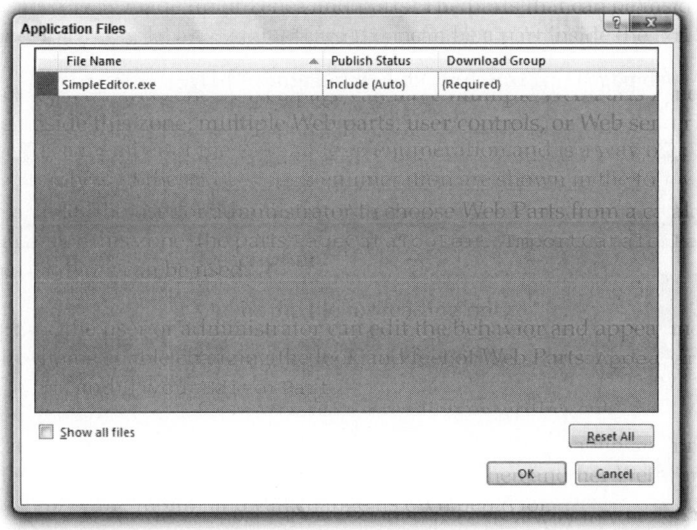

Figure 18-9

The prerequisites of the application are defined with the Prerequisites dialog (see Figure 18-10), accessed by clicking the Prerequisites button. With .NET 3.5 applications, the prerequisite .NET Framework 3.5 is automatically detected, as the figure shows. You can select other prerequisites with this dialog.

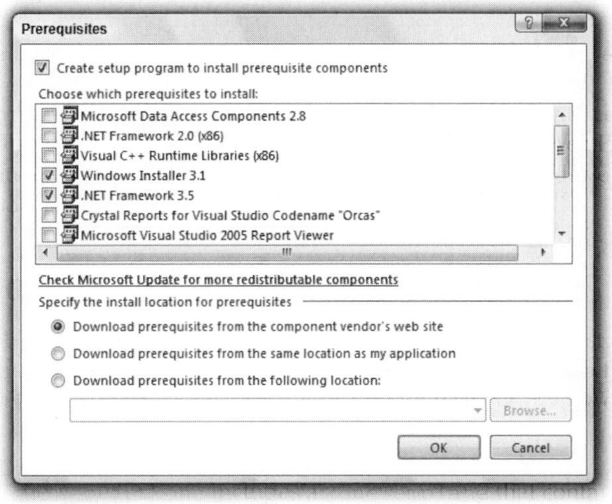

Figure 18-10

Now you can install the application by following the steps in the next Try It Out.

Try It Out — Installing the Application

1. Open the Web page `publish.htm`, shown in Figure 18-11.

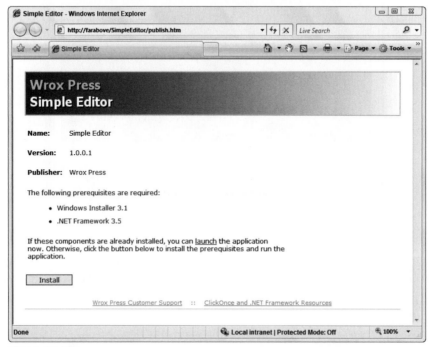

Figure 18-11

2. Click the Install button to install the application. A security warning will pop up (see Figure 18-12).

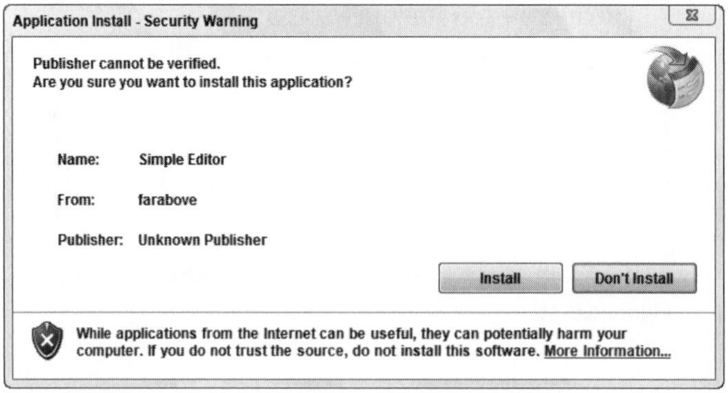

Figure 18-12

3. Click the More Information link to see the potential security issues with the application. Read the categories of this dialog, shown in Figure 18-13.

Application Install - More Information

🛡 **Publisher**
The publisher of this application cannot be verified. Only run applications from publishers that you trust.

🛡 **Machine Access**
This application will gain access to additional resources on your computer, such as your file system or your network connection. This may put your computer at risk. Do not approve unless you trust the application's publisher.

ⓘ **Installation**
This application will be installed on your computer. It will add a shortcut to your Start menu and will be added to the Add or Remove Programs list.

🛡 **Location**
This application comes from the Local Network. Only run applications from locations that you trust.

[Close]

Figure 18-13

4. After reading the dialog information, click the Close button and then click the Install button of the Application Install dialog.

How It Works

When the file `publish.htm` is opened, the target application is checked for version 3.5 of the .NET runtime. This check is done by a JavaScript function inside the HTML page. If the runtime is not there, it is installed together with the client application. With the default publish settings, the runtime is copied to the Web server.

By clicking the link to install the application, the deployment manifest is opened to install the application. Next, the user is informed about some possible security issues of the application. If the user clicks OK, the application is installed.

Updates

With the update options you configured earlier, the client application automatically checks the Web server for a new version. In the following Try It Out, you try such a scenario with the SimpleEditor application.

Try It Out   **Updating the Application**

1. Make a change to the SimpleEditor application that shows up immediately, such as setting the background color of the text box.

2. Build the application and click the Publish Now button with the Publish section of the project properties.

3. Do not click the `publish.htm` link on the Web page; instead, start the client application from the Start menu. When the application is started, the Update Available dialog shown in Figure 18-14 appears, asking whether a new version should be downloaded. Click OK to download the new version. When the new version launches, you can see the application with the colored text box.

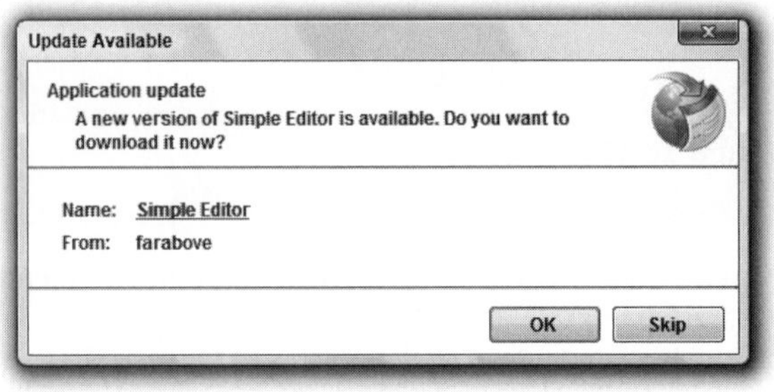

Figure 18-14

How It Works

The update policy is defined by a setting in the deployment manifest with the XML `<update>` element. You can change the update policy by clicking the Updates button with the Publish settings. Remember to access the Publish settings with the properties of the project. The Application Updates dialog is shown in Figure 18-15.

Use this dialog to specify whether the client should look for updates at all. If updates should be checked, then you can define whether the check should happen before the application starts or whether the update should occur in the background while the application is running. If the update should occur in the background, you can set the time interval between them: with every start of the application or with a specific number of hours, days, or weeks.

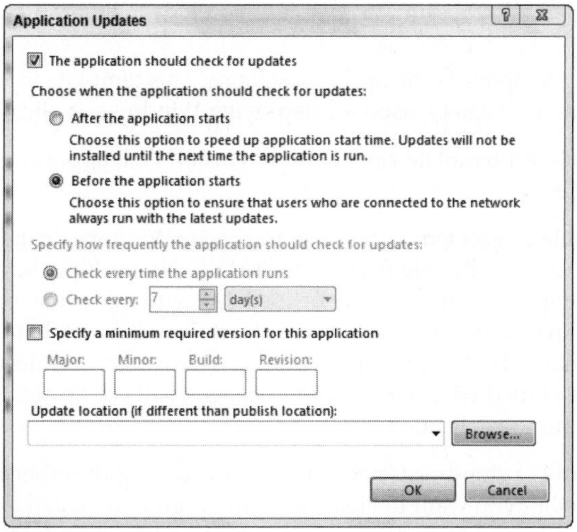

Application Updates

☑ The application should check for updates

Choose when the application should check for updates:

○ After the application starts

Choose this option to speed up application start time. Updates will not be installed until the next time the application is run.

◉ Before the application starts

Choose this option to ensure that users who are connected to the network always run with the latest updates.

Specify how frequently the application should check for updates:

◉ Check every time the application runs

○ Check every: 7 ▲▼ day(s) ▼

☐ Specify a minimum required version for this application

Major: Minor: Build: Revision:

[ ] [ ] [ ] [ ]

Update location (if different than publish location):

[ ] ▼ [Browse...]

[OK] [Cancel]

Figure 18-15

Visual Studio Setup and Deployment Project Types

Start the Visual Studio Add New Project dialog and select Setup and Deployment from the Project Types pane. The screen shown in Figure 18-16 is displayed.

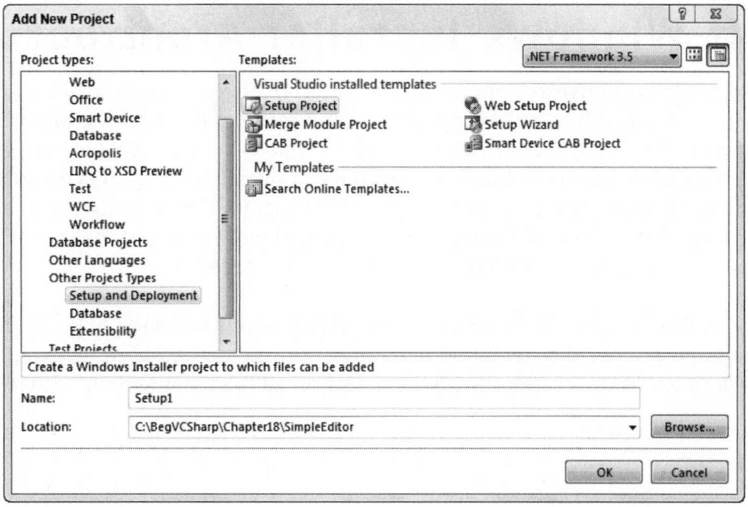

Add New Project

Project types:

- Web
- Office
- Smart Device
- Database
- Acropolis
- LINQ to XSD Preview
- Test
- WCF
- Workflow
- Database Projects
- Other Languages
- Other Project Types
  - **Setup and Deployment**
  - Database
  - Extensibility
- Test Projects

Templates: .NET Framework 3.5 ▼

Visual Studio installed templates

- Setup Project
- Merge Module Project
- CAB Project
- Web Setup Project
- Setup Wizard
- Smart Device CAB Project

My Templates

- Search Online Templates...

Create a Windows Installer project to which files can be added

Name: Setup1

Location: C:\BegVCSharp\Chapter18\SimpleEditor ▼ [Browse...]

[OK] [Cancel]

Figure 18-16

The following list describes the project types and what can be done with them:

❑ The Setup Project template is the one you will use. This template is used to create Windows Installer packages, so it can be used for deploying Windows applications.

❑ The Web Setup Project template can be used to install Web applications. This project template is used in Chapter 23.

❑ The Merge Module Project template is used to create Windows Installer merge modules. A merge module is an installer file that can be included in multiple Microsoft Installer installation packages. For components that should be installed with more than one installation program, a merge module can be created to include this module in the installation packages. One example of a merge module is the .NET runtime itself: It is delivered in a merge module, so the .NET runtime can be included with the installer package of an application. You will use a merge module in the sample application.

❑ The Setup Wizard is a step-by-step technique for choosing the other templates. You first need to ask yourself whether you want to create a setup program to install an application or a redistributable package. Depending on your choice, a Windows Installer package, a merge module, or a CAB file is created.

❑ The Cab Project template enables you to create cabinet files. Cabinet files can be used to merge multiple assemblies into a single file and compress it. Because the cabinet files can be compressed, a Web client can download a smaller file from the server.

Creating components is beyond the scope of this book, so you won't create cabinet projects here. See Professional C# 2008 (Wiley, 2008) for information on creating .NET components for download from a Web server.

❑ The Smart Device Cab Project template can be used to create an installer package for smart device applications.

Microsoft Windows Installer Architecture

Before the Windows Installer existed, programmers had to create custom installation programs. Not only was it more work to build such installation programs, but many of them didn't follow the Windows rules. Often, system DLLs were overwritten with older versions because the installation program didn't check the version. In addition, the directory to which the application files were copied was often wrong. If, for example, a hard-coded directory string such as C:\Program Files was used and the system administrator changed the default drive letter or an international version of the operating system was used where this directory is named differently, the installation failed.

The first version of the Windows Installer was released as part of Microsoft Office 2000 and as a distributable package that could be included with other application packages. Version 1.1 was first released with Windows 2000 and added support to register COM+ components. Version 1.2 added support for the file protection mechanism of Windows ME. Version 2.0 was the first version that included support to install .NET assemblies, and it has support for the 64-bit release of Windows as well. With Visual Studio 2008, version 3.1 is used.

Windows Installer Terms

In order to work with the Windows Installer, you need to be familiar with some terms that are used with the Windows Installer technology: packages, features, and components.

> In the context of the Windows Installer, a component is not the same as a component in the .NET Framework. A Windows Installer component is just a single file (or multiple files that logically belong together). Such a file can be an executable, a DLL, or even a simple text file.

As shown in Figure 18-17, a *package* consists of one or more features. A package is a single Microsoft Installer (MSI) database. A *feature* is the user's view of the capabilities of a product and can consist of features and components. A *component* is the developer's view of the installation; it is the smallest unit of installation and consists of one or more files. The differentiation between features and components exists because a single component can be included in multiple features (as shown in Component 2 in the figure). A single feature cannot be included within multiple features.

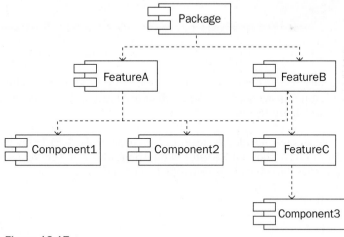

Figure 18-17

Let's look at the features of a real-world example that you should already have: Visual Studio 2008. Using the Add/Remove Programs option in the Control Panel, you can change the installed features of Visual Studio after installation by clicking the Uninstall/Change button, as shown in Figure 18-18.

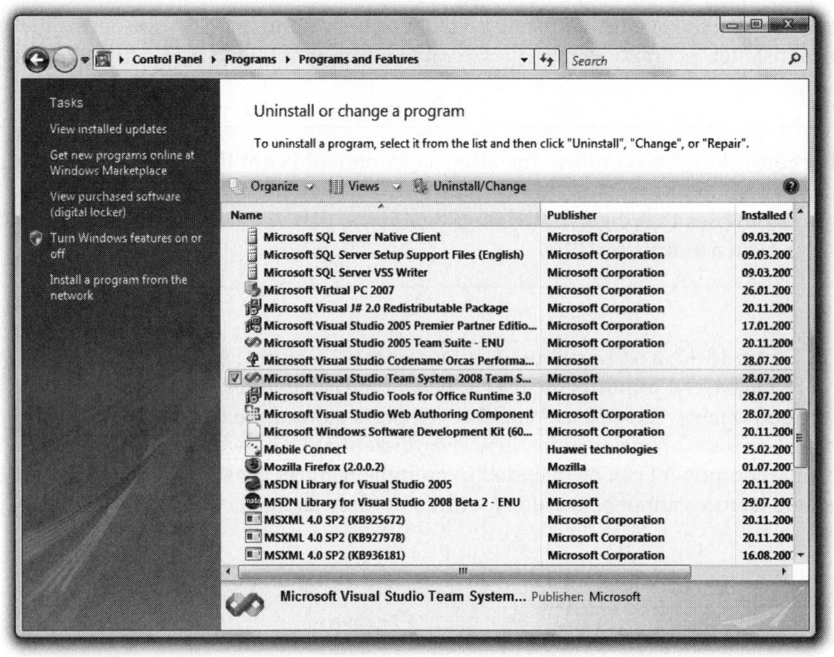

Figure 18-18

By clicking the Uninstall/Change button, you can visit the Visual Studio 2008 Maintenance Wizard. This is a good way to see features in action. Select Add or Remove Features to see the features of the Visual Studio 2008 package (see Figure 18-19).

The Visual Studio 2008 package includes the features Language Tools, .NET Framework SDK, Crystal Reports for Visual Studio 2008, Tools for Redistributing Applications, and Server Components. The Language Tools feature has the subfeatures Visual Basic, Visual C++, and Visual C#.

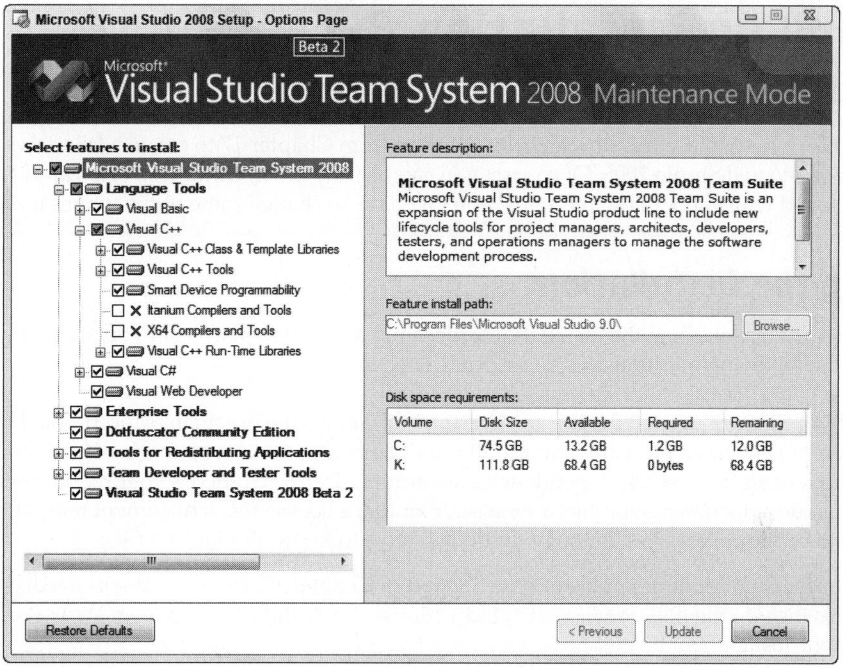

Figure 18-19

Advantages of the Windows Installer

The Windows Installer offers several advantages:

❑ Features can be installed, not installed, or advertised. With *advertisement*, a feature of the package is installed at first use. Maybe you have already seen the Windows Installer starting during your work with Microsoft Word. If you use an advertised feature of Word that was not installed, it will be installed automatically as soon as you use it.

❑ If an application becomes corrupt, it can *self-repair* through the repair feature of Windows Installer packages.

❑ An automatic *rollback* will be performed if the installation fails. After the installation fails, everything is left as before: no additional registry keys, files, and so on are left on the system.

❑ With an *uninstall*, all the relevant files, registry keys, and so on are removed — the application can be completely uninstalled. No temporary files are left out, and the registry is reinstated.

You can read the tables of the MSI database file to find information about such things as what files are copied and what registry keys are written.

Creating an Installation Package for the SimpleEditor

In this section, you will use the SimpleEditor solution from Chapter 17 to create a Windows Installer package using Visual Studio 2008. Of course, you can use any other Windows Forms application you have developed while you follow the steps; you just have to change some of the names used.

Planning the Installation

Before you can start building the installation program, you have to plan what you are going to put in it. Consider the following questions:

❏ **What files are needed for the application?** Of course, the executable and probably some component assemblies are required. It won't be necessary for you to identify all dependencies of these items because the dependencies are automatically included. Other required files might include a documentation file, a `readme.txt` file, a license file, a document template, pictures, and configuration files, among others. You have to know all required files.

For the SimpleEditor application developed in Chapter 17, an executable is needed, and you will also include the files `readme.rtf` and `license.rtf`, and a bitmap from Wrox Press to appear in the installation dialogs.

❏ **What directories should be used?** Application files should be installed in Program Files\ Application name. The Program Files directory is named differently for each language variant of the operating system. In addition, the administrator can choose different paths for this application. It is not necessary to know where this directory is, because there's an API function call to get this directory. With the installer, you can use a special predefined folder to put files in the Program Files directory.

> It's worth making this point again: Under no circumstances should the directories be hard-coded. With international versions, these directories are named differently! Even if your application only supports English versions of Windows (which isn't a good idea), the system administrator could have moved these directories to different drives.

The SimpleEditor application will have the executable in the default application directory unless the installing user selects a different path.

❏ **How should the user access the application?** You can put a shortcut to the executable in the Start menu, or place an icon on the desktop, for example. If you want to place an icon on the desktop, check whether the user is happy with that. With Windows XP, the guideline is to have the desktop as clean as possible. SimpleEditor should be accessible from the Start menu.

❏ **What is the distribution media?** Do you want to put the installation packages on a CD, floppy disks, or a network share?

❑ **What questions should users answer?** Should they accept license information, display a ReadMe file, or enter the path to install? Are some other options required for the installation?

The default dialogs supplied with the Visual Studio 2008 Installer are adequate for the Windows Installer project you create over the remainder of the chapter. You will ask for the directory where the program should be installed (the user may choose a path that is different from the default), show a ReadMe file, and ask the user to accept the license agreement.

Creating the Project

Now that you know what should be in the installation package, you can use the Visual Studio 2008 Installer to create an installer project and add all the files that should be installed. In the following Try It Out, you use the Project Wizard and configure the project.

Try It Out **Creating a Windows Installer Project**

1. Open the solution file of the SimpleEditor project you created in Chapter 17. You will add the installation project to the existing solution. If you didn't create the solution in Chapter 17 yourself (shame on you!), you'll find it in the downloadable code.

2. Add a Setup Project called "SimpleEditorSetup" to the solution with the File ⇨ Add Project ⇨ New Project menu, as shown in Figure 18-20, and click the OK button.

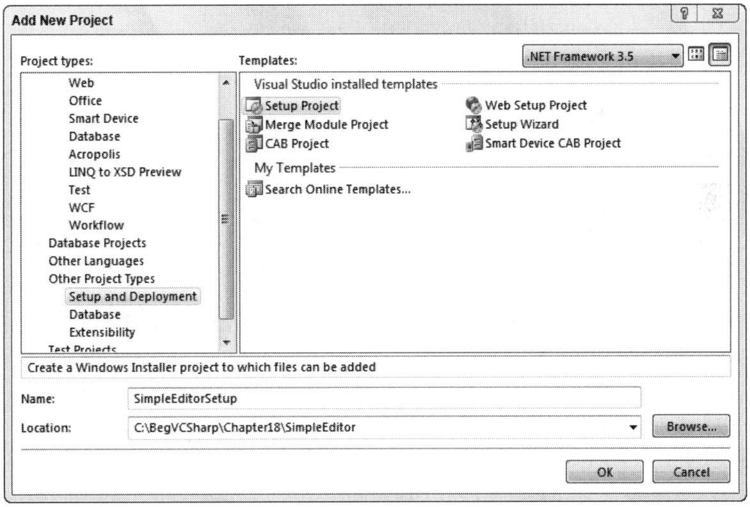

Figure 18-20

Project Properties

Up to this point, you have only a project file for the setup solution. The files to be installed must be defined, but you also have to configure the project properties. To do this, you have to know what the Packaging and Bootstrapper options mean.

Packaging

MSI is where the installation is started, but you can define how the files that are to be installed are packaged using the three options in the dialog shown in Figure 18-21. This dialog opens if you right-click on the SimpleEditorSetup project and select Properties.

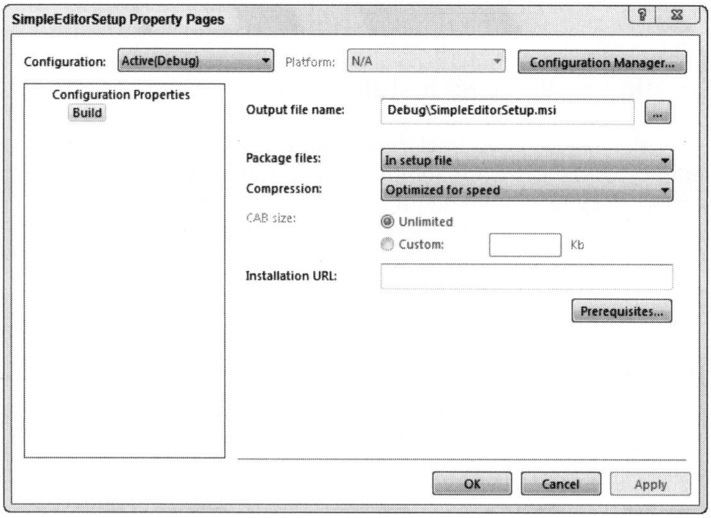

Figure 18-21

Look at the options in the Package Files drop-down list:

❑ The As Loose Uncompressed Files option stores all program and data files as they are. No compressing takes place.

❑ The In Setup File option merges and compresses all the files into the MSI file. This option can be overridden for single components in the package. If you put all your files into a single MSI file, then you have to ensure that the size of the installation program fits in the target you want to use, such as CDs or floppy disks. If you have so many files to install that they exceed the capacity of a single floppy, you can try to change the compression option by selecting the Optimized for Size option from the Compression drop-down list. If the files still don't fit, then choose the next option for packaging.

❑ The third way to package files is In Cabinet File(s). With this method, the MSI file is used just to load and install the CAB files. With CAB files, it is possible to set file sizes that enable installations on CDs or floppy disks (you can set sizes of 1440 KB for installations from floppy disks).

Prerequisites

In the same dialog, you can configure the prerequisites that must be installed before the application can be installed. When you click the Settings button near the Prerequisites URL text box, the Prerequisites dialog appears, as shown in Figure 18-22. As you can see, the .NET Framework 2.0 is selected by default as a prerequisite. If the client system doesn't have the .NET Framework installed, it will be installed from the setup program. You can also select other prerequisite options, as shown in the following list:

❑ **Windows Installer 3.1**: Windows Installer 3.1 is required for installer packages created with Visual Studio 2008. If the target system is Windows Vista or Windows Server 2008, the installer is already on the system. With older systems, the correct version of the Windows Installer might not be there, so you can select this option to include Windows Installer 3.1 with the installation program.

❑ **SQL Server 2005 Express Edition SP2**: If you need a database on the client system, then you can include the SQL Server 2005 Express Edition with the setup program. Accessing SQL Server with ADO.NET is covered in Chapter 24.

❑ **Visual C++ Runtime Libraries (x86)**: If the application uses native libraries that require the C++ runtime libraries, you can add this as a prerequisite.

❑ **Crystal Reports for .NET:** Crystal Reports enables you to create graphical reports. You can read more about Crystal Reports in David McAmis' *Professional Crystal Reports for Visual Studio .NET, Second Edition* (Wiley, 2004).

❑ **Microsoft Data Access Components 2.8**: Microsoft Data Access Components (MDAC) includes the OLE DB provider, ODBC drivers, and the Microsoft SQL Server Network Libraries that are used to access databases. MDAC version 8.0 is part of Windows Server 2003. With .NET 2.0, MDAC is no longer needed; if you are using the .NET Data Provider for SQL Server, only the OLEDB and ODBC data providers require MDAC to be installed.

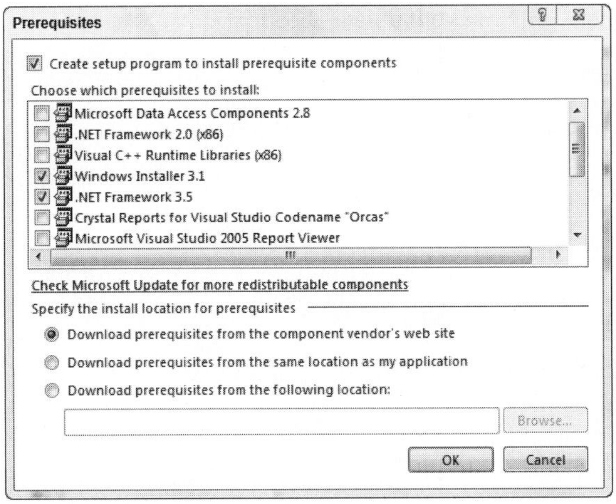

Figure 18-22

Try It Out   **Configuring the Project**

1. Change the Prerequisites option in the Property page that you just saw to include Windows Installer 3.1 so that the application can be installed on systems where Windows Installer 3.1 is not available. Also change the output filename to `WroxSimpleEditor.msi`, as shown in Figure 18-23. Then click OK.

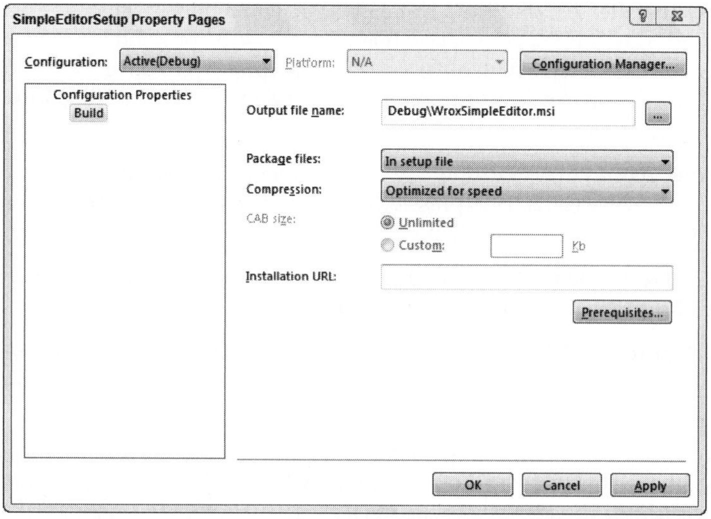

Figure 18-23

2. Using the Properties window, set the project properties to the values in the following table:

Property	Value
Author	Wrox Press
Description	Simple Editor to print and edit text files.
Keywords	Installer, Wrox Press, Simple Editor
Manufacturer	Wrox Press
ManufacturerUrl	http://www.wrox.com
Product Name	Simple Editor
SupportUrl	http://p2p.wrox.com
Title	Installation Demo for Simple Editor
Version	1.0.0

Setup Editors

With a Visual Studio 2008 Setup Project you have six editors available. You can select the editor by opening a deployment project and selecting View ⇨ Editor:

❑ The File System Editor is used to add files to the installation package.

❑ With the Registry Editor, you can create registry keys for the application.

❑ The File Types Editor enables you to register specific file extensions for an application.

❑ With the User Interface Editor you can add and configure dialogs that are shown during installation of the product.

❑ The Custom Actions Editor enables you to start custom programs during installation and uninstallation.

❑ With the Launch Conditions Editor, you can specify requirements for your application — for example, that the .NET runtime already has to be in place.

File System Editor

With the File System Editor, you can add files to the installation package and configure the locations where they should be installed. This editor is opened with the menu options View ⇨ Editor ⇨ File System. Some of the predefined special folders are automatically opened, as shown in Figure 18-24:

Figure 18-24

❑ The Application folder is used to store the executables and libraries. The location is defined as [ProgramFilesFolder]\[*Manufacturer*]\[*ProductName*]. On English language systems, [ProgramFilesFolder] is resolved to C:\Program Files. The directories for [*Manufacturer*] and [*ProductName*] are defined with the Manufacturer and ProductName project properties.

❑ If you want to place an icon on the desktop, the User's Desktop folder can be used. The default path to this folder is C:\Users*username*\Desktop or C:\Users\All Users\Desktop, depending on whether the installation is done for a single user or for all users.

❑ The user will usually start a program from the All Programs menu. The default path is C:\Documents and Settings*username*\Start Menu\Programs. You can put a shortcut to the application in this menu. The shortcut should have a name that includes the company and the application name, so that the user can easily identify the application, such as Microsoft Excel.

Some applications create a submenu where more than one application can be started — for example, Microsoft Visual Studio 2008. According to the Windows guidelines, many programs do this for the wrong reason, listing programs that are not necessary. You shouldn't put an uninstall program in these menus, because this feature is available from Add/Remove Programs in the Control Panel and should be used from there. Nor should a help file be placed in this menu because this should be available directly from the application. Thus, for many applications, it will be adequate to place a shortcut to the application directly in the All Programs menu. The goal of these restrictions is to ensure that the Start menu doesn't become cluttered with too many items.

A great reference to this information can be found in the application specifications paper for Microsoft Windows Vista. You can find these documents at www.microsoft.com/winlogo.

You can add other folders by right-clicking and selecting Add Special Folder. Some of these folders include the following:

❑   The Global Assembly Cache Folder refers to the folder in which you can install shared assemblies. The Global Assembly Cache (GAC) is used for assemblies that should be shared between multiple applications.

❑   The User's Personal Data Folder refers to the user's default folder for storing documents. C:\Users\[username]\My Documents is the default path. This path is the default directory used by Visual Studio to store projects.

❑   The shortcuts placed in the User's Send To Menu extend the Send To context menu when a file is selected. With this context menu the user can typically send a file to the target location, such as the floppy drive, a mail recipient, or the My Documents folder.

Adding Items to Special Folders

You can choose from a list to add items to a special folder by selecting a folder and choosing Action ⇨ Add Special Folder. You can select Project Output, Folder, File, or Assembly. Adding the output of a project to a folder automatically adds the generated output files and a .dll or .exe, depending on whether the added project is a component library or an application. Selecting either Project Output or Assembly automatically adds all dependencies (all referenced assemblies) to the folder.

File Properties

If you select the properties of a file in a folder, then you can set the following properties. Depending on the file types, some of these properties don't apply, and there are additional properties not listed in the following table:

Property	Description
Condition	A condition can be defined with this property to determine whether the selected file should be installed. This can be useful if you want to add this file only for specific operating system versions or if the user must make a selection in a dialog.
Exclude	Can be set to True if this file should not be installed. This way, the file can stay in the project but doesn't install. You can exclude a file if you are sure that it's not a dependency or that it already exists on every system on which the application is deployed.

Property	Description
PackageAs	With `PackageAs`, you can override the default way the file is added to the installer package. For example, if the project configuration says In Setup File, you can change the package configuration with this option to `Loose` for a specific file so that this file will not be added to the MSI database file. This is useful, for example, if you want to add a ReadMe file, which the user should read before starting the installation. Obviously, you would not compress this file even if all the others were compressed.
Permanent	Setting this property to `True` means that the file will stay on the target computer after uninstallation of the product. This can be used for configuration files. You might have already seen this when installing a new version of Microsoft Outlook: If you configure Microsoft Outlook, then uninstall the product and install it again. It's not necessary to configure it again because the configuration from the last install is not deleted.
ReadOnly	This sets the read-only file attribute at installation.
Vital	This property means that the file is essential for the installation of this product. If installation of this file fails, then the complete installation is aborted and a rollback occurs.

Try It Out   Adding Files to the Installer Package

1. Add the primary output of the SimpleEditor project to the Application folder of the installer project using the Project ⇨ Add ⇨ Project Output menu options. In the Add Project Output Group dialog, select Primary Output, as shown in Figure 18-25.

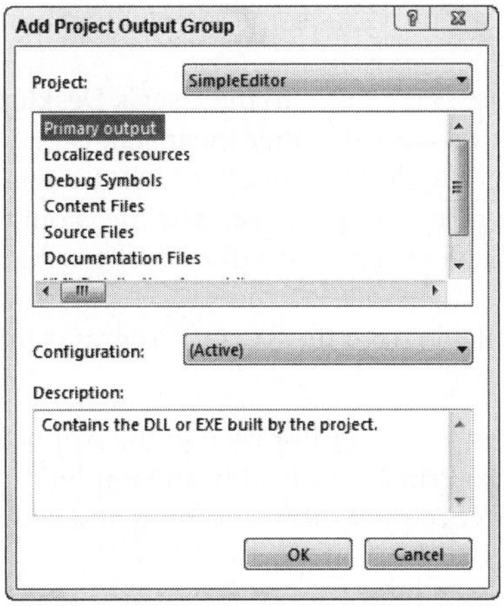

Figure 18-25

609

Click the OK button to add the primary output of the SimpleEditor project to the Application folder in the automatically opened File System Editor. In this case, the primary output is `SimpleEditor.exe`.

2. Additional files to add are a logo, a license, and a ReadMe file. In the File System Editor, create a subdirectory named Setup in the Application folder. You can do this by selecting the Application folder and then choosing the menu options Action ⇨ Add ⇨ Folder.

The Action menu in Visual Studio is available only if you select items in the setup editors. If an item in the Solution Explorer or Class View is selected, the Action menu is not available.

---

3. Add the files `wroxlogo.bmp`, `wroxsetuplogo.bmp`, `readme.rtf`, and `license.rtf` to the folder setup by right-clicking on the Setup folder and selecting Add ⇨ File. These files are available with the code download for this chapter, but you can easily create them yourself. You can fill the text files with license and ReadMe information. It is not necessary to change the properties of these files, which will be used in the dialogs of the installation program.

    The bitmap `wroxsetuplogo.bmp` should be sized 500 pixels wide and 70 pixels high. The left 420 pixels of the bitmap should only have a background graphic because the text of the installation dialogs will cover this range.

4. Add the file `readme.txt` to the Application folder. You want this file to be available for users to read before the installation is started. Set the property `PackageAs` to `vsdpaLoose` so that this file is not compressed into the Installer package. Set the `ReadOnly` property to `true` so this file can't be changed.

    The project now includes two ReadMe files, `readme.txt` and `readme.rtf`. The file `readme.txt` can be read by the user installing the application before the installation is started. The file `readme.rtf` provides some information in the installation dialogs.

5. Drag and drop the file `demo.wroxtext` to the User's Desktop folder. This file should be installed only after asking the user whether the install is really wanted, so set the `Condition` property of this file to `CHECKBOXDEMO`. `CHECKBOXDEMO` is the condition that can be set by the user. The value must be written in uppercase. The file is only installed if the `CHECKBOXDEMO` condition is set to `true`. Later you define a dialog where this property will be set.

6. To make the program available from the Start ⇨ Programs menu, you need a shortcut to the SimpleEditor program.

    Select Primary Output from SimpleEditor item in the Application folder and open the menu Action ⇨ Create Shortcut to Primary output from SimpleEditor. Set the `Name` property of the generated shortcut to Wrox Simple Editor, and drag and drop this shortcut to the User's Programs menu.

File Types Editor

If your application uses custom file types and you want to register file extensions for files that should start your application when a user double-clicks them, you can use the File Types Editor by selecting View ⇨ Editor ⇨ File Types. Figure 18-26 shows the File Types Editor with a custom file extension added.

Figure 18-26

With the File Types Editor, you can configure a file extension that should be handled from your application. The file extension has the properties shown in the following table:

Property	Description
Name	Add a useful name describing the file type. This name is displayed in the File Types Editor and written to the registry. Choose a unique name. An example for .doc file types is Word.Document.12. It's not necessary to use a ProgID as in the Word example; simple text like wordhtmlfile as used for the .dochtml file extension can also be used.
Command	With the Command property you can specify the executable that should be started when the user opens a file with this type.
Description	Add a description.
Extensions	This property is for the file extension where your application should be registered. The file extension will be registered in a section of the registry.
Icon	Specify an icon to display for the file extension.

Create Actions

After creating the file types in the File Types Editor, you can add actions. The default action that is automatically added is Open. You can add additional actions such as New and Print or whatever actions are appropriate for your program. Together with the actions, the Arguments and Verb properties must be defined. The Arguments property specifies the argument that is passed to the program, which is registered for the file extension. For example, %1 means that the filename is passed to the application. The Verb property specifies the action that should occur. With a print action, a /print can be added if supported by the application.

The next Try It Out adds an action to the SimpleEditor installation program. You want to register a file extension so that SimpleEditor can be used from Windows Explorer to open files with the extension .wroxtext. After this registration, you can double-click these files to open them, and the SimpleEditor application will start automatically.

Try It Out   Setting the File Extension

1. Start the File Types Editor with View ➪ Editor ➪File Types. Add a new file type using the menu Action ➪ Add File Type, with the properties set as shown in the following table. Because you don't want to change the ownership for Notepad of the .txt file extension, use the .wroxtext file extension.

Property	Value
(Name)	Wrox.SimpleEditor.Text
Command	Primary output from SimpleEditor
Description	Wrox Text Documents
Extensions	Wroxtext

You can also set the Icon property to define an icon for the opening of files, and a MIME type.

Leave the properties of the Open action with the default values so that the filename is passed as an application argument.

Launch Condition Editor

With the Launch Condition Editor you can specify some requirements that the target system must have before the installation can take place. Start the Launch Condition Editor by selecting View ➪ Editor ➪ Launch Conditions, as shown in Figure 18-27.

Figure 18-27

The editor has two sections to specify the requirements: Search Target Machine and Launch Conditions. In the first section, you can specify what specific file or registry key to search for. The second section defines the error message that occurs if the search is not successful. Following are some of the launch conditions that you can define using the Action menu:

❑ The File Launch Condition searches the target system for a file you define before the installation starts.

❑ The Registry Launch Condition enables you to require a check of registry keys before the installation starts.

❑ The Windows Installer Launch Condition makes it possible to search for Windows Installer components that must be present.

❑ The .NET Framework Launch Condition checks whether the .NET Framework is already installed on the target system.

❑ The Internet Information Services Launch Condition checks for installed Internet Information Services. Adding this launch condition adds a registry search for a specific registry key that is defined when Internet Information Services is installed, and adds a condition to check for a specific version.

By default, a .NET Framework Launch Condition is included, and its properties have been set to predefined values: the `Message` property is set to `[VSDNETMSG]`, which is a predefined error message. If the .NET Framework 3.5 is not installed, then a message informing the user to install the .NET Framework pops up. `InstallUrl`, by default, is set to `http://go.microsoft.com/fwlink/ ?linkid=76617`, so users can easily start the installation of the .NET Framework.

User Interface Editor

With the User Interface Editor, you can define the dialogs the user sees when configuring the installation. Here, you can inform users about license agreements and ask for installation paths and other information to configure the application.

In the next Try It Out, you start the User Interface Editor, which is used to configure the dialogs that appear when the application is installed.

Try It Out   **Starting the User Interface Editor**

1. Start the User Interface Editor by selecting View ➪ Editor ➪ User Interface.

2. Use the User Interface Editor to set properties for predefined dialog boxes. Figure 18-28 shows the automatically generated dialogs and two installation modes that you should see.

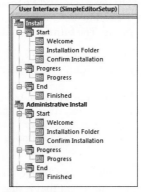

Figure 18-28

How It Works

As shown in Figure 18-28, there are two installation modes: Install and Administrative Install. The Install mode is typically used to install the application on a target system. With an Administrative Install, you can install an image of the application on a network share. Afterward, a user can install the application from the network.

Both installation modes have three phases during which dialogs can be shown: Start, Progress, and End. Let's look at the default dialogs:

- ❑ The Welcome dialog displays a welcome message to the user. You can replace the default welcome text with your own message. Users can only cancel the installation or click Next.

- ❑ With the second dialog, Installation Folder, users can choose the folder where the application should be installed. If you add custom dialogs (shown in a moment), then you have to add them before this one.

- ❑ The Confirm Installation dialog is the last dialog before the installation starts.

- ❑ The Progress dialog displays a progress control so users can see the progress of the installation.

- ❑ When installation is finished, the Finished dialog appears.

The default dialogs appear automatically at installation time, even if you never opened the User Interface Editor in the solution, but you should configure these dialogs to display useful messages for your application.

In the next Try It Out, you configure the default dialogs that are shown when the application is installed. Here, the Administrative Install path will be ignored; only the typical installation path is configured.

Try It Out   **Configuring the Default Dialogs**

1. Select the Welcome dialog. In the Properties window, you can see three properties for this dialog: `BannerBitmap`, `CopyrightWarning`, and `WelcomeText`. Select the `BannerBitmap` property by clicking Browse in the combo box, and select the `wroxsetuplogo.bmp` file in the folder `Application Folder\Setup`. The bitmap stored in this file will appear on top of this dialog.

   The default text for the property `CopyrightWarning` is as follows:

   ```
   WARNING: This computer program is protected by copyright law and international
   treaties. Unauthorized duplication or distribution of this program, or any
   portion of it, may result in severe civil or criminal penalties, and will be
   prosecuted to the maximum extent possible under the law.
   ```

   This text appears in the Welcome dialog also. Change this text if you want a stronger warning. The `WelcomeText` property defines more text that is displayed in the dialog. Its default value is as follows:

```
The installer will guide you through the steps required to install
[ProductName] on your computer.
```

You can change this text too. The string [ProductName] will be automatically replaced with the property ProductName that you defined in the properties of the project.

2. Select the Installation Folder dialog. This dialog has just two properties: BannerBitmap and InstallAllUsersVisible. The latter property has a default value of true. If this value is set to false, then the application can only be installed for the user who is logged on while the installation is running. Change the value of BannerBitmap to the wroxsetuplogo.bmp file, as you did with the Welcome dialog. As each dialog can display a bitmap with this property, change the BannerBitmap property for all the other dialogs too.

Additional Dialogs

If you design a custom dialog, you can't add it to the installation sequence with the Visual Studio Installer. A more sophisticated tool such as InstallShield or Wise for Windows is required — but with the Visual Studio Installer, you can add and customize many of the predefined dialogs by using the Add Dialog screen.

Selecting the Start sequence in the User Interface Editor and choosing the menu options Action ⇨ Add Dialog causes the Add Dialog dialog to be displayed (see Figure 18-29). All these dialogs are configurable.

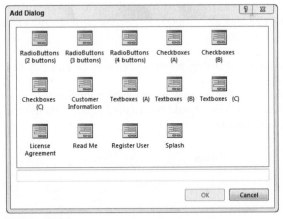

Figure 18-29

There are dialogs in which two, three, or four radio buttons appear, check box dialogs that show up to four check boxes, and text box dialogs that show up to four text boxes. You can configure these dialogs by setting their properties.

Here's a quick overview of some of the dialogs:

❑ The Customer Information dialog asks users for their name and company, and the product's serial number. If you don't provide a serial number with the product, you can hide the Serial Number text box by setting `ShowSerialNumber` to `false`.

❑ With the License Agreement dialog, users can accept a license before the installation starts. A license file is defined with the `LicenseFile` property.

❑ In the Register User dialog, users can click a Register Now button to launch a program defined with the `Executable` property. The custom program can send the data to an FTP server, or it can transfer the data by e-mail.

❑ The Splash dialog just displays a splash screen before the installation starts, using a bitmap specified by the `SplashBitmap` property.

In the next Try It Out, you add some additional dialogs such as Read Me, License Agreement, and a Checkboxes dialog.

Try It Out   Adding Other Dialogs

1. Add a Read Me, a License Agreement, and a Checkboxes (A) dialog to the Start sequence by selecting Action ⇨ Add Dialog. Define the order in the start sequence by dragging and dropping as follows:

```
Welcome - Read Me - License Agreement - Checkboxes (A) - Installation
Folder - Confirm Installation.
```

2. Configure the `BannerBitmap` property for all these dialogs as you did earlier. For the Read Me dialog, set the `ReadmeFile` property to `readme.rtf`, the file you added earlier to `Application Folder\Setup`.

3. For the License Agreement dialog, set the `LicenseFile` property to `license.rtf`.

4. Use the Checkboxes (A) dialog to ask users whether the file `demo.wroxtext` (which you put into the user's Desktop folder) should be installed or not. Change the properties of this dialog according to the following table:

Property	Values
BannerText	Optional Files
BodyText	Installation of optional files
Checkbox1Label	Do you want a demo file put on to the desktop?
Checkbox1Property	CHECKBOXDEMO
Checkbox2Visible	False
Checkbox3Visible	False
Checkbox4Visible	False

The Checkbox1Property property is set to the same value as the Condition property of the file demo.wroxtext — you set this Condition value earlier when you added the file to the package using the File System Editor. If the user checks this check box, the value of CHECKBOXDEMO will be true, and the file will be installed; otherwise, the value is false, and the file will not be installed.

The CheckboxXVisible property of the other check boxes is set to false, because you need only a single check box.

Building the Project

Now you can complete the following Try It Out to start the build of the installer project.

Try It Out   Building the Project

1. To create the Microsoft Installer Package, right-click the SimpleEditorSetup project and select Build.

2. With a successful build you will find the files setup.exe and WroxSimpleEditor.msi as well as a readme.txt file in the Debug or Release directory (depending on your build settings).

How It Works

Setup.exe starts the installation of the MSI database file WroxSimpleEditor.msi. All files that you have added to the installer project (with one exception) are merged and compressed into the MSI file because you set the project properties to Package Files in Setup File. The exception to this is the readme.txt file, for which the PackageAs property was changed so that it can be read immediately before the application is installed. You can also find the installation package of the .NET Framework in the DotNetFx subdirectory.

Installation

Now you can start installing the SimpleEditor application. Double-click the Setup.exe file or select the WroxSimpleEditor.msi file. Right-click to open the context menu and choose the Install option. You can also start the installation from within Visual Studio 2008 by right-clicking the opened installation project in the Solution Explorer and selecting Install.

As shown in the following sections, all the dialogs have the Wrox logo, and the inserted ReadMe and License Agreement dialogs appear with the configured files.

Let's walk through the installation sequence.

Welcome

The first dialog to appear is the Welcome dialog (see Figure 18-30). You can see the Wrox logo that was inserted by setting the value of the `BannerBitmap` property. The text that appears is defined with the `WelcomeText` and `CopyrightWarning` properties. The title of this dialog results from the `ProductName` property that you set with the project properties.

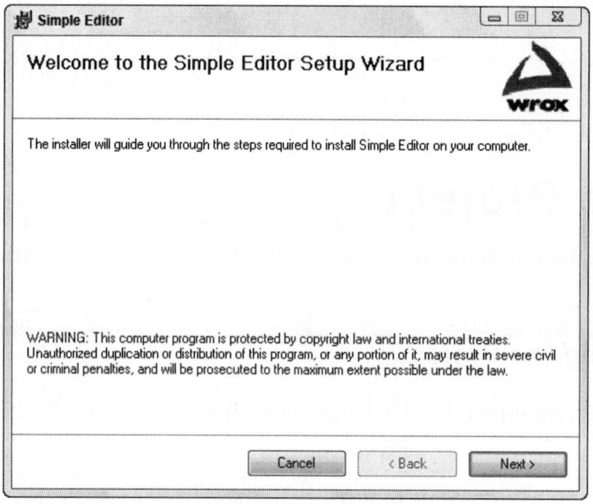

Figure 18-30

Read Me

After clicking the Next button, you can see the Read Me dialog (see Figure 18-31). It shows the Rich Text file `readme.rtf` that was configured by setting the `ReadmeFile` property.

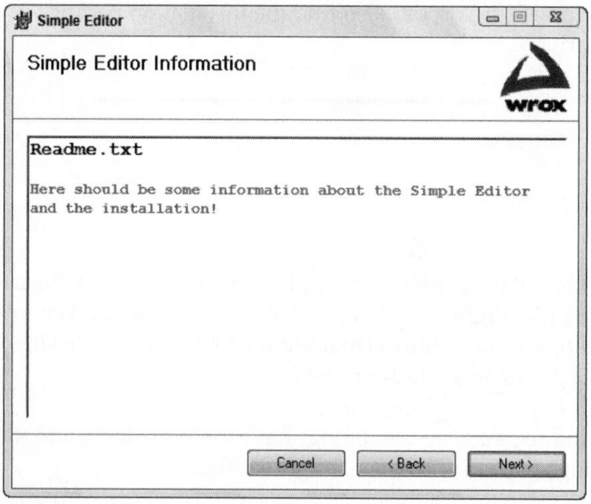

Figure 18-31

License Agreement

The third dialog to appear is the license agreement. Here, you have only configured the `BannerBitmap` and the `LicenseFile` properties. The radio buttons to agree to the license are added automatically. As shown in Figure 18-32, the Next button remains disabled until the I Agree button is pressed. This functionality is automatic with this dialog.

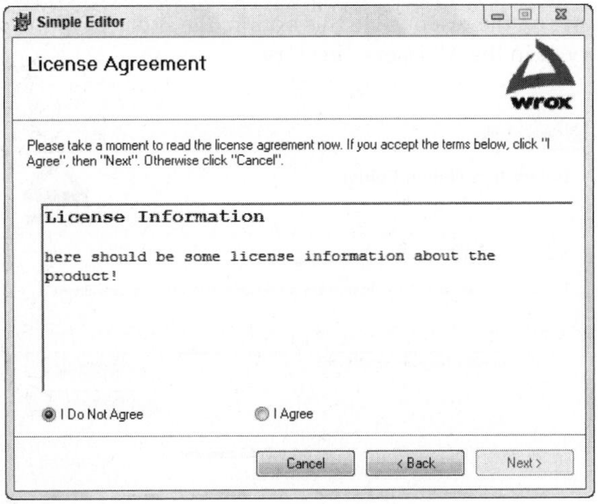

Figure 18-32

Optional Files

Agreeing to the license information and clicking the Next button displays the Checkboxes (A) dialog (see Figure 18-33). You should see the text that was defined with the `BannerText`, `BodyText`, and `Checkbox1Label` properties. The other check boxes are not visible because the specific `CheckboxVisible` property was set to `false`.

Selecting the check box will install the file `demo.wroxtext` to the desktop.

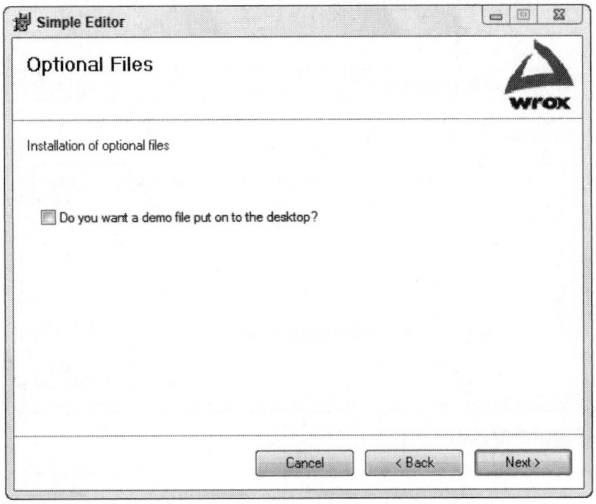

Figure 18-33

Select Installation Folder

In the Select Installation Folder dialog (see Figure 18-34), users can select the path where the application should be installed. This dialog allowed you to set only the `BannerBitmap` property. The default path shown is `[Program Files]\[Manufacturer]\[Product Name]`.

Users can also specify whether the application should be installed for everyone or just for the currently logged-on user. Depending on the response to this option, the shortcut to the program file will be put in the user-specific directory or in the All Users directory.

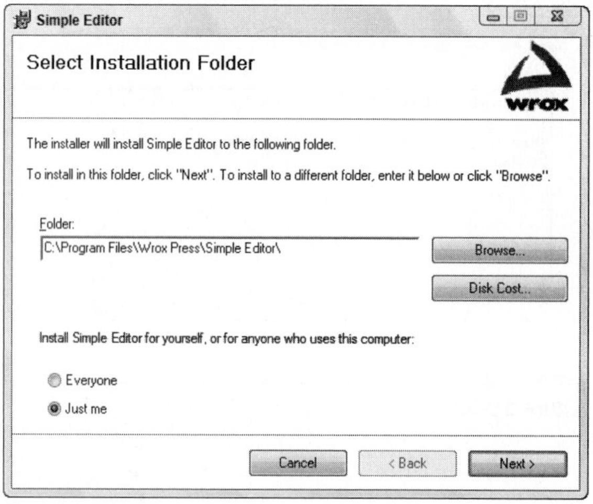

Figure 18-34

Disk Cost

Pressing the Disk Cost button opens the dialog shown in Figure 18-35. Here, the disk space of all hard drives is displayed, and the required space for every disk is calculated. This helps the user to choose a disk where the application should be installed.

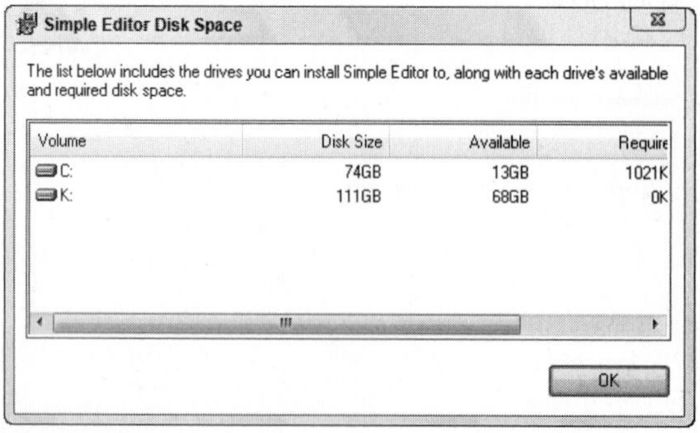

Figure 18-35

Confirm Installation

The Confirm Installation dialog (see Figure 18-36) is the last dialog to appear before the installation begins. No more questions are asked; this is just the last chance to cancel the installation before it begins.

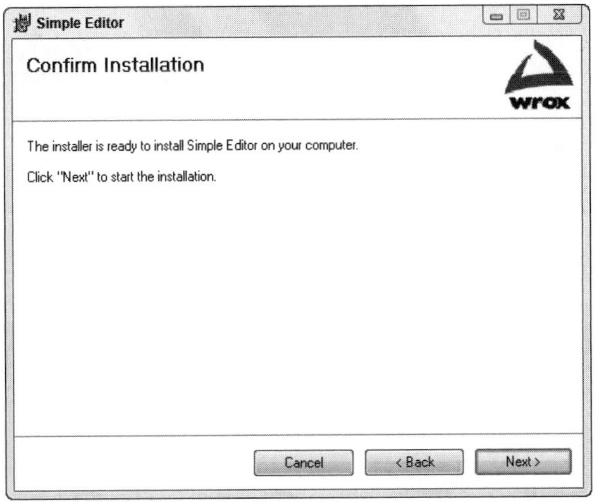

Figure 18-36

Progress

The Installing dialog (see Figure 18-37) shows a progress control during installation to indicate to users that the installation is continuing and to provide a rough idea of how long the installation will last. The editor is a small program, so this dialog finishes very fast.

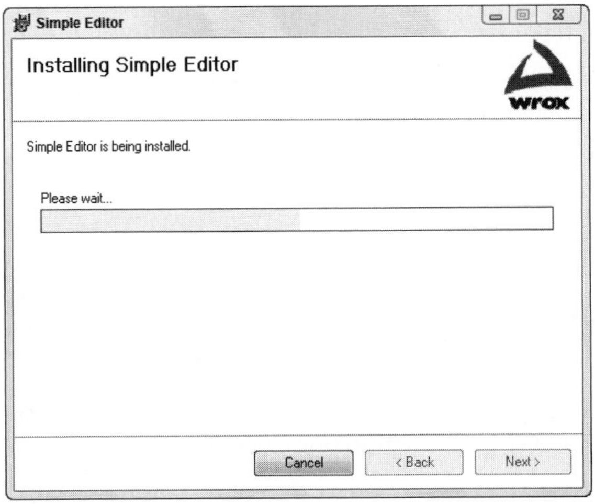

Figure 18-37

Installation Complete

After a successful installation, you will see the last dialog: Installation Complete (see Figure 18-38).

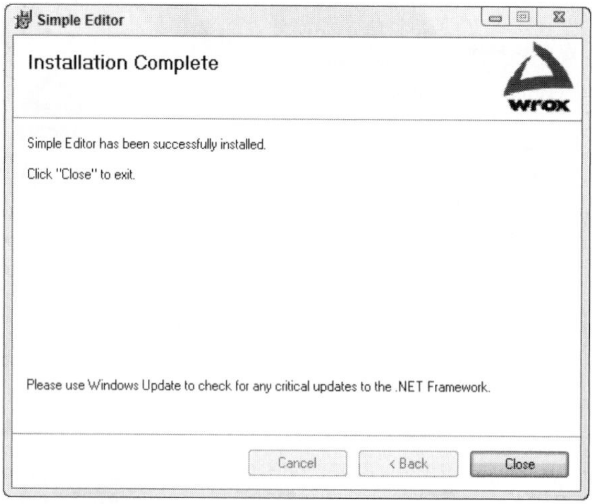

Figure 18-38

Running the Application

The editor can be started by selecting Start ⇨ All Programs ⇨ Wrox Simple Editor. Because you registered a file extension, there's another way to start the application: double-click a file with the file extension `.wroxtext`. If you selected the check box with the Optional Files dialog, you can find `demo.wroxtext` on your desktop; otherwise, you can create such a file with the now installed SimpleEditor tool.

Uninstall

If you want to get rid of the Wrox Simple Editor, you can use Add/Remove Programs from the Control Panel. Click the Remove button for SimpleEditor.

Summary

This chapter covered how to use ClickOnce deployment and the functionality of the Windows Installer, including how to create Installer packages using Visual Studio 2008. The Windows Installer makes it easy to do standardized installations, uninstalls, and repairs.

ClickOnce is a new technology that makes it easy to install Windows applications without the hassle of needing to be logged on as a system administrator. ClickOnce offers easy deployment as well as updates of client applications.

If more functionality than is available with ClickOnce is needed, the Windows Installer does a good job. The Visual Studio 2008 Installer is restricted in functionality and doesn't possess all the functionality of the Windows Installer, but for many applications the features of the Visual Studio 2008 Installer are more than enough. Several editors enable configuration of the generated Windows Installer file. With the File System Editor, you specify all files and shortcuts; the Launch Conditions Editor can define some mandatory prerequisites; the File Types Editor is used to register file extensions for applications; and the User Interface Editor makes it easy to adapt the dialogs used for the installation.

In this chapter, you learned the following:

- ❑ Features of and reasons to use ClickOnce deployment.
- ❑ How to configure ClickOnce deployment for Windows applications.
- ❑ How to create a setup project with Visual Studio.
- ❑ How to use the File System, File Types, Launch Condition, and User Interface editors of a setup project.

Exercises

1. What are the advantages of ClickOnce deployment?
2. How are the required permissions defined with ClickOnce deployment?
3. What is defined with a ClickOnce manifest?
4. When is it necessary to use the Windows Installer?
5. What different editors can you use to create a Windows Installer package using Visual Studio?

Part III
Web Programming

19

Basic Web Programming

Windows Forms is the technology for writing Windows applications; with ASP.NET, Web applications that are displayed in any browser can be built. ASP.NET enables you to write Web applications in a similar way to that in which Windows applications are developed. This is made possible by server-side controls that abstract the HTML code and mimic the behavior of the Windows controls. Of course, there are still many differences between Windows and Web applications because of the underlying technologies HTTP and HTML on which Web applications are based.

This chapter provides an overview of programming Web applications with ASP.NET, how to use Web controls, how to deal with state management (which is very different from how it's handled in Windows applications), how to perform authentication, and how to read and write data to and from a database.

Specifically, this chapter covers the following topics:

❑ What happens on the server when a HTML request is sent from the client

❑ How to create a simple Web page

❑ Using Web server controls in a Web page (and seeing the HTML code they generate)

❑ How to add event handlers to act on user actions

❑ Using validation controls to validate user input

❑ How to implement state management with different methods, such as ViewState, cookies, and `session`, `application`, and `cache` objects

❑ How to use authentication and authorization features offered by ASP.NET controls

❑ How to display and update database information

Overview

A Web application causes a Web server to send HTML code to a client. That code is displayed in a Web browser such as Internet Explorer. When a user enters a URL string in the browser, an HTTP request is sent to the Web server. The HTTP request contains the filename that is requested along with additional information such as a string identifying the client application, the languages that the client supports, and additional data belonging to the request. The Web server returns an HTTP response that contains HTML code, which is interpreted by the Web browser to display text boxes, buttons, and lists to the user.

You can read more about the HTTP protocol in Chapter 32.

ASP.NET is a technology for dynamically creating Web pages with server-side code. These Web pages can be developed with many similarities to client-side Windows programs. Instead of dealing directly with the HTTP request and response and manually creating HTML code to send to the client, you can use controls such as TextBox, Label, ComboBox and Calendar, which create HTML code themselves.

ASP.NET Runtime

Using ASP.NET for Web applications on the client system requires only a simple Web browser. You can use Internet Explorer, Opera, Netscape Navigator, Firefox, or any other Web browser that supports HTML. The client system doesn't require .NET to be installed.

On the server system, the ASP.NET runtime is needed. If you have Internet Information Services (IIS) on the system, the ASP.NET runtime is configured with the server when the .NET Framework is installed. During development, there's no need to work with Internet Information Services because Visual Studio delivers its own ASP.NET Web Development Server that you can use for testing and debugging the application.

Consider a typical Web request from a browser to show how the ASP.NET runtime goes into action (see Figure 19-1). The client requests a file, e.g., default.aspx, from the server. All ASP.NET Web pages usually have the file extension .aspx. Because this file extension is registered with IIS, or known by the ASP.NET Web Development Server, the ASP.NET runtime and the ASP.NET worker process enter the picture. With the first request to the file default.aspx, the ASP.NET parser is started, and the compiler compiles the file together with a C# file, which is associated with the .aspx file and creates an assembly. Then the assembly is compiled to native code by the JIT compiler of the .NET runtime. The assembly contains a Page class that is invoked to return HTML code to the client. Then the Page object is destroyed. The assembly is kept for subsequent requests, though, so it is not necessary to compile the assembly again.

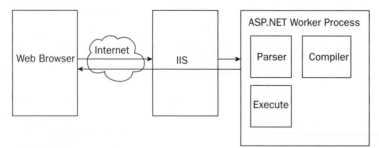

Figure 19-1

Creating a Simple Page

In the following Try It Out, you create a simple Web page. In the sample application used in this and the next chapter, a simple Event Web site will be created where attendees can register for events.

Creating a Simple Web Page

1. Create a new Web site by selecting File ⇨ New ⇨ Web Site within Visual Studio. In the New Web Site dialog (see Figure 19-2), select Visual C# as the language, and set the Location combo box to File System. With the location, selecting HTTP means that IIS is used and a virtual directory is created. (Selecting the File System results in the local file system being used.) Name the Web site **EventRegistrationWeb**.

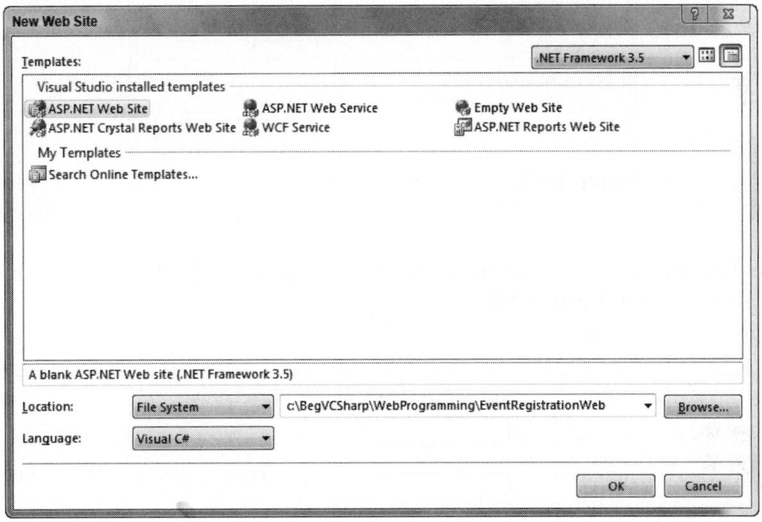

Figure 19-2

2. After creating the Web site, the file `default.aspx` is opened in the editor. One part shows the Source View, while the other shows the Design View.

3. A table is useful for arranging the controls. Click into the Design View and add a table by selecting Table ⇨ Insert Table. In the Insert Table dialog, set five rows and two columns, as shown in Figure 19-3.

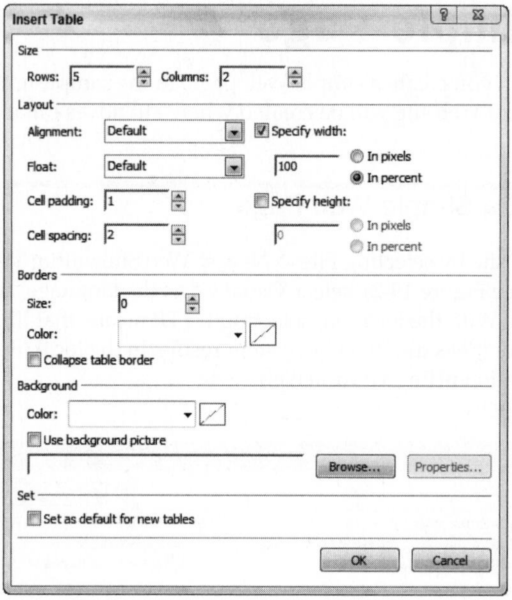

Figure 19-3

4. Add to the table four `Label` controls, three `TextBox` controls, a `DropDownList`, and a `Button`, as shown in Figure 19-4.

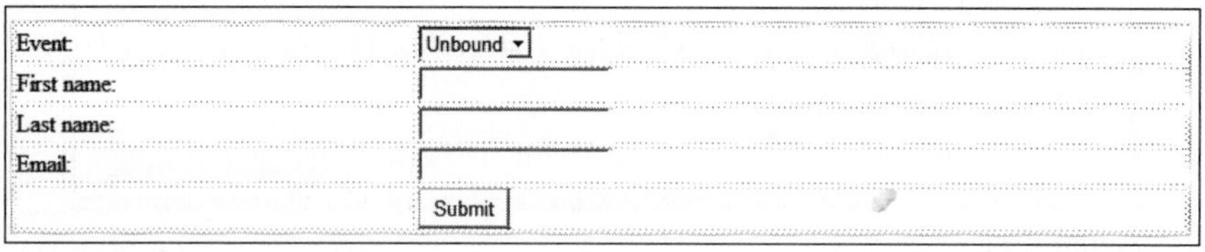

Figure 19-4

5. Set the control properties as shown in the following table:

Control Type	(ID)	Text
Label	labelEvent	Event:
Label	labelFirstName	First name:
Label	labelLastName	Last name:
Label	labelEmail	Email:
DropDownList	dropDownListEvents	

Control Type	(ID)	Text
TextBox	textFirstName	
TextBox	textLastName	
TextBox	textEmail	
Button	buttonSubmit	Submit

6. In the DropDownList, select the Items property in the Properties window, and enter the strings **SQL Server 2008 and XML**, **Office 2007 and XML**, and **Introduction to ASP.NET** in the ListItem Collection Editor, as shown in Figure 19-5.

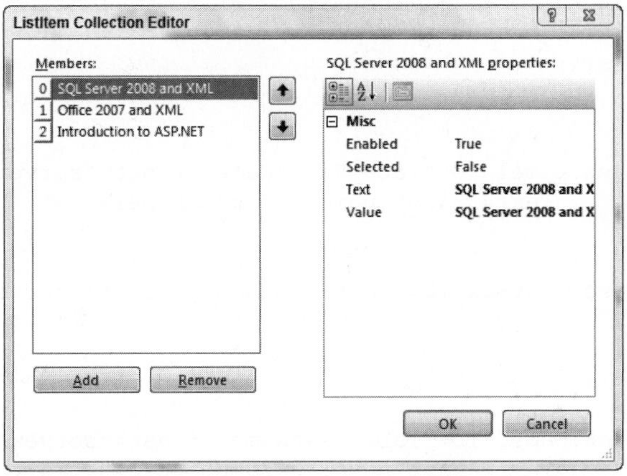

Figure 19-5

7. Switch the editor to the Source View and verify that the generated code looks similar to the following:

```
<%@ Page Language="C#" AutoEventWireup="true" CodeFile="Default.aspx.cs"
Inherits="_Default" %>

<!DOCTYPE html PUBLIC "-//W3C//DTD XHTML 1.0 Transitional//EN"
"http://www.w3.org/TR/xhtml1/DTD/xhtml1-transitional.dtd">

<html xmlns="http://www.w3.org/1999/xhtml">
<head runat="server">
   <title>Untitled Page</title>
       <style type="text/css">
          .style1
          {
              width: 100%;
          }
```

```
        </style>
    </head>
    <body>
        <form id="form1" runat="server">
        <div>

            <table class="style1">
                <tr>
                    <td>
                        <asp:Label ID="labelEvent" runat="server" Text="Event:">
</asp:Label>
                    </td>
                    <td>
                        <asp:DropDownList ID="dropDownListEvents" runat="server">
                            <asp:ListItem>SQL Server 2008 and XML</asp:ListItem>
                            <asp:ListItem>Office 2007 and XML</asp:ListItem>
                            <asp:ListItem>Introduction to ASP.NET</asp:ListItem>
                        </asp:DropDownList>
                    </td>
                </tr>
                <tr>
                    <td>
                        <asp:Label ID="labelFirstName" runat="server"
                            Text="First name:"></asp:Label>
                    </td>
                    <td>
                        <asp:TextBox ID="textFirstName" runat="server"></asp:TextBox>
                    </td>
                </tr>
                <tr>
                    <td>
                        <asp:Label ID="labelLastName" runat="server"
                            Text="Last name:"></asp:Label>
                    </td>
                    <td>
                        <asp:TextBox ID="textLastName" runat="server"></asp:TextBox>
                    </td>
                </tr>
                <tr>
                    <td>
                        <asp:Label ID="labelEmail" runat="server" Text="Email:">
</asp:Label>
                    </td>
                    <td>
                        <asp:TextBox ID="textEmail" runat="server"></asp:TextBox>
                    </td>
                </tr>
                <tr>
                    <td>
                         </td>
                    <td>
                        <asp:Button ID="buttonSubmit" runat="server" Height="26px"
                            Text="Submit" />
```

```
            </td>
          </tr>
        </table>

      </div>
      </form>
  </body>
  </html>
```

8. Start the Web application by selecting Debug ⇨ Start Without Debugging. When you start the application, the ASP.NET Web Development Server is automatically started. You will find an icon for the ASP.NET Web Development Server in the Windows Explorer taskbar. Double-click that icon to see a dialog similar to what is shown in Figure 19-6. This dialog shows the physical and logical paths of the Web server, and the port the Web server is listening to. This dialog can also be used to stop the Web server.

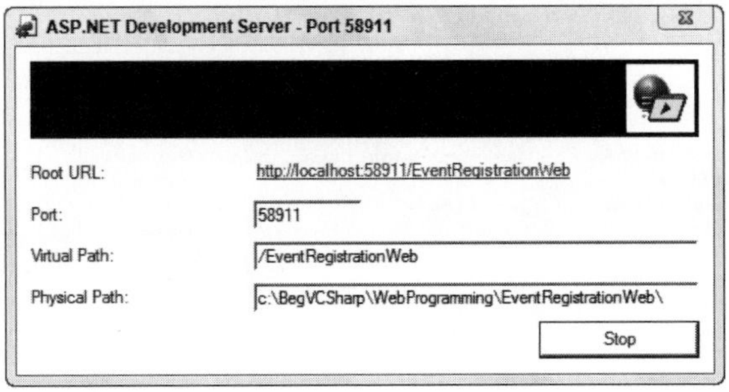

Figure 19-6

Starting the application causes Internet Explorer to show the Web page, as shown in Figure 19-7. You can view the HTML code by selecting View ⇨ Source. You'll see that the server-side controls are converted to pure HTML code.

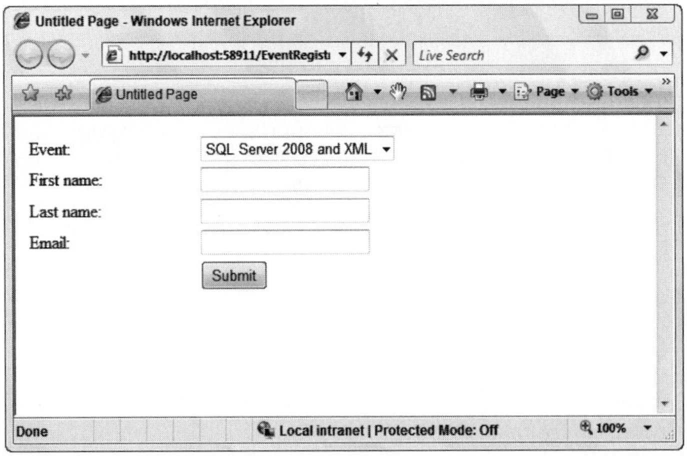

Figure 19-7

How It Works

The first line of the file `default.aspx` is the page directive:

```
<%@ Page Language="C#" AutoEventWireup="true" CodeFile="Default.aspx.cs" ↵
Inherits="_Default" %>
```

This directive defines the programming language and the classes that are used. The property
`AutoEventWireup="true"` automatically links the event handlers to specific method names, as
shown later. `Inherits="Default_aspx"` means that the class that is dynamically generated from
the ASPX file derives from the base class `_Default`. This base class is in the code-behind file
`Default.aspx.cs`, as defined with the `CodeFile` property.

Visual Studio allows code behind with separate CS files or inline code whereby the C# code can be
written directly into the ASPX file. When creating a new item with File ➪ New ➪ File, you can specify
whether the code should be put into a separate file (see Figure 19-8).

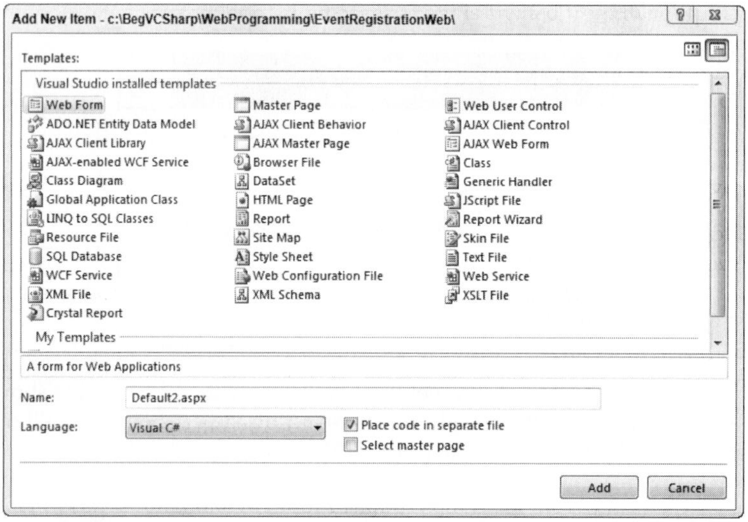

Figure 19-8

Separating the user interface and the code into ASPX and CS files enables better maintenance. The
code that is generated in the file `Default.aspx.cs` imports some namespaces and includes a
partial class: `_Default`. The automatically generated class in the file `Default.aspx` derives from
the class `_Default`. Later in the chapter, you add handler code to the CS file.

```
using System;
using System.Data;
using System.Configuration;
using System.Linq;
using System.Web;
using System.Web.Security;
using System.Web.UI;
using System.Web.UI.WebControls;
using System.Web.UI.WebControls.WebParts;
using System.Web.UI.HtmlControls;
```

```
using System.Xml.Linq;

public partial class _Default : System.Web.UI.Page
{
    protected void Page_Load(object sender, EventArgs e)
    {
    }
}
```

The `partial` *keyword used in the preceding code is discussed in Chapter 10.*

Here is the code of the ASPX page. The client receives simple HTML code as it is; just the `runat="server"` attribute is removed from the `<head>` tag:

```
<html xmlns="http://www.w3.org/1999/xhtml" >
<head runat="server">
  <title>Untitled Page</title>
    <style type="text/css">
        .style1
        {
            width: 100%;
        }
    </style>
</head>
<body>
```

You will also find other HTML elements with the attribute `runat=server`, such as the `<form>` element. With the `runat=server` attribute, an ASP.NET server control is associated with the HTML tag. The control can be used to write server-side code. Behind the `<form>` element is an object of type `System.Web.UI.HtmlControls.HtmlForm`. The object has the variable name `form1` as defined with the `id` attribute. `form1` can be used to invoke methods and properties of the `HtmlForm` class.

The `HtmlForm` object creates a `<form>` tag that is sent to the client:

```
<form id="form1" runat="server">
```

Of course, the `runat` attribute is not sent to the client.

The standard controls that you've dropped from the Toolbox to the Forms Designer have elements that begin with `<asp:`. `<asp:Label>` and `<asp:DropDownList>`. These are server-side ASP.NET Web controls that are associated with .NET classes in the namespace `System.Web.UI.WebControls`. `<asp:Label>` is represented by the class `Label`, and `<asp:DropDownList>` is represented by the class `DropDownList`:

```
<td>
  <asp:Label ID="labelEvent" runat="server" Text="Event:"></asp:Label>
</td>
<td>
  <asp:DropDownList ID="dropDownListEvents" runat="server">
    <asp:ListItem>SQL Server 2008 and XML</asp:ListItem>
    <asp:ListItem>Office 2007 and XML</asp:ListItem>
    <asp:ListItem>Introduction to ASP.NET</asp:ListItem>
  </asp:DropDownList>
</td>
```

`<asp:Label>` doesn't send an `<asp:Label>` element to the client because this is not a valid HTML element. Instead, `<asp:Label>` returns a `<span>` tag. Similarly, `<asp:DropDownList>` returns a `<select>` element, and `<asp:TextBox>` returns the element `<input type="text">`.

ASP.NET has UI control classes in the namespaces `System.Web.UI.HtmlControls` and `System.Web.UI.WebControls`. Both of these namespaces have some similar controls, also known as HTML server controls and Web server controls. Examples are the HTML server control `HtmlInputText` and the Web server control `TextBox`. The HTML server controls offer methods and properties that are similar to the HTML controls because they can be accessed from JavaScript in the HTML page on the client. The Web server controls offer methods and properties, as you know from Windows programming. Which control you use is partly a matter of taste. However, with the Web server controls, you will find much more complex controls such as `Calendar`, `DataGrid`, and `Wizard`.

Server Controls

The following table lists some of the principal Web server controls available with ASP.NET, and the HTML code returned by these controls:

Control	HTML	Description
Label	`<span>`	Returns a span element containing text.
Literal	`static text`	Returns simple static text. With this control, it is possible to transform the content depending on the client application.
TextBox	`<input type="text">`	Returns HTML `<input type="text">` whereby the user can enter some values. You can write a server-side event handler when the text changes.
Button	`<input type="submit">`	Sends form values to the server.
LinkButton	`<a href="javascript:__ dopostback()>`	Creates an anchor tag that includes JavaScript for doing a postback to the server.
ImageButton	`<input type="image">`	Generates an input tag of type image to show a referenced image.
HyperLink	`<a>`	Creates a simple anchor tag referencing a Web page.
DropDownList	`<select>`	Creates a select tag whereby the user sees one item and can select one of multiple items by clicking on the drop-down list.
ListBox	`<select size="">`	Creates a select tag with a size attribute that shows multiple items at once.

Control	HTML	Description
CheckBox	`<input type="checkbox">`	Returns an `input` element of type `check box` to show a button that can be selected or deselected. Instead of using the `CheckBox`, you could use a `CheckBoxList`, which creates a table consisting of multiple `check box` elements.
RadioButton	`<input type="radio">`	Returns an `input` element of type `radio`. With a radio button, just one button of a group can be selected. Similar to the `CheckBoxList`, `RadioButtonList` provides a list of buttons.
Image	`<img src="">`	Returns an `img` tag to display a GIF or JPG file on the client.
Calendar	`<table>`	Displays a complete calendar from which a date can be selected, the month can be changed, and so on.For output, an HTML table with JavaScript code is generated.
TreeView	`<div><table>`	Returns a `div` tag that includes multiple `table` tags, depending on its content. JavaScript is used to open and close the tree on the client.

Event Handlers

Web server controls can include event handlers that are invoked on the server. The `Button` control can include a `Click` event; the `DropDownList` offers the event `SelectedIndexChanged`, and the `TextBox` offers the event `TextChanged`.

The events occur on the server only when a postback occurs. When a value in a text box changes, the `TextChanged` event doesn't occur immediately; it occurs only when the form is submitted and sent to the server, which happens when the Submit button is clicked. The ASP.NET runtime verifies that the state of the control has changed before invoking the corresponding event handler. If the selection of the `DropDownList` has been changed, then the `SelectedIndexChanged` event is invoked; the `TextChanged` event is invoked accordingly when the value of a text box changes.

> *When you want a change event immediately posted to the server (e.g., when the selection of a `DropDownList` changes), you can set the `AutoPostback` property to `true`. That way, client-side JavaScript is used to submit the form data immediately to the server. Of course, network traffic is increased this way, so use this feature with care.*

Verification of the old values with the new values of the controls is done by the ViewState. ViewState is a hidden field that is sent with the page content to the browser. When sending the page to the client, the ViewState contains the same values as the controls within a form. With a postback to the server, the ViewState is sent to the server together with the new values of the controls. That way, it can be verified whether the values change, and the event handler can be invoked.

Until now, the sample application has sent only a simple page to the client. Now you need to deal with the result from the user input. In the first example, the user input is displayed in the same page, and then a different page is used. In the following Try It Out, you display the user input.

Displaying User Input

1.   Open the previously created Web application EventRegistrationWeb using Visual Studio.

2.   To display user input for the event registration, add a label with the name **labelResult** to the Web page `Default.aspx`.

3.   Double-click the Submit button to add a `Click` event handler to this button and add the following code to the handler in the file `Default.aspx.cs`:

```
public partial class _Default
{
    protected void buttonSubmit_Click(object sender, EventArgs e)
    {
        string selectedEvent = dropDownListEvents.SelectedValue;
        string firstName = textFirstName.Text;
        string lastName = textLastName.Text;
        string email = textEmail.Text;

        labelResult.Text = String.Format("{0} {1} selected the event {2}",
            firstName, lastName, selectedEvent);
    }
}
```

4.   Start the Web page using Visual Studio again. After you enter the data and click the Submit button, the same page displays the user input in the new label.

How It Works

Double-clicking the Submit button adds the `OnClick` attribute to the `<asp:Button>` element in the file `Default.aspx`:

```
<asp:Button ID="buttonSubmit" runat="server" Text="Submit"
    OnClick="buttonSubmit_Click" />
```

With the Web server control, `OnClick` defines the server-side `Click` event that will be invoked when the button is clicked.

Within the implementation of the `buttonSubmit_Click()` method, the values of the controls can be read by using properties. `dropDownListEvents` is the variable that references the `DropDownList` control. In the ASPX file, the ID is set to `dropDownListEvents`, so a variable is automatically created. The property `SelectedValue` returns the current selection. With the `TextBox` controls, the `Text` property returns the strings that have been entered by the user:

```
string selectedEvent = dropDownListEvents.SelectedValue;
string firstName = textFirstName.Text;
string lastName = textLastName.Text;
string email = textEmail.Text;
```

The label `labelResult` again has a `Text` property where the result is set:

```
labelResult.Text = String.Format("{0} {1} selected the event {2}",
    firstName, lastName, selectedEvent);
```

Instead of displaying the results on the same page, ASP.NET makes it easy to display the results in a different page, as shown in the following Try It Out.

Try It Out   **Displaying the Results in a Second Page**

1.   Create a new `WebForm` with the name `ResultsPage.aspx`.

2.   Add a label to the `ResultsPage` with the name **labelResult**.

3.   Add code to the `Page_Load` method to the class `_ResultsPage` as shown here:

```
public partial class _ResultsPage : System.Web.UI.Page
{
    protected void Page_Load(object sender, EventArgs e)
    {
        try
        {
            DropDownList dropDownListEvents =
                (DropDownList)PreviousPage.FindControl("dropDownListEvents");

            string selectedEvent = dropDownListEvents.SelectedValue;

            string firstName =
                ((TextBox)PreviousPage.FindControl("textFirstName")).Text;
            string lastName =
                ((TextBox)PreviousPage.FindControl("textLastName")).Text;
            string email = ((TextBox)PreviousPage.FindControl("textEmail")).Text;

            labelResult.Text = String.Format("{0} {1} selected the event {2}",
                firstName, lastName, selectedEvent);
        }
        catch
        {
            labelResult.Text = "The originating page must contain " +
                "textFirstName, textLastName, textEmail controls";
        }
    }
}
```

4.   Set the `Default.aspx` page's Submit button's `PostbackUrl` property to `ResultsPage.aspx`.

5. You can remove the Click event handler of the Submit button because it is not required anymore.

6. Start the Default.aspx page, fill in some data, and click the Submit button. You are redirected to the page ResultsPage.aspx, where the entered data is displayed.

How It Works

With ASP.NET, the Button control implements the property PostbackUrl to define the page that should be requested from the Web server. This property creates client-side JavaScript code to request the defined page with the client-side onclick handler of the Submit button:

```
<input type="submit" name="buttonSubmit" value="Submit"
    onclick="javascript:webForm_DoPostBackWithOptions(
        new WebForm_PostBackOptions(&quot;buttonSubmit&quot;,
            &quot;&quot;, false, &quot;&quot;, &quot;ResultPage.aspx&quot;,
            false, false))" id="buttonSubmit" />
```

The browser sends all the data from the form inside the first page to the new page. However, inside the newly requested page it is necessary to get the data from controls that have been defined with the previous page. To access the controls from a previous page, the Page class defines the property PreviousPage. PreviousPage returns a Page object, where the controls of this page can be accessed using the FindControl() method. FindControl() is defined to return a Control object, so you must cast the return value to the control type that is searched:

```
DropDownList dropDownListEvents =
    (DropDownList)PreviousPage.FindControl("dropDownListEvents");
```

Instead of using the FindControl() method to access the values of the previous page, access to the previous page can be strongly typed, which is less error prone during development. To make this possible, the next Try It Out defines a custom struct that is returned with a property from the default_aspx class.

Try It Out   **Creating a Strongly Typed PreviousPage**

1. Create the App_Code folder in the Web application by selecting the Web folder in the Solution Explorer and selecting Website ➪ Add Folder ➪ App_Code Folder.

2. In the Solution Explorer, select the App_Code folder and add a new C# file named RegistrationInformation.cs by selecting Website ➪ Add New Item ➪ Class.

3. Implement the struct RegistrationInformation in the file RegistrationInformation.cs as shown:

```
public struct RegistrationInformation
{
    public string FirstName { get; set; }
    public string LastName { get; set; }
```

```
    public string Email { get; set; }
    public string SelectedEvent { get; set; }
}
```

4. Add the public property `RegistrationInformation` to the class `_Default` in the file
`Default.aspx.cs`:

```
public RegistrationInformation RegistrationInformation
{
    get
    {
        return new RegistrationInformation()
        {
            FirstName = textFirstName.Text,
            LastName = textLastName.Text,
            Email = textEmail.Text,
            SelectedEvent = dropDownListEvents.SelectedValue
        };
    }
}
```

5. Add the `PreviousPageType` directive to the file `ResultPage.aspx` following the `Page`
directive:

```
<%@ Page Language="C#" AutoEventWireup="true" CodeFile="ResultPage.aspx.cs"
    Inherits="ResultPage_aspx" %>
<%@ PreviousPageType VirtualPath="~/Default.aspx" %>
```

6. Within the `Page_Load()` method of the class `_ResultsPage`, now the code can be simplified:

```
protected void Page_Load(object sender, EventArgs e)
{
    try
    {
        RegistrationInformation ri = PreviousPage.RegistrationInformation;

        labelResult.Text = String.Format("{0} {1} selected the event {2}",
            ri.FirstName, ri.LastName, ri.SelectedEvent);

    }
    catch
    {
        labelResult.Text = "The originating page must contain " +
            "textFirstName, textLastName, textEmail controls";
    }
}
```

Input Validation

When users enter data, it should be checked to confirm that the data is valid. The check can happen on the client and on the server. Checking the data on the client can be done by using JavaScript. However, if the data is checked on the client using JavaScript, it should also be checked on the server, because you can never fully trust the client. It is possible to disable JavaScript in the browser, and hackers can use different JavaScript functions that accept incorrect input. It is absolutely necessary to check the data on the server. Checking the data on the client as well leads to better performance, as no round-trips occur to the server until the data is validated on the client.

With ASP.NET it is not necessary to write the validation functions yourself. Many validation controls exist that create both client- and server-side validation.

The following example shows the `RequiredFieldValidator` validation control that is associated with the text box `textFirstname`. All validator controls have in common the properties `ErrorMessage` and `ControlToValidate`. If the input is not correct, then `ErrorMessage` defines the message that is displayed. By default, the error message is displayed where the validator control is positioned. The property `ControlToValidate` defines the control where the input is checked.

```
<asp:TextBox ID="textFirstname" runat="server"></asp:TextBox>
<asp:RequiredFieldValidator ID="RequiredFieldValidator1" runat="server"
    ErrorMessage="Enter your first name" ControlToValidate="textFirstName">
</asp:RequiredFieldValidator>
```

The following table lists and describes all the validation controls:

Control	Description
RequiredFieldValidator	Specifies that input is required with the control that is validated. If the control to validate has an initial value set, which the user has to change, you can set this initial value with the `InitialValue` property of the validator control.
RangeValidator	Defines a minimum and maximum value that the user is allowed to enter. The specific properties of the control are `MinimumValue` and `MaximumValue`.
RegularExpressionValidator	With the `ValidationExpression` property a regular expression using Perl 5 syntax can be set to check the user input.

Control	Description
CompareValidator	Compares multiple values (such as passwords). Not only does this validator support comparing two values for equality, additional options can be set with the Operator property. The Operator property is of type ValidationCompareOperator, which defines enumeration values such as Equal, NotEqual, GreaterThan, and DataTypeCheck. Using DataTypeCheck, the input value can be checked to determine whether it is of a specific data type, e.g., correct date input.
CustomValidator	If the other validator controls don't fulfill the requirements of the validation, the CustomValidator can be used. With the CustomValidator, both a client- and server-side validation function can be defined.
ValidationSummary	Writes a summary for a page instead of writing error messages directly to the input controls.

With the sample application that you've created until now, the user can input first name, last name, and e-mail address. In the following Try It Out, you extend the application by using validation controls.

Try It Out   Checking for Required Input and E-mail Address

1. Open the previously created project EventRegistrationWeb using Visual Studio.

2. Open the file default.aspx.

3. Add a new column to the table by selecting the right column in the Design View of the editor and choosing Table ⇨ Insert ⇨ Column to the Right.

4. First name, last name, and e-mail address are required inputs. A check is done to determine whether the e-mail address has the correct syntax. Add three RequiredFieldValidator controls and one RegularExpressionValidator control, as shown in Figure 19-9.

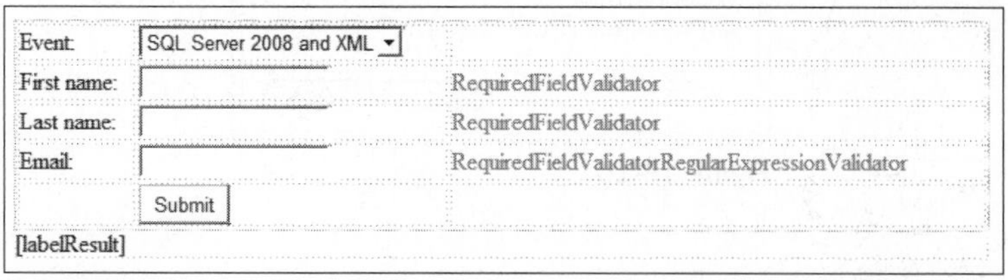

Event:	SQL Server 2008 and XML ▼	
First name:		RequiredFieldValidator
Last name:		RequiredFieldValidator
Email:		RequiredFieldValidatorRegularExpressionValidator
	Submit	
[labelResult]		

Figure 19-9

5. Configure the validation controls as defined in this table:

Validation Control	Property	Value
RequiredFieldValidator1	ErrorMessage	First name is required.
	ControlToValidate	textFirstName
RequiredFieldValidator2	ErrorMessage	Last name is required.
	ControlToValidate	textLastName
RequiredFieldValidator3	ErrorMessage	Email is required.
	ControlToValidate	textEmail
	Display	Dynamic
RegularExpressionValidator1	ErrorMessage	Enter a valid email.
	ControlToValidate	textEmail
	ValidationExpression	\w+([-+.']\w+)*@\w+([-.]\w+)*\.\w+([-.]\w+)*
	Display	Dynamic

6. It is not necessary to enter the regular expression manually. Instead, you can click the ellipsis button of the ValidationEpression property in the Properties window to start the Regular Expression Editor, shown in Figure 19-10. This editor provides some predefined regular expressions, including the regular expression to check for an Internet e-mail address.

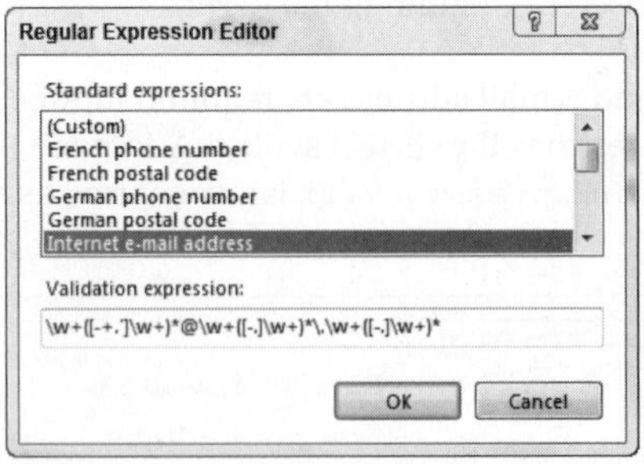

Figure 19-10

7. If a postback is done to a page that is different from the page that includes the validator controls (using the `PostBackUrl` property that was set earlier), in the new page you must verify that the result of the previous page was valid, using the `IsValid` property. Add this code to the `Page_Load()` method of the `_ResultsPage` class:

```
protected void Page_Load(object sender, EventArgs e)
{
    try
    {
        if (!PreviousPage.IsValid)
        {
            labelResult.Text = "Error in previous page";
            return;
        }
        //...
```

8. Now you can start the application. When data is not entered or not entered correctly, the validator controls show error messages, as shown in Figure 19-11.

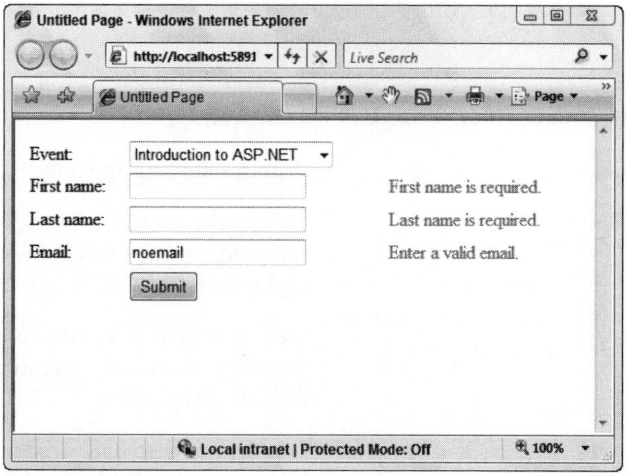

Figure 19-11

How It Works

The validator controls create both client-side JavaScript code to verify input on the client, and server-side code to validate input on the server. It is also possible to turn JavaScript off by setting the validator property `EnableClientScript` to `false`. Instead of changing the property with every validator control, you can also turn off JavaScript by setting the property `ClientTarget` of the `Page` class.

Depending on the client type, the ASP.NET controls might return JavaScript to the client. This behavior depends on the `ClientTarget` property. By default, the `ClientTarget` is set to `"automatic"`, where, depending on the Web browser's functionality, scripting code is returned or not. If the `ClientTarget` is set to `"downlevel"`, then scripting code is not returned for any clients, while setting the `ClientTarget` property to `"uplevel"` always returns scripting code.

Setting the property `ClientTarget` can be done inside the `Page_Load()` method of the `Page` class:

```
protected void Page_Load(object sender, EventArgs e)
{
    ClientTarget = "downlevel";
}
```

State Management

The HTTP protocol is stateless. The connection that is initiated from the client to the server can be closed after every request. However, normally it is necessary to remember some client information from one page to the other. There are several ways to accomplish this.

The main difference among the various ways to keep state is whether the state is stored on the client or on the server. The following table shows an overview of state management techniques and how long the state can be valid:

State Type	Client or Server Resource	Time Valid
ViewState	Client	Within a single page only.
Cookie	Client	Temporary cookies are deleted when the browser is closed; permanent cookies are stored on the disk of the client system.
Session	Server	Session state is associated with a browser session. The session is invalidated with a timeout (by default, 20 minutes).
Application	Server	Application state is shared among all clients. This state is valid until the server restarts.
Cache	Server	Similar to application state, cache is shared. However, when the cache should be invalidated, there's much better control.

Now let's take a more detailed look at these techniques.

Client-Side State Management

In this section, you are going to step into client-side state management by looking at two techniques: ViewState and cookies.

ViewState

One technique to store state on the client was already discussed: ViewState. ViewState is used automatically by the Web server controls to make events work. The ViewState contains the same state as the control when sent to the client. When the browser sends the form back to the server, the ViewState contains the original values, but the values of the controls that are sent contain the new values. If there's a difference, the corresponding event handlers are invoked.

The disadvantage to using ViewState is that data is always transferred from the server to the client, and vice versa, which increases network traffic. To reduce network traffic, ViewState can be turned off. To do so for all controls within the page, set the `EnableViewState` property to `false` with the `Page` directive:

```
<%@ Page Language="C#" AutoEventWireUp="true" CodeFile="Default.aspx.cs"
    Inherits="_Default" EnableViewState="false" %>
```

The ViewState can also be configured on a control by setting the `EnableViewState` property of a control. Regardless of what the page configuration says, when the `EnableViewState` property is defined for the control, the control value is used. The value of the page configuration is used only for these controls when the ViewState is not configured.

It is also possible to store custom data inside the ViewState. This can be done by using an indexer with the `ViewState` property of the `Page` class. You can define a name that is used to access the ViewState value with the `index` argument:

```
ViewState["mydata"] = "my data";
```

You can read the previously stored ViewState as shown here:

```
string mydata = (string)ViewState["mydata"];
```

In the HTML code that is sent to the client, you can see the ViewState of the complete page within a hidden field:

```
<input type="hidden" name="__VIEWSTATE"
    value="/wEPDwUKLTU4NzY5NTcwNw8WAh4HbXlzdGF0ZQUFbXl2YWwwWAgIDD2QWAg
    IFDw8WAh4EVGV4dAUFbXl2YWxkZGTCdCywUOcAW97aKpcjt1tzJ7ByUA==" />
```

Using hidden fields has the advantage that every browser can use this feature, and the user cannot turn it off.

The ViewState is only remembered within a page. If the state should be valid across different pages, then using cookies is an option for state on the client.

Cookies

A cookie is defined in the HTTP header. Use the `HttpResponse` class to send a cookie to the client. `Response` is a property of the `Page` class that returns an object of type `HttpResponse`. The `HttpResponse` class defines the `Cookies` property that returns an `HttpCookieCollection`. Multiple cookies can be returned to the client with the `HttpCookieCollection`.

The following sample code shows how a cookie can be sent to the client. First, an HttpCookie object is instantiated. In the constructor of this class, the name of the cookie is set — here it is mycookie. The HttpCookie class has a Values property to add multiple cookie values. If you just have one cookie value to return, you can use the Value property instead. However, if you plan to send multiple cookie values, it is better to add the values to a single cookie instead of using multiple cookies.

```
string myval = "myval";
HttpCookie cookie = new HttpCookie("mycookie");
cookie.Values.Add("mystate", myval);
Response.Cookies.Add(cookie);
```

Cookies can be temporary and valid within a browser session, or they can be stored on the client disk. To make the cookie permanent, the Expires property must be set with the HttpCookie object. With the Expires property, a date defines when the cookie is not valid anymore; here, it is set to a date three months from the current date.

Although a specific date can be set, there is no guarantee that the cookie is stored until the date is reached. The user can delete the cookie, and the browser application also deletes the cookie if too many cookies are stored locally. The browser has a limit of 20 cookies for a single server, and 300 cookies for all servers. When the limit is reached, the cookies that haven't been used for some time are deleted.

```
HttpCookie cookie = new HttpCookie("mycookie");
cookie.Values.Add("mystate", "myval");
cookie.Expires = DateTime.Now.AddMonths(3);
Response.Cookies.Add(cookie);
```

When the client requests a page from the server, and a cookie for this server is available on the client, the cookie is sent to the server as part of the HTTP request. Reading the cookie in the ASP.NET page can be done by accessing the cookies collection in the HttpRequest object.

Similarly to the HTTP response, the Page class has a Request property that returns an object of type HttpRequest. The property Cookies returns an HttpCookieCollection that can now be used to read the cookies sent by the client. A cookie can be accessed by its name with the indexer, and then the Values property of the HttpCookie is used to get the value from the cookie:

```
HttpCookie cookie = Request.Cookies["mycookie"];
string myval = cookie.Values["mystate"];
```

ASP.NET makes it easy to use cookies, but you must be aware of the cookie's restrictions. Recall that a browser accepts just 20 cookies from a single server and 300 cookies for all servers. There's also a restriction regarding the size of a cookie, which cannot store more than 4K of data. These restrictions ensure that the client disk won't be filled with cookies.

Server-Side State Management

Instead of remembering state with the client, it is also possible to remember state with the server. Using client-side state has the disadvantage that the data sent across the network increases. Using server-side state has the disadvantage that the server must allocate resources for its clients.

Let's look into the server-side state management techniques.

Session

Session state is associated with a browser session. A session starts when the client first opens an ASP.NET page on the server, and ends when the client doesn't access the server for 20 minutes.

You can define your own code that should run when a session starts or ends within the Global Application Class. To create a Global Application Class, select Website ⇨ Add New Item ⇨ Global Application Class. With this class, the file global.asax is created. Inside this file some event handler routines are defined:

```
<%@ Application Language="C#" %>

<script runat="server">

    void Application_Start(Object sender, EventArgs e) {
        // Code that runs on application startup
    }

    void Application_End(Object sender, EventArgs e) {
        //  Code that runs on application shutdown
    }

    void Application_Error(Object sender, EventArgs e) {
        // Code that runs when an unhandled error occurs
    }

    void Session_Start(Object sender, EventArgs e) {
        // Code that runs when a new session is started
    }

    void Session_End(Object sender, EventArgs e) {
        // Code that runs when a session ends.
        // Note: The Session_End event is raised only when the sessionstate mode
        // is set to InProc in the Web.config file. If session mode is set to
        // StateServer or SQLServer, the event is not raised.
    }

</script>
```

Session state can be stored within an HttpSessionState object. The session state object associated with the current HTTP context can be accessed with the Session property of the Page class. In the Session_Start() event handler, session variables can be initialized; in the example, the session state named mydata is initialized to 0:

```
    void Session_Start(Object sender, EventArgs e) {
        // Code that runs on application startup
        Session["mydata"] = 0;
    }
```

Reading session state, again, can be done with the `Session` property using the session state name:

```
void Button1_Click(object sender, EventArgs e)
{
    int val = (int)Session["mydata"];
    Label1.Text = val.ToString();
    val += 4;
    Session["mydata"] = val;
}
```

To associate the client with its session variables, by default ASP.NET uses a temporary cookie with a session identifier. ASP.NET also supports sessions without cookies, where URL identifiers are used to map the HTTP requests to the same session.

Application

If data should be shared between different clients, then application state can be used. Application state can be used in a manner that's very similar to the way session state is used. With application state, the class `HttpApplicationState` is used, and it can be accessed with the `Application` property of the `Page` class.

In the example, the application variable with the name `userCount` is initialized when the Web application is started. `Application_Start()` is the event handler method in the file `global.asax` that is invoked when the first ASP.NET page of the Web site is started. This variable is used to count every user accessing the Web site:

```
void Application_Start(Object sender, EventArgs e) {
    // Code that runs on application startup
    Application["userCount"] = 0;
}
```

In the `Session_Start()` event handler, the value of the application variable `userCount` is incremented. Before changing an application variable, the application object must be locked with the `Lock()` method; otherwise, threading problems can occur because multiple clients can access an application variable concurrently. After the value of the application variable is changed, the `Unlock()` method must be called. Be aware that the time between locking and unlocking is very short — you shouldn't read files or data from the database during that time. Otherwise, other clients must wait until the data access is completed.

```
void Session_Start(Object sender, EventArgs e) {
    // Code that runs when a new session is started
    Application.Lock();
    Application["userCount"] = (int)Application["userCount"] + 1;
    Application.UnLock();
}
```

Reading the data from the application state is as easy as it was with the session state:

```
Label1.Text = Application["userCount"].ToString();
```

Don't store too much data in the application state because the application state requires server resources until the server is stopped or restarted.

Cache

Cache is server-side state that is similar to application state insofar as it is shared with all clients. Cache is different from application state in that cache is much more flexible: There are many options to define when the state should be invalidated. Instead of reading a file with every request, or reading the database, the data can be stored inside the cache.

For the cache, the namespace `System.Web.Caching` and the class `Cache` are needed. Adding an object to the cache is shown in the following example:

```
Cache.Add("mycache", myobj, null, DateTime.MaxValue,
    TimeSpan.FromMinutes(10), CacheItemPriority.Normal, null);
```

The `Page` class has a `Cache` property that returns a `Cache` object. Using the `Add()` method of the `Cache` class, any object can be assigned to the cache. The first parameter of the `Add()` method defines the name of the cache item. The second parameter is the object that should be cached. With the third parameter, dependencies can be defined, e.g., the cache item can be dependent on a file. When the file changes, the cache object is invalidated. In the example there's no dependency because `null` is set with this parameter.

With parameters four and five, a time can be set specifying how long the cache item is valid. Parameter four defines an absolute time when the cache item should be invalidated, whereas parameter five requires a sliding time that invalidates the cache item after it hasn't been accessed for the time defined with the sliding expiration. Here, a sliding time span is used, invalidating the cache after the cache item hasn't been used for 10 minutes.

Parameter six defines a cache priority. `CacheItemPriority` is an enumeration for setting the cache priority. If the ASP.NET worker process has high memory usage, the ASP.NET runtime removes cache items according to their priority. Items with a lower priority are removed first. With the last parameter, it is possible to define a method that should be invoked when the cache item is removed. An example of where this can be used is when the cache is dependent on a file. When the file changes, the cache item is removed and the event handler is invoked. With the event handler, the cache can be reloaded by reading the file once more.

Cache items can be read by using the indexer, as you've already seen with the session and application state. Before using the object returned from the `Cache` property, always check whether the result is `null`, which happens when the cache is invalidated. When the returned value from the `Cache` indexer is not `null`, the returned object can be cast to the type that was used to store the cache item:

```
object o = Cache["mycache"];
if (o == null)
{
    // Reload the cache.
}
else
{
    // Use the cache.
    MyClass myObj = (MyClass)o;
    //...
}
```

Authentication and Authorization

To secure the Web site, authentication is used to verify that the user has a valid logon, while authorization checks whether the user who was authenticated is allowed to use the resource.

ASP.NET offers Windows and Forms authentication. The most frequently used authentication technique for Web applications is Forms authentication, which is covered here. ASP.NET also has some great new features for Forms authentication. Windows authentication makes use of Windows accounts and IIS to authenticate users.

ASP.NET has many classes for user authentication. Figure 19-12 shows the structure of the new architecture. With ASP.NET, many new security controls such as `Login` or `PasswordRecovery` are available. These controls make use of the Membership API. With the Membership API, it is possible to create and delete users, validate logon information, or get information about currently logged-in users. The Membership API itself makes use of a *membership provider*. With ASP.NET 2.0, different providers exist to access users in an Access database, the SQL Server database, or the Active Directory. It is also possible to create a custom provider that accesses an XML file or any custom store.

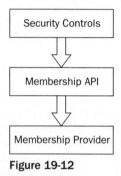

Figure 19-12

Authentication Configuration

This chapter demonstrates Forms authentication with a Membership provider. In the following Try It Out, you configure security for the Web application and assign different access lists to different folders.

Try It Out   **Configuring Security**

1. Open the previously created Web application EventRegistrationWeb using Visual Studio.

2. Create a new folder named Intro by selecting the Web directory in the Solution Explorer and then selecting Website ⇨ Add Folder ⇨ Regular Folder. This folder will be configured to be accessed by all users, while the main folder will be accessible only by authenticated users.

3. Start the ASP.NET Web Application Administration by selecting Website ⇨ ASP.NET Configuration in Visual Studio 2008.

4. Select the Security tab, as shown in Figure 19-13.

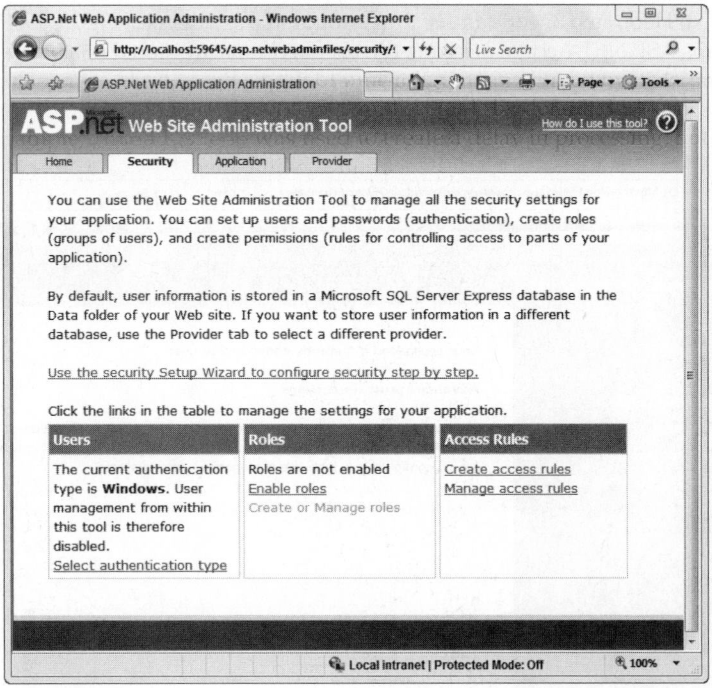

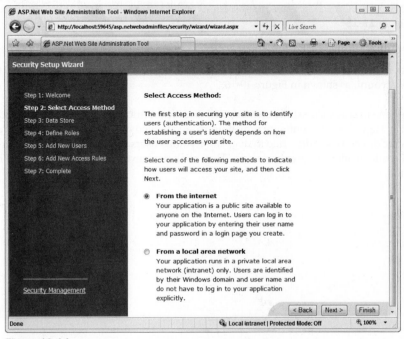

Figure 19-13

5. Click the link to the Security Setup Wizard. In the Welcome Screen, click the Next button. From step 2 of the wizard, select the access method From the Internet, as shown in Figure 19-14.

Figure 19-14

6. Click Next. Here, step 3, you can see the configured provider (see Figure 19-15). The default provider is ASP.NET Access, meaning the user accounts are stored in an Access database. This configuration cannot be changed in the Wizard mode, but you can change it afterward.

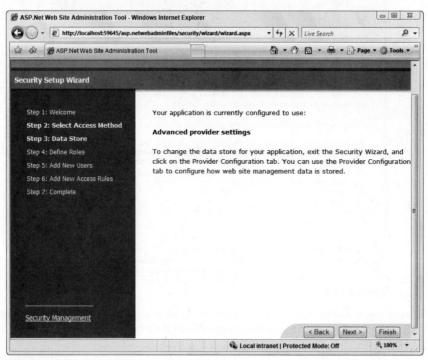

Figure 19-15

7. Click the Next button twice, which takes you to step 5, where you add new users. Create a new account, as shown in Figure 19-16.

8. After one user is successfully created, click the Next button for step 6 of the wizard (see Figure 19-17). Here, you can configure which users are allowed or denied access to the Web site or specific directories. Add a rule to deny anonymous users. Next, select the Intro directory and add a rule to allow anonymous users. Then click the Next button and finally the Finish button.

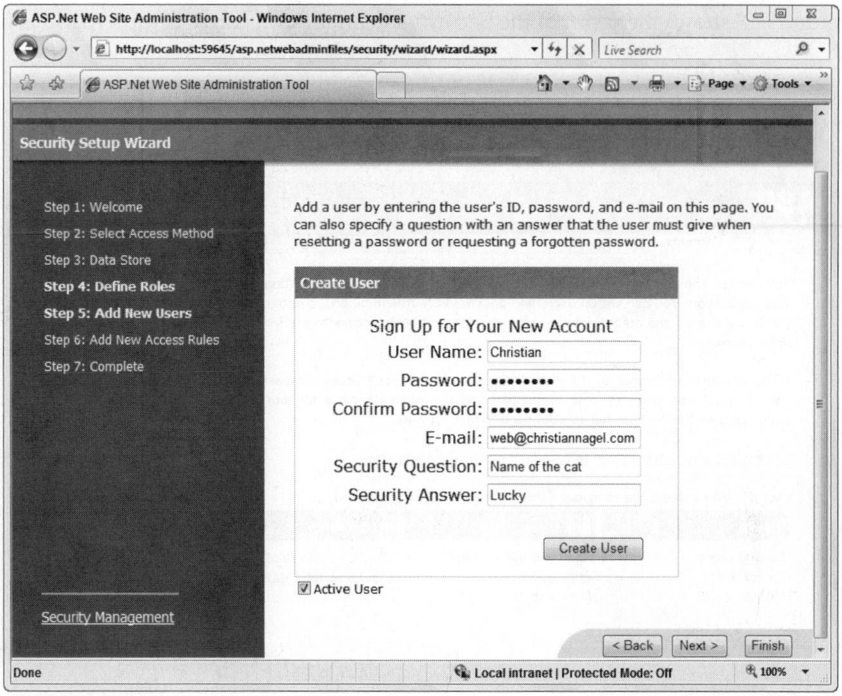

Figure 19-16

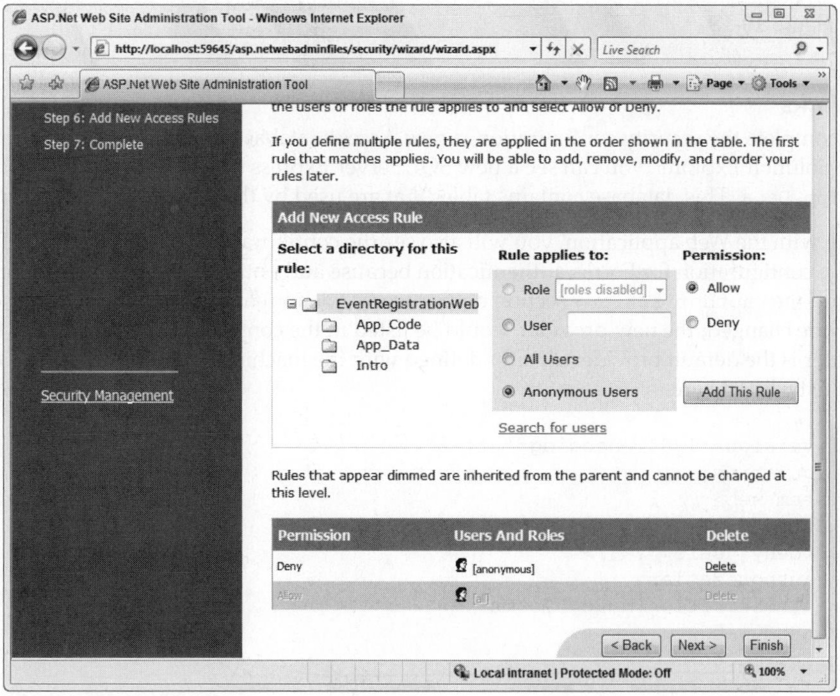

Figure 19-17

Figure 19-18 shows the result of the Security tab after the Security Setup Wizard is finished.

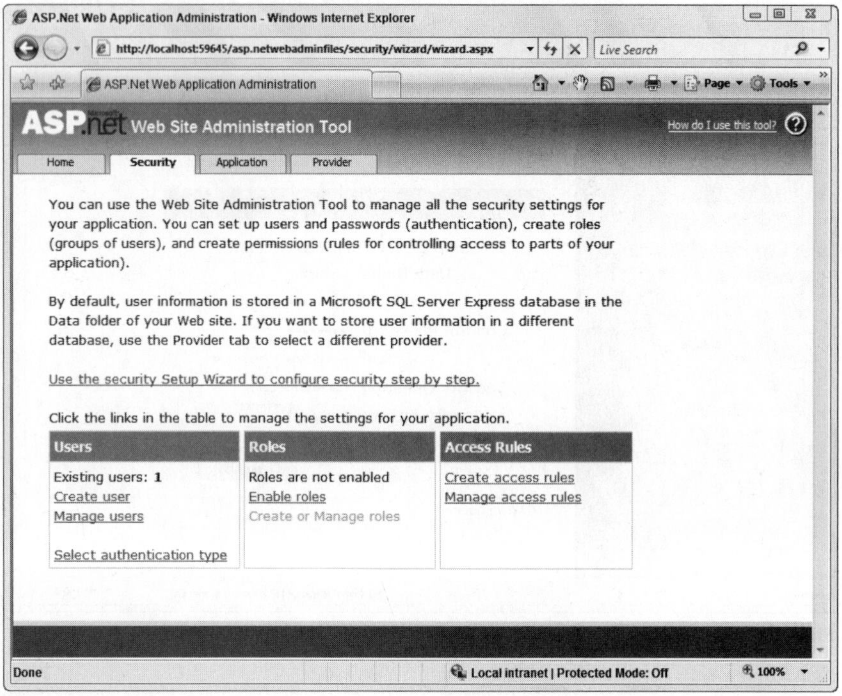

Figure 19-18

How It Works

After you complete the security configuration, a new Access database is created. Having refreshed the files in the Solution Explorer, you can see a new SQL Server Express database `ASPNETDB.mdf` in the directory `App_Data`. This database contains tables that are used by the SQL Membership provider.

Now, along with the Web application, you will also see the configuration file `web.config`. This file contains the configuration for Forms authentication because authentication across the Internet was selected, and the `<authorization>` section denies access to anonymous users. If the Membership provider were changed, the new provider would be listed in the configuration file. Because the SQL provider is the default provider already defined with the machine configuration file, there is no need for it to be listed here.

```xml
<?xml version="1.0" encoding="utf-8"?>
<configuration>
  <system.web>
    <authorization>
      <deny users="?" />
    </authorization>
    <authentication mode="Forms" />
  </system.web>
</configuration>
```

Within the Intro subfolder, you can see another configuration file, `web.config`. The authentication section is missing from this configuration file because the authentication configuration is taken from the parent directory. However, the authorization section is different. Here, anonymous users are allowed with `<allow users="?" />`:

```xml
<?xml version="1.0" encoding="utf-8"?>
<configuration>
  <system.web>
    <authorization>
      <allow users="?" />
    </authorization>
  </system.web>
</configuration>
```

Using Security Controls

ASP.NET includes many security controls. Instead of writing a custom form to ask the user for a username and password, a ready-to-use `Login` control is available. The security controls and their functionality are described in the following table:

Security Control	Description
Login	A composite control that includes controls to ask for username and password.
LoginStatus	Includes hyperlinks to log in or log out, depending on whether the user is logged in or not.
LoginName	Displays the name of the user.
LoginView	Different content can be displayed depending on whether the user is logged in or not.
PasswordRecovery	A composite control to reset forgotten passwords. Depending on the security configurations, the user is asked for the answer to a previously set secret question or the password is sent by e-mail.
ChangePassword	A composite control that allows logged in users to change their password.
CreateUserWizard	A wizard to create a new user and write the user information to the Membership provider.

The following Try It Out adds a login page to the Web application.

Creating a Login Page

If you tried to start the Web site after it was configured to deny anonymous users, you should have received an error because a `login.aspx` page is missing. If a specific login page is not configured with Forms authentication, `login.aspx` is used by default. You now create a `login.aspx` page:

1. Add a new Web Form and name it `login.aspx`.

2. Add the `Login` control to the form. In Design View, you see the control shown in Figure 19-19.

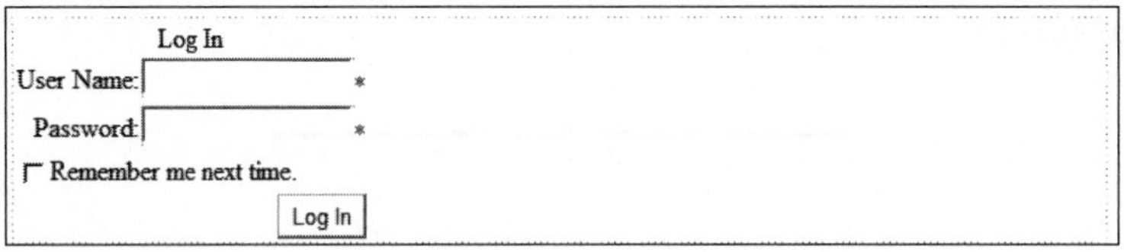

Figure 19-19

3. That's all that's necessary to create a login page. Now when you start the site `default.aspx`, you are redirected to `login.aspx`, where you can enter the user credentials for the user you created earlier.

How It Works

After adding the `Login` control, you can see this code in the Source View:

```
<asp:Login ID="Login1" runat="server">
</asp:Login>
```

The properties for this control enable you to configure the text for the header, username, and password labels, and for the login button, too. You can make the check box Remember Me Next Time visible by setting the `DisplayRememberMe` property.

If you want more control over the look and feel of the `Login` control, you can convert the control to a template. You can do this in the Design View by clicking the smart tag and selecting Convert to Template. Next, when you click Edit Templates, you get a view like that shown in Figure 19-20, where you can add and modify any controls.

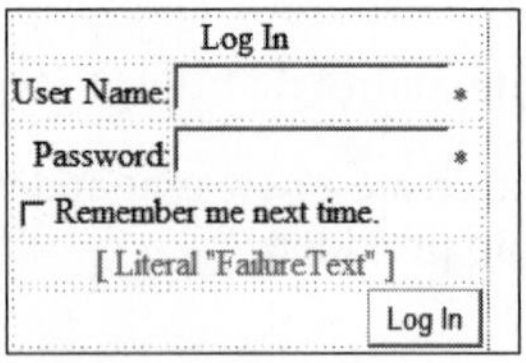

Figure 19-20

For verifying the user credentials, when the Login In button is clicked, the method `Membership`
`.ValidateUser()` is invoked by the control, and you don't have to do this yourself.

When users don't have an account to log in with the EventRegistration Website, they should create their own login. This can be done easily with the `CreateUserWizard` control, as shown in the next Try It Out.

Using the CreateUser Wizard

1. Add a new Web page named `RegisterUser.aspx` in the Intro folder previously created. This folder is configured to be accessed from anonymous users.

2. Add a `CreateUserWizard` control to this Web page.

3. Set the property `ContinueDestinationPageUrl` to `~/Default.aspx`.

4. Add a `LinkButton` control to the `Login.aspx` page. Set the content of this control to `Register User`, and the `PostBackUrl` property of this control to the Web page `Intro/RegisterUser.aspx`.

5. Now you can start the application. Clicking the link Register User on the `Login.aspx` page redirects to the page `RegisterUser.aspx` where a new account will be created with the entered data.

How It Works

The `CreateUserWizard` control is a wizardlike control that consists of multiple wizard steps, which are defined with the element `<WizardSteps>`:

```
<asp:CreateUserWizard ID="CreateUserWizard1" runat="server"
    ContinueDestinationPageUrl="~/Default.aspx">
  <WizardSteps>
    <asp:CreateUserWizardStep runat="server" />
    <asp:CompleteWizardStep runat="server" />
  </WizardSteps>
</asp:CreateUserWizard>
```

These wizard steps can be configured in the designer. The smart tag of the control enables you to configure each of these steps separately. Figure 19-21 shows configuration of the step Sign Up for Your New Account, and Figure 19-22 shows the step complete. You can also add custom steps with custom controls to add special requirements, such as having users accept a contract before signing up for an account.

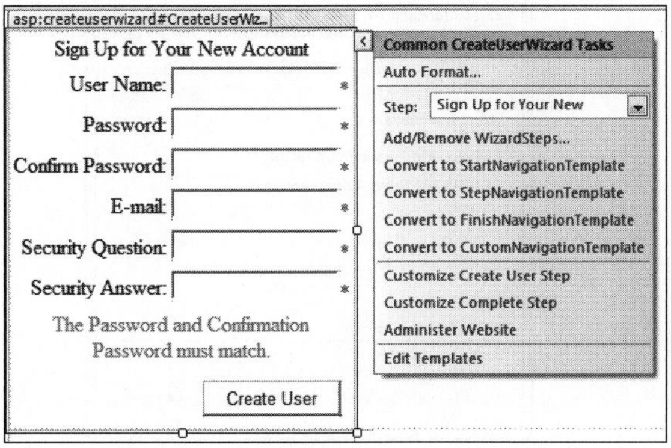

Figure 19-21

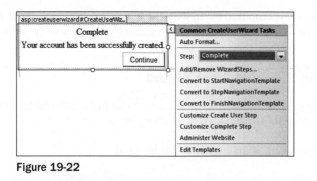

Figure 19-22

Reading and Writing to an SQL Server Database

Most Web applications need access to a database to read data from it and write data to it. In this section, you create a new database to store event information, and learn how to use this database from ASP.NET. First you create a new SQL Server database in the next Try It Out. This can be done directly from within Visual Studio 2008.

Creating a New Database

1. Open the previously created Web application EventRegistrationWeb.

2. Open the Server Explorer. If you cannot already see it in Visual Studio, you can open the window by selecting View ⇨ Other Windows ⇨ Server Explorer.

3. In the Server Explorer, select Data Connections, right-click to open the context menu, and select Create New SQL Server Database. The dialog shown in Figure 19-23 opens.

4. Enter **(local)** for the server name, and **BegVCSharpEvents** for the database name.

Figure 19-23

5. After the database is created, select the new database in Server Explorer.

6. Select the entry Tables below the database, and from Visual Studio select Data ⇨ Add New ⇨ Table.

7. Enter the following column names and data types (see Figure 19-24).

Column Name	Data Type
Id	int
Title	nvarchar(50)
Date	datetime
Location	nvarchar(50)

dbo.Table1: Ta...VCSharpEvents)*		
Column Name	Data Type	Allow Nulls
⌇ Id	int	☐
Title	nvarchar(50)	☐
Date	datetime	☐
Location	nvarchar(50)	☐
▶		☐

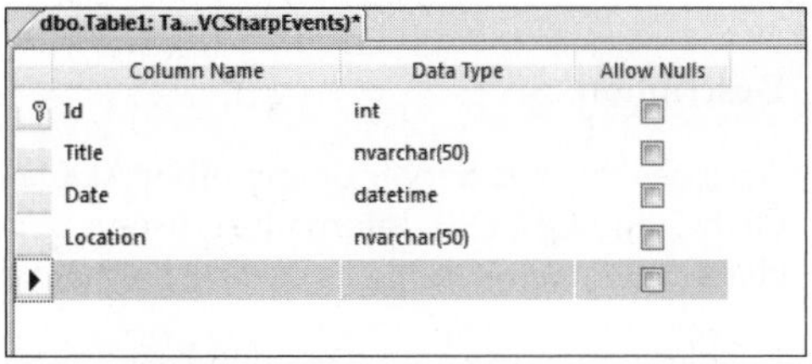

Figure 19-24

8. Configure the ID column as a primary key column with an identity increment of 1 and an identity seed of 1. Configure all columns to not allow `nulls`.

9. Save the table with the name **Events**.

10. Add a few events to the table with some sample titles, dates, and locations.

To display and edit data, there's a separate Data section in the Toolbox, representing data controls. The data controls can be categorized into two groups: data view and data source. A data source control is associated with a data source such as an XML file, a SQL database, or a .NET class; data views are connected with a data source to represent data.

The following table describes all the data controls:

Data Control	Description
GridView	Displays data with rows and columns.
DataList	Displays a single column to display all items.
DetailsView	Can be used together with a GridView if you have a master/detail relationship with your data.
FormView	Displays a single row of the data source.
Repeater	Template-based. You can define what HTML elements should be generated around the data from the data source.
ListView	New in .NET 3.5. This is template-based, similar to the Repeater control.

The data source controls and their functionality are listed in the following table:

Data Source Control	Description
SqlDataSource	Accesses the SQL Server or any other ADO.NET provider (e.g., Oracle, ODBC, and OLEDB). Internally, it uses a DataSet or a DataReader class.
AccessDataSource	Enables you to use an Access database.
LinqDataSource	New in .NET 3.5. Enables using LINQ providers as a data source.
ObjectDataSource	Enables you to use .NET classes as the data source.
XmlDataSource	Enables you to access XML files. Using this data source, hierarchical structures can be displayed.
SiteMapDataSource	Uses XML files to define a site structure for creating links and references with a Web site. This feature is discussed in Chapter 20.

In the next Try It Out, you use a GridView control to display and edit data from the previously created database.

Using a GridView Control to Display Data

1.   In the Solution Explorer, create a new regular folder Admin.

2.   Create a new Web page EventsManagement.aspx in the Admin folder.

3.   Add a GridView control to the Web page.

4.   In the Choose Data Source combo box of the control's smart tag, select <New data source . . .>. The dialog shown in Figure 19-25 opens.

5.   Select Database and enter the name **EventsDataSource** for this new data source.

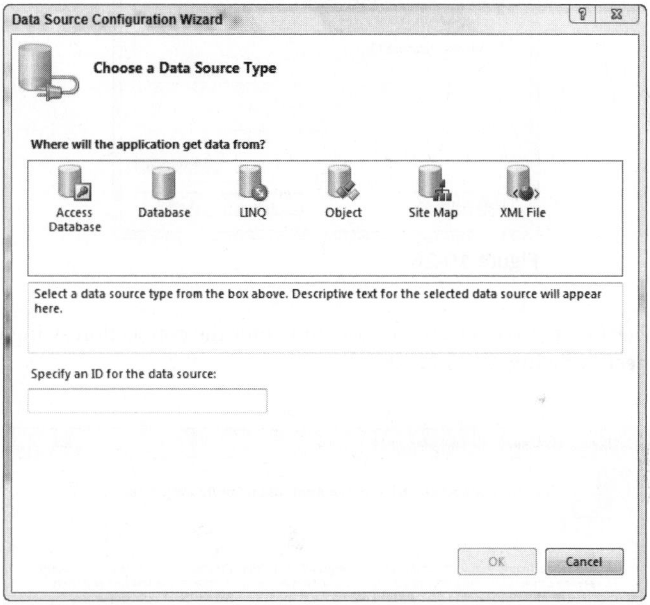

Figure 19-25

6.   Click OK to configure the data source. The Configure Data Source dialog opens. Click the New Connection button to create a new connection.

7.   In the Add Connection dialog shown in Figure 19-26, enter **(local)** as the server name, and select the previously created database BegVCSharpEvents. Click the Test Connection button to verify that the connection is correctly configured. When you're satisfied that it is, click OK. The next dialog (shown in Figure 19-27) opens, for storing the connection string.

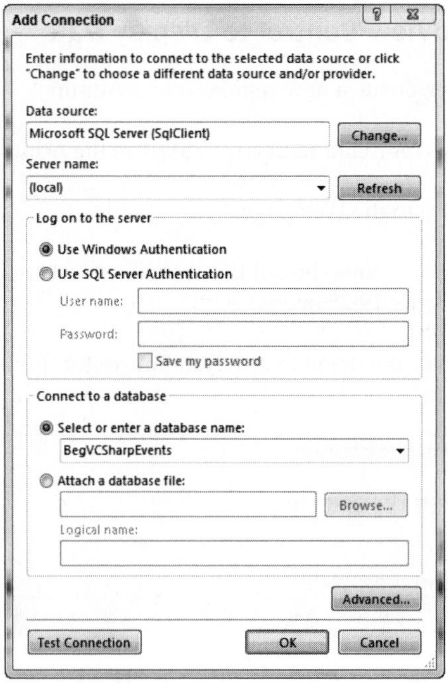

Figure 19-26

8. Click the check box to save the connection and enter the connection string name **EventsConnectionString**. Click Next.

Figure 19-27

9. In the next dialog, select the Events table to read the data from this table, as shown in Figure 19-28. Select the ID, Title, Date, and Location columns to define the SQL command shown in the figure. Click the Next button.

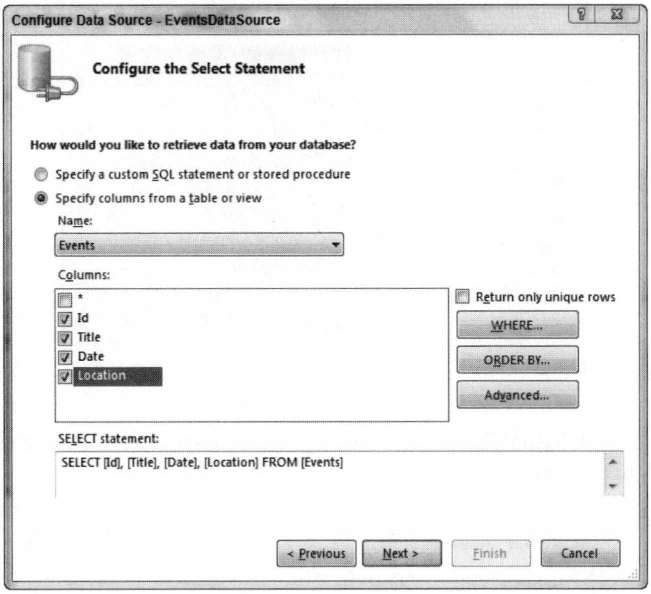

Figure 19-28

10. With the last window of the Configure Data Source dialog, you can test the query. Finally, click the Finish button.

11. In the designer, you can now see the `GridView` control with dummy data, and the `SqlDataSource` with the name `EventsDatasource`, as shown in Figure 19-29.

Id	Title	Date	Location
0	abc	02.10.2007 00:00:00	abc
1	abc	02.10.2007 00:00:00	abc
2	abc	02.10.2007 00:00:00	abc
3	abc	02.10.2007 00:00:00	abc
4	abc	02.10.2007 00:00:00	abc

SqlDataSource - EventsDataSource

Figure 19-29

12. For a more beautiful layout of the GridView control, select AutoFormat from the smart tag and select the scheme Lilacs in Mist, as shown in Figure 19-30.

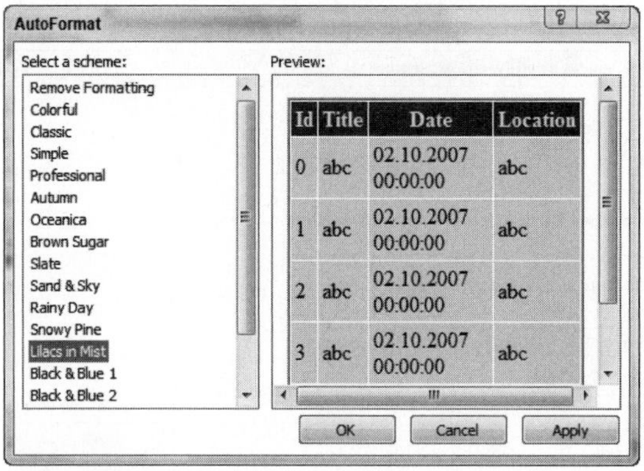

Figure 19-30

13. Start the page with Visual Studio, where you will see the events in a nice table like the one shown in Figure 19-31.

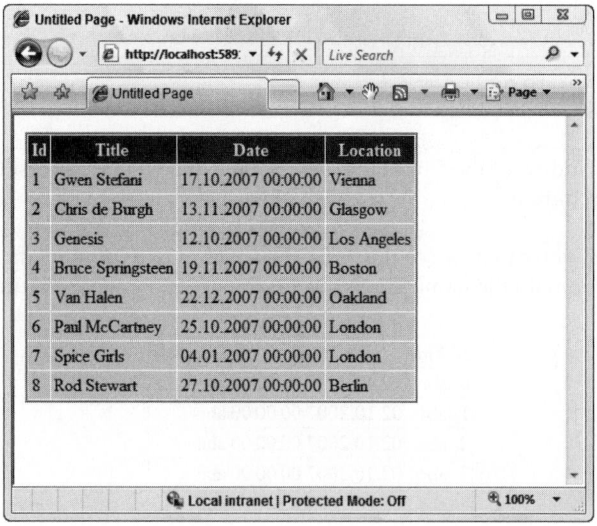

Figure 19-31

How It Works

After you add the GridView control, you can see its configuration in the source code. The DataSourceID attribute defines the association with the data source control that can be found after the grid control. Within the <Columns> element, all bound columns for displaying data are shown. HeaderText defines the text of the header and DataField defines the field name within the data source.

The data source is defined with the <asp:SqlDataSource> element, where the SelectCommand defines how the data is read from the database, and the ConnectionString defines how to connect with the database. Because you chose to save the connection string in the configuration file, <%$ is used to make an association with a dynamically generated class from the configuration file:

```
<asp:GridView AutoGenerateColumns="False" BackColor="White"
        BorderColor="White" BorderStyle="Ridge"

        BorderWidth="2px" CellPadding="3" CellSpacing="1" DataKeyNames="Id"
        DataSourceID="EventsDataSource"
        GridLines="None" ID="GridView1" runat="server">
    <footerstyle BackColor="#C6C3C6" forecolor="Black" />
    <rowStyle BackColor="#DEDFDE" forecolor="Black" />
    <Columns>
        <asp:boundfield DataField="Id" HeaderText="Id"
                InsertVisible="False" ReadOnly="True"
                SortExpression="Id"></asp:boundfield>
        <asp:boundfield DataField="Title" HeaderText="Title"
                SortExpression="Title"></asp:boundfield>
        <asp:boundfield DataField="Date" HeaderText="Date"
                SortExpression="Date"></asp:boundfield>
        <asp:boundfield DataField="Location" HeaderText="Location"
                SortExpression="Location"></asp:boundfield>
    </Columns>

    <pagerstyle backcolor="#C6C3C6" forecolor="Black"
            horizontalalign="Right" />
    <selectedrowstyle backcolor="#9471DE" font-bold="True"
            forecolor="White" />
    <headerstyle backcolor="#4A3C8C" font-bold="True" forecolor="#E7E7FF" />
    <editrowstyle font-bold="False" font-italic="False" />
</asp:GridView>

<asp:SqlDataSource
        ConnectionString="<%$ ConnectionStrings:EventsConnectionString %>"
        ID="EventsDataSource" runat="server" SelectCommand=
        "SELECT [Id], [Title], [Date], [Location] FROM [Events]">
</asp:SqlDataSource>
```

In the web.config configuration file, you can find the connection string to the database:

```
<connectionStrings>
  <add name="EventsConnectionString"
      connectionString="Data Source=(local);
      Integrated Security=True;Initial Catalog=BegVCSharpEvents;
      providerName="System.Data.SqlClient" />
</connectionStrings>
```

Now the GridView control should be configured differently. In the next Try It Out, the ID is no longer displayed to the user, and the date-time display shows only the date.

Configuring the GridView Control

1.   Select the smart tag of the GridView control and select the Edit Columns menu. The Fields
        dialog, shown in Figure 19-32, appears. Select the ID field, and change the Visible property
        to False. You can arrange the columns with this dialog, and you can change the colors and
        define the header text.

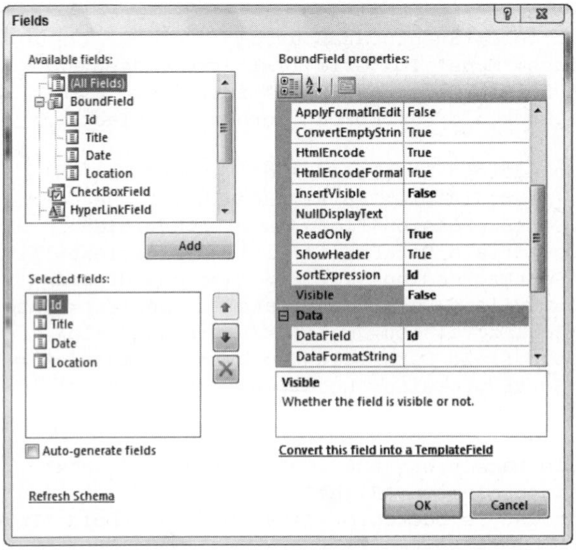

Figure 19-32

2.   For editing the GridView, an update command must be defined with the data source. Select
        the SqlDataSource control with the name EventsDataSource, and select Configure Data
        Source from the smart tag. In the Configure Data Source dialog, click the Next button until
        you can see the previously configured SELECT command. Click the Advanced button, and
        select the check box Generate INSERT, UPDATE, and DELETE statements, as shown in
        Figure 19-33. Click OK. Then click the Next and Finish buttons.

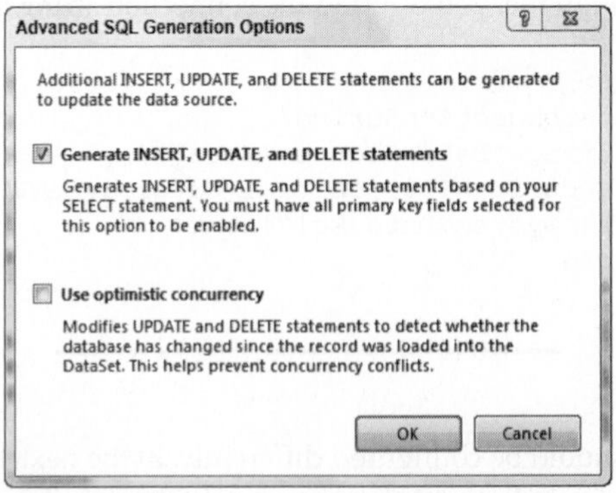

Figure 19-33

3. Select the smart tag of the `GridView` again. Now there's an Enable Editing item in the smart tag menu (see Figure 19-34). After you've selected the check box to enable editing, a new column is added to the `GridView` control. You can also edit the columns with the smart tag menu to arrange the new Edit button.

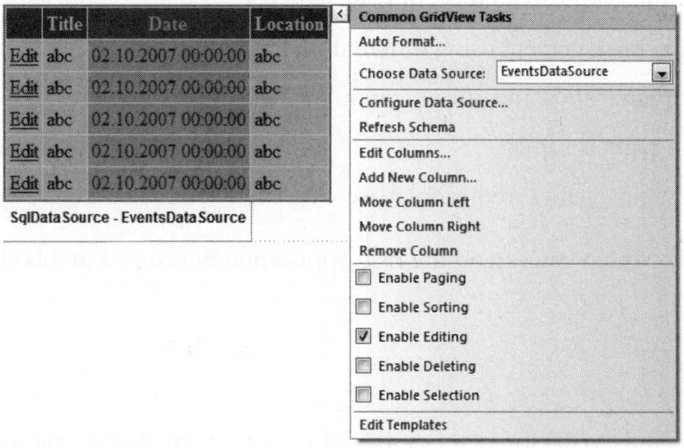

Figure 19-34

4. Start the application and edit the existing event records.

How It Works

No line of code had to be written manually in this example; everything was handled using ASP.NET Web controls. Behind the scenes, these controls make use of many features.

For example, the `SqlDataSource` control fills a `DataSet` with the help of a `SqlDataAdapter` with data from the database. The data used to fill the `DataSet` is defined with the connection string and the `SELECT` command. Just by changing a property of the `SqlDataSource`, the `SqlDataReader` can be used instead of the `DataSet`. Also, by setting the property `EnableCaching` to `true`, the `Cache` object (discussed earlier in the chapter) is used automatically.

Summary

This chapter described the architecture of ASP.NET, how to work with server-side controls, and some base features of ASP.NET. ASP.NET offers several controls for which not much code is necessary, as shown with the login and data controls.

After learning about the base functionality of ASP.NET with server controls and the event handling mechanism, you learned about input validation, several methods for state management, authentication, and authorization, and displaying data from the database.

Specifically, in this chapter you learned to do the following:

❑ Create a Web page with ASP.NET

❑ Use event handlers with Web server controls

❑ Verify user input with validation controls

❑ Deal with state management using different methods

❑ Configure authentication and authorization for Web applications

❑ Use ASP.NET login controls

❑ Access and display values from a database with the `SqlDataSource` and `GridView` controls

The exercises that follow help you extend the Web application developed in this chapter.

Exercises

1. Add the username to the top of the ASP.NET pages you created in this chapter. You can use the `LoginName` control for this task.

2. Add a page for password recovery. You can add a link to the Web page `login.aspx`, so that users can recover the password if the login fails.

3. Change the data source of the `Default.aspx` page so that it uses the Events database for displaying the events.

20

Advanced Web Programming

In Chapter 19, you learned about base features of ASP.NET, how server-side controls can be used to render HTML code to the client, input validation, and state management. You've also learned how security can be added, and how to read/write data from/to the database. This chapter looks at user interface elements and customization of Web pages with profiles and Web parts. Master pages are used to define a frame for multiple pages. You can use site navigation to define the structure of your Web site, making menus to access all the pages. To reuse controls within multiple pages on the same Web site, you can create user controls. The last section of the chapter describes Web parts, which you can use to create a portal Web site.

In this chapter, you learn about the following:

❑   Creating and using master pages

❑   Creating and using user controls

❑   Setting up navigation within Web sites

❑   Using profiles

❑   Using Web parts

❑   Coding with JavaScript

Master Pages

Most Web sites reuse part of their content on every page — things such as company logos and menus are often available on all pages. It's not necessary to repeat the common user interface elements with every page; instead, the common elements can be added to a *master page*. Master pages look like normal ASP.NET pages but define placeholders that are replaced by content pages.

A master page has the file extension `.master` and uses the `Master` directive in the first line of the file, as shown here:

```
<%@ Master Language="C#" AutoEventWireup="true" CodeFile="MasterPage.master.cs"
   Inherits="MasterPage" %>
```

Only the master pages in the Web site make use of `<html>`, `<head>`, `<body>`, and `<form>` HTML elements. The Web pages themselves contain only content that is embedded within the `<form>` element. The Web pages can embed their own content within the `ContentPlaceHolder` control. The master page can define default content for the `ContentPlaceHolder` if the Web page doesn't:

```
<html xmlns="http://www.w3.org/1999/xhtml">
<head runat="server">
  <title>Untitled Page</title>
      <asp:contentplaceholder id="head" runat="server">
      </asp:contentplaceholder>
</head>
<body>
  <form id="form1" runat="server">
    <div>
      <asp:contentplaceholder id="ContentPlaceHolder1" runat="server">
      </asp:contentplaceholder>
    </div>
  </form>
</body>
</html>
```

To use the master page, you must apply the `MasterPageFile` attribute to the `Page` directive. To replace the content of a master page, use the `Content` control. The `Content` control associates the `ContentPlaceHolder` with the `ContentPlaceHolderID`:

```
<%Page Language="C#" MasterPageFile="~/MasterPage.master"
    AutoEventWireUp="true" CodeFile="Default.aspx.cs" Inherits="default"
    Title="Untitled Page" %>
<asp:Content ID="Content1" ContentPlaceHolderID="head"
    Runat="Server"></asp:Content>
<asp:Content ID="Content2" ContentPlaceHolderID="ContentPlaceHolder1"
    Runat="Server"></asp:Content>
```

Instead of defining the master page with the `Page` directive, you can assign a default master page to all Web pages with the `<pages>` element in the Web configuration file, `web.config`:

```
<configuration>
    <system.web>
      <pages masterPageFile="~/MasterPage.master">
        <!-- ... -->
      </pages>
    </system.web>
</configuration>
```

With the master page file configured within `web.config`, the ASP.NET pages need a `Content` element configuration in the file as shown earlier; otherwise, the `masterPageFile` attribute would have no use. If you use both the `Page` directive's `MasterPageFile` attribute and the entry in `web.config`, the setting of the `Page` directive overrides the setting from `web.config`. This way, it's possible to define a default master page file (with `web.config`), but override the default setting for specific Web pages.

It is also possible to programmatically change the master page. By doing so, different master pages can be used for different devices or different browser types. The last place the master page can be changed is in the `Page_PreInit` handler method. In the following sample code, the `MasterPageFile` property of the `Page` class is set to `IE.master` if the browser sends the MSIE string with the browser name (which is done by Microsoft Internet Explorer) or to `Default.master` for all other browsers:

```csharp
public partial class ChangeMaster : System.Web.UI.Page
{
    void Page_Load(object sender, EventArgs e)
    {
    }

    void Page_PreInit(object sender, EventArgs e)
    {
        if (Request.UserAgent.Contains("MSIE"))
        {
            this.MasterPageFile = "~/IE.master";
        }
        else
        {
            this.MasterPageFile = "~/Default.master";
        }
    }
}
```

Now try creating your own master page in the following Try It Out. The sample master page here will have a heading and a body, and the main part of the master page will be replaced by individual pages.

Try It Out   Creating a Master Page

1. Open the Web site named EventRegistrationWeb that you created in the previous chapter.

2. Add a new Master Page item, as shown in Figure 20-1, and name it `EventRegistration .master`.

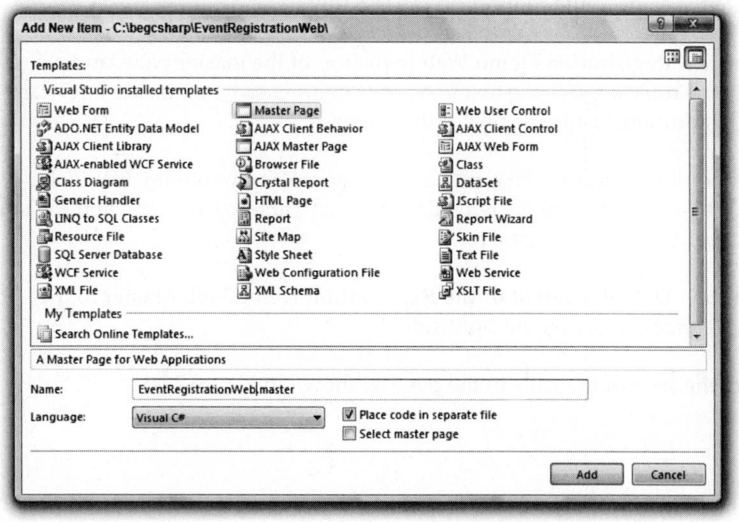

Figure 20-1

3. Remove the `ContentPlaceHolder` that was created automatically from the master page.

4. Insert a table in the page by selecting Table ➪ Insert Table. In the Insert Table dialog, select three rows and two columns as shown in Figure 20-2. The menu item Table is only available if you have the editor opened in Design View.

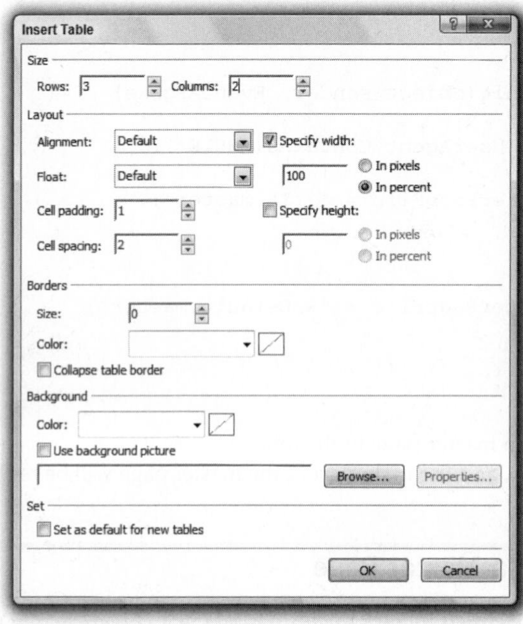

Figure 20-2

5. Select the two columns in the first row and merge them by selecting Table ➪ Modify ➪ Merge Cells. Do the same to the columns in the last row.

6. Add the text **Registration Demo Web** to the top of the master page, and a copyright notice to the bottom. You can place the text `Registration Demo Web` inside `<H1>` tags to make it larger. In addition, justify the text in the center.

7. In the second row, add a `ContentPlaceHolder` to every column. Name the `ContentPlaceHolder` on the left side `ContentPlaceHolderMenu` and the one on the right side `ContentPlaceHolderMain`.

8. Add the text **Default content of the Registration Demo Web Master** to the `ContentPlaceHolder` on the right side.

9. Arrange the sizes of the table in the page as shown in Figure 20-3.

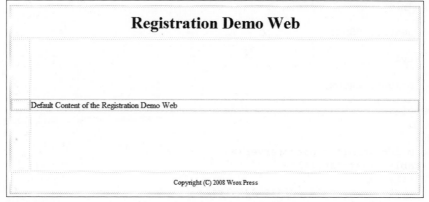

Figure 20-3

How It Works

As previously discussed, the master page contains the HTML, including the `<FORM>` tags that contain the content placeholders where the content will be replaced by the pages that use the master page. The HTML table defines the layout of the page:

```
<%@ Master Language="C#" AutoEventWireup="true"
      CodeFile="EventRegistration.master.cs" Inherits="EventRegistration" %>

<!DOCTYPE html PUBLIC "-//W3C//DTD XHTML 1.1//EN"
"http://www.w3.org/TR/xhtml11/DTD/xhtml11.dtd">

<html xmlns="http://www.w3.org/1999/xhtml" >
<head runat="server">
  <title>Untitled Page</title>
  <asp:ContentPlaceHolder id="head" runat="server">
  </asp:ContentPlaceHolder>
  <style type="text/css">
    .style1
    {
      width: 100%;
      height: 353px;
    }
    .style2
    {
      text-align: center;
    }
    .style3
    {
      font-size: smaller;
    }
```

```
      .style4
      {
        height: 58px;
      }
      .style5
      {
        height: 249px;
      }
    </style>
</head>
<body>
   <form id="form1" runat="server">
     <table class="style1">
       <tr>
         <td colspan="2" class="style4">
           <h1 class="style2">Registration Demo Web</h1>
         </td>
       </tr>
       <tr>
         <td class="style5">
           <asp:ContentPlaceHolder ID="ContentPlaceHolderMenu" runat="server">
           </asp:ContentPlaceHolder>
         </td>
         <td>
           <asp:ContentPlaceHolder ID="ContentPlaceHolderMain" runat="server">
               <p>Default content of the Registration Demo Web</p>
           </asp:ContentPlaceHolder>
         </td>
       </tr>
       <tr>
         <td class="style3" colspan="2" style="text-align: center">
             Copyright (C) 2008 Wrox Press</td>
       </tr>
     </table>
   </form>
</body>
</html>
```

After you have created the master page, you can use it from a Web page, as shown in the following Try It Out.

Try It Out   **Using a Master Page**

1.   Add a new item of type Web Form to the Web application and name it `EventList.aspx`.
     Click the Select Master Page check box (see Figure 20-4).

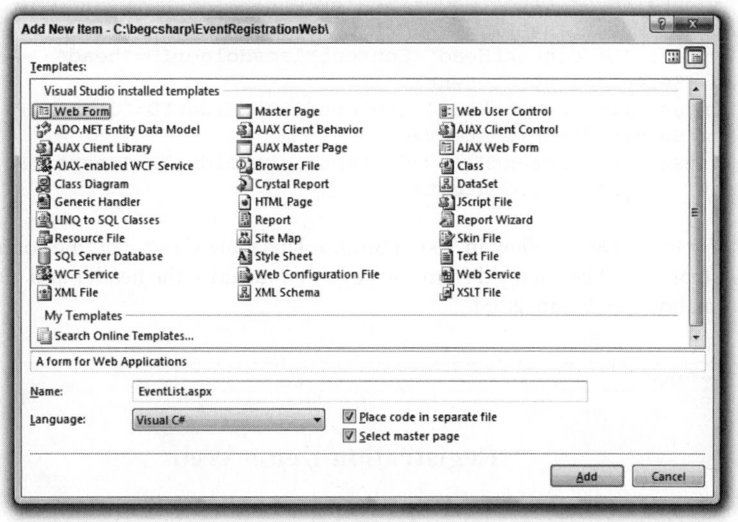

Figure 20-4

2.   Click the Add button to open the dialog Select a Master Page. Select the previously created
     master page `EventRegistration.master` (see Figure 20-5) and click OK.

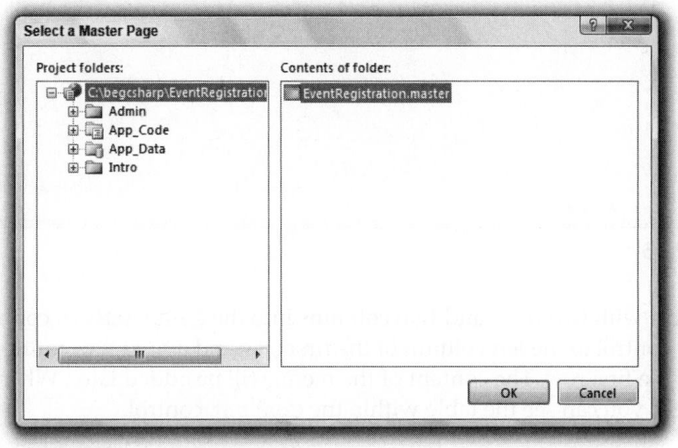

Figure 20-5

3. The Source View of the file `EventList.aspx` shows just three `Content` controls after the `Page` directive that references the `ContentPlaceHolder` controls from the master page. Change the `ID` properties of the `Content` controls to `ContentHead`, `ContentMenu`, and `ContentMain`:

```
<%@ Page Language="C#" MasterPageFile="~EventRegistration.master"
  AutoEventWireup="true" CodeFile="EventList.aspx.cs"
  Inherits="EventList" Title="Untitled Page" %>
<asp:Content ID="ContentHead" ContentPlaceHolderID="head"
  Runat="Server"><asp:Content>
<asp:Content ID="ContentMenu" ContentPlaceHolderID="ContentPlaceHolderMenu"
  Runat="Server"><asp:Content>
<asp:Content ID="ContentMain" ContentPlaceHolderID="ContentPlaceHolderMain"
  Runat="Server"><asp:Content>
```

4. Change to the Design View in Visual Studio. This view shows you the content of the master page that cannot be changed from the page that includes the header and copyright information (see Figure 20-6).

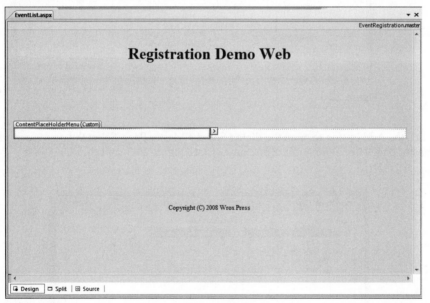

Figure 20-6

5. Insert a table with two rows and two columns into the `ContentMain` control. Add a `Calendar` control to the left column of the first row and a `ListBox` control to the right column of the first row. The content of the menu will be added later. When you open the Source View, you can see the table within the `Content` control.

6. View the page with the browser. The page includes the content from the Web page and the surroundings from the master page.

Site Navigation

For navigation between multiple pages on a Web site, you can define an XML file that contains the structure of the Web site, and use some UI controls to display the navigation options. The important navigation controls are listed in the following table:

Control	Description
SiteMapDataSource	SiteMapDataSource control is a data source control that references any site map data provider. In the Visual Studio Toolbox, you can find this control in the Data section.
Menu	The Menu control displays links to pages as defined with a site map data source. The Menu can be displayed horizontally or vertically, and it has many options to configure its style.
SiteMapPath	The SiteMapPath control uses a minimal space to display the current position of a page within the hierarchy of the Web site. You can display text or image hyperlinks.
TreeView	The TreeView control displays a hierarchical view of the Web site.

Try It Out   **Adding Navigation**

1. Open the Web site EventRegistrationWeb.

2. Add a new Site Map item to the Web site by right-clicking on the project in the Solution Explorer and selecting Add New Item. Keep the name Web.sitemap.

3. Change the content of the file as shown here:

```
<?xml version="1.0" encoding="utf-8" ?>
<siteMap xmlns="http://schemas.microsoft.com/AspNet/SiteMap-File-1.0" >
    <siteMapNode url="Default.aspx" title="Home">
        <siteMapNode url="Register.aspx" title="Register" />
        <siteMapNode url="EventList.aspx" title="Events" />
    </siteMapNode>
</siteMap>
```

4. Open the file EventRegistration.master.

5. Locate the SiteMapDataSource control under the Data Tab in your Toolbox and add it to the page.

6. Add a Menu control from the Navigation tab of your Toolbox below the title "Registration Demo Web." Set the data source to SiteMapDataSource1.

7. Add a SiteMapPath control below the Menu control.

8. Open the file EventList.aspx in the browser. Notice the menu and the path that displays the position of the current file in the Web site.

9. You can add other pages that are referenced in the file Web.sitemap as needed by referencing the same master page to show the defined menus.

How It Works

The structure of the Web site is defined by the Web pages listed in the file Web.sitemap. This XML file contains XML <siteMapNode> elements inside a <siteMap> root element. The <siteMapNode> element defines a Web page. The filename of the page is set with the url attribute, and the title attribute specifies the name as it should appear on menus. The hierarchy of the pages is defined by writing <siteMapNode> elements as child elements of the page where the link to the children should occur.

The SiteMapDataSource control is a data source control with similarities to the data source controls shown in the previous chapter. This control can use different providers. By default, the XmlSiteMapProvider class is used to get to the data. By default, the XmlSiteMapProvider class uses the page Web.sitemap, which is why you've never configured this filename. If you rename the XML file, the siteMapFile property of this provider must be set to a new filename.

With the Menu control you can edit menu items that appear in the ASPX source; or you can add menu items programmatically. The easiest way to add menu items is to use a site map data source by configuring the data source.

User Controls

If multiple Web controls that collaborate are used in several Web pages, you can create user controls. A user control has the file extension .ascx and contains parts of a form that can be included in several Web pages. Instead of creating the user interface and writing the code several times for every page where the same content is needed, the user control is implemented only once and used several times.

A user control can be added statically or dynamically to a Web page. Used dynamically, the controls shown can be changed during runtime.

A user control is represented by the Control directive in the first line of the source file. The CodeFile and Inherits attributes have the same usage as with the Page directive:

```
<%@ Control Language="C#" AutoEventWireup="true"
    CodeFile="DemoUserControl.ascx.cs" Inherits="DemoUserControl" %>
```

Normal HTML code that is part of a form follows the Control directive. The <HTML> and <FORM> tags are not used within the user control because the HTML code of the user control is embedded within a HTML form.

The user control can be added statically to the page as shown in the following ASPX code sample. It is referenced with the Register directive. The Src attribute references the ASCX file of the user control, named DemoUserControl.ascx in this example. TagPrefix and TagName define the names of the control used within the page. `TagPrefix` is set to `uc1` and `TagName` is set to `DemoUserControl`. That's why the control itself is referenced within the page using `<uc1:DemoUserControl>`. You can compare the `uc1` prefix to the `asp` prefix that is used with ASP.NET Web server controls.

```
<%@ Page Language="C#" AutoEventWireup="true" CodeFile="DemoPage.aspx.cs"
    Inherits="DemoPage" %>
<%@ Register tagprefix="uc1" tagname="DemoUserControl"
    src="DemoUserControl.ascx" %>

<html xmlns="http://www.w3.org/1999/xhtml" >
...
<uc1:DemoUserControl ID="DemoUserControl1" runat="server" />
...
```

Instead of declaring a user control statically, you can load it dynamically. To implement a dynamic user control, put a `PlaceHolder` control on the page. User controls can be added within the `Controls` collection of the placeholder. The `Page_Load` event handler shown demonstrates loading the user control `DemoUserControl.ascx` with the `LoadControl` method of the `Page` class. The returned control is added to the `Controls` collection of the `PlaceHolder` control named `PlaceHolder1`. Using such a technique, different user controls can be loaded according to user settings based on post data or URL strings:

```
void Page_Load(object sender, EventArgs e)
{
    Control c1 = LoadControl("DemoUserControl.ascx");
    PlaceHolder1.Controls.Add(c1);
}
```

It is easy to create and use user controls. You can immediately create one by following the instructions in the next Try It Out. Created here is a new custom user control that is used to show a calendar and countries for events in a drop-down list.

Try It Out   Creating a User Control

1. Open the previously created Web site EventRegistrationWeb.

2. Add a new user control by selecting Website ⇨ Add New Item; select the Web User Control template and name it `ListEvents.ascx`.

3. Add a table with two rows and one column to the user control.

4. Use the designer to add a `Calendar` control and a drop-down list to the user control, as shown in Figure 20-7. Name the calendar control `EventCalendar` and the drop-down list `DropDownListCountries`.

5. Set the `AutoPostback` property of the drop-down list to `true`.

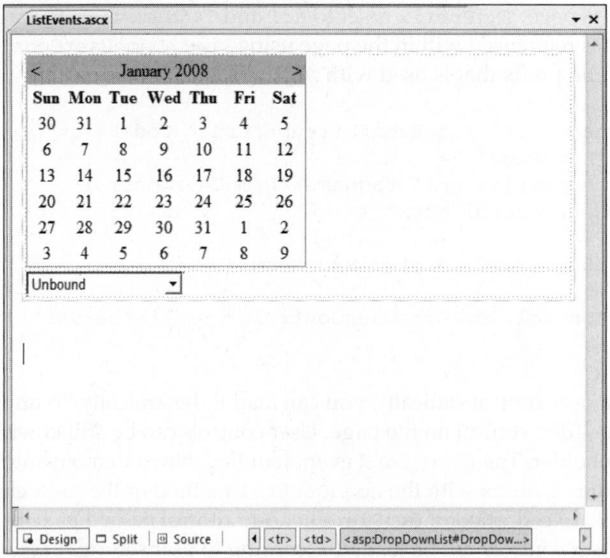

Figure 20-7

6. Open the source file of the user control, `ListEvents.ascx.cs`. Add a public
`Configure()` method as shown to initialize the elements of the user control. Public methods
and properties can be invoked from the Web pages using the control.

```
public void Configure(DateTime date, params string[] countries)
{
    DropDownListCountries.Items.Clear();

    EventCalendar.SelectedDate = date;
    ListItem[] items = new ListItem[countries.Length];
    for (int i = 0; i < countries.Length; i++)
    {
        items[i] = new ListItem(countries[i]);
    }
    DropDownListCountries.Items.AddRange(items);
}
```

The user control can now be used from within Web pages. In the next Try It Out, you create a Web page
that displays the user control as its content.

Try It Out   **Using a User Control**

1.   Create a new Web page `UseMyControl.aspx`.

2.   Open the Web page in Design View. Drag and drop the user control from the Solution Explorer to the design surface. The content of the user control immediately shows up in the designer. When you check the ASPX code, you will see the added `Register` directive and user control code.

3.   Open the source code to add initialization code for the user control by invoking the public method created earlier:

```
protected void Page_Load(object sender, EventArgs e)
{
    if (!Page.IsPostBack)
    {
        ListEvents1.Configure(DateTime.Today, "Italy",
            "France", "Germany", "Spain");
    }
}
```

4.   Start the Web page. The calendar shows the current date selected, and the drop-down list contains the list of countries available.

Profiles

Many commercial Web sites enable you to add products to a shopping cart, but if you feed your cat before submitting your order, the session times out. The lesson? It's not a good idea to store orders only in session variables because session state is lost after the session timeout occurs.

To keep state persistence, you can use profiles. Profiles are stored in the database, so they are also kept in cases where sessions end. Profiles have the following characteristics:

❑   They are stored persistently. The data store is managed by a profile provider. ASP.NET 3.5 includes profile providers for SQL Server and Access. Custom profile providers can be developed.

❑   They are strongly typed. Session and application variables use an indexer, and casting is required to access the data. When you use profiles, properties with the name of the profile are generated automatically. The name and type of the properties are defined in the configuration file.

❑   They can be used with both anonymous and authenticated users. With anonymous users, the user identification can be stored inside the cookie. As soon as the user logs on to the Web site, the state from the anonymous user can be converted to the state for the authenticated user.

In the next Try It Out, you create and use profile information.

Try It Out   Creating Profile Information

1. Open the previously created Web application EventRegistrationWeb.

2. Open the file `web.config` that was created in the previous chapter. If you don't see a `web.config` file the Solution Explorer, create a new one by selecting the menu option Add New Item and select Web Configuration File.

3. Add the `<profile>` XML element section containing the `Country`, `Visits`, and `LastVisit` properties to the file `web.config`, as shown. The `Country` property is of type `String` (the default), the property `Visits` is of type `Int32`, and the property `LastVisit` is of type `DateTime`:

```
<configuration xmlns="http://schemas.microsoft.com/.NetConfiguration/v2.0">
  <system.web>
  <!-- ... -->

    <profile>
      <properties>
        <add name="Country" />
        <add name="Visits" type="System.Int32" defaultValue="0" />
        <add name="LastVisit" type="System.DateTime" />
      </properties>
    </profile>

    <!-- ... -->
  </system.web>
</configuration>
```

4. Create a new Web page, `ProfileDemo.aspx`, and add three labels to display current values and a drop-down list to select a country. Set the name of the labels to `LabelLastVisit`, `LabelVisitCount`, and `LabelSelectedCountry`. Set the name of the drop-down list to `DropDownListCountries`, add some countries, and set `AutoPostBack` to true.

5. Add an event handler named `OnCountrySelection` to the `SelectedIndexChange` event of the drop-down list as follows:

```
protected void OnCountrySelection(object sender, EventArgs e)
{
    Profile.Country = this.DropDownListCountries.SelectedItem.Value;
    Profile.Save();
}
```

6. Add the following code to the `Page_Load()` event handler to display current values from the profile. `Profile` is a dynamically created property of the `Page` class that has properties defined within the configuration file. These properties are strongly typed — the name and type of the properties match those defined in the configuration file.

```
void Page_Load(object sender, EventArgs e)
{
    if (!Page.IsPostBack)
    {
        DropDownListCountries.SelectedValue = Profile.Country;
    }

    LabelLastVisit.Text = Profile.LastVisit.ToLongTimeString();
    LabelVisitCount.Text = Profile.Visits.ToString();
    LabelSelectedCountry.Text = Profile.Country;

    Profile.Visits++;
    Profile.LastVisit = DateTime.Now;
    Profile.Save();
}
```

7. Now you can start and view the Web page. Select a country from the list. Close the browser and start it again. The profile information is retained between sessions.

How It Works

The `Profile` property that you can use within the code of a Web page is dynamically created. You can't find this property in the `Page` class in the MSDN documentation because this property doesn't exist as part of the `Page` class. Instead, because of the property configuration in the `web.config` configuration file, the `Profile` property is created dynamically. The type of the `Profile` property is a dynamically created class that derives from `ProfileBase` and contains properties as defined with the configuration file.

Profile Groups

Profiles can keep track of a lot of information, and that information can be grouped. A group of properties is defined with the `<group>` element, as shown here:

```
<configuration xmlns="http://schemas.microsoft.com/.NetConfiguration/v2.0">
  <system.web>
    <profile>
      <properties>
        <add name="Country" />
        <add name="Visits" type="System.Int32" defaultValue="0" />
        <add name="LastVisit" type="System.DateTime" />
          <group name="EventSelection" >
            <add name="Country" />
            <add name="City" />
            <add name="StartDate" type="System.DateTime" />
            <add name="EndDate" type="System.DateTime" />
          </group>
      </properties>
    </profile>

    <!-- ... -->
  </system.web>
</configuration>
```

In order to access profile values defined within groups, a dynamic property is created that can be used to access the property values:

```
string country = Profile.EventSelection.Country;
string city = Profile.EventSelection.City;
DateTime startDate = Profile.EventSelection.StartDate;
DateTime endDate = Profile.EventSelection.EndDate;
```

Profiles with Components

Inside the code of the components, profile information cannot be accessed with a `Profile` property. Instead, the profile is accessed with the help of `HttpContext`. In addition, strong typing is not available. The following example accesses the `Country` profile string defined earlier. `Current` is a static property of the `HttpContext` class, which returns an `HttpContext` object associated with the client session. The property `Profile` returns an object of type `ProfileBase`, where every profile value can be accessed using an indexer. The indexer is defined to return objects of type `Object`, so a cast is needed to write the value to a variable.

```
string country = (string)HttpContext.Current.Profile["Country"];
```

Profiles with Custom Data Types

With profiles, you can store not only base data types such as `int`, `short`, `string`, and `DateTime`, but also custom data types. The data type just has to support one serialization mechanism. The following list explains the serialization mechanisms supported with profiles:

❑ **XML Serialization**: This is the default. With XML serialization, all public properties and fields are stored. This mechanism requires a default constructor. XML serialization is described in Chapter 23.

❑ **Binary Serialization**: With binary serialization, the class must be marked with the attribute `[Serializable]`. Here, all private fields are serialized. Runtime serialization is described in Chapter 22.

❑ **String Serialization**: With string serialization, a type converter class can be used to serialize the data. If there's no type converter class to do the serialization, the `ToString()` method is invoked to serialize the object as a string.

The serialization used is defined with the `serializeAs` attribute. If this attribute is not set, then XML serialization is used. The possible options with `serializeAs` are `Binary`, `Xml`, and `String`.

```
<profile>
  <properties>
    <add name="Demo" type="MyClass" serializeAs="Binary" />
  </properties>
</profile>
```

Profiles with Anonymous Users

By default, profiles are only enabled for authenticated users. To enable profiles for anonymous users, anonymous users must be enabled in the configuration file, and every profile property that should be available for anonymous users must be set individually:

```
<configuration>
  <system.web>
    <anonymousIdentification enabled="true" />
    <profile>
      <properties>
        <add name="Country" allowAnonymous="true" />
      </properties>
    </profile>
```

When a profile is accessed for an anonymous user, the anonymous user is created in the database of the profile provider. The anonymous user gets an ID similar to an authenticated user. By default, the ID of the anonymous user is stored inside a cookie, although it is also possible to use anonymous user identifiers within URL strings (*URL mungling*) instead of cookies.

Often, anonymous profile information must be migrated to authenticated users. For example, a user might be able to add products to a shopping basket without being logged on; but to send the order, the user must log on to the system. In such a case, all the profile information that was stored for the anonymous user must be migrated to the authenticated user.

For dealing with anonymous profiles, the following events can be acted on in `global.asax`:

Handler Name	Description
AnonymousIdentification_Create	When an anonymous user accesses the Web site for the first time, an anonymous profile is created. At this time the event handler `AnonymousIdentification_Create` is invoked.
AnonymousIdentification_Remove	When an authenticated user accesses the Web page and the request of the authenticated user contains a profile identifier of an anonymous user, the anonymous user profile is removed and the event handler `AnonymousIdentification_Remove` is invoked.
Profile_MigrateAnonymous	After the `AnonymousIdentification_Remove` event handler, the event handler `Profile_MigrateAnonymous` is invoked. With this event handler, an anonymous profile can be migrated to a profile for an authenticated user.

The implementation of the handler `Profile_MigrateAnonymous` in `global.asax` looks like the following sample. All profile values allowed for anonymous users can be migrated to the authenticated user configuration. The sample code migrates the `Country` profile value that is allowed for anonymous users in the configuration file. First, `Profile.Country` is checked to determine whether it already has a value. `Profile.Country` will have a value if the user was already logged on to the system when the profile value was created. It will not have a value if the user has been anonymous to the system before.

Here, the method `GetProfile()`, passing an ID of a user, helps to access profile information from other users. Although the same person sits on the client, an authenticated user and an anonymous user always have different user IDs. When an anonymous user logs on the system and becomes an authenticated user, the ID of the anonymous user is passed with the argument `ProfileMigrateEventArgs` of the method `Profile_MigrateAnonymous()`. The anonymous user ID (`e.AnonymousId`) is passed to the method `GetProfile()` to access the profile of the anonymous user. This profile information is then migrated to the profile information of the authenticated user by assigning profile value by value (such as the `Country` in the example).

```
void Profile_MigrateAnonymous(object sender, ProfileMigrateEventArgs e)
{
    if (Profile.Country == null)
    {
        Profile.Country = Profile.GetProfile(e.AnonymousId).Country;
    }
}
```

Web Parts

A very cool feature that enables customizing Web applications for every user is Web Parts. With Web Parts, portal-style Web applications can be created easily. Facebook.com (see Figure 20-8) is an example of a portal-style social-networking application that enables users to organize information as they like. Web Parts can be arranged to contact other users, get travel information, discuss topics in many groups, and so on. With a personalized Web portal, a user can configure what Web parts should be available.

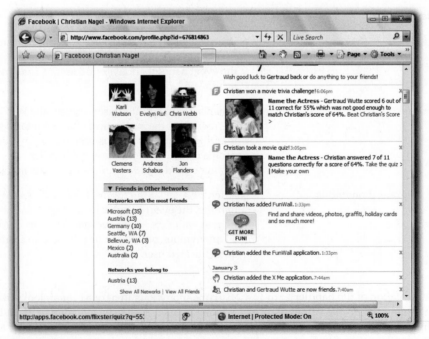

Figure 20-8

The Web Parts framework is made up of zones and parts. The parts that can be inside a zone depend on the type of the zone; for example, a LayoutEditorPart can be a part inside the EditorZone.

The major zone is the Web Parts zone. A Web page can have multiple Web Parts zones to define the layout of the page. Inside this zone, multiple Web parts, user controls, or Web server controls can be contained.

The Catalog zone enables the user or administrator to choose Web Parts from a catalog to be displayed within the Web page. For this zone, the parts PageCatalogPart, ImportCatalogPart, and DeclarativeCatalogPart can be used.

With the EditorZone, the user or administrator can edit the behavior and appearance of individual Web Parts. The following items enable changing the look and feel of Web Parts: AppearanceEditorPart, BehaviorEditorPart, and LayoutEditorPart.

The Connections zone is used to connect multiple Web Parts together, enabling communication between them. For example, if the user selects a month in one Web Part, then another Web Part displayed within the same page is aware of the month and can change its own behavior.

Web Parts Manager

A control required with every Web Parts-enabled site is the WebPartManager. This control is responsible for managing Web Parts. With the WebPartManager, Web Parts controls can be created, deleted, or moved.

The only requirement for a WebPartManager is that it be represented on a Web page, as shown with this ASPX code:

```
<asp:WebPartManager ID="WebPartManager1" runat="server"></asp:WebPartManager>
```

This control doesn't have a user interface at runtime, and it's not necessary to configure any properties. Its properties just enable you to configure some warning messages when Web Parts controls are closed and deleted. What's interesting about the WebPartManager are the methods you can optionally use to change the display mode, as shown later.

Web Parts Zone

To make use of the Web Parts framework, at least one WebPartZone must exist. A WebPartZone contains Web Parts controls and defines the layout and appearance of the Web Parts controls within the zone. As previously mentioned, the WebPartZone can contain user controls, Web parts, and Web server controls.

Within the ASPX page, the WebPartZone includes a ZoneTemplate that contains controls for display. The example here contains the previously created user control ListEvents:

```
<asp:WebPartZone ID="EventsZone" runat="server">
  <ZoneTemplate>
    <uc1:ListEvents ID="ListEvents1" runat="server" />
  </ZoneTemplate>
</asp:WebPartZone>
```

With the `WebPartZone` it is possible to define layout, color, and menus. The following sample shows the `WebPartZone` with the predefined professional layout to set colors and styles to the frame and the Web Parts menus:

```
<asp:WebPartZone BorderColor="#CCCCCC" Font-Names="Verdana"
    ID="EventZone" Padding="6" runat="server">
  <PartChromeStyle BackColor="#F7F6F3" BorderColor="#E2DED6"
      Font-Names="Verdana" ForeColor="White" />
  <MenuLabelHoverStyle ForeColor="#E2DED6" />
  <EmptyZoneTextStyle Font-Size="0.8em" />
  <MenuLabelStyle ForeColor="White" />
  <MenuVerbHoverStyle BackColor="#F7F6F3" BorderColor="#CCCCCC"
      BorderStyle="Solid" BorderWidth="1px" ForeColor="#333333" />
  <HeaderStyle Font-Size="0.7em" ForeColor="#CCCCCC"
      HorizontalAlign="Center" />
  <MenuVerbStyle BorderColor="#5D7B9D" BorderStyle="Solid"
      BorderWidth="1px" ForeColor="White" />
  <PartStyle Font-Size="0.8em" ForeColor="#333333" />
  <TitleBarVerbStyle Font-Size="0.6em" Font-Underline="False"
      ForeColor="White" />
  <MenuPopupStyle BackColor="#5D7B9D" BorderColor="#CCCCCC"
      BorderWidth="1px" Font-Names="Verdana" Font-Size="0.6em" />
  <PartTitleStyle BackColor="#5D7B9D" Font-Bold="True"
      Font-Size="0.8em" ForeColor="White" />
  <ZoneTemplate>
    <uc1:ListEvents ID="ListEvents1" runat="server" />
  </ZoneTemplate>
</asp:WebPartZone>
```

In the next Try It Out, you create the Web page `WebPartDemo.aspx` with the initial steps required to use the Web Parts framework. You will add two user controls to two different zones.

Try It Out   Creating a Web Application Using Web Parts

1. Open the previously created Web application EventRegistrationWeb.

2. Add a new page named `WebPartsDemo.aspx`.

3. Add a `WebPartManager` control to this page (found under the WebParts tab in your Toolbox).

4. Add a table with two columns and two rows to organize the layout of the Web Parts.

5. Within each column of the second row, add a `WebPartZone` control. Later, controls will be added to the first row. Set the ID of the first `WebPartZone` to `ZoneLeft`, and the ID of the second zone to `ZoneRight`.

6. Using the smart tag of the first `WebPartZone` control in Design View, select the Professional Auto Format. For easy differentiation of the second `WebPartZone`, select the Colorful Auto Format.

7. Set the `HeaderText` property of the first `WebPartZone` to `Events`, and set the same property of the second zone to `Weather`.

8. Add the user control `ListEvents.ascx`, created earlier, to the left `WebPartZone`.

9. Create a new Web user control `Weather.ascx` to show weather information based on a country. For now, the user control just needs one label named `LabelWeather`. You can use a random algorithm as shown if sun, cloudy, or rain should be displayed. Add this user control to the right `WebPartZone`.

```
public partial class Weather : System.Web.UI.UserControl
{
    protected void Page_Load(object sender, EventArgs e)
    {
        Random r = new Random();
        int n = r.Next(1, 3);

        switch (n)
        {
            case 1:
                LabelWeather.Text = "Sun";
                break;
            case 2:
                LabelWeather.Text = "Rain";
                break;
            case 3:
                LabelWeather.Text = "Cloudy";
                break;
        }
    }
}
```

10. Start the Web page. Figure 20-9 shows the user controls. Note the frame around the controls with the title Untitled and the small downward-pointing triangle (the Verb button) on the right side of the frame. This frame is known as the *chrome*. Click the Verb button to see the menu entries Minimize and Close. Try to minimize the control and restore it again, but don't click the Close menu entry because with no catalog configured, it is not possible to reopen the closed controls.

Figure 20-9

11. Now you are going to make it impossible to close the controls. Open the Web page again in the designer and select a Web Part. Open the `CloseVerb` property in the Property Editor. Set the `Enabled` option of this property to `false`. This makes it impossible to select the `Close` menu item. To remove the menu entry, set the `Visible` property to `false`, too.

12. Open the Web page in the browser again. Notice that the Close menu entry cannot be selected.

Editor Zone

The Editor zone is used to change the appearance, behavior, and layout of the Web Parts. For each of these activities, different editor parts are available. The editor parts are active when a Web Parts control is set to Edit mode.

The Layout editor part (see Figure 20-10) enables you to set the chrome state, the zone where the Web Part should be placed, and the order of a Web Part inside a zone. The chrome state can be Normal or Minimized. With Minimized chrome, the Web Part is displayed only with a small icon so that it won't take up a lot of space within the Web page. The user can restore the Web Part to a normal view by clicking this icon. The Zone combo box lists the names of all zones where the Web Parts controls can be placed.

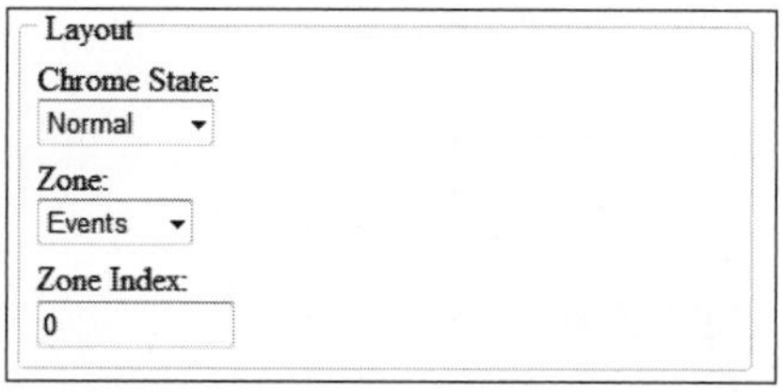

Figure 20-10

The Appearance editor part enables you to set the title, chrome type, and size. Figure 20-11 shows all the possible settings of the Appearance editor part. The title is used to give a Web Part a new header. The chrome type defines the visibility of the title and the border. The height and width of the Web Parts control can also be specified.

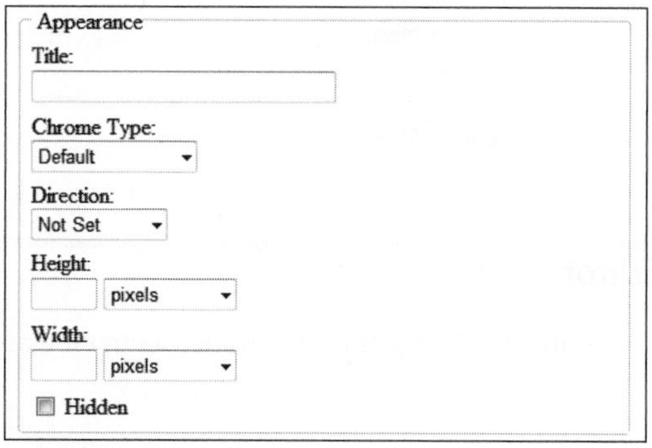

Figure 20-11

The Behavior editor part (see Figure 20-12) enables you to set title links and images, catalog links and images, and whether the Web Parts controls should be allowed to close, be edited, hide, and be minimized. The Export mode defines whether it is possible to export the Web Parts control information to the local disk of the user. Here, only the settings of the Web Parts control are exported to the local disk. This configuration can be used again to import the Web Parts control with any Web site that offers the same Web Parts controls.

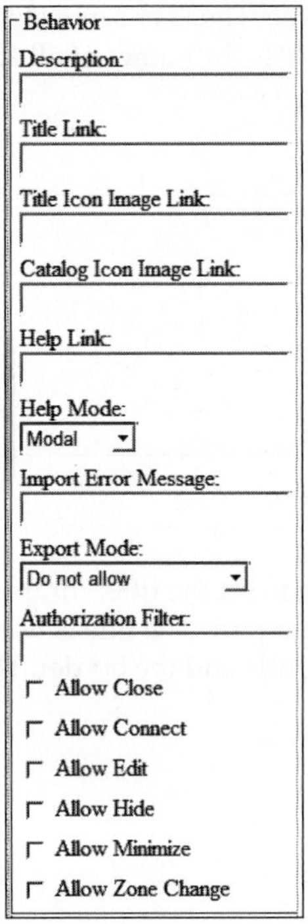

Figure 20-12

Try It Out   Adding an Editor Zone

Adding an Editor zone makes it possible to change the appearance, behavior, and layout of the Web parts:

1. Open the previously created Web page `WebPartDemo.aspx`.

2. Add an `EditorZone` control to the first row of the table within the page.

3. Add an `AppearanceEditorPart` and a `LayoutEditorPart` to the Editor zone.

4. Add a `DropDownList` control to the top of the page. This control will be used to change from Browse mode to Edit mode. Rename the `DropDownList` control to `DropDownListDisplayModes`.

5. Set the `AutoPostBack` property of the `DropDownListDisplayModes` control to `true`.

6. Add the following code to the class `WebPartsDemo` in the file `WebPartsDemo.aspx.cs`. Here, all the display modes that are supported by the actual configuration of the `WebPartManager` are shown in the drop-down list:

```
protected void Page_Init(object sender, EventArgs e)
{
    foreach (WebPartDisplayMode mode in WebPartManager1.SupportedDisplayModes)
    {
        if (mode.IsEnabled(WebPartManager1))
        {
            DropDownListDisplayModes.Items.Add(new ListItem(mode.Name));
        }
    }
}
```

7. Add the method `OnChangeDisplayMode` to the `SelectedIndexChanged` event of the drop-down list for `DropDownListDisplayModes`.

8. Add an implementation to the method `OnChangeDisplayMode()` to change the display mode of the `WebPartManager` to the mode that is selected in the drop-down list `DropDownListDisplayModes`:

```
protected void OnChangeDisplayMode(object sender, EventArgs e)
{
    string selectedMode = DropDownListDisplayModes.SelectedValue;
    WebPartDisplayMode mode = WebPartManager1.SupportedDisplayModes[selectedMode];
    if (mode != null)
    {
        WebPartManager1.DisplayMode = mode;
    }
}
```

9. Start the Web page in the browser. Because an Editor zone exists, there's an Edit selection in the drop-down list. Set the drop-down list to Edit the Page. Notice the Edit menu with the Web Parts chrome when you click the Verb button.

10. Select the Edit menu. The Editor zone appears. Change the title and chrome type of the Web Parts. Try to move the Web Parts to other zones, and change the zone order.

11. Instead of using the Editor parts of the Editor zone to change the Web Parts, you can also drag and drop a Web Part from one zone to another — if the mode is set to Edit mode.

Catalog Zone

The Catalog zone is a real catalog — you can select Web Parts from a catalog. Again, the Catalog zone is similar to the other zones that manage Web Parts. The Web Parts managed by a Catalog zone are Catalog parts. ASP.NET has three different kinds of catalogs: a page catalog, a declarative catalog, and an import catalog.

Figure 20-13 shows the `PageCatalogPart`. The page catalog lists all Web Parts available within a Web page. All Web Parts that have been closed by the user are listed within the `PageCatalogPart`. This way, the user can reopen closed controls.

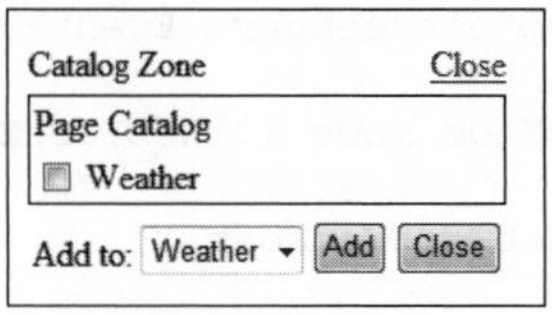

Figure 20-13

With the `DeclarativeCatalogPart`, shown in Figure 20-14, the controls that should be available for selection must be explicitly defined within a `<WebPartsTemplate>` element. With the Visual Studio Designer, this can be done by clicking the smart tag of the control and clicking Edit Templates.

```
<asp:CatalogZone ID="CatalogZone1" runat="server">
  <ZoneTemplate>
    <asp:DeclarativeCatalogPart runat="server" ID="DeclarativeCatalogPart1">
      <WebPartsTemplate>
        <uc1:ListEvents ID="ListEvents2" runat="server" />
        <asp:Calendar ID="Calendar1" runat="server" />
      </WebPartsTemplate>
    </asp:DeclarativeCatalogPart>
  </ZoneTemplate>
</asp:CatalogZone>
```

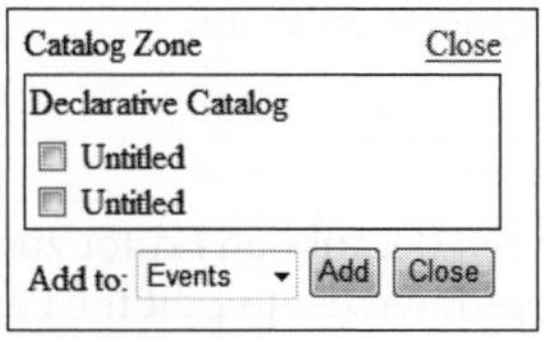

Figure 20-14

The `ImportCatalogPart` can be used to import Web Parts that have been stored on the client system. As shown in Figure 20-15, `ImportCatalogPart` includes Browse and Upload buttons. With the Browse button, a locally stored Web Part can be selected and uploaded to the user's personalized settings on the Web server.

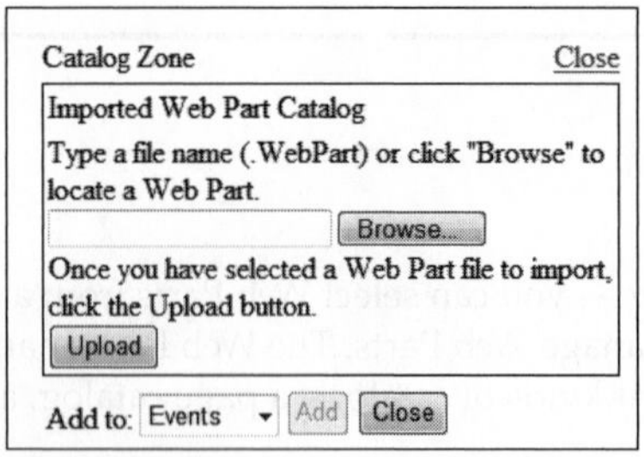

Figure 20-15

Adding a Catalog zone makes it possible to select Web Parts that should be included with the Web page from a catalog. In the next Try It Out, you create a Catalog zone that includes multiple catalogs.

Try It Out   **Adding a Catalog Zone**

1. Open the previously created Web page `WebPartDemo.aspx`.

2. Add a `CatalogZone` control to the second column of the first row of the table within the page.

3. Select a Professional Auto Format with the `CatalogZone` control.

4. Add a `PageCatalogPart` and a `DeclarativeCatalogPart` to the Catalog zone. Be sure to drop these controls directly on top of the `CatalogZone`, as these controls cannot exist directly on the page.

5. The `DeclarativeCatalogPart` requires some configuration. In the designer, click the smart tag of the `DeclarativeCatalogPart` control, and click Edit Templates. Now you can add several controls (user controls or Web server controls) to the control. After you've completed adding the controls, click the End Template Editing option.

6. Start the Web page in the browser. Close one or several Web Parts controls by clicking the Close menu. The Web Parts controls disappear. Of course, you can't close the controls of the zone where you've set the `Enabled` property of `CloseVerb` to `false`.

7. Set the `DropDownList` to Show the Catalog. Because of the existence of the `CatalogZone`, the Catalog menu is added to the drop-down list. The Catalog zone opens.

8. Select Page Catalog from the catalog list. In the page catalog, all Web Parts that have been closed appear in a list. Select Web Parts from the list and add it to a zone.

9. Select Declarative Catalog from the catalog list. With the declarative catalog, all configured Web Parts appear in the list. Select Web Parts from the list, add it to a zone, and close the Catalog zone.

Connections

Using the Connections zone, you can send data from one Web Parts control to another Web Parts control on the same page. For example, if the user selects a city for weather information from the Weather Web Part, the selected city can be sent to the News Web Part that shows news from the same city.

The `WebPartManager` is responsible for initiating and managing communication between the Web Parts. Communication between the Web Parts requires a consumer and a provider to be differentiated. The provider offers some data; the consumer uses the data. Figure 20-16 shows the interaction of the `WebPartManager` with the consumer and the provider. The `WebPartManager` calls methods from the providers to get interfaces that can be accessed to receive the data. The providers are identified with the attribute `[ConnectionProvider]`. The `WebPartManager` then passes these interfaces to the consumers. Consumers are identified with the attribute `[ConnectionConsumer]`. Now the consumer can invoke methods of the provider to receive data.

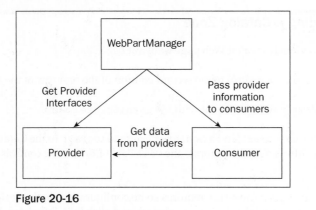

Figure 20-16

In the next Try It Out, you enable two Web Parts to communicate, passing a selected country from the `ListEvents` Web Part to another Web Part.

Try It Out   Creating a Connection between Web Parts

1.   Open the previously created Web site EventRegistrationWeb.

2.   Open the special folder `App_Code` in the Solution Explorer. If the folder does not exist, then create one by selecting Website ⇨ Add Folder ⇨ App_Code Folder.

3.   Create a new C# file `ICountry.cs` to define the `ICountry` interface:

```
public interface ICountry
{
    string GetCountry();
}
```

4.   Open the source code (`ListEvents.ascx.cs`) of the previously created user control `ListEvents`. With the `ListEvents` class, implement the interface `ICountry`. The `GetCountry()` method is implemented to return the selected country to the caller:

```
public partial class ListEvents : System.Web.UI.UserControl, ICountry
{
    public string GetCountry()
    {
        return DropDownListCountries.SelectedItem.Value;
    }

    //...
```

5.   The provider also needs a method that is marked with the attribute `[ConnectionProvider]`. The method must return an interface. Implement the method `GetCountryInterface()` to return a reference to the `ICountry` interface. The attribute `[ConnectionProvider]` defines a friendly name (Country) and an actual name (CountryProvider) for the provider. Add the following code to the ListEvents.ascx.cs file as well:

```
[ConnectionProvider("Country", "CountryProvider")]
public ICountry GetCountryInterface()
{
    return this;
}
```

6.   Create a new Web user control named Country.ascx that acts as a consumer. This user control just needs a simple label to display the country. Set the ID of the label to LabelCountry.

7.   Open the C# code of the user control Country to implement a consumer method that is marked with the attribute [ConnectionConsumer]. The method SetCountry() receives the ICountry interface, which it uses to receive the data from the provider by calling the GetCountry() method. The returned string is assigned to the Text property of the label:

```
[ConnectionConsumer("Country", "CountryConsumer")]
public void SetCountry(ICountry provider)
{
    string country = provider.GetCountry();
    if (!string.IsNullOrEmpty(country))
    {
        LabelCountry.Text = country;
    }
}
```

8.   Open the Web page WebPartDemo.aspx. Add the new Country.ascx user control to a Web Parts zone.

9.   Select the WebPartManager and click the Ellipsis button with the StaticConnections property in the Property Editor. Add a new connection with the following settings:

Connection Properties	Value
ConsumerConnectionPointID	CountryConsumer
ConsumerID	Country1
ID	CountryConnection
ProviderConnectionPointID	CountryProvider
ProviderID	ListEvents1

Configuring the connections with the Property Editor adds the <StaticConnections> element to the WebPartManager control, as shown:

```
<asp:WebPartManager ID="WebPartManager1" Runat="server">
  <StaticConnections>
    <asp:WebPartxConnection ID="CountryConnection" ProviderID="ListEvents1"
        ProviderConnectionPointID="CountryProvider" ConsumerID="Country1"
```

```
                    ConsumerConnectionPointID="ListEvents1" />
            </StaticConnections>
        </asp:WebPartManager>
```

10. Start the Web page. With the connection setup, if you select a country with the `ListEvents` control, the country shows up in the `Country` control.

11. Instead of using static connections, with the possibility to change the Web Parts shown during runtime, it is also necessary to configure connections during runtime. This can be done with the `ConnectionsZone` control. Add the `ConnectionsZone` control to the Web page and remove the static connections from the `WebPartManager`.

12. Start the Web page again. Select Connect in the drop-down list.

13. Setting the `WebPartManager` to `ConnectDisplayMode` (which happens when the drop-down list is changed), the `ConnectionsZone` is not immediately visible. Instead, with all provider and consumer controls, the Verb button offers the new verb Connect. Click this Connect entry of the `Country` control; this opens the `ConnectionsZone`. Create a dynamic connection with the `ListEvents` control (see Figure 20-17).

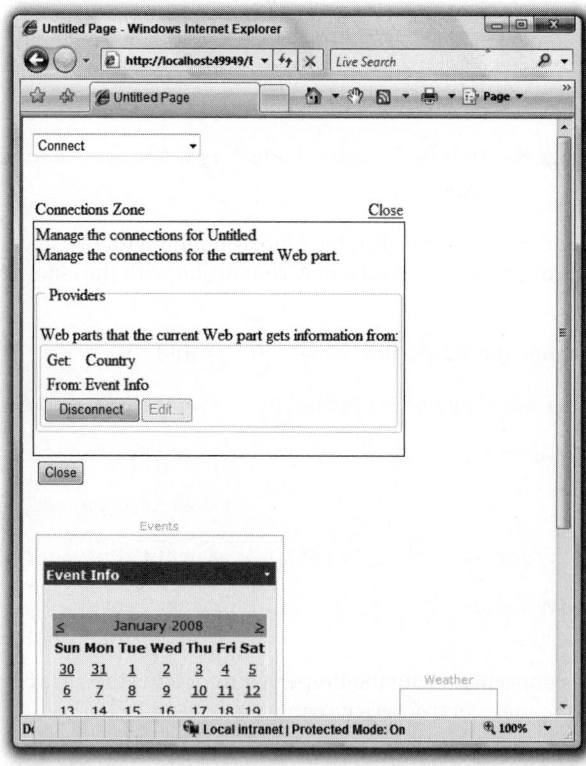

Figure 20-17

14. As before, select a country with the `ListEvents` control, enabling the selected country to appear in the `ListEvents` control.

JavaScript

To interact with the user on the client, you can add JavaScript code to the Web pages. JavaScript does not require a .NET installation on the client system and works with most browsers.

The original version of JavaScript comes from Netscape. JavaScript does not have anything other than the name in common with Java. The name JavaScript was created because of a cooperation between Sun and Netscape. Now you can see different flavors of JavaScript because other vendors are not allowed to use Java in the product name: ECMAScript is the standardized version of this scripting language, standardized by Ecma International (`www.ecma-international.org`). Microsoft's implementation of this standard is known by the term JScript.

Visual Studio 2008 is improved with the support of JavaScript, which includes IntelliSense and debugging functionality. JavaScript has some similarities with the syntax of C#, but behind the scenes it is very different. There's no compiler to create Intermediate Language (IL) code; instead, JavaScript is interpreted during runtime.

Let's get into the JavaScript syntax before some Try It Outs.

Script Element

Within the HTML code, you can add JavaScript code inside the `<script>` element:

```
<script language="javascript" type="text/javascript">
  <!--
  function foo()
  {
  }
  -->
</script>
```

You can also put the JavaScript functions in a separate `.js` file and reference this separate file from the script block with the `src` attribute:

```
<script language="javascript" type="text/javascript" src="SampleScripts.js" />
```

Separating the JavaScript functions helps with reuse and caches the scripts in the client browser. If the scripts are needed with different pages, the functions are loaded just once.

Declaration of Variables

Variables are declared with the var keyword. C# 3.0 also has the var keyword, but this is very different with JavaScript. With JavaScript, the variable can get any type. In the following example, the first line declares variable x to be a number. With the next line, the variable x references a string. Finally, the variable x references an object that has the properties FirstName and LastName. The properties are created dynamically, just as they are assigned:

```
var x = 3;

x = "text";

x = new Object();
x.FirstName = "Tom";
x.LastName = "Turbo";
```

You can also declare and initialize an object in one line:

```
var p = { "FirstName" : "Tom", "LastName" : "Turbo" };
```

The property values can be accessed with a property syntax you know from C#, but also with brackets:

```
var f = p.FirstName;
var l = p["LastName"];
```

Defining Functions

JavaScript functions are defined with the function keyword. Arguments are just defined by name:

```
function foo(arg1, arg2)
{
}
```

You can also define a variable to reference a function using the Function object. With the constructor of the Function object, the last parameter defines the implementation of the function; the parameters before that list the arguments of the function:

```
var add = new Function("x", "y", "return x + y");
```

Statements

Iteration statements are very similar to C#. With JavaScript you can use the keywords for, while, and do ... while. Instead of the C# foreach statement, you can use for ... in.

With for ... in, you can iterate not only arrays, but also all properties of an object, as shown here with the variable p, which has the properties FirstName, LastName, and Country assigned. The for ... in statement iterates through all properties and fills a string with property names and values:

```
var p = {"FirstName" : "Christian", "LastName" : "Nagel",
         "Country" : "Austria"};
var s = "";
for (key in p)
{
    s += key;
    s += ": ";
    s += p[key];
    s += "\t";
}
```

To conditionally perform some action, you can use the `if...else` and `switch` statements.

Objects

JavaScript offers some predefined objects with several methods. One example is the `String` object for working with strings. With strings, JavaScript defines the functions `toUpperCase()`, `toLowerCase()`, and `indexOf()` to return the first occurrence of a substring, `lastIndexOf()` to return the last occurrence of a substring, and `slice()` to return a substring by specifying a from and to position.

The `String` object also offers methods that surround the string with HTML code. For example, the `bold()` function adds a `<B>` element before the string and `</B>` after the string. Other functions are `anchor()`, to create a hyperlink, and `italics()`, to create an italics string.

The `Math` object enables you to do some calculations. `abs()`, `sin()`, `cos()`, `tan()`, `random()`, and `round()` are some methods of this object.

The `Date` object represents date and time. Several methods exist to access different parts of the date and time, such as `getYear()`, `getMonth()`, `getDay()`, `getHours()`, and `getMinutes()`.

Let's get into some examples that demonstrate how JavaScript can be used with Web pages.

Try It Out   Using the CustomValidator

The validator controls described in Chapter 19 included both client-side and server-side validation. With the `CustomValidator` control, you can define a custom JavaScript method to validate user input:

1. Open the previously created Web site EventRegistrationWeb.

2. Add a new Web Page named `ValidationDemo.aspx`.

3. Add `TextBox`, `Button`, and `CustomValidator` controls. For the `CustomValidator`, set the property `ControlToValidate` to **TextBox1**.

4. For the `CustomValidator`, set the event `ServerValidate` to the method `OnServerOddNumber` and implement the method with C#:

```
protected void OnServerOddNumber(object source, ServerValidateEventArgs args)
{
    if (int.Parse(args.Value) % 2 != 0)
    {
        args.IsValid = true;
    }
    else
    {
        args.IsValid = false;
    }
}
```

5. Add a JavaScript method named `oddNumberValidation()` to do the same validation you did in the previous step, this time using JavaScript:

```
<script language="javascript" type="text/javascript">
function oddNumberValidation(source, arguments)
{
    if (arguments.Value % 2 != 0)
    {
        arguments.IsValid = true;
    }
    else
    {
        arguments.IsValid = false;
    }
}
</script>
```

6. With the `CustomValidator` control, set the property `ClientValidationFunction` to `oddNumberValidation`. Then, start the page and debug the validation methods both on the client and on the server.

Try It Out   **Creating Objects**

1. Open the previously created Web site EventRegistrationWeb.

2. Add a new Web Page named `ObjectDemo.aspx`.

3. From the HTML category of the Toolbox, add a Div and an Input (Button) element to the page. The Div element should have the default identifier `div1` assigned.

4. Add the following script block to the HTML source. The function `Person(firstName, lastName)` behaves like a constructor because the `this` keyword is used inside the function to create properties `firstName` and `LastName`. The prototype syntax allows declaring a JavaScript version of a class. `Person.prototype` assigns the members of the `Person`

class. `Person.prototype.constructor` assigns the `Person` function as the constructor; `Person.prototype.toString` assigns the `toString` function as a member. The function `GetPerson()` creates a new `Person` object by calling the constructor with two arguments, and invokes the `toString` method. `document.getElementById()` finds the `div` tag to write the result there:

```
<script type="text/javascript">

function Person(firstName, lastName)
{
    this.firstName = firstName;
    this.lastName = lastName;
}

function toString()
{
    return this.firstName + " " + this.lastName;
}

Person.prototype.constructor = Person;
Person.prototype.toString = toString;

function getPerson()
{
    var p = new Person("Natalie", "Portman");
    var label = document.getElementById("div1");
    label.innerHTML = p.toString();
}
</script>
```

5. Add the `onclick` property to the button so that the function `getPerson()` is invoked when the `click` event occurs:

```
<input id="Button1" type="button" value="button" onclick="getPerson();" />
```

6. Now you can run and test the Web page.

Try It Out   Opening a Window

To open a Window on the client, you need to use JavaScript. You cannot open new Windows just from C# code-behind:

1. Open the previously created Web site EventRegistrationWeb.

2. Add a new Web page named `OpenWindow.aspx`. Add a HTML button to the page.

3. Add the JavaScript function `openWindow()` to open a page that has been created previously:

```
<script type="text/javascript">
function openWindow()
{
    window.open("ObjectDemo.aspx");
}
</script>
```

4. Add the `onclick` property to the button to invoke the `openWindow()` function:

```
<input id="Button1" type="button" value="button" onclick="openWindow();"/>
```

5. Now you can test the page and open a new window directly on the client.

The default settings of most browsers don't allow scripting code to open new windows without specific interaction from the user. (Many applications are annoying, opening window after window when the user closes one window.) As a general rule, opening a new window with JavaScript via user interaction is OK, but it is still possible for an overzealous pop-up blocker to catch these windows.

With the `open` method of the window, you can pass several parameters, as shown in the following snippet. The first parameter is the URL of the document that should be opened. The second parameter defines the name of the window. With the value `_blank`, a completely new window is opened, but you can also pass the target of a frame. The third parameter is a comma-separated list of features, whereby you can specify the size of the window and whether several options should be visible, such as the menu, title bar, and status bar:

```
window.open("ObjectDemo.aspx", "_blank",
    "menubar=no, resizable=no, status=no, titlebar=no, width=300, height=300");
```

Try It Out   Iterating through Controls

With the `window` object from the previous Try It Out, you already used an object that is not part of JavaScript, but part of DHTML instead. With DHTML, you can access all HTML elements from a page. Let's get into an example that retrieves some information about the HTML controls from a page:

1. Open the previously created Web site EventRegistrationWeb.

2. Add the new Web page `ScriptingDemo.aspx`. Add a table with five rows and two columns to the page. To the first four rows in the left column, add `Label` controls. Add three `TextBox` and one `DropDownList` controls to the right column. Add an HTML `Input` (Button) control to the last row of the right column.

3. Below the table, add an HTML `TextArea` control and resize it to occupy a large part of the page to show all the information about the elements.

4. Set the `onclick` property of the HTML button to invoke the `walktree()` method:

```
<input id="b1" type="button" value="Click"
    onclick="walktree(0, form1.childNodes);" />
```

5. Implement the `walktree()` method in a script block. This method calls itself recursively when iterating children of the elements. The result is written to the `TextArea1` element. You can access every element with the `getElementById()` method of the `document` object. When the method is called the first time, all the children of the `Form` are passed to the `tree` variable. From every item in the tree, the `tagName` property is written to the `TextArea`. If the item has children, `walktree` is invoked again, and the `childNodes` of the item are passed to the `tree` variable:

```
<script language="javascript" type="text/javascript">
function walktree(level, tree)
{
    var textArea = document.getElementById("TextArea1");

    var numItems = tree.length;

    for (var i = 0; i < numItems; i++)
    {
        var item = tree.item(i);
        textArea.value += level + " " + item.tagName + "\n";

        if (item.hasChildNodes)
        {
            walktree(level + 1, item.childNodes);
        }
    }
}
</script>
```

6. start the page to access all HTML elements from JavaScript.

Summary

This chapter covered many features of ASP.NET, including master pages, profiles, and Web Parts. Master pages enable you to define a common layout for all pages. Profiles are used to store user data persistently in a database. Unlike session variables, whereby the state is lost when the session timeout occurs, profiles are stored in the database. Because profiles are strongly typed, it is easy to access the value using properties and Visual Studio IntelliSense.

Web Parts are a powerful new feature of ASP.NET. They enable the creation of portal-style Web applications that can be customized by individual users with just a few clicks. With the Web Parts framework, you've looked at different zone types, including the `WebPartZone`, the Editor zone, Catalog zone, and the Connections zone.

User controls were also discussed, because these controls make it easy to reuse components with Web pages. User controls can also be used within Web zones.

JavaScript was also covered briefly in this chapter, because it enables interacting with the user on the client. JavaScript is a foundation of AJAX, as described in Chapter 22.

In this chapter, you've learned about the following:

❑   Creating and using master pages

❑   Creating a structure for your site to navigate different pages

❑   Creating user controls

❑   Storing user-specific data using profiles

❑   How to enable users to customize a Web application using Web Parts

❑   Using JavaScript with Web pages

In the exercises in this chapter, you create a new Web application that uses the ASP.NET features demonstrated in this chapter and the previous chapter. The next chapter gets you started with how to write Web services with ASP.NET.

Exercises

1.   Create a new portal-style personal Web application.

2.   Create a user control to display your résumé.

3.   Create a user control to display a list of links to your preferred Web sites.

4.   Define forms authentication as the authentication mechanism for the Web site.

5.   Create a user control whereby a user can register on the Web site.

6.   Create a master page that defines a common layout with top and bottom sections.

7.   Define a site map to create links to all the Web pages on the Web site.

8.   Create a Web page that uses the Web Parts framework, whereby users can define the layout of the page.

21

Web Services

You've certainly come across the term *Web services* before, although you may not be aware of what they are or how they fit into the way the Web operates — and will operate in the future. Suffice it to say that Web services provide the foundation of the new generation of Web applications. Whatever the client application is — whether it is a Windows application or an ASP.NET Web Forms application — and whatever operating system the client is running — Windows, Pocket Windows, or some other OS — they will regularly communicate over the Internet using a Web service.

Web services are server-side programs that listen for messages from client applications and return specific information. This information may come from the Web service itself, from other components in the same domain, or from other Web services. While the concept of the Web service is evolving continuously, there are several different types of Web services that carry out different functions: Some provide information specific to a particular industry such as manufacturing or healthcare; there are portal services that use services from different providers to offer information on a specific theme; there are services specific to single applications, and building block services that can be used by many different applications.

Web services give you the capability to combine, share, exchange, or plug in separate services from various vendors and developers to form entirely new services or custom applications created on-the-fly to meet the requirements of the client.

This chapter covers the following topics:

- ❑ Predecessors of Web services
- ❑ What a Web service is
- ❑ Protocols used for Web services
- ❑ Creating an ASP.NET Web service
- ❑ Testing a Web service
- ❑ Building a client to use Web services

❑   Calling a Web service asynchronously

❑   Sending and receiving messages

This chapter does not go into the inner workings of Web services, but you will get an overview of what these protocols are used for. After reading this chapter, you can start creating and consuming simple Web services with the help of Visual Studio.

Before Web Services

Connecting computers to transfer data was already an important concept in 1969 when just four computers were connected via telephone lines to form the ARPANET (Advanced Research Projects Agency Network). In 1976, the TCP/IP protocol was invented. To make this protocol easy to use, the University of Berkeley created the socket model for network programming.

When programming with the Sockets API, the client had to initiate a connection to the server and then send and receive data. To call some operations on the server to get results, additional protocols are needed to describe request and response codes. Examples of such so-called application protocols are File Transfer Protocol (FTP), Telnet, and Hypertext Transfer Protocol (HTTP). The FTP protocol is used to get files from the server and to put the files on the server. The FTP protocol supports request codes such as GET and PUT, which are sent across the wire from the client to the server. The server analyzes the data stream it receives, and, according to the request codes, invokes the corresponding method. The HTTP protocol works very similarly to the FTP protocol.

Remote Procedure Call (RPC)

With the Sockets API and the TCP/IP protocol calling custom methods on the server, the programmer would have had to create a means by which the server analyzes the data stream to invoke the corresponding method. To make all this work more easily, some companies created an RPC (remote procedure calls) protocol, an example of which is the still popular DCE-RPC protocol (Distributed Computing Environment – Remote Procedure Calls) from the Open Software Foundation (OSF), which later became the Open Group (www.opengroup.org). Using RPC, you defined methods in an IDL (Interface Definition Language) format, which the server has to implement, and which the client can call. You no longer have to define a custom protocol and parse the request codes to invoke the methods. This work is done by a special program, called a *stub*, generated by an interface compiler.

RPC is designed to invoke methods, which means that you have to do procedural programming. The RPC technology came in relatively late, when most developers had already started to work with the object-oriented paradigm. To bridge the technology gap, several technologies came into being, including CORBA and DCOM.

CORBA

In 1991, the Object Management Group (OMG) (www.omg.org) initiated CORBA (Common Object Request Broker Architecture) to add object-orientation to network programming. Many vendors such as Digital Equipment, HP, IBM, and others implemented CORBA servers. Because the OMG didn't define a reference implementation, however, only a specification, the servers of these vendors didn't really interoperate. The HP server needed an HP client, the IBM server an IBM client, and so on.

DCOM

With Windows NT 4, Microsoft extended the DCE-RPC protocol with object-oriented features. The DCOM (Distributed COM) protocol made it possible to call COM components across the network and is used in COM+ applications. After some years in which Microsoft operating systems were a requirement for DCOM, Microsoft opened the protocol for others with the Active Group. DCOM was made available for UNIX, VMS, and IBM systems. DCOM was heavily used in the Microsoft environments, but the initiative to bring it to other systems was not really successful. What IBM mainframe administrator wants to add Microsoft technology to his or her system?

RMI

Sun Microsystems took a different route with its Java technologies. In a pure Java world, the RMI (Remote Method Invocation) protocol can be used to call objects remotely. Sun added some bridges to the CORBA and COM world, but the major goal for Sun was to bring the masses to a Java-only solution.

SOAP

All the technologies that you've seen were used for application-to-application communication, but if you have a CORBA, a DCOM, and an RMI solution, it is hard to get these different technologies to talk together. Another problem with these technologies can be found in their architectures: Because they are not designed for thousands of clients, they can't achieve the scalability required for Internet solutions.

As a result, several companies, including Microsoft and UserLand Software (`www.userland.com`), created SOAP in 1999 as a completely new way of invoking objects over the Internet, one that builds upon already accepted standard protocols. SOAP uses an XML-based format to describe methods and parameters to make remote calls across the network. A SOAP server in the COM world could translate the SOAP messages to COM calls, whereas a SOAP server in the CORBA world translates them to CORBA calls. Originally, the SOAP definition made use of the HTTP protocol so that SOAP calls could be done across the Internet.

With SOAP 1.2, Web services are independent of the HTTP protocol. Any transport protocol can be used, but the most frequently used transport protocol for Web services is still HTTP. This chapter focuses on Web services that can be created with the Visual Studio 2008 Project Template, which makes use of SOAP and HTTP.

> *SOAP specifications can be found at* `www.w3.org/TR/SOAP`.

Where to Use Web Services

To get another view of what Web services are, you can distinguish between *user-to-application* communication and *application-to-application* communication. Let's start with a user-to-application communication example: getting some weather information from the Web. Several Web sites such as `weather.msn.com` and `www.weather.com` present weather information in an easy-to-digest format for a human reader. Normally, these pages are read directly by a user.

If you wanted to create a rich client application to display the weather (application-to-application communication), your application would have to connect to the Web site with a URL string containing the city for which you want to know the weather. You would have to parse the resulting HTML message returned from the Web site to get the temperatures and weather conditions, and then you could finally display the information in an appropriate format for the rich client application.

That's a lot of work, considering that you just want to get some temperature readings for a particular city, and the process of getting the data from the HTML is not trivial because HTML data is designed to be displayed in the Web browser; it's not meant to be used by any other client-side business application. Therefore, the data is embedded in the text and is not easily extracted, and you would have to rewrite or adapt the client application to retrieve different data information (such as rainfall) from the same Web page. Compared to using a Web browser, users can immediately pick out the data they need and can overlook what they don't need.

To get around the problem of processing HTML data, a Web service provides a useful means for returning only the data requested. Just call a method on the remote server and get the information needed, which can be used directly by the client application. At no point do you have to deal with the preformatted text that is meant for the user interface, because the Web service presents the information in XML format, and tools already exist to process XML data. All that is required from the client application is to call some methods of the .NET Framework XML classes to get the information. Better still, if you are writing a client in C# for a .NET Web service, you don't even need to write the code to do that — there are tools that will generate C# code for you!

This sort of weather application is one example of how Web services can be used, but there are a lot more.

A Hotel Travel Agency Application Scenario

How do you book your vacations? Instead of having a travel agency do all the work for you, you can book your holiday on the Internet. On an airline's Web site, you can look for possible flights and book them. A Web search engine can be used to look for a hotel in the desired city. Maybe you are lucky and find a map showing how to get to the hotel. When you find the hotel's home page, you navigate to the booking form page and book the room. Next you would search out a car rental firm, and so on.

A lot of the work you have to do today is to find the right Web sites with the help of search engines, and then to navigate these sites. Instead of going through that, you could create a Home Travel Agency application that uses Web services containing details about hotels, airlines, car rental firms, and so on. Then you can present the client with an easy-to-use interface to deal with all aspects of the vacation, including an early booking of a special musical event. With your Pocket PC on location during your holiday, you can use the same Web services to get a map to some leisure-time activities, and to get accurate information about cultural events or cinema programs, and so on.

A Book Distributor Application Scenario

Web services can also be useful for two companies that have a partnership. Assume that a book distributor wants to provide bookstores with information about books in stock. This can be accomplished with a Web service. An ASP.NET application using the Web service can be created to offer this service directly to users. Another client application of this service is a Windows application for the bookstore, which first checks the local stock and then that of the distributor. The salesperson can immediately answer questions about delivery dates without having to check different stock information in different applications.

Client Application Types

The client of a Web service can be a rich Windows application created using Windows Forms, or an ASP.NET application using Web Forms. A Windows PC, a UNIX system, or a Pocket PC can be used to consume (use) the Web service. With the .NET Framework, Web services can be consumed in every application type — Windows, Web, or console.

Smart client is a term for a rich client application that makes use of Web services. The smart client can operate without being connected to the Web service because it caches data locally. Microsoft Outlook is an example of a smart client, as all the mail data is stored on the client system, and when the Exchange server can be connected the data is synchronized.

Application Architecture

What does an application using Web services actually look like? Regardless of whether you develop ASP .NET or Windows applications, or applications for small devices (as described in the application scenarios presented here), Web services is an important technology.

Figure 21-1 illustrates a scenario showing how Web services can be used. Devices and browsers are connected through the Internet to an ASP.NET application developed with Web Forms. This ASP.NET application uses some local Web services and some other remote Web services that can be reached across the network: portal Web services, application-specific Web services, and building block Web services. The following list should help to elucidate the meaning of these service types:

❑ **Portal Web services**: Offer services from different companies with the same subject matter. This is an easy-to-use access point for multiple services.

❑ **Application-specific Web services**: Created just for the use of a single application.

❑ **Building block Web services**: Those that can easily be used within multiple applications.

The Windows applications in Figure 21-1 can use the Web services directly without going through the ASP.NET application.

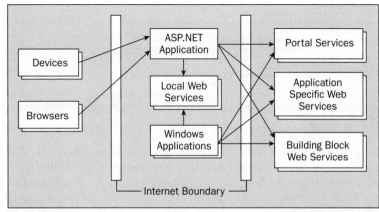

Figure 21-1

Web Services Architecture

Web services make use of the SOAP protocol, which is a standard defined by many companies. A big advantage of Web services is its platform-independence. However, Web services are not only a useful technology when multiple platforms need to cooperate. They are also a very useful technology for developing .NET applications on both the client and the server side. The advantage here is that the client and the server can emerge independently. A service description is created with a WSDL (Web Service Description Language) document that can be designed in a way to be independent of new versions of the Web service, and therefore the client needn't be changed.

Let's look into the steps of the sequence in more detail.

What Methods Can I Call?

A WSDL document has the information about the methods a Web service supports and how they can be called, parameter types passed to the service, and parameter types returned from the service. Figure 21-2 shows the WSDL that is generated from the ASP.NET runtime. Appending the string `?wsdl` to the `.asmx` file returns a WSDL document.

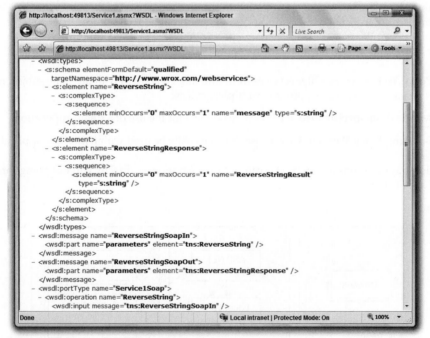

Figure 21-2

It is not necessary to deal with this information directly. The WSDL document will be generated dynamically with the `WebMethod` attribute; you look at this attribute later. Adding the Web reference to the client application with Visual Studio causes a WSDL document to be requested. This WSDL document, in turn, is used to create a client proxy with the same methods and arguments. With this proxy, the client application has the advantage that it only needs to call the methods as they are implemented in the server, because the proxy converts them to SOAP calls to make the call across the network.

The WSDL specification is maintained by the World Wide Web Consortium (W3C). You can read the specification at the W3C Web site (www.w3.org/TR/wsdl).

Calling a Method

To call a method on a Web service, the call must be converted to the SOAP message as defined in the WSDL document.

A SOAP message is the basic unit of communication between a client and a server. Figure 21-3 demonstrates the parts of a SOAP message. A SOAP message includes a SOAP envelope, which, as you might guess, wraps all the SOAP information in a single block. The SOAP envelope itself consists of two parts: a SOAP header and a SOAP body. The optional header defines how the client and server should process the body. The mandatory SOAP body includes the data that is sent. Usually, information within the body is the method that is called together with the serialized parameter values. The SOAP server sends back the return values in the SOAP body of the SOAP message.

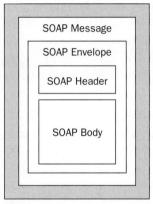

Figure 21-3

The following example shows what a SOAP message that is sent from the client to the server looks like. The client calls the Web service method ReverseString(). The string Hello World! is passed as an argument to this method. You can see that the method call is inside the SOAP body, within the XML element <soap:Body>. The body itself is contained within the envelope <soap:Envelope>. Before the start of the SOAP message, you can see the HTTP header, because the SOAP message is sent with an HTTP POST request.

It is not necessary to create such a message because that is done by the client proxy:

```
POST /Service1.asmx HTTP/1.1
Host: localhost
Content-Type: text/xml; charset=utf-8
Content-Length: 508
SOAPAction: "http://www.wrox.com/webservices/ReverseString"

<?xml version="1.0" encoding="utf-8"?>
<soap:Envelope xmlns:xsi="http://www.w3.org/2001/XMLSchema-instance"
```

```
        xmlns:xsd="http://www.w3.org/2001/XMLSchema"
        xmlns:soap="http://schemas.xmlsoap.org/soap/envelope/">
    <soap:Body>
        <ReverseString xmlns="http://www.wrox.com/webservices">
            <message>Hello World!</message>
    </ReverseString>
    </soap:Body>
    </soap:Envelope>
```

The server answers with the SOAP message !dlroW olleH, as shown with the ReverseStringResult XML element:

```
HTTP/1.1 200 OK
Content-Type: text/xml; charset=utf-8
Content-Length: 446

<?xml version="1.0" encoding="utf-8"?>
<soap:Envelope xmlns:xsi="http://www.w3.org/2001/XMLSchema-instance"
        xmlns:xsd="http://www.w3.org/2001/XMLSchema"
        xmlns:soap="http://schemas.xmlsoap.org/soap/envelope/">
    <soap:Body>
        <ReverseStringResponse xmlns="http://www.wrox.com/webservices">
            <ReverseStringResult>!dlroW olleH</ReverseStringResult>
    </ReverseStringResponse>
    </soap:Body>
    </soap:Envelope>
```

The SOAP specification is maintained by the XML Protocol Working Group of the W3C (www.w3.org/TR/soap).

SOAP and Firewalls

System administrators often ask whether the SOAP protocol breaks the security boundaries of the firewalls — in other words, does SOAP violate the concept of firewalls? In fact, there are no more security issues to consider than for normal Web servers. With normal Web server firewalls, the system administrator opens HTTP port 80 to allow the server to communicate with the outside world. Users on the Internet can have direct access to these servers even though they sit behind the firewall. A user can request an HTML file with an HTTP request and the server returns either a static page or a page created on-the-fly using ASP or CGI scripts. Web services are just another type of server-side application that communicates using HTTP, though instead of receiving simple HTTP GET or POST requests, it receives an HTTP POST request containing an embedded SOAP message, and instead of returning HTML, it returns an HTTP response containing the SOAP response message. As far as the firewall is concerned, the communication is through HTTP and hence it is allowed through port 80.

However, if this Web service does not behave as it should, such as leaking confidential data or breaking the server, then there is a problem, but such problems are common to all server-side applications whether they are traditional Web pages, server-side business objects, or Web services.

If the firewall's system administrator is still worried about the security implications of Web services, he or she can use an application filter to not allow SOAP calls with an HTTP request.

WS-I Basic Profile

The SOAP specification emerged over time. That's why sometimes it is hard to get interaction with Web services from different vendors. To cover this issue, the Web Services Interoperability Organization (http://ws-i.org) was formed. This organization defined the requirements for a Web service with the WS-I Basic Profile specification. You can read the WS-I Basic Profile specification at www.ws-i.org/Profiles/BasicProfile-1.1.html.

Web Services and the .NET Framework

The .NET Framework makes it easy to create and consume Web services, using three major namespaces that deal with Web services:

❑   System.Web.Services — Its classes are used to create Web services.

❑   System.Web.Services.Description — You can describe Web services via WSDL.

❑   System.Web.Services.Protocols — You can create SOAP requests and responses.

Creating a Web Service

To implement a Web service, you can derive the Web service class from System.Web.Services .WebService. The WebService class provides access to ASP.NET Application and Session objects. Using this class is optional, and you have to derive from it only if you need easy access to the properties the class offers.

Properties for the class WebService are explained in the following table:

WebService Property	Description
Application	Returns an HttpApplicationState object for the current request.
Context	Returns an HttpContext object that encapsulates HTTP-specific information. With this context, the HTTP header information can be read.
Server	Returns an HttpServerUtility object. This class has some helper methods to do URL encoding and decoding.
Session	Returns an HttpSessionState object to store some state for the client.
User	Returns a user object implementing the IPrincipal interface. With this interface, you can get the name of the user and the authentication type.
SoapVersion	Returns the SOAP version that is used with the Web service. The SOAP version is encapsulated in the enumeration SoapProtocolVersion.

When creating Web services with ASP.NET, it is not a requirement that they be derived from the base class WebService. *This base class is required only if you want to have easy access to the HTTP context with the properties of the* WebService *class.*

WebService Attribute

The subclass of `WebService` should be marked with the `WebService` attribute. The class `WebServiceAttribute` has the following properties:

Property	Description
Description	A description of the service that will be used in the WSDL document.
Name	Gets or sets the name of the Web service.
Namespace	Gets or sets the XML namespace for the Web service. The default value is `http://tempuri.org`, which is okay for testing, but before you make the service public you should change the namespace.

Attributes are covered in more detail in Chapter 30.

WebMethod Attribute

All methods available from the Web service must be marked with the `WebMethod` attribute. Of course, the service can have other methods that are not marked using `WebMethod`. Such methods can be called from the `WebMethods`, but they cannot be called from the client. With the attribute class `WebMethodAttribute`, the method will be callable from remote clients, and you can define whether the response is buffered, for how long the cache should be valid, and whether the session state should be stored with named parameters. The following table lists the properties of the `WebMethodAttribute` class:

Property	Description
BufferResponse	Gets or sets a flag indicating whether the response should be buffered. The default is `true`. With a buffered response, only the finished package is sent to the client.
CacheDuration	Set the length of time that the result should be cached. If the same request is made a second time, only the cached value will be returned if the request is made during the period set by this property. The default value is `0`, which means the result will not be cached.
Description	Used in the generation of service help pages for prospective consumers.
EnableSession	A Boolean value indicating whether the session state is valid. The default is `false`, so the `Session` property of the `WebService` class cannot be used for storing session state.
MessageName	By default, the name of the message is set to the name of the method.
TransactionOption	Indicates the transaction support for the method. The default value is `Disabled`.

WebServiceBinding Attribute

The attribute `WebServiceBinding` is used to mark the Web services interoperability conformance level of the Web service. Its properties are described in the following table:

Property	Description
ConformanceClaims	Set to a value of the `WsiClaims` enumeration. `WsiClaims` can have two values: `BasicProfile1_1` when the Web service conforms to Basic Profile 1.1, or `None` when no conformance is defined.
EmitConformanceClaims	A Boolean property that defines whether the conformance claims that are specified with the `ConformanceClaims` property should be transmitted to the generated WSDL documentation.
Name	Defines the name of the binding. By default, the name is the same as the name of the Web services with the string `Soap` appended.
Location	Defines the location of the binding information; for example, `http://www.wrox.com/DemoWebservice.asmx?wsdl`.
Namespace	Defines the XML namespace of the binding.

Client

To call a method, the client has to create an HTTP connection to the server of the Web service, and send an HTTP request to pass a SOAP message. The method call must be converted to a SOAP message. All this is done by the client proxy. The implementation of the client proxy is in the `SoapHttpClientProtocol` class.

SoapHttpClientProtocol

The class `System.Web.Services.Protocols.SoapHttpClientProtocol` is the base class for the client proxy. The `Invoke()` method converts the arguments to build a SOAP message that is sent to the Web service. Which Web service is called is defined with the `Url` property.

The `SoapHttpClientProtocol` class also supports asynchronous calls with the `BeginInvoke()` and `EndInvoke()` methods.

Alternative Client Protocols

Instead of using the `SoapHttpClientProtocol` class, other proxy classes can be used. `HttpGetClientProtocol` and `HttpPostClientProtocol` just do a simple HTTP GET or HTTP POST request without the overhead of a SOAP call.

> *The `HttpGetClientProtocol` and `HttpPostClientProtocol` classes can be used if your solution uses .NET on the client and the server. If you want to support different technologies, you have to use the SOAP protocol.*

Compare the following HTTP POST request with the SOAP call shown earlier in this chapter:

```
POST /WebServiceSample/Service1.asmx/ReverseString HTTP/1.1
Host: localhost
Content-Type: application/x-www-form-urlencoded
Content-Length: length

message=string
```

The HTTP GET request is even shorter. The disadvantage of the GET request is that the size of the parameters sent is limited. If the size goes beyond 1K, you should consider using POST:

```
GET /WebServiceSample/Service1.asmx/ReverseString?message=string HTTP/1.1
Host: localhost
```

The overhead of the HttpGetClientProtocol and the HttpPostClientProtocol is smaller than that of SOAP methods; the disadvantage here is that there is no support from Web services on other platforms and no support for sending anything other than simple data.

Creating a Simple ASP.NET Web Service

In the following Try It Out, you create a simple Web service with Visual Studio.

Try It Out   Creating a Web Service Project

1. Create a new Web Service project with File ⇨ New ⇨ Project, choose the ASP.NET Web Service Application template as shown in Figure 21-4, name the project WebServiceSample, and click OK.

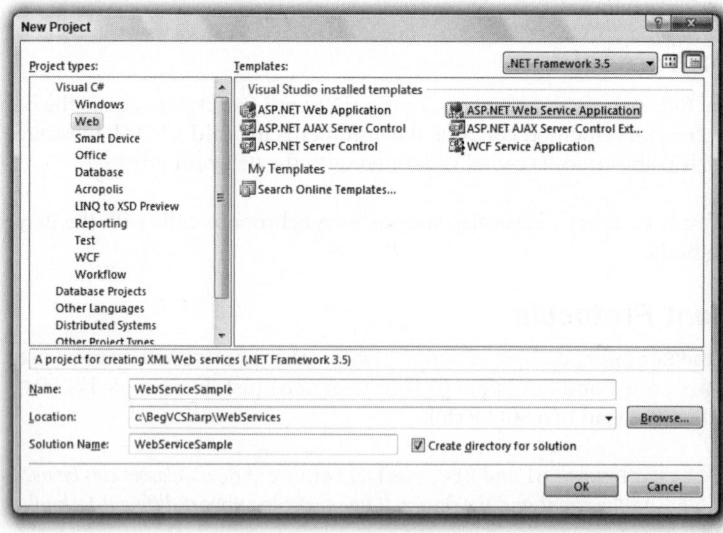

Figure 21-4

How It Works

The files generated by the project template are listed here:

❏ `Service1.asmx`: This file holds your Web service class. All ASP.NET Web services are identified with the `.asmx` extension. The file that has the source code is `Service.cs` because the code-beside feature is used with Visual Studio.

❏ `Service1.asmx.cs`: The project template generates a class `Service1` in the file `Service1 .asmx.cs` that derives from `System.Web.Services.WebService`. In this file, you can also see some sample code showing how a method for a Web service should be coded — it should be public and marked with the `WebMethod` attribute:

```
using System.Web;
using System.Web.Services;
using System.Web.Services.Protocols;

[WebService(Namespace = http://tempuri.org)]
[WebServiceBinding(ConformsTo=WsiProfile.BasicProfile1_1)]
[ToolboxItem(false)]
public class Service : System.Web.Services.WebService
{
    [WebMethod]
    public string HelloWorld()
    {
      return "Hello World";
    }
}
```

Adding a Web Method

The next thing to do is add a custom method to your Web service. In the following Try It Out, you add a simple method — `ReverseString()` — that receives a string and returns the reversed string to the client.

Try It Out   Adding a Method

1. Remove the method `HelloWorld()` with the complete implementation. Add the following code to the file `Service1.asmx.cs`. To use the `Array` class, you must import the `System` namespace.

```
[WebMethod]
public string ReverseString(string message)
{
  char[] arr = message.ToCharArray();
  Array.Reverse(arr);
  message = new string(arr);

  return message;
}
```

2. Modify the example code from the file `Service1.asmx.cs` as follows:

```
[WebService(Namespace="http://www.wrox.com/webservices")]
[WebServiceBinding(ConformsTo=WsiProfile.BasicProfile1_1)]
[ToolboxItem(false)]
public class Service : System.Web.Services.WebService
{
```

3. Compile the project.

How It Works

The ASP.NET runtime makes use of reflection to read some Web service–specific attributes such as `[WebMethod]` to offer the method as a Web service operation. The ASP.NET runtime also offers WSDL to describe the service.

To uniquely identify the XML elements in the generated description of the Web service, an XML namespace should be added. In the sample, the namespace `http://www.wrox.com/webservices` was added to the class `Service` by using the attribute `[WebService]`. Of course, you can use any other string that uniquely identifies the XML elements, such as the URL link to your company's page. It is not necessary for the Web link to really exist; it is just used for unique identification. If you use a namespace based on your company's Web address, you can almost guarantee that no other company is using the very same namespace.

If you don't change the XML namespace, the default namespace used is `http://tempuri.org`. For learning purposes, this default namespace is good enough, but you shouldn't deploy a production Web service using it.

Testing the Web Service

Now you can test the service. Opening the file `Service1.asmx` in the browser (you can start it from within Visual Studio 2008 by going to Debug ⇨ Start Without Debugging) lists all methods of the service, as shown in Figure 21-5. In your service the only method is `ReverseString()`.

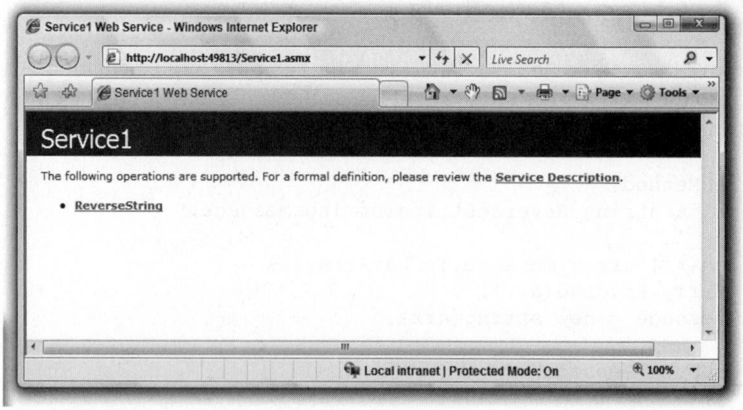

Figure 21-5

When you choose the link to the `ReverseString` method, you see a dialog to test the Web service. The test dialog has edit fields for every parameter you can pass with this method; here it is only a single parameter.

In this page, you also get information about what the SOAP calls from the client and what the responses from the server will look like (see Figure 21-6). The example shows SOAP and HTTP POST requests.

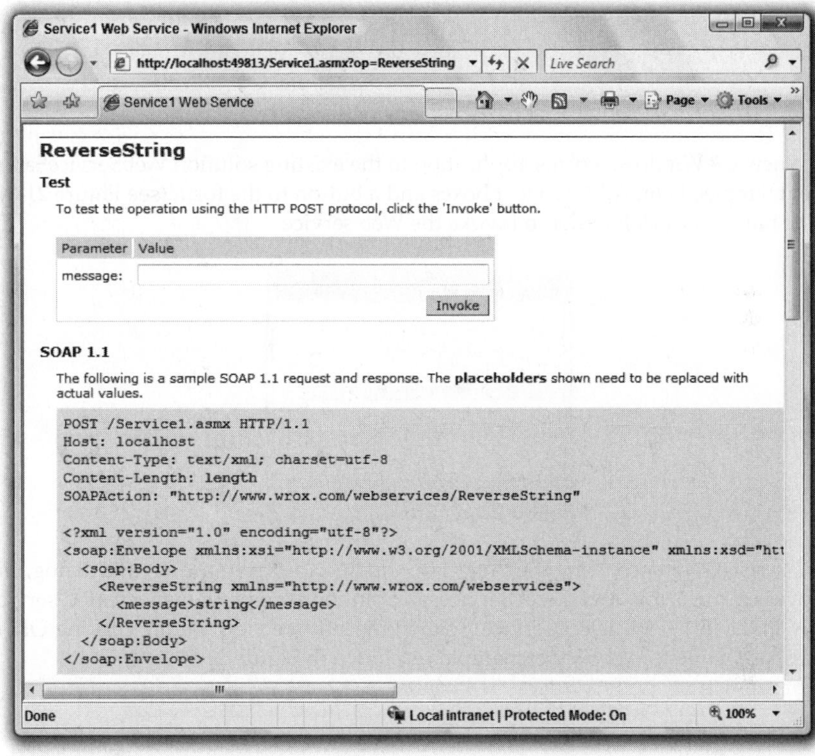

Figure 21-6

Clicking the Invoke button after entering the string **Hello Web Services!** into the text box, you receive the result shown in Figure 21-7 from the server.

Figure 21-7

The result is of type `string`, and, as expected, it is the reverse of the entered string.

Implementing a Windows Client

The test is working, but you want to create a Windows client that uses the Web service. The client must create a SOAP message that will be sent across an HTTP channel. It is not necessary to make this message yourself. Visual Studio 2008 creates a proxy class that uses an HTTP channel from Windows Communication Foundation (WCF) that does all the work behind the scenes.

You can read about WCF in Chapter 35.

Try It Out   Creating a Client Windows Application

1. Add a new C# Windows Forms application to the existing solution WebServiceSample and name it SimpleClient. Add two text boxes and a button to the form (see Figure 21-8). You will use the button's Click handler to invoke the Web service.

Figure 21-8

2. Add a service reference using the Project ⇨ Add Service Reference. In this dialog, click the Discover button arrow and select Services in Solution. The previously created service is shown in the left view. Select Service1Soap in the left tree view. Before clicking OK, change the Namespace name to WebServicesSample, as shown in Figure 21-9.

Figure 21-9

3. Until now you have not written a single line of code for the client. You designed a small user interface, and used the Add Web Reference menu to create a proxy class. Now you just have to create the link between the two. Add a `Click` event handler `button1_Click` to the button and add these two statements:

```
private void button1_Click(object sender, EventArgs e)
{
    WebServicesSample.Service1SoapClient client =
        new WebServicesSample.Service1SoapClient();
    textBox2.Text = client.ReverseString(textBox1.Text);
}
```

How It Works

In the Solution Explorer you can now see a new service reference, `WebServicesSample` (see Figure 21-10). Click the Show All Files button to see the WSDL document and the file `reference.cs` that includes the source code of the proxy. The Show All Files button is the second one in the toolbar of the Solution Explorer. When you move the mouse over the buttons, a tooltip gives you the information about each button.

Figure 21-10

What the Solution Explorer shows only when the Show All Files button is clicked can be seen more easily in the Class View (the new class that implements the client proxy). This class converts method calls to the SOAP format. In Class View (see Figure 21-11), you will find a new namespace with the name that was defined with the Web Reference name. In this case, `WebServicesSample` was created. The class `Service1SoapClient` derives from `ClientBase<Service1Soap>` and implements the method of the Web service, `ReverseString()`.

Figure 21-11

Double-click the `Service1SoapClient` class to open the auto-generated `reference.cs` file. Let's look into this generated code.

The `Service1SoapClient` class derives from the `ClientBase<Service1Soap>` class. This base class creates a SOAP message in the `Invoke()` method. The `WebServiceBindingAttribute` attribute sets binding values to the Web service:

```
[System.Diagnostics.DebuggerStepThroughAttribute()]
[System.ComponentModel.DesignerCategoryAttribute("code")]
[System.Web.Services.WebServiceBindingAttribute(Name="ServiceSoap",
    Namespace="http://www.wrox.com/webservices")]
public partial class Service :
    System.Web.Services.Protocols.SoapHttpClientProtocol {
```

In the constructor, the `Url` property is set to the Web service. It will be used from the `SoapHttpClientProtocol` class to request a service:

```
public Service() {
    this.Url =
SimpleClient.Properties.Settings.Default.SimpleClient_WebServicesSample_Service;
    }
```

The most important method is the method that the Web service supplies: `ReverseString()`. The method here has the same parameter that you implemented on the server. The implementation of the client-side version of `ReverseString()` calls the `Invoke()` method of the base class `SoapHttpClientProtocol`. `Invoke()` creates a SOAP message using the method name `ReverseString` and the parameter `message`. You can find this method in the file `reference.cs`:

```
public string ReverseString(string message) {
    ReverseStringRequest inValue = new ReverseStringRequest();
    inValue.Body = new ReverseStringRequestBody();
    inValue.Body.message = message;
    ReverseStringResponse retVal =
        ((Service1Soap)(this)).ReverseString(inValue);
    return retVal.Body.ReverseStringResult;
}
```

Sending a SOAP request across HTTP is defined in the automatically created application configuration file that defines a `basicHttpBinding`:

```
<?xml version="1.0" encoding="utf-8" ?>
<configuration>
  <system.serviceModel>
    <bindings>
      <basicHttpBinding>
        <binding name="Service1Soap" closeTimeout="00:01:00"
openTimeout="00:0 1:00"
            receiveTimeout="00:10:00" sendTimeout="00:01:00"
allowCookies="false"
            bypassProxyOnLocal="false" hostNameComparisonMode="StrongWildcard"
            maxBufferSize="65536" maxBufferPoolSize="524288"
            maxReceivedMessageSize="65536"
            messageEncoding="Text" textEncoding="utf-8" transferMode="Buffered"
            useDefaultWebProxy="true">
          <readerQuotas maxDepth="32" maxStringContentLength="8192"
              maxArrayLength="16384"
              maxBytesPerRead="4096" maxNameTableCharCount="16384" />
          <security mode="None">
            <transport clientCredentialType="None" proxyCredentialType="None"
                realm="" />
              <message clientCredentialType="UserName"
                  algorithmSuite="Default" />
          </security>
        </binding>
      </basicHttpBinding>
    </bindings>
    <client>
      <endpoint address="http://localhost:49813/Service1.asmx"
          binding="basicHttpBinding"
          bindingConfiguration="Service1Soap"
          contract="WebServicesSample.Service1Soap"
          name="Service1Soap" />
    </client>
  </system.serviceModel>
</configuration>
```

The call to the service is done in the following statement with the help of the generated proxy class. With the following statement, you create a new instance of the proxy class. As shown in the implementation of the constructor, the `Url` property is set to the Web service:

```
WebServicesSample.Service1SoapClient client =
        new WebServicesSample.Service1SoapClient();
```

As a result of calling the `ReverseString()` method of the proxy class, a SOAP message is sent to the server, and so the Web service is called:

```
textBox2.Text = client.ReverseString(textBox1.Text);
```

Running the program produces output like that shown in Figure 21-12.

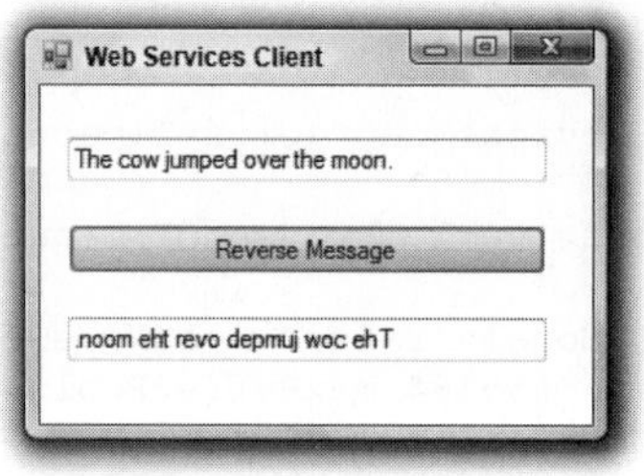

Figure 21-12

Calling the Service Asynchronously

When you send a message across the network, you always have to be aware of network latency. If the Web service is invoked synchronously, the client application is blocked until the call returns. This may be fast enough in a local network; however, you must pay attention to the production system's network infrastructure.

You can send messages to the Web service asynchronously. The client proxy creates not only synchronous methods but also asynchronous methods, but there's a special issue with Windows applications. Because every Windows control is bound to a single thread, methods and properties of Windows controls may only be called from within the creation thread. The proxy class of .NET 3.5 has some special features for this issue, as shown in the generated proxy code.

Try It Out   **Calling the Service Asynchronously**

Now let's use the asynchronous implementation of the proxy class. Here's what to do:

1.   Make a change to the generated proxy class by selecting the service reference WebServicesSample. Open the context menu and select Configure Service Reference. The dialog shown in Figure 21-13 opens.

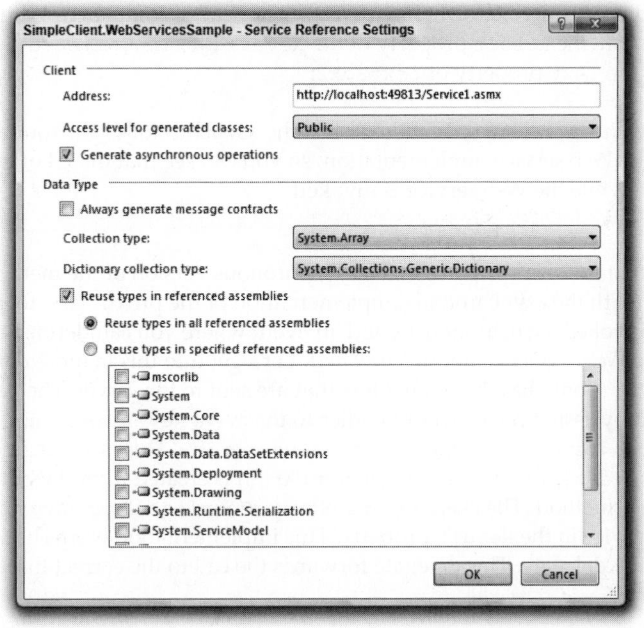

Figure 21-13

2. Check Generate asynchronous operations in the dialog Service Reference Settings.

3. To invoke the Web service asynchronously, change the implementation of the method `button1_Click` (code follows). After the proxy is instantiated, add an event handler named `client_ReverseStringCompleted` to the event `ReverseStringCompleted`. Next, invoke the asynchronous method of the proxy `ReverseStringAsync`, and pass the `Text` property from `textBox1`. With the `asnyc` method, a thread is created that makes the call to the Web service:

```
private void button1_Click(object sender, EventArgs e)
{
    // asynchronous version
    WebServicesSample.Service1SoapClient client =
        new WebServicesSample.Service1SoapClient();
    client.ReverseStringCompleted += new
        EventHandler<WebServicesSample.ReverseStringCompletedEventArgs>(
        client_ReverseStringCompleted);
    client.ReverseStringAsync(textBox1.Text);
}
```

4. Now implement the handler method `client_ReverseStringCompleted`:

```
private void client_ReverseStringCompleted(object sender,
    WebServicesSample.ReverseStringCompletedEventArgs e)
{
    textBox2.Text = e.Result;
}
```

This method will be invoked when the Web service call is completed. With the implementation, the `Result` property of the `ReverseStringComletedEventArgs` parameter is passed to the `Text` property of `textBox2`:

5. Now you can run the client once more to test the asynchronous call. You can also add a sleep interval to the Web service implementation, so you can see that the UI of the client application is not stalled while the Web service is invoked.

How It Works

In the code snippet that follows you can see the asynchronous version of the method `ReverseString()`. With the asynchronous implementation of the proxy class, there's always a method that can be invoked asynchronously, and an event where you can define what method should be invoked when the Web service method is finished. Let's get into this in more detail. The method `ReverseStringAsync()` only has the parameters that are sent to the server. The data received from the client can be read by assigning an event handler to the event `ReverseStringCompleted`, which is of type `EventHandler<ReverseStringCompletedEventArgs>`. This is a delegate whereby the second parameter (`ReverseStringCompletedEventArgs`) is created from the output parameters of the `ReverseString()` method. The class `ReverseStringCompletedEventArgs` contains the return data from the Web service in the `Result` property. This implementation works because of the `SendOrPostCallback` delegate. This delegate forwards the call to the correct thread of the Windows Forms control:

```csharp
public event System.EventHandler<ReverseStringCompletedEventArgs>
    ReverseStringCompleted;

public void ReverseStringAsync(string message) {
    this.ReverseStringAsync(message, null);
}

public void ReverseStringAsync(string message, object userState) {
    if ((this.onBeginReverseStringDelegate == null)) {
        this.onBeginReverseStringDelegate =
            new BeginOperationDelegate(this.OnBeginReverseString);
    }
    if ((this.onEndReverseStringDelegate == null)) {
        this.onEndReverseStringDelegate =
            new EndOperationDelegate(this.OnEndReverseString);
    }
    if ((this.onReverseStringCompletedDelegate == null)) {
        this.onReverseStringCompletedDelegate =
            new System.Threading.SendOrPostCallback(
            this.OnReverseStringCompleted);
    }
    base.InvokeAsync(this.onBeginReverseStringDelegate, new object[] {
            message}, this.onEndReverseStringDelegate,
            this.onReverseStringCompletedDelegate, userState);

}

public void OnReverseStringOperationCompleted(object arg) {
    if ((this.ReverseStringCompleted != null)) {
        InvokeAsyncCompletedEventArgs e =
```

```
                ((InvokeAsyncCompletedEventArgs)(state));
            this.ReverseStringCompleted(this,
                new ReverseStringCompletedEventArgs(e.Results, e.Error,
                e.Cancelled, e.UserState));
        }
    }


    public partial class ReverseStringCompletedEvenArgs :
        System.ComponentModel.AsyncCompletedEventArgs
    {

        private object[] results;

        internal ReverseStringCompletedEventArgs(object[] results,
            System.Exception exception, bool cancelled, object userState)
              : base(exception, cancelled, userState) {
            this.results = results;
        }

        public string Result
        {
            get {
                this.RaiseExceptionIfNecessary();
                return ((string)(ths.results[0]));
            }
        }
    }
}
```

Implementing an ASP.NET Client

The same service now can be used from an ASP.NET client application. Referencing the service can be done as it was with the Windows Forms application.

Try It Out   **Creating an ASP.NET Client Application**

1.   Open the previously created Web service WebServicesSample.

2.   Add a new C# ASP.NET Web site to the solution, call it ASPNETClient, and add two text boxes and a button to the Web form, as shown in Figure 21-14.

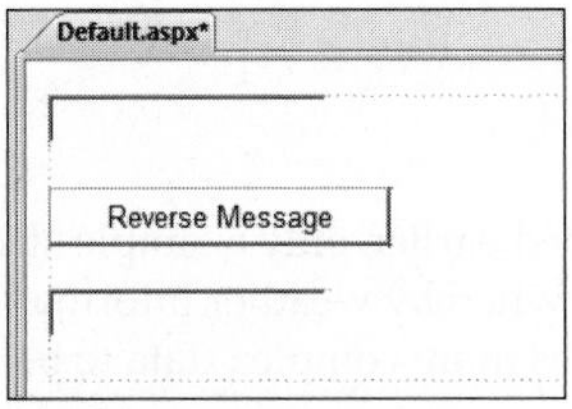

Figure 21-14

3. Add a service reference to `http://localhost/webservicesample/service.asmx` in the same way you did with the Windows application. Depending on your configuration, a port number might be required.

4. With the service reference added, a client proxy class is again generated. Add a click handler to the button and write the following lines of code for this handler:

```
private void Button1_Click(object sender, System.EventArgs e)
{
    WebServicesSample.Service1SoapClient client =
        new WebServicesSample.Service1SoapClient();
    TextBox2.Text = client.ReverseString(TextBox1.Text);
}
```

5. Build the project. With Debug ⇨ Start, you can start the browser and enter a test message in the first text box. When you press the button, the Web service is invoked, and you get the reversed message returned in the second text box, as shown in Figure 21-15. With a multiproject solution, you have to set the startup project to the project you want started.

Figure 21-15

How It Works

The functionality of the proxy class with the Windows application is exactly the same as with the Web application done earlier. Adding a service reference creates a proxy class that is based on the WSDL document. The proxy class makes the SOAP request to the service.

Passing Data

With the simple Web service developed earlier, only a simple string has been passed to the Web service. Now you are going to add a method whereby weather information is requested from the Web service. This information requires more complex data to be sent to and from the Web service.

Try It Out   Creating Passing Data with a Web Service

1. Open the previously created Web service project WebServicesSample using Visual Studio. With this Web service, define the types shown with the following code. The GetWeatherRequest and GetWeatherResponse classes define the documents to be sent to and from the Web service. The enumerations TemperatureType and TemperatureCondition are used within these classes.

ASP.NET Web services use XML serialization to convert objects to an XML representation. You can use attributes from the namespace System.Xml.Serialization to influence how the generated XML format should look. (You can read more about XML serialization in Chapter 25.)

```
public enum TemperatureType
{
    Fahrenheit,
    Celsius
}

public enum TemparatureCondition
{
    Rainy,
    Sunny,
    Cloudy,
    Thunderstorm
}

public class GetWeatherRequest
{
    public string City;
    public TemperatureType TemperatureType;
}

public class GetWeatherResponse
{
    public TemparatureCondition Condition;
    public int Temperature;
}
```

2. Add the Web service method GetWeather():

```
[WebMethod]
public GetWeatherResponse GetWeather(GetWeatherRequest req)
{
    GetWeatherResponse resp = new GetWeatherResponse();
    Random r = new Random();
    int celsius = r.Next(-20, 50);

    if (req.TemperatureType == TemperatureType.Celsius)
        resp.Temperature = celsius;
    else
        resp.Temperature = (212-32)/100 * celsius + 32;
```

```
if (req.City == "Redmond")
    resp.Condition = TemparatureCondition.Rainy;
else
    resp.Condition = (TemparatureCondition)r.Next(0, 3);

return resp;
}
```

This method receives the data defined with `GetWeatherRequest` and returns data defined with `GetWeatherResponse`. Within the implementation, a random weather condition is returned — with the exception of the home of Microsoft, Redmond, where it rains all week. For random weather generation, the class `Random` from the `System` namespace is used.

3. After building the Web service, create a new project using the Windows Forms template and name the application `WeatherClient`.

4. Modify the main dialog as shown in Figure 21-16. The control embeds two radio buttons from which the temperature type (Celsius or Fahrenheit) can be selected, and the city can be entered. Clicking the Get Weather button invokes the Web service, where the result is shown in the Weather Condition and the Temperature text box controls.

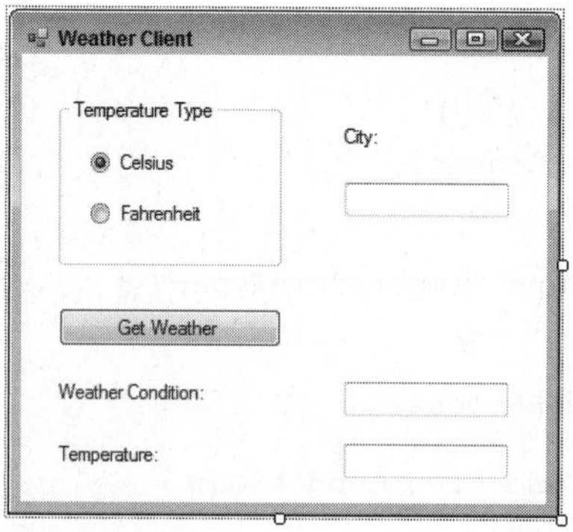

Figure 21-16

The controls, with their names and the value for the `Text` property, are listed in the following table:

Control	Name	Text Property
RadioButton	radioButtonCelsius	Celsius
RadioButton	radioButtonFahrenheit	Fahrenheit
Button	buttonGetWeather	Get Weather
Label	labelWeatherCondition	
TextBox	textCity	

Control	Name	Text Property
TextBox	textWeatherCondition	
TextBox	textTemperature	
Label	labelCity	City
Label	labelWeatherCondition	Weather Condition
Label	labelTemperature	Temperature
GroupBox	groupBox1	

5. Add a reference to the Web service, similar to how it was done with the earlier client application projects. Name the reference `WeatherService`.

6. Import the namespace `WeatherClient.WeatherService` with the client application.

7. Add a `Click` event handler to the button `buttonGetWeather` with the name `buttonGetWeather_Click` using the Properties dialog of the button.

8. Add the implementation to the `buttonGetWeather_Click()` method as shown:

```
private void OnGetWeather(object sender, EventArgs e)
{
    GetWeatherRequest req = new GetWeatherRequest();
    if (radioButtonCelsius.Checked)
        req.TemperatureType = TemperatureType.Celsius;
    else
        req.TemperatureType = TemperatureType.Fahrenheit;
    req.City = textCity.Text;

    Service1SoapClient client = new Service1SoapClient();

    GetWeatherResponse resp = client.GetWeather(req);

    textWeatherCondition.Text = resp.Condition.ToString();
    textTemperature.Text = resp.Temperature.ToString();
}
```

Here, a `GetWeatherRequest` object is created that defines the request sent to the Web service. The Web service is invoked by calling the `GetWeather()` method. This method returns a `GetWeatherResponse` object with values that are read for display in the user interface.

9. Start the client application. Enter a city and click the Get Weather button. If you are lucky, the real weather is shown (see Figure 21-17).

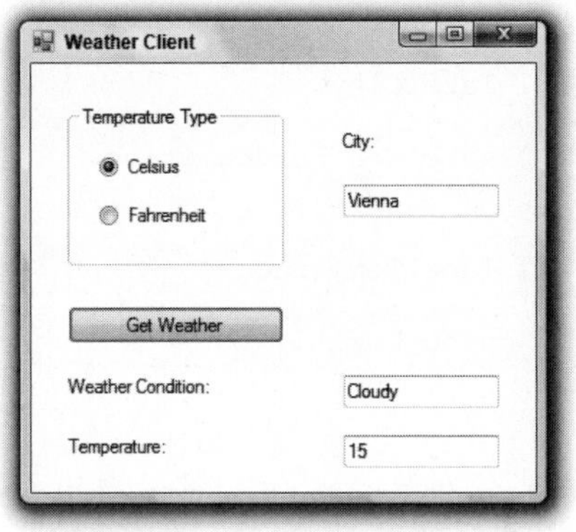

Figure 21-17

Summary

In this chapter you learned what Web services are, and you briefly looked at the protocols used with them. To locate and run Web services, you have to use some or all of the following:

❏ **Directory**: Find a Web service by UDDI.

❏ **Description**: WSDL describes the methods and arguments.

❏ **Calling**: Platform-independent method calls are done with the SOAP protocol.

You saw how easy it is to create Web services with Visual Studio, where the WebService class is used to define some methods with the WebMethod attribute. Creating the client that consumes Web services is as easy as creating Web services — you add a Web reference to the client project and use the proxy. The heart of the client is the SoapHttpClientProtocol class, which converts the method call to a SOAP message. The client proxy you created offers both asynchronous and synchronous methods. The client interface is not blocked when you use asynchronous methods until the Web service method completes. You also learned how to create custom classes that define the data passed when you want to transfer more than simple data. The next chapter shows how Web applications and Web services can be deployed.

Exercises

The following exercises help you use the knowledge you gained in this chapter to create a new Web service that offers a seat reservation system for a cinema.

1. Create a new Web service named CinemaReservation.

2. The ReserveSeatRequest and ReserveSeatResponse classes are needed to define the data sent to and from the Web service. The ReserveSeatRequest class needs a member Name of type string to send a name and two members of type int to send a request for a seat defined with Row and Seat. The class ReserveSeatResponse defines the data to be sent back to the client — that is, the name for the reservation and the seat that is really reserved.

3. Create a Web method ReserveSeat that requires a ReserveSeatRequest as a parameter and returns a ReserveSeatResponse. Within the implementation of the Web service, you can use a Cache object (see Chapter 19) to remember the seats that already have been reserved. If the requested seat is available, return the seat and reserve it in the Cache object. If it is not available, then take the next free seat. For the seats in the Cache object, use a two-dimensional array, as was shown in Chapter 5.

4. Create a Windows client application that uses the Web service to reserve a seat in the cinema.

Ajax Programming

Users want Web applications that are as interactive as Windows applications are. Asynchronous JavaScript and XML — Ajax — is a technology that makes it easy to create interactive Web applications.

In this chapter, you

- ❑ Get an overview of Ajax.
- ❑ Use the ASP.NET UpdatePanel control.
- ❑ Use the ASP.NET AJAX Timer control.
- ❑ Use the UpdateProgress control.
- ❑ Create a Web service and call it from client script.
- ❑ Explore the extender controls that you get in the ASP.NET AJAX Control Toolkit.

Ajax Overview

ASP.NET is based on postbacks. When the user clicks a button or makes a selection in a list box that has AutoPostBack enabled, a request is sent to the server, and the complete page is sent back to the client. For the user this doesn't give the feeling of a "normal" application, because the complete page is redrawn. The user interface should stay active on the client, and only additional data to display should be requested from the server.

In reality, the technology that Ajax is based on is not new. With Internet Explorer and Web applications this has been possible for many years. Internet Explorer has included the XmlHttpRequest object from version 5; this object makes it possible to send a request from within JavaScript while the page remains active. This was used in Outlook Web Access 2000 to give the user a better interactive experience. The problem with this technology was that it wasn't easy to use.

Ajax makes it easy to use the `XmlHttpRequest` object, and nowadays this feature is also offered by other browsers.

Ajax is based on the following technologies:

❑ DHTML: On the client side, the HTML elements must be accessed and modified programmatically, which was made possible by Dynamic HTML.

❑ JavaScript: Nearly all browsers support JavaScript. JavaScript is the scripting language used to access the DOM (Document Object Model) from DHTML.

❑ `XmlHttpRequest`: This object is used to make an asynchronous call from JavaScript to the server to request additional data.

❑ JSON (JavaScript Object Notation): Instead of passing XML around from the client to the server, typically a format that requires less data and is optimized for JavaScript is used: JSON.

Microsoft's implementation of Ajax is ASP.NET AJAX, which consists of a client-side JavaScript library and server-side ASP.NET controls that use the library. Unlike ASP.NET 2.0, which required you to download the ASP.NET AJAX library and controls, ASP.NET 3.5 includes ASP.NET AJAX., so you can begin working with that library immediately.

Microsoft offers some additional kits that can be useful in developing your ASP.NET AJAX applications:

❑ ASP.NET AJAX Control Toolkit — A community-based toolkit that includes several controls to extend Web pages. The last section in this chapter makes use of this kit.

❑ Microsoft ASP.NET 3.5 Extensions Preview — This kit provides a pre-release version of functionality that might be available in a future version of ASP.NET.

You can download these kits from `http://ajax.asp.net`.

The server-side controls that you can use with your ASP.NET applications are described in the following table:

ASP.NET AJAX Control	Description
ScriptManager	Loads client scripts. One instance of this control is required with every ASP.NET AJAX page.
UpdatePanel	Allows for partial rendering updates of the page via an ASP.NET AJAX postback.
Timer	Invokes a function after a specified interval.
UpdateProgress	Displays some progress information while a request is being made.

Instead of using the server-side controls, you can use JavaScript functions directly. The name of the classes and methods are very similar to classes and methods of the .NET Framework, so you will feel at home immediately.

Some of the ASP.NET AJAX client script extensions are described in the following table:

Client Script Extensions	Description
`Array` type extensions	The client script library adds functions to the JavaScript `Array` type. Methods such as `add()`, `addRange()`, `clear()`, `contains()`, `insert()`, and `remove()` are very similar to methods of the .NET `Array` type.
`Date` type extensions	The client script library adds functions to the JavaScript `Date` type. With the `format` method you can pass format strings like those used with the .NET `DateTime` structure.
`String` type extensions	The client script library adds functions to the JavaScript `String` type. Methods that are available here include `startsWith()`, `endsWith()`, `trim()`, and `trimEnd()`.
`Sys` namespace	The `Sys` namespace gives you the `StringBuilder` class, which is similar to the .NET class `StringBuilder`. The `Application` class exposes global client events such as `init`, `load`, and `unload`.
`Sys.Net` namespace	The `Sys.Net` namespace includes classes that are used by client script to invoke Web services.

Let's look at how you can use ASP.NET AJAX in your ASP.NET applications, starting with a partial rendering update of a Web page.

Update Panel

In the following Try It Out, you create a simple Web page that makes use of the ASP.NET Update Panel.

Try It Out   Using the Update Panel

1. Create a new Web site with File ⇨ New Web Site, and select ASP.NET Web Site. Give the Web site the name AJAXWebsite.

2. Add a new Web Form named `UpdatePanelDemo.aspx` and make it the start page for the application.

3. From the AJAX Extensions category in the Toolbox, add a `ScriptManager` to the page:

```
<asp:ScriptManager ID="ScriptManager1" runat="server">
</asp:ScriptManager>
```

4. Add an `UpdatePanel` to the page:

```
<asp:UpdatePanel ID="UpdatePanel1" runat="server">
</asp:UpdatePanel>
```

5. Add a `Label` and a `Button` within the `UpdatePanel`, and another `Label` and `Button` outside of the `UpdatePanel`. Set the `Text` property of the `Button` within the `UpdatePanel` and the `Button` outside of the `UpdatePanel` to `AJAX Postback` and `ASP.NET Postback`, respectively (see Figure 22-1).

```
<form id="form1" runat="server">
<div>
    <asp:ScriptManager ID="ScriptManager1" runat="server">
    </asp:ScriptManager>
</div>
<asp:UpdatePanel ID="UpdatePanel1" runat="server">
    <ContentTemplate>
        <asp:Label ID="Label1" runat="server" Text="Label"></asp:Label>
        <asp:Button ID="Button1" runat="server" Text="AJAX Postback" />
    </ContentTemplate>
</asp:UpdatePanel>
<asp:Label ID="Label2" runat="server" Text="Label"></asp:Label>
<asp:Button ID="Button2" runat="server" Text="ASP.NET Postback" />
</form>
```

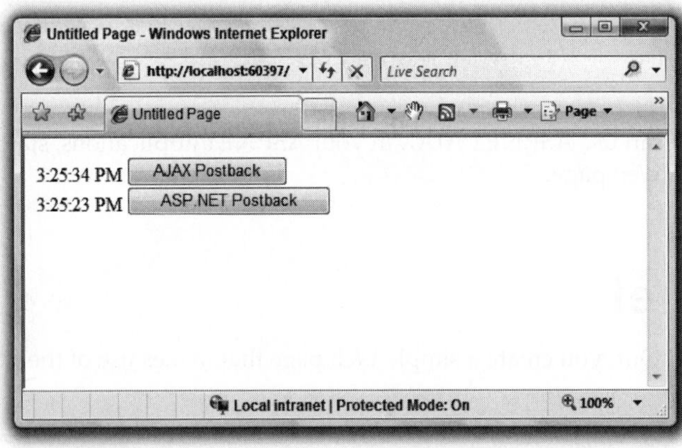

Figure 22-1

6. Assign a `Click` event handler named `OnButtonClick` to both buttons and implement it as shown:

```
protected void OnButtonClick(object sender, EventArgs e)
{
    Label1.Text = DateTime.Now.ToLongTimeString();
    Label2.Text = DateTime.Now.ToLongTimeString();
}
```

7. Start the application and click both buttons. Clicking the AJAX Postback button refreshes only the first label. With the ASP.NET Postback button, the entire page is refreshed.

How It Works

With an ASP.NET page, one `ScriptManager` object is required. This class loads JavaScript functions for several features. You can also use this class to load your own custom scripts. `ScriptManager` properties are explained in the following table:

ScriptManager Property	Description
EnablePageMethods	Defines whether public static methods defined in the ASPX page should be callable from client script as Web service methods.
EnablePartialRendering	To enable partial rendering with the `UpdatePanel`, this property must be set to `true`, which is the default.
LoadScriptsBeforeUI	Defines the position where the scripts are included in the returned HTML page. By placing them inside the `<head>` element, the scripts are loaded before the UI is loaded.
ScriptMode	Specifies whether the debug or release version of scripts should be used.
ScriptPath	Specifies the root path of the directory where custom scripts are located.
Scripts	Contains a collection of custom script files that should be rendered to the client.
Services	Contains a collection of Web service references that can be called from within client script.

The ASP.NET `Button` controls on the page result in the client creating HTML Submit buttons. `Button2` makes a normal HTTP `POST` request to the server. Because `Button1` is within an `UpdatePanel`, client script attaches to the `Click` event of the button to do an Ajax `POST` request. The Ajax `POST` request makes use of the `XmlHttpRequest` object to send a request to the server. The server returns only the data required to update the UI. The data is interpreted, and JavaScript code modifies HTML controls within the `UpdatePanel` for a new UI:

```
<form id="form1" runat="server">
<div>
    <asp:ScriptManager ID="ScriptManager1" runat="server">
    </asp:ScriptManager>
</div>
<asp:UpdatePanel ID="UpdatePanel1" runat="server">
    <ContentTemplate>
        <asp:Label ID="Label1" runat="server" Text="Label"></asp:Label>
        <asp:Button ID="Button1" runat="server" Text="AJAX Postback"
            onclick="OnButtonClick" />
    </ContentTemplate>
</asp:UpdatePanel>
<asp:Label ID="Label2" runat="server" Text="Label"></asp:Label>
<asp:Button ID="Button2" runat="server" Text="ASP.NET Postback"
    onclick="OnButtonClick" />
</form>
```

You can have multiple update panels in a page. Let's try that with the next Try It Out.

Try It Out   **Update Panel with Triggers**

1. Open the previously created Web site AJAXWebsite.

2. Add a new AJAX Web Form named UpdatePanelWithTrigger.aspx and make it the start
    page for the application. This template already includes a ScriptManager control.

3. Add two UpdatePanel controls.

4. Add a Label and a Button control in each of the UpdatePanel controls.

5. Assign the Click event handler of both Button controls to the OnButtonClick method and
    implement the method as shown here:

    ```
    protected void OnButtonClick(object sender, EventArgs e)
    {
        Label1.Text = DateTime.Now.ToLongTimeString();
        Label2.Text = DateTime.Now.ToLongTimeString();
    }
    ```

6. Run the application. Both Labels change regardless of which Button control is clicked (see
    Figure 22-2).

Figure 22-2

7. Change the property UpdateMode for both UpdatePanels from Always to Conditional.

8. Run the application again. Now only the Label inside the UpdatePanel where the Button is
    clicked changes.

9. Select the first `UpdatePanel`, and click the ellipsis with the `Triggers` property that opens the dialog shown in Figure 22-3. Add an `AsyncPostback` trigger, set the `ControlID` property to the button of the second `UpdatePanel`, `Button2`, and set the `EventName` to `Click`.

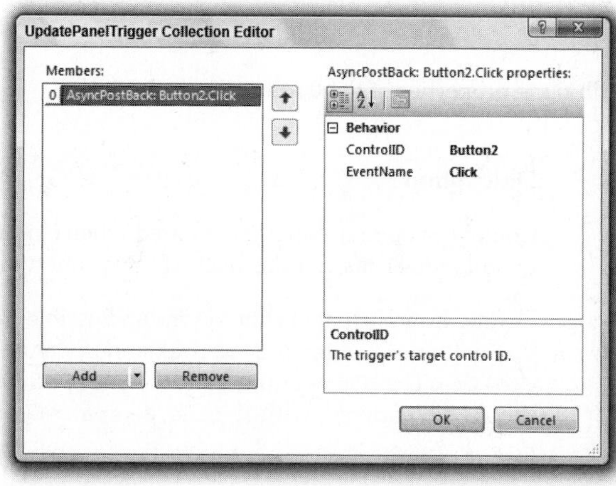

Figure 22-3

10. Run the application. Clicking `Button2` updates the content of both `UpdatePanels`; clicking `Button1` updates only the content of the first `UpdatePanel`.

How It Works

The update behavior of the `UpdatePanel` can be influenced. By default, it is updated every time an Ajax postback occurs. You can change the update so that controls are updated just when an update occurs from within the panel, or is fired from controls outside of the panel by defining a trigger.

Here is the ASPX code to define an `AsyncPostBackTrigger` for `UpdatePanel1`:

```
<form id="form1" runat="server">
<div>
    <asp:ScriptManager ID="ScriptManager1" runat="server">
    </asp:ScriptManager>

    <asp:UpdatePanel ID="UpdatePanel1" runat="server" UpdateMode="Conditional">
        <ContentTemplate>
            <asp:Label ID="Label1" runat="server" Text="Label"></asp:Label>
            <asp:Button ID="Button1" runat="server" OnClick="OnButtonClick"
                Text="Button" />
        </ContentTemplate>
        <Triggers>
        <asp:AsyncPostBackTrigger ControlID="Button2"EventName="Click" />
        </Triggers>
    </asp:UpdatePanel>
</div>
<asp:UpdatePanel ID="UpdatePanel2" runat="server" UpdateMode="Conditional">
```

```
    <ContentTemplate>
        <asp:Label ID="Label2" runat="server" Text="Label"></asp:Label>
        <asp:Button ID="Button2" runat="server" OnClick="OnButtonClick"
            Text="Button" />
    </ContentTemplate>
</asp:UpdatePanel>
</form>
```

The following table describes the properties of the UpdatePanel control:

UpdatePanel Property	Description
ChildrenAsTriggers	Content of UpdatePanel is updated when children controls of the UpdatePanel make a postback, if this property is set to true.
RenderMode	Defines how the panel should render. Possible values are UpdatePanelRenderMode.Block and UpdatePanelRenderMode.Inline. The Block enumeration value specifies that a <div> tag should be rendered; with Inline, a <span> tag is rendered.
UpdateMode	Set to one of the UpdatePanelUpdateMode enumeration values. Always updates the panel with every Ajax postback, Conditional only depending on the triggers.
Triggers	Specifies a collection of AsyncPostbackTrigger and PostbackTrigger elements to define when the content of the panel should update.

Timer Control

The ASP.NET AJAX Timer control can be used to repeatedly execute a method after a specified interval.

Try It Out   **Using the Timer Control**

1. Open the previously created Web site AJAXWebsite.

2. Add a new AJAX Web Form named TimerDemo.aspx and make it the start page for the application.

3. Add an UpdatePanel control to the Web Form.

4. Add a Label and a Timer control inside the UpdatePanel.

5. Set the `Timer` control's `Interval` property to 5000, and add the `OnTick` method to the `Tick` event.

6. Implement the `OnTick()` method to update the `Label`:

```
protected void OnTick(object sender, EventArgs e)
{
    Label1.Text = DateTime.Now.ToLongTimeString();
}
```

7. Start the Web Form and verify that the label is updated every five seconds (see Figure 22-4).

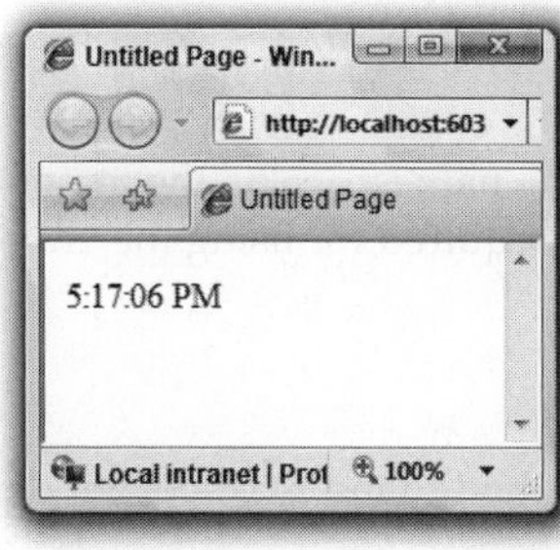

Figure 22-4

How It Works

The `Timer` control uses client-side JavaScript to perform postbacks at the specified interval. If the `Timer` control is positioned within an `UpdatePanel` as in this example, partial rendering updates can be done.

Update Progress

With the `UpdateProgress` control, you can give users some indication of how much time is left for a lengthy process.

Try It Out   Using the UpdateProgress Control

1. Open the previously created Web site AJAXWebsite.

2. Add a new AJAX Web Form named `UpdateProgressDemo.aspx` and make it the start page for the application.

3. Add an `UpdateProgress` control to the page. Within this control add the text `Wait....`

4. Add an `UpdatePanel` to the page. Within the `UpdatePanel`, add ASP.NET `TextBox` and `Button` controls.

5. Set the property `AssociatedUpdatePanelId` of the `UpdateProgress` control to the `UpdatePanel1`.

6. Set the `Text` property of the `TextBox` to `1000`.

7. Import the `System.Threading` namespace on the top of the file `UpdateProgressDemo` `.aspx.cs`. This namespace is required for using the `Thread` class in the next step.

   ```
   using System.Threading;
   ```

8. Assign the `Button_Click` method to the `Click` event of the `Button` control and implement the method:

   ```
   protected void Button_Click(object sender, EventArgs e)
   {
       System.Threading.Thread.Sleep(int.Parse(TextBox1.Text));
   }
   ```

9. Start the Web Form and verify that the content of the `UpateProgress` control is shown when the `Button` is clicked (see Figure 22-5) and stays visible until the process is completed. Observe the behavior of the page when you enter smaller and larger values in the `TextBox` before clicking the `Button` control.

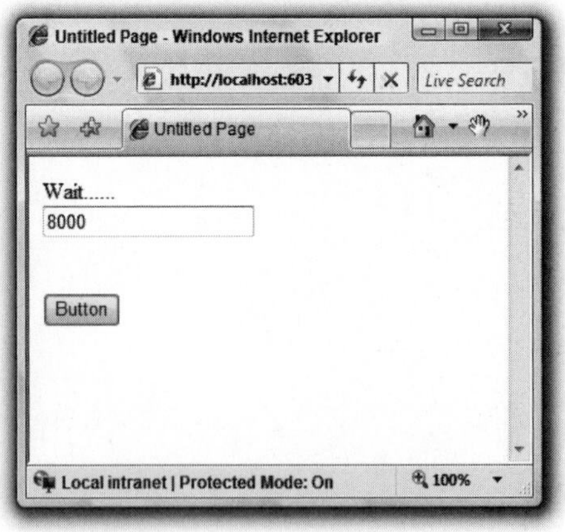

Figure 22-5

How It Works

The UpateProgress control displays the content of its <ProgressTemplate> template if a background operation is occurring for a length of time longer than defined by its DisplayAfter property. The DisplayAfter property is set to 500 milliseconds by default. It doesn't matter what the process is. In the sample, Thread.Sleep was used to create a delay in processing, but you can also invoke a Web service or do some other lengthy action.

```
<form id="form1" runat="server">
 <div>
     <asp:ScriptManager ID="ScriptManager1" runat="server"
         EnablePageMethods="True">
     </asp:ScriptManager>
     <asp:UpdateProgress ID="UpdateProgress1" runat="server"
         AssociatedUpdatePanelID="UpdatePanel1">
         <ProgressTemplate>
             Wait......
         </ProgressTemplate>
     </asp:UpdateProgress>
 </div>
 <asp:UpdatePanel ID="UpdatePanel1" runat="server">
     <ContentTemplate>
         <asp:TextBox ID="TextBox1" runat="server">1000</asp:TextBox>
         <br />
         <br />
         <br />
         <asp:Button ID="Button1" runat="server" Text="Button"
             onclick="Button_Click" />
         <br />
     </ContentTemplate>
 </asp:UpdatePanel>
</form>
```

With the Try It Outs you've done so far, you've used server-side ASP.NET controls. With ASP.NET AJAX, you can also use the client script library — for example, you can invoke a Web service directly from the client. The next section shows you how.

Web Services

Web services are used for platform-independent communication. In Chapter 21 you learned how to create and call ASP.NET Web services. Chapter 35 provides details about creating Web services with Windows Communication Foundation (WCF).

In the following Try It Out you create a new Web service and call it directly from client script.

Calling a Web Service

1.   Open the previously created Web site AJAXWebsite.

2.   Add an AJAX-enabled WCF Service (see Figure 22-6) and name it `HelloService.svc`.

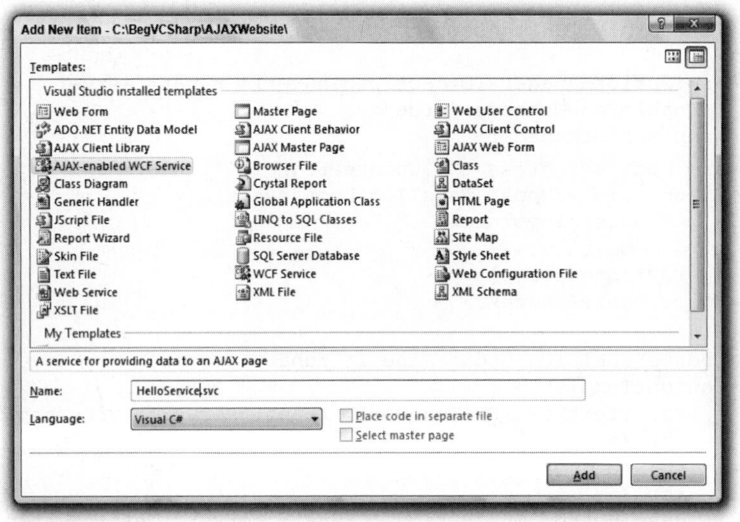

Figure 22-6

3.   Open the file `HelloService.cs` and add the `Greeting()` method:

```
using System.ServiceModel;
using System.ServiceModel.Activation;
using System.ServiceModel.Web;

[ServiceContract(Namespace = "")]
[AspNetCompatibilityRequirements(RequirementsMode =
        AspNetCompatibilityRequirementsMode.Allowed)]
public class HelloService
{
    [WebGet]
    [OperationContract]
    public string Greeting(string name)
    {
        return "Hello, " + name;
    }
}
```

4.   Add a new AJAX Web Form named `CallService.aspx`.

5.   Open the property editor for the `ScriptManager` control in the ASPX page. Click the ellipsis button of the `Services` property that opens dialog shown in Figure 22-7. Add a service reference with the `Add` button, and change its `Path` property to `HelloService.svc`.

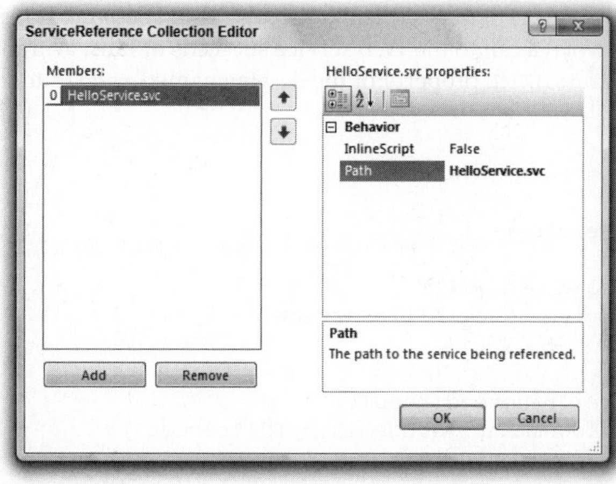

Figure 22-7

6. Add three HTML controls — an Input (Text), an Input (Button) and a Div control — to the page.

7. Set the identifier of the Div control to result.

8. Set the identifier of the Input (Text) control to input.

9. Change the Value property of button1 to Invoke Service...

10. Modify the script block in the page by first declaring a variable helloService within the script block as shown here:

```
<script type="text/javascript">

    var helloService;

    function pageLoad() {
    }
</script>
```

11. Within the pageLoad method, create an instance of the variable helloService. The type is the same as defined by the Services property of the ScriptManager defined earlier. HelloService is a proxy to access the Web service:

```
<script type="text/javascript">

    var helloService;

    function pageLoad() {
      helloService = new HelloService();
    }
```

12. Create the functions `helloSucceed` and `helloFailed`. These methods are invoked asynchronously when a call to the Web service succeeds or fails. Within the `helloSucceeded` method, set the `innerHTML` property of the `div` tag named `result` to the result from the Web service:

```
<script type="text/javascript">

  var helloService;

  function pageLoad() {
    helloService = new HelloService();
  }

  function helloSucceed(result) {
      var d = document.getElementById("result");
      d.innerHTML = result;
  }

  function helloFailed(error, userContext, methodName) {
  }

</script>
```

13. Within the `pageLoad` function, invoke the `set_defaultSucceededCallback` and `set_defaultFailedCallback` methods of the proxy object to define that the functions `helloSucceed` and `helloFailed` are invoked when an asynchronous Web service call succeeds or fails:

```
<script type="text/javascript">

  var helloService;

  function pageLoad() {
    helloService = new HelloService();
    helloService.set_defaultSucceededCallback(helloSucceed);
    helloService.set_defaultFailedCallback(helloFailed);
  }

  function helloSucceed(result) {
      var d = document.getElementById("result");
      d.innerHTML = result;
  }

  function helloFailed(error, userContext, methodName) {
  }

  function callService() {
    var l = document.getElementById("input");

    helloService.Greeting(l.value);
  }

</script>
```

14. Add the function `callService`, which uses the proxy variable `hello` to invoke the `Greeting` operation of the Web service. To send a value from the input field, the input field is accessed with the `getElementById` function of the `document` object. `input` is the name that was assigned to the input field:

```
<script type="text/javascript">

    var helloService;

    function pageLoad() {
      helloService = new HelloService();
      helloService.set_defaultSucceededCallback(helloSucceed);
      helloService.set_defaultFailedCallback(helloFailed);
    }

    function helloSucceed(result) {
        var d = document.getElementById("result");
        d.innerHTML = result;
    }

    function helloFailed(error, userContext, methodName) {
    }

    function callService() {
      var l = document.getElementById("input");

      helloService.Greeting(l.value);
    }

</script>
```

15. Define that the `callService` function is invoked by clicking the `Invoke Service` button. Assign the `onclick` event on `button1` to invoke the function as shown:

```
<input id="button1" type="button" value="Invoke Service..."
        onclick="callService();" />
```

16. Start the Web page, enter a name in the text control, and invoke the Web service by clicking the button.

How It Works

Creating the AJAX-enabled WCF service adds the following configuration section to `web.config`. The behavior element `enableWebScript` adds JSON support to the Web service and thus the Web service directly receives and returns JSON objects that can optimally be used by JavaScript clients:

```
<system.serviceModel>
  <behaviors>
    <endpointBehaviors>
      <behavior name="HelloServiceAspNetAjaxBehavior">
        <enableWebScript />
      </behavior>
```

```
      </endpointBehaviors>
    </behaviors>
    <serviceHostingEnvironment aspNetCompatibilityEnabled="true" />
    <services>
     <service name="HelloService">
        <endpoint address="" behaviorConfiguration="HelloServiceAspNetAjaxBehavior"
           binding="webHttpBinding" contract="HelloService" />
     </service>
    </services>
 </system.serviceModel>
```

The Web service is configured in the ASPX page with the `Services` property of the `ScriptManager`. You've assigned the service by using the Service Reference Collection Editor. The editor adds `Services` elements to the `ScriptManager`, which contain `ServiceReference` elements that reference the Web service with the `Path` property.

```
<asp:ScriptManager ID="ScriptManager1" runat="server">
    <Services>
        <asp:ServiceReference Path="HelloService.svc" />
    </Services>
</asp:ScriptManager>
```

With client script, the Web service is invoked asynchronously. Here, the Web service is invoked by calling the `Greeting` method, and is passed a string that was defined by the `Greeting` operation of the Web service:

```
helloService.Greeting(l.value);
```

The result arrives asynchronously. The method to be invoked when the Web service is finished is defined by the `set_defaultSucceededCallback` method. In case the Web service returns a failure, the method invoked is defined by `set_defaultFailedCallback`.

```
helloService.set_defaultSucceededCallback(helloSucceed);
helloService.set_defaultFailedCallback(helloFailed);
```

By using `set_defaultSucceedCallback` and `set_defaultFailedCallback`, the functions assigned to these methods are invoked every time a Web service operation succeeds or fails — no matter what operation you invoke with the Web service. Instead of using these defaults, you can also assign a succeed and failed function directly to the call where you invoke the Web service. In the example, the Web service offers the operation `Greeting()`. The `Greeting()` function of the proxy object sends the Greeting request to the Web service. Instead of just passing the input parameters to the Web service, you can pass the `helloSucceed` and `helloFailed` functions as shown here:

```
helloService.Greeting(l.value, helloSucceed, helloFailed, null);
```

This way, you can create different succeed and failed functions depending on the operation invoked.

Extender Controls

ASP.NET AJAX offers great advantages in extending existing controls. It provides a framework for creating new extender controls; there are no extender controls out of the box. However, with the ASP.NET AJAX Control Toolkit you get many extender controls. This section is based on using the ASP.NET AJAX Control Toolkit.

Try It Out   **Using an Extender Control**

1. Download the ASP.NET AJAX Control Toolkit (`AjaxControlToolkit-Framework3.5-NoSource.zip`) from `www.asp.net/ajax/downloads` and store it in a directory on your system. Extract the zip file.

2. Open the previously created Web site AJAXWebsite with Visual Studio 2008.

3. In the Toolbox, right-click and select `Add Tab` to create a new category, and name it AJAX Control Toolkit.

4. Right-click in the content of the new category and select Choose Items. The Choose Toolbox Items dialog opens. Click the Browse button and select the assembly `AjaxControlToolkit.dll` (you'll find this in the `SampleWebsite/bin/` directory in the zip file you extracted in Step 1).

5. Extender controls now show up in the new category in the Toolbox.

6. Add the `ajaxToolkit tagPrefix` to the `web.config` file referencing the assembly AjaxControlToolkit:

```
<pages>
  <controls>
    <add tagPrefix="asp" namespace="System.Web.UI"
        assembly="System.Web.Extensions, Version=3.5.0.0, Culture=neutral,
        PublicKeyToken=31BF3856AD364E35"/>
    <add tagPrefix="asp" namespace="System.Web.UI.WebControls"
        assembly="System.Web.Extensions, Version=3.5.0.0, Culture=neutral,
        PublicKeyToken=31BF3856AD364E35"/>
    <add namespace="AjaxControlToolkit" assembly="AjaxControlToolkit"
        tagPrefix="ajaxToolkit"/>
  </controls>
</pages>
```

7. Add a new AJAX Web Form named `TextBoxWatermark.aspx` and make it the start page for the application

8. Add two ASP.NET `TextBox` controls.

9. In the designer, click the smart tag of the first TextBox control and select Add Extender from the menu. (The smart tag appears when you move the mouse over the TextBox control.) The Extender Wizard dialog, shown in Figure 22-8, opens. Select TextBoxWatermarkExtender and click OK.

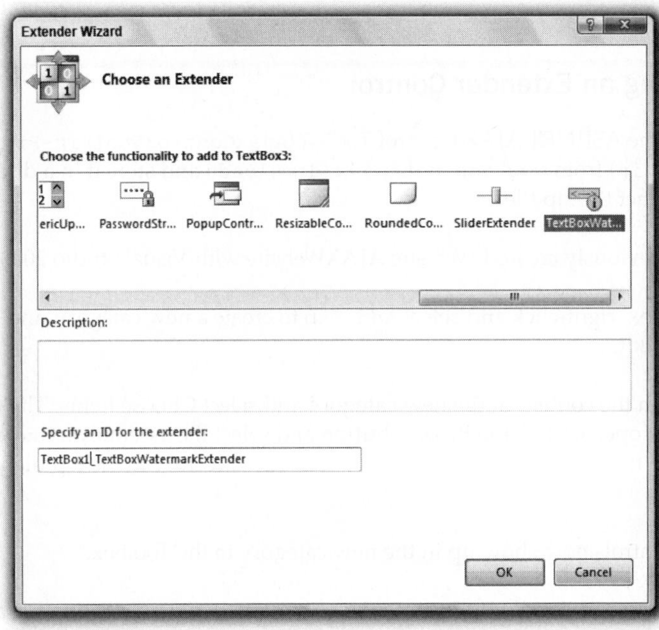

Figure 22-8

10. Repeat step 9 with the second TextBox control to add another TextBoxWatermarkExtender.

11. Select the first TextBox. With the Properties editor, expand the group TextBox1_ TextBoxWatermarkExtender. Set the WatermarkText property to Enter your first name.

12. Select the second TextBox. With the Properties editor, expand the group TextBox2_ TextBoxWatermarkExtender. Set the WatermarkText property to Enter your last name.

13. Start the Web page. You can see the watermark text in the TextBox controls before some other text is added.

How It Works

`TextBoxWatermarkExtender` is an extender control to extend the `TextBox` with a watermark. When you use the Extender Wizard, the extender control is added to the ASPX file and associates to the `TextBox` control with the property `TargetControlID`. The control defines the properties `WatermarkText` and `WatermarkCssClass`.

```
<asp:TextBox ID="TextBox1" runat="server"></asp:TextBox>
<ajaxToolkit:TextBoxWatermarkExtender
    ID="TextBox1_TextBoxWatermarkExtender"
    runat="server" Enabled="True" TargetControlID="TextBox1"
    WatermarkText="Enter your firstname">
</ajaxToolkit:TextBoxWatermarkExtender>
```

Summary

In this chapter you learned how to add interactivity to ASP.NET Web pages with ASP.NET AJAX. With ASP.NET AJAX, you can stay with the ASP.NET programming model by using new server-side controls such as the `UpdatePanel` to do partial updates of the Web page. You used the `Timer` control to update the page after specified intervals. `UpdateProgess` is the control to use to show some lengthy progress information to the user.

You've also seen how to use client scripting to invoke a Web service not from the code-behind but directly from within JavaScript. The ASP.NET Control Toolkit offers extender controls such as the `TextBoxWatermarkExtender` as an extender of the `TextBox` control. Several other controls are available with this toolkit.

The next chapter shows how Web applications and Web services can be deployed.

Exercises

1. What control can you use to update only part of a Web page?

2. If a Web page contains multiple `UpatePanel` controls, how do you prevent every region contained by an `UpdatePanel` control from being updated during a partial postback?

3. How can you display an animated GIF that should only be seen when a lengthy action is in progress?

4. What do you need to do to invoke a Web service directly from client script?

Deploying Web Applications

In the previous three chapters you learned to develop Web applications and Web services with ASP.NET. For all these application types, different deployment options exist. You can copy the Web pages, publish the Web site, or create an installation program. This chapter covers the advantages and disadvantages of the different options, and how to accomplish these tasks.

In this chapter, you learn about the following:

- ❑ Internet Information Services (IIS)
- ❑ IIS configuration
- ❑ Copying Web sites
- ❑ Publishing Web sites
- ❑ Windows Installer

Internet Information Services

Internet Information Services (IIS) needn't be installed for developing Web applications with Visual Studio 2008 because Studio 2008 has its own Web server: the Visual Web Developer Web Server. This is a simple Web server that runs only on the local machine. On the production system, IIS is needed to run the Web application.

IIS is not available with Windows Vista Home Edition. On other editions, you can install IIS in the same way that you install other Windows components. In the Control Panel, click Programs. Here you can find a category Programs and Features with a link Turn Windows features on or off. Click this link. One of the features of Windows is Internet Information Services, which needs to be selected to install Internet Information Services. You can also ask your system administrator to install IIS on your system.

The ASP.NET runtime needs to be configured with IIS to allow it to run ASP.NET Web applications. You can easily verify whether the ASP.NET runtime is configured by checking handler mappings (see Figure 23-1) with the IIS Manager tool. If IIS is installed, you can find this tool in the Administrative Tools with the menu entry Internet Information Services (IIS) Manager. In case Administrative Tools is not configured to be directly available from your Start button, you can find the Administrative Tools in the Control Panel. With the Internet Information Services (IIS) Manager, double-click to Handler Mappings. Scrolling through the information, you can see that the *.aspx path is configured two times, once as IsapiModule and once with the System.Web.UI.PageHandlerFactory.

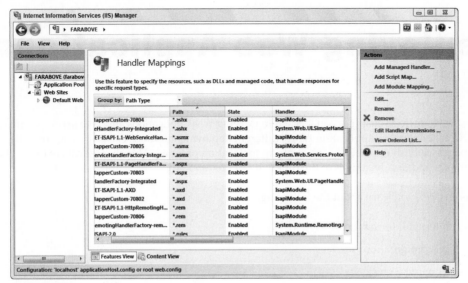

Figure 23-1

If the handler mappings to the ASP.NET runtime are not configured on your system, you can start the program aspnet_regiis -i to install the file extensions and modules with IIS.

The main process of IIS is inetinfo.exe. It runs high-privileged with the System account. With the IsapiModule configured, a request to an ASPX file is forwarded to a worker process (w3wp.exe). Different worker processes can be configured to run different versions of the .NET runtime. You can also configure the user identity under which this process is running, and specify recycling options.

IIS Configuration

IIS must be configured before you run a Web application with it. In the following Try It Out, you create a Web site with the Internet Information Services (IIS) Manager. To begin, your Web site needs a virtual directory, which is the directory used by the client accessing the Web application. For example, in http://server/mydirectory, mydirectory is a virtual directory. The virtual directory is completely independent of the physical directory where the files are stored on the disk. For example, the physical directory for mydirectory can be D:\someotherdirectory.

Try It Out   **Creating a New Application Pool**

1. Start the IIS Manager tool (see Figure 23-2). You can find this tool in the Control Panel, under Administrative Tools.

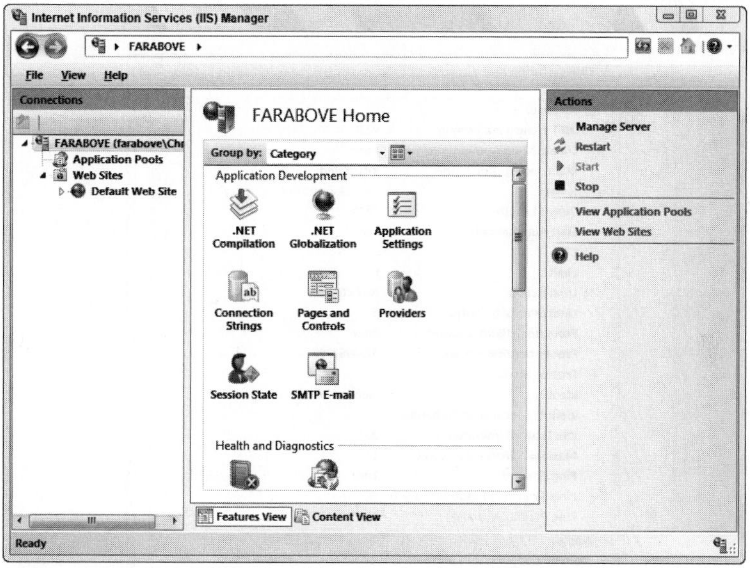

Figure 23-2

2. In the tree view, select Application Pools, right-click it, and choose Add Application Pool from the context menu.

3. The Add Application Pool dialog opens (see Figure 23-3). In the Name text box, enter **Beg C# App Pool**, and then select the .NET Framework version v2.0.50727. Click the OK button. In fact, you configure the version of the .NET runtime. Because ASP.NET 3.5 is using the same runtime as ASP.NET 2.0, version 2.0.50727 works for both ASP.NET 2.0 and ASP.NET 3.5 applications.

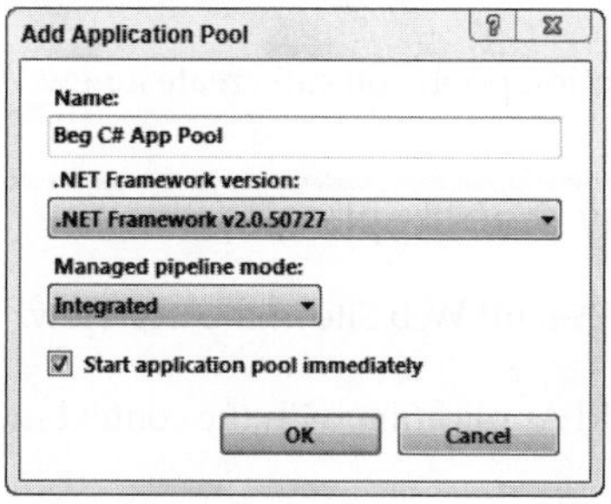

Figure 23-3

4. After the application pool is created, you can configure advanced settings (see Figure 23-4) to define the identity under which the process is running; whether, on a multi-CPU system, just specific CPUs should be used; and the number of worker processes that should run in this pool. Advanced settings are available after you've selected the application pool either from the Actions category on the right side of Internet Information Services (IIS) Manager, or from the context menu.

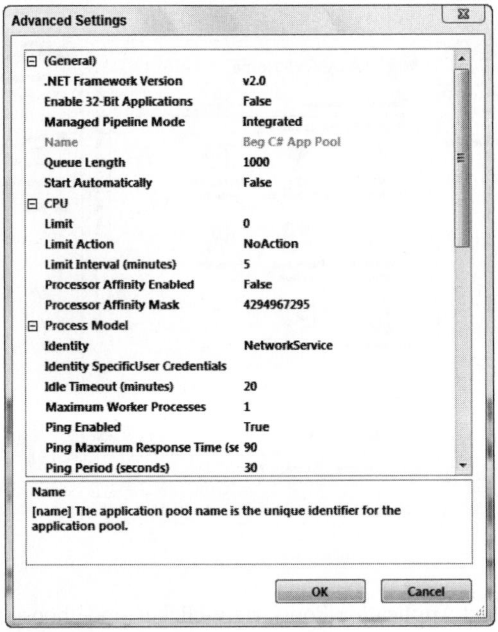

Figure 23-4

How It Works

Application pools make it possible for different Web sites to run different versions of the ASP.NET runtime, and to have different user accounts and different stability.

After you've configured an application pool, you can create a new Web application.

Try It Out   **Creating a New Web Application**

1. In the IIS Manager, select Default Web Site in the tree view.

2. Right-click and choose Add Application with the context menu. The Add Application dialog opens (see Figure 23-5).

3. Enter the physical path for the Website and the alias name **BegVCSharpWebsite**. Select the application pool Beg C# App Pool that you just created.

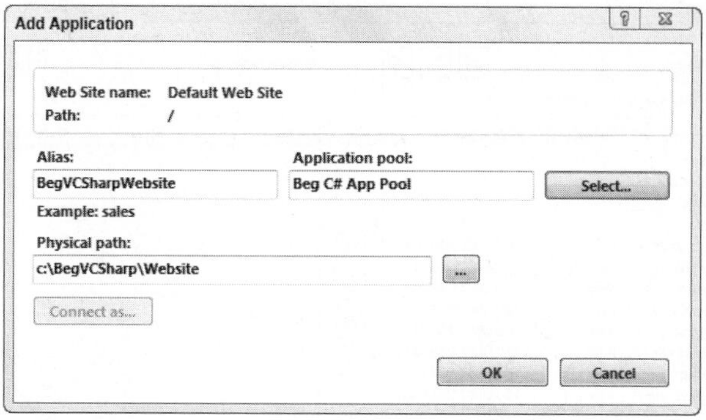

Figure 23-5

4. Click the OK button.

Now the Web application is configured, and you can copy or publish Web applications from Visual Studio to this Web site.

Copying a Web Site

With Visual Studio 2008, you can copy files from a source Web site to a remote Web site. The source Web site is the Web site of your Web application, which has been opened with Visual Studio. It is accessed either from the local file system or from IIS — depending on how the Web application was created. The remote Web site to which the files should be copied can be accessed using the file system, the FTP protocol, or FrontPage Server Extensions on IIS.

Copying files can happen in both directions: from the source Web site to the remote Web site and vice versa. In the next Try It Out, you use Visual Studio to copy the Web application from Chapter 20 to the Web site you configured earlier.

Try It Out   Copying a Web Site

1. With Windows Vista, start Visual Studio 2008 with elevated admin rights. Copying a Web site to the local IIS requires administrator rights. With Windows XP, you can start Visual Studio normally if you've logged on to an account with administrative rights.

2. Open the Web application from Chapter 20.

3. Select Website ⇨ Copy Web Site. The dialog shown in Figure 23-6 appears.

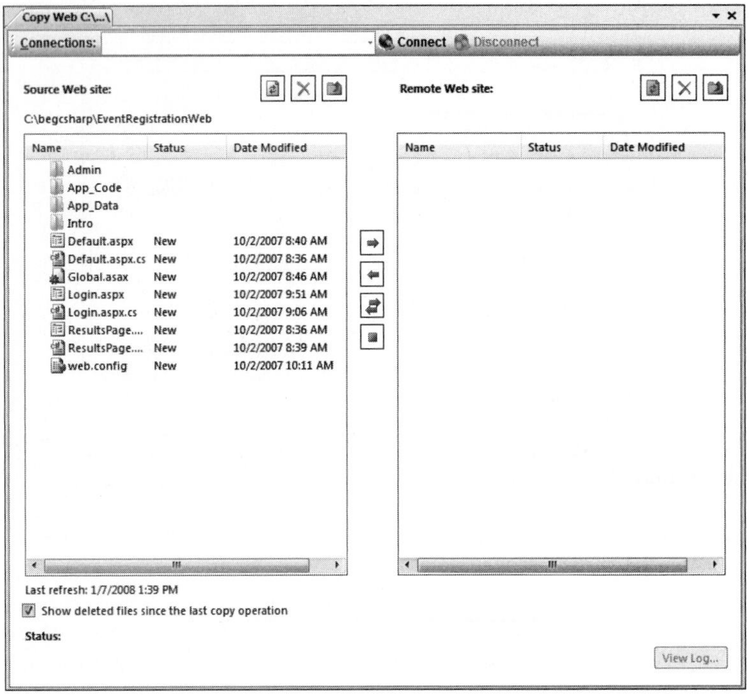

Figure 23-6

4. Click the Connect button at the top of the window shown in Figure 23-6. The Open Web Site dialog opens (see Figure 23-7).

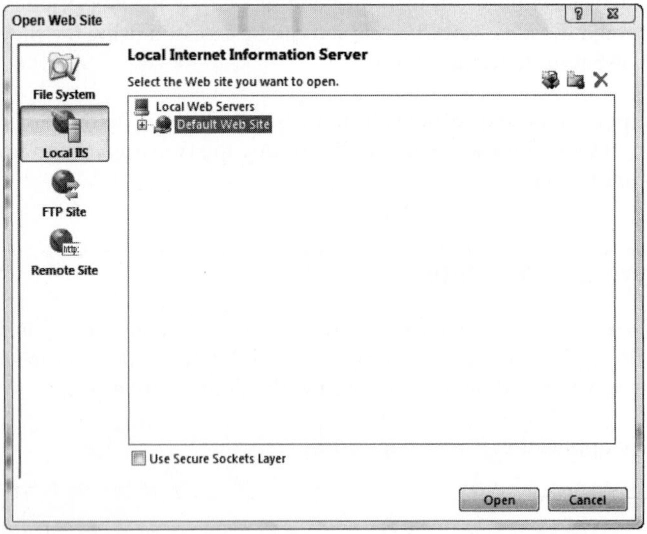

Figure 23-7

5. Here you can select files to copy to the local file system, local IIS, FTP sites, and remote sites (that have FrontPage Server Extensions installed). Select Local IIS, and select the previously created Web site, BegVCSharpWebsite. If you're running a Windows Vista Home Edition, you can only copy the files to the local file system because IIS is not available.

6. In the Source Web site list, select the files you want to copy from Source Web Site to Remote Web Site.

7. Click the Copy Selected Files button. This button is located in the middle between the Source Web Site view and the Remote Web Site view and has an arrow. If you move the mouse over the buttons, a tooltip appears that explains what button this is. The direction of the arrow shows in which direction the files are copied, from the source to the remote site or vice versa. The button with arrows pointing in both directions verifies which files are newer and copies the newer files to the other side.

8. Now all the selected files have been copied to the new Web site.

With the Copy Web Site tool, you can also select files to copy from the remote Web site to the source Web site. Selecting the button Synchronize Selected Files shows arrows pointing in both directions; the newer files from the remote Web site are copied to the source Web site, and the newer files from the source Web site are copied to the remote Web site. This is a very useful option if you have a team Web server on which other developers synchronize files. Synchronizing in both directions copies your newer files to the team Web server and the files from your colleagues' remote Web server to your local site.

When the files are just copied, you cannot be sure if the files can be compiled. Compilation happens when the files are accessed by a browser. You can perform a precompilation of the Web site using the command-line utility `aspnet_compiler.exe`.

Enter the command **aspnet_compiler –v /BegVCSharpWebsite** and the Web site BegVCSharpWebsite is precompiled. This way, the first user doesn't have to wait until the ASPX pages are compiled because they already are.

You can find this utility in the directory of the .NET runtime.

Publishing a Web Site

Instead of copying all of your source files (`.cs`) to the target Web site, you can precompile the Web site with the publishing option. With publishing, the assemblies are created first. Then the presentation files (`.aspx`, `.ascx`, etc.) are copied to the target Web site. This way, `.cs` source files are not copied to the target Web site.

In the next Try It Out, you use Visual Studio to publish the Web application from Chapter 20.

Try It Out   **Publishing a Web Site for Deployment**

1.   Open the Web application EventRegistrationWeb from Chapter 20 with Visual Studio.

2.   Create a new directory for the precompiled Web site on your C: drive. Name it precompiledWeb.

3.   Select Build ⇨ Publish Web Site. The Publish Web Site dialog opens (see Figure 23-8).

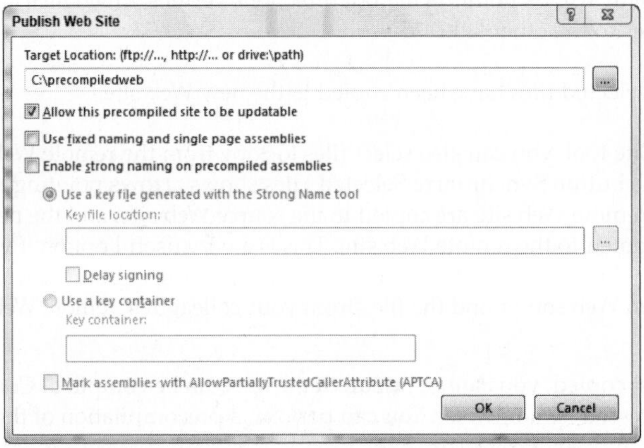

Publish Web Site   ? ⊠

Target Location: (ftp://..., http://... or drive:\path)

C:\precompiledweb   [...]

☑ Allow this precompiled site to be updatable

☐ Use fixed naming and single page assemblies

☐ Enable strong naming on precompiled assemblies

   ◉ Use a key file generated with the Strong Name tool
     Key file location:

     [   ] [...]

     ☐ Delay signing

   ◯ Use a key container
     Key container:

     [   ]

☐ Mark assemblies with AllowPartiallyTrustedCallerAttribute (APTCA)

                         [OK]   [Cancel]

Figure 23-8

Here's a quick look at the options you can configure:

❑   Allow this precompiled site to be updatable — The code-behind files are compiled to assemblies, but the ASPX files are published in source. If you do not want the Web site administrator (or customer purchasing your Web site) to update the layout (the ASPX files), deselect this option. That way, ASPX files are still published, but with the content of these files you'll find only this text:

```
This is a marker file generated by the precompilation tool,
and should not be deleted!
```

The content of the ASPX files is compiled into assemblies.

❑ Use fixed naming and single page assemblies — One assembly is created for every page, and this assembly has a fixed name that will be the same the next time publishing. Setting this option allows for partial updates of the Web site and updating or adding assemblies.

❑ Enable strong naming on precompiled assemblies — This allows you to specify a key file to sign the generated assemblies.

4. Click OK to publish the Web site.

> **Precompiling Web sites has the advantage that the source files are not copied to the target Web site, which means that the Web administrator cannot change the source files on the server.**

Windows Installer

You can also create a Windows installer program to install your Web application. Creating installation programs is required if shared assemblies are needed by the application. Using installation programs has the advantage that the virtual directory is configured with IIS, and you're not required to create a virtual directory manually. The person installing the Web application can start a `setup.exe` program, and the complete setup is done automatically. Of course, administrative privileges are required to start this program.

Creating a Setup Program

Visual Studio 2008 ships with the project type Web Setup Project to create installation programs for Web applications. With Web Setup Project, the following editors are available: File System, Registry, File Types, User Interface, and Custom Action and Launch Conditions. These editors were introduced in Chapter 18 with Windows applications, so only those editors needed for Web applications are discussed here.

In the following Try It Out, you create a setup program that installs a Web application.

Try It Out   Creating a Setup Program

1. Open the Web application EventRegistrationWeb from Chapter 20 using Visual Studio 2008.

2. Add a new project of type Web Setup Project, as shown in Figure 23-9. Name the project **EventRegistrationWebSetup** and click OK.

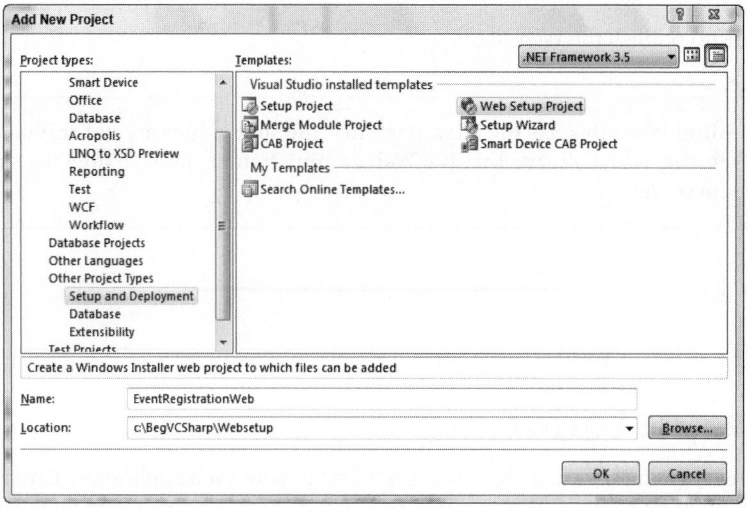

Figure 23-9

3. The File System Editor displays. Select File System on Target Machine, and select Project ⇨ Add ⇨ Project Output. From the Project Output dialog, select Content Files of the Web application and click OK.

4. In the File System Editor, select Web Application Folder. You can now configure the Web application with the properties editor. The following table describes the properties:

Web Application Folder Property	Description
AllowDirectoryBrowsing	An IIS configuration option. Setting this to `true` allows browsing for files on the Web site. The default value is `false`.
AllowReadAccess	Set by default to `true`. To access ASPX pages, read access is required.

Web Application Folder Property	Description
AllowScriptSourceAccess	By default, script source access is denied with this property set to `false`.
AllowWriteAccess	Write access is denied by default.
DefaultDocument	Sets the home page of the Website — for example, `Default.aspx`.
ExecutePermissions	The default value is set to `vsdepScriptsOnly`, which allows access to ASP.NET pages, but does not allow custom executables to run on the server. If custom executables should be allowed to run on the server, then this option can be set to `vsdepScriptsAndExecutables`.
LogVisits	Set to `true`, client access logging is configured.
VirtualDirectory	Sets the name of the virtual directory that is configured with IIS.

5. Open the Launch Conditions Editor by selecting View ➪ Editor ➪ Launch Conditions. Launch conditions define what products must be installed on the target system before the installation can be done.

6. Check the launch conditions that are configured. The Search for IIS configuration verifies whether IIS is installed on the target system by checking the registry key SYSTEM\ CurrentControlSet\Services\W3SVC\Parameters to get the IIS version. The launch condition IIS Condition confirms that the IIS version is at least 4. For ASP.NET 3.5 Web applications, you can change this value to 5 to require at least IIS 5.

7. Build the setup application by selecting Build ➪ Build EventRegistrationWebSetup.

8. In the directory of the setup project you will find the `setup.exe` file and an installation package named `EventRegistrationWebSetup.msi`.

Installing the Web Application

By starting the `setup.exe` program, you can install the Web application.

Try It Out   **Installing a Web Application**

1.   Click `setup.exe` to start installing the Web application. The Setup Wizard opens (see Figure 23-10). Click Next.

Figure 23-10

2.   On the Select Installation Address page (see Figure 23-11), rename the Virtual Directory to a name that's not already configured with IIS. Select the Application Pool (Beg C# App Pool) that you created previously, and click Next.

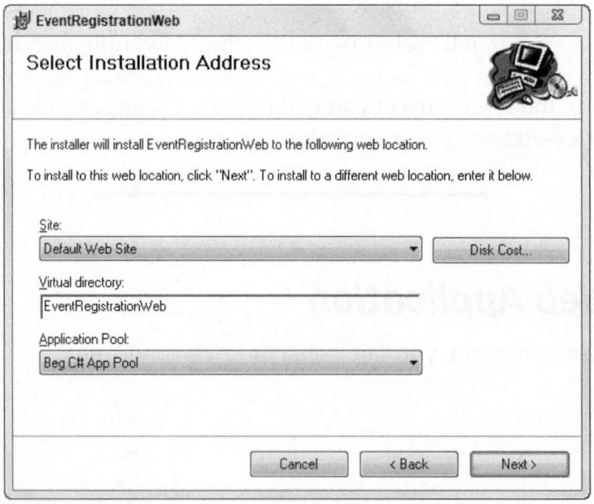

Figure 23-11

3. Confirm the installation (see Figure 23-12) by clicking Next.

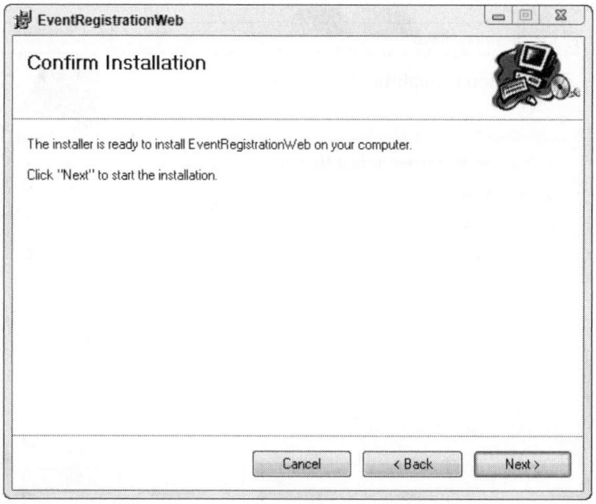

Figure 23-12

4. A progress bar displays while the installation is running (see Figure 23-13).

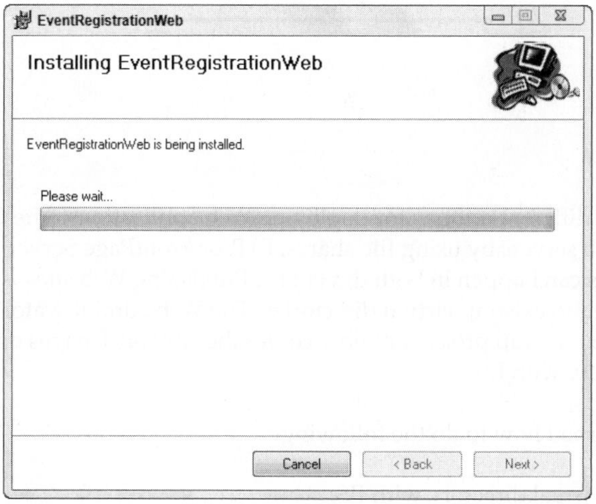

Figure 23-13

5. The Installation Complete page (see Figure 23-14) opens after a successful installation. Click Close.

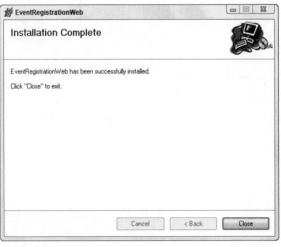

Figure 23-14

6. Now you can start the Web site from the new virtual directory.

Summary

This chapter described different options for deploying Web applications. The Copy Web Site tool enables you to copy files to Web servers by using file shares, FTP, or FrontPage Server Extensions. Synchronization of files can happen in both directions. Publishing Web sites is a feature whereby just the assemblies are deployed to existing virtual directories. The Web administrator no longer has access to the sources. Finally, creating a setup project not only copies the ASP.NET pages and assemblies, but also creates a virtual directory with IIS.

In this chapter, you learned how to do the following:

❑ Create a new virtual directory with IIS.

❑ Copy a Web site with Visual Studio.

❑ Publish a Web site with Visual Studio.

❑ Create a setup program for the installation of a Web application.

The next chapter is the first chapter in a series that deals with data access, starting with the file system.

Exercises

1. What is the difference between copying and precompiling a Web application? When should you use each?

2. When is using a setup program preferable to copying a site?

3. What must be done before a Web site can be published?

4. Publish the Web service from Chapter 21 to a virtual directory that you define with IIS.

Part IV

Data Access

File System Data

Reading and writing files are essential aspects of many .NET applications. This chapter shows you how, touching on the major classes used to create, read from, and write to files, and the supporting classes used to manipulate the file system from C# code. Although you won't examine all of the classes in detail, this chapter goes into enough depth to give you a good idea of the concepts and fundamentals.

Files can be a great way to store data between instances of your application, or they can be used to transfer data between applications. User and application configuration settings can be stored to be retrieved the next time your application is run. Delimited text files, such as comma-separated files, are used by many legacy systems, and to interoperate with such systems you need to know how to work with delimited data. As you will see, the .NET Framework provides you with the necessary tools to use files effectively in your applications.

By the end of this chapter, you will have learned the following:

- ❑ What a stream is and how .NET uses stream classes to access files.
- ❑ How to use the `File` object to manipulate the file structure.
- ❑ How to write to, and read from, a file.
- ❑ How to read and write formatted data from and to files.
- ❑ How to read and write compressed files.
- ❑ How to serialize and deserialize objects.
- ❑ How to monitor files and directories for changes.

Streams

All input and output in the .NET Framework involves the use of *streams*. A stream is an abstract representation of a *serial device*. A serial device is something that stores data in a linear manner and is accessed the same way: one byte at a time. This device can be a disk file, a network channel, a memory location, or any other object that supports reading and writing to it in a linear manner. Keeping the device abstract means that the underlying destination/source of the stream can be hidden. This level of abstraction enables code reuse, and enables you to write more generic routines because you don't have to worry about the specifics of how data transfer actually occurs. Therefore, similar code can be transferred and reused when the application is reading from a file input stream, a network input stream, or any other kind of stream. Because you can ignore the physical mechanics of each device, you don't need to worry about, for example, hard disk heads or memory allocation when dealing with a file stream.

There are two types of streams:

❑ **Output:** Output streams are used when data is written to some external destination, which can be a physical disk file, a network location, a printer, or another program. Understanding stream programming opens many advanced possibilities. This chapter focuses on file system data, so you'll only be looking at writing to disk files.

❑ **Input:** Input streams are used to read data into memory or variables that your program can access. The most common form of input stream you have worked with so far is the keyboard. An input stream can come from almost any source, but this chapter focuses on reading disk files. The concepts applied to reading/writing disk files apply to most devices, so you'll gain a basic understanding of streams and see a proven approach that can be applied to many situations.

The Classes for Input and Output

The `System.IO` namespace contains almost all of the classes that you will be covering in this chapter. `System.IO` contains the classes for reading and writing data to and from files, and you can reference this namespace in your C# application to gain access to these classes without fully qualifying type names. Quite a few classes are contained in `System.IO`, as shown in Figure 24-1, but you will only be working with the primary classes needed for file input and output.

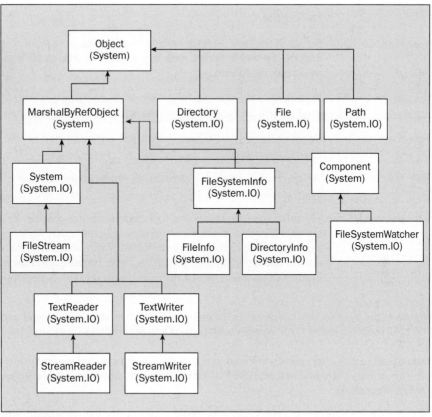

Figure 24-1

The classes covered in this chapter are described in the following table:

Class	Description
File	A static utility class that exposes many static methods for moving, copying, and deleting files.
Directory	A static utility class that exposes many static methods for moving, copying, and deleting directories.
Path	A utility class used to manipulate path names.
FileInfo	Represents a physical file on disk, and has methods to manipulate this file. For any reading and writing to the file, a Stream object must be created.
DirectoryInfo	Represents a physical directory on disk and has methods to manipulate this directory.

(continued)

Class	Description
FileSystemInfo	Serves as the base class for both FileInfo and DirectoryInfo, making it possible to deal with files and directories at the same time using polymorphism.
FileStream	Represents a file that can be written to or read from, or both. This file can be written to and read from asynchronously or synchronously.
StreamReader	Reads character data from a stream and can be created by using a FileStream as a base.
StreamWriter	Writes character data to a stream and can be created by using a FileStream as a base.
FileSystemWatcher	The most advanced class you will examine in this chapter. It is used to monitor files and directories, and exposes events that your application can catch when changes occur in these locations. This functionality has always been missing from Windows programming, but now the .NET Framework makes it much easier to respond to file system events.

You'll also look at the System.IO.Compression namespace, which enables you to read and write compressed files, by using either GZIP compression or the Deflate compression scheme:

❑   DeflateStream — Represents a stream in which data is compressed automatically when writing, or uncompressed automatically when reading. Compression is achieved using the Deflate algorithm.

❑   GZipStream — Represents a stream in which data is compressed automatically when writing, or uncompressed automatically when reading. Compression is achieved using the GZIP algorithm.

Finally, you'll explore object serialization using the System.Runtime.Serialization namespace and its child namespaces. You'll primarily be looking at the BinaryFormatter class in the System.Runtime.Serialization.Formatters.Binary namespace, which enables you to serialize objects to a stream as binary data, and deserialize them again.

The File and Directory Classes

The File and Directory utility classes expose many static methods for manipulating, surprisingly enough, files and directories. These methods make it possible to move files, query and update attributes, and create FileStream objects. As you learned in Chapter 8, static methods can be called on classes without having to create instances of them.

Some of the most useful static methods of the `File` class are shown in the following table:

Method	Description
Copy()	Copies a file from a source location to a target location.
Create()	Creates a file in the specified path.
Delete()	Deletes a file.
Open()	Returns a `FileStream` object at the specified path.
Move()	Moves a specified file to a new location. You can specify a different name for the file in the new location.

Some useful static methods of the `Directory` class are shown in the next table:

Method	Description
CreateDirectory()	Creates a directory with the specified path.
Delete()	Deletes the specified directory and all the files within it.
GetDirectories()	Returns an array of `string` objects that represent the names of the directories below the specified directory.
GetFiles()	Returns an array of `string` objects that represent the names of the files in the specified directory.
GetFileSystemEntries()	Returns an array of `string` objects that represent the names of the files and directories in the specified directory.
Move()	Moves the specified directory to a new location. You can specify a new name for the folder in the new location.

The FileInfo Class

Unlike the `File` class, the `FileInfo` class is not static and does not have static methods. This class is only useful when instantiated. A `FileInfo` object represents a file on a disk or a network location, and you can create one by supplying a path to a file:

```
FileInfo aFile = new FileInfo(@"C:\Log.txt");
```

Because you will be working with strings representing the path of a file throughout this chapter, which means a lot of \ characters in your strings, remember that the @ that prefixes the preceding string means that this string will be interpreted literally. Thus, \ will be interpreted as \, and not as an escape character. Without the @ prefix, you would need to use \\ instead of \ to avoid having this character be interpreted as an escape character. In this chapter you'll stick to the @ prefix for your strings.

You can also pass the name of a directory to the `FileInfo` constructor, although in practical terms that isn't particularly useful, as it causes the base class of `FileInfo`, which is `FileSystemInfo`, to be initialized with all the directory information, but none of the `FileInfo` methods or properties relating specifically to files will work.

Many of the methods exposed by the `FileInfo` class are similar to those of the `File` class, but because `File` is a static class, it requires a string parameter specifying the file location for every method call. Therefore, the following calls do the same thing:

```
FileInfo aFile = new FileInfo("Data.txt");

if (aFile.Exists)
    Console.WriteLine("File Exists");

if (File.Exists("Data.txt"))
    Console.WriteLine("File Exists");
```

In this code a check is made to see whether the file `Data.txt` exists. Note that no directory information is specified here, meaning that the current *working directory* is the only location examined. This directory is the one containing the application that calls this code. You'll look at this in more detail a little later, in the section "Path Names and Relative Paths."

Most of the `FileInfo` methods mirror the `File` methods in this manner. In most cases it doesn't matter which technique you use, although the following criteria may help you to decide which is more appropriate:

❑ It makes sense to use methods on the static `File` class if you are only making a single method call — the single call will be faster because the .NET Framework will not have to go through the process of instantiating a new object and then calling the method.

❑ If your application is performing several operations on a file, it makes more sense to instantiate a `FileInfo` object and use its methods — this saves time because the object will already be referencing the correct file on the file system, whereas the static class will have to find it every time.

The `FileInfo` class also exposes properties relating to the underlying file, some of which can be manipulated to update the file. Many of these properties are inherited from `FileSystemInfo`, and thus apply to both the `File` and `Directory` classes. The properties of `FileSystemInfo` are shown in the following table:

Property	Description
`Attributes`	Gets or sets the attributes of the current file or directory, using the `FileAttributes` enumeration.
`CreationTime`	Gets or sets the creation date and time of the current file.
`Extension`	Retrieves the extension of the file. This property is read-only.

Property	Description
Exists	Determines whether a file exists. This is a read-only abstract property, and is overridden in FileInfo and DirectoryInfo.
FullName	Retrieves the full path of the file. This property is read-only.
LastAccessTime	Gets or sets the date and time that the current file was last accessed.
LastWriteTime	Gets or sets the date and time that the current file was last written to.
Name	Retrieves the full path of the file. This is a read-only abstract property, and is overridden in FileInfo and DirectoryInfo.

The properties specific to FileInfo are shown in the next table:

Property	Description
Directory	Retrieves a DirectoryInfo object representing the directory containing the current file. This property is read-only.
DirectoryName	Returns the path to the file's directory. This property is read-only.
IsReadOnly	Shortcut to the read-only attribute of the file. This property is also accessible via Attributes.
Length	Gets the size of the file in bytes, returned as a long value. This property is read-only.

A FileInfo object doesn't in itself represent a stream. To read or write to a file, a Stream object has to be created. The FileInfo object aids you in doing this by exposing several methods that return instantiated Stream objects.

The DirectoryInfo Class

The DirectoryInfo class works exactly like the FileInfo class. It is an instantiated object that represents a single directory on a machine. Like the FileInfo class, many of the method calls are duplicated across Directory and DirectoryInfo. The guidelines for choosing whether to use the methods of File or FileInfo also apply to DirectoryInfo methods:

❑ If you are making a single call, use the static Directory class.

❑ If you are making a series of calls, use an instantiated DirectoryInfo object.

The `DirectoryInfo` class inherits most of its properties from `FileSystemInfo`, as does `FileInfo`, although these properties operate on directories instead of files. There are also two `DirectoryInfo`-specific properties, shown in the following table:

Property	Description
Parent	Retrieves a `DirectoryInfo` object representing the directory containing the current directory. This property is read-only.
Root	Retrieves a `DirectoryInfo` object representing the root directory of the current volume — for example, the C:\ directory. This property is read-only.

Path Names and Relative Paths

When specifying a path name in .NET code, you can use either absolute or relative path names. An *absolute* path name explicitly specifies a file or directory from a known location — such as the C: drive. An example of this would be C:\Work\LogFile.txt — this path defines exactly where the file is, with no ambiguity.

Relative path names are relative to a starting location. By using relative path names, no drive or known location needs to be specified. You saw this earlier, where the current working directory was the starting point, which is the default behavior for relative path names. For example, if your application is running in the C:\Development\FileDemo directory and uses the relative path LogFile.txt, the file references would be C:\Development\FileDemo\LogFile.txt. To move "up" a directory, the . . string is used. Thus, in the same application, the path . .\Log.txt points to the file C:\Development\Log.txt.

As shown earlier, the working directory is initially set to the directory in which your application is running. When you are developing with VS or VCE, this means the application is several directories beneath the project folder you created. It is usually located in *ProjectName*\bin\Debug. To access a file in the root folder of the project, then, you have to move up *two* directories with . .\. .\ — you will see this happen often throughout the chapter.

Should you need to, you can determine the working directory by using `Directory.GetCurrentDirectory()`, or you can set it to a new path by using `Directory.SetCurrentDirectory()`.

The FileStream Object

The `FileStream` object represents a stream pointing to a file on a disk or a network path. While the class does expose methods for reading and writing bytes from and to the files, most often you will use a `StreamReader` or `StreamWriter` to perform these functions. That's because the `FileStream` class operates on bytes and byte arrays, whereas the `Stream` classes operate on character data. Character data is easier to work with, but certain operations, such as random file access (access to data at some point in the middle of a file), can only be performed by a `FileStream` object. You'll learn more about this later in the chapter.

There are several ways to create a `FileStream` object. The constructor has many different overloads but the simplest takes just two arguments: the filename and a `FileMode` enumeration value:

```
FileStream aFile = new FileStream(filename, FileMode.Member);
```

The `FileMode` enumeration has several members that specify how the file is opened or created. You'll see the possibilities shortly. Another commonly used constructer is as follows:

```
FileStream aFile = new FileStream(filename, FileMode.Member, FileAccess.Member);
```

The third parameter is a member of the `FileAccess` enumeration and is a way of specifying the purpose of the stream. The members of the `FileAccess` enumeration are shown in the following table:

Member	Description
Read	Opens the file for reading only.
Write	Opens the file for writing only.
ReadWrite	Opens the file for reading or writing only.

Attempting to perform an action other than that specified by the `FileAccess` enumeration member will result in exception being thrown. This property is often used as a way to vary user access to the file based on the authorization level of the user.

In the version of the `FileStream` constructor that doesn't use a `FileAccess` enumeration parameter, the default value is used, which is `FileAccess.ReadWrite`.

The `FileMode` enumeration members are shown in the next table. What actually happens when each of these values is used depends on whether the filename specified refers to an existing file. Note that the entries in this table refer to the position in the file that the stream points to when it is created, a topic you'll learn more about in the next section. Unless otherwise stated, the stream points to the beginning of a file.

Member	File Exists Behavior	No File Exists Behavior
Append	The file is opened, with the stream positioned at the end of the file. Can only be used in conjunction with `FileAccess.Write`.	A new file is created. Can only be used in conjunction with `FileAccess.Write`.
Create	The file is destroyed, and a new file is created in its place.	A new file is created.
CreateNew	An exception is thrown.	A new file is created.
Open	The file is opened, with the stream positioned at the beginning of the file.	An exception is thrown.
OpenOrCreate	The file is opened, with the stream positioned at the beginning of the file.	A new file is created.
Truncate	The file is opened and erased. The stream is positioned at the beginning of the file. The original file creation date is retained.	An exception is thrown.

Both the `File` and `FileInfo` classes expose `OpenRead()` and `OpenWrite()` methods that make it easier to create `FileStream` objects. The first opens the file for read-only access, and the second allows write-only access. These methods provide shortcuts, so you do not have to provide all the information required in the form of parameters to the `FileStream` constructor. For example, the following line of code opens the `Data.txt` file for read-only access:

```
FileStream aFile = File.OpenRead("Data.txt");
```

The following code performs the same function:

```
FileInfo aFileInfo = new FileInfo("Data.txt");
FileStream aFile = aFileInfo.OpenRead();
```

File Position

The `FileStream` class maintains an internal file pointer that points to the location within the file where the next read or write operation will occur. In most cases, when a file is opened it points to the beginning of the file, but this pointer can be modified. This enables an application to read or write anywhere within the file, which in turn enables random access to a file and the capability to jump directly to a specific location in the file. This can save a lot of time when dealing with very large files because you can instantly move to the location you want.

The method that implements this functionality is the `Seek()` method, which takes two parameters. The first parameter specifies how far to move the file pointer, in bytes. The second parameter specifies where to start counting from, in the form of a value from the `SeekOrigin` enumeration. The `SeekOrigin` enumeration contains three values: `Begin`, `Current`, and `End`.

For example, the following line would move the file pointer to the eighth byte in the file, starting from the very first byte in the file:

```
aFile.Seek(8, SeekOrigin.Begin);
```

The following line would move the file pointer two bytes forward, starting from the current position. If this were executed directly after the previous line, then the file pointer would now point to the tenth byte in the file:

```
aFile.Seek(2, SeekOrigin.Current);
```

When you read from or write to a file, the file pointer changes as well. After you have read 10 bytes, the file pointer will point to the byte after the tenth byte read.

You can also specify negative seek positions, which could be combined with the `SeekOrigin.End` enumeration value to seek near the end of the file. The following seeks to the fifth byte from the end of the file:

```
aFile.Seek(-5, SeekOrigin.End);
```

Files accessed in this manner are sometimes referred to as *random access files* because an application can access any position within the file. The `Stream` classes described later access files sequentially and do not allow you to manipulate the file pointer in this way.

Reading Data

Reading data using the FileStream class is not as easy as using the StreamReader class, which you will look at later in this chapter. That's because the FileStream class deals exclusively with raw bytes. Working in raw bytes makes the FileStream class useful for any kind of data file, not just text files. By reading byte data, the FileStream object can be used to read files such as images or sound files. The cost of this flexibility is that you cannot use a FileStream to read data directly into a string as you can with the StreamReader class. However, several conversion classes make it fairly easy to convert byte arrays into character arrays and vice versa.

The FileStream.Read() method is the primary means to access data from a file that a FileStream object points to. This method reads the data from a file and then writes this data into a byte array. There are three parameters, the first being a byte array passed in to accept data from the FileStream object. The second parameter is the position in the byte array to begin writing data to — this is normally zero, to begin writing data from the file at the beginning of the array. The last parameter specifies how many bytes to read from the file.

The following Try It Out demonstrates reading data from a random access file. The file you will read from is actually the class file you create for the example.

Try It Out   Reading Data from Random Access Files

1. Create a new console application called ReadFile and save it in the directory C:\BegVCSharp\Chapter24.

2. Add the following using directive to the top of the Program.cs file:

```
using System;
using System.Collections.Generic;
using System.Linq;
using System.Text;
using System.IO;
```

3. Add the following code to the Main() method:

```
static void Main(string[] args)
{
    byte[] byData = new byte[200];
    char[] charData = new Char[200];

    try
    {
        FileStream aFile = new FileStream("../../Program.cs", FileMode.Open);
        aFile.Seek(113, SeekOrigin.Begin);
        aFile.Read(byData, 0, 200);
    }
    catch(IOException e)
    {
        Console.WriteLine("An IO exception has been thrown!");
        Console.WriteLine(e.ToString());
```

```
        Console.ReadKey();
        return;
    }

    Decoder d = Encoding.UTF8.GetDecoder();
    d.GetChars(byData, 0, byData.Length, charData, 0);

    Console.WriteLine(charData);
    Console.ReadKey();
}
```

4. Run the application. The result is shown in Figure 24-2.

Figure 24-2

How It Works

This application opens its own `.cs` file to read from. It does so by navigating two directories up the file structure with the `..` string in the following line:

```
FileStream aFile = new FileStream("../../Program.cs", FileMode.Open);
```

The two lines that implement the actual seeking and reading from a specific point in the file are as follows:

```
aFile.Seek(135, SeekOrigin.Begin);
aFile.Read(byData, 0, 200);
```

The first line moves the file pointer to byte number 113 in the file. This is the `"n"` of `namespace` in the `Program.cs` file; the 113 characters preceding it are the `using` directives. The second line reads the next 200 bytes into the `byte` array `byData`.

Note that these two lines were enclosed in `try...catch` blocks to handle any exceptions that may be thrown:

```
try
{
    aFile.Seek(135, SeekOrigin.Begin);
    aFile.Read(byData,0,100);
}
catch(IOException e)
```

```
    {
        Console.WriteLine("An IO exception has been thrown!");
        Console.WriteLine(e.ToString());
        Console.ReadKey();
        return;
    }
```

Almost all operations involving file I/O can throw an exception of type IOException. All production code should contain error handling, especially when dealing with the file system. The examples in this chapter all include a basic form of error handling.

Once you have the byte array from the file, you need to convert it into a character array so that you can display it to the console. To do this, use the Decoder class from the System.Text namespace. This class is designed to convert raw bytes into more useful items, such as characters:

```
Decoder d = Encoding.UTF8.GetDecoder();
d.GetChars(byData, 0, byData.Length, charData, 0);
```

These lines create a Decoder object based on the UTF-8 encoding schema, which is the Unicode encoding schema. Then the GetChars() method is called, which takes an array of bytes and converts it to an array of characters. After that has been done, the character array can be written to the console.

Writing Data

The process for writing data to a random access file is very similar. A byte array must be created; the easiest way to do this is to first build the character array you wish to write to the file. Next, use the Encoder object to convert it to a byte array, very much like you used the Decoder object. Last, call the Write() method to send the array to the file.

Here's a simple example to demonstrate how this is done.

Try It Out   Writing Data to Random Access Files

1. Create a new console application called WriteFile and save it in the directory C:\BegVCSharp\Chapter24.

2. Add the following using directive to the top of the Program.cs file:

```
using System;
using System.Collections.Generic;
using System.Linq;
using System.Text;
using System.IO;
```

3. Add the following code to the `Main()` method:

```
static void Main(string[] args)
{
    byte[] byData;
    char[] charData;

    try
    {
        FileStream aFile = new FileStream("Temp.txt", FileMode.Create);
        charData = "My pink half of the drainpipe.".ToCharArray();
        byData = new byte[charData.Length];
        Encoder e = Encoding.UTF8.GetEncoder();
        e.GetBytes(charData, 0, charData.Length, byData, 0, true);

        // Move file pointer to beginning of file.
        aFile.Seek(0, SeekOrigin.Begin);
        aFile.Write(byData, 0, byData.Length);
    }
    catch (IOException ex)
    {
        Console.WriteLine("An IO exception has been thrown!");
        Console.WriteLine(ex.ToString());
        Console.ReadKey();
        return;
    }
}
```

4. Run the application. It should run briefly and then close.

5. Navigate to the application directory — the file will have been saved there because you used a relative path. This is located in the WriteFile\bin\Debug folder. Open the `Temp.txt` file. You should see text in the file, as shown in Figure 24-3.

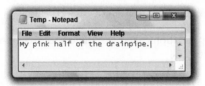

Figure 24-3

How It Works

This application opens a file in its own directory and writes a simple string to it. In structure, this example is very similar to the previous example, except you use `Write()` instead of `Read()`, and `Encoder` instead of `Decoder`.

The following line creates a character array by using the `ToCharArray()` static method of the `String` class. Because everything in C# is an object, the text "My pink half of the drainpipe." is actually a string object (albeit a slightly odd one), so these static methods can be called even on a string of characters:

```
CharData = "My pink half of the drainpipe.".ToCharArray();
```

The following lines show how to convert the character array to the correct byte array needed by the FileStream object:

```
Encoder e = Endoding.UTF8.GetEncoder();
e.GetBytes(charData, 0, charData.Length, byData, 0, true);
```

This time, an Encoder object is created based on the UTF-8 encoding. You used Unicode for the decoding as well, and this time you need to encode the character data into the correct byte format before you can write to the stream. The GetBytes() method is where the magic happens. It converts the character array to the byte array. It accepts a character array as the first parameter (charData in your example), and the index to start in that array as the second parameter (0 for the start of the array). The third parameter is the number of characters to convert (charData.Length — the number of elements in the charData array). The fourth parameter is the byte array to place the data into (byData), and the fifth parameter is the index to start writing from in the byte array (0 for the start of the byData array).

The sixth and final parameter determines whether the Encoder object should flush its state after completion. This reflects the fact that the Encoder object retains an in-memory record of where it was in the byte array. This aids in subsequent calls to the Encoder object, but is meaningless when only a single call is made. The final call to the Encoder must set this parameter to true to clear its memory and free the object for garbage collection.

After that it is a simple matter of writing the byte array to the FileStream by using the Write() method:

```
aFile.Seek(0, SeekOrigin.Begin);
aFile.Write(byData, 0, byData.Length);
```

Like the Read() method, the Write() method has three parameters: the array to write from, the index in the array to start writing from, and the number of bytes to write.

The StreamWriter Object

Working with arrays of bytes is not most people's idea of fun — having worked with the FileStream object, you may be wondering whether there is an easier way. Fear not, for once you have a FileStream object, you will usually wrap it in a StreamWriter or StreamReader and use its methods to manipulate the file. If you don't need the capability to change the file pointer to any arbitrary position, these classes make working with files much easier.

The StreamWriter class enables you to write characters and strings to a file, with the class handling the underlying conversions and writing to the FileStream object for you.

There are many ways to create a `StreamWriter` object. If you already have a `FileStream` object, then you can use this to create a `StreamWriter`:

```
FileStream aFile = new FileStream("Log.txt", FileMode.CreateNew);
StreamWriter sw = new StreamWriter(aFile);
```

A `StreamWriter` object can also be created directly from a file:

```
StreamWriter sw = new StreamWriter("Log.txt", true);
```

This constructor takes the filename and a Boolean value that specifies whether to append to the file or create a new one:

❑ If this is set to `false`, then a new file is created or the existing file is truncated and then opened.

❑ If it is set to `true`, the file is opened and the data is retained. If there is no file, then a new one is created.

Unlike creating a `FileStream` object, creating a `StreamWriter` does not provide you with a similar range of options — other than the Boolean value to append or create a new file, you have no option for specifying the `FileMode` property as you did with the `FileStream` class. Nor do you have an option to set the `FileAccess` property, so you will always have read/write privileges to the file. To use any of the advanced parameters, you must first specify them in the `FileStream` constructor and then create a `StreamWriter` from the `FileStream` object, as you do in the following Try It Out.

Try It Out   Output Stream

1.   Create a new console application called StreamWrite and save it in the directory C:\BegVCSharp\Chapter24.

2.   You will be using the `System.IO` namespace again, so add the following using directive near the top of the `Program.cs` file:

```
using System;
using System.Collections.Generic;
using System.Linq;
using System.Text;
using System.IO;
```

3.   Add the following code to the `Main()` method:

```
static void Main(string[] args)
{
    try
    {
        FileStream aFile = new FileStream("Log.txt", FileMode.OpenOrCreate);
        StreamWriter sw = new StreamWriter(aFile);

        bool truth = true;
        // Write data to file.
```

```
        sw.WriteLine("Hello to you.");
        sw.WriteLine("It is now {0} and things are looking good.",
                  DateTime.Now.ToLongDateString());
        sw.Write("More than that,");
        sw.Write(" it's {0} that C# is fun.", truth);
        sw.Close();
    }
    catch(IOException e)
    {
        Console.WriteLine("An IO exception has been thrown!");
        Console.WriteLine(e.ToString());
        Console.ReadLine();
        return;
    }
}
```

4. Build and run the project. If no errors are found, it should quickly run and close. Because you are not displaying anything on the console, it is not a very exciting program to watch.

5. Go to the application directory and find the Log.txt file. It is located in the StreamWrite\ bin\Debug folder because you used a relative path.

6. Open the file. You should see the text shown in Figure 24-4.

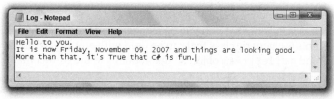

Figure 24-4

How It Works

This simple application demonstrates the two most important methods of the StreamWriter class, Write() and WriteLine(). Both of them have many overloaded versions for performing more advanced file output, but you used basic string output in this example.

The WriteLine() method writes the string passed to it, followed immediately by a newline character. You can see in the example that this causes the next write operation to begin on a new line.

Just as you can write formatted data to the console, so can you also do this to files. For example, you can write out the value of variables to the file using standard format parameters:

```
        sw.WriteLine("It is now {0} and things are looking good.",
                  DateTime.Now.ToLongDateString());
```

DateTime.Now holds the current date; the ToLongDateString() method is used to convert this date into an easy-to-read form.

The `Write()` method simply writes the string passed to it to the file, without a newline character appended, enabling you to write a complete sentence or paragraph using more than one `Write()` statement:

```
sw.Write("More than that,");
sw.Write(" it's {0} that C# is fun.", truth);
```

Here, again, you use format parameters, this time with `Write()` to display the Boolean value `truth` — you set this variable to `true` earlier, and its value is automatically converted into the string `"True"` for the formatting.

You can use `Write()` and format parameters to write comma-separated files:

```
[StreamWriter object].Write("{0},{1},{2}", 100, "A nice product", 10.50);
```

In a more sophisticated example, this data could come from a database or other data source.

The StreamReader Object

Input streams are used to read data from an external source. Often this will be a file on a disk or network location, but remember that this source could be almost anything that can send data, such as a network application, a Web service, or even the console.

The `StreamReader` class is the one that you will be using to read data from files. Like the `StreamWriter` class, this is a generic class that can be used with any stream. In the next Try It Out, you again construct it around a `FileStream` object so that it points to the correct file.

`StreamReader` objects are created in much the same way as `StreamWriter` objects. The most common way to create one is to use a previously created `FileStream` object:

```
FileStream aFile = new FileStream("Log.txt", FileMode.Open);
StreamReader sr = new StreamReader(aFile);
```

Like `StreamWriter`, the `StreamReader` class can be created directly from a string containing the path to a particular file:

```
StreamReader sr = new StreamReader("Log.txt");
```

Try It Out   Stream Input

1. Create a new console application called StreamRead and save it in the directory C:\BegVCSharp\Chapter24.

2. Import the `System.IO` namespace by placing the following line of code near the top of Program.cs:

```
using System;
using System.Collections.Generic;
using System.Linq;
using System.Text;
using System.IO;
```

3. Add the following code to the `Main()` method:

```
static void Main(string[] args)
{
    string strLine;

    try
    {
        FileStream aFile = new FileStream("Log.txt", FileMode.Open);
        StreamReader sr = new StreamReader(aFile);
        strLine = sr.ReadLine();
        // Read data in line by line.
        while(strLine != null)
        {
            Console.WriteLine(strLine);
            strLine = sr.ReadLine();
        }
        sr.Close();
    }
    catch(IOException e)
    {
        Console.WriteLine("An IO exception has been thrown!");
        Console.WriteLine(e.ToString());
        return;
    }
    Console.ReadKey();
}
```

4. Copy the `Log.txt` file, created in the previous example, into the `StreamRead\bin\Debug` directory. If you don't have a file named `Log.txt`, the `FileStream` constructor will throw an exception when it doesn't find it.

5. Run the application. You should see the text of the file written to the console, as shown in Figure 24-5.

Figure 24-5

How It Works

This application is very similar to the previous one, with the obvious difference being that it is reading a file, rather than writing one. As before, you must import the `System.IO` namespace to be able to access the necessary classes.

You use the `ReadLine()` method to read text from the file. This method reads text until a new line is found, and returns the resulting text as a string. The method returns a `null` when the end of the file has been reached, which you use to test for the end of the file. Note that you use a `while` loop, which ensures that the line read isn't null before any code in the body of the loop is executed — that way, only the genuine contents of the file are displayed:

```
strLine = sr.ReadLine();
while(strLine != null)
{
    Console.WriteLine(strLine);
    strLine = sr.ReadLine();
}
```

Reading Data

The `ReadLine()` method is not the only way you have of accessing data in a file. The `StreamReader` class has many methods for reading data.

The simplest of the reading methods is `Read()`. It returns the next character from the stream as a positive integer value or a -1 if it has reached the end. This value can be converted into a character by using the `Convert` utility class. In the preceding example, the main parts of the program could be rewritten as follows:

```
StreamReader sr = new StreamReader(aFile);
int nChar;
nChar = sr.Read();
while(nChar != -1)
{
    Console.Write(Convert.ToChar(nChar));
    nChar = sr.Read();
}
sr.Close();
```

A very convenient method to use with smaller files is the `ReadToEnd()` method. It reads the entire file and returns it as a string. In this case, the earlier application could be simplified to the following:

```
StreamReader sr = new StreamReader(aFile);
strLine = sr.ReadToEnd();
Console.WriteLine(strLine);
sr.Close();
```

While this may seem easy and convenient, be careful. By reading all the data into a string object, you are forcing the data in the file to exist in memory. Depending on the size of the data file, this can be prohibitive. If the data file is extremely large, then it is better to leave the data in the file and access it with the methods of the `StreamReader`.

Delimited Files

Delimited files are a common form of data storage and are used by many legacy systems. If your application must interoperate with such a system, then you will often encounter the delimited data format. A particularly common form of delimiter is the comma — for example, the data in an Excel spreadsheet, an Access database, or a SQL Server database can be exported as a comma-separated value (CSV) file.

You've seen how to use the `StreamWriter` class to write such files using this approach — it is also easy to read comma-separated files. You may remember from Chapter 5 the `String` class's `Split()` method, which is used to convert a string into an array based on a supplied separator character. If you specify a comma as the separator, it creates a correctly dimensioned string array containing all of the data in the original comma-separated string.

The next Try It Out shows how useful this can be. The example uses comma-separated values, loading them into a `List<Dictionary<string, string>>` object. This useful example is quite generic, and you may find yourself using the technique in your own applications if you need to work with comma-separated values.

Try It Out   Comma-Separated Values

1. Create a new console application called CommaValues and save it in the directory C:\BegVCSharp\Chapter24.

2. Place the following line of code near the top of `Program.cs`. You need to import the `System.IO` namespace for your file handling:

```
using System;
using System.Collections.Generic;
using System.Linq;
using System.Text;
using System.IO;
```

3. Add the following `GetData()` method into the body of `Program.cs`, before the `Main()` method:

```
private static List<Dictionary<string, string>> GetData(out List<string>
columns)
{
    string strLine;
    string[] strArray;
    char[] charArray = new char[] {','};
    List<Dictionary<string, string>> data = new List<Dictionary<string,
string>>();
    columns = new List<string>();

    try
```

```
{
    FileStream aFile = new FileStream(@"..\..\SomeData.txt", FileMode.Open);
    StreamReader sr = new StreamReader(aFile);

    // Obtain the columns from the first line.

    // Split row of data into string array
    strLine = sr.ReadLine();
    strArray = strLine.Split(charArray);

    for (int x = 0; x <= strArray.GetUpperBound(0); x++)
    {
        columns.Add(strArray[x]);
    }

    strLine = sr.ReadLine();
    while (strLine != null)
    {
        // Split row of data into string array
        strArray = strLine.Split(charArray);
        Dictionary<string, string> dataRow = new Dictionary<string, string>();

        for (int x = 0; x <= strArray.GetUpperBound(0); x++)
        {
            dataRow.Add(columns[x], strArray[x]);
        }

        data.Add(dataRow);

        strLine = sr.ReadLine();
    }

    sr.Close();
    return data;
}
catch (IOException ex)
{
    Console.WriteLine("An IO exception has been thrown!");
    Console.WriteLine(ex.ToString());
    Console.ReadLine();
    return data;
}
}
```

4. Add the following code to the `Main()` method:

```
static void Main(string[] args)
{
    List<string> columns;
    List<Dictionary<string, string>> myData = GetData(out columns);

    foreach (string column in columns)
    {
```

```
        Console.Write("{0,-20}", column);
    }
    Console.WriteLine();

    foreach (Dictionary<string, string> row in myData)
    {
        foreach (string column in columns)
        {
            Console.Write("{0,-20}", row[column]);
        }
        Console.WriteLine();
    }
    Console.ReadKey();
}
```

5. Add a new text file called SomeData.txt by choosing Text File from the Project ⇨ Add New Item dialog.

6. Enter the following text into this new text file:

```
ProductID,Name,Price
1,Spiky Pung,1000
2,Gloop Galloop Soup,25
4,Hat Sauce,12
```

7. Run the application. You should see the text of the file written to the console, as shown in Figure 24-6.

Figure 24-6

How It Works

Like the previous example, this application reads the file line by line into a string. However, because you know this is a file containing comma-separated text values, you are going to handle it differently. Not only that, but you will actually store the values you read in a data structure.

First, you need to look at some of the comma-separated data itself:

```
ProductID,Name,Price
1,Spiky Pung,1000
```

The first line holds the names of the columns of data; subsequent lines hold the data. Thus, your procedure is to obtain the column names from the first line of the file and then retrieve the data in the remaining lines.

The GetData() method is declared as static, so you can call this method without creating an instance of your class. This method returns a List<Dictionary<string, string>> object that you will create and then populate with data from the comma-separated text file. It also returns a List<string> object containing the header names. The following lines initialize these objects:

```
List<Dictionary<string, string>> data = new List<Dictionary<string, string>>();
columns = new List<string>();
```

columns will contain the column names from the first row of the comma-separated text file, and data will hold the values on subsequent rows.

You start by creating a FileStream object and then construct a StreamReader around that, as you did in earlier examples. Now you can read the first line of the file and create an array of strings from that one string:

```
strLine = sr.ReadLine();
strArray = strLine.Split(charArray);
```

The Split() method you saw in Chapter 5 accepts a character array, in this case consisting of just ", " so that strArray will hold the array of strings formed from splitting strLine at each instance of ", ". Because you are currently reading from the first line of the file, and this line holds the names of the columns of data, you need to loop through each string in strArray and add it to columns:

```
for (int x = 0; x <= strArray.GetUpperBound(0); x++)
{
    columns.Add(strArray[x]);
}
```

Now that you have the names of the columns for your data, you can read in the data. The code for this is essentially the same as that for the earlier StreamRead example, except for the presence of the code required to add Dictionary<string, string> objects to data:

```
strLine = sr.ReadLine();
while (strLine != null)
{
    // Split row of data into string array.
    strArray = strLine.Split(charArray);
    Dictionary<string, string> dataRow = new Dictionary<string, string>();

    for (int x = 0; x <= strArray.GetUpperBound(0); x++)
    {
        dataRow.Add(columns[x], strArray[x]);
    }

    data.Add(dataRow);

    strLine = sr.ReadLine();
}
```

For each line in the file, you create a new Dictionary<string, string> object and fill it with a row of data. Each entry in this collection has a key corresponding to a column name and a value that is the value of the column for that row. The keys are extracted from the columns object you created earlier, and the values come from the string array obtained using Split() for the line of text extracted from the data file.

Once you've read all the data in from the file, you close the StreamReader and return your data. The code in the Main() method obtains the data from the GetData() method in variables called myData and columns, and displays this information to the console. First, the name of each column is displayed:

```
foreach (string column in columns)
{
    Console.Write("{0,-20}", column);
}
Console.WriteLine();
```

The -20 part of the formatting string {0,-20} ensures that the name you display is left-aligned in a column of 20 characters — this helps to format the display.

Finally, you loop through each Dictionary<string, string> object in the myData collection and display the values in that row, once again using the formatting string to format your output:

```
foreach (Dictionary<string, string> row in myData)
{
    foreach (string column in columns)
    {
        Console.Write("{0,-20}", row[column]);
    }
    Console.WriteLine();
}
```

As you can see, it is simple to extract meaningful data from comma-separated value (CSV) files using the .NET Framework. This technique is also easy to combine with the data access techniques you will see in later chapters, meaning that data from a CSV file can be manipulated just like any other data source (such as a database). However, no information about the data types of the data is extracted from the CSV file. Currently, you've just been treating all data as strings. For an enterprise-level business application, you need to go the extra step of adding type information to the data you extract. This could come from additional information stored in the CSV file, it could be configured manually, or it could be inferred from the strings in the file, all depending on the specific application.

Even though XML, described in the next chapter, is a superior method of storing and transporting data, CSV files are still quite common and will be for a long time. Delimited files such as comma-separated files also have the advantage of being very terse and, therefore, smaller than their XML counterparts.

Reading and Writing Compressed Files

Often when dealing with files, quite a lot of space is used up on the hard disk. This is particularly true for graphics and sound files. You've probably come across utilities that enable you to compress and decompress files, which are handy when you want to move them around or e-mail them. The `System.IO.Compression` namespace contains classes that enable you to compress files from your code, either using the GZIP or Deflate algorithm — both of which are publicly available and free for anyone to use.

There is a little bit more to compressing files than just compressing them, though. Commercial applications enable multiple files to be placed in a single compressed file, and so on. What you'll be looking at in this section is much simpler: saving text data to a compressed file. You are unlikely to be able to access this file in an external utility, but the file will be much smaller than its uncompressed equivalent!

The two compression stream classes in the `System.IO.Compression` namespace that you'll look at here, `DeflateStream` and `GZipStream`, work very similarly. In both cases, you initialize them with an existing stream, which in the case of files will be a `FileStream` object. After this you can use them with `StreamReader` and `StreamWriter` just like any other stream. All you need to specify in addition to that is whether the stream will be used for compression (saving files) or decompression (loading files) so that the class knows what to do with the data that passes through it. This is best illustrated with the following example.

Try It Out   Compressed Data

1. Create a new console application called Compressor and save it in the directory
C:\BegVCSharp\Chapter24.

2. Place the following lines of code near the top of `Program.cs`. You need to import the
`System.IO` namespace for your file handling and `System.IO.Compression` to use the
compression classes:

```
using System;
using System.Collections.Generic;
using System.Linq;
using System.Text;
using System.IO;
using System.IO.Compression;
```

3. Add the following methods into the body of `Program.cs`, before the `Main()` method:

```
static void SaveCompressedFile(string filename, string data)
{
    FileStream fileStream =
        new FileStream(filename, FileMode.Create, FileAccess.Write);
    GZipStream compressionStream =
        new GZipStream(fileStream, CompressionMode.Compress);
    StreamWriter writer = new StreamWriter(compressionStream);
    writer.Write(data);
    writer.Close();
}

static string LoadCompressedFile(string filename)
```

```
{
    FileStream fileStream =
        new FileStream(filename, FileMode.Open, FileAccess.Read);
    GZipStream compressionStream =
        new GZipStream(fileStream, CompressionMode.Decompress);
    StreamReader reader = new StreamReader(compressionStream);
    string data = reader.ReadToEnd();
    reader.Close();
    return data;
}
```

4.   Add the following code to the `Main()` method:

```
static void Main(string[] args)
{
    try
    {
        string filename = "compressedFile.txt";

        Console.WriteLine(
            "Enter a string to compress (will be repeated 100 times):");
        string sourceString = Console.ReadLine();
        StringBuilder sourceStringMultiplier =
            new StringBuilder(sourceString.Length * 100);
        for (int i = 0; i < 100; i++)
        {
            sourceStringMultiplier.Append(sourceString);
        }
        sourceString = sourceStringMultiplier.ToString();
        Console.WriteLine("Source data is {0} bytes long.", sourceString.Length);

        SaveCompressedFile(filename, sourceString);
        Console.WriteLine("\nData saved to {0}.", filename);

        FileInfo compressedFileData = new FileInfo(filename);
        Console.WriteLine("Compressed file is {0} bytes long.",
                        compressedFileData.Length);

        string recoveredString = LoadCompressedFile(filename);
        recoveredString = recoveredString.Substring(0, recoveredString.Length
 / 100);
        Console.WriteLine("\nRecovered data: {0}", recoveredString);

        Console.ReadKey();
    }
    catch (IOException ex)
    {
        Console.WriteLine("An IO exception has been thrown!");
        Console.WriteLine(ex.ToString());
        Console.ReadKey();
    }
}
```

5.   Run the application and enter a suitably long string. An example result is shown in
     Figure 24-7.

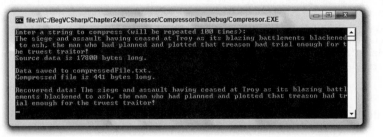

Figure 24-7

6.   Open `compressedFile.txt` in Notepad. The text is shown in Figure 24-8.

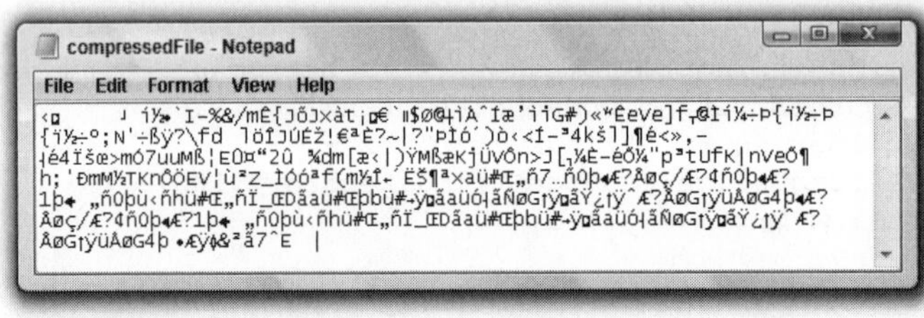

Figure 24-8

How It Works

In this example, you define two methods for saving and loading a compressed text file. The first of
these, `SaveCompressedFile()`, is as follows:

```
static void SaveCompressedFile(string filename, string data)
{
    FileStream fileStream =
        new FileStream(filename, FileMode.Create, FileAccess.Write);
    GZipStream compressionStream =
        new GZipStream(fileStream, CompressionMode.Compress);
    StreamWriter writer = new StreamWriter(compressionStream);
    writer.Write(data);
    writer.Close();
}
```

The code starts by creating a `FileStream` object, and then uses it to create a `GZipStream` object. Note
that you could replace all occurrences of `GZipStream` in this code with `DeflateStream` — the classes
work in the same way. You use the `CompressionMode.Compress` enumeration value to specify that
data is to be compressed, and then use a `StreamWriter` to write data to the file.

`LoadCompressedFile()` mirrors the `SaveCompressedFile()` method. Instead of saving to a filename, it loads a compressed file into a string:

```
static string LoadCompressedFile(string filename)
{
    FileStream fileStream =
        new FileStream(filename, FileMode.Open, FileAccess.Read);
    GZipStream compressionStream =
        new GZipStream(fileStream, CompressionMode.Decompress);
    StreamReader reader = new StreamReader(compressionStream);
    string data = reader.ReadToEnd();
    reader.Close();
    return data;
}
```

The differences are as you would expect — different `FileMode`, `FileAccess`, and `CompressionMode` enumeration values to load and uncompress data, and the use of a `StreamReader` to get the uncompressed text out of the file.

The code in `Main()` is a simple test of these methods. It simply asks for a string, duplicates the string 100 times to make things interesting, compresses it to a file, and then retrieves it. In the example, the opening stanza of Sir Gawain and the Green Knight repeated 100 times is 17,800 characters long, but when compressed it only takes up 441 bytes — that's a compression ration of around 40:1. Admittedly, this is a bit of a cheat — the GZIP algorithm works particularly well with repetitive data, but it does illustrate compression in action.

You also looked at the text stored in the compressed file. Obviously, it isn't easily readable, which has implications should you want to share data between applications, for example. However, because the file was compressed with a known algorithm, at least you know that it is possible for applications to uncompress it.

Serialized Objects

Applications, as you have seen, often need to store data on a hard disk. So far in this chapter, you've looked at constructing text and data files piece by piece, but often that isn't the most convenient way of doing things. Sometimes it's better to store data in the form that it is used in — namely, objects.

The .NET Framework provides the infrastructure to serialize objects in the `System.Runtime` `.Serialization` and `System.Runtime.Serialization.Formatters` namespaces, with specific classes implementing this infrastructure in namespaces below the latter. Two implementations are available to you in the framework:

❑   `System.Runtime.Serialization.Formatters.Binary` — This namespace contains the class `BinaryFormatter`, which is capable of serializing objects into binary data, and vice versa.

❑   `System.Runtime.Serialization.Formatters.Soap` — This namespace contains the class `SoapFormatter`, which is capable of serializing objects into SOAP format XML data, and vice versa.

In this chapter, you only look at `BinaryFormatter` because you have yet to learn about XML data. However, because these classes implement the `IFormatter` interface, much of the discussion applies equally to both.

The `IFormatter` interface provides the following methods:

Method	Description
`void Serialize(Stream stream, object source)`	Serializes source into stream.
`object Deserialize(Stream stream)`	Deserializes the data in stream and returns the resultant object.

Importantly, and conveniently for this chapter, these methods work with streams. That makes it easy to tie these methods into the file access techniques already shown in this chapter — you can use `FileStream` objects.

Serializing using `BinaryFormatter` is as simple as this:

```
IFormatter serializer = new BinaryFormatter();
serializer.Serialize(myStream, myObject);
```

Deserializing is equally easy:

```
IFormatter serializer = new BinaryFormatter();
MyObjectType myNewObject = serializer.Deserialize(myStream) as MyObjectType;
```

Obviously, you need streams and objects to work with, but the preceding holds true for pretty much all circumstances. The following Try It Out shows how this works in practice.

Try It Out   Object Serialization

1. Create a new console application called ObjectStore and save it in the directory
   C:\BegVCSharp\Chapter24.

2. Add a new class called `Product` to the project, and modify the code as follows:

```
namespace ObjectStore
{
    public class Product
    {
        public long Id;
        public string Name;
        public double Price;

        [NonSerialized]
```

```
        string Notes;

        public Product(long id, string name, double price, string notes)
        {
            Id = id;
            Name = name;
            Price = price;
            Notes = notes;
        }

        public override string ToString()
        {
            return string.Format("{0}: {1} (${2:F2}) {3}", Id, Name, Price,
Notes);
        }
    }
}
```

3. Place the following lines of code near the top of `Program.cs`. You need to import the `System.IO` namespace for your file handling, and the other namespaces for serialization:

```
using System;
using System.Collections.Generic;
using System.Linq;
using System.Text;
using System.IO;
using System.Runtime.Serialization;
using System.Runtime.Serialization.Formatters.Binary;
```

4. Add the following code to the `Main()` method in `Program.cs`:

```
static void Main(string[] args)
{
    try
    {
        // Create products.
        List<Product> products = new List<Product>();
        products.Add(new Product(1, "Spiky Pung", 1000.0, "Good stuff."));
        products.Add(new Product(2, "Gloop Galloop Soup", 25.0, "Tasty."));
        products.Add(new Product(4, "Hat Sauce", 12.0, "One for the kids."));

        Console.WriteLine("Products to save:");
        foreach (Product product in products)
        {
            Console.WriteLine(product);
        }
        Console.WriteLine();

        // Get serializer.
        IFormatter serializer = new BinaryFormatter();

        // Serialize products.
```

```
        FileStream saveFile =
            new FileStream("Products.bin", FileMode.Create, FileAccess.Write);
        serializer.Serialize(saveFile, products);
        saveFile.Close();

        // Deserialize products.
        FileStream loadFile =
            new FileStream("Products.bin", FileMode.Open, FileAccess.Read);
        List<Product> savedProducts =
            serializer.Deserialize(loadFile) as List<Product>;
        loadFile.Close();

        Console.WriteLine("Products loaded:");
        foreach (Product product in savedProducts)
        {
            Console.WriteLine(product);
        }
    }
    catch (SerializationException e)
    {
        Console.WriteLine("A serialization exception has been thrown!");
        Console.WriteLine(e.Message);
    }
    catch (IOException e)
    {
        Console.WriteLine("An IO exception has been thrown!");
        Console.WriteLine(e.ToString());
    }

    Console.ReadKey();
}
```

5. Run the application. The result is shown in Figure 24-9.

Figure 24-9

6. Modify the code in `Product.cs` as follows:

```
namespace ObjectStore
{
    [Serializable]
    public class Product
    {
        ...
    }
```

7. Run the application again. The result is shown in Figure 24-10.

Figure 24-10

8. Open `Products.bin` in Notepad. The text is shown in Figure 24-11.

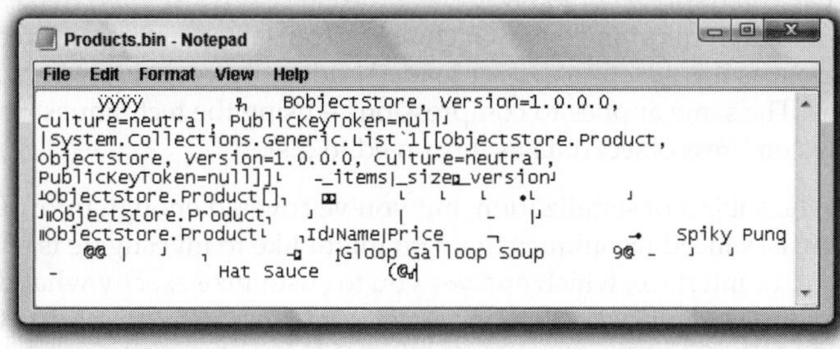

Figure 24-11

How It Works

This example created a collection of `Product` objects, saved the collection to disk, and then reloaded it. The first time you ran the application, though, an exception was thrown because the `Product` object was not marked as *serializable*.

The .NET Framework forces you to mark objects as serializable to enable them to be serialized. There are several reasons for this, including the following:

❑ Some objects don't serialize very well. They may require references to local data that only exists while they are in memory, for example.

❑ Some objects might contain sensitive data that you wouldn't want to be saved in an insecure way or transferred to another process.

As shown in the example, marking an object as serializable is straightforward, using the `Serializable` attribute:

```
namespace ObjectStore
{
    [Serializable]
    public class Product
    {
        ...
    }
}
```

Note that this attribute is not inherited by derived classes. It must be applied to each and every class that you want to be able to serialize. It is also worth noting that the List<T> class you used to generate a collection of Product objects has this attribute — otherwise, applying it to Product wouldn't have helped to make the collection serializable.

When the products collection was successfully serialized and deserialized (on the second attempt), another important fact came to light. Only the Id, Name, and Price fields were reconstituted. This is because of another attribute being used, NonSerialized:

```
[NonSerialized]
string Notes;
```

Any member can be marked with this attribute and it will not be saved with other members. This can be useful if, for example, just one field or property contains sensitive data.

You also looked at the resultant saved data in the example. Some of the data here is human-readable, which may not be what you desire — or expect. The BinaryFormatter class makes no serious attempt to shield your data from prying eyes. Of course, because you are using streams it relatively easy to intercept the data as it is saved to disk or loaded and apply your own obfuscating or encryption algorithms. The same applies to compression — using the techniques from the last section you could quite easily compress object data as it is saved to disk.

There is a lot more to the subject of serialization, but you've covered enough information to get the basics. One of the more advanced techniques that you might like to investigate is custom serialization using the ISerializable interface, which enables you to customize exactly what data is serialized. This can be important, for example, when upgrading classes subsequent to release. Changing the members exposed to serialization can cause existing saved data to become unreadable, unless you provide your own logic to save and retrieve data.

Monitoring the File Structure

Sometimes an application must do more than just read and write files to the file system. For example, it may be important to know when files or directories are being modified. The .NET Framework has made it easy to create custom applications that do just that.

The class that helps you to do this is the FileSystemWatcher class. It exposes several events that your application can catch. This enables your application to respond to file system events.

The basic procedure for using the FileSystemWatcher is simple. First you must set a handful of properties, which specify where to monitor, what to monitor, and when it should raise the event that your application will handle. Then you give it the addresses of your custom event handlers, so that it can call these when significant events occur. Finally, you turn it on and wait for the events.

The properties that must be set before a `FileSystemWatcher` object is enabled are shown in the following table:

Property	Description
Path	Must be set to the file location or directory to monitor.
NotifyFilter	A combination of `NotifyFilters` enumeration values that specify what to watch for within the monitored files. These represent properties of the file or folders being monitored. If any of the specified properties change, then an event is raised. The possible enumeration values are `Attributes`, `CreationTime`, `DirectoryName`, `FileName`, `LastAccess`, `LastWrite`, `Security`, and `Size`. Note that these can be combined using the binary OR operator.
Filter	A filter specifying which files to monitor — for example, `*.txt`.

Once these are set, you must write event handlers for the four events, `Changed`, `Created`, `Deleted`, and `Renamed`. As you saw in Chapter 13, this is simply a matter of creating your own method and assigning it to the object's event. By assigning your own event handler to these methods, your method will be called when the event is fired. Each event will fire when a file or directory matching the `Path`, `NotifyFilter`, and `Filter` property is modified.

Once you have set the properties and the events, set the `EnableRaisingEvents` property to `true` to begin the monitoring. In the following Try It Out, you use `FileSystemWatcher` in a simple client application to keep tabs on a directory of your choice.

Try It Out   Monitoring the File System

Here's a more sophisticated example using much of what you have learned in this chapter.

1. Create a new Windows application called FileWatch and save it in the directory C:\BegVCSharp\Chapter24.

2. Set the various form properties using those shown in the following table:

Property	Setting
FormBorderStyle	FixedDialog
MaximizeBox	False
MinimizeBox	False
Size	302, 160
StartPosition	CenterScreen
Text	File Monitor

3. Using the properties from the following table, add the required controls to the form and set the appropriate properties:

Control	Name	Location	Size	Text
TextBox	txtLocation	8, 26	184,20	
Button	cmdBrowse	208, 24	64, 24	Browse...
Button	cmdWatch	88, 56	80, 32	Watch!
Label	lblWatch	8, 104	0, 13	

Ensure that you set the Enabled property of the cmdWatch Button to False because you can't watch a file before one has been specified, and set the AutoSize property of lblWatch to True so you can see its contents. Also add an OpenFileDialog control to the form, setting its Name to FileDialog and its Filter to All Files|*.*. When you are finished, your form should look like the one in Figure 24-12.

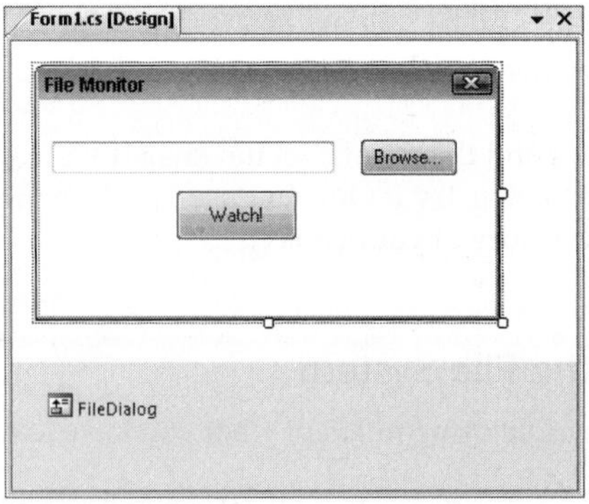

Figure 24-12

4. Now that the form looks good, you can add some code to make it do some work. First, add your usual using directive for the System.IO namespace to the existing list of using directives:

```
using System;
using System.Collections.Generic;
using System.ComponentModel;
using System.Data;
using System.Drawing;
using System.Linq;
using System.Text;
using System.Windows.Forms;
using System.IO;
```

5. Add the `FileSystemWatcher` class to the `Form1` class, as well as a delegate to facilitate changing the text of `lblWatch` from different threads. Add the following code to `Form1.cs`:

```
namespace FileWatch
{
    partial class Form1 : Form
    {
        // File System Watcher object.
        private FileSystemWatcher watcher;
        private delegate void UpdateWatchTextDelegate(string newText);
```

6. You need to add some code to the form constructor. Just after the `InitializeComponent()` method call, add the following code. This code is needed to initialize the `FileSystemWatcher` object and associate the events to methods that you are going to create next:

```
public Form1()
{
    InitializeComponent();

    this.watcher = new System.IO.FileSystemWatcher();
    this.watcher.Deleted +=
        new System.IO.FileSystemEventHandler(this.OnDelete);
    this.watcher.Renamed +=
        new System.IO.RenamedEventHandler(this.OnRenamed);
    this.watcher.Changed +=
        new System.IO.FileSystemEventHandler(this.OnChanged);
    this.watcher.Created +=
        new System.IO.FileSystemEventHandler(this.OnCreate);
}
```

7. Add the following five methods to the `Form1` class. The first method is used to update the text in `lblWatch` asynchronously from the threads that will run the event handlers for the `FileSystemWatcher` events. The other methods are the event handlers themselves.

```
// Utility method to update watch text.
public void UpdateWatchText(string newText)
{
    lblWatch.Text = newText;
}

// Define the event handlers.
public void OnChanged(object source, FileSystemEventArgs e)
{
    try
    {
        StreamWriter sw =
            new StreamWriter("C:/FileLogs/Log.txt", true);
        sw.WriteLine("File: {0} {1}", e.FullPath,
                    e.ChangeType.ToString());
```

```
            sw.Close();
            this.BeginInvoke(new UpdateWatchTextDelegate(UpdateWatchText),
                "Wrote change event to log");
        }
        catch (IOException)
        {
            this.BeginInvoke(new UpdateWatchTextDelegate(UpdateWatchText),
                "Error Writing to log");
        }
    }
    public void OnRenamed(object source, RenamedEventArgs e)
    {
        try
        {
            StreamWriter sw =
                new StreamWriter("C:/FileLogs/Log.txt", true);
            sw.WriteLine("File renamed from {0} to {1}", e.OldName,
                        e.FullPath);
            sw.Close();
            this.BeginInvoke(new UpdateWatchTextDelegate(UpdateWatchText),
                "Wrote renamed event to log");
        }
        catch (IOException)
        {
            this.BeginInvoke(new UpdateWatchTextDelegate(UpdateWatchText),
                "Error Writing to log");
        }
    }
    public void OnDelete(object source, FileSystemEventArgs e)
    {
        try
        {
            StreamWriter sw =
                new StreamWriter("C:/FileLogs/Log.txt", true);
            sw.WriteLine("File: {0} Deleted", e.FullPath);
            sw.Close();
            this.BeginInvoke(new UpdateWatchTextDelegate(UpdateWatchText),
                "Wrote delete event to log");
        }
        catch (IOException)
        {
            this.BeginInvoke(new UpdateWatchTextDelegate(UpdateWatchText),
                "Error Writing to log");
        }
    }

    public void OnCreate(object source, FileSystemEventArgs e)
    {
        try
        {
            StreamWriter sw =
                new StreamWriter("C:/FileLogs/Log.txt", true);
```

```
        sw.WriteLine("File: {0} Created", e.FullPath);
        sw.Close();
        this.BeginInvoke(new UpdateWatchTextDelegate(UpdateWatchText),
            "Wrote create event to log");
    }
    catch (IOException)
    {
        this.BeginInvoke(new UpdateWatchTextDelegate(UpdateWatchText),
            "Error Writing to log");
    }
}
```

8. Add the `Click` event handler for the `Browse` button. The code in this event handler opens the Open File dialog, enabling the user to select a file to monitor. Double-click the `Browse` button and enter the following:

```
private void cmdBrowse_Click(object sender, EventArgs e)
{
    if (FileDialog.ShowDialog() != DialogResult.Cancel )
    {
        txtLocation.Text = FileDialog.FileName;
        cmdWatch.Enabled = true;
    }
}
```

The `ShowDialog()` method returns a `DialogResult` enumeration value reflecting how the user exited the File Open dialog (The user could have clicked OK or pressed the Cancel button.) You need to confirm that the user did not click the Cancel button, so you compare the result from the method call to the `DialogResult.Cancel` enumeration value before saving the user's file selection to the `TextBox`. Finally, you set the `Enabled` property of the Watch button to `true` so that you can watch the file.

9. Follow the same procedure as above with the Watch button. Add the following code to launch the `FileSystemWatcher`:

```
private void cmdWatch_Click(object sender, EventArgs e)
{
    watcher.Path =Path.GetDirectoryName(txtLocation.Text);
    watcher.Filter = Path.GetFileName(txtLocation.Text);
    watcher.NotifyFilter = NotifyFilters.LastWrite |
        NotifyFilters.FileName | NotifyFilters.Size;
    lblWatch.Text = "Watching " + txtLocation.Text;
    // Begin watching.
    watcher.EnableRaisingEvents = true;
}
```

10. Make sure the `FileLogs` directory exists for you to write data to. Add the following code to the `Form1` constructor that will check whether the directory exists, and create the directory if it does not already exist:

```
public Form1()
{
    . . .

    DirectoryInfo aDir = new DirectoryInfo(@"C:\FileLogs");
    if (!aDir.Exists)
        aDir.Create();
}
```

11. Create a directory called C:\TempWatch and a file in this directory called `temp.txt`.

12. Run the application. If everything builds successfully, click the Browse button and select C:\TempWatch\temp.txt.

13. Click the Watch button to begin monitoring the file. The only change you will see in your application is the label control showing the file is being watched.

14. Using Windows Explorer, navigate to C:\TempWatch. Open `temp.txt` in Notepad, add some text to the file, and save it.

15. Rename the file.

16. You can now check the log file to see the changes. Navigate to C:\FileLogs\Log.txt and open the file in Notepad. You should see a description of the changes to the file you selected to watch, as shown in Figure 24-13.

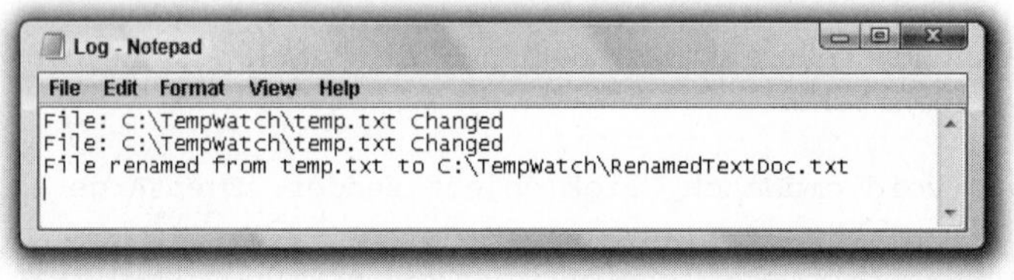

Figure 24-13

How It Works

This application is fairly simple, but it demonstrates how the `FileSystemWatcher` works. Try playing with the string you put into the monitor text box. If you specify *.* in a directory, it will monitor all changes in the directory.

Most of the code in the application is related to setting up the `FileSystemWatcher` object to watch the correct location:

```
watcher.Path =Path.GetDirectoryName(txtLocation.Text);
watcher.Filter = Path.GetFileName(txtLocation.Text);
watcher.NotifyFilter = NotifyFilters.LastWrite |
    NotifyFilters.FileName | NotifyFilters.Size;
lblWatch.Text = "Watching " + txtLocation.Text;
// Begin watching.
watcher.EnableRaisingEvents = true;
```

The code first sets the path to the directory to monitor. It uses a new object you have not looked at yet: `System.IO.Path`. This is a static class, much like the static `File` object. It exposes many static methods to manipulate and extract information out of file location strings. You first use it to extract the directory name the user typed in the text box, using the `GetDirectoryName()` method.

The next line sets the filter for the object. This can be an actual file, in which case it would only monitor the file, or it could be something like `*.txt`, in which case it would monitor all the `.txt` files in the directory specified. Again, you use the `Path` static object to extract the information from the supplied file location.

The `NotifyFilter` is a combination of `NotifyFilters` enumeration values that specify what constitutes a change. In this example, you have indicated that if the last write time stamp, the filename, or the size of the file changes, your application should be notified of the change. After updating the UI, you set the `EnableRaisingEvents` property to `true` to begin monitoring.

Before that, however, you have to create the object and set the event handlers:

```
this.watcher = new System.IO.FileSystemWatcher();
this.watcher.Deleted +=
    new System.IO.FileSystemEventHandler(this.OnDelete);
this.watcher.Renamed +=
    new System.IO.RenamedEventHandler(this.OnRenamed);
this.watcher.Changed +=
    new System.IO.FileSystemEventHandler(this.OnChanged);
this.watcher.Created +=
    new System.IO.FileSystemEventHandler(this.OnCreate);
```

That's how you hook up the event handlers for the watcher object with the private methods you have created. Here, you will have event handlers for the event raised by the watcher object when a file is deleted, renamed, changed, or created. In your own methods, you decide how to handle the actual event. Note that you are notified *after* the event takes place.

In the actual event handler methods, you simply write the event to a log file. Obviously, this could be a more sophisticated response, depending on your application. When a file is added to a directory, you could move it somewhere else or read the contents and fire off a new process using the information. The possibilities are endless!

Summary

In this chapter, you learned about streams and why they are used in the .NET Framework to access files and other serial devices. You looked at the basic classes in the System.IO namespace, including the following:

- ❑ File
- ❑ FileInfo
- ❑ FileStream

You saw that the File class exposes many static methods for moving, copying, and deleting files; and FileInfo represents a physical file on disk, and has methods to manipulate this file. A FileStream object represents a file that can be written to, or read from, or both. You also explored StreamReader and StreamWriter classes and saw how useful they are for writing to streams, and learned to read and write to random files using the FileStream class. Building on that knowledge, you used classes in the System.IO.Compression namespace to compress streams as you write them to disk, and learned how to serialize objects to files. Finally, you built an entire application to monitor files and directories using the FileSystemWatcher class.

In summary, you learned all of the following in this chapter:

- ❑ How to open a file, read from a file, and write to a file.
- ❑ The difference between the StreamWriter and StreamReader classes and the FileStream class.
- ❑ How to work with delimited files to populate a data structure.
- ❑ Compressing and decompressing streams.
- ❑ How to serialize and deserialize objects.
- ❑ Monitoring the file system with the FileSystemWatcher class.

Exercises

1. Which namespace enables an application to work with files?

2. When would you use a FileStream object to write to a file instead of using a StreamWriter object?

3. What methods of the StreamReader class enable you to read data from files and what does each one do?

4. What class would you use to compress a stream by using the Deflate algorithm?

5. How would you prevent a class you have created from being serialized?

6. What events does the FileSystemWatcher class expose and what are they for?

7. Modify the FileWatch application you built in this chapter by adding the capability to turn the file system monitoring on and off without exiting the application.

XML

Extensible Markup Language (XML) is a technology that has been receiving great attention for the past few years. XML is not new, and it was certainly not invented by Microsoft for use in the .NET environment, but Microsoft recognized the possibilities of XML early in its development. Because of that you will see it performing a large number of duties in .NET, from describing the configuration of your applications to transporting information between Web services.

XML is a way of storing data in a simple text format, which means that it can be read by nearly any computer. As you've seen in some of the earlier chapters about Web programming, this makes it a perfect format for transferring data over the Internet. It's even not too difficult for humans to read!

The ins and outs of XML can be very complicated, so you won't look at every single detail here. However, the basic format is very simple, and most tasks don't require a detailed knowledge of XML because Visual Studio typically takes care of most of the work — you will rarely have to write an XML document by hand. Having said that, XML is hugely important in the .NET world because it's used as the default format for transferring data, so it's vital to understand the basics.

In this chapter, you learn about the following:

❑ The structure and elements of XML

❑ XML Schema

❑ Using XML in your applications

For a more detailed look at XML, check out Beginning XML, Fourth Edition *(Wrox, 2007).*

XML Documents

A complete set of data in XML is known as an *XML document*. An XML document could be a physical file on your computer or just a string in memory. However, it has to be complete in itself, and it must obey certain rules (described shortly). An XML document is made up of a number of different parts. The most important of these are XML elements, which contain the actual data of the document.

XML Elements

XML elements consist of an opening tag (the name of the element enclosed in angled brackets, such as `<myElement>`), the data within the element, and a closing tag (the same as the opening tag, but with a forward slash after the opening bracket: `</myElement>`).

For example, you might define an element to hold the title of a book like this:

```
<book>Tristram Shandy</book>
```

If you already know some HTML, you might be thinking that this looks very similar — and you'd be right. In fact, HTML and XML share much of the same syntax. The big difference is that XML doesn't have any predefined elements — you choose the names of our own elements, so there's no limit to the number of elements you can have. The most important point to remember is that XML — despite its name — isn't actually a language at all. Rather, it's a standard for defining languages (known as *XML applications*). Each language has its own distinct vocabulary — a specific set of elements that can be used in the document and the structure these elements are allowed to take. As you'll shortly see, you can explicitly limit the elements allowed in the XML document. Alternatively, you can allow any elements, and have the program using the document determine for itself what the structure is.

Element names are case sensitive, so `<book>` and `<BOOK>` are considered different elements. This means that if you attempt to close a `<book>` element using a closing tag that doesn't have identical case (for example, `</BOOK>`), your XML document won't be legal. Programs that read XML documents and analyze them by examining their individual elements are known as *XML parsers*, and they reject any document that contains illegal XML.

Elements can also contain other elements, so you could modify the `<book>` element to include the author as well as the title by adding two sub-elements:

```
<book>
    <title>Tristram Shandy</title>
    <author>Lawrence Sterne</author>
</book>
```

Overlapping elements aren't allowed, so you must close all sub-elements before the closing tag of the parent element. This means, for example, that you can't do this:

```
<book>
    <title>Tristram Shandy
    <author>Lawrence Sterne
    </title></author>
</book>
```

This is illegal because the `<author>` element is opened within the `<title>` element, but the closing `</title>` tag comes before the closing `</author>` tag.

There's one exception to the rule that all elements must have a closing element. It's possible to have "empty" elements, with no nested data or text. In this case, you can simply add the closing tag immediately after the opening element, as shown in the preceding code, or you can use a shorthand syntax, adding the slash of the closing element to the end of the opening element:

```
<book />
```

This is identical to the full syntax:

```
<book></book>
```

Attributes

As well as storing data within the body of the element, you can also store data within attributes, which are added within the opening tag of an element. Attributes are in the form

```
name="value"
```

where the value of the attribute *must* be enclosed in either single or double quotes. For example:

```
<book title="Tristram Shandy"></book>
```

or

```
<book title='Tristram Shandy'></book>
```

The preceding are both legal, but this is not:

```
<book title=Tristram Shandy></book>
```

At this point, you may be wondering why you need both ways of storing data in XML. What is the difference between the following?

```
<book>
    <title>Tristram Shandy</title>
</book>
```

and

```
<book title="Tristram Shandy"></book>
```

In fact, there isn't any earth-shattering, fundamental difference between the two. There isn't really any big advantage to using one over the other. Elements are a better choice if there's a possibility that you'll need to add more information about that piece of data later — you can always add a sub-element or an attribute to an element, but you can't do that for attributes. Arguably, elements are more readable and more elegant (but that's really a matter of personal taste). Conversely, attributes consume less bandwidth if the document is sent over a network without compression (with compression there's not much difference) and are convenient for holding information that isn't essential to every user of the document. Probably the best advice is to use both, selecting whichever you're most comfortable with for storing a particular item of data, but there are no hard-and-fast rules.

The XML Declaration

In addition to elements and attributes, XML documents can contain a number of constituent parts. These individual parts of an XML document are known as *nodes*; elements, the text within elements, and attributes are all nodes of the XML document. Many of these are important only if you really want to delve deeply into XML. However, one type of node occurs in almost every XML document. It is the *XML declaration*, and if you include it, it must occur as the first node of the document.

The XML declaration is similar in format to an element, but has question marks inside the angled brackets. It always has the name xml, and it always has an attribute named version; currently, the only possible value for this is "1.0". The simplest possible form of the XML declaration is therefore as follows:

```
<?xml version="1.0"?>
```

As of February 2004, the W3C (www.w3c.org) released a recommendation for XML 1.1, but at the time of this writing there are few or no real-life implementations of this recommendation.

Optionally, it can also contain the attributes encoding (with a value indicating the character set that should be used to read the document, such as "UTF-16" to indicate that the document uses the 16-bit Unicode character set) and standalone (with the value "yes" or "no" to indicate whether the XML document depends on any other files). However, these attributes are not required, and you will probably include only the version attribute in your own XML files.

Structure of an XML Document

One of the most important things about XML is that it offers a way of structuring data that is very different from relational databases. Most modern database systems store data in tables that are related to each other through values in individual columns. The tables store data in rows and columns — each row represents a single record, and each column a particular item of data about that record. In contrast, XML data is structured hierarchically, a little like the folders and files in Windows Explorer. Each document must have a single *root element* within which all elements and text data is contained. If there is more than one element at the top level of the document, then the document is not legal XML. However, you can include other XML nodes at the top level — notably the XML declaration. Therefore, this is a legal XML document:

```
<?xml version="1.0"?>
<books>
    <book>Tristram Shandy</book>
    <book>Moby Dick</book>
    <book>Ulysses</book>
</books>
```

The following, however, is not:

```
<?xml version="1.0"?>
<book>Tristram Shandy</book>
<book>Moby Dick</book>
<book>Ulysses</book>
```

Under this root element, you have a great deal of flexibility regarding how you structure the data. Unlike relational data, in which every row has the same number of columns, there's no restriction on the number of sub-elements an element can have. In addition, although XML documents are often structured similarly to relational data, with an element for each record, XML documents don't need any predefined structure at all. This is one of the major differences between traditional relational databases and XML. Whereas relational databases always define the structure of the information before any data can be added, information can be stored in XML without this initial overhead, which makes it a very convenient way to store small blocks of data. As you will see shortly, it is quite possible to provide a structure for your XML, but unlike the relational databases, no one will enforce this structure unless you ask for it explicitly.

XML Namespaces

As you learned in Chapter 9, anyone can define their own C# classes, and anyone can define their own XML elements, which leads to the obvious problem — how do you know which elements belong to which vocabulary? In a word, namespaces. Just as you define namespaces to organize your C# types, you use XML namespaces to define your XML vocabularies. This enables you to include elements from a number of different vocabularies within a single XML document, without the risk of misinterpreting elements because (for example) two different vocabularies define a `<customer>` element.

XML namespaces can be quite complex, so this section doesn't go into great detail here, but the basic syntax is simple. Specific elements or attributes are associated with a specific namespace using a prefix, followed by a colon. For example, `<wrox:book>` represents a `<book>` element that resides in the `wrox` namespace. How do you know what namespace `wrox` represents? For this approach to work, you need to be able to guarantee that every namespace is unique. The easiest way to do this is to map the prefixes to something already known to be unique, which is exactly what happens: Somewhere in your XML document you need to associate any namespace prefixes with a *Uniform Resource Identifier (URI)*. URIs come in several flavors, but the most common type is simply a Web address, such as `www.wrox.com`.

To identify a prefix with a specific namespace, use the `xmlns:prefix` attribute within an element, setting its value to the unique URI that identifies that namespace. The prefix can then be used anywhere within that element, including any nested child elements:

```
<?xml version="1.0"?>
<books>
    <book xmlns:wrox="http://www.wrox.com">
        <wrox:title>Beginning C#</wrox:title>
        <wrox:author>Karli Watson</wrox:author>
    </book>
</books>
```

Here, you can use the `wrox:` prefix with the `<title>` and `<author>` elements because they are within the `<book>` element, where the prefix is defined. However, if you tried to add this prefix to the `<books>` element, the XML would be illegal, as the prefix isn't defined for this element.

You can also define a default namespace for an element using the `xmlns` attribute:

```
<?xml version="1.0"?>
<books>
    <book xmlns="http://www.wrox.com">
        <title>Beginning Visual C#</title>
        <author>Karli Watson</author>
        <html:img src="begvcsharp.gif"
                  xmlns:html="http://www.w3.org/1999/xhtml" />
    </book>
</books>
```

Here, the default namespace for the `<book>` element is defined as `"http://www.wrox.com"`. Everything within this element will, therefore, belong to this namespace, unless you explicitly specify otherwise by adding a different namespace prefix, as you do for the `<img>` element (when you set it to the namespace used by XML-compatible HTML documents).

Well-Formed and Valid XML

So far, we've been talking about *legal* XML. In fact, XML distinguishes between two forms of legality. Documents that obey all the rules required by the XML standard itself are said to be *well-formed*. If an XML document is not well-formed, parsers will be unable to interpret it correctly, and will reject the document. To be well-formed, a document must conform to the following:

❑ Have one and only one root element.

❑ Have closing tags for every element (except for the shorthand syntax mentioned previously).

❑ Not have any overlapping elements — all child elements must be fully nested within the parent.

❑ Have all attributes enclosed in quotes.

This isn't a complete list, by any means, but it does highlight the most common pitfalls made by programmers who are new to XML. However, XML documents can obey all these rules and still not be *valid*. Remember that earlier it was mentioned that XML is not itself a language, but a standard for defining XML applications. Well-formed XML documents simply comply with the XML standard; to be valid, they also need to conform to any rules specified for the XML application. Not all parsers check whether documents are valid; those that do are said to be *validating parsers*. To check whether a document adheres to the rules of the application, you first need a way to specify what those rules are.

Validating XML Documents

XML supports two ways of defining which elements and attributes can be placed in a document and in what order: *Document Type Definitions (DTDs)* and *schemas*. DTDs use a non-XML syntax inherited from the parent of XML and are gradually being replaced by schemas. DTDs don't allow you to specify the data types of the elements and attributes and so are relatively inflexible and not used that much in the context of the .NET Framework. Schemas, conversely, are used frequently — they allow you to specify data types, and they are written in an XML-compatible syntax. Unfortunately, schemas are very complex, and there are different formats for defining them — even within the .NET world!

Schemas

There are two separate formats for schemas supported by .NET — XML Schema Definition language (XSD) and XML-Data Reduced schemas (XDR). The XDR schema definition is an older standard that is proprietary to Microsoft and is not generally used or recognized by non-Microsoft parsers. XSD is an open standard, recommended by the W3C, and so it is the definition presented here. Schemas can be either included within your XML document or kept in a separate file. You actually need to be very familiar with XML before you attempt to write a schema, but it is useful to be able to recognize a schema's main elements, so the basic principles are explained here. To aid in your understanding, you look at a sample XSD schema for this simple XML document, which contains basic details about a couple of Wrox's C# books. This XML can be found in the download code for this book as `book.xml`:

```
<?xml version="1.0"?>
<books>
    <book>
        <title>Beginning Visual C#</title>
        <author>Karli Watson</author>
        <code>7582</code>
```

```
        </book>
        <book>
            <title>Professional C# 2nd Edition</title>
            <author>Simon Robinson</author>
            <code>7043</code>
        </book>
    </books>
```

XSD Schemas

Elements in XSD schemas must belong to the namespace `http://www.w3.org/2001/XMLSchema`. If this namespace isn't included, the schema elements won't be recognized.

To associate the XML document with an XSD schema in another file, you need to add a `schemalocation` element to the root element:

```
<?xml version="1.0"?>
<books schemalocation="file://C:\Beginning Visual C#\Chapter 25\books.xsd">
    ...
</books>
```

Take a quick look at an example XSD schema:

```
<schema xmlns="http://www.w3.org/2001/XMLSchema">
    <element name="books">
        <complexType>
            <choice maxOccurs="unbounded">
                <element name="book">
                    <complexType>
                        <sequence>
                            <element name="title" />
                            <element name="author" />
                            <element name="code" />
                        </sequence>
                    </complexType>
                </element>
            </choice>
            <attribute name="schemalocation" />
        </complexType>
    </element>
</schema>
```

The first thing to notice here is that the default namespace is set to the XSD namespace. This tells the parser that all the elements in the document belong to the schema. If you don't specify this namespace, the parser will think that the elements are just normal XML elements and won't realize that it needs to use them for validation.

The entire schema is contained within an element called <schema> (with a lowercase "s" — remember that case is important!). Each element that can occur within the document must be represented by an <element> element. This element has a name attribute that indicates the name of the element. If the element is to contain nested child elements, then you must include the <element> tags for these within a <complexType> element. Inside this, you specify how the child elements must occur.

For example, you use a <choice> element to specify that any selection of the child elements can occur, or <sequence> to specify that the child elements must appear in the same order as they are listed in the schema. If an element can appear more than once (as the <book> element does), then you need to include a maxOccurs attribute within its parent element. Setting this to "unbounded" means that the element can occur unlimited times. Finally, any attributes must be represented by <attribute> elements, including your schemalocation attribute, which tells the parser where to find the schema. Place this after the end of the list of child elements.

Now you've covered the basic theory behind XML, in the following Try It Out you can have a go at creating XML documents. Fortunately, VS does a lot of the hard work for you. It even creates an XSD schema based on your XML document without you having to write a single line of code!

Try It Out   Creating an XML Document in Visual Studio

Follow these steps to create an XML document:

1. Open VS and select File ⇨ New ⇨ File from the menu. If you don't see this option, please create a new project, right-click the project in the Solution Explorer, and choose to add a new item. Then select XML File from the dialog.

2. In the New File dialog, select XML File and click Open. VS creates a new XML document for you. As Figure 25-1 shows, VS adds the XML declaration, complete with an encoding attribute (it also colors the attributes and elements, but this won't show up very well in black-and-white print):

```
XMLFile1.xml   Start Page
    <?xml version="1.0" encoding="utf-8"?>
```

Figure 25-1

3. Save the file by pressing Ctrl+S or by selecting File ⇨ Save XMLFile1.xml from the menu. VS asks you where to save the file and what to call the file; save it in the Beginning Visual C#\Chapter25 folder as GhostStories.xml.

4. Move the cursor to the line underneath the XML declaration, and type the text <stories>. Notice how VS automatically puts the end tag in as soon as you type the greater than sign to close the opening tag.

5. Type this XML file and then click Save:

```
<stories>
    <story>
        <title>A House in Aungier Street</title>
        <author>
            <name>Sheridan Le Fanu</name>
            <nationality>Irish</nationality>
        </author>
        <rating>eerie</rating>
    </story>
    <story>
        <title>The Signalman</title>
        <author>
            <name>Charles Dickens</name>
            <nationality>English</nationality>
        </author>
        <rating>atmospheric</rating>
    </story>
    <story>
        <title>The Turn of the Screw</title>
        <author>
            <name>Henry James</name>
            <nationality>American</nationality>
        </author>
        <rating>a bit dull</rating>
    </story>
</stories>
```

6. It is now possible to let Visual Studio create a schema that fits the XML you have written. Do this by selecting the Create Schema menu option from the XML menu. Save the resulting XSD file by clicking Save as GhostStories.XSD.

7. Return to the XML file and type the following XML before the ending </stories> tag:

```
<story>
    <title>Number 13</title>
    <author>
        <name>MR James</name>
        <nationality>English</nationality>
    </author>
    <rating>mysterious</rating>
</story>
```

Note that you are now getting IntelliSense hints when you begin typing the starting tags. That's because Visual Studio knows to connect the newly created XSD schema to the XML file you are typing.

8. It is possible to create this link between XML and one or more schemas in Visual Studio. Select XML ⇨ Schemas. That brings up the dialog shown in Figure 25-2. At the top of the long list of schemas that Visual Studio recognizes, you will see GhostStories.XSD. To the left of it is a green check mark, which indicates that this schema is being used on the current XML document.

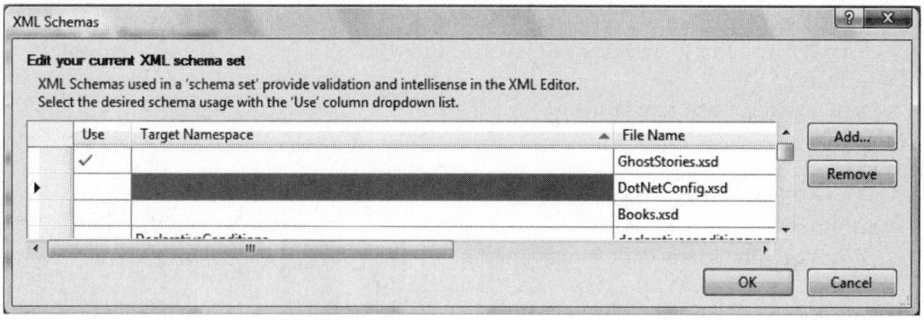

XML Schemas

Edit your current XML schema set

XML Schemas used in a 'schema set' provide validation and intellisense in the XML Editor.
Select the desired schema usage with the 'Use' column dropdown list.

Use	Target Namespace	File Name	
✓		GhostStories.xsd	Add...
▶		DotNetConfig.xsd	Remove
		Books.xsd	
	DeclarativeConditions	declarativeconditionsm...	

OK   Cancel

Figure 25-2

Using XML in Your Application

Now that you know how to create XML documents, it is time to put this knowledge to use. The .NET Framework includes a number of namespaces and classes that make it quite simple to read, manipulate, and write XML. The following pages cover a number of these classes and examine how you can use them to create and manipulate XML programmatically.

XML Document Object Model

The XML Document Object Model (XML DOM) is a set of classes used to access and manipulate XML in a very intuitive way. The DOM is perhaps not the quickest way to read XML data, but as soon as you understand the relationship between the classes and the elements of an XML document, you are going to find it very easy to use.

The classes that make up the DOM can be found in the namespace System.Xml. There are several classes and namespaces in this namespace, but this chapter focuses on only a few of the classes that enable you to easily manipulate XML. These classes are described in the following table:

Class	Description
XmlNode	Represents a single node in a document tree. It is the base of many of the classes shown in this chapter. If this node represents the root of an XML document, you can navigate to any position in the document from it.
XmlDocument	Extends the XmlNode class, but is often the first object you use when using XML. That's because this class is used to load and save data from disk or elsewhere.

Class	Description
XmlElement	Represents a single element in the XML document. XmlElement is derived from XmlLinkedNode, which in turn is derived from XmlNode.
XmlAttribute	Represents a single attribute. Like the XmlDocument class, it is derived from the XmlNode class.
XmlText	Represents the text between a starting tag and a closing tag.
XmlComment	Represents a special kind of node that is not regarded as part of the document other than to provide information to the reader about parts of the document.
XmlNodeList	Represents a collection of nodes.

XmlDocument Class

Usually, the first thing your application will want to do with XML is read it from disk. As described in the preceding table, this is the domain of the XmlDocument class. You can think of the XmlDocument as an in-memory representation of the file on disk. Once you have used the XmlDocument class to load a file into memory, you can obtain the root node of the document from it and start reading and manipulating the XML:

```
using System.Xml;
.
.
.

XmlDocument document = new XmlDocument();
document.Load(@"C:\Beginning Visual C#\Chapter 25\books.xml");
```

The two lines of code create a new instance of the XmlDocument class and load the file books.xml into it. Remember that the XmlDocument class is located in the System.Xml namespace, and you should insert a using System.Xml; in the using section at the beginning of the code.

In addition to loading and saving the XML, the XmlDocument class is also responsible for maintaining the XML structure itself. Therefore, you will find numerous methods on this class that are used to create, alter, and delete nodes in the tree. You will look at some of those methods shortly, but to present the methods properly, you need to know a bit more about another class, XmlElement.

XmlElement Class

Now that the document has been loaded into memory, you want to do something with it. The DocumentElement property of the XmlDocument instance you created in the preceding code returns an instance of an XmlElement that represents the root element of the XmlDocument. This element is important because it gives you access to every bit of information in the document:

```
XmlDocument document = new XmlDocument();
document.Load(@"C:\Beginning Visual C#\Chapter 25\books.xml");
XmlElement element = document.DocumentElement;
```

After you've got the root element of the document, you are ready to use the information. The `XmlElement` class contains methods and properties for manipulating the nodes and attributes of the tree. Let's examine the methods for navigating the XML elements first:

Property	Description

FirstChild	Returns the first child element after this one. If you recall the `books.xml` file from earlier in the chapter, the root node of the document was called "books" and the next node after that was "book." In that document, then, the first child of the root node "books" is "book."
	
	 `<books>      @@la Root node`
	 `    <book>     @@la FirstChild`
	
	 node`FirstChild` returns an `XmlNode` object, and you should test for the type of the returned node because it is unlikely to always be an `XmlElement` instance. In the books example, the child of the `Title` element is, in fact, an `XmlText` node that represents the text `Beginning Visual C#`.

LastChild	Operates exactly like the `FirstChild` property except that it returns the last child of the current node. In the case of the books example, the last child of the "books" node will still be a "book" node, but it will be the node representing the "Professional C# 2nd Edition" book.
	
	 `<books> @@la Root node`
	 `    <book> @@la FirstChild`
	 `        <title>Beginning Visual C#</title>`
	 `        <author>Karli Watson</author>`
	 `        <code>7582</code>`
	 `    </book>`
	 `    <book> @@la LastChild`
	 `        <title>Professional C# 2nd Edition</title>`
	 `        <author>Simon Robinson</author>`
	 `        <code>7043</code>`
	 `    </book>`
	 `</books>`

ParentNode	Returns the parent of the current node. In the books example, the "books" node is the parent of both of the "book" nodes.
NextSibling	Where `FirstChild` and `LastChild` properties return the leaf node of the current node, the `NextSibling` node returns the next node that has the same parent node. In the case of the books example, that means getting the `NextSibling` of the title element will return the author element, and calling `NextSibling` on that will return the code element.
HasChildNodes	Enables you to check whether the current element has child elements without actually getting the value from `FirstChild` and examining that against `null`.

Using the four properties from the preceding table, it is possible to run through an entire XmlDocument, as shown in the following Try It Out.

Try It Out   Looping through All Nodes in an XML Document

In this example, you are going to create a small Windows Forms application that loops through all the nodes of an XML document and prints out the name of the element or the text contained in the element in the case of an XmlText element. This code uses book.xml, which you saw in the "Schemas" section earlier; if you didn't create that file as you worked through that section, you can find it in this book's downloaded code.

1. Begin by creating a new Windows Form project by selecting File ⇨ New ⇨ Project. In the dialog, select Windows Application. Name the project **LoopThroughXmlDocument** and press Enter.

2. Design the form as shown in Figure 25-3 by dragging a ListBox control and a Button control onto the form.

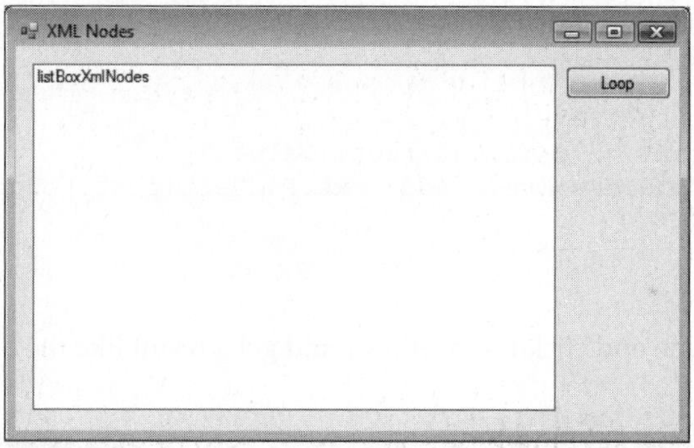

Figure 25-3

3. Name the ListBox **listBoxXmlNodes** and the button **buttonLoopThroughDocument**.

4. Double-click the button and enter the code that follows. Don't forget to add using System.Xml; to the using section at the top of the file:

```
private void buttonLoopThroughDocument_Click(object sender, EventArgs e)
{
    // Clear ListBox
    listBoxXmlNodes.Items.Clear();

    // Load the XML document
    XmlDocument document = new XmlDocument();
    document.Load(@"C:\Beginning Visual C#\Chapter 25\Books.xml");

    // Use recursion to loop through the document.
    RecurseXmlDocument((XmlNode)document.DocumentElement, 0);
```

831

```
    }

    private void RecurseXmlDocument(XmlNode root, int indent)
    {
        // Make sure we don't do anything if the root is null.
        if (root == null)
            return;

        if (root is XmlElement) // Root is an XmlElement type
        {
            // first, print the name
            listBoxXmlNodes.Items.Add(root.Name.PadLeft(root.Name.Length + indent));

            // Then check if there are any child nodes and if there are, call this
            // method again to print them.
            if (root.HasChildNodes)
                RecurseXmlDocument(root.FirstChild, indent + 2);

            // Finally check to see if there are any siblings and if there are
            // call this method again to have them printed.
            if (root.NextSibling != null)
                RecurseXmlDocument(root.NextSibling, indent);
        }
        else if (root is XmlText)
        {
            // Print the text.
            string text = ((XmlText)root).Value;
            listBoxXmlNodes.Items.Add(text.PadLeft(text.Length + indent));
        }
    }
```

5. Run the application and click Loop. You should get a result like the one shown in Figure 25-4.

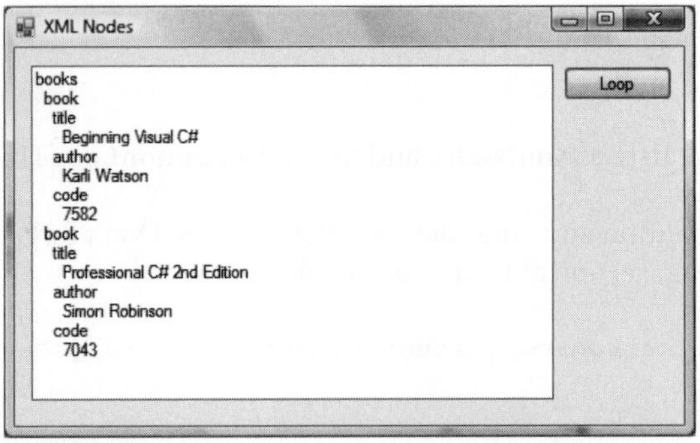

Figure 25-4

The output doesn't look like it is valid XML, and obviously it isn't. The thing to notice is that when you ran through the elements of the XML document, you didn't encounter a single closing tag. In other words, you never have to worry whether the current element is a starting tag or a closing tag — the `XmlNode` or `XmlElement` instance represents the entire node, not just the text representation of a tag.

How It Works

When you click the button, the first thing that happens is the XmlDocument method Load is called. This method loads the XML from a file into the XmlDocument instance, which can then be used to access the elements of the XML. Then you call a method that enables you to loop through the XML recursively, passing the root node of the XML document to the method. The root element is obtained with the property DocumentElement of the XmlDocument class. Aside from the check for null on the root parameter that is passed into the RecurseXmlDocument method, the first line to note is the if sentence:

```
if (root is XmlElement) // Root is an XmlElement type
{
  . . .
}
else if (root is XmlText)
{
  . . .
}
```

Recall that the is operator enables you to examine the type of an object and returns true if the instance is of the specified type. Even though the root node is declared as an Xmlnode, that is merely the base type of the objects you are going to work with. By using the is operator to test the type of the objects, you are able to determine the type of the object's runtime and behave accordingly.

Inside the two if blocks you add the appropriate text to the list view. You have to know the type of the current instance of root because the information you want to display is obtained differently for different elements: You want to display the name of XmlElements and the value of XmlText elements. The reason you only call RecurseXmlDocument recursively if the node is an XmlElement is that XmlText nodes never have child nodes.

Changing the Values of Nodes

Before you examine how to change the value of a node, it is important to realize that very rarely is the value of a node a simple thing. In fact, you will find that although all of the classes that derive from XmlNode include a property called Value, it very rarely returns anything useful to you. While this can feel like a bit of a letdown at first, you'll find it is actually quite logical. Examine the books example from earlier:

```
<books>
  <book>
    <title>Beginning Visual C#</title>
    <author>Karli Watson</author>
    <code>7582</code>
  </book>
  <book>
</books>
```

Every single tag pair in the document resolves into a node in the DOM. Remember that when you looped through all the nodes in the document, you encountered a number of XmlElement nodes and three XmlText nodes. The XmlElement nodes in this XML are <books>, <book>, <title>, <author>, and `<code>`. The `XmlText` nodes are the text between the starting and closing tags of title, author, and code. Though it could be argued that the value of title, author, and code is the text between the tags, that text is itself a node and it is that node that actually holds the value. The other tags clearly have no value associated with them other than other nodes.

If you look toward the bottom of the code in the earlier `RecurseXmlDocument` method, you will find the following line in the `if` block that executes when the current node is an `XmlText` node:

```
string text = ((XmlText)root).Value;
```

Here, you see that the `Value` property of the `XmlText` node instance is used to get the value of the node.

Nodes of the type `XmlElement` return `null` if you use their `Value` property, but it is possible to get the information between the starting and closing tags of an `XmlElement` if you use one of two other methods: `InnerText` and `InnerXml`. That means you are able to manipulate the value of nodes using two methods and a property, as described in the following table:

Property	Description
InnerText	Gets the text of all the child nodes of the current node and returns it as a single concatenated string. This means that if you get the value of `InnerText` from the book node in the preceding XML, the string `Beginning Visual C#Karli Watson7582` returned. If you get the `InnerText` of the title node, only `"Beginning Visual C#"` is returned. You can set the text using this method, but be careful if you do so because if you set the text of a wrong node you may overwrite information you did not want to change.
InnerXml	Returns the text like `InnerText`, but it also returns all of the tags. Therefore, if you get the value of `InnerXml` on the book node, the result is the following string: `<title>Beginning Visual C#</title><author>Karli Watson </author><code>7582</code>` As you can see, this can be quite useful if you have a string containing XML that you want to inject directly into your XML document. However, you are entirely responsible for the string yourself, and if you insert badly formed XML, the application will generate an exception.
Value	The "cleanest" way to manipulate information in the document, but as mentioned earlier, only a few of the classes actually return anything useful to you when you get the value. The classes that will return the desired text are as follows: `XmlText` `XmlComment` `XmlAttribute`

Inserting New Nodes

Now that you've seen that you can move around in the XML document and even get the values of the elements, let's examine how to change the structure of the document by adding nodes to the books document you've been using until now.

To insert new elements in the list, you need to examine the new methods that are placed on the XmlDocument and XmlNode classes, shown in the following table. The XmlDocument class has methods that enable you to create new XmlNode and XmlElement instances, which is nice because both of these classes have only a protected constructor, which means you cannot create an instance of either directly with new.

Method	Description
CreateNode	Creates any kind of node. There are three overloads of the method, two of which enable you to create nodes of the type found in the XmlNodeType enumeration and one that enables you to specify the type of node to use as a string. Unless you are quite sure about specifying a node type other than those in the enumeration, I strongly recommend using the two overloads that use the enumeration. The method returns an instance of XmlNode that can then be cast to the appropriate type explicitly.
CreateElement	A version of CreateNode that creates only nodes of the XmlDocument variety.
CreateAttribute	A version of CreateNode that creates only nodes of the XmlAttribute variety.
CreateTextNode	Creates — yes, you guessed it — nodes of the type XmlTextNode.
CreateComment	This method is included here to highlight the diversity of node types that can be created. This method doesn't create a node that is actually part of the data represented by the XML document, but rather it is a comment meant for any human eyes that might have to read the data. You can pick up comments when reading the document in your applications as well.

The methods in the preceding table are all used to create the nodes themselves, but after calling any of them you have to do something with them before they become interesting. Immediately after creation, the nodes have no additional information about them, and they are not yet inserted into the document. To do either, you should use methods that are found on any class derived from XmlNode (including XmlDocument and XmlElement). The following table describes those methods:

Method	Description
AppendChild	Appends a child node to a node of type XmlNode or a derived type. Remember that the node you append appears at the bottom of the list of children of the node on which the method is called. If you don't care about the order of the children, there's no problem; if you do care, remember to append the nodes in the correct sequence.
InsertAfter	Controls exactly where you want to insert the new node. The method takes two parameters — the first is the new node and the second is the node after which the new node should be inserted.
InsertBefore	Works exactly like InsertAfter, except that the new node is inserted before the node you supply as a reference.

In the Following Try It Out, you build on the previous example and insert a book node in the `books.xml` document. There is no code in the example to clean the document (yet), so if you run it several times you will probably end up with a lot of identical nodes.

Creating Nodes

Follow these steps to add a node to the `books.xml` document:

1.   Add a button beneath the existing button on the form and name it **buttonCreateNode**. Change its `Text` property to `Create Node`.

2.   Double-click the new button and enter the following code:

```csharp
private void buttonCreateNode_Click(object sender, EventArgs e)
{
    // Load the XML document.
    XmlDocument document = new XmlDocument();
    document.Load(@"C:\Beginning Visual C#\Chapter 25\Books.xml");

    // Get the root element.
    XmlElement root = document.DocumentElement;

    // Create the new nodes.
    XmlElement newBook = document.CreateElement("book");
    XmlElement newTitle = document.CreateElement("title");
    XmlElement newAuthor = document.CreateElement("author");
    XmlElement newCode = document.CreateElement("code");
    XmlText title = document.CreateTextNode("Beginning Visual C# 3rd Edition");
    XmlText author = document.CreateTextNode("Karli Watson et al");
    XmlText code = document.CreateTextNode("1234567890");
    XmlComment comment = document.CreateComment("This book is the book you
are reading");

    // Insert the elements.
    newBook.AppendChild(comment);
    newBook.AppendChild(newTitle);
    newBook.AppendChild(newAuthor);
    newBook.AppendChild(newCode);
    newTitle.AppendChild(title);
    newAuthor.AppendChild(author);
    newCode.AppendChild(code);
    root.InsertAfter(newBook, root.FirstChild);

    document.Save(@"C:\Beginning Visual C#\Chapter 25\Books.xml");
}
```

3.   Add the following code to the end of the `RecurseXmlDocument` method:

```csharp
else if (root is XmlComment)
{
    // Print text.
    string text = root.Value;
```

```
listBoxXmlNodes.Items.Add(text.PadLeft(text.Length + indent));

    // Then check if there are any child nodes, and if there are call this
    // method again to print them.
    if (root.HasChildNodes)
      RecurseXmlDocument(root.FirstChild, indent + 2);

    // Finally, check to see if there are any siblings, and if there are
    // call this method again to have them printed.
    if (root.NextSibling != null)
      RecurseXmlDocument(root.NextSibling, indent);
}
```

4.   Run the application and click Create Node. Then click Loop, and you should see the dialog shown in Figure 25-5.

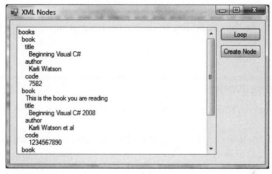

Figure 25-5

There is one important type of node that you didn't create in the preceding example: the XmlAttribute. This is left as an exercise at the end of the chapter.

How It Works

The code in the buttonCreateNode_Click method is where all the creation of nodes happens. It creates eight new nodes, four of which are of type XmlElement, three of type XmlText, and finally one of type XmlComment.

All of the nodes are created with the method of the encapsulating XmlDocument instance. The XmlElement nodes are created with the CreateElement method, the XmlText nodes are created with the CreateTextNode method, and the XmlComment node is created with the CreateComment method.

After the nodes have been created, they still need to be inserted into the XML tree. This is done with the AppendChild method on the element to which the new node should become a child. The only exception to this is the book node, which is the root node of all of the new nodes. This node is inserted into the tree using the InsertAfter method of the root object. Whereas all of the nodes that are inserted using AppendChild always become the last of the nodes in the list of child nodes, InsertAfter enables you to position the node where you want it.

Deleting Nodes

Now that you've seen how to create new nodes, all that is left is to learn how to delete them again. All classes derived from XmlNode include a number of methods, shown in the following table, that enable you to remove nodes from the document:

Method	Description
RemoveAll	Removes all child nodes in the node on which it is called. What is slightly less obvious is that it also removes all attributes on the node because they are regarded as child nodes as well.
RemoveChild	Removes a single child in the node on which it is called. The method returns the node that has been removed from the document, but you can reinsert it if you change your mind.

The following short Try It Out extends the Windows Forms application you've been creating over the past two examples to include the capability to delete nodes. For now, it only finds the last instance of the book node and removes it.

Try It Out   Removing Nodes

The following steps enable you to find and remove the final instance of the book node:

1.   Add a new button below the two that already exist and name it **buttonDeleteNode**. Set its Text property to Delete Node.

2.   Double-click the new button and enter the following code:

```
private void buttonDeleteNode_Click(object sender, EventArgs e)
{
    // Load the XML document.
    XmlDocument document = new XmlDocument();
    document.Load(@"C:\Beginning Visual C#\Chapter 25\Books.xml");

    // Get the root element.
    XmlElement root = document.DocumentElement;

    // Find the node. root is the <books> tag, so its last child
    // which will be the last <book> node.
    if (root.HasChildNodes)
    {
        XmlNode book = root.LastChild;

        // Delete the child.
        root.RemoveChild(book);

        // Save the document back to disk.
        document.Save(@"C:\Beginning Visual C#\Chapter 25\Books.xml");
    }
}
```

3. Run the application. When you click the Delete Node button and then the Loop button, the last node in the tree will disappear.

How It Works

After the initial steps to load the XML into the `XmlDocument` object, you examine the root element to see whether there are any child elements in the XML you loaded. If there are, you use the `LastChild` property of the `XmlElement` class to get the last child. After that, removing the element is as simple as calling `RemoveChild`, passing in the instance of the element that you wish to remove — in this case, the last child of the root element.

Selecting Nodes

You now know how to move back and forth in an XML document, how to manipulate the values of the document, how to create new nodes, and how to delete them again. Only one thing remains in this chapter: how to select nodes without having to traverse the entire tree.

The `XmlNode` class includes two methods commonly used to select nodes from the document without running through every node in it: `SelectSingleNode` and `SelectNodes` (described in the following table), both of which use a special query language, called XPath, to select the nodes. You learn about that shortly.

Method	Description
`SelectSingleNode`	Selects a single node. If you create a query that fetches more than one node, only the first node will be returned.
`SelectNodes`	Returns a node collection in the form of an `XmlNodesList` class.

XPath

XPath is a query language for XML documents much as SQL is for relational databases. It is used by the two methods described in the previous table to enable you to avoid the hassle of walking the entire tree of an XML document. It does take a little getting used to, however, because the syntax is nothing like SQL or C#.

> XPath is quite extensive, and only a small part of it is covered here so you can start selecting nodes. If you are interested in learning more, take a look at www.w3.org/TR/xpath and the Visual Studio help pages.

To properly see XPath in action, you are going to use a slightly extended version of the `books.xml` file. It is listed in its entirety in the "Selecting Nodes" Try It Out example later in the chapter, and it can be found in the download code for this chapter on this book's Web site as `XPathQuery.xml`.

The following table lists some of the most common operations you can perform with XPath. If nothing else is stated, the XPath query example makes a selection that is relative to the node on which it is performed. Where it is necessary to have a name of a node, you can assume that the current node is the `<book>` node in the XML document.

Purpose	XPath Query Example
Select the current node.	`.`
Select the parent of the current node.	`..`
Select all child nodes of the current node.	`*`
Select all child nodes with a specific name — in this case, `title`.	`title`
Select an attribute of the current node.	`@pages`
Select all attributes of the current node.	`@*`
Select a child node by index — in this case, the second author node.	`author[2]`
Select all the text nodes of the current node.	`text()`
Select one or more grandchildren of the current node.	`author/text()`
Select all nodes in the document with a particular name — in this case, all `title` nodes.	`//title`
Select all nodes in the document with a particular name and particular parent name — in this case, the parent name is `book` and the node name is `title`.	`//book/title`
Select a node where a value criterion is met — in this case, the books where the author `Jacob Hammer Pedersen` participated.	`//book[author='Jacob Hammer Pedersen']`
Select a node where an attribute value criteria is met — in this case, the `pages` attribute = 1000.	`//book[@pages='1000']`

In the following Try It Out, you'll create a small application that enables you to execute and see the results of a number of predefined queries, as well as enter your own queries.

Try It Out **Selecting Nodes**

As previously mentioned, this example uses a new XML file called `XPathQuery.XML`. You can download the file from the book's Web site or type it in from the listing here:

```xml
<?xml version="1.0"?>
<books>
  <book pages="944">
    <title>Beginning Visual C#</title>
    <author>Karli Watson</author>
    <author>Jacob Hammer Pedersen</author>
    <author>Christian Nagel</author>
    <author>David Espinosa</author>
    <author>Zach Greenvoss</author>
    <author>Jon D. Reid</author>
    <author>Matthew Reynolds</author>
    <author>Morgan Skinner</author>
    <author>Eric White</author>
    <code>7582</code>
  </book>
  <book pages="1000">
    <title>Beginning Visual C# 2008</title>
    <author>Karli Watson</author>
    <author>Jacob Hammer Pedersen</author>
    <author>Christian Nagel</author>
    <author>Jon D. Reid</author>
    <author>Morgan Skinner</author>
    <author>Eric White</author>
    <code>1234567890</code>
  </book>
  <book pages="1272">
    <title>Professional C# 2nd Edition</title>
    <author>Simon Robinson</author>
    <author>Scott Allen</author>
    <author>Ollie Cornes</author>
    <author>Jay Glynn</author>
    <author>Zach Greenvoss</author>
    <author>Burton Harvey</author>
    <author>Christian Nagel</author>
    <author>Morgan Skinner</author>
    <author>Karli Watson</author>
    <code>7043</code>
  </book>
</books>
```

Save the XML file as `XPathQuery.xml`. Remember to change the path to the file in the code that follows.

Follow these steps to create a Windows Forms application with querying capability:

1. Create a new Windows Forms application and name it **XmlQueryExample**.

2. Create the dialog shown in Figure 25-6. Name the `TextBox` **textBoxQuery**. All the other controls should be named with their type followed by their text property (that is, the name of

the radio button "Set Book as current" is `radioButtonSetBookAsCurrent` and the Close button is `buttonClose`).

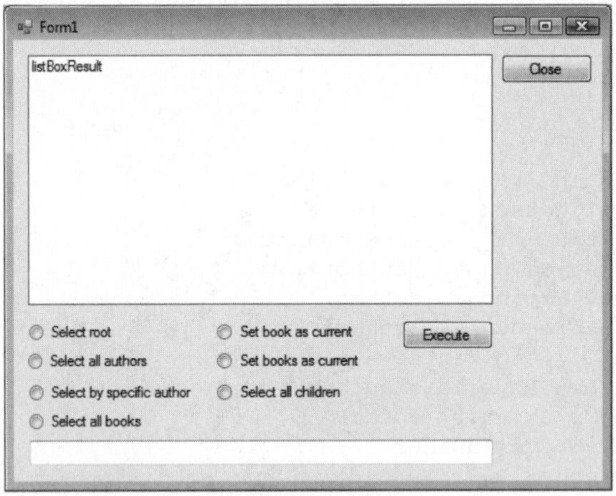

Figure 25-6

3. Right-click the form and choose View Code. Include the `using` directive:

```
using System.Xml;
```

4. Add two private fields to hold the document and current node, and initialize them in the constructor:

```
private XmlDocument mDocument;
private XmlNode mCurrentNode;

public Form1()
{
    InitializeComponent();

    mDocument = new XmlDocument();
    mDocument.Load(@"C:\Beginning Visual C#\Chapter 25\XPathQuery.xml");
    mCurrentNode = mDocument.DocumentElement;
    ClearListBox();
}
```

5. You need a few helper methods to display the result of the queries in the list box:

```
private void DisplayList(XmlNodeList nodeList)
{
    foreach (XmlNode node in nodeList)
    {
        RecurseXmlDocumentNoSiblings(node, 0);
    }
}

private void RecurseXmlDocumentNoSiblings(XmlNode root, int indent)
```

```
{
    // Make sure we don't do anything if the root is null.
    if (root == null)
      return;

    if (root is XmlElement) // Root is an XmlElement type
    {
      // First, print the name.
      listBoxResult.Items.Add(root.Name.PadLeft(root.Name.Length + indent));

      // Then check if there are any child nodes and if there are, call this
      // method again to print them.
      if (root.HasChildNodes)
        RecurseXmlDocument(root.FirstChild, indent + 2);
    }
    else if (root is XmlText)
    {
      // Print the text.
      string text = ((XmlText)root).Value;
      listBoxResult.Items.Add(text.PadLeft(text.Length + indent));
    }
    else if (root is XmlComment)
    {
      // Print text.
      string text = root.Value;
      listBoxResult.Items.Add(text.PadLeft(text.Length + indent));

      // Then check if there are any child nodes and if there are, call this
      // method again to print them.
      if (root.HasChildNodes)
        RecurseXmlDocument(root.FirstChild, indent + 2);
    }
}

private void RecurseXmlDocument(XmlNode root, int indent)
{
    // Make sure we don't do anything if the root is null.
    if (root == null)
      return;

    if (root is XmlElement) // Root is an XmlElement type.
    {
      // First, print the name.
      listBoxResult.Items.Add(root.Name.PadLeft(root.Name.Length + indent));

      // Then check if there are any child nodes and if there are, call this
      // method again to print them.
      if (root.HasChildNodes)
        RecurseXmlDocument(root.FirstChild, indent + 2);

      // Finally check to see if there are any siblings, and if there are
      // call this method again to have them printed.
      if (root.NextSibling != null)
        RecurseXmlDocument(root.NextSibling, indent);
    }
```

```
      else if (root is XmlText)
      {
        // Print the text.
        string text = ((XmlText)root).Value;
        listBoxResult.Items.Add(text.PadLeft(text.Length + indent));
      }
      else if (root is XmlComment)
      {
        // Print text.
        string text = root.Value;
        listBoxResult.Items.Add(text.PadLeft(text.Length + indent));

        // Then check if there are any child nodes. and if there are call this
        // method again to print them.
        if (root.HasChildNodes)
          RecurseXmlDocument(root.FirstChild, indent + 2);

        // Finally, check to see if there are any siblings, and if there are
        // call this method again to have them printed.
        if (root.NextSibling != null)
          RecurseXmlDocument(root.NextSibling, indent);
      }
    }

    private void ClearListBox()
    {
      listBoxResult.Items.Clear();
    }

    private void buttonClose_Click(object sender, EventArgs e)
    {
      Application.Exit();
    }
```

6. Insert the code to perform the queries on the XML into the `SelectionChange` event of the radio buttons. Insert each of the events by double-clicking on the radio buttons:

```
    private void radioButtonSelectRoot_CheckedChanged(object sender,
EventArgs e)
    {
      mCurrentNode = mDocument.DocumentElement.SelectSingleNode("//books");
      ClearListBox();
      RecurseXmlDocument(mCurrentNode, 0);
    }

    private void radioButtonSelectAllAuthors_CheckedChanged(object sender,
EventArgs e)
    {
      if (mCurrentNode != null)
      {
        XmlNodeList nodeList = mCurrentNode.SelectNodes("//book/author");
        ClearListBox();
        DisplayList(nodeList);
```

```
      }
      else
        ClearListBox();
    }

    private void radioButtonSelectBySpecificAuthor_CheckedChanged(object ⏎
sender, EventArgs e)
    {
      if (mCurrentNode != null)
      {
        XmlNodeList nodeList = mCurrentNode.SelectNodes("//book[author= ⏎
'Jacob Hammer Pedersen']");
        ClearListBox();
        DisplayList(nodeList);
      }
      else
        ClearListBox();
    }

    private void radioButtonSelectAllBooks_CheckedChanged(object sender, ⏎
EventArgs e)
    {
      if (mCurrentNode != null)
      {
        XmlNodeList nodeList = mCurrentNode.SelectNodes("//book");
        ClearListBox();
        DisplayList(nodeList);
      }
      else
        ClearListBox();
    }

    private void radioButtonSetBookAsCurrent_CheckedChanged(object sender, ⏎
EventArgs e)
    {
      if (mCurrentNode != null)
      {
        mCurrentNode = mCurrentNode.SelectSingleNode("book[title='Beginning ⏎
Visual C#']");
        ClearListBox();
        RecurseXmlDocumentNoSiblings(mCurrentNode, 0);
      }
      else
        ClearListBox();
    }

    private void radioButtonSetBooksAsCurrent_CheckedChanged(object ⏎
sender, EventArgs e)
    {
      if (mCurrentNode != null)
      {
        mCurrentNode = mCurrentNode.SelectSingleNode("//books");
        ClearListBox();
```

```
                RecurseXmlDocumentNoSiblings(mCurrentNode, 0);
        }
        else
           ClearListBox();
    }

    private void radioButtonSelectAllChildren_CheckedChanged(object sender,
EventArgs e)
    {
        if (mCurrentNode != null)
        {
           XmlNodeList nodeList = mCurrentNode.SelectNodes("*");
           ClearListBox();
           DisplayList(nodeList);
        }
        else
           ClearListBox();
    }
```

7. Finally, insert the code that executes whatever the user has entered in the text box and the code that closes the application when the buttonClose button is clicked:

```
    private void buttonExecute_Click(object sender, EventArgs e)
    {
        if (textBoxQuery.Text == "")
           return;

        try
        {
           XmlNodeList nodeList = mCurrentNode.SelectNodes(textBoxQuery.Text);
           ClearListBox();
           DisplayList(nodeList);
        }
        catch (System.Exception err)
        {
           MessageBox.Show(err.Message);
        }
    }
    private void buttonClose_Click(object sender, EventArgs e)
    {
        Application.Exit();
    }
```

8. Run the application. Note how the values change as you click the radio buttons.

How It Works

The first two methods, RecurseXmlDocumentNoSiblings and RecurseXmlDocument, and DisplayList are used to make the listings in the list box. The reason you need more than one of these methods is that you want to be able to more tightly control the output.

The code that does the actual searching in the XML is all found in steps 6 and 7. The method SelectNodes of the XmlNode class is used to execute searches that can or should return multiple nodes. This method returns an XmlNodeList object, which is then passed to the DisplayList helper method.

The other method that is used to search through the XML is SelectSingleNode. This method, as the name suggests, returns a single node, which you pass to the RecurseXmlNodeNoSiblings helper method to display the current node and its child nodes.

The following table describes the XPath queries that are used in the methods:

XPath Query	Description
//book/author	Selects all the nodes in the XML that have the name author and the parent book.
//book[author='Jacob Hammer Pedersen']	Selects all the book nodes in the XML that have a child node with the name author that has the value Jacob Hammer Pedersen.
//book	Selects all the book nodes in the XML.
book[title='Beginning Visual C#']	Selects the book node with the title node that equals Beginning Visual C#.
//books	Selects all books nodes.
*	Selects all child nodes of the current node.

Summary

In this chapter you learned about Extensible Markup Language (XML), a text format for storing and retrieving data. You looked at the rules you need to obey to ensure that XML documents are well-formed, and you learned how to validate them against XSD and XDR schemas.

After learning about the basics of XML, you saw how XML can be utilized through code using C# and Visual Studio. Finally, you learned how to use XPath to make queries in the XML.

The following topics were covered in this chapter:

❑ How to read and write Extensible Markup Language (XML).

❑ The rules that apply to well-formed XML.

❑ How to validate your XML documents against two types of schema: XSD and XDR.

❑ How to use .NET to use XML in your programs.

❑ How to search through XML documents using XPath queries.

In the next chapter you will learn how to access databases in .NET using ADO.NET. Before you move on, however, try to complete the following exercises.

Exercises

1. Change the Insert example in the "Creating Nodes" Try It Out section to insert an attribute called `Pages` with the value `1000` on the book node.

2. Currently, the last XPath example doesn't have a built-in capability to search for an attribute. Add a radio button and make a query for all books where the `pages` attribute of the book node equals 1000.

3. Change the methods that write to the list box (`RecurseXmlDocument` and `RecurseXmlDocumentNoSiblings`) in the XPath example so that they're able to display attributes.

26

Introduction to LINQ

This chapter introduces Language-Integrated Query (LINQ), a new extension to the C# language just added for C# 3.0, which is the C# language supported in Visual C# 2008. LINQ solves the problem of dealing with very large collections of objects, where you typically need to select a subset of the collection for the task your program is performing.

In the past, this sort of work required writing a lot of looping code, and additional processing such as sorting or grouping the found objects required even more code. LINQ frees you from having to write this extra looping code to filter and sort. It enables you to focus on the objects that matter to your program, providing a query.

In addition to providing an elegant query language that enables you to specify exactly what objects you are searching for, LINQ offers many extension methods that make it easy to sort, group, and calculate statistics on your query results.

LINQ also enables you to query large databases or complex XML documents in which millions or even billions of objects need to be searched or manipulated efficiently. Traditionally, this problem was usually solved with a specialized class library or even using a different language, such as database query language SQL. However, class libraries are not easy to extend for many different types of objects, and mixing languages causes problems with mismatched types, as well as making programs hard to understand for developers not familiar with both languages, *entiende*? LINQ provides a mechanism built into the C# language itself that solves each of these problems.

This chapter introduces you to the varieties of LINQ, including LINQ to Objects, LINQ to SQL, and LINQ to XML, and covers the following topics:

❑   Coding a LINQ query and the parts of a LINQ query statement.

❑   Using LINQ method syntax versus LINQ query syntax.

❑   Using lambda expressions with LINQ.

❑   Ordering query results, including ordering on multiple levels.

❑   How to use LINQ aggregate operators — and when to use them.

❑   Using projection to create new objects in queries.

❑   Using the `Distinct()`, `Any()`, `All()`, `First()`, `FirstOrDefault()`, `Take()`, and `Skip()` operators.

❑   Group queries.

❑   Set operators and joins.

While this chapter focuses on LINQ to Objects, the concepts apply to all the varieties of LINQ and are necessary background for later chapters on LINQ to SQL and LINQ to XML.

LINQ is large enough that complete coverage of all its facilities and methods is beyond the scope of a beginning book. However, you will see examples of all of the different types of operators and statements you are likely to need as a user of LINQ, and you will be pointed to resources for more in-depth coverage as appropriate.

LINQ Varieties

Visual Studio 2008 comes with three built-in LINQ varieties that provide query solutions for different types of data: LINQ to Objects, LINQ to SQL, and LINQ to XML:

❑   **LINQ to Objects** — Provides queries on any kind of C# in-memory object, such as arrays, lists, and other collection types. All of the examples in this chapter use LINQ to Objects. However, you can use the techniques you learn in this chapter with all of varieties of LINQ.

❑   **LINQ to SQL** — Provides queries to relational databases that use the standard SQL database query language, such as Microsoft SQL Server, Oracle, and others. In the past, C# access to these databases required the developer to learn at least some SQL, but now the query capability is built into C# itself through LINQ and you can let LINQ to SQL handle the SQL translation for you. LINQ to SQL is covered in detail in Chapter 27.

❑   **LINQ to XML** — Provides creation and manipulation of XML documents using the same syntax and general query mechanism as the other LINQ varieties. LINQ to XML is described in detail in Chapters 27 and 29.

❑   **LINQ Providers** — LINQ can be extended for other varieties of data sources beyond objects, SQL databases, and XML. You merely need to write a LINQ provider for that type of data source. The design of a LINQ provider is an advanced topic beyond the scope of this book, but it is important for all C# developers to know that new LINQ providers can and will be written (both by Microsoft and by third parties), so expect to hear about other LINQ varieties in the future.

First LINQ Query

Let's get started with an example. In the following Try It Out, you create a query to find some data in a simple in-memory array of objects using LINQ and print it to the console.

Try It Out   **First LINQ Program**

Follow these steps to create the example in Visual Studio 2008:

1. Create a new console application called 26-1-FirstLINQquery in the directory C:\BegVCSharp\Chapter26, and then open the main source file `Program.cs`.

2. Notice that Visual C# 2008 includes the LINQ namespace by default in `Program.cs`:

```
using System;
using System.Collections.Generic;
using System.Linq;
using System.Text;
```

3. Add the following code to the `Main()` method in `Program.cs`:

```
static void Main(string[] args)
{
        string[] names = { "Alonso", "Zheng", "Smith", "Jones", "Smythe", ⏎
"Small", "Ruiz", "Hsieh", "Jorgenson", "Ilyich", "Singh", "Samba", "Fatimah" };

        var queryResults =
            from n in names
            where n.StartsWith("S")
            select n;

        Console.WriteLine("Names beginning with S:");

        foreach (var item in queryResults) {
            Console.WriteLine(item);
        }

        Console.Write("Program finished, press Enter/Return to continue:");
        Console.ReadLine();
}
```

4. Compile and execute the program (you can just press F5 for Start Debugging). You will see the names in the list beginning with S in the order they were declared in the array, as shown here:

```
Names beginning with S:
Smith
Smythe
Small
Singh
Samba
Program finished, press Enter/Return to continue:
```

Simply press Enter/Return to finish the program and make the console screen disappear. If you used Ctrl+F5 (Start Without Debugging), you may need to press Enter/Return twice. That finishes the program run.

How It Works

The first step is to reference the `System.Linq` namespace, which is done automatically by Visual C# 2008 when you create a project:

```
using System.Linq;
```

All the base underlying system support classes for LINQ reside in the `System.Linq` namespace. If you create a C# source file outside of Visual C# 2008 or edit a previously existing Visual C# 2005 project, you may have to add the `using System.Linq` statement manually.

The next step is to create some data, which is done in this example by declaring and initializing the array of `names`:

```
string[] names = { "Alonso", "Zheng", "Smith", "Jones", "Smythe", "Small", ↩
"Ruiz", "Hsieh", "Jorgenson", "Ilyich", "Singh", "Samba", "Fatimah" };
```

This is a trivial set of data, but it is good to start with an example where the result of the query is obvious. The actual LINQ query statement is the next part of the program:

```
var queryResults =
            from n in names
            where n.StartsWith("S")
            select n;
```

This is an odd-looking statement, isn't it? It almost looks like something from a language other than C#, and indeed the `from...where...select` syntax is deliberately similar to that of the SQL database query language. However, this statement is not SQL; it is indeed C#, as you saw when you typed in the code in Visual Studio 2008 — the `from, where,` and `select` were highlighted as keywords and the odd-looking syntax is perfectly fine to the compiler.

The LINQ query statement in this program uses the LINQ declarative query syntax:

```
            var queryResults =
                from n in names
                where n.StartsWith("S")
                select n;
```

The statement has four parts: the result variable declaration beginning with `var`, which is assigned using a *query expression* consisting of the `from` clause, the `where` clause, and the `select` cause. Let's look at each of these parts in turn.

Declaring a Variable for Results Using the var Keyword

The LINQ query starts by declaring a variable to hold the results of the query, which is usually done by declaring a variable with the `var` keyword:

```
var queryResult =
```

As described in Chapter 14, var is a new keyword in C# 3.0 created to declare a general variable type that is ideal for holding the results of LINQ queries. The var keyword tells the C# compiler to infer the type of the result based on the query. That way you don't have to declare ahead of time what type of objects will be returned from the LINQ query — the compiler take care of it for you. If the query can return multiple items, then it will act like a collection of the objects in the query data source (technically it is not a collection; it just looks that way).

> *If you want to know the details, the query result will be a type that implements the* IEnumerable<> *interface. In this particular case, the compiler creates an instance of* System.Linq *.*OrderedSequence<string, string>, *a special LINQ data type that provides an ordered list of strings (strings because the data source is a collection of strings).*

By the way, the name queryResult is arbitrary — you can name the result anything you want. It could be namesBeginningWithS or anything else that makes sense in your program.

Specify Data Source: from Clause

The next part of the LINQ query is the from clause, which specifies the data you are querying:

```
from n in names
```

Your data source in this case is names, the array of strings declared earlier. The variable n is just a stand-in for an individual element in the data source, similar to the variable name following a foreach statement. By specifying from you are saying you are going to *query* a subset of the collection rather than iterate through all the elements.

Speaking of iteration, a LINQ data source must be *enumerable* — that is, it must be an array or collection of items from which you can pick one or more elements to iterate through.

> *Technically, this means the data source must support the* IEnumerable<> *interface, which is supported for any C# array or collection of items.*

The data source cannot be a single value or object, such as a single int variable. You already have such a single item, so there would be no point in querying it!

Specify Condition: where Clause

In the next part of the LINQ query you specify the condition for your query using the where clause, which looks like this:

```
where n.StartsWith("S")
```

Any Boolean (true or false) expression that can be applied to the items in the data source can be specified in the where clause. Actually, the where clause is optional and can even be omitted, but in almost all cases you will want to specify a where condition to limit the results to only the data you want. The where clause is called a *restriction operator* in LINQ because it restricts the results of the query.

Here you specify that the name string starts with the letter S, but you could specify anything else about the string instead — for example, a length greater than 10 (where n.Length > 10) or containing a Q (where n.Contains("Q")).

Select Items: select Clause

Finally, the `select` clause specifies which items appear in the result set. The `select` clause looks like this:

```
select n
```

The `select` clause is required because you must specify which items from your query appear in the result set. For this set of data, it is not very interesting because you have only one item, the name, in each element of the result set. You'll look at some examples with more complex objects in the result set where the usefulness of the `select` clause will be more apparent, but first let's finish the example.

Finishing Up: Using the foreach Loop

Now you print out the results of the query. Like the array used as the data source, the results of a LINQ query like this are *enumerable*, meaning you can iterate through the results with a `foreach` statement:

```
Console.WriteLine("Names beginning with S:");

foreach (var item in queryResults) {
        Console.WriteLine(item);
}
```

In this case you matched four names, Singh, Small, Smythe, and Samba, so that is what you display in the `foreach` loop.

Deferred Query Execution

You may be thinking that the `foreach` loop really isn't part of LINQ itself — it's only looping through your results. While it's true that the `foreach` construct is not itself part of LINQ, nevertheless it is the part of your code that actually executes the LINQ query! The assignment of the query results variable only saves a plan for executing the query; with LINQ the data itself is not retrieved until the results are accessed. This is called *deferred query execution* or lazy evaluation of queries. Execution will be deferred for any query that produces a sequence — that is, a list — of results.

Now, back to your code. Because you've printed out the results, let's finish the program:

```
Console.Write("Program finished, press Enter/Return to continue:");
Console.ReadLine();
```

These lines just ensure that the results of the console program stay on the screen until you press a key, even if you press F5 instead of Ctrl+F5. You'll use this construct in most of the other LINQ examples as well.

Using the LINQ Method Syntax and Lambda Expressions

There are multiple ways of doing the same thing with LINQ, as is often the case in programming. As noted, the previous example was written using the LINQ *query syntax*; in the next example you will write the same program using LINQ's *method syntax* (also called *explicit syntax* but we'll use the term method syntax here).

LINQ Extension Methods

LINQ is implemented as a series of extension methods to collections, arrays, query results, and any other object that implements the `IEnumerable` interface. You can see these methods with the Visual Studio IntelliSense feature. For example, in Visual Studio 2008 open the `Program.cs` file in the `FirstLINQquery` program you just completed and type in a new reference to the `names` array just below it:

```
string[] names = { "Alonso", "Zheng", "Smith", "Jones", "Smythe", "Small", ↵
"Ruiz", "Hsieh", "Jorgenson", "Ilyich", "Singh", "Samba", "Fatimah" };

names.
```

Just as you type the period following `names`, you will see the methods available for `names` listed by the Visual Studio 2008 IntelliSense feature, as shown in Figure 26-1.

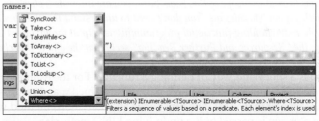

Figure 26-1

The `Where<>` method and most of the other available methods are extension methods (as shown in the documentation appearing to the right of the `Where<>` method, it begins with `extension`). You can see that they are LINQ extensions by commenting out the `using System.Linq` directive at the top; you will find that `Where<>`, `Union<>`, `Take<>`, and most of the other methods in the list no longer appear. The `for...where...select` query expression you used in the previous example is translated by the C# compiler into a series of calls to these methods. When using the LINQ method syntax, you call these methods directly.

Query Syntax versus Method Syntax

The query syntax is the preferred way of programming queries in LINQ, as it is generally easier to read and is simpler to use for the most common queries. However, it is important to have a basic understanding of the method syntax because some LINQ capabilities either are not available in the query syntax or are just easier to use in the method syntax.

> As the Visual C# 2008 online help recommends, use query syntax whenever possible and method syntax whenever necessary.

In this chapter you will mostly use the query syntax, but I'll point out situations where the method syntax is needed, and show you how to use the method syntax to solve the problem.

Lambda Expressions

Most of the LINQ methods that use the method syntax require that you pass a method or function to evaluate the query expression. The method/function parameter is passed in the form of a delegate, which typically references an anonymous method.

Luckily, LINQ makes doing this much easier than it sounds! You create the method/function by using a special C# 3.0 construct called a *lambda expression*. A lambda expression is a short, concise way of writing an anonymous method that is used to evaluate the query expression. Here is a simple lambda expression:

```
n => n < 1000
```

The operator => is called the *lambda operator*.

> *"Lambda" comes from the lambda calculus, the mathematical formalism underlying functional programming languages, which are the kind of programming on which LINQ is based. Explaining the details behind this is beyond the scope of this book, but if you are interested, check out sources such as the Wikipedia article on lambda calculus. You don't need to understand the mathematics to use lambda functions, although understanding functional programming is helpful for advanced LINQ programming. See the "Resources and Further Reading" section at the end of this chapter.*

A lambda expression is a shorthand way of defining a function. For the example n => n < 1000, the lambda expression defines a function that takes a parameter named n and returns true if n is less than 1000 and false if n is greater than 1000. The function is an anonymous method with no name, used only where the lambda expression is passed to the underlying LINQ method.

The Visual C# 2008 online help advises that this lambda expression should be read as "n *goes to* n greater than 1000," although for a true/false lambda expression like this I find it much more useful to read the expression as "n *such that* n is less than 1000."

The lambda expression for the query in the first program example might be written as

```
n => n.StartsWith("S"));
```

which would be read as "n such that n starts with S."

Try this out in an actual program to see this more clearly.

Try It Out   **Using LINQ Method Syntax and Lambda Expressions**

Follow these steps to create the example in Visual C# 2008:

1.   You can either modify the FirstLINQQuery example or create a new console application called 26-2-LINQMethodSyntax in the directory C:\BegVCSharp\Chapter26. Open the main source file `Program.cs`.

2.   Again, Visual C# 2008 includes the LINQ namespace automatically in `Program.cs`:

```
using System.Linq;
```

3.   Add the following code to the `Main()` method in `Program.cs`. Only the code differing from the first example is highlighted:

```
static void Main(string[] args)
{
        string[] names = { "Alonso", "Zheng", "Smith", "Jones", "Smythe",
"Small", "Ruiz", "Hsieh", "Jorgenson", "Ilyich", "Singh", "Samba", "Fatimah"
};

        var queryResults = names.Where(n => n.StartsWith("S"));

        Console.WriteLine("Names beginning with S:");

        foreach (var item in queryResults) {
            Console.WriteLine(item);
        }

        Console.Write("Program finished, press Enter/Return to continue:");
        Console.ReadLine();
}
```

4.   Compile and execute the program (you can just press F5). You will see the same output of names in the list beginning with S in the order they were declared in the array, as shown here:

```
Names beginning with S:
Smith
Smythe
Small
Singh
Samba
Program finished, press Enter/Return to continue:
```

How It Works

As before, the `System.Linq` namespace is referenced automatically by Visual C# 2008:

```
using System.Linq;
```

The same source data as before is created again by declaring and initializing the array of names:

```
string[] names = { "Alonso", "Zheng", "Smith", "Jones", "Smythe", "Small",
"Ruiz", "Hsieh", "Jorgenson", "Ilyich", "Singh", "Samba", "Fatimah" };
```

The part that is different is the LINQ query, which is now a call to the `Where()` method instead of a query expression:

```
var queryResults = names.Where(n => n.StartsWith("S"));
```

The C# compiler compiles the lambda expression `n => n.StartsWith("S")` into an anonymous method that is executed by `Where()` on each item in the names array. If the lambda expression returns `true` for an item, that item is included in the result set returned by `Where()`. The C# compiler infers that the `Where()` method should accept `string` as the input type for each item from the definition of the input source (the names array, in this case).

Well, a lot is going on in that one line, isn't it? For the simplest type of query like this, the method syntax is actually shorter than the query syntax because you do not need the `from` or `select` clauses; however, most queries are more complex than this.

The rest of the example is the same as the previous one — you print out the results of the query in a `foreach` loop and pause the output so you can see it before the program finishes execution:

```
foreach (var item in queryResults) {
        Console.WriteLine(item);
}

Console.Write("Program finished, press Enter/Return to continue:");
Console.ReadLine();
```

An explanation of these lines isn't repeated here because that was covered in the How It Works section following the first example in the chapter. Let's move on now and explore how to use more of LINQ's capabilities.

Ordering Query Results

Once you have located some data of interest with a `where` clause (or `Where()` method invocation), LINQ makes it easy to perform further processing — such as re-ordering the results — on the resulting data. In the following Try It Out, you put the results from your first query in alphabetical order.

Try It Out   **Ordering Query Results**

Follow these steps to create the example in Visual Studio 2008:

1. You can either modify the FirstLINQQuery example or create a new console application project called 26-3-OrderQueryResults in the directory C:\BegVCSharp\Chapter26.

2. Open the main source file `Program.cs`. As before, Visual C# 2008 includes the `using System.Linq;` namespace directive automatically in `Program.cs`.

3. Add the following code to the `Main()` method in `Program.cs`. Only the code differing from the first example is highlighted:

```
static void Main(string[] args)
{
        string[] names = { "Alonso", "Zheng", "Smith", "Jones", "Smythe",
"Small", "Ruiz", "Hsieh", "Jorgenson", "Ilyich", "Singh", "Samba", "Fatimah" };

        var queryResults =
            from n in names
            where n.StartsWith("S")
            orderby n
            select n;

        Console.WriteLine("Names beginning with S ordered alphabetically:");

        foreach (var item in queryResults) {
            Console.WriteLine(item);
        }

        Console.Write("Program finished, press Enter/Return to continue:");
        Console.ReadLine();
}
```

4. Compile and execute the program. You will see the names in the list beginning with S in alphabetical order, as shown here:

```
Names beginning with S:
Samba
Singh
Small
Smith
Smythe
Program finished, press Enter/Return to continue:
```

How It Works

This program is nearly identical to the previous example except for one additional line added to the query statement:

```
var queryResults =
            from n in names
            where n.StartsWith("S")
            orderby n
            select n;
```

orderby Clause

The `orderby` clause looks like this:

```
orderby n
```

Like the `where` clause, the `orderby` clause is optional. Just by adding one line you can order the results of any arbitrary query, which would otherwise require at least several lines of additional code and probably additional methods or collections to store the results of the reordered result depending on the sorting algorithm you chose to implement. If you had multiple types that needed to be sorted you would need to implement a set of ordering methods for each one. With LINQ you don't need to worry about any of that; just add one additional clause in the query statement and you're done.

By default, `orderby` orders in ascending order (A to Z), but you can specify descending order (from Z to A) simply by adding the `descending` keyword:

```
orderby n descending
```

This orders the example results as follows:

```
Smythe
Smith
Small
Singh
Samba
```

Plus, you can order by any arbitrary expression without having to rewrite the query; for example, to order by the last letter in the name instead of normal alphabetical order, you just change the `orderby` clause to the following:

```
orderby n.Substring(n.Length - 1)
```

This results in the following output:

```
Samba
Smythe
Smith
Singh
Small
```

Note that the last letters are in alphabetical order (a e h h l).

Ordering Using Method Syntax

To add capabilities such as ordering to a query using the method syntax, you simply add a method call for each LINQ operation you want to perform to your method-based LINQ query. Again, this is simpler than it sounds.

Try It Out   **Ordering Using Method Syntax**

Follow these steps to create the example in Visual Studio 2008:

1. You can either modify the 26-2-LINQMethodSyntax example or create a new console application project called 26-4-OrderMethodSyntax in the directory C:\BegVCSharp\Chapter26.

2. Add the following code to the `Main()` method in `Program.cs`. As in all the examples Visual C# 2008 automatically includes the reference to the `System.Linq` namespace.

3. Only the code differing from the previous method syntax example is highlighted:

```
static void Main(string[] args)
{
        string[] names = { "Alonso", "Zheng", "Smith", "Jones", "Smythe",
"Small", "Ruiz", "Hsieh", "Jorgenson", "Ilyich", "Singh", "Samba", "Fatimah" };

        var queryResults = names.OrderBy(n => n).Where(n => n.StartsWith("S"));

        Console.WriteLine("Names beginning with S:");

        foreach (var item in queryResults) {
            Console.WriteLine(item);
        }

        Console.Write("Program finished, press Enter/Return to continue:");
        Console.ReadLine();
}
```

4. Compile and execute the program. You will see the names in the list beginning with S in alphabetical order, as in the output from the previous example.

How It Works

This example is nearly identical to the previous method syntax example except for the addition of the call to the LINQ `OrderBy()` method preceding the call to the `Where()` method:

```
        var queryResults = names.OrderBy(n => n).Where(n => n.StartsWith("S"));
```

As you may have seen from the IntelliSense when you typed the code in, the `OrderBy()` method returns an `IOrderedEnumerable`, which is a superset of the `IEnumerable` interface, so you can call `Where()` on it just as you can with any other `IEnumerable`.

The compiler infers that you are working with `string` *data, so the data types appear in IntelliSense as* `IOrderedEnumerable<string>` *and* `IEnumerable<string>`.

You need to pass a lambda expression to `OrderBy()` to tell it which function to use for ordering. You pass the simplest possible lambda, `n => n`, because you do not need to order by anything other than the item itself. In the query syntax, you do not need to create this extra lambda expression.

To order the items in the reverse order, call the `OrderByDescending()` method:

```
var queryResults = names.OrderByDescending(n => n).Where(n => n.StartsWith("S"));
```

This produces the same results as the `orderby n descending` clause you used in the query syntax version.

To order by something other than the value of the item itself, you can change the lambda expression passed to `OrderBy()`. For example, to order by the last letter in each name, you would use the lambda `n => n.Substring(n.Length-1)` and pass it to `OrderBy` as shown here:

```
var queryResults =
        names.OrderBy(n => n.Substring(n.Length-1)).Where(n => n.StartsWith("S"));
```

This produces the same results ordered by the last letter in each name, as with the previous example.

Querying a Large Data Set

All this LINQ syntax is well and good, you may be saying, but what is the point? You can see the expected results clearly just by looking at the source array, so why go to all this trouble to query something that is obvious by just looking? As mentioned earlier, sometimes the results of a query are not so obvious. In the following Try It Out, you create a very large array of numbers and query it using LINQ.

Try It Out   Querying a Large Data Set

Follow these steps to create the example in Visual Studio 2008:

1. Create a new console application called 26-5-LargeNumberQuery in the directory
    C:\BegVCSharp\Chapter26. As before, when you create the project, Visual Studio 2008
    already includes the LINQ namespace method in `Program.cs`:

```
using System;
using System.Collections.Generic;
using System.Linq;
using System.Text;
```

2. Add the following code to the `Main()` method:

```
static void Main(string[] args)
{
        int[] numbers = generateLotsOfNumbers(12345678);

        var queryResults =
            from n in numbers
```

```
                    where n < 1000
                    select n
                  ;

        Console.WriteLine("Numbers less than 1000:");
        foreach (var item in queryResults)
        {
            Console.WriteLine(item);
        }
        Console.Write("Program finished, press Enter/Return to continue:");
        Console.ReadLine();
}
```

3. Add the following method to generate the list of random numbers:

```
        private static int[] generateLotsOfNumbers(int count)
        {
            Random generator = new Random(0);
            int[] result = new int[count];
            for (int i = 0; i < count; i++)
            {
                result[i] = generator.Next();
            }
            return result;
        }
```

4. Compile and execute the program. You will see a list of numbers less than 1000, as shown here:

```
Numbers less than 1000:
714
24
677
350
257
719
584
Program finished, press Enter/Return to continue:
```

How It Works

As before, the first step is to reference the `System.Linq` namespace, which is done automatically by Visual C# 2008 when you create the project:

```
using System.Linq;
```

The next step is to create some data, which is done in this example by creating and calling the `generateLotsOfNumbers()` method:

```
        int[] numbers = generateLotsOfNumbers(12345678);

        private static int[] generateLotsOfNumbers(int count)
        {
            Random generator = new Random(0);
```

```
                int[] result = new int[count];
                for (int i = 0; i < count; i++)
                {
                    result[i] = generator.Next();
                }
                return result;
        }
```

This is not a trivial set of data — there are 12 million numbers in the array! In one of the exercises at the end of the chapter, you will change the `size` parameter passed to the `generateLotsOfNumbers()` method to generate variously sized sets of random numbers and see how this affects the query results. As you will see when doing the exercises, the size shown here of 12,345,678 is just large enough to have some random numbers less than 1000 to have results to show for this first query.

The values should be randomly distributed over the range of a signed integer (from zero to more than two billion). By creating the random number generator with a seed of 0, you ensure that the same set of random numbers is created each time and is repeatable so you get the same query results as shown here, but what those query results are neither I nor you know until you try some queries. Luckily, LINQ makes those queries easy!

The query statement itself is similar to what you did with the names before, selecting some numbers that meet a condition (in this case, numbers less than 1000):

```
            var queryResults =
                from n in numbers
                where n < 1000
                select n
```

The `orderby` clause isn't needed this time and would add extra processing time (not noticeably for this query but more so as you vary the conditions in the next example).

You print out the results of the query with a `foreach` statement, just as in the previous example:

```
    Console.WriteLine("Numbers less than 1000:");

    foreach (var item in queryResults) {
            Console.WriteLine(item);
    }
```

Again, output to the console and read a character to pause the output:

```
    Console.Write("Program finished, press Enter/Return to continue:");
    Console.ReadLine();
```

The pause code is in all the following examples but isn't shown again because it is the same for each one.

It is very easy with LINQ to change the query conditions to explore different characteristics of the data set. However, depending on how many results the query returns, it may not make sense to print all the results each time. In the next section you'll look at how LINQ provides aggregate operators to deal with that issue.

Aggregate Operators

Often a query gives more results than you might expect. For example, if you were to change the condition of the large number query program you just created to list the numbers greater than 1000, rather than the numbers less than 1000, there would be so many query results that the numbers would not stop printing!

Luckily, LINQ provides a set of *aggregate operators* that enable you to analyze the results of a query without having to loop through all the results. The following aggregate operators are the most commonly used ones for a set of numeric results such as the results from the large-number query, and may be familiar to you if you have used a database query language such as SQL:

Operator	Description
Count()	Count of results
Min()	Minimum value in results
Max()	Maximum value in results
Average()	Average value of numeric results
Sum()	Total of all of numeric results

There are more aggregate operators, such as Aggregate(), to execute arbitrary code in a manner that enables you to code your own aggregate function. However, those are for advanced users and are beyond the scope of this book.

Because the aggregate operators return a simple scalar type instead of a sequence for their results, their use forces immediate execution of query results with no deferred execution.

In the following Try It Out, you modify the large-number query and use aggregate operators to explore the result set from the greater-than version of the large-number query using LINQ.

Try It Out   Numeric Aggregate Operators

Follow these steps to create the example in Visual Studio 2008:

1. For this example you can either modify the LargeNumberQuery example you just made or create a new console project named 26-6-NumericAggregates in the directory C:\BegVCSharp\Chapter26.

2. As before, when you create the project, Visual Studio 2008 includes the LINQ namespace method in Program.cs. You just need to modify the Main() method as shown in the following code and in the rest of this Try It Out. As with the previous example, the orderby clause is not used in this query. However, the condition on the where clause is the opposite of the previous example (the numbers are greater than one thousand (n > 1000), instead of less than one thousand).

```
        static void Main(string[] args)
        {
            int[] numbers = generateLotsOfNumbers(12345678);

            Console.WriteLine("Numeric Aggregates");

            var queryResults =
                from n in numbers
                where n > 1000
                select n
                ;

            Console.WriteLine("Count of Numbers > 1000");
            Console.WriteLine(queryResults.Count());

            Console.WriteLine("Max of Numbers > 1000");
            Console.WriteLine(queryResults.Max());

            Console.WriteLine("Min of Numbers > 1000");
            Console.WriteLine(queryResults.Min());

            Console.WriteLine("Average of Numbers > 1000");
            Console.WriteLine(queryResults.Average());

            Console.WriteLine("Sum of Numbers > 1000");
            Console.WriteLine(queryResults.Sum(n => (long) n));

            Console.Write("Program finished, press Enter/Return to continue:");
            Console.ReadLine();
        }
```

3. If it is not already present, add the same `generateLotsOfNumbers()` method used in the previous example:

```
        private static int[] generateLotsOfNumbers(int count)
        {
            Random generator = new Random(0);
            int[] result = new int[count];
            for (int i = 0; i < count; i++)
            {
                result[i] = generator.Next();
            }
            return result;
        }
```

4. Compile and execute. You will see the count, minimum, maximum, and average values as shown here:

```
Numeric Aggregates
Count of Numbers > 1000
12345671
Maximum of Numbers > 1000
2147483591
```

```
Minimum of Numbers > 1000
1034
Average of Numbers > 1000
1073643807.50298
Sum of Numbers > 1000
13254853218619179
Program finished, press Enter/Return to continue:
```

This query produces many more results than the previous example (more than 12 million). Using `orderby` on this result set would definitely have a noticeable impact on performance! The largest number (maximum) in the result set is over two billion and the smallest (minimum) is just over one thousand, as expected. The average is around one billion, near the middle of the range of possible values. Looks like the `Rand()` function generates a good distribution of numbers!

How It Works

The first part of the program is exactly the same as the previous example, with the reference to the `System.Linq` namespace, and the use of the `generateLotsOfNumbers()` method to generate the source data:

```
int[] numbers = generateLotsOfNumbers(12345678);
```

The query is the same as the previous example except for changing the `where` condition from less-than to greater-than:

```
var queryResults =
    from n in numbers
    where n > 1000
    select n;
```

As noted before, this query using the greater-than condition produces many more results than the less-than query (with this particular data set). By using the aggregate operators, you are able to explore the results of the query without having to print out each result or do a comparison in a `foreach` loop. Each one appears as a method that can be called on the result set, similar to methods on a collection type.

Let's look at the use of each aggregate operator:

❑   `Count()`:

```
Console.WriteLine("Count of Numbers > 1000");
Console.WriteLine(queryResults.Count());
```

`Count()` returns the number of rows in the query results — in this case, 12,345,671 rows.

❑   `Max()`:

```
Console.WriteLine("Max of Numbers > 1000");
Console.WriteLine(queryResults.Max());
```

`Max()` returns the maximum value in the query results — in this case, a number larger than 2 billion: 2,147,483,591, which is very close to the maximum value of an `int` (int.MaxValue or 2,147,483,647).

❑   Min():

```
            Console.WriteLine("Min of Numbers > 1000");
            Console.WriteLine(queryResults.Min());
```

Min() returns the maximum value in the query results — in this case, 1034.

❑   Average():

```
            Console.WriteLine("Average of Numbers > 1000");
            Console.WriteLine(queryResults.Average());
```

Average() returns the average value of the query results, which in this case is 1073643807.50298, a value very close to the middle of the range of possible values from 1000 to over 2 billion. This is rather meaningless with an arbitrary set of large numbers, but it shows the kind of analysis of the query results that is possible. We'll look at a more practical use of these operators with some business-oriented data in the last part of the chapter.

❑   Sum():

```
            Console.WriteLine("Sum of Numbers > 1000");
            Console.WriteLine(queryResults.Sum(n => (long) n));
```

Note that you passed the lambda expression n => (long) n to the Sum() method call in order to get the sum of all the numbers. While Sum() has a no-parameter overload, like Count(), Min(), Max(), and so on, using that version of the method call would cause an overflow error because there are so many large numbers in the data set that the sum of all of them would be too large to fit into a standard 32-bit int, which is what the no-parameter version of Sum() returns. The lambda expression enables you to convert the result of Sum() to a long 64-bit integer, which is what you need to hold the total of over 13 quadrillion without overflow: 13,254,853,218,619,179 lambda expressions enable you to perform this kind of fixup easily.

In addition to Count(), *which returns a 32-bit* int, *LINQ also provides a* LongCount() *method that returns the count of query results in a 64-bit integer. That is a special case, however — all the other operators require a lambda or a call to a conversion method if a 64-bit version of the number is needed.*

Querying Complex Objects

The previous examples show how LINQ queries can work with lists of simple types such as numbers and strings. Now you will look at how to use LINQ queries with more complex objects. You'll create a simple Customer class with just enough information to create some interesting queries.

Try It Out   Querying Complex Objects

Follow these steps to create the example in Visual C# 2008:

1.   Create a new console application called 26-7-QueryComplexObjects in the directory
C:\BegVCSharp\Chapter26.

2.   Before the start of the `Program` class in `Program.cs`, add the following short class definition
for the `Customer` class:

```csharp
class Customer
{
    public string ID { get; set; }
    public string City { get; set; }
    public string Country { get; set; }
    public string Region { get; set; }
    public decimal Sales { get; set; }

    public override string ToString()
    {
        return "ID: " + ID + " City: " + City + " Country: " + Country +
               " Region: " + Region + " Sales: " + Sales;
    }
}
```

3.   Add the following code to the `Main()` method of the `Program` class of `Program.cs`:

```csharp
static void Main(string[] args)
{
    List <Customer> customers = new List<Customer> {
        new Customer { ID="A", City="New York", Country="USA",
                                    Region="North America", Sales=9999},
        new Customer { ID="B", City="Mumbai", Country="India",
                                    Region="Asia", Sales=8888 },
        new Customer { ID="C", City="Karachi", Country="Pakistan",
                                    Region="Asia", Sales=7777 },
        new Customer { ID="D", City="Delhi", Country="India",
                                    Region="Asia", Sales=6666 },
        new Customer { ID="E", City="São Paulo", Country="Brazil",
                                    Region="South America", Sales=5555 },
        new Customer { ID="F", City="Moscow", Country="Russia",
                                    Region="Europe", Sales=4444 },
        new Customer { ID="G", City="Seoul", Country="Korea", Region="Asia",
                                    Sales=3333 },
        new Customer { ID="H", City="Istanbul", Country="Turkey",
                                    Region="Asia", Sales=2222 },
        new Customer { ID="I", City="Shanghai", Country="China", Region="Asia",
                                    Sales=1111 },
        new Customer { ID="J", City="Lagos", Country="Nigeria",
                                    Region="Africa", Sales=1000 },
        new Customer { ID="K", City="Mexico City", Country="Mexico",
                                    Region="North America", Sales=2000 },
        new Customer { ID="L", City="Jakarta", Country="Indonesia",
```

```
                                        Region="Asia", Sales=3000 },
            new Customer { ID="M", City="Tokyo", Country="Japan",
                                        Region="Asia", Sales=4000 },
            new Customer { ID="N", City="Los Angeles", Country="USA",
                                        Region="North America", Sales=5000 },
            new Customer { ID="O", City="Cairo", Country="Egypt",
                                        Region="Africa", Sales=6000 },
            new Customer { ID="P", City="Tehran", Country="Iran",
                                        Region="Asia", Sales=7000 },
            new Customer { ID="Q", City="London", Country="UK",
                                        Region="Europe", Sales=8000 },
            new Customer { ID="R", City="Beijing", Country="China",
                                        Region="Asia", Sales=9000 },
            new Customer { ID="S", City="Bogotá", Country="Colombia",
                                        Region="South America", Sales=1001 },
            new Customer { ID="T", City="Lima", Country="Peru",
                                        Region="South America", Sales=2002 }
        };
        var queryResults =
            from c in customers
            where c.Region == "Asia"
            select c
            ;
        Console.WriteLine("Customers in Asia:");
        foreach (Customer c in queryResults)
        {
            Console.WriteLine(c);
        }
        Console.Write("Program finished, press Enter/Return to continue:");
        Console.ReadLine();
    }
}
```

4. Compile and execute the program. The result is a list of the customers from Asia:

```
Customers in Asia:
ID: B City: Mumbai Country: India Region: Asia Sales: 8888
ID: C City: Karachi Country: Pakistan Region: Asia Sales: 7777
ID: D City: Delhi Country: India Region: Asia Sales: 6666
ID: G City: Seoul Country: Korea Region: Asia Sales: 3333
ID: H City: Istanbul Country: Turkey Region: Asia Sales: 2222
ID: I City: Shanghai Country: China Region: Asia Sales: 1111
ID: L City: Jakarta Country: Indonesia Region: Asia Sales: 3000
ID: M City: Tokyo Country: Japan Region: Asia Sales: 4000
ID: P City: Tehran Country: Iran Region: Asia Sales: 7000
ID: R City: Beijing Country: China Region: Asia Sales: 9000
Program finished, press Enter/Return to continue:
```

How It Works

In the `Customer` class definition you use the C# 3.0 automatic properties feature to declare public properties (`ID`, `City`, `Country`, `Region`, `Sales`) for the `Customer` class without having to explicitly code private instance variables and get/set code for each property:

```
class Customer
{
      public string ID { get; set; }
      public string City { get; set; }
      . . .
```

The only extra method you bother to code for the `Customer` class is an override for the `ToString()` method to provide a string representation for a `Customer` instance:

```
public override string ToString()
{
      return "ID: " + ID + " City: " + City + " Country: " + Country +
            " Region: " + Region + " Sales: " + Sales;
}
```

You will use this `ToString()` method to simplify printing out the results of the query, which is shown a bit later in the How It Works section.

In the `Main()` method of the `Program` class, you create a strongly typed collection of type `Customer` using the C# 3.0 collection/object initialization syntax, to avoid having to code a constructor method and call the constructor to make each list member:

```
List <Customer> customers = new List<Customer> {
      new Customer { ID="A", City="New York", Country="USA",
                                       Region="North America", Sales=9999},
      new Customer { ID="B", City="Mumbai", Country="India",
                                       Region="Asia", Sales=8888 },
      . . .
```

Your customers are located all over the world, with enough geographical information in your data to make interesting selection criteria and groups for queries.

Still in the `Main()` method, you create the query statement — in this case, selecting the customers from Asia:

```
var queryResults =
      from c in customers
      where c.Region == "Asia"
      select c
   ;
```

This query should be very familiar to you by now — it's the same from ... where ... select LINQ query you have used in the other examples, except that each item in the result list is a full-fledged object (a `Customer`), rather than a simple `string` or `int`. Next, you print out the results in a `foreach` loop:

```
Console.WriteLine("Customers in Asia:");
foreach (Customer c in queryResults)
{
      Console.WriteLine(c);
}
```

871

This `foreach` loop is a little different from the ones in previous examples. Because you know you are querying `Customer` objects, you explicitly declare the iteration variable `c` as type `Customer`:

```
foreach (Customer c in queryResults)
```

You could have declared `c` with the variable keyword `var` and the compiler would have inferred that the iteration variable should be of type `Customer`, but explicitly declaring it makes the code clearer to a human reader.

Within the loop itself you simply write

```
{
    Console.WriteLine(c);
}
```

instead of explicitly printing out the fields of `Customer` because you added an override to the `Customer` class for the `ToString()` method. If you had not provided a `ToString()` override, then the default `ToString()` method would have simply printed the name of the type, like this:

```
Customers in Asia:
BegVCSharp_26_7_QueryComplexObjects.Customer
BegVCSharp_26_7_QueryComplexObjects.Customer
BegVCSharp_26_7_QueryComplexObjects.Customer
BegVCSharp_26_7_QueryComplexObjects.Customer
BegVCSharp_26_7_QueryComplexObjects.Customer
BegVCSharp_26_7_QueryComplexObjects.Customer
BegVCSharp_26_7_QueryComplexObjects.Customer
BegVCSharp_26_7_QueryComplexObjects.Customer
BegVCSharp_26_7_QueryComplexObjects.Customer
BegVCSharp_26_7_QueryComplexObjects.Customer
Program finished, press Enter/Return to continue:
```

Not what you want at all! Of course, you could always explicitly print the properties of `Customer` that you are interested in:

```
Console.WriteLine("Customer {0}: {1}, {2}", c.ID, c.City, c.Country);
```

However, if you are only interested in a few properties of an object, it is inefficient to pull the entire object into the query. Luckily, LINQ makes it simple to create query results that contain only the items you need — via *projection,* which you will experiment with in the next section.

Projection: Creating New Objects in Queries

Projection is the technical term for creating a new data type from other data types in a LINQ query. The `select` keyword is the projection operator, which you have used in previous examples. If you are familiar with the SELECT keyword in the SQL data query language, you will be familiar with the operation of selecting a specific field from a data object, as opposed to selecting the entire object itself. In LINQ you can do this as well; for example, to select only the `City` field from the `Customer` list in the previous example, simply change the `select` clause in the query statement to reference only the `City` property:

```
var queryResults =
    from c in customers
    where c.Region == "Asia"
    select c.City
    ;
```

That produces the following output:

```
Mumbai
Karachi
Delhi
Seoul
Istanbul
Shanghai
Jakarta
Tokyo
Tehran
Beijing
```

You can even transform the data in the query by adding an expression to the `select`, as shown here

```
select n + 1
```

for a numeric data type, or

```
select s.ToUpper()
```

for a string data type query. However, unlike in SQL, LINQ does not allow multiple fields in a `select` clause. That means the line

```
select c.City, c.Country, c.Sales
```

produces a compile error (semicolon expected) because the `select` clause takes only one item in its parameter list.

What you do in LINQ instead is create a new object on-the-fly in the `select` clause to hold the results you want for your query. You'll do this in the following Try It Out.

Try It Out   Projection: Creating New Objects in Queries

Follow these steps to create the example in Visual Studio 2008:

1. Modify 26-7-QueryComplexObjects or create a new console application called 26-8-ProjectionCreateNewObjects in the directory C:\BegVCSharp\Chapter26.

2. If you chose to create a new project, copy the code to create the `Customer` class and the initialization of the customers list (`List<Customer> customers`) from the 26-7-QueryComplexObjects example; this code is exactly the same as the code previously shown.

3. In the `Main()` method following the initialization of the `customers` list, enter (or modify) the query and results processing loop as shown here:

```
var queryResults =
    from c in customers
    where c.Region == "North America"
    select new { c.City, c.Country, c.Sales }
    ;
foreach (var item in queryResults)
{
    Console.WriteLine(item);
}
```

4. The remaining code in the `Main()` method is the same as it was in previous examples.

5. Compile and execute the program. You will see the selected fields from the customers in North America listed, like this:

```
{ City = New York, Country = USA, Sales = 9999 }
{ City = Mexico City, Country = Mexico, Sales = 2000 }
{ City = Los Angeles, Country = USA, Sales = 5000 }
Program finished, press Enter/Return to continue:
```

How It Works

The `Customer` class and `customers` list initialization are the same as in the previous example. In the query, you changed the requested region to North America just to mix things up a bit. The interesting change in terms of projection is the parameter to the `select` clause:

```
select new { c.City, c.Country, c.Sales }
```

You use the C# 3.0 anonymous type creation syntax directly in the `select` clause to create a new unnamed object type having the `City`, `Country`, and `Sales` properties. The `select` clause creates the new object. This way, only these three properties are duplicated and carried through the different stages of processing the query.

When you print out the query results, you use the same generic `foreach` loop code that you have used in all the previous examples except for the `Customers` query:

```
foreach (var item in queryResults)
{
    Console.WriteLine(item);
}
```

This code is entirely generic; the compiler infers the type of the query result and calls the right methods for the anonymous type without you having to code anything explicitly. You did not even have to provide a `ToString()` override, as the compiler provided a default `ToString()` implementation that prints out the property names and values in a manner similar to the object initialization itself.

Projection: Method Syntax

The method syntax version of a projection query is accomplished by chaining a call to the LINQ `Select()` method along with the other LINQ methods you are calling. For example, you can get the same query result if you add the `Select()` method call to a `Where()` method call, as shown here:

```
var queryResults = customers.Where(c => c.Region == "North America")
                            .Select(c => new { c.City, c.Country, c.Sales });
```

While the `select` clause is required in the query syntax, you haven't seen the `Select()` method before because it isn't needed in the LINQ method syntax unless you are actually doing a projection (changing the type in the result set from the original type being queried).

The order of the method calls is not fixed because the return types from the LINQ methods all implement `IEnumerable` — you can call `Select()` on a `Where()` result or vice versa. However, the order may be important depending on the specifics of your query. For example, you could not reverse the order of `Select()` and `Where()` like this:

```
var queryResults = customers.Select(c => new { c.City, c.Country, c.Sales })
                            .Where(c => c.Region == "North America");
```

The `Region` property is not included in the anonymous type `{c.City, c.Country, c.Sales }` created by the `Select()` projection, so your program would get a compile error on the `Where()` method, indicating that the anonymous type does not contain a definition for `Region`.

However, if the `Where()` method were restricting the data based on a field included in the anonymous type, such as `City`, there would be no problem — for example, the following query compiles and executes with no problem:

```
var queryResults = customers.Select(c => new {c.City, c.Country, c.Sales })
                            .Where(c => c.City == "New York");
```

Select Distinct Query

Another type of query that those of you familiar with the SQL data query language will recognize is the `SELECT DISTINCT` query, in which you search for the unique values in your data — that is, values that are not repeated. This is a fairly common need when working with queries.

Suppose you need to find the distinct regions in the customer data used in the previous examples. There is no separate region list in the data you just used, so you need to find the unique, non-repeating list of regions from the customer list itself. LINQ provides a `Distinct()` method that makes it easy to find this data. You'll use it in the following Try It Out.

Projection: Select Distinct Query

Follow these steps to create the example in Visual Studio 2008:

1. Modify the previous example, 26-8-ProjectionCreateNewObjects, or create a new console application called 26-9-SelectDistinctQuery in the directory C:\BegVCSharp\Chapter26.

2. Copy the code to create the `Customer` class and the initialization of the `customers` list (`List<Customer> customers`) from the 26-7-QueryComplexObjects example; the code is the same.

3. In the `Main()` method following the initialization of the `customers` list, enter (or modify) the query as shown here:

```
var queryResults = customers.Select(c => c.Region).Distinct();
```

4. The remaining code in the `Main()` method is the same as in the previous example.

5. Compile and execute the program. You will see the unique regions where customers exist:

```
North America
Asia
South America
Europe
Africa
Program finished, press Enter/Return to continue:
```

How It Works

The `Customer` class and `customers` list initialization are the same as in the previous example. In the query statement, you call the `Select()` method with a simple lambda expression to select the region from the `Customer` objects, and then call `Distinct()` to return only the unique results from `Select()`:

```
var queryResults = customers.Select(c => c.Region).Distinct();
```

Because `Distinct()` is only available in method syntax, you make the call to `Select()` using method syntax. However, you can call `Distinct()` to modify a query made in the query syntax as well:

```
var queryResults = (from c in customers select c.Region).Distinct();
```

Because query syntax is translated by the C# 3.0 compiler into the same series of LINQ method calls as used in the method syntax, you can mix and match if it makes sense for readability and style.

Any and All

Another type of query that you often need is determining whether any of your data satisfies a certain condition, or ensuring that all data satisfies a condition. For example, you may need to know whether a product is out of stock (quantity is zero), or whether a transaction happens.

LINQ provides two Boolean methods — `Any()` and `All()` — that can quickly tell you whether a condition is `true` or `false` for your data. That makes it easy to find the data, which you will do in the following Try It Out.

Try It Out   Using Any and All

Follow these steps to create the example in Visual Studio 2008:

1. Modify the previous example, 26-9-SelectDistinctQuery, or create a new console application called 26-10-AnyAndAll in the directory C:\BegVCSharp\Chapter26.

2. Copy the code to create the `Customer` class and the initialization of the `customers` list (`List<Customer> customers`) from the 26-7-QueryComplexObjects example; this code is the same.

3. In the `Main()` method following the initialization of the `customers` list and query declaration, remove the processing loop and enter the code as shown here:

```
bool anyUSA = customers.Any(c => c.Country == "USA");
if (anyUSA)
{
    Console.WriteLine("Some customers are in the USA");
}
else
{
    Console.WriteLine("No customers are in the USA");
}

bool allAsia = customers.All(c => c.Region == "Asia");
if (allAsia)
{
    Console.WriteLine("All customers are in Asia");
}
else
{
    Console.WriteLine("Not all customers are in Asia");
}
```

4. The remaining code in the `Main()` method is the same as in the previous example.

5. Compile and execute the program. You will see the messages indicating that some customers are in the U.S.A. but not all customers are in Asia:

```
Some customers are in the USA
Not all customers are in Asia
Program finished, press Enter/Return to continue:
```

How It Works

The Customer class and customers list initialization are the same as in previous examples. In the first query statement, you call the Any() method with a simple lambda expression to check whether the Customer Country field has the value USA:

```
bool anyUSA = customers.Any(c => c.Country == "USA");
```

The LINQ Any() method applies the lambda expression you pass to it — c => c.Country == "USA" — against all the data in the customers list, and returns true if the lambda expression is true for any of the customers in the list.

Next, you check the Boolean result variable returned by the Any() method and print out a message indicating the result of the query (even though the Any() method is simply returning true or false, it is performing a query to obtain the true/false result):

```
if (anyUSA)
{
    Console.WriteLine("Some customers are in the USA");
}
else
{
    Console.WriteLine("No customers are in the USA");
}
```

While you could make this message more compact with some clever code, it is more straightforward and readable as shown here. As you would expect, the anyUSA variable is set to true because there are indeed customers located in the U.S.A. in the data set, so you see the message "Some customers are in the USA".

In the next query statement you call the All() method with another simple lambda expression to determine whether all the customers are located in Asia:

```
bool allAsia = customers.All(c => c.Region == "Asia");
```

The LINQ All() method applies the lambda expression against the data set and returns false as you would expect because some customers are outside of Asia. You then print the appropriate message based on the value of allAsia.

Ordering By Multiple Levels

Now that you are dealing with objects with multiple properties you might be able to envision a situation where ordering the query results by a single field is not enough. What if you wanted to query your customers and order the results alphabetically by region, but then order alphabetically by country or city name within a region? LINQ makes this very easy, as you will see in the following Try It Out.

Try It Out   **Ordering By Multiple Levels**

Follow these steps to create the example in Visual Studio 2008:

1. Modify the previous example, 26-8-ProjectionCreateNewObjects, or create a new console application called 26-11-MultiLevelOrdering in the directory C:\BegVCSharp\Chapter26.

2. Create the Customer class and the initialization of the customers list (List<Customer> customers) as shown in the 26-7-QueryComplexObjects example; this code is exactly the same as in previous examples.

3. In the Main() method following the initialization of the customers list, enter the following query:

```
var queryResults =
    from c in customers
    orderby c.Region, c.Country, c.City
    select new { c.ID, c.Region, c.Country, c.City }
    ;
```

4. The results processing loop and the remaining code in the Main() method are the same as in previous examples.

5. Compile and execute the program. You will see the selected properties from all customers ordered alphabetically by region first, then by country, and then by city, as shown here:

```
{ ID = O, Region = Africa, Country = Egypt, City = Cairo }
{ ID = J, Region = Africa, Country = Nigeria, City = Lagos }
{ ID = R, Region = Asia, Country = China, City = Beijing }
{ ID = I, Region = Asia, Country = China, City = Shanghai }
{ ID = D, Region = Asia, Country = India, City = Delhi }
{ ID = B, Region = Asia, Country = India, City = Mumbai }
{ ID = L, Region = Asia, Country = Indonesia, City = Jakarta }
{ ID = P, Region = Asia, Country = Iran, City = Tehran }
{ ID = M, Region = Asia, Country = Japan, City = Tokyo }
{ ID = G, Region = Asia, Country = Korea, City = Seoul }
{ ID = C, Region = Asia, Country = Pakistan, City = Karachi }
{ ID = H, Region = Asia, Country = Turkey, City = Istanbul }
{ ID = F, Region = Europe, Country = Russia, City = Moscow }
{ ID = Q, Region = Europe, Country = UK, City = London }
{ ID = K, Region = North America, Country = Mexico, City = Mexico City }
```

```
{ ID = N, Region = North America, Country = USA, City = Los Angeles }
{ ID = A, Region = North America, Country = USA, City = New York }
{ ID = E, Region = South America, Country = Brazil, City = Sao Paulo }
{ ID = S, Region = South America, Country = Colombia, City = Bogotá }
{ ID = T, Region = South America, Country = Peru, City = Lima }
Program finished, press Enter/Return to continue:
```

How It Works

The Customer class and customers list initialization are the same as in previous examples. In this query you have no where clause because you want to see all the customers, but you simply list the fields you want to sort by in order in a comma-separated list in the orderby clause:

```
orderby c.Region, c.Country, c.City
```

Couldn't be easier, could it? It seems a bit counterintuitive that a simple list of fields is allowed in the orderby clause but not in the select clause, but that is how LINQ works. It makes sense if you realize that the select clause is creating a new object but the orderby clause, by definition, operates on a field-by-field basis.

You can add the descending keyword to any of the fields listed to reverse the sort order for that field. For example, to order this query by ascending region but descending country, simply add descending following Country in the list, like this:

```
orderby c.Region, c.Country descending, c.City
```

With descending added, you see following output:

```
{ ID = J, Region = Africa, Country = Nigeria, City = Lagos }
{ ID = O, Region = Africa, Country = Egypt, City = Cairo }
{ ID = H, Region = Asia, Country = Turkey, City = Istanbul }
{ ID = C, Region = Asia, Country = Pakistan, City = Karachi }
{ ID = G, Region = Asia, Country = Korea, City = Seoul }
{ ID = M, Region = Asia, Country = Japan, City = Tokyo }
{ ID = P, Region = Asia, Country = Iran, City = Tehran }
{ ID = L, Region = Asia, Country = Indonesia, City = Jakarta }
{ ID = D, Region = Asia, Country = India, City = Delhi }
{ ID = B, Region = Asia, Country = India, City = Mumbai }
{ ID = R, Region = Asia, Country = China, City = Beijing }
{ ID = I, Region = Asia, Country = China, City = Shanghai }
{ ID = Q, Region = Europe, Country = UK, City = London }
{ ID = F, Region = Europe, Country = Russia, City = Moscow }
{ ID = N, Region = North America, Country = USA, City = Los Angeles }
{ ID = A, Region = North America, Country = USA, City = New York }
{ ID = K, Region = North America, Country = Mexico, City = Mexico City }
{ ID = T, Region = South America, Country = Peru, City = Lima }
{ ID = S, Region = South America, Country = Colombia, City = Bogotá }
{ ID = E, Region = South America, Country = Brazil, City = Sao Paulo }
Program finished, press Enter/Return to continue:
```

Note that the cities in India and China are still in ascending order even though the country ordering has been reversed.

Multi-Level Ordering Method Syntax: ThenBy

Under the covers, things get a bit more complicated when you look at multi-level ordering using the method syntax, which uses the `ThenBy()` method as well as `OrderBy()`.

For instance, you get the same query result as the example you just created with the following:

```
var queryResults = customers.OrderBy(c => c.Region)
                            .ThenBy(c => c.Country)
                            .ThenBy(c => c.City)
                            .Select(c => new { c.ID, c.Region, c.Country, c.City });
```

Now it is more apparent why a multi-field list is allowed in the `orderby` clause in the query syntax; you can see it is translated into a series of `ThenBy()` method invocations on a field-by-field basis. The order is important in writing these method calls: you must begin with `OrderBy()` because the `ThenBy()` method is only available on an `IOrderedEnumerable` interface, which is produced by `OrderBy()`. However, the `ThenBy()` method can be chained to other `ThenBy()` method calls as many times as necessary. This is a clear case where the query syntax is easier to write than the method syntax.

The descending sort order is specified by calling either `OrderByDescending()` if the first field is to be sorted in descending order or `ThenByDescending()` if any of the remaining fields are to be sorted in descending order. To sort the country in descending order as in this example, the method syntax query would be as follows:

```
var queryResults = customers.OrderBy(c => c.Region)
                            .ThenByDescending(c => c.Country)
                            .ThenBy(c => c.City)
                            .Select(c => new { c.ID, c.Region, c.Country, c.City });
```

Group Queries

A group query divides the data up into groups and enables you to sort, calculate aggregates, and compare by group. These are often the most interesting queries in a business context (the ones that really drive decision-making). For example, you may want to compare sales by country or by region to decide where to open another store or hire more staff. You'll do that in the next Try It Out.

Group Query

Follow these steps to create the example in Visual Studio 2008:

1.   Create a new console application called 26-12-GroupQuery in the directory
C:\BegVCSharp\Chapter26.

2.   Create the `Customer` class and the initialization of the `customers` list (`List<Customer>`
`customers`) as shown in the 26-7-QueryComplexObjects example; this code is exactly the
same as in previous examples.

3.   In the `Main()` method following the initialization of the `customers` list, enter two queries:

```
var queryResults =
    from c in customers
    group c by c.Region into cg
    select new { TotalSales = cg.Sum(c => c.Sales), Region = cg.Key }
    ;
var orderedResults =
    from cg in queryResults
    orderby cg.TotalSales descending
    select cg
  ;
```

4.   Continuing in the `Main()` method, add the following print statement and `foreach` processing
loop:

```
Console.WriteLine("Total\t: By\nSales\t: Region\n-----\t  ------");
foreach (var item in orderedResults)
{
    Console.WriteLine(item.TotalSales + "\t: " + item.Region);
}
```

5.   The results processing loop and the remaining code in the `Main()` method are the same as in
previous examples. Compile and execute the program. Here are the group results:

```
Total   : By
Sales   : Region
-----   ------
52997   : Asia
16999   : North America
12444   : Europe
8558    : South America
7000    : Africa
```

How It Works

The `Customer` class and `customers` list initialization are the same as in previous examples.

The data in a group query is grouped by a *key* field, the field for which all the members of each group
share a value. In this example the key field is the `Region`:

```
group c by c.Region
```

You want to calculate a total for each group, so you group `into` a new result set named `cg`:

```
group c by c.Region into cg
```

In the `select` clause you project a new anonymous type whose properties are the total sales (calculated by referencing the `cg` result set) and the key value of the group, which you reference with the special group `Key`:

```
select new { TotalSales = cg.Sum(c => c.Sales), Region = cg.Key }
```

The group result set implements the LINQ `IGrouping` interface, which supports the `Key` property. You almost always want to reference the `Key` property in some way in processing group results because it represents the criteria by which each group in your data was created.

You want to order the result in descending order by `TotalSales` field so you can see which region has the highest total sales, next highest, and so on. To do that, you create a second query to order the results from the group query:

```
var orderedResults =
    from cg in queryResults
    orderby cg.TotalSales descending
    select cg
;
```

The second query is a standard `select` query with an `orderby` clause, as you have seen in previous examples; it does not make use of any LINQ group capabilities except that the data source comes from the previous group query.

Next, you print out the results, with a little bit of formatting code to display the data with column headers and some separation between the totals and the group names:

```
Console.WriteLine("Total\t: By\nSales\t: Region\n-----\t  ------");
foreach (var item in orderedResults)
{
    Console.WriteLine(item.TotalSales + "\t: " + item.Region);
};
```

This could be formatted in a more sophisticated way with field widths and right-justifying the totals, but this is just an example so you don't need to bother — you can see the data clearly enough to understand what the code is doing.

Take and Skip

Suppose you need to find the top five customers by sales in your data set. You don't know ahead of time what amount of sales qualifies a customer to be in the top five so you can't use a `where` condition to find them.

Some SQL databases such as Microsoft SQL Server implement a TOP operator, so you can issue a command like SELECT TOP 5 FROM ... to get the top five customers.

The LINQ equivalent to this operation is the Take() method, which takes the first *n* results in the query output. In practical use this needs to be combined with orderby in order to get the top *n* results. However, the orderby is not required, as there may be situations where you the know the data is already in the order you want, or for some reason you want the first *n* results without caring about their order.

The inverse of Take() is Skip(), which skips the first *n* results, returning the remainder. Take() and Skip() are called *partitioning operators* in LINQ documentation because they partition the result set into the first *n* results (Take()) and/or its remainder (Skip()).

In the following Try It Out you use both Take() and Skip() with the customers list data.

Try It Out   Working with Take and Skip

Follow these steps to create the example in Visual Studio 2008:

1. Create a new console application called 26-13-TakeAndSkip in the directory C:\BegVCSharp\Chapter26.

2. Copy the code to create the Customer class and the initialization of the customers list (List<Customer> customers) from the 26-7-QueryComplexObjects example.

3. In the Main() method following the initialization of the customers list, enter this query:

```
//query syntax
var queryResults =
    from c in customers
    orderby c.Sales descending
    select new { c.ID, c.City, c.Country, c.Sales }
    ;
```

4. Enter two results processing loops, one using Take() and another using Skip():

```
Console.WriteLine("Top Five Customers by Sales");
foreach (var item in queryResults.Take(5))
{
    Console.WriteLine(item);
}

Console.WriteLine("Customers Not In Top Five");
foreach (var item in queryResults.Skip(5))
{
    Console.WriteLine(item);
}
```

5. Compile and execute the program. You will see the top five customers and the remaining customers listed as shown here:

```
Top Five Customers by Sales
{ ID = A, City = New York, Country = USA, Sales = 9999 }
{ ID = R, City = Beijing, Country = China, Sales = 9000 }
{ ID = B, City = Mumbai, Country = India, Sales = 8888 }
{ ID = Q, City = London, Country = UK, Sales = 8000 }
{ ID = C, City = Karachi, Country = Pakistan, Sales = 7777 }
Customers Not In Top Five
{ ID = P, City = Tehran, Country = Iran, Sales = 7000 }
{ ID = D, City = Delhi, Country = India, Sales = 6666 }
{ ID = O, City = Cairo, Country = Egypt, Sales = 6000 }
{ ID = E, City = Sao Paulo, Country = Brazil, Sales = 5555 }
{ ID = N, City = Los Angeles, Country = USA, Sales = 5000 }
{ ID = F, City = Moscow, Country = Russia, Sales = 4444 }
{ ID = M, City = Tokyo, Country = Japan, Sales = 4000 }
{ ID = G, City = Seoul, Country = Korea, Sales = 3333 }
{ ID = L, City = Jakarta, Country = Indonesia, Sales = 3000 }
{ ID = H, City = Istanbul, Country = Turkey, Sales = 2222 }
{ ID = T, City = Lima, Country = Peru, Sales = 2002 }
{ ID = K, City = Mexico City, Country = Mexico, Sales = 2000 }
{ ID = I, City = Shanghai, Country = China, Sales = 1111 }
{ ID = S, City = Bogotá, Country = Colombia, Sales = 1001 }
{ ID = J, City = Lagos, Country = Nigeria, Sales = 1000 }
Program finished, press Enter/Return to continue:
```

How It Works

The `Customer` class and `customers` list initialization are the same as in previous examples.

The main query consists of a `from...orderby...select` statement in the query syntax, like the ones you have created previously in this chapter, except that there is no `where` clause restriction because you want to get all of the customers (ordered by sales from highest to lowest):

```
var queryResults =
                from c in customers
                orderby c.Sales descending
                select new { c.ID, c.City, c.Country, c.Sales }
```

This example works a bit differently than previous examples in that you do not apply the operator until you actually execute the `foreach` loop on the query results because you want to reuse the query results. First you apply `Take(5)` to get the top five customers:

```
foreach (var item in queryResults.Take(5))
```

Then you apply `Skip(5)` to skip the first five items (what you already printed) and print the remaining customers from the same original set of query results:

```
foreach (var item in queryResults.Skip(5))
```

The code to print out the results and pause the screen is the same as in previous examples, except for minor changes to the messages, so it isn't repeated here.

First and FirstOrDefault

Suppose you need to find an example of a customer from Africa in your data set. You need the actual data itself, not a true/false value or the result set of all matching values.

LINQ provides this capability via the `First()` method, which returns the first element in a result set that matches the criteria given. If there isn't a customer from Africa, then LINQ also provides a method to handle that contingency without additional error handling code: `FirstOrDefault()`.

In the following Try It Out, you use both `First()` and `FirstOrDefault()` with the `customers` list data.

Try It Out   Using First and FirstOrDefault

Follow these steps to create the example in Visual Studio 2008:

1. Create a new console application called 26-14-FirstOrDefault in the directory C:\BegVCSharp\Chapter26.

2. Copy the code to create the `Customer` class and the initialization of the `customers` list (`List<Customer> customers`) from the 26-7-QueryComplexObjects example.

3. In the `Main()` method following the initialization of the `customers` list, enter this query:

```
var queryResults = from c in customers
                   select new { c.City, c.Country, c.Region }
                   ;
```

4. Enter the following queries using `First()` and `FirstOrDefault()`:

```
Console.WriteLine("A customer in Africa");
Console.WriteLine(queryResults.First(c => c.Region == "Africa"));

Console.WriteLine("A customer in Antarctica");
Console.WriteLine(queryResults.FirstOrDefault(c => c.Region == "Antarctica"));
```

5. Compile and execute the program. Here's the resulting output:

```
A customer in Africa
{ City = Lagos, Country = Nigeria, Region = Africa }
A customer in Antarctica

Program finished, press Enter/Return to continue:
```

How It Works

The `Customer` class and `customers` list initialization are the same as in previous examples.

The main query consists of a `from...orderby...select` statement in the query syntax, like the ones you have created previously in this chapter, with no `where` or `orderby` clauses. You project the fields of interest with the `select` statement — in this case, the `City`, `Country`, and `Region` properties:

```
var queryResults = from c in customers
            select new { c.City, c.Country, c.Region }
        ;
```

Because the `First()` operator returns a single object value, not a result set, you do not need to create a `foreach` loop; instead, you print out the result directly:

```
Console.WriteLine(queryResults.First(c => c.Region == "Africa"));
```

This finds a customer and the result `City = Lagos, Country = Nigeria, Region = Africa` is printed out. Next, you query for the Antarctica region using `FirstOrDefault()`:

```
Console.WriteLine(queryResults.FirstOrDefault(c => c.Region == "Antarctica"));
```

This does not find any results so a null (empty result) is returned and the output is blank. What would have happened if you had used the `First()` operator instead of `FirstOrDefault()` for the Antarctica query? You would have received the following exception:

```
System.InvalidOperationException: Sequence contains no matching element
```

Instead of `FirstOrDefault()`, it returns the default element for the list if the search criteria are not met, which is a `null` for this anonymous type. For the Antarctica query, you would have received the exception.

The code to print out the results and pause the screen is the same as in previous examples, except for minor changes to the messages.

Set Operators

LINQ provides standard set operators such as `Union()` and `Intersect()` that operate on query results. You used one of the set operators when you wrote the `Distinct()` query earlier.

In the following Try It Out you add a simple list of orders that have been submitted by hypothetical customers and use the standard set operators to match the orders up with the existing customers.

Set Operators

Follow these steps to create the example in Visual Studio 2008:

1. Create a new console application called 26-15-SetOperators in the directory
   C:\BegVCSharp\Chapter26.

2. Copy the code to create the Customer class and the initialization of the customers list
   (List<Customer> customers) from the 26-7-QueryComplexObjects example.

3. Following the Customer class, add the following Order class:

```
class Order
{
    public string ID { get; set; }
    public decimal Amount { get; set; }
}
```

4. In the Main() method following the initialization of the customers list, create and initialize
   an orders list with the data shown here:

```
List<Order> orders = new List<Order> {
    new Order { ID="P", Amount=100 },
    new Order { ID="Q", Amount=200 },
    new Order { ID="R", Amount=300 },
    new Order { ID="S", Amount=400 },
    new Order { ID="T", Amount=500 },
    new Order { ID="U", Amount=600 },
    new Order { ID="V", Amount=700 },
    new Order { ID="W", Amount=800 },
    new Order { ID="X", Amount=900 },
    new Order { ID="Y", Amount=1000 },
    new Order { ID="Z", Amount=1100 }
};
```

5. Following the initialization of the orders list, enter these queries:

```
var customerIDs =
    from c in customers
    select c.ID
    ;
var orderIDs =
    from o in orders
    select o.ID
    ;
```

6. Enter the following query using `Intersect()`:

```
var customersWithOrders = customerIDs.Intersect(orderIDs);
Console.WriteLine("Customer IDs with Orders:");
foreach (var item in customersWithOrders)
{
    Console.Write("{0} ", item);
}
Console.WriteLine();
```

7. Next, enter the following query using `Except()`:

```
Console.WriteLine("Order IDs with no customers:");
var ordersNoCustomers = orderIDs.Except(customerIDs);
foreach (var item in ordersNoCustomers)
{
    Console.Write("{0} ", item);
}
Console.WriteLine();
```

8. Finally, enter the following query using `Union()`:

```
Console.WriteLine("All Customer and Order IDs:");
var allCustomerOrderIDs = orderIDs.Union(customerIDs);
foreach (var item in allCustomerOrderIDs)
{
    Console.Write("{0} ", item);
}
Console.WriteLine();
```

9. Compile and execute the program. Here's the output:

```
Customers IDs with Orders:
P Q R S T
Order IDs with no customers:
U V W X Y Z
All Customer and Order IDs:
P Q R S T U V W X Y Z A B C D E F G H I J K L M N O
Program finished, press Enter/Return to continue:
```

How It Works

The `Customer` class and `customers` list initialization are the same as previous examples. The new `Order` class is similar to the `Customer` class, using the C# 3.0 automatic properties feature to declare public properties (`ID`, `Amount`):

```
class Order
{
    public string ID { get; set; }
    public decimal Amount { get; set; }
}
```

Like the `Customer` class, this is a simplified example with just enough data to make the query work.

You use two simple `from...select` queries to get the ID fields from the `Customer` and `Order` classes, respectively:

```
var customerIDs =
    from c in customers
    select c.ID
    ;
var orderIDs =
    from o in orders
    select o.ID
    ;
```

Next, you use the `Intersect()` set operator to find only the customer IDs that also have orders in the `orderIDs` result. Only the IDs that appear in both result sets are included in the intersect set:

```
var customersWithOrders = customerIDs.Intersect(orderIDs);
```

The set operators require the set members to have the same type in order to ensure the expected results. Here you take advantage of the fact that the IDs in both object types are strings and have the same semantics (like foreign keys in a database).

The printout of the result set takes advantage of the fact that the IDs are only a single character, so you use `Console.Write()` with no `WriteLine()` call until the end of the `foreach` loop to make the output compact and neat:

```
Console.WriteLine("Customer IDs with Orders:");
foreach (var item in customersWithOrders)
{
    Console.Write("{0} ", item);
}
Console.WriteLine();
```

You use this same print logic in the remaining `foreach` loops.

Next, you use the `Except()` operator to find the order IDs that have no matching customer:

```
Console.WriteLine("Order IDs with no customers:");
var ordersNoCustomers = orderIDs.Except(customerIDs);
```

Finally, you use the `Union()` operator to find the union of all the customer ID and order ID fields:

```
Console.WriteLine("All Customer and Order IDs:");
var allCustomerOrderIDs = orderIDs.Union(customerIDs);
```

Note that the IDs are output in the same order as they appear in the customer and order lists, with duplicates removed.

The code to pause the screen is the same as in previous examples.

The set operators are useful but the practical benefit of using them is limited by the requirement that all the objects being manipulated have the same type. The operators are useful in certain narrow situations where you need to manipulate sets of similarly typed results, but in the more typical case where you need to work with different related object types, you need a more practical mechanism designed to work with different object types, such as the `join` statement.

Joins

A data set such as the `customers` and `orders` list you just created with a shared key field (ID) enables a `join` query, whereby you can query related data in both lists with a single query, joining the results together with the key field. This is similar to the `JOIN` operation in the SQL data query language; and as you might expect, LINQ provides a `join` command in the query syntax, which you will use in the following Try It Out.

Try It Out   **Join Query**

Follow these steps to create the example in Visual Studio 2008:

1. Create a new console application called 26-16-JoinQuery in the directory
    C:\BegVCSharp\Chapter26.

2. Copy the code to create the `Customer` class, the `Order` class, and the initialization of the
    `customers` list (`List<Customer> customers`) and `orders` list (`List<Order> orders`)
    from the previous example; this code is the same.

3. In the `Main()` method following the initialization of the `customers` and `orders` list, enter this
    query:

```
var queryResults =
    from c in customers
    join o in orders on c.ID equals o.ID
    select new { c.ID, c.City, SalesBefore = c.Sales, NewOrder = o.Amount,
                            SalesAfter = c.Sales+o.Amount };
```

4. Finish the program using the standard `foreach` query processing loop you used in earlier
    examples:

```
foreach (var item in queryResults)
{
    Console.WriteLine(item);
}
```

5. Compile and execute the program. Here's the output:

```
{ ID = P, City = Tehran, SalesBefore = 7000, NewOrder = 100, SalesAfter = 7100 }
{ ID = Q, City = London, SalesBefore = 8000, NewOrder = 200, SalesAfter = 8200 }
{ ID = R, City = Beijing, SalesBefore = 9000, NewOrder = 300, SalesAfter = 9300 }
{ ID = S, City = Bogotá, SalesBefore = 1001, NewOrder = 400, SalesAfter = 1401 }
{ ID = T, City = Lima, SalesBefore = 2002, NewOrder = 500, SalesAfter = 2502 }
Program finished, press Enter/Return to continue:
```

How It Works

The code declaring and initializing the Customer class, the Order class, and the customers and orders lists is the same as in the previous example.

The query uses the join keyword to unite each customer with their corresponding orders using the ID fields from the Customer and Order classes, respectively:

```
var queryResults =
    from c in customers
    join o in orders on c.ID equals o.ID
```

The on keyword is followed by the name of the key field (ID), and the equals keyword indicates the corresponding field in the other collection. The query result only includes the data for objects having the same ID field value as the corresponding ID field in the other collection.

The select statement projects a new data type with properties named so that you can clearly see the original sales total, the new order, and the resulting new total:

```
select new { c.ID, c.City, SalesBefore = c.Sales, NewOrder = o.Amount,
                          SalesAfter = c.Sales+o.Amount };
```

While you do not increment the sales total in the customer object in this program, you could easily do so in the business logic of your program.

The logic of the foreach loop and the display of the values from the query are exactly the same as in previous programs in this chapter.

Resources and Further Reading

There are too many LINQ methods in the method syntax to cover them all in a beginning book. For more details and examples, explore the Microsoft online documentation on LINQ. For short examples of every LINQ method, check out the "101 LINQ Samples" topic in the MSDN help (or online at http://msdn2 .microsoft.com/en-us/vcsharp/aa336746.aspx).

Eric White's tutorial on functional programming at http://blogs.msdn.com/ericwhite/pages/ FP-Tutorial.aspx is a good source for functional programming in the context of LINQ. Also offered is a comprehensive tutorial on the LINQ method syntax.

Summary

In this chapter, you learned the following:

❑ The different varieties of LINQ, including LINQ to Objects, LINQ to SQL, and LINQ to XML.

❑ How to code a LINQ query for LINQ to Objects and the parts of a LINQ query statement, including the `from`, `where`, `select`, and `orderby` clauses.

❑ How to use a `foreach` statement to iterate through the results from a LINQ query and how query execution can be deferred until the `foreach` statement is executed.

❑ That LINQ is built on the concept of extension methods. You learned how to use the method syntax and lambda expressions.

❑ How to use LINQ aggregate operators to obtain information about a large data set without having to iterate through every result.

❑ How to use projection to change the data types and create new objects in queries.

❑ How to use the `Distinct()`, `Any()`, `All()`, `First()`, `FirstOrDefault()`, `Take()`, and `Skip()` operators.

❑ Group queries and ordering on multiple levels.

❑ Set operators and joins.

As you have seen, LINQ makes queries written in native C# quite easy and powerful. In the next chapter, you will learn how to use LINQ to SQL to query relational databases and work effectively with large data sets.

Exercises

1. Modify the first example program (`26-1-FirstLINQquery`) to order the results in descending order.

2. Modify the number passed to the `generateLotsOfNumbers()` method in the large number program example (`26-5-LargeNumberQuery`) to create result sets of different sizes and see how query results are affected.

3. Add an `orderby` clause to the query in the large number program example (`26-5-LargeNumberQuery`) to see how this affects performance.

4. Modify the query conditions in the large number program example (`26-5-LargeNumberQuery`) to select large and smaller subsets of the number list. How does this affect performance?

5. Modify the method syntax example (`26-2-LINQMethodSyntax`) to eliminate the `where` clause entirely. How much output does it generate?

6. Modify the query complex objects program example (`26-7-QueryComplexObjects`) to select a different subset of the query fields with a condition appropriate to that field.

7. Add aggregate operators to the first example program (`26-1-FirstLINQquery`). Which simple aggregate operators are available for this non-numeric result set?

27

LINQ to SQL

The previous chapter introduced LINQ (Language-Integrated Query) and showed how to use LINQ to Objects, the version of LINQ that works with objects in memory. This chapter explores LINQ to SQL, the version of LINQ that provides access to SQL (pronounced "sequel") databases such as Microsoft SQL Server and Oracle.

These databases use the SQL database language (SQL stands for *Structured Query Language*) to query and manipulate their data. Traditionally, working with such a database required knowing at least some SQL, either embedding SQL statements in your programming language or passing strings containing SQL statements to API calls or methods in a SQL-oriented database class library.

Sounds complicated, doesn't it? Well, the good news is that LINQ to SQL handles all the details of communicating with the SQL database for you! It translates your LINQ queries to SQL statements automatically and enables you and your programs to work simply with C# objects.

Visual C# 2008 provides designers that create LINQ to SQL classes for you from the existing database, and provides a simple way to bind the controls in your forms to your databases graphically, so that a full database application can be created quickly and easily with very little handwritten code.

You will see how this works as you step through the examples in this chapter. In particular, you look at the following:

❑   The concept of *object-relational mapping (ORM)* and how LINQ to SQL provides it.

❑   How to install SQL Server Express as a relational database to use with LINQ to SQL.

❑   How to install the Northwind sample database to use with the example code.

❑   How to use the O/R Designer in Visual C# 2008 to create objects for a specific database.

❑   How to use LINQ to SQL queries with the objects created by the O/R Designer.

❑   How to navigate relationships between database objects using LINQ to SQL.

❑   How to use group queries and other advanced LINQ features with LINQ to SQL.

❑   How to tie LINQ to SQL objects to graphical controls.

❑   How to update and insert new objects in a database using LINQ to SQL.

Object-Relational Mapping (ORM)

SQL databases such as Microsoft SQL Server are also called *relational databases*. Relational databases store similar data in *tables*, which conceptually are simple groups of rows and columns, like a spreadsheet, stored on your hard disk or other permanent storage.

Conversely, C# (as well as other object-oriented languages) stores data in objects in memory. Objects are more complex than tables because they have code (methods) associated with them, may contain other objects, and so on.

LINQ to SQL creates an *object-relational mapping (ORM)* layer between the tables in the relational database and the objects in your C# program, as shown in Figure 27-1.

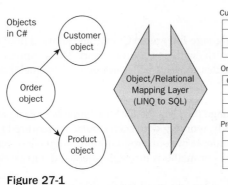

Relational Tables in SQL Database

Customer Table

ID	Name	City	Country
A	Zhang	New York	USA
B	Smythe	London	UK
C	Singh	Mumbai	India

Order Table

Order #	Customer ID	Product ID	Quantity
11	A	1	2
22	B	2	5
23	C	3	1

Product Table

ID	Product	Price
1	Widget	$25.00
2	Wax	$3.00
3	Cable	$50.00

Figure 27-1

As you saw in Chapter 26, to model the concept of a customer in C#, you create a class called `Customer` with properties such as customer name, city, and country. To store several customers, you create a collection of `Customer` objects.

Creating the code to make a set of classes and collections that matches the structure of an existing relational table structure is tedious and time-consuming, but with LINQ to SQL object-relational mapping, the classes that match the database table are created automatically from the database itself so you don't have to, and you can start using the classes immediately.

Installing SQL Server and the Northwind Sample Data

To run the examples shown in this chapter, you must install Microsoft SQL Server Express 2005, the lightweight version of Microsoft SQL Server.

*If you are familiar with SQL Server and have access to an instance of Microsoft SQL Server 2005
Standard or Enterprise Edition with the Northwind sample database installed, you may skip this
installation, although you will have to change the connection information to match your SQL Server
instance. If you have never worked with SQL Server, then go ahead and install SQL Server Express.*

Install SQL Server Express 2005

Visual Studio 2008 and Visual C# 2008 Express Edition both include a copy of SQL Server Express 2005,
the lightweight desktop engine version of SQL Server 2005.

To install SQL Server Express 2005, simply check its option box in the Visual C# 2008 setup, as shown in
Figure 27-2.

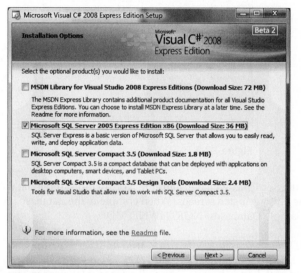

Figure 27-2

If you have already installed Visual Studio 2008 or Visual C# 2008 Express but have not installed SQL
Server 2005 Express Edition, you can rerun the setup to add SQL Server 2005 Express Edition as an
additional component. You can also download and install SQL Server Express using the following
URL: `http://microsoft.com/sql/editions/express/default.mspx`.

> You cannot use Microsoft SQL Server Compact Edition with LINQ to SQL. You must
> use SQL Server 2005 Express Edition instead.

Installing the Northwind Sample Database

The Northwind sample database for SQL Server is required for the examples in this chapter. It is not included with Visual C# 2008 or SQL Server 2005 Express, but is available as a separate download from Microsoft. You can find it by searching for "northwind sample database download" on Google or a similar search site, or just go to the following URL:

```
www.microsoft.com/downloads/details.aspx?familyid=06616212-0356-46a0-8da2-
eebc53a68034&displaylang=en
```

The link downloads the installation file `SQL2000SampleDb.msi` (see Figure 27-3).

Figure 27-3

Click Run to execute the `.msi` file, which installs the Northwind sample database files. Accept the default options for the various install screens. When complete, the database files will be installed at C:\SQL Server 2000 Sample Databases\NORTHWND.MDF.

The Northwind MDF filename is NORTHWND.MDF, *with no "I."*

Keep this filename and path handy because you will refer to it later when creating the connection to the database. That completes the installation of SQL Express and the sample data needed for this chapter. Now you can have some fun with LINQ to SQL!

First LINQ to SQL Query

In the following Try It Out, you create a simple query to find a subset of customer objects in the Northwind SQL Server sample data using LINQ to SQL, and print it to the console.

Try It Out **First LINQ to SQL Query**

Follow these steps to create the example in Visual C# 2008:

1. Create a new console application project called BegVCSharp_27_1_FirstLINQtoSQLQuery in the directory C:\BegVCSharp\Chapter27, as shown in Figure 27-4.

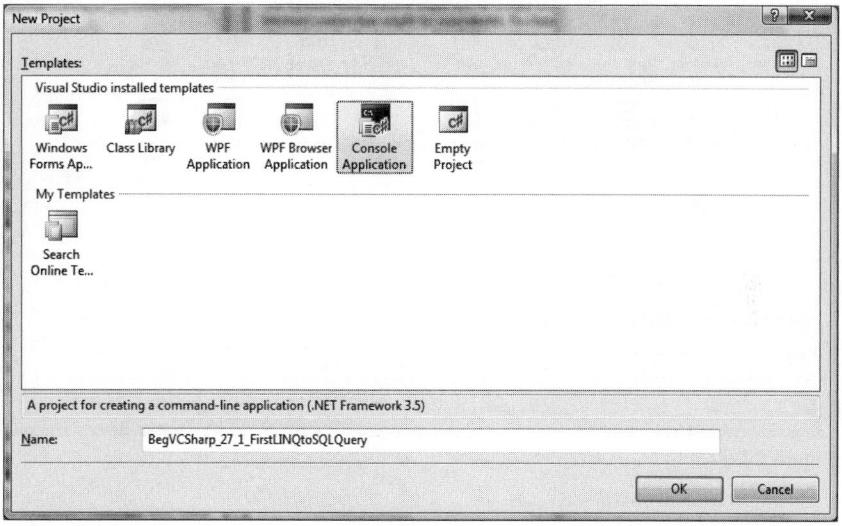

Figure 27-4

2. Press OK to create the project.

3. To add the LINQ to SQL mapping class for the Northwind database, go to the Solution Explorer pane, right-click on the BegVCSharp_27_1_FirstLINQtoSQLQuery C# project, and select Add ➪ New Item, as shown in Figure 27-5.

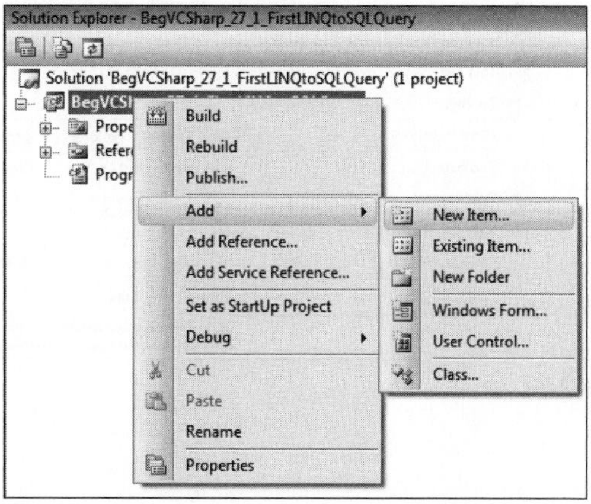

Figure 27-5

4. In the New Item dialog, choose LINQ to SQL Classes as the template for the new class and change the name of the class from the default name `DataClasses1.dbml` (dbml = data base mapping language) to `Northwind.dbml`, as shown in Figure 27-6.

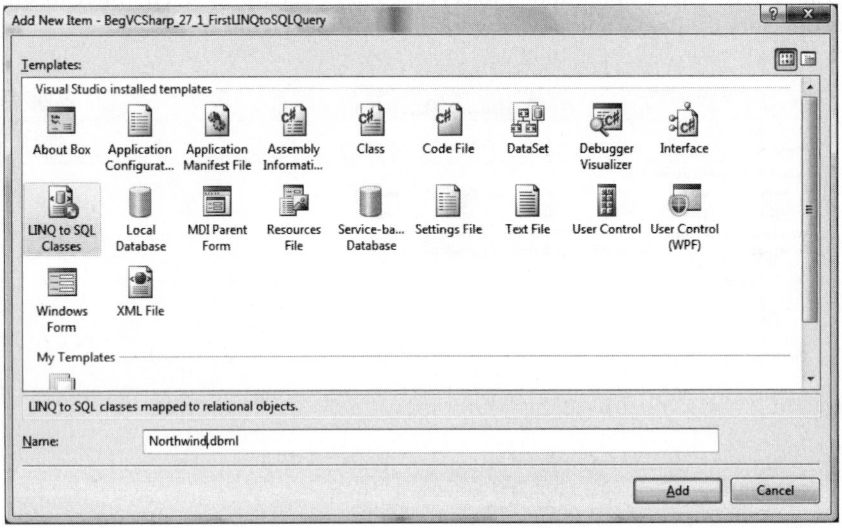

Figure 27-6

5. Add a database connection for your project to the Northwind sample database. Open the Database Explorer window by selecting View ⇨ Other Windows ⇨ Database Explorer, as shown in Figure 27-7.

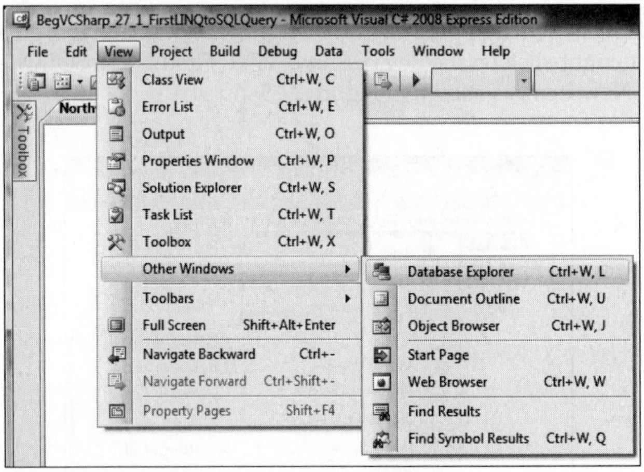

Figure 27-7

6. In the Database Explorer window, click the Connect to Database icon (see Figure 27-8).

Figure 27-8

7. In the Choose Data Source dialog, select Microsoft SQL Server Database File in the Data Source list (see Figure 27-9). Click Continue.

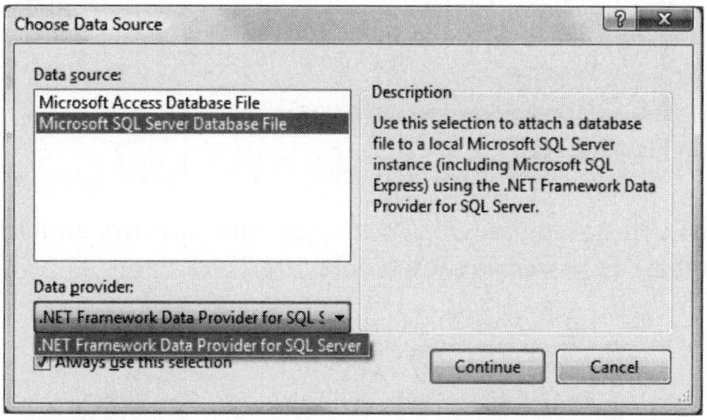

Figure 27-9

8. In the Add Connection dialog, enter the path to the Northwind database file as shown in Figure 27-10. Click the Test Connection button to confirm that the connection to the database is working.

If Test Connection does not work, make sure that SQL Server is running. If the exception indicates that user instances are not enabled, then start SSMS, open a query window, and run the following database command:

```
exec sp_configure 'user instances enabled', 1
Reconfigure
```

This will enable user instances and automatically restart SQL Server.

Click OK to finish and move to the next step.

Figure 27-10

The SQL Server Express database NORTHWND.MDF now appears under the Data Connections node in the Database Explorer, as shown in Figure 27-11.

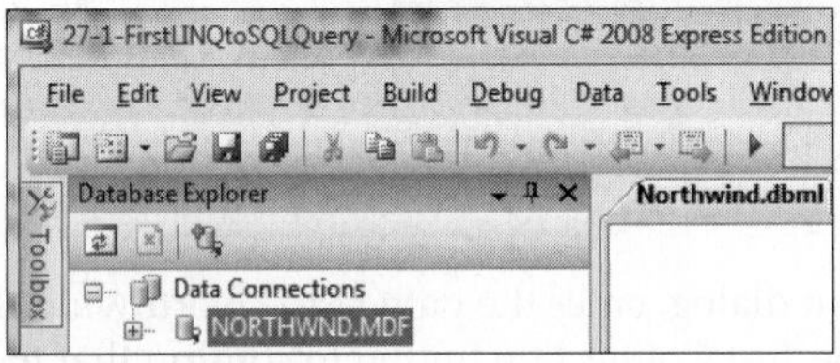

Figure 27-11

9. Expand the NORTHWND.MDF node so that you can see the items beneath it.

10. Now expand the Tables node so that you can see the list of database tables beneath the node, as shown in Figure 27-12.

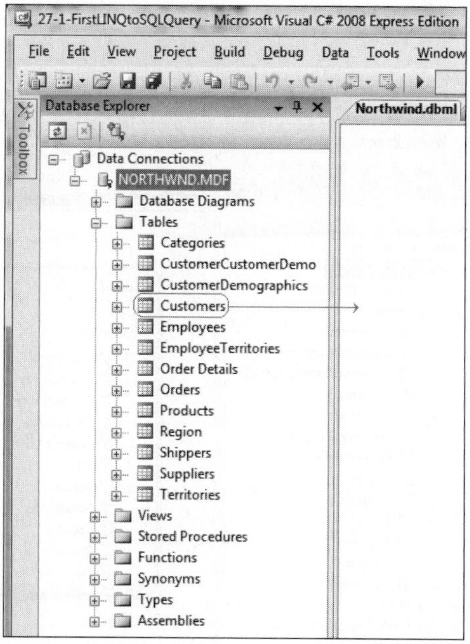

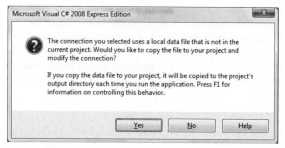

Figure 27-12

11. Click and drag the `Customers` table to the `Northwind.dbml` pane as shown in Figure 27-12.

12. A dialog opens (see Figure 27-13) asking if you want to copy the local database file to your project.

Figure 27-13

Click the No button to ensure that duplicate copies of `Northwnd.MDF` are not created.

13. The Customer object now appears in the Northwind.dbml pane, as shown in Figure 27-14.

Figure 27-14

14. Compile the project now so that the Customer object will be available when you start entering code in the next step.

You can see the code for classes generated by the O/R Designer by looking in the Northwind .designer.cs file, which appears underneath the Northwind.dbml source file in the Solution Explorer, similar to the way a form's generated code is placed in <formname>.designer.cs. However, just as with a form's generated code, you should not modify the designer-generated code, so it best not to open this code in the editor except when you want to verify a class name or check a generated data type.

15. Open the main source file Program.cs and add the following code to the Main() method:

```csharp
static void Main(string[] args)
{
        NorthwindDataContext northWindDataContext = new NorthwindDataContext();

        var queryResults = from c in northWindDataContext.Customers
                        where c.Country == "USA"
                        select new {
                                     ID=c.CustomerID,
                                     Name=c.CompanyName,
                                     City=c.City,
```

```
                                    State=c.Region
                      };
        foreach (var item in queryResults) {
            Console.WriteLine(item);
        };


        Console.WriteLine("Press Enter/Return to continue...");
        Console.ReadLine();
    }
```

16.   Compile and execute the program (you can just press F5 for Start Debugging). You will see the information for customers in the U.S.A. appear as shown here:

```
{ ID = GREAL, Name = Great Lakes Food Market, City = Eugene, State = OR }
{ ID = HUNGC, Name = Hungry Coyote Import Store, City = Elgin, State = OR }
{ ID = LAZYK, Name = Lazy K Kountry Store, City = Walla Walla, State = WA }
{ ID = LETSS, Name = Let's Stop N Shop, City = San Francisco, State = CA }
{ ID = LONEP, Name = Lonesome Pine Restaurant, Ci.ty = Portland, State = OR }
{ ID = OLDWO, Name = Old World Delicatessen, City = Anchorage, State = AK }
{ ID = RATTC, Name = Rattlesnake Canyon Grocery, City = Albuquerque, State = NM
}
{ ID = SAVEA, Name = Save-a-lot Markets, City = Boise, State = ID }
{ ID = SPLIR, Name = Split Rail Beer & Ale, City = Lander, State = WY }
{ ID = THEBI, Name = The Big Cheese, City = Portland, State = OR }
{ ID = THECR, Name = The Cracker Box, City = Butte, State = MT }
{ ID = TRAIH, Name = Trail's Head Gourmet Provisioners, City = Kirkland,
    State = WA }
{ ID = WHITC, Name = White Clover Markets, City = Seattle, State = WA }
Press Enter/Return to continue...
```

Simply press Enter/Return to finish the program and make the console screen disappear. If you used Ctrl+F5 (Start Without Debugging), you may need to press Enter/Return twice. That finishes the program run. Now let's look at how it works in detail.

How It Works

The code for this and all other examples in this chapter are similar to the examples described in the introduction to LINQ in the previous chapter, using extension classes from the System.Linq namespace, which is referenced by a using statement inserted automatically by Visual C# 2008 when you create the project:

```
using System.Linq;
```

The first step in using the LINQ to SQL classes is to create an instance of the DataContext object for the particular database you are accessing, which is the class compiled from the .dbml file created in the O/R Designer. This object is the gateway to your database, providing all the methods you need to control it from your program. It also acts as a factory for creating the business objects that correspond to the conceptual entities stored in your database (for example, customers and products).

In your project, the data context class is called `NorthwindDataContext`, compiled from the `Northwind.dbml` file. Your first step in the `Main()` method is to create an instance of `NorthwindDataContext` as shown here:

```
NorthwindDataContext northWindDataContext = new NorthwindDataContext();
```

When you dragged the `Customers` table into the O/R Designer pane, a `Customer` object was added to the LINQ to SQL class in `Northwind.dbml` and a `Customers` member was added to the `NorthwindDataContext` object to enable you to query the `Customer` objects in the Northwind database.

Pluralization in the O/R Designer

The O/R Designer detects that the table name `Customers` is an English plural form and automatically generates the singular name `Customer` for the generated object. You can control this pluralization behavior by going to Tools ➪ Options ➪ Database Tools ➪ O/R Designer, as shown in the following figure.

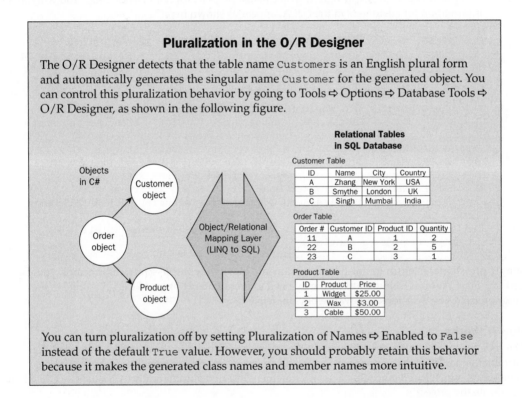

You can turn pluralization off by setting Pluralization of Names ➪ Enabled to `False` instead of the default `True` value. However, you should probably retain this behavior because it makes the generated class names and member names more intuitive.

The actual LINQ query statement makes a query using the `Customers` member of the `NorthwindDataContext` as the data source:

```
var queryResults = from c in northWindDataContext.Customers
                   where c.Country == "USA"
                   select new {
                           ID=c.CustomerID,
                           Name=c.CompanyName,
                           City=c.City,
                           State=c.Region
                   };
```

`Customers` is a typed LINQ table (`System.Data.Linq.Table<Customer>`), which is similar to a typed collection of `Customer` objects (like a `List<Table>`), but implemented for LINQ to SQL and filled from the database automatically. It implements the `IEnumerable/IQueryable` interfaces so it can be used as a LINQ data source in the `from` clause just like any collection or array.

The `where` clause restricts the results to customers only in the U.S.A. The `select` clause is a projection, similar to the examples you developed in the preceding chapter, that creates a new object having members `ID`, `Name`, `City`, and `State`. Because you know the results are for the U.S.A. only, you can rename the `Region` to `State` for more precise display of the results. Finally, you create a standard `foreach` loop like the ones you wrote in Chapter 26:

```
foreach (var item in queryResults) {
    Console.WriteLine(item);
};
```

This code uses the default generated `ToString()` method for each `item` to format the output for the `Console.WriteLine(item)` so you see the values for each projected member instance in curly braces:

```
{ ID=WHITC, Name=White Clover Markets, City=Seattle, State=WA }
```

Finally, the example ends with code to pause the display so you can see the results:

```
        Console.WriteLine("Press Enter/Return to continue...");
        Console.ReadLine();
    };
```

Now you have created a basic LINQ to SQL query that you can use as a base to build on for more complex queries.

Navigating LINQ to SQL Relationships

One of the most powerful aspects of the Visual Studio O/R Designer is its capability to automatically create LINQ to SQL objects to help you navigate relationships between related tables in the database. In the following Try It Out, you add a related table to the LINQ to SQL class, add code to navigate through the related data objects in the database, and print out their values

Try It Out   **Navigating LINQ to SQL Relationships**

Follow these steps to create the example in Visual C# 2008:

1. Modify the project for the previous example BegVCSharp_27_1_FirstLINQtoSQLQuery in the directory C:\BegVCSharp\Chapter27 as shown in the following steps.

2. Click on the `Orders` table in the Database Explorer window and drag it into the `Northwind.dbml` pane as shown in Figure 27-15.

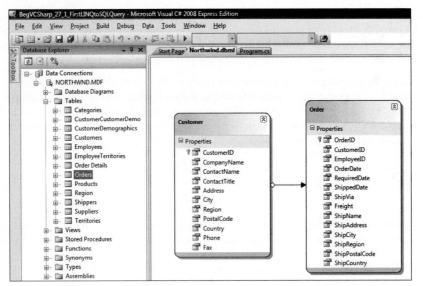

Figure 27-15

3. Compile the project so that the Orders object appears in IntelliSense when you start entering code in the next step.

4. Open the main source file Program.cs. In the Main() method, add an Orders field to the select clause in the LINQ query (don't forget to add a comma following c.Region to separate the added field from the rest of the list):

```
static void Main(string[] args)
{
    NorthwindDataContext northWindDataContext = new NorthwindDataContext();

    var queryResults = from c in northWindDataContext.Customers
                       where c.Country == "USA"
                       select new {
                                ID=c.CustomerID,
                                Name=c.CompanyName,
                                City=c.City,
                                State=c.Region,
                                Orders=c.Orders

                       };
```

5. Modify the foreach clause to print the query results as shown:

```
        foreach (var item in queryResults) {

            Console.WriteLine(
                "Customer: {0} {1}, {2}\n{3} orders:\tOrder ID\tOrder Date",
                    item.Name, item.City, item.State, item.Orders.Count
```

```
            );
            foreach (Order o in item.Orders) {
                Console.WriteLine("\t\t{0}\t{1}", o.OrderID, o.OrderDate);
            }
```

```
        };

        Console.WriteLine("Press Enter/Return to continue...");
        Console.ReadLine();
    }
```

6. Compile and execute the program (you can just press F5 for Start Debugging). You will see the information for customers in the U.S.A. and their orders as follows (this is the last part of the output; the first part scrolls off the top of the console window):

```
Customer: Trail's Head Gourmet Provisioners Kirkland, WA
3 orders:          Order ID          Order Date
                10574   6/19/1997 12:00:00 AM
                10577   6/23/1997 12:00:00 AM
                10822   1/8/1998 12:00:00 AM
Customer: White Clover Markets Seattle, WA
14 orders:         Order ID          Order Date
                10269   7/31/1996 12:00:00 AM
                10344   11/1/1996 12:00:00 AM
                10469   3/10/1997 12:00:00 AM
                10483   3/24/1997 12:00:00 AM
                10504   4/11/1997 12:00:00 AM
                10596   7/11/1997 12:00:00 AM
                10693   10/6/1997 12:00:00 AM
                10696   10/8/1997 12:00:00 AM
                10723   10/30/1997 12:00:00 AM
                10740   11/13/1997 12:00:00 AM
                10861   1/30/1998 12:00:00 AM
                10904   2/24/1998 12:00:00 AM
                11032   4/17/1998 12:00:00 AM
                11066   5/1/1998 12:00:00 AM
Press Enter/Return to continue...
```

As before, press Enter/Return to finish the program and make the console screen disappear.

How It Works

You modified your previous program instead of creating a new program from scratch so you did not have to repeat all the steps to create the `Northwind.dbml` LINQ to SQL mapping source file (note that the sample code has separate projects, each with its own instance of `Northwind.dbml`).

By dragging the `Orders` table in from the Database Explorer window, you added the `Order` class to the `Northwind.dbml` source file to represent the `Orders` table in your mapping of the Northwind database.

The O/R Designer also detected the relationship in the database between Customers and Orders, adding an `Orders` collection member to the `Customer` class to represent the relationship. All this was done automatically, as when you add new controls to a form.

If you look before and after you add a database object to the O/R Designer pane, you will see that the class definition for the added object(s) appears in the `Northwind.designer.cs` *generated source file. As noted before, do not modify this generated source file; use it only for reference purposes.*

Next, you added the newly available `Orders` member to the `select` clause of the query:

```
select new {
            ID=c.CustomerID,
            Name=c.CompanyName,
            City=c.City,
            State=c.Region,
            Orders=c.Orders
            };
```

`Orders` is a special typed LINQ set (`System.Data.Linq.EntitySet<Order>`) that represents the relationship between two tables in the relational database. It implements the `IEnumerable`/ `IQueryable` interfaces so it can be used as a LINQ data source itself or iterated with a `foreach` statement just like any collection or array.

Like the `Table` object shown in the previous example, the `EntitySet` is similar to a typed collection of `Order` objects (like a `List<Order>`), but only those orders submitted by a particular customer will appear in the `EntitySet` member for a particular `Customer` instance.

The `Order` *objects in the customer's* `EntitySet` *member correspond to the order rows in the database having the same customer ID as that customer's ID.*

Navigating the relationship simply involves building a nested `foreach` statement to iterate through each customer and then each customer's orders:

```
foreach (var item in queryResults) {

        Console.WriteLine(
            "Customer: {0} {1}, {2}\n{3} orders:\tOrder ID\tOrder Date",
                item.Name, item.City, item.State, item.Orders.Count
        );
        foreach (Order o in item.Orders) {
            Console.WriteLine("\t\t{0}\t{1}", o.OrderID, o.OrderDate);
        }
};
```

Rather that just use the default `ToString()` formatting, you format the output for readability so you can show the hierarchy properly with the list of orders under each customer. The format string `"Customer: {0} {1}, {2}\n{3} orders:\tOrder ID\tOrder Date"` has a placeholder for the name, city, and state of each customer on the first line, and then prints a column header for that customer's orders on the next line. You use the LINQ aggregate `Count()` method to print the count of the number of that customer's orders, and then print out the order ID and order date on each line in the nested `foreach` statement:

```
Customer: White Clover Markets Seattle, WA
14 orders:      Order ID        Order Date
                10269   7/31/1996 12:00:00 AM
                10344   11/1/1996 12:00:00 AM
```

The formatting is still a bit rusty in that you see the time of the order when all that really matters is the date. However, you will get a chance to clean that up in the next example.

Drilling Down Further with LINQ to SQL

To get to the interesting data of how much each customer is spending, you need to add one more level of detail and drill down into the details of each order, using the `Order Details` table. Again, LINQ to SQL and the O/R Designer make this very easy to do, as you will see in the following Try It Out.

Drilling Down Further LINQ to SQL

In Visual C# 2008, modify the project for the previous example, BegVCSharp_27_1_ FirstLINQtoSQLQuery, in the directory C:\BegVCSharp\Chapter27 as shown in the following steps:

1.   Click on the `Order Details` table in the Database Explorer window and drag it into the `Northwind.dbml` pane as shown in Figure 27-16.

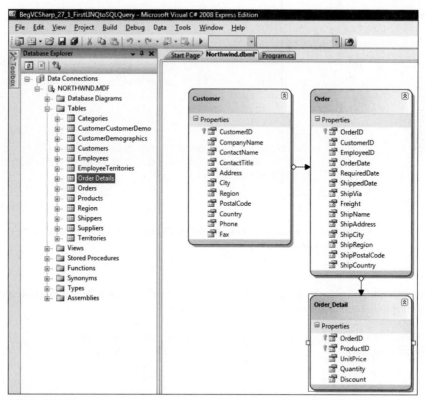

Figure 27-16

2. Compile the project so that the `Order_Detail` object appears when you start entering code in the next step.

3. Open the main source file `Program.cs`. In the `Main()` method the query should appear like this:

```
static void Main(string[] args)
{
    NorthwindDataContext northWindDataContext = new NorthwindDataContext();

    var queryResults = from c in northWindDataContext.Customers
                       where c.Country == "USA"
                       select new {
                                      ID=c.CustomerID,
                                      Name=c.CompanyName,
                                      City=c.City,
                                      State=c.Region,
                                      Orders=c.Orders
                                  };
```

4. Modify the `foreach` clause to print the query results:

```
foreach (var item in queryResults) {
        Console.WriteLine(
        "Customer: {0} {1}, {2}\n{3} orders:  Order ID\tOrder Date\tTotal
Amount",
                    item.Name, item.City, item.State, item.Orders.Count);
        foreach (Order o in item.Orders) {
            Console.WriteLine(
            "\t{0,10}\t{1,10}\t{2,10}",
            o.OrderID,
            o.OrderDate.Value.ToShortDateString(),
            o.Order_Details.Sum(od => od.Quantity * od.UnitPrice)
                .ToString("C2"));
        }
    };

            Console.WriteLine("Press Enter/Return to continue...");
            Console.ReadLine();
}
```

5. Compile and execute the program (you can just press F5 for Start Debugging). Again, the result shown here is just the last part of the output):

```
Customer: Trail's Head Gourmet Provisioners Kirkland, WA
3 orders:  Order ID     Order Date      Total Amount
              10574      6/19/1997        $764.30
              10577      6/23/1997        $569.00
              10822       1/8/1998        $237.90
```

```
Customer: White Clover Markets Seattle, WA
14 orders:  Order ID    Order Date      Total Amount
            10269       7/31/1996         $676.00
            10344       11/1/1996       $2,856.00
            10469       3/10/1997       $1,125.50
            10483       3/24/1997         $704.00
            10504       4/11/1997       $1,388.50
            10596       7/11/1997       $1,476.10
            10693       10/6/1997       $2,334.00
            10696       10/8/1997         $996.00
            10723       10/30/1997        $468.45
            10740       11/13/1997      $1,770.00
            10861       1/30/1998       $3,523.40
            10904       2/24/1998       $1,924.25
            11032       4/17/1998       $8,902.50
            11066       5/1/1998          $928.75
Press Enter/Return to continue
```

As you did before, press Enter/Return to finish the program and make the console screen disappear.

How It Works

You modified your previous program instead of creating a new program from scratch so you did not have to repeat all the steps to create the Northwind.dbml LINQ to SQL mapping source file.

You dragged the Order Details table in from the Database Explorer window, adding the Order_Detail class to the Northwind.dbml source file and adding an Order_Details_ collection member to the Order class to represent the relationship between Orders and Order Details.

> *Because class names and members in C# cannot contain spaces, the O/R Designer added an underscore to form the names* Order_Detail *and* Order_Details.

Like the Orders member of Customer itself, the Order_Details member of Orders is an EntitySet representing the relationship.

You did not have to modify the from . . . where . . . select clauses of the previous LINQ query at all; instead, all the changes are confined to the foreach processing loop:

```
foreach (var item in queryResults) {
```

```
        Console.WriteLine(
        "Customer: {0} {1}, {2}\n{3} orders:  Order ID\tOrder Date\tTotal
Amount",
                    item.Name, item.City, item.State, item.Orders.Count);
        foreach (Order o in item.Orders) {
            Console.WriteLine(
                "\t{0,10}\t{1,10}\t{2,10}",
                o.OrderID,
                o.OrderDate.Value.ToShortDateString(),
                o.Order_Details.Sum(od => od.Quantity * od.UnitPrice)
                    .ToString("C2"));
        }
```

```
};
```

You added "Total Amount" to the end of the header for each customer in the first line of the outer `foreach` loop. In the inner `foreach` loop you cleaned up the formatting of each entry by adding a field width of 10 to each `Console.Writeline()` placeholder so that it reads `"\t{0,10}\t{1,10}\t{2,10}"`. In the list of fields, you passed the `OrderID`, and the `OrderDate` formatted as a short date string to eliminate the unused time portion of the `OrderDate`.

The total for each order is calculated from the `Order_Details`. Things get a bit interesting here, but you've already seen each element in the previous chapter.

To get the sum of all the order details for a single order, you use the LINQ `Sum()` aggregate operator, passing a lambda expression (`od => od.Quantity * od.UnitPrice`) that calculates the total price of each order (the subtotal for each order detail is the quantity times the unit price (that is, three widgets @ $2 each = $6)). You format this total as currency with two decimal places (`"C2"`), and that finishes the example.

Grouping, Ordering, and Other Advanced Queries in LINQ to SQL

Now that you know how the total spending for each customer is calculated, you may begin to have questions at a higher level. Which customers are buying the most? What regions or countries are they located in? What products are selling best? To answer decision support questions such as these, grouping and ordering are required. The `group` and `orderby` operations are the same in your code in LINQ to SQL as they are in LINQ to Objects, but use SQL data sources for which LINQ can take advantage of the underlying `group` and `orderby` capabilities in the SQL database, depending on your query construction. In the next example, you try this out by constructing a query to find what countries have had the largest total sales.

Try It Out   **Grouping, Ordering, and Other Advanced Queries**

In Visual C# 2008, modify the project for the previous example, BegVCSharp_27_1_FirstLINQtoSQLQuery, in the directory C:\BegVCSharp\Chapter27 as shown in the following steps:

1. Open the main source file `Program.cs`. Replace the LINQ query in the `Main()` method with the following queries:

```
static void Main(string[] args)
{
    NorthwindDataContext northWindDataContext = new NorthwindDataContext();
    var totalResults =
        from c in northWindDataContext.Customers
        select new
        {
            Country = c.Country,
            Sales =
                c.Orders.Sum(o =>
```

```
                    o.Order_Details.Sum(od => od.Quantity * od.UnitPrice)
                )
        };

    var groupResults =
        from c in totalResults
        group c by c.Country into cg
        select new { TotalSales = cg.Sum(c => c.Sales), Country = cg.Key }
        ;

    var orderedResults =
        from cg in groupResults
        orderby cg.TotalSales descending
        select cg
        ;
```

2. Continue to modify the `Main()` method in `Program.cs` by replacing the `foreach` loop following the LINQ query with the code shown here:

```
Console.WriteLine("Country\t\tTotal Sales\n--------\t------------");

foreach (var item in orderedResults) {
        Console.WriteLine("{0,-15}{1,12}",
        item.Country, item.TotalSales.ToString("C2"));
}

Console.WriteLine("Press Enter/Return to continue...");
Console.ReadLine();
}
```

3. Compile and execute the program (you can just press F5 for Start Debugging). You will see the total sales by country in descending order as follows:

```
Country         Total Sales
--------        ------------
USA             $263,566.98
Germany         $244,640.63
Austria         $139,496.63
Brazil          $114,968.48
France           $85,498.76
Venezuela        $60,814.89
UK               $60,616.51
Sweden           $59,523.70
Ireland          $57,317.39
Canada           $55,334.10
Belgium          $35,134.98
Denmark          $34,782.25
Switzerland      $32,919.50
Mexico           $24,073.45
Finland          $19,778.45
```

```
Spain               $19,431.89
Italy               $16,705.15
Portugal            $12,468.65
Argentina            $8,119.10
Norway               $5,735.15
Poland               $3,531.95
Press Enter/Return to continue...
```

As before, press Enter/Return to finish the program and make the console screen disappear.

How It Works

Again you modified your previous program to reuse the Northwind.dbml LINQ to SQL mapping. For this example you did not have to add any classes to Northwind.dbml because you used the existing mapping classes for Customer, Order, and Order_Details.

You replaced the previous LINQ query with three new queries using the same data source as before but processing the results very differently.

The first LINQ query is similar to previous queries in this chapter, using northWindDataContext.Customers as the data source:

```
var totalResults =
    from c in northWindDataContext.Customers
    select new
    {
        Country = c.Country,
        Sales =
         c.Orders.Sum(o =>
            o.Order_Details.Sum(od => od.Quantity * od.UnitPrice)
         )
    };
```

For this query you do not want to restrict the results to the U.S.A. only, so there is no where clause. Instead of the Region property, you select Country because this queries groups and orders by country. You do not select the customer ID, Name, or City because these are not used in the result and it is inefficient to ask for more data from the database than you are going to use. The Sum() operation using the lambda expression od => od.Quantity * od.UnitPrice to get the sum of all the order details is now moved to the LINQ query itself.

Next, you specify a group query to group the total sales by country, using the preceding query results as the data source:

```
var groupResults =
    from c in totalResults
    group c by c.Country into cg
    select new { TotalSales = cg.Sum(c => c.Sales), Country = cg.Key }
    ;
```

This query is very similar to the group query you created for LINQ to Objects in the previous chapter, using the country as the key to group results and by summing the total sales (in this case, Sum() is adding up the customer total sales for all customers within a country) the operation is nested inside another Sum() to sum up the sales for all the Orders of each Customer.

For the last query, you order the results with the ordered results query, using the group query as the data source. A separate query is needed for this because group queries can be ordered only by the key field:

```
var orderedResults =
    from cg in groupResults
    orderby cg.TotalSales descending
    select cg
;
```

Finally, you do some output formatting, printing a header for the Country and Total Sales columns in the result, and then in the foreach processing loop printing the two columns in justified format (left-justified in a 15-character-wide field for the Country, right-justified in a 12-character-wide field for the Total Sales:

```
Console.WriteLine("Country\t\tTotal Sales\n--------\t------------");

foreach (var item in orderedResults) {
    Console.WriteLine("{0,-15}{1,12}",
        item.Country, item.TotalSales.ToString("C2"));
}
```

Displaying Generated SQL

If you are familiar with SQL databases you may be wondering what SQL database commands are being generated by LINQ to SQL. Even if you are not familiar with SQL, it is sometimes instructive to look at the generated SQL to understand how LINQ to SQL is interacting with the database (and perhaps to appreciate what LINQ to SQL is doing by taking care of writing the complex SQL for you!).

In the following Try It Out, you will modify the previous group query example to display the generated SQL, and then look at how it is executed.

Try It Out   **Displaying Generated SQL**

Follow these steps to create the example in Visual C# 2008:

1. Modify the project for the previous example, BegVCSharp_27_1_FirstLINQtoSQLQuery, in the directory C:\BegVCSharp\Chapter27 as shown in the following steps.

2. Open the main source file Program.cs. Add the highlighted lines to the Main() method:

```
static void Main(string[] args)
{
    NorthwindDataContext northWindDataContext = new NorthwindDataContext();
    var totalResults =
        from c in northWindDataContext.Customers
        select new
```

```
        {
            Country = c.Country,
            Sales =
                    c.Orders.Sum(o =>
                        o.Order_Details.Sum(od => od.Quantity * od.UnitPrice)
                    )
        };
    Console.WriteLine("------ SQL for totalResults query --------");;
    Console.WriteLine(totalResults);
    Console.WriteLine("Press Enter/Return to continue...");
    Console.ReadLine();

    var groupResults =
        from c in totalResults
        group c by c.Country into cg
        select new { TotalSales = cg.Sum(c => c.Sales), Country = cg.Key }
        ;
    Console.WriteLine("------ SQL for groupResults query --------");;
    Console.WriteLine(groupResults);
    Console.WriteLine("Press Enter/Return to continue...");
    Console.ReadLine();

    var orderedResults =
        from cg in groupResults
        orderby cg.TotalSales descending
        select cg
        ;
    Console.WriteLine("------ SQL for orderedResults query --------");;
    Console.WriteLine(groupResults);
    Console.WriteLine("Press Enter/Return to continue...");
    Console.ReadLine();

            Console.WriteLine("Country\t\tTotal Sales\n--------\t------------");

            foreach (var item in orderedResults) {
                    Console.WriteLine("{0,-15}{1,12}",
                    item.Country, item.TotalSales.ToString("C2"));
            }

            Console.WriteLine("Press Enter/Return to continue...");
            Console.ReadLine();
    }
```

3. Compile and execute the program (you can just press F5 for Start Debugging). You will see the following SQL output for the first query on the console screen:

```
------ SQL for totalResults query --------
SELECT [t0].[Country], (
    SELECT SUM([t4].[value])
    FROM (
        SELECT SUM([t3].[value])(
            SELECT SUM((CONVERT(Decimal(29,4),[t2].[Quantity])) *
[t2].[UnitPrice])
```

```
        FROM [dbo].[Order Details] AS [t2]
          WHERE [t2].[OrderID] = [t1].[OrderID]
      ) AS [value], [t1].[CustomerID]
    FROM [dbo].[Orders] AS [t1]
  ) AS [t3]
  WHERE [t3].[CustomerID] = [t0].[CustomerID]
) AS [value]
FROM [dbo].[Customers] AS [t0]
Press Enter/Return to continue...
```

Do not press Enter yet; leave the console screen up and read the How It Works section to follow the output as it is generated.

How It Works

The default ToString() method for a LINQ to SQL query prints the generated SQL, so what you are seeing is the output from the call to Console.WriteLine(totalResults); aren't you glad you didn't have to write this SQL yourself?

This SQL command will be passed to SQL Server to return the results to LINQ to SQL. LINQ to SQL translates the LINQ select, from, and where clauses into SQL SELECT, FROM, and WHERE clauses. It also translates the LINQ Sum() aggregate operator into an invocation of the SQL SUM() aggregate operator.

The operation of these SQL functions is similar enough to the equivalent LINQ functions that they are not explained in detail; however, be aware that not every LINQ clause or method translates into an exact SQL equivalent. It just so happens that this query has a fairly literal SQL translation, with a few extras such as calling the SQL CONVERT() function to get the correct decimal data type for the Sales column in the result, and adding SQL WHERE clauses to join the Order Details, Orders, and Customer table results on the OrderID and CustomerID fields — messy SQL details that LINQ to SQL takes care of for you.

Note also that this SQL query has not executed yet — because of LINQ's deferred execution, this displays what SQL commands LINQ to SQL *will* send to SQL Server when the query is actually executed (when you loop through the results with a foreach loop). Now press Enter/Return to see the next screen of generated SQL, for the group results query:

```
------ SQL for groupResults query --------
SELECT SUM([t4].[value]) AS [value], [t4].[Country]
FROM (
    SELECT [t0].[Country], (
    SELECT SUM([t4].[value])
    FROM (
      SELECT SUM([t3].[value])(
        SELECT SUM((CONVERT(Decimal(29,4),[t2].[Quantity])) *
[t2].[UnitPrice])
        FROM [dbo].[Order Details] AS [t2]
          WHERE [t2].[OrderID] = [t1].[OrderID]
      ) AS [value], [t1].[CustomerID]
      FROM [dbo].[Orders] AS [t1]
```

```
       ) AS [t3]
         WHERE [t3].[CustomerID] = [t0].[CustomerID]
       ) AS [value]
       FROM [dbo].[Customers] AS [t0]
  ) AS [t4]
  GROUP BY [t4].[Country]
  Press Enter/Return to continue...
```

Note that the SQL for the group query contains the same SQL you just saw for the total results query inside it; because its data source is the `totalResults` query as specified in the `from` clause (`from c in totalResults`), it wraps the SQL for the `totalResults` query in a nested SQL query with a GROUP BY clause:

```
SELECT SUM([t4].[value]) AS [value], [t4].[Country]
FROM (
... SQL for totaResults ...
) AS [t4]
GROUP BY [t4].[Country]
```

Again, this has not been sent to the server yet; because you pass these results to yet another nested query you are essentially building up a single complex SQL command with multiple LINQ to SQL queries. Now press Enter/Return to see the next screen of generated SQL:

```
------ SQL for orderedResults query --------
SELECT [t5].[value] AS [TotalSales], [t5].[Country]
FROM (
  SELECT SUM([t4].[value]) AS [value], [t4].[Country]
  FROM (
     SELECT [t0].[Country], (
       SELECT SUM([t3].[value])
       FROM (
         SELECT (
           SELECT SUM((CONVERT(Decimal(29,4),[t2].[Quantity])) *
[t2].[UnitPrice])
             FROM [dbo].[Order Details] AS [t2]
             WHERE [t2].[OrderID] = [t1].[OrderID]
           ) AS [value], [t1].[CustomerID]
         FROM [dbo].[Orders] AS [t1]
       ) AS [t3]
       WHERE [t3].[CustomerID] = [t0].[CustomerID]
     ) AS [value]
     FROM [dbo].[Customers] AS [t0]
  ) AS [t4]
  GROUP BY [t4].[Country]
) AS [t5]
ORDER BY [t5].[value] DESC
Press Enter/Return to continue
```

As before, this SQL query contains the SQL for the preceding queries inside it. It wraps the GROUP BY results in an ORDER BY query:

```
SELECT [t5].[value] AS [TotalSales], [t5].[Country]
FROM (
...SQL for groupResults...
) AS [t5]
ORDER BY [t5].[value] DESC
```

This has still not been sent to the server yet; however, when you press Enter/Return next, you execute the `foreach` loop over the results of the `orderby` query, causing this SQL query to be the one actually executed. Because of deferred execution, only one SQL query is actually sent to the database server, which is almost always more efficient than processing the results of multiple queries.

Whether the SQL is executed efficiently is up to the *query optimizer* built into almost all modern SQL database servers — it will analyze the nested queries and build a query plan that executes the query in the most optimal manner possible. While some SQL query optimizers are better than others, most modern ones do a better job than the average application programmer — so it is OK to let LINQ to SQL and the SQL database do the heavy lifting together.

It is good to be aware of what SQL is being generated and be able to tell the SQL experts in your organization what SQL your program is generating, but with LINQ to SQL you don't have to create the SQL yourself.

If you have a special need to execute specific SQL queries against your data, see the ADO.NET classes described in the next chapter, which are designed to enable you to specify the SQL you send to the server. LINQ to SQL also provides an `ExecuteQuery()` method in the `DataContext` class for your database, for situations when you primarily want to use the SQL generated by LINQ to SQL classes but have an occasional need to send a specific SQL command to the SQL database.

Next you will learn another way in which Visual C# 2008 and LINQ to SQL make your work easier, when you look at how you can generate user interfaces bound to database queries with very little work required on your part.

Data Binding with LINQ to SQL

In order for end users to interact with a database application, you need to design a set of forms for data entry and reports.

It traditionally required much tedious coding to update business objects from the GUI forms and then make method calls to the business layer to query and update the database as users browse it and update or enter new data.

Previously you saw how the O/R Designer generates LINQ to SQL classes to handle reading the database and navigating relationships. Well, there's more good news for you!

Visual C# 2008 includes data binding in the forms designers that works with LINQ to SQL so that you don't have to have write detailed code to get data from your end-user forms to the database classes. You can point-and-click in Visual C# 2008 to generate code for a sophisticated graphical database application that works pretty much right out of the Forms Designer with practically no hand-coding required. You will see how this works in the next Try It Out.

Data Binding with LINQ To SQL

Follow these steps to create the example in Visual C# 2008:

1.   Create a new Windows Forms project called BegVCSharp_27_2_LINQtoSQLDataBinding in the directory C:\BegVCSharp\Chapter27.

2.   Add the LINQ to SQL class Northwind.dbml and connect to the Northwind database as you did in the first LINQ to SQL query example at the beginning of the chapter.

   If you need a reminder of how to do this, go back to the "First LINQ to SQL Query" Try It Out at the beginning of this chapter and repeat steps 3 through 13.

3.   Drag the Customers and Orders tables into Northwind.dbml using the O/R Designer. Your project screen should now look like the one shown in Figure 27-17.

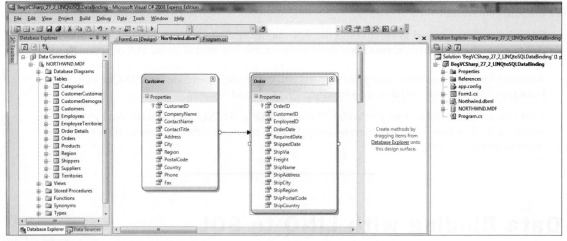

Figure 27-17

4.   Compile the project so that the classes defined in Northwind.dbml objects will be available in the following steps.

5.   Add a new data source to your project by selecting Data ⇨ Add New Data Source as shown in Figure 27-18.

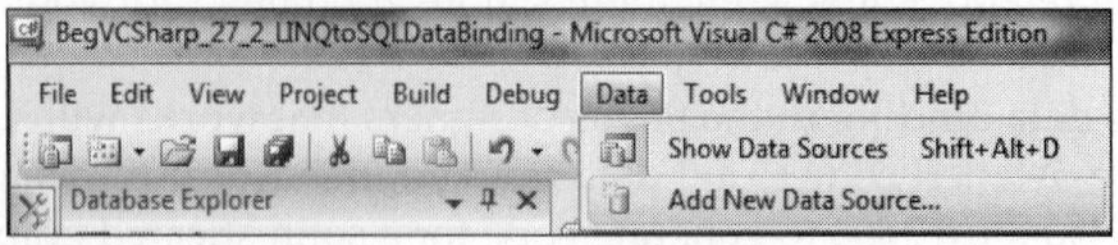

Figure 27-18

922

6. In the Data Source Configuration Wizard dialog, click Object as the data source type as shown in Figure 27-19. Then click Next.

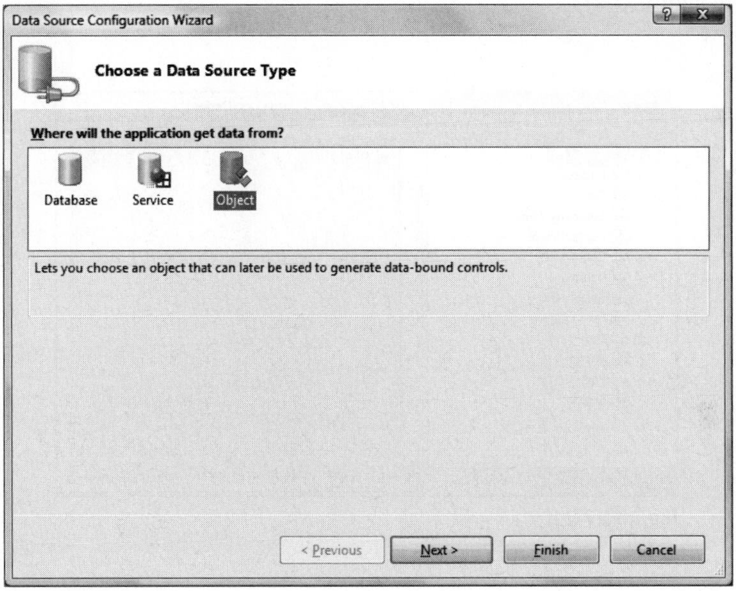

Figure 27-19

7. Choose the Customer object (see Figure 27-20) and then click Finish.

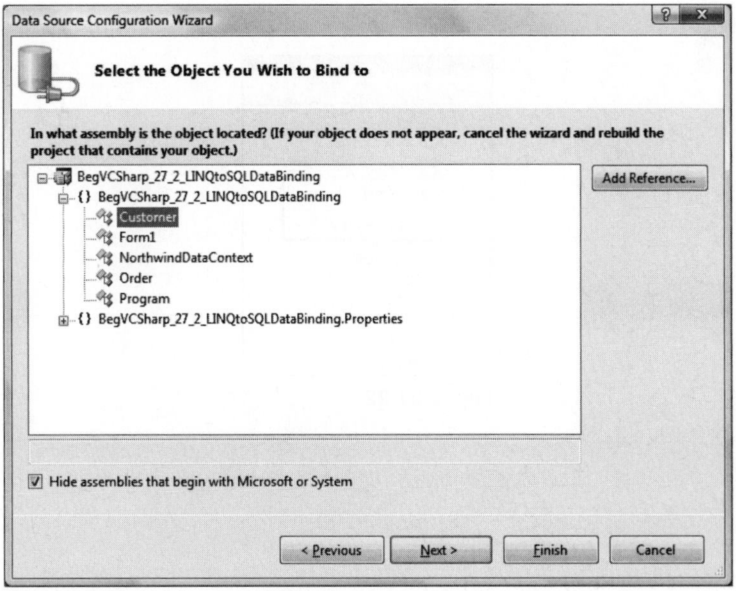

Figure 27-20

8. Click on the design pane for `Form1.cs` so it appears in the foreground of your project code windows. Show your newly added data source by selecting Data ⇨ Show Data Sources (see Figure 27-18 if you do not find it), and expand the `Customer` node in the data source as shown in Figure 27-21.

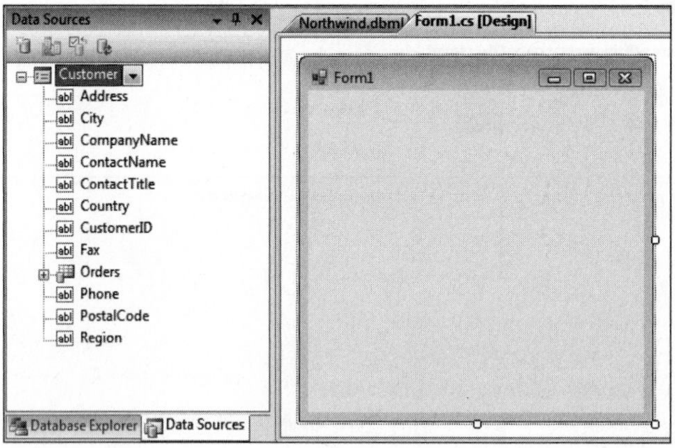

Figure 27-21

9. Expand the size of `Form1.cs` a bit because you are going to add a number of controls to it.

10. Click on the `Customer` node drop-down box (see Figure 27-22) and choose Details as the default control type to create for this table.

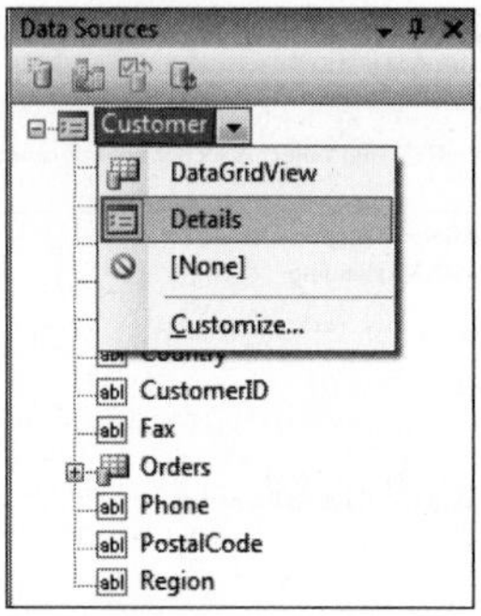

Figure 27-22

11. Click on the `Customer` node and drag it into the `Form1.cs` design window (see Figure 27-23).

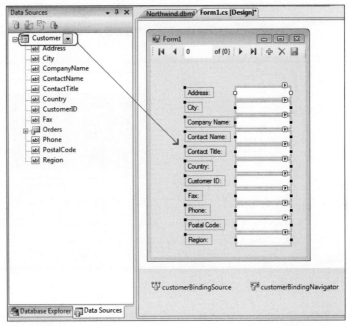

Figure 27-23

A series of data entry fields will appear on the form (refer to Figure 27-23) as well as two new objects: `customerBindingSource` and `customerBindingNavigator`.

What are these strange pseudo-controls at the bottom of your form? They do not seem to appear on the screen if you run the application.

Actually, one of the new objects *does* appear on the form. This is the `customerBindingNavigator`, a navigation bar at the top of your form for moving through the rows in the database, as shown at the top of Figure 27-23.

The `customerBindingSource` object controls the binding of the controls on the form to the Customer LINQ to SQL source. While not actually visible on the form, it interacts with the controls and your LINQ to SQL classes to keep them synchronized with the database.

12. Click on the Orders node and drag it into the design window for Form1.cs to the right the Customer data entry fields (see Figure 27-24).

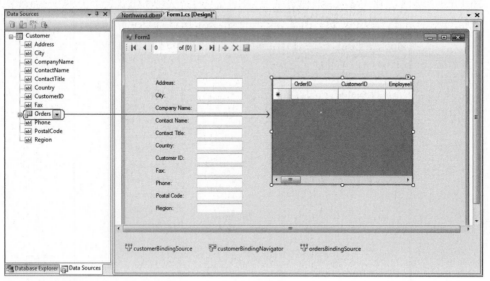

Figure 27-24

A data grid control will appear on the form (refer to Figure 27-24) as well as a new binding source, the orderBindingSource. No navigator was added because Orders is a dependent member of the Customer object and its navigation is controlled by the position in the parent Customers table.

13. Double-click on the title bar of Form1 in the Form1.cs designer window to create an event handler for Form1's Form_Load event. The code view of Form1.cs appears, with the stub of the event handler ready to be filled in.

14. Add the following lines to the Form1 class in Form1.cs in the code editor:

```csharp
public partial class Form1 : Form
{
    NorthwindDataContext northwindDataContext = new NorthwindDataContext();

    public Form1()
    {
        InitializeComponent();
    }

    private void Form1_Load(object sender, EventArgs e)
    {
        customerBindingSource.DataSource = northwindDataContext.Customers;
    }
}
```

15. Compile and execute the program (you can just press F5 for Start Debugging). You will see the information for customers in the U.S.A. and their orders, similar to that shown in Figure 27-25 for Germany.

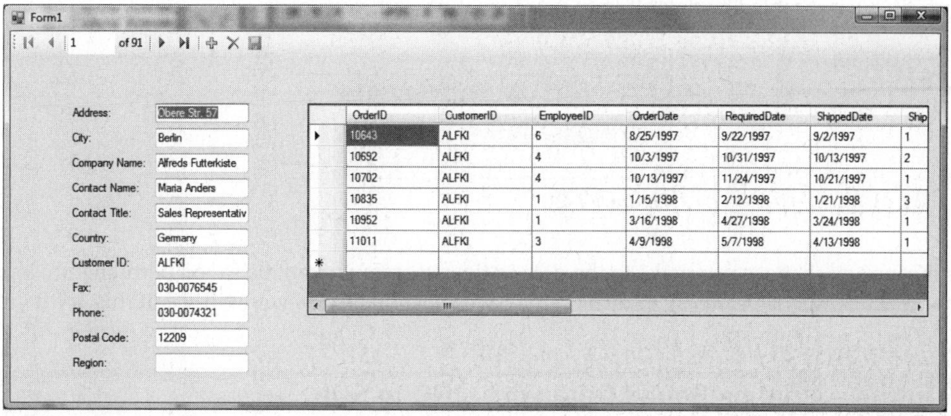

	OrderID	CustomerID	EmployeeID	OrderDate	RequiredDate	ShippedDate	Ship
▶	10643	ALFKI	6	8/25/1997	9/22/1997	9/2/1997	1
	10692	ALFKI	4	10/3/1997	10/31/1997	10/13/1997	2
	10702	ALFKI	4	10/13/1997	11/24/1997	10/21/1997	1
	10835	ALFKI	1	1/15/1998	2/12/1998	1/21/1998	3
	10952	ALFKI	1	3/16/1998	4/27/1998	3/24/1998	1
	11011	ALFKI	3	4/9/1998	5/7/1998	4/13/1998	1

Figure 27-25

Use the navigation buttons in the upper-left corner to move through the customer records. You can see the customer fields change values and each customer's orders display in the data grid as you scroll through the data. Pretty good functionality for just having to write two lines of code!

How It Works

The process for creating and using the `Northwind.dbml` LINQ to SQL mapping is the same as in previous examples. Just as with previous console examples, you must create an instance of the `NorthwindDataContext` class through which access to the other LINQ to SQL objects is obtained. Here, you made this instance a part of the `Form1` class instead of adding it to a `Main()` method:

```
public partial class Form1 : Form
{
    NorthwindDataContext northwindDataContext = new NorthwindDataContext();
```

The key line of code that connects the bound data-entry fields to the `NorthwindDataContext` class is the code you added to the `Form_Load()` method:

```
private void Form1_Load(object sender, EventArgs e)
{
    customerBindingSource.DataSource = northwindDataContext.Customers;
```

Although the data controls were generated for your LINQ to SQL class when you specified an object as the data source, the assignment to the `DataSource` member is what tells C# from which object instance to fill the controls.

However, once the initial instance is bound, the rest of the behavior happens automatically behind the scenes when users interact with the controls on the screen, and you don't have to code any of it yourself! What could be easier?

Updating Bound Data with LINQ to SQL

One piece of functionality that you may notice is missing in the preceding example is making changes to the database. The Save button, indicated by a floppy disk icon at the right of the navigator bar (see Figure 27-26), is disabled by default until you turn it on with your code.

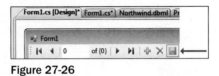

Figure 27-26

This means any changes you make to the data in the program will not be saved permanently in the database. Luckily, it is very easy to turn on the Save functionality, as you will see in this Try It Out.

<hr/>

Try It Out   **Updating Bound Data with LINQ to SQL**

Follow these steps to create the example in Visual C# 2008:

1. Modify the existing Windows forms project BegVCSharp_27_2_LINQtoSQLDataBinding in the directory C:\BegVCSharp\Chapter27.

2. In the Form1.cs design window, double-click on the Save button in the navigator bar.

3. An empty event handler for the customerBindingNavigatorSaveItem_Click event appears in the Form1.cs code window. Add the following line to the handler method:

```
private void customerBindingNavigatorSaveItem_Click(object sender, EventArgs e)
{
        northwindDataContext.SubmitChanges();
}
```

4. Back in the Form1.cs design window, set the Enabled property for the customerBindingNavigatorSaveItem control to True.

5. If you chose "No" to not copy the Northwnd.MDF database file as recommended in previous examples, skip to step 6. If you chose "Yes," click on Northwnd.MDF in the Solution Explorer. In the Properties window, set the Copy to Output Directory property to Copy if Newer, as shown in Figure 27-27. This ensures that Visual C# 2008 does not overwrite your changed local copy when starting your project.

6. Compile and execute the program (press F5 for Start Debugging).

7. Modify a field (e.g., enter a value for Region on the first customer record, ALKFI). After making the change, navigate to the next record with the right arrow, and then press the Save button. Navigate back to the first record and you will find that the change persists. It will also persist if you exit the program and restart.

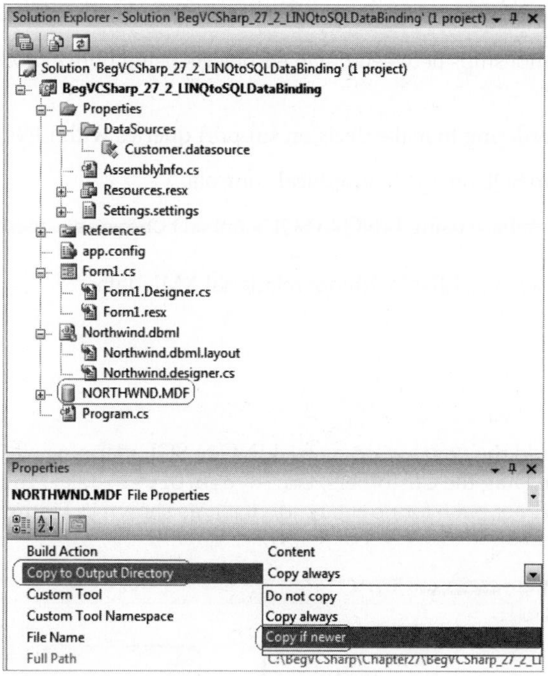

Figure 27-27

How It Works

The `SubmitChanges()` method you call in the Save button event handler will save all pending changes in the memory of the `DataContext` instance to the database:

```
northwindDataContext.SubmitChanges();
```

This includes all database objects loaded into memory and their related rows. It does not include data entered in a field but not saved to memory yet; that is why you need to navigate to the next record before clicking Save. Appropriate SQL insert and update statements are executed against the database based on the changes you made to your objects.

Summary

That completes your tour of LINQ to SQL. Highlights of this chapter included the following:

❑   The concept of *object-relational mapping (ORM)* and how LINQ to SQL implements this concept for C#.

❑   Learning to use the O/R Designer in Visual C# 2008 to create objects for a specific database.

❑ Using LINQ to SQL queries with the objects created by the O/R Designer.

❑ Navigating relationships between database objects using both explicit query code and generated code.

❑ Grouping and ordering to make decision support queries with LINQ to SQL.

❑ Binding LINQ to SQL objects to graphical controls.

❑ Updating the database using LINQ to SQL's `SubmitChanges()` method.

In the next chapter you will use LINQ with nonrelational XML data.

Exercises

For each exercise here, add the `Northwind.dbml` LINQ to SQL mapping class to your solution as described in the chapter. Drag the Customers, `Employees`, `Order Details`, `Orders`, and `Products` tables into the O/R Designer pane for `Northwind.dbml`, as shown in Figure 27-28.

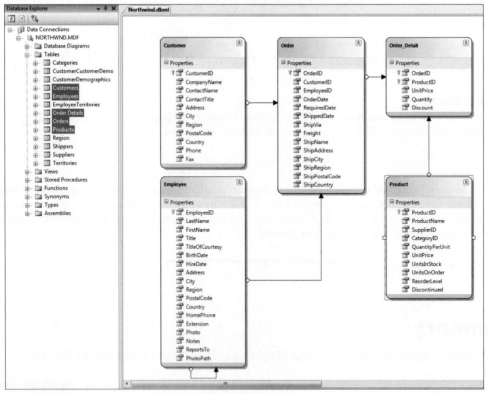

Figure 27-28

1. Use LINQ to SQL to display detail information from the `Products` and `Employees` tables in the Northwind database.

2. Create a LINQ to SQL query to show the top-selling products in the Northwind database.

3. Create a group query to show top-selling products by country.

4. Create a set of data-bound controls to edit product information for the Northwind data.

ADO.NET and LINQ over DataSet

The previous chapter introduced LINQ (Language-Integrated Query) and showed how it works with objects. This chapter introduces ADO.NET, which is the traditional way of accessing databases with previous versions of C# and .NET, and then it introduces LINQ over DataSet, which is the version of LINQ that cooperates with ADO.NET.

> *All examples in this chapter use the SQL Server Northwind example database (except where specifically noted). See the previous chapter for instructions on installing the SQL Server Northwind example database.*

In particular, this chapter looks at the following:

- ❑ An overview of ADO.NET and the structure of its main classes.
- ❑ Reading data with a `DataReader` and with a `DataSet`.
- ❑ Updating the database, adding records, and deleting records.
- ❑ Working with relationships in ADO.NET.
- ❑ Reading and writing XML documents in ADO.NET.
- ❑ Executing SQL commands directly from ADO.NET.
- ❑ Executing stored procedures from ADO.NET.
- ❑ Querying ADO.NET objects with LINQ over DataSet.

After an overview of ADO.NET, you will learn the concepts behind it. Then you can create some simple projects and start using the ADO.NET classes.

What Is ADO.NET?

ADO.NET is the name for the set of classes you use with C# and the .NET Framework to access data in a relational, table-oriented format. This includes relational databases such as Microsoft SQL Server and Microsoft Access, as well as other databases and even nonrelational data sources. ADO.NET is integrated into the .NET Framework and is designed to be used with any .NET language, especially C#.

ADO.NET includes the `System.Data` namespace and its nested namespaces, such as `System.Data` `.SqlClient` and `System.Data.Linq`, plus some specific data-related classes from the `System.Xml` namespace. You looked at XML in Chapter 25; this chapter describes ADO.NET's support for XML. Physically, the ADO.NET classes are contained in the `System.Data.dll` assembly and related `System.Data.xxx.dll` assemblies, again with some exceptions such as XML.

Why Is It Called ADO.NET?

You might be wondering why this part of the .NET Framework gets its own weird moniker, ADO.NET. Why not just call it `System.Data` and be done with it? ADO.NET takes its name from ActiveX Data Objects (ADO), a widely used set of classes used for data access in the previous generation of Microsoft technologies. The ADO.NET name is used because Microsoft wanted to make it clear that this set of classes replaces ADO and is the preferred data access interface in the .NET programming environment, at least until LINQ to SQL.

ADO.NET serves the same purpose as ADO, providing an easy-to-use set of classes for data access, updated and enhanced for the .NET programming environment. While it fulfills the same role as ADO, the classes, properties, and methods in ADO.NET are quite different from those in ADO.

If you are interested in more details about how this developed historically and where it fits in with other Microsoft database interfaces such as ODBC and OLE DB, see the following brief history. Otherwise, skip to the next section to start learning about ADO.NET!

A (Very) Brief History of Data Access

When the first database systems, such as Oracle and IBM's DB2, were written, any developers who wanted their programs to access the data in them needed to use sets of functions that were specific to that database system. Each system had its own library of functions, such as the Oracle Call Interface (OCI) for Oracle, or DBLib for Sybase's SQL Server (later bought by Microsoft). This enabled the programs to have fast access to the data, because their programs communicated directly with the database. However, it meant that programmers had to be familiar with a different library for every database they worked with, so the task of writing data-driven applications was very complicated. It also meant that if a company changed the database system it used, its applications had to be completely rewritten.

This problem was solved by Open Database Connectivity (ODBC). ODBC was developed by Microsoft in collaboration with other companies in the early 1990s. ODBC provided a common set of functions that developers could use against any database system. These functions were translated into database-specific function calls by drivers for that specific database system.

This solved the main problems of the proprietary database libraries — developers only needed to know how to use one set of functions (the ODBC functions); and if a company changed its database system, all it needed to change in its applications was the code to connect to the database. However, there was still one problem. While the paperless office is still largely a dream, companies do have a vast amount of electronic data stored in a large variety of places — e-mails, Web pages, Project 2000 files, and so on. ODBC was fine for accessing data in traditional databases, but it couldn't access other types of data that aren't stored in nice neat columns and rows and don't necessarily have a coherent structure at all.

The answer to this problem was provided by OLE DB. OLE DB works in a similar way to ODBC, providing a layer of abstraction between the database and the applications that need access to the data. Client applications communicate with the data source, which can be a traditional database or any other place where data is held, through an OLE DB provider for that data source. Data from any source is exposed to the application in table format — just as if it came from a database. In addition, because OLE DB allows access to data exposed by the existing ODBC drivers, it can be used to access all the databases supported by ODBC. As you will see shortly, ADO.NET supports both OLE DB and ODBC in a very similar way.

The last non-.NET legacy data access technology to mention is ActiveX Data Objects (ADO). ADO is simply a thin layer that sits on top of OLE DB, enabling programs written in high-level languages such as Visual Basic to access OLE DB data.

ADO.NET was introduced with the .NET Framework 1.0 and has evolved through the various .NET versions with additional data providers and incremental improvements. LINQ over SQL is the first major paradigm shift in data access since the .NET Framework was introduced. ADO.NET will continue to evolve alongside LINQ, with new facilities such as the forthcoming ADO.NET for Entities, which will ship after Visual Studio 2008.

ADO.NET for Entities is an advanced interface targeted at expert ADO.NET developers and is a subject beyond the scope of this book. Still evolving, it is not officially part of Visual Studio 2008.

Design Goals of ADO.NET

Let's quickly look at the design goals of ADO.NET:

❑ Simple access to relational and nonrelational data.

❑ Extensibility to support even more data sources than its predecessor technologies.

❑ Support for multitier applications across the Internet.

❑ Unification of XML and relational data access.

Simple Access to Relational Data

The primary goal of ADO.NET is to provide simple access to relational data. Straightforward, easy-to-use classes represent the tables, columns, and rows within relational databases. Additionally, ADO.NET introduces the `DataSet` class, which represents a set of data from related tables encapsulated as a single unit, preserving the integrity of the relationships between them. This is a new concept in ADO.NET that significantly extends the capabilities of the data access interface.

Extensibility

ADO.NET is *extensible* — it provides a framework for plug-in .NET data providers (also called *managed providers*) that can be built to read and write data from any data source. ADO.NET comes with several built-in .NET data providers, including one for the Microsoft SQL Server database, one for Oracle, and one each for the generic database interfaces: the Microsoft Open DataBase Connectivity database (ODBC) API and Microsoft's COM-based Object Linking and Embedding DataBase (OLE DB) API. Almost every database and data file format has an ODBC or OLE DB provider available for it, including Microsoft Access, third-party databases, and nonrelational data; thus, ADO.NET can be used to interface to almost any database or data format through one of the built-in data providers. Many database vendors such as MySQL and Oracle also provide native .NET data providers for their offerings.

Support for Multitier Applications

ADO.NET is designed for multitier applications. This is the most common architecture today for business and e-commerce applications. In multitier architecture, different parts of the application logic are separated into layers, or tiers, and communicate only with the layer around them.

One of the most common approaches is the three-tier model, which consists of the following:

❑ **Data tier**: Contains the database and data access code.

❑ **Business tier**: Contains the business logic, which defines the unique functionality of the application, and abstracts this away from other tiers. This tier is sometimes referred to as the *middle tier*.

❑ **Presentation tier**: Provides the user interface and control of process flow to the application, as well as such things as the validation of user input.

ADO.NET uses the open Internet-standard XML format for communications between the tiers, enabling data to pass through Internet firewalls and allowing the possibility of a non-Microsoft implementation of one or more tiers.

Unification of XML and Relational Data Access

Another important goal of ADO.NET is to provide a bridge between relational data in rows and columns, and XML documents, which have a hierarchical data structure. The .NET technology is built around XML, and ADO.NET makes extensive use of it.

Now that you've seen what ADO.NET's goals are, let's look at the actual ADO.NET classes themselves.

Overview of ADO.NET Classes and Objects

The diagram in Figure 28-1 shows the basic classes in ADO.NET. Note that this is not an inheritance diagram. It shows the relationships between the most commonly used classes.

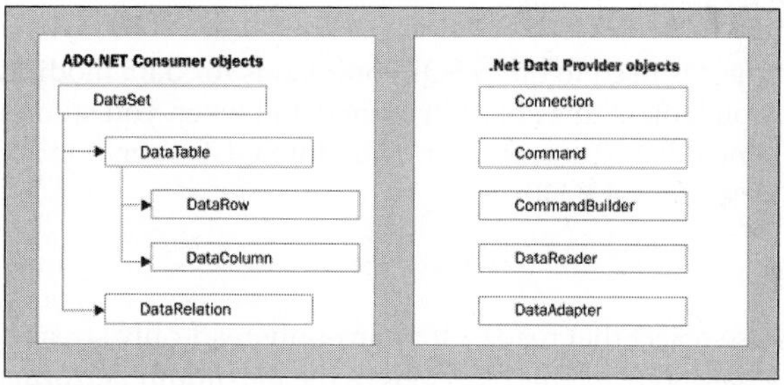

Figure 28-1

The classes are divided into .NET data provider objects and consumer objects:

❑ *Provider objects* are specific to each type of data source — the actual reading and writing to and from the data source is done with the provider-specific objects.

❑ *Consumer objects* are what you use to access and manipulate the data once you have read it into memory.

The provider objects require an active connection. You use these first to read the data, and then depending on your needs you may work with the data in memory using the consumer objects. You can also update the data in the data source using the provider objects to write the changes back to the data source. Thus, the consumer objects operate in a disconnected fashion; you can work with the data in memory even if the database connection is down.

Provider Objects

`Provider` objects are defined in each .NET data provider. The names are prefaced with a name unique to the provider; for example, the actual connection object for the OLE DB provider is `OleDbConnection`; the class for the SQL Server .NET provider is `SqlConnection`.

Connection Object

The `Connection` object is typically the first object that you use, before using most of the other ADO.NET objects — it provides the basic connection to your data source. If you are using a database that requires a username and password or one on a remote network server, then the `Connection` object takes care of the details of establishing the connection and logging in.

If you are familiar with classic ADO, note that `Connection` and other objects that serve a similar function in classic ADO have similar names in ADO.NET.

Command Object

You use the `Command` object to give a command to a data source, such as `SELECT * FROM Customers` to query the data in the `Customers` table. The provider-specific names include `SqlCommand` for SQL Server, `OdbcCommand` for ODBC, and `OleDbCommand` for OLE DB.

CommandBuilder Object

The `CommandBuilder` object is used to build SQL commands for data modification from objects based on a single-table query. You look at this object in more detail when you study how to update data. The provider-specific names include `SqlCommandBuilder` for SQL Server, `OdbcCommandBuilder` for ODBC, and `OleDbCommandBuilder` for OLE DB.

DataReader Object

This is a fast, simple-to-use object that reads a forward-only read-only stream of data, such as the set of customers found from a data source. This object gives the maximum performance for simply reading data; the first example will demonstrate how to use this object. The provider-specific objects include `SqlDataReader` for SQL Server, `OdbcDataReader` for ODBC, and `OleDbDataReader` for OLE DB.

DataAdapter Object

This is a general-purpose class that performs various operations specific to the data source, including updating changed data, filling `DataSet` objects (see the "DataSet Object" section) and other operations, shown in the following examples. Provider-specific names include `SqlDataAdapter` for SQL Server, `OdbcDataAdapter` for ODBC, and `OleDbAdapter` for OLE DB.

Consumer Objects

These are the objects defined for the disconnected, consumer side of ADO.NET. These aren't related to any specific .NET data provider and live within the `System.Data` namespace.

DataSet Object

The `DataSet` is the king of consumer objects. The `DataSet` represents a set of related tables referenced as one unit in your application. For example, `Customers`, `Orders`, and `Products` might all be tables in one `DataSet` representing each customer and the products he or she ordered from your company. With this object, you can get all the data you need from each table quickly, examine and change it while you're disconnected from the server, and then update the server with the changes in one efficient operation.

The `DataSet` has features that enable you to access lower-level objects that represent individual tables and relationships. These objects, the `DataTable` object and the `DataRelation` object, are covered in the following sections.

DataTable Object

This object represents one of the tables in the `DataSet`, such as `Customers`, `Orders`, or `Products`. The `DataTable` object has features that enable you to access its rows and columns:

❑ **DataColumn object**: This represents one column in the table, such as `OrderID` or `CustomerName`.

❑ **DataRow object**: This represents one row of related data from a table, such as a particular customer's `CustomerID`, name, address, and so on.

DataRelation Object

The `DataRelation` object represents the relationship between two tables via a shared column; for example, the `Orders` table might have a `CustomerID` column identifying the customer who placed the order. A `DataRelation` object might be created representing the relationship between `Customers` and `Orders` via the shared column `CustomerID`.

That should give you an idea of the overall structure of the objects in ADO.NET. There are more objects than the ones just listed, but let's skip the details for now and get into some examples that show how this all works.

Using the System.Data Namespace

The first step in using ADO.NET within your C# code is to reference the `System.Data` namespace, in which all the ADO.NET classes are located. Put the following `using` directive at the beginning of any program using ADO.NET:

```
using System.Data;
```

Next, you need to reference the .NET data provider for the specific data source you'll be using.

SQL Server .NET Data Provider

If you are using the SQL Server database (version 7 or later), including the desktop engine (SQL Express or MSDE), the best performance and most direct access to the underlying features is available with the native (SQL Server–specific) .NET data provider, referenced with this `using` directive:

```
using System.Data.SqlClient;
```

Oracle .NET Data Provider

If you are using the Oracle database, a native Oracle .NET driver is the best choice; one is provided with the .NET Framework, referenced with this `using` directive:

```
using System.Data.OracleClient;
```

Oracle itself also provides a .NET data provider, referenced as `Oracle.DataAccess.Client`. This is a separate download that you have to get from Oracle. Whether you use a .NET data provider from the database vendor or use the one provided with the .NET Framework is your choice. Generally, a provider from the vendor makes more use of the database product's special features, but for basic or beginning usage this is unlikely to matter much. Either provider will work; use the one that you prefer.

OLE DB .NET Data Provider

For data sources other than SQL Server or Oracle (such as Microsoft Access), you can use the OLE DB .NET data provider, referenced with this `using` directive:

```
using System.Data.OleDb;
```

This provider uses an OLE DB provider DLL for the specific database you are accessing; OLE DB providers for many common databases are installed with Windows, notably Microsoft Access, which you use in the following examples.

ODBC .NET Data Provider

If you have a data source for which no native or OLE DB provider is available, the ODBC .NET data provider is a good alternative because most databases provide an ODBC interface. It is referenced with this `using` directive:

```
using System.Data.Odbc;
```

Other Native .NET Data Providers

If there is a native .NET data provider available specifically for your database, then you may want to use that .NET data provider instead. Many other database vendors and third-party companies provide native .NET data providers; the choice between using the native provider and using something generic like the ODBC provider depends on your circumstances. If you value portability over performance, then go generic. If you want to get the best performance or make the best use of a particular database's features, then go native.

Reading Data with the DataReader

In the following Try It Out, you just get some data from one table, the `Customers` table in the SQL Server/MSDE Northwind sample database (also covered in Chapter 25). The `Customers` table contains rows and columns with data about the customers of Northwind traders. The first example here uses a `DataReader` to retrieve the `CustomerID` and `CompanyName` columns from this table.

Try It Out   Reading Data with the DataReader

Follow these steps to create the example in Visual Studio 2008:

1. Create a new console application called DataReading in the directory C:\BegVCSharp\Chapter28.

2. Begin by adding the `using` directives for the ADO.NET classes you will be using:

```
#region Using Directives
using System;
using System.Data;              // Use ADO.NET namespace
using System.Data.SqlClient;   // Use SQL Server data provider namespace
using System.Collections.Generic;
using System.Text;
#endregion
```

3. Add the following code to the `Main()` method:

```
static void Main(string[] args)
{
    // Specify SQL Server-specific connection string
    SqlConnection thisConnection = new SqlConnection(
            @"Data Source=.\SQLEXPRESS;"+
```

```
        @"AttachDbFilename='C:\SQL Server 2000 Sample Databases\NORTHWND
.MDF';" +
        @"Integrated Security=True;Connect Timeout=30;User Instance=true" );

    // Open connection
    thisConnection.Open();

    // Create command for this connection
    SqlCommand thisCommand = thisConnection.CreateCommand();

    // Specify SQL query for this command
    thisCommand.CommandText =
        "SELECT CustomerID, CompanyName from Customers";

    // Execute DataReader for specified command
    SqlDataReader thisReader = thisCommand.ExecuteReader();

    // While there are rows to read
    while (thisReader.Read())
    {
        // Output ID and name columns
        Console.WriteLine("\t{0}\t{1}",
        thisReader["CustomerID"], thisReader["CompanyName"]);
    }

    // Close reader
    thisReader.Close();

    // Close connection
    thisConnection.Close();

    Console.Write("Program finished, press Enter/Return to continue:");
    Console.ReadLine();
}
```

4. Compile and execute this program. You should see a list of customer IDs and company names, as shown in the following code. If you don't see this output, don't worry; you can troubleshoot any problems in a moment.

```
        RICAR    Ricardo Adocicados
        RICSU    Richter Supermarkt
        ROMEY    Romero y tomillo
        SANTG    Santé Gourmet
        SAVEA    Save-a-lot Markets
        SEVES    Seven Seas Imports
        SIMOB    Simons bistro
        SPECD    Spécialités du monde
        SPLIR    Split Rail Beer & Ale
        SUPRD    Suprêmes délices
        THEBI    The Big Cheese
        THECR    The Cracker Box
        TOMSP    Toms Spezialitäten
```

```
         TORTU    Tortuga Restaurante
         TRADH    Tradiçao Hipermercados
         TRAIH    Trail's Head Gourmet Provisioners
         VAFFE    Vaffeljernet
         VICTE    Victuailles en stock
         VINET    Vins et alcools Chevalier
         WARTH    Wartian Herkku
         WELLI    Wellington Importadora
         WHITC    White Clover Markets
         WILMK    Wilman Kala
         WOLZA    Wolski  Zajazd
    Program finished, press Enter/Return to continue:
```

How It Works

The first step is to reference the System.Data namespace and your provider as described before. You're going to use the SQL Server .NET provider in these examples, so you need the following lines at the start of your program:

```
using System.Data;
using System.Data.SqlClient;
```

Five steps are required to retrieve the data from the program:

1. Connect to the data source.

2. Open the connection.

3. Issue a SQL query.

4. Read and display the data with the DataReader.

5. Close the DataReader and the connection.

The following section describes each of these steps in turn.

First, you need to connect to your data source. This is done by creating a connection object using a connection string. The connection string is just a character string containing the name of the provider for the database you want to connect to, the login information (database user, password, and so on), and the name of the particular database you want to use. Let's look at the specific elements of this connection string; however, keep in mind that these strings differ significantly between data providers, so you need to look up the specific connection information for your data provider if it is different from this example (the connection information for Access is shown a little later in the chapter).

The line where you create the connection object looks like this:

```
SqlConnection thisConnection = new SqlConnection(
    @"Data Source=.\SQLEXPRESS;"+
    @"AttachDbFilename='C:\SQL Server 2000 Sample Databases\NORTHWND.MDF';" +
    @"Integrated Security=True;Connect Timeout=30;User Instance=true" );
```

`SqlConnection` is the name of the connection object for the SQL .NET data provider; if you were using OLE DB, then you would create an `OleDbConnection`. The connection string consists of named entries separated by semicolons. The first is as follows:

```
@"Data Source=.\SQLEXPRESS;"
```

This is just the name of the SQL Server you are accessing, in the form `computername\instancename`. The period is a handy SQL Server shorthand name that refers to the server instance running on the current machine. You can also substitute the name `(local)` or the actual network name of your computer; for example, my laptop computer is `\\roadrunner`, so I could also use `roadrunner\` `sqlexpress` as my server name.

`SQLEXPRESS` is the SQL Server *instance* name. There can be multiple copies of SQL Server installed on one machine, and the instance name, set at installation time, is how you tell SQL Server which one you want. `SQLEXPRESS` is the default instance name used when you install SQL Express. If you have another version of SQL Server installed, then the instance name will differ — there may be no instance name (in which case you would use `(local)` or your machine name by itself), or it may be a different name, such as `local)\NetSDK` used for the MSDE installations with previous versions of the .NET Framework.

Note that the @ sign prefacing the connection string indicates a string literal, making the backslash in this name work; otherwise, double backslashes (`\\`) are necessary to escape the backslash character inside a C# string.

If you installed the SQL Server you are working with, then you know the name of the SQL Server instance. Otherwise, you have to check with your SQL Server or network administrator to find out what name to use.

The next entry is as follows:

```
AttachDbFilename='C:\SQL Server 2000 Sample Databases\NORTHWND.MDF';
```

This is same `.MDF` file you downloaded in Chapter 27, containing the Northwind sample data. If you placed the file in different directory, change the path to match the setup on your computer.

The next part of the connection string specifies how to log in to the database; here, you use the integrated security of the Windows login so no separate user and password need to be specified:

```
Integrated Security=True;
```

This clause specifies the standard built-in security for SQL Server and Windows. Alternatively, instead of the `Integrated Security` clause, you could specify a username and password clause, as in `User=sa;PWD=secret`. Using the built-in security of your Windows login is preferable to using hard-coded usernames and passwords in connection strings!

The next part of the connection string specifies the connect timeout — how long the program waits for a connection to the SQL Server database before returning an error. The value shown is 30 seconds; for production applications it may take this long to establish a connection over a network, talking to a busy server.

```
Connect Timeout=30;
```

The last part of the connection string specifies whether a user instance is used for your connection:

```
User Instance=true;
```

A user instance is a local SQL Server Express instance that runs under your Windows login on your local computer. The user instance enables you to run a local copy of SQL Server for program development even if your Windows login does not have Windows administrator or database administrator privileges. For more information on user instances, see the web links http://technet .microsoft.com/en-us/library/bb264564.aspx and http://technet.microsoft.com/ en-us/library/ms143684.aspx.

> *If you get an exception indicating that user instances are not enabled, open a query window and run the following database command:*

```
exec sp_configure 'user instances enabled', 1
Reconfigure
```

> *This will enable user instances and will automatically restart SQL Server.*

You should now have a connection object that is configured for your machine and database (the connection is not yet active; to do this you must open it).

After you have a connection object, you can move on to the second step, opening it, which establishes the connection to the database:

```
thisConnection.Open();
```

If the Open() method fails — for example, if the SQL Server cannot be found — a SqlException exception will be thrown and you will see a message like that shown in Figure 28-2.

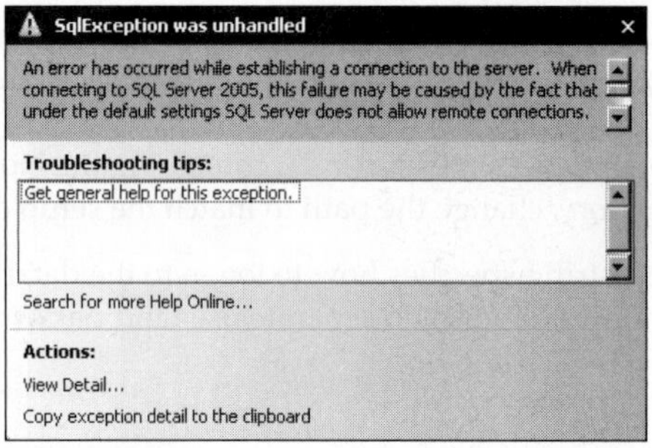

Figure 28-2

This particular message indicates that the program couldn't find the SQL Server database or server. Check that the server name in the connection string is correct and that the server is running.

The third step is to create a command object and give it a SQL command to perform a database operation (such as retrieving some data). The code is as follows:

```
SqlCommand thisCommand = thisConnection.CreateCommand();
thisCommand.CommandText = "SELECT CustomerID, CompanyName from Customers";
```

The connection object has a method called CreateCommand() to create a command associated with this connection, so you use this to get your command object. The command itself is assigned to the

`CommandText` property of the command object. You're going to get a list of the customer IDs and the company names from the Northwind database, so that is the basis for your SQL query command:

```
SELECT CustomerID, CompanyName from Customers
```

The `SELECT` command is the SQL command to get the data from one or more tables. A common error is to mistype the name of one of the tables, resulting in another exception:

```
thisCommand.CommandText = "SELECT CustomerID, CompanyName from Customer";
```

Oops! I forgot the "s" in `Customers`, so I get the exception shown in Figure 28-3.

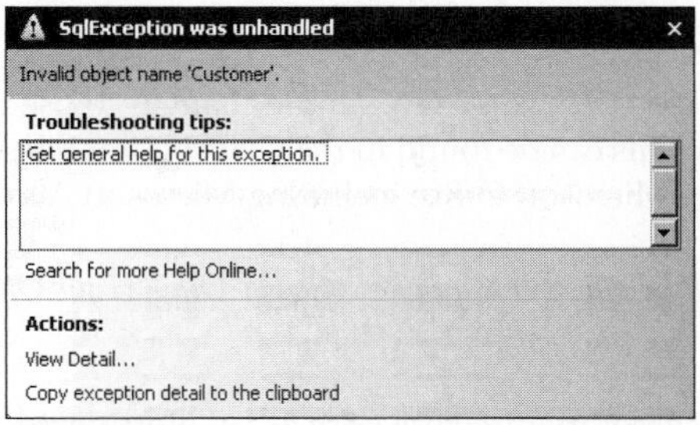

Figure 28-3

Fix the typo, rebuild, and move on.

The fourth step is to read and display the data. First, you read the data with a `DataReader`. The `DataReader` is a lightweight, fast object for quickly getting the results of a query. It is read-only, so you can't use it to update data — you get to that after you finish this example. As you saw in the previous section, you use a method from the last object you created, the command object, to create an associated instance of the object you need next — in this case, the `DataReader`:

```
SqlDataReader thisReader = thisCommand.ExecuteReader();
```

`ExecuteReader()` executes the SQL command at the database, so any database errors are generated here; it also creates the reader object for reading the generated results — here you assign it to `thisReader`.

There are several methods for getting the results out of the reader, but the following is the usual process. The `Read()` method of `DataReader` reads a single row of the data resulting from the query, returning `true` while there is more data to read, `false` if there is not. Therefore, you set up a `while` loop to read data with the `Read()` method and print out the results as you get them on each iteration:

```
while (thisReader.Read())
{
    Console.WriteLine("\t{0}\t{1}",
                      thisReader["CustomerID"], thisReader["CompanyName"]);
}
```

While `Read()` returns `true`, `Console.WriteLine("\t{0}\t{1}"`, `...)` writes out a line with two pieces of data separated by tab characters (`\t`). The `DataReader` object provides an `indexer` property (see Chapter 11 for a discussion of indexers). The indexer is overloaded, and enables you to reference the columns as an array reference by column name: `thisReader["CustomerID"]`, `thisReader["CompanyName"]`, or by an integer: `thisReader[0]`, `thisReader[1]`.

When `Read()` returns `false` at the end of the results, the `while` loop ends.

The fifth and final step is to close the objects you opened, which include the reader object and the connection object. Each of these objects has a `Close()` method, which you call before exiting the program:

```
thisReader.Close();
thisConnection.Close();
```

That's all there is to accessing a single table!

The same program can be written with just a few simple changes to use the Microsoft Access version of this database (`nwind.mdb`). This can be found in the C:\Program Files\Microsoft Office\OfficeXX\ Samples directory (if you have Microsoft Office including Microsoft Access).

The XX in OfficeXX is a placeholder for a number, such as Office11 for Office 2003 or Office12 for Office 2007.

Make a copy of the file (in a temporary directory such as C:\Northwind\nwind.mdb), so you can always go back to the original.

If you do not have Office already, download `Nwind.exe` from the following:

```
http://microsoft.com/downloads/details.
aspx?familyid=c6661372-8dbe-422b-8676-c632d66c529c&displaylang=en
```

Execute `Nwind.exe` to install the sample database; it prompts you for a directory, so you can place it wherever you want, such as in c:\Northwind. Except for the details of the connection string, the changes you make in the following Try It Out will work for any other OLE DB data source.

Try It Out   Reading from an Access Database

1. Create a new console application called ReadingAccessData in the directory C:\BegVCSharp\Chapter28.

2. Begin by adding the `using` directives for the OLE DB provider classes you will be using:

```
#region Using Directives
using System;
using System.Data;              // Use ADO.NET namespace
using System.Data.OleDb;        // Use namespace for OLE DB .NET Data Provider
using System.Collections.Generic;
using System.Text;
#endregion
```

3. Add the following code to the `Main()` method:

```
static void Main(string[] args)
{

    // Create connection object for Microsoft Access OLE DB Provider;
    // note @ sign prefacing string literal so backslashes in path name;
    // work
    OleDbConnection thisConnection = new OleDbConnection(
        @"Provider=Microsoft.Jet.OLEDB.4.0;Data Source=C:\Northwind\nwind.mdb");

    // Open connection object
    thisConnection.Open();

    // Create SQL command object on this connection
    OleDbCommand thisCommand = thisConnection.CreateCommand();

    // Initialize SQL SELECT command to retrieve desired data
    thisCommand.CommandText =
        "SELECT CustomerID, CompanyName FROM Customers";

    // Create a DataReader object based on previously defined command object
    OleDbDataReader thisReader = thisCommand.ExecuteReader();

    while (thisReader.Read())
    {
        Console.WriteLine("\t{0}\t{1}",
        thisReader["CustomerID"], thisReader["CompanyName"]);
    }
    thisReader.Close();
    thisConnection.Close();

    Console.Write("Program finished, press Enter/Return to continue:");
    Console.ReadLine();

}
```

How It Works

Instead of the `SqlConnection`, `SqlCommand`, and `SqlDataReader` objects, you create
`OleDbConnection`, `OleDbCommand`, and `OleDbDataReader` objects. These objects work essentially
the same way as their SQL Server counterparts.

Accordingly, you change the `using` directive that specifies the data provider from

```
using System.Data.SqlClient;
```

to

```
using System.Data.OleDb;
```

The only other difference is in the connection string, which you need to change completely. The first
part of an OLE DB connection string, the `Provider` clause, specifies the name of the OLE DB provider

for this type of database. For Microsoft Access databases, this is always the following name (Jet is the name of the database engine included in Access):

```
Provider=Microsoft.Jet.OLEDB.4.0;
```

If you are using a different OLE DB provider for a different database or data format, then specify the name of that provider in the Provider clause.

The second part of the connection string is the Data Source clause. For OLE DB/Microsoft Access, this simply specifies the name of the Microsoft Access database file (.mdb file) you are going to open:

```
Data Source=C:\Northwind\nwind.mdb
```

Again, the @ sign preceding the connection string specifies a string literal so that the backslashes in the path name work; otherwise, double backslashes (\\) would be necessary to escape the filename in C#.

Reading Data with the DataSet

You've just seen how to read data with a DataReader, so now you'll see how to accomplish the same task with the DataSet. First, let's take a detailed look at the structure of the DataSet. The DataSet is the central object in ADO.NET; all operations of any complexity use it. A DataSet contains a set of DataTable objects representing the database tables that you are working with.

It can be just one DataTable.

Each DataTable object has children DataRow and DataColumn objects representing the rows and columns of the database table. You can get to all the individual elements of the tables, rows, and columns through these objects, as described in a moment.

Filling the DataSet with Data

Your favorite activity with the DataSet will probably be to fill it with data using the Fill() method of a data adapter object.

Fill() is a method of the data adapter and not the DataSet because the DataSet is an abstract representation of data in memory, whereas the data adapter is the object that ties the DataSet to a particular database. Fill() has many overloads, but the one you use in this chapter takes two parameters — the first specifies the DataSet you want filled, and the second is the name of the DataTable within the DataSet that will contain the data you want loaded.

Accessing Tables, Rows, and Columns in the DataSet

The DataSet object has a property named Tables that is a collection of all the DataTable objects within the DataSet. Tables is of type DataTableCollection and has an overloaded indexer, which means that you can access each individual DataTable in one of two possible ways:

❏ **By table name:** `thisDataSet.Tables["Customers"]` specifies the `DataTable` called Customers.

❏ **By index (the index is zero-based):** `thisDataSet.Tables[0]` specifies the first `DataTable` in the `DataSet`.

Within each `DataTable` is a `Rows` property that is a collection of the individual `DataRow` objects. `Rows` is of type `DataRowCollection`, and is an ordered list, indexed by row number. Thus,

```
myDataSet.Tables["Customers"].Rows[n]
```

specifies row number n - 1 (remember the index is zero-based) in the `Customers DataTable` of `thisDataSet`. (Of course, you could have used the alternative index syntax to specify the `DataTable` as well.)

You might expect `DataRow` to have a property of type `DataColumnCollection`, but it's not as simple as that, because you want to take advantage of the data type of the individual columns in each row, so that a column containing character data becomes a string, a column containing an integer becomes an integer object, and so on.

The `DataRow` object itself has an indexer property that is overloaded, enabling you to access individual columns by name, and by number. Thus

```
thisDataSet.Tables["Customers"].Rows[n]["CompanyName"]
```

specifies the `CompanyName` column of row number n - 1 in the `Customers DataTable` of `thisDataSet` — the `DataRow` object here is `thisDataSet.Tables["Customers"].Rows[n]`.

The following Try It Out demonstrates all of this in practice by creating a program that uses the DataSet and its child classes. Let's start with a program that simply reads data. It is similar in function to the DataReading program, but accomplishes its task via the DataSet instead.

Try It Out   Reading Data with the DataSet

Follow these steps to create the DataSetRead program in Visual Studio 2008:

1. Create a new console application called DataSetRead in the directory C:\BegVCSharp\Chapter28.

2. Add the `using` directives for the ADO.NET classes you need:

```
#region Using Directives
using System;
using System.Data;              // Use ADO.NET namespace
using System.Data.SqlClient;    // Use SQL Server data provider namespace
using System.Collections.Generic;
using System.Text;
#endregion
```

3. Add the following code to the `Main()` method:

```csharp
static void Main(string[] args)
{
    // Specify SQL Server-specific connection string
    SqlConnection thisConnection = new SqlConnection(
        @"Data Source=.\SQLEXPRESS;"+
        @"AttachDbFilename='C:\SQL Server 2000 Sample Databases\
NORTHWND.MDF';" +
        @"Integrated Security=True;Connect Timeout=30;User Instance=true" );


    // Create DataAdapter object
    SqlDataAdapter thisAdapter = new SqlDataAdapter(
        "SELECT CustomerID, ContactName FROM Customers", thisConnection);

    // Create DataSet to contain related data tables, rows, and columns
    DataSet thisDataSet = new DataSet();

    // Fill DataSet using query defined previously for DataAdapter
    thisAdapter.Fill(thisDataSet, "Customers");
    foreach (DataRow theRow in thisDataSet.Tables["Customers"].Rows)
    {
        Console.WriteLine(theRow["CustomerID"] + "\t" +
                                        theRow["ContactName"]);
    }

    thisConnection.Close();
    Console.Write("Program finished, press Enter/Return to continue:");
    Console.ReadLine();
}
```

4. Compile and execute this program. You should see the list of customer IDs and company names, like this:

```
RICSU    Michael Holz
ROMEY    Alejandra Camino
SANTG    Jonas Bergulfsen
SAVEA    Jose Pavarotti
SEVES    Hari Kumar
SIMOB    Jytte Petersen
SPECD    Dominique Perrier
SPLIR    Art Braunschweiger
SUPRD    Pascale Cartrain
THEBI    Liz Nixon
THECR    Liu Wong
TOMSP    Karin Josephs
TORTU    Miguel Angel Paolino
TRADH    Anabela Domingues
TRAIH    Helvetius Nagy
VAFFE    Palle Ibsen
```

```
VICTE    Mary Saveley
VINET    Paul Henriot
WANDK    Rita Müller
WARTH    Pirkko Koskitalo
WELLI    Paula Parente
WHITC    Karl Jablonski
WILMK    Matti Karttunen
WOLZA    Zbyszek Piestrzeniewicz
Program finished, press Enter/Return to continue:
```

How It Works

You first create a connection and then use this connection to create a `SqlDataAdapter` object:

```
SqlConnection thisConnection = new SqlConnection(
                @"Data Source=.\SQLEXPRESS;"+
        @"AttachDbFilename='C:\SQL Server 2000 Sample Databases\
NORTHWND.MDF';" +
        @"Integrated Security=True;Connect Timeout=30;User Instance=true" );
```

```
SqlDataAdapter thisAdapter = new SqlDataAdapter(
        "SELECT CustomerID, ContactName FROM Customers", thisConnection);
```

The next step is to create the `DataSet` that you want filled with data:

```
DataSet thisDataSet = new DataSet();
```

Now that you have your `DataSet` and your data adapter object in place (`SqlDataAdapter` here, because you are using the SQL Server provider), you can proceed to fill a `DataTable` in the `DataSet`:

```
thisAdapter.Fill(thisDataSet, "Customers");
```

A `DataTable` named `Customers` will be created in this `DataSet`. Note that this occurrence of the word `Customers` does not refer to the `Customers` table in the Northwind database — it specifies the name of the `DataTable` in the `DataSet` to be created and filled with data.

Now that the `DataSet` has been filled, you can access the individual rows and columns. The process for this is straightforward — you loop through all the `DataRow` objects in the `Rows` collection of the `Customers DataTable`. For each `DataRow`, you retrieve the values in the `CustomerID` and `ContactName` columns:

```
foreach (DataRow theRow in thisDataSet.Tables["Customers"].Rows)
{
    Console.WriteLine(theRow["CustomerID"] + "\t" +
                            theRow["ContactName"]);
}
```

It was mentioned earlier that the `DataRow` object has an indexer property that enables you to access its individual columns by name and by number. Thus, `theRow["CustomerID"]` specifies the `CustomerID` column of `theRow DataRow`, and `theRow["ContactName"]` specifies the `ContactName`

column of `theRow` DataRow. Alternatively, you could have referred to the columns by number —
`CustomerID` would be `theRow[0]` (it is the first column retrieved from the database), and
`ContactName` as `theRow[1]`. However, it is generally better to refer to the column by name, as your
query may change in the future, or the columns may appear in a different order.

You may have noticed that you have not explicitly opened or closed a connection in this example —
the data adapter takes care of this for you. The data adapter object opens a connection as needed and
closes it again once it has finished its work. The data adapter leaves the state of the connection
unchanged — so if the connection was open before the data adapter started its work, it is still open
after the data adapter has finished.

At this point, you've learned how to read in data from a database. You've used a `DataReader`, which
requires a connection to the database to be maintained while it is doing its work. You've also just used
the data adapter to fill a `DataSet` — with this method the data adapter deals with the connection for
you, opening it and closing it as needed. The `DataReader` also reads in a forward-only manner — it
can navigate through records or jump to a given record. As its name suggests, the `DataReader` only
reads data — the `DataSet` offers tremendous flexibility for *reading* and *writing* data, and working with
data from different sources. You will see the power of the `DataSet` unfold as you move through the
chapter.

Reading data is only going to be half of what you want — you usually want to modify data, add new
data, or delete data, so let's move on to that.

Updating the Database

Now that you can read data from databases, how do you change it? This section provides a very simple
example, again using just one table, and at the same time introduces a few new objects you will use later
in the chapter.

All the actions you typically want to perform on the database (updating, inserting, and deleting records)
can be accomplished with the same pattern:

1. Fill a `DataSet` with the data from the database you wish to work with.

2. Modify the data held in the `DataSet` (update, insert, or delete records, for example).

3. After all the modifications are made, persist the `DataSet` changes back to the database.

You see this theme recurring as you move through the examples — there is no need to worry about the
exact SQL syntax for updating the database, for example, and all the modifications to the data in the
database can be performed at one time.

In the following Try It Out, you begin by looking at how to update data in a database before moving on
to add and delete records.

Try It Out   **Updating the Database**

Imagine that one of your customers, Bottom-Dollar Markets, has changed its name to Acme, Inc. You need to change the company's name in your databases. Again, you will use the SQL Server/MSDE version of the Northwind database.

1.   Create a new console application called UpdatingData in the directory
C:\BegVCSharp\Chapter28.

2.   Begin by adding the using directives for the ADO.NET classes you will be using:

```
#region Using Directives
using System;
using System.Data;                 // Use ADO.NET namespace
using System.Data.SqlClient;       // Use SQL Server data provider namespace
using System.Collections.Generic;
using System.Text;
#endregion
```

3.   Add the following code to the Main() method:

```
static void Main(string[] args)
{
    // Specify SQL Server-specific connection string
    SqlConnection thisConnection = new SqlConnection(
            @"Data Source=.\SQLEXPRESS;"+
        @"AttachDbFilename='C:\SQL Server 2000 Sample Databases\
NORTHWND.MDF';" +
        @"Integrated Security=True;Connect Timeout=30;User Instance=true" );


    // Create DataAdapter object for update and other operations
    SqlDataAdapter thisAdapter = new SqlDataAdapter(
        "SELECT CustomerID, CompanyName FROM Customers", thisConnection);

    // Create CommandBuilder object to build SQL commands
    SqlCommandBuilder thisBuilder = new SqlCommandBuilder(thisAdapter);
    // Create DataSet to contain related data tables, rows, and columns
    DataSet thisDataSet = new DataSet();

    // Fill DataSet using query defined previously for DataAdapter
    thisAdapter.Fill(thisDataSet, "Customers");

    // Show data before change
    Console.WriteLine("name before change: {0}",
        thisDataSet.Tables["Customers"].Rows[9]["CompanyName"]);

    // Change data in Customers table, row 9, CompanyName column
    thisDataSet.Tables["Customers"].Rows[9]["CompanyName"] = "Acme, Inc.";
```

```
          // Call Update command to mark change in table
          thisAdapter.Update(thisDataSet, "Customers");

          Console.WriteLine("name after change: {0}",
               thisDataSet.Tables["Customers"].Rows[9]["CompanyName"]);

          thisConnection.Close();
          Console.Write("Program finished, press Enter/Return to continue:");
          Console.ReadLine();
     }
```

4.   Running the program produces the output shown here:

```
name before change: Bottom-Dollar Markets
name after change: Acme, Inc.
Program finished, press Enter/Return to continue:
```

How It Works

The first part of the program is similar to the previous SQL Server example; you create a connection object using a connection string:

```
SqlConnection thisConnection = new SqlConnection(
          @"Data Source=.\SQLEXPRESS;"+
          @"AttachDbFilename='C:\SQL Server 2000 Sample Databases\
NORTHWND.MDF';" +
          @"Integrated Security=True;Connect Timeout=30;User Instance=true" );
```

Then you create a `SqlDataAdapter` object with the following statement:

```
SqlDataAdapter thisAdapter = new SqlDataAdapter(
     "SELECT CustomerID, CompanyName FROM Customers", thisConnection);
```

Next, you want to create the correct SQL statements to update the database — you don't have to do this yourself, the `SqlCommandBuilder` takes care of this:

```
SqlCommandBuilder thisBuilder = new SqlCommandBuilder(thisAdapter);
```

Note that you pass `thisAdapter` to the `SqlCommandBuilder` constructor as an argument. The correct SQL commands are generated and associated with the passed data adapter by the constructor when the `SqlCommandBuilder` object is created. A bit later in the chapter you look at different SQL statements; but for now the SQL has been taken care of for you.

Now you create your illustrious `DataSet` object and fill it with data:

```
DataSet thisDataSet = new DataSet();
thisAdapter.Fill(thisDataSet, "Customers");
```

In this case, it is the `Customers` table you want, so you call the associated `DataTable` in the `DataSet` by the same name. With the `DataSet` filled, you can access the individual rows and columns.

Before changing the data, you output a *before* picture of the data you want to change:

```
Console.WriteLine("name before change: {0}",
    thisDataSet.Tables["Customers"].Rows[9]["CompanyName"]);
```

Here, you are printing the value in the `CompanyName` column in the row with index number nine in the `Customers` table. This whole line outputs the following:

```
name before change: Bottom-Dollar Markets
```

You're cheating a little bit here; you just happen to know that you are interested in the row with index number nine (which is actually the tenth row because the indexer is zero-based — the first row is `Rows[0]`). In a real program, rather than an example, you would have probably put a qualifier in your SQL query to select just the rows you were interested in, rather than knowing to go to the row with an index number of nine. The next example explains how to find only the rows you are interested in.

Another way to understand what is going on with all of this is to look at an equivalent example that breaks out each separate object in the expression:

```
// Example using multiple objects
DataTable customerTable = thisDataSet.Tables["Customers"];
DataRow rowTen = customerTable.Rows[9];
object companyName = rowTen["CompanyName"];
Console.WriteLine("name before change: {0}", companyName);
```

In this example, you declare `customerTable` as a `DataTable` and assign the `Customers` table from the `Tables` property of `thisDataSet`. You declare `rowTen` as a `DataRow` and to it you assign the tenth element of the `Rows` property of `customerTable`. Finally, you declare `companyName` as an `object` and use the indexer property of `rowTen` to assign the `CompanyName` field to it.

This example helps you understand the process as you follow the chain of related objects, but it is often simpler to use the one-line expression, which gives the same result:

```
Console.WriteLine("name before change: {0}",
        thisDataSet.Tables["Customers"].Rows[9]["CompanyName"]);
```

If the code using multiple objects is more understandable to you, by all means use this method. For a one-time reference like this one, it is potentially inefficient to create variables for each object and assign to them every time; however, if the objects are going to be reused, then the multiple-object method may be more efficient. The compiler's optimizer may compensate for any inefficiency in one way of coding over another, so it's often best to code in the most readable manner.

Back to the example: You've displayed the value of the column before you make a change, so now let's make a change to the column. To change the value of a `DataColumn`, simply assign to it, as in the next line of the example:

```
thisDataSet.Tables["Customers"].Rows[9]["CompanyName"] = "Acme, Inc.";
```

This line changes the value of the `CompanyName` column in the row with index number nine of `Customers` to `"Acme, Inc."`.

This change only changes the value of the column in the `DataSet` *in memory, not in the database itself.*

The `DataSet`, `DataTable`, `DataRow`, and `DataColumn` are in-memory representations of the data in the table. To update the database, you need to call the `Update()` method.

`Update()` is a method of the data adapter object. To call it, specify the `DataSet` you want the update to be based on and the name of the `DataTable` in the `DataSet` to update. It's important that the `DataTable` name (`"Customers"`) match the one you used when calling the `Fill()` method previously:

```
thisAdapter.Update(thisDataSet, "Customers");
```

The `Update()` method automatically goes through the rows in the `DataTable` to check for changes that need to be made to the database. Each `DataRow` object in the `Rows` collection has a property, `RowState`, that tracks whether this row is deleted, added, modified, or unchanged. Any changes made are reflected in the database.

Now you confirm the change by printing out the *after* state of the data:

```
Console.WriteLine("name after change: {0}",
    thisDataSet.Tables["Customers"].Rows[9]["CompanyName"]);
```

That's all there is to it!

Before moving on, here is a quick recap of the new characters you met here:

❑ `SqlCommandBuilder`: The `SqlCommandBuilder` object takes care of the correct SQL statements for updating the database — you don't have to craft these statements yourself.

❑ `SqlDataAdapter.Update()`: This method goes through the rows in a `DataTable` to check for changes that need to be made to the database. Each `DataRow` object in the `Rows` collection has a property, `RowState`, tracking whether the row is deleted, added, modified, or unchanged. Any changes made are reflected in the database.

These, of course, are the SQL Server provider versions — there are corresponding OLE DB provider versions that work in the same way.

Adding Rows to the Database

In the previous example you updated values in existing rows; your next step is to add an entirely new row. The procedure you'll follow to add a new record to the database involves, exactly like the update example, adding a new row to an existing `DataSet` (this is where most of the work is required), and then persisting this change back to the database:

1. Create a new `DataRow`.
2. Populate it with some data.
3. Add it to the `Rows` collection of the `DataSet`.
4. Persist this change back to the database by calling the `Update()` method of the data adapter.

Sounds like a perfectly sensible scheme. In the following Try It Out, you see exactly how it's done.

Try It Out   Adding Rows

Follow these steps to create the AddingData example in Visual Studio 2008:

1. Create a new console application called AddingData in the directory C:\BegVCSharp\Chapter28.

2. Begin by adding the usual `using` directives for the ADO.NET classes you will be using:

```
#region Using Directives
using System;
using System.Data;            // Use ADO.NET namespace
using System.Data.SqlClient;  // Use SQL Server data provider namespace
using System.Collections.Generic;
using System.Text;
#endregion
```

3. Add the following code to the `Main()` method:

```
static void Main(string[] args)
{
    // Specify SQL Server-specific connection string
    SqlConnection thisConnection = new SqlConnection(
                @"Data Source=.\SQLEXPRESS;"+
        @"AttachDbFilename='C:\SQL Server 2000 Sample Databases\
NORTHWND.MDF';" +
        @"Integrated Security=True;Connect Timeout=30;User Instance=true" );

    // Create DataAdapter object for update and other operations
    SqlDataAdapter thisAdapter = new SqlDataAdapter(
        "SELECT CustomerID, CompanyName FROM Customers", thisConnection);

    // Create CommandBuilder object to build SQL commands
    SqlCommandBuilder thisBuilder = new SqlCommandBuilder(thisAdapter);

    // Create DataSet to contain related data tables, rows, and columns
    DataSet thisDataSet = new DataSet();
    // Fill DataSet using query defined previously for DataAdapter
    thisAdapter.Fill(thisDataSet, "Customers");

    Console.WriteLine("# rows before change: {0}",
                    thisDataSet.Tables["Customers"].Rows.Count);

    DataRow thisRow = thisDataSet.Tables["Customers"].NewRow();
    thisRow["CustomerID"] = "ZACZI";
    thisRow["CompanyName"] = "Zachary Zithers Ltd.";
```

```
        thisDataSet.Tables["Customers"].Rows.Add(thisRow);

        Console.WriteLine("# rows after change: {0}",
                        thisDataSet.Tables["Customers"].Rows.Count);

        // Call Update command to mark change in table
        thisAdapter.Update(thisDataSet, "Customers");

        thisConnection.Close();
        Console.Write("Program finished, press Enter/Return to continue:");
        Console.ReadLine();
    }
```

4.   On executing, the output of this example is as shown here:

```
# rows before change: 91
# rows after change: 92
Program finished, press Enter/Return to continue:
```

How It Works

The lines of interest here are the lines between the `thisAdapter.Fill()` and `thisAdapter` `.Update()` method calls.

First, to see the *before* picture, you introduce a new property of the Rows collection: `Count`. This gives you a count of how many rows are in this table:

```
Console.WriteLine("# rows before change: {0}",
      thisDataSet.Tables["Customers"].Rows.Count);
```

Next, you create the new row object, using the `NewRow()` method of the `DataTable` object:

```
DataRow thisRow = thisDataSet.Tables["Customers"].NewRow();
```

Note that this creates a new row object using the same columns as the `Customers` table, but does not actually add it to the `DataSet`; you need to assign some values to the columns before that can be done:

```
thisRow["CustomerID"] = "ZACZI";
thisRow["CompanyName"] = "Zachary Zithers Ltd.";
```

Now you can actually add the row using the `Add()` method of the Rows collection:

```
thisDataSet.Tables["Customers"].Rows.Add(thisRow);
```

If you check the `Count` property again after calling `Add()`, you see that you have indeed added one row:

```
Console.WriteLine("# rows after change: {0}",
                thisDataSet.Tables["Customers"].Rows.Count);
```

The output shows 92 rows, one more than the before change output. As with the previous example, the call to `Update()` is needed to actually add the new row to the database on disk:

```
thisAdapter.Update (thisDataSet, "Customers");
```

Remember that the `DataSet` is an in-memory, disconnected copy of the data; it is the `DataAdapter` that is actually connected to the database on disk. Therefore, its `Update()` method needs to be called to synchronize the in-memory data in the `DataSet` with the database on disk.

Only the `Customer ID` and `Company Name` columns are filled, because that's all you used in your program. The remaining columns are blank (actually, they contain the value `NULL` in SQL terms). You might assume that filling in, say, `Contact Name` is simply a matter of adding the following line to the code:

```
thisRow["ContactName"] = "Zylla Zithers";
```

However, this is not the only step you must perform. Recall that when you made the original query, you built the `DataSet` specifying just two columns, `CustomerID` and `CompanyName`:

```
SqlDataAdapter thisAdapter = new SqlDataAdapter(
    "SELECT CustomerID, CompanyName FROM Customers", thisConnection);
```

The reference to `ContactName` would cause an error because there is no such column in the `DataSet` that you built. You could rectify this by adding the `ContactName` column to the original SQL query:

```
SqlDataAdapter thisAdapter = new SqlDataAdapter(
    "SELECT CustomerID, ContactName, CompanyName FROM Customers",
    thisConnection);
```

Alternately, you could select all the columns from `Customers` using this command:

```
SqlDataAdapter thisAdapter = new SqlDataAdapter("SELECT * FROM Customers",
                                                thisConnection);
```

The asterisk (*) in a SQL `SELECT` command is shorthand for all the columns in the table; with this change, you can add values for any of the columns in the database. However, getting all the columns when you are working with only two or three is inefficient, and something you should generally avoid.

Finding Rows

If you tried to run the previous example more than once, you would have seen a message like the one shown in Figure 28-4.

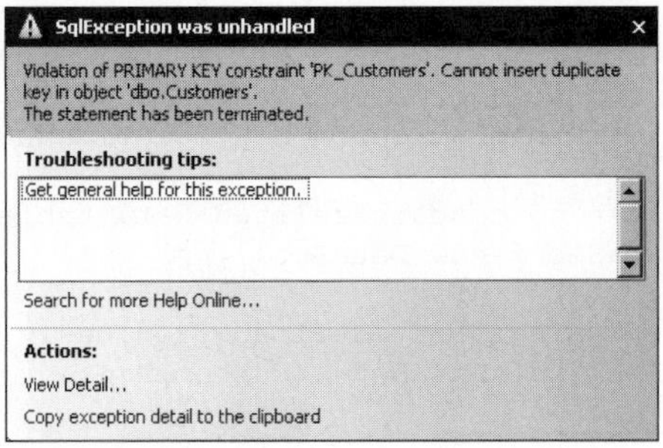

Figure 28-4

This indicates that `Add()` failed because it attempted to create a duplicate primary key. The definition of the `Customers` table requires that the `CustomerID` field contain unique values, which is required when a column is designated the primary key. The value `"ZACZI"` was already present when you tried to run the code for the second time because it was placed in the table the first time you ran the sample.

Let's change the logic so that you search for the row first, before you try to add it. The `DataTable Rows` collection provides a method called `Find()` that is very useful for this purpose. In the following Try It Out, you rewrite the logic surrounding your row addition to use `Find()` instead of counting rows.

Try It Out   Finding Rows

Follow these steps to create the FindingData example in Visual Studio 2008:

1. Create a new console application called FindingData in the directory C:\BegVCSharp\Chapter28.

2. Begin by adding the usual `using` directives for the ADO.NET classes you will be using:

```
#region Using Directives
using System;
using System.Data;              // Use ADO.NET namespace
using System.Data.SqlClient;    // Use SQL Server data provider namespace
using System.Collections.Generic;
using System.Text;
#endregion
```

3. Add the following code to the `Main()` method:

```
static void Main(string[] args)
{
    // Specify SQL Server-specific connection string
    SqlConnection thisConnection = new SqlConnection(
                @"Data Source=.\SQLEXPRESS;"+
        @"AttachDbFilename='C:\SQL Server 2000 Sample Databases\
NORTHWND.MDF';" +
            @"Integrated Security=True;Connect Timeout=30;User Instance=true" );


    // Create DataAdapter object for update and other operations
    SqlDataAdapter thisAdapter = new SqlDataAdapter(
        "SELECT CustomerID, CompanyName FROM Customers", thisConnection);
    // Create CommandBuilder object to build SQL commands
    SqlCommandBuilder thisBuilder = new SqlCommandBuilder(thisAdapter);

    // Create DataSet to contain related data tables, rows, and columns
    DataSet thisDataSet = new DataSet();

    // Fill DataSet using query defined previously for DataAdapter
    thisAdapter.Fill(thisDataSet, "Customers");
```

```
    Console.WriteLine("# rows before change: {0}",
        thisDataSet.Tables["Customers"].Rows.Count);

    // Set up keys object for defining primary key
    DataColumn[] keys = new DataColumn[1];
    keys[0] = thisDataSet.Tables["Customers"].Columns["CustomerID"];
    thisDataSet.Tables["Customers"].PrimaryKey = keys;

    DataRow findRow = thisDataSet.Tables["Customers"].Rows.Find("ZACZI");

    if (findRow == null)
    {
        Console.WriteLine("ZACZI not found, will add to Customers table");

        DataRow thisRow = thisDataSet.Tables["Customers"].NewRow();
        thisRow["CustomerID"] = "ZACZI";
        thisRow["CompanyName"] = "Zachary Zithers Ltd.";
        thisDataSet.Tables["Customers"].Rows.Add(thisRow);
        if ((findRow =
              thisDataSet.Tables["Customers"].Rows.Find("ZACZI")) != null)
        {
            Console.WriteLine("ZACZI successfully added to Customers table");
        }
    }
    else
    {
        Console.WriteLine("ZACZI already present in database");
    }

    thisAdapter.Update(thisDataSet, "Customers");

    Console.WriteLine("# rows after change: {0}",
    thisDataSet.Tables["Customers"].Rows.Count);

    thisConnection.Close();
    Console.Write("Program finished, press Enter/Return to continue:");
    Console.ReadLine();
}
```

How It Works

The beginning of the program up to the `Fill()` method call is the same as previous examples. You use the `Count` property to output the number of rows currently existing, and then proceed to use `Find()` to confirm that the row you want to add is already present.

Before you can use `Find()` you need to set up a primary key. The primary key is what you use when searching; it is one or more of the table columns and contains a value or set of values that uniquely identifies this particular row in the table, so that when you search by the key you will find one and only one row. The `Customers` table in the Northwind database uses the `CustomerID` column as its primary key:

```
DataColumn[] keys = new DataColumn[1];
keys[0] = thisDataSet.Tables["Customers"].Columns["CustomerID"];
thisDataSet.Tables["Customers"].PrimaryKey = keys;
```

First, you create a DataColumn array. Because the key can consist of one or more columns (known as a composite key), an array is the natural structure to use; you call your DataColumn array keys. Next, you assign the first element of the keys array, keys[0], to the CustomerID column in your Customers table. Finally, you assign keys to the PrimaryKey property of the Customers DataTable object.

Alternatively, it is possible to load primary key information directly from the database, which is not done by default. You can explicitly tell ADO.NET to load the primary key information by setting the DataAdapter MissingSchemaAction property before filling the DataSet, as follows:

```
thisAdapter.MissingSchemaAction = MissingSchemaAction.AddWithKey;
thisAdapter.Fill(thisDataSet, "Customers");
```

This accomplishes the same primary key setup by initializing the PrimaryKey property of the DataTable implicitly.

In any case, now you're ready to find a row:

```
DataRow findRow = thisDataSet.Tables["Customers"].Rows.Find("ZACZI");
```

Find() returns a DataRow, so you set up a DataRow object named findRow to get the result. Find() takes a parameter, which is the value to look up; this can be an array of objects for a multicolumn primary key, but in this case, with only one primary key column, you need just one value, which you pass as a string containing the value ZACZI — this is the CustomerID you want to look up.

If Find() locates a matching row, then it returns the DataRow matching that row; if it doesn't find a match, then it returns a null reference, which you can check for:

```
if (findRow == null)
{
    Console.WriteLine("ZACZI not found, will add to Customers table");

    DataRow thisRow = thisDataSet.Tables["Customers"].NewRow();
    thisRow["CustomerID"] = "ZACZI";
    thisRow["CompanyName"] = "Zachary Zithers Ltd.";
    thisDataSet.Tables["Customers"].Rows.Add(thisRow);
    if ((findRow = thisDataSet.Tables["Customers"].Rows.Find("ZACZI")) != null)
    {
        Console.WriteLine("ZACZI successfully added to Customers table");
    }
}
else
{
    Console.WriteLine("ZACZI already present in database");
}
```

If findRow is null, then you go ahead and add the row as in the previous example. Just to make sure that the Add() was successful, you do a Find() again immediately after the add operation to prove that it worked.

As mentioned at the start of this section, this version using `Find()` is repeatable; you can run it multiple times without errors. However, it never executes the `Add()` code after the `"ZACZI"` row is in the database. Let's look at how to make it repeat that part of the program also.

Deleting Rows

After you can add rows to the `DataSet` and to the database, it is logical to follow with the opposite action, removing rows.

The `DataRow` object has a `Delete()` method that deletes the current row. The following Try It Out changes the sense of the `if` statement on `findRow` so that you test for `findRow` *not* equal to `null` (in other words, the row you were searching for was found). Then you remove the row by calling `Delete()` on `findRow`.

Try It Out   Deleting Rows

Follow these steps to create the DeletingData example in Visual Studio 2008:

1. Create a new console application called DeletingData in the directory
    C:\BegVCSharp\Chapter28.

2. As usual, begin by adding the `using` directives for the ADO.NET classes you will be using:

```
#region Using Directives
using System;
using System.Data;              // Use ADO.NET namespace
using System.Data.SqlClient;    // Use SQL Server data provider namespace
using System.Collections.Generic;
using System.Text;
#endregion
```

3. Add the following code to the `Main()` method:

```
static void Main(string[] args)
{
    // Specify SQL Server-specific connection string
    SqlConnection thisConnection = new SqlConnection(
                @"Data Source=.\SQLEXPRESS;"+
        @"AttachDbFilename='C:\SQL Server 2000 Sample Databases\
NORTHWND.MDF';" +
        @"Integrated Security=True;Connect Timeout=30;User Instance=true" );


    // Create DataAdapter object for update and other operations
    SqlDataAdapter thisAdapter = new SqlDataAdapter(
```

```
            "SELECT CustomerID, CompanyName FROM Customers", thisConnection);

    // Create CommandBuilder object to build SQL commands
    SqlCommandBuilder thisBuilder = new SqlCommandBuilder(thisAdapter);

    // Create DataSet to contain related data tables, rows, and columns
    DataSet thisDataSet = new DataSet();

    // Fill DataSet using query defined previously for DataAdapter
    thisAdapter.Fill(thisDataSet, "Customers");

    Console.WriteLine("# rows before change: {0}",
        thisDataSet.Tables["Customers"].Rows.Count);
    // Set up keys object for defining primary key
    DataColumn[] keys = new DataColumn[1];
    keys[0] = thisDataSet.Tables["Customers"].Columns["CustomerID"];
    thisDataSet.Tables["Customers"].PrimaryKey = keys;

    DataRow findRow = thisDataSet.Tables["Customers"].Rows.Find("ZACZI");

    if (findRow != null)
    {
        Console.WriteLine("ZACZI already in Customers table");
        Console.WriteLine("Removing ZACZI  . . .");

        findRow.Delete();

        thisAdapter.Update(thisDataSet, "Customers");
    }

    Console.WriteLine("# rows after change: {0}",
        thisDataSet.Tables["Customers"].Rows.Count);
    thisConnection.Close();
    Console.Write("Program finished, press Enter/Return to continue:");
    Console.ReadLine();
}
```

How It Works

The code to create the DataSet and the data adapter objects is standard — you've seen it before several times in this chapter so it isn't repeated here.

The difference between this code and the previous example is that if the row is found, it is deleted! Note that when Delete() is called it doesn't remove the row in the database until Update is called to commit the change.

The Delete() method doesn't actually delete a row, it just marks it for deletion.

Each DataRow object in the Rows collection has a property, RowState, that tracks whether the row is deleted, added, modified, or unchanged. The Delete() method sets the RowState of the row to

`Deleted`, and then `Update()` deletes any rows it finds in the `Rows` collection marked as `Deleted` from the database.

This same issue applies to the `Remove()` method; call this only if you want to remove rows from the `Rows` collection of the `DataSet`, but not from the database itself.

Accessing Multiple Tables in a DataSet

One of the big advantages of the ADO.NET model over previous data access models is that the `DataSet` object tracks multiple tables and the relationships between them all within itself. This means that you can pass an entire set of related data between parts of your program in one operation, and the architecture inherently maintains the integrity of the relationships between the data.

Relationships in ADO.NET

The `DataRelation` object is used to describe the relationships between multiple `DataTable` objects in a `DataSet`. Each `DataSet` has a `Relations` collection of `DataRelations` that enables you to find and manipulate related tables.

Let's start with just the `Customers` and `Orders` tables. Each customer may place several orders; how can you see the orders placed by each customer? Each row of the `Orders` table contains the `CustomerID` of the customer placing the order; you match all the order rows containing a particular `CustomerID` with that customer's row in the `Customers` table.

The matching `CustomerID` fields in the two tables define a one-to-many relationship between the `Customers` table and the `Orders` table. You can use that relationship in ADO.NET by creating a `DataRelation` object to represent it.

Creating a DataRelation Object

The `DataSet` has a `Relations` property that is a collection of all the `DataRelation` objects representing relationships between tables in this `DataSet`.

To create a new `DataRelation`, use the `Add()` method of `Relations`, which accepts a string name for the relationship and two `DataColumns` — the parent column, followed by the child column. Thus, to create the relationship described previously between the `CustomerID` column of the `Customers` table and the `CustomerID` table of the `Orders` table, you would use the following syntax, giving the relationship the name `CustOrders`:

```
DataRelation custOrderRel = thisDataSet.Relations.Add("CustOrders",
    thisDataSet.Tables["Customers"].Columns["CustomerID"],
    thisDataSet.Tables["Orders"].Columns["CustomerID"]);
```

You see this syntax again in the next example.

Navigating with Relationships

To use the relationship, you need to go from a row of one of your tables to the related rows in the other table. This is called *navigating* the relationship. Often navigations consist of traveling from a parent row in the first table to the related children in the other table. In the Northwind database, the row in the Customers table can be considered the parent row and each of the related rows in the Orders table can be considered children. Navigations can also go in the opposite direction.

Fetching the Child Rows

Given a row in the parent table, how do you obtain all the rows in the child table that correspond to this row? You can retrieve this set of rows with the GetChildRows() method of the DataRow object. The DataRelation object that you have created between the parent and child tables is passed to the method, and a DataRowCollection object is returned, which is a collection of the related DataRow objects in the child DataTable.

For example, with the DataRelation that you created earlier, if the given DataRow in the parent DataTable (Customers) is customerRow, then

```
customerRow.GetChildRows(custOrderRel);
```

returns the collection of corresponding DataRow objects from the Orders table. You see how to handle this set of objects in the following Try It Out.

Try It Out   **Getting Related Rows**

Follow these steps to create the DataRelationExample program in Visual Studio 2008:

1. Create a new console application called DataRelationExample in the directory
    C:\BegVCSharp\Chapter28.

2. Begin by adding the using directives for the ADO.NET classes you will be using:

    ```
    #region Using Directives
    using System;
    using System.Data;              // Use ADO.NET namespace
    using System.Data.SqlClient;    // Use SQL Server data provider namespace
    using System.Collections.Generic;
    using System.Text;
    #endregion
    ```

3. Add the following code to the Main() method:

    ```
    static void Main(string[] args)
    {
        // Specify SQL Server-specific connection string
        SqlConnection thisConnection = new SqlConnection(
                    @"Data Source=.\SQLEXPRESS;"+
            @"AttachDbFilename='C:\SQL Server 2000 Sample Databases\
    NORTHWND.MDF';" +
    ```

```
                 @"Integrated Security=True;Connect Timeout=30;User Instance=true" );


        // Create DataAdapter object for update and other operations
        SqlDataAdapter thisAdapter = new SqlDataAdapter(
            "SELECT CustomerID, CompanyName FROM Customers", thisConnection);
        // Create CommandBuilder object to build SQL commands
        SqlCommandBuilder thisBuilder = new SqlCommandBuilder(thisAdapter);

        // Create DataSet to contain related data tables, rows, and columns
        DataSet thisDataSet = new DataSet();

        // Set up DataAdapter objects for each table and fill
        SqlDataAdapter custAdapter = new SqlDataAdapter(
            "SELECT * FROM Customers", thisConnection);
        SqlDataAdapter orderAdapter = new SqlDataAdapter(
            "SELECT * FROM Orders", thisConnection);
        custAdapter.Fill(thisDataSet, "Customers");
        orderAdapter.Fill(thisDataSet, "Orders");

        // Set up DataRelation between customers and orders
        DataRelation custOrderRel = thisDataSet.Relations.Add("CustOrders",
            thisDataSet.Tables["Customers"].Columns["CustomerID"],
            thisDataSet.Tables["Orders"].Columns["CustomerID"]);

        // Print out nested customers and their order ids
        foreach (DataRow custRow in thisDataSet.Tables["Customers"].Rows)
        {
            Console.WriteLine("Customer ID: " + custRow["CustomerID"] +
                            " Name: " + custRow["CompanyName"]);
            foreach (DataRow orderRow in custRow.GetChildRows(custOrderRel))
            {
                Console.WriteLine(" Order ID: " + orderRow["OrderID"]);
            }
        }
        thisConnection.Close();
        Console.Write("Program finished, press Enter/Return to continue:");
        Console.ReadLine();
    }
}
```

4. Execute the application. You will see the output shown here:

```
    Order ID: 10696
    Order ID: 10723
    Order ID: 10740
    Order ID: 10861
    Order ID: 10904
    Order ID: 11032
    Order ID: 11066
 Customer ID: WILMK Name: Wilman Kala
    Order ID: 10615
    Order ID: 10673
    Order ID: 10695
```

```
      Order ID: 10873
      Order ID: 10879
      Order ID: 10910
      Order ID: 11005
Customer ID: WOLZA Name: Wolski   Zajazd
    Order ID: 10374
    Order ID: 10611
    Order ID: 10792
    Order ID: 10870
    Order ID: 10906
    Order ID: 10998
    Order ID: 11044
Customer ID: ZACZI Name: Zachary Zithers Ltd.
Program finished, press Enter/Return to continue:
```

How It Works

Before constructing the DataRelation, you need to create the DataSet object and link the database tables you are going to use with it, as shown here:

```
DataSet thisDataSet = new DataSet();
SqlDataAdapter custAdapter = new SqlDataAdapter(
     "SELECT * FROM Customers", thisConnection);
SqlDataAdapter orderAdapter = new SqlDataAdapter(
     "SELECT * FROM Orders", thisConnection);
custAdapter.Fill(thisDataSet, "Customers");
orderAdapter.Fill(thisDataSet, "Orders");
```

You create a DataAdapter object for each table you will reference. You then fill the DataSet with data from the columns you're going to work with; in this case, you're not worried about efficiency, so you just use all of the available columns (SELECT * FROM <table>).

Next, you make the DataRelation object and link it to the DataSet:

```
DataRelation custOrderRel = thisDataSet.Relations.Add("CustOrders",
     thisDataSet.Tables["Customers"].Columns["CustomerID"],
     thisDataSet.Tables["Orders"].Columns["CustomerID"]);
```

Now you're ready to find the customers and orders. First, set up a foreach loop to display the customer information for each customer:

```
foreach (DataRow custRow in thisDataSet.Tables["Customers"].Rows)
{
    Console.WriteLine("Customer ID: " + custRow["CustomerID"] +
                  " Name: " + custRow["CompanyName"]);
```

You're just looping through the Rows collection of the Customers table, printing the CustomerID and CompanyName for each customer. Once you've displayed the customer, you'd like to display the related orders for that customer.

To do that, add a nested foreach loop, initialized by calling the GetChildRows() method of DataRow. You pass your DataRelation object to GetChildRows(), and it returns a DataRowCollection containing just the related rows in the Orders table for this customer. To display these related rows, simply loop through each DataRow in this collection with your foreach loop:

```
    foreach (DataRow orderRow in custRow.GetChildRows(custOrderRel))
    {
        Console.WriteLine(" Order ID: " + orderRow["OrderID"]);
    }
}
```

Now you repeat the process for each customer. You added some leading spaces to the display of the OrderID, so the orders for each customer are displayed indented underneath the customer information. With the indented display, you can see the parent-child relationship between each customer and its orders more clearly. Customer ID "Zachary Zithers Ltd." has no Orders because you just added it to the table in the previous examples.

That's one relation between two tables — now consider relations between more tables by extending this program to see what specific items each customer is placing in each order and what the names of the products are. This information is available through the other tables in the Northwind database. Let's review these relationships; an easy way to see these is to look at a database diagram for the Northwind database, as shown in Figure 28-5.

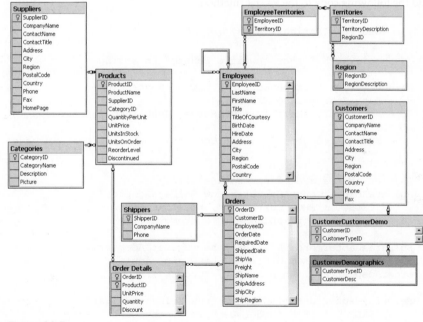

Figure 28-5

The lines between the tables represent the relationships, with the line on each side going to the column that identifies the relationship. A primary key-foreign key relationship is shown with a key symbol by the parent column and an infinity symbol by the child column.

In the next Try It Out, you're going to display the details of each customer order, including the product names, by following the relationships between four tables shown in Figure 28-5: Customers, Orders, Order Details, and Products.

Try It Out   **Working with Multiple Relations**

Follow these steps to create the ManyRelations program in Visual Studio 2008:

1. Create a new console application called ManyRelations in the directory
C:\BegVCSharp\Chapter28.

2. Add the using directives for the ADO.NET classes you will use:

```
#region Using Directives
using System;
using System.Data;                // Use ADO.NET namespace
using System.Data.SqlClient;   // Use SQL Server data provider namespace
using System.Collections.Generic;
using System.Text;
#endregion
```

3. Add the following code to the Main() method:

```
static void Main(string[] args)
{
    // Specify SQL Server-specific connection string

    SqlConnection thisConnection = new SqlConnection(
        @"Data Source=.\SQLEXPRESS;"+
        @"AttachDbFilename='C:\SQL Server 2000 Sample Databases\
NORTHWND.MDF';" +
        @"Integrated Security=True;Connect Timeout=30;User Instance=true" );


    DataSet thisDataSet = new DataSet();
    SqlDataAdapter custAdapter = new SqlDataAdapter(
        "SELECT * FROM Customers", thisConnection);
    custAdapter.Fill(thisDataSet, "Customers");

    SqlDataAdapter orderAdapter = new SqlDataAdapter(
        "SELECT * FROM Orders", thisConnection);
    orderAdapter.Fill(thisDataSet, "Orders");

    SqlDataAdapter detailAdapter = new SqlDataAdapter(
        "SELECT * FROM [Order Details]", thisConnection);
    detailAdapter.Fill(thisDataSet, "Order Details");

    SqlDataAdapter prodAdapter = new SqlDataAdapter(
        "SELECT * FROM Products", thisConnection);
    prodAdapter.Fill(thisDataSet, "Products");

    DataRelation custOrderRel = thisDataSet.Relations.Add("CustOrders",
                thisDataSet.Tables["Customers"].Columns["CustomerID"],
                thisDataSet.Tables["Orders"].Columns["CustomerID"]);

    DataRelation orderDetailRel = thisDataSet.Relations.Add("OrderDetail",
                thisDataSet.Tables["Orders"].Columns["OrderID"],
```

```
                            thisDataSet.Tables["Order Details"].Columns["OrderID"]);

            DataRelation orderProductRel = thisDataSet.Relations.Add(
                "OrderProducts",thisDataSet.Tables["Products"].Columns["ProductID"],
                thisDataSet.Tables["Order Details"].Columns["ProductID"]);

            foreach (DataRow custRow in thisDataSet.Tables["Customers"].Rows)
            {
                Console.WriteLine("Customer ID: " + custRow["CustomerID"]);

                foreach (DataRow orderRow in custRow.GetChildRows(custOrderRel))
                {
                    Console.WriteLine("\tOrder ID: " + orderRow["OrderID"]);
                    Console.WriteLine("\t\tOrder Date: " + orderRow["OrderDate"]);

                    foreach (DataRow detailRow in
                            orderRow.GetChildRows(orderDetailRel))
                    {
                        Console.WriteLine("\t\tProduct: " +
                        detailRow.GetParentRow(orderProductRel)["ProductName"]);
                        Console.WriteLine("\t\tQuantity: " + detailRow["Quantity"]);
                    }
                }
            }
            thisConnection.Close();
            Console.Write("Program finished, press Enter/Return to continue:");
            Console.ReadLine();
    }
```

4. Execute the application. You will see output like the following (an abbreviated version is shown here, with only the last part of the output):

```
Customer ID: WOLZA
        ...
        Order ID: 10998
                Order Date: 4/3/1998 12:00:00 AM
                Product: Guaraná Fantástica
                Quantity: 12
                Product: Sirop d'érable
                Quantity: 7
                Product: Longlife Tofu
                Quantity: 20
                Product: Rhönbräu Klosterbier
                Quantity: 30
        Order ID: 11044
                Order Date: 4/23/1998 12:00:00 AM
                Product: Tarte au sucre
                Quantity: 12
Customer ID: ZACZI
```

How It Works

As usual, you begin by initializing a connection and then creating a new `DataSet`. Next, you create a data adapter for each of the four tables that will be used:

```
SqlDataAdapter custAdapter = new SqlDataAdapter(
    "SELECT * FROM Customers", thisConnection);
custAdapter.Fill(thisDataSet, "Customers");

SqlDataAdapter orderAdapter = new SqlDataAdapter(
    "SELECT * FROM Orders", thisConnection);
orderAdapter.Fill(thisDataSet, "Orders");

SqlDataAdapter detailAdapter = new SqlDataAdapter(
    "SELECT * FROM [Order Details]", thisConnection);
detailAdapter.Fill(thisDataSet, "Order Details");

SqlDataAdapter prodAdapter = new SqlDataAdapter(
    "SELECT * FROM Products", thisConnection);
prodAdapter.Fill(thisDataSet, "Products");
```

Next, you build `DataRelation` objects for each of the relationships between the four tables:

```
DataRelation custOrderRel = thisDataSet.Relations.Add("CustOrders",
            thisDataSet.Tables["Customers"].Columns["CustomerID"],
            thisDataSet.Tables["Orders"].Columns["CustomerID"]);

DataRelation orderDetailRel = thisDataSet.Relations.Add("OrderDetail",
            thisDataSet.Tables["Orders"].Columns["OrderID"],
            thisDataSet.Tables["Order Details"].Columns["OrderID"]);

DataRelation orderProductRel = thisDataSet.Relations.Add(
    "OrderProducts",thisDataSet.Tables["Products"].Columns["ProductID"],
    thisDataSet.Tables["Order Details"].Columns["ProductID"]);
```

The first relationship is exactly the same as in the previous example. The next one adds the relationship between `Orders` and `Order Details`, using the `OrderID` as the linking column. The last relationship is the one between `Order Details` and `Products`, using `ProductID` as the linking column. Notice that in this relationship, `Products` is actually the parent table (the second of the three parameters). This is because it is the *one* side of the one-to-many relation (one `Product` may appear in many `Orders`).

Now that you've set up the relationships, you can do processing with them. Again, the basic structure is a nested `foreach` loop, this time with three nested levels:

```
foreach (DataRow custRow in thisDataSet.Tables["Customers"].Rows)
{
    Console.WriteLine("Customer ID: " + custRow["CustomerID"]);

    foreach (DataRow orderRow in custRow.GetChildRows(custOrderRel))
    {
        Console.WriteLine("\tOrder ID: " + orderRow["OrderID"]);
        Console.WriteLine("\t\tOrder Date: " + orderRow["OrderDate"]);

        foreach (DataRow detailRow in
                orderRow.GetChildRows(orderDetailRel))
```

```
        {
            Console.WriteLine("\t\tProduct: " +
            detailRow.GetParentRow(orderProductRel)["ProductName"]);
            Console.WriteLine("\t\tQuantity: " + detailRow["Quantity"]);
        }
    }
}
```

As before, you output the data for the parent row, and then use GetChildRows() to obtain the child rows related to this parent. The outer loop is the same as the previous example. Print out the additional detail of the OrderDate to the OrderID and then get the OrderDetails for this OrderID.

The innermost loop is different; to get the Product row, you call GetParentRow(), which gets the parent object, going from the *many* side to the *one* side of the relationship. Sometimes this navigation from child to parent is called navigating *upstream*, as opposed to the normal parent-to-child *downstream* navigation. Upstream navigation requires the GetParentRow() call.

The output of the program shows details of the orders processed for each customer, indented to show the parent and child hierarchy. Again, the Customer ID ZACZI has no orders because you just added it to the table in the previous examples.

XML and ADO.NET

As stated in the introduction, XML support is one of the major design goals of ADO.NET and it is also central to ADO.NET's internal implementation. Therefore, it makes sense that ADO.NET would have a lot of support for XML built into its object model. XML was introduced in Chapter 23, and you are now going to learn about ADO.NET's support for it.

XML Support in ADO.NET DataSets

The XML support in ADO.NET is centered around the DataSet object, because XML is all about relationships and hierarchically structured data. The DataSet has several methods that process XML, and one of the easiest to use is WriteXml(), which writes out the contents of the DataSet as an XML document.

To use WriteXml(), simply construct a DataSet from existing data using the same code as in the previous examples; use the Fill() method of a data adapter to load the data, define DataRelation objects for the relationships, and so on. Then, simply call WriteXml() on the DataSet you have constructed:

```
thisDataSet.WriteXml("nwinddata.xml");
```

WriteXml() can write to various targets; this version of the method simply writes the XML to a file. An external program that accepts XML as an input format can easily read and process the XML.

A ReadXml() method is available to read the contents of an XML file into a DataSet.

The next example takes the code from the DataRelationExample and simply writes the data in the DataSet to an XML file — the nested foreach loops are just replaced by the single call to WriteXml(). You need to ensure that you have a directory named C:\Northwind before running this program.

Try It Out   **Writing XML from a DataSet**

Follow these steps to modify the DataRelationExample program to write XML:

1. Open the DataRelationExample project and replace the `foreach` loop

```
// Print out nested customers and their order IDs
foreach (DataRow custRow in thisDataSet.Tables["Customers"].Rows)
{
    ...
}
```

with the following code:

```
custOrderRel.Nested = true;

thisDataSet.WriteXml(@"c:\northwind\nwinddata.xml");
Console.WriteLine(
    @"Successfully wrote XML output to file c:\Northwind\nwinddata.xml");
```

2. Run the modified example.

3. Open Internet Explorer and browse to the C:\Northwind\nwinddata.xml file, as shown in Figure 28-6.

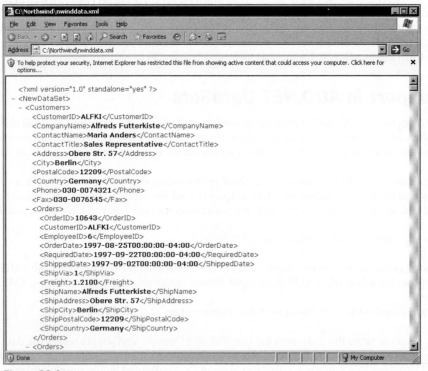

Figure 28-6

How It Works

The Nested property of the DataRelation objects tells the WriteXml() method to nest the order details and orders underneath each parent customer in the XML output. The file nwinddata.xml contains all the data in your tables (including all the columns because you specified SELECT * FROM when filling the DataSet). It is in human-readable, easy-to-parse XML format, and the file can be browsed directly in Microsoft Internet Explorer.

Just as the DataSet has a WriteXml(), it also has a ReadXml() method. The ReadXml() method creates and populates a DataTable in a DataSet with the data from an XML file. Furthermore, the DataTable created is given the name of the root element in the XML document.

Having just created an XML file in the previous example, in the next Try It Out you read it back in and display it.

Try It Out   Reading XML into a DataSet

Follow these steps to create the ReadingXML example in Visual Studio 2008:

1. Create a new console application called ReadingXML in the directory C:\BegVCSharp\Chapter28.

2. Add a using directive for the System.Data namespace to the top of the code:

```
using System.Data;
```

3. Add the following code to the Main() method:

```
static void Main(string[] args)
{
    DataSet thisDataSet = new DataSet();
    thisDataSet.ReadXml(@"c:\Northwind\nwinddata.xml");

    foreach (DataRow custRow in thisDataSet.Tables["Customers"].Rows)
    {
        Console.WriteLine("Customer ID: " + custRow["CustomerID"] +
                          " Name: " + custRow["CompanyName"]);
    }

    Console.WriteLine("Table created by ReadXml is called {0}",
                      thisDataSet.Tables[0].TableName);

    Console.Write("Program finished, press Enter/Return to continue:");
    Console.ReadLine();
}
```

4. Execute the application. You should see output like that shown next, provided that you ran the previous example to create the C:\Northwind\nwinddata.xml file:

```
Customer ID: SANTG Name: Santé Gourmet
Customer ID: SAVEA Name: Save-a-lot Markets
Customer ID: SEVES Name: Seven Seas Imports
Customer ID: SIMOB Name: Simons bistro
Customer ID: SPECD Name: Spécialités du monde
Customer ID: SPLIR Name: Split Rail Beer & Ale
Customer ID: SUPRD Name: Suprêmes délices
Customer ID: THEBI Name: The Big Cheese
Customer ID: THECR Name: The Cracker Box
Customer ID: TOMSP Name: Toms Spezialitäten
Customer ID: TORTU Name: Tortuga Restaurante
Customer ID: TRADH Name: Tradiçao Hipermercados
Customer ID: TRAIH Name: Trail's Head Gourmet Provisioners
Customer ID: VAFFE Name: Vaffeljernet
Customer ID: VICTE Name: Victuailles en stock
Customer ID: VINET Name: Vins et alcools Chevalier
Customer ID: WANDK Name: Die Wandernde Kuh
Customer ID: WARTH Name: Wartian Herkku
Customer ID: WELLI Name: Wellington Importadora
Customer ID: WHITC Name: White Clover Markets
Customer ID: WILMK Name: Wilman Kala
Customer ID: WOLZA Name: Wolski  Zajazd
Customer ID: ZACZI Name: Zachary Zithers Ltd.
Table created by ReadXml is called Customers
Program finished, press Enter/Return to continue:
```

How It Works

Note that you are only using one data namespace here — `System.Data`. You aren't using any database access so you don't have any need for `System.Data.SqlClient` or `System.Data.OleDb`. All you do is create a new `DataSet` and then use the `ReadXml()` method to load the data from the C:\Northwind\nwinddata.xml file. The overload of `ReadXml()` that you use here simply requires you to specify the name of the XML file:

```
DataSet thisDataSet = new DataSet();
thisDataSet.ReadXml(@"c:\Northwind\nwinddata.xml");
```

Next, you output the contents of the `Customers` table — this code should be familiar from the `DataRelationExample` code — and you loop through each `DataRow` in the `Rows` collection of the `Customers` table, displaying the value of the `CustomerID` and `CompanyName` columns:

```
foreach (DataRow custRow in thisDataSet.Tables["Customers"].Rows)
{
    Console.WriteLine("Customer ID: " + custRow["CustomerID"] +
                      " Name: " + custRow["CompanyName"]);
}
```

How did you know the table was called `Customers`? As mentioned earlier, the `DataTable` is named from the root node of the XML document that is read in — if you refer back to the preceding figure for the `WriteXml()` method, you will see that the root node of the XML document produced is indeed `Customers`. Just to prove the point, write the name of the first `DataTable` in the `Tables` collection of the `DataSet`, using the `TableName` property of the `DataTable`:

```
Console.WriteLine("Table created by ReadXml is called {0}",
                  thisDataSet.Tables[0].TableName);
```

SQL Support in ADO.NET

This chapter has covered the basic ADO.NET operations without your having to know anything about the SQL database query language. All ADO.NET commands that read and write from the data source are translated to SQL commands that execute the raw database operations.

Practical use of ADO.NET in real-life working situations requires some knowledge of SQL; for a much more complete introduction to SQL than there is space for here, refer to a good book on SQL such as Robert Viera's *Beginning SQL Server 2008 Programming* or *Professional SQL Server 2005 Programming*. Alternately, use LINQ so you can stick with C#!

That said, there are a few basics to cover here.

SQL Commands in Data Adapters

In the examples given earlier, you used SQL SELECT commands that return all the rows of a table, such as the following:

```
SqlDataAdapter thisAdapter = new SqlDataAdapter(
    "SELECT * FROM Customers", thisConnection);
```

This SELECT command returns all the rows and columns of the customer table when the `Fill()` method is called, and loads them into the memory of your program. This is fine for a small table like the `Customers` table of Northwind, which has only 11 columns and less than 100 rows of data; however, it is not likely to work well for the large tables typically encountered in many business applications, with 100,000 or even 1,000,000 rows.

You need to construct the SELECT command so that it brings in only the data you actually need to process. One way is to limit the number of columns used if your program only interacts with some of the columns, with a SELECT statement specifying only the desired columns:

```
SELECT CustomerID, CompanyName FROM Customers
```

However, you typically don't want to do this when adding rows, because you want to specify values for all columns.

Using WHERE with SELECT

Another technique for minimizing the amount of data loaded into memory is to always specify a WHERE clause on the SQL SELECT statement, which limits the number of rows selected. For example, the statement

```
SELECT * FROM Customers WHERE CustomerID = 'ZACZI'
```

loads only the one row containing Zachary Zithers into memory, using a fraction of the memory required to load the entire table. A range can be specified with WHERE clauses as well, so the statement

```
SELECT * FROM Orders WHERE OrderID BETWEEN 10900 AND 10999
```

loads only the rows with OrderID in the range shown.

If you can limit the number of rows being loaded from a large table with a WHERE clause, always do so. Never load all the rows of a table into your DataSet and then search them with a foreach loop; use the SELECT statement with WHERE to do this kind of search instead.

Your goal is to find the most effective balance between processing data locally on the client where your ADO.NET program is executing and processing on the server where the SQL is executed. The ADO.NET object model and C# are better suited than SQL for complex calculations or navigational logic. Fill your DataSet with the data from the tables you want to process, and execute this kind of logic on the client. However, limiting the number of rows selected from each table with appropriate conditions will greatly increase performance (especially if the data is being transferred across a network), and reduce memory usage.

Viewing SQL SELECT, UPDATE, INSERT, and DELETE Commands

SQL uses four basic commands for querying, updating, adding, and deleting rows from a table. These are, respectively, the SELECT, UPDATE, INSERT, and DELETE commands. In earlier examples, you used the CommandBuilder object to create the SQL commands used to update the database:

```
SqlDataAdapter thisAdapter =
    new SqlDataAdapter("SELECT CustomerID from Customers", thisConnection);

SqlCommandBuilder thisBuilder = new SqlCommandBuilder(thisAdapter);
```

The command builder generates the SQL commands for modifying the data (UPDATE, INSERT, and DELETE) based on the SELECT command.

In the program you create in the following Try It Out, you can see the generated commands with the GetUpdateCommand(), GetInsertCommand(), and GetDeleteCommand() methods of the CommandBuilder object.

Try It Out   **Show SQL Example**

Follow these steps to create the ShowSQL example in Visual Studio 2008:

1.   Create a new console application called ShowSQL in the C:\BegVCSharp\Chapter28
directory, and add the usual using directives to the top of the code:

```
#region Using Directives
using System;
using System.Data;                    // Use ADO.NET namespace
using System.Data.SqlClient;   // Use SQL Server data provider namespace
using System.Collections.Generic;
using System.Text;
#endregion
```

2.   Now add the following code to the Main() method:

```
static void Main(string[] args)
{
    // Specify SQL Server-specific connection string
    SqlConnection thisConnection = new SqlConnection(
                @"Data Source=.\SQLEXPRESS;"+
        @"AttachDbFilename='C:\SQL Server 2000 Sample Databases\
NORTHWND.MDF';" +
        @"Integrated Security=True;Connect Timeout=30;User Instance=true" );



    thisConnection.Open();

    SqlDataAdapter thisAdapter = new
      SqlDataAdapter("SELECT CustomerID from Customers", thisConnection);

    SqlCommandBuilder thisBuilder = new SqlCommandBuilder(thisAdapter);

    Console.WriteLine("SQL SELECT Command is:\n{0}\n",
                thisAdapter.SelectCommand.CommandText);

    SqlCommand updateCommand = thisBuilder.GetUpdateCommand();
    Console.WriteLine("SQL UPDATE Command is:\n{0}\n",
                updateCommand.CommandText);

    SqlCommand insertCommand = thisBuilder.GetInsertCommand();
    Console.WriteLine("SQL INSERT Command is:\n{0}\n",
                insertCommand.CommandText);

    SqlCommand deleteCommand = thisBuilder.GetDeleteCommand();
    Console.WriteLine("SQL DELETE Command is:\n{0}",
                deleteCommand.CommandText);
```

```
        thisConnection.Close();

        Console.Write("Program finished, press Enter/Return to continue:");
        Console.ReadLine();
    }
```

The output of this example is shown here:

```
SQL SELECT Command is:
SELECT CustomerID from Customers

SQL UPDATE Command is:
UPDATE [Customers] SET [CustomerID] = @p1 WHERE (([CustomerID] = @p2))

SQL INSERT Command is:
INSERT INTO [Customers] ([CustomerID]) VALUES (@p1)

SQL DELETE Command is:
DELETE FROM [Customers] WHERE (([CustomerID] = @p1))
Program finished, press Enter/Return to continue:
```

How It Works

Note that the UPDATE and DELETE commands use a WHERE clause that was generated by the CommandBuilder object.

The question marks (?) are markers for parameters, where the ADO.NET runtime will substitute an actual value into the command; for example, when you used the Delete() method to delete the row containing CustomerID ZACZI, at the time Update() was called, the command

```
DELETE FROM Customers WHERE ( CustomerID = 'ZACZI' )
```

was executed to remove the ZACZI row.

Notice that to output the SELECT command you used the SelectCommand property to get the command directly from the DataAdapter. The DataAdapter also has the UpdateCommand, InsertCommand, and DeleteCommand properties to get or set the SQL commands used at update time directly. A developer familiar with SQL can optimize these commands to perform better than the commands automatically generated by CommandBuilder, especially when all columns are included in the SQL SELECT statement.

Direct Execution of SQL Commands

If your program needs to perform a set-oriented operation such as deleting or updating all rows meeting a certain condition, it is much more efficient, especially for large tables, to do this as a single SQL command than to do extended processing in C# code.

ADO.NET provides the SqlCommand or OleDbCommand objects for executing SQL commands. These objects provide methods for executing SQL commands directly. You used the ExecuteReader() method at the beginning of the chapter when you looked at the `DataReader` object. Here, you look at the other methods for executing SQL statements — `ExecuteScalar()` and `ExecuteNonQuery()`.

Retrieving Single Values

On many occasions, it is necessary to return a single result from a SQL query, such as the number of records in a given table. The `ExecuteScalar()` method enables you to achieve this — this method is used to execute SQL commands that return only a scalar (a single value), as opposed to returning multiple rows, as with `ExecuteReader()`.

In the next Try It Out, you use the `ExecuteScalar()` method of `SqlCommand` to execute the query.

Try It Out   **Retrieving Single Values with ExecuteScalar()**

As a first example, consider a program that gets a count of the rows in the `Customers` table. This is similar to the DataReader example earlier, but it uses a different SQL statement and method of execution.

1. Create a new console application called ExecuteScalarExample in the C:\BegVCSharp\ Chapter28 directory, and add the usual `using` directives to the top of the code:

```
#region Using Directives
using System;
using System.Data;          // Use ADO.NET namespace
using System.Data.SqlClient; // Use SQL Server data provider namespace
. . .
```

2. Add the following code to the `Main()` method:

```
static void Main(string[] args)
{
    SqlConnection thisConnection = new
    SqlConnection(        @"Data Source=.\SQLEXPRESS;"+
        @"AttachDbFilename='C:\SQL Server 2000 Sample Databases\
NORTHWND.MDF';" +
        @"Integrated Security=True;Connect Timeout=30;User Instance=true" );

    thisConnection.Open();
    SqlCommand thisCommand = thisConnection.CreateCommand();
    thisCommand.CommandText = "SELECT COUNT(*) FROM Customers";
    Object countResult = thisCommand.ExecuteScalar();
    Console.WriteLine("Count of Customers = {0}", countResult);

    thisConnection.Close();
    Console.Write("Program finished, press Enter/Return to continue:");
    Console.ReadLine();
}
```

How It Works

This program uses the SQL Server .NET data provider. The core of the program is the same as the first example in this chapter, opening a connection to SQL Server on the local machine with integrated security and the Northwind database.

You create a `SqlCommand` object and assign the `SELECT COUNT(*)` command to its `CommandText` property. `COUNT()` is a SQL function that returns the count of rows that match the `WHERE` condition. Then you call the `ExecuteScalar()` method of `SqlCommand` to execute the query to retrieve the count. You display the count and exit. When executed against the Northwind database, the program displays the following (provided that you've deleted Zachary Zithers Ltd!):

```
Count of Customers = 91
```

This is equivalent to loading the `Customers` table into the `DataTable` object and using the `Count` property of the `Rows` object as in earlier examples. Why would you want to do the job this way? It depends on the structure of your data and what else you are doing in your program. If you have a small amount of data, or are loading all the rows into your `DataSet` for any other reason, it makes sense to just use `DataTable.Rows.Count`. However, if you want to count the exact number of rows in a very large table with 1,000,000 rows, it is much more efficient to issue a `SELECT COUNT(*)` query with the `ExecuteScalar()` method, rather than try to load 1,000,000 rows into memory.

Retrieving No Data

A rather strange heading, but bear in mind that data modification operations such as SQL `INSERT`, `UPDATE`, and `DELETE` do not return data. What is interesting for these commands is the number of rows affected. This number is returned by the `ExecuteNonQuery()` method.

Assume that one of your suppliers has increased prices by 5 percent for all of its products. The following Try It Out shows how to use the `SqlCommand` object to execute a SQL `UPDATE` command to increase all the prices by 5 percent for products supplied by that supplier:

Try It Out   Data Modification with ExecuteNonQuery

Follow these steps to create the ExecuteNonQueryExample in Visual Studio 2008:

1. Create a new console application called ExecuteNonQueryExample in the C:\BegVCSharp\ Chapter28 directory, and add the usual `using` directives to the top of the code:

    ```
    #region Using Directives
    using System;
    using System.Data;             // Use ADO.NET namespace
    using System.Data.SqlClient;   // Use SQL Server data provider namespace

    . . .
    ```

2. Add the following code to the `Main()` method:

```
static void Main(string[] args)
{
    SqlConnection thisConnection = new SqlConnection(
                @"Data Source=.\SQLEXPRESS;"+
        @"AttachDbFilename='C:\SQL Server 2000 Sample Databases\
NORTHWND.MDF';" +
        @"Integrated Security=True;Connect Timeout=30;User Instance=true" );


    thisConnection.Open();

    SqlCommand thisCommand = thisConnection.CreateCommand();
    thisCommand.CommandText = "UPDATE Products SET " +
        "UnitPrice=UnitPrice*1.05 WHERE SupplierId=12";
    int rowsAffected = thisCommand.ExecuteNonQuery();
    Console.WriteLine("Rows Updated = {0}", rowsAffected);
    thisConnection.Close();

    Console.Write("Program finished, press Enter/Return to continue:");
    Console.ReadLine();
}
```

How It Works

This program opens the connection just as in the previous example. You create a `SqlCommand` object and assign the UPDATE command shown as the text of the command. Then you call the `ExecuteNonQuery()` method of `SqlCommand` to execute the query, returning the number of rows affected in the database. You display the number of rows and exit. When executed against the Northwind database, the program displays the following:

```
Rows Updated = 5
```

This indicates that prices were adjusted for five products.

Calling a SQL Stored Procedure

Finally, here's an example of calling a SQL stored procedure, which is a procedure written in SQL and stored in the database. Stored procedures encapsulate complex SQL queries and database procedures in a single unit that can be called by multiple application programs or directly by users; the database administrator can be sure that the exact same steps are followed whenever a stored procedure is called, ensuring consistent use of the database. Users and application developers don't have to remember complex SQL query syntax; they only have know the name of the stored procedure and what it does. Northwind contains several stored procedures.

This example calls the Ten Most Expensive Products procedure, which is included in the Northwind sample database. This procedure returns two columns: `TenMostExpensiveProducts` and `UnitPrice`. Try it out.

Try It Out   Calling a Stored Procedure

Essentially, this program is a variation on the very first example in this chapter, DataReading. Just like SQL commands, stored procedures can return single values, in which case you would use ExecuteScalar or ExecuteNonQuery, as you just saw with regular SQL commands. Alternately, they can return query results that are read with a DataReader, as in this example:

1.   Create a new console application called SQLStoredProcedure in the C:\BegVCSharp\ Chapter28 directory, and add the usual using directives to the top of the code:

```
#region Using Directives
using System;

using System.Data;         // Use ADO.NET namespace
using System.Data.SqlClient;  // Use SQL Server data provider namespace

. . .
```

2.   Make the Main() method look as follows (it is the same as DataReading except for the highlighted differences):

```
static void Main(string[] args)
{
    // Specify SQL Server-specific connection string
    SqlConnection thisConnection = new SqlConnection(
        @"Data Source=.\SQLEXPRESS;"+
        @"AttachDbFilename='C:\SQL Server 2000 Sample Databases\
NORTHWND.MDF';" +
        @"Integrated Security=True;Connect Timeout=30;User Instance=true" );


    // Open connection
    thisConnection.Open();

    // Create command for this connection
    SqlCommand thisCommand = thisConnection.CreateCommand();

    // Set command to Stored Procedure type.
    thisCommand.CommandType = CommandType.StoredProcedure;
    thisCommand.CommandText =
        "Ten Most Expensive Products";

    // Execute DataReader for specified command
    SqlDataReader thisReader = thisCommand.ExecuteReader();

    // While there are rows to read
    while (thisReader.Read())
    {
        // Output product name and price columns
        Console.WriteLine("\t{0}\t{1}",
            thisReader["TenMostExpensiveProducts"], thisReader["UnitPrice"]);
    }
```

```
// Close reader
thisReader.Close();

// Close connection
thisConnection.Close();
Console.Write("Program finished, press Enter/Return to continue:");
Console.ReadLine();
}
```

3. Press F5 to execute in the debugger; you should see the results shown here (the exact values may vary depending on which version of the Northwind database you are using):

```
Côte de Blaye     263.5000
Thüringer Rostbratwurst 123.7900
Mishi Kobe Niku 97.0000
Sir Rodney's Marmalade  81.0000
Carnarvon Tigers        62.5000
Raclette Courdavault    55.0000
Manjimup Dried Apples   53.0000
Tarte au sucre  49.3000
Ipoh Coffee     46.0000
Rössle Sauerkraut       45.6000
Program finished, press Enter/Return to continue:
```

How It Works

This program opens the connection as in previous examples. You create a SqlCommand object, setting the CommandType parameter to CommandType.StoredProcedure, an enumeration within ADO.NET for the purpose of supporting stored procedure calls. When CommandType is set to StoredProcedure, the CommandText holds the name of the stored procedure, not a SQL command. The rest of the program is exactly the same as if a SQL command were executed. The columns returned have different names, so the printout of the values differs slightly.

Using LINQ over DataSet with ADO.NET

In the previous chapter you learned about LINQ to SQL and its advantages for simplifying database access and queries. You can also use LINQ in conjunction with ADO.NET by using the LINQ over DataSet facility, which you will try out in this section.

When to Use LINQ over DataSet

If you have legacy code that already uses ADO.NET DataSets, LINQ over DataSet adds the full set of LINQ query operators to the limited query facilities that are part of the original DataSet class without requiring you to recode the entire application using LINQ to SQL classes. LINQ over DataSet is also useful if your application requires extended manipulation of disconnected subsets of data.

Using LINQ over DataSet

Follow these steps to create the LINQoverDataSet program in Visual Studio 2008:

1. Create a new console application project called LINQoverDataSet in the directory C:\BegVCSharp\Chapter28.

2. Add a reference to the `System.Data.Linq` component as shown in Figure 28-7.

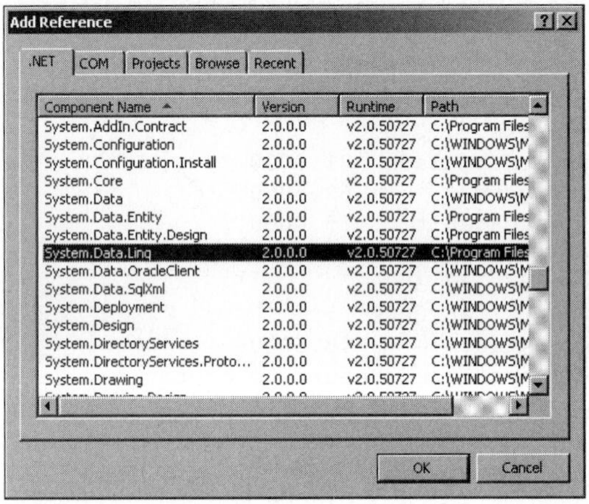

Figure 28-7

> Note that LINQ over DataSet also uses the `System.Data.DataSetExtensions` namespace, which is automatically added by Visual Studio.

When you use LINQ over DataSet you are using a small part of the LINQ to Entity facility mentioned at the start of this chapter. While LINQ to Entity in its entirety is beyond the scope of a beginning book like this one, LINQ to DataSet is a simple part of LINQ to Entity that you can use immediately based on what you have already learned about LINQ.

3. Begin by adding the `using` directives for the ADO.NET and LINQ classes you will be using:

```
#region Using Directives
using System;
using System.Collections.Generic;
using System.Linq;
using System.Data;              // Use ADO.NET namespace
using System.Data.SqlClient;    // Use SQL Server data provider namespace
using System.Data.Linq;         // Use LINQ / ADO.NET connector
using System.Data.Common;
using System.Text;

#endregion
```

4. Add the following code to the Main() method. Because this code is the same as the start of the code from the DataRelationExample program, you may find it convenient to cut and paste from that source file:

```
static void Main(string[] args)
{

    // Specify SQL Server-specific connection string
    SqlConnection thisConnection = new SqlConnection(
        @"Data Source=.\SQLEXPRESS;"+
        @"AttachDbFilename='C:\SQL Server 2000 Sample Databases\
NORTHWND.MDF';" +
        @"Integrated Security=True;Connect Timeout=30;User Instance=true" );

    // Create DataAdapter object for update and other operations
    SqlDataAdapter thisAdapter = new SqlDataAdapter(
            "SELECT CustomerID, CompanyName FROM Customers", thisConnection);
    // Create CommandBuilder object to build SQL commands
    SqlCommandBuilder thisBuilder = new SqlCommandBuilder(thisAdapter);

    // Create DataSet to contain related data tables, rows, and columns
    DataSet thisDataSet = new DataSet();

    // Set up DataAdapter objects for each table and fill
    SqlDataAdapter custAdapter = new SqlDataAdapter(
                "SELECT * FROM Customers", thisConnection);
    SqlDataAdapter orderAdapter = new SqlDataAdapter(
                "SELECT * FROM Orders", thisConnection);
    custAdapter.Fill(thisDataSet, "Customers");
    orderAdapter.Fill(thisDataSet, "Orders");

    // Set up DataRelation between customers and orders
    DataRelation custOrderRel = thisDataSet.Relations.Add("CustOrders",
                thisDataSet.Tables["Customers"].Columns["CustomerID"],
                thisDataSet.Tables["Orders"].Columns["CustomerID"]);
```

5. Now add the following code that uses LINQ:

```
    var customers = thisDataSet.Tables["Customers"].AsEnumerable();
    var orders = thisDataSet.Tables["Orders"].AsEnumerable();

    var preferredCustomers =
        from c in customers
        where c.GetChildRows("CustOrders").Length > 10
        orderby c.GetChildRows("CustOrders").Length
        select c;

    Console.WriteLine("Customers with > 10 orders:");
    foreach (var customer in preferredCustomers)
    {
        Console.WriteLine("{0} orders: {1} {2}, {3} {4}",
        customer.GetChildRows("CustOrders").Length,
        customer["CustomerID"], customer["CompanyName"],
        customer["City"], customer["Region"] );
    }
```

6. Finish the `Main()` method with the standard closing logic used in our other examples:

```
        thisConnection.Close();
        Console.Write("Program finished, press Enter/Return to
continue:");
        Console.ReadLine();
```

7. Compile and execute the application. You should see this output:

```
12 orders: LINOD LINO-Delicateses, I. de Margarita Nueva Esparta
12 orders: REGGC Reggiani Caseifici, Reggio Emilia
12 orders: SUPRD Suprêmes délices, Charleroi
13 orders: AROUT Around the Horn, London
13 orders: MEREP Mère Paillarde, Montréal Québec
13 orders: QUEEN Queen Cozinha, Sao Paulo SP
14 orders: BOTTM Bottom-Dollar Markets, Tsawassen BC
14 orders: HANAR Hanari Carnes, Rio de Janeiro RJ
14 orders: KOENE Königlich Essen, Brandenburg
14 orders: LAMAI La maison d'Asie, Toulouse
14 orders: LILAS LILA-Supermercado, Barquisimeto Lara
14 orders: WHITC White Clover Markets, Seattle WA
15 orders: FRANK Frankenversand, München
15 orders: LEHMS Lehmanns Marktstand, Frankfurt a.M.
15 orders: WARTH Wartian Herkku, Oulu
17 orders: BONAP Bon app', Marseille
18 orders: BERGS Berglunds snabbköp, Luleå
18 orders: HILAA HILARION-Abastos, San Cristóbal Táchira
18 orders: RATTC Rattlesnake Canyon Grocery, Albuquerque NM
19 orders: FOLKO Folk och fä HB, Bräcke
19 orders: HUNGO Hungry Owl All-Night Grocers, Cork Co. Cork
28 orders: QUICK QUICK-Stop, Cunewalde
30 orders: ERNSH Ernst Handel, Graz
31 orders: SAVEA Save-a-lot Markets, Boise ID
Program finished, press Enter/Return to continue:
```

How It Works

Before you construct the `DataRelation`, you need to create the `DataSet` object and link the database tables you are going to use with it, as shown here:

```
DataSet thisDataSet = new DataSet();
SqlDataAdapter custAdapter = new SqlDataAdapter(
    "SELECT * FROM Customers", thisConnection);
SqlDataAdapter orderAdapter = new SqlDataAdapter(
    "SELECT * FROM Orders", thisConnection);
custAdapter.Fill(thisDataSet, "Customers");
orderAdapter.Fill(thisDataSet, "Orders");
```

You create a `DataAdapter` object for each table you will reference. You then fill the `DataSet` with data from the columns you're going to work with; in this case, you're not worried about efficiency, so you just use all of the available columns (`SELECT * FROM <table>`).

Next, you make the `DataRelation` object and link it to the `DataSet`:

```
DataRelation custOrderRel = thisDataSet.Relations.Add("CustOrders",
        thisDataSet.Tables["Customers"].Columns["CustomerID"],
        thisDataSet.Tables["Orders"].Columns["CustomerID"]);
```

Now you're ready to find the customers and orders. You first set up a `foreach` loop to display the customer information for each customer:

```
foreach (DataRow custRow in thisDataSet.Tables["Customers"].Rows)
{
    Console.WriteLine("Customer ID: " + custRow["CustomerID"] +
                    " Name: " + custRow["CompanyName"]);
```

You're just looping through the `Rows` collection of the `Customers` table, printing the `CustomerID` and `CompanyName` for each customer. Once you've displayed the customer, you'd like to display the related orders for that customer.

To do that, you add a nested `foreach` loop, initialized by calling the `GetChildRows()` method of `DataRow`. You pass your `DataRelation` object to `GetChildRows()`, and it returns a `DataRowCollection` containing just the related rows in the `Orders` table for this customer. To display these related rows, simply loop through each `DataRow` in this collection with your `foreach` loop:

```
namespace LINQtoDataSet
{

    class Program
    {
        static void Main(string[] args)
        {



            var customers = thisDataSet.Tables["Customers"].AsEnumerable();
            var orders = thisDataSet.Tables["Orders"].AsEnumerable();

            var preferredCustomers =
                from c in customers
                where c.GetChildRows("CustOrders").Length > 10
                orderby c.GetChildRows("CustOrders").Length
                select c;
```

Now you repeat the process for each customer. You added some leading spaces to the display of the `OrderID`, so the orders for each customer are displayed indented underneath the customer information. With the indented display, you can see the parent-child relationship between each customer and its orders more clearly. Customer ID `"Zachary Zithers Ltd."` has no `Orders` because you just added it to the table in the previous examples.

Summary

This chapter covered the following:

❑ ADO.NET is the part of the .NET Framework that enables access to relational databases and other data sources. ADO.NET is designed to provide a simple, flexible framework for data access. It is designed for multitier application architectures and integrates relational data with XML.

❑ ADO.NET classes are contained in the System.Data namespace. You reviewed the object model of ADO.NET and learned the roles of its major objects, including the connection, command, DataReader, data adapter, DataSet, DataTable, DataRow, and DataColumn objects.

❑ .NET data providers offer access to specific data sources, and ADO.NET can be extended to new data sources by writing .NET data providers for the new data source. You examined the .NET data providers included with ADO.NET for Microsoft SQL Server and OLE DB data sources, and learned that these are contained in the System.Data.SqlClient and System.Data.OleDb namespaces, respectively.

❑ You learned how to implement quick read-only access to data via the DataReader object, and how to write an equivalent program for both the SqlClient and OleDb .NET data providers. You learned how to update data and add rows via the DataSet, data adapter, and CommandBuilder objects. You also learned how to find rows using the primary key, and how to delete rows.

❑ It is easy to access multiple tables in a DataSet via the DataRelation object and to generate an XML view of that data. Finally, you looked briefly at how to take advantage of the SQL database language support within ADO.NET, including display of automatically generated SQL commands, direction execution of SQL, and how to call a SQL stored procedure.

As you have seen, creating database code can be quite complex as you start to build more than a simple application. In the next chapter, you look at the tools in Visual Studio 2008 that create much of this complex code for you and make database development much more fun!

Exercises

1. Modify the program given in the first sample to use the Employees table in the Northwind database. Retrieve the EmployeeID and LastName columns.

2. Modify the first program showing the Update() method to change the company name back to Bottom-Dollar Markets.

3. Write a program that asks the user for a Customer ID.

4. Write a program to create some orders for the customer Zachary Zithers; use the sample programs to view the orders.

5. Write a program to display a different part of the relationship hierarchies in the Northwind database than the one used in this chapter, such as Products, Suppliers, and Categories.

6. Write out the data generated in the previous exercise as an XML document.

7. Change the program used to print all customer order details and products to use a WHERE clause in the SELECT statement for Customers, limiting the customers processed.

8. Modify the program shown to print out UPDATE, INSERT, and DELETE statements to use "SELECT * FROM Customers" as the SQL SELECT command. Note the complexity of the generated statements.

9. Modify the LINQoverDataSet sample to use the Employees table in the Northwind database as with exercise 1. Again, retrieve the EmployeeID and LastName columns.

29

LINQ to XML

The previous two chapters introduced LINQ (Language-Integrated Query) and showed how LINQ works with objects and databases. This chapter introduces LINQ to XML, which is the version of LINQ that enables you to use LINQ to query and manipulate XML (Extensible Markup Language).

You learned about XML in Chapter 25, so that is not covered again here. You should be familiar with XML documents, elements, attributes, and so on before proceeding further in this chapter, so if you haven't read the introduction to XML at the beginning of Chapter 25, do so now.

LINQ to XML is not intended to replace the standard XML APIs such as XML DOM (Document Object Model), XPath, XQuery, XSLT, and so on. If you are familiar with these APIs or currently need to use them or learn them, you should continue to do so.

LINQ to XML supplements these standard XML classes and makes working with XML easier. LINQ to XML gives you extra options for creating and querying XML data, resulting in simpler code and quicker development for many common situations, especially if you are already using LINQ to Objects or LINQ to SQL in other parts of your programs.

In learning LINQ to XML, in particular you will look at the following:

❑   How to easily create XML documents with LINQ to XML functional constructor methods.

❑   How to format, load, and save XML documents with LINQ to XML.

❑   How use LINQ to XML to work with incomplete XML documents (fragments).

❑   How to generate an XML document from a LINQ to SQL or LINQ to Objects query.

❑   How to query an XML document with LINQ to XML using standard LINQ query syntax.

❑   How use LINQ aggregate operators with LINQ to XML.

LINQ to XML Functional Constructors

As shown in previous chapters, one of the themes in C# 3.0 is easier construction of objects, with features such as object initializers and anonymous types. LINQ to XML continues this theme by introducing a new, easier way to create XML documents called *functional construction* in which the constructor calls can be nested in a way that naturally reflects the structure of the XML document. In the following Try It Out, you use functional constructors to make a simple XML document containing customers and orders.

Try It Out   LINQ to XML Constructors

Follow these steps to create the example in Visual Studio 2008:

1. Create a new console application called BegVCSharp_29_1_LinqToXmlConstructors in the directory C:\BegVCSharp\Chapter29.

2. Open the main source file `Program.cs`.

3. Add a reference to the `System.Xml.Linq` namespace to the beginning of `Program.cs` as shown:

```
using System;
using System.Collections.Generic;
using System.Linq;
using System.Xml.Linq;
using System.Text;
```

4. Add the following code to the `Main()` method in `Program.cs`:

```
static void Main(string[] args)
{
            XDocument xdoc = new XDocument(
                new XElement("customers",
                    new XElement("customer",
                        new XAttribute("ID", "A"),
                        new XAttribute("City", "New York"),
                        new XAttribute("Region", "North America"),
                        new XElement("order",
                            new XAttribute("Item", "Widget"),
                            new XAttribute("Price", 100)
                        ),
                        new XElement("order",
                            new XAttribute("Item", "Tire"),
                            new XAttribute("Price", 200)
                        )
                    ),
                    new XElement("customer",
                        new XAttribute("ID", "B"),
                        new XAttribute("City", "Mumbai"),
                        new XAttribute("Region", "Asia"),
```

```
                        new XElement("order",
                            new XAttribute("Item", "Oven"),
                            new XAttribute("Price", 501)
                        )
                    )
                )
            );
            Console.WriteLine(xdoc);

            Console.Write("Program finished, press Enter/Return to continue:");
            Console.ReadLine();
    }
```

5. Compile and execute the program (you can just press F5 for Start Debugging). You will see the output shown here:

```
<customers>
  <customer ID="A" City="New York" Region="North America">
    <order Item="Widget" Price="100" />
    <order Item="Tire" Price="200" />
  </customer>
  <customer ID="B" City="Mumbai" Region="Asia">
    <order Item="Oven" Price="501" />
  </customer>
</customers>
Program finished, press Enter/Return to continue:
```

The XML document shown on the output screen contains a very simplified version of the customer/order data you have seen in previous examples. Note that the root element of the XML document is <customers>, which contains two nested <customer> elements. These in turn contain a number of nested <order> elements. The <customer> elements have two attributes, <City> and <Region>, and the <order> elements have <Item> and <Price> attributes.

Press Enter/Return to exit the program and make the console screen disappear. If you used Ctrl+F5 (Start Without Debugging), you may need to press Enter/Return twice.

How It Works

The first step is to reference the System.Xml.Linq namespace. All the examples following in this chapter require that you add this line to your program:

```
using System.Xml.Linq;
```

While the System.Linq namespace is included by default when you create a project, the System.Xml.Linq namespace is not included; you must add this line explicitly.

Next are the calls to the LINQ to XML constructors XDocument(), XElement(), and XAttribute(), which are nested inside one another as shown here:

```
XDocument xdoc = new XDocument(
    new XElement("customers",
        new XElement("customer",
            new XAttribute("ID", "A"),
            ...
```

Note that the code here looks like the XML itself, where the document contains elements, and each element contains attributes and other elements. Let's look at each of these constructors in turn:

❑ XDocument() — The highest-level object in the LINQ to XML constructor hierarchy is XDocument(), which represents the complete XML document. This appears in your code here:

```
static void Main(string[] args)
{
        XDocument xdoc = new XDocument(
   . . .
            );
```

The parameter list for XDocument() is omitted in the previous code fragment so you can see where the XDocument() call begins and ends. Like all the LINQ to XML constructors, XDocument() takes an array of objects (object[]) as one of its parameters so that a number of other objects created by other constructors can be passed to it. All the other constructors you call in this program are parameters in the one call to the XDocument() constructor. The first (and only) parameter you pass in this program is the XElement() constructor.

❑ XElement () — an XML document must have a root element, so in most cases the parameter list of XDocument() will begin with an XElement object . The XElement() constructor takes the name of the element as a string, followed by a list of the XML objects contained within that element. Here, the root element is "customers", which in turn contains a list of "customer" elements:

```
new XElement("customers",
    new XElement("customer",
. . .
        ),
. . .
    )
```

❑ The "customer" element does not contain any other XML elements. Instead, it contains three XML attributes, which are constructed with the XAttribute() constructor.

❑ XAttribute() — Here you add three XML attributes to the "customer" element, named "ID", "City" and "Region":

```
new XAttribute("ID", "A"),
new XAttribute("City", "New York"),
new XAttribute("Region", "North America"),
```

❑ Because an XML attribute is by definition a leaf XML node containing no other XML nodes, the XAttribute() constructor takes only the name of the attribute and its value as parameters. In this case, the three attributes generated are ID="A", City="New York", and Region="North America".

❑ Other LINQ to XML constructors — While you do not call them in this program, there are other LINQ to XML constructors for all the XML node types, such as XDeclaration() for the XML declaration at the start of an XML document, XComment() for an XML comment, and so on. These other constructors are not used often, but are available if you need them for precise control over formatting an XML document.

Finishing Up How It Works

Finishing up the explanation of the first example, you add two child `"order"` elements to the `"customer"` element following the `"ID"`, `"City"` and `"Region"` attributes:

```
new XElement("order",
    new XAttribute("Item", "Widget"),
    new XAttribute("Price", 100)
),
new XElement("order",
    new XAttribute("Item", "Tire"),
    new XAttribute("Price", 200)
)
```

These order elements have `"Item"` and `"Price"` attributes but no other children.

Next, you display its contents to the console screen:

```
Console.WriteLine(xdoc);
```

This prints out the text of the XML document using the default `ToString()` method of `XDocument()`.

Finally, you pause the screen so you can see the console output, and then wait until the user presses Enter:

```
Console.Write("Program finished, press Enter/Return to continue:");
Console.ReadLine();
```

After that your program exits the `Main()` method, which ends the program.

Constructing XML Element Text with Strings

The example you just performed formatted the XML with no text content in the elements. Often your XML needs to have text content as well; this is very easy to do with the LINQ to XML `XElement()` constructor. For example, to make the ID the text of the `<customer>` element instead of an attribute, just pass a string in the parameters of the `XElement()` constructor instead of a nested `XAttribute`:

```
XDocument xdoc = new XDocument(
    new XElement("customers",
        new XElement("customer",
        "AAAAAA",
        new XAttribute("City", "New York"),
        new XAttribute("Region", "North America")
    ),
    new XElement("customer",
        "BBBBBB",
        new XAttribute("City", "Mumbai"),
        new XAttribute("Region", "Asia")
    )
);
```

This produces an XML document that looks like this:

```
<customers>
  <customer City="New York" Region="North America">AAAAAA</customer>
  <customer City="Mumbai" Region="Asia">BBBBBB</customer>
</customers>
```

The `XElement()` constructor concatenates all strings in the parameter list into the text section of the element.

Saving and Loading an XML Document

You may have noticed that when the XML document was displayed to the console screen with `Console.WriteLine()`, it did not display the normal XML declaration that begins with `<?xml version="1.0"`. While you can create such a declaration explicitly with the `XDeclaration()` constructor, you normally do not need to do so, as it is created automatically when you save an XML document to a file with the LINQ to XML `Save()` method.

In addition, while constructing XML documents in your program is useful for understanding how constructors work, it is not something you will do often. More typically, you load XML documents from an external source such as a file.

You try both of these operations in the following Try It Out.

Try It Out   Saving and Loading an XML Document

Follow these steps to create the example in Visual Studio 2008:

1. Either modify the previous example or create a new console application called BegVCSharp_29-2-SaveLoadXML in the directory C:\BegVCSharp\Chapter29.

2. Open the main source file `Program.cs`.

3. Add a reference to the `System.Xml.Linq` namespace to the beginning of `Program.cs` as shown:

```
using System;
using System.Collections.Generic;
using System.Linq;
using System.Xml.Linq;
using System.Text;
```

This will already be present if you are modifying the previous example.

4. If not already present, add the XML document constructor and its nested XML element and attribute calls from the preceding example to the Main() method in Program.cs:

```
static void Main(string[] args)
{
            XDocument xdoc = new XDocument(
                new XElement("customers",
                    new XElement("customer",
                        new XAttribute("ID", "A"),
                        new XAttribute("City", "New York"),
                        new XAttribute("Region", "North America"),
                        new XElement("order",
                            new XAttribute("Item", "Widget"),
                            new XAttribute("Price", 100)
                        ),
                        new XElement("order",
                            new XAttribute("Item", "Tire"),
                            new XAttribute("Price", 200)
                        )
                    ),

                new XElement("customer",
                    new XAttribute("ID", "B"),
                    new XAttribute("City", "Mumbai"),
                    new XAttribute("Region", "Asia"),
                    new XElement("order",
                        new XAttribute("Item", "Oven"),
                        new XAttribute("Price", 501)
                    )
                )
            )
        );
```

5. After the XML document constructor code added in the previous step, add the following code to save, load, and display the XML document at the end of the Main() method in Program.cs:

```
            string xmlFileName = @"c:\BegVCSharp\Chapter29\Xml\example2.xml";

            xdoc.Save(xmlFileName);

            XDocument xdoc2 = XDocument.Load(xmlFileName);

            Console.WriteLine("Contents of xdoc2:");
            Console.WriteLine(xdoc2);

            Console.Write("Program finished, press Enter/Return to continue:");
            Console.ReadLine();
}
```

6. Compile and execute the program (you can just press F5 for Start Debugging). You should see the following output in the console window:

```
Contents of xdoc2:
<customers>
  <customer ID="A" City="New York" Region="North America">
    <order Item="Widget" Price="100" />
    <order Item="Tire" Price="200" />
  </customer>
  <customer ID="B" City="Mumbai" Region="Asia">
    <order Item="Oven" Price="501" />
  </customer>
</customers>
Program finished, press Enter/Return to continue:
```

Press Enter/Return to finish the program and make the console screen disappear. If you used Ctrl+F5 (Start Without Debugging) you may need to press Enter/Return twice.

How It Works

As before, the first step is to reference the System.Xml.Linq namespace. Next are the nested calls to the LINQ to XML constructors XDocument(), XElement(), and XAttribute(). See the first example for an explanation of these parts and other code repeated from the first example.

Following the creation of your XDocument() object, you specify a filename as a string and save the XML document to a file with this call to the Save() method:

```
string xmlFileName = @"c:\BegVCSharp\Chapter29\Xml\example2.xml";

xdoc.Save(xmlFileName);
```

While in this particular case you save to a specified filename, the Save() method also has overloads to save to a System.IO.TextWriter or a System.Xml.XmlWriter, which may be appropriate if you are writing another program in which you are already using one of those classes to write to a file.

The Save() method also has an overload whereby you can specify SaveOptions to disable formatting (by default, the XML document is saved with indentation and whitespace to make it look "pretty").

Now that you've saved the document to a file, you load it into a new XDocument instance called xdoc2:

```
XDocument xdoc2 = XDocument.Load(xmlFileName);
```

The XDocument.Load() method is static because it is a factory-type method that creates an new instance of an XDocument; you can use this to load a document created by a completely different program.

Next, you display the document just as you did before, only this time using the xdoc2 instance that you loaded from the file. The rest of the program is the same as the previous example:

```
Console.WriteLine("Contents of xdoc2:");
Console.WriteLine(xdoc2);

Console.Write("Program finished, press Enter/Return to continue:");
Console.ReadLine();
```

Loading XML from a String

Sometimes instead of loading XML from a file, you receive XML sent from another application as a string. through one or more of your methods. You can create XML documents from strings in LINQ to XML by using the `Parse()` method:

```
XDocument xdoc = XDocument.Parse(@"
            <customers>
                <customer ID=""A"" City=""New York"" Region=""North America"">
                    <order Item=""Widget"" Price=""100"" />
                    <order Item=""Tire"" Price=""200"" />
                 </customer>
                <customer ID=""B"" City=""Mumbai"" Region=""Asia"">
                    <order Item=""Oven"" Price=""501"" />
                </customer>
            </customers>
            ");
```

This produces the same result that loading the document from a file does. Just as with `Load()`, `Parse()` is a class-level method that creates a new instance of an `XDocument`; you do not need to construct a new `XDocument` object before calling the `Parse()` method.

> *While the string literal for the XML in the preceding example has double quotation marks (" "), in the actual contents of the string the quotation marks are not double. The double quotation marks are just the convention for including quotation marks in an @-quoted string literal.*

Contents of a Saved XML Document

Use Internet Explorer to open the document you just saved with the previous example. Specify the full path name C:\BegVCSharp\Chapter29\Xml\example2.xml in the address bar. You will see the document as shown in Figure 29-1.

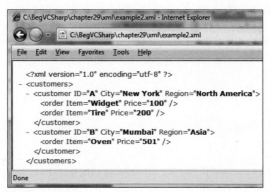

Figure 29-1

Note that the XML document declaration `<?xml version="1.0" encoding="utf-8" ?>` appears at the beginning of the saved document even though it is not displayed when you simply print the `XDocument` object to the screen using `Console.Writeline()`. You needn't worry about the declaration and many other XML details using the defaults supplied by LINQ to XML.

The default encoding for XML documents in Windows is UTF-8 (8-bit Unicode Transformation Format). You shouldn't change this except in a very unusual situation, such as creating an ASCII-encoded XML document that would be consumed by a legacy program that doesn't understand UTF-8. In that case, you can either add an XDeclaration() *object with the encoding set to ASCII to the beginning of the parameter list for the* XDocument() *constructor, or set the* Declaration *property of the* XDocument:

```
xdoc.Declaration = new XDeclaration("1.0", "us-ascii", "yes");
```

Working with XML Fragments

Unlike some XML APIs, LINQ to XML works with XML fragments (partial or incomplete XML documents) in very much the same way as complete XML documents. When working with a fragment, you simply work with XElement as the top-level XML object instead of XDocument.

The only restriction on this is that you cannot add some of the more esoteric XML node types that apply only the XML documents to XElement, *such as* XComment *for XML comments,* XDeclaration *for the XML document declaration, and* XProcessingInstruction *for XML processing instructions.*

In the following Try It Out, you load, save, and manipulate an XML element and its child nodes, just as you did for an XML document.

Try It Out   Working with XML Fragments

Follow these steps to create the example in Visual Studio 2008:

1. Either modify the previous example or create a new console application called BegVCSharp_29-3-XMLFragments in the directory C:\BegVCSharp\Chapter29.

2. Open the main source file Program.cs.

3. Add a reference to the System.Xml.Linq namespace to the beginning of Program.cs as shown:

```
using System;
using System.Collections.Generic;
using System.Linq;
using System.Xml.Linq;
using System.Text;
```

This will already be present if you are modifying the previous example.

4. Add the XML element without the containing XML document constructor used in the previous examples to the Main() method in Program.cs:

```
static void Main(string[] args)
{
        XElement xcust =
            new XElement("customers",
                new XElement("customer",
                    new XAttribute("ID", "A"),
                    new XAttribute("City", "New York"),
                    new XAttribute("Region", "North America"),
                    new XElement("order",
                        new XAttribute("Item", "Widget"),
                        new XAttribute("Price", 100)
                    ),
                    new XElement("order",
                        new XAttribute("Item", "Tire"),
                        new XAttribute("Price", 200)
                    )
                ),
                new XElement("customer",
                    new XAttribute("ID", "B"),
                    new XAttribute("City", "Mumbai"),
                    new XAttribute("Region", "Asia"),
                    new XElement("order",
                        new XAttribute("Item", "Oven"),
                        new XAttribute("Price", 501)
                    )
                )
            )
        ;
```

5. After the XML element constructor code you added in the previous step, add the following code to save, load, and display the XML element:

```
        string xmlFileName = @"c:\BegVCSharp\Chapter29\Xml\example3.xml";
        xcust.Save(xmlFileName);

        XElement xcust2 = XElement.Load(xmlFileName);

        Console.WriteLine("Contents of xcust:");
        Console.WriteLine(xcust);

        Console.Write("Program finished, press Enter/Return to continue:");
        Console.ReadLine();
}
```

6. Compile and execute the program (you can just press F5 for Start Debugging). You should see the following output in the console window:

```
Contents of XElement xcust2:
<customers>
  <customer ID="A" City="New York" Region="North America">
    <order Item="Widget" Price="100" />
    <order Item="Tire" Price="200" />
  </customer>
  <customer ID="B" City="Mumbai" Region="Asia">
    <order Item="Oven" Price="501" />
  </customer>
</customers>
Program finished, press Enter/Return to continue:
```

Press Enter/Return to finish the program and make the console screen disappear. If you used Ctrl+F5 (Start Without Debugging), you may need to press Enter/Return twice.

How It Works

Both XElement and XDocument inherit from the LINQ to XML XContainer class, which implements an XML node that can contain other XML nodes. Both classes also implement Load() and Save() so that most operations that can be performed on an XDocument() in LINQ to XML can also be performed on an XElement instance and its children.

You simply create an XElement instance that has the same structure as the XDocument used in previous examples but omits the containing XDocument. All the operations for this particular program work the same with the XElement fragment.

XElement also supports the Load() and Parse() methods for loading XML from files and strings, respectively.

Generating XML from LINQ to SQL

Often XML is used to communicate data between client and server machines or between "tiers" in a multitier application. It is quite common to query for some data in a database, and then produce an XML document or fragment from that data to pass to another tier. In the following Try It Out, you create a query to find some data in the Northwind sample database, use LINQ to SQL to query the data, and then use LINQ to XML classes to convert the data to XML.

This example requires the Northwind sample database, described at the beginning of Chapter 27, "LINQ to SQL."

Try It Out   Generating XML from LINQ to SQL

Follow these steps to create the example in Visual Studio 2008:

1. Create a new console application called BegVCSharp_29_4_XMLfromLINQtoSQL in the directory C:\BegVCSharp\Chapter29.

2. As described in steps 3–12 of the "First LINQ to SQL Query" example at the start of Chapter 27, add a new LINQ to SQL class named `Northwind.dbml` to the project, and then add a connection to the Northwind sample database.

3. Drag the `Customers`, `Orders`, and `Order Details` tables to the O/R Designer view of `Northwind.dbml`. Your O/R Designer view should now look like Figure 29-2, showing the three tables and their relationships:

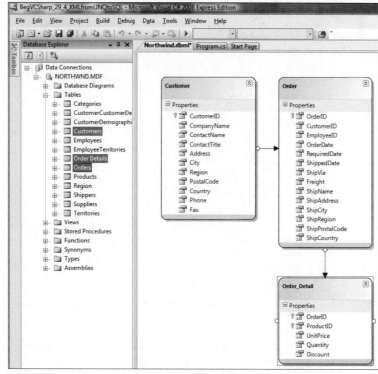

Figure 29-2

4. Compile your program so that the classes and properties defined in `Northwind.dbml` will be available via IntelliSense when editing the code in the next steps.

5. Open the main source file `Program.cs`.

6. Add a reference to the `System.Xml.Linq` namespace to the beginning of `Program.cs` as shown:

```
using System;
using System.Collections.Generic;
using System.Linq;
using System.Xml.Linq;
using System.Text;
```

7. Add the following code to the `Main()` method in `Program.cs`:

```
static void Main(string[] args)
{
        NorthwindDataContext northWindDataContext = new
    NorthwindDataContext();

        XElement northwindCustomerOrders =
            new XElement("customers",
             from c in northWindDataContext.Customers
             select new XElement("customer",
                new XAttribute("ID", c.CustomerID),
                new XAttribute("City", c.City),
                new XAttribute("Company", c.CompanyName),
                 from o in c.Orders
                 select new XElement("order",
                    new XAttribute("orderID", o.OrderID),
                    new XAttribute("orderDay",
                            o.OrderDate.Value.Day),
                    new XAttribute("orderMonth",
                            o.OrderDate.Value.Month),
                    new XAttribute("orderYear",
                            o.OrderDate.Value.Year),
                    new XAttribute("orderTotal",
                        o.Order_Details.Sum(od => od.Quantity * od.UnitPrice))
                 ) //end order
            ) // end customer
        ); // end customers

        string xmlFileName =
                @"C:\BegVCSharp\Chapter29\Xml\NorthwindCustomerOrders.xml";
        northwindCustomerOrders.Save(xmlFileName);

        Console.WriteLine("Successfully saved Northwind customer orders to:");
        Console.WriteLine(xmlFileName);
        Console.Write("Program finished, press Enter/Return to continue:");
        Console.ReadLine();
}
```

8. Compile and execute the program (you can just press F5 for Start Debugging). You will see the following output:

```
Successfully saved Northwind customer orders to:
C:\BegVCSharp\Chapter29\Xml\NorthwindCustomerOrders.xml
Program finished, press Enter/Return to continue:
```

Simply press Enter/Return to exit the program and make the console screen disappear. If you used Ctrl+F5 (Start Without Debugging), you may need to press Enter/Return twice.

How It Works

In `Program.cs` you added the reference to the `System.Xml.Linq` namespace in order to call the LINQ to XML constructor classes.

As described in Chapter 27, you created a connection to the Northwind sample database and then used the O/R Designer to create a LINQ to SQL mapping for the Northwind data. In the main program, you created an instance of the Northwind data context class to use the following mapping:

```
NorthwindDataContext northWindDataContext = new NorthwindDataContext();
```

Your LINQ to SQL query is very similar to the one used in the Drill Down example in Chapter 27. It uses the Northwind data context `Customers` member as a data source and drills down through the `Customers`, `Orders`, and `Order Details` tables to produce a list of all customer orders. However, the query results are projected in the `select` clause of the query into a nested set of LINQ to XML elements and attributes:

```
XElement northwindCustomerOrders =
    new XElement("customers",
      from c in northWindDataContext.Customers
      select new XElement("customer",
        new XAttribute("ID", c.CustomerID),
        new XAttribute("City", c.City),
        new XAttribute("Company", c.CompanyName),
        from o in c.Orders
          select new XElement("order",
            new XAttribute("orderID", o.OrderID),
            new XAttribute("orderDay",
                    o.OrderDate.Value.Day),
            new XAttribute("orderMonth",
                    o.OrderDate.Value.Month),
            new XAttribute("orderYear",
                    o.OrderDate.Value.Year),
            new XAttribute("orderTotal",
              o.Order_Details.Sum(od => od.Quantity * od.UnitPrice))
          ) //end order
      ) // end customer
);  // end customers
```

To grab all the orders for a customer, you use a second LINQ to SQL query (`from o in c.Orders...`) nested inside the first one (`from c in northWindDataContext.Customers...`).

You divide the OrderDate field into its month, date, and year components to make the XML easier to query; you will see how this is used in the next example.

Finally, you save the generated XML to file as in the previous example:

```
string xmlFileName =
            @"C:\BegVCSharp\Chapter29\Xml\NorthwindCustomerOrders.xml";
northwindCustomerOrders.Save(xmlFileName);

Console.WriteLine("Successfully saved Northwind customer orders to:");
Console.WriteLine(xmlFileName);
```

Now you will look at the contents of that file in preparation for writing a query against it.

Displaying the Northwind Customer Orders XML Document

Open Internet Explorer and choose File ⇨ Open, and then enter the path to the XML file you just created: C:\BegVCSharp\Chapter29\Xml\NorthwindCustomerOrders.xml.

The XML will display in Internet Explorer as shown in Figure 29-3.

Figure 29-3

This document contains all the customers in the Northwind sample database and their orders. In the next section you will write a LINQ to XML program to query this data.

How to Query an XML Document

Why would you need to do LINQ queries on an XML document? If your program receives XML generated by another program, you may be looking for specific XML elements or attributes within the received XML to determine how to process it. Your program may be concerned only with a subset of the XML content, or you may need to count elements within the document, or you may need to search for elements or attributes that satisfy a specific condition. LINQ queries are a powerful solution for situations like these.

To query an XML document, the LINQ to XML classes such as XDocument and XElement provide member properties and methods that return LINQ-queryable collections of the LINQ to XML objects contained within the XML document or fragment represented by that LINQ to XML class.

In the following Try It Out, you use these queryable member methods and properties on the XML document you created in the previous example.

Try It Out   Querying an XML Document

Follow these steps to create the example in Visual Studio 2008:

1. Create a new console application called BegVCSharp_29-5-QueryXML in the directory C:\BegVCSharp\Chapter29.

2. Open the main source file Program.cs.

3. Add a reference to the System.Xml.Linq namespace to the beginning of Program.cs as shown:

```
using System;
using System.Collections.Generic;
using System.Linq;
using System.Xml.Linq;
using System.Text;
```

4. Add the following code to the Main() method in Program.cs:

```
static void Main(string[] args)
{
    string xmlFileName = @"C:\BegVCSharp\Chapter29\Xml\NorthwindCustomerOrders.xml";
    XDocument customers = XDocument.Load(xmlFileName);

    Console.WriteLine("Elements in loaded document:");
    var queryResult = from c in customers.Elements()
                      select c.Name;
```

```
foreach (var item in queryResult)
{
    Console.WriteLine(item);
}
Console.Write("Press Enter/Return to continue:");
Console.ReadLine();
}
```

5. Compile and execute the program (you can just press F5 for Start Debugging). You will see the following output:

```
Elements in loaded document:
customers
Press Enter/Return to continue:
```

6. Press Enter/Return to finish the program and make the console screen disappear. If you used Ctrl+F5 (Start Without Debugging), you may need to press Enter/Return twice.

How It Works

As you read through the explanation for each query method, you modify the LINQ to XML query example you just created to use it. Each of these queries returns a collection of LINQ to XML elements or attribute objects having a `Name` property, so your `select` clause simply returns this name to be printed out in the `foreach` loop:

```
var queryResult = from c in customers.Elements()
                  select c.Name;
foreach (var item in queryResult)
{
    Console.WriteLine(item);
}
```

This type of code is what you might first use when developing or debugging a program to see what the queries return. Later, you modify the output to display business results that would be more meaningful to end users.

Using Query Members

This section looks at the LINQ to XML query members that are available to you. Then you can try them out in turn, using the `NorthwindCustomerOrders.xml` file as a data source.

Elements()

The first LINQ to XML query method you used is the `Elements()` member of the `XDocument` class. This member is also available in the `XElement` class.

`Elements()` returns the set of all first-level elements in the XML document or fragment. For a valid XML document, such as the `NorthwindCustomerOrders.xml` file you just created, there is only one first-level element, the root element, which is named `customers`:

```
<?xml version="1.0" encoding="utf-8" ?>
<customers>
  ...
</customers>
```

All other elements are children of customers, so `Elements()` returns just one element:

```
Elements in loaded document:
customers
```

An XML fragment may contain multiple first-level elements, but it is usually more useful to query the child elements, which you look at next with the `Descendants()` member.

Descendants()

The next LINQ to XML query method you look at is the `Descendants()` member of the `XDocument` class. This member is also available in the `XElement` class.

`Descendants()` returns a flattened list of all the child elements (at all levels) in the XML document or fragment. Try modifying the BegVCSharp_29-5-QueryXML example as follows:

```
Console.WriteLine("All descendants in document:");
queryResult =
    from c in customers.Descendants()
    select c.Name;
foreach (var item in queryResult)
{
    Console.WriteLine(item);
}
```

Compile and execute. You will see the `customer` and `order` element names repeated in order as found in the document:

```
All descendants in document:
customer
order
order
...
customer
order
...
customer
order
...
order
order
Press Enter/Return to continue:
```

The output will scroll off the screen, so you may not see the first part of it. This reflects the fact that the NorthwindCustomerOrders.xml file contains only customer and order elements beneath the root customers element:

```
<?xml version="1.0" encoding="utf-8" ?>
<customers>
 <customer ...[{[SPACE]}]>
  <order ... />
  <order ... />
  ...
 </customer>
 <customer ...>
  <order ... />
  ...
```

You can make the output more manageable by adding the LINQ Distinct() operator to the results processing:

```
Console.WriteLine("All distinct descendants in document:");
var queryResult =
    from c in customers.Descendants()
    select c.Name;
foreach (var item in queryResult.Distinct())
```

This results in a list of only the distinct element names:

```
All distinct descendants in document:
customers
customer
order
Press Enter/Return to continue:
```

This is very useful for exploring a document structure the first time you start to work with it, but finding all elements is not a problem you will often need to solve in finished production applications.

A more common scenario is needing to look for descendant elements with a particular name. The Descendants() method has an overload that takes the desired element name as a string parameter, as shown here:

```
Console.WriteLine("Descendants named 'customer':");
var queryResult =
    from c in customers.Descendants("customer")
    select c.Name;
foreach (var item in queryResult) // remove Distinct()
{
    Console.WriteLine(item);
}
```

This returns just the `customer` elements:

```
Descendants named 'customer':
customer
customer
customer
...
customer
customer
Press Enter/Return to continue:
```

Clearly, this is a more generally useful query. By querying a list of elements of a known type, you can then search for specific attributes, which you will look at next.

For completeness sake, you should know that LINQ to XML also provides an `Ancestors()` method that is the converse of the `Descendants()` method, returning the flattened list of all elements higher than the source element in the tree structure of the XML document. This is not used nearly as often as the `Descendants()` method because developers tend to start processing XML documents at the root and descend from there to the leaf levels of the tree of elements and attributes. The `Parent` property, which points to the single ancestor one level up, is used more often.

Attributes()

The next LINQ to XML query method you look at is the `Attributes()` member. This returns all the attributes of the currently selected element. To see how this method works, try modifying the BegVCSharp_29-5-QueryXML example as follows:

```
Console.WriteLine("Attributes of descendants named 'customer':");
var queryResult =
    from c in customers.Descendants("customer").Attributes()
    select c.Name;
foreach (var item in queryResult)
{
    Console.WriteLine(item);
}
```

Compile and execute. You should see the names of the attributes of the `customer` elements:

```
Attributes of descendants named 'customer':
ID
City
Company
ID
City
Company
...
ID
City
Company
ID
City
Company
Press Enter/Return to continue:
```

Again the output scrolls off the screen. This query has found the names of the attributes of the `customer` elements:

```
<customer ID= ... City= ... Company= ... >
<customer ID= ... City= ... Company= ... >
<customer ID= ... City= ... Company= ... >
   ...
```

As you can with the `Descendants()` method, you can pass a specific name to `Attributes()` to search for. In addition, you don't have to restrict the display to the name; you can display the attribute itself. Here is a query that displays the attributes of a customer named `Company`:

```
Console.WriteLine("customer attributes named 'Company':");
var queryResult =
    from c in customers.Descendants("customer").Attributes("Company")
    select c;
foreach (var item in queryResult)
{
    Console.WriteLine(item);
}
```

Compile and execute. You will see the attributes containing the companies for the `customer` elements:

```
...
Company="Toms Spezialitäten"
Company="Tortuga Restaurante"
Company="Tradiçao Hipermercados"
Company="Trail's Head Gourmet Provisioners"
Company="Vaffeljernet"
Company="Victuailles en stock"
Company="Vins et alcools Chevalier"
Company="Die Wandernde Kuh"
Company="Wartian Herkku"
Company="Wellington Importadora"
Company="White Clover Markets"
Company="Wilman Kala"
Company="Wolski  Zajazd"
Press Enter/Return to continue:
```

Here is another example, this time with the `orders` elements and the `orderYear` attribute:

```
Console.WriteLine("order attributes named 'orderYear':");
var queryResult =
    from c in customers.Descendants("order").Attributes("orderYear")
    select c;
foreach (var item in queryResult)
{
    Console.WriteLine(item);
}
```

Compile and execute. Now you see the following:

```
...
orderYear="1998"
orderYear="1998"
orderYear="1998"
orderYear="1996"
orderYear="1997"
orderYear="1997"
orderYear="1998"
orderYear="1998"
orderYear="1998"
orderYear="1998"
Press Enter/Return to continue:
```

You can also get the value of the attribute specifically (here, the year) with the `Value` property:

```
Console.WriteLine("Values of order attributes named 'orderYear':");
var queryResult =
    from c in customers.Descendants("order").Attributes("orderYear")
    select c.Value;
foreach (var item in queryResult)
{
    Console.WriteLine(item);
}
```

Compile and execute. You should see the following:

```
...
1996
1997
1997
1998
1998
1998
1998
Press Enter/Return to continue:
```

Now you can begin to ask specific questions: For example, what was the earliest year in which orders were placed? You can answer that by using the same query but applying the `Min()` aggregate operator on the result instead of the usual `foreach` loop:

```
var queryResult =
    from c in customers.Descendants("order").Attributes("orderYear")
    select c.Value;
Console.WriteLine("Earliest year in which orders were placed: {0}",
                                            queryResults.Min());
```

Compile and execute. Now you see the answer, 1996:

```
Earliest year in which orders were placed: 1996
Press Enter/Return to continue:
```

You can explore more specific questions in the exercises for this chapter.

Summary

That finishes our exploration of LINQ to XML. As you have seen, LINQ to XML integrates the concepts of LINQ with an easy-to-use alternative XML API that enables quick integration of XML into other programs that use LINQ. This makes queries on XML documents simple and natural for programmers already familiar with LINQ in its other forms.

In this chapter, you learned how to construct XML documents with LINQ to XML functional constructors, and then how to load and save XML documents with LINQ to XML.

You mastered using LINQ to XML to work with incomplete XML documents (fragments), and learned how to easily generate an XML document from a LINQ to SQL or LINQ to Objects query.

Finally, you learned how to query an existing XML document with LINQ to XML, and used advanced LINQ features such as LINQ aggregate operators with LINQ to XML.

Exercises

1. Create the following XML document using LINQ to XML constructors:

```
<employees>
  <employee ID="1001" FirstName="Fred" LastName="Lancelot">
    <Skills>
      <Language>C#</Language>
      <Math>Calculus</Math>
    </Skills>
  </employee>
  <employee ID="2002" FirstName="Jerry" LastName="Garcia">
    <Skills>
      <Language>French</Language>
      <Math>Business</Math>
    </Skills>
  </employee>
</employees>
```

2. Write a query against the `NorthwindCustomerOrders.xml` file you created to find the oldest customers (those with orders placed in the first year of Northwind operation, 1996).

3. Write a query against the `NorthwindCustomerOrders.xml` file to find customers who have placed individual orders over $10,000.

4. Write a query against the `NorthwindCustomerOrders.xml` file to find the lifetime highest-selling customers — for example, companies with all orders totaling more than $100,000.

Part V

Additional Techniques

Attributes

This chapter introduces the subject of attributes, describing what they are and what they can be used for. Also included are examples demonstrating several of the attributes available with the .NET Framework. Custom attributes — attributes you can write yourself to extend the system — are covered as well, along with several working examples. You'll also learn how the Intermediate Language Disassembler (Ildasm) can be used to discover the attributes of existing assemblies.

Attributes are one of the most useful features of the .NET Framework, and they are used frequently by Microsoft. To use them effectively, you need to make a significant investment of time, but it is worth the effort. In this chapter, you'll learn how to do the following:

❑   Use attributes to define sections of code that are only included in Debug builds.

❑   Use attributes to define information about an assembly, such as copyright information.

❑   Use attributes to mark sections of code as obsolete, so that over time you can revise your assemblies.

❑   Create your own attributes and use these to maintain a change history.

The final section of this chapter describes in detail how to write your own attributes that extend the system, and it provides a working example of a custom attribute that can be used to maintain change history of your code. By the end of the chapter, you should have enough knowledge of attributes to apply these to your own projects.

What Is an Attribute?

It's difficult to define an attribute in a single sentence — it's best to learn by examining how they are used. A simple definition might describe an attribute as extra information that can be applied to chunks of code within an assembly — such as a class, method, or property. This information is accessible to any other class that uses the assembly.

Try It Out   Using Assembly Attributes

When you create a .NET project, Visual Studio adds an `AssemblyInfo.cs` file. Let's have a look at this file: Create a new Windows application called AttributePeek in the C:\BegVCSharp\Chapter30 folder, and open the Solution Explorer. Expand the Properties node, as shown in Figure 30-1.

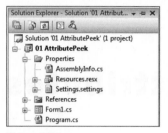

Figure 30-1

Double-click on the `AssemblyInfo.cs` file to see some code created by Visual Studio. Part of this code is shown here:

```
using System.Reflection;
using System.Runtime.CompilerServices;

//
// General Information about an assembly is controlled through the following
// set of attributes. Change these attribute values to modify
// the information associated with an assembly.
//
[assembly: AssemblyTitle("AttributePeek")]
[assembly: AssemblyDescription("")]
[assembly: AssemblyConfiguration("")]
[assembly: AssemblyCompany("MorganSkinner.com")]
[assembly: AssemblyProduct("AttributePeek")]
[assembly: AssemblyCopyright("Copyright Morgan Skinner 2008")]
[assembly: AssemblyTrademark("")]
[assembly: AssemblyCulture("")]
```

Within this file are a number of lines beginning `[assembly:` — these are attribute definitions. When the file is compiled, any attributes defined are saved into the resulting assembly — this process is known as *pickling*. To see this in action, modify one of the preceding attributes — such as the `AssemblyTitle` attribute — and compile your assembly:

```
[assembly: AssemblyTitle("AttributePeek - by ME")]
```

After it is compiled, right-click the assembly (which you can find in the project \bin\Debug directory) in Windows Explorer and select Properties. Figure 30-2 shows the Details tab in Windows Vista. The File Description field contains the description contained in the `AssemblyTitle` attribute.

Figure 30-2

The assembly attributes and their corresponding names on the Details tab are listed in the following table:

Attribute	Property Name
AssemblyTitle	File description
AssemblyTrademark	Legal trademarks
AssemblyFileVersion	File version and product version
AssemblyCopyright	Copyright
AssemblyProduct	Product name

You may have noticed that the list of attributes available through the assembly property sheet is fewer than the list of attributes defined within the assembly — one example being the AssemblyConfiguration attribute. Microsoft has mapped some of the most common attributes onto the Details property page, but to get at the other attributes you have to either write some code (shown in the upcoming "Reflection" section) or use Ildasm or the Reflector tool. To find all attributes on a given assembly, you can use Ildasm to inspect the assembly and look for the attribute(s) defined. To add ILDASM as a tool within Visual Studio 2008, invoke the External Tools option from the Tools menu, click Add, and set the title to ILDASM and the command to C:\Program Files\Microsoft SDKs\Windows\v6.0A\bin\ildasm.exe.

With this added to your tools menu you can then open `Ildasm` and select the assembly by using the File Open dialog. Double-clicking the highlighted MANIFEST section opens a secondary window containing the assembly manifest. Scrolling down the file a little reveals some lines of strange-looking code — this code is the IL (Intermediate Language) produced from the C# compiler:

```
.assembly AttributePeek
{
    ...
    .custom instance void
    [mscorlib]System.Reflection.AssemblyTitleAttribute::.ctor(string)
        = ( 01 00 15 41 74 74 72 69 62 75 74 65 50 65 65 6B    // ...AttributePeek
            20 2D 20 62 79 20 4D 45 00 00 )                     //  - by ME..

    .custom instance void
    [mscorlib]System.Reflection.AssemblyCopyrightAttribute::.ctor(string)
        = ( 01 00 20 43 6F 70 79 72 69 67 68 74 20 C2 A9 20    // .. Copyright ..
            4D 6F 72 67 61 6E 20 53 6B 69 6E 6E 65 72 20 32    // Morgan Skinner 2
            30 30 37 00 00 )                                    // 007..
    ...
    .hash algorithm 0x00008004
    .ver 1:0:0:0
}
```

Looking down through the file, you'll notice a number of declarations that look something like type declarations:

```
[mscorlib]System.Reflection.AssemblyTitleAttribute::.ctor(string) =
    ( 01 00 15 41 74 74 72 69 62 75 74 65 50 65 65 6B    // ...AttributePeek
```

The `AssemblyTitle` that you typed in has been persisted into the assembly manifest — if you get your hex/ASCII conversion tables out, you'll see that the set of characters after `01 00 15` are the ASCII codes for the text `AttributePeek`. Just in case you are curious, the prolog bytes `01 00` are a two-byte ID, and `15` is the length of the string (21 characters) — this may be a two-byte value if the length of the data is more than 256 characters. As mentioned earlier, this process of storing the attribute within the assembly is known as pickling, and you may come across this if you look at some of the background material on .NET available on the Web.

You may have noticed that in the code snippet from `AssemblyInfo.cs`, the term `AssemblyTitle` was used; however, in the IL code you just looked at, this is shown as `AssemblyTitleAttribute`. The C# compiler looks up an attribute class called `AssemblyTitle` first, and if it is not found it then appends the word `Attribute` and searches again. Therefore, whether you type the whole class name or omit the final `Attribute`, the same code is generated. Throughout this chapter, the `Attribute` suffix has been dropped.

The attribute declaration persisted (pickled) into the manifest looks suspiciously like an object and its constructor. The bytes in parentheses are the parameters passed to the constructor.

Having examined the background, you can now understand the following attribute definition: An *attribute* is a class that can include additional data within an assembly, concerning the assembly or any type within that assembly. Given that an attribute is a class, and in the manifest the attribute is stored in the format shown above, let's revisit the attribute definition from earlier in the chapter:

```
[assembly: AssemblyTitle("AttributePeek - by ME")]
```

The syntax is a little different from normal C# because there are square brackets enclosing the attribute. The `assembly:` tag defines the scope of the attribute (which is covered later in the chapter), and the rest of the code declares the attribute. The `AssemblyTitle` attribute has a constructor that takes only one argument — a string value. The compiler includes this value in the assembly. This value can be accessed by the standard Windows Explorer Properties sheet, by viewing the assembly within `Ildasm`, or programmatically by *reflection* — discussed in the following section.

In addition to the simple attributes dealing with assembly information, the .NET Framework defines several hundred attributes used for things as diverse as debugging, design-time control behavior, serialization, and much more. You'll look at some standard attributes after the next section and then learn how to extend .NET with your own custom attributes.

Reflection

Unless you have a grounding in Java, reflection is probably a new topic for you, so I will spend a couple of pages defining it and showing how it can be used.

Reflection enables you to programmatically inspect and get information about an assembly, including all object types contained within it. This information includes the attributes you have added to those types. The reflection classes reside within the `System.Reflection` namespace.

In addition to reading the types defined within a given assembly, you can also generate (emit) your own assemblies and types using the services of `System.Reflection.Emit` or `System.CodeDom`. This topic is a bit advanced for a beginning book on C#, but if you are interested, the MSDN contains information on emitting dynamic assemblies.

The first example in this section inspects an assembly and displays a list of all attributes defined on the assembly — this should produce a list similar to that shown earlier.

This chapter is a bit more relaxed about the format of the code examples because if you've gotten to this point in the book, you must be pretty confident of what you're doing! All of the code can be found in the Chapter30 folder of the download. Some examples in this chapter show only the most important parts of the code, so be sure to look through the downloaded code to get the whole picture.

This first example can be found in the Chapter30\02 FindAttributes directory. The entire source file is reproduced here:

```
// Import types from the System and System.Reflection assemblies
using System;
using System.Reflection;

namespace FindAttributes
{
    class Program
    {
        /// <summary>
        /// Main .exe entry point
        /// </summary>
```

```
        /// <param name="args">Command line args - the name of an assembly</
param>
        static void Main(string[] args)
        {
            // Output usage information if necessary.
            if (args.Length == 0)
                Usage();
            else if ((args.Length == 1) && (args[0] == "/?"))
                Usage();
            else
            {
                // Loop through the arguments passed to the console application.
                // I'm doing this as if you specify a full path name including
                // spaces you end up with several arguments - I'm just stitching
                // them back together again to make one filename...
                StringBuilder sb = null;

                for (int pos = 0; pos < args.Length; pos++)
                {
                    if (null == sb)
                        sb = new StringBuilder(args[pos]);
                    else
                        sb.AppendFormat(" {0}", args[pos]);
                }

                string assemblyName = sb.ToString();

                try
                {
                    // Attempt to load the named assembly.
                    Assembly a = Assembly.LoadFrom(assemblyName);

                    // Now find the attributes on the assembly.
                    // The parameter is ignored, so I chose true.
                    object[] attributes = a.GetCustomAttributes(true);

                    // If there were any attributes defined...
                    if (attributes.Length > 0)
                    {
                        Console.WriteLine("Assembly attributes for '{0}'...",
                                          assemblyName);

                        // Dump them out...
                        foreach (object o in attributes)
                            Console.WriteLine(" {0}", o.ToString());
                    }
                    else
                        Console.WriteLine("Assembly {0} contains no Attributes.",
                                          assemblyName);
                }
```

```
            catch (Exception ex)
            {
                Console.WriteLine("Exception thrown loading assembly {0}...",
                                    assemblyName);
                Console.WriteLine();
                Console.WriteLine(ex.ToString());
            }
        }
    }

    /// <summary>
    /// Display usage information for the .exe.
    /// </summary>
    static void Usage()
    {
        Console.WriteLine("Usage:");
        Console.WriteLine(" FindAttributes <Assembly>");
    }
    }
}
```

To run the FindAttributes application, you need to supply the name of an assembly to inspect. For now, you can use the `FindAttributes.exe` assembly itself, which is shown in Figure 30-3.

Figure 30-3

The example code first checks the parameters passed to the command line — if none are supplied, or if the user types `FindAttributes /?`, then the `Usage()` method is called. It displays a simple command usage summary:

```
if (args.Length == 0)
    Usage ();
else if ((args.Length == 1) && (args[0] == "/?"))
    Usage ();
```

Next, the code reconstitutes the command-line arguments into a single string. This is because it's common to have spaces in directory names, such as Program Files, and the space would cause it to be considered as two arguments. Therefore, the code iterates through all the arguments, stitching them back into a single string, and this is used as the name of the assembly to load:

```
StringBuilder sb = null;

for (int pos = 0; pos < args.Length; pos++)
{
    if (null == sb)
        sb = new StringBuilder(args[pos]);
    else
        sb.AppendFormat(" {0}", args[pos]);
}

string assemblyName = sb.ToString();
```

The code then attempts to load the assembly and retrieve all custom attributes defined on that assembly with the GetCustomAttributes() method:

```
Assembly a = Assembly.LoadFrom (assemblyName);

// Now find the attributes on the assembly.
object[]  attributes = a.GetCustomAttributes(true);
```

Any attributes found are output to the console. When you tested the program against the FindAttributes.exe file, an attribute called DebuggableAttribute was displayed. Although you have not specified the DebuggableAttribute it has been added by the C# compiler, and you will find that any of your executables built for debug have this attribute.

In order to view attributes on a given assembly, you will have to either run the example from the command line or alter the command-line parameters to include an assembly to inspect.

We will return to reflection later in the chapter, to see how to retrieve attributes on classes and methods defined within an assembly.

Built-in Attributes

You saw in previous sections that the .NET Framework includes a number of attributes, such as DebuggableAttribute and AssemblyTitleAttribute. This section discusses some of the more common attributes defined in the .NET Framework, and when you might want to use them.

The attributes covered in this section are as follows:

❑   System.Diagnostics.ConditionalAttribute

❑   System.ObsoleteAttribute

❑   System.SerializableAttribute

❑   System.Reflection.AssemblyDelaySignAttribute

You can find more information about the other attributes that ship with the .NET Framework in the .NET Framework SDK documentation.

Another extremely useful tool when working with .NET is a program called *Reflector* that is downloadable from www.aisto.com/roeder/dotnet. This tool enables you to inspect assemblies and view all of the types defined within these assemblies. You can use it to find, with a few mouse clicks, all classes that derive from System.Attribute. It's one tool you shouldn't be without. In addition, Reflector enables you to decompile methods and convert the IL back into C#, which can be very useful when you want to know the internal workings of some .NET code.

System.Diagnostics.ConditionalAttribute

This is one of the most useful attributes of all because it permits sections of code to be included or excluded based on the definition of a symbol at compilation time. This attribute is contained within the System.Diagnostics namespace, which includes classes for debug and trace output, event logging, performance counters, and process information. The following Try It Out demonstrates how to use this attribute.

```
using System;
using System.Diagnostics;

namespace TestConditional
{
    class Program
    {
        static void Main(string[] args)
        {
            // Call a method only available if DEBUG is defined...
            Program.DebugOnly();
        }

        // This method is atributed and will ONLY be included in
        // the emitted code if the DEBUG symbol is defined when
        // the program is compiled.
        [Conditional("DEBUG")]
        public static void DebugOnly()
        {
            // This line will only be displayed in debug builds...
            Console.WriteLine("This string only displays in Debug");
        }
    }
}
```

The source code for this example is available in the Chapter30/03 Test Conditional directory. The code calls the static DebugOnly() method, which is attributed with the Conditional attribute, as shown with [Conditional("DEBUG")] above. This function just displays a line of text on the console.

When a C# source file is compiled, you can define symbols on the command line. The Conditional attribute omits calls to code marked with a symbol during the compilation phase, so if you have a method marked as [Conditional("DEBUG")], then calls to that method exist only if the DEBUG symbol is defined during compiling.

The DEBUG symbol is set automatically for you if you compile a Debug build in Visual Studio 2008. If you want to define or refine the symbols for a particular project, then display the project Properties dialog and navigate to the Build option of Configuration Properties, as shown in Figure 30-4.

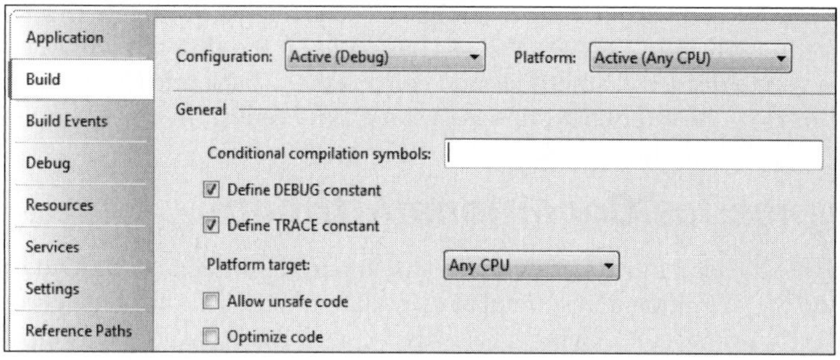

Figure 30-4

Notice that the defaults for a Debug build are to define both the DEBUG and TRACE symbols.

To define a symbol on the command line, you use the /d: switch (the short form for /define: — or you can type the entire string):

```
>csc /d:DEBUG TestConditional.cs
```

If you compile and run the file, you'll see the output string This string only displays in Debug. If you change the build target to Release and execute the application, you will not see this string within the console window.

To get a clearer picture of what is happening, use Ildasm to view the generated code, as shown in Figure 30-5.

Figure 30-5

When the DEBUG symbol is not defined, the IL generated for the Main() method is as follows:

```
.method private hidebysig static void  Main(string[] args) cil managed
{
  .entrypoint
  // Code size       1 (0x1)
  .maxstack  8
  IL_0000:  ret
} // end of method Program::Main
```

This code simply returns from the Main method.

If, however, you compile the file with the /d:DEBUG switch, you'll see the following code:

```
.method private hidebysig static void  Main(string[] args) cil managed
{
  .entrypoint
  // Code size       8 (0x8)
  .maxstack  8
  IL_0000:  nop
  IL_0001:  call           void TestConditional.Program::DebugOnly()
  IL_0006:  nop
  IL_0007:  ret
} // end of method Program::Main
```

The line highlighted is the call to the conditionally compiled method. Using Conditional() removes calls to a method, but not the method itself.

> The Conditional attribute can be used only on methods that return void — otherwise, removing the call would mean that no value was returned. However, you can attribute a method that has out or ref parameters — the variables will retain their original value.

To recap, the Conditional attribute omits calls to methods marked with that attribute when a symbol is defined during compilation.

In the System.Diagnostics namespace, the Debug class has a number of static methods attributed with [Conditional("DEBUG")], which are used to output debug information when running your application. If you switch to a release build, then all of the calls to these methods are omitted from the resulting assembly. This is a great way to add debugging information and have it automatically removed when you build the final release version of your product.

System.ObsoleteAttribute

This attribute shows the attention to detail that the Microsoft engineers have put into the .NET Framework. The Obsolete attribute can be used to mark a class, method, or any other entry in an assembly as being no longer used.

This attribute would be useful, for example, when publishing a library of classes. It is inevitable that through the course of developing a set of classes, some of those classes/methods/properties will be superseded. This attribute can be used to prepare the users of your code for the eventual withdrawal of a particular feature.

Suppose that in version one of your application, you have a class like this:

```
public class Coder
{
    public Coder ()
    {
    }

    public void CodeInCPlusPlus ()
    {
    }
}
```

You compile and use this class for several years, but then something new comes along to replace the old functionality:

```
public void CodeInCSharp ()
{
}
```

Naturally, you want to enable the users of your library to use `CodeInCPlusPlus()` for some time, but you would also like to alert them to the fact that there is a newer method by displaying a warning message at compile time, informing them of the existence of `CodeInCSharp()`. To do this, all you need to add is the `Obsolete` attribute, as shown here:

```
[Obsolete("CodeInCSharp instead.")]
public void CodeInCPlusPlus ()
{
}
```

When you compile again, for debug or release, you'll receive a warning from the C# compiler that you are using an obsolete (or soon to be obsolete) method, as shown in Figure 30-6. Warnings will not normally halt the compiler unless you have set the "Treat warnings as errors" option on the Build tab of the project configuration settings — this tab can be reached by selecting the Properties menu item of the project.

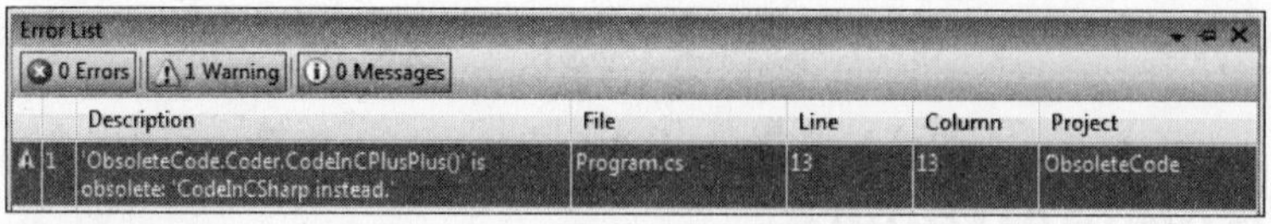

Figure 30-6

Over time, users will get tired of seeing this warning message each time the code is compiled, so eventually everyone (well, almost everyone) will utilize `CodeInCSharp()`. Ultimately, you want to entirely drop support for `CodeInCPlusPlus()`, so you add an extra parameter to the `Obsolete` attribute:

```
[Obsolete("You must CodeInCSharp instead.", true)]
public void CodeInCPlusPlus()
{
}
```

This way, when users attempt to compile their code that calls this method, the compiler will now generate an error and halt the compilation with an error message. Using this attribute provides users of your class with help in modifying applications that use your class as the class evolves.

For binary classes, such as components that you purchase without source code, this isn't a good way to do versioning — the .NET Framework has excellent built-in versioning capabilities. However, the `Obsolete` attribute does provide a useful way to hint that a particular feature of your classes should no longer be used.

System.SerializableAttribute

Serialization is the name for storing and retrieving an object, either in a disk file, memory, or anywhere else you can think of. When serialized, all instance data is persisted to the storage medium, and when deserialized, the object is reconstructed and is effectively the same as its original instance.

For any of you who have programmed in MFC, ATL, or VB before, and had to worry about storing and retrieving instance data, this attribute will save you a great deal of typing. Suppose that you have a C# class that you would like to store in a file, such as the following:

```
public class Person
{
    public Person ()
    {
    }

    public int Age { get; set; };
    public int WeightInPounds { get; set; };
}
```

In C# (and indeed in any of the languages built on the .NET Framework), you can serialize an instance's members without writing any code — well, almost. All you need to do is add the `Serializable` attribute to the class, and the .NET runtime does the rest for you.

When the runtime receives a request to serialize an object, it checks whether the object's class implements the `ISerializable` interface. If it does not, then the runtime checks whether the class is attributed with the `Serializable` attribute. `ISerializable` isn't discussed any further here — it is an advanced way to alter what data is serialized.

If the `Serializable` attribute is found on the class, then .NET uses reflection to get all instance data — whether public, protected, or private — and to store this as the representation of the object. Deserialization is the opposite process — data is read from the storage medium, and this data is assigned to instance variables of the class.

The following code shows a class marked with the `Serializable` attribute:

```
[Serializable]
public class Person
{
    public Person ()
    {
    }

    public int Age { get; set; };
    public int WeightInPounds { get; set; };
}
```

The entire code for this example is available in the Chapter30/05 Serialize subdirectory. To store an instance of this `Person` class, it is necessary to use a `Formatter` object — this object converts the data stored within your class into a stream of bytes. The system comes with two default formatters, `BinaryFormatter` and `SoapFormatter` (these have their own namespaces below `System.Runtime` `.Serialization.Formatters`). The following code shows how to use the `BinaryFormatter` to store a person object:

```
using System;
using System.Runtime.Serialization.Formatters.Binary;
using System.IO;

  public static void Serialize ()
  {
    // Construct a person object.
    Person  me = new Person ();

    // Set the data that is to be serialized.
    me.Age = 40;
    me.WeightInPounds = 200;

    // Create a disk file to store the object to...
    Stream  s = File.Open ("Me.dat" , FileMode.Create);

    // And use a BinaryFormatted to write the object to the stream...
    BinaryFormatter bf = new BinaryFormatter ();

    // Serialize the object.
    bf.Serialize (s , me);

    // And close the stream.
    s.Close ();
  }
```

The code first creates the person object and sets the Age and WeightInPounds data, and then it constructs a stream on a file called Me.dat. The binary formatter utilizes the stream to store the instance of the person class into Me.dat and finally the stream is closed.

The default serialization code stores all the public contents of the object, which in most cases is what you would want. However, in some circumstances, you may want to define one or more fields that should not be serialized. That's easy, too — just add a [NonSerialized] attribute to the data that you want to omit from serialization. This attribute applies to fields only, so in the example, the WeightInPounds property has been modified to use a backing field:

```
[Serializable]
public class Person
{
  public Person ()
  {
  }

  public int Age { get; set; };
  [NonSerialized]
  private int _weightInPounds;

  public int WeightInPounds
  {
    get { return _weightInPounds; }
    set { _weightInPounds = value; }
  }
}

        [NonSerialized()]
        public int weight;
        public int WeightInPounds
        {
            get
            {
                return weight;
            }
            set
            {
                weight = value;
            }
        }
```

When this class is serialized, only the Age member will be stored — the WeightInPounds member will not be persisted and so will not be retrieved on deserialization.

Deserialization is basically the opposite of the preceding serialization code. The example that follows opens a stream on the Me.dat file created earlier, constructs a BinaryFormatter to read the object, and calls its `Deserialize` method to retrieve the object. It then casts this into a `Person` and writes the age and weight to the console:

```
public static void DeSerialize ()
{
  // Open the file this time.
  Stream  s = File.Open ("Me.dat" , FileMode.Open);

  // And use BinaryFormatted to read object(s) from the stream.
  BinaryFormatter bf = new BinaryFormatter ();

  // Deserialize the object.
  object  o = bf.Deserialize (s);

  // Ensure it is of the correct type...
  Person  p = o as Person;

  if (p != null)
    Console.WriteLine ("DeSerialized Person aged: {0} weight: {1}" ,
                       p.Age , p.WeightInPounds);

  // And close the stream.
  s.Close ();
}
```

Typically, you would use the `NonSerialized` attribute to mark data that does not need to be serialized, such as data that can be recomputed or calculated when necessary. An example is a class that computes prime numbers — you may well cache primes to speed up response times while using the class; however, serializing and deserializing a list of primes is unnecessary because they can simply be recomputed on request. At other times, the member may be relevant only to that specific use of the object. For example, in an object representing a word processor document, you would want to serialize the content of the document but usually not the position of the insertion point — when the document next loads you simply place the insertion point at the start of the document.

If you want yet more control over how an object is serialized, you can implement the `ISerializable` interface, but this is an advanced topic not covered in this book.

System.Reflection.AssemblyDelaySignAttribute

The `System.Reflection` namespace provides a number of attributes, some of which were shown earlier in the chapter. One of the more complex to use is the `AssemblyDelaySign` attribute, which enables you to delay-sign an assembly so that you can register it in the Global Assembly Cache (GAC) for testing without a private key.

One scenario in which you might use delayed signing is when developing commercial software. Each assembly that is developed in-house needs to be signed with your company's private key before being shipped to your customers — this provides your customers with some guarantee that the assembly was actually created by your company. When you compile your assembly, you reference the key file before you can register the assembly in the GAC. A key file contains two keys — a public key and a private key.

However, many organizations would not want their private key to be on every developer's machine. For this reason, the runtime enables you to partially sign the assembly and tweak a few settings so that your assembly can be registered within the GAC. When fully tested, it can be signed by whomever holds the private key file. This may be your QA department, one or more trusted individuals, or the marketing department.

The following Try It Out shows how you can delay-sign a typical assembly, register it in the GAC for testing, and finally complete the signing by adding in the private key.

Try It Out **Delay Signing**

1. Create a key file with the `sn.exe` utility. If you are using the Express version of Visual Studio, then you also need to download the .NET Framework 2.0 SDK, which includes this tool. The key file will contain the public and private keys and is typically named after your company. The file extension for key files is `.snk` by convention:

    ```
    >sn -k Company.snk
    ```

2. Extract the public key portion for use by developers with the –p option:

    ```
    >sn -p Company.snk CompanyPublic.snk
    ```

    This command produces a key file `CompanyPublic.snk` with only the public part of the key. This public key file can be copied onto all machines and doesn't need to be kept safe — it's the private key file that needs to be secure. Store the `Company.snk` file somewhere safe, because it only needs to be used when you want to finally sign your assemblies.

3. To delay-sign an assembly and register that assembly within the GAC, you also need to obtain the public key token — this is basically a shorter version of the public key, used when registering assemblies. You can obtain the token in one of two ways:

    ❑   From the public key file itself:

    ```
    >sn -t CompanyPublic.snk
    ```

    ❑   From any assembly signed with the `CompanyPublic.snk` key file:

    ```
    >sn -T <assembly>
    ```

    Both of these methods display a hashed version of the public key and are case sensitive. You'll learn more about this when you register the assembly. With the key file included in the 06 DelaySign folder accompanying this chapter, this produces a public key token value of `a1ad1a5619382d41`. This value is needed later in the chapter — and will be different on your machine if you have constructed a new key file.

Delay-Signing the Assembly

The following code shows how to attribute an assembly for delayed signing. It is available in the Chapter30/06 DelaySign directory:

```
using System;
using System.Reflection;

// Define the file that contains the public key.
[assembly: AssemblyKeyFile ("CompanyPublic.snk") ]
// And that this assembly is to be delay signed.
[assembly: AssemblyDelaySign (true) ]
public class DelayedSigning
{
  public DelayedSigning ()
  {
  }
}
```

The `AssemblyKeyFile` attribute defines the file where the key is to be found. This can be either the public key file or, for more trusted individuals, the file containing both public and private keys. The `AssemblyDelaySign` attribute defines whether the assembly is fully signed (`false`) or delay-signed (`true`). Note that you can also set the key file and delay-sign option from the user interface in Visual Studio 2008, as shown in Figure 30-7 — this is a portion of the project Properties window.

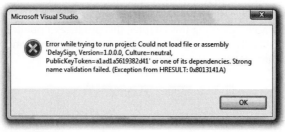

Figure 30-7

When compiled, the assembly will contain an entry in the manifest for the public key. In fact, the manifest will also contain enough room for the private key too, so re-signing the assembly will not change it in any way (other than writing a few extra bytes into the manifest). If you try to debug the assembly, then you will receive the error shown in Figure 30-8.

Figure 30-8

This is because, by default, the .NET runtime will only load unsigned assemblies (where no key file has been defined) or run fully signed assemblies that contain both the public and private key pairs. In effect, .NET is not allowing partially signed assemblies to be loaded, which is why the error message in Figure 30-8 is displayed. The section that follows on registering an assembly in the GAC also shows how to permit partially signed assemblies to load using a process called *skip verification*.

Registering in the GAC

Attempting to use the Gacutil tool (also available in the .NET 2.0 Framework SDK) to register a delay-signed assembly in the GAC generates an error message similar to this:

```
Microsoft (R) .NET Global Assembly Cache Utility.  Version 3.5.20706.1
Copyright (C) Microsoft Corporation. All rights reserved.

Failure adding assembly to the cache: Strong name signature could not be
verified.  Was the assembly built delay-signed?
```

The assembly is only partially signed at the moment, and by default the GAC and Visual Studio .NET will only accept assemblies with a complete strong name. You can, however, instruct .NET to skip verification of the strong name on a delay-signed assembly by using the sn utility. Remember the public key token from earlier? This is where it comes into play.

```
>sn -Vr *,a1ad1a5619382d41
```

This instructs .NET to permit any assemblies with a public key token of a1ad1a5619382d41 to be registered in the GAC, and, more important, for the current example it allows DelaySign.exe to run from within Visual Studio. Typing the previous code at the command prompt generates the following message:

```
Microsoft (R) .NET Framework Strong Name Utility  Version 3.5.20706.1
Copyright (C) Microsoft Corporation. All rights reserved.

Verification entry added for assembly '*,a1ad1a5619382d41'
```

Attempting to install the assembly into the GAC with Gacutil now succeeds. You don't need to use the public key value when adding a verification entry for your assembly — you could alternatively specify that all assemblies can be registered by using the following:

```
>sn -Vr *
```

Or you can define a specific assembly by typing its full name, like this:

```
>sn -Vr DelaySign.exe
```

This data is permanently held in what is called the *verification skip table,* which is a file stored on disk. To obtain a list of the entries in the verification skip table, type the following (these commands are case sensitive):

```
>sn -Vl
```

1037

This is the output on my machine:

```
Microsoft (R) .NET Framework Strong Name Utility   Version 3.5.20706.1
Copyright (C) Microsoft Corporation. All rights reserved.

Assembly/Strong Name                    Users
===========================================
*,a1ad1a5619382d41                      All users
```

Notice the Users column — you can define that a given assembly can be loaded into the GAC by a subset of all users. Check out the sn.exe documentation for further details of this and other assembly naming options.

Completing the Strong Name

The last stage in the process is to compile the public and private keys into the assembly — an assembly with both entries is said to be strongly named and can be registered in the GAC without a skip verification entry.

Again, use the sn.exe utility, this time with the –R switch. The –R switch means that you want to re-sign the assembly and add in the private key portion:

```
>sn -R delaysign.dll Company.snk
```

This displays the following:

```
Microsoft (R) .NET Framework Strong Name Utility   Version 3.5.20706.1
Copyright (C) Microsoft Corporation. All rights reserved.

Assembly 'delaysign.dll' successfully re-signed
```

The other parameters along with the –R switch are the name of the assembly to be re-signed and the key file that contains the public and private keys.

Custom Attributes

Up to this point, this chapter has concentrated on some of the attributes contained within the .NET Framework. That's not the whole story, though — you can also create your own attributes.

As an example of a custom attribute, in this section you create the BugFixAttribute, which could be used to record in the source code who made changes to a given area of functionality.

A custom attribute is simply a special class that must comply with two specifications:

❑   A custom attribute must derive from System.Attribute.

❑   The constructor(s) for an attribute may only contain types that can be resolved at compile time — such as strings and integers.

The restriction on the types of parameters allowed on the attribute constructor(s) is due to the way that attributes are persisted into the assembly metadata. When you use an attribute within code, you are using the attribute's constructor inline, as shown here:

```
[assembly: AssemblyKeyFile ("CompanyPublic.snk") ]
```

This attribute is persisted into the assembly metadata as an instruction to call a constructor of `AssemblyKeyFileAttribute`, which accepts a string. In the preceding example, that string is `CompanyPublic.snk`. If you define a custom attribute, users of the attribute are basically writing parameters to the constructor of the class.

BugFixAttribute

When writing production code, it would be nice to be able to automatically produce a list of fixes that have been made between versions of an application. Typically, this would be done by looking at the bug database to check which bugs and enhancements have been added between two dates and then generating a report from this data.

Another, and possibly better, way is to embed the details of the changes within the code itself, as then the report can be produced based solely on the code (and the code doesn't lie!). In this section you create the `BugFix` attribute. Another benefit of including details of bug fixes in the code is that these attributes are available in the compiled assembly, and can therefore be found at runtime.

The full source code is available in the Chapter30/07 BugFix directory.

To create a custom attribute class, you must do the following:

❑ Create a class derived from `System.Attribute`.

❑ Create the constructor(s) and public properties as required.

❑ Attribute the class to define where it is valid to use your custom attribute.

Each of these steps is discussed in turn in the following sections.

Creating the Custom Attribute Class

This is the simplest step. All you need to do here is create a class derived from `System.Attribute`:

```
public class BugFixAttribute : Attribute
{
}
```

Creating Constructors and Properties

As mentioned earlier, when users use an attribute, they are effectively calling the attribute's constructor. For the `BugFix` attribute, you probably want to record a bug number and some comments:

```
using System;
public class BugFixAttribute : Attribute
{
    public BugFixAttribute(string bugNumber, string comments)
    {
        BugNumber = bugNumber;
        Comments = comments;
    }

    public readonly string BugNumber;
    public readonly string Comments;
}
```

This defines a single constructor and two read-only member variables `BugNumber` and `Comments`.

Attributing the Class for Usage

The last thing you need to do is mark your attribute class and indicate where it can be used. For the `BugFix` attribute, you want to specify "this attribute is only valid on classes, properties, methods, and constructors." You can decide where an attribute that you create is valid. This is explained in more detail later in the chapter.

```
[AttributeUsage(AttributeTargets.Class | AttributeTargets.Property |
             AttributeTargets.Method | AttributeTargets.Constructor,
    AllowMultiple = true, Inherited=false)]
public class BugFixAttribute : Attribute
...
```

The `AttributeUsage` attribute has a single constructor, which takes a value from the `AttributeTargets` enum (described in full later in this section).

The definition of the attribute here also utilizes two properties of that attribute — `AllowMultiple` and `Inherited`. These properties are covered more fully later in the section.

With the definition of the `BugFix` attribute in place, you can now start adorning code with it. The following snippet shows a section of code that has had a number of bug fixes applied to it:

```
[BugFix("101", "Created some methods")]
public class MyBuggyCode
{
    [BugFix("90125", "Removed call to base()")]
    public MyBuggyCode()
    {
    }

    [BugFix("2112", "Returned a non null string")]
    [BugFix("38382", "Returned OK")]
```

```
        public string DoSomething()
        {
            return "OK";
        }
    }
```

You revisit the `BugFix` attribute again later in the chapter to add some extra functionality.

System.AttributeUsageAttribute

When you're defining a custom attribute class, you must define the type or types on which the attribute can be used. In the preceding example, the `BugFix` attribute is valid only for use on classes, methods, properties, and constructors. To define where an attribute can be placed, you add another attribute — `AttributeUsage`.

In its simplest form, this can be used as shown here:

```
[AttributeUsage(AttributeTargets.Class | AttributeTargets.Property
            | AttributeTargets.Method | AttributeTargets.Constructor )]
```

The single parameter is an enumeration defining where your attribute is valid. If you attempt to attribute a field with the `BugFix` attribute, then you receive an error message from the compiler.

The `AttributeTargets` enum defines the following members, which can be combined using the logical or operator (|) to define a set of elements on which the attribute is valid:

AttributeTargets Value	Description
All	Attribute is valid on anything within the assembly.
Assembly	Attribute is valid on the assembly — an example is the `AssemblyTitle` attribute shown earlier in the chapter.
Class	Attribute is valid on a class definition. The `TestCase` attribute used this value. Another example is the `Serializable` attribute.
Constructor	Attribute is valid only on class constructors.
Delegate	Attribute is valid only on a delegate.
Enum	Attribute can be added to enumerated values. One example of this attribute is the `System.FlagsAttribute`, which when applied to an enum defines that the user can use the bitwise or operator to combine values from the enumeration. The `AttributeTargets` enum uses this attribute.
Event	Attribute is valid on event definitions.
Field	Attribute can be placed on a field, such as an internal member variable. An example of this is the `NonSerialized` attribute, which was used earlier to define that a particular value should not be stored when the class was serialized.

(continued)

AttributeTargets Value	Description
Interface	Attribute is valid on an interface. One example of this is the GuidAttribute defined within System.Runtime.InteropServices, which permits you to explicitly define the GUID for an interface.
Method	Attribute is valid on a method. The OneWay attribute from System.Runtime.Remoting.Messaging uses this value.
Module	Attribute is valid on a module. An assembly may be created from a number of code modules, so you can use this to place the attribute on an individual module and not the whole assembly.
Parameter	Attribute can be applied to a parameter within a method definition.
Property	Attribute can be applied to a property.
ReturnValue	Attribute is associated with the return value of a function.
Struct	Attribute is valid on a structure.

Attribute Scope

In earlier examples in the chapter you saw the Assembly* attributes, which all included syntax similar to the following:

```
[assembly: AssemblyTitle("AttributePeek")]
```

The assembly: string defines the scope of the attribute, which in this case tells the compiler that the AssemblyTitle attribute should be applied to the assembly itself. You only need to use the scope modifier when the compiler cannot work out the scope itself. For example, you may want to add an attribute to the return value of a function:

```
[MyAttribute ()]
public long DoSomething ()
{
   ...
}
```

When the compiler reaches this attribute, it takes an educated guess that you are applying the attribute to the method itself, which is not what you want here, so you can add a modifier to indicate exactly what the attribute is attached to:

```
[return:MyAttribute ()]
public long DoSomething ()
{
   ...
}
```

To define the scope of the attribute, choose one of the following values:

❑   `assembly` — The attribute applies to the assembly.

❑   `field` — The attribute applies to a field of an `enum` or class.

❑   `event` — The attribute applies to an event.

❑   `method` — The attribute applies to the method it precedes.

❑   `module` — The attribute is stored in the module.

❑   `param` — The attribute applies to a parameter.

❑   `property` — The attribute is stored against the property.

❑   `return` — Apply the attribute to the return value of a function.

❑   `type` — The attribute applies to a class, interface, or struct.

Many of these are rarely used because the scope is not normally ambiguous. However, for `assembly`, `module`, and `return` values you have to use the scope flag. If there is some ambiguity as to where the attribute is defined, then the compiler chooses which object the attribute will be assigned to. This is most common when attributing the return value of a function, as shown here:

```
[SomeAttribute]
public string DoSomething ();
```

Here, the compiler guesses that the attribute applies to the method and not the return value. You need to define the scope in the following way to get the desired effect:

```
[return:SomeAttribute]
public string DoSomething ();
```

AttributeUsage.AllowMultiple

This attribute defines whether users can add one or more of the same attributes to the element. The syntax for setting the `AllowMultiple` flag is a little strange. The constructor for `AttributeUsage` takes only a single parameter — the list of flags where the attribute can be used. `AllowMultiple` is a property on the `AttributeUsage` attribute, and so the syntax that follows means "construct the attribute, and then set the value of the `AllowMultiple` property to `true`":

```
[AttributeUsage (AttributeTargets.Class | AttributeTargets.Property |
                 AttributeTargets.Method | AttributeTargets.Constructor ,
                 AllowMultiple=true)]
public class BugFixAttribute : Attribute
{
   ...
}
```

A similar method is used to set the `Inherited` property. If a custom attribute has properties, then you can set these in the same manner. One example might be to add the name of the person who fixed the bug:

```
public readonly string BugNumber;
public readonly string Comments;
public readonly string Author;

public override string ToString ()
{
   if (string.IsNullOrEmpty(Author))
      return string.Format ("BugFix {0} : {1}" ,
                            BugNumber , Comments);
   else
      return string.Format ("BugFix {0} by {1} : {2}" ,
                            BugNumber , Author , Comments);
}
```

This adds the `Author` field and an overridden `ToString()` implementation that displays the full details if the `Author` field is set. If the `Author` property is not defined when you attribute your code, then the output from the `BugFix` attribute just shows the bug number and comments. The `ToString()` method would be used to display a list of bug fixes for a given section of code — perhaps to print and file away somewhere. Once you have written the `BugFix` attribute, you need some way to report the fixes made on a class and the members of that class.

The way to report bug fixes for a class is to pass the class type (again a `System.Type`) to the following `DisplayFixes` function. This also uses reflection to find any bug fixes applied to the class, and then iterates through all methods of that class looking for `BugFix` attributes:

```
public static void DisplayFixes (System.Type t)
{
  // Get all bug fixes for the given type,
  // which is assumed to be a class.
  object[]  fixes = t.GetCustomAttributes (typeof (BugFixAttribute) , false);

  Console.WriteLine ("Displaying fixes for {0}" , t);

  // Display the big fix information.
  foreach (BugFixAttribute bugFix in fixes)
    Console.WriteLine (" {0}" , bugFix);

  // Now get all members (i.e., functions) of the class.
  foreach (MemberInfo member in t.GetMembers (BindingFlags.Instance |
                                             BindingFlags.Public |
                                             BindingFlags.NonPublic |
                                             BindingFlags.Static))
  {
    // And find any big fixes applied to these too.
    object[] memberFixes = member.GetCustomAttributes(typeof(BugFixAttribute)
                                                      , false);

    if (memberFixes.Length > 0)
    {
```

```
          Console.WriteLine (" {0}" , member.Name);

          // Loop through and display these.
          foreach (BugFixAttribute memberFix in memberFixes)
            Console.WriteLine (" {0}" , memberFix);
      }
    }
  }
```

The code first retrieves all `BugFix` attributes from the type itself:

```
object[] fixes = t.GetCustomAttributes (typeof (BugFixAttribute),
false);
```

These are enumerated and displayed. The code then loops through all members defined on the class, by using the `GetMembers()` method:

```
foreach (MemberInfo member in t.GetMembers (
          BindingFlags.Instance | BindingFlags.Public |
          BindingFlags.NonPublic | BindingFlags.Static))
```

`GetMembers` retrieves properties, methods, and fields from a given type. To limit the list of members that are returned, the `BindingFlags` enum is used (which is defined within `System.Reflection`).

The binding flags passed to this method indicate which members you are interested in — in this case, you'd like all instance and static members, regardless of visibility, so you specify `Instance` and `Static`, together with `Public` and `NonPublic` members.

After getting all members, you loop through these, finding any `BugFix` attributes associated with the particular member, and output these to the console. To output a list of bug fixes for a given class, you just call the static `DisplayFixes()` method, passing in the class type:

```
          BugFixAttribute.DisplayFixes (typeof (MyBuggyCode));
```

For the `MyBuggyCode` class presented earlier, this results in the following output:

```
Displaying fixes for MyBuggyCode
   BugFix 101 : Created some methods
   DoSomething
      BugFix 2112 : Returned a non-null string
      BugFix 38382 : Returned OK
   .ctor
      BugFix 90125 : Removed call to base()
```

If you wanted to display fixes for all classes in a given assembly, you could use reflection to get all the types from the assembly, and pass each one to the static `BugFixAttribute.DisplayFixes` method.

AttributeUsage.Inherited

An attribute may be defined as inheritable by setting this flag when defining the custom attribute:

```
[AttributeUsage (AttributeTargets.Class,
                  Inherited = true)]
public class BugFixAttribute { ... }
```

This indicates that the BugFix attribute will be inherited by any subclasses of the class using the attribute, which may or may not be desirable. In the case of the BugFix attribute, this behavior would probably not be desirable, because a bug fix normally applies to a single class and not the derived classes.

Suppose you have the following abstract class with a bug fix applied:

```
[BugFix("38383","Fixed that abstract bug")]
public abstract class GenericRow : DataRow
{
    public GenericRow (System.Data.DataRowBuilder builder) : base (builder)
    {
    }
}
```

If you created a subclass from this class, you wouldn't want the same BugFix attribute to be reflected in the subclass — the subclass has not had that fix done on it. However, if you were defining a set of attributes that linked members of a class to fields in a database table, then you probably would want to inherit these attributes.

Armed with the knowledge you now have about custom attributes, you can probably think of several places where adding extra information to assemblies is useful. You could take the BugFix attribute defined here and extend it too — one example would be to define the version number of the software that the bug was fixed in. That would enable you to display to end users all bugs fixed for a given version of your application simply by using reflection to find the BugFix attributes and then checking the version number of that fix against the versions that the end user has asked to see.

This would also be great for producing documentation at the end of a product cycle to list all fixes made in the latest version. Obviously, you have to rely on the developers to add in these attributes, but it could be made part of the code review cycle to ensure that all fixes were documented within the code.

Summary

This chapter described what attributes are and discussed some of the attributes defined within the .NET Framework. There are many more attribute classes within the framework, and the best way to find out what they are used for is to look through the .NET Framework SDK documentation. To find all attributes in an assembly, just load it into Reflector, browse for the System.Attribute class, and then display the derived types. You may be surprised at just how many attributes are defined within .NET.

In this chapter, you learned about the following attribute-related topics:

❑ Using the Conditional attribute to exclude debugging code from release mode binaries.

❑ Using the Obsolete attribute to revise libraries over time.

❑ How serialization uses attributes to specify what should and what should not be serialized.

❑ How to delay-sign an assembly.

❑ How to create custom attributes.

Attributes are a powerful way to add extra, out-of-band information to your assemblies. You can create your own attributes to add extra information to your classes as appropriate. This chapter described how to create a BugFix attribute, which could be used to provide a link between the source code that was fixed and the bug originally raised by an end user. There are many other uses of attributes — and you are encouraged to look into the .NET Framework for other attribute classes.

31

XML Documentation

Up to this point in this book, you've seen the entire C# language and a great many things you can do with it, including both Web and Windows programming. Along the way, you've seen and made extensive use of the IntelliSense feature in Visual Studio. This helpful tool dramatically reduces the amount of typing you have to do, because it suggests keywords, type names, variable names, and parameters as you type. It also makes it easier to remember what methods and properties you have at your disposal and often tells you exactly how to use them.

However, the classes you have made have suffered slightly here. While the classes and member names are suggested for you, no handy hints pop up telling you how to do things. To achieve the kind of behavior that you see with the .NET Framework types, you need to use *XML documentation*. XML documentation enables you to include syntax, help, and examples for the classes you create at the source-code level. This information may then be used to provide IntelliSense information for Visual Studio as discussed previously, but there are other possibilities. You can use XML documentation as a starting point for full, MSDN-link documentation of your projects. You can also style the XML documentation using XSLT to obtain instant HTML documentation with very little effort. You have seen in earlier chapters just how versatile XML is, and you can use all of its power in the development and production life cycle of your applications.

Documentation is particularly important when you are working as part of a team, as it enables you to show exactly how your types work. It can also be very useful to end users if you are creating an SDK or similar product where you expect people to use your classes from their code. Having the facility to create this documentation built into the tool you use to develop code is a very powerful feature. Although adding XML documentation to your code can be a time-consuming process, the result is well worth it. Dropping text in as you develop can make things easier in the long run and provide you with a handy quick reference that will help to avoid confusion when the amount of classes in your project starts getting out of hand.

In this chapter, you will learn two main things:

❑ How to add and view basic XML documentation

❑ How to use XML documentation

Adding XML Documentation

Adding XML documentation to your code is a remarkably simple thing to do. As with attributes, which you examined in the previous chapter, you can apply XML documentation to any type or member by placing it on lines just before the member. XML documentation is added by using an extended version of C# comment syntax, with three front slashes instead of two. For example, the following code shows how to place XML documentation in a source code file for a class called `MyClass`, and a method of that class, `MyMethod()`:

```
/// (XML Documentation goes here.)
class MyClass
{
    /// (And here.)
    public void MyMethod()
    {
        ...
    }
    ...
}
```

XML documentation cannot be applied to namespace declarations.

Typically, XML documentation will span multiple lines and be marked up by using the XML documentation vocabulary:

```
/// <XMLDocElement>
/// Content.
/// More content.
/// </XMLDocElement>
class MyClass
{
    ...
```

Here, `<XMLDocElement>` is one of several available elements, and may contain nested elements, some of which use attributes to further specify functionality. Note that the `///` parts of the lines of code containing XML documentation are completely ignored and treated as whitespace. They are necessary to prevent the compiler from thinking that the lines of documentation can be interpreted as code, which would lead to compiler errors.

The most basic element for XML documentation is `<summary>`, and it provides a short description of a type or member. Before moving on to anything more complicated, you should take a look at the following example, which illustrates this element and how the results become visible.

Try It Out   **Adding and Viewing Basic XML Documentation**

1. Create a new console application called FirstXMLDocumentation and save it in the directory C:\BegVCSharp\Chapter31.

2. Add a class called `DocumentedClass`.

3. Open the code for `DocumentedClass`, make the class definition public, add a new line before the class declaration, and type `///` (three forward slashes).

4. Note that the IDE auto-completion adds the following code, placing the cursor inside the `<summary>` element:

```
namespace FirstXMLDocumentation
{
    /// <summary>
    ///
    /// </summary>
    public class DocumentedClass
    {
```

5. Add the following text to the `<summary>` element:

```
namespace FirstXMLDocumentation
{
    /// <summary>
    /// This is a summary description for the DocumentedClass class.
    /// </summary>
    public class DocumentedClass
    {
```

6. In `Program.cs`, type **doc** in the `Main()` method and note the IntelliSense information that pops up, shown in Figure 31-1.

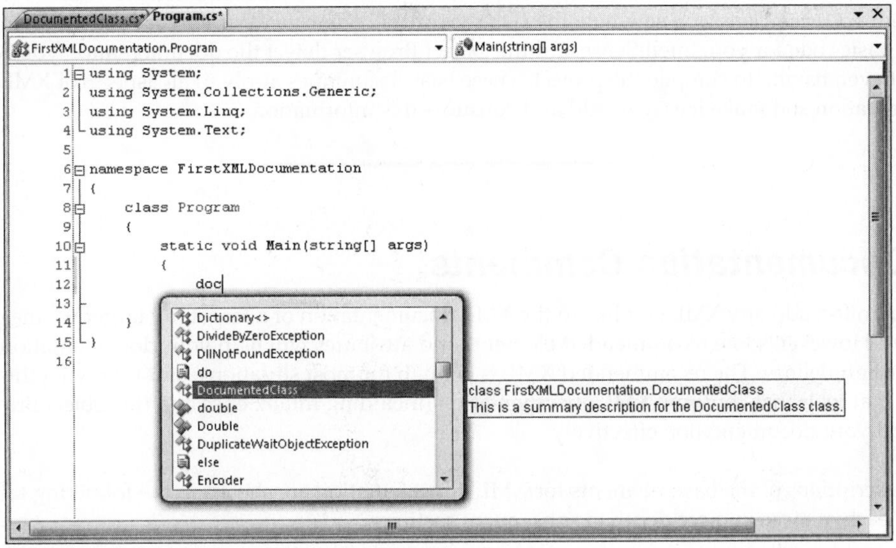

Figure 31-1

7. Open the Object Browser widow and expand the entry for the FirstXMLDocumentation project until you can click `DocumentedClass`. Note the summary information displayed in the bottom-right pane, as shown in Figure 31-2.

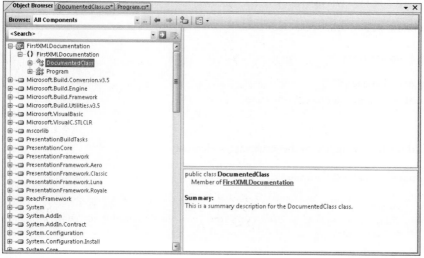

Figure 31-2

How It Works

This example demonstrates the basic technique for adding XML documentation and how this documentation is used in the IDE. When adding the basic summary information for your `DocumentedClass` class, you saw how the IDE dynamically detects what you have in mind and fills out the basic code for you. IntelliSense and the Object Browser detect the documentation you added without even having to compile the project. These basic techniques apply to all aspects of XML documentation and make it easy to add and consume this information.

XML Documentation Comments

You can in fact add any XML you like to the XML documentation of a target (by target we mean *type* or *member*). However, some recommended elements and attributes will help your documentation to meet standard guidelines. The recommended XML is enough for most situations, and following this standard means that tools that consume XML documentation (including IntelliSense and the Object Browser) can interpret your documentation effectively.

Brief descriptions of the basic elements for XML documentation are shown in the following table. You'll look at each of these in more depth in subsequent sections.

Element	Description
`<c>`	Formats text in code font. Use this for individual code words embedded in other text.
`<code>`	Formats text in code font. Use this for multiple lines of code, not embedded in other text.
`<description>`	Marks text as being an item description. Used as a child element of `<item>` or `<listheader>` in lists.
`<example>`	Marks text as an example usage of the target.
`<exception>`	Specifies an exception that may be thrown by the target.
`<include>`	Gets XML documentation from an external file.
`<item>`	Represents an item in a list. Used as a child of `<list>`, and can have `<description>` and `<term>` children.
`<list>`	Defines a list. Can have `<listheader>` and `<item>` children.
`<listheader>`	Represents the header row of a tabular list. Used as a child of `<list>`, and can have `<description>` and `<term>` children.
`<para>`	Used to break text into separate paragraphs.
`<param>`	Describes a parameter of the target.
`<paramref>`	References a method parameter.
`<permission>`	Specifies the permissions required for the target.
`<remarks>`	Includes additional information concerning the target.
`<returns>`	Describes the return value of the target; used with methods.
`<see>`	References another target used in the body of an element such as `<summary>`.
`<seealso>`	References another target, usually used outside of other elements, or at the end of, for example, `<summary>`.
`<summary>`	Holds summary information concerning the target.
`<term>`	Marks text as being an item definition. Used as a child element of `<item>` or `<listheader>` in lists.
`<typeparam>`	Describes a type parameter for a generic target.
`<typeparamref>`	References a type parameter.
`<value>`	Describes the return value of the target; used with properties.

Text Formatting Elements

Many of the elements shown in the preceding table are intended for formatting the text within other elements. A `<summary>` element, for example, might contain a combination of other elements that specify the text to display. The text formatting elements are `<c>`, `<code>`, `<list>`, and its associated elements, `<para>`, `<paramref>`, and `<see>`. `<seealso>` is a special case that you can also include in this list, as it can be included in a body of text, although it usually occurs at the end.

<para>

The `<para>` element is used to separate text into paragraphs:

```
/// <summary>
/// <para>1st paragraph of summary.</para>
/// <para>2nd paragraph of summary.</para>
/// </summary>
```

<c> and <code>

The `<c>` and `<code>` elements are both used to format text in a code font, typically a monospaced font such as Courier. The difference is that `<c>` can be thought of as "code in text," that is, code words that appear in the middle of sentences, whereas `<code>` is used for sections of code outside of text. `<c>` and `<code>` might be used as follows:

```
/// <summary>
/// <para>
/// This summary is about a <c>class</c> that does interesting things. Try this:
/// </para>
/// <code>
/// MyPoet poet = new MyPoet("Homer");
/// poet.AddMuse("Thalia");
/// poet.WriteMeAnEpic();
///</code>
/// </summary>
```

<see>, <seealso>, <paramref>, and <typeparamref>

These four elements are all used to refer to other entries in the XML documentation for a project or to external MSDN entries. Commonly, each of these will be rendered as a hyperlink, enabling documentation browsers to jump to other entries.

`<see>` and `<seealso>` specify their target via a `cref` attribute, where the target can be any type or member of any class, in the project or elsewhere. `<paramref>` and `<typeparamref>` use a `name` attribute to reference a parameter of the current target:

```
/// <summary>
/// <para>
/// This method uses <paramref name="museName" /> to choose a muse.
/// For more details, see <see cref="MyPoet" />.
/// </para>
/// <seealso cref="MyParchment" />
/// <seealso cref="MyTheme" />
/// </summary>
```

<see> can be particularly useful to refer to C# keywords using an alternative attribute, langword:

```
/// <summary>
/// For more information, see <see langword="null" />.
/// </summary>
```

The benefit here is that because you have specified a language-specific keyword, it is possible to refactor the documentation for other languages, such as Visual Basic. The null keyword in C# is equivalent to Nothing in Visual Basic, so it would be possible to cater to both languages — assuming that the tool you use to format the XML documentation is aware of such things.

Note that the elements don't include the text to display, which will typically be constructed from the name, cref, or langword attribute. You should bear this in mind to avoid repetition of text, for example:

```
/// This method uses <paramref name="museName" /> museName to choose a muse.
```

Here the word museName is likely to be repeated.

<list> and Associated Elements

The <list> element is the most complicated text formatting element because it can be used in different ways. It has an attribute called type that can be any of the following:

- ❏ **bullet** — Formats a bulleted list
- ❏ **number** — Formats a numbered list
- ❏ **table** — Formats a table

A <list> element typically has a single <listheader> element child and several <item> children. Each of these may have <term> and <description> children. The exact choice of which children to use will depend on the type of the list and the way your chosen tool formats lists. <term>, for example, is optional in table format lists, while <listheader> might make sense only in a table. For bulleted lists you could use something like the following:

```
/// <summary>
/// <para>
/// This method uses <paramref name="museName" /> to choose a muse.
/// </para>
/// <para>
/// Try the following muses:
/// <list type="bullet">
/// <listheader>
/// <term>Muse name</term>
/// <description>Muse's favorite pizza</description>
/// </listheader>
/// <item>
/// <term>Calliope</term>
/// <description>Ham &amp; Mushroom</description>
/// </item>
/// <item>
/// <term>Clio</term>
/// <description>Four Seasons</description>
/// </item>
```

```
///    <item>
///    <term>Erato</term>
///    <description>Meat Feast</description>
///    </item>
///    </list>
///    </para>
///    </summary>
```

Because the exact behavior of the formatting with these elements may vary, it's best to experiment a bit. Note that whatever you do with these elements, you won't see any difference in the Object Browser, which ignores them.

Major Structural Elements

Several of the elements in the previous table are intended for use as top-level elements in the description of a given target. <summary> is a good example of this, as you saw in the earlier example. The <summary> element should never be contained in another element, and it is always used to provide summary information about the target. The other elements that fit this description are <example>, <exception>, <param>, <permission>, <remarks>, <returns>, and <value>. <seealso> is a special case that can be either a top-level element or a child of another element. <include> is another special case, because it effectively overrides other elements by fetching XML from an external file.

You'll look at each of these elements in turn.

<summary>, <example>, and <remarks>

Each of these three elements provides general information about the target. You've already seen <summary>, which you can use to provide basic information about a target. Because this information appears in tooltips, it's a good idea to keep this information short; put additional information in <example> and <remarks>.

Often when you are introducing a class, it can be helpful to give an example of how that class should be used. The same applies to methods, properties, and so on. Rather than include this information in <summary>, it can make sense to separate it into a new section, <example>:

```
///    <summary>
///    <para>
///    This summary is about a <c>class</c> that does interesting things.
///    </para>
///    </summary>
///    <example>
///    <para>
///    Try this:
///    </para>
///    <code>
///    MyPoet poet = new MyPoet("Homer");
///    poet.AddMuse("Thalia");
///    poet.WriteMeAnEpic();
///    </code>
///    </example>
```

Similarly, `<remarks>` is often used to provide a longer description of a target, and it may include more `<see>` and `<seealso>` elements for cross-referencing.

`<param>` and `<typeparam>`

These elements describe a parameter, either a standard method parameter or a type parameter, for generic targets. The parameter being referenced is set by using a `name` attribute. These elements may occur several times if several parameters are used, as shown here:

```
/// <summary>
/// Method to add a muse.
/// </summary>
/// <param name="museName">
/// A <see langword="string" /> parameter specifying the name of a muse.
/// </param>
/// <param name="museMood">
/// A <see cref="MuseMood" /> enumeration value specifying the mood of a muse.
/// </param>
```

The `name` attribute of a `<param>` or `<typeparam>` element not only specifies the name of the parameter, but also will match the `name` attribute of any `<paramref>` or `<typeparamref>` elements that reference the parameter.

`<returns>` and `<value>`

These two elements are similar in that they both refer to a return value: `<returns>` is used for the return value for methods, and `<value>` is used for the value of a property, which can also be thought of as a return value. Neither of these elements uses any attributes.

For methods, you might use `<returns>` as follows:

```
/// <summary>
/// Method to add a muse.
/// </summary>
/// <param name="museName">
/// A <see langword="string" /> parameter specifying the name of a muse.
/// </param>
/// <param name="museMood">
/// A <see cref="MuseMood" /> enumeration value specifying the mood of a muse.
/// </param>
/// <returns>
/// The return value of this method is <see langword="void" />.
/// </returns>
```

For properties, here is an example of `<value>`:

```
/// <summary>
/// Property for getting / setting a muse.
/// </summary>
/// <value>
/// The type of this property is <see langword="string" />.
/// </value>
```

<permission>

This element is used to describe the permissions associated with a target. Actually setting the permissions is performed by other means, such as applying a `PermissionSetAttribute` attribute to a method; the `<permission>` element merely enables you to inform others about these permissions.

The `<permission>` element includes a `cref` attribute, so you can, if you wish, reference a class that includes additional information, such as `System.Security.PermissionSet`. Here is an example:

```
/// <permission cref="System.Security.PermissionSet">
/// Only administrators can use this method.
/// </permission>
```

<exception>

This element is used to describe any exceptions that might be thrown during the use of the target. It has a `cref` attribute that you can use to cross-reference an exception type. You might, for example, use this element to state the range of allowed values for a property, and what would happen if someone attempted to set the property to a value that isn't allowed:

```
/// <exception cref="System.ArgumentException">
/// This exception will be thrown if you set <paramref name="Width" /> to a
/// negative value.
/// </exception>
```

<seealso>

As previously mentioned, you can use the `<seealso>` element as a top-level element. You can use several of these, which, depending on the tool you use, may be formatted as a list of references at the end of an entry for a target:

```
/// <summary>
/// This is a summary for the MyPoet class.
/// </summary>
/// <seealso cref="MyParchment" />
/// <seealso cref="MyTheme" />
/// <seealso cref="MyToenails" />
```

<include>

Including a lot of XML documentation in your source files can get a little messy, and you might want to consider placing it in completely separate files. This can also be desirable, for example, if someone else is providing the documentation for your code, as you don't have to give that person access to the source files themselves.

The `<include>` element enables you to do this, via its two attributes, `file` and `path`. `file` specifies the external XML file that contains the XML documentation you want to include, and `path` is used to locate the specific section of XML within the document by using XPath syntax.

For example, you could reference some external XML as follows:

```
/// <include file="ExternalDoc.xml" path="documentation/classes/MyClass/*" />
public class MyClass
```

Here a file called `ExternalDoc.xml` is referenced. This may contain code such as the following:

```
<?xml version="1.0" encoding="utf-8" ?>
<documentation>
  <classes>
    <MyClass>
      <summary>
        Summary in an external file.
      </summary>
      <remarks>
        Nice, eh?
      </remarks>
    </MyClass>
  </classes>
</documentation>
```

This could then be equivalent to the following:

```
/// <summary>
/// Summary in an external file.
/// </summary>
/// <remarks>
/// Nice, eh?
/// </remarks>
public class MyClass
```

Adding XML Documentation Using a Class Diagram

In Chapter 9, you were introduced to class diagrams, and since then you've seen how you can use class diagrams to create classes diagrammatically, with changes reflected in your code in real time. You've also learned how to add classes and members, modify the signatures of methods, and so on. It should, therefore, come as no surprise that you can use class diagrams to add XML documentation to your classes, without getting bogged down in source code.

Recall that class diagrams are available only in VS, and are not included in VCE. You need VS in order to work through this example.

Unfortunately, as you will see, adding XML documentation in this way isn't as flexible as adding it manually, but you do get the advantage of being able to do things very quickly, without having to remember any XML syntax.

You'll see the capabilities in the following Try It Out.

Try It Out   Adding XML Documentation in a Class Diagram

1. Create a new class library application called DiagrammaticDocumentation and save it in the directory C:\BegVCSharp\Chapter31.

2. When the project has loaded, click the View Class Diagram button in the Solution Explorer window. You should see a diagram containing just the Class1 class that is generated for you when you create a class library application.

3. Add a class called DocumentedClass and modify its members as shown in Figure 31-3 and the following table.

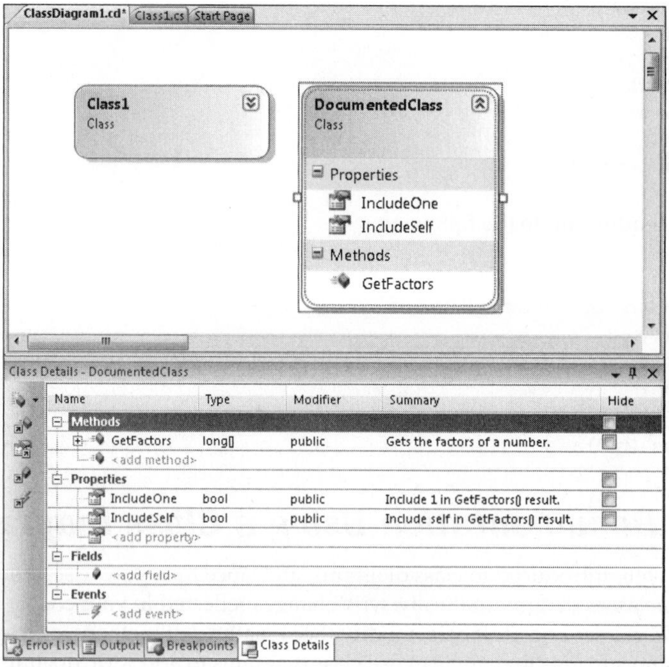

Figure 31-3

Member Type	Name	Type	Modifier	Summary
Method	GetFactors	long[]	public	Gets the factors of a number.
Property	IncludeOne	bool	public	Include 1 in GetFactors() result.
Property	IncludeSelf	bool	public	Include self in GetFactors() result.

4. Click in the Summary box for the `GetFactors()` method, and then click the . . . (ellipses) button. Modify the text in the Description dialog as shown in Figure 31-4 and the following table.

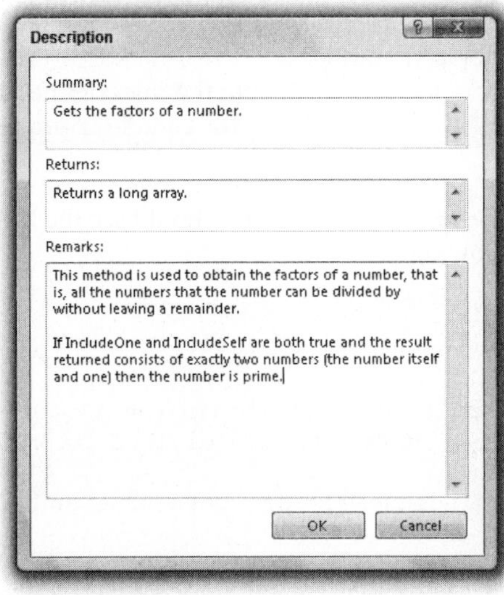

Figure 31-4

Field	Value
Summary	Gets the factors of a number.
Returns	Returns a `long` array.
Remarks	This method is used to obtain the factors of a number — that is, all the numbers that the number can be divided by without leaving a remainder. If `IncludeOne` and `IncludeSelf` are both `true` and the result returned consists of exactly two numbers (the number itself and one), then the number is prime.

5. Similarly, modify the Value and Remarks text for the `IncludeOne` and `IncludeSelf` properties, as shown in the following table:

Property	Value Text	Remarks Text
`IncludeOne`	A `bool` value	If this property is set to `true`, then `GetFactors()` will include 1 in its `long[]` result.
`IncludeSelf`	A `bool` value	If this property is set to `true`, then `GetFactors()` will include its `numberToFactor` parameter in its `long[]` result.

6. Click the class in the class diagram, and in the properties for the class, modify the Summary and Remarks for the class as shown in the next table:

Summary Text	Remarks Text
This class enables you to factorize a number according to certain rules.	Use `GetFactor()` to factorize a number according to the rules defined by the `IncludeOne` and `IncludeSelf` properties.

7. Examine the code for `DocumentedClass`. You should see the XML comments you have added in place, such as the following:

```
/// <summary>
/// Gets the factors of a number.
/// </summary>
/// <remarks>This method is used to obtain the factors of a number, that is, all
/// the numbers that the number can be divided by without leaving a
    remainder.
/// If IncludeOne and IncludeSelf are both true and the result returned
    consists of
/// exactly two numbers (the number itself and one) then the number is
/// prime.</remarks>
/// <param name="numberToFactor">The number to factor.</param>
/// <returns>Returns a long array.</returns>
public long[] GetFactors(long numberToFactor)
{
    throw new System.NotImplementedException();
}
```

How It Works

This example demonstrates how you can use a class diagram to set the XML documentation for a project. After reading the preceding section, you may be wondering why you haven't included cross-references between methods and the like. For example, why wasn't the Remarks text for `GetFactors()` set as follows:

```
This method is used to obtain the factors of a number, that is, all the
numbers that the number can be divided by without leaving a remainder.

If <see cref="IncludeOne" /> and <see cref="IncludeSelf" /> are both <see
langword="true" /> and the result returned consists of exactly two numbers
(the number itself and one) then the number is prime.
```

The reason is because the text editor in the class diagram automatically escapes text that is entered into the `Description` dialog, so the result of entering the previous code is actually the following:

```
/// <summary>
/// Gets the factors of a number.
/// </summary>
/// <remarks>This method is used to obtain the factors of a number, that is, all
/// the numbers that the number can be divided by without leaving a remainder.
```

```
/// If &lt;see cref="IncludeOne" /&gt; and &lt;see cref="IncludeSelf" /&gt; are
/// both &lt;see langword="true" /&gt; and the result returned consists of exactly
/// two numbers (the number itself and one) then the number is prime.</remarks>
/// <param name="numberToFactor">The number to factor.</param>
/// <returns>Returns a long array.</returns>
public long[] GetFactors(long numberToFactor)
{
    throw new System.NotImplementedException();
}
```

This is unfortunately one of the inconveniences you have to cope with if you add XML documentation by using a class diagram. It's great for adding text, but to embed XML documentation markup, you have to modify the code manually.

Generating XML Documentation Files

So far, all the XML documentation you have added has been confined to the development environment while you are working with a project. If you want to actually do anything with the documentation you add, you have to set the project to output the documentation as an XML file.

To do this, you need to modify the build settings for your project, as shown in Figure 31-5.

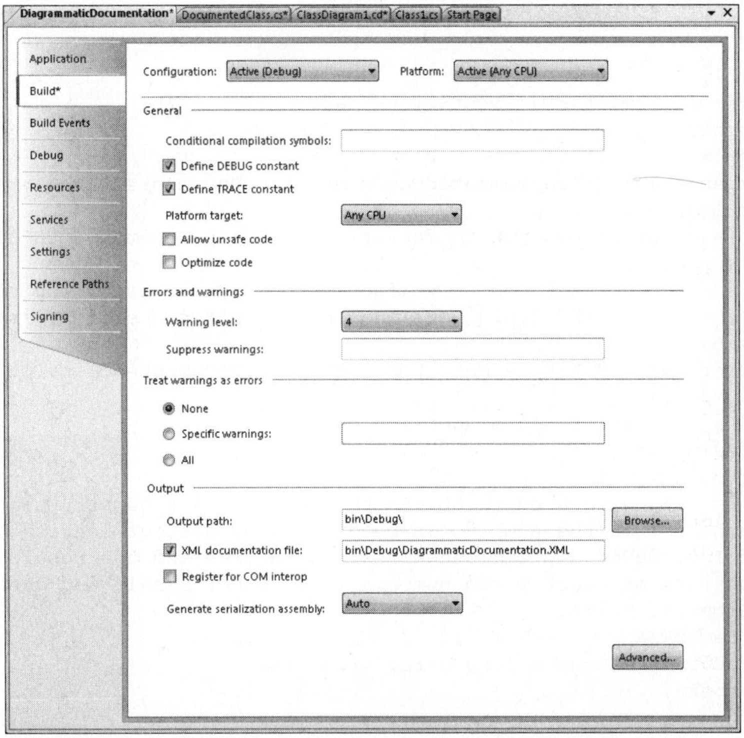

Figure 31-5

The only changes to make are to check the XML Documentation File box and supply an output filename. It is generally a good idea to save the XML documentation file in the same directory as the assembly because that is where the IDE searches for it. If you have a client application to a documented assembly in a different solution, you get the benefits of IntelliSense and help in the Object Browser only if the IDE can find the XML documentation file.

Once the build setting for XML documentation is turned on, the compiler will be configured to actively search for XML documentation in your classes. While it isn't necessarily an error to omit XML documentation for a given class or method, the IDE will alert you to anything missing, in the form of warnings in the Error List window. An example is shown in Figure 31-6.

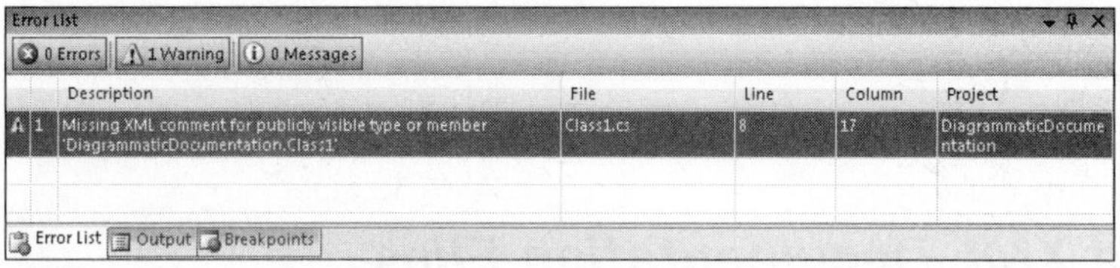

Figure 31-6

This warning, obtained from the previous example, indicates that documentation is missing for the `Class1` class (which you left unchanged).

Here's the XML documentation file created for the previous example:

```
<?xml version="1.0"?>
<doc>
  <assembly>
    <name>DiagrammaticDocumentation</name>
  </assembly>
  <members>
    <member name="T:DiagrammaticDocumentation.DocumentedClass">
      <summary>
      This class allows you to factorize a number according to certain rules.
      </summary>
      <remarks>Use GetFactor() to factorize a number according to the rules
        defined by the IncludeOne and IncludeSelf properties.</remarks>
    </member>
    <member name="M:DiagrammaticDocumentation.DocumentedClass.GetFactors">
      <summary>
      Gets the factors of a number.
      </summary>
      <remarks>
      This method is used to obtain the factors of a number, that is, all the
      numbers that the number can be divided by without leaving a remainder.
      If IncludeOne and IncludeSelf are both true and the result returned
      consists of exactly two numbers (the number itself and one) then the
      number is prime.
      </remarks>
      <returns>Returns a long array.</returns>
    </member>
```

```
<member name="P:DiagrammaticDocumentation.DocumentedClass.IncludeOne">
  <summary>
  Include 1 in GetFactors() result.
  </summary>
  <remarks>If this property is set to true, then GetFactors() will include
    1 in its long[] result.</remarks>
  <value>A bool value.</value>
</member>
<member name="P:DiagrammaticDocumentation.DocumentedClass.IncludeSelf">
  <summary>
  Include self in GetFactors() result.
  </summary>
  <remarks>If this property is set to true, then GetFactors() will include
    its numberToFactor parameter in its long[] result.</remarks>
  <value>A bool value.</value>
</member>
    </members>
  </doc>
```

This document contains the following:

❑ A root level <doc> element containing all other documentation information.

❑ An <assembly> element containing a <name> element containing the name of the assembly to which the XML documentation applies.

❑ A <members> element containing the XML documentation for each member in the assembly.

❑ Several <member> elements, each with a name attribute stating to which type or member the XML documentation contained by the <member> element applies.

The name attributes of the <member> elements follow a consistent naming scheme. They are all names belonging to one of the following namespaces — that is, they all start with one of the following letters:

❑ T — Specifies that the member is a type (class, interface, strut, enumeration, or delegate).

❑ M — Specifies that the member is a method.

❑ P — Specifies that the member is a property or indexer.

❑ F — Specifies that the type is a field or enumeration member (not shown in the example).

❑ E — Specifies that the member is an event (not shown in the example).

Any errors in the XML documentation for a type are shown in the generated file as a commented <member> element:

```
<!-- Badly formed XML comment ignored for member
  "T:DiagrammaticDocumentation.DocumentedClass" -->
```

Within a <member> element, the XML documentation for a target is inserted exactly as is (unless there is a problem with the XML).

Example Application with XML Documentation

For the remainder of this chapter, you'll look at ways to use XML documentation files; and to make this easier, you'll be using a fully functional example class library called DocumentedClasses, which comes packed with XML documentation of almost all types.

The classes in the DocumentedClasses library are shown in Figure 31-7.

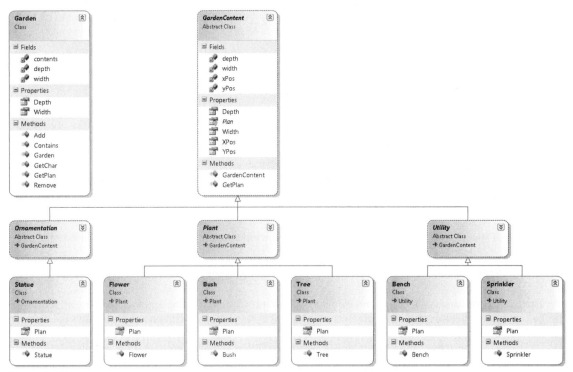

Figure 31-7

The idea behind this class library is that a client application can create an instance of a `Garden` class and then add instances of classes derived from `GardenContent` to the garden. This can then be used to obtain a simple graphical representation of the garden. The classes effectively form a very basic garden design tool.

The downloadable code for this chapter includes this class library, should you want to investigate the code for yourself, but there is no real need to present it all here. Also included in the downloadable code is a simple client application called DocumentedClassesClient, with code as follows:

```
static void Main(string[] args)
{
    int gardenWidth = 40;
    int gardenDepth = 20;

    Garden myGarden = new Garden(gardenWidth, gardenDepth);
```

```
myGarden.Add(new Bench(4, 2));
myGarden.Add(new Bench(10, 2));
myGarden.Add(new Sprinkler(20, 10));
myGarden.Add(new Tree(3, 13));
myGarden.Add(new Tree(25, 7));
myGarden.Add(new Tree(35, 15));
myGarden.Add(new Flower(36, 0));
myGarden.Add(new Flower(37, 0));
myGarden.Add(new Flower(38, 0));
myGarden.Add(new Flower(39, 0));
myGarden.Add(new Flower(37, 1));
myGarden.Add(new Flower(38, 1));
myGarden.Add(new Flower(39, 1));
myGarden.Add(new Flower(37, 2));
myGarden.Add(new Flower(38, 2));
myGarden.Add(new Flower(39, 2));
myGarden.Add(new Statue(16, 3));
myGarden.Add(new Bush(20, 17));

char[,] plan = myGarden.GetPlan();

for (int y = 0; y < gardenDepth; y++)
{
    for (int x = 0; x < gardenWidth; x++)
    {
        Console.Write(plan[x, y]);
    }
    Console.WriteLine();
}
Console.ReadKey();
}
```

This illustrates how to use the classes in DocumentedClasses, and results in the output shown in Figure 31-8.

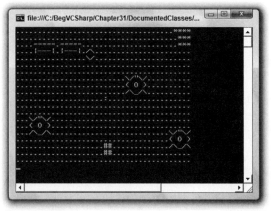

Figure 31-8

As you can see, very basic indeed! (Luckily, if you are a garden designer, there are better tools available.) Of course, here you are merely interested in the XML documentation contained in DocumentedClasses.

Making Use of XML Documentation

This chapter has mentioned in several places that there is much more that you can do with XML documentation than simply use it to supply IntelliSense information to the IDE — which isn't to say that customized IntelliSense isn't an extremely useful feature.

Perhaps the simplest thing you can do with XML documentation is ship it with your assemblies and leave it up to other people to make use of it, but this is far from ideal. In this section, you look at some of the possibilities for getting the most out of your documentation.

Programmatically Processing XML Documentation

The most obvious thing to do with XML documentation is to make use of the wealth of XML tools in the .NET namespaces. Using the techniques and classes you saw in Chapter 25, it is possible to load XML documentation into an XmlDocument object. The following Try It Out is a simple console application that does just that.

> *This Try It Out requires the XML documentation output from the example project, DocumentedClasses. Before starting this Try It Out, download and build the DocumentedClasses solution.*

Try It Out   Processing XML Documentation

1. Create a new console application called XMLDocViewer in the directory C:\BegVCSharp\Chapter31.

2. Add a using statement for the System.Xml namespace to Program.cs:

```
using System;
using System.Collections.Generic;
using System.Linq;
using System.Text;
using System.Xml;
```

3. Modify the code in Main() as follows:

```
static void Main(string[] args)
{
    // Load XML documentation file
    XmlDocument documentation = new XmlDocument();
    documentation.Load(@"..\..\..\..\DocumentedClasses"
        + @"\DocumentedClasses\bin\debug\DocumentedClasses.xml");

    // Get <member> elements.
```

```
        XmlNodeList memberNodes = documentation.SelectNodes("//member");

        // Extract <member> elements for types.
        List<XmlNode> typeNodes = new List<XmlNode>();
        foreach (XmlNode node in memberNodes)
        {
            if (node.Attributes["name"].Value.StartsWith("T"))
            {
                typeNodes.Add(node);
            }
        }

        // Write types to the console.
        Console.WriteLine("Types:");
        foreach (XmlNode node in typeNodes)
        {
            Console.WriteLine("- {0}", node.Attributes["name"].Value.Substring(2));
        }

        Console.ReadKey();
    }
```

4. Execute the application. The result is shown in Figure 31-9.

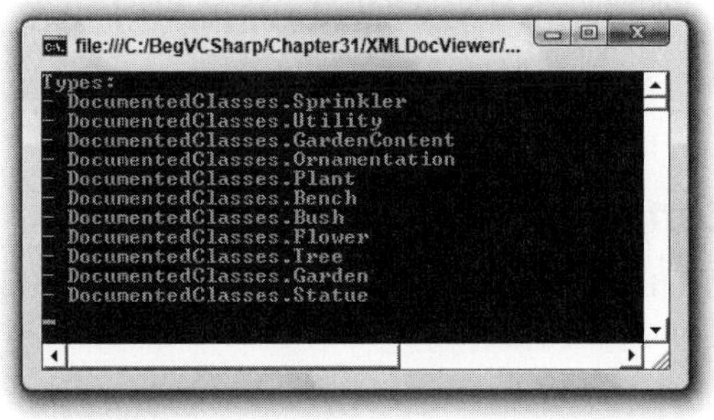

Figure 31-9

How It Works

This example demonstrates the basics of loading and processing an XML documentation file in C#
code. You start by loading in a documentation file, which in this case is the one generated by the
DocumentedClasses type library:

```
XmlDocument documentation = new XmlDocument();
documentation.Load(@"..\..\..\..\DocumentedClasses"
    + @"\DocumentedClasses\bin\debug\DocumentedClasses.xml");
```

Note that the string concatenation used here isn't necessary, but makes the code easier to read on a
narrow page. Next, you get a list of all the <member> elements by using the simple XPath expression
//member:

```
XmlNodeList memberNodes = documentation.SelectNodes("//member");
```

When you have a list of `<member>` elements, you can search through them, looking for those that start with a `T` to get the elements that refer to types, and placing them into a `List<XmlNode>` collection:

```
List<XmlNode> typeNodes = new List<XmlNode>();
foreach (XmlNode node in memberNodes)
{
    if (node.Attributes["name"].Value.StartsWith("T"))
    {
        typeNodes.Add(node);
    }
}
```

You could, of course, achieve this in a single step using a more advanced XPath expression that included an attribute check, but why overcomplicate things? Finally, you output the names of the types found to the console:

```
Console.WriteLine("Types:");
foreach (XmlNode node in typeNodes)
{
    Console.WriteLine("- {0}", node.Attributes["name"].Value.Substring(2));
}
```

There's a lot more that you could do here, as navigating and processing XML files in .NET isn't a complicated process. However, because there are better ways of handling XML documentation, as you'll see in the next two sections, there is no real need to take this example further.

Styling XML Documentation with XSLT

Because XML documentation is, by definition, XML, there is plenty of scope for using XSLT transformations to convert your XML into HTML, or even to use XSLT formatting objects to create printable documentation.

At this point, we'd like to defer to the true master of (and driving force behind) C# — Anders Hejlsberg. He has published an XSLT document and associated CSS file to turn XML documentation files into stylish HTML. These two files, `doc.xsl` and `doc.css`, can be found in the downloadable code for this chapter in the directory `XSLTStyledXMLDocumentation`. In order to use these files, simply add a processing directive to your XML documentation files as follows:

```
<?xml version="1.0"?>
<?xml:stylesheet href="doc.xsl" type="text/xsl"?>
<doc>
   ...
</doc>
```

You'll also find a version of `DocumentedClasses.xml` in the `XSLTStyledXMLDocumentation` directory that includes this directive. A sample of the result is shown in Figure 31-10.

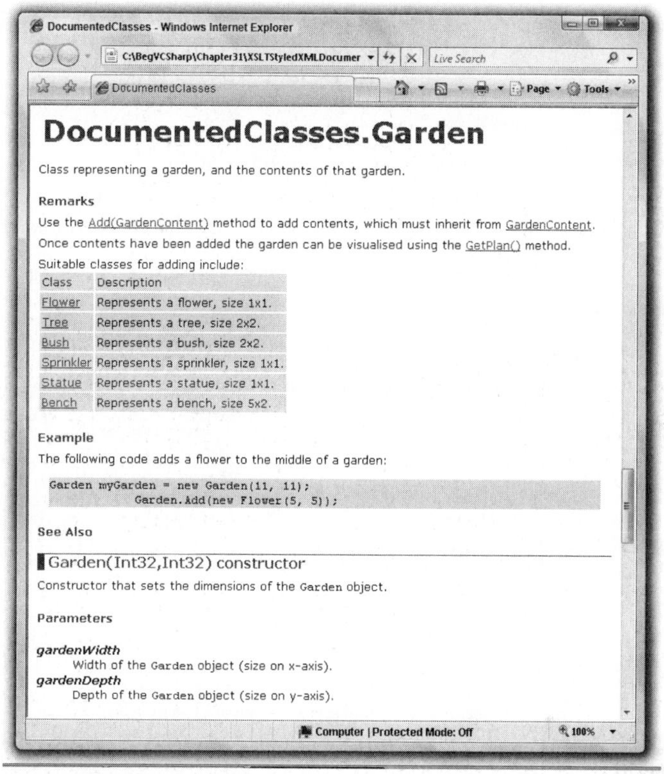

Figure 31-10

The styling isn't perfect — `<seealso>` elements in particular don't come out right, and you can see in the screenshot that there are problems with `<code>` formatting — but overall it's pretty impressive. The files make an excellent starting point should you wish to make a Web page of your documentation. The way that the `<see>` elements link to anchors on the page is particularly good.

Perhaps the biggest problem with doing things this way is that everything appears in a single HTML page, which could get very large indeed.

Documentation Tools

An alternative way of processing XML documentation is to use a tool. Until recently, the tool of choice for XML documentation styling was NDoc. NDoc is a third-party tool that is capable of converting your documentation into a number of formats, including MSDN-style help files. Unfortunately, development on NDoc is (at the time of writing) stalled.

To obtain the most recent version of NDoc (which is free), head to `http://ndoc.sourceforge.net`. Although it hasn't been upgraded for some time, it's still functional (as long as you use the .NET

Framework 1.x version). It is possible that the project may become live again at some point in the future, so it's worth a look. Figure 31-11 shows an example of NDoc documentation in a help-style format.

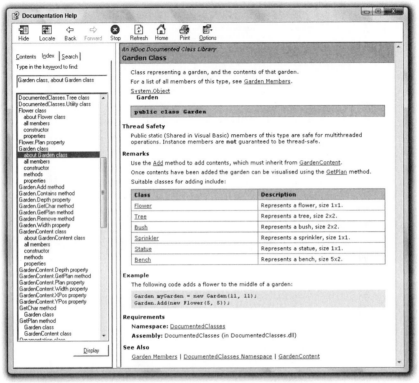

Figure 31-11

With the possible demise of NDoc, it is worth looking at Sandcastle, an alternative tool. It's the tool that Microsoft uses to generate API documentation, so it is as fully featured as you would expect it to be. It has full support for the latest .NET Framework version and C# language features, including support for example generics that NDoc does not support.

However, as Sandcastle is effectively an internal tool, it is not the easiest thing to use. Several GUIs exist for the tool, most of which have been created by its users.

You can find out more at www.sandcastledocs.com or http://blogs.msdn.com/sandcastle. You can also download a popular GUI for Sandcastle at www.codeplex.com/SHFB.

Summary

In this chapter, you looked at all aspects of XML documentation, from how to create it to what you can do with it. Specifically, you have learned the following:

- ❏ XML documentation syntax.
- ❏ How to include external XML documentation.
- ❏ How XML documentation is used in VS IntelliSense and the Object Browser.
- ❏ How to use class diagrams to add XML documentation.
- ❏ How to generate XML documentation files.
- ❏ How to process XML documentation files in C#.
- ❏ How to style XML documentation with XSLT.
- ❏ How to use tools such as NDoc and Sandcastle to compile help files from XML documentation.

Admittedly, adding XML documentation to your projects can be a time-consuming process, and it can make your source code look a bit messy; but in large-scale projects, it is an essential part of development, and the result is well worth the effort — especially when you use a tool designed for the purpose.

Exercises

1. Which of the following elements can you use in XML documentation?

    - ❏ `<summary>`
    - ❏ `<usage>`
    - ❏ `<member>`
    - ❏ `<seealso>`
    - ❏ `<typeparamref>`

2. Which top-level XML documentation tags would you use to document a property?

3. XML documentation is contained in C# source files. True or false?

4. What is the major disadvantage of adding XML documentation using a class diagram?

5. What do you need to do to ensure that other projects can make use of XML documentation in your class libraries?

Networking

Chapter 21 dealt with a high-level technology to communicate across the network: Web Services. You learned how to send messages from the client to the server in a platform-independent way with the SOAP and .NET-specific protocols. In this chapter, you step into lower networking layers, programming with classes from the namespace System.Net. Web Services itself uses this technology.

This chapter begins with an overview of programming client and server applications with classes from the namespaces System.Net and System.Net.Sockets, which make use of protocols such as HTTP, TCP, and UDP. You explore both connection-oriented applications with TCP and connectionless applications with the UDP protocol.

This chapter includes the following topics:

- ❑ An overview of networking
- ❑ Networking programming options
- ❑ Using WebRequest
- ❑ TcpListener and TcpClient
- ❑ Socket programming

Networking Overview

Networking is about communicating with applications on other systems. The communication happens by sending messages. Messages can be sent to a single system where a connection is initiated before the message, as shown in Figure 32-1, or messages can be sent to multiple systems by a *broadcast*, as shown in Figure 32-2. With a broadcast, connections are not initiated; the messages are just sent to the network instead.

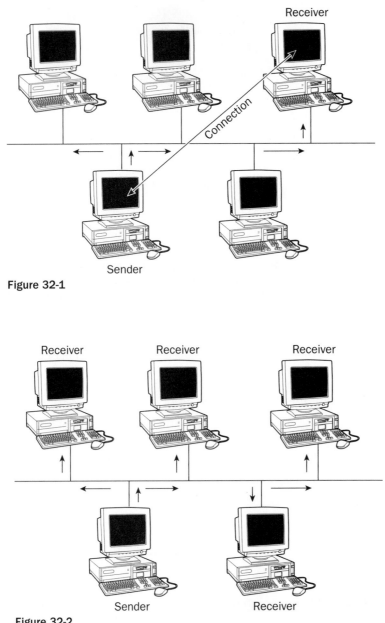

Figure 32-1

Figure 32-2

Networking can be best illustrated by showing the seven OSI layers. Figure 32-3 shows the stack of the OSI layers with their corresponding TCP/IP layers. Often the layers are also defined by numbers that are simply increments of the layers — from the bottom, where the physical layer is number 1, to the top, where the application layer is number 7.

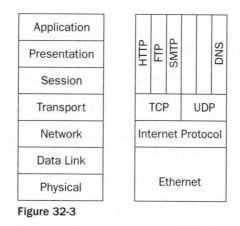

Figure 32-3

The lowest OSI layer is the physical layer. At the physical layer, physical devices (such as networking cards and cables) are defined. The data link layer accesses the physical network with physical addresses. The data link layer performs error correction, flow control, and hardware addressing. The address of your Ethernet network card shows up when you use the `ipconfig /all` command. The system shown here has the MAC address 00-13-02-38-0D-5C:

```
C:\> ipconfig /all

Windows IP Configuration

        Host Name . . . . . . . . . . . . : farabove
        Primary Dns Suffix  . . . . . . . : explorer.local
        Node Type . . . . . . . . . . . . : Hybrid
        IP Routing Enabled  . . . . . . . : No
        WINS Proxy Enabled  . . . . . . . : No
        DNS Suffix Search List  . . . . . : explorer.local
                                            kabsi.at

Wireless LAN adapter Wireless Network Connection:
        Connection-specific DNS Suffix  . : kabsi.at
        Description . . . . . . . . . . . : Intel(R) PRO/Wireless 3945ABG Network
Connection
        Physical address  . . . . . . . . : 00-13-02-38-0D-5C
        DHCP Enabled  . . . . . . . . . . : Yes
        Autoconfiguration Enabled . . . . : Yes
        Link-local IPv6 Address   . . . . : fe80:bd:3d27:4106:9f4c%10(Preferred)
        IPv4 Address  . . . . . . . . . . : 192.168.0.31(Preferred)
        Subnet Mask . . . . . . . . . . . : 255.255.255.0
        Lease Obtained  . . . . . . . . . : Sunday, July 29, 2007, 3:10:08 PM
        Lease Expires . . . . . . . . . . : Wednesday, August 01, 2007, 3:10:08 PM
        Default Gateway . . . . . . . . . : 192.168.0.6
        DHCP Server . . . . . . . . . . . : 192.168.0.6
        DHCPv6 IAID . . . . . . . . . . . : 167777026
        DNS Servers . . . . . . . . . . . : 192.168.0.10
                                            195.202.128.2
        NetBIOS over Tcpip. . . . . . . . : Enabled
```

The network layer uses a logical address to address systems in a WAN. The Internet Protocol (IP) is a layer 3 protocol; at layer 3, an IP address is used to address other systems. In IPv4, the IP address consists of 4 bytes — for example, 192.14.5.12.

The transport layer is used to identify the applications that communicate. The applications can be identified by endpoints. The server application waiting for clients to connect has a known endpoint to connect to. Both the Transmission Control Protocol (TCP) and User Datagram Protocol (UDP) are layer 4 protocols that use a port number (the endpoint) to identify an application. The TCP protocol is used for reliable communication in which a connection is set up before data is sent; whereas with the UDP protocol, communication is unreliable because data is sent without a guarantee that it will be received.

Above layer 4, the OSI layers define a session, presentation, and application layer. The session layer defines services for an application, such as logging in to and out of an application. The session layer enables a virtual connection between applications. You can compare this with ASP.NET sessions, discussed in Chapter 18. The presentation layer is about data formatting — it is within this layer that encryption, decryption, and compression can happen. Finally, the application layer is the highest layer to offer networking features to applications, such as file transfers, e-mail, Web browsing, and so on.

With the TCP/IP protocol suite, the application-level protocols cover layers 4 to 7 of the OSI layer model. A few examples of these protocols are Hypertext Transfer Protocol (HTTP), File Transfer Protocol (FTP), and Simple Mail Transfer Protocol (SMTP). At the transport layer, endpoints are used to reach other applications; these application protocols define how the data that is sent to the other system looks. Later you will see what data is sent with HTTP.

Name Resolution

The Internet Protocol requires IP addresses. Because the IP addresses aren't easy to remember (and are even more difficult with IPv6, where the IP address consists of 128 bits instead of 32 bits), a *hostname* is used. For communication between the systems, however, the IP address is required, as discussed earlier. To map the hostname to the IP address, Domain Name System (DNS) servers are used.

Windows has a command-line tool, nslookup, that can do name lookups (resolve IP addresses from hostnames) or reverse lookups (resolve hostnames from IP addresses). Reverse lookups are interesting because by analyzing the log files where the IP address of client systems can be found, you can determine the origin of the client system.

With .NET, you can perform name lookups with the Dns class in the System.Net namespace. With the Dns class, a hostname can be resolved to its IP addresses, or an IP address can be resolved to its hostname. Let's try it out with a simple project.

Try It Out   **Using DNS**

1.   Create a new C# console application project named DnsLookup in the directory C:\BegVCSharp\Chapter32.

2.   Import the namespace System.Net.

3. Invoke the `GetHostEntry()` method of the `Dns` class, as shown here, after checking the arguments from the `Main()` method:

```
static void Main(string[] args)
{
    if (args.Length != 1)
    {
        Console.WriteLine("Usage: DnsLookup hostname/IP Adddress");
        return;
    }

    IPHostEntry ipHostEntry = Dns.GetHostEntry(args[0]);
```

4. Add the following code to the `Main()` method that follows the call to the `GetHostEntry()` method to write information about the resolved host to the console:

```
Console.WriteLine("Host: {0}", ipHostEntry.HostName);

if (ipHostEntry.Aliases.Length > 0)
{
    Console.WriteLine("\nAliases:");
    foreach (string alias in ipHostEntry.Aliases)
    {
        Console.WriteLine(alias);
    }
}

Console.WriteLine("\nAddress(es):");
foreach (IPAddress address in ipHostEntry.AddressList)
{
    Console.WriteLine("Address: {0}", address.ToString());
}
}
```

5. Compile the application and start the program. Pass a hostname as a command-line argument — for example, www.microsoft.com. To start it from Visual Studio, you can set the command-line arguments with the Debug configuration, as shown in Figure 32-4. You can also start a command prompt, change to the directory of the executable, and start the application with dnslookup www.microsoft.com. You should get output that looks similar to the following:

```
Host: lb1.www.ms.akadns.net

Address(es):
Address: 207.46.193.254
Address: 207.46.19.190
Address: 207.46.19.254
Address: 207.46.192.254
```

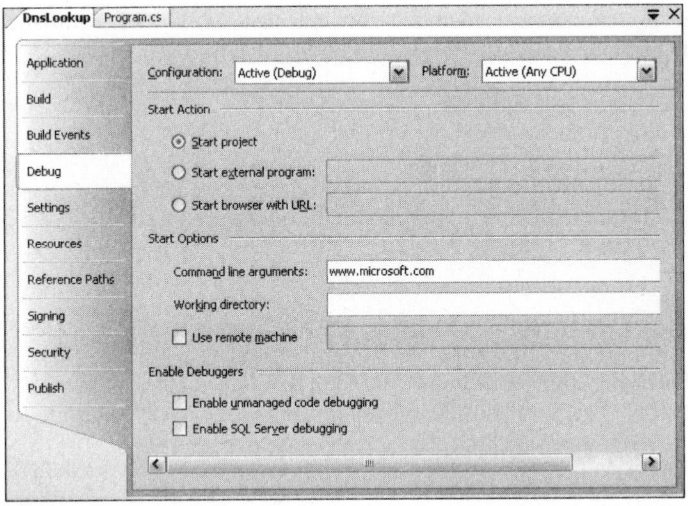

Figure 32-4

How It Works

The Dns class queries the DNS server to resolve hostnames to IP addresses and to do reverse lookups to get a hostname from an IP address. To do this, the Dns class uses the GetHostEntry() method, with which you can pass a hostname, and an IPHostEntry will be returned. For reverse lookups, the GetHostByAddress() method can be called.

In all cases, the Dns class returns an IPHostEntry. This class wraps information about a host. The IPHostEntry class has three properties: HostName returns the name of the host, Aliases returns a list of all alias names, and AddressList returns an array of IPAddress elements. The ToString() method of the IPAddress class returns the Internet address in a standard notation.

Uniform Resource Identifier

The resources that can be accessed across the network are described by a URI (Uniform Resource Identifier). You use URIs every day when you enter Web addresses, such as http://www .thinktecture.com, in your Web browser. The class Uri encapsulates a URI and has properties and methods for parsing, comparing, and combining URIs.

A Uri object can be created by passing a URI string to the constructor:

```
Uri uri = new Uri("http://www.wrox.com/go/p2p");
```

If you go to different pages on the same site, you can use a base URI and construct out of it URIs that contain the directories:

```
Uri baseUri = new Uri("http://msdn.microsoft.com");
Uri uri = new Uri(baseUri, "downloads");
```

You can access parts of the URI by using properties of the Uri class. The following table shows a few examples of what you can get out of an Uri object that is initialized with the URI http://www.wrox.com/marketbasket.cgi?isbn=0470124725.

Uri Property	Result
Scheme	http
Host	www.wrox.com
Port	80
LocalPath	/marketbasket.cgi
Query	?isbn=0470124725

TCP and UDP

Now that you know how to get an IP address from a hostname, you're ready to step into the functionality of the TCP and UDP protocols. Both TCP and UDP are transport-layer protocols, as shown in Figure 32-3. Both of these protocols use a port number to identify the application that will receive the data. The TCP protocol is connection-oriented, while the UDP protocol is connectionless.

The TCP protocol requires the server application to create a socket with a well-known port number, so that the client application can connect to the server. The client creates a socket with a freely available port number. When the client connects to the server, the client passes its port number to the server so that the server knows the path to the client. After the connection is established, the client can send data that is received by the server, and then the server can send some data that is received by the client. Of course, sending and receiving can also happen the other way around. With the QOTD (quote of the day) protocol (a QOTD server is part of the Windows component Simple TCP/IP Services), the server just sends some data after the client connects and then closes the connection.

The UDP protocol is similar in that the server must create a socket with a well-known port number, and the client uses a freely available port number. The difference is that the client doesn't initiate a connection. Instead, the client can send the data without making a connection first. Without a connection, there's no guarantee that the data is received at all, but the overall transfer is faster. The UDP protocol has the big advantage that broadcasts can be done with it — sending information to all systems in the LAN by using a broadcast address.

Broadcast addresses are IP addresses for which all bits of the host part of the IP address are set to 1.

Application Protocols

This section looks at application protocols that make use of TCP or UDP. HTTP is an application protocol that is layered on top of TCP. The HTTP protocol defines the message that is sent across the network.

Using the HTTP protocol to request data from a Web server, a TCP connection is opened, and then an HTTP request is sent. An example of an HTTP request initiated by a browser looks like this:

```
GET /default.aspx HTTP/1.1
Accept: image/gif, image/x-xbitmap, image/jpeg, image/pjpeg,
application/x-ms-application, application/vnd.ms-xpsdocument,
application/xaml+xml, application/x-xbap, application/x-shockwave-flash,
*/*
Accept-Language: de-AT,en-US;q=0.7
Accept-Encoding: gzip, deflate
User-Agent: Mozilla/4.0 (compatible; MSIE 7.0; Windows NT 6.0; .NET CLR
2.0.50727; Media Center PC 5.0; Tablet PC 2.0; .NET CLR 1.1.4322; .NET CLR
3.5.20706; .NET CLR 3.0.590)
Host: localhost:80
Connection: Keep-Alive
```

This sample request shows a GET command. Some of the most frequently used HTTP commands are GET, POST and HEAD. GET is used to request a file from the server. With the POST command, a file is requested from the server, too, but unlike with the GET command, with the POST command additional data is sent after the HTTP header. With the HEAD command, the server returns only the file's header information, so that the client can determine whether the file is different from data already in the cache.

The GET command requests the file on the server. Here, the server should return the file /default .aspx. The last section of the first line defines the HTTP version. If both the client and server support version 1.1, then this version is used for the communication. Otherwise, HTTP 1.0 is used. With HTTP 1.1 it is possible to keep the same connection (see the HTTP header information Connection: Keep-Alive).

After the first line of the request with the GET command, HTTP header information follows. The browser sends information about itself with the request. In the example, you can see the Accept information, where mime types of supported programs are sent. The Accept-Language header defines the languages that are configured on the browser. The server can use this information to return different information to the client, depending on the supported files and languages. With the User-Agent header, the browser sends information about the client application used to request the page from the server. Here, Internet Explorer 7.0 is used with Windows Vista. Windows Vista has the identifier Windows NT 6.0. The server can also read whether the .NET runtime is installed on the client system. Here, .NET 1.1, .NET 2.0, .NET 3.0, and .NET 3.5 appear as supported .NET versions.

After the server receives a GET request, a response message is returned. An example of a response message is shown in the following example. If the request succeeds, then the first line of the response shows an OK status and the HTTP version used. Then HTTP header information follows, which includes the Server, the Date, and the Content-Type and the length that follows the header. The header and the content are separated by two lines:

```
HTTP/1.1 200 OK
Server: Microsoft-IIS/7.0
Date: Sun, 29 Jul 2007 20:14:59 GMT
X-Powered-By: ASP.NET
```

```
X-AspNet-Version: 2.0.50727
Cache-Control: private
Content-Type: text/html; charset=utf-8
Content-Length: 991


<!DOCTYPE HTML PUBLIC "-//W3C//DTD HTML 4.0 Transitional//EN" >
<HTML>
 <HEAD>
  <title>Demo</title>
```

You can easily simulate an HTTP request by using the telnet utility, which you do with the next Try It Out.

Try It Out **Simulate an HTTP Request**

1. Start the telnet client by typing `telnet.exe` at a command prompt. The prompt `Microsoft Telnet>` appears. With Windows Vista, the telnet client is not installed by default. If it is missing on your system, then select Control Panel ⇨ Programs ⇨ Turn Windows Features On or Off; and select the check box for the Telnet Client to install it.

2. To see the commands you type and send to the server, enter `set localecho` in the telnet session.

3. Create a connection to the Web server in your LAN. If you have a Web server on the local system, enter **open localhost 80**. 80 is the default port number used with the Web server.

4. Send a request to the Web server by typing the command **GET / HTTP/1.1**, and then press Return twice. With the /, the default page from the server is returned — for example, `default.htm`. Instead of using the /, you can request specific filenames. Sending two newline characters marks the end of the transmission. Now you get a response from the server that looks similar to the response shown earlier.

Networking Programming Options

The `System.Net` and `System.Net.Sockets` namespaces offer several options for networking programming. Figure 32-5 shows those options. The easiest way to do network programming is by using the `WebClient` class. Just a single method of this class is needed to get files from a Web server or to transfer files to an FTP server. However, the functionality of this class is limited. With .NET 3.5, you can use it only with the HTTP and the FTP protocols, and to access files. Of course, you can also plug in custom classes to support other protocols.

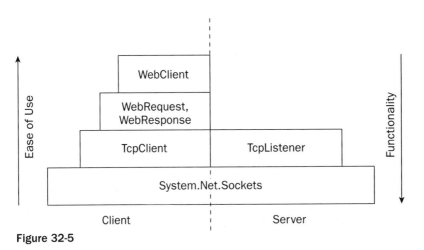

Figure 32-5

The WebClient class itself makes use of the WebRequest and WebResponse classes. These classes have more functionality but are more complex to use.

If you need to create a server, then you can't use WebClient or WebRequest; you have to use the TcpListener class from the namespace System.Net.Sockets. The TcpListener class can be used to create a server for the TCP protocol, while the TcpClient class is used for writing client applications. With these classes, you are not bound to the HTTP and TCP protocols; you can use any TCP-based protocol.

If you have to use the UDP protocol, then you use the UdpListener and UdpClient classes (which are similar to the TcpListener and the TcpClient classes) to write UDP servers and clients.

If you want to be independent of the protocol or you require more control over the TCP and UDP protocols, you can do socket programming with .NET. Classes for socket programming are located in the System.Net.Sockets namespace.

WebClient

Let's start with the class that is easiest to use: the WebClient class. This class is a component that can be dragged and dropped from the Toolbox to a Windows Forms application. You can use it with client applications to access HTTP or FTP servers or use it to access files in the file system.

The following table describes the major properties and methods of the WebClient class:

WebClient Properties	Description
BaseAddress	The property BaseAddress defines the base address of a request that is made by the WebClient.
Credentials	With the Credentials property you can pass authentication information — for example, by using the NetworkCredential class.

WebClient Properties	Description
UseDefaultCredentials	If the credentials of the currently logged on user should be used, then set the property UseDefaultCredentials to true.
Encoding	The Encoding property can be used to set the encoding of strings to upload and download.
Headers	With the Headers property you can define a WebHeaderCollection that can contain header information specifically for the protocol that is used.
Proxy	By default, the proxy configured with Internet Explorer is used to access the Internet. If a different proxy is needed, then you can define a WebProxy object with the Proxy property.
QueryString	If a query string needs to be sent to the Web server, you can do this by setting a NameValueCollection with the QueryString property.
ResponseHeaders	After sending the request, you can read the header information of the response within the WebHeaderCollection class that is associated with the ResponseHeaders class.

The WebClient class has simple methods to upload and download files, as described in the following table:

WebClient Properties	Description
DownloadData()	With the DownloadData() method, you can pass a string for the Web address that is appended to the BaseAddress, and a byte array containing the data from the server is returned.
DownloadString()	DownloadString() is similar to DownloadData(); the only difference is that the returned data is stored inside a string.
DownloadFile()	If the data returned from the server should be stored inside a file, then the method DownloadFile() does all the work for you. The arguments to set with this method are the Web address and the filename.
OpenRead()	With the OpenRead() file, you also download data from the server, but the data downloaded can be read from a stream returned by this method.
UploadFile()	To upload files to an FTP or Web server, the method UploadFile() can be used. This method also allows passing the HTTP method that should be used with the upload.

(continued)

WebClient Properties	Description
UploadData()	Whereas UploadFile() enables uploading files from the local file system, UploadData() sends a byte array to the server.
UploadString()	With UploadString(), you can upload a string to the server.
UploadValues()	With UploadValues(), you can upload a NameValueCollection to the server.
OpenWrite()	The method OpenWrite() sends content to a server by using a stream.

In the following Try It Out, you download a file from the Web with the WebClient class.

Try It Out   **Using the WebClient Class**

1. Create a new Console Application project named WebClientDemo in the directory C:\BegVCSharp\Chapter32.

2. Import the namespace System.Net.

3. Add the following code to the Main() method:

```
static void Main()
{
    WebClient client = new WebClient();
    client.BaseAddress = "http://www.microsoft.com";
    string data = client.DownloadString("Office");
    Console.WriteLine(data);
    Console.ReadLine();
}
```

4. Compile and run the application.

How It Works

After instantiating the WebClient class, the property BaseAddress is set to http://www.microsoft .com. This is the left part of the address that is used with all the following requests. The method DownloadString("Office") requests the page http://www.microsoft.com/Office. All the returned data is stored in the variable data and written to the console.

WebRequest and WebResponse

Instead of using the WebClient class, you can use the WebRequest class to communicate with a Web or a FTP server; it is also possible to read files. Behind the scenes, the WebClient class itself makes use of WebRequest.

The WebRequest class is always used in combination with the WebResponse class. First, you have to define the request that will be sent to the server by configuring a WebRequest object. Next, you can invoke the method GetResponse, which sends the request to the server and returns the response from the server in the WebResponse class.

The WebRequest and WebResponse classes are abstract classes, and thus not directly used. These classes are base classes, as shown in Figure 32-6, and the namespace System.Net offers concrete implementations for the HTTP, FTP, and file protocols. Concrete implementations of these base classes are HttpWebRequest, FtpWebRequest, FileWebRequest, HttpWebResponse, FtpWebResponse, and FileWebResponse. The HTTP protocol is used by the HttpWebXXX classes, the FtpWebXXX classes make use of the FTP protocol, and the FileWebXXX classes enable you to access the file system.

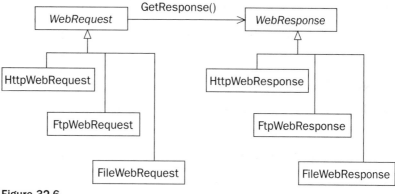

Figure 32-6

Writing an FTP client is a simple task with the help of the FtpWebRequest class. In the next Try It Out, you create a Windows application that downloads files from an FTP server.

Try It Out   Getting a File from an FTP Server

1.   Create a new WPF application named FtpClient in the directory C:\BegVCSharp\Chapter32.

2.   Rename the file Window1.xaml to FtpClientWindow.xaml. Rename the class Window1 to FtpClientWindow. In the file App.xaml, change the reference to FtpClientWindow.xaml.

3.   Add the controls shown in Figure 32-7 to the main window.

Figure 32-7

The controls from this form and their property settings are shown in the following table:

Control Type	Name	Property
FtpClientWindow		Title="FTP Client"
ListBox	listFiles	ItemsSource="{Binding}"
Label	labelServer	Content="Server:"
Label	labelUserName	Content ="Username:"
Label	labelPassword	Content ="Password:"
TextBox	textServer	Text="ftp://"
TextBox	textUserName	Text="Anonymous"
PasswordBox	passwordBox	
Button	buttonOpen	Content="Open"
Button	buttonOpenDirectory	Content="Open Directory"
Button	buttonGetFile	Content="Get File"
CheckBox	checkBoxBinary	Content="Binary Mode"

Here's the XAML code to define the window:

```
<Window x:Class="FtpClient.FtpClientWindow"
    xmlns="http://schemas.microsoft.com/winfx/2006/xaml/presentation"
    xmlns:x="http://schemas.microsoft.com/winfx/2006/xaml"
    Title="FTP Client" Height="300" Width="800">
  <Grid>
     <Grid.ColumnDefinitions>
        <ColumnDefinition Width="150" />
        <ColumnDefinition Width="*" />
        <ColumnDefinition Width="*" />
     </Grid.ColumnDefinitions>
     <Grid.RowDefinitions>
        <RowDefinition Height="40" />
        <RowDefinition Height="40" />
        <RowDefinition Height="40" />
        <RowDefinition />
        <RowDefinition />
        <RowDefinition />
     </Grid.RowDefinitions>
     <Label HorizontalAlignment="Right" Grid.Column="0" Grid.Row="0"
         Name="labelServer" Margin="6,6,6,6">Server:</Label>
     <Label HorizontalAlignment="Right" Grid.Column="0" Grid.Row="1"
         Name="labelUserName" Margin="6,6,6,6">Username:</Label>
```

```
<Label HorizontalAlignment="Right" Grid.Column="0" Grid.Row="2"
        Name="labelPassword" Margin="6,6,6,6">Password:</Label>
<TextBox Grid.Column="1" Grid.Row="0" Name="textServer" Text="ftp://"
        Margin="6,6,6,6" />
<TextBox Grid.Column="1" Grid.Row="1" Name="textUserName" Text="Anonymous"
        Margin="6,6,6,6" />
<PasswordBox Grid.Column="1" Grid.Row="2" Name="passwordBox"
        Margin="6,6,6,6" />

<ListBox ItemsSource="{Binding}" Margin="12,12,12,12" x:Name="listFiles"
        Grid.Column="0" Grid.Row="3" Grid.ColumnSpan="2" Grid.RowSpan="3" />

<Button Grid.Column="2" Grid.Row="0" x:Name="buttonOpen"
        Margin="6,6,6,6">Open</Button>
<Button Grid.Column="2" Grid.Row="1" x:Name="buttonOpenDirectory"
        IsEnabled="False" Margin="6,6,6,6">Open Directory</Button>
<Button Grid.Column="2" Grid.Row="2" x:Name="buttonGetFile" IsEnabled="False"
        Margin="6,6,6,6">Get File</Button>
<CheckBox HorizontalAlignment="Left" VerticalAlignment="Center"
        Grid.Column="2" Grid.Row="3" x:Name="checkBoxBinary"
        Margin="8,8,8,8">Binary Mode</CheckBox>
    </Grid>
</Window>
```

4. Using the Property Editor, set the IsEnabled property of the buttons buttonGetFile and buttonOpenDirectory to false. These buttons are only active when a file is selected.

5. In the code-behind file, import the System.Net, System.IO and Microsoft.Win32 namespaces.

6. Add the variable serverDirectory as a private member to the class FtpClientWindow:

```
public partial class FtpClientWindow : Window
{
    private string serverDirectory;
```

7. Add the helper method FillDirectoryList to the class FtpClientWindow. This method fills the listBox with all the data that is inside the stream argument:

```
private void FillDirectoryList(Stream stream)
{
    StreamReader reader = new StreamReader(stream);
    string content = reader.ReadToEnd();
    string[] files = content.Split('\n');
    this.DataContext = files;
    reader.Close();
}
```

8. To make an initial connection to the server, add a `Click` event handler to the button `buttonOpen` with the name `buttonOpen_Click`. Add the implementation to this handler as shown here:

```
private void buttonOpen_Click(object sender, RoutedEventArgs e)
{
    Cursor currentCursor = this.Cursor;
    FtpWebResponse response = null;
    Stream stream = null;
    try
    {
        this.Cursor = Cursors.Wait;

        // Create the FtpWebRequest object.
        FtpWebRequest request =
            (FtpWebRequest)WebRequest.Create(textServer.Text);
        request.Credentials = new NetworkCredential(textUserName.Text,
            passwordBox.Password);
        request.Method = WebRequestMethods.Ftp.ListDirectory;

        // Send the request to the server.
        response = (FtpWebResponse)request.GetResponse();

        // Read the response and fill the list box.
        stream = response.GetResponseStream();
        FillDirectoryList(stream);

        serverDirectory = null;
        buttonOpenDirectory.IsEnabled = false;
        buttonGetFile.IsEnabled = false;
    }
    catch (WebException ex)
    {
        MessageBox.Show(ex.Message, "Error FTP Client",
            MessageBoxButton.OK, MessageBoxImage.Error);
    }
    catch (IOException ex)
    {
        MessageBox.Show(ex.Message, "Error FTP Client",
            MessageBoxButton.OK, MessageBoxImage.Error);
    }
    finally
    {
        if (response != null)
            response.Close();
        if (stream != null)
            stream.Close();
        this.Cursor = currentCursor;
    }
}
```

9. To open a specific directory on the server, add a `Click` event handler to the button `buttonOpenDirectory` with the name `buttonOpenDirectory_Click`. Add the code to this handler as shown here:

```
private void buttonOpenDirectory_Click(object sender, RoutedEventArgs e)
{
    Cursor currentCursor = this.Cursor;

    FtpWebResponse response = null;
    Stream stream = null;
    try
    {
        this.Cursor = Cursors.Wait;

        string subDirectory = listFiles.SelectedValue.ToString().Trim();
        if (serverDirectory != null)
        {
            serverDirectory += "/" + subDirectory;
        }
        else
        {
            serverDirectory = subDirectory;
        }

        Uri baseUri = new Uri(textServer.Text);
        Uri uri = new Uri(baseUri, serverDirectory);

        FtpWebRequest request = (FtpWebRequest)WebRequest.Create(uri);
        request.Credentials = new NetworkCredential(textUserName.Text,
            passwordBox.Password);

        request.Method = WebRequestMethods.Ftp.ListDirectory;
        response = (FtpWebResponse)request.GetResponse();

        stream = response.GetResponseStream();
        FillDirectoryList(stream);
    }
    catch (WebException ex)
    {
        MessageBox.Show(ex.Message, "Error FTP Client",
            MessageBoxButton.OK, MessageBoxImage.Error);
    }
    finally
    {
        if (response != null)
            response.Close();
        if (stream != null)
            stream.Close();

        this.Cursor = currentCursor;
    }
}
```

10. For downloading a file from the server, add a `Click` event handler named `buttonGetFile_Click` to the `buttonGetFile` button. Add the following code to this event handler method:

```
private void buttonGetFile_Click(object sender, RoutedEventArgs e)
{
    Cursor currentCursor = this.Cursor;

    FtpWebResponse response = null;
    Stream inStream = null;
    Stream outStream = null;
    try
    {
        this.Cursor = Cursors.Wait;

        Uri baseUri = new Uri(textServer.Text);

        string filename = listFiles.SelectedValue.ToString().Trim();
        string fullFilename = serverDirectory + @"/" + filename;

        Uri uri = new Uri(baseUri, fullFilename);

        FtpWebRequest request = (FtpWebRequest)WebRequest.Create(uri);
        request.Credentials = new NetworkCredential(textUserName.Text,
                passwordBox.Password);
        request.Method = WebRequestMethods.Ftp.DownloadFile;
        request.UseBinary = checkBoxBinary.IsChecked ?? false;

        response = (FtpWebResponse)request.GetResponse();

        inStream = response.GetResponseStream();

        SaveFileDialog saveFileDialog = new SaveFileDialog();
        saveFileDialog.FileName = filename;

        if (saveFileDialog.ShowDialog() == true)
        {
            outStream = File.OpenWrite(saveFileDialog.FileName);
            byte[] buffer = new byte[8192];
            int size = 0;
            while ((size = inStream.Read(buffer, 0, 8192)) > 0)
            {
                outStream.Write(buffer, 0, size);
            }
        }
    }
    catch (WebException ex)
    {
        MessageBox.Show(ex.Message, "Error FTP Client",
                MessageBoxButton.OK, MessageBoxImage.Error);
    }
    finally
    {
        if (inStream != null)
            inStream.Close();
```

```
                        if (outStream != null)
                            outStream.Close();
                        if (response != null)
                            response.Close();

                        this.Cursor = currentCursor;
                    }
            }
```

11. To enable the Open Directory and Get File buttons, you must add an event handler for the
`SelectionChanged` event of the `listFiles` list box. Name the event handler
`listFiles_SelectionChanged`:

```
private void listFiles_SelectionChanged(object sender, RoutedEventArgs e)
{
    buttonGetFile.IsEnabled = true;
    buttonOpenDirectory.IsEnabled = true;
}
```

12. After compiling the application, you can try it out. Start the application, which presents a
screen like the one shown in Figure 32-8. Enter an FTP server to connect to (for example,
`ftp://ftp.microsoft.com`), and click the Open button. FTP servers that support
anonymous users accept the username Anonymous. Some FTP servers that allow anonymous
users check for a password that is in valid e-mail address format. This behavior is not used for
security reasons but to write the file requests to a log file.

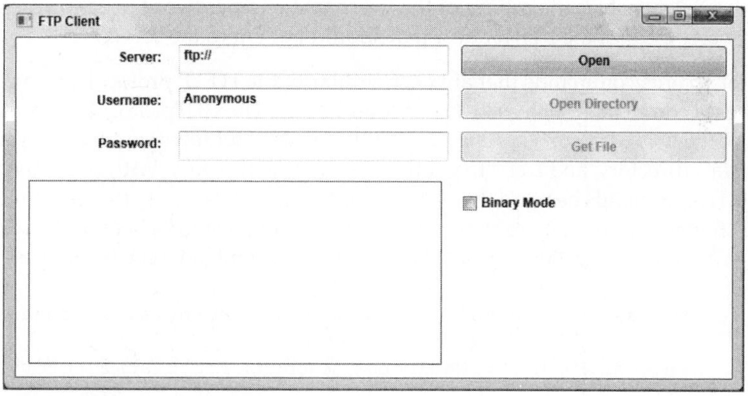

Figure 32-8

After a successful connection, the server's files and directories appear in the list box, as shown
in Figure 32-9. Now you can open other directories by clicking the Open Directory button, or
download files by clicking the Get File button.

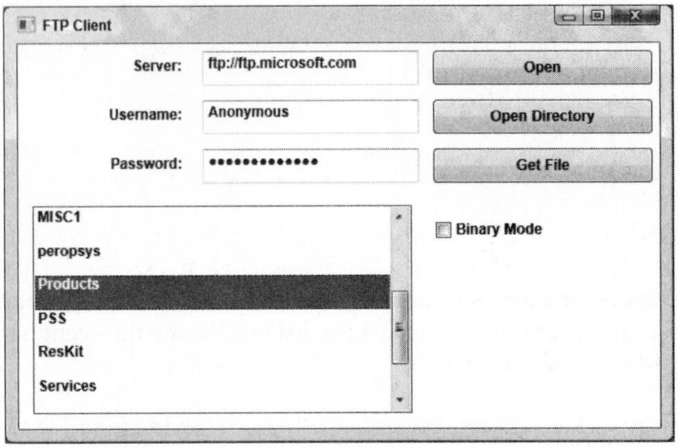

Figure 32-9

How It Works

When you send a request to an FTP server, an `FtpWebRequest` object must be created. The `FtpWebRequest` object is created by the factory method `WebRequest.Create()`. This method creates either an `FtpWebRequest` object, an `HttpWebRequest` object, or a `FileWebRequest` object, depending on the URL string that is passed to the method:

```
FtpWebRequest request =
        (FtpWebRequest)WebRequest.Create(textServer.Text);
```

After the `FtpWebRequest` object is created, you must configure it by setting its properties. The property `Credentials` enables the setting of the username and password used to access the server. The `Method` property defines the FTP request that should be sent to the server.

The FTP protocol accepts commands that are very similar to the HTTP protocol's commands. The HTTP protocol uses commands such as GET, HEAD, and POST. The FTP protocol's commands are defined in RFC 959 (www.ietf.org/rfc/rfc0959.txt): RETR to download files, STOR to upload files, MKD to create a directory, and LIST to get the files from a directory. With .NET, there's no need to know all these FTP commands because the `WebRequestMethods` class has these commands defined. `WebRequestMethods.Ftp.ListDirectory` creates a LIST request to be sent to the server, and `WebRequestMethods.Ftp.DownloadFiles` is used to download a file from the server:

```
request.Credentials = new NetworkCredential(textUsername.Text,
        passwordBox.Password);
request.Method = WebRequestMethods.Ftp.ListDirectory;
```

When the request is defined, it can be sent to the server. The `GetResponse()` method sends the request to the server and waits until a response is received:

```
response = (FtpWebResponse)request.GetResponse();
```

To access the data from the response, the `GetResponseStream()` method returns a stream. In response to the `WebRequestMethods.Ftp.ListDirectory` request, the response stream contains all

the filenames from the requested server directory. After a `WebRequestMethods.Ftp.DownloadFile`
request, the response stream contains the content of the requested file:

```
stream = response.GetResponseStream();
```

The returned stream containing the server directory's file listing is dealt with in the `FillDirectoryList()`
method. The stream is read by using a `StreamReader`. The method `ReadToEnd()` returns a string of all
the filenames that have been returned by the server. The filenames are separated by the newline
character, which is used to create a string array containing all filenames. This string array is set as the
data context of the Window so that the files are displayed with the `ListBox` control:

```
private void FillDirectoryList(Stream stream)
{
    StreamReader reader = new StreamReader(stream);
    string content = reader.ReadToEnd();
    string[] files = content.Split('\n');
    this.DataContext = files;
    reader.Close();
}
```

The stream received from the download file request is dealt with in the `OnDownloadFile()` method.
A `SaveFileDialog` is opened so the user can specify in which directory to store the file. The
`SaveFileDialog FileName` property returns the directory and filename selected by the user. The `File`
class `OpenWrite()` method returns the stream indicating where the file from the server can be stored.
The stream returned from the FTP server is read in a `while` loop and written into the stream of the
local file:

You can read more about dialogs in Chapter 17.

```
inStream = response.GetResponseStream();

SaveFileDialog saveFileDialog = new SaveFileDialog();
saveFileDialog.FileName = fileName;

if (saveFileDialog.ShowDialog() == true)
{
    outStream = File.OpenWrite(saveFileDialog.FileName);
    byte[] buffer = new byte[8192];
    int size = 0;
    while ((size = inStream.Read(buffer, 0, 8192)) > 0)
    {
        outStream.Write(buffer, 0, size);
    }
}
```

Now you have seen how .NET classes can be used with well-known application protocols. If you want
to create your own application protocol based on TCP, you can use the `TcpListener` and `TcpClient`
classes.

TcpListener and TcpClient

Classes from the `System.Net.Sockets` namespace provide much more control for network programming. Classes from these namespaces enable you to write your own server and define a custom protocol to transfer information from the client to the server and from the server to the client.

The `TcpListener` class can be used with the server. You can define a port number that the server should listen to with the constructor of the class. With the `Start()` method, the listening begins. However, to communicate with a client, the server must invoke the method `AcceptTcpClient()`. This method blocks until a client connects. The return value of this method is a `TcpClient` object that contains information about the connection to the client. Using this `TcpClient` object, the server can receive data that is sent from the client, and send data back to the client.

The client itself makes use of the `TcpClient` class. The client can initiate the connection to the server with the `Connect()` method, and afterward it can send and receive data by using a stream associated with the `TcpClient` object.

In the following two Try It Outs, you create a simple server and a client application with the `TcpListener` and `TcpClient` classes. The server sends a list of picture files to the client, and the client can choose a file from this list to request that file from the server. With this application, the client can make two requests: the `LIST` request returns the file list, while the `PICTURE:filename` request returns the picture in a byte stream.

Try It Out   **Creating a TCP Server**

Start by creating the server application:

1.   Create a new console application project in the directory C:\BegVCSharp\Chapter32 with Visual Studio. Name the application PictureServer.

2.   Select the project properties. Open the Settings tab and create a default settings file by clicking the link "This Project Does Not Contain A Default Settings File. Click Here To Create One."

3.   With the `Settings.settings` file, add a property named `PictureDirectory` of type `string` and a property named `Port` of type `int`, as shown in Figure 32-10. Set the value of the `PictureDirectory` to a directory on your system where you have pictures, such as c:\pictures. Set the value of the `Port` property to `8888` to define the server's port number.

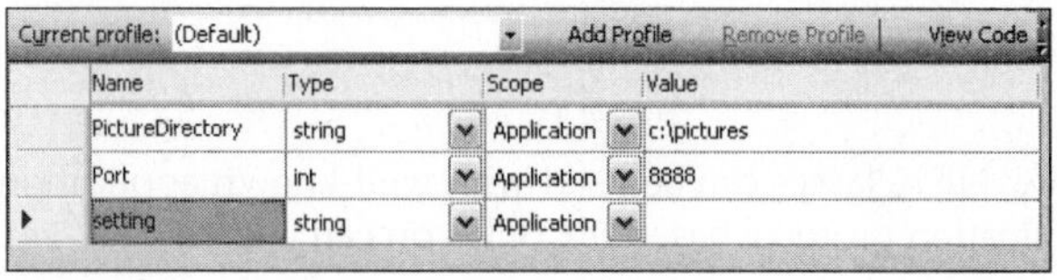

Current profile:	(Default)		▼	Add Profile	Remove Profile	View Code
	Name	Type		Scope		Value
	PictureDirectory	string	▼	Application	▼	c:\pictures
	Port	int	▼	Application	▼	8888
▶	setting	string	▼	Application	▼	

Figure 32-10

4. Add the internal helper class `PictureHelper` to the console application using Add ⇨ Class in the Solution Explorer. The static methods offered by this class return a list of all files (`GetFileList()` method), and return the list of the filenames in a byte array (`GetFileListBytes()` method). This class uses file I/O to get filenames and to read a file:

You can read more about file I/O in Chapter 24.

```csharp
using System;
using System.Collections.Generic;
using System.Linq;
using System.IO;
using System.Text;

namespace PictureServer
{
    internal static class PictureHelper
    {
        internal static IEnumerable<string> GetFileList()
        {
            // Remove the directory path from the filename
            return from file in Directory.GetFiles(
                    Properties.Settings.Default.PictureDirectory)
                select Path.GetFileName(file);
        }

        internal static byte[] GetFileListBytes()
        {
            try
            {
                // LIST request - return list
                IEnumerable<string> files = PictureHelper.GetFileList();
                StringBuilder responseMessage = new StringBuilder();
                foreach (string s in files)
                {
                    responseMessage.Append(s);
                    responseMessage.Append(":");
                }
                return Encoding.ASCII.GetBytes(
                    responseMessage.ToString());
            }
            catch (DirectoryNotFoundException ex)
            {
                Console.WriteLine(ex.Message);
                throw;
            }
        }
    }
}
```

5. Import the namespaces System.Net, System.Net.Sockets, and System.IO in the file Program.cs.

6. In the Main() method of the server application, add the code shown here:

```
class Program
{
    static void Main()
    {
        TcpListener listener = new TcpListener(IPAddress.Any,
                Properties.Settings.Default.Port);
        listener.Start();
        Console.WriteLine("Server running...");

        while (true)
        {
            const int bufferSize = 8192;

            TcpClient client = listener.AcceptTcpClient();
            NetworkStream clientStream = client.GetStream();

            byte[] buffer = new byte[bufferSize];
            int readBytes = 0;
            readBytes = clientStream.Read(buffer, 0, bufferSize);

            string request = Encoding.ASCII.GetString(buffer).Substring(
                    0, readBytes);

            if (request.StartsWith("LIST", StringComparison.Ordinal))
            {
                // LIST request - return list
                byte[] responseBuffer = PictureHelper.GetFileListBytes();

                clientStream.Write(responseBuffer, 0, responseBuffer.Length);
            }
            else if (request.StartsWith("FILE", StringComparison.Ordinal))
            {
                // FILE request - return file

                // get the filename
                string[] requestMessage = request.Split(':');
                string filename = requestMessage[1];

                byte[] data = File.ReadAllBytes(Path.Combine(
                        Properties.Settings.Default.PictureDirectory, filename));

                // Send the picture to the client.
                clientStream.Write(data, 0, data.Length);
            }
            clientStream.Close();
        }
    }
}
```

How It Works

To create a server application that waits for connecting clients using the TCP protocol, you can use the `TcpListener` class. To create a `TcpListener` object, you must define a port number for the server. Here, the port number is read from the configuration file with `Properties.Settings.Default` `.Port`. Then the `Start()` method is invoked to start listening for incoming requests:

```
TcpListener listener = new TcpListener(IPAddress.Any,
        Properties.Settings.Default.Port);
listener.Start();
```

After starting the listener, the server waits in the `AcceptTcpClient()` method until a client connects. The connection to the client is defined in the `TcpClient` object returned by `AcceptTcpClient()`:

```
TcpClient client = listener.AcceptTcpClient();
```

After the connection is initiated, the client sends a request to the server. The request is read in the stream. `client.GetStream()` returns a `NetworkStream` object. The data from this network stream is read into the byte array buffer and then converted to a string that is stored in the variable `request`:

```
NetworkStream clientStream = client.GetStream();

byte[] buffer = new byte[bufferSize];
int readBytes = 0;
readBytes = clientStream.Read(buffer, 0, bufferSize);

string request = Encoding.ASCII.GetString(buffer).Substring(
        0, readBytes);
```

Depending on the request string, either a list of picture files or the bytes of a picture are returned to the client. The request string is checked with the `String` method `StartsWith`:

```
if (request.StartsWith("LIST", StringComparison.Ordinal))
```

The server sends data back to the client by writing the return data to the network stream:

```
byte[] responseBuffer = PictureHelper.GetFileListBytes();
clientStream.Write(responseBuffer, 0, responseBuffer.Length);
```

Try It Out   Creating a TCP Client

The client application is a Windows forms application that shows the picture files available on the server. When the user selects a picture file, the picture is shown in the client application.

1.   Create a new WPF project named PictureClient in the directory C:\BegVCSharp\Chapter32.

2.   Delete the file `Window1.xaml` and add a new WPF window named `PictureClientWindow` `.xaml`. In the file `App.xaml`, change the reference to `PictureClientWindow.xaml`.

3. Add the server name and server port number to the application's property settings as you did with the server application. The server name has the property name `Server`, and the port number has the property name `ServerPort`. Set the value of the server to the name of your server, and the port number to the port number of the server. In the example, server port number 8888 has been used.

4. Add controls as shown in Figure 32-11 to the main window.

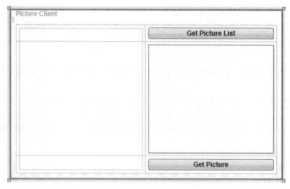

Figure 32-11

The main controls of this dialog are shown in the following table:

Control Type	Name	Property
PictureBox	pictureBox	
Button	buttonListPictures	Content="List Pictures"
ListBox	listFiles	ItemsSource="{Binding}"
Button	buttonGetPicture	Content="Get Picture"

Here's the code for `PictureClientWindow.xaml`:

```
<Window x:Class="PictureClient.PictureClientWindow"
    xmlns="http://schemas.microsoft.com/winfx/2006/xaml/presentation"
    xmlns:x="http://schemas.microsoft.com/winfx/2006/xaml"
    Title="Picture Client" Height="300" Width="500">
    <Grid>
        <Grid.RowDefinitions>
            <RowDefinition Height="30" />
            <RowDefinition />
            <RowDefinition Height="30" />
        </Grid.RowDefinitions>
        <Grid.ColumnDefinitions>
            <ColumnDefinition />
```

```
            <ColumnDefinition />
        </Grid.ColumnDefinitions>
        <Image x:Name="pictureBox" Grid.Row="0" Grid.Column="0" Grid.RowSpan="3"
            Margin="6,6,6,6" />
        <Button Grid.Row="0" Grid.Column="1" Margin="5,5,5,5"
            x:Name="buttonGetPictureList">Get Picture List</Button>
        <Button Grid.Row="2" Grid.Column="1" Margin="5,5,5,5"
            x:Name="buttonGetPicture">Get Picture</Button>
        <ListBox ItemsSource="{Binding}" Grid.Row="1" Grid.Column="1"
            Margin="5,5,5,5" x:Name="listFiles" />
    </Grid>
</Window>
```

5. Import the namespaces `System.Net`, `System.Net.Sockets`, and `System.IO` in the file `PictureClientWindow.xaml.cs`.

6. Add a const `bufferSize` to the class `PicutreClientWindow`:

```
public partial class PictureClientWindow : Window
{
    private const int bufferSize = 8192;
```

7. Add the helper method `ConnectToServer()` with the implementation shown here:

```
private TcpClient ConnectToServer()
{
    // Connect to the server.
    TcpClient client = new TcpClient();

    IPHostEntry host = Dns.GetHostEntry(
        Properties.Settings.Default.Server);
    var address= (from h in host.AddressList
                  where h.AddressFamily == AddressFamily.InterNetwork
                  select h).First();
    client.Connect(address.ToString(),
        Properties.Settings.Default.ServerPort);

    return client;
}
```

8. Add a `Click` event handler to the button `buttonListPictures` to include this code:

```
private void buttonGetPictureList_Click(object sender, RoutedEventArgs e)
{
    TcpClient client = ConnectToServer();

    // Send a request to the server.
    NetworkStream clientStream = client.GetStream();
    string request = "LIST";
    byte[] requestBuffer = Encoding.ASCII.GetBytes(request);
    clientStream.Write(requestBuffer, 0, requestBuffer.Length);
```

```
// Read the response from the server.
byte[] responseBuffer = new byte[bufferSize];
MemoryStream memStream = new MemoryStream();
int bytesRead = 0;
do
{
    bytesRead = clientStream.Read(responseBuffer, 0, bufferSize);
    memStream.Write(responseBuffer, 0, bytesRead);
} while (bytesRead > 0);
clientStream.Close();
client.Close();

byte[] buffer = memStream.GetBuffer();
string response = Encoding.ASCII.GetString(buffer);
this.DataContext = response.Split(':');
}
```

9. Add a `Click` event handler to the `buttonGetPicture` button, and add this code:

```
private void buttonGetPicture_Click(object sender, RoutedEventArgs e)
{
    TcpClient client = ConnectToServer();

    NetworkStream clientStream = client.GetStream();

    string request = "FILE:" + this.listFiles.SelectedItem.ToString();
    byte[] requestBuffer = Encoding.ASCII.GetBytes(request);
    clientStream.Write(requestBuffer, 0, requestBuffer.Length);

    byte[] responseBuffer = new byte[bufferSize];
    MemoryStream memStream = new MemoryStream();
    int bytesRead = 0;
    do
    {
        bytesRead = clientStream.Read(responseBuffer, 0, bufferSize);
        memStream.Write(responseBuffer, 0, bytesRead);
    } while (bytesRead > 0);
    clientStream.Close();
    client.Close();

    BitmapImage bitmapImage = new BitmapImage();
    memStream.Seek(0, SeekOrigin.Begin);
    bitmapImage.BeginInit();
    bitmapImage.StreamSource = memStream;
    bitmapImage.EndInit();
    pictureBox.Source = bitmapImage;
}
```

10. Now you can start the server application and then the client application (see Figure 32-12). When you click the first button (List Pictures), a list of all pictures in the pictures directory (which has been configured on the server) appears. Selecting a picture and clicking the Get Picture button transfers the picture to the client and the picture is displayed in the picture box.

If you have the Windows Vista firewall enabled, you are asked to unblock the program. In order for the server to listen on a specific port, you have to allow this. With the firewall settings, you can also configure an exception for specific port numbers used during development.

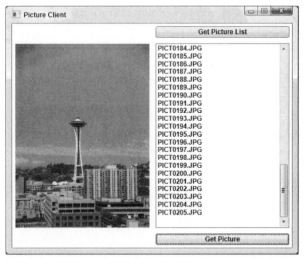

Figure 32-12

How It Works

The `TcpClient` class is used with the client to connect to the server. After creating the `TcpClient` object, the `Connect()` method initiates a connection to the server. The `Connect()` method requires an IP address and a port number. The IP address is read from the `IPHostEntry` variable host. The `IPHostEntry` that contains all IP addresses of the server is returned from the `Dns` class's `GetHostEntry()` method. The server's name is read from the application configuration file with `Properties.Settings.Default.Server`:

```
TcpClient client = new TcpClient();
IPHostEntry host = Dns.GetHostEntry(
        Properties.Settings.Default.Server);
client.Connect(host.AddressList[0],
        Properties.Settings.Default.ServerPort);
```

Using a `NetworkStream`, data can now be sent to the server. The `NetworkStream` object can be accessed using the `GetStream()` method of the `TcpClient` object. Data to be written can now be sent to the server with the `NetworkStream` method. Because the `Write()` method requires a byte array, the string `"LIST"` is converted to a byte array with the `Encoding` class. `Encoding.ASCII` returns an ASCII `Encoding` object. With this object, the `GetBytes()` method is used to convert the string to a byte array:

```
NetworkStream clientStream = client.GetStream();
string request = "LIST";
byte[] requestBuffer = Encoding.ASCII.GetBytes(request);
clientStream.Write(requestBuffer, 0, requestBuffer.Length);
```

The data returned from the server is read with the `clientStream` object's `Read()` method. Because the amount of data to be received from the server is unknown, a `do while` loop is used to read data as long as there is any. The data read is appended to a `MemoryStream`, which automatically resizes:

```
byte[] responseBuffer = new byte[bufferSize];
MemoryStream memStream = new MemoryStream();
int bytesRead = 0;
do
{
    bytesRead = clientStream.Read(responseBuffer, 0, bufferSize);
    memStream.Write(responseBuffer, 0, bytesRead);
} while (bytesRead > 0);
```

The picture is read in a similar way as the file data. The memory stream that contains the picture data is converted to an image with the WPF `BitmapImage` class. The image is then assigned to the `Source` property of the `PictureBox`, so it is displayed in the form:

```
BitmapImage bitmapImage = new BitmapImage();
memStream.Seek(0, SeekOrigin.Begin);
bitmapImage.BeginInit();
bitmapImage.StreamSource = memStream;
bitmapImage.EndInit();

pictureBox.Source = bitmapImage;
```

Summary

In this chapter, you learned how to use classes from the `System.Net` and `System.Net.Sockets` namespaces to create networking applications. The `WebClient` class can be used to access Web servers. The simple FTP client you created illustrated how to use the `FtpWebRequest` and `FtpWebResponse` classes, which provide more control than the `WebClient` class. You also saw that, in addition to the `FtpWebRequest` class, the `HttpWebRequest` and `FileWebRequest` classes can be used.

Because writing a server is not possible with the `FtpWebRequest` and `FtpWebResponse` classes, you need classes from the `System.Net.Sockets` namespace instead. You learned how to create a TCP server with the `TcpListener` class and a client application with the `TcpClient` class.

In this chapter, you learned the following:

❑ How to use the `Dns` class for name lookups.

❑ What the client sends with a HTTP request.

❑ How to do HTTP requests with the `WebClient` class.

❑ How to work with the `WebRequest` class, and in particular how to get files from an FTP server with the `FtpWebRequest` class.

❑ How to use a custom protocol with classes from the namespace `System.Net.Sockets`.

Exercises

1. Extend the FTP client application that makes use of the `FtpWebRequest` and `FtpWebResponse` classes so that it not only downloads files from the FTP server, but also allows uploading files to the server. Add one more button to the form with the `Text` property set to `Upload File`, use the `OpenFileDialog` to ask the user for a file to upload, and then send a request to the server. For uploading files, the `WebRequestMethods` class offers the `Ftp.UploadFile` member.

2. Modify the Picture server and client applications that use the `TcpListener` and `TcpClient` classes so that it is possible to upload picture files from the client to the server.

Introduction to GDI+

In the previous chapter, the term GDI+ was briefly introduced when you looked at printing in the .NET Framework. This chapter provides a real introduction to programming using the Graphics Device Interface classes (GDI+), the drawing technology of the .NET Framework. Mapping applications, games, computer-aided design/computer-aided manufacturing (CAD/CAM), drawing programs, charting programs, and many other types of applications require developers to write graphics code for their Windows Forms applications. Writing custom controls can also require graphics code. With this latest class library, Microsoft has made writing graphics code easier than ever.

Writing graphics code is one of the most enjoyable programming tasks. It is very rewarding to change your code and immediately see the results in a visible form. Whether you are writing a custom graphics window that presents something in your application in a new and different way or writing a custom control that makes your application more stylish and more usable, your application will be well received by the general public.

This chapter first explains the mechanics of drawing using GDI+, and you write a few simple graphical example programs. Then you take a high-level look at some of the extensive capabilities of GDI+ such as clipping. After an overview of each of these topics, you look at the classes you can use to implement the features. Knowing what you can do and understanding the class hierarchy is half the battle.

This chapter covers the following:

- ❑ Drawing surfaces as encapsulated by the Graphics class.
- ❑ Colors as defined by the Color structure.
- ❑ Drawing lines and shapes.
- ❑ Drawing text and images.
- ❑ Drawing into images (double-buffering).

Overview of Graphical Drawing

The first thing to learn about writing graphics code is that Windows does not remember what an open window looks like if that window is obscured by other windows. When a covered window becomes visible, Windows in effect tells your application, "Your window (or some portion of it) has now become visible. Will you please draw it?" You only need to draw the contents of your window. Windows itself takes care of the border of the window, the title bar, and all the other window features.

When you create a window into which you want to draw, you typically declare a class that derives from `System.Windows.Forms.Form`. If you are writing a custom control, you declare a class that derives from `System.Windows.Forms.UserControl`. In either case, you override the virtual function `OnPaint()`. Windows calls this function whenever any portion of your window needs to be repainted.

With this event, a `PaintEventArgs` class is passed as an argument. There are two pertinent pieces of information in `PaintEventArgs`: a `Graphics` object and a `ClipRectangle`. You explore the `Graphics` class first and touch on clipping near the end of the chapter.

The Graphics Class

The `Graphics` class encapsulates a GDI+ drawing surface. There are three basic types of drawing surfaces:

❑ Windows and controls on the screen.

❑ Pages being sent to a printer.

❑ Bitmaps and images in memory.

The `Graphics` class provides functions to draw on any of these drawing surfaces. Among other capabilities, you can use it to draw arcs, curves, Bezier curves, ellipses, images, lines, rectangles, and text.

You can get a `Graphics` object for the window in two different ways. The first is to override the `OnPaint()` method. The `Form` class inherits the `OnPaint()` method from `Control`, and this method is the event handler for the `Paint` event that is raised whenever the control is redrawn. You can get the `Graphics` object from the `PaintEventArgs` class that is passed in with the event:

```
protected override void OnPaint(PaintEventArgs e)
{
    Graphics g = e.Graphics;

    // Do our drawing here.

}
```

At other times, you might want to draw directly into your window without waiting for the `Paint` event to be raised. This would be the case if you were writing code for selecting some graphical object on the window (similar to selecting icons in Windows Explorer) or dragging some object with the mouse. You can get a Graphics object by calling the CreateGraphics() method on the form, which is another method that Form inherits from Control:

```
protected void Form1_Click (object sender, System.EventArgs e)
{
    Graphics g = this.CreateGraphics();

    // Do our drawing here.

    g.Dispose();    // this is important
}
```

Building an application that handles dragging and dropping is a somewhat involved affair and is beyond the scope of this chapter. In any case, this is a less common technique. You will do almost all of your drawing in response to an OnPaint() method.

Disposing of Objects

Everybody is familiar with the behavior of Windows when it runs out of resources. It starts to run very slowly, and sometimes applications are not drawn correctly. Well-behaved applications free up their resources after they are done with them. When developing applications using the .NET Framework, there are several data types on which it is important to call the Dispose() method; otherwise, some resources will not be freed. These classes implement the IDisposable interface, and Graphics is one of these classes.

When you get a Graphics object from the OnPaint() method, it was not created by you, so it is not your responsibility to call Dispose(). But if you call CreateGraphics(), this is your responsibility.

> It is important to call the Dispose() method if you get a Graphics object by calling CreateGraphics().

The Dispose() method is automatically called in the destructor for the various classes that implement IDisposable. You might think that this removes your responsibility to call Dispose(), but it does not. That's because only the garbage collector (GC) ever calls the destructor, and you cannot guarantee when the GC will run. In particular, on a Windows 9X operating system with a lot of memory, the GC may run very infrequently, and all resources may very well be used up before the GC runs. Although running out of memory triggers the GC to run, running out of resources does not. Windows 2000 and Windows XP are much less sensitive to running out of resources, and according to their specifications, these two operating systems do not have any finite limits on these types of resources; however, I have seen Windows 2000 misbehave when too many applications were open, and closing some applications quickly restored correct behavior. In any case, it is better coding practice to manually dispose of any resource-hungry objects correctly and in a timely fashion.

There is another, easier way to deal with objects that need to be disposed of properly. You can use the `using` construct, which automatically calls `Dispose()` when an object goes out of scope. The following code shows the correct use of the `using` keyword in this context:

```
using (Graphics g = this.CreateGraphics())
{
    g.DrawLine(Pens.Black, new Point(0, 0), new Point(3, 5));
}
```

According to the documentation, the preceding code is precisely equivalent to the following:

```
Graphics g = this.CreateGraphics();
try
{
    g.DrawLine(Pens.Black, new Point(0, 0), new Point(3, 5));
}
finally
{
    if (g != null)
        ((IDisposable)g).Dispose();
}
```

Don't confuse this use of the `using` keyword with the `using` directive that creates an alias for a namespace or that permits the use of types in a namespace, such that you do not need to fully qualify the use of the type. This is an entirely separate use of the `using` keyword — if you like, the block of code enclosed by the `using` keyword can be referred to as a `using` block.

Examples in this chapter handle calls to `Dispose()` using both styles. Sometimes, you call `Dispose()` directly, and other times you use the `using` block. The latter is a much cleaner solution, as you can see from the preceding code snippets, but there is no preferred method.

Before jumping into the first example, there are two other aspects of drawing graphics to examine — the coordinate system and colors.

Coordinate System

When designing a program that draws a complicated, intricate graphic, it is very important that your code draws exactly what you intend, and nothing but what you intend. It is possible for a single misplaced pixel to have a negative influence on the visual impact of a graphic, so it is important to understand exactly what pixels are drawn when invoking drawing operations. This is most important when creating custom controls, which include a lot of rectangles and horizontal and vertical lines. A line that runs one pixel too long or falls one pixel short is very noticeable. However, this is somewhat less important with curves, diagonal lines, and other graphical operations.

GDI+ has a coordinate system based on imaginary grid lines that run through the center of the pixels. These lines are numbered starting at zero — the intersection of these grid lines in the upper-left pixel in any coordinate space is point X = 0, Y = 0. As a shorter notation, we can say point 1, 2, which is shorthand for saying X = 1, Y = 2. Each window into which you draw has its own coordinate space. If you create a custom control that can be used in other windows, this custom control itself has its own coordinate space. In other words, the upper-left pixel of the custom control is point 0, 0 when drawing in that custom control. You don't need to worry about where the custom control is placed on its containing window.

When drawing lines, GDI+ centers the pixels drawn on the grid line that you specify. When drawing a horizontal line with integer coordinates, you can consider half of each pixel to fall above the imaginary grid line, and half of each pixel to fall below it. When you draw a horizontal line that is one-pixel wide from point 1,1 to point 4,1, the pixels shown in Figure 33-1 will be drawn.

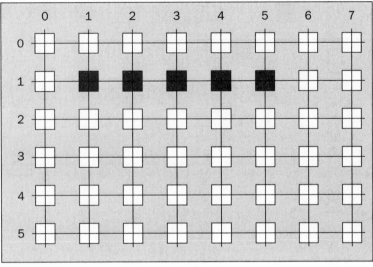

Figure 33-1

When you draw a vertical line that is one-pixel wide and four pixels long, from point 1, 1 to point 1, 4, the pixels shown in Figure 33-2 are colored in.

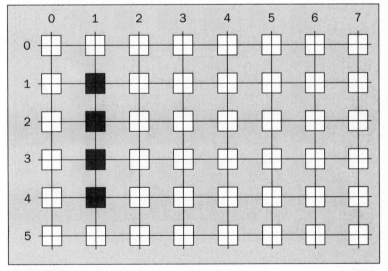

Figure 33-2

When you draw a diagonal line from point 1, 0 to point 4, 3, the pixels shown in Figure 33-3 are to be drawn.

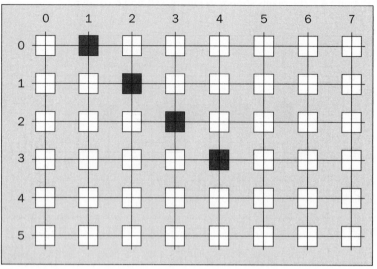

Figure 33-3

When you draw a rectangle with the upper-left corner at 1, 0 and a size of 5, 4, the rectangle shown in Figure 33-4 is drawn.

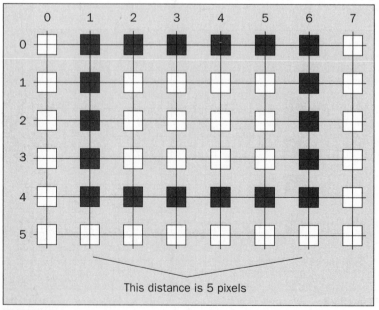

This distance is 5 pixels

Figure 33-4

Note something interesting here. A width of 5 was specified, and there are 6 pixels drawn in the horizontal direction. However, if you consider the grid lines running through the pixels, this rectangle is only 5 pixels wide, and the line drawn falls half a pixel outside and half a pixel inside of the grid line that you specified.

There is more to the story than this. If you draw with anti-aliasing, other pixels will be *half* colored in, creating the appearance of a smooth line, and partially avoiding having a *stair step* appearance on diagonal lines.

Figure 33-5 shows a line drawn without anti-aliasing.

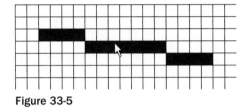

Figure 33-5

Figure 33-6 shows the same line drawn with anti-aliasing.

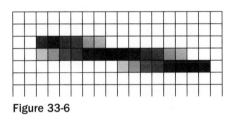

Figure 33-6

When viewed at a high resolution, this line will appear much smoother, without a stair step effect. Understanding the relationship between the coordinates passed to drawing functions and the resulting effect on the drawing surface makes it easy to visualize exactly which pixels will be affected by a given call to a drawing function.

There are three structs that you will use often to specify coordinates when drawing: Point, Size, and Rectangle.

Point

GDI+ uses Point to represent a single point with integer coordinates. This is a point in a two-dimensional plane — a specification of a single pixel. Many GDI+ functions, such as DrawLine(), take a Point as an argument. You declare and construct a Point struct as follows:

```
Point p = new Point(1, 1);
```

There are public properties, X and Y, to get and set the X and Y coordinates of a Point.

Size

GDI+ uses `Size` to represent a size in pixels. A `Size` struct contains both width and height. You declare and construct a `Size` as follows:

```
Size s = new Size(5, 5);
```

There are public properties, `Height` and `Width`, to get and set the height and width of a `Size`.

Rectangle

GDI+ uses this structure in many different places to specify the coordinates of a rectangle. A `Point` structure defines the upper-left corner of the rectangle and a `Size` structure defines its size. There are two constructors for `Rectangle`. One takes as arguments the X position, the Y position, the width, and the height. The other takes a `Point` and a `Size` structure. Two examples of declaring and constructing a `Rectangle` are as follows:

```
Rectangle r1 = new Rectangle(1, 2, 5, 6);

Point p = new Point(1, 2);
Size s = new Size(5, 6);
Rectangle r2 = new Rectangle(p, s);
```

There are public properties to get and set all aspects of the location and size of a `Rectangle`. In addition, there are other useful properties and methods to perform such tasks as determining whether the rectangle intersects with another rectangle, taking the intersection of two rectangles, and taking the union of two rectangles.

GraphicsPaths

There are two more important data types that you can use as arguments to various drawing functions in GDI+. The `GraphicsPath` class represents a series of connected lines and curves. When constructing a path, you can add lines, Bezier curves, arcs, pie shapes, polygons, rectangles, and more. After constructing a complex path, you can draw the path with one operation: a call to `DrawPath()`. You can fill the path with a call to `FillPath()`.

You construct a `GraphicsPath` using an array of points and `PathTypes`. `PathTypes` is a byte array, where each element in the array corresponds to an element in the array of points and provides additional information about how the path is to be constructed through each particular point. The information about the path through a point can be gleaned by using the `PathPointType` enumeration. For instance, if the point is the beginning of the path, the path type for that point is `PathPointType.Start`. If the point is a junction between two lines, the path type for that point is `PathPointType.Line`. If the point is used to construct a Bezier curve from the points before and after, then the path type is `PathPointType.Bezier`.

In the following Try It Out, you create a `GraphicsPath` object, and draw it to a window.

Try It Out   **Creating a Graphics Path**

Follow these steps to create and draw a `GraphicsPath` object:

1. Create a new Windows application called DrawingPaths in the directory
    C:\BegVCSharp\Chapter33.

2. Add the following `using` directive for `System.Drawing.Drawing2D` to the top of the code:

```
using System;
using System.Collections.Generic;
using System.ComponentModel;
using System.Data;
using System.Drawing;
using System.Text;
using System.Windows.Forms;
using System.Drawing.Drawing2D;
```

3. Enter the following code into the body of `Form1`:

```
protected override void OnPaint (PaintEventArgs e)
{
    GraphicsPath path;
    path = new GraphicsPath(new Point[]{ new Point(10, 10),
                                         new Point(150, 10),
                                         new Point(200, 150),
                                         new Point(10, 150),
                                         new Point(200, 160)},
                   new byte[] {(byte)PathPointType.Start,
                               (byte)PathPointType.Line,
                               (byte)PathPointType.Line,
                               (byte)PathPointType.Line,
                               (byte)PathPointType.Line });
    e.Graphics.DrawPath(Pens.Black, path);
}
```

4. Run the application. You should see the path shown in Figure 33-7.

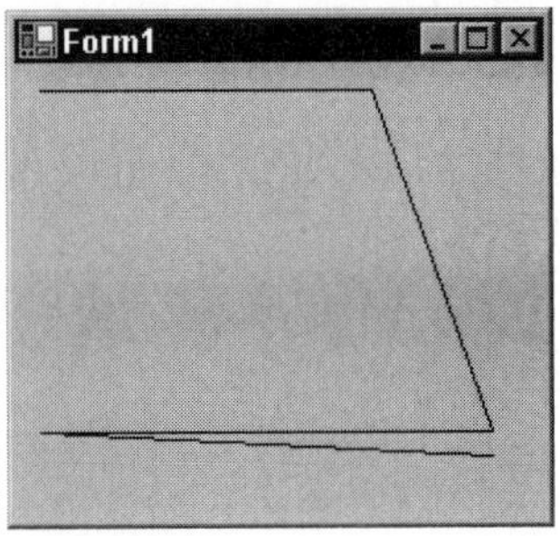

Figure 33-7

How It Works

The code to construct this path is quite complex. The constructor for `GraphicsPath` takes two arguments. The first argument is a `Point` array; here, you use C# syntax for declaring and initializing the array in the same place, and create each new `Point` object as you go:

```
new Point[]{
    new Point(10, 10),
    new Point(150, 10),
    new Point(200, 150),
    new Point(10, 150),
    new Point(200, 160)
}
```

The second argument is an array of bytes that you also construct right in place:

```
new byte[] {
    (byte)PathPointType.Start,
    (byte)PathPointType.Line,
    (byte)PathPointType.Line,
    (byte)PathPointType.Line,
    (byte)PathPointType.Line
}
```

Finally, you call the `DrawPath()` method:

```
e.Graphics.DrawPath(Pens.Black, path);
```

Regions

The `Region` class is a complex graphical shape comprising rectangles and paths. After constructing a `Region`, you can draw that region using the method `FillRegion()`. In the following Try It Out, you create a `Region` object and draw it to a window.

Try It Out   Creating a Region

The following code creates a region and adds a `Rectangle` and a `GraphicsPath` to it, and then fills that region with the color blue:

1. Create a new Windows application called DrawingRegions in the directory C:\BegVCSharp\Chapter33.

2. Add a `using` directive for `System.Drawing.Drawing2D` to the top of the code:

```
using System;
using System.Collections.Generic;
using System.ComponentModel;
using System.Data;
```

```
using System.Drawing;
using System.Text;
using System.Windows.Forms;
using System.Drawing.Drawing2D;
```

3. Enter the following code into the body of `Form1`:

```
protected override void OnPaint ( PaintEventArgs e)
{
    Rectangle r1 = new Rectangle(10, 10, 50, 50);
    Rectangle r2 = new Rectangle(40, 40, 50, 50);
    Region r = new Region(r1);
    r.Union(r2);

    GraphicsPath path = new GraphicsPath(new Point[] {
                                new Point(45, 45),
                                new Point(145, 55),
                                new Point(200, 150),
                                new Point(75, 150),
                                new Point(45, 45)
                                }, new byte[] {
                                    (byte)PathPointType.Start,
                                    (byte)PathPointType.Bezier,
                                    (byte)PathPointType.Bezier,
                                    (byte)PathPointType.Bezier,
                                    (byte)PathPointType.Line
                                });
    r.Union(path);
    e.Graphics.FillRegion(Brushes.Blue, r);
}
```

4. When you run this code, it will display as shown in Figure 33-8.

Figure 33-8

How It Works

The code to construct a region is also quite complex, though the most complex part of the example is constructing any paths that will go into the region, and you have already seen how to construct these from the previous example.

Constructing regions consists of constructing rectangles and paths, before calling the Union() method. If you wanted the intersection of a rectangle and a path, you could have used the Intersection() method instead of the Union() method.

Further information on paths and regions is not needed for an introduction to GDI+, so you will not explore them in any more detail here.

Colors

Many of the drawing operations in GDI+ involve a color. When drawing a line or rectangle, you need to specify what color it should be.

In GDI+, colors are encapsulated in the Color structure. You can create a color by passing red, green, and blue values to a function of the Color structure, but this is almost never necessary. The Color structure contains approximately 150 properties that get a large variety of preset colors. Forget about red, green, blue, yellow, and black — if you need to do some drawing in the color of LightGoldenrodYellow or LavenderBlush, there is a predefined color made just for you! You declare a variable of type Color and initialize it with a color from the Color structure as follows:

```
Color redColor = Color.Red;
Color anotherColor = Color.LightGoldenrodYellow;
```

You're almost ready to do some drawing, but here are a couple of notes before continuing.

Another way to represent a color is to break it into three components: hue, saturation, and brightness. The Color structure contains utility methods to do this — namely, GetHue(), GetSaturation(), and GetBrightness().

At this point, you can create a color selection dialog that you can use to see the relationship between colors defined using red, green, and blue, and colors defined using hue, saturation, and brightness. Here's how:

1. In a new Windows application, drag a ColorDialog control onto your form, and add a call to this.colorDialog1.ShowDialog(), after the InitializeComponent() call:

```
public Form1()
{
  InitializeComponent();
  this.colorDialog1.ShowDialog();
}
```

When you put up the form, the color selection dialog will also be put up.

2. Run the application and click the Define Custom Colors button. A dialog will appear from which you can pick a color using the mouse and see the RGB values for the color. You can also get the hue, saturation, and luminosity values for the color (where luminosity corresponds to brightness). You can also directly enter the RGB values and see the resulting color.

Colors in GDI+ have a fourth component, alpha. Using this component, you can set the opacity of the color, which enables you to create fade in/fade out effects such as the menu effects in Windows 2000 and Windows XP/Vista. Explaining how to use the alpha component is beyond the scope of this chapter.

Drawing Lines Using the Pen Class

The first example here draws lines. In the following Try It Out, you draw lines using the Pen class, which enables you to define the color, width, and pattern of the line that your code is drawing. The color and width properties are obvious, but the pattern of a line indicates whether the line is a solid line or is composed of dashes and dots. The Pen class is in the System.Drawing namespace.

Try It Out   **Using the Pen**

Follow these steps to draw some lines in a window using the Pen class:

1. Create a new Windows application called DrawingLines in the directory C:\BegVCSharp\Chapter33.

2. Enter the following code into the body of Form1:

```
protected override void OnPaint(PaintEventArgs e)
{
    Graphics g = e.Graphics;

    using (Pen blackPen = new Pen(Color.Black, 1))
    {
        if (ClientRectangle.Height/10>0)
        {
            for (int y = 0; y < ClientRectangle.Height;
                y += ClientRectangle.Height / 10)
            {
                g.DrawLine(blackPen, new Point(0, 0),
                        new Point(ClientRectangle.Width, y));
            }
        }
    }
}
```

3. Press F5 to compile and run the code. When you run it, it will create the window shown in Figure 33-9.

Figure 33-9

How It Works

The `Graphics` class was introduced earlier in the chapter. The first thing that you do in the `OnPaint()` method is get the `Graphics` object from the `PaintEventArgs` parameter:

```
Graphics g = e.Graphics;
```

Because you are passed the reference to the `Graphics` object, and you did not create it, you do not need to (and should not) manually call `Dispose()` on it. However, because you are using a potentially resource-hungry `Pen` object for this example, I have wrapped the rest of the code in a `using` block, as described earlier, which will ensure that the object is destroyed as soon as possible.

When you construct the pen, you pass as parameters to the constructor a color and a width for the pen. In this example, the color is black, and the width is one. This is the line of code to construct the pen:

```
using (Pen blackPen = new Pen(Color.Black, 1))
```

Every window into which you can draw has a client area, which is a rectangle that exists within the border and defines the exact area into which you can draw. You can get the client area from `ClientRectangle`, which is a public, read-only property of the form (inherited from `Control`). It contains the size (that is, the width and height) of the client area of the window into which you are drawing. The following code starts a loop that goes from zero up to the height of the client area (given by `ClientRectangle.Height`) in increments of 10. Note that you first check that `ClientRectangle.Height/10` is bigger than zero — without this, the loop will run indefinitely if the form is resized below a certain height. (Because `ClientRectangle.Height/10` is the loop increment, if this is zero, you'll loop forever.)

```
if (ClientRectangle.Height/10>0)
{
    for (int y = 0; y < ClientRectangle.Height;
        y += ClientRectangle.Height / 10)
```

Now you can draw the lines — when you draw each line, you pass the Pen that you just created, along with the starting point and ending point of the line:

```
g.DrawLine(blackPen, new Point(0, 0),
             new Point(ClientRectangle.Width, y));
```

> **Always call** Dispose() **on Pen objects.**

Just as for Graphics objects, it is important to either call Dispose() on Pen objects when you are finished with them or use the using block; otherwise, your application can deplete the Windows resources.

In this example, you constructed a Pen, but there is an easier way to get a Pen. The Pens class contains properties for getting approximately 150 pens, one for each of the predefined colors that you learned about previously. The following version of the example works identically to the previous one, but instead of constructing a Pen, you get it from the Pens class:

```
protected override void OnPaint(PaintEventArgs e)
{
    if (ClientRectangle.Height/10>0)
    {
        for (int y = 0; y < ClientRectangle.Height;
            y += ClientRectangle.Height / 10)
        {
            e.Graphics.DrawLine(Pens.Black, new Point(0, 0),
                                new Point(ClientRectangle.Width, y));
        }
    }
}
```

In this case, you did not create the Pen, so it is not necessary to call Dispose().

There are many more features of the Pen class. You could create a pen to draw a dashed line, or you could create a pen with a width thicker than one pixel. There is an Alignment property of the Pen class that enables you to define whether the pen is drawn to the left or right of (or above or below) the line that you specify. By setting the StartCap and EndCap properties, you can specify that your line should end with an arrow, a diamond, a square, or should be rounded off. You can even program a custom start cap and end cap using the CustomStartCap and CustomEndCap properties. After learning about images, you will learn how to specify a Brush with a Pen so that you can draw the line using a bitmap instead of a solid color.

Drawing Shapes Using the Brush Class

The next example uses the `Brush` class to draw shapes such as rectangles, ellipses, pie charts, and polygons. The `Brush` class is an abstract base class. To instantiate a `Brush` object, you use classes derived from `Brush` such as `SolidBrush`, `TextureBrush`, and `LinearGradientBrush`.

The `Brush` and `SolidBrush` classes are in the `System.Drawing` namespace. However, the `TextureBrush` and `LinearGradientBrush` are in the `System.Drawing.Drawing2D` namespace. This is what each brush class achieves:

❑   `SolidBrush` fills a shape with a solid color.

❑   `TextureBrush` fills a shape with a bitmap. When constructing this brush, you also specify a bounding rectangle and a wrap mode. The bounding rectangle specifies what portion of the bitmap to use for the brush — you don't need to use the entire bitmap if you don't want to. The wrap mode has a number of options, including `Tile`, which tiles the texture, and `TileFlipX`, `TileFlipY`, and `TileFlipXY`, which tile while flipping the image for successive tiles. You can create very interesting and imaginative effects using the `TextureBrush`.

❑   `LinearGradientBrush` encapsulates a brush that draws a gradient of two colors, with the first color transitioning to the second color at a specified angle. You specify angles in terms of degrees. An angle of zero specifies that the colors will transition from left to right. An angle of 90 degrees means that the colors will transition from top to bottom.

One more brush to mention is the `PathGradientBrush`, which creates an elaborate shading effect whereby the shading runs from the center of the path to the edge of the path. This brush reminds me of when I was a child, and I would shade maps with colored pencils, making the color darker at the boundary between different states or countries.

> **Always call** `Dispose()` **on** `Brush` **objects.**

Just as for `Graphics` objects and `Pen` objects, it is important to call `Dispose()` on `Brush` objects that you create, or use the `using` block; otherwise, your application may deplete the Windows resources. In the following Try It Out, you will fill some shapes using brushes.

Try It Out   Using a Brush

Follow these steps to see brushes in action:

1. Create a new Windows application called UsingBrushes in the directory C:\BegVCSharp\Chapter33.

2. Add a using directive for `System.Drawing.Drawing2D` for the `LinearGradientBrush` to the top of the code:

```
using System;
using System.Collections.Generic;
using System.ComponentModel;
```

```
using System.Data;
using System.Drawing;
using System.Text;
using System.Windows.Forms;
using System.Drawing.Drawing2D;
```

3.   In the constructor of the Form1 class, add a call to SetStyle() after the call to
     InitializeComponent():

```
public Form1()
{
    InitializeComponent();
    SetStyle(ControlStyles.Opaque, true);

}
```

4.   Add an OnPaint() method to your class:

```
protected override void OnPaint(PaintEventArgs e)
{
    Graphics g = e.Graphics;
    g.FillRectangle(Brushes.White, ClientRectangle);
    g.FillRectangle(Brushes.Red, new Rectangle(10, 10, 50, 50));

    Brush linearGradientBrush = new LinearGradientBrush(
            new Rectangle(10, 60, 50, 50), Color.Blue, Color.White, 45);
    g.FillRectangle(linearGradientBrush, new Rectangle(10, 60, 50, 50));

    // Manually call Dispose().
    linearGradientBrush.Dispose();

    g.FillEllipse(Brushes.Aquamarine, new Rectangle(60, 20, 50, 30));
    g.FillPie(Brushes.Chartreuse, new Rectangle(60, 60, 50, 50), 90, 210);
    g.FillPolygon(Brushes.BlueViolet, new Point[] {
                            new Point(110, 10),
                            new Point(150, 10),
                            new Point(160, 40),
                            new Point(120, 20),
                            new Point(120, 60),
                            });
}
```

5.   When you compile and run this program, it will display as shown in Figure 33-10.

Figure 33-10

How It Works

The first thing to note is the call to `SetStyle()` in the form's constructor. `SetStyle()` is a method of the `Form` class:

```
SetStyle(ControlStyles.Opaque, true);
```

This method changes the behavior of the `Form` class so that it will not automatically draw the background of the window. If you include this line but don't draw the background of the window yourself, then anything underneath the window at the time of creation shows through, which is not what you want. Thus, your next task is to draw your own background onto the client area of the window.

Just as with the `Pens` class, there is a `Brushes` class that contains properties for getting approximately 150 brushes, one for each predefined color. You use this class to get most of the brushes in this example, with the exception of the `LinearGradientBrush`, which you create yourself.

The first call to `FillRectangle()` draws the background of the client area of your window:

```
g.FillRectangle(Brushes.White, ClientRectangle);
```

The creation of the `LinearGradientBrush` takes a rectangle, specifying its size, the two colors to be used for the gradient, and the angle (in this case, 45):

```
Brush linearGradientBrush = new LinearGradientBrush(
        new Rectangle(10, 60, 50, 50), Color.Blue, Color.White, 45);
g.FillRectangle(linearGradientBrush, new Rectangle(10, 60, 50, 50));
linearGradientBrush.Dispose();
```

When you specified the rectangle for the brush, you used a rectangle of width 50 and height 50, which is the same size as the rectangle used when you defined the brush. The result is that the brush area just fits the rectangle. Try changing the rectangle defined in the creation of the brush so that the width and height are 10 and see what happens. Also try changing the angle to different values to see the change in effect.

Drawing Text Using the Font Class

The next example uses the `Font` class to draw text. The `Font` class encapsulates the three main characteristics of a font, which are the font family, the font size, and the font style. The `Font` class is in the `System.Drawing` namespace.

According to the .NET documentation, a font family "abstracts a group of type faces having a similar basic design." This is a fancy way of saying that font families are things like Courier, Arial, or Times New Roman.

The font `Size` property represents the size of the font type. However, in the .NET Framework, this size is not strictly the point size. It can be the point size, but you can change a property called the `GraphicsUnit` via the `Unit` property, which defines the unit of measure for the font. To refresh your memory, one point is equal to 1/72 of an inch, so a 10-point font is 10/72 of an inch high. Based on the `GraphicsUnit` enumeration, you can specify the unit for the font as one of the following:

- ❏ point (1/72 of an inch)
- ❏ display (1/75 of an inch)
- ❏ document (1/300 of an inch)
- ❏ inch
- ❏ millimeter
- ❏ pixel

This means you have unprecedented flexibility in specifying the desired size of your font. One possible use for this might be if you are writing a text drawing routine that needs to work in an acceptable way on very high-resolution displays, low-resolution displays, and printers.

When drawing text, given a specific font, and given a specific drawing surface, you often need to know the width in pixels of a specified string of text. It is pretty clear why different fonts will have an effect on the width in pixels of a string — a smaller font will result in a width of fewer pixels. However, it is equally as important to know the drawing surface, because the pixel resolutions of different drawing surfaces are different. Typically, the screen has 72 pixels per inch. Printers can be 300 pixels per inch, 600 pixels per inch, and sometimes even more. Use the `MeasureString()` method of the `Graphics` object to calculate the width of a string for a given font.

The font `Style` property refers to whether the type is italicized, emboldened, struck-through, or underlined.

> **Always call** `Dispose()` **on** `Font` **objects.**

It is important to call `Dispose()` on `Font` objects that you create, or use the `using` block: otherwise, your application may deplete Windows resources.

When drawing text, you use a `Rectangle` to specify the bounding coordinates of the text to be drawn. Typically, the height of this rectangle should be the font's height or a multiple of the font's height. This would be different only when drawing some special effect using clipped text.

The `StringFormat` class encapsulates text layout information, including alignment and line spacing. The following example shows right and centered text justification using the `StringFormat` class. In this Try It Out, you create a `Font` object and draw some text with it.

Try It Out   **Drawing Text**

Follow these steps to practice drawing text in a variety of ways:

1. Create a new Windows application called DrawText in the directory
   C:\BegVCSharp\Chapter33.

2. In the constructor of the `Form1` class, add a call to `SetStyle()` after the call to
   `InitializeComponent()`. You also change the bounds of the window to provide enough
   room to display the text you want to display. The modified constructor is as follows:

```csharp
public Form1()
{
    InitializeComponent();
    SetStyle(ControlStyles.Opaque, true);
    Bounds = new Rectangle(0, 0, 500, 300);

}
```

3. Add an `OnPaint()` method to your class:

```csharp
protected override void OnPaint(PaintEventArgs e)
{
    Graphics g = e.Graphics;
    int y = 0;

    g.FillRectangle(Brushes.White, ClientRectangle);

    // Draw left-justified text.
    Rectangle rect = new Rectangle(0, y, 400, Font.Height);
    g.DrawRectangle(Pens.Blue, rect);
    g.DrawString("This text is left justified.", Font,
                 Brushes.Black, rect);
    y += Font.Height + 20;

    // Draw right-justified text.
    Font aFont = new Font("Arial", 16, FontStyle.Bold | FontStyle.Italic);
    rect = new Rectangle(0, y, 400, aFont.Height);
    g.DrawRectangle(Pens.Blue, rect);

    StringFormat sf = new StringFormat();
    sf.Alignment = StringAlignment.Far;
    g.DrawString("This text is right justified.", aFont, Brushes.Blue,
                 rect, sf);
    y += aFont.Height + 20;
    // Manually call Dispose().
    aFont.Dispose();

    // Draw centered text.
    Font cFont = new Font("Courier New", 12, FontStyle.Underline);
    rect = new Rectangle(0, y, 400, cFont.Height);
    g.DrawRectangle(Pens.Blue, rect);
    sf = new StringFormat();
```

```
    sf.Alignment = StringAlignment.Center;
    g.DrawString("This text is centered  and underlined.", cFont,
                 Brushes.Red, rect, sf);
    y += cFont.Height + 20;

    // Manually call Dispose().
    cFont.Dispose();

    // Draw multiline text.
    Font trFont = new Font("Times New Roman", 12);
    rect = new Rectangle(0, y, 400, trFont.Height * 3);
    g.DrawRectangle(Pens.Blue, rect);
    String longString = "This text is much longer, and drawn ";
    longString += "into a rectangle that is higher than ";
    longString += "one line, so that it will wrap.  It is ";
    longString += "very easy to wrap text using GDI+.";
    g.DrawString(longString, trFont, Brushes.Black, rect);

    // Manually call Dispose().
    trFont.Dispose();
}
```

4. When you compile and run the code, it will create the window shown in Figure 33-11.

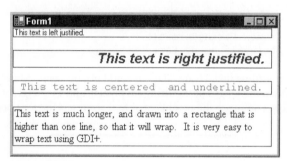

Figure 33-11

How It Works

This example contains a few of the most common text drawing operations. As usual, you assign a reference to the `Graphics` object to a local variable, for your convenience. You also paint the background of the window white.

When drawing the text, you calculate the bounding rectangle for your text. You get the height of the font using the `Height` property. For illustrative purposes, you draw this rectangle in blue so that the bounding rectangle of your text is very clear. When you draw the text, you pass the text, the font, a brush, and a bounding rectangle:

```
    // Draw left-justified text.
    Rectangle rect = new Rectangle(0, y, 400, Font.Height);
    g.DrawRectangle(Pens.Blue, rect);
    g.DrawString("This text is left justified.", Font,
                 Brushes.Black, rect);
```

You specify only the rectangle in which the text will appear. The baseline of a font is the imaginary line that most of the characters of the font "sit" on. GDI+ and the font itself determine where the actual baseline will go — you have no control over that.

When you draw the text, you pass a brush to the `DrawString()` function. In this example, you pass only brushes that have a solid color. You could just as easily have passed other types of brushes, such as a gradient brush. After you look at working with images in the next section, I will demonstrate drawing text using a `TextureBrush`.

The first time that you draw text in this example, you use the default font for the form. This font is referenced in the `Font` property, which is inherited from `Control`:

```
g.DrawString("This is a left justified string.", Font,
             Brushes.Black, rect);
```

The next time you draw text in this example, you create a new instance of a `Font`:

```
Font aFont = new Font("Arial", 16, FontStyle.Bold | FontStyle.Italic);
```

This example shows not only how to create a new instance of a font, but also how to give it a style. In this case, the style is bold and italic.

The example also shows creating a `StringFormat` object, so that you can draw right-justified and centered text. In GDI+, right-justified text alignment is referred to as `Far` alignment. Left-justified text is `Near` alignment:

```
StringFormat sf = new StringFormat();
sf.Alignment = StringAlignment.Far;
```

Finally, you draw some multiline text. Using GDI+, it could not be easier. Merely specify a rectangle where the width is less than the length of the string (in pixels), and the height is sufficient to draw multiple lines. In this case, you made the height equal to three times the font height.

Drawing Using Images

Images have many uses in GDI+. Of course, you can draw images into your windows, but you can also create a brush (`TextureBrush`) with an image and draw shapes that are then filled in with the image. You can create a pen from the `TextureBrush` and draw lines using the image. You can supply a `TextureBrush` when drawing text, and the text will then be drawn using the image. The `Image` class is in the `System.Drawing` namespace.

Sometimes the drawing you wish to create is very elaborate and intricate and takes quite a bit of time to draw, even with today's fast machines. It is not a pleasing effect to see the graphic "creep" onto the screen as it is being drawn. Examples of these types of applications are mapping applications and complex CAD/CAM applications. In this technique, instead of drawing into a window, you draw into an image, and after drawing into the image is completed, you draw the image to the window. This technique is known as *double-buffering*. Certain other graphics techniques involve drawing in layers, where first you draw the background, then you draw objects on top of the background, and finally you draw some text on top of the objects. If this drawing is done directly to the screen, users will see a flickering effect. Double-buffering eliminates this flickering effect. You look at a double-buffering example a bit later.

`Image` itself is an abstract class. It has two descendants: `Bitmap` and `Metafile`. The `Bitmap` class is a general-purpose image, with height and width properties. The examples in this section use the `Bitmap` class. You will load a `Bitmap` image from a file and draw it. You will also create a brush from it and use that brush to create a pen to draw lines, and use the brush to draw some text. You look at the `Metafile` class near the end of this chapter, when you get an overview of the advanced capabilities of GDI+.

> **Always call** `Dispose()` **on** `Image` **objects.**

Remember that it is important to call `Dispose()` on `Image` objects that you create, or use the `using` blocks; otherwise, your application may deplete the Windows resources.

There are several possible sources for a bitmap. You can load the bitmap from a file or create the bitmap from another existing image, or it can be created as an empty image onto which you can draw. When you read the image from a file, it can be in the JPEG, GIF, or BMP format. The following Try It Out demonstrates how to read an image from a file and draw it in a window.

Try It Out   Reading and Drawing an Image

The following, very simple example reads an image from a file and draws it in a window:

1. Create a new Windows application called DrawImage in the directory C:\BegVCSharp\Chapter33.

2. Declare a private variable in your `Form1` class to hold the image after you read it from a file. After the declaration of the components variable, add the declaration of `theImage` as follows:

```
partial class Form1 : Form
{
    private Image theImage;
```

3. Modify the constructor so that it appears as follows:

```
public Form1()
{
    InitializeComponent();
    SetStyle(ControlStyles.Opaque, true);
    theImage = new Bitmap("Person.bmp");
}
```

4. Now add an `OnPaintEvent()` method to your class:

```
protected override void OnPaint(PaintEventArgs e)
{
    Graphics g = e.Graphics;

    g.DrawImage(theImage, ClientRectangle);
}
```

5. Dispose of the `Image` that is stored in a member variable of your class. Modify the `Dispose()` method of the form class. Note that with Visual Studio 2008, the `Dispose()` method is in the file `Form1.Designer.cs`. The easiest way to open the file is to click the Show All Files button on the toolbar at the top of the Solution Explorer window. Here is the function:

```
protected override void Dispose( bool disposing )
{
    if (disposing)
    {
        theImage.Dispose();
    }
    if (disposing && (components != null))
    {
        components.Dispose();
    }
    base.Dispose(disposing);
}
```

Before running this example, you must get the BMP file called `Person.bmp` and place it in the DrawImage\bin\Debug directory. The `Person.bmp` file can be found in the code download, or you can use another bitmap you have, but remember to change the line

```
theImage = new Bitmap("Person.bmp");
```

that you added in step 3 to hold the filename of your own bitmap. When you compile and run this code, you should see the image shown in Figure 33-12.

Figure 33-12

How It Works

In the constructor, you instantiate a `Bitmap` object and assign it to the `Image` variable you declared. Then, in the `OnPaint()` method, you draw the image. When you draw the image, you pass a `Rectangle` as one of the arguments to the `DrawImage()` method. If the image is not the same size as the rectangle that you pass to `DrawImage()`, GDI+ automatically resizes the image to fit in the specified rectangle. To ensure that GDI+ will not resize the image, pass the size of the image, retrieved from the `Width` and `Height` properties, to the `DrawImage()` method.

Drawing with a Texture Brush

You will now create a `TextureBrush` from the image you have just used, and look at the following three different examples of its use:

❑ Drawing an ellipse

❑ Creating a `Pen`

❑ Drawing text

In the following Try It Out, you start with the previous code example and make a few modifications to it.

Try It Out   **Drawing an Ellipse with an Image**

Follow these steps to draw some text using a `TextureBrush`:

1. Starting with the code in the previous DrawImage example, add another `Image` variable declaration to the `Form1` class:

```
partial class Form1 : Form
{
    private Image theImage;
    private Image smallImage;
```

2. In the form's constructor, create `smallImage` from `theImage`. When you create it, you specify a rectangle that is half the height and half the width of `theImage`. This creates a smaller version of the original image:

```
public Form1()
{
    InitializeComponent();
    SetStyle(ControlStyles.Opaque, true);
    theImage = new Bitmap("Person.bmp");
    smallImage = new Bitmap(theImage,
            new Size(theImage.Width / 2, theImage.Height / 2));

}
```

3. Replace the `OnPaint()` method with this one:

```
protected override void OnPaint(PaintEventArgs e)
{
    Graphics g = e.Graphics;

    g.FillRectangle(Brushes.White, ClientRectangle);

    Brush tBrush = new TextureBrush(smallImage, new Rectangle(0, 0,
                    smallImage.Width, smallImage.Height));
    g.FillEllipse(tBrush, ClientRectangle);
    tBrush.Dispose();
}
```

4. Dispose of the two images that are stored in the member variables of your class. Modify the `Dispose()` method of the class (in `Form1.Designer.cs`) as follows:

```
protected override void Dispose( bool disposing )
{
    if (disposing)
    {
        theImage.Dispose();
        smallImage.Dispose();
    }
    if (disposing && (components != null))
    {
        components.Dispose();
    }
    base.Dispose(disposing);
}
```

5. When you run this application, the window should look like the one shown in Figure 33-13.

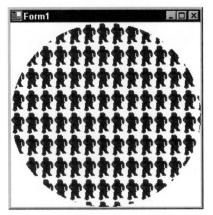

Figure 33-13

How It Works

When you create the `TextureBrush`, you pass a rectangle to the constructor to specify what part of the image will be used for the brush. In this case, you specify that you will use the entire image. Whatever is drawn using the `TextureBrush` uses the bitmap instead of a solid color.

Most of the code for this example has already been explained in this chapter. The difference here is that you call the `FillEllipse()` method of the `Graphics` class, passing your newly created texture brush, and the `ClientRectangle` draws the ellipse in the window:

```
g.FillEllipse(tBrush, ClientRectangle);
```

In the following Try It Out, you will create a `TextureBrush` and then create a pen from the `TextureBrush`.

Try It Out   Creating a Pen from an Image

Now that you have created a `TextureBrush`, you can create a pen using that brush:

1. Starting with the code in the DrawImage example that you modified in the previous Try It Out, change the `OnPaint()` method so that it looks like this:

```
protected override void OnPaint(PaintEventArgs e)
{
    Graphics g = e.Graphics;

    g.FillRectangle(Brushes.White, ClientRectangle);

    Brush tBrush = new TextureBrush(smallImage, new Rectangle(0, 0,
                    smallImage.Width, smallImage.Height));
    Pen tPen = new Pen(tBrush, 40);
    g.DrawRectangle(tPen, 0, 0,
                    ClientRectangle.Width, ClientRectangle.Height);
    tPen.Dispose();
    tBrush.Dispose();
}
```

2. When you run this code, it should look like what is shown in Figure 33-14.

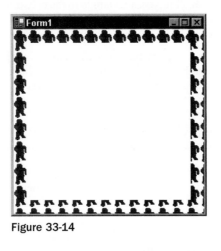

Figure 33-14

In the following Try It Out, having created a `TextureBrush`, you will draw some text with it.

Try It Out   Drawing Text with an Image

You can draw text using the `TextureBrush`:

1. Continuing with the code from the previous Try It Out, modify the `OnPaint` method as follows:

```
protected override void OnPaint(PaintEventArgs e)
{
    Graphics g = e.Graphics;
    g.FillRectangle(Brushes.White, ClientRectangle);

    Brush tBrush = new TextureBrush(smallImage, new Rectangle(0, 0,
                smallImage.Width, smallImage.Height));
    Font trFont = new Font("Times New Roman", 32,
                FontStyle.Bold | FontStyle.Italic);
    g.DrawString("Hello from Beginning Visual C#",
                trFont, tBrush, ClientRectangle);
    tBrush.Dispose();
    trFont.Dispose();
}
```

2. For this example, you'll actually use a different bitmap — change the line in the form constructor that sets the source for theImage to the following:

```
theImage = new Bitmap("Tile.bmp");
```

The Tile.bmp file can also be found in the download code.

3. When you run this code, it appears as shown in Figure 33-15.

Figure 33-15

The call to the DrawString() method is similar to previous uses of that method. It takes as arguments the text, the font, your texture brush, and a bounding rectangle:

```
g.DrawString("Hello from Beginning Visual C#",
             trFont, tBrush, ClientRectangle);
```

Double-Buffering

Recall that it can be problematic when drawing takes too long and the user has to wait a long time to see the graphics drawn. As explained earlier, the solution is to draw into an image, and when you have completed all drawing operations, draw the complete image to the window.

In the following Try It Out, you can see the performance benefits of double-buffering. By not drawing to the screen until fully ready, you can improve the performance profile of your application.

Try It Out   Double-Buffering

Follow these steps to create an application with performance issues:

1. Create a new Windows application called DoubleBuffer and add the following
    OnPaint() method, which draws a large number of lines in random colors:

```
protected override void OnPaint(PaintEventArgs e)
{
    Graphics g = e.Graphics;
    Random r = new Random();

    g.FillRectangle(Brushes.White, ClientRectangle);

    for (int x = 0; x < ClientRectangle.Width; x++)
    {
        for (int y = 0; y < ClientRectangle.Height; y += 10)
        {
            Color c = Color.FromArgb(r.Next(255), r.Next(255), r.Next(255));
            using (Pen p = new Pen(c, 1))
            {
                g.DrawLine(p, new Point(0, 0), new Point(x, y));
            }
        }
    }
}
```

2. When you run this, you can see the drawing take place before your eyes (that is, if your
    machine is not *too* fast). After all the drawing is completed, the window looks like what is
    shown in Figure 33-16.

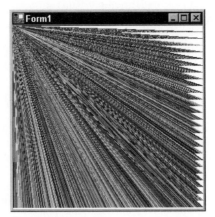

Figure 33-16

3. Now you add the double-buffering — if you replace the `OnPaint()` method with this version, the graphics are drawn all at once, after a second or two:

```
protected override void OnPaint(PaintEventArgs e)
{
    Graphics displayGraphics = e.Graphics;
    Random r = new Random();
    Image i = new Bitmap(ClientRectangle.Width, ClientRectangle.Height);
    Graphics g = Graphics.FromImage(i);

    g.FillRectangle(Brushes.White, ClientRectangle);

    for (int x = 0; x < ClientRectangle.Width; x++)
    {
        for (int y = 0; y < ClientRectangle.Height; y += 10)
        {
            Color c = Color.FromArgb (r.Next(255), r.Next(255), r.Next(255));
            Pen p = new Pen(c, 1);
            g.DrawLine(p, new Point(0, 0), new Point(x, y));
            p.Dispose();
        }
    }
    displayGraphics.DrawImage(i, ClientRectangle);
    i.Dispose();
}
```

How It Works

The part of the code responsible for drawing the lines is straightforward — you saw the `DrawLine()` method earlier in the chapter. The only item of note in this part of the code is the `FromArgb()` static `Color` method, which creates a `Color` struct from the three supplied integer values, corresponding to the red, green, and blue parts of the color.

In the double-buffering code (step 3), you create a new image that has the same height and width of the `ClientRectangle` with the following line:

```
Image i = new Bitmap(ClientRectangle.Width, ClientRectangle.Height);
```

You then get a `Graphics` object from the image using the following line:

```
Graphics g = Graphics.FromImage(i);
```

All of the drawing operations are the same as the previous code, except that they now draw into the image instead of directly onto the window. Finally, at the end of the function, you draw the image to the window:

```
displayGraphics.DrawImage(i, ClientRectangle);
```

Because the lines are drawn first to an invisible image, you do have to wait a short while before you see anything.

Advanced Capabilities of GDI+

We have only just touched on the many capabilities of GDI+. There is much more that you can do with it — far more than can be achieved in a single chapter. However, to round off this chapter, I will introduce several areas of these advanced capabilities.

Clipping

There are three contexts in which clipping is important. First, when the `OnPaint()` method is called, in addition to the `Graphics` object, the event is passed a clipping rectangle. For simple drawing routines, you don't need to pay much attention to this clipping rectangle, but if you have a very elaborate drawing routine that takes a lot of time, you can reduce the drawing time by testing against this clipping rectangle before you draw. You know the bounding rectangle of whatever graphic or figure that you need to draw. If this bounding rectangle does not intersect with the clipping rectangle, then you can skip the drawing operation.

Figure 33-17 shows one window containing a bar chart that is partially obscured by another window.

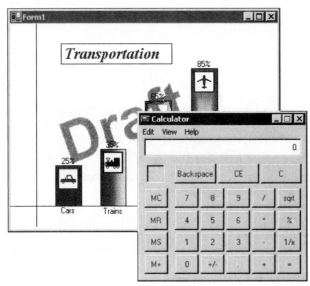

Figure 33-17

After the calculator has been closed, and after the Windows operating system has drawn the border of the window, the bar chart window looks like the one in Figure 33-18.

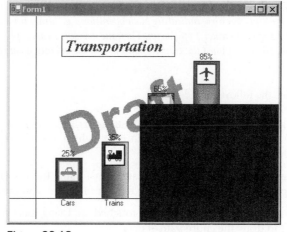

Figure 33-18

At this point, the OnPaint() method for the bar chart window would be called, with the clipping rectangle set to the area exposed by the closed window, shown in black in Figure 33-18. The bar chart would now need to draw the portions of its window that were previously underneath the overlying window. It would not need to redraw the car or train bars, and in fact, even if the OnPaint() method tried to draw into the window in an area other than the exposed area, it could not. Any drawing that it did would be ignored. The bar chart window knows the bounding rectangle for the cars bar, and can determine whether this rectangle intersects with the exposed portion of the window. Having determined that it does not intersect, the drawing routine does not redraw the part of the display covering the cars bar.

Sometimes when you need to draw only part of a figure or graphic, it is more convenient to draw the entire figure and clip the drawing to just what you want to see. You might have an image and want to draw just a portion of it. Rather than create a new image to represent a portion of the original image, you can set the clipping rectangle and then draw the image such that just the portion you want to see shows through the clipping area. When creating a marquee, this is the technique you would use. By successively changing where you draw the text, and at the same time setting a clipping region, you can create the effect of horizontally moving text.

Finally, there is a technique whereby you can create a *view port* into a larger graphic. The user can move this view port around by dragging the mouse on the graphic or by manipulating scroll bars. The view port also can be moved programmatically based on other actions that the user takes. In this case, setting a clipping region and drawing so that only what you want to see shows through is a good technique.

See the Clip property of the Graphics class in the .NET documentation for more information.

System.Drawing.Drawing2D

The classes in this namespace provide advanced two-dimensional and vector graphics functionality. You could use these classes to build a sophisticated drawing and image-processing application.

Vector graphics are a technique in which the programmer doesn't address pixels at all. Rather, the programmer records multiple vectors, *indicating such operations as "draw from one point to another," "draw a rectangle at a certain location," and so on. Then the developer can apply scaling, rotation, and other transformations. Having applied the transformations, all the operations are rendered at once to the window.*

This namespace includes the following:

❏ Advanced brushes: You have already seen the `LinearGradientBrush`, and I touched on the `PathGradientBrush`. There is also a `HatchBrush`, which draws using a hatch style, a foreground color, and a background color.

❏ The `Matrix` class: This defines geometric transforms. Using this class, you can do transforms on the drawing operations. For instance, using the `Matrix` class, you can draw an oval at a slant.

❏ The `GraphicsPath` class: This was already touched on. Using this class, you can define a complex path and draw the entire path at once.

System.Drawing.Imaging

The classes in this namespace provide advanced imaging support, such as support for metafiles. A *metafile* describes a sequence of graphics operations that can be recorded and later played back, and there are classes within the `System.Drawing.Imaging` namespace that enable you to extend GDI+ to support other image formats.

Summary

This chapter covered some of the classes in the `System.Drawing` namespace. You saw how the `Graphics` class encapsulates a drawing surface, and you reviewed the mechanics of drawing, in which the `OnPaint` event is called whenever your window needs to be redrawn.

You explored colors and coordinate systems, and looked at the `Point`, `Size`, and `Rectangle` structures used to specify positions and sizes on your drawing surface. Next, you saw some examples of drawing lines, shapes, text, and images.

In this chapter, you learned about the following:

❏ The `Graphics` class

❏ The `Color` structure

❏ Drawing lines using the `Pen` class

❏ Drawing shapes using the `Brush` class

❏ Drawing text using the `Font` class

❏ Drawing images using the `Bitmap` class

❏ Drawing into images (double-buffering)

You also learned that it is very important to call `Dispose()` on the following classes when you are done with them:

❏ `Graphics`

❏ `Pen`

❏ `Brush`

❏ `Font`

❏ `Image`

Finally, you took a short look at additional graphical capabilities in the .NET Framework.

Exercises

1. Write a small application that attempts to inappropriately dispose of a `Pen` object that was obtained from the `Pens` class. Note the error message that results.

2. Create an application that displays a three-color traffic light. Have the traffic light change color when the user clicks on it.

3. Write an application that inputs RGB values. Display the color in a rectangle. Display the HSB values of the color.

Windows Presentation Foundation

In this book you have seen two main types of application: desktop applications, which users run directly, and Web applications, which users access through a browser. You have created these with two different sections of the .NET Framework: Windows Forms and ASP.NET pages. These application types have their advantages and disadvantages. While desktop applications give you more flexibility and responsiveness, Web applications can be accessed remotely by many users at once.

However, in today's computing environment, the boundaries between applications are becoming increasingly blurred. With the advent of Web services and now the Windows Communication Foundation (WCF, which you'll look at in Chapter 35), both desktop and Web applications can operate in a more distributed way, exchanging data across local and global networks. In addition, Web client applications (that is, browsers such as Internet Explorer or Firefox) can no longer be seen as so-called "thin" clients that lack any functionality other than the simple display of information. The latest browsers, and the computers that run them, are capable of far more than this.

In recent years there has been a gradual convergence toward a user experience singularity. Web applications now typically use technologies such as JavaScript, Flash, Java applications, and others, and increasingly behave like desktop applications. You only have to look at the capabilities of, for example, Google Docs to see this in action. Conversely, desktop applications have become increasingly "connected," with capabilities ranging from the simple (automatic updates, online help, and so on) through to the advanced (such as online data sources and peer-to-peer networking). This is illustrated in Figure 34-1.

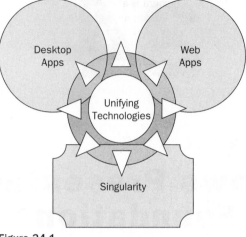

Figure 34-1

Windows Presentation Foundation (WPF) is a unifying technology that enables you to write applications that bridge the desktop/Internet gap. A WPF application, as you will see in this chapter, can run as a desktop application or inside a browser as a Web application. There is also a slimmed down version of WPF, *Silverlight,* that you can use to add dynamic content to Web applications.

In this chapter you learn about WPF and how you can use it to create the next generation of applications. You look at the following topics:

❏   What is WPF?

❏   The anatomy of a basic WPF application

❏   WPF fundamentals

❏   Programming with WPF

What Is WPF?

WPF (formerly known as Avalon) is a technology that enables you to write platform-independent applications with a clearly defined split between design and functionality. It borrows and extends concepts and classes from many previous technologies, including Windows Forms, ASP.NET, XML, data binding techniques, GDI+, and more. If you have any experience building Web applications with the .NET Framework, then when you first look at the code for a WPF application you will immediately notice many of these similarities. In particular, WPF applications use a markup plus code-behind model similar to the one used in ASP.NET. However, under the covers, there are as many differences as similarities, which combine to make WPF an entirely new experience for developers as well as users.

One of the key concepts of WPF development is an almost total separation of design and functionality. This separation enables designers and C# developers to work together on projects with a degree of freedom that has previously required advanced design concepts or third-party tools. This functionality is to be welcomed by all — by small teams and hobbyist developers as well as huge teams of developers and designers that work together on large-scale projects.

In the following sections you'll see how WPF benefits designers and developers and enables them to work together.

WPF for Designers

The language used for user interface design in WPF is Extensible Application Markup Language (XAML, pronounced *zammel*). This is similar to the markup language used in ASP.NET in that it uses XML syntax and enables controls to be added to a user interface in a declarative, hierarchical way. That is to say, you can add controls in the form of XML elements, and specify control properties with XML attributes. You can also have controls that contain other controls, which is essential for both layout and functionality.

XAML is, however, a much more powerful language than ASP.NET, and is not limited by the capabilities of HTML when it is rendered for display to a user. XAML is designed with today's powerful graphics cards in mind, and as such it enables you to use all the advanced capabilities that these graphics cards offer through DirectX 7 or later. The following lists some of these capabilities:

❑ Floating-point coordinates and vector graphics to provide layout that can be scaled, rotated, and otherwise transformed with no loss of quality.

❑ 2D and 3D capabilities for advanced rendering.

❑ Advanced font processing and rendering.

❑ Solid, gradient, and texture fills with optional transparency for UI objects.

❑ Animation storyboarding that can be used in all manner of situations, including user-triggered events such as mouse clicks on buttons.

❑ Reusable resources that you can use to dynamically style controls.

Much of this functionality is specifically targeted at Microsoft Vista operating systems, which have advanced graphical capabilities accessible through the Aero interface. However, WPF applications can run on other operating systems such as Windows XP. A fallback rendering system built into the .NET Framework 3.5 runtime can render XAML (with an associated loss of performance) if the graphics card cannot for some reason.

VS and VCE include capabilities for creating and styling XAML code, but the tool of choice for designers is Microsoft Expression Blend (EB). This is a design and layout package that you can use to create XAML files, which can then be used by developers to build applications. In fact, EB uses the same solution and project files as VS and VCE, so you can create a project in any of these environments and then edit it in any of the others. In EB, all you need to do to edit a code-behind file is double-click on it in the Files window — the equivalent of the Solution Explorer in VS and VCE. Figure 34-2 shows the EB interface.

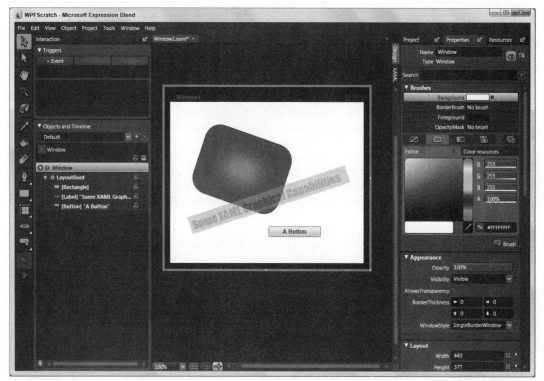

Figure 34-2

You can find out more and download a trial version of EB (and EB2, in development at the time of writing) at `microsoft.com/expression/products/overview.aspx?key=blend`. However, remember that you do not need EB to write WPF applications or edit XAML. Figure 34-3 shows the exact same project shown in Figure 34-2, but loaded in VCE.

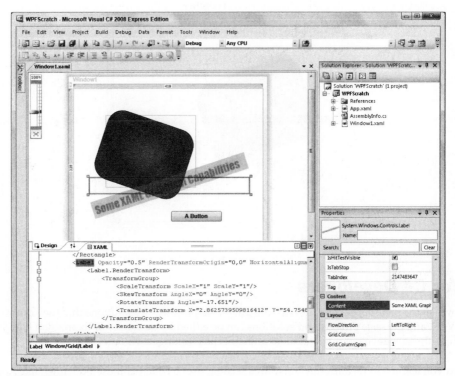

Figure 34-3

Unfortunately, a difference between the solution files in the 2005 and 2008 versions of VS and VCE prevents you from working with the current version of EB. However, there is a configuration tool that you can use to reconfigure EB to work with VS 2008 and VCE 2008. This app is available at
`http://blogs.msdn.com/expression/archive/2007/05/29/working-with-visual-studio-code-name-orcas-and-expression-blend.aspx`.

When you run the configuration app (`BlendConfiguration.exe`*), select the option to configure EB for Visual Studio Code Name "Orcas."*

It is hoped that this problem will be addressed in future releases of EB and EB2.

In VCE, the default display shows the XAML (don't worry too much about the code shown in the XAML view for now) and a preview of the rendered XAML in two panes. The property editor is a little less intuitive, and when you select objects there are some slightly strange features of this editor. In Figure 34-3, the `Label` control is selected, but the selection marquee doesn't match up with the control particularly well.

The application can be launched from both environments with the same result, shown in Figure 34-4.

Figure 34-4

WPF for C# Developers

As shown in the previous section, developers can create projects and solutions that they can work on in VS or VCE, and the *same* projects and solutions can be edited by designers in Expression Blend. Unlike designers, though, developers spend most of their time working in VS or VCE.

WPF, as you learned in the introduction to this section, uses a code-behind mode much like ASP.NET. For example, you can add an event handler to a `Button` control by adding a `Click` attribute to the XML element representing the control. This attribute specifies the name of an event handler in the code-behind file for the XAML page, which you can write in C#.

Note that you can also manipulate controls in a WPF application similarly to how Windows Forms applications use programmatic techniques to layout user interfaces. You can use code behind to instantiate a control, set its properties, add event handlers, and add the control to a window. This effectively bypasses XAML completely. The code to do this will typically be a lot more long-winded than the associated XAML declarative code, and you will lose the separation between design and functionality. While the programmatic way of doing things is necessary in some situations, in general you should use XAML to lay out controls in a user interface.

This chapter concentrates on the C# developer's perspective. WPF is a subject that entire books have been written about, so you will mostly be getting a quick initiation and a summary of possibilities.

Anatomy of a Basic WPF Application

WPF is quite intuitive to use, and the best way to learn about it is to dive straight in and play. Many of the techniques will instantly be familiar to you if you have worked through the rest of this book.

In the following Try It Out you create a simple WPF application and in the How It Works section that follows you examine the code and results to learn more about how things fit together.

Try It Out   **Creating a Basic WPF Application**

1.   Create a new WPF application called Ch34Ex01 and save it in the directory
C:\BegVCSharp\Chapter34.

2.   Modify the code in `Window1.xaml` as follows:

```
<Window
  xmlns="http://schemas.microsoft.com/winfx/2006/xaml/presentation"
  xmlns:x="http://schemas.microsoft.com/winfx/2006/xaml"
  x:Class="Ch34Ex01.Window1"
  Title="Color Spinner" Height="370" Width="270">
  <Window.Resources>
    <Storyboard x:Key="Spin">
      <DoubleAnimationUsingKeyFrames BeginTime="00:00:00"
        Storyboard.TargetName="ellipse1"
        Storyboard.TargetProperty=
"(UIElement.RenderTransform).(TransformGroup.Children)[0].(RotateTransform.Angle)"
        RepeatBehavior="Forever">
        <SplineDoubleKeyFrame KeyTime="00:00:10" Value="360"/>
      </DoubleAnimationUsingKeyFrames>
      <DoubleAnimationUsingKeyFrames BeginTime="00:00:00"
        Storyboard.TargetName="ellipse2"
        Storyboard.TargetProperty=
"(UIElement.RenderTransform).(TransformGroup.Children)[0].(RotateTransform.Angle)"
        RepeatBehavior="Forever">
        <SplineDoubleKeyFrame KeyTime="00:00:10" Value="-360"/>
      </DoubleAnimationUsingKeyFrames>
      <DoubleAnimationUsingKeyFrames BeginTime="00:00:00"
        Storyboard.TargetName="ellipse3"
        Storyboard.TargetProperty=
"(UIElement.RenderTransform).(TransformGroup.Children)[0].(RotateTransform.Angle)"
        RepeatBehavior="Forever">
        <SplineDoubleKeyFrame KeyTime="00:00:05" Value="360"/>
      </DoubleAnimationUsingKeyFrames>
      <DoubleAnimationUsingKeyFrames BeginTime="00:00:00"
        Storyboard.TargetName="ellipse4"
        Storyboard.TargetProperty=
"(UIElement.RenderTransform).(TransformGroup.Children)[0].(RotateTransform.Angle)"
        RepeatBehavior="Forever">
        <SplineDoubleKeyFrame KeyTime="00:00:05" Value="-360"/>
      </DoubleAnimationUsingKeyFrames>
    </Storyboard>
  </Window.Resources>
  <Window.Triggers>
    <EventTrigger RoutedEvent="FrameworkElement.Loaded">
      <BeginStoryboard Storyboard="{StaticResource Spin}"
        x:Name="Spin_BeginStoryboard"/>
    </EventTrigger>
    <EventTrigger RoutedEvent="ButtonBase.Click" SourceName="goButton">
      <ResumeStoryboard BeginStoryboardName="Spin_BeginStoryboard"/>
    </EventTrigger>
    <EventTrigger RoutedEvent="ButtonBase.Click" SourceName="stopButton">
      <PauseStoryboard BeginStoryboardName="Spin_BeginStoryboard"/>
```

```
    </EventTrigger>
  </Window.Triggers>
  <Window.Background>
    <LinearGradientBrush EndPoint="0.5,1" StartPoint="0.5,0">
      <GradientStop Color="#FFFFFFFF" Offset="0"/>
      <GradientStop Color="#FFFFC45A" Offset="1"/>
    </LinearGradientBrush>
  </Window.Background>
  <Grid>
    <Ellipse Margin="50,50,0,0" Name="ellipse5" Stroke="Black" Height="150"
      HorizontalAlignment="Left" VerticalAlignment="Top" Width="150">
      <Ellipse.BitmapEffect>
        <BlurBitmapEffect Radius="10"/>
      </Ellipse.BitmapEffect>
      <Ellipse.Fill>
        <RadialGradientBrush>
          <GradientStop Color="#FF000000" Offset="1"/>
          <GradientStop Color="#FFFFFFFF" Offset="0.306"/>
        </RadialGradientBrush>
      </Ellipse.Fill>
    </Ellipse>
    <Ellipse Margin="15,85,0,0" Name="ellipse1" Stroke="{x:Null}" Height="80"
      HorizontalAlignment="Left" VerticalAlignment="Top" Width="120" Fill="Red"
      Opacity="0.5" RenderTransformOrigin="0.92,0.5" >
      <Ellipse.BitmapEffect>
        <BevelBitmapEffect/>
      </Ellipse.BitmapEffect>
      <Ellipse.RenderTransform>
        <TransformGroup>
          <RotateTransform Angle="0"/>
        </TransformGroup>
      </Ellipse.RenderTransform>
    </Ellipse>
    <Ellipse Margin="85,15,0,0" Name="ellipse2" Stroke="{x:Null}" Height="120"
      HorizontalAlignment="Left" VerticalAlignment="Top" Width="80" Fill="Blue"
      Opacity="0.5" RenderTransformOrigin="0.5,0.92" >
      <Ellipse.BitmapEffect>
        <BevelBitmapEffect/>
      </Ellipse.BitmapEffect>
      <Ellipse.RenderTransform>
        <TransformGroup>
          <RotateTransform Angle="0"/>
        </TransformGroup>
      </Ellipse.RenderTransform>
    </Ellipse>
    <Ellipse Margin="115,85,0,0" Name="ellipse3" Stroke="{x:Null}" Height="80"
      HorizontalAlignment="Left" VerticalAlignment="Top" Width="120" Opacity="0.5"
      Fill="Yellow" RenderTransformOrigin="0.08,0.5" >
      <Ellipse.BitmapEffect>
        <BevelBitmapEffect/>
      </Ellipse.BitmapEffect>
      <Ellipse.RenderTransform>
        <TransformGroup>
          <RotateTransform Angle="0"/>
```

```
        </TransformGroup>
      </Ellipse.RenderTransform>
    </Ellipse>
    <Ellipse Margin="85,115,0,0" Name="ellipse4" Stroke="{x:Null}" Height="120"
      HorizontalAlignment="Left" VerticalAlignment="Top" Width="80" Opacity="0.5"
      Fill="Green" RenderTransformOrigin="0.5,0.08" >
      <Ellipse.BitmapEffect>
        <BevelBitmapEffect/>
      </Ellipse.BitmapEffect>
      <Ellipse.RenderTransform>
        <TransformGroup>
          <RotateTransform Angle="0"/>
        </TransformGroup>
      </Ellipse.RenderTransform>
    </Ellipse>
    <Button Height="23" HorizontalAlignment="Left" Margin="20,0,0,56"
      Name="goButton" VerticalAlignment="Bottom" Width="75" Content="Go"/>
    <Button Height="23" HorizontalAlignment="Left" Margin="152,0,0,56"
      Name="stopButton" VerticalAlignment="Bottom" Width="75" Content="Stop"/>
    <Button Height="23" HorizontalAlignment="Left" Margin="85,0,86,16"
        Name="toggleButton" VerticalAlignment="Bottom" Width="75" Content="Toggle"/>
  </Grid>
</Window>
```

3. Double-click the Toggle button in the Design View (shown highlighted in Figure 34-5, which has the XAML view collapsed).

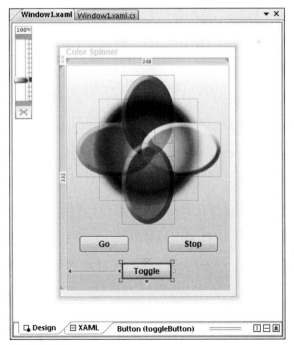

Figure 34-5

4. Modify the code in `Window1.xaml.cs` as follows (both the `using` statement and the new code in the `toggleButton_Click()` event handler that was added when you double-clicked the button):

```csharp
using System;
using System.Collections.Generic;
using System.Linq;
using System.Text;
using System.Windows;
using System.Windows.Controls;
using System.Windows.Data;
using System.Windows.Documents;
using System.Windows.Input;
using System.Windows.Media;
using System.Windows.Media.Imaging;
using System.Windows.Navigation;
using System.Windows.Shapes;
using System.Windows.Media.Animation;

namespace Ch34Ex01
{
    /// <summary>
    /// Interaction logic for Window1.xaml
    /// </summary>
    public partial class Window1 : Window
    {
        public Window1()
        {
            InitializeComponent();
        }

        private void toggleButton_Click(object sender, RoutedEventArgs e)
        {
            Storyboard spinStoryboard = Resources["Spin"] as Storyboard;
            if (spinStoryboard != null)
            {
                if (spinStoryboard.GetIsPaused(this))
                {
                    spinStoryboard.Resume(this);
                }
                else
                {
                    spinStoryboard.Pause(this);
                }
            }
        }
    }
}
```

5. Execute the application and experiment with starting, stopping, and toggling the animation. An example is shown in Figure 34-6.

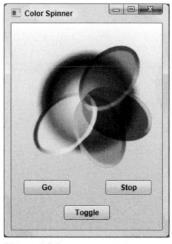

Figure 34-6

6. Create a new WPF Browser application called Ch34Ex01Web and save it in the directory C:\BegVCSharp\Chapter34.

7. Change the value of the `Title` attribute of the `<Page>` element in `Page1.xaml` to `Color Spinner Web`.

8. Open the `Window1.xaml` file from the Ch34Ex01 application and copy all the code from the `<Window>` element in that file into the `<Page>` element in `Page1.xaml`.

9. Change the `<Window.Resources>`, `<Window.Triggers>`, and `<Window.Background>` elements to `<Page.Resources>`, `<Page.Triggers>`, and `<Page.Background>` elements, respectively (remember to change both the start and end tags for these elements).

10. Remove the five `<Ellipse.BitmapEffect>` elements and their contents from `Page1.xaml`.

11. Copy the `toggleButton_Click()` event handler and the `using` statement for the `System.Windows.Media.Animation` namespace from `Window1.xaml.cs` to `Page1.xaml.cs`.

12. Execute the Ch34Ex01Web application. The result is shown in Figure 34-7.

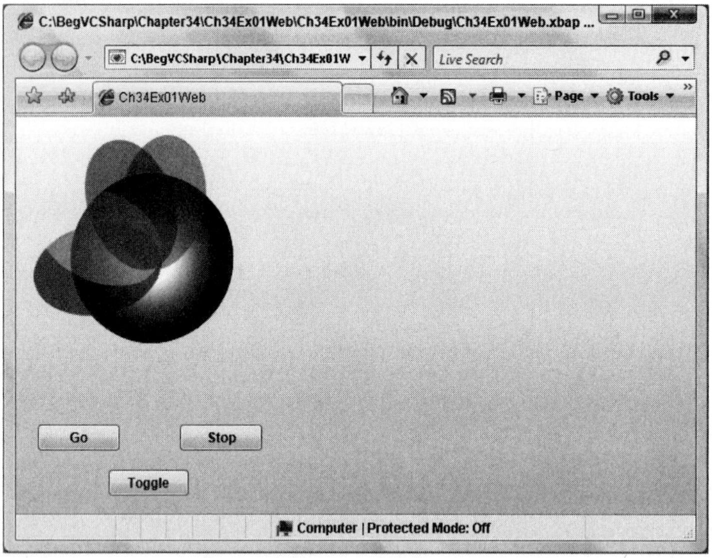

Figure 34-7

How It Works

In this example you created a simple application that results in spinning ellipses of color that you can start or stop. Unfortunately, the black-and-white screenshots don't convey the full effect, but when you run the code yourself you should find the application at least partly aesthetically pleasing.

You added quite a lot of XAML code to achieve this result, but if you look a little closer you will notice that a lot of it was repetitive code — required because there are four ellipses to animate. You may also have noticed that you hardly added any C# code in the code-behind file, and that code was for only one of the three buttons. The code was designed this way to illustrate two important points:

❏   Designers can create compelling user interfaces involving advanced graphical capabilities, animation, and user interaction with nothing but XAML code.

❏   When required, you can achieve complete control over a XAML user interface from code behind.

You also saw how you can use the same code in a Web application as in a desktop application. A few modifications were necessary, which you'll look at later, but the essential functionality was the same in both environments.

The code in this application demonstrates many features of WPF to introduce you to some key techniques. To begin, you'll look at the desktop application; then you look at the changes required for Web applications. First, look at the XAML for the desktop application, `Window1.xaml`, and the top-level element of this code:

```
<Window
  xmlns="http://schemas.microsoft.com/winfx/2006/xaml/presentation"
  xmlns:x="http://schemas.microsoft.com/winfx/2006/xaml"
  x:Class="Ch34Ex01.Window1"
```

```
      Title="Color Spinner" Height="370" Width="270">

      ...

  </Window>
```

The `<Window>` element is used, unsurprisingly, to define a window. An application might consist of several windows, each of which would be contained in a separate XAML file. This isn't to say that a XAML file always defines a window, though; XAML files can contain user controls, brushes, and other resources, Web pages, and more. There is even a XAML file in the Ch34Ex01 project that defines the application itself — `App.xaml`. You'll look at applications and the `App.xaml` file a little later in this chapter.

Back to `Window1.xaml`, notice that the `<Window>` element contains some fairly self-explanatory attributes. There are two namespace declarations, one for the global namespace to be used for the XML and one for the x namespace. Both of these are essential for WPF functionality and define the vocabulary for the XAML syntax. Next is a `Class` attribute, taken from the x namespace. This attribute links the XAML `<Window>` element to a partial class definition in the code behind, in this case `Ch34Ex01.Window`. This is similar to the way things work in ASP.NET, with a class used for a page, and enables code behind to share the same code model as the XAML file, including controls defined by XAML elements and so on. Note that the `x:Class` attribute can be used only on the root element of a XAML file.

Three other attributes, `Title`, `Height`, and `Width`, specify the text to display in the title of the window and the dimensions (in pixels) to use for the window. These attributes map to properties of the `System.Windows.Window` class, which the `Ch34Ex01.Window` class derives from.

There are several other properties of the `System.Windows.Window` class that enable you to define additional functionality. Many of these properties are more complex than the three used on the `<Window>` element — that is, they aren't, for example, simple strings or numbers. XAML syntax enables you to use nested elements to specify values for these properties.

> *The syntax used for XAML to define objects, properties, and content is discussed in more detail in the section "XAML Syntax."*

For example, the `Background` property is defined in this code with a nested `<Window.Background>` element as follows:

```
  <Window.Background>
    <LinearGradientBrush EndPoint="0.5,1" StartPoint="0.5,0">
      <GradientStop Color="#FFFFFFFF" Offset="0"/>
      <GradientStop Color="#FFFFC45A" Offset="1"/>
    </LinearGradientBrush>
  </Window.Background>
```

This code sets the `Background` property to an instance of the `LinearGradientBruch` class. WPF uses brushes in a similar way to GDI+, discussed in Chapter 33. In this case, the brush defines a gradient that changes from white to a peachlike color from top to bottom.

There are two other "complex" properties defined in nested elements in this code: `<Window.Resources>`, which defines the animation, and `<Window.Triggers>`, which defines triggers that control the animation. Both of these properties, `Resources` and `Triggers`, are capable of far more than this, and you will look at them in more detail later in the chapter.

Before looking at the implementation of these properties, it's worth jumping ahead to the `<Grid>` element. The `<Grid>` element defines an instance of the `System.Windows.Controls.Grid` control. This is one of several controls that you can use for layout in a WPF application. It enables you to position nested controls using coordinates that can be relative to any of the four edges of a rectangle. Other controls enable you to position controls in different ways. All the layout controls are described in the "Control Layout" section later in this chapter.

The `<Grid>` element contains five `<Ellipse>` elements (`System.Windows.Shapes.Ellipse` controls) and three `<Button>` elements (`System.Windows.Controls.Button` controls). These elements define the ellipses used to display the spinning graphics in the application and the buttons used to control the application, respectively.

The first `<Ellipse>` element is as follows:

```
<Ellipse Margin="50,50,0,0" Name="ellipse5" Stroke="Black" Height="150"
  HorizontalAlignment="Left" VerticalAlignment="Top" Width="150">
  <Ellipse.BitmapEffect>
    <BlurBitmapEffect Radius="10"/>
  </Ellipse.BitmapEffect>
  <Ellipse.Fill>
    <RadialGradientBrush>
      <GradientStop Color="#FF000000" Offset="1"/>
      <GradientStop Color="#FFFFFFFF" Offset="0.306"/>
    </RadialGradientBrush>
  </Ellipse.Fill>
</Ellipse>
```

This element defines an instance of the `System.Windows.Shapes.Ellipse` class, which is used to display an ellipse shape, and sets several properties of this instance as follows:

❑ **Name:** An identifier to use for the control.

❑ **Margin:** Specifies the location of the shape defined by the `Ellipse` control in the grid that contains it by specifying the margin around the shape. These measurements are given in pixels in this code. The way that this property maps to the actual location of the shape depends on the `HorizontalAlignment` and `VerticalAlignment` properties.

❑ **HorizontalAlignment and VerticalAlignment:** Used to specify which edges of the rectangle defined by `Grid` are used to lay out the shape. For example, values of `Left` and `Bottom` causes the shape to be positioned relative to the bottom left of the grid.

❑ **Height and Width:** The dimensions of the shape.

❑ **Stroke:** The brush to use for the outline of the shape defined by the `Ellipse` control.

❑ **Fill:** The brush to use for the interior of the shape defined by the `Ellipse` control.

❑ **BitmapEffect:** A special effect to use when displaying the `Ellipse` control.

The brush used for the Fill property is a RadialGradientBrush. You have seen similar brushes in GDI+ code. In this case, the brush specifies a gradient from white (near the center of the ellipse) to black (at the edge).

The BitmapEffect property is set to use BlurBitmapEffect. This is one of several effects that you can apply to graphics in WPF. This effect blurs the shape with a magnitude defined by the BlurBitmapEffect.Radius property. This effect is not available to Web applications, which is why you removed it in step 11. This is one of several differences between desktop and Web applications.

Four more <Ellipse> elements in the code are very similar. Each of these elements defines one of the four colored ellipses that are animated. The first of these elements is as follows:

```
<Ellipse Margin="15,85,0,0" Name="ellipse1" Stroke="{x:Null}" Height="80"
  HorizontalAlignment="Left" VerticalAlignment="Top" Width="120" Fill="Red"
  Opacity="0.5" RenderTransformOrigin="0.92,0.5" >
  <Ellipse.BitmapEffect>
    <BevelBitmapEffect/>
  </Ellipse.BitmapEffect>
  <Ellipse.RenderTransform>
    <TransformGroup>
      <RotateTransform Angle="0"/>
    </TransformGroup>
  </Ellipse.RenderTransform>
</Ellipse>
```

This code looks a lot like the code for the previous ellipse, with the following differences:

❑ The Stroke property is set to {x:null}. In XAML, values enclosed in curly braces such as this are called *markup extensions* and are used to provide values for properties that cannot be reduced to simple strings in the XAML syntax. In this case, {x:null} specifies a null value for the property, meaning that no brush is to be used for Stroke.

❑ An Opacity property is specified with a value of 0.5. This specifies that the ellipse is semi-transparent.

❑ The BitmapEffect property uses a BevelBitmapEffect, which results in the beveled edges shown in Figure 34-5, earlier.

❑ A RenderTransform property is specified. This property is set to a TransformGroup object with a single transformation, RotateTransform. This transformation is used when the ellipse is animated. It has a single property specified, Angle. This is the angle, in degrees, through which the ellipse is rotated, and is initially set to 0.

❑ RenderTransformOrigin is used to set a center point around which the ellipse will be rotated by the RotateTransform transformation.

These last two properties relate to the animation defined in the XAML, which is defined by a System.Windows.Media.Animation.Storyboard object. This object is defined in the <Window.Resources> element, meaning that the Storyboard object will be available through the `Resources` collection of the window. The code also defines a `x:Key` attribute, which enables the `Storyboard` object to be referenced through `Resources` using a key:

```
<Window.Resources>
  <Storyboard x:Key="Spin">
    . . .
  </Storyboard>
</Window.Resources>
```

The `Storyboard` object contains four `DoubleAnimationUsingKeyFrames` objects. These objects enable you to specify that a property that contains a `double` value should change over time, along with details to further define this behavior. Each of the elements in this code defines the animation used by one of the colored ellipses. For example, the animation for the `ellipse1` ellipse examined earlier is as follows:

```
<DoubleAnimationUsingKeyFrames BeginTime="00:00:00"
   Storyboard.TargetName="ellipse1"
   Storyboard.TargetProperty=
"(UIElement.RenderTransform).(TransformGroup.Children)[0].(RotateTransform.Angle)"
   RepeatBehavior="Forever">
   <SplineDoubleKeyFrame KeyTime="00:00:10" Value="360"/>
</DoubleAnimationUsingKeyFrames>
```

Without going into this element too deeply at this point, this specifies that the `Angle` property of the `RotateTransform` transformation described previously should change from its initial value to a value of `360` over a time period of 10 seconds, and that this change should be repeated once complete. You'll look at animation in more detail in the "Animation" section of this chapter.

After the ellipse definitions there are three `<Button>` elements that define buttons (note that the `Click` attribute was not shown in the code in the example; it was added by the IDE when you double-clicked the button in step 3):

```
<Button Height="23" HorizontalAlignment="Left" Margin="20,0,0,56" Name="goButton"
   VerticalAlignment="Bottom" Width="75" Content="Go"/>
<Button Height="23" HorizontalAlignment="Left" Margin="152,0,0,56"
   Name="stopButton" VerticalAlignment="Bottom" Width="75" Content="Stop"/>
<Button Height="23" HorizontalAlignment="Left" Margin="85,0,86,16"
   Name="toggleButton" VerticalAlignment="Bottom" Width="75" Content="Toggle"
   Click="toggleButton_Click"/>
```

Each of these elements specifies the name, position, and dimensions of a `Button` object using the same properties as the `<Ellipse>` elements shown earlier. They also have `Content` properties that determine what is displayed in the content of the button — in this case, the string to display for the text on the button. Buttons aren't limited to displaying simple strings in this way, though; you could use embedded shapes or other graphical content if you prefer. You'll look at this in more detail in the "Control Styling" section later in this chapter.

The `Click` attribute on the `toggleButton` button defines an event handler method for the `Click` event. This method, `toggleButton_Click()`, is actually a *routed event* handler. You'll look at routed events in the "Routed Events" section later in this chapter. For now, all you need to know is that this event fires when you click the button, and the event hander is then called.

In the event handler code, you start by obtaining a reference to the Storyboard object that defines the animation. Earlier you saw that this object is contained in the Resources property of the containing Window object, and that it uses the key Spin. The code that retrieves the storyboard should therefore come as no surprise:

```
private void toggleButton_Click(object sender, RoutedEventArgs e)
{
    Storyboard spinStoryboard = Resources["Spin"] as Storyboard;
```

Once obtained, and if the previous code doesn't obtain a null value, the Storyboard .GetIsPaused() method is used to determine whether the animation is currently paused or not. If it is, then a call to Resume() is made; otherwise, Pause() is called. These methods resume or pause the animation, respectively:

```
if (spinStoryboard != null)
{
    if (spinStoryboard.GetIsPaused(this))
    {
        spinStoryboard.Resume(this);
    }
    else
    {
        spinStoryboard.Pause(this);
    }
}
}
```

Note that all these methods require a reference to the object that contains the storyboard. This is because storyboards themselves do not keep track of time. The window that contains a storyboard has its own clock, which is used by the storyboard. By passing a reference to the window (using this), the storyboard is able to gain access to this clock.

The other two buttons, goButton and stopButton, are not linked to any event handler methods in the code behind. Instead, their functionality is determined by triggers. In this example, three triggers are defined as follows:

```
<Window.Triggers>
  <EventTrigger RoutedEvent="FrameworkElement.Loaded">
    <BeginStoryboard Storyboard="{StaticResource Spin}"
      x:Name="Spin_BeginStoryboard"/>
  </EventTrigger>
  <EventTrigger RoutedEvent="ButtonBase.Click" SourceName="goButton">
    <ResumeStoryboard BeginStoryboardName="Spin_BeginStoryboard"/>
  </EventTrigger>
  <EventTrigger RoutedEvent="ButtonBase.Click" SourceName="stopButton">
    <PauseStoryboard BeginStoryboardName="Spin_BeginStoryboard"/>
  </EventTrigger>
</Window.Triggers>
```

The first of these is a trigger that links the `FrameworkElement.Loaded` event (which fires when the application is loaded) with a `BeginStoryboard` action. This action starts the `Spin` animation. Notice how the `Spin` animation is referenced by using markup extension syntax with the code `{StaticResource Spin}`. This syntax, used to reference resources in the containing window, is used frequently in WPF applications. The `BeginStoryboard` action is given the name `Spin_BeginStoryboard` and is referenced in the other two triggers, which link up the `Click` events of `goButton` and `stopButton`, respectively. These triggers use the `ResumeStoryboard` and `PauseStoryboard` actions, which do exactly what their names suggest.

This code worked fine as a desktop application, but when you converted it to a Web application there were several changes to be made. In fact, the example hid a few of these details from you by creating a new WPF Browser application. For example, because there are certain security restrictions associated with running code in a browser, the WPF Browser application is equipped with a temporary key that you can use to sign your application. This is necessary if you want to permit the application to perform actions that might otherwise be forbidden in browser applications, such as accessing the local file system.

You probably also noticed that the `<Window>` root element of the desktop application is replaced with a `<Page>` element in the Web application. This is because the capabilities exposed by a browser differ slightly from the capabilities exposed by the host application that is used to run desktop applications. WPF therefore used different classes to represent these differing hosts. However, as you saw in the code, for a lot of things you can use identical code in the same environments. You'll look at this in more detail later in this chapter.

This completes the analysis of this example application. You've covered a lot of ground here, and have learned a lot of new concepts very quickly, so it might be a good idea to take a breather at this point. The remainder of this chapter describes the techniques you've seen here in more depth, formalizes the syntax required, and looks at a few new things.

WPF Fundamentals

It is hoped that the example in the first part of this chapter has filled you with enthusiasm for WPF programming. Although there are a lot of new concepts to get to a grip on, you have seen how the combination of XAML and .NET code enables you to create dynamic applications very quickly. You have also seen that it is possible, if you wish, to leave a lot of functionality, including the UI of your applications, in the hands of designers who don't require any knowledge of C#. Finally, you saw how you can create desktop and Web applications with (more or less) the same code.

However, before you begin to create WPF applications for yourself, you should spend a little longer on the fundamentals. This section covers several topics that are fundamental to WPF applications, and looks at the syntax required to implement them. You also learn about many additional possibilities that you can investigate further in your own applications.

This section covers the following:

- ❏ XAML syntax
- ❏ Desktop and Web applications
- ❏ The `Application` object
- ❏ Control basics, including dependency properties, attached properties, routed events, and attached events
- ❏ Control layout and styling
- ❏ Triggers
- ❏ Animation
- ❏ Static and dynamic resources

XAML Syntax

The example in the first part of this chapter introduced you to a lot of XAML syntax without formally describing it. Many of the rules and possibilities were omitted there so you could focus on the general structure and functionality. In this section you look at XAML in a little more detail so that you understand how XAML files are assembled.

Object Element Syntax

The basic structure of a XAML file uses *object element syntax* to describe a hierarchy of objects with a single root object that contains everything else. Object element syntax, as its name suggests, describes an object (or struct) represented by an XML element. For example, you saw in the example how the `<Button>` element was used to represent a `System.Windows.Controls.Button` object.

The root element of a XAML file always uses object element syntax, although as you saw in the earlier example, the class used for the root object is defined not by the element name (`<Window>` or `<Page>`) but by the `x:Class` attribute. This syntax is only used in the root element. For desktop applications, the root element must inherit from `System.Windows.Window`, and for Web applications, it must inherit from `System.Windows.Controls.Page`.

Many of the objects that you define using object element syntax are, in fact, controls, such as the `Button` control used in the example.

Attribute Syntax

You have seen that in many cases where an element is used to represent an object (using object element syntax), attributes are used to specify properties and events. For example, the `<Button>` element shown earlier used attributes as follows:

```
<Button Height="23" HorizontalAlignment="Left" Margin="85,0,86,16"
   Name="toggleButton" VerticalAlignment="Bottom" Width="75" Content="Toggle"
   Click="toggleButton_Click"/>
```

Here, each attribute sets the value of a property of the `toggleButton` object, apart from `Click`, which assigns a routed event handler to the `Click` event of `toggleButton`, and `Name`. These are all examples of *attribute syntax*.

The `Name` attribute used here is a special case: It defines the identifier for the control so that you can reference it from code behind and other XAML code.

Attributes may be qualified with the base class that they refer to by using a period. For example, the `Button` control inherits its `Click` event from `ButtonBase`, so you could rewrite the previous code as follows:

```
<Button Height="23" HorizontalAlignment="Left" Margin="85,0,86,16"
   Name="toggleButton" VerticalAlignment="Bottom" Width="75" Content="Toggle"
   ButtonBase.Click="toggleButton_Click"/>
```

Note that this same syntax is also used for *attached properties*, which you'll look at in the "Control Basics" section of this chapter.

Property Element Syntax

In many cases you will want to use something more complicated than a simple string to initialize the value of a property. In the example application, that was the case for the `Fill` properties you used, which you set to various brush objects:

```
<Ellipse ...>
  ...
  <Ellipse.Fill>
    <RadialGradientBrush>
      <GradientStop Color="#FF000000" Offset="1"/>
      <GradientStop Color="#FFFFFFFF" Offset="0.306"/>
    </RadialGradientBrush>
  </Ellipse.Fill>
</Ellipse>
```

Here, the property is set by a child element that is named according to the following convention:

```
[Parent Element Name].[Property Name]
```

This is referred to as *property element syntax*.

Content Syntax

Many controls are in fact *content presenters*. This means that you supply the controls with content that is displayed according to the control template. For example, the content you supply for a `Button` control is displayed on the surface of the button. This can be text, as in the example, or it could be something graphical.

With *content syntax,* you specify the content for a control simply by adding it as the content of the element representing the control:

```
<Button ...>Go</Button>
```

This code is for a `Button` control that will display the text Go on itself when rendered. The example used a simpler, but less flexible, way of doing this: It used an attribute called `Content`. The full content syntax used here is necessary for more complex content such as the graphical content discussed in the introduction to this section.

When you use complex content for a control, you can end up with complex nested hierarchies of XAML code. For this reason, XAML enables controls to be styled by other, more subtle means. You learn more about content presenters and styling in the "Control Styling" section.

Mixing Property Element Syntax and Content Syntax

A control on a XAML page that is formatted using object element syntax may include both property element syntax and content syntax. If this is the case, then you must respect the following syntactic rules:

❑ The elements used for property element syntax do not have to be contiguous — that is, you can have an element that uses property element syntax followed by one that uses content syntax followed by a third element that uses property element syntax.

❑ The elements (and text content, if applicable) used for content syntax must be contiguous — that is, you cannot have text or an element that uses content syntax followed by one that uses property element syntax followed by a third element that uses text or content syntax.

The following code is therefore fine:

```
<Button ...>
  <Button.BitmapEffect>
    <OuterGlowBitmapEffect GlowColor="Blue" GlowSize="10"/>
  </Button.BitmapEffect>
  Go
  <Button.RenderTransform>
    <RotateTransform Angle="20"/>
  </Button.RenderTransform>
</Button>
```

However, the next bit of code won't work because there are two places where content syntax is used that are separated by an element that uses property element syntax:

```
<Button ...>
  Don't
  <Button.BitmapEffect>
    <OuterGlowBitmapEffect GlowColor="Red" GlowSize="10"/>
  </Button.BitmapEffect>
  Go
</Button>
```

Markup Extensions

The example showed how markup extensions can also be used for property values — for example, the value {x:null}. Wherever curly braces ({}) are used, you are using *markup extensions*. These can be used in both attribute syntax and property element syntax code.

All of the markup extensions in this chapter are specific to WPF. WPF-specific extensions include those used for referencing resources and for data binding.

Desktop and Web Applications

The example shown earlier in this chapter demonstrated how a WPF application can run as both a standalone desktop application and a Web application. You looked at both the WPF Application and WPF Browser Application project templates as a starting point and added XAML and C# code to complete your application. The WPF Application template compiled your project to a `.exe` file, and the WPF Browser application compiled your project to a `.xbap` file.

> XBAP (pronounced ex-bap) is an acronym for XAML Browser Application, and Web applications that are created using WPF are often referred to as XBAP applications.

Most of the differences between these application types are differences between the project (`.csproj`) files. WPF Browser applications have some extra settings defined here, including settings to sign both the application and the manifest for the application (for the security reasons mentioned earlier), and to enable debugging in the browser. There is also, as mentioned earlier, a test certificate that you can use for this signing. In a production environment you replace this certificate with one from your certification authority.

Converting between desktop WPF and Web WPF applications can be a fiddly business, as you must change quite a few settings, and (as shown in the example) certain changes are required to the XAML code. These changes include changing `<Window>` elements to `<Page>` elements and removing functionality such as bitmap effects. The best approach is usually to create separate projects, as in the previous example. However, there are alternatives. Perhaps the best solution so far has been implemented by Karen Corby, and is available at her blog at `http://scorbs.com/2006/06/04/ vs-template-flexible-application/`. Karen has created a flexible application template that you can use instead of the default WPF Application and WPF Browser Application templates. This template enables you to switch between desktop and Web applications using the configuration drop-down in the IDE. The template is well worth a look if you anticipate switching between application types frequently, although in practice you are likely to pick one environment and stick with it.

Figure 34-8 shows how to switch to XBAP output using Karen's flexible application template.

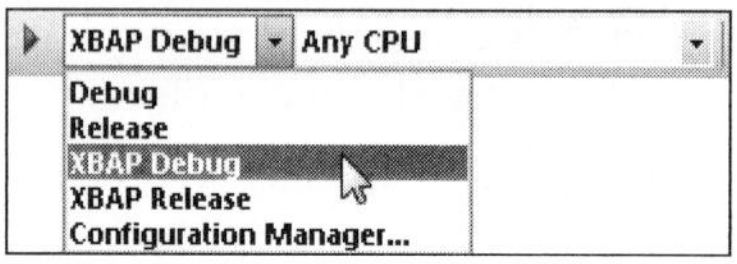

Figure 34-8

One thing that you will have to do manually is disable features that are not available in XBAP applications that run in partial trust. For example, you cannot use bitmap effects. For a full list of features that you can and can't use in a partial trust environment, see the topic "Windows Presentation Foundation Partial Trust Security" in the MSDN documentation.

The Application Object

In WPF, most applications (including all XBAP applications as well as desktop applications that use the WPF Application template) include an instance of a class derived from `System.Windows.Application`. In the example application you saw earlier, this object is defined by the `App.xaml` and `App.xaml.cs` files. `App.xaml` for Ch34Ex01 is as follows:

```
<Application x:Class="Ch34Ex01.App"
    xmlns="http://schemas.microsoft.com/winfx/2006/xaml/presentation"
    xmlns:x="http://schemas.microsoft.com/winfx/2006/xaml"
    StartupUri="Window1.xaml">
    <Application.Resources>

    </Application.Resources>
</Application>
```

The syntax for the `<Application>` element is similar to the `<Window>` element discussed earlier, and uses the `x:Class` attribute in the same way, to link the code to a partial class definition in the code behind.

The object defined by this code is the entry point for the WPF application. There can be only one instance of this object, and it is accessible throughout your code by using the static `Application.Current` property. The application object for an application is extremely useful for the following reasons:

❑ It exposes numerous events that are raised at specific points during the lifetime of an application. This includes the `LoadCompleted` event you saw earlier, which is raised when an application is loaded and rendered, the `DispatcherUnhandledException` event that occurs when an unhandled exception is thrown, and many more.

❑ It contains methods that you can use to set or load cookies, locate and load resources, and more.

❑ It has several properties that you can use to access, for example, application-scoped resources (see the "Static and Dynamic Resources" section) and the windows in the application.

The events raised by the application object are probably the most useful feature in this list, and probably the things you will use most often.

Control Basics

WPF supplies you with a wide array of controls that you can use to create applications. This chapter provides a broad overview of WPF and what you can do with it, so rather than examine each of the WPF controls in detail, you learn about them by seeing them in action.

The following is a list of the controls supplied by WPF:

Border	Image	ScrollViewer
BulletDecorator	Label	Separator
Button	ListBox	Slider
CheckBox	ListView	StatusBar
ComboBox	Menu	TabControl
ContextMenu	PasswordBox	TextBlock
DocumentViewer	Popup	TextBox
Expander	ProgressBar	ToolBar
FlowDocumentPageViewer	PrintDialog	ToolTip
FlowDocumentReader	RadioButton	TreeView
FlowDocumentScrollViewer	RepeatButton	Viewbox
Frame	RichTextBox	
GroupBox	ScrollBar	

This list does not include the WPF controls that are used for layout, described later in this chapter.

Some of the controls shown here have very familiar names, and in fact they do very similar things compared to their counterparts in Windows Forms and ASP.NET applications. For example, you have already seen how the `Button` control can be used to render a button. Others are less familiar, and it is worth experimenting to see what is possible.

These controls initially have a very basic look. To get the most out of them you have to style them, which is arguably where the true power of WPF becomes evident, as you will see later in this chapter. Apart from styling, there are several other features that WPF controls use. In this section you look at the following:

❑   Dependency properties

❑   Attached properties

❑   Routed events

As with other desktop and Web application development, you can (and almost certainly will) create your own controls. When you create a control you can use all of the features described here. In the following sections you see implementation examples.

Dependency Properties

A *dependency property* is a type of property used throughout WPF, in particular on controls, that gives you functionality that extends ordinary .NET properties. To illustrate this, consider an ordinary .NET property. When you create classes in .NET, you typically implement properties using very simple code such as the following:

```
private string aStringProperty;

public string AStringProperty
{
    get
    {
        return aStringProperty;
    }
    set
    {
        aStringProperty = value;
    }
}
```

Here you have a public property that is backed by a private field. This simple implementation is absolutely fine for most purposes, but it doesn't include much functionality other than basic access to state. For example, if you wanted to add the `AStringProperty` to a control (`ControlA`) and you also wanted another control (`ControlB`) to respond to changes to the property, you would have to do the following:

1.   Add the `AStringProperty` to `ControlA` using the code shown earlier.

2.   Add an event to `ControlA`.

3.   Add a method to `ControlA` to raise the event.

4.   Add code to the `set` accessor of `AStringProperty` in `ControlA` to call the event raising method.

5.   Add code to `ControlB` to subscribe to the event exposed by `ControlA`.

There is no need to look at the code required to do this here as you have seen it several times in this book.

The problem with this approach is that there are no defined standards that you can follow to achieve this result. Different developers might add code that achieves the same result in different ways. Moreover, this requires you to identify all the properties that you might want notifications for at the time you develop the controls.

The WPF approach to this problem is to replace the simple property definition used in the earlier code with a dependency property, and then to use formalized, structured techniques to expose property change notifications. A dependency property is a property that is registered with the WPF property system in such a way as to allow extended functionality. This extended functionality includes, but is not limited to, automatic property change notifications. Specifically, dependency properties have the following features:

❑   You can use styles to change the values of dependency properties.

❑   You can set the value of a dependency property by using resources or by data binding.

❑   You can change dependency property values in an animation.

❑   You can set dependency properties hierarchically in XAML — that is, a value for a dependency property that you set on a parent element can be used to set the default value for the same dependency property of its child elements.

❑   You can configure notifications for property value changes using a well-defined coding pattern.

❑   You can configure sets of related properties so that they all update in response to a change to one of them. This is known as *coercion*. The changed property is said to *coerce* the values of the other properties.

❑   You can apply metadata to a dependency property to specify other behavior characteristics. For example, you might specify that if a given property changes, then there may be a need to rearrange the user interface.

In practice, because of the way in which dependency properties are implemented, you may not notice much of a difference compared to ordinary properties at first. However, when you create your own controls, you will quickly find that a lot of functionality suddenly disappears when you use ordinary .NET properties.

Because dependency properties are so prevalent in WPF, you will learn how to implement them later in this chapter.

Attached Properties

An *attached property* is a property that is made available to each child object of an instance of the class that defines the property. For example, imagine you have a class called `Recipe` that can contain child objects that represent ingredients. You could define an attached property called `Quantity` in the `Recipe` class definition that could then be used by each child. Note that child objects do not have to specify values for attached properties.

The main reason you'd want to do this is that the XAML code you use to set values for attached properties is very easy to understand:

```
<Recipe Name="Simple Vegetable Chili">
  <TinOfKidneyBeans Recipe.Quantity="2" Mashed="true" />
  <TinOfChoppedTomatoes Recipe.Quantity="2" />
  <FreshChili Recipe.Quantity="5" Notes="Chopped fine, vary to taste." />
  <Onion Recipe.Quantity="1" Notes="Chopped and fried in olive oil." />
  <LBVPort Notes="Just a dash." />
</Recipe>
```

The syntax used here is a form of attribute syntax that you looked at earlier. Here, the attached property is referred to using the name of the parent element, a period, and the name of the attached property.

In WPF, attached properties serve a variety of uses. You will see a lot of attached properties shortly, when you look at how to position controls in the "Control Layout" section. You will learn how container controls define attached properties that enable child controls to define, for example, which edges of the container to dock to.

Routed Events

Because of its hierarchical nature, WPF applications often consist of controls that contain other controls, which contain more controls, and so on. A *routed event* is a mechanism by which an event that affects one control in a hierarchy can also be made to affect other events in the hierarchy, without requiring complex code.

One excellent example of this is when you enable users to interact with your applications with the mouse, which is of course extremely common. When a user clicks a button in your application, you typically want to respond to the click event. One way to do this is familiar to you from Windows Forms and ASP.NET development: Provide an event handler for an event that is exposed by the button, and respond to the mouse click there.

While it might not seem so at first, this technique is actually quite limiting, and has led to some quite confusing code — for example, in some Windows Forms applications. The reason is because some mechanism is required to identify which control should respond to the mouse click by raising its click event, and this may not immediately be obvious. In the simple example given here, should the click event of the button be raised, or should the click event of the Window that contains the button be raised? If both the button and the Window have event handlers and only one of these events is to be raised, you probably want the button to raise the event. However, what if you want *both* events to be raised, and to be raised in a specific order? With Windows Forms applications, you probably have to write (possibly complex) custom code to achieve this.

The mouse click event for WPF controls, including `Button` and `Window`, is implemented as a *routed event*, which circumvents this problem. Routed events are raised by all objects in a hierarchy in a specific order, giving you complete control over how to respond to them.

For example, consider a `Window` that contains a `Grid`, which in turn contains a `Rectangle`. When you click on the `Rectangle`, the following sequence of events occurs:

1. The mouse down event is raised on the `Window`.

2. The mouse down event is raised on the `Grid`.

3. The mouse down event is raised on the `Rectangle`.

    (You might expect things to finish here, but the sequence continues. . .)

4. Another mouse down event is raised on the `Rectangle`.

5. Another mouse down event is raised on the `Grid`.

6. Another mouse down event is raised on the `Window`.

You can respond to the event at any point in the preceding sequence by adding an appropriate event handler method. You can also choose to interrupt the sequence at any point in an event handler method, but event handlers don't interrupt the sequence by default. This means that you can trigger multiple event handler methods from a single event (in this case, a single mouse down event).

When describing the sequence of events shown here, WPF introduces some useful terminology. As an event moves down through the hierarchy of controls it is said to be *tunneling*. On the way back up through the hierarchy it is *bubbling*.

In addition, wherever routed events are used in WPF, the event names enable you to tell whether the event is a tunneling or bubbling event. All tunneling events start with the prefix `Preview`. For example, the Window control has both a `PreviewMouseDown` and a `MouseDown` event. You can add handlers to one, both, or none of these events as desired.

Figure 34-9 shows the preceding sequence in terms of which events are fired when, and how the event is tunneled and bubbled through the control hierarchy.

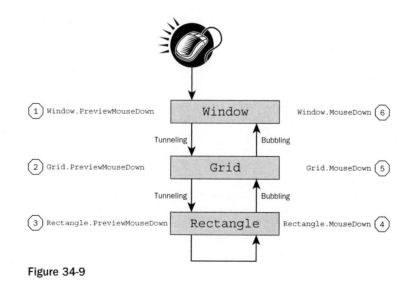

Figure 34-9

Routed event handlers have two parameters: the source of the event, and an instance of `RoutedEventArgs` or a class that derives from `RoutedEventArgs`.

When you implement an event handler for a routed event, you can, if desired, set the `Handled` property of the `RoutedEventArgs` object to `true`. If you do so, then no further processing takes place — that is, no more event handlers will fire for the event.

`RoutedEventArgs` also exposes a property called `Source`, which enables you to tell which control raised the event to start off with. This control is the one in which WPF initially detected the event, so in the scenario illustrated in Figure 34-9, it will be the `Rectangle` control. This can be very useful, as parent controls can determine which child control, if any, was clicked. Note that this "hit testing" is quite sophisticated. WPF is capable of ignoring clicks on transparent regions of controls, for example, without you having to do anything to enable this. Alternatively, you can create transparent controls that do respond to mouse clicks, so you have a great deal of flexibility.

Note also that routed events cover far more than just mouse clicks; you can use them for a wide array of purposes, including keyboard interaction, data binding, timers, and more. Attached events, which you'll look at shortly, make routed events even more useful.

The following Try It Out illustrates the situation described in this section and covers some additional information about routed events.

Try It Out Working with Routed Events

1. Create a new WPF application called Ch34Ex02 and save it in the directory C:\BegVCSharp\Chapter34.

2. Modify the code in `Window1.xaml` as follows:

```
<Window
    xmlns="http://schemas.microsoft.com/winfx/2006/xaml/presentation"
    xmlns:x="http://schemas.microsoft.com/winfx/2006/xaml"
    x:Class="Ch34Ex02.Window1"
    Title="Routed Events" Height="400" Width="800"
    MouseDown="Generic_MouseDown" PreviewMouseDown="Generic_MouseDown"
    MouseUp="Window_MouseUp">

    <Grid Name="contentGrid" MouseDown="Generic_MouseDown"
      PreviewMouseDown="Generic_MouseDown" Background="Azure">
      <Rectangle Name="clickMeRectangle" Margin="10,10,0,0" Height="23"
        HorizontalAlignment="Left" VerticalAlignment="Top" Width="70" Stroke="Black"
        MouseDown="Generic_MouseDown" PreviewMouseDown="Generic_MouseDown"
        Fill="CadetBlue" />
      <Button Name="clickMeButton" Margin="0,10,10,0" Height="23"
        HorizontalAlignment="Right" VerticalAlignment="Top" Width="70"
        MouseDown="Generic_MouseDown" PreviewMouseDown="Generic_MouseDown"
        Click="clickMeButton_Click">Click Me</Button>
      <TextBlock Name="outputText" Margin="10,40,10,10" Background="Cornsilk" />
    </Grid>
</Window>
```

3. Modify the code in `Window1.xaml.cs` as follows (note that depending on which IDE you are using and how you entered the XAML code, empty event handler methods may have been added for you automatically):

```
public partial class Window1 : Window
{
    private void Generic_MouseDown(object sender, MouseButtonEventArgs e)
    {
        outputText.Text = string.Format(
            "{0}Event {1} raised by control {2}. e.Source={3}\n",
            outputText.Text,
            e.RoutedEvent.Name,
            sender.ToString(),
            ((FrameworkElement)e.Source).Name);
    }

    private void Window_MouseUp(object sender, MouseButtonEventArgs e)
    {
        outputText.Text = string.Format(
            "{0}==========\n\n",
            outputText.Text);
    }

    private void clickMeButton_Click(object sender, RoutedEventArgs e)
    {
        outputText.Text = string.Format(
            "{0}Button clicked!\n==========\n\n",
            outputText.Text);
    }
}
```

4. Run the application. When the application is running, click once on the rectangle in the top, left corner, once in the light-blue area between the rectangle and the button, and once on the button. Figure 34-10 shows the result.

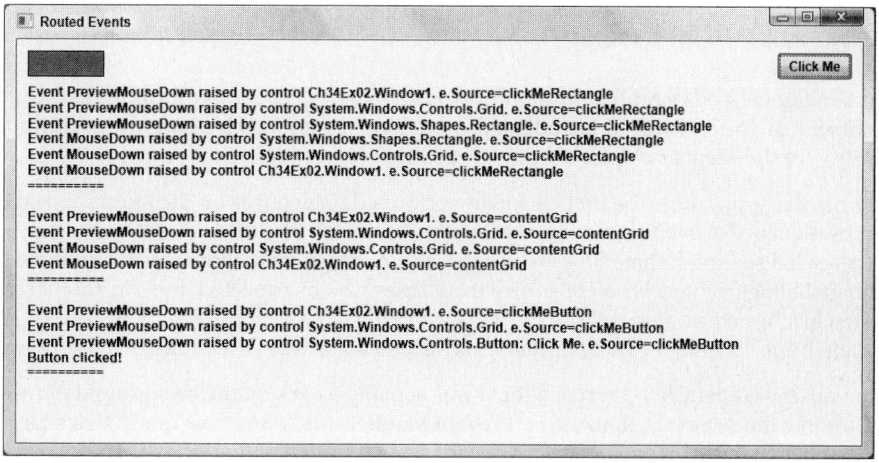

Figure 34-10

How It Works

This example demonstrated how routed events are processed by highlighting the MouseDown and PreviewMouseDown events that are exposed by all WPF controls. You also looked at what happens when you include a button in the chain of events. The XAML code you used was already very simple, but to examine the essential parts (in the context of this example) consider the following:

```
<Window
    x:Class="Ch34Ex02.Window1" MouseDown="Generic_MouseDown"
    PreviewMouseDown="Generic_MouseDown" MouseUp="Window_MouseUp">

    <Grid Name="contentGrid" MouseDown="Generic_MouseDown"
      PreviewMouseDown="Generic_MouseDown">
      <Rectangle Name="clickMeRectangle" MouseDown="Generic_MouseDown"
        PreviewMouseDown="Generic_MouseDown" />
      <Button Name="clickMeButton" MouseDown="Generic_MouseDown"
        PreviewMouseDown="Generic_MouseDown" Click="clickMeButton_Click" />
      <TextBlock Name="outputText" />
    </Grid>
</Window>
```

Here, all the properties that don't affect functionality have been removed so that you can concentrate on the code that relates to routed event handling. Three event handlers are used, configured for events as shown in the following table:

Event Handler	Events Handled
Generic_MouseDown()	Window.PreviewMouseDown Window.MouseDown Grid.PreviewMouseDown Grid.MouseDown Rectangle.PreviewMouseDown Rectangle.MouseDown
Window_MouseUp()	Window.MouseUp
clickMeButton_Click()	Button.Click

The event handler methods simply output information to the TextBlock control so that you can see what is happening. The text output includes the event name, the control raising the event, and the source control for the event as obtained from RoutedEventArgs.Source.

When you run the application, the first click you performed, which was on the Rectangle control, gave you the sequence of events described before the Try It Out. The Generic_MouseDown() event handler was called six times: three times for PreviewMouseDown tunneling events and three times for MouseDown bubbling events. The event source in all cases was, as expected, the control that satisfied the hit test, which was the Rectangle, clickMeRectangle. The Window_MouseUp() event handler was also called, after the other event handlers, and added some text to separate this test from the next.

After that, you clicked between controls, which was actually a click on the background of the Grid control. This time the Generic_MouseDown() event handler was called four times: twice for PreviewMouseDown tunneling events and twice for MouseDown bubbling events. The event source here was the Grid control, contentGrid, in all cases. Again, the Window_MouseUp() event handler was called after the Generic_MouseDown() calls.

Finally, you clicked on the Button control. This time Generic_MouseDown() was called only three times. Next, the Button.Click event fired, resulting in a call to clickMeButton_Click(). Finally, the Window_MouseUp() event handler was called.

What happened in this final chain of events is that the MouseDown event was handled by the button, and used to trigger its Click event. The underlying implementation of the MouseDown event hander for the button set the Handled property of the RoutedEventArgs event arguments parameter to true. This interrupted the flow of events such that the MouseDown event was not bubbled back up the control hierarchy.

In case you were wondering, the way the Button control interrupts event routing is the reason why you looked at clicking on the Rectangle control before the Try It Out.

Attached Events

The preceding example added a Button.Click event to the Button control on a page. You didn't add handlers to the Click event of Grid or Window because these two controls don't have a Click event. However, sometimes you might wish that they did.

For example, imagine you have a window containing a thousand buttons and you want to handle the Click event of each. You could have a thousand event handlers, or you could simplify things by having a single, shared event handler. Even with a single event handler, though, you have to associate it with each and every Button.Click event.

WPF provides an alternative (better) way of dealing with this situation: *attached events*. By using the attached events system, you can handle events on controls that don't expose them, so in the example discussed here you could handle the Button.Click event on the Grid that contains the buttons — even though the Grid control doesn't have a Click event. In fact, you handle ButtonBase.Click, as ButtonBase is the class that defines the Click event that the Button control inherits.

The syntax for this is the same attribute syntax used for attached properties:

```
<Grid Name="contentGrid" ButtonBase.Click="contentGrid_Click" ...>
   <Button Name="button1" ...>Button1</Button>
   <Button Name="button2" ...>Button2</Button>
   ...
   <Button Name="button1000" ...>Button1000</Button>
</Grid>
```

In the event handler you get a reference to the Grid control in the sender parameter, and you can use the RoutedEventArgs.Source property to determine which button was clicked, and respond accordingly. This event is raised only when a button is clicked, not when you click the Grid control background, because the Grid control has no Click event to raise.

Control Layout

So far in this chapter you have used the Grid element to lay out controls, primarily because that is the control supplied by default when you create a new WPF application. However, you haven't yet examined the full capabilities of this class, nor have you learned about the other layout containers that you can use to achieve alternative layouts. This section looks at control layout in more detail, as it is a fundamental concept to grasp in WPF.

All content layout controls derive from the abstract Panel class. This class simply defines a container that can contain a collection of objects that derive from UIElement. All WPF controls derive from UIElement. You cannot use the Panel class directly for control layout, but you can derive from it if you want to. Alternatively, you can use one of the following layout controls that derive from Panel:

❑ **Canvas:** This control enables you to position child controls any way you see fit. It doesn't place any restrictions on child control positioning, but nor does it provide any assistance in child control positioning.

❑ **DockPanel:** This control enables you to dock child controls against one of its four edges. The last child control fills the remaining space.

❑ **Grid:** You have seen how this control enables flexible positioning of child controls. What you haven't seen is how you can divide the layout of this control into rows and columns, which enables you to align controls in a grid layout.

❑ **StackPanel:** This control positions its child controls in a sequential horizontal or vertical layout.

❑ **WrapPanel:** This control positions its child controls in a sequential horizontal or vertical layout as StackPanel, but rather than a single row or column of controls, this control wraps its children into multiple rows or columns according to the space available.

You'll look at how to use these controls in more detail shortly. First, however, there are a few basic concepts to understand:

❑ How controls appear in stack order

❑ How to use alignment, margins, and padding to position controls and their content

❑ How to use the Border control

Stack Order

When a container control contains multiple child controls, they are drawn in a specific stack order. You may be familiar with this concept from drawing packages. The best way to think of stack order is to imagine that each control is contained in a plate of glass, and the container contains a stack of these plates of glass. The appearance of the container, therefore, is what you would see if you looked down from the top through these layers of glass. The controls contained by the container overlap, so what you see is determined by the order of the glass plates. If a control is higher up the stack, then it will be the control that you see in the overlap area. Controls lower down may be partially or completely hidden by controls above them.

This also affects hit testing when you click on a window with the mouse. The target control will always be the one that is uppermost in the stack when considering overlapping controls. The stack order of controls is determined by the order in which they appear in the list of children for a container. The first child in a container is placed on the lowest layer in the stack, and the last child on the topmost layer. The children between the first and last child are placed on increasingly higher layers. The stack order of controls has additional implications for some of the layout controls that you can use in WPF, as you will see shortly.

Alignment, Margins, Padding, and Dimensions

Earlier examples showed how a combination of `Margin`, `HorizontalAlignment`, and `VerticalAlignment` enables you to position controls in a `Grid` container. You have also seen how you can use `Height` and `Width` to specify dimensions. These properties, along with `Padding`, which you haven't looked at yet, are useful for all of the layout controls (or most of them, as you will see), but in different ways. Different layout controls can also set default values for these properties. You'll see a lot of this by example in subsequent sections, but before doing that it is worth covering the basics.

The two alignment properties determine how the control is aligned, but you haven't yet looked at all the values for these properties. `HorizontalAlignment`, for example, can be set to `Left`, `Right`, `Center`, or `Stretch`. `Left` and `Right` tend to position controls to the left or right edges of the container, `Center` positions controls in the middle, and `Stretch` changes the width of the control so that its edges reach to the sides of the container. `VerticalAlignment` is similar, and has the values `Top`, `Bottom`, `Center`, or `Stretch`.

`Margin` and `Padding` specify the space to leave blank around the edges of controls and inside the edges of controls, respectively. Earlier examples used `Margin` to position controls relative to, for example, the top-left corner of a `Grid`. This worked because with `HorizontalAlignment` set to `Left` and `VerticalAlignment` set to `Top`, the control is positioned tight against the top-left corner, and `Margin` inserted a gap around the edge of the control. `Padding` is used similarly, but spaces out the content of a control from its edges. This is particularly useful for `Border`, as you will see in the next section. Both `Padding` and `Margin` can be specified in four parts (in the form `leftAmount`, `topAmount`, `rightAmount`, `bottomAmount`) or as a single value (a `Thickness` value).

Later, you will see how `Height` and `Width` are often controlled by other properties. For example, with `HorizontalAlignment` set to `Stretch`, the `Width` property of a control changes as the width of its container changes.

Border

The `Border` control is a very simple, and very useful, container control. It holds a single child, not multiple children like the more complicated controls you'll look at in a moment. This child will be sized to completely fill the `Border` control. This may not seem particularly useful, but remember that you can use the `Margin` and `Padding` properties to position the `Border` within its container, and the content of the `Border` within the edges of the `Border`. You can also set, for example, the `Background` property of a `Border` so that it is visible. You will see this control in action shortly.

Canvas

The `Canvas` control, as previously noted, provides complete freedom over control positioning. Another thing about `Canvas` is that `HorizontalAligment` and `VerticalAlignment` properties used with a child element will have no effect whatsoever over the positioning of those elements.

You can use `Margin` to position elements in a `Canvas` as per earlier examples, but a better way is to use the `Canvas.Left`, `Canvas.Top`, `Canvas.Right`, and `Canvas.Bottom` attached properties that the `Canvas` class exposes:

```
<Canvas ...>
  <Button Canvas.Top="10" Canvas.Left="10" ...>Button1</Button>
</Canvas>
```

The preceding code positions a `Button` so that its top edge is 10 pixels from the top edge of the `Canvas`, and its left edge is 10 pixels from the left edge of the `Canvas`. Note that the `Top` and `Left` properties take precedence over `Bottom` and `Right`. For example, if you specify both `Top` and `Bottom`, then the `Bottom` property is ignored.

Figure 34-11 shows two `Rectangle` controls positioned in a `Canvas` control, with the window resized to two sizes.

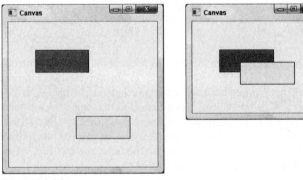

Figure 34-11

All of the example layouts in this section can be found in the `LayoutExamples` *project in the downloadable code for this chapter.*

One `Rectangle` is positioned relative to the top-left corner, and one is positioned relative to the bottom-right corner. As you resize the window, these relative positions are maintained. You can also see the importance of the stacking order of the `Rectangle` controls. The bottom-right `Rectangle` is higher up in the stacking order, so when they overlap this is the control that you see.

The code for this example is as follows:

```
<Canvas Background="AliceBlue">
  <Rectangle Canvas.Left="50" Canvas.Top="50" Height="40" Width="100"
    Stroke="Black" Fill="Chocolate" />
  <Rectangle Canvas.Right="50" Canvas.Bottom="50" Height="40" Width="100"
    Stroke="Black" Fill="Bisque" />
</Canvas>
```

DockPanel

The DockPanel control, as its name suggests, enables you to dock controls to one of its edges. This sort of layout should be familiar to you, even if you've never stopped to notice it before. It is how, for example, the Ribbon control in Word remains at the top of the Word window, or how the various windows in VS and VCE are positioned. In VS and VCE you may also (intentionally or accidentally) change the docking of windows by dragging them around.

DockPanel has a single attached property that child controls can use to specify the edge that controls dock to: DockPanel.Dock. You can set this property to Left, Top, Right, or Bottom.

The stack order of controls in a DockPanel is extremely important, as every time you dock a control to an edge you also reduce the available space of subsequent child controls. For example, you might dock a toolbar to the top of a DockPanel and then a second toolbar to the left of the DockPanel. The first control would stretch across the entire top of the DockPanel display area, but the second control would only stretch from the bottom of the first toolbar to the bottom of the DockPanel along the left edge.

The last child control you specify will (usually) fill the area that remains after all the previous children have been positioned. (You can control this behavior, which is why this statement is qualified.)

When you position a control in a DockPanel, the area occupied by the control may be smaller than the area of the DockPanel that is reserved for the control. For example, if you dock a Button with a Width of 100, a Height of 50, and a HorizontalAlingment of Left to the top of a DockPanel, then there will be space to the right of the Button that isn't used by other docked children. In addition, if the Button control has a Margin of 20, then a total of 90 pixels at the top of the DockPanel will be reserved (the height of the control plus the top and bottom margins). You need to take this behavior into account when you use DockPanel for layout; otherwise, you may end up with unexpected results.

Figure 34-12 shows a sample DockPanel layout.

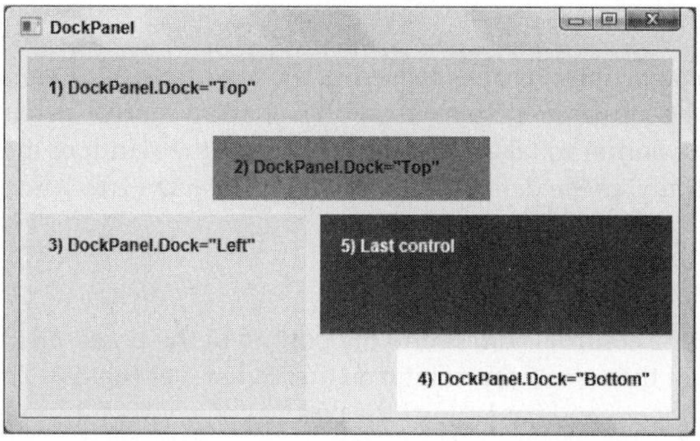

Figure 34-12

The code for this layout is as follows:

```
<DockPanel Background="AliceBlue">
  <Border DockPanel.Dock="Top" Padding="10" Margin="5" Background="Aquamarine"
    Height="45">
    <Label>1) DockPanel.Dock="Top"</Label>
  </Border>
  <Border DockPanel.Dock="Top" Padding="10" Margin="5" Background="PaleVioletRed"
    Height="45" Width="200">
    <Label>2) DockPanel.Dock="Top"</Label>
  </Border>
  <Border DockPanel.Dock="Left" Padding="10" Margin="5" Background="Bisque"
    Width="200">
    <Label>3) DockPanel.Dock="Left"</Label>
  </Border>
  <Border DockPanel.Dock="Bottom" Padding="10" Margin="5" Background="Ivory"
    Width="200" HorizontalAlignment="Right">
    <Label>4) DockPanel.Dock="Bottom"</Label>
  </Border>
  <Border Padding="10" Margin="5" Background="BlueViolet">
    <Label Foreground="White">5) Last control</Label>
  </Border>
</DockPanel>
```

This code uses the `Border` control introduced earlier to clearly mark out the docked control regions in the example layout, along with `Label` controls to output simple informative text. To understand the layout, you must read it from top to bottom, looking at each control in turn:

1. The first `Border` control is docked to the top of the `DockPanel`. The total area taken up in the `DockPanel` is the top 55 pixels (`Height` + 2 × `Margin`). Note that the `Padding` property does not affect this layout, as it is inside the edge of the `Border`, but this property does control the positioning of the embedded `Label` control. The `Border` control fills any available space along the edge it is docked to if not constrained by `Height` or `Width` properties, which is why it stretches across the `DockPanel`.

2. The second `Border` control is also docked to the top of the `DockPanel`, and takes up another 55 pixels from the top of the display area. This `Border` control also includes a `Width` property, which causes the border to take up only a portion of the width of the `DockPanel`. It is positioned centrally, as the default value for `HorizonalAlignement` in a `DockPanel` is `Center`.

3. The third `Border` control is docked to the left of the `DockPanel` and takes up 210 pixels of the left of the display.

4. The fourth `Border` control is docked to the bottom of the `DockPanel` and takes up 30 pixels plus the height of the `Label` control it contains (whatever that is). This height is determined by the `Margin`, `Padding`, and contents of the border control, as it is not specified explicitly. The `Border` control is locked to the bottom-right corner of the `DockPanel`, as it has a `HorizontalAlignment` of `Right`.

5. The fifth and final `Border` fills the remaining space.

Run this example and experiment with resizing content. Note that the further up the stacking order a control is, the more priority is given to its space. By shrinking the window, the fifth `Border` control can quickly be completely obscured by controls further up the stacking order. Be careful when using `DockPanel` control layout to avoid this, perhaps by setting minimum dimensions for the window.

Grid

`Grid` controls can have multiple rows and columns that you can use to lay out child controls. You have used `Grid` controls several times already in this chapter, but in all cases you used a `Grid` with a single row and a single column. To add more rows and columns, you must use the `RowDefinitions` and `ColumnDefinitions` properties, which are collections of `RowDefinition` and `ColumnDefinition` objects, respectively, and are specified using property element syntax:

```
<Grid>
  <Grid.RowDefinitions>
    <RowDefinition />
    <RowDefinition />
  </Grid.RowDefinitions>
  <Grid.ColumnDefinitions>
    <ColumnDefinition />
    <ColumnDefinition />
  </Grid.ColumnDefinitions>
  ...
</Grid>
```

This code defines a `Grid` control with three rows and two columns. Note that no extra information is required here; with this code, each row and column is dynamically resized automatically as the `Grid` control resizes. Each row will be a third of the height of the `Grid`, and each column will be half the width. You can display lines between cells in a `Grid` by setting the `Grid.ShowGridlines` property to `true`.

You can control the resizing with `Width`, `Height`, `MinWidth`, `MaxWidth`, `MinHeight`, and `MaxHeight` properties. For example, setting the `Width` property of a column ensures that the column stays at that width. You can also set the `Width` property of a column to `*`, which means "fill the remaining space after calculating the width of all other columns." This is actually the default. When you have multiple columns with a `Width` of `*`, then the remaining space is divided between them equally. The `*` value can also be used with the `Height` property of rows. The other possible value for `Height` and `Width` is `Auto`, which sizes the row or column according to its content. You can also use `GridSplitter` controls to enable users to customize the dimensions of rows and columns by clicking and dragging.

Child controls of a `Grid` control can use the attached `Grid.Column` and `Grid.Row` properties to specify what cell they are contained in. Both these properties default to 0, so if you omit them, then the child control is placed in the top-left cell. Child controls can also use `Grid.ColumnSpan` and `Grid.RowSpan` to be positioned over multiple cells in a table, where the upper-left cell is specified by `Grid.Column` and `Grid.Row`.

Figure 34-13 shows a `Grid` control containing multiple ellipses and a `GridSplitter` with the window resized to two sizes.

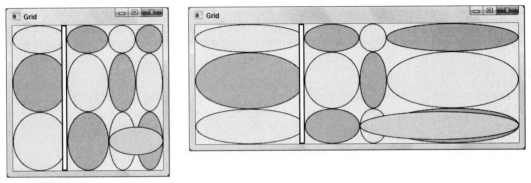

Figure 34-13

The code used here is as follows:

```xml
<Grid Background="AliceBlue">
  <Grid.ColumnDefinitions>
    <ColumnDefinition MinWidth="100" MaxWidth="200" />
    <ColumnDefinition MaxWidth="100" />
    <ColumnDefinition Width="50" />
    <ColumnDefinition Width="*" />
  </Grid.ColumnDefinitions>
  <Grid.RowDefinitions>
    <RowDefinition Height="50" />
    <RowDefinition MinHeight="100" />
    <RowDefinition />
  </Grid.RowDefinitions>
  <Ellipse Grid.Row="0" Grid.Column="0" Fill="BlanchedAlmond" Stroke="Black" />
  <Ellipse Grid.Row="0" Grid.Column="1" Fill="BurlyWood" Stroke="Black" />
  <Ellipse Grid.Row="0" Grid.Column="2" Fill="BlanchedAlmond" Stroke="Black" />
  <Ellipse Grid.Row="0" Grid.Column="3" Fill="BurlyWood" Stroke="Black" />
  <Ellipse Grid.Row="1" Grid.Column="0" Fill="BurlyWood" Stroke="Black" />
  <Ellipse Grid.Row="1" Grid.Column="1" Fill="BlanchedAlmond" Stroke="Black" />
  <Ellipse Grid.Row="1" Grid.Column="2" Fill="BurlyWood" Stroke="Black" />
  <Ellipse Grid.Row="1" Grid.Column="3" Fill="BlanchedAlmond" Stroke="Black" />
  <Ellipse Grid.Row="2" Grid.Column="0" Fill="BlanchedAlmond" Stroke="Black" />
  <Ellipse Grid.Row="2" Grid.Column="1" Fill="BurlyWood" Stroke="Black" />
  <Ellipse Grid.Row="2" Grid.Column="2" Fill="BlanchedAlmond" Stroke="Black" />
  <Ellipse Grid.Row="2" Grid.Column="3" Fill="BurlyWood" Stroke="Black" />
  <Ellipse Grid.Row="2" Grid.Column="2" Grid.ColumnSpan="2" Fill="Gold"
    Stroke="Black" Height="50"/>
  <GridSplitter Grid.RowSpan="3" Width="10" BorderThickness="2">
    <GridSplitter.BorderBrush>
      <SolidColorBrush Color="Black" />
    </GridSplitter.BorderBrush>
  </GridSplitter>
</Grid>
```

This code uses various combinations of properties on the row and column definitions to achieve an interesting effect when you resize the display, so it's worth testing for yourself.

First, consider the rows. The top row has a fixed height of 50 pixels, the second row has a minimum height of 100, and the third row fills the remaining space. This means that if the Grid has a height of less than 150 pixels, then the third row will not be visible. When the Grid has a height of between 150 and 250 pixels, only the size of the third row will change, from 0 to 100 pixels. This is because the remaining space is calculated as the total height minus the combined heights of rows that have a fixed height. This remaining space is allocated between the second and third rows, but because the second row has a minimum height of 100 pixels, it will not change its height until the total height of the Grid reaches 250 pixels. Finally, when the height of the Grid is greater than 250, both the second and third rows will share the remaining space, so their height will be both equal to and greater than 100 pixels.

Next, look at the columns. Only the third column has a fixed size, of 50 pixels. The first and second columns share up to a maximum of 300 pixels. The fourth column will therefore be the only one to increase in size when the total width of the Grid control exceeds 550 pixels. To work this out for yourself, consider how many pixels are available to the columns and how they are distributed. First, 50 pixels are allocated to the third column, leaving 500 for the rest of the columns. The third column has a maximum width of 100 pixels, leaving 400 between the first and fourth columns. The first column has a maximum width of 200, so even if the width increases beyond this point, it will not consume any more space. Instead, the fourth column will increase in size.

Note two additional points in this example. First, the final ellipse defined spans the third and fourth columns to illustrate Grid.ColumnSpan. Second, a GridSplitter is provided to enable resizing of the first and second columns. However, once the total width of the Grid control exceeds 550 pixels, this GridSplitter will not be able to size these columns, as neither the first nor the second column can increase in size.

The GridSplitter control is useful, but it has a very dull appearance. This is one control that really needs to be styled, or at least made invisible by setting its Background property to Transparent, for you to make the most of it.

If you have multiple Grid controls in a window, you can also define shared size groups for rows or columns by using the ShareSizeGroup property in row and/or column definitions, which you just set to a string identifier of your choice. For example, if a column in a shared size group changes in one Grid control, then a column in another Grid control in the same size group will change to match this size. You can enable or disable this functionality through the Grid.IsSharedSizeScope property.

StackPanel

After the complexity of Grid, you may be relieved to discover that StackPanel is a relatively simple layout control. You can think of StackPanel as being a slimmed down version of DockPanel, where the edge to which child controls are docked is fixed for those controls. The other difference between these controls is that the last child control of a StackPanel doesn't fill the remaining space. However, controls will, by default, stretch to the edges of the StackPanel control.

The direction in which controls are stacked is determined by three properties. Orientation can be set to Horizontal or Vertical, and HorizontalAlignment and VerticalAlignement can be used to determine whether control stacks are positioned next to the top, bottom, left, or right edge of the StackPanel. You can even make the stacked controls stack at the center of the StackPanel using the Center value for the alignment property you use.

Figure 34-14 shows two `StackPanel` controls, each of which contains three buttons. The `StackPanel` controls are positioned using a `Grid` control with two rows and one column.

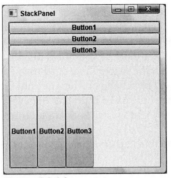

Figure 34-14

The code used here is as follows:

```
<Grid Background="AliceBlue">
  <Grid.RowDefinitions>
    <RowDefinition />
    <RowDefinition />
  </Grid.RowDefinitions>
  <StackPanel Grid.Row="0">
    <Button>Button1</Button>
    <Button>Button2</Button>
    <Button>Button3</Button>
  </StackPanel>
  <StackPanel Grid.Row="1" Orientation="Horizontal">
    <Button>Button1</Button>
    <Button>Button2</Button>
    <Button>Button3</Button>
  </StackPanel>
</Grid>
```

When you use `StackPanel` layout, you often need to add scroll bars so that it is possible to view all the controls contained in the `StackPanel`. This is another area where WPF does a lot of the heavy lifting for you. You can use the `ScrollViewer` control to achieve this — simply enclose the `StackPanel` in this control:

```
<Grid Background="AliceBlue">
  <Grid.RowDefinitions>
    <RowDefinition />
    <RowDefinition />
  </Grid.RowDefinitions>
  <ScrollViewer>
    <StackPanel Grid.Row="0">
      <Button>Button1</Button>
      <Button>Button2</Button>
```

```
      <Button>Button3</Button>
    </StackPanel>
  </ScrollViewer>
  <StackPanel Grid.Row="1" Orientation="Horizontal">
    <Button>Button1</Button>
    <Button>Button2</Button>
    <Button>Button3</Button>
  </StackPanel>
</Grid>
```

You can use more complicated techniques to scroll in different ways, or to scroll programmatically, but often this is all you need to do.

WrapPanel

WrapPanel is essentially an extended version of StackPanel where controls that "don't fit" are moved to additional rows (or columns). Figure 34-15 shows a WrapPanel control containing multiple shapes, with the window resized to two sizes.

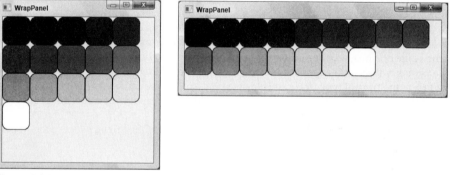

Figure 34-15

An abbreviated version of the code to achieve this is shown here:

```
<WrapPanel Background="AliceBlue">
  <Rectangle Fill="#FF000000" Height="50" Width="50" Stroke="Black" RadiusX="10"
    RadiusY="10" />
  <Rectangle Fill="#FF111111" Height="50" Width="50" Stroke="Black" RadiusX="10"
    RadiusY="10" />
  <Rectangle Fill="#FF222222" Height="50" Width="50" Stroke="Black" RadiusX="10"
    RadiusY="10" />
  ...
  <Rectangle Fill="#FFFFFFFF" Height="50" Width="50" Stroke="Black" RadiusX="10"
    RadiusY="10" />
</WrapPanel>
```

`WrapPanel` controls are a great way to create a dynamic layout that enables users to control exactly how content should be viewed.

Control Styling

One of the best features of WPF is the complete control it provides designers over the look and feel of user interfaces. Central to this is the ability to style controls however you want, in two or three dimensions. Until now, you have been using the basic styling for controls that is supplied with .NET 3.5, but the actual possibilities are endless.

This section describes two basic techniques:

❑ **Styles**: Sets of properties that are applied to a control as a batch

❑ **Templates**: The controls that are used to build the display for a control

There is some overlap here, as styles can contain templates.

Styles

WPF controls have a property called `Style` (inherited from `FrameworkElement`) that can be set to an instance of the `Style` class. The `Style` class is quite complex and is capable of advanced styling functionality, but at its heart it is essentially a set of `Setter` objects. Each `Setter` object is responsible for setting the value of a property according to its `Property` property (the name of the property to set) and its `Value` property (the value to set the property to). You can either fully qualify the name you use in `Property` to the control type (for example, `Button.Foreground`) or you can set the `TargetType` property of the `Style` object (for example, `Button`) so that it is capable of resolving property names.

The following code, then, shows how to use a `Style` object to set the `Foreground` property of a `Button` control:

```
<Button>
  Click me!
  <Button.Style>
    <Style TargetType="Button">
      <Setter Property="Foreground">
        <Setter.Value>
          <SolidColorBrush Color="Purple" />
        </Setter.Value>
      </Setter>
    </Style>
  </Button.Style>
</Button>
```

Obviously, in this case it would be far easier simply to set the `Foreground` property of the button in the usual way. Styles become much more useful when you turn them into resources, because resources can be reused. You will learn how to do this later in the chapter.

Templates

Controls are constructed using templates, which you can customize. A template consists of a hierarchy of controls used to build the display of a control, which may include a content presenter for controls such as buttons that display content.

The template of a control is stored in its `Template` property, which is an instance of the `ControlTemplate` class. The `ControlTemplate` class includes a `TargetType` property that you can set to the type of control for which you are defining a template, and it can contain a single control. This control can be a container such as `Grid`, so this doesn't exactly limit what you can do.

Typically, you set the template for a class by using a style. This simply involves providing controls to use for the `Template` property in the following way:

```
<Button>
   Click me!
   <Button.Style>
      <Style TargetType="Button">
         <Setter Property="Template">
            <Setter.Value>
               <ControlTemplate TargetType="Button">
                  ...
               </ControlTemplate>
            </Setter.Value>
         </Setter>
      </Style>
   </Button.Style>
</Button>
```

Some controls may require more than one template. For example, `CheckBox` controls use one template for a check box (`CheckBox.Template`) and one template to output text next to the check box (`CheckBox.ContentTemplate`).

Templates that require content presenters can include a `ContentPresenter` control at the location where you want to output content. Some controls, in particular those that output collections of items, use alternative techniques, which aren't covered in this chapter.

Again, replacing templates is most useful when combined with resources. However, as control styling is a very common technique, it is worth looking at how to do it in a Try It Out.

Using Styles and Templates

1.   Create a new WPF application called Ch34Ex03 and save it in the directory
      C:\BegVCSharp\Chapter34.

2.   Modify the code in Window1.xaml as follows:

```xaml
<Window x:Class="Ch34Ex03.Window1"
  xmlns="http://schemas.microsoft.com/winfx/2006/xaml/presentation"
  xmlns:x="http://schemas.microsoft.com/winfx/2006/xaml"
  Title="Nasty Button" Height="150" Width="550">
  <Grid Background="Black">
    <Button Margin="20" Click="Button_Click">
      Would anyone use a button like this?
      <Button.Style>
        <Style TargetType="Button">
          <Setter Property="FontSize" Value="18" />
          <Setter Property="FontFamily" Value="arial" />
          <Setter Property="FontWeight" Value="bold" />
          <Setter Property="Foreground">
            <Setter.Value>
              <LinearGradientBrush StartPoint="0.5,0" EndPoint="0.5,1">
                <LinearGradientBrush.GradientStops>
                  <GradientStop Offset="0.0" Color="Purple" />
                  <GradientStop Offset="0.5" Color="Azure" />
                  <GradientStop Offset="1.0" Color="Purple" />
                </LinearGradientBrush.GradientStops>
              </LinearGradientBrush>
            </Setter.Value>
          </Setter>
          <Setter Property="Template">
            <Setter.Value>
              <ControlTemplate TargetType="Button">
                <Grid>
                  <Grid.ColumnDefinitions>
                    <ColumnDefinition Width="50" />
                    <ColumnDefinition />
                    <ColumnDefinition Width="50" />
                  </Grid.ColumnDefinitions>
                  <Grid.RowDefinitions>
                    <RowDefinition MinHeight="50" />
                  </Grid.RowDefinitions>
                  <Ellipse Grid.Column="0" Height="50">
                    <Ellipse.Fill>
                      <RadialGradientBrush>
                        <RadialGradientBrush.GradientStops>
                          <GradientStop Offset="0.0" Color="Yellow" />
                          <GradientStop Offset="1.0" Color="Red" />
                        </RadialGradientBrush.GradientStops>
                      </RadialGradientBrush>
                    </Ellipse.Fill>
                  </Ellipse>
```

```
                    <Grid Grid.Column="1">
                      <Rectangle RadiusX="10" RadiusY="10">
                        <Rectangle.Fill>
                          <RadialGradientBrush>
                            <RadialGradientBrush.GradientStops>
                              <GradientStop Offset="0.0" Color="Yellow" />
                              <GradientStop Offset="1.0" Color="Red" />
                            </RadialGradientBrush.GradientStops>
                          </RadialGradientBrush>
                        </Rectangle.Fill>
                      </Rectangle>
                      <ContentPresenter Margin="20,0,20,0"
                        HorizontalAlignment="Center" VerticalAlignment="Center" />
                    </Grid>
                    <Ellipse Grid.Column="2" Height="50">
                      <Ellipse.Fill>
                        <RadialGradientBrush>
                          <RadialGradientBrush.GradientStops>
                            <GradientStop Offset="0.0" Color="Yellow" />
                            <GradientStop Offset="1.0" Color="Red" />
                          </RadialGradientBrush.GradientStops>
                        </RadialGradientBrush>
                      </Ellipse.Fill>
                    </Ellipse>
                  </Grid>
                </ControlTemplate>
              </Setter.Value>
            </Setter>
          </Style>
        </Button.Style>
      </Button>
    </Grid>
</Window>
```

3. Modify the code in `Window1.xaml.cs` as follows:

```
public partial class Window1 : Window
{
    ...
```

```
    private void Button_Click(object sender, RoutedEventArgs e)
    {
        MessageBox.Show("Button clicked.");
    }
}
```

4. Run the application and click once on the button. Figure 34-16 shows the result.

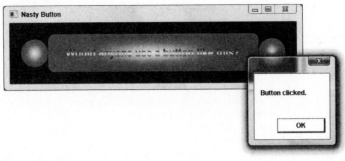

Figure 34-16

How It Works

First, let me apologize for the truly nasty-looking button shown in this example. However, aesthetic considerations aside, this example does show that you can completely change how a button looks in WPF without a lot of effort. In changing the button template, though, note that the functionality of the button remains unchanged. That is, you can click on the button and respond to that click in an event handler.

You probably noticed that certain things you associate with Windows buttons aren't implemented in the template used here. In particular, there is no visual feedback when you roll over the button or when you click it. This button also looks exactly the same whether it has focus or not. To achieve these effects you need to learn about *triggers*, which are the subject of the next section.

Before doing that, though, consider the example code in a little more detail, focusing on styles and templates and looking at how the template was created.

The code starts with ordinary code that you would use to display a Button control:

```
<Button Margin="20" Click="Button_Click">
   Would anyone use a button like this?
```

This provides basic properties and content for the button. Next, the Style property is set to a Style object, which begins by setting three simple font properties of the Button control:

```
<Button.Style>
  <Style TargetType="Button">
    <Setter Property="FontSize" Value="18" />
    <Setter Property="FontFamily" Value="arial" />
    <Setter Property="FontWeight" Value="bold" />
```

Next, the Button.Foreground property is set using property element syntax because a brush is used:

```
<Setter Property="Foreground">
  <Setter.Value>
    <LinearGradientBrush StartPoint="0.5,0" EndPoint="0.5,1">
      <LinearGradientBrush.GradientStops>
        <GradientStop Offset="0.0" Color="Purple" />
        <GradientStop Offset="0.5" Color="Azure" />
```

```
            <GradientStop Offset="1.0" Color="Purple" />
          </LinearGradientBrush.GradientStops>
        </LinearGradientBrush>
      </Setter.Value>
    </Setter>
```

The remainder of the code for the `Style` object sets the `Button.Template` property to a `ControlTemplate` object:

```
        <Setter Property="Template">
          <Setter.Value>
            <ControlTemplate TargetType="Button">
              ...
            </ControlTemplate>
          </Setter.Value>
        </Setter>
      </Style>
    </Button.Style>
  </Button>
```

The template code can be summarized as a `Grid` control that contains three cells in a single row. In turn, these cells contain an `Ellipse`, a `Rectangle`, along with the `ContentPresenter` for the template, and another `Ellipse`:

```
      <Grid>
        <Ellipse Grid.Column="0" Height="50">
          ...
        </Ellipse>
        <Grid Grid.Column="1">
          <Rectangle RadiusX="10" RadiusY="10">
            ...
          </Rectangle>
          <ContentPresenter Margin="20,0,20,0"
            HorizontalAlignment="Center"
            VerticalAlignment="Center" />
        </Grid>
        <Ellipse Grid.Column="2" Height="50">
          ...
        </Ellipse>
      </Grid>
```

None of this code is particularly complicated, and you can analyze it further at your leisure.

Triggers

In the first example of this chapter you saw how triggers can be used to link events to actions. Events in WPF can include all manner of things, including button clicks, application startup and shutdown events, and so on. There are, in fact, several types of triggers in WPF, all of which inherit from a base `TriggerBase` class. The type of trigger shown in the example was an `EventTrigger`. The `EventTrigger` class contains a collection of actions, each of which is an object that derives from the base `TriggerAction` class. These actions are executed when the trigger is activated.

Not a lot of classes inherit from `TriggerAction` in WPF, but you can, of course, define your own. You can use `EventTrigger` to trigger animations using the `BeginStoryboard` action, manipulate storyboards using `ControllableStoryboardAction`, and trigger sound effects with `SoundPlayerAction`. As this latter trigger is mostly used in animations, you'll look at it in the next section.

Every control has a `Triggers` property that you can use to define triggers directly on that control. You can also define triggers further up the hierarchy — for example, on a `Window` object as shown earlier. The type of trigger you will use most often when you are styling controls is `Trigger` (although you will still use `EventTrigger` to trigger control animations). The `Trigger` class is used to set properties in response to changes to other properties, and is particularly useful when used in `Style` objects.

Trigger objects are configured as follows:

- ❑ To define what property a `Trigger` object monitors, you use the `Trigger.Property` property.
- ❑ To define when the `Trigger` object activates, you set the `Trigger.Value` property.
- ❑ To define the actions taken by a `Trigger`, you set the `Trigger.Setters` property to a collection of `Setter` objects.

The `Setter` objects referred to here are exactly the same objects that you saw in the "Styles" section earlier.

For example, the following trigger would examine the value of a property called `MyBooleanValue`, and when that property is `true` it would set the value of the `Opacity` property to 0.5:

```
<Trigger Property="MyBooleanValue" Value="true">
  <Setter Property="Opacity" Value="0.5" />
</Trigger>
```

On its own this code doesn't tell you very much, as it is not associated with any control or style. The following code is much more explanatory, as it shows a `Trigger` as you would use it in a `Style` object:

```
<Style TargetType="Button">
  <Style.Triggers>
    <Trigger Property="IsMouseOver" Value="true">
      <Setter Property="Foreground" Value="Yellow" />
    </Trigger>
  </Style.Triggers>
</Style>
```

This code would change the `Foreground` property of a `Button` control to `Yellow` when the `Button.IsMouseOver` property is `true`. `IsMouseOver` is one of several extremely useful properties that you can use as a shortcut to find out information about controls and control state. As its name suggests, it is `true` if the mouse is over the control. This enables you to code for mouse rollovers. Other properties like this include `IsFocused`, to determine whether a control has focus; `IsHitTestVisible`, which indicates whether it is possible to click on a control (that is, it is not obscured by controls further up the stacking order); and `IsPressed`, which indicates whether a button is pressed. The last of these only applies to buttons that inherit from `ButtonBase`, whereas the others are available on all controls.

As well as the `Style.Triggers` property, you can also achieve a lot by using the `ControlTemplate`
`.Triggers` property. This enables you to create templates for controls that include triggers. This is how
the default `Button` template is able to respond to mouse rollovers, clicks, and focus changes with its
template. This is also what you must modify to implement this functionality for yourself.

Animation

Animations are created by using storyboards. The absolute best way to define animations is, without a
doubt, to use a designer such as Expression Blend. However, you can also define them by editing
XAML code directly, and by implication from code behind (as XAML is simply a way to build a WPF
object model).

A storyboard is defined using a `Storyboard` object, which contains one or more timelines. You can
define timelines by using key frames or by using one of several simpler objects that encapsulate entire
animations. Complex storyboards may even contain nested storyboards.

As shown in the example, a `Storyboard` is contained in a resource dictionary, so you must identify it
with an `x:Key` property.

Within the timeline of a storyboard, you can animate properties of any element in your application that
is of type `double`, `Point`, or `Color`. This covers most of the things that you may want to change, so it's
quite flexible. There are some things that you can't do, such as completely replace one brush with
another, but there are ways to achieve pretty much any effect you can imagine given these three types.

Each of these three types has two associated timeline controls that you can use as children of
`Storyboard`. These six controls are `DoubleAnimation`, `DoubleAnimationUsingKeyFrames`,
`PointAnimation`, `PointAnimationUsingKeyFrames`, `ColorAnimation`, and
`ColorAnimationUsingKeyFrames`. Every timeline control can be associated with a specific
property of a specific control by using the attached properties `Storyboard.TargetName` and
`Storyboard.TargetProperty`. For example, you would set these properties to `MyRectangle` and
`Width` if you wanted to animate the `Width` property of a `Rectangle` control with a `Name` property of
`MyRectangle`. You would use either `DoubleAnimation` or `DoubleAnimationUsingKeyFrames` to
animate this property.

The `Storyboard.TargetProperty` property is capable of interpreting quite advanced syntax so that
you can locate the property you are interested in animating. In the example at the beginning of this
chapter, you used the following values for the two attached properties:

```
Storyboard.TargetName="ellipse1"
Storyboard.TargetProperty=
"(UIElement.RenderTransform).(TransformGroup.Children)[0].(RotateTransform.Angle)"
```

The control `ellipse1` was of type `Ellipse`, and the `TargetProperty` specified the angle that the
ellipse was rotated through in a transformation. This angle was located through the `RenderTransform`
property of `Ellipse`, inherited from `UIElement`, and the first child of the `TransformGroup` object that
was the value of this property. This first child was a `RotateTransform` object, and the angle was the
`Angle` property of this object.

Although this syntax can be long-winded, is straightforward to use. The most difficult thing is determining what base class a given property is inherited from, although the object browser can help you with that.

Next, you'll look at the simple, nonkey-frame animation timelines, and then move on to look at the timelines that use key frames.

Timelines Without Key Frames

The timelines without key frames are `DoubleAnimation`, `PointAnimation`, and `ColorAnimation`. These timelines have identical property names, although the types of these properties vary according to the type of the timeline (note that all duration properties are specified in the form `[days.]hours: minutes:seconds` in XAML code):

Property	Usage
Name	The name of the timeline, so that you can refer to it from other places.
BeginTime	How long after the storyboard is triggered before the timeline starts.
Duration	How long the timeline lasts.
AutoReverse	Whether the timeline reverses when it completes and returns properties to their original values. This property is a Boolean value.
RepeatBehavior	Set this to a specified duration to make the timeline repeat as indicated — an integer followed by x (for example, 5x) to repeat the timeline a set number of times; or use `Forever` to make the timeline repeat until the storyboard is paused or stopped.
FillBehavior	How the timeline behaves if it completes while the storyboard is still continuing. You can use `HoldEnd` to leave properties at the values they are at when the timeline completes (the default), or `Stop` to return them to their original values.
SpeedRatio	Controls the speed of the animation relative to the values specified in other properties. The default value is 1, but you can change it from other code to speed up or slow down animations.
From	The initial value to set the property to at the start of the animation. You can omit this value to use the current value of the property.
To	The final value for the property at the end of the animation. You can omit this value to use the current value of the property.
By	Use this value to animate from the current value of a property to the sum of the current value and the value you specify. You can use this property on its own or in combination with `From`.

For example, the following timeline will animate the `Width` property of a `Rectangle` control with a `Name` property of `MyRectangle` between 100 and 200 over 5 seconds:

```
<Storyboard x:Key="RectangleExpander">
  <DoubleAnimation Storyboard.TargetName="MyRectangle"
    Storyboard.TargetProperty="Width" Duration="00:00:05" From="100" To="200" />
</Storyboard>
```

Timelines with Key Frames

The timelines with key frames are `DoubleAnimationUsingKeyFrames`, `PointAnimationUsingKeyFrames`, and `ColorAnimationUsingKeyFrames`. These timeline classes use the same properties as the timeline classes in the previous section, except that they don't have `From`, `To`, or `By` properties. Instead, they have a `KeyFrames` property that is a collection of key frame objects.

These timelines can contain any number of key frames, each of which can cause the value being animated to behave in a different way. There are three types of key frames for each type of timeline:

❑ **Discrete:** A discrete key frame causes the value being animated to jump to a specified value with no transition.

❑ **Linear:** A linear key frame causes the value being animated to animate to a specified value in a linear transition.

❑ **Spline:** A spline key frame causes the value being animated to animate to a specified value in a nonlinear transition defined by a cubic Bezier curve function.

There are therefore nine types of key frame objects: `DiscreteDoubleKeyFrame`, `LinearDoubleKeyFrame`, `SplineDoubleKeyFrame`, `DiscreteColorKeyFrame`, `LinearColorKeyFrame`, `SplineColorKeyFrame`, `DiscretePointKeyFrame`, `LinearPointKeyFrame`, and `SplinePointKeyFrame`.

The key frame classes have the same three properties as the timeline classes examined in the previous section, apart from the spline key frames, which have one additional property:

Property	Usage
Name	The name of the key frame, so that you can refer to it from other places
KeyTime	The location of the key frame expressed as an amount of time after the timeline starts
Value	The value that the property will reach or be set to when the key frame is reached
KeySpline	Two sets of two numbers in the form cp1x, cp1y cp2x, cp2y that define the cubic Bezier function to use to animate the property. *(Spline key frames only.)*

For example, you could animate the position of an `Ellipse` in a square by animating its `Center` property, which is of type `Point`, as follows:

```
<Storyboard x:Key="EllipseMover">
  <PointAnimationUsingKeyFrames Storyboard.TargetName="MyEllipse"
    Storyboard.TargetProperty="Center" RepeatBehavior="Forever">
    <LinearPointKeyFrame KeyTime="00:00:00" Value="50,50" />
    <LinearPointKeyFrame KeyTime="00:00:01" Value="100,50" />
    <LinearPointKeyFrame KeyTime="00:00:02" Value="100,100" />
    <LinearPointKeyFrame KeyTime="00:00:03" Value="50,100" />
    <LinearPointKeyFrame KeyTime="00:00:04" Value="50,50" />
  </PointAnimationUsingKeyFrames>
</Storyboard>
```

Point values are specified in `x,y` form in XAML code.

Static and Dynamic Resources

Another great feature of WPF is the capability to define resources, such as control styles and templates, which you can reuse throughout your application. You can even use resources across multiple applications if you define them in the right place.

Resources are defined as entries in a `ResourceDictionary` object. As its name suggests, this is a keyed collection of objects. This is why you've used `x:Key` attributes in example code so far in this chapter when you have defined resources: to specify the key associated with a resource. You can access `ResourceDictionary` objects in a variety of locations. You could include resources local to a control, local to a window, local to your application, or in an external assembly.

There are two ways to reference resources: statically or dynamically. Note that this distinction doesn't mean that the resource itself is in any way different — that is, you don't *define* a resource as static or dynamic. The difference is in how you use it.

Static Resources

You use static resources when you know exactly what the resource will be at design time, and you know that the reference won't change over the application's lifetime. For example, if you define a button style that you want to use for the buttons in your application, then you probably won't want to change it while the application runs. In this case, you should reference the resource statically. In addition, when you use a static resource, the resource type is resolved at compile time, so performance is very fast.

To reference a static resource, you use the following markup extension syntax:

```
{StaticResource resourceName}
```

For example, if you had a style defined for `Button` controls with a `x:Key` attribute of `MyStyle`, then you could reference it from a control as follows:

```
<Button Style="{StaticResource MyStyle}" ...>...</Button>
```

Dynamic Resources

A property defined by using a dynamic resource can be changed at runtime to another dynamic resource. This can be useful in a number of circumstances. Sometimes you want to give users control over the general theme of your application, in which case you want resources to be allocated dynamically. In addition, sometimes you are not aware of the key you require for a resource at runtime — for example, if you dynamically attach to a resource assembly.

Dynamic resources therefore give you more flexibility than static resources do. However, there is a downside. There is slightly more overhead related to the use of dynamic resources, so you should use them sparingly if you want to optimize the performance of your applications.

The syntax required to reference a resource dynamically is very similar to that required to reference a resource statically:

```
{DynamicResource resourceName}
```

For example, if you have a style defined for `Button` controls with a `x:Key` attribute of `MyDynamicStyle`, you could reference it from a control as follows:

```
<Button Style="{DynamicResource MyDynamicStyle}" ...>...</Button>
```

Referencing Style Resources

Earlier, you saw how to reference a `Style` resource from a `Button` control, both statically and dynamically. The `Style` resource used here might be in the `Resources` property of the local `Window` control, for example:

```
<Window ...>
  <Window.Resources>
    <Style x:Key="MyStyle" TargetType="Button">
      ...
    </Style>
  </Window.Resources>
  ...
</Window>
```

Every `Button` control that you want to use this control must then refer to it in its `Style` property (statically or dynamically). Alternatively, you could define a style resource that is *global* to a given control type. That is, the `Style` object will be applied to *every* control of a given type in your application. To do this, all you have to do is omit the `x:Key` attribute:

```
<Window ...>
  <Window.Resources>
    <Style TargetType="Button">
      ...
    </Style>
  </Window.Resources>
  ...
</Window>
```

This is a great way to theme your applications. You can define a set of global styles for the various control types that you use and they will be used everywhere.

You've covered a lot of ground in the last few sections, so it's time to tie things together with an example. In the next Try It Out, you modify the `Button` control from the previous Try It Out to use triggers and animations, and define the style as a global, reusable resource.

Try It Out   Triggers, Animations, and Resources

1. Create a new WPF application called Ch34Ex04 and save it in the directory C:\BegVCSharp\Chapter34.

2. Copy the code from `Window1.xaml` in Ch34Ex03 into `Window1.xaml` in Ch34Ex04, but change the namespace reference on the `Window` element as follows:

```
<Window x:Class="Ch34Ex04.Window1"
```

3. Copy the `Button_Click()` event handler from `Window1.xaml.cs` in Ch34Ex03 into `Window1.xaml.cs` in Ch34Ex04.

4. Add a `<Window.Resources>` child to the `<Window>` element and move the `<Style>` definition from the `<Button.Style>` element to the `<Window.Resources>` element. Remove the empty `<Button.Style>` element. The result is shown here (abbreviated):

```
<Window x:Class="Ch34Ex04.Window1"
   xmlns="http://schemas.microsoft.com/winfx/2006/xaml/presentation"
   xmlns:x="http://schemas.microsoft.com/winfx/2006/xaml"
   Title="Nasty Button" Height="150" Width="550">
  <Window.Resources>
    <Style TargetType="Button">
      ...
    </Style>
  </Window.Resources>
  <Grid Background="Black">
    <Button Margin="20" Click="Button_Click">
      Would anyone use a button like this?
    </Button>
  </Grid>
</Window>
```

5. Run the application and verify that the result is the same as in the previous example.

6. Add `Name` attributes to the main `Grid` in the template and the `Rectangle` that contains the `ContentPresenter` element as follows:

```
<Setter Property="Template">
  <Setter.Value>
    <ControlTemplate TargetType="Button">
      <Grid Name="LayoutGrid">
        <Grid.ColumnDefinitions>
          ...
        <Grid Grid.Column="1">
          <Rectangle RadiusX="10" RadiusY="10" Name="BackgroundRectangle">
```

```
        <Rectangle.Fill>
          ...
        </Rectangle.Fill>
      </Rectangle>
      ...
    </Grid>
    ...
  </Grid>
      </ControlTemplate>
    </Setter.Value>
  </Setter>
```

7. Add the following code to the `<ControlTemplate>` element, just before the
    `</ControlTemplate>` tag:

```
        </Grid>
        <ControlTemplate.Resources>
          <Storyboard x:Key="PulseButton">
            <ColorAnimationUsingKeyFrames BeginTime="00:00:00"
              RepeatBehavior="Forever"
              Storyboard.TargetName="BackgroundRectangle"
              Storyboard.TargetProperty=
  "(Shape.Fill).(RadialGradientBrush.GradientStops)[1].(GradientStop.Color)">
              <LinearColorKeyFrame Value="Red" KeyTime="00:00:00" />
              <LinearColorKeyFrame Value="Orange" KeyTime="00:00:01" />
              <LinearColorKeyFrame Value="Red" KeyTime="00:00:02" />
            </ColorAnimationUsingKeyFrames>
          </Storyboard>
        </ControlTemplate.Resources>
        <ControlTemplate.Triggers>
          <Trigger Property="IsMouseOver" Value="True">
            <Setter TargetName="LayoutGrid" Property="BitmapEffect">
              <Setter.Value>
                <OuterGlowBitmapEffect GlowColor="Red" GlowSize="20" />
              </Setter.Value>
            </Setter>
          </Trigger>
          <Trigger Property="IsPressed" Value="True">
            <Setter TargetName="LayoutGrid" Property="BitmapEffect">
              <Setter.Value>
                <OuterGlowBitmapEffect GlowColor="Yellow" GlowSize="40" />
              </Setter.Value>
            </Setter>
          </Trigger>
          <EventTrigger RoutedEvent="UIElement.MouseEnter">
            <BeginStoryboard Storyboard="{StaticResource PulseButton}"
              x:Name="PulseButton_BeginStoryboard" />
          </EventTrigger>
          <EventTrigger RoutedEvent="UIElement.MouseLeave">
            <StopStoryboard
              BeginStoryboardName="PulseButton_BeginStoryboard" />
          </EventTrigger>
        </ControlTemplate.Triggers>
      </ControlTemplate>
```

8. Run the application and hover the mouse over the button, as shown in Figure 34-17. The button pulses and glows.

Figure 34-17

9. Click the button, as shown in Figure 34-18. The glow changes.

Figure 34-18

How It Works

In this example you have done two things. First, you defined a global resource that is used to format all buttons in the application (there's only one button, but that's not the point). Second, you added some features to the style created in the previous Try It Out that make it almost respectable. Specifically, you have made it glow and pulsate in response to mouse rollover and click interaction.

Making the style a global resource was simply a matter of moving the `<Style>` element to the resources section of the `Window`. You could have added an `x:Key` attribute, but because you didn't there was no need to set the `Style` property of the `Button` control on the page; the style was instantly global.

After making the style a resource, you proceeded to modify it. First, you added `Name` attributes to two of the controls in the style. This was necessary so that you could refer to them from other code, which you do in the animation and triggers for the control template that is part of the style.

Next, you added an animation as a local resource for the control template specified in the style. The animation `Storyboard` object was identified using the `x:Key` value of `PulseButton`:

```
<ControlTemplate.Resources>
  <Storyboard x:Key="PulseButton">
```

The storyboard contains a `ColorAnimationUsingKeyFrames` element, as it will animate a color used in the control template. The property to animate was the red color used as the outer color in the radial fill used in the `BackgroundRectangle` control. Locating this property from the control required fairly complex syntax for the `Storyboard.TargetProperty` attached property:

```
<ColorAnimationUsingKeyFrames BeginTime="00:00:00"
    RepeatBehavior="Forever"
    Storyboard.TargetName="BackgroundRectangle"
    Storyboard.TargetProperty=
 "(Shape.Fill).(RadialGradientBrush.GradientStops)[1].(GradientStop.Color)">
```

The timeline for the animation consisted of three key frames to animate the color from `Red` to `Orange` and then back again over two seconds:

```
            <LinearColorKeyFrame Value="Red" KeyTime="00:00:00" />
            <LinearColorKeyFrame Value="Orange" KeyTime="00:00:01" />
            <LinearColorKeyFrame Value="Red" KeyTime="00:00:02" />
        </ColorAnimationUsingKeyFrames>
    </Storyboard>
</ControlTemplate.Resources>
```

Adding the animation as a resource does not cause it to be performed. To do that you added two `EventTrigger` triggers:

```
            <EventTrigger RoutedEvent="UIElement.MouseEnter">
              <BeginStoryboard Storyboard="{StaticResource PulseButton}"
                x:Name="PulseButton_BeginStoryboard" />
            </EventTrigger>
            <EventTrigger RoutedEvent="UIElement.MouseLeave">
              <StopStoryboard
                BeginStoryboardName="PulseButton_BeginStoryboard" />
            </EventTrigger>
```

This code uses the `MouseEnter` and `MouseLeave` events of the `UIElement` base class of the `Button` control to control the operation of the animation. `MouseEnter` causes animation to start through a `BeginStoryboard` element, and `MouseLeave` causes it to stop through the `StopStoryboard` element.

Note that the storyboard resource is located using a static resource reference. This makes perfect sense here because the storyboard is defined local to the control and you have no intention of changing it at runtime.

You also defined two other triggers to provide a rollover and click glow by using the `OuterGlowBitmapEffect` bitmap effect. You made use of the `IsMouseOver` and `IsPressed` properties shown earlier in the chapter to achieve this:

```
            <Trigger Property="IsMouseOver" Value="True">
              <Setter TargetName="LayoutGrid" Property="BitmapEffect">
                <Setter.Value>
                  <OuterGlowBitmapEffect GlowColor="Red" GlowSize="20" />
                </Setter.Value>
              </Setter>
            </Trigger>
            <Trigger Property="IsPressed" Value="True">
```

```
<Setter TargetName="LayoutGrid" Property="BitmapEffect">
  <Setter.Value>
    <OuterGlowBitmapEffect GlowColor="Yellow" GlowSize="40" />
  </Setter.Value>
</Setter>
</Trigger>
```

Here, the defined glow is small and red when the mouse hovers over the button, and larger and yellow when the button is clicked.

Programming with WPF

Now that you have covered all of the basic WPF programming techniques you can begin to create applications of your own. Unfortunately, there isn't enough space here to cover some of the other great features of WPF, including the details of data binding and some great ways to format the display of lists. However, it wouldn't be right to stop here just when you are becoming familiar with WPF programming. Therefore, you look at two more topics before finishing this chapter, chosen not for their complexity but because they reflect tasks you are likely to often perform in WPF applications:

❑   How to create and use your own controls

❑   How to implement dependency properties on your controls

You also work through a final example that illustrates more of the techniques covered in this chapter, and just a small taste of WPF data binding.

WPF User Controls

WPF provides a set of controls that are useful in many situations. However, as with all the .NET development frameworks, it also enables you to extend this functionality. Specifically, you can create your own controls by deriving your classes from classes in the WPF class hierarchy.

One of the most useful controls you can derive from is UserControl. This class gives you all the basic functionality that you are likely to require from a WPF control, and enables your control to snap in beside the existing WPF control suite seamlessly. Everything you might hope to achieve with a WPF control, such as animation, styling, templating, and so on, can be achieved with user controls.

You can add user controls to your project by using the Project ⇨ Add User Control menu item. This gives you a blank canvas (well, actually a blank Grid) to work from. User controls are defined using the top-level UserControl element in XAML, and the class in the code behind derives from the System.Windows.Controls.UserControl class.

Once you have added a user control to your project, you can add controls to lay out the control and code behind to configure the control. When you have finished doing that, you can use it throughout your application, and even reuse it in other applications.

One of the crucial things you need to know when creating user controls is how to implement dependency properties. As shown earlier in this chapter, dependency properties are an essential part of WPF programming. You won't want to miss out on the functionality these properties give you when you create your own controls.

Implementing Dependency Properties

You can add dependency properties to any class that inherits from `System.Windows` `.DependencyObject`. This class is in the inheritance hierarchy for many classes in WPF, including all the controls and `UserControl`.

To implement a dependency property to a class, you add a public, static member to your class definition of type `System.Windows.DependencyProperty`. The name of this member is up to you, but best practice is to follow the naming convention `<PropertyName>Property`:

```
public static DependencyProperty MyStringProperty;
```

It may seem odd that this property is defined as static, since you end up with a property that can be uniquely defined for each instance of your class. The WPF property framework keeps track of things for you, so you don't have to worry about this for the moment.

The member you add must be configured by using the static `DependencyProperty.Register()` method:

```
public static DependencyProperty MyStringProperty =
DependencyProperty.Register(...);
```

This method takes between three and five parameters, as shown in the following table (in order, with the first three parameters being the mandatory ones):

Parameter	Usage
`string name`	The name of the property.
`Type propertyType`	The type of the property.
`Type ownerType`	The type of the class containing the property.
`PropertyMetadata typeMetadata`	Additional property settings: the default value of the property and callback methods to use for property change notifications and coercion.
`ValidateValueCallback validateValueCallback`	The callback method to use to validate property values.

There are other methods that you can use to register dependency properties, such as
`RegisterAttached()`, *which you can use to implement an attached property. You won't look at these other methods in this chapter, but it's worth reading up on them.*

For example, you could register the `MyStringProperty` dependency property using three parameters as follows:

```
public class MyClass : DependencyObject
{
   public static DependencyProperty MyStringProperty = DependencyProperty.Register(
      "MyString",
      typeof(string),
      typeof(MyClass)
...);
}
```

You can also include a .NET property that can be used to access dependency properties directly (although this isn't mandatory, as you will see shortly). However, because dependency properties are defined as static members, you cannot use the same syntax you would use with ordinary properties. To access the value of a dependency property, you have to use methods that are inherited from `DependencyObject`, as follows:

```
public class MyClass : DependencyObject
{
   public static DependencyProperty MyStringProperty =
DependencyProperty.Register(
      "MyString",
      typeof(string),
      typeof(MyClass)
...);

      public string MyString
      {
         get { return (string)GetValue(MyStringProperty); }
         set { SetValue(MyStringProperty, value); }
      }
}
```

Here, the `GetValue()` and `SetValue()` methods get and set the value of the `MyStringProperty` dependency property for the current instance, respectively. These two methods are public, so client code can use them directly to manipulate dependency property values. This is why adding a .NET property to access a dependency property is not mandatory.

If you want to set metadata for a property, then you must use an object that derives from `PropertyMetadata`, such as `FrameworkPropertyMetadata`, and pass this instance as the fourth parameter to `Register()`. There are 11 overloads of the `FrameworkPropertyMetadata` constructor, and they take one or more of the parameters shown in the following table:

Parameter Type	Usage
`object defaultValue`	The default value for the property.
`FrameworkPropertyMetadataOptions flags`	A combination of the flags (from the `FrameworkPropertyMetadataOptions` enum) that you can use to specify additional metadata for a property. For example, you might use `AffectsArrange` to declare that changes to the property might affect control layout. This would cause the layout engine for a window to recalculate control layout if the property changed. See the MSDN documentation for a full list of the options available here.
`PropertyChangedCallback propertyChangedCallback`	The callback method to use when the property value changes.
`CoerceValueCallback coerceValueCallback`	The callback method to use if the property value is coerced.
`bool isAnimationProhibited`	Specifies whether this property can be changed by an animation.
`UpdateSourceTrigger defaultUpdateSourceTrigger`	When property values are databound, this property determines when the data source is updated, according to values in the `UpdateSourceTrigger` enum. The default value is `PropertyChanged`, which means that the binding source is updated as soon as the property changes. This is not always appropriate — for example, the `TextBox.Text` property uses a value of `LostFocus` for this property. This ensures that the binding source is not updated prematurely. You can also use the value `Eplicit` to specify that the binding source should only be updated when requested (by calling the `UpdateSource()` method of a class derived from `DependancyObject`).

A simple example of using `FrameworkPropertyMetadata` would be to use it simply to set the default value of a property:

```
public class MyClass : DependencyObject
{
    public static DependencyProperty MyStringProperty = DependencyProperty.
    Register(
        "MyString",
        typeof(string),
        typeof(MyClass),
        new FrameworkPropertyMetadata("Default value")
    ...);
}
```

You have so far learned about three callback methods that you can specify, for property change notification, property coercion, and property value validation. These callbacks, like the dependency property itself, must all be implemented as public, static methods. Each callback has a specific return type and parameter list that you must use on your callback method.

In the following Try It Out, you create and use a user control that has two dependency properties. You will see how to implement callback methods for these properties in the user control code.

Try It Out   User Controls

1. Create a new WPF application called Ch34Ex05 and save it in the directory C:\BegVCSharp\Chapter34.

2. Add a new user control to the application called `Card` and modify the code in `Card.xaml` as follows:

```
<UserControl
    xmlns="http://schemas.microsoft.com/winfx/2006/xaml/presentation"
    xmlns:x="http://schemas.microsoft.com/winfx/2006/xaml"
    x:Class="Ch34Ex05.Card"
    Height="150" Width="100" x:Name="UserControl"
    FontSize="16" FontWeight="Bold">
    <UserControl.Resources>
      <DataTemplate x:Key="SuitTemplate">
        <TextBlock Text="{Binding}"/>
      </DataTemplate>
    </UserControl.Resources>
    <Grid>
      <Rectangle Stroke="{x:Null}" RadiusX="12.5" RadiusY="12.5">
        <Rectangle.Fill>
          <LinearGradientBrush EndPoint="0.47,-0.167" StartPoint="0.86,0.92">
            <GradientStop Color="#FFD1C78F" Offset="0"/>
            <GradientStop Color="#FFFFFFFF" Offset="1"/>
          </LinearGradientBrush>
        </Rectangle.Fill>
        <Rectangle.BitmapEffect>
```

```xml
            <DropShadowBitmapEffect/>
          </Rectangle.BitmapEffect>
        </Rectangle>
        <Label x:Name="SuitLabel"
          Content="{Binding Path=Suit, ElementName=UserControl, Mode=Default}"
          ContentTemplate="{DynamicResource SuitTemplate}" HorizontalAlignment="Center"
          VerticalAlignment="Center" Margin="8,51,8,60" />
        <Label x:Name="RankLabel"
          Content="{Binding Path=Rank, ElementName=UserControl, Mode=Default}"
          ContentTemplate="{DynamicResource SuitTemplate}" HorizontalAlignment="Left"
          VerticalAlignment="Top" Margin="8,8,0,0" />
        <Label x:Name="RankLabelInverted"
          Content="{Binding Path=Rank, ElementName=UserControl, Mode=Default}"
          ContentTemplate="{DynamicResource SuitTemplate}" HorizontalAlignment="Right"
          VerticalAlignment="Bottom" Margin="0,0,8,8" RenderTransformOrigin="0.5,0.5">
          <Label.RenderTransform>
            <RotateTransform Angle="180"/>
          </Label.RenderTransform>
        </Label>
        <Path Fill="#FFFFFFFF" Stretch="Fill" Stroke="{x:Null}"
          Margin="0,0,35.218,-0.077" Data="F1 M110.5,51 L123.16457,51 C116.5986,
            76.731148 115.63518,132.69684 121.63533,149.34013 133.45299,
            182.12018 152.15821,195.69803 161.79765,200.07669 L110.5,200 C103.59644,
            200 98,194.40356 98,187.5 L98,63.5 C98,56.596439 103.59644,51 110.5,51 z">
          <Path.OpacityMask>
            <LinearGradientBrush EndPoint="0.957,1.127" StartPoint="0,-0.06">
              <GradientStop Color="#FF000000" Offset="0"/>
              <GradientStop Color="#00FFFFFF" Offset="1"/>
            </LinearGradientBrush>
          </Path.OpacityMask>
        </Path>
      </Grid>
    </UserControl>
```

3. Modify the code in `Card.xaml.cs` as follows:

```csharp
public partial class Card : UserControl
{
    public static string[] Suits = { "Club", "Diamond", "Heart", "Spade" };

    public static DependencyProperty SuitProperty = DependencyProperty.Register(
      "Suit",
      typeof(string),
      typeof(Card),
      new PropertyMetadata("Club", new PropertyChangedCallback(OnSuitChanged)),
      new ValidateValueCallback(ValidateSuit)
      );
```

```
public static DependencyProperty RankProperty = DependencyProperty.Register(
  "Rank",
  typeof(int),
  typeof(Card),
  new PropertyMetadata(1),
  new ValidateValueCallback(ValidateRank)
);

public Card()
{
  InitializeComponent();
}

public string Suit
{
  get { return (string)GetValue(SuitProperty); }
  set { SetValue(SuitProperty, value); }
}

public int Rank
{
  get { return (int)GetValue(RankProperty); }
  set { SetValue(RankProperty, value); }
}

public static bool ValidateSuit(object suitValue)
{
  string suitValueString = (string)suitValue;
  if (suitValueString != "Club" && suitValueString != "Diamond"
    && suitValueString != "Heart" && suitValueString != "Spade")
  {
    return false;
  }
  return true;
}

public static bool ValidateRank(object rankValue)
{
  int rankValueInt = (int)rankValue;
  if (rankValueInt < 1 || rankValueInt > 12)
  {
    return false;
  }
  return true;
}

private void SetTextColor()
{
```

```
    if (Suit == "Club" || Suit == "Spade")
    {
      RankLabel.Foreground = new SolidColorBrush(Color.FromRgb(0, 0, 0));
      SuitLabel.Foreground = new SolidColorBrush(Color.FromRgb(0, 0, 0));
      RankLabelInverted.Foreground = new SolidColorBrush(Color.FromRgb(0, 0, 0));
    }
    else
    {
      RankLabel.Foreground = new SolidColorBrush(Color.FromRgb(255, 0, 0));
      SuitLabel.Foreground = new SolidColorBrush(Color.FromRgb(255, 0, 0));
      RankLabelInverted.Foreground = new SolidColorBrush(Color.FromRgb(255, 0, 0));
    }
  }

  public static void OnSuitChanged(DependencyObject source,
    DependencyPropertyChangedEventArgs args)
  {
    ((Card)source).SetTextColor();
  }
}
```

4. Modify the code in `Window1.xaml` as follows:

```xml
<Window x:Class="Ch34Ex05.Window1"
  xmlns="http://schemas.microsoft.com/winfx/2006/xaml/presentation"
  xmlns:x="http://schemas.microsoft.com/winfx/2006/xaml"
  Title="Card Dealer" Height="600" Width="800">

  <Grid Name="contentGrid" MouseLeftButtonDown="Grid_MouseLeftButtonDown"
    MouseLeftButtonUp="Grid_MouseLeftButtonUp" MouseMove="Grid_MouseMove">
    <Grid.Background>
      <LinearGradientBrush EndPoint="0.364,0.128" StartPoint="0.598,1.042">
        <GradientStop Color="#FF0D4F1A" Offset="0"/>
        <GradientStop Color="#FF448251" Offset="1"/>
      </LinearGradientBrush>
    </Grid.Background>
  </Grid>
</Window>
```

5. Modify the code in `Window1.xaml.cs` as follows:

```csharp
public partial class Window1 : Window
{
  private Card currentCard;
  private Point offset;
  private Random random = new Random();

  public Window1()
  {
    InitializeComponent();
  }
```

```
    private void Grid_MouseLeftButtonDown(object sender, MouseButtonEventArgs e)
    {
      if (e.Source is Card)
      {
        currentCard = (Card)e.Source;
        offset = Mouse.GetPosition(currentCard);
        contentGrid.Children.Remove(currentCard);
      }
      else
      {
        currentCard = new Card
        {
          Suit = Card.Suits[random.Next(0, 4)],
          Rank = random.Next(1, 13)
        };
        currentCard.HorizontalAlignment = HorizontalAlignment.Left;
        currentCard.VerticalAlignment = VerticalAlignment.Top;
        offset = new Point(50, 75);
      }
      contentGrid.Children.Add(currentCard);
      PositionCard();
    }

    private void Grid_MouseLeftButtonUp(object sender, MouseButtonEventArgs e)
    {
      currentCard = null;
    }

    private void Grid_MouseMove(object sender, MouseEventArgs e)
    {
      if (currentCard != null)
      {
        PositionCard();
      }
    }

    private void PositionCard()
    {
      Point mousePos = Mouse.GetPosition(this);
      currentCard.Margin =
        new Thickness(mousePos.X - offset.X, mousePos.Y - offset.Y, 0, 0);
    }
  }
}
```

6. Run the application. Click the surface of the window to add random cards, click and drag to reposition cards. When you click an existing card, it jumps to the top of the stack order. The result is shown in Figure 34-19.

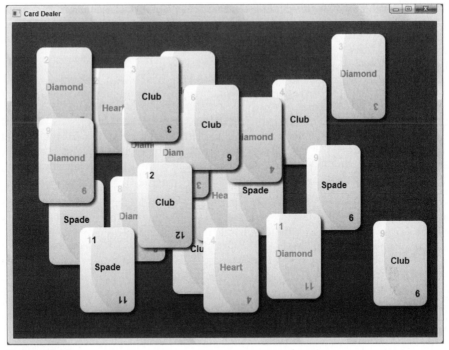

Figure 34-19

How It Works

This example created a user control with two dependent properties, and included client code to use the control. This example covered plenty of ground, and the place to start looking at the code is the Card control.

The Card control consists mostly of code that will be familiar to you from code you've seen earlier in this chapter. The layout code uses nothing new, although you might agree that the result is a bit prettier than the lurid button in the previous two examples. One thing that is completely new, though, is that this control uses a small amount of *data binding*. Data binding is where the property of a control is bound to a data source, and as such encompasses a wide array of techniques. WPF makes it easy to bind properties to all manner of data sources, such as database data, XML data, and (as used in this example) dependency property values.

Specifically, the code in Card exposes two dependency properties, Suit and Rank, to client code, and binds these properties to visual elements in the control layout. The result is that when you set Suit to Club, the word Club is displayed in the center of the card. Similarly, the value of Rank is displayed in two corners of the card.

You'll look at the implementation of Suit and Rank in a moment. For now it is enough to know that these properties are string and int values, respectively. It would have been possible to use, for example, enumeration values for these properties, although that would have required a little more new code, so this example keeps things as simple as possible by using basic properties.

To bind a value to a property you use binding syntax, which is a markup extension. This syntax means that you specify the value of a property as {Binding ...}. There are various ways to configure binding in this way. In the example, the binding for the SuitLabel label is configured as follows:

```
<Label x:Name="SuitLabel"
  Content="{Binding Path=Suit, ElementName=UserControl, Mode=Default}"
  ContentTemplate="{DynamicResource SuitTemplate}" HorizontalAlignment="Center"
  VerticalAlignment="Center" Margin="8,51,8,60" />
```

Here, three properties are specified for the binding: Path (the name of the property), ElementName (the element with the property), and Mode (how to perform the binding). Path and Element are quite straightforward; for now you can ignore Mode. The important point is that this specification binds the Label.Content property to the Card.Suit property.

When you bind property values, you must also specify how to render the bound content, by using a *data template*. In this example, the data template is SuitTemplate, referenced as a dynamic resource (although in this case a static resource binding would also work fine). This template is defined in the user control resources section as follows:

```
<UserControl.Resources>
  <DataTemplate x:Key="SuitTemplate">
    <TextBlock Text="{Binding}"/>
  </DataTemplate>
</UserControl.Resources>
```

The string value of Suit is therefore used as the Text property of a TextBlock control. This same DataTemplate definition is reused for the two rank labels — it doesn't matter that Rank is an int; it is transformed into a string when bound to the TextBlock.Text property.

Obviously, much more could be said about data binding and data templates, but there simply isn't space in this book to fill in the details. The chapter summary will point you toward places where you can learn more about this subject. As a final note, if you are using Expression Blend, you will find that you can bind to data effectively without having to worry too much about the XAML syntax, as it will take care of it for you.

For this data binding to work, you had to define two dependency properties using techniques you learned in the previous section. These are defined in the code behind for the user control as follows (they both have simple .NET property wrappers, which there is no need to show here because of the simplicity of the code):

```
public static DependencyProperty SuitProperty = DependencyProperty.Register(
  "Suit",
  typeof(string),
  typeof(Card),
  new PropertyMetadata("Club", new PropertyChangedCallback(OnSuitChanged)),
  new ValidateValueCallback(ValidateSuit)
  );

public static DependencyProperty RankProperty = DependencyProperty.Register(
  "Rank",
  typeof(int),
  typeof(Card),
  new PropertyMetadata(1),
  new ValidateValueCallback(ValidateRank)
  );
```

Both dependency properties use a callback method to validate values, and the Suit property also has a callback method for when its value changes. Validation callback methods have a return type of bool and a single parameter of type object, which is the value that client code is attempting to set the property to. If the value is OK, then you should return true; otherwise, return false. In the example code, the Suit property is restricted to one of four strings:

```
public static bool ValidateSuit(object suitValue)
{
  string suitValueString = (string)suitValue;
  if (suitValueString != "Club" && suitValueString != "Diamond"
    && suitValueString != "Heart" && suitValueString != "Spade")
  {
    return false;
  }
  return true;
}
```

This is quite brutal, and obviously an enumeration would be better here, but it has been avoided for reasons outlined earlier. Similarly, the Rank property is restricted to a value between 1 (ace) and 12 (king):

```
public static bool ValidateRank(object rankValue)
{
  int rankValueInt = (int)rankValue;
  if (rankValueInt < 1 || rankValueInt > 12)
  {
    return false;
  }
  return true;
}
```

When the value of Suit changes, the OnSuitChanged() callback method is called. This method is responsible for setting the text color to red (for hearts and diamonds) or black (for clubs and spades). It does this by calling a utility method on the source of the method call. This is necessary because the callback method is implemented as a static method, but it is passed the instance of the user control that raised the event as a parameter so that it can interact with it. The method called is SetTextColor():

```
public static void OnSuitChanged(DependencyObject source,
  DependencyPropertyChangedEventArgs args)
{
  ((Card)source).SetTextColor();
}
```

The SetTextColor() method is private but is obviously still accessible from OnSuitChanged(), as they are both members of the same class, despite being instance and static methods, respectively. SetTextColor() simply sets the Foreground property of the various labels of the control to a solid color brush that is either black or red, depending on the Suit value:

```
private void SetTextColor()
{
  if (Suit == "Club" || Suit == "Spade")
  {
    RankLabel.Foreground = new SolidColorBrush(Color.FromRgb(0, 0, 0));
    SuitLabel.Foreground = new SolidColorBrush(Color.FromRgb(0, 0, 0));
    RankLabelInverted.Foreground = new SolidColorBrush(Color.FromRgb(0, 0, 0));
  }
  else
  {
    RankLabel.Foreground = new SolidColorBrush(Color.FromRgb(255, 0, 0));
    SuitLabel.Foreground = new SolidColorBrush(Color.FromRgb(255, 0, 0));
    RankLabelInverted.Foreground = new SolidColorBrush(Color.FromRgb(255, 0, 0));
  }
}
```

This is all you need to look at in the Card control. The client code, in Window1.xaml and Window1.xaml.cs, is fairly simple. It uses some basic styling to give you a gradiated green background, and plenty of event handling (using routed and attached routed events) to enable user interaction. There a couple of tricks — for example, how margins are used to position cards and how an offset is used so that existing cards can be dragged from the point on which you click — but nothing that you shouldn't be able to figure out for yourself by reading through the code.

Summary

In this chapter you have learned everything you need to know to start programming with WPF. You have also seen, albeit briefly, some more advanced techniques that have given you a taste of what more advanced WPF programming has to offer. WPF is a subject that is far too big to cover in a single chapter, and if you are interested you will probably want to look at additional resources on this subject. A good place to start is *Professional WPF Programming: .NET Development with the Windows Presentation Foundation* (Wrox, 2007) or *Silverlight 1.0* (Wrox, 2007) if you are interested in more details about XAML in the Web environment.

Of course, you may prefer simply to play around with the available tools — in particular, Expression Blend — and see what you can achieve. The MSDN documentation will also assist you, although as WPF is still so new there are noticeable gaps in this resource that you will have to look elsewhere to fill.

There are some great Web sites around that you can also check out for additional information. In particular, see the community site for WPF at `http://wpf.netfx3.com/`, and it is always worth keeping an eye on Scott Guthrie's blog at `http://weblogs.asp.net/scottgu`.

In this chapter you have covered the following:

❑ What WPF is and the impact it could potentially have on both desktop and Web software development.

❑ How WPF is designed so that designers and developers can work together on projects by using both Expression Blend and VS or VCE.

❑ What XAML is and how the basic syntax for XAML works, along with some terminology.

❑ How to use the `Application` object.

❑ How controls in WPF work, including concepts about dependency and attached properties and routed and attached events.

❑ How the layout system in WPF works and how you can use the various layout containers to position controls.

❑ Using styles and templates to customize how controls look and behave.

❑ How to use triggers and animations to enhance the user experience.

❑ How to define resources in internal or external resource dictionaries, and how to access resources statically and dynamically.

❑ How to create user controls with dependency properties.

In the next chapter you'll look at another technology that is new to .NET 3.0 and 3.5: the Windows Communication Foundation.

Exercises

1. You can use exactly the same XAML code for WPF desktop applications and WPF browser applications. True or false?

2. What technique would you use to enable child controls to set individual values for a property defined on a parent? What syntax would you use in XAML to achieve this? Give an XAML example where two child `Branch` controls set different values for a `LeafCount` property defined by a parent `Tree` control.

3. Which of the following statements about dependency properties are true?

a. Dependency properties must be accessible through an associated .NET property.

b. Dependency properties are defined as public, static members.

    c.   You can only have one dependency property per class definition.

    d.   Dependency properties must be named using the naming convention `[PropertyName]Property`.

    e.   You can validate the values assigned to a dependency property with a callback method.

4. Which layout control would you use to display controls in a single row or column?

5. Tunneling events in WPF are named in a specific way so that you can identify them. What is this naming convention?

6. What property types can be animated?

7. When would you use a dynamic resource reference rather than a static resource reference?

Windows Communication Foundation

In Chapter 21 you learned about Web services and how you can use them to provide simple communication between applications. You saw how you could use HTTP GET and POST techniques to exchange data with Web services, and how to use SOAP. Over the years since Web services were first made available to .NET developers, it has become apparent that although Web services are great, there is scope to extend this technology. Microsoft released the Web Service Enhancements (WSE) add-on to address this. WSE enabled Web service developers to include security for messages, routing techniques, and various other policies to improve Web services. Again, though, there was room for improvement.

Another .NET technology, remoting, makes it possible to create instances of objects in one process and use them from another process. Remoting makes this possible even if the object is on a different computer from the one that is using it. However, this technology, despite being a great improvement over previous technologies such as DCOM, still has its problems. Remoting is limited, and it isn't the easiest thing for a beginner programmer to learn.

Windows Communication Foundation (WCF) is essentially a replacement for both Web services and remoting technology. It takes concepts such as services and platform-independent SOAP messaging from Web services, and combines these with concepts such as host server applications and advanced binding capabilities from remoting. The result is a technology that you can think of as a superset that includes both Web services and remoting, but that is much more powerful that Web services and much easier to use than remoting. By using WCF, you can move from simple applications to applications that use a service-oriented architecture (SOA). SOA means that you decentralize processing and make use of distributed processing by connecting to services and data as you need them across local networks and the Internet.

In this chapter you learn about the principles behind WCF and how you can create and consume WCF services from your application code. Included are the following topics:

- ❑ What is WCF?
- ❑ WCF concepts
- ❑ WCF programming

You cannot create WCF services in VCE, but you can in the full version of VS. You can also create IIS-hosted WCF services in Visual Web Developer 2008 Express Edition, but in this chapter you'll use VS in order to see the full range of options.

What Is WCF?

WCF is a technology that enables you to create services that you can access from other applications across process, machine, and network boundaries. You can use these services to share functionality across multiple applications, to expose data sources, or to abstract complicated processes.

As with Web services, the functionality that WCF services offer is encapsulated as individual methods that are exposed by the service. Each method — or, in WCF terminology, each *operation* — has an endpoint that you exchange data with in order to use it. At this point, WCF differs from Web services. With Web services, you can only communicate with an endpoint with SOAP over HTTP. With WCF services, you have a choice of protocols that you can use. You can even have endpoints that communicate through more than one protocol, depending on the network that you connect to the service through and your specific requirements.

In WCF, an endpoint can have multiple *bindings*, each of which specifies a means of communication. Bindings can also specify additional information, such as what security requirements must be met to communicate with the endpoint. A binding might require username and password authentication or a Windows user account token, for example. When you connect to an endpoint, the protocol that the binding uses affects the address that you use, as you will see shortly.

Once you have connected to an endpoint, you can communicate with it by using SOAP messages. The form of the messages that you use depends on the operation that you are using, and the data structures that are required to send messages to and receive messages from that operation. WCF uses *contracts* to specify all of this. You can discover contracts through metadata exchange with a service. This is analogous to the way Web services use WSDL to describe their functionality. In fact, you can get information about a WCF service in WSDL format, although WCF services can also be described in other ways.

When you have identified a service and endpoint that you want to use, and after you know what binding you use and what contracts to adhere to, you can communicate with a WCF service as easily as with an object that you have defined locally. Communications with WCF services can be simple, one-way transactions, request/response messages, or full-duplex communications that can be initiated from either end of the communication channel. You can also use message payload optimization techniques, such as Message Transmission Optimization Mechanism (MTOM) to package data if required.

The WCF service itself may be running in one of a number of different processes on the computer where it is hosted. Unlike Web services, which always run in IIS, you can choose a host process that is appropriate to your situation. You can use IIS to host WCF services, but you can also use Windows services or executables. If you are using TCP to communicate with a WCF service over a local network, there is no need even to have IIS installed on the PC that is hosting the service.

The WCF framework has been designed to enable you to customize nearly everything you have read about in this section. However, this is an advanced subject and you will only be using the techniques provided by default in .NET 3.5 in this chapter.

Now that you have covered the basics about WCF services, you will look in more detail at these concepts in the following sections.

WCF Concepts

This section describes the following aspects of WCF:

- ❑   WCF communication protocols
- ❑   Addresses, endpoints, and bindings
- ❑   Contracts
- ❑   Message patterns
- ❑   Behaviors
- ❑   Hosting

WCF Communication Protocols

As described earlier, you can communicate with WCF services through a variety of transport protocols. In fact, four are defined in the .NET 3.5 Framework:

- ❑   **HTTP:** This enables you to communicate with WCF services from anywhere, including across the Internet. You can use HTTP communications to create WCF Web services.

- ❑   **TCP:** This enables you to communicate with WCF services on your local network or across the Internet if you configure your firewall appropriately. TCP is more efficient than HTTP and has more capabilities, but it can be more complicated to configure.

- ❑   **Named pipe:** This enables you to communicate with WCF services on the same machine as the calling code but residing in a separate process.

- ❑   **MSMQ:** This is a queuing technology that enables messages sent by an application to be routed through a queue to arrive at a destination. MSMQ is a reliable messaging technology that ensures that a message sent to a queue will reach that queue. MSMQ is also inherently asynchronous, so a queued message will only be processed when messages ahead of it in the queue have been processed and a processing service is available.

These protocols often enable you to establish secure connections. For example, you can use the HTTPS protocol to establish a secure SSL connection across the Internet. TCP offers extensive possibilities for security in a local network by using the Windows security framework.

Figure 35-1 illustrates how these transport protocols can connect an application to WCF services in various locations. This chapter describes all of these protocols except for MSMQ, which is a subject requiring a more in-depth discussion.

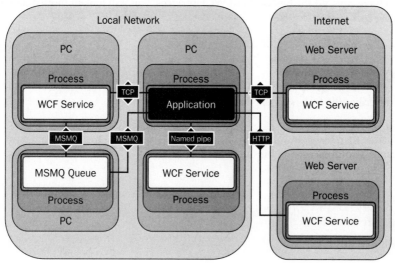

Figure 35-1

In order to connect to a WCF service, you must know where it is. In practice, this means knowing the address of an endpoint.

Addresses, Endpoints, and Bindings

The type of address you use for a service depends on the protocol that you are using. Service addresses are formatted for the three protocols described in this chapter as follows:

❑ **HTTP:** Addresses for the HTTP protocol are URLs of the familiar form
   `http://<server>:<port>/<service>`. For SSL connections, you can also use
   `https://<server>:<port>/<service>`. If you are hosting a service in IIS, `<service>` will be
   a file with a .svc extension. (.svc files are analogous to the .asmx files used in Web services.)
   IIS addresses will probably include more subdirectories than this example — that is, more
   sections separated by / characters before the .svc file.

❑ **TCP:** Addresses for TCP are of the form `net.tcp://<server>:<port>/<service>`.

❑ **Named pipe:** Address for named pipe connections are similar but have no port number. They
   are of the form `net.pipe://<server>/<service>`.

The address for a service is a base address that you can use to create addresses for endpoints
representing operations. For example, you might have an operation at
`net.tcp://<server>:<port>/<service>/operation1`.

For example, imagine you create a WCF service with a single operation that has bindings for all three of the protocols listed here. You might use the following base addresses:

```
http://www.mydomain.com/services/amazingservices/mygreatservice.svc
net.tcp://myhugeserver:8080/mygreatservice
net.pipe://localhost/mygreatservice
```

You could then use the following addresses for operations:

```
http://www.mydomain.com/services/amazingservices/mygreatservice.svc/greatop
net.tcp://myhugeserver:8080/mygreatservice/greatop
net.pipe://localhost/mygreatservice/greatop
```

Bindings, as mentioned earlier, specify more than just the transport protocol that will be used by an operation. You can also use them to specify the security requirements for communication over the transport protocol, transactional capabilities of the endpoint, message encoding, and much more.

Because bindings offer such a great degree of flexibility, the .NET Framework provides some predefined bindings that you can use. You can also use these bindings as starting points, and tweak them to obtain exactly the type of binding you want — up to a point. The predefined bindings have certain capabilities to which you must adhere. Each binding type is represented by a class in the `System.ServiceModel` namespace. The following table lists these bindings along with some basic information about them:

Binding	Description
BasicHttpBinding	The simplest HTTP binding, and the default binding used by Web services. It has limited security capabilities and no transactional support.
WSHttpBinding	A more advanced form of HTTP binding that is capable of using all the additional functionality that was introduced in WSE.
WSDualHttpBinding	Extends WSHttpBinding capabilities to include duplex communication capabilities. With duplex communication, the server can initiate communications with the client in addition to ordinary message exchange.
WSFederationHttpBinding	Extends WSHttpBinding capabilities to include federation capabilities. Federation enables third parties to implement single sign-on and other proprietary security measures. This is an advanced topic not covered in this chapter.
NetTcpBinding	Used for TCP communications, and enables you to configure security, transactions, and so on.
NetNamedPipeBinding	Used for named pipe communications, and enables you to configure security, transactions, and so on.
NetPeerTcpBinding	Enables broadcast communications to multiple clients, and is another advanced class not covered in this chapter.
NetMsmqBinding and MsmqIntegrationBinding	These bindings are used with MSMQ, which is not covered in this chapter.

Many of the binding classes listed in this table have similar properties that you can use for additional configuration. For example, they have properties that you can use to configure timeout values. You'll learn more about this when you look at code later in this chapter.

Contracts

Contracts define how WCF services can be used. Several types of contract can be defined:

❑ **Service contract:** Contains general information about a service and the operations exposed by a service. This includes, for example, the namespace used by service. Services have unique namespaces that are used when defining the schema for SOAP messages in order to avoid possible conflicts with other services.

❑ **Operation contract:** Defines how an operation is used. This includes the parameter and return types for an operation method along with additional information, such as whether a method will return a response message.

❑ **Message contract:** Enables you to customize how information is formatted inside SOAP messages — for example, whether data should be included in the SOAP header or SOAP message body. This can be useful when creating a WCF service that must integrate with legacy systems.

❑ **Fault contract:** Defines faults that an operation may return. When you use .NET clients, faults result in exceptions that you can catch and deal with in the normal way.

❑ **Data contract:** If you use complex types such as user-defined structs and objects as parameters or return types for operations, then you must define data contracts for these types. Data contracts define the types in terms of the data that they expose through properties.

You typically add contracts to service classes and methods by using attributes, as you will see later in this chapter.

Message Patterns

In the previous section you saw that an operation contract can define whether an operation returns a value. You've also read about duplex communications that are made possible by the `WSDualHttpBinding` binding. These are both forms of message patterns, of which there are three types:

❑ **Request/response messaging:** The "ordinary" way of exchanging messages, whereby every message sent to a service results in a response being sent back to the client. This doesn't necessarily mean that the client waits for a response, as you can call operations asynchronously in the usual way.

❑ **One-way, or simplex, messaging:** Messages are sent from the client to the WCF operation but no response is sent. This is useful when no response is required. For example, you might create a WCF operation that results in the WCF host server rebooting, in which case you wouldn't really want or need to wait for a response.

❑ **Two-way, or duplex, messaging:** A more advanced scheme whereby the client effectively acts as a server as well as a client, and the server as a client as well as a server. Once set up, duplex messaging enables both the client and the server to send messages to each other, which may or may not have responses. This is analogous to creating an object and subscribing to events exposed by that object.

You'll see how these message patterns are used in practice later in this chapter.

Behaviors

Behaviors are a way to apply additional configuration that is not directly exposed to a client to services and operations. By adding a behavior to a service, you can control how it is instantiated and used by its hosting process, how it participates in transactions, how multithreading issues are dealt with in the service, and so on. Operation behaviors can control whether impersonation is used in the operation execution, how the individual operation affects transactions, and more.

As this chapter is intended to give you a basic understanding of WCF services, you will only see the most basic functionality of behaviors.

Hosting

In the introduction to this chapter you learned that WCF services can be hosted in several different processes. These possibilities are as follows:

❑ **Web server:** IIS-hosted WCF services are the closest thing to Web services that WCF offers. However, you can use advanced functionality and security features in WCF services that are much more difficult to implement in Web services. You can also integrate with IIS features such as IIS security.

❑ **Executable:** You can host a WCF service in any application type that you can create in .NET, such as console applications, Windows Forms applications, and WPF applications.

❑ **Windows service:** You can host a WCF service in a Windows service, which means that you can use the useful features that Windows services provide. This includes automatic startup and fault recovery.

❑ **Windows Activation Service (WAS):** Designed specifically to host WCF services, it is basically a simple version of IIS, which you can use where IIS is not available.

Two of the options in the preceding list — IIS and WAS — provide useful features for WCF services such as activation, process recycling, and object pooling. If you use either of the other two hosting options, the WCF service is said to be *self-hosted*. This isn't necessarily a bad thing, as you might not require the additional functionality that the hosted environments offer. However, self-hosted services do require you to write more code.

WCF Programming

Now that you have covered all the basics, it is time to get started with some code. In this section you'll start by looking as a simple Web server-hosted WCF service and a console application client. After looking at the structure of the code created, you'll learn about the basic structure of WCF services and client applications. Then you will look at some key topics in a bit more detail:

❑ Defining WCF service contracts

❑ Self-hosted WCF services

Try It Out   **A Simple WCF Service and Client**

1. Create a new WCF Service Application project called Ch35Ex01 in the directory
    C:\BegVCSharp\Chapter35.

2. Add a console application called Ch35Ex01Client to the solution.

3. On the Build menu, click Build Solution.

4. Right-click the Ch35Ex01Client project in the Solution Explorer and select Add Service
    Reference.

5. In the Add Service Reference dialog, click Discover.

6. When the development Web server has started and information about the WCF service has
    been loaded, expand the reference to look at its details, as shown in Figure 35-2 (you may
    have a different port number).

Figure 35-2

7. Click OK to add the service reference.

8. Modify the code in Program.cs in the Ch35Ex01Client application as follows:

```
using System;
using System.Collections.Generic;
using System.Linq;
using System.Text;
using Ch35Ex01Client.ServiceReference1;

namespace Ch35Ex01Client
```

```
{
    class Program
    {
        static void Main(string[] args)
        {
            string numericInput = null;
            int intParam;
            do
            {
                Console.WriteLine(
                    "Enter an integer and press enter to call the WCF service.");
                numericInput = Console.ReadLine();
            }
            while (!int.TryParse(numericInput, out intParam));
            Service1Client client = new Service1Client();
            Console.WriteLine(client.GetData(intParam));
            Console.WriteLine("Press an key to exit.");
            Console.ReadKey();
        }
    }
}
```

9. Right-click the solution in the Solution Explorer and select Set StartUp Projects.

10. Set both projects as startup projects as shown in Figure 35-3 and click OK.

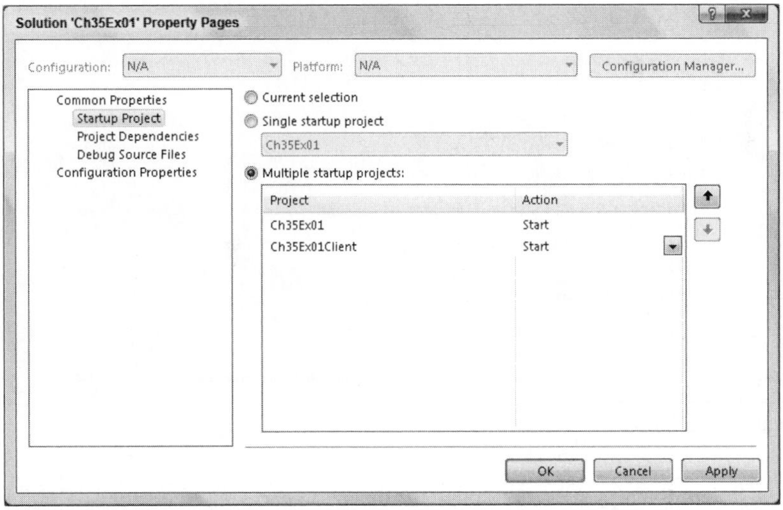

Figure 35-3

11. Right-click Service1.svc in Ch35Ex01 and click Set as Startup Page.

12. Run the application. If prompted, click OK to enable debugging in `Web.config`. Enter a number in the console application window and press Enter. The result is shown in Figure 35-4.

Figure 35-4

13. Review the information in the window (see Figure 35-5).

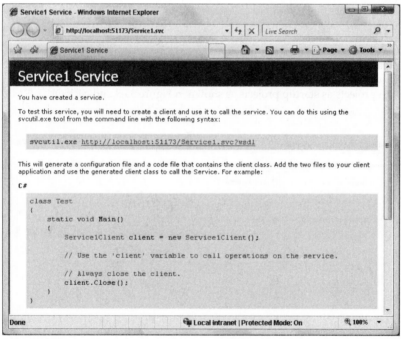

Figure 35-5

14. Click the link at the top of the Web page for the service to view the WSDL. Don't panic — you don't need to know what all the stuff in the WSDL file means!

How It Works

In this example you created a simple Web server–hosted WCF service and console application client. You used the default VS template for a WCF service project, which meant that you didn't have to add any code. Instead, you used one of the operations defined in this default template, `GetData()`. For the purposes of this example, the actual operation used isn't important; you will instead focus on the structure of the code and the plumbing that makes things work.

First, look at the server project, Ch35Ex01. This consists of the following:

❑ A `Service1.svc` file that defines the hosting for the service.

❑ A class definition, `CompositeType`, that defines a data contract used by the service.

❑ An interface definition, `IService1`, that defines the service contract and two operation contracts for the service.

❑ A class definition, `Service1`, that implements `IService1` and defines the functionality of the service.

❑ A `<system.serviceModel>` configuration section (in `Web.config`) that configures the service.

The `Service1.svc` file contains the following line of code (to see this code, right-click the file in the Solution Explorer and click View Markup):

```
<%@ ServiceHost Language="C#" Debug="true" Service="Ch35Ex01.Service1"
    CodeBehind="Service1.svc.cs" %>
```

This is a `ServiceHost` instruction that is used to tell the Web server (the development Web server in this case, although this also applies to IIS) what service is hosted at this address. The class that defines the service is declared in the `Service` attribute, and the code file that defines this class is declared in the `CodeBehind` attribute. This instruction is necessary in order to get the hosting features of the Web server as defined in the previous sections.

Obviously, this file is not required for WCF services that aren't hosted in a Web server. You'll learn how to self-host WCF services later in this chapter.

Next, the data contract `CompositeType` is defined in the `IService1.cs` file. You can see from the code that the data contract is simply a class definition that includes the `DataContract` attribute on the class definition and `DataMember` attributes on class members:

```
[DataContract]
public class CompositeType
{
    bool boolValue = true;
    string stringValue = "Hello ";

    [DataMember]
    public bool BoolValue
    {
        get { return boolValue; }
        set { boolValue = value; }
    }

    [DataMember]
    public string StringValue
    {
        get { return stringValue; }
        set { stringValue = value; }
    }
}
```

This data contract is exposed to the client application through metadata (if you looked through the WSDL file in the example you may have seen this). This enables client applications to define a type that can be serialized into a form that can be deserialized by the service into a `CompositeType` object. The client doesn't need to know the actual definition of this type; in fact, the class used by the client may have a different implementation. This simple way of defining data contracts is surprisingly powerful, and enables the exchange of complex data structures between the WCF service and its clients.

The `IService1.cs` file also contains the service contract for the service, which is defined as an interface with the `ServiceContract` attribute. Again, this interface is completely described in the metadata for the service, and can be recreated in client applications. The interface members constitute the operations exposed by the service, and each is used to create an operation contract by applying the `OperationContract` attribute. The example code includes two operations, one of which uses the data contract you looked at earlier:

```
[ServiceContract]
public interface IService1
{

    [OperationContract]
    string GetData(int value);

    [OperationContract]
    CompositeType GetDataUsingDataContract(CompositeType composite);
}
```

All four of the contract-defining attributes that you have seen so far can be further configured with attributes, as shown in the next section. The code that implements the service looks much like any other class definition:

```
public class Service1 : IService1
{
    public string GetData(int value)
    {
        return string.Format("You entered: {0}", value);
    }

    public CompositeType GetDataUsingDataContract(CompositeType composite)
    {
        if (composite.BoolValue)
        {
            composite.StringValue += "Suffix";
        }
        return composite;
    }
}
```

Note that this class definition doesn't need to inherit from a particular type, and doesn't require any particular attributes. All it needs to do is implement the interface that defines the service contract. In fact, you can add attributes to this class and its members to specify behaviors, but these aren't mandatory.

The separation of the service contract (the interface) from the service implementation (the class) works fantastically well. The client doesn't need to know anything about the class, which could include much more functionality than just the service implementation. A single class could even implement more than one service contract.

Finally, you come to the configuration in the `Web.config` file. Configuration of WCF services in config files is a feature that has been taken from .NET remoting, and works with all types of WCF services (hosted or self-hosted), and (as shown in a moment) clients of WCF services. The vocabulary of this configuration is such that you can apply pretty much any configuration that you can think of to a service, and you can even extend this syntax.

WCF configuration code is contained in the `<system.serviceModel>` configuration section of `Web.config` or `app.config` files. In the `Web.config` file in this example, the configuration section consists of two subsections:

❑   `<services>`: Defines the services in the project. Each service is defined in a `<service>` child section.

❑   `<behaviors>`: Defines behaviors that are used by various elements in the `<services>` section. Behaviors defined here in `<behavior>` child sections can be reused on multiple other elements.

There is only one service in this example. In the configuration code it is given a name and associated with a named behavior that is defined in the `<behaviors>` section:

```
<configuration>
   ...
  <system.serviceModel>
    <services>
      <service name="Ch35Ex01.Service1"
        behaviorConfiguration="Ch35Ex01.Service1Behavior">
```

The `<service>` element contains two child `<endpoint>` elements, each of which (you guessed it) defines an endpoint for the service. In fact, these endpoints are base endpoints for the service. Endpoints for operations are inferred from these.

Endpoint addresses are defined in `address` attributes. In Web server–hosted services, the address is relative to the .svc file for the service. Endpoint bindings are defined in `binding` attributes, and service contracts for bindings are specified with interface names. The first endpoint is the main one for the service so it uses the `IService1` interface as its service contract. It also uses the default address and the `WSHttpBinding` binding type:

```
<endpoint address="" binding="wsHttpBinding" contract="Ch35Ex01.IService1">
  <identity>
    <dns value="localhost"/>
  </identity>
</endpoint>
```

Various additional elements are possible inside `<endpoint>` elements, such as the `<identity>` element used here, which specifies the base server address for the endpoint. As this is a development service, it uses `localhost`.

The example service includes a second endpoint, at an address of mex. This is short for metadata exchange, and is used to enable clients to obtain descriptions of WCF services. WCF services, unlike

Web services, do not expose service descriptions be default. By adding an endpoint that uses the `IMetadataExchange` contract, you can make service descriptions available. Service description endpoints use one of the bindings `mexHttpBinding`, `mexHttpsBinding`, `mexNamedPipeBinding`, or `mexTcpBinding` depending on the protocol being used:

```
        <endpoint address="mex" binding="mexHttpBinding"
          contract="IMetadataExchange"/>
      </service>
    </services>
```

In this example, as you saw, a WSDL description is available. This is obtained by appending `?wsdl` to the address of the service, and is in fact exposed by a behavior, not through the metadata exchange endpoint. This behavior, which is applied to the service as a whole, is defined as follows:

```
    <behaviors>
      <serviceBehaviors>
        <behavior name="Ch35Ex01.Service1Behavior">
          <serviceMetadata httpGetEnabled="true"/>
```

The same behavior also exposes exception details in any faults that are transmitted to the client, which is something you would usually allow only in development:

```
          <serviceDebug includeExceptionDetailInFaults="false"/>
        </behavior>
      </serviceBehaviors>
    </behaviors>
  </system.serviceModel>
</configuration>
```

This completes the definition of the server.

In the client application, you added a reference to the service by using the Add Service Reference tool, which uses the metadata that a service exposes (that is, the WSDL for the service) to construct proxy classes. This is not the only way to get access to WCF services, but it is one of the easiest. Another common way is to define the contracts for a WCF service in a separate assembly, which is referenced by both the hosting project and the client project. The client can then generate a proxy by using these contracts directly, rather than through exposed metadata.

You can browse through the code that is generated by the Add Service Reference tool if you want (by displaying all files in the project, including the hidden ones), although at this point it's probably best not to, as there is quite a lot of confusing code in there.

The important thing to note here is that the tool creates all the classes you require to access the service. This includes a proxy class for the service that includes methods for all the operations exposed by the service (`Service1Client`), and a client-side class generated from the data contract (`CompositeType`).

The tool also adds a configuration file to the project, `app.config`. This configuration defines two things:

❑   Binding information for the service endpoint.

❑   The address and contract for the endpoint.

The binding information is taken from the service description, and in the client every single configurable option is copied to the configuration file:

```
<configuration>
  <system.serviceModel>
    <bindings>
      <wsHttpBinding>
        <binding name="WSHttpBinding_IService1" closeTimeout="00:01:00"
          openTimeout="00:01:00" receiveTimeout="00:10:00" sendTimeout="00:01:00"
          bypassProxyOnLocal="false" transactionFlow="false"
          hostNameComparisonMode="StrongWildcard" maxBufferPoolSize="524288"
          maxReceivedMessageSize="65536" messageEncoding="Text"
          textEncoding="utf-8" useDefaultWebProxy="true" allowCookies="false">
          <readerQuotas maxDepth="32" maxStringContentLength="8192"
            maxArrayLength="16384" maxBytesPerRead="4096"
            maxNameTableCharCount="16384" />
          <reliableSession ordered="true" inactivityTimeout="00:10:00"
            enabled="false" />
          <security mode="Message">
            <transport clientCredentialType="Windows" proxyCredentialType="None"
              realm="" />
            <message clientCredentialType="Windows"
              negotiateServiceCredential="true" algorithmSuite="Default"
              establishSecurityContext="true" />
          </security>
        </binding>
      </wsHttpBinding>
    </bindings>
```

This binding is used in the endpoint configuration, along with the base address of the service (which is the address of the .svc file for Web server–hosted services) and the client-side version of the contract IService1:

```
    <client>
      <endpoint address="http://localhost:51173/Service1.svc"
        binding="wsHttpBinding"
        bindingConfiguration="WSHttpBinding_IService1"
        contract="ServiceReference1.IService1" name="WSHttpBinding_IService1">
        <identity>
          <dns value="localhost" />
        </identity>
      </endpoint>
    </client>
  </system.serviceModel>
</configuration>
```

The Add Service Reference tool has been very thorough here. In fact, most of this information isn't required, as you've used the default WSHttpBinding binding. You could replace this configuration file with the following:

```
<configuration>
  <system.serviceModel>
    <client>
      <endpoint address="http://localhost:51173/Service1.svc"
          binding="wsHttpBinding" contract="ServiceReference1.IService1"
          name="WSHttpBinding_IService1">
        <identity>
          <dns value="localhost" />
        </identity>
      </endpoint>
    </client>
  </system.serviceModel>
</configuration>
```

Here, the bindingConfiguration attribute of the <endpoint> element has been removed, which means that the client will use the default binding configuration.

However, for the purpose of learning about WCF services, the thoroughness of the tool is quite useful. It has shown you all of the settings that are included in the default WSHtttpBinding binding. You won't look at WCF service configuration in great depth in this chapter, but you can already see that some of them, such as the timeout settings, are quite easy to understand due to their explicit naming.

This example has covered a lot of ground, and it is worth summarizing what you have learned before moving on:

❑ WCF service definitions:

    ❑ Services are defined by a service contract interface that includes operation contract members.

    ❑ Services are implemented in a class that implements the service contract interface.

    ❑ Data contracts are simply type definitions that use data contract attributes.

❑ WCF service configuration:

    ❑ You can use configuration files (Web.config or app.config) to configure WCF services.

❑ WCF Web server hosting:

    ❑ Web server hosting uses .svc files as service base addresses.

❑ WCF client configuration:

    ❑ You can use configuration files (Web.config or app.config) to configure WCF service clients.

In the following section you explore contracts in more detail.

Defining WCF Service Contracts

The example showed how the WCF infrastructure makes it easy for you to define contracts for WCF services with a combination of classes, interfaces, and attributes. This section takes a deeper look at this technique.

Data Contracts

To define a data contract for a service, you apply the `DataContractAttribute` attribute to a class definition. This attribute is found in the `System.Runtime.Serialization` namespace. You can configure this attribute with the following properties:

Property	Usage
Name	Names the data contract with a different name than the name you use for the class definition. This name will be used in SOAP messages and client-side data objects that are defined from service metadata.
Namespace	Defines the namespace that the data contract uses in SOAP messages.

Both of these properties are useful when you need interoperability with existing SOAP message formats (as are the similarly named properties for other contracts), but otherwise you will probably not require them.

Each class member that is part of a data contract must use the `DataMemberAttribute` attribute, which is also found in the `System.Runtime.Serialization` namespace. This attribute has the following properties:

Property	Usage
Name	Specifies the name of the data member when serialized (the default is the member name).
IsRequired	Specifies whether the member must be present in a SOAP message.
Order	An `int` value specifying the order of serializing or deserializing the member, which may be required if one member must be present before another can be understood. Lower `Order` members are processed first.
EmitDefaultValue	Set this to `false` to prevent members from being included in SOAP messages if their value is the default value for the member.

Service Contracts

Service contracts are defined by applying the `System.ServiceModel.ServiceContractAttribute` attribute to an interface definition. You can customize the service contract with the following properties:

Property	Usage
Name	Specifies the name of the service contract as defined in the `<portType>` element in WSDL.
Namespace	Defines the namespace of the service contract used by the `<portType>` element in WSDL.
ConfigurationName	The name of the service contract as used in the configuration file.
HasProtectionLevel	Determines whether messages used by the service have explicitly defined protection levels. Protection levels enable you to sign, or sign and encrypt, messages.
ProtectionLevel	The protection level to use for message protection.
SessionMode	Determines whether sessions are enabled for messages. If you use sessions, then you can ensure that messages sent to different endpoints of a service are correlated — that is, they use the same service instance and so can share state, etc.
CallbackContract	For duplex messaging the client exposes a contract as well as the service. This is because, as discussed earlier, the client in duplex communications also acts as a server. This property enables you to specify which contract the client uses.

Operation Contracts

Within interfaces that define service contracts, you define members as operations by applying the `System.ServiceModel.OperationContractAttribute` attribute. This attribute has the following properties:

Property	Usage
Name	Specifies the name of the service operation. The default is the member name.
IsOneWay	Specifies whether the operation returns a response. If you set this to `true`, then clients won't wait for the operation to complete before continuing.
AsyncPattern	Set to `true`, the operation is implemented as two methods that you can use to call the operation asynchronously: `Begin<methodName>` and `End<methodName>`.
HasProtectionLevel	See the previous section.

Property	Usage
ProtectionLevel	See the previous section.
IsInitiating	If sessions are used, then this property determines whether calling this operation can start a new session.
IsTerminating	If sessions are used, then this property determines whether calling this operation terminates the current session.
Action	If you are using addressing (an advanced capability of WCF services), then an operation has an associated action name, which you can specify with this property.
ReplyAction	As above, but specifies the action name for the operation response.

Message Contracts

The earlier example didn't use message contract specifications. If you use these, then you do so by defining a class that represents the message, and apply the MessageContractAttribute attribute to the class. You then apply MessageBodyMemberAttribute, MessageHeaderAttribute, or MessageHeaderArrayAttribute attributes to members of this class. All these attributes are in the System.ServiceModel namespace. You are unlikely to want to do this unless you want a very high degree of control over the SOAP messages used by WCF services, so you won't see the details here.

Fault Contracts

If you have a particular exception type — for example, a custom exception — that you want to make available to client applications, then you can apply the System.ServiceModel .FaultContractAttribute attribute to the operation that might generate this exception. Again, this isn't something you will want to do in ordinary WCF use.

Try It Out   WCF Contracts

1. Create a new WCF Service Application project called Ch35Ex02 in the directory C:\BegVCSharp\Chapter35.

2. Add a class library project called Ch35Ex01Contracts to the solution and remove the Class1.cs file.

3. Add references to the System.Runtime.Serialization.dll and System.ServiceModel .dll assemblies to the Ch35Ex01Contracts project.

4. Add a class called Person to the Ch35Ex01Contracts project and modify the code in Person.cs as follows:

```
using System;
using System.Collections.Generic;
using System.Linq;
using System.Text;
```

```csharp
using System.Runtime.Serialization;

namespace Ch35Ex02Contracts
{
    [DataContract]
    public class Person
    {
        [DataMember]
        public string Name { get; set; }

        [DataMember]
        public int Mark { get; set; }
    }
}
```

5. Add a class called `IAwardService` to the Ch35Ex01Contracts project and modify the code in `IAwardService.cs` as follows:

```csharp
using System;
using System.Collections.Generic;
using System.Linq;
using System.Text;
using System.ServiceModel;

namespace Ch35Ex02Contracts
{
    [ServiceContract(SessionMode=SessionMode.Required)]
    public interface IAwardService
    {
        [OperationContract(IsOneWay=true, IsInitiating=true)]
        void SetPassMark(int passMark);

        [OperationContract]
        Person[] GetAwardedPeople(Person[] peopleToTest);
    }
}
```

6. To the Ch35Ex01 project, add a reference to the Ch35Ex01Contracts.

7. Remove `IService1.cs` and `Service1.svc` from the Ch35Ex01 project.

8. Add a new WCF service called `AwardService` to Ch35Ex01.

9. Remove the `IAwardService.cs` file from the Ch35Ex01 project.

10. Modify the code in `AwardService.svc.cs` as follows:

```
using System;
using System.Collections.Generic;
using System.Linq;
using System.Runtime.Serialization;
using System.ServiceModel;
using System.Text;
using Ch35Ex02Contracts;

namespace Ch35Ex02
{
    public class AwardService : IAwardService
    {
        private int passMark;

        public void SetPassMark(int passMark)
        {
            this.passMark = passMark;
        }

        public Person[] GetAwardedPeople(Person[] peopleToTest)
        {
            List<Person> result = new List<Person>();
            foreach (Person person in peopleToTest)
            {
                if (person.Mark > passMark)
                {
                    result.Add(person);
                }
            }
            return result.ToArray();
        }
    }
}
```

11. Modify the service configuration section in `Web.config` as follows:

```
<system.serviceModel>
  <services>
    <service name="Ch35Ex02.AwardService">
      <endpoint address="" binding="wsHttpBinding"
        contract="Ch35Ex02Contracts.IAwardService" />
    </service>
  </services>
</system.serviceModel>
```

12. Set the startup page of Ch35Ex02 to `AwardService.svc`.

13. Run the Ch35Ex02 project in debug mode and make a note of the URL used in the browser (include the port number, which you will require shortly).

14. Stop debugging and add a new console project called Ch35Ex02Client to the solution.

15. Add references to the `System.ServiceModel.dll` assembly and the Ch35Ex02Contracts project to the Ch35Ex01Client project.

16. Modify the code in `Program.cs` in Ch35Ex01Client as follows:

```
using System;
using System.Collections.Generic;
using System.Linq;
using System.Text;
using System.ServiceModel;
using Ch35Ex02Contracts;

namespace Ch35E02Client
{
    class Program
    {
        static void Main(string[] args)
        {
            Person[] people = new Person[]
            {
                new Person { Mark = 46, Name="Jim" },
                new Person { Mark = 73, Name="Mike" },
                new Person { Mark = 92, Name="Stefan" },
                new Person { Mark = 84, Name="George" },
                new Person { Mark = 24, Name="Arthur" },
                new Person { Mark = 58, Name="Nigel" }
            };

            Console.WriteLine("People:");
            OutputPeople(people);

            IAwardService client = ChannelFactory<IAwardService>.CreateChannel(
                new WSHttpBinding(),
                new EndpointAddress("http://localhost:51425/AwardService.svc"));
            client.SetPassMark(70);
            Person[] awardedPeople = client.GetAwardedPeople(people);

            Console.WriteLine();
            Console.WriteLine("Awarded people:");
            OutputPeople(awardedPeople);

            Console.ReadKey();
        }

        static void OutputPeople(Person[] people)
        {
            foreach (Person person in people)
            {
                Console.WriteLine("{0}, mark: {1}", person.Name, person.Mark);
            }
        }
    }
}
```

17. Run the application. The result is shown in Figure 35-6.

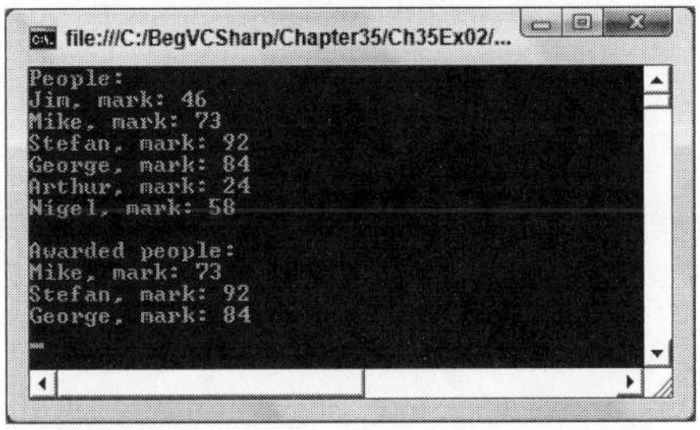

Figure 35-6

How It Works

In this example you have created a set of contracts in a class library project and used that class library in both a WCF service and a client. The service, as in the previous example, is hosted in a Web server. The configuration for this service was reduced to the bare minimum.

The main difference in this example is that no metadata was required by the client, as the client had access to the contract assembly. Instead of generating a proxy class from metadata, the client obtained a reference to the service contract interface through an alternative method. Another point to note about this example is the use of a session to maintain state in the service.

The data contract used in this example was for a simple class called `Person`, which has a `string` property called `Name` and an `int` property called `Mark`. You used the `DataContractAttribute` and `DataMemberAttribute` attributes with no customization, and there is no need to reiterate the code for this contract here.

The service contract was defined by applying the `ServiceContractAttribute` attribute to the `IAwardService` interface. The `SessionMode` property of this attribute was set to `SessionMode.Required`, as this service requires state:

```
[ServiceContract(SessionMode=SessionMode.Required)]
public interface IAwardService
{
```

The first operation contract, `SetPassMark()`, is the one that sets state, and therefore has the `IsInitiating` property of `OperationContractAttribute` set to `true`. This operation doesn't return anything, so it is defined as a one-way operation by setting `IsOneWay` to `true`:

```
[OperationContract(IsOneWay=true,IsInitiating=true)]
void SetPassMark(int passMark);
```

The other operation contract, `GetAwardedPeople()`, does not require any customization and uses the data contract defined earlier:

```
[OperationContract]
Person[] GetAwardedPeople(Person[] peopleToTest);
}
```

Remember that these two types, `Person` and `IAwardService`, are available to both the service and the client. The service implements the `IAwardService` contract in a type called `AwardService`, which doesn't contain any remarkable code. The only difference between this class and the service class you saw earlier is that it is stateful. This is permissible, as a session is defined to correlate messages from a client.

The client is more interesting, primarily because of this line of code:

```
IAwardService client = ChannelFactory<IAwardService>.CreateChannel(
    new WSHttpBinding(),
    new EndpointAddress("http://localhost:51425/AwardService.svc"));
```

The client application has no `app.config` file to configure communications with the service, and has no proxy class defined from metadata to communicate with the service. Instead, a proxy class is created through the `ChannelFactory<T>.CreateChannel()` method. This method creates a proxy class that implements the `IAwardService` client, although behind the scenes the generated class communicates with the service just like the metadata-generated proxy you saw earlier.

> *If you create a proxy class in this way, the communication channel will, by default, time out after a minute, which can lead to communication errors. There are ways to keep connections alive, but they are beyond the scope of this chapter.*

Creating proxy classes in this way is an extremely useful technique that you can use to quickly generate a client application on-the-fly.

Self-Hosted WCF Services

So far in this chapter you have seen WCF services that are hosted in Web servers. This enables you to communicate across the Internet, but for local network communications it is not the most efficient way of doing things. For one thing, you need a Web server on the computer that hosts the service. In addition, the architecture of your applications may be such that having an independent WCF service may not be desirable.

Instead, you might want to use a *self-hosted* WCF service. A self-hosted WCF service is a service that exists in a process that you create, rather than in the process of a specially made hosting application such as a Web server. This means, for example, that you can use a console application or Windows application to host your service.

To self-host a WCF service you use the `System.ServiceModel.ServiceHost` class. You instantiate this class with either the type of the service you want to host or an instance of the service class. You can configure a service host through properties or methods or (and this is the clever part) through a configuration file. In fact, host processes, such as Web servers, use a `ServiceHost` instance to do their hosting. The difference when self-hosting is that you interact with this class directly. However, the configuration you place in the `<system.serviceModel>` section of the `app.config` file for your host application uses exactly the same syntax as the configuration sections you've already seen in this chapter.

You can expose a self-hosted service through any protocol that you like, although typically you will use TCP or named pipe binding in this type of application. Services accessed through HTTP are more likely to live inside Web server processes, because you get the additional functionality that Web servers offer, such as security and so on.

If you want to host a service called `MyService`, you could use code as follows to create an instance of `ServiceHost`:

```
ServiceHost host = new ServiceHost(typeof(MyService));
```

If you want to host an instance of `MyService` called `myServiceObject`, you could code as follows to create an instance of `ServiceHost`:

```
MyService myServiceObject = new MyService();
ServiceHost host = new ServiceHost(myServiceObject);
```

Note that this latter technique works only if you configure the service so that calls are always routed to the same object instance. To do this you must apply a `ServiceBehaviorAttribute` attribute to the service class and set the `InstanceContextMode` property of this attribute to `InstanceContextMode.Single`.

After creating a `ServiceHost` instance you can configure the service and its endpoints and binding through properties. Alternatively, if you put your configuration in a `.config` file, the `ServiceHost` instance will be configured automatically.

To start hosting a service once you have a configured `ServiceHost` instance, you use the `ServiceHost.Open()` method. Similarly, you stop hosting the service through the `ServiceHost.Close()` method. When you first start hosting a TCP-bound service you may, if you have it enabled, receive a warning from the Windows Firewall service, as it will block the TCP port by default. You must open the TCP port for the service to begin listening on the port.

In the following Try it Out you use self-hosting techniques to expose some functionality of a WPF application through a WCF service.

Try It Out   Self-Hosted WCF Services

1. Create a new WPF application called Ch35Ex03 in the directory C:\BegVCSharp\Chapter35.

2. Add a new WCF Service to the project called AppControlService by using the Add New Item Wizard.

3. Modify the code in `Window1.xaml` as follows:

```xml
<Window
  xmlns="http://schemas.microsoft.com/winfx/2006/xaml/presentation"
  xmlns:x="http://schemas.microsoft.com/winfx/2006/xaml"
  x:Class="Ch35Ex03.Window1"
  Title="Solar Evolution" Height="450" Width="430" Loaded="Window_Loaded"
  Closing="Window_Closing">
  <Grid Height="400" Width="400" HorizontalAlignment="Center"
    VerticalAlignment="Center">
    <Rectangle Fill="Black" RadiusX="20" RadiusY="20" StrokeThickness="10" >
```

```xml
        <Rectangle.Stroke>
          <LinearGradientBrush EndPoint="0.358,0.02" StartPoint="0.642,0.98">
            <GradientStop Color="#FF121A5D" Offset="0"/>
            <GradientStop Color="#FFB1B9FF" Offset="1"/>
          </LinearGradientBrush>
        </Rectangle.Stroke>
      </Rectangle>
      <Ellipse Name="AnimatableEllipse" Stroke="{x:Null}" Height="0" Width="0"
        HorizontalAlignment="Center" VerticalAlignment="Center">
        <Ellipse.Fill>
          <RadialGradientBrush>
            <GradientStop Color="#FFFFFFFF" Offset="0"/>
            <GradientStop Color="#FFFFFFFF" Offset="1"/>
          </RadialGradientBrush>
        </Ellipse.Fill>
        <Ellipse.BitmapEffect>
          <OuterGlowBitmapEffect GlowColor="#FFFFFFFF" GlowSize="16"/>
        </Ellipse.BitmapEffect>
      </Ellipse>
    </Grid>
</Window>
```

4. Modify the code in `Window1.xaml.cs` as follows:

```csharp
...
using System.Windows.Shapes;
using System.ServiceModel;
using System.Windows.Media.Animation;

namespace Ch35Ex03
{
    /// <summary>
    /// Interaction logic for Window1.xaml
    /// </summary>
    public partial class Window1 : Window
    {
        private AppControlService service;
        private ServiceHost host;

        public Window1()
        {
            InitializeComponent();
        }

        private void Window_Loaded(object sender, RoutedEventArgs e)
        {
            service = new AppControlService(this);
            host = new ServiceHost(service);
            host.Open();
```

```
        }

        private void Window_Closing(object sender,
            System.ComponentModel.CancelEventArgs e)
        {
            host.Close();
        }

        internal void SetRadius(double radius, string foreTo, TimeSpan duration)
        {
            if (radius > 200)
            {
                radius = 200;
            }
            Color foreToColor = Colors.Red;
            try
            {
                foreToColor = (Color)ColorConverter.ConvertFromString(foreTo);
            }
            catch
            {
                // Ignore color conversion failure.
            }
            Duration animationLength = new Duration(duration);

            DoubleAnimation radiusAnimation = new DoubleAnimation(
                radius * 2, animationLength);
            ColorAnimation colorAnimation = new ColorAnimation(
                foreToColor, animationLength);
            AnimatableEllipse.BeginAnimation(Ellipse.HeightProperty,
radiusAnimation);
            AnimatableEllipse.BeginAnimation(Ellipse.WidthProperty,
radiusAnimation);
            ((RadialGradientBrush)AnimatableEllipse.Fill).GradientStops[1]
                .BeginAnimation(GradientStop.ColorProperty, colorAnimation);
        }
    }
}
```

5.   Modify the code in `IAppControlService.cs` as follows:

```
[ServiceContract]
public interface IAppControlService
{
    [OperationContract]
    void SetRadius(int radius, string foreTo, int seconds);
}
```

6. Modify the code in `AppControlService.cs` as follows:

```
[ServiceBehavior(InstanceContextMode=InstanceContextMode.Single)]
public class AppControlService : IAppControlService
{
    private Window1 hostApp;

    public AppControlService(Window1 hostApp)
    {
        this.hostApp = hostApp;
    }

    public void SetRadius(int radius, string foreTo, int seconds)
    {
        hostApp.SetRadius(radius, foreTo, new TimeSpan(0, 0, seconds));
    }
}
```

7. Modify the code in `app.config` as follows:

```
<configuration>
  <system.serviceModel>
    <services>
      <service name="Ch35Ex03.AppControlService">
        <endpoint address="net.tcp://localhost:8081/AppControlService"
          binding="netTcpBinding" contract="Ch35Ex03.IAppControlService" />
      </service>
    </services>
  </system.serviceModel>
</configuration>
```

8. Add a new console application to the project called Ch35Ex03Client.

9. Configure the solution to have multiple startup projects, with both projects being started simultaneously.

10. Add references to `System.ServiceModel.dll` and Ch35Ex03 to the Ch35Ex03Client project.

11. Modify the code in `Program.cs` as follows:

```
using System;
using System.Collections.Generic;
using System.Linq;
using System.Text;
using Ch35Ex03;
using System.ServiceModel;

namespace Ch35Ex03Client
{
    class Program
```

```
{
    static void Main(string[] args)
    {
        Console.WriteLine("Press enter to begin.");
        Console.ReadLine();
        Console.WriteLine("Opening channel...");
        IAppControlService client =
            ChannelFactory<IAppControlService>.CreateChannel(
                new NetTcpBinding(),
                new EndpointAddress("net.tcp://localhost:8081/AppControlService"));
        Console.WriteLine("Creating sun...");
        client.SetRadius(100, "yellow", 3);
        Console.WriteLine("Press enter to continue.");
        Console.ReadLine();
        Console.WriteLine("Growing sun to red giant...");
        client.SetRadius(200, "Red", 5);
        Console.WriteLine("Press enter to continue.");
        Console.ReadLine();
        Console.WriteLine("Collapsing sun to neutron star...");
        client.SetRadius(50, "AliceBlue", 2);
        Console.WriteLine("Finished. Press enter to exit.");
        Console.ReadLine();
    }
}
}
```

12. Run the solution. If prompted, unblock the Windows Firewall TCP port so that the WCF can listen for connections.

13. When both the Solar Evolution window and the console application window are displayed, press Enter in the console window. The result is shown in Figure 35-7.

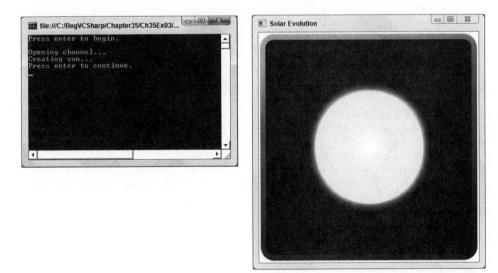

Figure 35-7

14. Continue pressing Enter in the console window to continue the solar evolution cycle.

How It Works

In this example you have added a WCF service to a WPF application and used it to control the animation of an `Ellipse` control. You have created a simple client application to test the service. Don't worry too much about the XAML code in this example if you are not too familiar with WPF yet; it's the WCF plumbing that interests us here.

The WCF service, `AppControlService`, exposes a single operation, `SetRadius()`, which clients call to control the animation. This method communicates with an identically named method defined in the `Window1` class for the WPF application. For this to work, the service must have a reference to the application, so you must host an object instance of the service. As discussed previously, this means that the service must use a behavior attribute:

```
[ServiceBehavior(InstanceContextMode=InstanceContextMode.Single)]
public class AppControlService : IAppControlService
{
    ...
}
```

In `Window1.xaml.cs`, the service instance is created in the `Windows_Loaded()` event handler. This method also starts hosting by creating a `ServiceHost` object for the service and calling its `Open()` method:

```
public partial class Window1 : Window
{
    private AppControlService service;
    private ServiceHost host;

    ...

    private void Window_Loaded(object sender, RoutedEventArgs e)
    {
        service = new AppControlService(this);
        host = new ServiceHost(service);
        host.Open();
    }
}
```

Hosting is terminated when the application closes, in the `Window_Closing()` event handler.

The configuration file is again about as simple as it can be. It defines a single endpoint for the WCF service that listens at a `net.tcp` address, on port 8081, and uses the default `NetTcpBinding` binding:

```
<service name="Ch35Ex03.AppControlService">
  <endpoint address="net.tcp://localhost:8081/AppControlService"
    binding="netTcpBinding" contract="Ch35Ex03.IAppControlService" />
</service>
```

This matches up with code in the client app, as in the previous example (although TCP binding is used here):

```
IAppControlService client =
    ChannelFactory<IAppControlService>.CreateChannel(
        new NetTcpBinding(),
        new EndpointAddress("net.tcp://localhost:8081/AppControlService"));
```

When the client has created a client proxy class it can call the `SetRadius()` method with radius, color, and animation duration parameters, and these will be forwarded to the WPF application through the service. Simple code in the WPF application then defines and uses animations to change the size and color of the ellipse.

This code would work across a network if you used a machine name rather than localhost, and if the network permitted traffic on the specified port. Alternatively, you could separate the client and host application further, and connect across the Internet. Either way, WCF services provide an excellent means of communication that really doesn't take much effort to set up.

Summary

In this chapter you looked at the basic techniques for using WCF services to communicate between applications, processes, and computers. You started by learning what a WCF service is and how it differs from a Web service or a remoting implementation, and the concepts that you need to know about to use WCF services. You then looked at how to program WCF services, how to consume WCF services in clients, and how to host WCF services in various ways.

Specifically, you learned the following:

- ❑ What WCF services are.
- ❑ How WCF services are configured with addresses, endpoints, bindings, contracts, and behaviors.
- ❑ Different ways you can host WCF services.
- ❑ The classes, attributes, interfaces, and configuration required to create a WCF service.
- ❑ How to create proxy classes for client applications through WCF metadata.
- ❑ How to define and use data, service, and operation contracts.
- ❑ How to generate proxy client classes from WCF contracts.
- ❑ How to self-host WCF services

This is the absolute minimum that you need in order to use WCF services in your applications. You have barely scratched the surface of what is possible here, in particular with `.config` file configuration and behaviors. The WCF framework enables you to integrate with advanced security infrastructures, and communication can be customized in pretty much any way you can imagine.

If you want to learn more about WCF services, you might like to read Scott Klein's *Professional WCF Programming* (Wrox, 2007). In the next chapter, you look at the last of the major new technologies introduced with .NET 3.5: Workflow Foundation.

Exercises

1. Which of the following applications can host WCF services?

    a. Web applications

    b. Windows Forms applications

    c. Windows services

    d. COM+ applications

    e. Console applications

2. Which type of contract would you implement if you wanted to exchange parameters of type `MyClass` with a WCF service? Which attributes would you require?

3. If you host a WCF service in a Web application, what extension will the base endpoint for the service use?

4. When self-hosting WCF services you must configure the service by setting properties and calling methods of the `ServiceHost` class. True or false?

5. Provide the code for a service contract, `IMusicPlayer`, with operations defined for `Play()`, `Stop()`, and `GetTrackInformation()`. Use one-way methods where appropriate. What other contracts might you define for this service to work?

Windows Workflow Foundation

Welcome to the final chapter of the book — and I would like to think that we've saved the best for last! Many applications need some form of configuration or customization capability, and traditionally this was done by adding in some form of hook to the application so that a third party could add in extra code. A common method was to define an interface in .NET and then ensure that each plug-in supported that interface. The only trouble with this is that it's all code based, and users without a programming background would find this daunting, if not impossible, to do.

Another way to extend applications is using some form of scripting language — such as VBA (Visual Basic for Applications), which is included in Microsoft Word, Excel, and many other applications. The issue here is the barrier to entry — there are licensing costs for VBA, and integrating it with your application isn't a trivial task.

In .NET 3.0 and above there is another — and in my opinion much better — way to permit end users to customize an application: Windows Workflow Foundation (referred to as WF throughout the rest of this chapter).

A workflow can be considered simply as a function in C#, which consists of a number of statements (known as *activities*), optional parameters, and optional return values. That, however, is where the similarity ends — a workflow is defined using a set of graphical building blocks, rather than code.

Activities are the building blocks from which a workflow is constructed — there are 30 built-in activities, some of which are discussed in this chapter. An activity is just a .NET class that is derived from a particular base class, so you can construct your own activities to perform your own processing. Constructing a workflow is similar to designing a form or an ASP.NET page — you can drag and drop activities from the Toolbox onto the design surface and wire these up into a complete workflow.

When you run a workflow, there is a runtime engine (known as the *WorkflowRuntime*) that executes the activities in that workflow. This engine knows how to schedule workflows and is used to communicate with running workflow instances. A workflow can be considered in a similar way to a Word template — the workflow is the template and the running workflow instance is like the document created from that template.

In this chapter you learn the following:

❑   How to create workflows.

❑   What an activity is, and how to use several of the built-in activities.

❑   How to handle faults in a workflow.

❑   How to use the Workflow Persistence Service.

❑   How to pass parameters to a workflow.

Try It Out   Hello World (Workflow Style)

No description of a new programming paradigm is complete without the "Hello World" example, so rather than break with tradition, here's an implementation of the canonical example that is built using Windows Workflow Foundation:

1.   Several new project types are available in Visual Studio 2008, so to create a new workflow project, choose the Workflow item in the Project types tree view, and then select the Sequential Workflow Console Application template, shown in Figure 36-1.

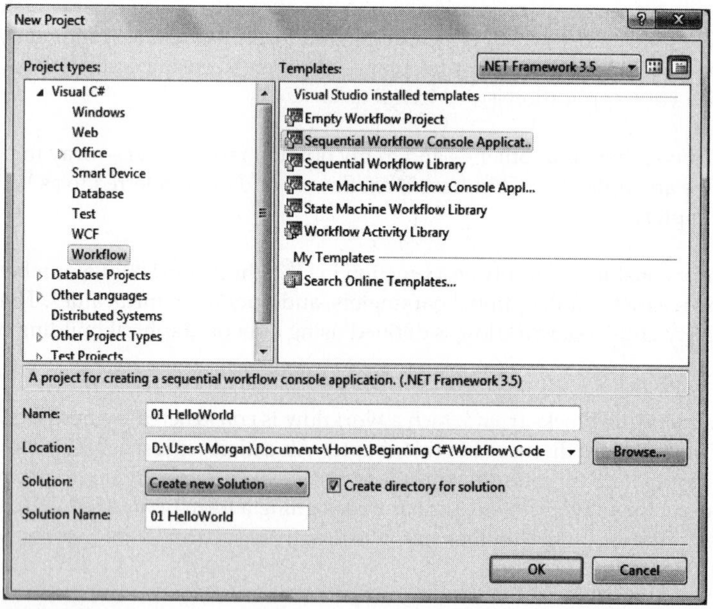

Figure 36-1

Note the drop-down in the top right part of Figure 36-1 — this new feature in Visual Studio 2008 enables you to target multiple versions of the .NET Framework from the same copy of Visual Studio.

The project created in this first step constructs a number of files that are discussed in this section. The most interesting is the workflow itself, which is shown in Figure 36-2. This type of workflow is similar to a flowchart in that there is a start shape and an end shape, and an area in the middle into which you can drag activities.

Figure 36-2

2. To continue with the Hello World example, you need to add an activity — in this case, the Code activity available on the Toolbox. Figure 36-3 shows the workflow once the Code activity has been added.

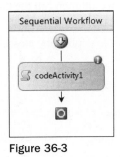

Figure 36-3

Notice that the activity has an exclamation mark in its top corner — this indicates that a mandatory property of the activity has not been set, which in this case is the method that is called when the activity executes.

3. Double-clicking the Code activity generates the method for you, shown in the following code snippet:

```
public sealed partial class Workflow1: SequentialWorkflowActivity
{
    public Workflow1()
    {
        InitializeComponent();
    }
```

```
private void codeActivity1_ExecuteCode(object sender, EventArgs e)
{

}
}
```

Here, the `codeActivity1_ExecuteCode` method has been created for you. Note also that the workflow is derived from the `SequentialWorkflowActivity` class — so a workflow itself is just another type of activity.

4.   Now add in a call to `Console.WriteLine` to output the customary Hello World greeting:

```
private void codeActivity1_ExecuteCode(object sender, EventArgs e)
{
    Console.WriteLine("Hello World");
}
```

Compile and run the application to see the text on the console.

How It Works

The main program created when you chose the Sequential Workflow Console application project is an instance of the `WorkflowRuntime`. This object coordinates all workflows and can be used to run workflow instances. In this example, it creates an instance of the `Workflow1` class and executes this instance.

The runtime executes the first activity in the workflow (which in this case is the workflow itself). Each activity is then executed in turn, so this would then call the `CodeActivity`, which in turn executes the method in which the call to `Console.WriteLine` was added.

When the workflow completes, the console application closes. The full code of the main application is shown here:

```
static void Main(string[] args)
{
    using(WorkflowRuntime workflowRuntime = new WorkflowRuntime())
    {
        AutoResetEvent waitHandle = new AutoResetEvent(false);

        workflowRuntime.WorkflowCompleted +=
            delegate(object sender, WorkflowCompletedEventArgs e)
            {waitHandle.Set();};

        workflowRuntime.WorkflowTerminated +=
            delegate(object sender, WorkflowTerminatedEventArgs e)
            {
                Console.WriteLine(e.Exception.Message);
                waitHandle.Set();
            };

        WorkflowInstance instance =
            workflowRuntime.CreateWorkflow
```

```
                    (typeof(_1_HelloWorld.Workflow1));

        instance.Start();

        waitHandle.WaitOne();
    }
}
```

The `WorkflowRuntime` is created within a `using` block and `AutoResetEvent`, which will be used to signal that the workflow has completed, or is constructed. The code hooks up event handlers to the `WorkflowCompleted` and `WorkflowTerminated` events to set this wait handle.

A `WorkflowInstance` is then constructed and told to execute — this schedules the instance and the runtime and then executes this instance by calling the `Start()` method.

Finally, the console application waits for the event to be signaled — either by the workflow completing successfully or, if the workflow is terminated, unexpectedly (i.e., if an exception is thrown when running an activity within that workflow).

You revisit the `WorkflowRuntime` class later in the chapter.

Activities

The building blocks of a workflow (and indeed the workflow itself) are activities. An activity is a .NET class that typically derives from the `System.Workflow.ComponentModel.Activity` class. Several other classes can augment the behavior of an activity — such as changing the onscreen design-time experience or validating that all mandatory properties have been defined.

Thirty activities ship with .NET 3.5, and this section describes some of these activities and how they could be used in an application.

You have already seen the `CodeActivity`, which was used in the previous section to display some output to the console. In most cases, you should create custom activities, rather than use `CodeActivity`, as this enables you to reuse these in other workflows. Reuse of the `CodeActivity` is limited to copying the code-behind file.

There are two type of activities in WF: simple activities and composite activities. A simple activity such as the `CodeActivity` derives from the `Activity` base class as explained, and appears as a single entry in the workflow designer. A composite activity, conversely, is essentially a container for other activities. This section first deals with some of the simple activities, and then describes some of the composite activities. You will then be in a position to write your own.

DelayActivity

The `DelayActivity` can be used in a workflow to wait for a specified time period. This could be useful if, for example, the workflow were used for insurance policy reminders. At the start of a new policy, you could start a reminder workflow that had an 11-month delay as its first activity. After this delay, you might want to prepare renewal documents and automatically send these out to the policyholder.

Figure 36-4 shows the properties available for the `DelayActivity`. If you want to set the duration to a known figure (such as two hours), then you can alter the `TimeoutDuration` property and specify a time in the form `{days} HH:MM:SS` — here, the `{days}` portion is optional.

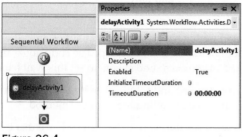

Figure 36-4

When the activity executes, it effectively suspends the workflow for the defined period, and then resumes at the next activity after the delay has completed.

You can control the length of the delay by using the `InitializeTimeoutDuration` property, which binds to an event handler in your code-behind file. Double-click the `DelayActivity` to add an event handler, as shown here:

```
private void delayActivity1_InitializeTimeoutDuration
    (object sender, EventArgs e)
{

}
```

Here, the first argument is `DelayActivity`, so you could add code like the following to initialize the `TimeoutDuration` property to any value you wish. In this example, it is set to ten seconds:

```
private void delayActivity1_InitializeTimeoutDuration
    (object sender, EventArgs e)
{
    DelayActivity delay = sender as DelayActivity;

    if (null != delay)
        delay.TimeoutDuration = new TimeSpan(0, 0, 0, 10);
}
```

Note that it is necessary to cast the `sender` argument to an instance of `DelayActivity`.

When a workflow is in a delay state it doesn't actually do anything — a timer facility within the workflow runtime knows how to deal with delays and can "wake up" a dormant workflow when the delay expires. You'll learn more about this in the section "The Workflow Runtime" later in this chapter.

SuspendActivity

When a workflow is executing it may be necessary to suspend its execution — for example, a database service may be currently unavailable and so the workflow needs to suspend its execution until that system has been brought back online again. The suspend activity shown in Figure 36-5 has an `Error` property that can be set to a string describing why the workflow was suspended.

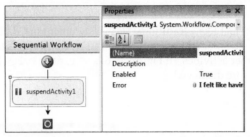

Figure 36-5

When a workflow is suspended, the `WorkflowSuspended` event is raised on the `WorkflowRuntime`, and here you may use the error message to decide what action should be taken. A suspended workflow cannot resume execution itself — you must obtain the workflow instance and call the `Resume()` method on that.

Given that there may be many instances of the same workflows executing at any one time, this raises the question of how to get hold of the particular workflow instance that was suspended.

When a workflow is started, it is given a unique ID in the form of a `Guid`. This `Guid` can be set when you start the workflow instance, as shown in the following code; however, in the absence of this code, the `WorkflowRuntime` constructs a unique ID for you.

```
Guid theInstanceId = Guid.NewGuid();
Dictionary<string, object> parms = new Dictionary<string,object> ();

WorkflowInstance instance = workflowRuntime.CreateWorkflow
   (typeof(_3_Suspend.Workflow1), parms, theInstanceId);

instance.Start();
```

Here, the `Guid.NewGuid()` function creates a new unique identifier for the workflow that is passed as the third parameter to the `CreateWorkflow` call. The `dictionary<>` parameter passes data into a workflow instance, as described later in the chapter.

Given this unique identifier, you can then ask the `WorkflowRuntime` for the `WorkflowInstance` based on this identifier:

```
WorkflowInstance wf = workflowRuntime.GetWorkflow(theInstanceId);
wf.Resume();
```

The GetWorkflow() method takes a Guid parameter and attempts to find that workflow instance. If you pass in an invalid Guid, a System.InvalidOperationException is thrown.

The TerminateActivity works in a similar manner, but it immediately aborts the execution of the workflow instance and raises the WorkflowTerminated event on the runtime. Once a workflow has terminated it is not possible to resume it.

WhileActivity

The WhileActivity works just like a traditional while statement in C#. It enables you to execute several activities in a loop. The main difference with a WhileActivity is that it is a *composite activity* — i.e., one that can contain other activities. In Figure 36-6, a WhileActivity has been dragged onto the designer, and its properties are displayed.

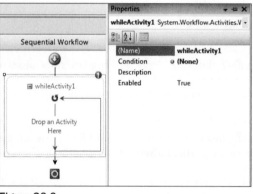

Figure 36-6

The Condition property of the WhileActivity is mandatory — this defines the criteria used when deciding whether to enter the loop for another iteration. A Condition can be defined in code or in a declarative manner, and both of these types are explained here.

To declare a code condition, click the drop-down next to the Condition property and choose Code Condition. Then enter the name of a method that will be used to evaluate this condition at runtime. This generates a code-behind method, as shown here:

```
private void NotFinished(object sender, ConditionalEventArgs e)
{
    e.Result = _howManyTimes++ < 5;
}
```

This method is passed the ConditionalEventArgs parameter, which is used to return true or false to the WhileActivity. You set the Result property of the ConditionalEventArgs object to true to continue looping, whereas returning false exits the loop. The preceding code assumes the presence of an integer variable _howManyTimes that is used to count up to five iterations.

To define a declarative condition, choose the Declarative Rule Condition item from the drop-down next to the `Condition` property, and then click on the ellipses (. . .) next to the `Condition Name` property. That opens the Select Condition dialog (see in Figure 36-7), where you can define the condition based on properties of the current workflow.

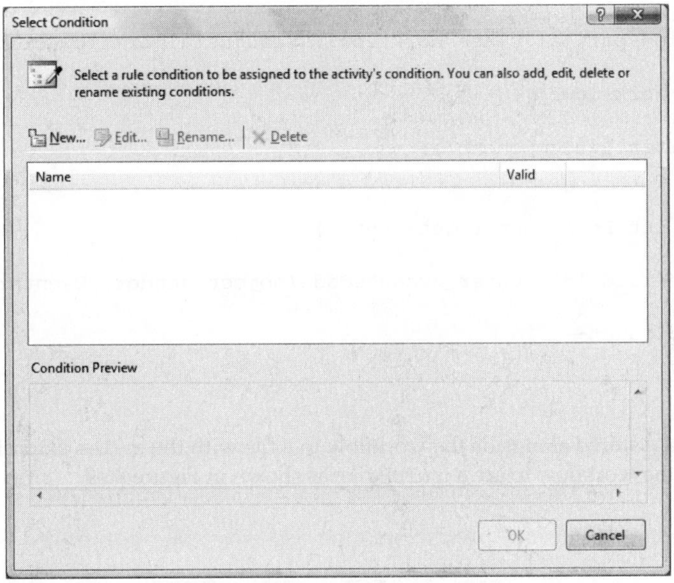

Figure 36-7

To create a new condition, click the New button to open the Rule Condition Editor dialog shown in Figure 36-8 and type in the condition.

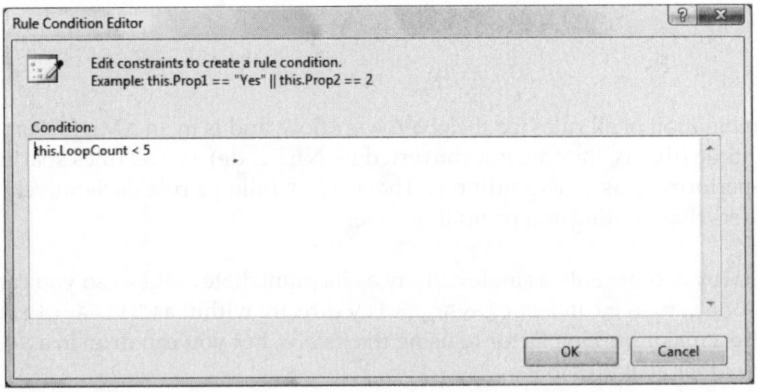

Figure 36-8

This dialog enables you to enter code expressions that are evaluated at runtime. In this example, a property called `LoopCount` is defined on the workflow to check whether the count is less than 5. If you were to compile this code, you would find that the loop never exits, because currently there is nothing updating the value of the `LoopCounter` property.

You need to add to the workflow a `CodeActivity` that updates this value each time around the loop. The code for the workflow would then be as follows:

```
public sealed partial class Workflow1: SequentialWorkflowActivity
{
    public Workflow1()
    {
        InitializeComponent();
    }

    public int LoopCount { get; set; }

    private void incCounter_ExecuteCode(object sender, EventArgs e)
    {
        LoopCount++;
    }
}
```

Declarative rules are stored alongside the workflow in a file with the `.rules` extension. In the Solution Explorer, expand the workflow to see a `.rules` file, as shown in Figure 36-9.

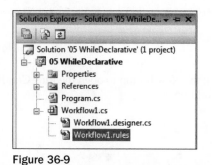

Figure 36-9

This file is a combination of all rules for the given workflow, and is in an XML format. These rules are evaluated at runtime (that is, they are not converted to .NET code), so use rules sparingly because they are not as high-performing as code conditions. That said, defining a rule declaratively is somewhat easier for end users than writing and compiling code.

The `WhileActivity` accepts only a single activity as its immediate child — so you can't, for example, include both a `CodeActivity` and a `DelayActivity` directly within a `WhileActivity`. This might seem at first to be a major limiting factor to using the `While`, but you can drop in a `SequenceActivity` and then add the other activities to it.

SequenceActivity

SequenceActivity is another composite activity that enables any number of child activities to be added within it. As the name implies, it executes these activities in a sequential order. In the code example for the WhileActivity, a SequenceActivity was used to contain all the activities that were executed within the body of the loop.

In common with other composite activities, the SequenceActivity also has two other views. These are accessed by clicking the drop-down available with any composite activity. Figure 36-10 shows the location of this for the SequenceActivity.

Figure 36-10

This drop-down provides three options: View Sequence, View Cancel Handler, and View Fault Handlers. Figure 36-11 shows a view of both the Cancel handler and the Fault handler.

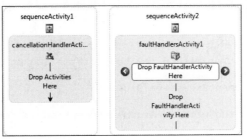

Figure 36-11

When writing .NET code, it is common to surround code in a try/catch block. Within the try block you execute some code that might throw an exception, and with a catch block (or set of catch blocks) you define what happens when an exception is thrown.

The corollary to this in WF is using the fault handlers on a given composite activity. The try block in this instance is composed of the activity or activities within the main body of the composite activity — for a SequentialActivity this is the set of activities within the default view, and similarly for a WhileActivity it is the set of activities within the while block.

Handling Faults

To define a catch block (or set of catch blocks), you can display the fault handlers view and then drag any number of FaultHandlerActivity instances into the list marked Drop FaultHandlerActivity Here (refer to Figure 36-11). In the example shown in Figure 36-12, handlers are defined for two exceptions that might be thrown from within the SequenceActivity: System.ArgumentException and System.Exception.

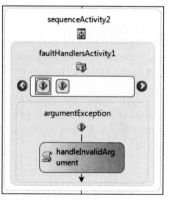

Figure 36-12

When you drop a `FaultHandlerActivity` onto the design surface, you need to specify the `FaultType` property — this defines the type of exception you are catching. Within the body of the activity you can then define the activity or activities that are to be executed when an exception of this type is thrown.

In effect, what you have created is a `try/catch` block, as shown in the following code snippet:

```
try
{
  // Execute activities within the body of the SequentialActivity
}
catch ( System.ArgumentException argex )
{
  // Activities to run when an ArgumentException is thrown
}
catch ( System.Exception ex )
{
  // Activities to run when an Exception is raised
}
```

The code example 06 CancellationAndFaults, available in the download for this book, defines a workflow as shown in Figure 36-13. In the body of the `tryAndCatch` activity (a `SequentialActivity`) is a code activity that displays a message on the console saying that an exception is about to be thrown. `ThrowActivity` is then used to generate a `System.ArgumentException`. The last activity (`afterThrow`) shouldn't be executed because by this point an exception has been created.

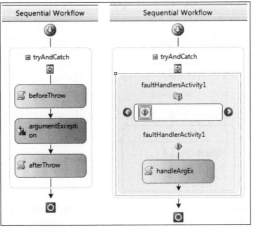

Figure 36-13

The `ArgumentException` is caught within the fault handler and a code activity is added that again writes to the console to state that an exception has been caught. With this code in place, the workflow continues to execute at the point immediately after the sequence activity because the exception raised has been handled and processed. You can define fault handlers on any composite activity, so it is possible, for example, to define a fault handler on the workflow itself to catch any exceptions that bubble up from activities running within it.

If you don't have a fault handler at this top level, the exception will propagate outside of the workflow and be caught by `WorkflowRuntime` — and this will cause the workflow instance to terminate and raise the `WorkflowTerminated` event. The default code added to the console application for this event simply writes the exception message to the console, as shown in the following code snippet:

```
workflowRuntime.WorkflowTerminated +=
    delegate(object sender, WorkflowTerminatedEventArgs e)
{
    Console.WriteLine(e.Exception.Message);
    waitHandle.Set();
};
```

Here, the `WorkflowTerminatedEventArgs` parameter contains the exception that was raised, as well as the `WorkflowInstance` that caused the exception.

Providing Cleanup Code

The preceding section showed how exceptions can be raised and handled by composite activities, but there is another class of problems that needs to be addressed — providing a style of undo logic in a workflow. This example uses the `ParallelActivity`, which enables you to execute several sequences in parallel. Figure 36-14 shows an example.

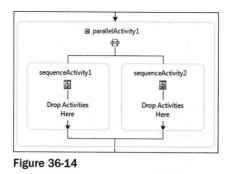

Figure 36-14

This activity consists of at least two SequentialActivity branches — you can add more by using the activity's context menu. Within these branches you may have multiple activities — but what happens when an exception is raised from the second branch and some work has already been executed on the first branch that needs to be undone?

This is where the use of a cancellation handler can be worthwhile. When an exception is raised in one branch of the ParallelActivity, all other branches are notified of this fact by being cancelled. If a cancellation handler has been defined, then this will be called — and because a cancellation handler is just another set of activities, that effectively schedules these activities to execute. You can provide whatever logic you require within a cancellation handler — if, for example, you sent an e-mail on the left branch of the ParallelActivity, you might send another in the cancellation handler telling the recipient to ignore the earlier e-mail.

On the subject of the ParallelActivity, note that this activity is ill-named. If you assumed that this activity runs its children in parallel, and maybe uses threads to schedule the activities on each branch, you would be wrong. (I thought that too when I first saw this.) ParallelActivity actually uses only one thread of execution, and effectively runs the first activity on the first branch, then the second on the second branch, and so on. This is an important concept to understand — the designers of WF chose this method to simplify programming workflows so that end users don't need to understand anything about threading and locks. If you want to execute parts of a workflow in true parallel, then you can use the InvokeWorkflowActivity to create a new workflow (or set of workflows). The runtime will schedule multiple workflows on different threads (and potentially different processors on a multiprocessor machine).

Custom Activities

So far in this chapter you've examined built-in activities. In this section you create your own activity that can be used to assist in debugging workflows by writing output to the console. In the previous examples, CodeActivity was used to display console messages, but it would be better to define an activity that has a string property defining the message to output — then you wouldn't need any code behind to display messages because the activity could do this itself.

All activities ultimately derive from `System.Workflow.ComponentModel.Activity`, and you will use this as the base class for the next activity.

Creating a Custom Activity

1. Create a new Sequential Workflow Console application and add a new class called `DebugActivity` to that project. The class needs to derive from the `Activity` base class, so type in the following code and then add a `using` clause for `System.Workflow` `.ComponentModel`:

```
public class DebugActivity : Activity
{
}
```

2. Define a property on this activity that will hold the message to be displayed when the activity is executed. Add a string property called `Message`, as shown in the following code:

```
public class DebugActivity : Activity
{
    public string Message { get; set; }
}
```

3. When an activity is scheduled for execution by the workflow runtime, its `Execute` method is called. Add an implementation of this method as follows — you can just type in **override Execute** and press the Tab key to have the method constructed for you. This method must return a value to the workflow runtime to indicate that it has completed execution, and the base class `Execute` method already does this, which is why it's called at the end of the method:

```
public class DebugActivity : Activity
{
    public string Message { get; set; }

    protected override ActivityExecutionStatus Execute
        (ActivityExecutionContext executionContext)
    {
        return base.Execute(executionContext);
    }
}
```

4. Now add the code that displays the message during debugging, but omits the message when running without a debugger attached. You could use the `Debug.WriteLine()` method to output the text, but this method is conditionally compiled in release builds, so if you were to build a release version of the library containing `DebugActivity`, no output would be displayed. Instead, you need some way to determine whether the workflow is running with a debugger attached. The `Debugger` class in the `System.Diagnostics` namespace has a property `IsAttached` that is only set to `true` if the current application is being debugged, so you can simply check this property and output the message only if this property is `true`. Here's the completed `DebugActivity` code:

```
public class DebugActivity : Activity
{
    public string Message { get; set; }

    protected override ActivityExecutionStatus Execute
        (ActivityExecutionContext executionContext)
    {
        if (Debugger.IsAttached)
        {
            Console.WriteLine(Message);
            Trace.WriteLine(Message);
        }

        return base.Execute(executionContext);
    }
}
```

This code uses both `Console.WriteLine()` and `Trace.WriteLine()` to output the message. It logs a message to the console and to the output window in Visual Studio. When you drag and drop the `DebugActivity` from the tool palette onto the workflow design surface, you will see an activity as shown in Figure 36-15.

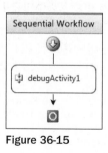

Figure 36-15

The activity looks a bit plain compared to the standard activities, and it doesn't mark the `Message` property as mandatory — so you could easily forget to set this and wonder why no output was being shown during debugging. You solve both of these problems in the next Try It Out section.

Activity Validation

Many of the built-in activities include mandatory properties, signified on the designer surface by an exclamation mark in the top-right corner of the activity. To add this capability to your custom activities, you need to construct an activity validator class.

This class derives from `System.Workflow.ComponentModel.Compiler.ActivityValidtor`, and needs to implement the `Validate` method. This method is called when the activity is initially dropped onto the designer surface, and when properties are modified on the activity. The `Validate` method can return any number of validation errors — as there may be several mandatory properties on the activity in question.

Once the validator has been written it is associated with the activity by using the `ActivityValidator` attribute. This is applied to the activity as shown in the following example on adding an activity validator.

Adding an Activity Validator

The following code shows the implementation of a validator for the `DebugActivity`. When the `Validate` method is called, you are passed the activity as the second parameter to the function; and because this should be a `DebugActivity`, a check is made and an exception thrown if the validator has been attached to another class by mistake:

```
public class DebugActivityValidator : ActivityValidator
{
    public override ValidationErrorCollection Validate
        (ValidationManager manager, object obj)
    {
        DebugActivity act = obj as DebugActivity;

        if (null == act)
            throw new ArgumentException("This validator is only designed to
                                        validate DebugActivity instances");

        // Get any errors from the base class
        ValidationErrorCollection errors = base.Validate(manager, obj);

        // Now check if I have a parent
        if (null != act.Parent)
        {
            // OK - check the Message property
            if (string.IsNullOrEmpty(act.Message))
                errors.Add(
                    ValidationError.GetNotSetValidationError("Message"));
        }

        return errors;
    }
}
```

After checking that the `obj` parameter is valid, the base class `Validate` method is called. This ensures that validation for any inherited properties has also been executed.

Validators are actually executed when the code compiles, and without a check to verify that the activity has a parent you can actually get validation errors when simply compiling this class — which are none too helpful. As an activity always has a parent, the code checks for this first before doing any further validation.

You need to verify that the user has entered something into the Message property of the DebugActivity, so here you test for a null or empty string for this property. If no message has been specified, you call the static ValidationError.GetNotSetValidationError() method and pass in the name of the property that hasn't been defined.

Finally, you need to link this validator to the DebugActivity by adding an attribute to the activity itself. Enter the following code to define this attribute on the activity:

```
[ActivityValidator(typeof(DebugActivityValidator))]
public class DebugActivity : Activity
{
    ...
}
```

With this in place you can now compile the application and confirm that validation of the Message property occurs. Drag a new DebugActivity onto the design surface — you should see the exclamation mark against the activity, as shown in Figure 36-16.

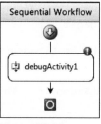

Figure 36-16

Click the validation error. A drop-down menu will be displayed, listing the error (or errors) with the activity. Because you used the GetNotSetValidationError() method, you can click this menu option and it will move you to the appropriate property within the property grid. Note that the validation error is also displayed in the property grid, and hovering the mouse over the exclamation mark in the property grid displays a ToolTip containing the error message.

If you now define a value for the Message property, the validator will be called again, and it will verify that all mandatory properties have been defined and remove the validation error from the UI. Note that if any activities have validation errors, then you won't be able to successfully compile your application either.

Enhancing Design Time

In comparing the design-time look of the DebugActivity with the built-in activities, it looks distinctly plain — the background is white and a generic icon has been associated with it. In this section, you enhance this by adding code to draw a different color background and change the outline to a dashed pen.

Changing the drawing behavior of an activity is done in a similar manner to adding a validator — you need to create a couple of classes and associate these with the DebugActivity by using attributes.

The two classes responsible for the rendering of an activity are ActivityDesigner and ActivityDesignerTheme. The designer class enables you to have complete control over all aspects of rendering — typical uses are to augment the generic design-time behavior by adding extra glyphs to the surface of the activity. You could completely change the rendering of an activity by writing a designer, but for our purposes the theme class is all you need to change the background color and other simple aspects of the activity.

Try It Out   **Adding a Designer and Theme**

Follow these steps to add a designer and a theme to the DebugActivity to enhance the design-time experience of the activity:

1. Create the theme class as shown in the following code:

```
public class DebugActivityTheme : ActivityDesignerTheme
{
    public DebugActivityTheme(WorkflowTheme theme)
        : base(theme)
    {
        this.BackColorStart = Color.Green;
        this.BackColorEnd = Color.Yellow;
        this.BackgroundStyle = LinearGradientMode.ForwardDiagonal;
        this.BorderStyle = DashStyle.Dot;
    }
}
```

Here you create a class that derives from ActivityDesignerTheme, and all theme classes need to include a constructor that takes as a single argument an instance of the WorkflowTheme class. Within your constructor, you set properties of the theme such as the background start and end colors and the style. This renders the background of the activity using a gradient brush and changes the border style of the activity to use a dotted pen.

2. With the theme class written you now need a designer class. This is nothing more than an empty class because there is no need to override any of the designer methods to provide a theme for an activity. The class, however, is necessary. Create it as follows:

```
[ActivityDesignerTheme(typeof(DebugActivityTheme))]
public class DebugActivityDesigner : ActivityDesigner
{
}
```

Note that this includes the `ActivityDesignerTheme` attribute, which ensures that the workflow design surface can find the appropriate theme class at design time.

3. Finally, link the custom designer with the activity itself. Again, you do this using an attribute:

```
[ActivityValidator(typeof(DebugActivityValidator))]
[Designer(typeof(DebugActivityDesigner))]
public class DebugActivity : Activity
{
    . . .
}
```

Here, you added the `Designer` attribute and defined the type to be the `DebugActivityDesigner`. If you now compile the application and drag a `DebugActivity` onto the design surface (or just open an existing workflow that contains this activity), you will see an enhanced activity as shown in Figure 36-17.

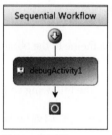

Figure 36-17

If you make changes to the theme and recompile your activity, you may wonder why those changes are not immediately reflected inside Visual Studio. When Visual Studio finds a designer for a particular type, it caches it internally, so the only way to update this is to restart Visual Studio. If you remove the `Designer` attribute from the activity and recompile, you will still see the old designer in the UI, so restarting is your only option.

The Workflow Runtime

The `WorkflowRuntime` can be hosted in a console application as shown throughout the chapter so far, but you can host the runtime in any .NET application. One common example would be to host the runtime within a Windows Forms application on the client machine. Another would be hosting the runtime within an ASP.NET site so that workflows can be executed based on actions a user takes on a Web site. The runtime is designed to be used in all of these environments and has specific support for each type of application.

In addition to hosting workflows, the runtime also hosts a set of services that it uses and that can also be used by workflows as they execute. A service is simply an instance of a .NET class that has been registered with the runtime.

Arguably, the most useful of these services is the *persistence service,* which takes an idle workflow and persists it to disk. This typically happens when you have a delay in the workflow, as there's no need to have a workflow in memory while it is dormant, so the persistence service can package up the state of the workflow and store this on disk.

The persistence service follows a common model in .NET programming — that of an abstract class that can be derived from to provide a specific implementation. In this case the abstract class is the `WorkflowPersistenceService` class, and a concrete implementation of this, which stores persistence data to SQL Server, is `SqlWorkflowPersistenceService`. If you want to persist workflows to another storage medium, you can write your own persistence service and plug that into the workflow runtime either in code or by using the configuration file.

In the following Try It Out, you create a workflow that includes a `DelayActivity` and see how the workflow is persisted to a SQL Server database. You first create a new database and then execute two scripts that are provided with WF to create the tables and stored procedures used by the persistence service.

Try It Out   **Using the Persistence Service**

There are several different ways to create a new SQL Server database, but this example assumes that you only have SQL Express installed, so you create the database and run the scripts from within Visual Studio.

1.   From the Data Connections node in the Server Explorer window, choose Create New SQL Server Database. This opens the dialog shown in Figure 36-18.

Figure 36-18

2. Type **.\sqlexpress** for the name of the database server and **WF** for the name of the database. After this, you will see an item in the Server Explorer window matching the database you have just created.

3. Execute two scripts against that database — these are stored in `%windir%\Microsoft.NET\Framework\v3.5\SQL\EN`. Within Visual Studio, open the two files shown in the dialog in Figure 36-19: `SqlPersistenceProviderSchema.sql` and `SqlPersistenceProviderLogic.sql`. One contains the schema for the persistence service and the other contains the logic (i.e., stored procedures).

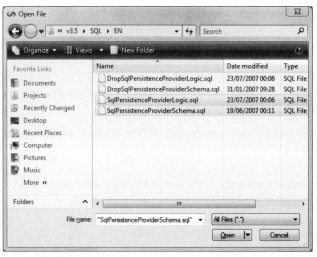

Figure 36-19

4. With these files open within Visual Studio, you can then execute them in order. First, run the `SqlPersistenceProviderSchema.sql` file: Just select F5 and choose the WF database created in the previous step. Then execute the `SqlPersistenceProviderLogic.sql` file in the same manner.

5. With the SQL database set up, you can now create a new project and use the persistence service within this project. Create a new Sequential Workflow Console application and drag in a `DelayActivity` and set its `TimeoutDuration` to five seconds — later you will update this to a longer duration.

6. You need to add some event handlers to the main program so that you can view the state of the workflow as it is executing. Open the `Program.cs` file and add event handlers as follows for the `WorkflowIdled`, `WorkflowUnloaded`, `WorkflowPersisted`, and `WorkflowLoaded` events. The handlers just write information to the console:

```
static void Main(string[] args)
{
    using(WorkflowRuntime workflowRuntime = new WorkflowRuntime())
    {
        ...

        workflowRuntime.WorkflowIdled +=
            new EventHandler<WorkflowEventArgs> (WorkflowIdled);
        workflowRuntime.WorkflowPersisted +=
            new EventHandler<WorkflowEventArgs> (WorkflowPersisted);
        workflowRuntime.WorkflowLoaded +=
            new EventHandler<WorkflowEventArgs> (WorkflowLoaded);
        workflowRuntime.WorkflowUnloaded +=
            new EventHandler<WorkflowEventArgs> (WorkflowUnloaded);

        ...
    }
}

static void WorkflowLoaded(object sender, WorkflowEventArgs e)
{
    Console.WriteLine("Workflow {0} Loaded",
        e.WorkflowInstance.InstanceId);
}

static void WorkflowUnloaded(object sender, WorkflowEventArgs e)
{
    Console.WriteLine("Workflow {0} Unloaded",
        e.WorkflowInstance.InstanceId);
}

static void WorkflowPersisted(object sender, WorkflowEventArgs e)
{
    Console.WriteLine("Workflow {0} Persisted",
        e.WorkflowInstance.InstanceId);
}

static void WorkflowIdled(object sender, WorkflowEventArgs e)
{
    Console.WriteLine("Workflow {0} Idled",
        e.WorkflowInstance.InstanceId);
}
```

Each of the events simply writes output to the console. If you run the application now you should see the following message:

```
Workflow 9223fe0b-5a3f-4e93-a5e0-f5852b11b006 Idled
```

This includes the unique workflow instance ID and the event that occurred. Without a persistence service this is all you get — a notification that a workflow has become idle. If you now add code to add a persistence service to the runtime, you will see the workflow persist and be unloaded from memory, and a short while later that workflow will be reloaded and continue execution.

There are two ways you can add a service to the workflow runtime — either in code or by using a configuration file. Both methods are shown here, but I recommend adding all services to the runtime by using the configuration file approach. This makes it much easier to change services later without having to recompile the application.

The SqlWorkflowPersistenceService has a number of constructors, but the most useful one takes four parameters: the connection string, a Boolean indicating whether the service should unload idle instances, and two time-span values — instanceOwnershipDuration and loadingInterval. The unloadOnIdle parameter should generally be true — it determines whether idle workflows will be unloaded from memory, and is only settable using this four-parameter constructor. If it's false (the default), then workflows are only persisted when they complete or when an activity specifically requests a persistence point. The instanceOwnershipDuration is used to define how long a workflow is permitted to run in a multi-machine environment.

When you have multiple machines processing workflows, you need to define this value to indicate whether a workflow node has failed while processing a workflow. When a machine picks up a schedulable workflow from the database, it is marked as locked for this period. If the workflow does not persist again until after this time span, then another node can unlock the workflow and process it itself. loadingInterval specifies how often the persistence service will poll the database looking for workflows whose timers have expired (i.e., that are ready to execute). The default for instanceOwnershipDuration is TimeSpan.MaxValue, and for loadInterval is two minutes.

7. Now add the following code to the application. It adds the persistence service to the workflow runtime. The database connection string is hard-coded here, whereas you should define this within the configuration file to make it easier to change:

```
static void Main(string[] args)
{
    using(WorkflowRuntime workflowRuntime = new WorkflowRuntime())
    {
        string conn = @"Data Source=.\sqlexpress;Initial Catalog=WF;
                        Integrated Security=True";
        workflowRuntime.AddService(new SqlWorkflowPersistenceService
            (conn, true, TimeSpan.FromMinutes(2), TimeSpan.FromSeconds(30)));

        ...

    }
}
```

Here you have constructed the SqlWorkflowPersistenceService and specified the connection string, true for the unloadOnIdle parameter, two minutes for the instance ownership duration, and 30 seconds for the loading interval.

8. To define the same using a configuration file, add a reference to the `System.Configuration` assembly and then add an application configuration file to your solution, as follows:

```
<?xml version="1.0" encoding="utf-8" ?>
<configuration>

  <configSections>
    <section name="WF"
      type="System.Workflow.Runtime.Configuration.WorkflowRuntimeSection,
            System.Workflow.Runtime, Version=3.0.0.0, Culture=neutral,
            PublicKeyToken=31bf3856ad364e35" />
  </configSections>

  <WF>
    <CommonParameters>
      <add name="ConnectionString"
           value="Initial Catalog=WF;Data Source=.\sqlexpress;
                  Integrated Security=SSPI;" />
    </CommonParameters>
    <Services>
     <add type="System.Workflow.Runtime.Hosting.SqlWorkflowPersistenceService,
                System.Workflow.Runtime, Version=3.0.0.0, Culture=neutral,
                PublicKeyToken=31bf3856ad364e35"
         UnloadOnIdle="true"/>
    </Services>
  </WF>

</configuration>
```

This file includes a definition for the `WorkflowRuntimeSection` configuration section handler, which is used to read the section called WF. In the WF section, you defined the `ConnectionString` as a shared parameter and then defined the persistence service within the `Services` section by adding the `SqlWorkflowPersistenceService`. You also specified the value of `true` for the `UnloadOnIdle` attribute.

9. Within the application code, one small change is needed to get the workflow runtime to read data from this configuration section:

```
static void Main(string[] args)
{
    // Read the config section to configure services
    using (WorkflowRuntime workflowRuntime = new WorkflowRuntime("WF"))
    {
    }
}
```

With these change in place, when the application executes you'll see the following output to the console:

```
Workflow 755348bc-3e86-46c4-99a0-3552a2ba7e5f Idled
Workflow 755348bc-3e86-46c4-99a0-3552a2ba7e5f Persisted
Workflow 755348bc-3e86-46c4-99a0-3552a2ba7e5f Unloaded
Workflow 755348bc-3e86-46c4-99a0-3552a2ba7e5f Loaded
Workflow 755348bc-3e86-46c4-99a0-3552a2ba7e5f Persisted
```

The first message indicates that the DelayActivity is executing, as when this runs the workflow reverts to an idle state. Because there is now a persistence service installed with UnloadOnIdle set, the workflow is persisted, which is where the current state of the workflow is packaged up and stored within the database. The next event is an Unload of the workflow — so at this point the workflow is no longer in memory and exists solely on disk in the database. This also adds an entry to the database to define when the workflow should be woken up to continue processing.

If at this point you were to look into the InstanceState table in the database, you would see a row for the workflow instance (see Figure 36-20).

	uidInstanceID	state	status	unlocked	blocked	info	modified	ownerID	ownedUntil	nextTimer
▶	755348bc-3e86-46c4-99a0-3552a2ba7e5f	<Binary data>	0	1	1		26/10/2007 19:47:49	NULL	NULL	26/10/2007 19:48:49
*	NULL	NULL	NULL	NULL	NULL	NULL	NULL	NULL	NULL	NULL

Figure 36-20

The primary key for this row is the workflow identifier, and the second column holds the binary serialized state of the workflow when it was persisted. The nextTimer column indicates when the delay activity will complete, and at this point (or sometime shortly after this time based on the polling interval) the workflow will be reloaded.

After the period defined by the DelayActivity, the workflow is reloaded, as indicated by the Loaded message — the workflow then completes, which forces another persistence event to be raised. When a completed workflow is persisted, the row in the InstanceState table is deleted.

If you want to force a persistence point in a custom activity such as the DebugActivity presented earlier, then you can add the PersistOnCloseAttribute to the activity:

```
[ActivityValidator(typeof(DebugActivityValidator))]
[Designer(typeof(DebugActivityDesigner))]
[PersistOnClose]
public class DebugActivity : Activity
{
    ...
}
```

Adding two debug activities to the workflow, with one above and one below the DelayActivity, will then output the following to the console:

```
Workflow 005f5924-fb49-4d60-a8bd-f572a19a1d39 Persisted   ← A
Workflow 005f5924-fb49-4d60-a8bd-f572a19a1d39 Idled
Workflow 005f5924-fb49-4d60-a8bd-f572a19a1d39 Persisted
Workflow 005f5924-fb49-4d60-a8bd-f572a19a1d39 Unloaded
Workflow 005f5924-fb49-4d60-a8bd-f572a19a1d39 Loaded
Workflow 005f5924-fb49-4d60-a8bd-f572a19a1d39 Persisted   ← B
Workflow 005f5924-fb49-4d60-a8bd-f572a19a1d39 Persisted
```

This shows the two extra persistence events (marked A and B) that correspond to the debug activities added into the workflow. Use this attribute with care — too many persistence points in a workflow can harm the performance of that workflow. Note that if you use an activity with the `PersistOnClose` attribute defined, then you must have a persistence service defined.

The main benefit of having a persistence service is to be able to continue the workflow after an interruption — such as a power outage on the server hosting the workflows. When the workflow runtime starts up again which might be in a few minutes, hours, or even days — the persistence service will look for runnable workflows and load any that can be executed. Therefore, if you had a set of workflows in memory when the power went off, each would revert to its previous persistence point and start running from there again. This enables you to have programs (as a workflow is in effect a program) that can carry on from their last positions after interruption. This is a very powerful concept!

Data Binding

To end this chapters, let's take a look at the concept of data binding and workflows. A typical scenario when running a workflow is that some state needs to be carried along with that workflow as it executes. Consider the example of the insurance policy workflow described earlier in the chapter — it is likely that you would want to pass some information into the workflow, such as a unique policy number, so that activities within the workflow can use this data.

To pass parameters into a workflow, you need to make two changes to the code. First, you need to define properties on the workflow for each parameter you want to pass in. Second, you need to pass in these parameters when you start the workflow.

One other concept that we've ignored up to this point is how to define properties on a workflow. Because a workflow is just a .NET class, you could use the regular property syntax in C#. But another technique in workflows enables you to do some additional things with the data, beyond what is available with regular properties. Using what's called a `DependencyProperty`, you can bind data coming into the workflow to other activities in that workflow.

The syntax for defining a property for a workflow is fairly complex, but a code snippet included with .NET will do this for you. In the following Try It Out, you add a property to a workflow and pass a value to this property when you start the workflow. You'll also be able to data-bind to this property.

Try It Out   Defining Bound Properties

1. Create another new workflow project and display the code for that workflow. Then display
    the context menu within the code window and choose Insert Snippet. From the displayed list
    of types, choose Workflow. Then choose Dependency Property — Property from the pop-up
    menu. This adds the following code. (As an alternative to choosing this from the menu, if you
    type in **wdp** and then press the Tab key twice, this snippet will also be created for you.)

```
public static DependencyProperty {NAME}Property =
DependencyProperty.Register("{NAME}", typeof({TYPE}), typeof(Workflow1));

[DescriptionAttribute("{NAME}")]
[CategoryAttribute("{NAME} Category")]
[BrowsableAttribute(true)]
[DesignerSerializationVisibility(DesignerSerializationVisibility.Visible)]
public {TYPE} {NAME}
{
    get
    {
        return ((string)(base.GetValue(Workflow1.{NAME}Property)));
    }
    set
    {
        base.SetValue(Workflow1.{NAME}Property, value);
    }
}
```

The snippet includes two regions where you can type: {NAME} and {TYPE}. The {NAME} is the
name that you will use for the property; for this example use **PolicyId**. The {TYPE} is the data
type of the property; in this example assume that this is a string.

You'll notice in the code for the property that rather than use a member variable to store that
value, a call is made to a base class GetValue() or SetValue() function. The Activity class
(from which a workflow derives) is itself derived from a class called DependencyObject and
it is this class that defines these methods. In effect, a DependencyObject contains a dictionary
of key/value pairs and this dictionary is used to store the actual value of a property.

While this may seem like a lot of code to define a property, the benefit is the data binding
support that this provides.

2. You revisit the DebugActivity again in this section, as the Message property was originally
    defined as a regular .NET property. But to support data binding, you need to update this
    definition. Remove the Message property from DebugActivity and then change this to a
    dependency property. Here's the completed code:

```
[ActivityValidator(typeof(DebugActivityValidator))]
[Designer(typeof(DebugActivityDesigner))]
[PersistOnClose]
public class DebugActivity : Activity
{
    public static DependencyProperty MessageProperty =
        DependencyProperty.Register("Message", typeof(string),
```

```
                                    typeof(DebugActivity));

    [DescriptionAttribute("Message")]
    [CategoryAttribute("Details")]
    [BrowsableAttribute(true)]
    [DesignerSerializationVisibility(DesignerSerializationVisibility.Visible)]
    public string Message
    {
        get
        {
            return ((string)(base.GetValue(DebugActivity.MessageProperty)));
        }
        set
        {
            base.SetValue(DebugActivity.MessageProperty, value);
        }
    }

    ...
}
```

This code simply replaces the definition of the Message property with a dependency property of the same name and data type. One more slight change is needed before you can use this in a workflow, and that is to the validator code.

3. Because a dependency property is used to data-bind one item in a workflow to another, you can no longer just check whether the Message property is non-null. Instead, you need to first check whether the property is bound to another in the workflow — and only if it is not do you check its textual value. Remove the logic within the if (null != act.Parent) section and replace it with the following:

```
public class DebugActivityValidator : ActivityValidator
{
    public override ValidationErrorCollection Validate
        (ValidationManager manager, object obj)
    {
        ...

        if (null != act.Parent)
        {
            // OK - check the Message property
            if (!act.IsBindingSet(DebugActivity.MessageProperty))
            {
                if (string.IsNullOrEmpty(act.Message))
                    errors.Add(
                        ValidationError.GetNotSetValidationError("Message"));
            }
        }

        return errors;
    }
}
```

Here, you call the `IsBindingSet` method prior to checking whether the message property is empty or null. If a binding has been made, then there is no need to raise the validation error.

With all this defined, you can now hook the `Message` property of the `DebugActivity` to any other string property on the workflow. When a property is defined as a dependency property, it is indicated as such in the property grid as a small icon, as shown in Figure 36-21.

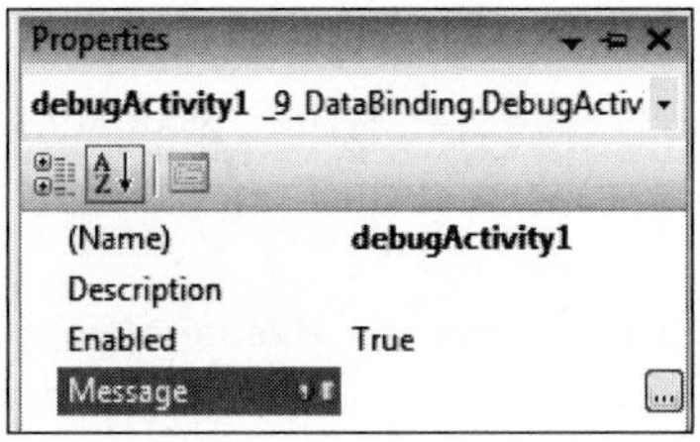

Figure 36-21

4. After compiling your solution and adding the `DebugActivity` to your workflow, click on the activity to display the properties, and select the `Message` property. In addition to the icon next to the property name, you will also see ellipses. Type in a value for the property or click the ellipses (or double-click on the binding icon), which will then display the dialog shown in Figure 36-22.

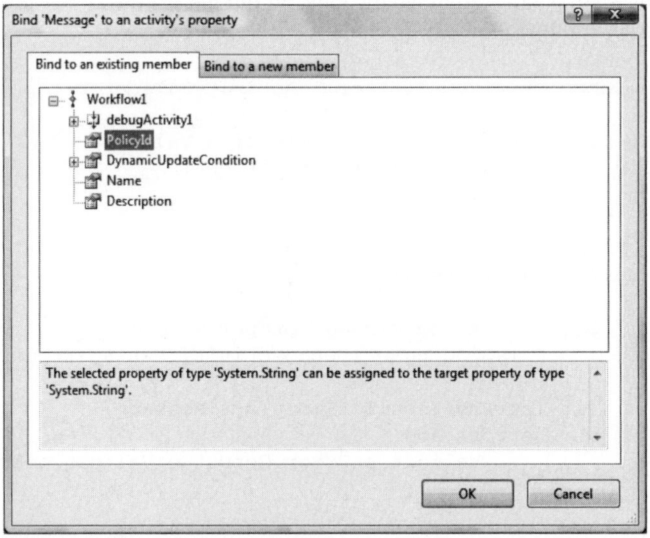

Figure 36-22

Here you can choose a property of the same data type as that which you are binding, so I have bound the value of the Message property to the PolicyId property defined on the workflow. At runtime these two properties will be linked, so when the Message property is used by the DebugActivity, it will match the value of the PolicyId property on the workflow. No copying of data occurs here — the Message property is in effect the same as the PolicyId property.

Figure 36-23 shows what is displayed in the property grid for a bound property. This includes the name of the object where the bound property is defined and the path to that property — in this case, the property name.

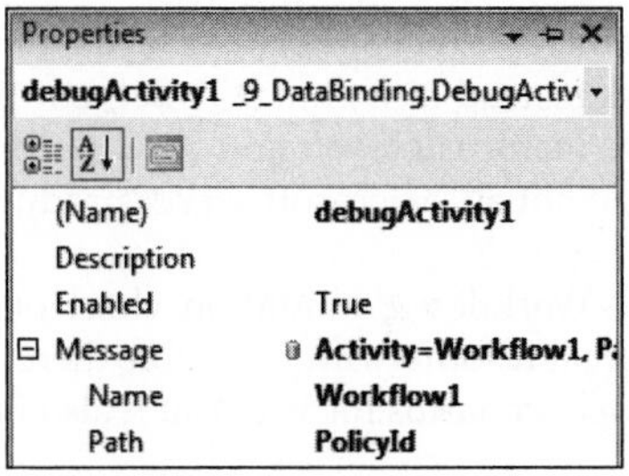

Figure 36-23

5. Now you need to pass in the PolicyId to the workflow. To do so, it is necessary to create a dictionary of name-value pairs and pass this to the CreateWorkflow call on the WorkflowRuntime. Enter the following code to construct this dictionary and start the workflow:

```
Dictionary<string, object> parms = new Dictionary<string, object>();

parms.Add("PolicyId", "xx-99-2293382");

WorkflowInstance instance = workflowRuntime.CreateWorkflow
    (typeof(_9_DataBinding.Workflow1), parms);

instance.Start();
```

This code defines the parms dictionary and adds the PolicyId value to it. The workflow is constructed and passed this parameter dictionary as the second parameter to the CreateWorkflow method. With this you can pass parameters into a workflow and use them within the workflow.

Summary

In this chapter you learned about Windows Workflow Foundation, and how to create workflows and execute them by using the `WorkflowRuntime`. Workflows can be used as a way to extend applications and provide a simplified user experience whereby activities can be added to a workflow in a drag-and-drop manner.

A workflow contains a number of activities — these are the building blocks of WF — and custom activities can be written to extend the behavior of workflows to add extra functionality. For example, you can create activities that send e-mail or update sales information in a database, and the end user of the activity can simply drop it onto a workflow and hook up its properties.

WF also has many extensibility points — you could create a custom persistence service that stores the state of running workflows on disk instead of within SQL Server. WF is at the heart of SharePoint Server 2007 already and is being built into many Microsoft and third-party products, and you are likely to see it adopted across the board in most, if not all, Microsoft server products.

For more information on Windows Workflow Foundation, check out the WF site at `http://wf.netfxe.com`. Some great resources are available there, including an excellent set of screencasts that demonstrate various scenarios for WF. You'll also find details of custom activities that can be downloaded.

Adding in workflow capability to your own applications is relatively simple — and your end users will love you for it.

Index